PHIL

STR

London

Contents

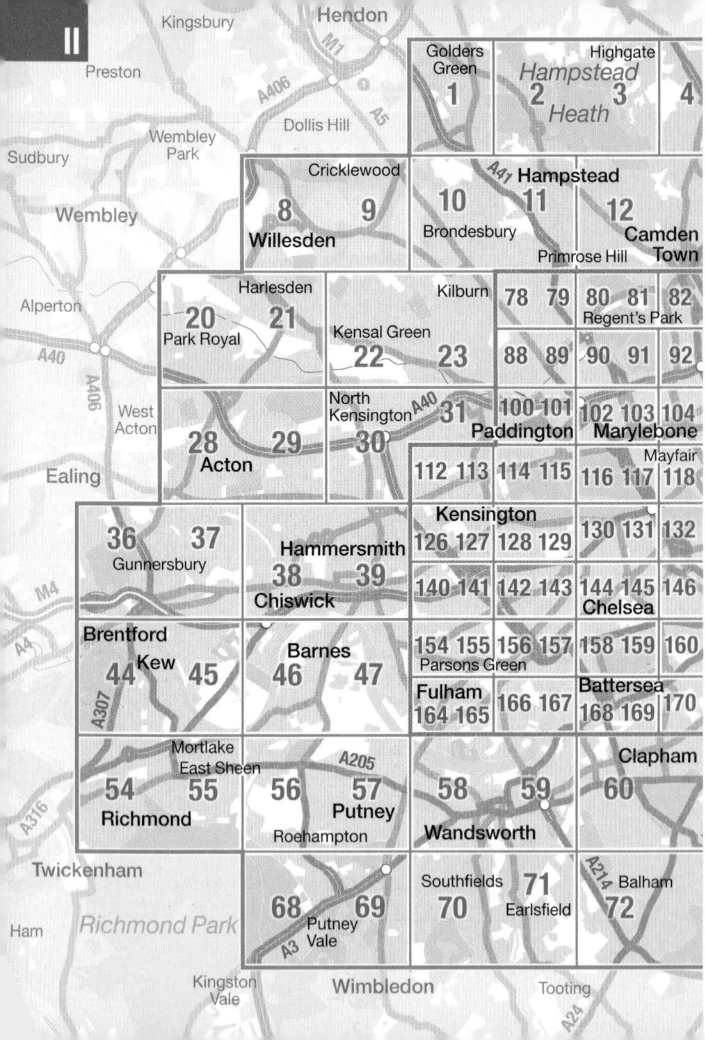

II

Kingsbury
Hendon
Preston

Golders
Green
1

Highgate
Hampstead
2 **3** **4**
Heath

A406
M1
Dollis Hill
A5

Wembley
Park

Sudbury

Cricklewood

Hampstead
A41

10
8 **9**
Willesden

Brondesbury
11

12
Camden
Primrose Hill Town

Wembley

Alperton

Harlesden
Kilburn

78 79 **80 81 82**
Regent's Park

20 **21**
Park Royal
Kensal Green
22 **23**

88 89 **90 91 92**

A40

West
Acton

North
Kensington A40
30 31
28 29
Acton

100 101 **102 103 104**
Paddington Marylebone

Ealing

112 113 **114 115** **116 117 118**
Mayfair

Kensington
126 127 **128 129** **130 131 132**

36 37
Gunnersbury
Hammersmith
38 39
Chiswick

140 141 **142 143** **144 145 146**
Chelsea

M4

Brentford
44 **Kew** **45**
A307

Barnes
46 47

154 155 **156 157** **158 159 160**
Parsons Green

Fulham
164 165 **166 167**
Battersea
168 169 170

Mortlake
East Sheen

A205

Clapham

54 55
Richmond

56 57
Putney
Roehampton

58 59
60
Wandsworth

A316

Twickenham

Southfields
71
Balham
A214
70
Earlsfield
72

Ham

Richmond Park

68 69
Putney
Vale
A3

Kingston
Vale

Wimbledon

Tooting

A24

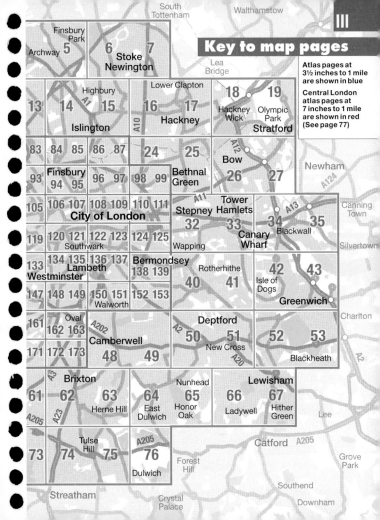

III

Key to map pages

Atlas pages at
3½ inches to 1 mile
are shown in blue

Central London
atlas pages at
7 inches to 1 mile
are shown in red
(See page 77)

South
Tottenham

Walthamstow

Finsbury
Park

Archway **5**

6 **7**
Stoke
Newington

Lea
Bridge

Highbury

13 **14** **15**
Islington
A1

Lower Clapton

16 **17**
Hackney
A10

18 **19**
Hackney Olympic
Wick Park
Stratford

83 **84** **85** **86** **87** **24** **25**
Finsbury
93 **94** **95** **96** **97** **98** **99**
Bethnal
Green

Bow
26 **27**
A12

Newham
A124

105 **106** **107** **108** **109** **110** **111**
City of London

Tower
Stepney Hamlets
32 **33** **34** **35**
Canary Blackwall
Wharf

Canning
Town
A13

Silvertown

119 **120** **121** **122** **123** **124** **125**
Southwark
Wapping

133 **134** **135** **136** **137**
Westminster Lambeth
Bermondsey
138 **139**
Rotherhithe
40 **41**
Isle of
Dogs

42 **43**

Greenwich

Charlton

147 **148** **149** **150** **151** **152** **153**
Walworth

Deptford
50 **51** **52** **53**
New Cross
Blackheath
A2

161 **162** **163**
Oval
A202

A2
Camberwell
171 **172** **173** **48** **49**

61 **62** **63**
Brixton
A43
Herne Hill
A23
A205

64 **65**
East Honor
Dulwich Oak
Nunhead

66 **67**
Lewisham
Ladywell Hither
Green

Lee

73 **74** **75**
Tulse
Hill

76
Dulwich
A205

Forest
Hill

Catford A205

Grove
Park

Streatham
Crystal
Palace

Southend

Downham

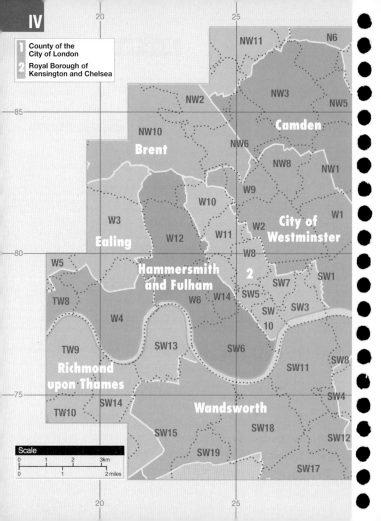

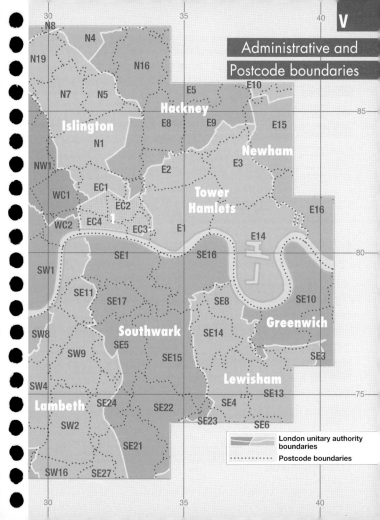

Administrative and
Postcode boundaries

London unitary authority
boundaries
.... Postcode boundaries

VI

Key to map symbols

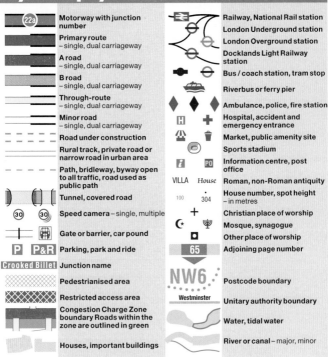

	Motorway with junction number
	Primary route – single, dual carriageway
	A road – single, dual carriageway
	B road – single, dual carriageway
	Through-route – single, dual carriageway
	Minor road – single, dual carriageway
	Road under construction
	Rural track, private road or narrow road in urban area
	Path, bridleway, byway open to all traffic, road used as public path
	Tunnel, covered road
	Speed camera – single, multiple
	Gate or barrier, car pound
	Parking, park and ride
Crooked Billet	Junction name
	Pedestrianised area
	Restricted access area
	Congestion Charge Zone boundary Roads within the zone are outlined in green
	Houses, important buildings
	Woods, parkland/common

	Railway, National Rail station
	London Underground station
	London Overground station
	Docklands Light Railway station
	Bus / coach station, tram stop
	Riverbus or ferry pier
	Ambulance, police, fire station
	Hospital, accident and emergency entrance
	Market, public amenity site
	Sports stadium
	Information centre, post office
VILLA House	Roman, non-Roman antiquity
100 304	House number, spot height – in metres
	Christian place of worship
	Mosque, synagogue
	Other place of worship
65	Adjoining page number
NW6	Postcode boundary
Westminster	Unitary authority boundary
	Water, tidal water
	River or canal – major, minor

The map scale on the pages numbered in blue is 3½ inches to 1 mile
5.52 cm to 1 km • 1:18 103

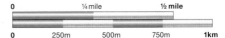

0	¼ mile	½ mile
0	250m 500m 750m	1km

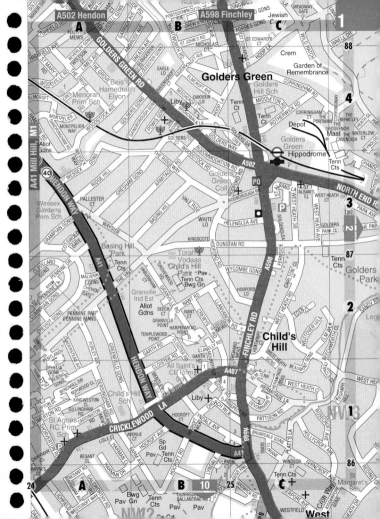

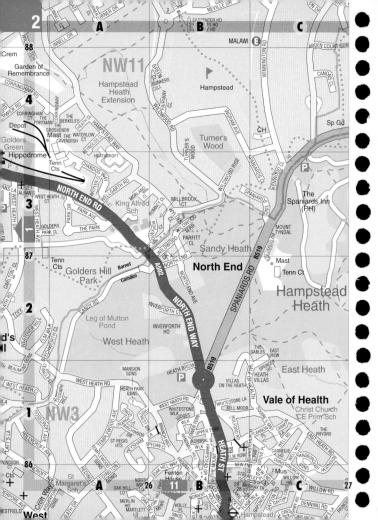

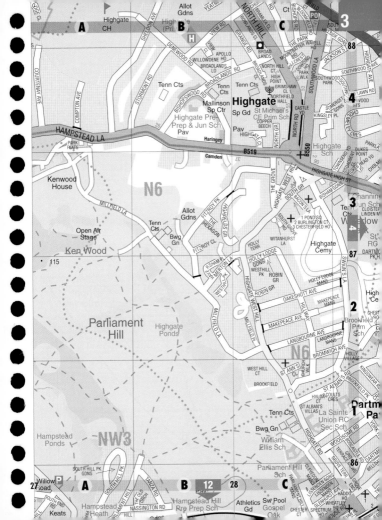

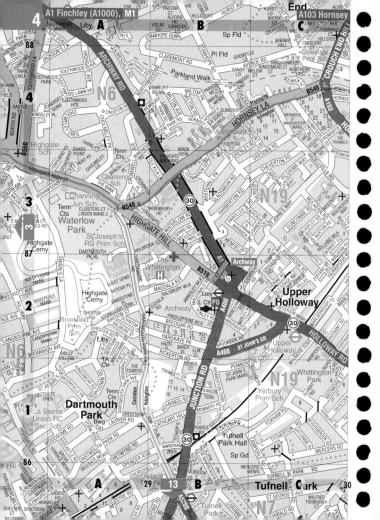

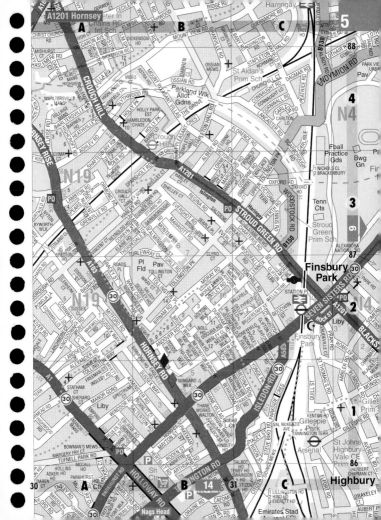

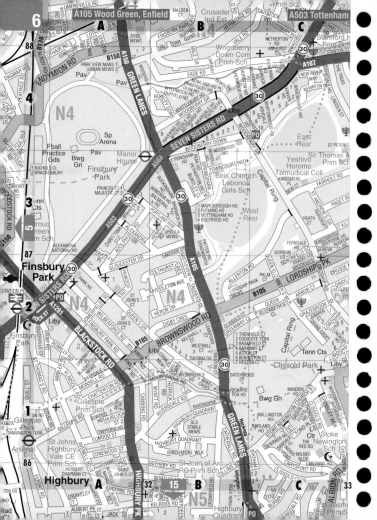

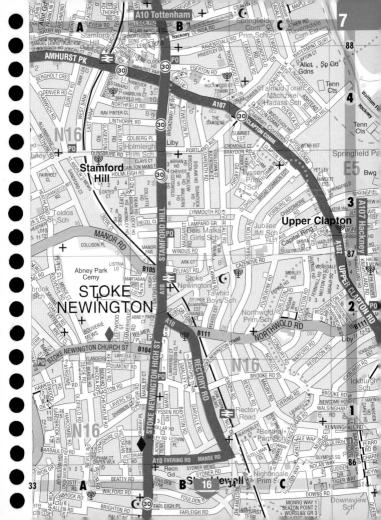

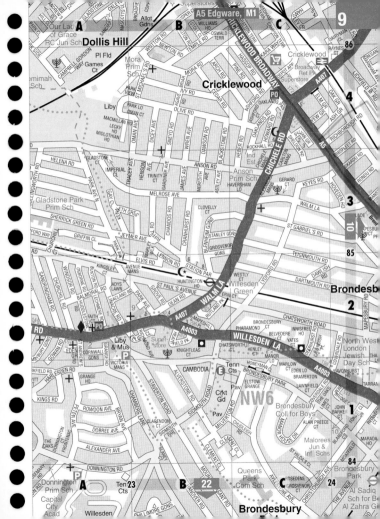

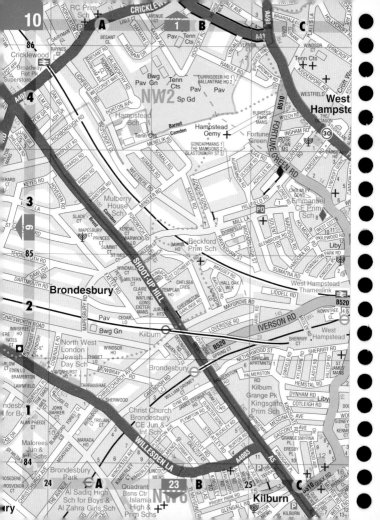

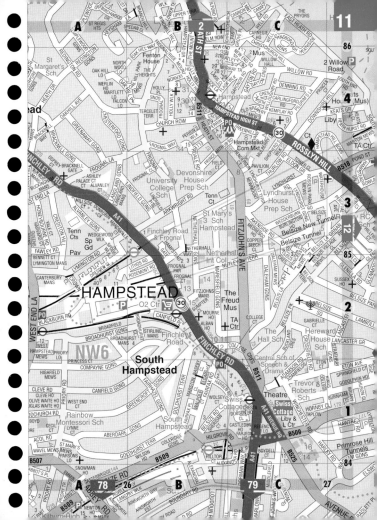

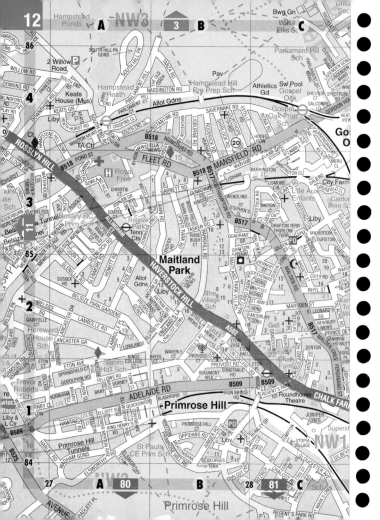

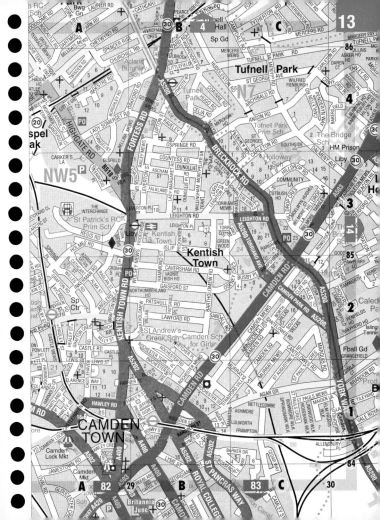

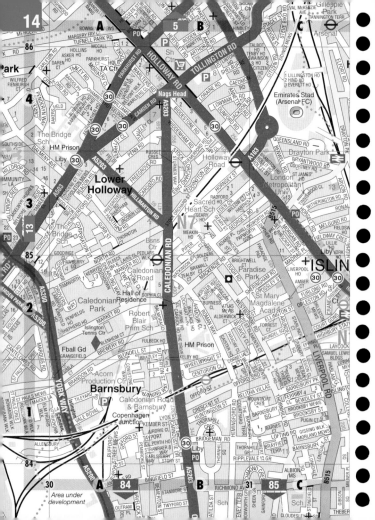

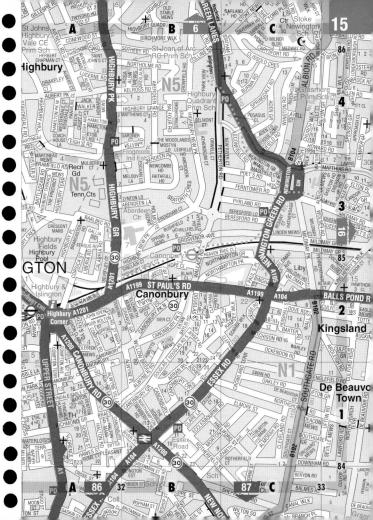

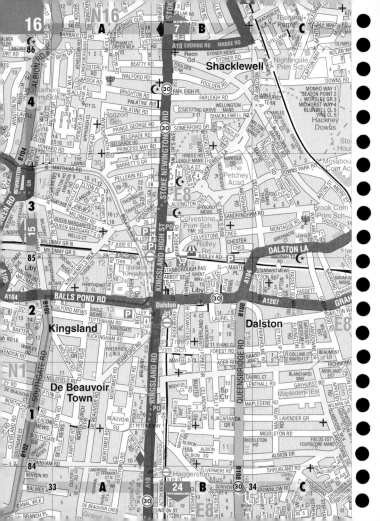

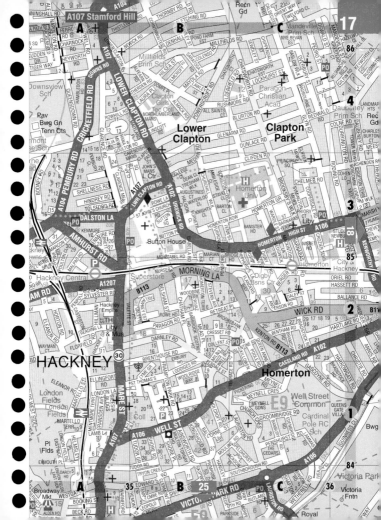

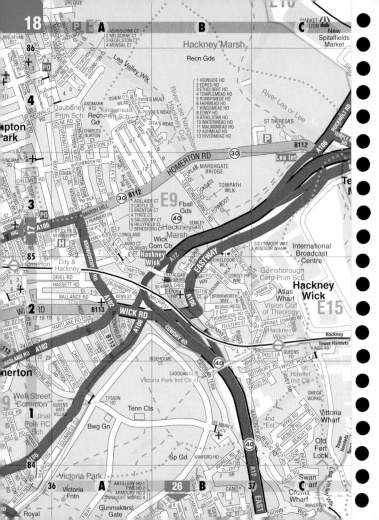

Hackney Marsh

Recn Gds

New Spitalfields Market

MARKET LION

C

B112

A106

TEMPLE MILL RD

RUCKHOLT RD

Lea Int

Te

Ml

1 ASHBOURNE CT
2 MELBORNE CT
3 KEDLESTON CT
4 MONSAL CT

A

NYE BEVAN

86

PO

4

Daubeney
Prim Sch

Kingsmead
Prim Sch

LANDMARK
HTS

Recn
Gd

CHARLES
BURTON

OSWALD'S ST

EDWIN'S MEAD

PENDA'S MEAD

OFFA'S MEAD

KINGS MEAD

MEESON ST

River Lee Navigation

River Lea or Lee

River Lee Hackney Cut

1 IRONSIDE HO
2 EDRED HO
3 ETHELBERT HO
4 TEMPLEMEAD HO
5 RUNNYMEDE HO
6 FAIRMEAD HO
7 KINGSMEAD HO
8 EDWY HO
9 ATHELSTAN HO
10 WATERMEAD HO
11 MALMSMEAD HO
12 MERSMEAD HO
13 RIVERMEAD HO

ST THERESA'S
CL

HOMERTON RD

POPLAR

MARSHGATE
BRIDGE

30

P

B112

30

E9

Fball
Gds

LEA CONSERVANCY RD

CLOCKGATE

CROWFOOT

TOWPATH
WLK

40

SEMLEY

Hackney
Marsh

Wick
Com Ctr

1 ADELAIDE CT
2 CASTLE CL
3 BRENTON CT
4 TYNTE CT
5 SALISBURY CT
6 HILLYFIELD CL
7 BERESFORD CT

LONGLAND
CT

OLDBURY

MARSH HILL

HUMBERTON

CHELMER RD

B112

3

PO

17

A106

HIG

85

H

Homerton

City &
Hackney

ORIEL RD

HASSETT RD

BALLANCE RD

KENWORTHY RD

EDMESTON

BUSHBERRY RD

BENN ST

A12

EASTWAY

Hackney
Wick

CHISELDON

CORSLEY

SOUTHMOOR WAY

WINDSOR WHARF

Gainsborough
Com Prim Sch

International
Broadcast
Centre

Atlas
Wharf

Vision Col
of Theology

Hackney
Wick

E15

2

WICK RD

A102

B113

WICK RD

A106

TRAFALGAR
MEWS

COUNTRY
WAY

BUXHALL CRES

ETON

BARTRIP

LAWINGTON

BRINKWORTH
WAY

BEANACRE CL

TROWBRIDGE RD

FELSTEAD ST

WHITE POST LA

QUEENS
YD

Hackney
Wick

Hackney
Tower Hamlets

113

HARTLAKE RD

BLOCKFIELD RD

ANNIS RD

CADOGAN TERR

COWDRY RD

40

RISEHOLME

CADOGAN CL

Victoria Park Ind Ctr

WHITE POST LA

ROTHBURY RD

TREGO RD

Hamlet
Ind Ctr

OMEGA
WORKS

Vittoria
Wharf

Old
Fort
Lock

9

Well Street
Common

Cardinal
Pole RC
Sch

QUEENS
GATE
VILLAS

GUINNESS CL

TYSSON RD

Tenn Cts

Bwg Gn

ST MARK'S
GATE

WINFORD HO

Sp Gd

40

WANSBECK RD

WYKE RD

MONIER RD

ROACH RD

PEACH RD

SHED RD

STOUR RD

DACE RD

BREAM

Swan
Wharf

Crown
Wharf

84

Victoria Park

36

Victoria
Fntn

A

ARTILLERY HO 1
PINE HO 2
ARMOURY HO 3
CONNAUGHT WORKS 4

26

B

37

C

CANDY

RUSTON

SYCAMORE

EAST

CROWN

MAVERTON
RD

Lea Valley Wk

Gunmakers
Gate

Royal

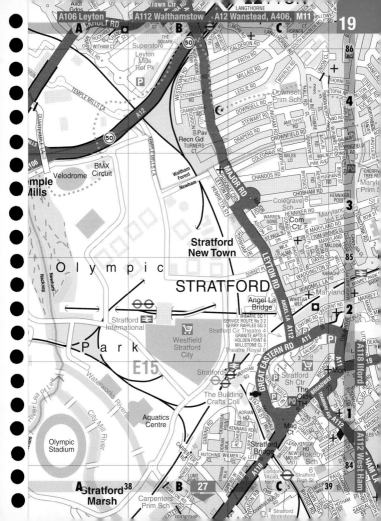

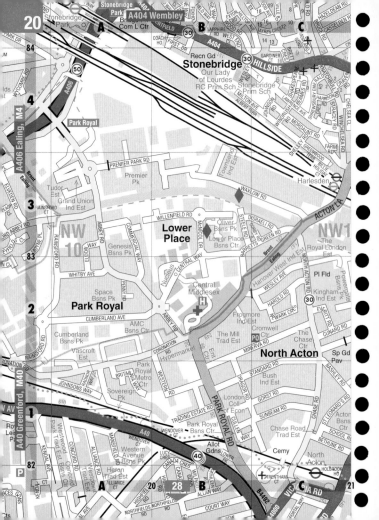

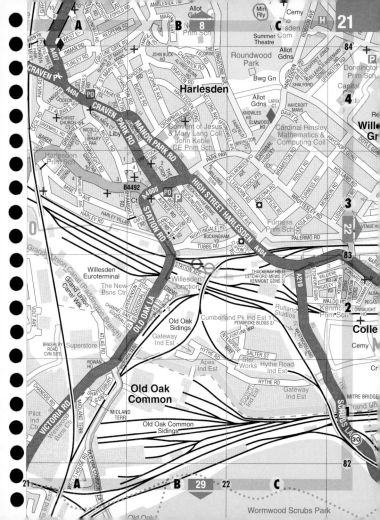

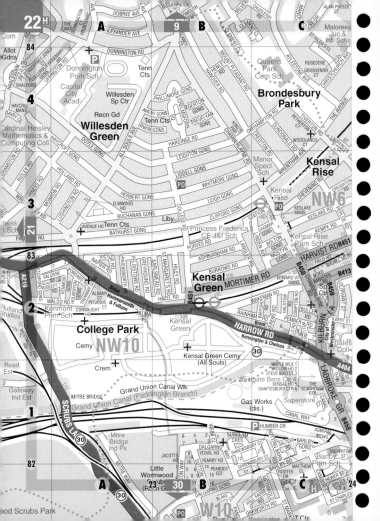

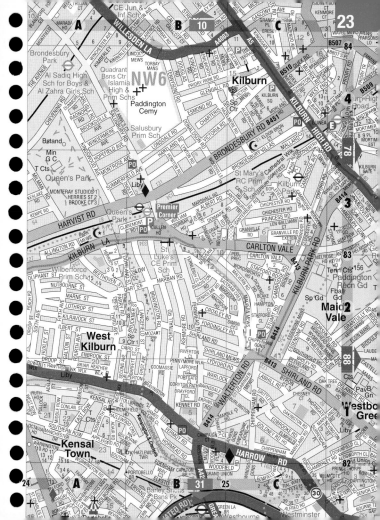

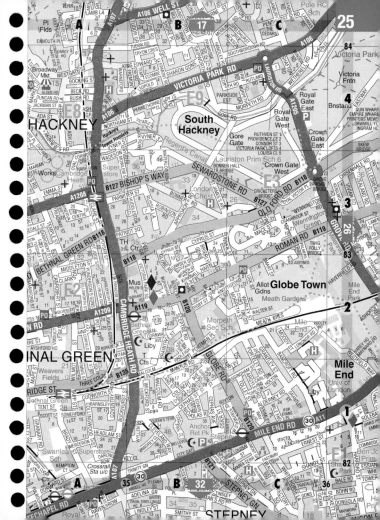

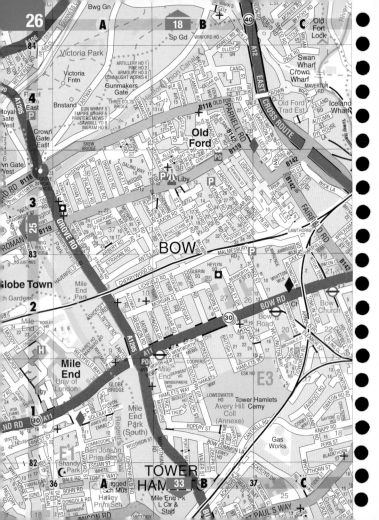

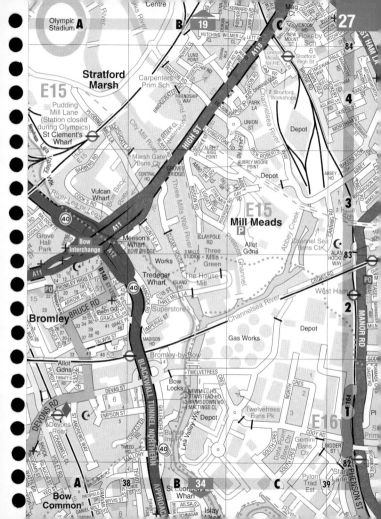

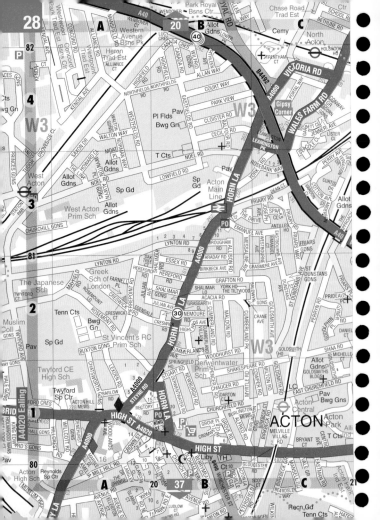

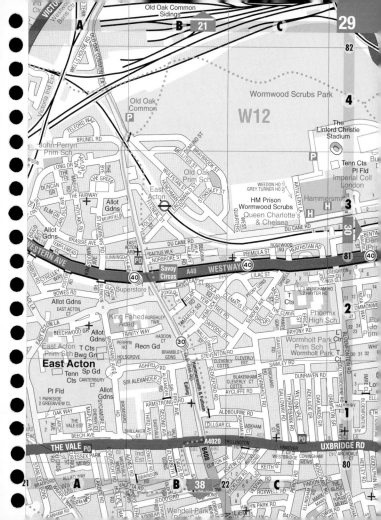

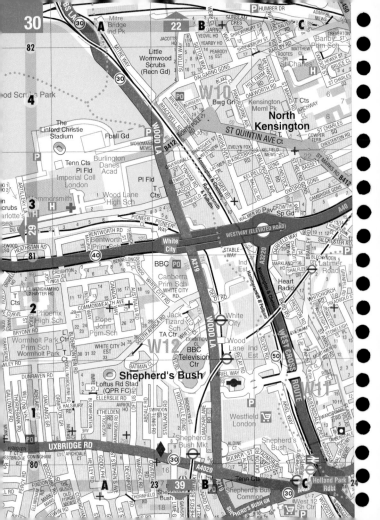

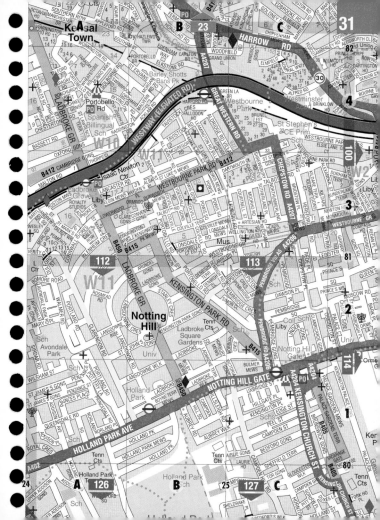

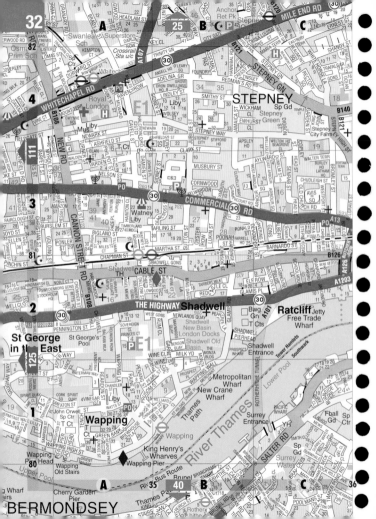

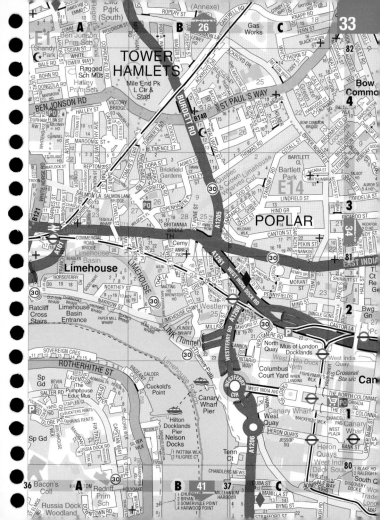

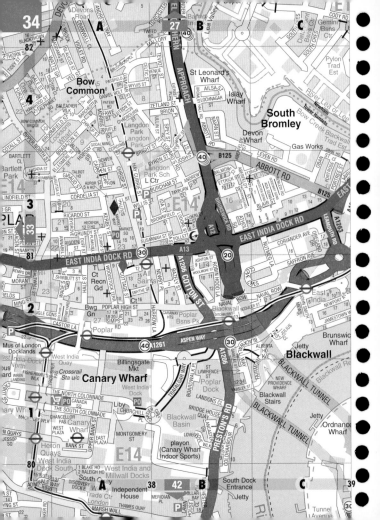

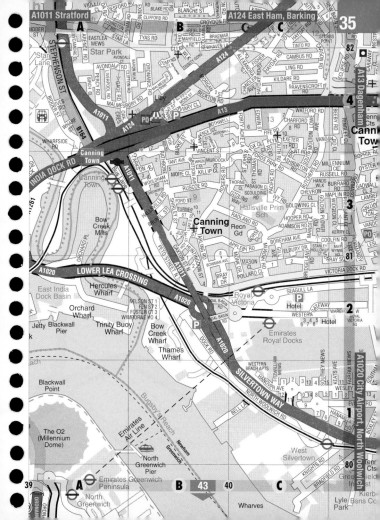

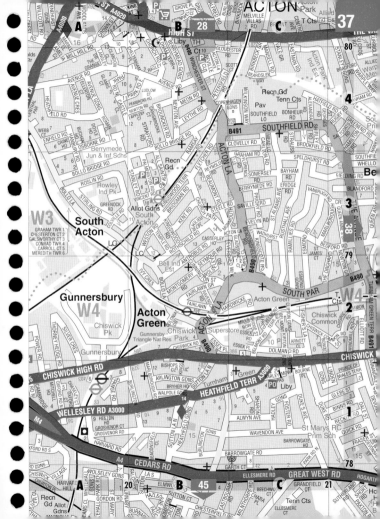

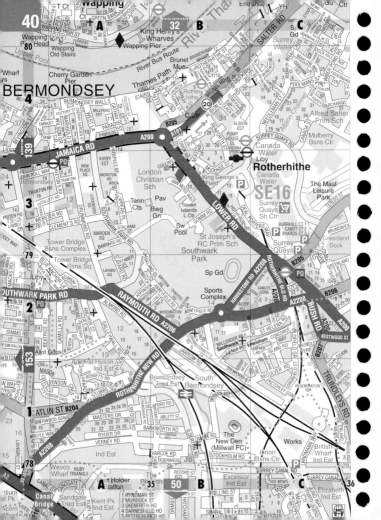

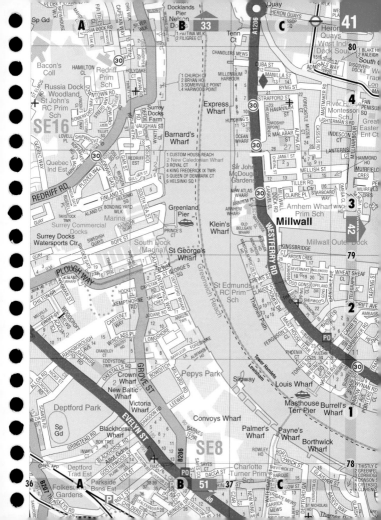

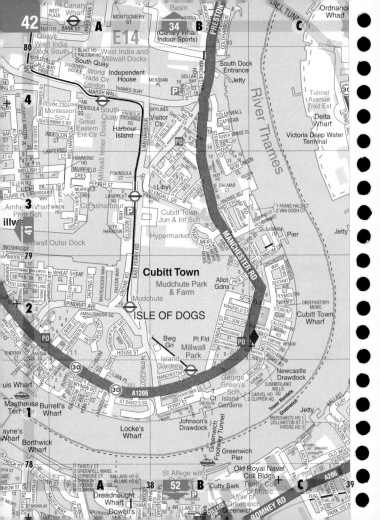

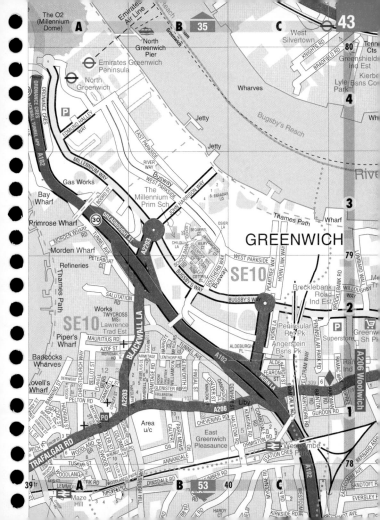

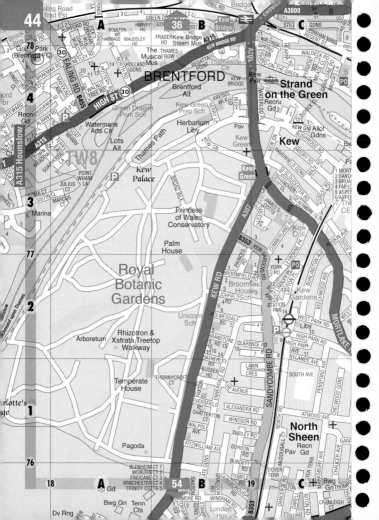

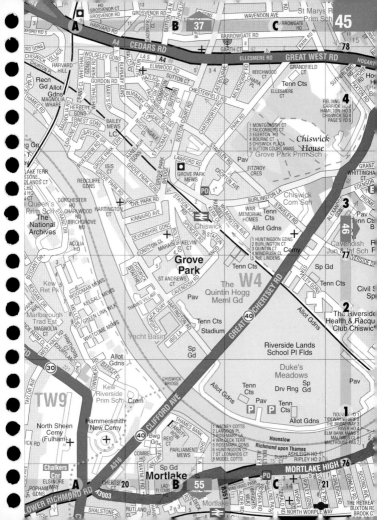

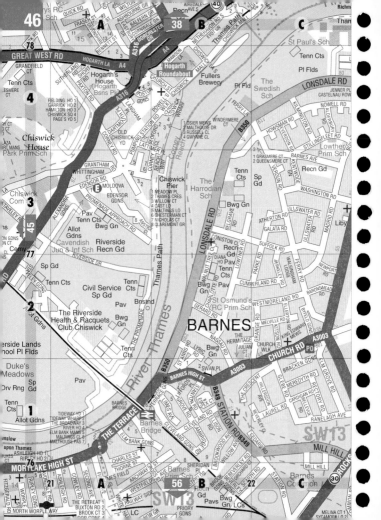

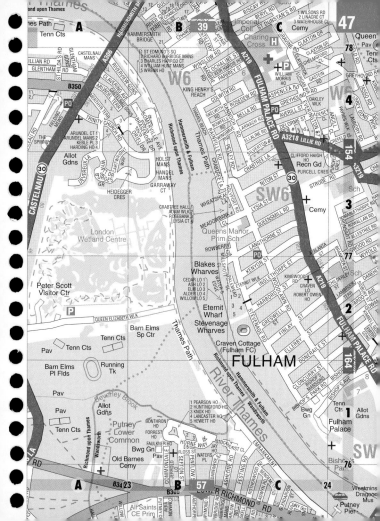

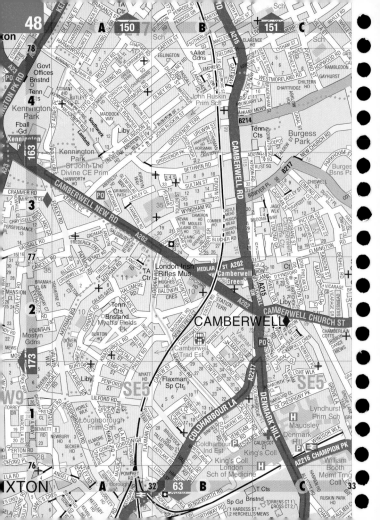

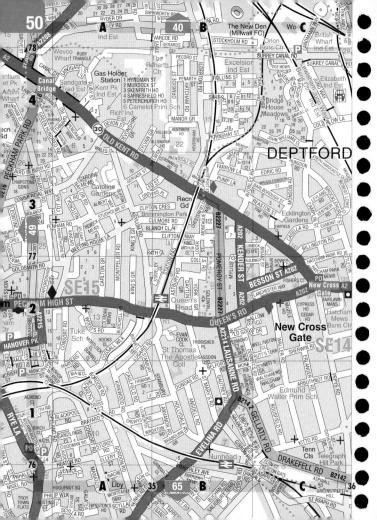

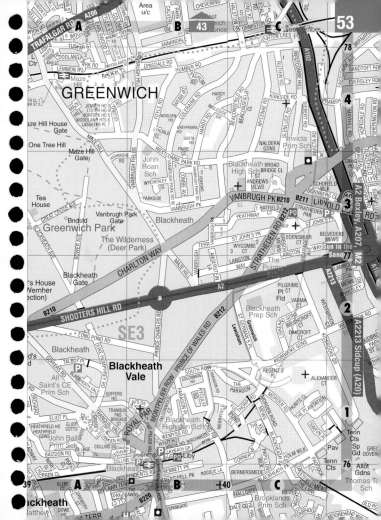

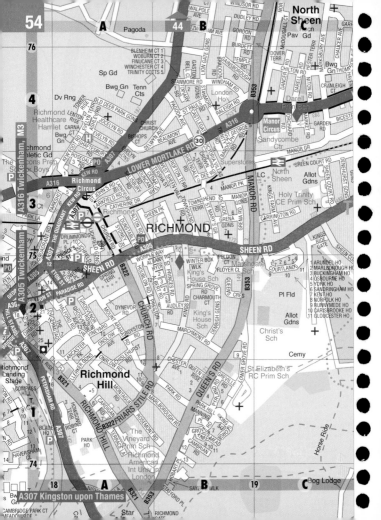

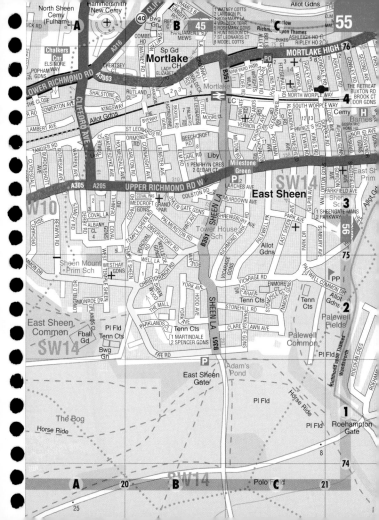

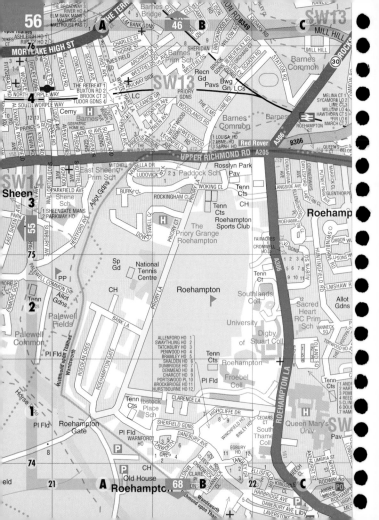

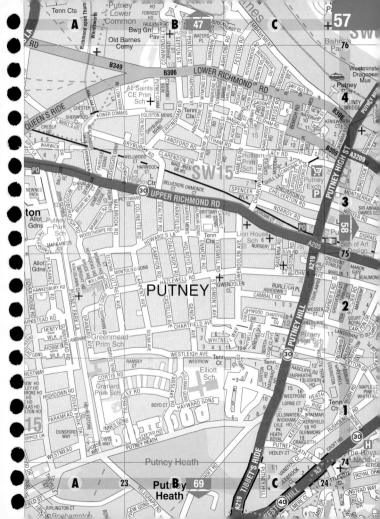

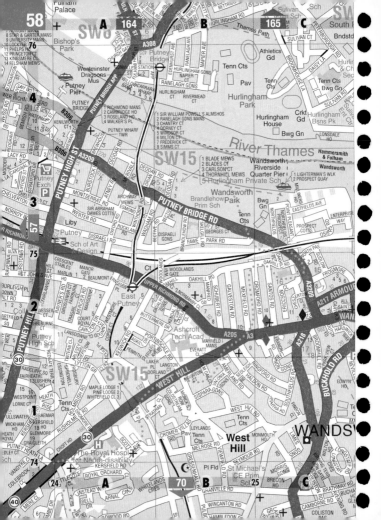

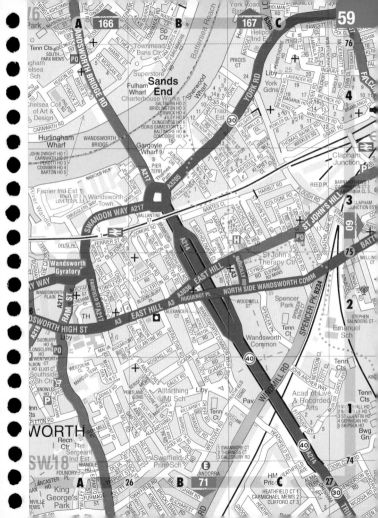

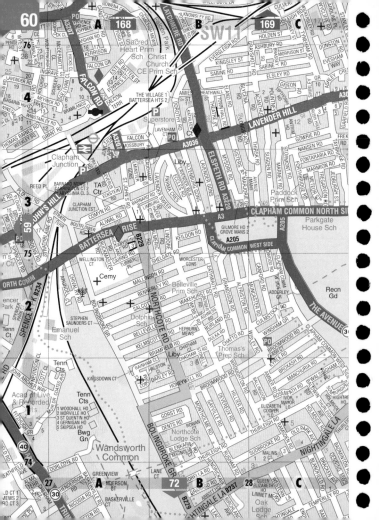

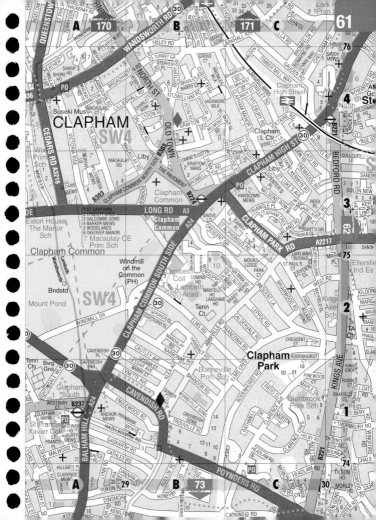

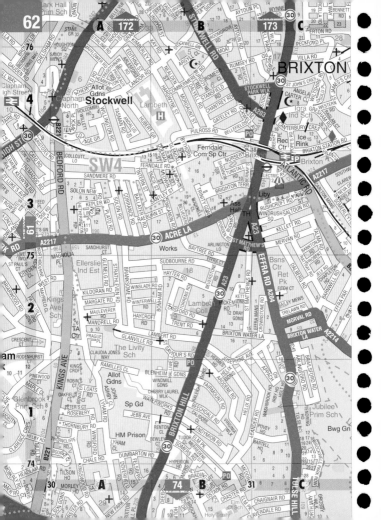

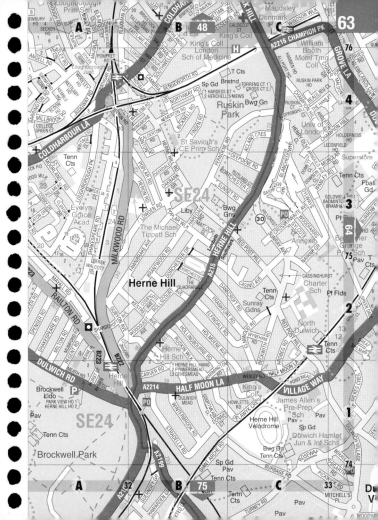

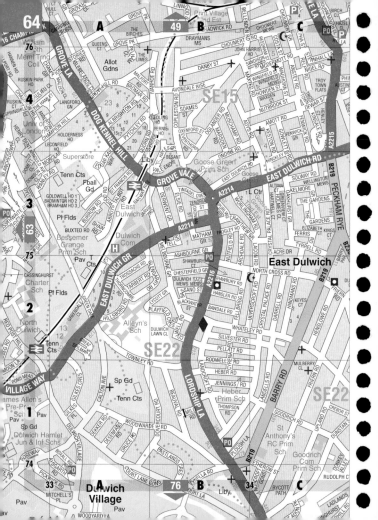

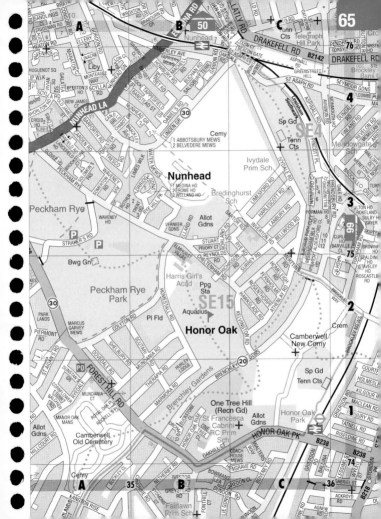

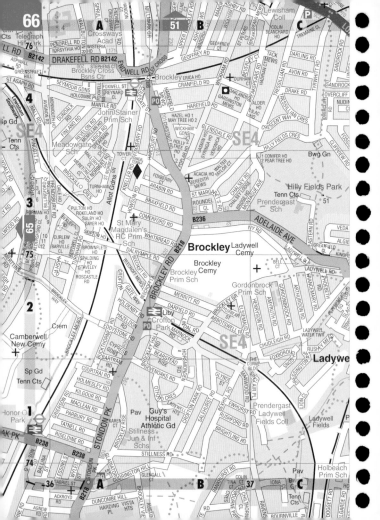

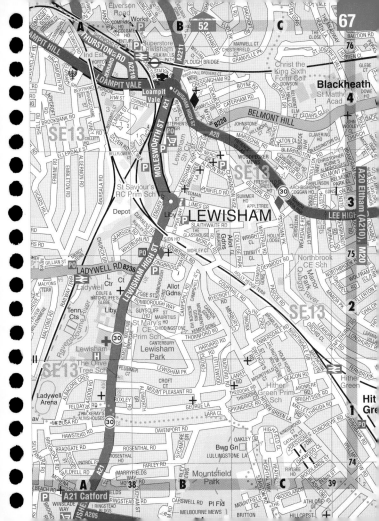

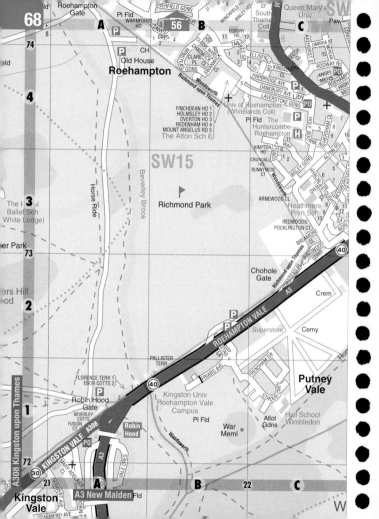

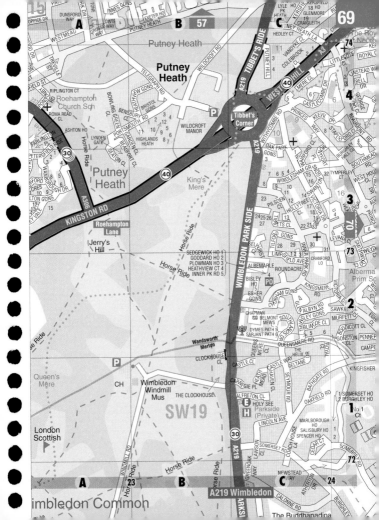

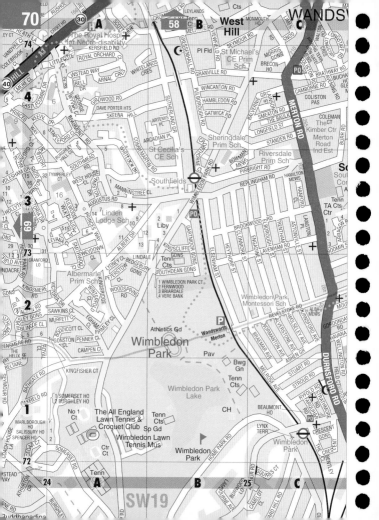

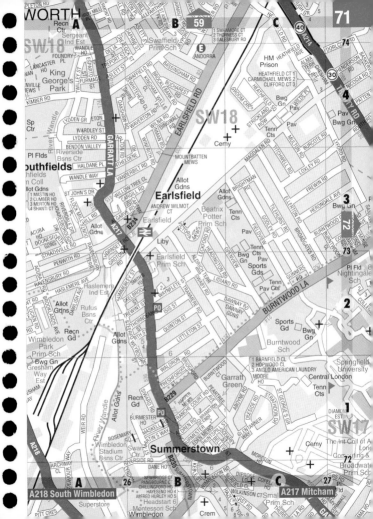

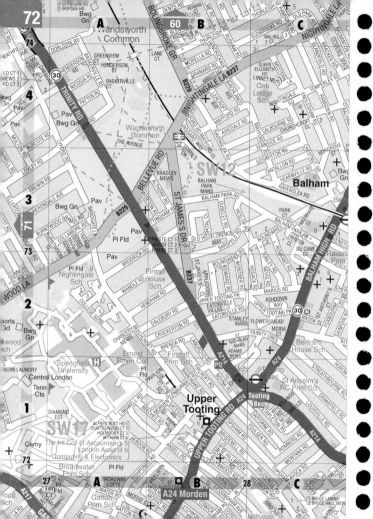

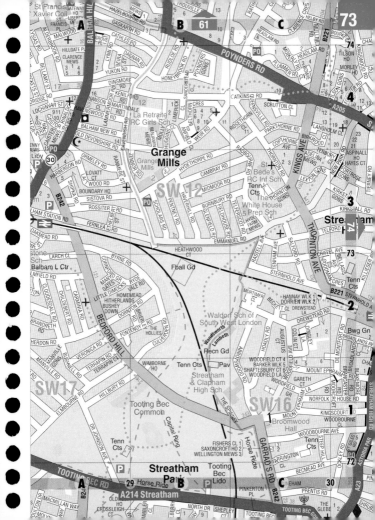

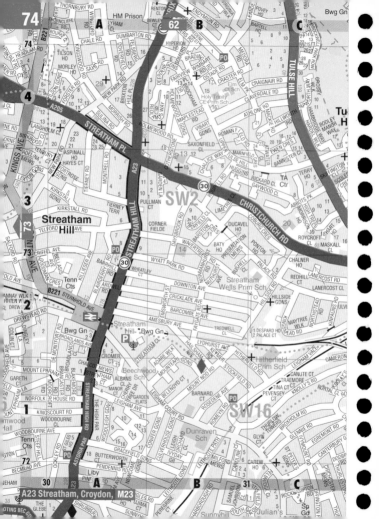

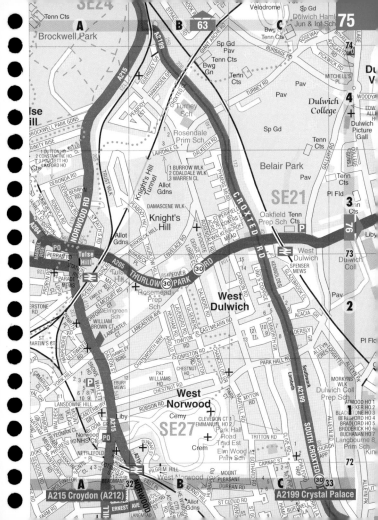

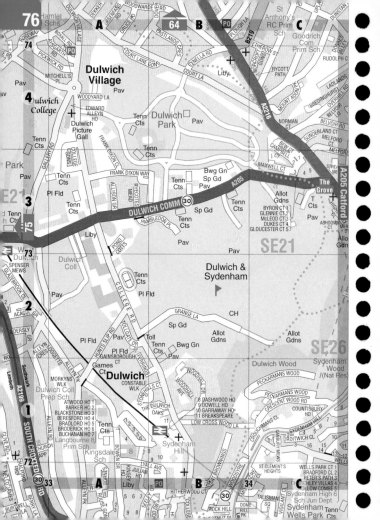

Key to central London map pages

78 79 St John's Wood	Primrose Hill **80 81** Regent's Park	**82 83** Somers Town	**Islington** **84 85** King's Cross	**86 87**
Maida Vale **88 89** Westbourne Green	Lisson Grove **90 91**	**92 93** Bloomsbury	St Pancras **Finsbury Shoreditch** **94 95**	**96 97** **98 99** **Bethnal Green**
Paddington **100 101**	**Marylebone** **102 103**	Fitzrovia **104 105** St Giles	Holborn **106 107** Strand	**108 109** **City** **110 111** Whitechapel Spitalfields
Notting Hill **112 113** Bayswater	**Kensington Gardens** **114 115** Knightsbridge	Mayfair **116 117** Hyde Park	**118 119** St James	Green Park **120 121** South Bank **122 123** **Southwark** **124 125** St George in the East
Kensington Holland Pk **126 127** West Kensington	South Kensington **128 129** Brompton	**Westminster** **130 131**	**132 133**	Waterloo **134 135** The Borough **136 137** **138 139** **Bermondsey**
140 141 Earl's Ct	**142 143** Belgravia	Victoria **144 145** Pimlico	**Lambeth** **146 147** Vauxhall	**Lambeth** Newington **148 149** **150 151** Kennington **152 153** Walworth
West Brompton **Chelsea** **154 155** Parsons Green Walham Green	**156 157** Battersea Park	**158 159** Nine Elms	**160 161**	South Lambeth **162 163**
Fulham **164 165**	**Battersea** **166 167**	**168 169**	**170 171**	**172 173** Stockwell

A10 A11 A13 A40 A3220 A4 A2 A202

Congestion Charge Zone

Additional symbols on enlarged maps

All other symbols may be found on page VI

Primary route – single, dual carriageway	**Congestion Charge Zone** boundary Streets within the zone are outlined in green – for further information call 0845 900 1234
A road – single, dual carriageway	
B road	**Public building**
Through route	**Railway or bus station building**
Minor road	
One way street	**Place of interest**
No access in direction shown	**E 🏛 🎭** Embassy, museum, theatre

The map scale on the pages numbered in red is 7 inches to 1 mile
11.04 cm to 1 km • 1:9051

0	220yds	½ mile

0	125m	250m	375m	**500m**

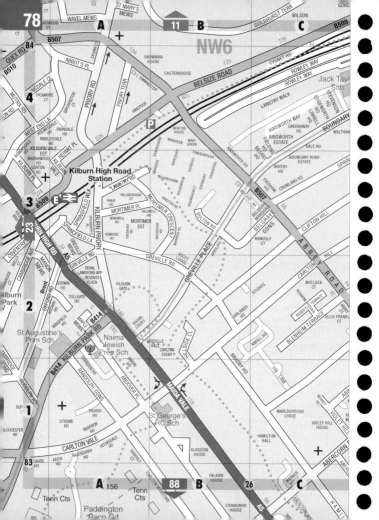

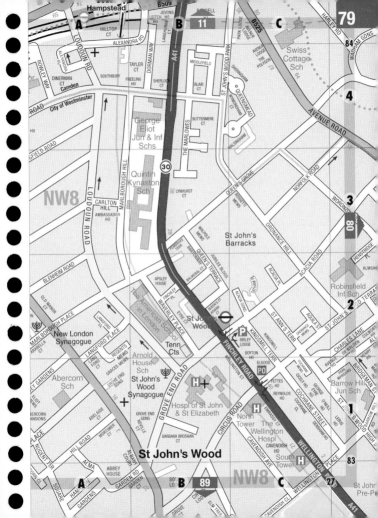

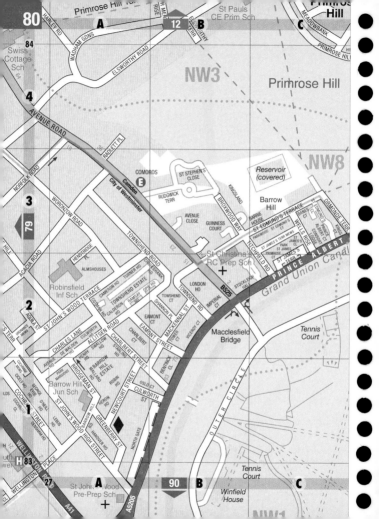

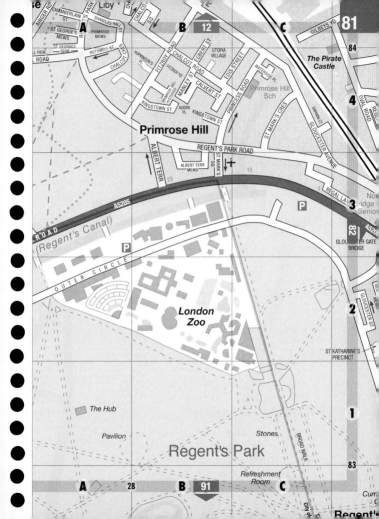

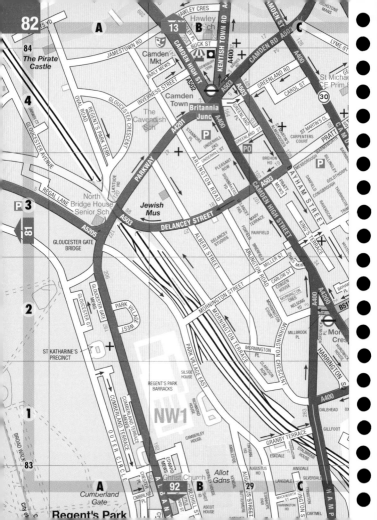

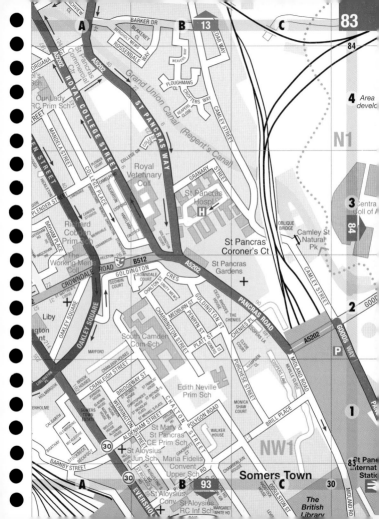

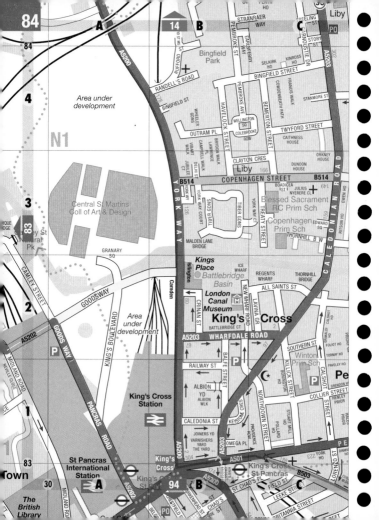

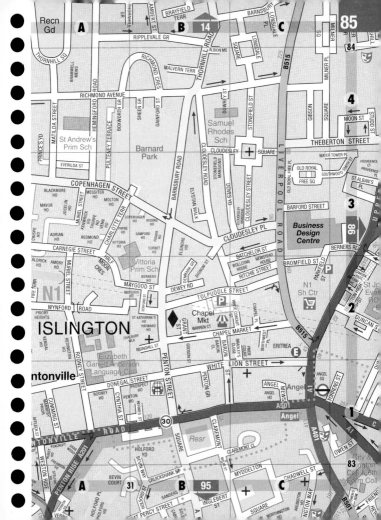

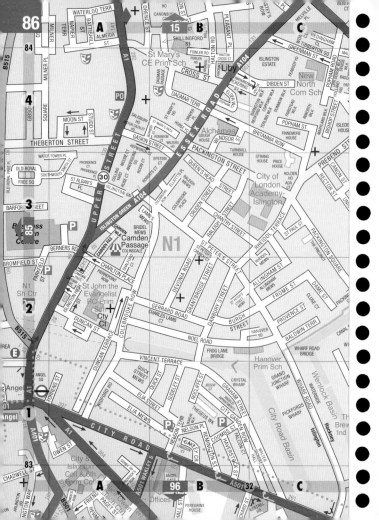

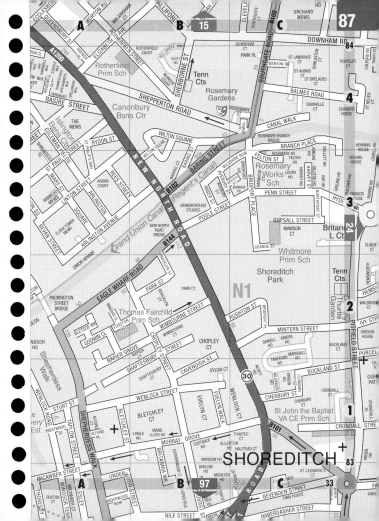

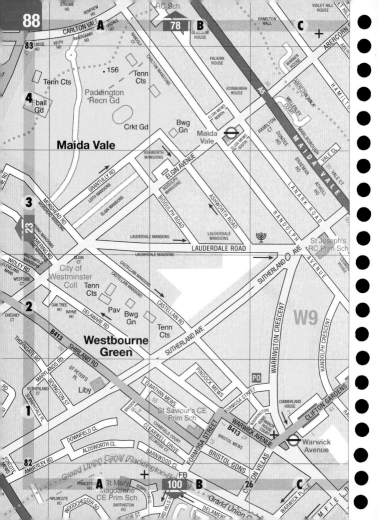

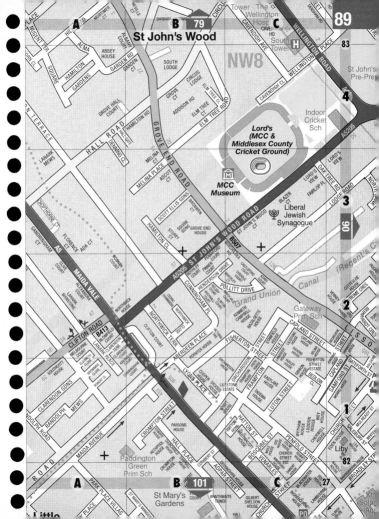

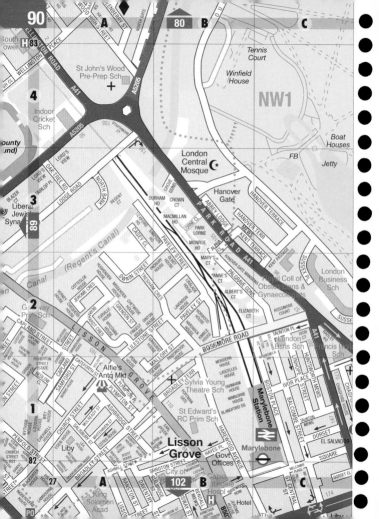

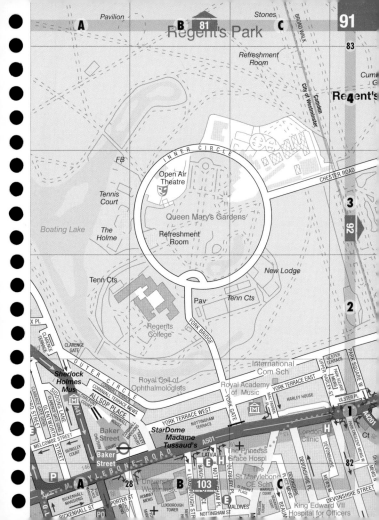

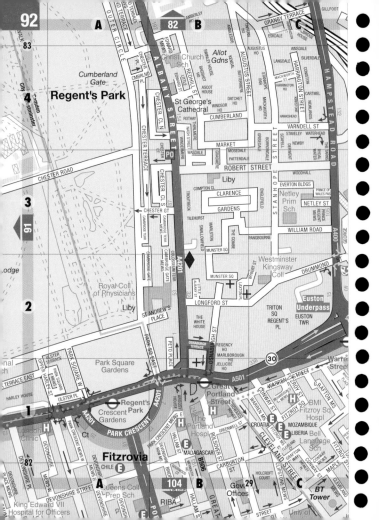

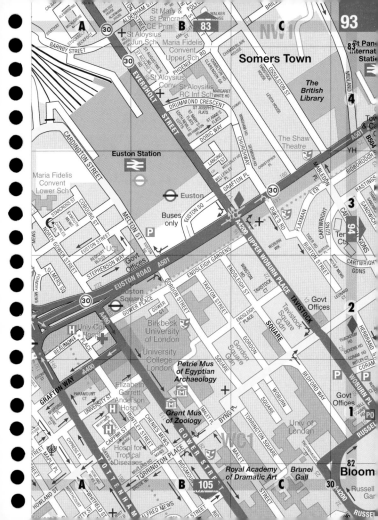

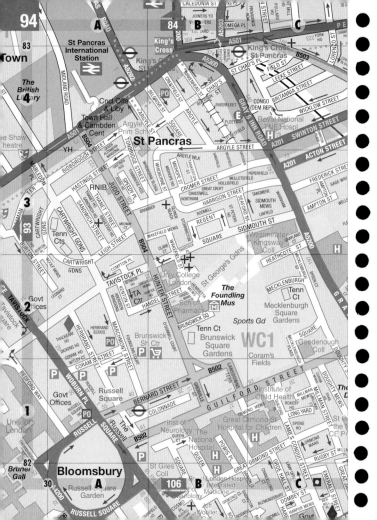

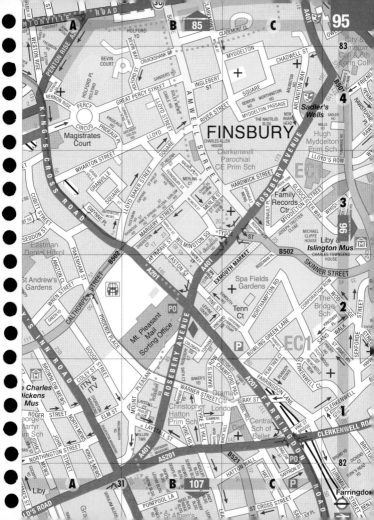

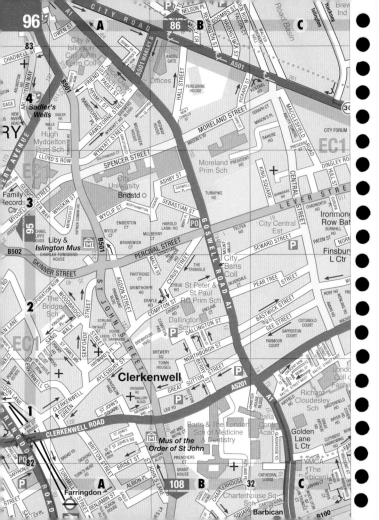

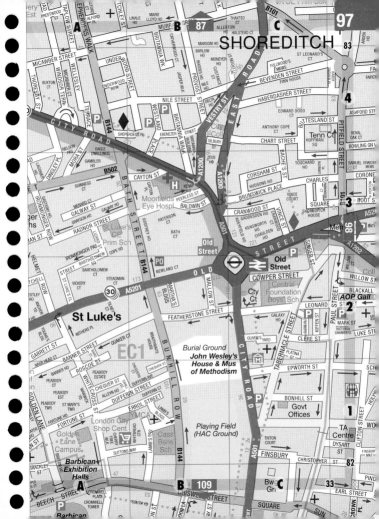

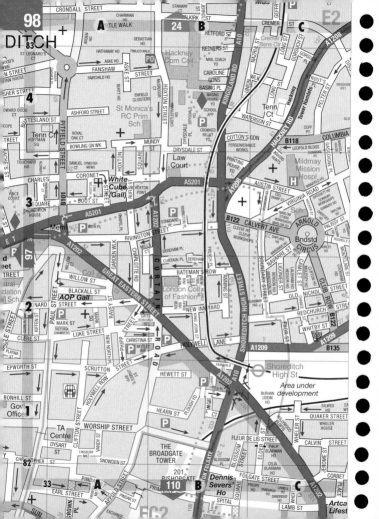

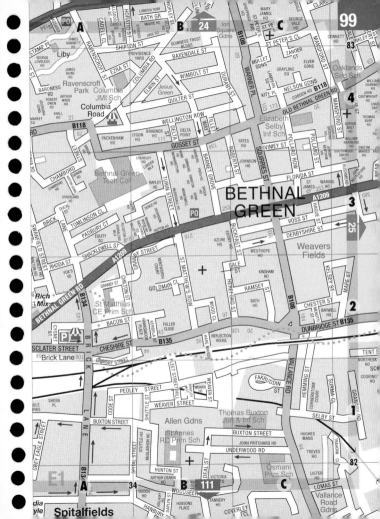

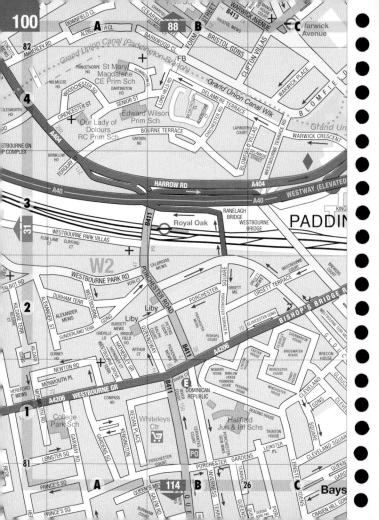

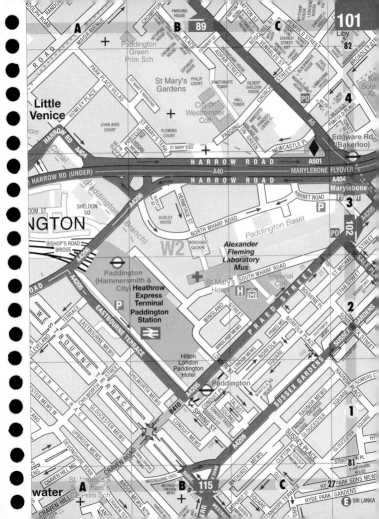

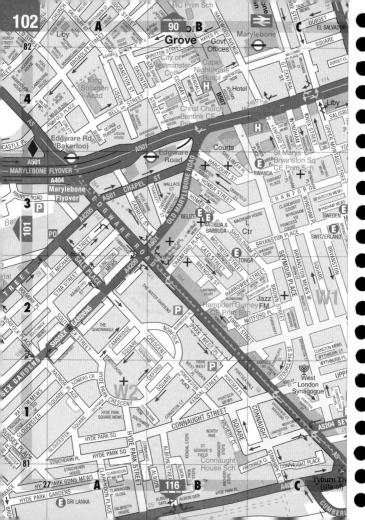

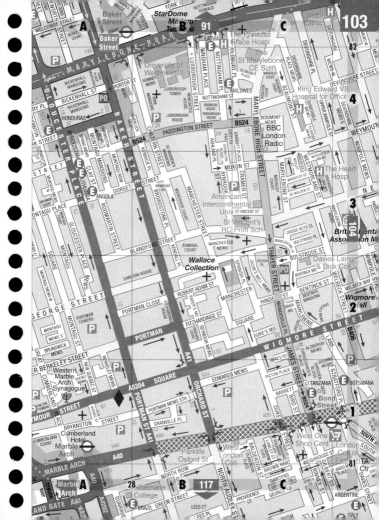

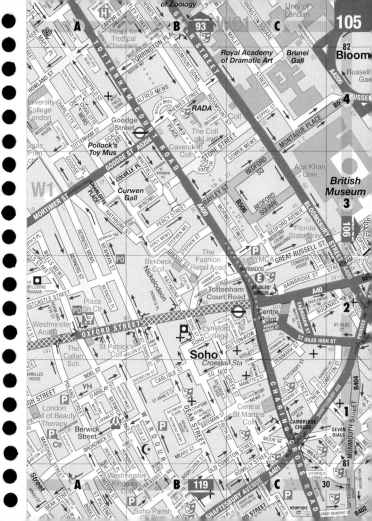

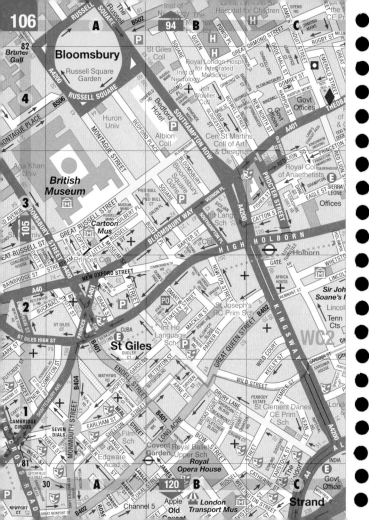

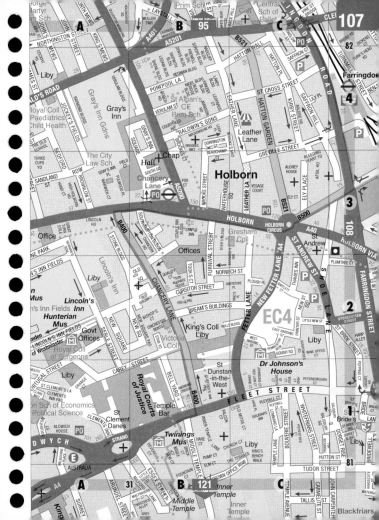

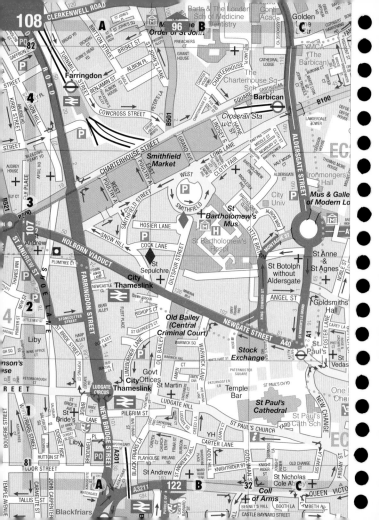

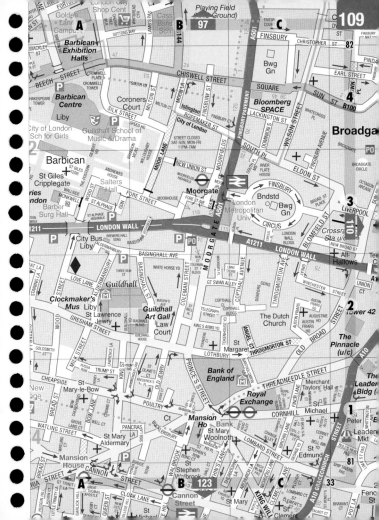

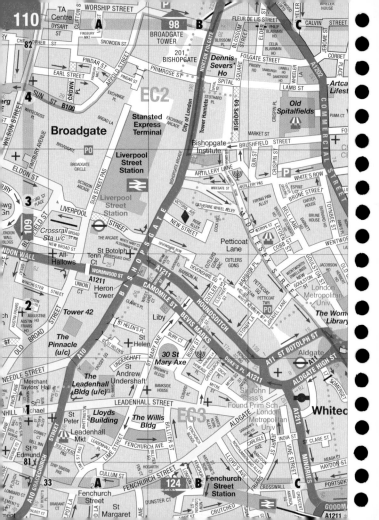

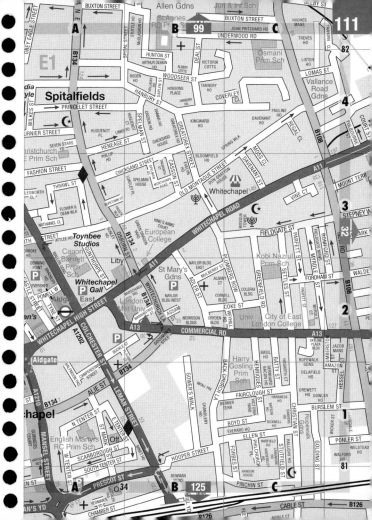

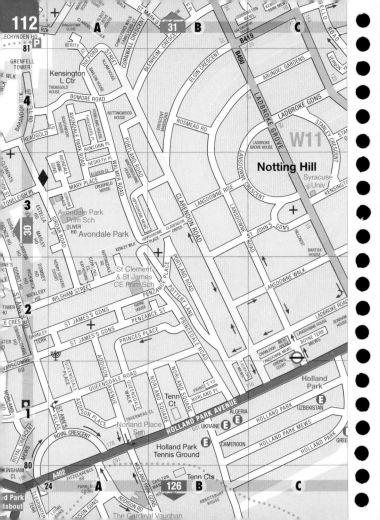

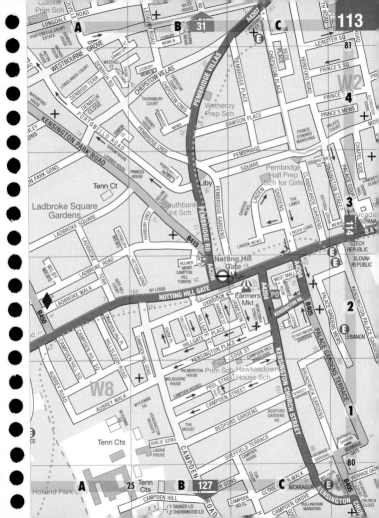

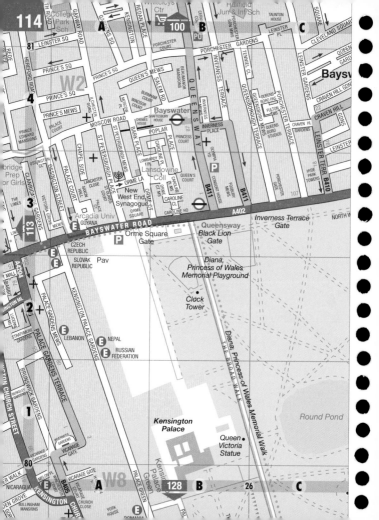

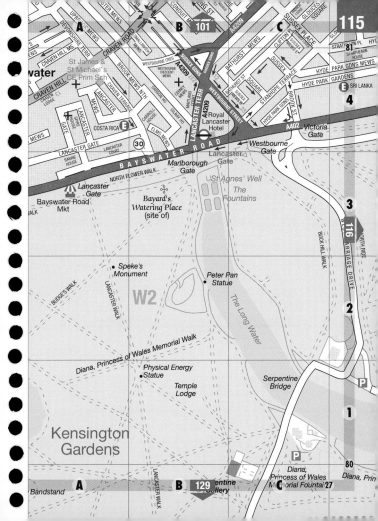

A B 101 C SUSSEX PLACE GLOUCES. SQUARE

UPPER R MEWS

DEVONSHIRE TERR.

CRAVEN HILL MS

CRAVEN ROAD CRAVEN ROAD

SMALLBROOK MEWS

CONDUIT ING ST.

A4209 A4209

BATHURST MEWS

STRATH 81 HYC

STRATHEARN HOUSE

ater

St James &
St Michael's
CE Prim Sch

CRAVEN HILL

CRAVEN
LODGE

BROOK MEWS NTH

CRAVEN TERRACE

WESTBOURNE CRES

GARSON RD

WESTBOURNE
CRESCENT
MEWS

SUSSEX GDNS

LANCASTER TERR

BATHURST ST

SUSSEX
SQUARE

CLIFTON
MEWS

SUSSEX MEWS W.

HYDE PARK GDNS MEWS

STANHOPE TERRACE

HYDE PARK GARDENS

E SRI LANKA

LANCASTER
MEWS

LANCASTER
GATE

COSTA RICA E

ELMS MEWS

LANCASTER TERR

WESTBOURNE STREET

HYDE PARK GDNS

BROOK ST.

4

LANCASTER GATE LANCASTER
COURT

BAYRIE
HOUSE

30

Royal Lancaster
Hotel

A402 Victoria
Gate

Westbourne
Gate

BAYSWATER ROAD

Lancaster
Gate

Lancaster
Gate

Marlborough
Gate

Westbourne
Gate

NORTH FLOWER WALK

St Agnes' Well

The
Fountains

Lancaster
Gate

Bayswater Road
Mkt

WALK

Bayard's
Watering Place
(site of)

3

BUCK HILL WALK

116

W CARRIAGE DRIVE

NORTH RIDE

BUDGE'S WALK

LANCASTER WALK

Speke's
Monument

W2

Peter Pan
Statue

The Long Water

2

Diana, Princess of Wales Memorial Walk

Physical Energy
Statue

Serpentine
Bridge

P

Temple
Lodge

Kensington
Gardens

1

LANCASTER WALK

Diana,
Princess of Wales
Memorial Fountai

P

80

Diana, Prin

Bandstand

A B 129 entine
Gallery

C 27

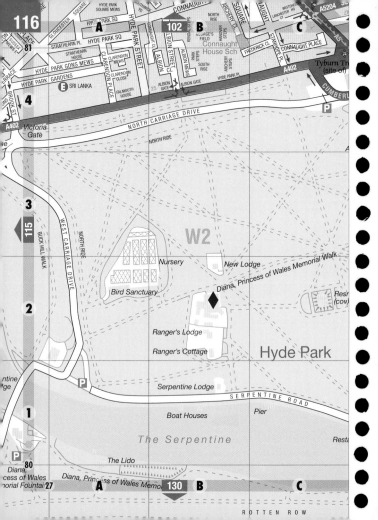

GLOUCESTER SQUARE

HYDE PARK SQUARE MEWS

PLACE

81

A

HYDE PK SQ

HYDE PARK SQUARE

STRATHEARN PL

STRATHEARN HOUSE

HYDE PARK STREET

CLARENDON MEWS

CLARENDON CLOSE

CLARENDON PLACE

HYDE PARK GDNS MEWS

HYDE PARK GARDENS

BROOK ST

E SRI LANKA

FALMOUTH HOUSE

CONNAUGHT

102

B

ALBION STREET

ALBION CLOSE

ALBION MEWS

25

ALBION GATE

SOUTH RISE

KENDAL STREET

NORTH RISE

ALBION GATE

ALBION STREET

HYDE PARK PL

4

GEORGE'S FIELD

HANOVER STEPS

ARCHERY CL

SQUARE

AUGHT

WESTMINSTER

LANCASTER HO

CONNAUGHT PLACE

FREDERICK CL

STANHOPE STEPS

ARCHERY STEPS

C

A5204

A45

Connaught
House Sch

Tyburn Tr
(site of)

A402

CUMBER

Victoria
Gate

A402

P

NORTH CARRIAGE DRIVE

NORTH RIDE

3

115

WEST CARRIAGE DRIVE

BUCK HILL WALK

NORTH RIDE

W2

Nursery

Bird Sanctuary

New Lodge

Diana, Princess of Wales Memorial Walk

Resr
(cov)

2

Ranger's Lodge

Ranger's Cottage

Hyde Park

ntine
ge

P

Serpentine Lodge

SERPENTINE ROAD

1

Boat Houses

Pier

The Serpentine

Resta

P

80

Diana,
cess of Wales
norial Fountai 27

The Lido

Diana, Princess of Wales Memo

A

130

B

C

ROTTEN ROW

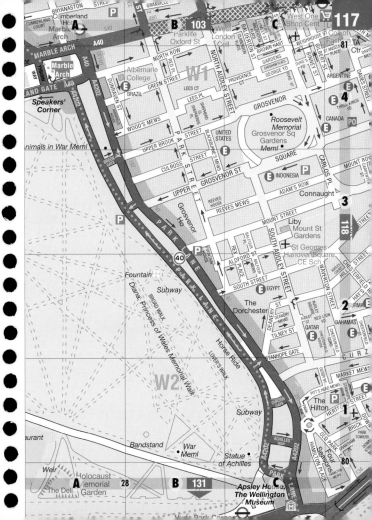

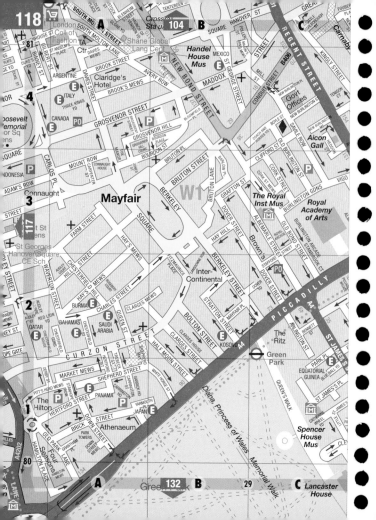

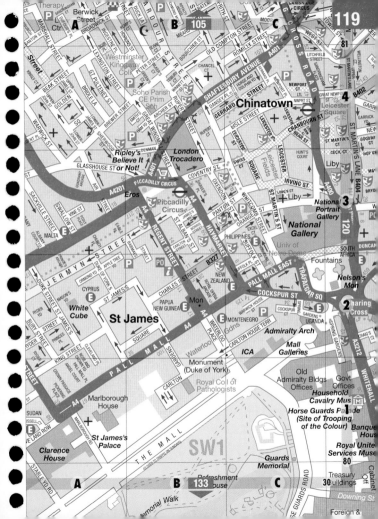

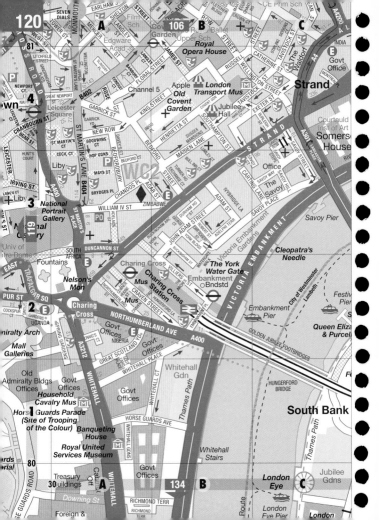

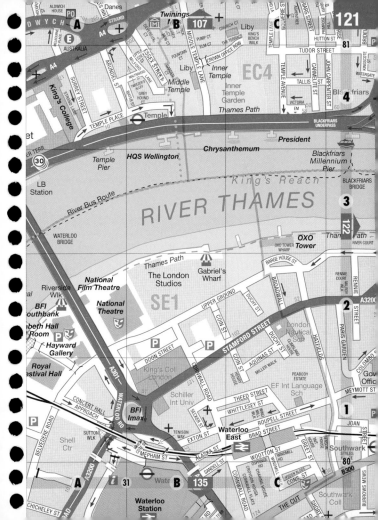

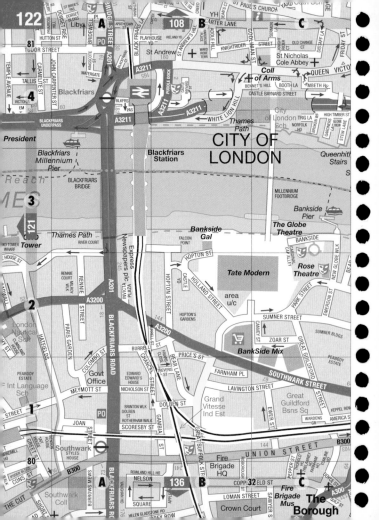

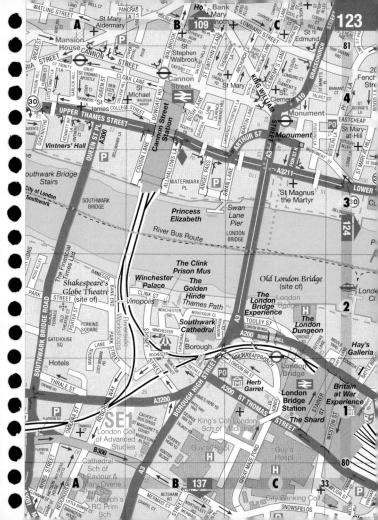

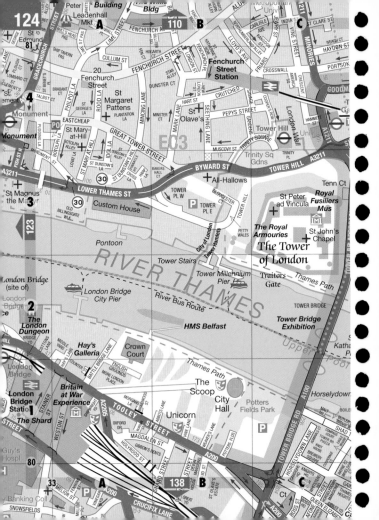

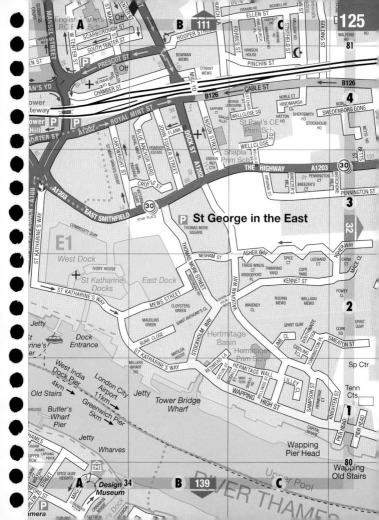

St George in the East

E1

West Dock

St Katharine Docks

East Dock

Hertmitage Basin

Hermitage Prim Sch

River Thames

Upper Pool

Wapping Pier Head

Wapping Old Stairs

80

Tower Bridge Wharf

London City Airport 11km

Greenwich Pier 5km

West India Dock Pier 4km

Old Stairs

Butler's Wharf Pier

Jetty

Wharves

Design Museum 34

Spice Quay Heights

Dock Entrance

St Katharine's Way

Mews Street

Cloysters Green

Saint Anthony's Cl.

Mauldins Green

Burr Close

Matilda House

Millers Wharf

Stockholm Way

Redmead La

Hermitage Wall

Wapping High St

Lilley Cl.

Sampson St

Hermitage

Knighten St

Pier Head

Tenn Cts

1

2

3

4

32

30

Asher Way

China Ct

Mace Cl.

Fowey Cl.

Cork Sq

Spirit Quay

Smeaton St

Lime Cl.

Roding Mews

Welland Mews

Waveney Cl.

Kennet St

Spice Ct

Leeward Ct

Cope Yard

Tamarind Yard

Trade Winds Ct

Bridgeport Pl.

Vaughan Way

Nesham St

Thomas More Square

Thomas More Street

Star Place

East Smithfield

A1203

The Highway A1203

Pennington St

Pennington Hill

Breezer's Hill

Breezer's Ct

Virginia St

Antrobus St

Betts St

Shapla Prim Sch

Ensign Ind Ctr

Wellclose St

St Paul's CE Prim Sch

Hindmarsh Cl.

Noble Ct

Swedenborg Gdns

Stockholm Ho

Shearsmith Ho

Hatton Ho

George Leybourne Ho

Sapphire Ct

Graces Alley

Fletcher Ho

Wellclose Sq

Cable St

B126

Royal Mint St

A1202

John Fisher St

Blue Anchor Yard

Peabody Estate

Swan Passage

Royal Mint Pl.

Victoria Pl.

Crofts St

Cartwright St

St Mark's Court

Ensign St

Dock St

A1202

Millpond

Chamber St

Prescot St

Yeoman's Row

Royal Mint St

Mansel Street

St Tenter St

W Tenter St

Scarborough St

South Tenter St

Guinness Court

Mansel St

English Martyrs RC Prim Sch

Hooper Street

Pinchin St

Cable St

Conant Mews

Bowman Mews

Ellen St

Forbes St

Hanson House

Hill Ho

Stutfield St

Golding St

Walford Ho

111

81

139

A

B

C

A

B

C

30

Tower Gateway

Tower Hill

Porter St

A100

St Katharine's Way

Commodity Quay

Ivory House

St Katharine Docks

Jetty

Catherine's

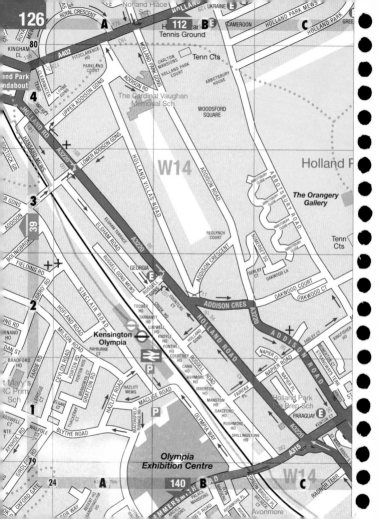

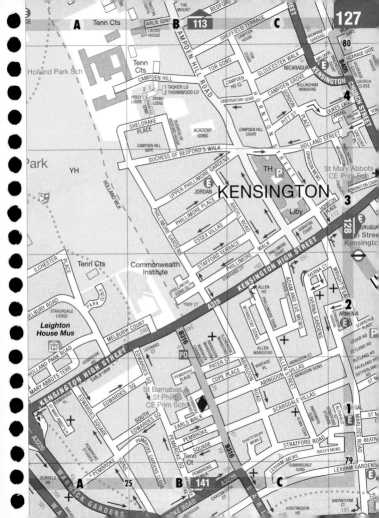

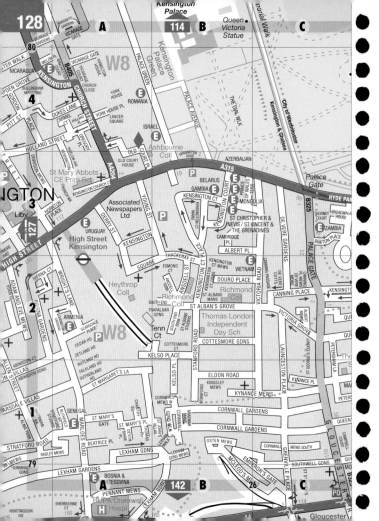

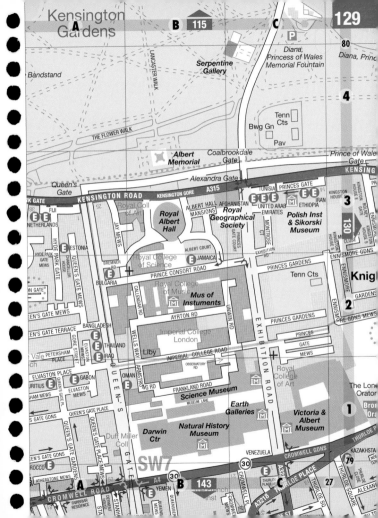

80

Bandstand

LANCASTER WALK

Serpentine Gallery

P

Diana, Princess of Wales Memorial Fountain

Diana, Princ

4

THE FLOWER WALK

Tenn Cts

Bwg Gn

Pav

Albert Memorial

Coalbrookdale Gate

Queen's Gate

Alexandra Gate

Prince of Wale Gate

KENSING

K GATE

FIJI

E

KENSINGTON ROAD

KENSINGTON GORE

A315

TUNISIA PRINCES GATE

Royal Coll of Art

ALBERT HALL MANSIONS

AFGHANISTAN

UNITED ARAB EMIRATES

E E E

Royal Geographical Society

IRAN ETHIOPIA

E E

KINGSTON HOUSE E

3

NETHERLANDS

E

JAY MEWS

Royal Albert Hall

Polish Inst & Sikorski Museum

130

CLOSE

ESTONIA

E

BREMNER RD

Royal College of Science

ALBERT COURT

MONTROSE CT

PRINCES COURT

EXHIBITION RD

PRINCES GARDENS

ENNISMORE GDNS

HYDE PARK GATE MEWS

QUEEN'S GATE

E

JAMAICA

BULGARIA

PRINCE CONSORT ROAD

Royal College of Music

Tenn Cts

Knig

CALENDAR RD

Mus of Instuments

ENNISMORE

GARDENS

QUEEN'S GATE MEWS

BANGLADESH

E

AYRTON RD

UNWIN RD

PRINCES GARDENS

E GONS MEWS

2

THAILAND

E

IRAQ

WELLS WAY

Imperial College London

E

X

H

I

B

I

T

I

O

N

R

O

A

D

PRINCES GATE MEWS

QUEEN'S GATE TERRACE

Liby

IMPERIAL COLLEGE ROAD

Vale PETERSHAM PLACE

ELVASTON PLACE

GABON

E

ARMSTRONG RD

OBSERVATORY RD

Royal College of Art

+

AURITIUS

E

QUEEN'S GATE PLACE

ELVASTON MEWS

OMAN

FRANKLAND ROAD

The Lon Orator

1

SHAM MEWS

O

M

A

N

Science Museum

MUSEUM LANE

Bro Ora

'S GATE GDNS

ELVASTON PLACE

Q

U

E

E

N

'

S

Earth Galleries

Victoria & Albert Museum

MOROCCO

E

QUEEN'S GATE PLACE MEWS

Duff Miller Coll

Darwin Ctr

Natural History Museum

VENEZUELA

E

CROMWELL GDNS

THURLOE

KAZAKHSTA

79

EN'S GATE GARDENS

SW7

THURLOE PLACE

E

THURLOE CLOSE

ATHERSTONE MEWS

FAIRBRIAR RESIDENCE

DERWENT STANHOPE

CROMWELL ROAD

A4

30

YEMEN

30

A3

CROMWELL PL

QUEENS

A3218

THURLOE SQ

ALEXA

ench Inst

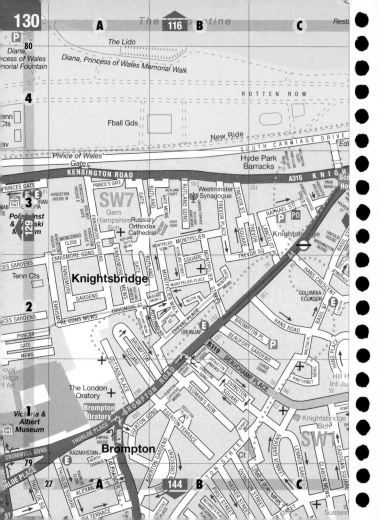

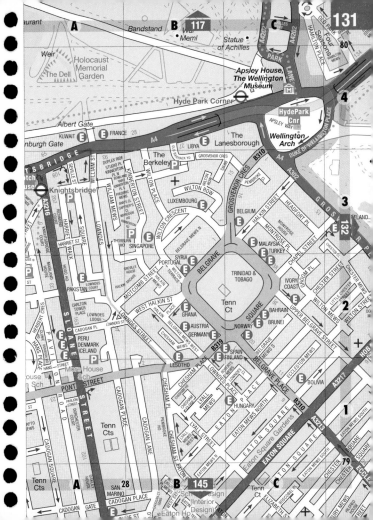

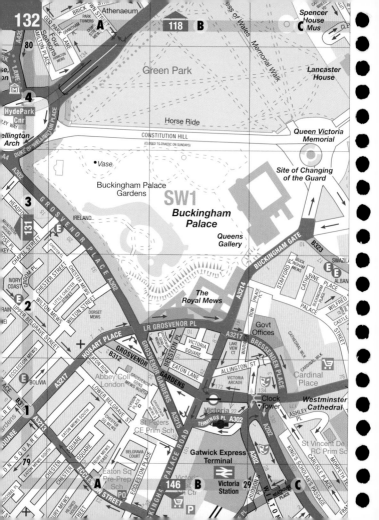

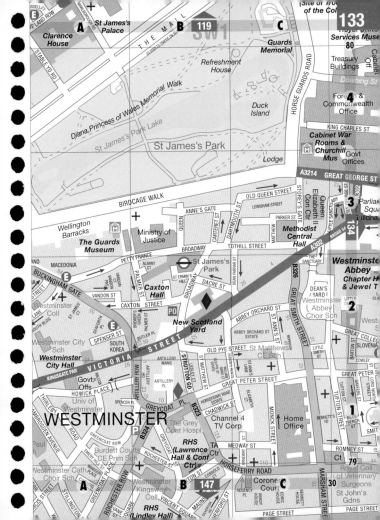

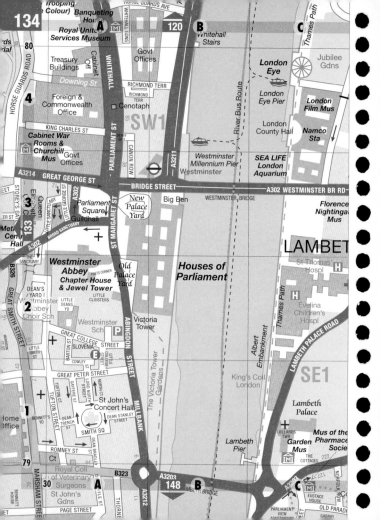

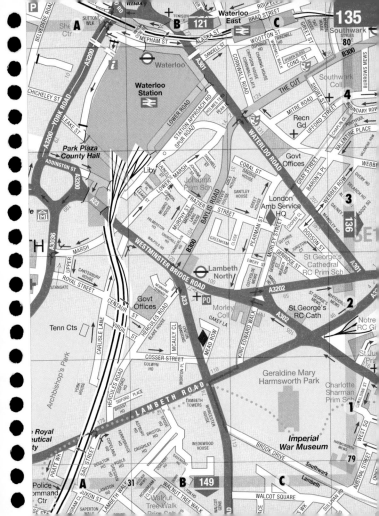

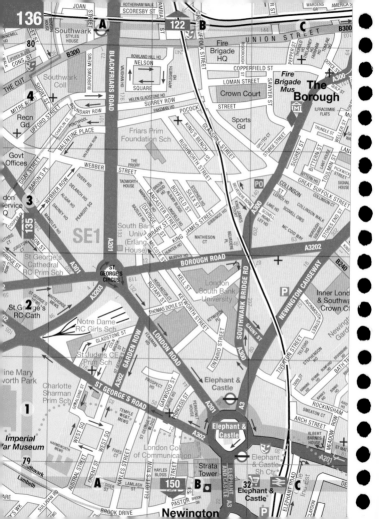

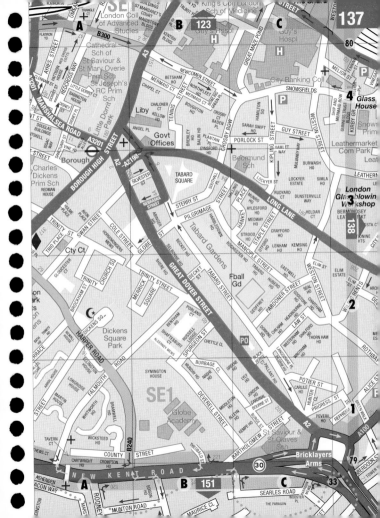

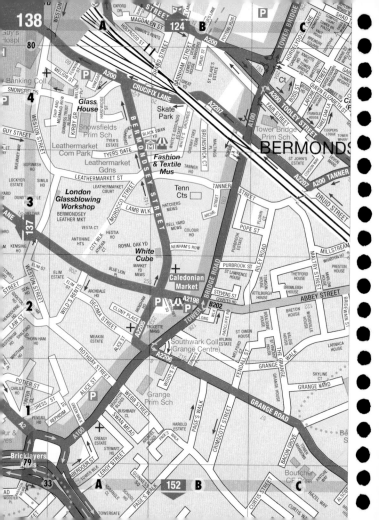

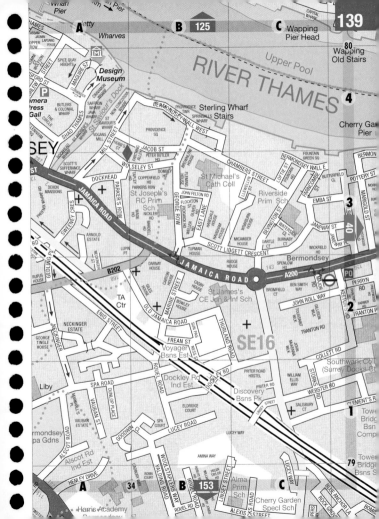

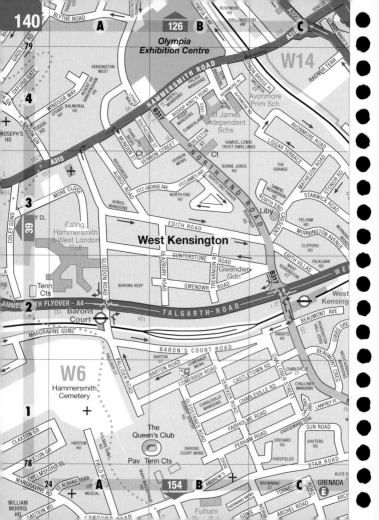

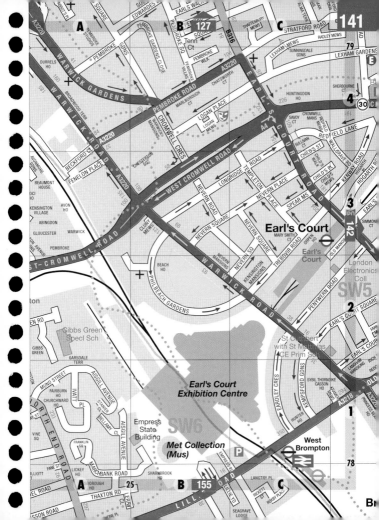

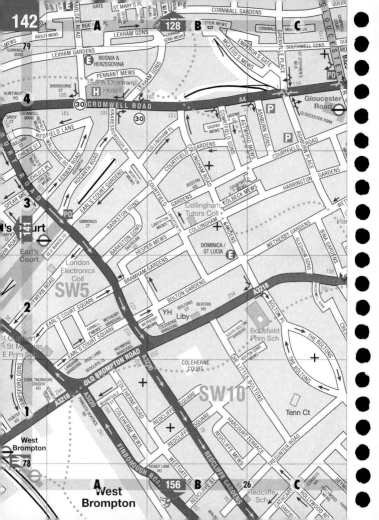

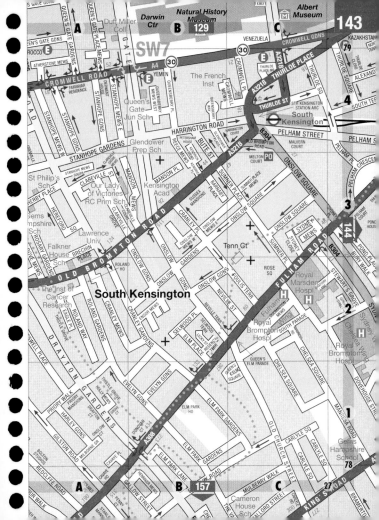

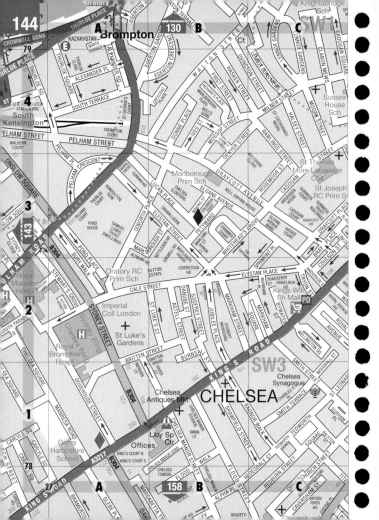

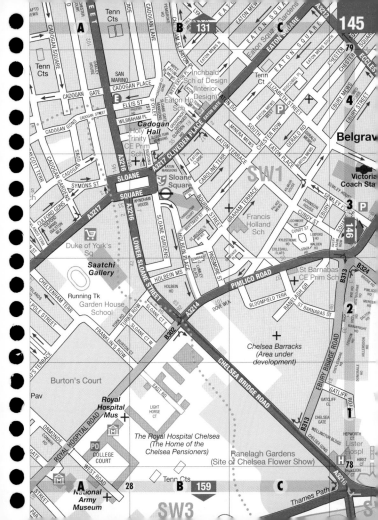

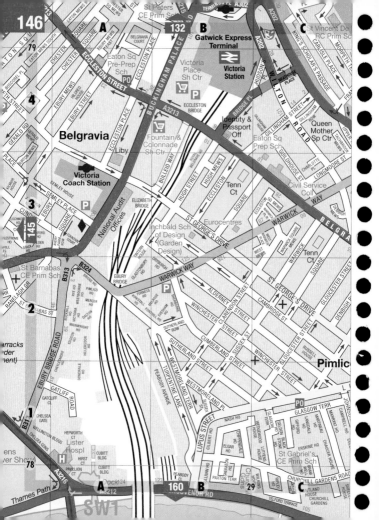

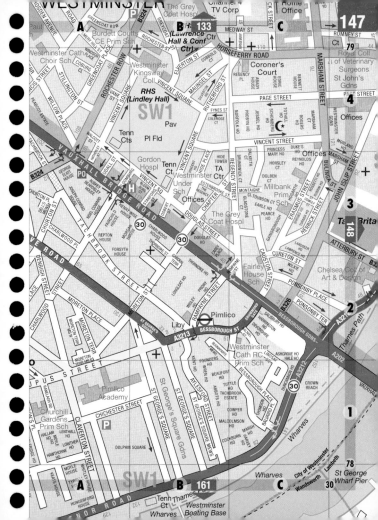

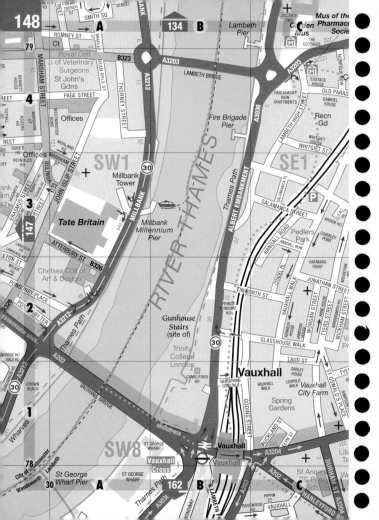

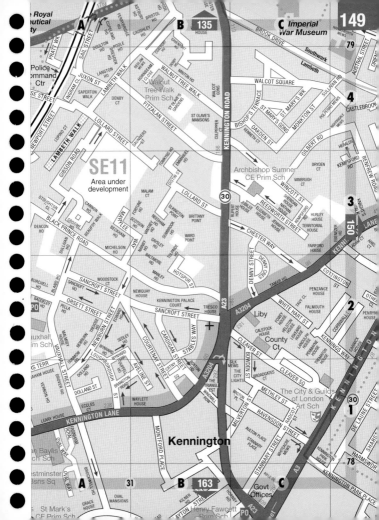

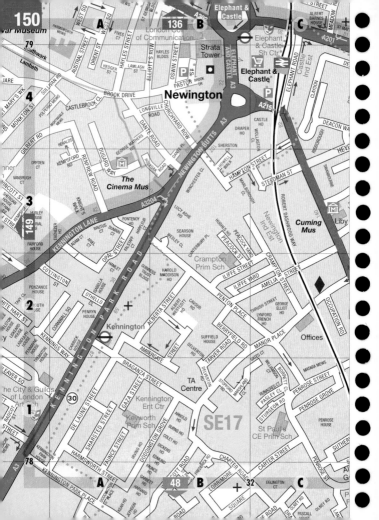

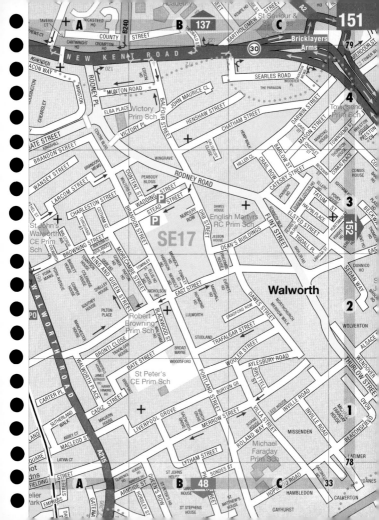

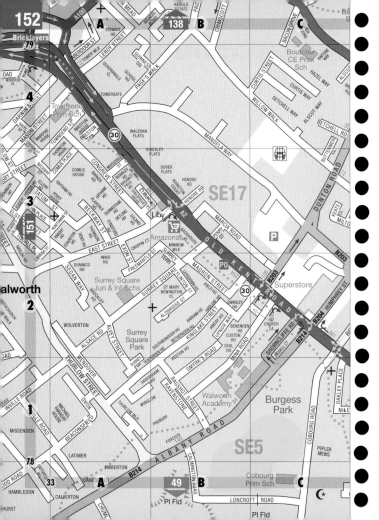

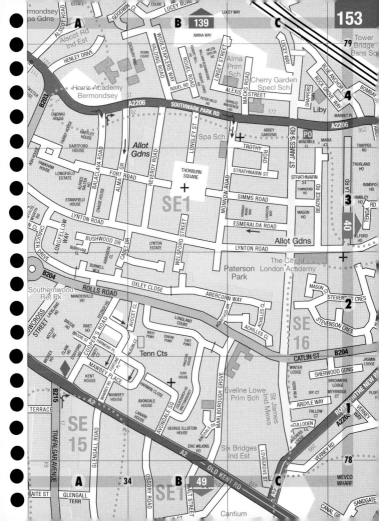

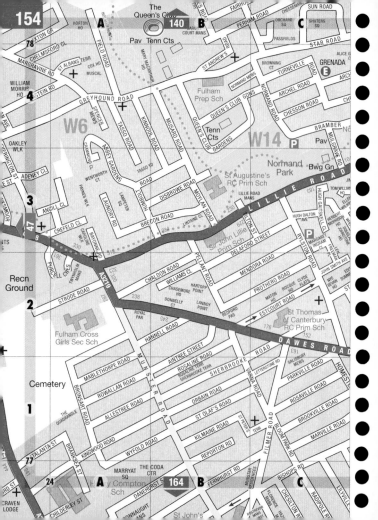

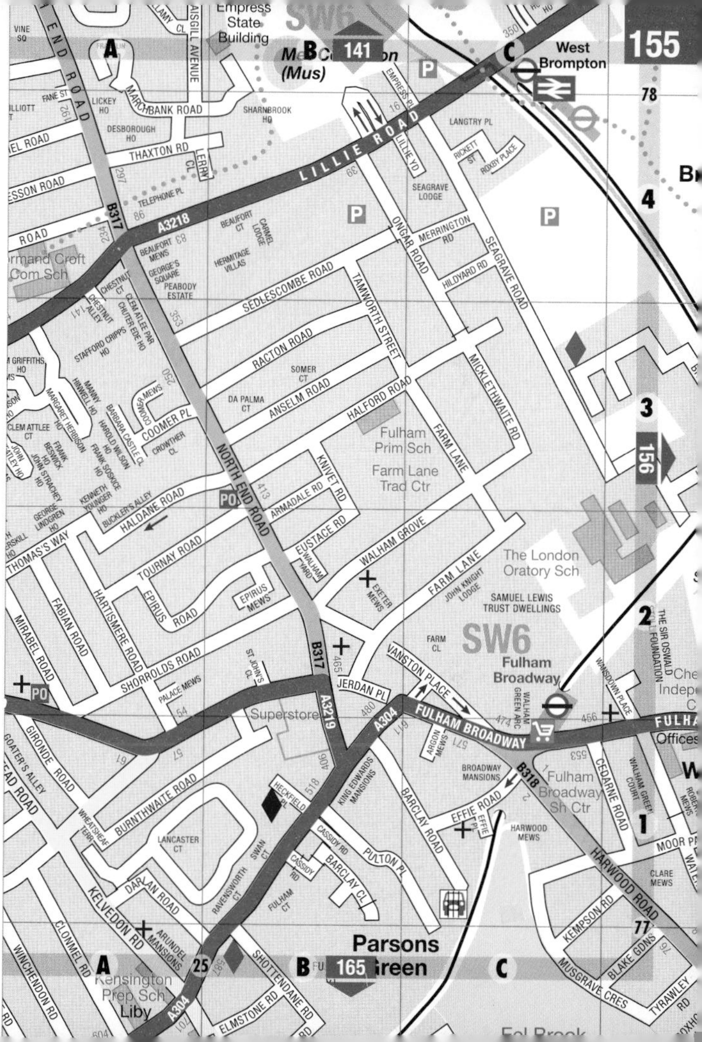
Empress State Building
A
B
C
141
West Brompton
78
SW6
VINE SQ
LAMY CL
AISGILL AVENUE
FANE ST
LICKEY HO
MARCHBANK ROAD
SHARNBROOK HO
DESBOROUGH HO
THAXTON RD
LERRY CL
EMPRESS PL
LILLIE ROAD
LILLIE YD
LANGTRY PL
RICKETT ST
ROXBY PLACE
SEAGRAVE LODGE
TELEPHONE PL
B317
A3218
BEAUFORT CT
CARMEL LODGE
BEAUFORT MEWS
GEORGE'S SQUARE
PEABODY ESTATE
HERMITAGE VILLAS
MERRINGTON RD
ONGAR ROAD
SEAGRAVE ROAD
HILDYARD RD
4
Ormand Croft Com Sch
CHESTNUT CT
CHESTNUT ALLEY
CLEM ATLEE PAR
CHUTER EDE HO
SEDLESCOMBE ROAD
TAMWORTH STREET
STAFFORD CRIPPS HO
RACTON ROAD
SOMER CT
MICKLETHWAITE RD
ANSELM ROAD
DA PALMA CT
HALFORD ROAD
COOMER MEWS
COOMER PL
CROWTHER CL
BARBARA CASTLE CL
HAROLD WILSON HO
FRANK SOSKICE HO
MARGARET HERBISON HO
MANNY HINWELL HO
CLEM ATTLEE CT
FRANK BESWICK HO
JOHN STRACHEY HO
Fulham Prim Sch
Farm Lane Trad Ctr
FARM LANE
3
156
NORTH END ROAD
KNIVET RD
ARMADALE RD
KENNETH YOUNGER HO
GEORGE LINDGREN HO
BUCKLER'S ALLEY
HALDANE ROAD
PO
EUSTACE RD
WALHAM GROVE
THOMAS'S WAY
TOURNAY ROAD
WALHAM YARD
EXETER MEWS
FARM LANE
JOHN KNIGHT LODGE
The London Oratory Sch
SAMUEL LEWIS TRUST DWELLINGS
MIRABEL ROAD
FABIAN ROAD
HARTISMERE ROAD
EPIRUS ROAD
EPIRUS MEWS
SHORROLDS ROAD
ST JOHN'S CL
FARM CL
SW6
Fulham Broadway
VANSTON PLACE
2
THE SIR OSWALD STOLL FOUNDATION
WANSDOWN PLACE
JERDAN PL
PALACE MEWS
Superstore
A3219
A304
FULHAM BROADWAY
WALHAM GREEN ARC
ARGON MEWS
Offices
GIRONDE ROAD
GOATER'S ALLEY
BURNTHWAITE ROAD
HECKFIELD PL
KING EDWARDS MANSIONS
BROADWAY MANSIONS
B318
Fulham Broadway Sh Ctr
CEDARNE ROAD
WALHAM GREEN COURT
WHEATSHEAF TERR
LANCASTER CT
CASSIDY RD
BARCLAY ROAD
EFFIE ROAD
EFFIE PL
HARWOOD MEWS
1
MOOR PK
DARLAN ROAD
SWAN CT
CASSIDY RD
BARCLAY CL
PULTON PL
HARWOOD ROAD
CLARE MEWS
KELVEDON RD
RAVENSWORTH CT
FULHAM CT
KEMPSON RD
77
ARUNDEL MANSIONS
Parsons Green
CLONMEL RD
WINCHENDON RD
25
165
SHOTTENDANE RD
BLAKE GDNS
MUSGRAVE CRES
TYRAWLEY RD
Kensington Prep Sch
Liby
ELMSTONE RD

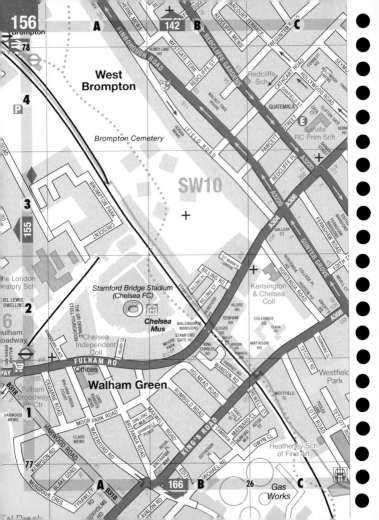

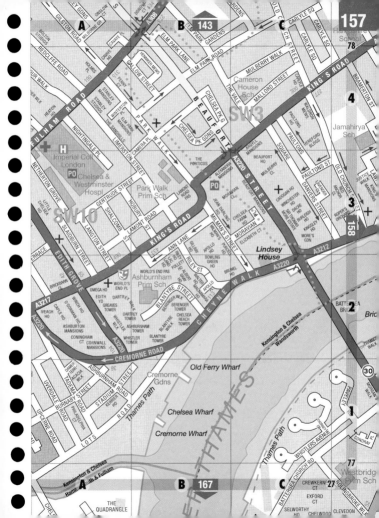

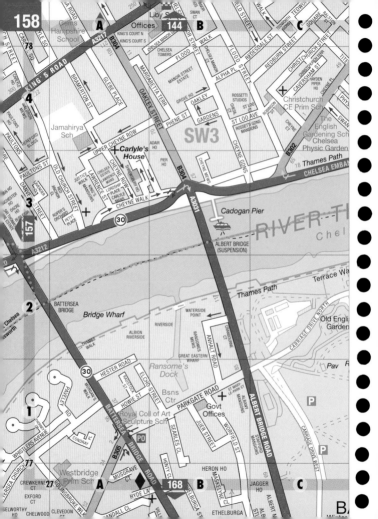

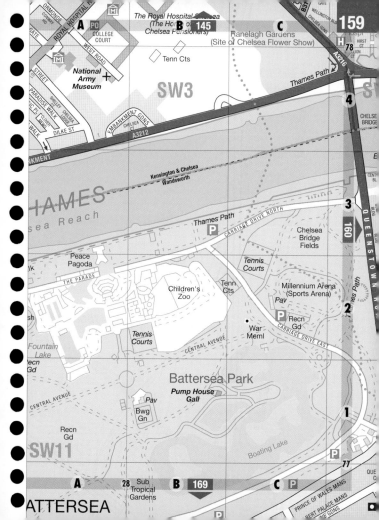

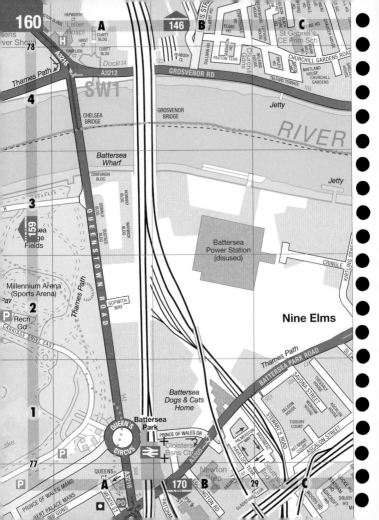

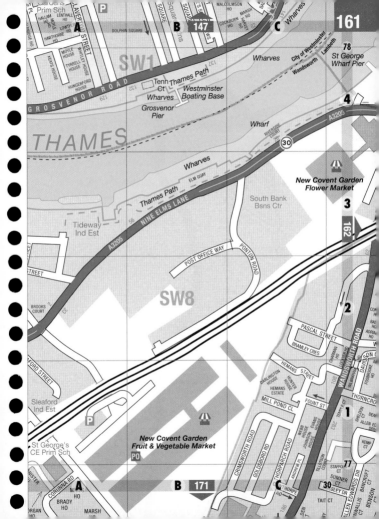

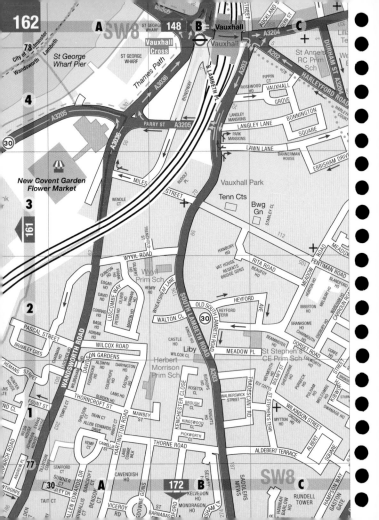

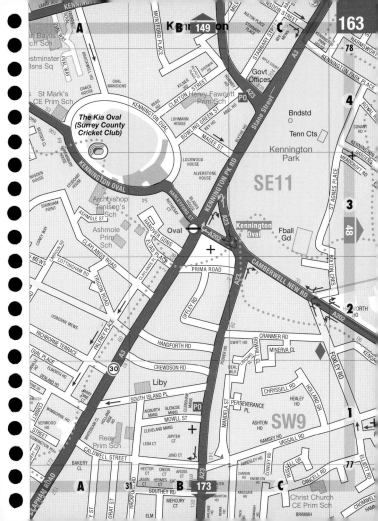

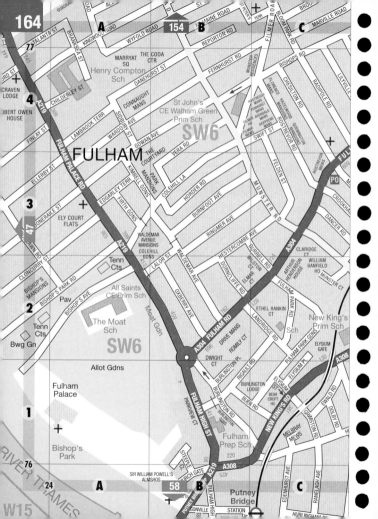

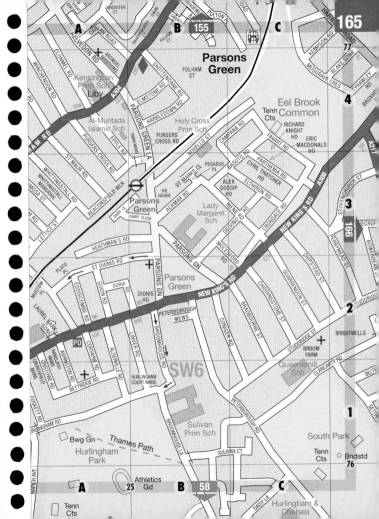

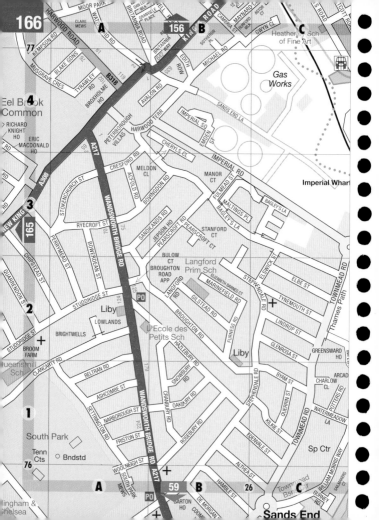

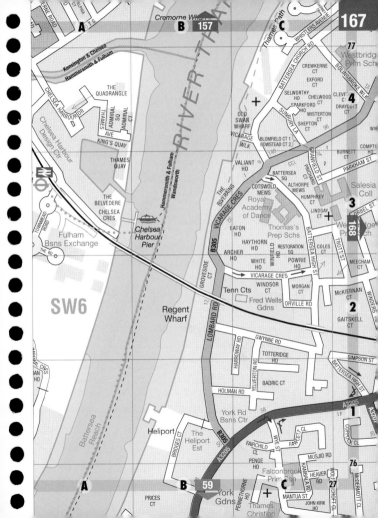

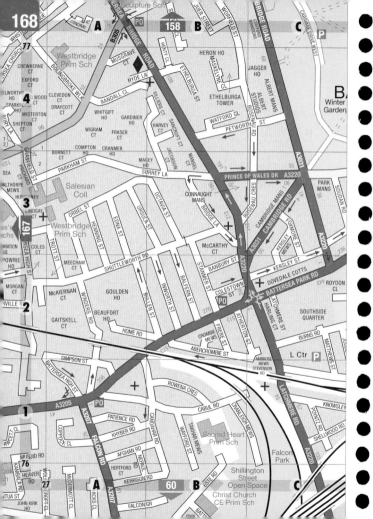

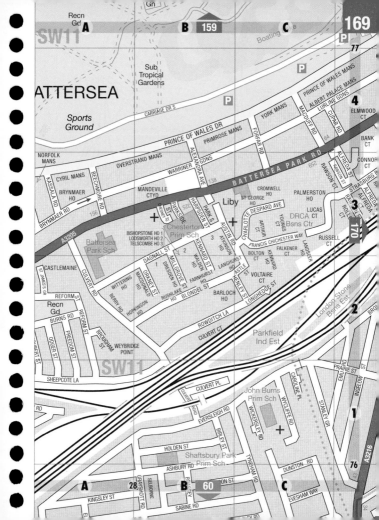

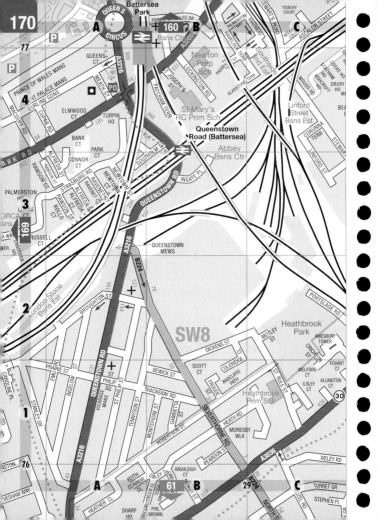

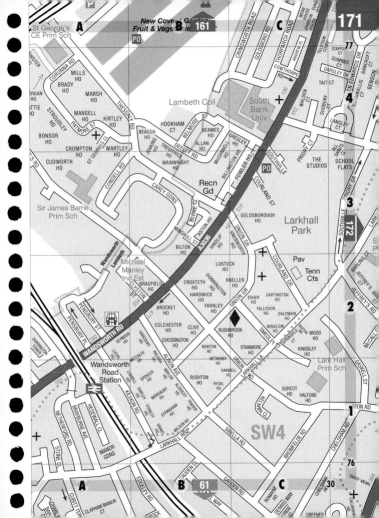

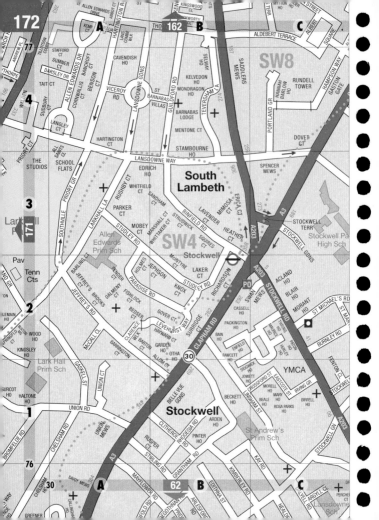

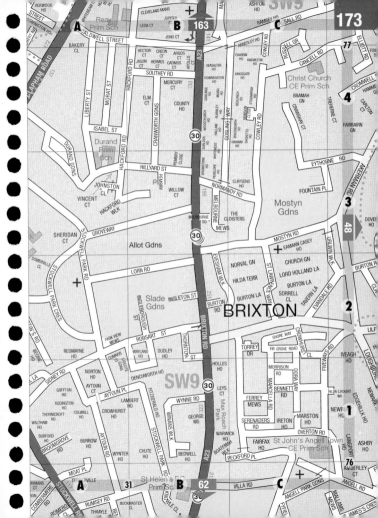

Index

Church Rd [6] **Beckenham BR2**..........**53** C6 **228** C6

Place name	**Location number**	**Locality, town or village**	**Postcode district**	**Standard scale reference**	**Enlarged scale reference**
May be abbreviated on the map	Present when a number indicates the place's position in a crowded area of mapping	Shown when more than one place (outside London postal districts) has the same name	District for the indexed place	Page number and grid reference for the standard mapping	Page number and grid reference for the central London enlarged mapping, underlined in red

Public and commercial buildings are highlighted in magenta.
Places of interest are highlighted in blue
Cities, towns and villages are listed in CAPITAL LETTERS

Abbreviations used in the index

Acad	Academy	Ct	Court	Int	International	Prom	Promenade
App	Approach	Ctr	Centre	Intc	Interchange	RC	Roman Catholic
Arc	Arcade	Crkt	Cricket	Jun	Junior	Rd	Road
Art Gall	Art Gallery	Ctry Pk	Country Park	Junc	Junction	Rdbt	Roundabout
Ave	Avenue	Cty	County	La	Lane	Ret Pk	Retail Park
Bglws	Bungalows	Ctyd	Courtyard	L Ctr	Leisure Centre	Sch	School
Bldgs	Buildings	Dr	Drive	Liby	Library	Sec	Secondary
Bsns Ctr	Business Centre	Ent Ctr	Enterprise Centre	Mans	Mansions	Sh Ctr	Shopping Centre
Bsns Pk	Business Park	Ent Pk	Enterprise Park	Mdw/s	Meadow/s	Sp	Sports
Bvd	Boulevard	Est	Estate	Meml	Memorial	Specl	Special
Cath	Cathedral, Catholic	Ex Ctr	Exhibition Centre	Mid	Middle	Sports Ctr	Sports Centre
CE	Church of England	Ex Hall	Exhibition Hall	Mix	Mixed	Sq	Square
Cemy	Cemetery	Fst	First	Mkt	Market	St	Street, Saint
Cir	Circus	Gdn	Garden	Mon	Monument	Sta	Station
Circ	Circle	Gdns	Gardens	Mus	Museum	Stad	Stadium
Cl	Close	Gn	Green	Obsy	Observatory	Tech	Technical Technology
Cnr	Corner	Gr	Grove	Orch	Orchard	Terr	Terrace
Coll	College	Gram	Grammar	Par	Parade	Trad Est	Trading Estate
Com	Community	Her Ctr	Heritage Centre	Pas	Passage	Twr/s	Tower/s
Comm	Common	Ho	House	Pav	Pavilion	Univ	University
Comp	Comprehensive	Hospl	Hospital	Pk	Park	Wlk	Walk
Con Ctr	Conference Centre	Hts	Heights	Pl	Place	Yd	Yard
Cotts	Cottages	Ind Est	Industrial Estate	Prec	Precinct		
Cres	Crescent	Inf	Infant	Prep	Preparatory		
Cswy	Causeway	Inst	Institute	Prim	Primary		

2 Willow Rd NW3...12 A4
3 Mills Studios E14...27 B2
30 St Mary Axe (The Gherkin) EC2...110 B2
176 Gall NW5...12 C2
201 Bishopsgate EC2...110 B4

A

Abady Ho W14...147 C4
Abberley Mews 9 SW8...61 A4
Abbess Cl SW2...75 A3
Abbeville Mews 3 SW4...61 C3
Abbeville Rd SW4...61 C2
Abbey Bsns Ctr SW8...170 B4
Abbey Coll London SW1...132 A1
Abbey Ct
6 Bedford Pk W12...38 A3
Camberwell SE17...151 A1
St John's Wood NW8...78 C2
Abbeyfield Rd SE16...40 B2
Abbey Gdns
10 Bermondsey SE16...153 C4
St John's Wood NW8...79 A1
West Kensington W6...154 A3
Abbey Ho NW8...89 A4
Abbey Lo NW8...90 B3
Abbey Orchard St SW1...133 C2
Abbey Orchard Street Est SW1...133 C2
Abbey Rd
St John's Wood NW8...78 C2
Wembley NW10...20 A3
Abbot St E8...16 B2
Abbots Cl SW8...138 C2
Abbot Ho 7 E14...34 A2
Abbotsbury Ho W14...126 B4
Abbotsbury Mews SE15...65 B4
Abbotsbury Rd W14...126 B3
Abbotshade Rd 15 SE16...32 C1
Abbots Ho
Kensington W14...126 C1
Pimlico SW1...147 B1
Abbots La SE1...124 B1
Abbots Pk SW2...74 C3
Abbot's Pl NW6...78 A4
Abbot St E8...16 B2
Abbotstone Ho 4 E5...7 C2
Abbotstone Rd SW15...57 B4
Abbotswell Rd SE4...66 B2

Abbotswood Rd
London SE22...64 A3
Streatham SW16...73 C1
Abbott Ho SW12...72 B4
Abbott Rd E14...34 C3
Abbotts Cl N1...15 B2
Abbotts Wharf 4 E14...33 C3
Abchurch La EC2, EC4...123 C4
Abchurch Yd EC4...123 B4
Abdale Rd W12...30 A1
Abel Ho 9 SE11...163 B4
Aberavon Rd E3...26 A2
Abercorn Cl NW8...88 C4
Abercorn Mans NW8...79 A1
Abercorn Mews TW10...54 B3
Abercorn Pl NW8...79 A1
Abercorn Sch NW8...79 A1
Abercorn Way SE1...153 B2
Abercrombie Ho 1 W12...30 A2
Abercrombie St SW11...168 B2
Aberdale Ct 22 SE16...40 C4
Aberdeen Ct NW6...1 A1
Aberdeen Ct
Canonbury N5...15 B3
Paddington W2...89 B1
Aberdeen La N5...15 B3
Aberdeen Mans WC1...94 A2
Aberdeen Pk N5...15 B3
Aberdeen Pl NW8...89 B2
Aberdeen Rd
Canonbury N5...15 B4
Dudden Hill NW10...8 B3
Aberdeen Terr SE3...52 C1
Aberdour St SE1...152 A4
Aberfeldy Ho SE5...48 A3
Aberfeldy St E14...34 B3
Abersham Rd E8...16 B3
Ability Plaza 8 E8...16 B1
Ability Twrs EC1...96 C4
Abingdon W14...141 A3
Abingdon Cl
Fulham SE1...153 A2
Kentish Town NW1...13 C2
Abingdon Gdns W8...127 C1
Abingdon Ho E2...24 B1 98 C2
Abingdon Mans W8...127 B2
Abingdon Rd W8...127 C1
Abingdon St SW1...134 A2
Abingdon Villas W8...127 C1
Abinger Gr SE8...51 B4
Abinger Ho SE1...137 B3
Abinger Mews W9...23 C1
Abinger Rd W4...38 A3
Ablett St SE16...40 B1
Abney Gdns 5 N16...7 B2
Abney Park Cemetery N16...7 A2

Abney Park Ct N16...7 B2
Aborfield 6 NW5...13 B3
Aboyne Rd SW17...71 C1
Abyssinia Cl SW11...60 A3
Abyssinia Rd SW11...60 A3
Acacia Cl SE8...41 A2
Acacia Gdns NW8...79 C2
Acacia Gr SE21...75 C2
Acacia Ho
Brockley SE4...66 B3
Stoke Newington...
Acacia Pl NW8...79 C2
Acacia Rd
Acton W3...28 B2
St John's Wood NW8...79 C2
Acacia Wlk SW10...157 A1
Academy Ct 13 E2...25 B2
Academy Gdns W8...127 B4
Academy Sch The 8 NW3...11 C4
Academy The 2 N19...4 C1
Acad of Live & Recorded Arts SW18...59 C1
Acanthus Dr SE1...153 B2
Acanthus Rd SW11...60 C4
Accommodation Rd NW11...1 B3
Acer Ct 2 NW2...10 A3
Acer Rd E8...16 B1
Acfold Rd SW6...166 A3
Achilles Cl SE1...153 C2
Achilles Ho 16 E2...25 A3
Achilles Rd NW6...10 C3
Achilles St SE14...51 A3
Achilles Way W1...117 C1
Acklam Rd W10...31 B4
Ackmar Rd SW6...165 B3
Ackroyd Dr E3...33 C4
Acland Burghley Sch NW5...13 A4
Acland Cres SE5...63 C4
Acland Ho SW9...172 C2
Acland Rd NW2...9 A2
Acol Ct 3 NW6...10 C1
Acol Rd NW6...11 A1
Acorn Ct 5 E3...26 C3
Acorn Gdns W3...28 C4
Acorn Par 7 SE15...50 A3
Acorn Production Ctr N7...14 A1
Acorns The 21 SW19...
Acorn Wharf SE15...49 C4
Acorn Wlk SE16...33 A1
Acqua Ho TW9...45 A3
Acre Dr SE22...64 C3
Acre La SW2...62 B3
Acris St SW18...59 B2
ACTON...28 C1
Acton Bsns Ctr NW10...20 C1
Acton Central Ind Est W3...28 A1
Acton Central Sta...
Acton High Sch W3...36 C4

Acton Hill Mews W3...28 A1
Acton Ho
Acton W3...28 B3
10 Haggerston E8...24 B4
Acton La
Acton Green W4...37 B2
Acton W3...28 B1
Harlesden NW10...21 B3
Acton Main Line Sta W3...28 B3
Acton Mews E8...24 B4
Acton Park Ind Est W3...37 B4
Acton St WC1...94 C3
Acton Town Sta W3...36 C4
Acton Vale Ind Pk W3...29 B1
Acton & West London Coll 18 W3...28 A1
Acuba Ho SW18...71 A3
Acuba Rd SW18...71 A2
Ada Ct
Islington N1...86 C3
St John's Wood W9...89 A3
Ada Ho 23 E2...24 C4
Adair Ho SW3...158 B4
Adair Rd W10...23 A1
Adair Twr 7 W10...23 A1
Ada Kennedy Ct 6 SE10...52 B3
Adam Ct SE11...150 A3
Adam & Eve Ct W1...105 A2
Adam & Eve Mews W8...127 C2
Adamfields SW11...11 C1
Adams Gardens Est 5 SE16...40 B4
Adams Ho 3 E14...34 C3
Adams Mews SW17...72 B2
Adamson Rd
Hampstead NW3...11 C1
Newham E16...35 C3
Adams Pi N7...14 B3
Adam's Row W1...117 C3
Adam St WC2...120 B3
Adam Wlk SW6...47 B3
Ada Pl E2...24 C4
Ada Rd SE5...49 A3
Adare Wlk SW16...
Ada St E8...25 A4
Adderley Gr SW11...60 C2
Adderley St E14...34 B3
Addey Ho SE8...51 B3
Addey & Stanhope Sch SE14...51 C2
Addington Ct W14...55 C4
Addington Ho 13 SW9...173 A1
Addington Rd E3...26 C2
Addington Sq SE5...48 C3
Addington St SE1...135 A3
Addis Ho 12 E1...32 B4
Addison Ave W11...31 A1 112 A1
Addison Bridge Pl W14...140 C4
Addison Cres W14...126 B2

2 Wi–Adr 175

Addison Gdns W14...39 C3
Addison Gr W4...38 A3
Addison Ho NW8...89 B4
Addison Park Mans 12 W14...39 C3
Addison Pl W11...31 A1 112 A1
Addison Prim Sch W14...39 C3
Addison Rd W14...126 C2
Addle Hill EC4...108 B1
Addlestone Ho W10...30 B4
Addy Ho SE16...40 B2
Adela Ho 9 W6...39 B1
Adelaide Ave SE4...66 C3
Adelaide Cl SW9...62 C3
Adelaide Ct
Hackney E5...18 A3
St John's Wood NW8...79 A1
Adelaide Gr W12...29 C1
Adelaide Rd
Primrose Hill NW3...12 A1
Richmond TW9...54 B3
2 Wandsworth SW18...58 C2
Adelaide St WC2...120 A3
Adela St W10...23 A1
Adelina Gr E1...32 B4
Adelina Mews SW12...73 C3
Adeline Pl WC1...105 C3
Adelphi Ct 20 SE16...40 C4
Adelphi Terr WC2...120 B3
Adeney Cl W6...47 C4
Aden Gr N16...15 C4
Aden Ho 16 E1...32 C4
Aden Lo N16...15 C4
Adeyfield Ho EC1...97 C3
Adie Rd W6...39 B3
Adisham Ho 4 E5...17 A3
Adler St E1...111 B2
Adley St E5...18 A3
Admiral Ct
Chelsea SW3...167 A4
Marylebone W1...103 B3
Admiral Ho SW1...147 A1
Admirals Ct
Bermondsey SE1...124 C1
32 Putney SW19...69 C3
Admirals Gate SE10...52 A2
Admiral Sq SW10...167 A4
Admiral St SE8...51 C2
Admirals Way E14...41 C4
Admiral's Wlk NW3...2 B1
Admiralty Arch SW1...119 C2
Admiralty Cl 1 SE8...51 C2
Admiral Wlk W9...31 C4
Adolphus Rd N4...6 A3
Adolphus St SE8...51 B3
Adpar St W2...101 B4
Adrian Bolt Ho 2 E2...25 A2

Adrian Ho
  Islington N1.....85 A3
  South Lambeth
  SW8.....162 A2
  Stratford E15.....19 C1
Adrian Mews
  SW10.....156 B4
Adriatic Bldg 18
  E14.....33 A2
Adriatic Ho 1 E1.....25 C1
Adron Ho 3 SE16.....40 B2
Adstock Ho 5 N1.....5 A1
Adventurers Ct 17
  E14.....34 C2
Adys Lawn NW2.....9 A2
Adys Rd SE15.....64 B4
Aegean Apts 7
  E16.....35 C2
Aegon Ho 8 E14.....42 A3
Affleck St N1.....85 A1
Afghan Rd SW11.....59 C4
Africa Ho WC2.....106 C2
Afsil Ho EC1.....107 C3
Aga Khan Univ
  WC1.....105 C3
Agamemnon Rd
  NW6.....10 B3
Agar Gr NW1.....13 C1
Agar Pl NW1.....13 B1
Agar St WC2.....120 B3
Agate Rd W6.....39 B3
Agatha Cl E1.....32 B1
Agave Rd NW2.....9 B4
Agdon St EC1.....96 A2
Agincourt Rd NW3.....12 B4
Agnes Ct 11 SW18.....59 C3
Agnes Ho 13 W11.....30 C2
Agnes Rd W3.....29 B1
Agnes St E14.....33 B3
Aicon Gall SW1.....118 C3
Aigburth Mans 5
  SW9.....163 B1
Ailsa St E14.....34 B4
Ainger Rd NW3.....12 B1
Ainsdale NW1.....92 C4
Ainsdale Dr SE1.....153 B1
Ainsley St E2.....25 A2
Ainslie Wlk
  SW12.....73 A4
Ainsty St 20 SE16.....40 B4
Ainsworth Cl SE5.....49 A1
Ainsworth Est
  NW8.....78 C4
Ainsworth Ho NW8.....78 B3
Ainsworth Rd E9.....17 B1
Ainsworth Way
  NW8.....78 C4
Aintree St SW6.....154 B2
Aird Ho SE1.....136 C1
Airdrie Cl N1.....14 B1
Airedale Ave W4.....38 B1
Airedale Ave S W4.....38 A1
Airedale Rd SW12.....72 B4
Airlie Gdns
  W8.....31 C1 113 B1
Air St W1.....119 A3
Aisgill Ave SW5.....141 A1
Aiten Pl W6.....38 C2
Aithan Ho 15 E14.....33 B3
Aitken Cl E8.....24 C4
Ajax Ho 16 E2.....25 A3
Ajax Rd NW6.....10 C3
Akbar Ho 7 E14.....42 A2
Akehurst St SW15.....68 C4

Akenside Ct 3
  NW3.....11 C3
Akenside Rd NW3.....11 C3
Akerman Rd SW9.....48 A2
Akintaro Ho 7
  SE8.....51 B4
Alamaro Lo 5
  SE10.....43 B3
Aland Ct SE16.....41 A3
Alan Preece Ct
  NW6.....9 C1
Alaska Bldg 12
  SE13.....52 A2
Alaska St SE1.....121 B1
Alastor Ho 10 E14.....42 B3
Albacore Cres
  SE13.....67 A1
Alba Mews SW18,
  SW19.....70 C2
Alban Ho
  Hampstead NW3.....11 B2
  New Cross SE14.....51 B2
Albans Cl SW16.....74 A1
Albany W1.....118 C3
Albany Cl SW14.....55 A3
Albany Ct
  College Pk NW10.....22 A2
  NW8.....79 B1
  Westminster SW1.....133 B2
  8 Whitechapel E1.....111 B2
Albany Ctyd W1.....119 A3
Albany Ho 13 TW8.....44 A4
Albany Mans
  SW11.....158 B1
Albany Mews
  Camberwell SE5.....48 B4
  Islington N1.....14 C1
Albany Par 4
  TW8.....44 A4
Albany Pas 12
  TW10.....54 A2
Albany Rd
  Camberwell SE5.....49 A4
  Richmond TW10.....54 A2
Albany St NW1.....92 B4
Albany Terr 8
  TW10.....54 A2
Alba Pl W11.....31 B3
Albemarle SW19.....69 C2
Albemarle Ho
  2 Brixton SW9.....62 C4
  Rotherhithe SE16.....41 B2
Albemarle Mans
  NW3.....11 A3
Albemarle Prim Sch
  SW19.....70 A2
Albemarle St W1.....118 C3
Albemarle Way
  EC1.....96 A1
Alberta Ct 1
  TW10.....54 B2
Alberta Ho E14.....34 B1
Alberta St SE17.....150 B2
Albert Ave SW8.....162 C1
Albert Barnes Ho
  SE1.....136 C1
Albert Bigg Point
  E15.....27 B4
Albert Bridge Rd
  SW11.....168 C3
Albert Cl 11 E9.....25 A4
Albert Cotts 2
  E1.....111 B4

Albert Ct
  Knightsbridge
  SW7.....129 B3
  5 Putney SW19.....70 A3
Albert Dr SW19.....70 A3
Albert Emb SE1.....148 B3
Albert Gate Ct
  SW1.....130 C3
Albert Gdns E1.....32 C3
Albert Gray Ho
  SW10.....157 B2
Albert Hall Mans
  SW7.....129 B3
Albert Mans
  Battersea SW11.....168 C4
  Hornsey N8.....5 A4
Albert Meml SW7.....129 B3
Albert Pl W8.....128 B3
Albert Rd
  Finsbury Pk N4.....5 B4
  Kilburn NW6.....23 B3
  Richmond TW10.....54 A2
Albert's Ct NW1.....90 B2
Albert St NW1.....82 B3
Albert Starr Ho 7
  SE8.....40 C2
Albert Studios
  SW11.....168 C4
Albert Terr
  Camden Town
  NW1.....81 B3
  Stonebridge NW10.....20 B4
Albert Terr Mews
  NW1.....81 B3
Albert Way SE15.....50 A3
Albert Westcott Ho
  SE17.....150 B2
Albion Ave SW8.....171 B1
Albion Cl W2.....116 B4
Albion Coll W10.....106 B3
Albion Ct 9 W6.....39 A2
Albion Dr E8.....16 C1
Albion Est SE16.....40 B4
Albion Gate W2.....116 B4
Albion Gdns 1
  W6.....39 A2
Albion Ho
  17 Deptford SE8.....51 C3
  EC1.....108 A4
Albion Mews
  Bayswater W2.....116 B4
  6 Hammersmith
  W6.....39 A2
  Islington N1.....85 B4
Albion Pl
  Broadgate EC2.....109 C3
  Clerkenwell EC1.....108 A4
  Hammersmith W6.....39 A2
Albion Prim Sch 34
  SE16.....40 B4
Albion Rd N16.....15 C4
Albion Riverside
  SW11.....158 A2
Albion Sq E8.....16 B1
Albion St
  Bayswater W2.....116 B4
  Rotherhithe SE16.....40 B4
Albion Terr E8.....16 B1
Albion Way
  Barbican EC2.....108 C3
  Lewisham SE13.....67 B3

Albion Wlk N1.....84 B1
Albion Works Studios
  10 E8.....18 B3
Albion Yd N1.....84 B1
Albon Ho SW18.....59 A1
Albrighton Rd SE5,
  SE22.....64 A4
Albury Bldgs SE1.....136 B3
Albury Ct SE8.....51 C4
Albury Lo 7 SW2.....74 B4
Albury St SE8.....51 C4
Alchemea Coll of
  Audio Engineering
  N1.....86 B3
Alconbury Rd E5.....7 C2
Aldbourne Rd
  W12.....29 C1
Aldbridge St SE17.....152 B2
Aldburgh Mews
  W1.....103 C2
Aldbury Ho SW3.....144 A3
Aldebert Terr
  SW8.....162 C1
Aldeburgh Pl SE10.....43 C3
Aldeburgh St SE10.....43 C1
Aldenham Ho NW1.....83 A1
Aldenham St NW1.....83 B1
Alden Ho E8.....25 A4
Aldensley Rd W6.....39 A3
Alderbrook Prim Sch
  12 SW12.....73 A4
Alderbrook Rd
  SW12.....61 A1
Alderbury Rd
  SW13.....46 C4
Aldergrove Ho 3
  E5.....7 C2
Alder Ho
  Camberwell SE15.....49 B4
  11 Maitland Pk
  NW3.....12 B2
  St Johns SE4.....66 C4
Alderley Ho 36
  SW8.....171 B1
Alder Lo SW6.....47 C2
Aldermanbury
  EC2.....109 A2
Aldermanbury Sq
  EC2.....109 A3
Alderman's Wlk
  EC2.....110 A3
Alderney Ho 20
  N1.....15 B2
Alderney Mews
  SE1.....137 B2
Alderney Rd E1.....25 C1
Alderney St SW1.....146 B2
Alder Rd SW14.....55 C4
Aldersford Cl SE4.....65 C3
Aldersgate Ct EC1.....108 C3
Aldersgate St EC1.....108 C3
Aldershot Rd NW6.....23 B4
Alderson St W10.....23 A1
Alderton Rd SE24.....63 B4
Alderville Rd SW6.....165 A2
Alderwick Ct N7.....14 B2
Aldford St W1.....117 C2
Aldgate EC3.....110 B1
Aldgate East Sta
  E1.....111 A2
Aldgate High St
  EC3.....110 C1
Aldgate Sta EC3.....110 C1
Aldham Ho SE4.....51 B2

Aldine Ct W12.....30 B1
Aldine St W12.....39 B4
Aldington Ct 8
  E8.....16 C1
Aldred Rd NW6.....10 C3
Aldren Rd SW17.....71 B1
Aldrich Terr SW18.....71 B2
Aldrick Ho N1.....85 A2
Aldridge Ct W11.....31 B4
Aldridge Rd Villas
  W11.....31 B4
Aldsworth Cl W9.....88 A1
Aldwich Ho WC2.....107 A1
Aldworth Gr SE13.....67 B1
Aldwych WC2.....107 A1
Aldwych Bldgs
  WC2.....106 B2
Aldwyn Ho SW8.....162 A1
Alexander Ave
  NW10.....9 A1
Alexander Ct
  SW18.....59 B2
Alexander Fleming
  Laboratory Mus
  W2.....101 C2
Alexander Ho 16
  E14.....41 C3
Alexander Mews 2
  W2.....100 A2
Alexander Pl SW7.....144 A4
Alexander Rd N19.....5 A2
Alexander Sq
  SW3.....144 A4
Alexander St W2.....31 C3
Alexandra Ave
  SW11.....169 B3
Alexandra Cl SE8.....51 B4
Alexandra Cotts
  SE14.....51 B2
Alexandra Ct
  Paddington W9.....89 A2
  4 Shacklewell N16.....16 B4
  5 Shepherd's Bush
  W12.....38 C4
Alexandra Gdns
  W4.....46 A3
Alexandra Gr N4.....6 A3
Alexandra Ho 16
  W6.....39 B1
Alexandra Mans
  Chelsea SW3.....157 B3
  Cricklewood NW2.....9 C3
  6 Hampstead
  NW6.....10 C3
  5 Shepherd's Bush
  W12.....38 C4
Alexandra National Ho
  N4.....6 A2
Alexandra Pl NW8.....79 A4
Alexandra Rd
  Acton W4.....37 C4
  Hampstead NW8.....11 C1
  Mortlake SW14.....55 C4
  Richmond TW9.....44 B1
Alexandra St
  5 Deptford SE14.....51 A3
  Newham E16.....35 C4
Alex Gossip Ho
  SW6.....165 B3
Alexis St SE16.....153 C4
Alfearn Rd E5.....17 B4
Alfie's Antique Mkt
  NW8.....90 A1
Alford Ct N1.....87 A1
Alford Pl N1.....87 A1
Alfreda Ct SW11.....170 A3
Alfreda St SW11.....170 A3

Alfreda St SW11 . . . **170** A3
Alfred Butt Ho
SW17 . . . . .72 B1
Alfred Cl W4 . . . . .37 C2
Alfred Ho E9 . . . . .18 A3
Alfred Mews W1,
WC1 . . . . **105** B4
Alfred Nunn Ho
NW10 . . . . .21 B4
Alfred Pl WC1 . . . . **105** B4
Alfred Rd
Acton W3 . . . . .28 B1
Paddington W2 . . . . .31 C4
Alfred Salter Ho
SE1 . . . . **153** A3
Alfred Salter Prim Sch
SE16 . . . . .40 C4
Alfred St E3 . . . . .26 B2
Alfreton Cl SW19 . . . . . . .69 C1
Alfriston Rd SW11 . . . . . .60 B2
Algar Ho SE1 . . . . **136** A3
Algarve Rd SW18 . . . . . . .71 A3
Algernon Rd
Kilburn NW6 . . . . .23 C4
Lewisham SE13 . . . . .67 A3
Algiers Rd SE13 . . . . .66 C3
Alice Gilliott Ct
W14 . . . . **155** A4
Alice La E3 . . . . .26 B4
Alice Owen Tech Ctr
EC1 . . . . .96 A4
Alice Shepherd Ho 12
E14 . . . . .42 B4
Alice St SE1 . . . . **138** A1
Alice Walker Cl 3
SE24 . . . . .63 A3
Alie St E1 . . . . **111** A1
Aliwal Rd SW11 . . . . .60 A3
Alkerden Rd W4 . . . . .38 A1
Alkham Rd N16 . . . . .7 B2
Allam Ho
W11 . . . . .31 A2 **112** A4
Allanbridge N16 . . . . .7 A4
Allan Ho SW8 . . . . **171** B4
Allan Way W3 . . . . .28 B4
Allard Gdns SW4 . . . . . . .61 C2
Allardyce St SW4,
SW9 . . . . .62 B3
Allbrook Ho 4
SW15 . . . . .68 C4
Allcroft Rd NW5 . . . . .12 C2
Allendale Cl SE5 . . . . .48 C2
Allen Edwards Dr
SW8 . . . . **172** A4
Allen Edwards Prim
Sch SW4 . . . . **172** A3
Allenford Ho
SW15 . . . . .56 B1
All England Lawn
Tennis & Croquet
Club The SW19 . . . . .70 A1
Allen Ho W8 . . . . **127** C2
Allen Mans W8 . . . . **127** C2
Allen Rd
Old Ford E3 . . . . .26 B3
Stoke Newington
N16 . . . . .16 A4
Allensbury Pl
7 Camden Town
NW1 . . . . .13 C1
Camden Town NW1 . .14 A1
Allen St W8 . . . . **127** C1
Allenswood 12
SW19 . . . . .70 A3
Allerdale Ho 7 N4 . .6 C4
Allerton Ho N1 . . . . .87 C1

Allerton Rd N16 . . . . .6 B2
Allerton St N1 . . . . .97 C4
Allerton Wlk 11 N7 . . .5 B2
Allestree Rd SW6 . . . . . **154** A1
Alleyn Cres SE21 . . . . . . .75 C2
Alleyn Ho
Bermondsey SE1 . . . **137** B1
St Luke's EC1 . . . . .97 A1
Alleyn Pk SE21 . . . . .76 A1
Alleyn Rd SE21 . . . . .76 A1
Alleyn's Sch SE22 . . . . . .64 A2
Allfarthing JMI Sch
SW18 . . . . .59 B1
Allfarthing La
SW18 . . . . .59 B1
Allgood St 10 E2 . . . . . .24 B3
Allhallows La EC4 . . . . . **123** B3
Allington Rd W10 . . . . . . .23 A3
Allington St SW1 . . . . . **132** B1
Allison Cl SE10 . . . . .52 B2
Allison Gr SE21 . . . . .76 A3
Allison Rd W3 . . . . .28 B2
Alliston Ho 27
E2 . . . . .24 B2 **99** A3
Allitsen Rd NW8 . . . . . . .80 A2
All Nations Ho 10
E8 . . . . .17 A1
Allnutt Way SW4 . . . . . . .61 C2
Allom Cl 11 SW4 . . . . . **172** B1
Allonby Ho E14 . . . . .33 A4
Alloway Rd E3 . . . . .26 A2
Allport Ho SE5 . . . . .63 C4
Allport Mews 44
E1 . . . . .25 B1
All Saints CE Prim Sch
6 Fulham SW6 . . . . **164** A2
Putney SW15 . . . . .57 B4
All Saints' CE Prim
Sch
Blackheath Vale
SE3 . . . . .53 A1
Child's Hill NW2 . . . . .1 B1
All Saints Church 1
N19 . . . . .4 C1
All Saints Ct
Lower Clapton E5 . . .17 B4
1 Shadwell E1 . . . . . . .32 B2
All Saints Dr SE3 . . . . . . .53 B1
All Saints Ho 2
W11 . . . . .31 B4
All Saints Pas
SW18 . . . . .58 C2
All Saints Rd W11 . . . . . . .31 B3
All Saints' Rd W3 . . . . . . .37 B3
All Saints St N1 . . . . .84 C2
All Saints Sta E14 . . . . . . .34 A2
Allsop Pl NW1 . . . . .91 A1
All Souls Ave
NW10 . . . . .22 A4
All Souls CE Prim Sch
W1 . . . . **104** C4
All Souls Pl W1 . . . . . . **104** B3
Alma Birk Ho 1
NW6 . . . . .10 B1
Almack Rd E5 . . . . .17 B4
Alma Gr SE1 . . . . **153** A3

Alma Ho 7 TW8 . . . . .44 A4
Alma Pl NW10 . . . . .22 A2
Alma Prim Sch 24
SE16 . . . . **153** C4
Alma Rd SW18 . . . . .59 B2
Alma Sq NW8 . . . . .89 A4
Alma St
Camden Town
NW5 . . . . .13 A3
Stratford New Town
E15 . . . . .19 C2
Alma Terr
Earl's Ct W8 . . . . . . **127** C1
Wandsworth SW18 . . .71 C4
Almeida St 10 N1 . . . . . . .15 A1
Almeric Rd SW11 . . . . . . .60 B3
Almington St N4 . . . . .5 B3
Almond Ave W5 . . . . .36 A3
Almond Cl SE15 . . . . .49 C1
Almond Ho SE4 . . . . .51 B1
Almond Rd SE16 . . . . .40 A2
Almorah Rd N1 . . . . .15 C1
Al-Muntada Islamic
Sch SW6 . . . . **165** A4
Alperton St W10 . . . . .23 B1
Alphabet Sq E3 . . . . .33 C4
Alpha Cl NW8 . . . . .90 B3
Alpha Gr E14 . . . . .41 C4
Alpha Ho
6 Brixton SW4 . . . . . .62 B3
Kilburn NW6 . . . . .23 C3
Lisson Gr NW8 . . . . .90 B1
Alpha Pl
Chelsea SW3 . . . . . . **158** B4
Kilburn NW6 . . . . .23 C3
Alpha Rd SE14 . . . . .51 B2
Alpha St SE15 . . . . .49 C1
Alpine Gr 88 E9 . . . . .17 B1
Alpine Rd SE16 . . . . .40 C1
Alroy Rd N4 . . . . .5 C4
Alsace Rd SE17 . . . . . . **152** A2
Al Sadiq High Sch for
Boys & Al Zahra
Girls Sch NW6 . . . . . . .23 A4
Alscot Rd SE1 . . . . **139** A1
Alscot Road Ind Est
SE1 . . . . **138** C1
Alscot Way SE1 . . . . . . **152** C4
Altair Ct N1 . . . . .15 C2
Altenburg Gdns
SW11 . . . . .60 C3
Althea St SW6 . . . . .59 A4
Althorpe Mews
SW11 . . . . **167** C3
Althorp Rd SW17 . . . . . . .72 B3
Altima Ct SE22 . . . . .64 C3
Alton Ho 3 E3 . . . . .27 A2
Alton Rd
Richmond TW10,
TW9 . . . . .54 A3
Roehampton SW15 . . . .68 C3
Alton St E14 . . . . .34 A4
Alumni Ct SE1 . . . . **139** A4
Alvanley Ho SW9 . . . . .11 A3
Alvanley Gdns
NW6 . . . . .11 A3
Alvanley Ho 14
SW9 . . . . **173** B4
Alverstone Ho SW18,
SW19 . . . . .70 C2
Alverstone Ho
SE11 . . . . **163** B3
Alverstone Rd NW2 . .9 B1
Alverton St SE8 . . . . .51 B4
Alvey St SE17 . . . . **152** A2

Alvington Cres E16 . . .B3
Alwold Cres SE12 . . . . . . .A4
Alwyn Ave W4 . . . . .37 C1
Alwyne La N1 . . . . .15 A1
Alwyne Pl N1 . . . . .15 B1
Alwyne Rd N1 . . . . .15 B1
Alwyne Sq N1 . . . . .15 B2
Alwyne Villas N1 . . . .15 A1
Alwyn Gdns W3 . . . . .28 A3
Alzette Ho 11 E2 . . . . . . .25 C3
Aman Dalvi Ho 2
SW18 . . . . .70 A4
Amazonas SE1 . . . . **152** B3
Amazon St E1 . . . . .32 A3
Ambassador Ct 9
NW6 . . . . .10 C3
Ambassador Ho
NW8 . . . . .79 A3
Ambassador Sq
E14 . . . . .42 A2
Amber Ct N7 . . . . .14 C2
Ambergate St
SE17 . . . . **150** B2
Amberley Ct 2
SW9 . . . . .63 A4
Amberley Rd W9 . . . . . . .31 C4
Amber Wharf 29
E2 . . . . .24 B4
Ambler Prim Sch
N4 . . . . .6 A2
Ambler Rd N4 . . . . .6 A1
Ambleside
18 Putney SW19 . . . . .70 A3
Regent's Pk NW1 . . . **82** B1
Ambleside Cl E9 . . . . .17 B3
Ambleside Point 1
SE15 . . . . .50 B3
Ambleside Rd
NW10 . . . . .8 B1
Ambrosden Ave
SW1 . . . . **133** A1
Ambrose Ho 5
E14 . . . . .33 C4
Ambrose Mews 2
SW11 . . . . **168** C2
Ambrose St SE16 . . . . . . .40 A2
Ambrose Wlk E3 . . . . . . .26 C3
AMC Bsns Ctr
NW10 . . . . .20 A3
Amelia Cl W3 . . . . .37 A4
Amelia Ho 6 W6 . . . . . . .39 B1
Amelia St SE17 . . . . . . **150** C2
Amen Cnr EC4 . . . . **108** B1
Amen Ct EC4 . . . . **108** B1
American
Intercontinental
Univ W1 . . . . **103** C3
American Sch in
London The W8 . . . **79** B2
American Univ in
London The 3 N7 . .5 B1
America Sq EC3 . . . . . **124** C4
America St SE1 . . . . . . **122** C1
Amerland Rd
SW18 . . . . .58 B1
Amersham Gr
SE14 . . . . .51 B3
Amersham Rd
SE14 . . . . .51 B3
Amersham Vale SE14,
SE8 . . . . .51 B3
Amery Gdns NW10 . .22 A4
Amery Ho SE17 . . . . . **152** B2
Amesbury Ave
SW2 . . . . .74 B2
Amesbury Twr 4
SW8 . . . . **170** C2

Ames Cotts 12 E3 . .33 A4
Ames Ho E2 . . . . .25 C3
Amethyst Rd E15 . . . . .19 C4
Amhurst Ct N4 . . . . .6 C4
Amhurst Par N16 . . . . .7 B4
Amhurst Pk N4, N16 . .7 A4
Amhurst Rd E8,
N16 . . . . .16 C4
Amhurst Terr E8 . . . . . . .16 C4
Amias Ho EC1 . . . . .96 C2
Amiel St 18 E1 . . . . .25 B1
Amies St SW11 . . . . .60 B4
Amigo Ho SE1 . . . . **135** C2
Amina Way SE16 . . . . . **139** B1
Amner Rd SW11 . . . . .60 C1
Amor Rd W6 . . . . .39 B3
Amory Ho N1 . . . . .85 A2
Amott Rd SE15 . . . . .64 C4
Amoy Pl E14 . . . . .33 C2
Ampton Pl WC1 . . . . .94 C3
Ampton St WC1 . . . . .94 C3
Amstel Ct 12 SE15 . . . . . .49 B3
Amsterdam Rd
E14 . . . . .42 B3
Amundsen Ct 7
E14 . . . . .41 C1
Amwell St EC1 . . . . .95 B4
Amyruth Rd SE4 . . . . .66 C2
Anatola Rd N19 . . . . .4 B2
Anchorage Point 1
E14 . . . . .41 C4
Anchor Ho EC1 . . . . .96 C2
Anchor Mews
SW12 . . . . .61 A1
Anchor Ret Pk E1 . . . . . . .25 B1
Anchor St SE16 . . . . .40 A2
Anchor Terr SE1 . . . . . **123** A2
Anchor Yd EC1 . . . . .97 A2
Ancill Cl W6 . . . . **154** A3
Ancona Rd NW10 . . . . . . .22 A3
Andalus Rd SW9 . . . . .62 A4
Andaman Ho 3
E1 . . . . .33 A4
Andersens Wharf 9
E14 . . . . .33 B3
Anderson Cl W3 . . . . .28 C3
Anderson Ho 10
E14 . . . . .34 B2
Anderson Rd E9 . . . . .17 C2
Andersons Sq N1 . . . . . **86** A3
Anderson St SW3 . . . . . **144** C2
Anderton Cl SE5 . . . . .63 C4
Andover Ho 5 N7 . .5 B2
Andover PI NW6 . . . . . . .78 A1
Andover Rd N7 . . . . .5 B2
Andoversford Ct 2
SE15 . . . . .49 A4
Andre St E8 . . . . .16 C3
Andrew Borde St
WC2 . . . . **105** C2
Andrewes Ho EC2 . . . **109** A3
Andrew Ho
New Cross SE14 . . . .51 B1
Putney SW15 . . . . .56 C2
Andrew Logan's
Glasshouse SE1 . . . **138** A4
Andrew Marvell Ho 12
N16 . . . . .16 A4
Andrew PI SW8 . . . . . . **171** C4
Andrew Reed Ho 3
SW18 . . . . .70 A4
Andrews Crosse
WC2 . . . . **107** B1
Andrew's Rd E8 . . . . .25 A4

Andrew St E14 .... 34 B3
Andrews Wharf **14**
E8 .... 25 A4
Andrews Wlk SE17 ..48 A4
Andrew Wilmot Ct
SW18 .... 71 B3
Anfield Cl SW12 ...73 B4
Angel EC1 .... 86 B1
Angela Carter Cl
SW9 .... 62 C4
Angela Davis Ind Est
20 SW9 .... 63 A3
Angel Ct
  Broadgate EC2 .. 109 C2
  St James SW1 .... 119 A1
  5 Willesden NW2 ...8 C2
Angel Gate EC1 .... 96 B4
Angel Ho N1 .... 85 C1
Angelina Ho **2**
SE15 .... 49 C2
Angelis Appartments
N1 .... 86 B1
Angel La E15 .... 19 C2
Angell Park Gdns **4**
SW9 .... 62 C4
Angell Rd SW9 ..... 63 A4
Angel Mews
  Finsbury N1 .... 85 C1
  Putney SW15 ...... 68 C4
  Stepney E1 .... 32 A2
Angel Pas EC4 ..... 123 B3
Angel Pl SE1 .... 137 B4
Angel Sq N1 .... 85 C1
Angel St EC1 .... 108 C2
Angel Sta EC1 ...... 85 C1
Angel Wlk W6 ...... 39 B2
Angerstein Bsns Pk
SE10 .... 43 C2
Angerstein La SE3 .53 B2
Anglebury **5** W2 ...31 C3
Anglers La NW5 ....13 A2
Anglesey Ho **11**
E14 .... 33 C3
Anglia Ho **13** E14 ..33 A3
Anglo American
Laundry SW17 .....71 B1
Anglo Rd **11** E3 ....26 B3
Angrave Ct **4** E8 ..24 B4
Angrave Pas **5** E8 .24 B4
Angus Ho **12**
SW12 .... 73 C4
Angus St SE14 ..... 51 A3
Anhalt Rd SW11 ...158 B2
Animals in War Meml
W1 .... 117 A4
Anley Rd **11** W14 ..39 C4
Annabel Cl E14 .....34 A3
Anna Cl E8 .... 24 B4
Annandale Rd
  Chiswick W4 .... 38 A1
  Greenwich SE10 ...43 B1
Anne Goodman Ho **3**
E1 .... 32 B3
Anne Kerr Ct **18**
SW15 .... 57 C1
Anne's Ct NW8 .... 90 B2
Annesley Ho **15**
SW9 .... 173 B4
Annesley Wlk N19 ..4 B2
Annette Cres **16**
N1 .... 15 B1
Annette Ct N7 ...... 5 B1
Annette Rd N7 .....14 B4

Annie Besant Cl
E3 .... 26 B4
Anning St
EC2 ....24 A1 98 B2
Annis Rd E9 .... 18 A2
Ann La SW10 ...... 157 B3
Ann Moss Way
SE16 .... 40 B3
Ann's Cl SW1 ...... 131 B3
Ann's Pl E1 .... 110 C3
Ansdell Rd SE15 ...50 B1
Ansdell St W8 ..... 128 B2
Ansdell Terr W8 ...128 B2
Ansell Ho E1 .... 32 B4
Ansell Rd SW17 ...72 B1
Ansleigh Pl W11 ...30 C2
Anson Ho
  Pimlico SW1 ...... 160 C4
  1 Tower Hamlets
  E1 .... 26 A1
Anson Prim Sch
NW2 .... 9 C3
Anson Rd
  Cricklewood NW2 ..9 B3
  Tufnell Pk N7 ..... 13 C4
Anstey Ct **8** W3 ...37 A4
Anstey Ho **9** E9 ...25 B4
Anstice Cl W4 ..... 46 A3
Antenor Ho **10** E2 .25 A3
Anthony Cope Ct
N1 .... 97 C4
Anthony Ho NW8 ..90 A1
Anthony St E1 ..... 32 A3
Antilles Bay **19**
E14 .... 42 B4
Antilles Ho W3 .....28 C3
Antill Rd E3 .... 26 A2
Antill Terr **5** E1 ....32 C3
Antonine Hts SE1 ..138 A3
Anton St E8 .... 16 C3
Antony Ho
  4 Deptford SE14 ..50 C3
  2 Rotherhithe
  SE16 .... 40 B2
Antrim Gr NW3 ....12 B2
Antrim Ho SW11 ..60 C4
Antrim Mans NW3 ..12 B2
Antrim Rd NW3 ....12 B2
Antrobus Rd W4 ...37 B2
AOP Gall EC2 ...... 98 A2
Apex Ind Est NW10 ..21 B1
Aphrodite Ct **11**
E14 .... 41 C2
Apollo Bldg **2**
E14 .... 41 C2
Apollo Ct
  5 Chelsea SW10 ..157 B3
  32 Hackney E8 ....25 A3
  Highgate N6 .... 4 C4
Apollo Ind Bsns Ctr **9**
SE15 .... 49 A3
Apollo Pl SW10 ...157 B2
Apollo Studios **18**
NW5 .... 13 C3
Apothecary St
EC4 .... 108 A1
Appach Rd SW2 ...62 C1
Appleby Ct W3 .....37 B4
Appleby Rd
  Hackney E8 .... 16 C1
  Newham E16 ...... 35 C3
Appleby St E2 ..... 24 B3
Appledore Cl SW12,
SW17 .... 72 B2

Appleford **8** NW5 ..13 B3
Appleford Ho **8**
W10 .... 23 A1
Appleford Rd W10 ..23 A1
Applegarth Ho
  Borough SE1 ..... 136 B4
  9 Camberwell
  SE15 .... 49 C3
Applegarth Rd
W14 .... 39 C3
Apple Mkt WC2 ....120 B4
Appleshaw Ho **4**
SE5 .... 64 A4
Appleton Ct SE10 88 ..17 A3
Appletree Ct SE13 ..67 C3
Apple Tree Yd
SW1 .... 119 A2
Appold St EC2 ..... 110 A4
Appollo Ct **7**
SW9 .... 173 B4
Apprentice Way **5**
E5 .... 17 A4
Approach Cl N16 ..16 A4
Approach Rd E2 ...25 B3
Approach The W3 ..28 C3
April Ct **20** E2 ......24 C3
April St E8 .... 16 B4
Apsley Ho
  Stepney E1 .... 32 B4
  St John's Wood
  NW8 .... 79 B2
Apsley Ho, The
Wellington Mus
SW1 .... 131 C4
Apsley Way W1 ....131 C4
Aquila St NW8 .....79 C2
Aquinas St SE1 ....121 C1
Arabella Ct NW8 ..79 A2
Arabella Dr SW15 ..56 A3
Arabian Ho **11** E1 ..26 A1
Arabin Rd SE4 .....66 B3
Aragon Twr SE8 ...41 B2
Arakan Ho **4** N16 ..15 C4
Aral Ho **14** E1 ......25 C1
Arapiles Ho **6**
E14 .... 34 C3
Arbery Rd E3 ...... 26 A3
Arbon Ct N1 .... 87 A3
Arbor Ct N16 ...... 6 C2
Arborfield Cl SW2 ..74 B3
Arborfield Ho **7**
E14 .... 33 C2
Arbour Ho **8** E1 ...32 C3
Arbour Sq E1 ...... 32 C3
Arbuthnot Rd
SE14 .... 50 C1
Arbutus St E8 ......24 B4
Arcade The
  Broadgate EC2 .. 110 A3
  1 Tufnell Pk N7 ...14 A4
Arcadian Ho **5** W6 ..167 A1
Arcadian Pl SW18 ..70 A4
Arcadia St E14 .....33 C3
Arcadia Univ W2 ..114 A3
Archangel St SE16 ..40 C4
Archbishop Coggan
Ho SE13 .... 67 C3
Archbishop's Pl **11**
SW2 .... 74 B4
Archbishop Sumner
CE Prim Sch
SE11 .... 149 B3
Archbishop Tenison's
Sch SE11 .... 163 A3
Archdale Ct W12 ...30 A1
Archdale Ho SE1 ..138 C2

Archdale Rd SE22 ..64 B3
Archel Rd W14 ....154 C4
Archer Ho
  1 Battersea
  SW11 .... 167 C2
  24 Hoxton N1 .....24 A4
  1 New Cross SE14 ..51 A2
  Notting Hill
  W11 ....31 B2 113 A4
Archers Lo **22**
SE1 .... 153 C1
Archer Sq SE14 ....51 A4
Archer St W1 ...... 119 B4
Archery Cl W2 ..... 102 B1
Archery Fields Ho
WC1 .... 95 B4
Archery Stps SW2 ..116 B4
Arches The WC2 ...120 B2
Archibald Mews
W1 .... 118 A3
Archibald Rd E3 ...26 C2
Archibald St E3 ....26 C2
Archie St SE1 ...... 138 B3
Arch St SE1 .... 136 C1
Archway N19 ...... 4 B2
Archway Bsns Ctr **3**
N19 .... 4 C1
Archway Cl
  North Kensington
  W10 .... 30 C4
  2 Upper Holloway
  N19 .... 4 B2
Archway Hts **5** N19 ..4 B3
Archway L Ctr N19 ..4 B2
Archway Mews
SW15 .... 58 A3
Archway Rd N6 ....4 A4
Archway St SW13,
SW14 .... 56 A4
Archway Sta N19 ..4 B2
Arcola St E8 .... 16 B3
Arctic St NW5 ..... 13 A3
Ardbeg Rd SE24 ...63 C2
Arden **17** SW19 ....69 C3
Arden Cres E14 ....41 C2
Arden Ho
  21 Hoxton N1 .....24 A3
  22 Stockwell SW9 ..172 B1
  Vauxhall SE11 ....148 C3
Ardent Ho **20** E3 ...26 A3
Ardilaun Rd N5 ....15 B4
Ardleigh Rd N1 ....16 A2
Ardlui Rd SE27 ....75 B2
Ardmere Rd SE13 ..67 C1
Ardshiel Cl **8**
SW15 .... 57 C4
Ardwell Rd SW2 ...74 A2
Ardwick Rd NW2 ..10 C4
Ares Ct **18** E14 ....41 C2
Arethusa Ho **8**
E14 .... 42 A2
Argo Bsns Ctr **7**
NW6 .... 23 C2
Argos Ct **5** SW9 ..173 B4
Argos Ho **8** E2 .....25 A3
Argosy Ho
  Fitzrovia W1 ...... 92 B1
  Rotherhithe SE8 ..41 A2
Argyle Ho E14 .....42 B3
Argyle Mans **4**
NW2 .... 1 B2
Argyle Pl W6 ...... 39 A2
Argyle Prim Sch
WC1 .... 94 A4
Argyle Rd E1 ...... 25 C1

Argyle Sq WC1 ....94 B4
Argyle St WC1 .....94 B4
Argyle Way SE16 ..153 C1
Argyll Cl SW9 ......62 B4
Argyll Ct **15** SW2 ..74 A4
Argyll Mans
  Chelsea SW3 ..... 157 C4
  West Kensington
  W14 .... 140 B4
Argyll Rd W8 ...... 127 C3
Argyll St W1 .... 104 C1
Arica Ho SE16 .....40 A3
Arica Rd SE4 ...... 66 A4
Ariel Ct
  5 Hammersmith
  W12 .... 38 C3
  Newington SE11 ..150 A3
Ariel Rd NW6 ......10 C2
Ariel Way W11,
W12 .... 30 B1
Aristotle Rd SW4 ..61 C4
Arizona Bldg **10**
SE13 .... 52 A2
Arkansas Ho **21**
N19 .... 4 C4
Ark Ct N16 .... 7 B2
Arklow Ho SE17 ...48 C4
Arklow Rd SE14 ...51 B4
Arklow Road Trad Est
SE14 .... 51 B4
Arkwright Ho **23**
SW2 .... 74 A4
Arkwright Mans **1**
NW3 .... 11 B3
Arkwright Rd NW3 ..11 B3
Arlesey Cl SW15 ..58 A2
Arlesford Rd SW9 ..62 A4
Arlidge Ho EC1 ....107 C4
Arlingford Rd
SW2 .... 62 C1
Arlington Ave N1 ..87 A3
Arlington Cl SE13 ..67 C2
Arlington Ct **13**
W3 .... 28 A1
Arlington Gdns
W4 .... 37 B1
Arlington Ho
  3 Deptford SE8 ...51 B4
  Finsbury EC1 ..... 95 C4
  1 Shepherd's Bush
  W12 .... 30 A1
Arlington Lo **2** SW2 ..62 B3
Arlington Park Mans
1 W4 .... 37 B1
Arlington Pl **7**
SE10 .... 52 B3
Arlington Rd NW1 ..82 B3
Arlington Sq N1 ...87 A3
Arlington St SW1 ..118 C2
Arlington Way EC1 ..95 C4
Armada Ct
  3 Deptford SE8 ...51 C4
Armadale Rd
SW6 .... 155 B3
Armada St **10** SE8 ..51 C4
Armagh Rd E3 .....26 B4
Arminger Rd W12 ..30 A1
Armitage Ho NW1 ..102 B4
Armitage Rd
  Golders Green
  NW11 .... 1 B3
  Greenwich SE10 ..43 B1
Armour Cl N7 ......14 B2
Armoury Ho E3 ....26 A4
Armoury Rd SE8 ..52 A1

Armoury Way
SW18 . . . . 58 C2
Armsby Ho 17 E1 . . . 32 B4
Armstrong Ho 8
SW15 . . . . 57 C1
Armstrong Rd
East Acton W3 . . . . . . 29 B1
Knightsbridge
SW7 . . . . 129 B1
10 Willesden NW10 . . 8 A1
Arnal Cres SW18 . . . 70 A4
Arncliffe Ho 6 . . . . . 78 B3
Arndale Wlk 6
SW18 . . . . 59 A2
Arne Ho SE11 . . . . . 148 C2
Arne St WC2 . . . . . 106 B1
Arneway St SW1 . . . 133 C1
Arnewood Cl
SW15 . . . . 68 C3
Arnham Pl E14 . . . . 41 C3
Arnham Way 3
SE22 . . . . 64 A3
Arnham Wharf
E14 . . . . 41 C3
Arnham Wharf Prim
Sch E14 . . . . 41 C3
Arnold Cl 7
E2 . . . . 24 B2 98 C3
Arnold Ho
Newington SE17 . . . . 150 B1
2 Stoke Newington
N16 . . . . 7 A1
Arnold House Sch
NW8 . . . . 79 B1
Arnold Rd E3 . . . . . . 26 C2
Arnot Ho 97 SE5 . . . 48 B3
Arnott Cl W4 . . . . . . 37 C2
Arnould Ave SE5 . . . 63 C3
Arnside Ho 3
SE17 . . . . 48 C4
Arnside St SE17 . . . . 48 B4
Arodene Rd SW2 . . . 62 B1
Arragon Rd SW18 . . . 70 C3
Arran Ho
5 Canary Wharf
E14 . . . . 34 B1
Stoke Newington N16 . . 7 B3
Arran Wlk N1 . . . . . . 15 B1
Arrol Ho SE1 . . . . . 137 A1
Arrowe Ct 6 E5 . . . . . 17 A4
Arrow Ho 23 N1 . . . . 24 A4
Arrow Rd E3 . . . . 27 A2
Arrowsmith Ho
SE11 . . . . 148 C2
Arsenal Sta N5 . . . . . . 5 C1
Arta Ho 20 E1 . . . . . 32 B3
Artcadia Lifestyle
EC2 . . . . 110 C4
Artemis Ct 14 E14 . . . 41 C2
Artemis Pl SW18 . . . 70 B4
Artesian Rd W2 . . . . 31 C3
Arthur Ct
Battersea SW11 . . . . . 169 C3
10 North Kensington
W10 . . . . 30 C3
Paddington W2 . . . . . 100 A4
Arthur Deakin Ho 1
E1 . . . . 111 B4
Arthur Rd N7 . . . . . . 14 B4

Arthur St EC4 . . . . . 123 C4
Arthur Wade Ho 7
E2 . . . . 24 B2 99 A4
Artichoke Hill 3
E1 . . . . 32 A2
Artichoke Mews 3
SE5 . . . . 48 C2
Artichoke Pl SE5 . . . . 48 C2
Artillery Ho
Bow E3 . . . . 26 A4
Westminster SW1 . . . 133 B1
Artillery La
Broadgate E1 . . . . . . 110 B3
North Kensington
W12 . . . . 29 C3
Artillery Pas E1 . . . . 110 B3
Artillery Row SW1 . . 133 B1
Artillery Row
SW1 . . . . 133 B1
Artisan Ct E8 . . . . 16 C2
Artisan Mews 9
NW10 . . . . 22 C2
Artisan Quarter 10
NW10 . . . . 22 C2
Artizan St E1 . . . . . . 110 B2
Arton Wilson Ho 8
SW15 . . . . 56 C2
Arts Educational Sch
The W4 . . . . 38 A2
Arundel Bldgs
SE1 . . . . 138 B1
Arundel Cl SW11 . . . 60 A2
Arundel Ct
Barnes SW13 . . . . 47 A4
Chelsea SW3 . . . . . . 144 B2
Putney SW15 . . . . 57 C2
Arundel Gdns
W11 . . . . . 31 B2 112 C4
Arundel Gr N16 . . . . 16 A3
Arundel Ho
Islington N1 . . . . 86 B4
Richmond TW10 . . . . . 54 C2
3 South Acton W3 . . . 37 A4
Arundel Lo 9 N19 . . . . 5 A2
Arundel Mans
Barnes SW13 . . . . 47 A4
Fulham SW6 . . . . . . 165 A4
Arundel Pl N1, N7 . . . 14 C2
Arundel Sq N7 . . . . . . 14 C2
Arundel St WC2 . . . 121 A4
Arundel Terr
SW13 . . . . 47 A4
Arungford Mews 5
SW2 . . . . 62 C2
Arvon Rd N5 . . . . 14 C3
Asaph Ho SE14 . . . . . 51 B2
Ascalon Ct 6
SW2 . . . . 74 B4
Ascalon Ho SW8 . . . 160 C1
Ascalon St SW8 . . . 160 C1
Ascham St NW5 . . . . 13 B3
Ascot Ct
3 Brixton SW4 . . . . . 62 A3
St John's Wood
NW8 . . . . 89 B3
Ascot Ho
2 Acton Green
W4 . . . . 37 B1
1 Paddington W9 . . . 31 C4
Regent's Pk NW1 . . . . 92 B4
Ascot Lo NW6 . . . . . . 78 B2
Ascot Par 5 SW4 . . . . 62 A3
Ascott Ave W5 . . . . . 36 A4
Ashbourne Coll
W8 . . . . 128 A3
Ashbourne Ct E5 . . . . 18 A4

Ashbourne Gr
Chiswick W4 . . . . 38 A1
East Dulwich SE22 . . . 64 B3
Ashbridge Ct 1
W6 . . . . 39 A3
Ashbridge St NW8 . . 90 A1
Ashbrook Rd N19 . . . 4 C2
Ashburn Gdns
SW7 . . . . 142 C4
Ashburnham Gr
SE10 . . . . 52 A3
Ashburnham Pl
SE10 . . . . 52 A3
Ashburnham Prim Sch
SW10 . . . . 157 A1
Ashburnham Rd
Chelsea SW10 . . . . . 157 A1
Kensal Rise NW10 . . . 22 B3
Ashburnham Retreat
4 SE10 . . . . 52 A3
Ashburnham Twr
SW10 . . . . 157 B2
Ashburn Pl SW7 . . . 142 C3
Ashburton Mans
SW10 . . . . 157 A2
Ashburton Rd E16 . . 35 C3
Ashbury Rd SW11 . . . 60 C4
Ashby Ct NW8 . . . . . . 89 C2
Ashby Gr N1 . . . . 15 B1
Ashby Ho
6 Brixton SW9 . . . . . 48 A1
5 Islington N1 . . . . . 15 B1
Ashby Mews
4 Clapham Pk
SW2 . . . . 62 A2
New Cross SE4 . . . . . 51 B1
Ashby Rd SE4 . . . . . . 51 B1
Ashby St EC1 . . . . . . 96 B3
Ashchurch Ct 2
W12 . . . . 38 C3
Ashchurch Gr
W12 . . . . 38 C3
Ashchurch Park Villas
W12 . . . . 38 C3
Ashchurch Terr
W12 . . . . 38 C3
Ashcombe Ct 3
SW15 . . . . 57 C2
Ashcombe Ho 30
E3 . . . . 27 A2
Ashcombe St
SW6 . . . . 166 A1
Ashcroft Ho SW8 . . 170 C4
Ashcroft Sq 8 W6 . . . 39 B2
Ashcroft Tech Acad
SW15 . . . . 58 B2
Ash Ct
Clapham SW11 . . . . . . 59 C4
Marylebone W1 . . . . 102 C2
6 Rotherhithe
SE16 . . . . 33 A1
St John's Wood
NW8 . . . . 90 A3
Ashdale Ho N4 . . . . . . 6 C4
Ashdene 6 SE15 . . . . 50 A3
Ashdon Rd NW10 . . . 21 B4
Ashdown Cres
NW5 . . . . 12 C3
Ashdown Ho 7 E5 . . . . 7 C2
Ashdown Way
SW17 . . . . 72 C2
Ashdown Wlk 20
E14 . . . . 41 C2
Ashenden SE17 . . . . 151 A4

Ashenden Rd E5 . . . 18 A3
Ashen Gr SW19 . . . . . 70 C2
Ashentree Ct EC4 . . 107 C1
Asher Way 1 E1 . . . . 125 C3
Ashfield Ho 5 N5 . . . 15 B3
Ashfield Rd W3 . . . . . 29 B1
Ashfield St
E1 . . . . 32 B4
4 Whitechapel E1 . . . 32 A4
Ashfield Yd 2 E1 . . . 32 B4
Ashford Ct NW2 . . . . . 9 C4
Ashford Ho
14 Brixton SW9 . . . . 63 A3
11 Deptford SE8 . . . . 51 B4
Ashford Rd NW2 . . . . . 9 C4
Ashford St
N1 . . . . 24 A2 98 A4
Ash Gr
Cricklewood NW2 . . . 10 A4
Ealing W5 . . . . 36 A3
Hackney E8 . . . . 25 A4
Ashgrove Ct 2
W9 . . . . 31 C4
Ashgrove Ho SW1 . . 147 C2
Ash Ho
8 Canary Wharf
E14 . . . . 42 B4
Fulham SE1 . . . . 153 A3
Ashington 1 NW5 . . . 13 A2
Ashington Ho 18
E1 . . . . 25 A1
Ashington Rd
SW6 . . . . 165 A1
Ashland Pl W1 . . . . . 103 B4
Ashleigh Ho SW14 . . 56 A4
Ashleigh Rd SW14 . . 56 A4
Ashley Cres SW11 . . . 60 C4
Ashley Ct
Hampstead NW3 . . . . 11 A3
19 Kingsland N16 . . . 16 A4
Ashley Pl SW1 . . . . . 132 C1
Ashley Rd
Hornsey N19 . . . . 5 A4
Richmond TW9 . . . . . . 54 A4
8 Lo S5 SW6 . . . . . . 19 C4
Ashlin Rd E15 . . . . . . 19 C4
Ashlone Rd SW15 . . . 57 C4
Ashmead Bsns Ctr 2
E16 . . . . 27 C1
Ashmead Ho 9 E9 . . . 18 A3
Ashmead Mews 1
SE8 . . . . 51 C1
Ashmead Prim Sch
SE8 . . . . 51 C1
Ashmere Gr 19 SW2,
SW4 . . . . 62 A3
Ashmere Ho 10
SW2 . . . . 62 A3
Ashmill St NW8 . . . . 102 A4
Ashmole Prim Sch
SW8 . . . . 163 A3
Ashmole St SW8 . . . 163 A3
Ashmore NW1 . . . . . . 83 B3
Ashmore Cl SE15 . . . 49 B3
Ashmore Ho W14 . . 126 B2
Ashmore Rd W9 . . . . 23 B2
Ashmount Prim Sch
N19 . . . . 4 B4
Ashmount Rd N19 . . . 4 C4
Ashness Rd SW11 . . . 60 B2
Ashpark Ho 4
E14 . . . . 33 A3
Ashtead Rd E5 . . . . . . 7 C4

Ashton Ho
15 Kennington
SW9 . . . . 163 C1
Roehampton SW15 . . 69 A4
Ashton Rd E15 . . . . . . 19 C3
Ashton St E14 . . . . . . 34 B2
Ashurst Lo 4 N5 . . . . 15 A3
Ashwin St E8 . . . . 16 B2
Ashworth Cl SE5 . . . . 48 C1
Ashworth Mans
W9 . . . . 88 B3
Ashworth Rd W9 . . . . 88 B3
Aske Ho 3
N1 . . . . 24 A2 98 A4
Asker Ho N7 . . . . 14 A4
Aske St N1 . . 24 A2 98 A4
Askew Cres W12 . . . . 38 C4
Askew Mans 14
W12 . . . . 38 C4
Askew Rd W12 . . . . . . 38 C4
Askham Ct W12 . . . . . 29 C1
Askham Rd W12 . . . . 29 C1
Askill Dr SW15 . . . . . 58 A2
Asland Rd E15 . . . . . . 27 C4
Aslett St SW18 . . . . . 71 B4
Asmara Rd NW2 . . . . 10 A3
Asolando Dr SE17 . . 151 A3
Aspect Ho 2 E14 . . . . 42 B4
Aspen Cl
Ealing W5 . . . . 36 B4
13 Upper Holloway
N19 . . . . 4 B2
Aspen Ct
Acton W3 . . . . 28 B3
12 Hackney E8 . . . . . 16 C3
Richmond TW9 . . . . . . 44 C3
Aspen Gdns 2
W6 . . . . 39 A1
Aspen Ho
5 Deptford SE15 . . . 50 B4
4 Maitland Pk
NW3 . . . . 12 B2
Richmond TW9 . . . . . . 44 C3
Aspen Way E14 . . . . . 34 B2
Aspern Gr NW3 . . . . . 12 A3
Aspinall Ho SW12 . . . 74 A3
Aspinall Rd SE4 . . . . 65 C4
Aspinden Rd SE16 . . 40 A2
Aspire Bld 10
SW15 . . . . 58 B2
Aspley Rd SW18 . . . . 59 A2
Assam St E1 . . . . 111 B2
Assam St E1 . . . . 111 B2
Assata Mews N1 . . . . 15 A2
Assembly Pas 1
E1 . . . . 32 B4
Assisi Ct SW12 . . . . . 72 B3
Astbury Bsns Pk 5
SE15 . . . . 50 B2
Astbury Ho SE11 . . . 135 B1
Astbury Rd SE15 . . . . 50 B2
Astell St SW3 . . . . . 144 B2
Aster Ho 3 SE13 . . . . 52 B1
Aste St E14 . . . . 42 B4
Astey's Row 1 N1 . . 15 B1
Astle St SW11 . . . . . 169 C2
Astley Ave NW2 . . . . . 9 B3
Astley Ho
Fulham SE1 . . . . 153 A2
Paddington W2 . . . . . 31 C4
2 West Norwood
SE27 . . . . 75 A2
Aston Ct N4 . . . . 6 B2
Aston Ho
Notting Hill
W11 . . . . . 31 B2 113 A4

Aston Ho continued
South Lambeth
SW8 . . . . **171 B3**
Aston St E14 . . . . . . 33 A4
Astonville St
SW18 . . . . .70 C3
Astor Ct SW6 . . . . . . **156** C1
Astoria Mans **13**
SW16 . . . . .74 A1
Astoria Par SW16 . . .74 A1
Astoria Wlk SW9 . . . .62 C4
Astra Ho
4 Bow E3 . . . . 26 B2
Hornsey N4. . . . . 5 B4
Astrop Mews W6 . . .39 B3
Astrop Terr W6 . . . . .39 B3
Astwood Mews
SW7 . . . . **142** C4
Asylum Rd SE15 . . . .50 A3
Atalanta St
SW6 . . . . . 47 C3 **154** A1
Atheldene Rd
SW18 . . . . .71 B3
Athelstan Gr **3** E3. .26 B3
Athelstane Mews
N4. . . . . 5 C3
Athelstan Gdns **3**
NW6 . . . . .10 A1
Athelstan Ho
Hackney Wick E9 . . . .18 B3
Stoke Newington
N16. . . . . .16 A4
Athena Ct
Bermondsey SE1 . . **138** A3
St John's Wood
NW8 . . . . .79 B2
Athenia Ho **7** E14. .34 C3
Athenlay Rd SE15. . .65 C2
Atheneoum Ct N5 . .15 B4
Athens Gdns W9 . . . .23 C1
Atherden Rd E5 . . . .17 B4
Atherfield Rd
SW18 . . . . .59 A1
Atherfold Rd SW9 . .62 A4
Atherstone Ct W2 . **100** B4
Atherstone Mews
SW7 . . . . **143** A4
Atherton Rd SW13. .46 C3
Atherton St SW11 . . **168** B2
Athlone Cl **24** E5 . . .17 A3
Athlone Ho
16 Camden Town
NW5. . . . . .12 C2
9 Stepney E1 . . . . . .32 B3
Athlone Rd SW2 . . . .74 C4
Athlone St NW5 . . . .12 C2
Athol Ct **15** N4 . . . . . . .5 B2
Atholl Ho W9 . . . . . . **88** C3
Athol Sq E14 . . . . . . .34 B3
Atkins Ct **15** E3 . . . . .26 B4
Atkins Lo W8 . . . . . **127** B4
Atkinson Ho
Battersea SW11. . . **169** B3
18 Hackney E2 . . . . .25 A3
Walworth SE17 . . . **151** C3
Atkins Rd SW4,
SW12 . . . . .73 C4
Atlanta Bldg **8**
SE13 . . . . .52 A2
Atlantic Ct **19** E14 . .34 C2
Atlantic Ho
5 Putney SW15 . . .58 B2
4 Tower Hamlets
E1 . . . . .33 A4

Atlantic Rd SW2, SW9,
SE24 . . . . .62 C3
Atlas Mews
Dalston E8 . . . . .16 B2
Islington N7 . . . . .14 B2
Atlas Rd NW10 . . . . .21 A2
Atney Rd SW15 . . . . .58 A3
Atterbury St SW1 . **148** A3
Attilburgh Ho SE1 . **138** C2
Attlee Ho E1 . . . . . . **111** A3
Attneave St WC1 . . . **95** B3
Atwater Cl SW2 . . . .74 C3
Atwell Rd **6** SE15 . . .49 C1
Atwood Ave TW9 . . .44 C1
Atwood Ho SE21. . . .76 A1
Atwood Rd W6 . . . . .39 A2
Aubert Ct N5 . . . . . . .15 A4
Aubert Pk N5 . . . . . . .15 A4
Aubert Rd N5 . . . . . .15 A4
Aubrey Beardsley Ho
SW1 . . . . **147** A3
Aubrey Mans
NW1 . . . . **102** A4
Aubrey Moore Point
E15 . . . . .27 B3
Aubrey Pl NW8 . . . . . **78** C1
Aubrey Rd
W14 . . . . . . 31 B1 **113** A1
Aubrey Wlk
W14 . . . . . . 31 B1 **113** A1
Auburn Cl SE14. . . . .51 A3
Aubyn Sq SW15 . . . .56 C2
Auckland Ho **11**
W12 . . . . .30 A2
Auckland Rd
SW11 . . . . .60 A3
Auckland St SE11 . **148** C1
Auden Pl NW1. . . . . . **81** B4
Audley Cl **8** SW11 . .60 C4
Audley Ct W2 . . . . . **118** A2
Audley Rd TW10 . . . .54 B2
Audley Sq W1 . . . . . **117** C2
Audley St W1 . . . . . **117** C2
Audrey Ho EC1 . . . . **107** C3
Audrey St E2 . . . . . . .24 C3
Augusta St E14 . . . . .34 A3
Augustine Ho
Broadgate EC2 . . . **109** C2
New Cross SE4. . . . . .51 B2
Augustine Rd W14. .39 C3
Augustines Ct E9 . . .17 B3
Augustus Cl W12 . . .39 A3
Augustus Ho
33 Putney SW19 . . .69 C3
Putney SW19 . . . . . . .70 A3
Augustus Rd
SW19 . . . . .69 C3
Augustus St NW1 . . **92** B4
Aulton Pl SE11 . . . . **149** C1
Aura Ho **3** TW9 . . . .45 A2
Auriga Mews N1 . . . .15 C3
Auriol Mans W14 . . **140** A3
Auriol Rd W14 . . . . **140** A3
Aurora Bldg **4**
E14. . . . . .34 B1
Aurora Ho E14 . . . . .34 A3
Austen Ho **5** NW6 . .23 C2
Austin Friars EC2 . **109** C2
Austin Friars Ho
EC2 . . . . **109** C2
Austin Friars Sq
EC2 . . . . **109** C2
Austin Ho
6 Brixton SW2 . . . .62 B2

Austin Ho continued
1 New Cross SE14. . .51 B3
Austin Rd SW11 . . . **169** B3
Austins Ct SE15. . . . .64 C4
Austin St E2. . .24 B2 **98** C3
Australia Rd W12 . . .30 A2
Austral St SE11 . . . **150** A4
Autumn Rise **9**
W4 . . . . .37 C1
Autumn St E3 . . . . . .26 C4
Avalon Rd SW6 . . . **166** A4
Avebury Ct N1. . . . . . **87** B3
Avebury Rd N1. . . . . . **87** B3
Aveline St SE11 . . . **149** B1
Aveling Ho **12** N19. . . .4 B1
Ave Maria La EC4 . **108** B1
Avenell Mans N5 . . .15 A4
Avenell Rd N5 . . . . . . .6 A1
Avenfield Ho W1 . . **117** A4
Avening Ct SW18. . . .70 C4
Avening Terr
SW18 . . . . .70 C4
Avenue Cl NW8 . . . . **80** B3
Avenue Cres **3**. 37 A4
Avenue Ct
Chelsea SW3 . . . . . **144** C3
Cricklewood NW2 . . . . .1 A1
Avenue Gdns
Mortlake SW14 . . . . .56 A4
South Acton W3 . . . . .37 A4
Avenue Ho
St John's Wood
NW8 . . . . **80** A1
Upper Clapton N16 . . . 7 C2
Willesden Green
NW10 . . . . .22 A3
Avenue Lo **12**
NW8 . . . . .11 C1
Avenue Mans
Clapham SW11. . . . . .60 C3
Hampstead NW3 . . . .11 A3
Willesden NW2 . . . . . . 9 A2
Avenue Park Rd SE21,
SE27 . . . . .75 A2
Avenue Rd
Crouch End N6 . . . . 4 C4
Harlesden NW10 . . . .21 B3
Primrose Hill NW8 . . .80 A4
South Acton W3 . . . . .37 A4
Avenue The
Bedford Pk W4 . . . . .38 A3
Brondesbury Pk
NW6 . . . . .23 A4
Clapham SW4. . . . . . .60 C2
Greenwich SE10 . . . .52 C3
Richmond TW9 . . . . . .44 B2
Wandsworth SW18,
SW12 . . . . .72 A4
Averill St W6 . . . . . . .47 C4
Avery Farm Row
SW1 . . . . **146** A3
Avery Hill Coll (Mile
End Annexe) E3 . . .26 B1
Avery Row W1 . . . **118** B4
Aviary Cl E16. . . . . . .35 B4
Avignon Rd SE4 . . . .65 C4
Avington Ct **16**
SE1 . . . . .25 C2
Avington Gr SE20 . . .76 A4
Avis Sq E1 . . . . .32 C3
Avocet Cl SE1 . . . . . **153** B2
Avon Ct
1 Acton W3 . . . . . .28 B3
10 Putney SW15 . . .58 A2
Avondale Ct E16. . . . .35 A4
Azania Mews NW5. .13 A2

Avondale Ho
11 Bermondsey
SE1 . . . . **153** B1
6 Mortlake SW14 . .55 C4
Avondale Mans
SW6 . . . . **164** C4
Avondale Park Gdns
W11 . . . . . . 31 A2 **112** A3
Avondale Park Prim
Sch W11 . . 31 A2 **112** A3
Avondale Park Rd
W11 . . . . . . 31 A2 **112** A4
Avondale Rd
Mortlake SW14 . . . . .55 C4
Newham E16 . . . . . . .35 A4
Avondale Rise
SE15 . . . . .64 B4
Avondale Sq SE1 . . **153** B1
Avon Ho
2 Islington N1 . . . .14 C1
14 Stoke Newington
N16. . . . . .15 C4
West Kensington
W14 . . . . **141** A3
Avonhurst Ho
NW6 . . . . .10 A1
Avonley Rd SE14. . . .50 B3
Avonmore Gdns
W14 . . . . **141** A3
Avonmore Pl W14 **140** B4
Avonmore Prim Sch
W14 . . . . **140** B4
Avonmore Rd
W14 . . . . **140** C4
Avonmouth St
SE1 . . . . **136** C2
Avon Pl SE1 . . . . . . **137** A3
Avon Rd SE4 . . . . . . .66 C4
Avriol Ho W12 . . . . . .30 A1
Avro Ct E9 . . . . .18 A3
Axford Ho SW2 . . . . .75 A3
Axis St SE10 . . . . . . .53 A4
Axminster Rd N7 . . . . 5 B1
Aybrook St W1 . . . . **103** B3
Aycliffe Rd W12 . . . .29 C1
Aylesbury Ho **13**
SE15 . . . . .49 C4
Aylesbury Rd
SE17 . . . . **151** C1
Aylesbury St
Clerkenwell EC1 . . . . .96 A1
Willesden NW10 . . . . . 8 A3
Aylesford Ho SE1 . **137** C3
Aylesford St SW1 . **147** B1
Aylesham Sh Ctr
SE15 . . . . .49 C2
Aylestone Ave
NW6 . . . . .22 C4
Aylmer Ho SE10 . . . .42 C1
Aylmer Rd W12 . . . .38 B4
Aylton Est **23** SE16. .40 B4
Aylward St E1 . . . . . .32 C3
Aylwin Est SE1 . . . **138** B2
Aynhoe Mans W14 . .39 C2
Aynhoe Rd W14 . . . .39 C2
Ayres St SE1 . . . . . **137** A4
Ayrsome Rd N16 . . . . 7 A1
Ayrton Gould Ho **8**
E2 . . . . .25 C2
Ayrton Rd SW7 . . . **129** B2
Aysgarth Rd SE21. . .76 A4
Ayshford Ho E2 . . . .25 A2
Ayston Ho **19** SE8. . .40 C2
Aytoun Ct **17** SW9 **173** A1
Aytoun Pl SW9 . . . **173** A1
Aytoun Rd SW9 . . . **173** A1
Azalea Ho SE14. . . . .51 B3

Azenby Rd SE15 . . . .49 B1
Azof St SE10 . . . . . . .43 B2
Azov Ho **10** E1. . . . . .26 A1
Aztec Ct **3** N16 . . . . .16 A2
Azure Ho **3**
E2 . . . . .24 C2 **99** B3

B

Baalbec Rd N5 . . . . .15 A3
Babington Ct
WC1 . . . . **106** B4
Babington Ho
SE1 . . . . **137** A4
Babmaes St SW1 . **119** B3
Bacchus Wlk **12**
N1. . . . . .24 A3
Bache's St N1 . . . . . . **97** C3
Back Church La
E1 . . . . **111** B1
Back Hill EC1 . . . . . . **95** C1
Backhouse Pl SE1 **152** B3
Back La NW3 . . . . . . .11 B4
Bacon Gr SE1 . . . . **138** C2
Bacon's Coll SE16 . .41 A4
Bacon's La N6 . . . . . . 3 C3
Bacton NW5. . . . . . . .12 C3
Bacton St E2 . . . . . . .25 B2
Baddeley Ho SE11 **149** A2
Baddow Wlk N1 . . . . **86** C4
Baden Pl SE1 . . . . . **137** B4
Badminton Ct **7**
N4 . . . . 6 B4
Badminton Ho
SE22 . . . . .64 A3
Badminton Mews **9**
E16. . . . . .35 C1
Badminton Rd
SW12 . . . . .60 C1
Badric Ct SW11. . . . **167** C1
Badsworth Rd **3**
SE5 . . . . .48 B2
Bagley's La SW6. . . **166** B3
Bagnigge Ho WC1 . . **95** B3
Bagshot Ho NW1 . . . **92** B4
Bagshot St SE17 . . **152** B1
Baildon **27** E2 . . . . . .25 B3
Baildon St SE8 . . . . .51 B3
Bailey Ct **9** W12 . . .38 C4
Bailey Ho SW10 . . **156** B2
Bailey Mews
Brixton SW2 . . . . . . .62 C2
Chiswick W4 . . . . . . .45 A4
Bainbridge St
WC1 . . . . **105** C2
Bain Ho **23** SW9 . . **172** B2
Baird Ho **20** W12 . . .30 A2
Baird St EC1. . . . . . . .97 A2
Baizdon Rd SE3 . . . .53 A1
Baker Ho **13** E3. . . . .27 A2
Baker Rd NW10. . . . .21 A4
Bakers Field N7 . . . .14 A4
Bakers Hall Ct
EC3 . . . . **124** B3
Baker's Mews W1 **103** B2
Bakers Pas **22**
NW3 . . . . .11 B4
Bakers Rents **13**
E2 . . . . .24 B2 **98** C3
Baker's Row EC1 . . . **95** B1
Baker St W1 . . . . . **103** A4
Baker Street Sta
NW1 . . . . **91** A1

Baker's Yd EC1 . . . . . 95 B1
Bakery Cl SW9 . . . 163 A1
Balaclava Rd SE1 153 A3
Balchier Rd SE22 . . 65 A1
Balcombe Ho
  Lisson Gr NW1 . . . . . 90 C2
  3 Streatham SW2 . . 74 B3
Balcombe St NW1 . 90 C1
Balcorne St E9 . . . . . 17 B1
Balderton Flats
  W1 . . . . 103 C1
Balderton St W1 . . . 103 C1
Baldock St E3 . . . . . . 27 A3
Baldrey Ho 1
  SE10 . . . . 43 B1
Baldwin Cres SE5 . . 48 B2
Baldwin Ho 5
  SW2 . . . . 74 C1
Baldwin Rd SW12 . . 60 C1
Baldwin's Gdns
  EC1 . . . . 107 B4
Baldwin St EC1 . . . . 97 B3
Baldwin Terr N1 . . . 86 C2
Baldwyn Gdns W3 . . 28 C2
Balearic Apts 8
  E16 . . . . 35 C2
Bale Rd E1 . . . . 33 A4
Bales Coll W10 . . . . 22 C2
Balfern Gr W4 . . . . . 38 A1
Balfern St SW11 . . . 168 B2
Balfe St N1 . . . . 84 B1
Balfour Ho 4
  W10 . . . . 30 C4
Balfour Mews W1 117 C2
Balfour Pl
  Mayfair W1 . . . . . . 117 C3
  Putney SW15 . . . . . 57 A3
Balfour Rd
  Highbury N5 . . . . . 15 B4
  North Acton W3 . . . 28 B4
Balfour St SE17 . . . 151 B4
Balfron Twr 4
  E14 . . . . 34 B3
BALHAM 72 C3
Balham Gr SW12 . . . 72 C4
Balham High Rd SW12,
  SW17 . . . . 72 C3
Balham Hill SW12 . . 61 A1
Balham L Ctr
  SW12 . . . . 73 A2
Balham New Rd
  SW12 . . . . 73 A4
Balham Park Mans
  SW12 . . . . 72 B3
Balham Park Rd SW12,
  SW17 . . . . 72 B3
Balham Sta SW12 . . 73 A3
Balham Station Rd
  SW12 . . . . 73 A3
Balin Ho SE1 . . . . . 137 B4
Balkan Wlk E1 . . . . . 32 A2
Balladier Wlk E14 . . 34 A4
Ballance Rd E9 . . . . 18 A2
Ballantine St
  SW18 . . . . 59 B3
Ballantrae Ho
  NW2 . . . . 10 B4
Ballard Ho SE10 . . . 52 A4
Ballast Quay SE10 . 42 C1
Ballater Rd SW2,
  SW4 . . . . 62 A3
Ball Ct EC3 . . . . 109 C1
Ballin Ct 14 E14 . . . 42 B4
Ballingdon Rd
  SW11 . . . . 60 C1

Ballinger Point 18
  E3 . . . . 27 A2
Balliol Ho 11
  SW15 . . . . 57 C1
Balliol Rd W10 . . . . . 30 C3
Ballogie Ave NW10 . . 8 A4
Ballow Cl 15 SE5 . . . 49 A3
Ball's Pond Pl 3
  N1 . . . . 15 C2
Ball's Pond Rd N1 . . 16 A2
Balman Ho 8
  SE16 . . . . 40 C2
Balmer Rd E3 . . . . . 26 B3
Balmes Rd N1 . . . . . 87 C4
Balmoral Cl 4
  SW15 . . . . 57 C1
Balmoral Ct
  21 Rotherhithe
  SE16 . . . . 32 C1
  St John's Wood
  NW8 . . . . 79 B2
Balmoral Gr N7 . . . . 14 B2
Balmoral Ho
  2 Isle of Dogs
  E14 . . . . 42 A3
  Stoke Newington N4 . 6 B3
  West Kensington
  W14 . . . . 140 A4
Balmoral Mews
  W12 . . . . 38 B3
Balmoral Rd NW2 . . 9 A2
Balmore Cl E14 . . . . 34 B3
Balmore St N19 . . . . 4 A2
Balmuir Gdns
  SW15 . . . . 57 B3
Balnacraig Ave
  NW10 . . . . 8 A4
Balniel Gate SW1 . 147 C2
Balsam Ho 6 E14 . . 34 A2
Baltic Apts 5 E16 . . 35 C2
Baltic Ho 7 SE5 . . . 48 B1
Baltic St E EC1 . . . . 96 C1
Baltic St W EC1 . . . . 96 C1
Baltimore Ho
  Clapham SW18 . . . . 59 B3
  Kennington SE11 . . 149 B2
Balvaird Pl SW1 . . . 147 C1
Balvernie Gr SW18 . 70 C4
Bamber Rd 5
  SE15 . . . . 49 B2
Bamborough Gdns 12
  W12 . . . . 39 B4
Banbury Ct WC2 . . . 120 A4
Banbury Ho 6 E9 . . 17 C1
Banbury Rd E9 . . . . 17 C1
Banbury St 3
  SW11 . . . . 168 B2
Bancroft Ct SW8 . . 172 A4
Bancroft Ho 11 E1 . 25 B1
Bancroft Rd E1 . . . . 25 C1
Banff Ho 11 NW3 . . 12 A2
Bangabandhu Prim
  Sch 22 E2 . . . . 25 B2
Bangalore St
  SW15 . . . . 57 C4
Banim St W6 . . . . . . 39 A2
Banister Ho
  Hackney E9 . . . . 17 C3
  Nine Elms SW8 . . . 171 A4
  6 West Kilburn
  W10 . . . . 23 A2
Banister Rd W10 . . . 22 C2
Bank La SW15 . . . . . 170 A4
Bank End SE1 . . . . . 123 A2
Bank La SW15 . . . . . 56 A2

Bank of England
  EC2 . . . . 109 B1
Bank of England Mus
  EC2 . . . . 109 B1
Banks Ho SE1 . . . . . 136 C1
Bankside
  Borough The SE1 . . 122 C3
  Borough The SE1 . . 123 A2
Bankside Ave 1
  SE13 . . . . 67 B4
Bankside Gall
  SE1 . . . . 122 C3
Bankside Ho EC3 . . 110 B1
Bankside Mix SE1 . 122 C3
Bankside Pier
  SE1 . . . . 122 C3
Bank St E14 . . . . 34 A1
Bank Sta EC3 . . . . . 109 C1
Bankton Rd SW2 . . 62 C3
Banner Ct 5 SE16 . . 40 B2
Banner Ho 3
  EC1 . . . . 97 A1
Bannerman Ho
  SW8 . . . . 162 C3
Banner St EC1 . . . . . 97 A2
Banning Ho 4
  SW19 . . . . 69 C3
Banning St SE10 . . . 43 A1
Bannister Cl SW2 . . 74 C3
Bannister Ho 28
  SE14 . . . . 50 C4
Banqueting Ho
  SW1 . . . . 120 A1
Banstead Ct
  East Acton W12 . . . 29 B2
  Stoke Newington N4 . 6 B3
Banstead St SE15 . . 65 B4
Bantock Ho 8
  W10 . . . . 23 A2
Bantry Ho 13 E1 . . . 25 C1
Bantry St SE5 . . . . . 48 C3
Banville Ho SW8 . . 163 A1
Banyan Ho 2
  NW3 . . . . 11 A2
Banyard Rd 12 SE16 40 A3
Baptist Gdns NW5 . 12 C2
Barandon Wlk 6
  W11 . . . . 30 C2
Barbanel Ho 20 E1 . 25 B1
Barbara Brosnan Ct
  NW8 . . . . 79 B1
Barbara Castle Cl
  SW6 . . . . 155 A3
Barbara Rudolph Ct
  5 N19 . . . . 5 A4
Barbauld Rd N16 . . . 7 A1
Barber Beaumont Ho
  2 E1 . . . . 25 C2
Barbers Rd E15 . . . . 27 A3
BARBICAN 109 A3
Barbican Ctr EC2 . . 109 A3
Barb Mews W6 . . . . 39 B3
Barbon Alley EC3 . . 110 B2
Barbrook Ho E9 . . . 17 B2
Barchard St SW18 . 59 A2
Barchester St E14 . . 34 A4
Barclay Cl SW6 . . . 155 B1
Barclay Ho 21 E9 . . 17 B1
Barclay Rd SW6 . . . 155 C1
Barcombe Ave
  SW2 . . . . 74 B2
Bardell Ho 17 SE1 . 139 B3
Bardolph Rd
  Richmond TW9 . . . . 54 B4
  Tufnell Pk N7 . . . . . 14 A4

Bard Rd W10 . . . . . . 30 C2
Bardsey Pl 41 E1 . . . 25 B1
Bardsey Wlk 5
  N1 . . . . 15 B2
Bardsley Ho 6
  SE10 . . . . 52 B4
Bardsley La SE10 . . 52 B4
Barents Ho 10 E1 . . 25 C1
Barfett St W10 . . . . . 23 B1
Barfleur La SE8 . . . . 41 B2
Barford Ho 23 E3 . . . 26 B3
Barford St N1 . . . . . . 85 C3
Barforth Rd SE15 . . 65 A4
Barge House St
  SE1 . . . . 121 C2
Barge La 10 E3 . . . . 26 B4
Barham Ho SE17 . . 152 B2
Baring Ct N1 . . . . . . 87 B3
Baring Ho 15 E14 . . 33 C3
Baring St N1 . . . . . . 87 B3
Barker Cl TW9 . . . . . 45 A1
Barker Dr NW1 . . . . 13 C1
Barker Ho
  Dulwich SE21 . . . . . 76 A1
  Walworth SE17 . . . 152 A3
Barker Mews SW4 . . 61 A3
Barker St SW10 . . . 156 C4
Bark Pl W2 . . . . 114 A4
Barkston Gdns
  SW5 . . . . 142 A3
Barkway Ct N4 . . . . . 6 B2
Barkwith Ho 27
  SE14 . . . . 50 C4
Barkworth Rd
  SE16 . . . . 40 B1
Barlborough St
  SE14 . . . . 50 C3
Barlby Gdns W10 . . 22 C1
Barlby Prim Sch
  W10 . . . . 22 C1
Barlby Rd W10 . . . . 30 C4
Barleycorn Way
  E14 . . . . 33 B2
Barley Mow Pas
  Chiswick W4 . . . . . . 37 C1
  Clerkenwell EC1 . . . 108 B3
Barley Shotts Bsns Pk
  W10 . . . . 31 B4
Barling 6 NW1 . . . . 13 A1
Barling St 1
  SW4 . . . . 172 A2
Barlings Ho 2
  SE4 . . . . 65 C3
Barloch Ho 14
  SW11 . . . . 169 B2
Barlow Ho
  14 Bermondsey
  SE16 . . . . 40 A2
  Notting Hill
  W11 . . . . 31 A2 112 A4
  Shoreditch N1 . . . . 97 B4
Barlow Pl W1 . . . . . 118 B3
Barlow Rd
  Acton W3 . . . . 28 A1
  Brondesbury NW6 . . 10 B2
Barlow St SE17 . . . . 151 C3
Barmouth Ho 6 N7 . 14 B2
Barmouth Rd
  SW18 . . . . 59 B1
Barnabas Ho EC1 . . 96 C3
Barnabas Lo SW8 . 172 B4
Barnabas Rd E9 . . . 17 C3
Barnaby Pl SW7 . . . 143 B3
Barnard Ct SE16 . . . 74 B1
Barnard Ho 17 E2 . . 25 A2

Barnard Lo 10 W9 . . 31 C4
Barnard Mews
  SW11 . . . . 60 A3
Barnardo Gdns 1
  E1 . . . . 32 C2
Barnardo St E1 . . . . 32 C3
Barnard Rd SW11 . . 60 A3
Barnard's Inn EC4 . 107 C2
Barnbrough NW1 . . 82 C3
Barnby St NW1 . . . . 93 A4
Barn Cl 12 NW5 . . . . 13 C3
Barn Elms Sp Ctr
  SW15 . . . . 47 B2
Barnersbury Ho
  N7 . . . . 14 A4
BARNES 46 B2
Barnes Ave SW13 . . 46 C3
Barnes Bridge Sta
  SW13 . . . . 46 A1
Barnes Common
  SW13 . . . . 56 C4
Barnes Ct N1 . . . . . . 14 C1
Barnes High St
  SW13 . . . . 46 B1
Barnes Ho
  14 Bethnal Green
  E2 . . . . 25 B3
  Camden Town NW1 . 82 B4
  26 Deptford SE14 . . 50 C4
  Hornsey N19 . . . . . . 5 A4
Barnes Hospl
  SW14 . . . . 56 A4
Barnes Prim Sch
  SW13 . . . . 56 B4
Barnes St E14 . . . . . 33 A3
Barnes Sta SW13 . . 56 C4
Barnes Terr SE8 . . . 41 B1
Barnet Gr
  E2 . . . . 24 C2 99 B3
Barnet Ho 55 SE5 . . 48 B1
Barnett Ho 11 E1 . . 110 C3
Barnett St 8 E1 . . . . 32 A3
Barn Field NW3 . . . . 12 B3
Barnfield Cl
  London N4 . . . . 5 A4
  Wandsworth SW17 . 71 B1
Barnfield Pl E14 . . . 41 C2
Barnham St SE1 . . . 138 B4
BARNSBURY 14 A1
Barnsbury Gr N7 . . . 14 B1
Barnsbury Ho 4
  SW4 . . . . 61 C1
Barnsbury Pk N1 . . . 14 C1
Barnsbury Rd N1 . . 85 B3
Barnsbury Sq N1 . . . 14 C1
Barnsbury St N1 . . . 14 C1
Barnsbury Terr N1 . 14 B1
Barnsdale Ave E14 . 41 C2
Barnsdale Rd W9 . . 23 B1
Barnsley St 11 E1 . . 25 A1
Barnstable La 1
  SE13 . . . . 67 B3
Barnston Wlk N1 . . . 86 C4
Barnwell Ho 1
  SE5 . . . . 49 A2
Barnwell Rd SW2 . . 62 C2
Barnwood Cl W9 . . . 88 B1
Barnes Rd 41
  SW18 . . . . 59 B1
Baroness Rd 2
  E2 . . . . 24 B2 99 A4
Barons Court Mans
  W14 . . . . 140 B1

Baron's Court Rd
W14 . . . . **140** B2
Barons Court Sta
W14 . . . . **140** A2
Barons Gate 🔟
W4 . . . . 37 B3
Barons Lo 🟨 E14 . . . 42 B2
Baronsmead Rd
SW13 . . . . 46 C2
Baronsmede W5 . . . . 36 B4
Baron's PI SE1 . . . . **135** C3
Baron St N1 . . . . 85 B2
Baron Wlk E16 . . . . . 35 B4
Barque Mews SE8 . . 51 C4
Barradell Ho 🔟
W14 . . . . 39 C3
Barratt Ho 🔟 N1 . . 15 A1
Barratt Ind Pk E3 . . 27 B1
Barret Ho NW6 . . . . 23 C4
Barrett Ct 🟨
NW10 . . . . 21 A3
Barrett's Gr N16 . . 16 A3
Barretts Green Rd
NW10 . . . . 20 C3
Barrett St W1 . . . . **103** C1
Barrhill Rd SW2 . . . . 74 A2
Barriedale SE14 . . . 51 A1
Barrie Ho
Acton W3 . . . . 37 B4
Bayswater W2 . . . . . **115** A3
Primrose Hill NW8 . . **80** B3
🟨 Stoke Newington
N16 . . . . 7 A2
Barrington CI
NW5 . . . . 12 C3
Barrington Ct
🟨 Acton W3 . . . . 37 A4
Kentish Town NW5 . . 12 C3
🟩 South Lambeth
SW9 . . . . **172** B1
Barrington Rd
SW9 . . . . 63 A4
Barrowgate Ho
W4 . . . . 37 C1
Barrowgate Rd
W4 . . . . 37 C1
Barrow Hill Est
NW8 . . . . **80** A1
Barrow Hill Jun Sch
NW8 . . . . **80** A1
Barrow Hill Rd
NW8 . . . . **80** A1
Barry Ct SW4 . . . . . 61 B1
Barry Ho 🟨 SE16 . . 40 A1
Barry Lo N4 . . . . 5 A4
Barry Par SE22 . . . . 64 C3
Barry Rd SE22 . . . . 64 C2
Barset Rd SE15 . . . . 65 B4
Barston Rd SE27 . . 75 B1
Barstow Cres SW2 . 74 B3
Bartell Ho SW2 . . . . 62 C1
Barter St WC1 . . . . **106** B3
Bartholomew CI
Barbican EC1 . . . . . . **108** C3
Wandsworth SW18 . . 59 B3
Bartholomew Ct
🟨 Blackwall E14 . . . 34 C2
St Luke's EC1 . . . . . . **97** A2
Bartholomew Ho 🟨
SE5 . . . . 48 B1
Bartholomew La
EC2 . . . . **109** C1

Bartholomew Pas
EC1 . . . . **108** B3
Bartholomew PI
EC1 . . . . **108** C3
Bartholomew Rd
NW5 . . . . 13 B2
Bartholomew Sq
🔟 Bethnal Green
E1 . . . . 25 A1
St Luke's EC1 . . . . . . **97** A2
Bartholomew St
SE1 . . . . **137** C1
Bartholomew Villas
NW5 . . . . 13 B2
Bartle Rd W11 . . . . 31 A3
Bartlett Cl E14 . . . . 33 C3
Bartlett Ct EC4 . . . **107** C2
Bartok Ho
W11 . . . . . 31 B2 **112** C3
Barton Cl
Hackney E9 . . . . 17 B3
Peckham SE15 . . . . . 65 A4
Barton Ct
🔟 South Lambeth
SW4 . . . . **172** A2
West Kensington
W14 . . . . **140** B2
Barton Ho
🟨 Bromley E3 . . . . 27 A2
Islington N1 . . . . 15 A1
Sands End SW6 . . . . 59 A4
Barton Rd W14 . . . **140** B1
Barton St SW1 . . . **134** A2
Bartonway NW8 . . 79 B2
Bartram Rd SE4 . . . 66 A1
Bartrip St E9 . . . . . 18 B2
Barts & The London
Sch of Medicine &
Dentistry EC1 . . . **96** B1
Barville CI SE4 . . . . 66 A3
Barwell Ho 🟨
E2 . . . . 24 C1 **99** C2
Barwick Ho 🟨 W3 . 37 B4
Bascome St 🔟 W3 . . . .
SW2 . . . . 62 C1
Base Apartments 🟨
N1 . . . . 15 B1
Baseline Business
Studios 🔟 W11 . . 30 C2
Basevi Way SE8 . . . . 52 A4
Bashley Rd NW10 . . 20 C1
Basildon Ct W1 . . **103** C4
Basil Ho
South Lambeth
SW8 . . . . **162** A2
🟨 Whitechapel E1 . **111** C2
Basil Mans SW1 . . **130** C3
Basil St
Knightsbridge
SW1 . . . . **130** C3
Knightsbridge SW1,
SW3 . . . . **130** C2
Basin App 🔟 E14 . . 33 A3
Basing Ct 🟨 SE15 . 49 B2
Basingdon Way
SE5 . . . . 63 C3
Basinghall Ave
EC2 . . . . **109** B2
Basinghall St EC2 . **109** B2
Basing Hill NW11 . . 1 B3
Basing House 🟨 E2 . . . .
E2 . . . . 24 A2 **98** B4
Basing PI E2 . . 24 A2 **98** B4
Basing St W11 . . . . 31 B3
Basire St N1 . . . . . . 87 A4

Baskerville Ct
SW18 . . . . 72 A4
Baskerville Gdns
NW10 . . . . 8 A4
Baskerville Rd
SW18 . . . . 72 A4
Baslow Wlk E5 . . . . . 17 C4
Basnett Rd 🟨
SW11 . . . . 60 C4
Basque Ct 🟨 SE16 . 40 C4
Bassano St SE22 . . 64 B2
Bassein Park Rd
W12 . . . . 38 B4
Bassett House Sch 🟨
W10 . . . . 30 C3
Bassett Rd W10 . . . 30 C3
Bassett St NW5 . . . 12 C2
Bassingbourn Ho 🟨
N1 . . . . 15 A1
Bassingham Rd
SW18 . . . . 71 B4
Bassishaw Highwalk
EC2 . . . . **109** B3
Basswood CI 🟨
SE15 . . . . 65 A4
Basterfield Ho 🟨 EC1 . . . .
EC1 . . . . **96** C1
Bastion Highwalk
EC2 . . . . **108** C3
Bastwick St EC1 . . . **96** C2
Basuto Rd SW6 . . . **165** C3
Batavia Ho 🟨
SE14 . . . . 51 A3
Batavia Mews 🟨
SE14 . . . . 51 A3
Batavia Rd SE14 . . . 51 A3
Batchelor St N1 . . . **85** C3
Bateman Ho 🟨
SE17 . . . . 48 A4
Bateman's Bldgs
W1 . . . . **105** B1
Bateman's Row
EC2 . . . . . . 24 A1 **98** B2
Bate St 🔟 E14 . . . . 33 B2
Bath Cl SE15 . . . . . . 50 A3
Bath Ct
Finsbury EC1 . . . . . . **95** B3
🟨 Forest Hill SE26 . 76 C1
Holborn EC1 . . . . . . **95** B1
Bathgate Ho 🟨
SW9 . . . . 48 A2
Bathgate Rd SW19 . 69 C1
Bath Gr E2 . . . . 24 C3
Bath Ho
Bethnal Green
E2 . . . . 24 C1 **99** C2
Borough The SE1 . . . **137** A2
Bath PI
🔟 Hammersmith
W6 . . . . 39 B1
🔟 Shoreditch
EC2 . . . . . . 24 A2 **98** A3
Bath Rd W4 . . . . . . 38 A2
Bath St EC1 . . . . . . **97** B3
Bath Terr SE1 . . . . **136** C2
Bathurst Gdns
NW10 . . . . 22 A3
Bathurst Ho 🟨
W12 . . . . 30 A2
Bathurst Mews
W2 . . . . **115** C4
Bathurst St W2 . . . **115** C4
Batley PI 🟨 N16 . . . 7 B1
Batley Rd N16 . . . . . 7 B1
Batman CI W12 . . . 30 A1
Batoum Gdns W6 . . 39 B3

Batson Ho 🟨 E1 . **111** C1
Batson St W12 . . . . 38 C4
Batten Ho
🔟 London W4 . . . . 61 B2
🔟 West Kilburn
W10 . . . . 23 A2
Batten St SW11 . . . 60 A4
BATTERSEA **169** A4
Battersea Bridge Rd
SW11 . . . . **158** A1
Battersea Bsns Ctr
SW11 . . . . 60 C3
Battersea Church Rd
SW11 . . . . **167** C4
Battersea Dogs & Cats
Home SW8 . . . . **160** B1
Battersea High St
SW11 . . . . **167** B1
Battersea Hts
SW11 . . . . 60 B4
Battersea Park
SW11 . . . . **159** B1
Battersea Park Rd
SW8, SW11 . . . . **169** A3
Battersea Park Sta
SW8 . . . . **160** C1
Battersea Power
Station(dis)
SW8 . . . . **160** B4
Battersea Rise
SW11 . . . . 60 A3
Battersea Sq 🟨
SW11 . . . . . . 32 B4 **167** C3
Battishill St 🟨 N1 . 15 A1
Battlebridge Ct
NW1 . . . . **84** B2
Battle Bridge La
SE1 . . . . **124** A1
Battledean Rd N5 . . 15 A3
Battle Ho 🟨 SE15 . 49 C4
Batty St E1 . . . . **111** C2
Baty Ho SW2 . . . . . 74 B3
Baulk The SW18 . . . 70 C4
Bavaria Rd N19 . . . . 5 A2
Bavent Rd SE5 . . . . 48 B1
Bawdale Rd SE22 . . 64 B2
Bawtree Rd SE14 . . 51 A3
Baxendale
E2 . . . . 24 C2 **99** B4
Baxter Ho 🔟 E3 . . . 27 A2
Baxter Rd N1 . . . . . 15 C2
Baycliffe Ho 🟨 E9 . 17 C2
Bay Ct
Ealing W5 . . . . 36 A3
🟨 Stepney E1 . . . . 25 C1
Bayer Ho EC1 . . . . . **96** C1
Bayes Ct NW3 . . . . 12 B1
Bayfield Ho 🟨
SE4 . . . . 65 C3
Bayford Rd NW10 . . 22 C2
Bayford St Ind Ctr 🟨
E8 . . . . 17 A1
Bayford St 🟨 E8 . . 17 A1
Bayham PI NW1 . . . 83 A3
Bayham Rd W4 . . . . 37 C3
Bayham St NW1 . . . **82** C3
Bayhurst Ho N4 . . . . 6 B4
Bayley St WC1 . . . . **105** B3
Baylis Rd SE1 . . . . **135** B3
Baynes Mews 🟨
NW3 . . . . 11 C2
Baynes St NW1 . . . 13 B1
Bayon Ho 🟨 N19 . . . 4 C4
Bayonne Rd W6 . . . **154** A3

Bayston Rd N16 . . . . 7 B1
BAYSWATER **114** C4
Bayswater Rd W2 . **115** B3
Bayswater Sta
W2 . . . . **115** A3
Bayswater Sta
W2 . . . . **114** B4
Bayton Ct 🟨 E8 . . **16** C1
Baytree Rd SW2 . . . 62 B3
Bazalgette Ho
NW8 . . . . **89** C2
Bazeley Ho SE1 . . **136** A3
Bazely St E14 . . . . . 34 B2
BBC Television Ctr
W12 . . . . 30 B1
Beach Ho SW5 . . . **141** B2
Beachy Rd E3 . . . . . 18 C1
Beaconfield Terrace
Rd W14 . . . . **126** A1
Beacon Gate SE14 . 65 C4
Beacon Hill N7 . . . 14 A3
Beacon Ho
🟨 Camberwell
SE5 . . . . 49 A3
🟨 Isle of Dogs
E14 . . . . 42 A1
South Lambeth
SW8 . . . . **171** B4
Beacon Rd SE13 . . . 67 C1
Beaconsfield Cl
Acton Green W4 . . . 37 B1
Greenwich SE3 . . . . 53 C4
Beaconsfield Rd
Acton W4 . . . . 37 C3
Greenwich SE3 . . . . 53 C3
Walworth SE17 . . . . **152** A1
Willesden NW10 . . . . 8 B2
Beaconsfield Wlk
SW6 . . . . **165** A3
Beadon Rd W6 . . . . 39 B2
Beak St W1 . . . . **119** A4
Beale PI E3 . . . . 26 B3
Beale Rd E3 . . . . 26 B4
Beames Ho SW8 . . **171** B4
Beames Rd NW10 . . 20 C4
Beaminster Ho
SW8 . . . . **162** C2
Beamish Ho 🟨
SE16 . . . . 40 B2
Beanacre Cl E9 . . . . 18 B2
Bear Alley EC4 . . . **108** A2
Bear Croft Ho 🟨
SW6 . . . . **164** C1
Beardsley Way
W3 . . . . 37 C4
Bear Gdns SE1 . . . **122** C2
Bear La SE1 . . . . . . **122** B1
Bear St WC2 . . . . . **119** C4
Bearstead Rise
SE4 . . . . 66 B2
Beaton Cl SE15 . . . 49 B2
Beatrice Ho
🟨 Brixton SW2 . . . 62 B2
🟨 Hammersmith
W6 . . . . 39 B1
🟨 Stepney E1 . . . . 32 C4
Beatrice PI W8 . . . **128** A1
Beatrice Rd
Bermondsey SE1 . . **153** C3
Finsbury Pk N4 . . . . . 5 C4
🟨 Richmond TW10 . 54 B2
Beatrice Tate Sch 🟨
E2 . . . . 25 A2
Beatrice Webb Ho 🟨
E3 . . . . 26 A3

Beatrix Ho SW5 . . . 142 B2
Beatrix Potter Prim
Sch SW18 . . . . 71 B3
Beatson Wlk 28
SE16 . . . . 32 C1
Beattie Ho SW8 . . . 171 A4
Beatty Ho 12 E14 . . . 41 C4
Beatty Rd N16 . . . . . 16 A4
Beauchamp Cl 7
W4 . . . . 37 B3
Beauchamp Pl
SW3 . . . . 130 B1
Beauchamp Rd
SW11 . . . . 60 B3
Beauchamp St
EC1 . . . . 107 B3
Beauchamp Terr
SW15 . . . . 57 A4
Beauclerc Rd W6 . . . 39 A3
Beauclerk Ho 10
SW16 . . . . 74 A1
Beaufort Cl SW19 . . . 69 A4
Beaufort Ct SW6 . . . 155 B4
Beaufort Gdns
SW3 . . . . 130 B2
Beaufort Ho
Battersea SW11 . . . 168 A2
Chelsea SW3 . . . . . 157 C3
20 Millwall E14 . . . . 41 C4
Pimlico SW1 . . . . . 147 B1
Beaufort Mans
SW3 . . . . 157 C3
Beaufort Mews
SW6 . . . . 155 A4
Beaufort St SW3 . . 157 B4
Beaufoy Ho
South Lambeth
SW8 . . . . 162 C2
3 West Norwood
SE27 . . . . 75 A1
Beaufoy Rd 11
SW8 . . . . 61 A4
Beaufoy Wlk SE11 . 149 A3
Beaulieu Cl SE5 . . . . 63 C4
Beaulieu Pl W4 . . . . 37 B3
Beaumanor Mans
W2 . . . . 114 B4
Beaumaris Twr 2
W3 . . . . 37 A4
Beaumont SW15 . . . 58 B2
Beaumont Ave
Richmond TW9 . . . . . 54 B4
West Kensington
W14 . . . . 140 C2
Beaumont Bldgs
WC2 . . . . 106 B1
Beaumont Cres
W14 . . . . 140 C1
Beaumont Ct
10 Acton Green
W4 . . . . 37 B1
Marylebone W1 . . . 103 C4
3 Mile End E1 . . . . 26 A2
Beaumont Gdns
NW3 . . . . 1 C1
Beaumont Gr E1 . . . 25 C1
Beaumont Ho
1 Streatham
SW2 . . . . 74 A3
West Kensington
W14 . . . . 141 A3
Wimbledon SW19 . . . 70 C1
Beaumont Lo E8 . . . 16 C2
Beaumont Pl NW1, NW1,
W1 . . . . 93 A2

Beaumont Rd
Putney SW15,
SW19 . . . . 70 A4
South Acton W4 . . . 37 B3
Beaumont Rise N19 . 4 C3
Beaumont Sq E1 . . . 32 C4
Beaumont St W1 . . 103 C4
Beaumont Wlk
NW3 . . . . 12 B1
Beauvale 6 NW1 . . . 12 C1
Beauval Rd SE22 . . . 64 B1
Beavis Ho N16 . . . . . 7 A1
Beavor La W6 . . . . . 38 C1
Beccles St E14 . . . . 33 B3
Beck Ct SE13 . . . . . 52 A2
Beckers The N16 . . 16 C4
Becket Ho SE1 . . . . 137 B3
Becket St SE1 . . . . 137 B2
Beckett Cl
Streatham SW16 . . . 73 C2
Willesden NW10 . . . . 8 A2
Beckett Ho
28 London SW9 . . . 172 B1
11 Stepney E1 . . . . 32 B4
Beckfoot NW1 . . . . 83 A1
Beckford Cl W14 . . 141 A3
Beckford Ho 15
N16 . . . . 16 A3
Beckford Prim Sch
NW6 . . . . 10 A1
Beckham Ho
SE11 . . . . 149 A3
Beck Ho N16 . . . . . . 7 A1
Beckington 15
NW5 . . . . 12 C2
Beckley Ho E3 . . . . . 26 B1
Becklow Gdns
Chiswick W12 . . . . . 38 B4
1 Shepherd's Bush
W12 . . . . 38 C4
Becklow Mews 7
W12 . . . . 38 B4
Becklow Rd W12 . . 38 C4
Beck Rd E8 . . . . 25 A4
Beckton Rd E16 . . . 35 B4
Beckway St SE17 . . 152 A3
Beckwith Ho 22
E2 . . . . 25 A3
Beckwith Rd SE24 . . 63 C2
Bective Pl SW15 . . . 58 B3
Bective Rd SW15 . . 58 B3
Bedale St SE1 . . . . 123 B1
Bedefield WC1 . . . . 94 B3
Bede Ho
London SE14 . . . . . . 51 B2
8 Putney SW15 . . . 57 C1
Bedford Ave WC1 . . 105 C3
Bedfordbury WC2 . 120 A3
Bedford Cl W4 . . . . 46 B4
Bedford Cnr 3
W4 . . . . 38 A2
Bedford Court Mans
WC1 . . . . 105 C3
Bedford Ct 5
6 Richmond
TW9 . . . . 54 B3
St James WC2 . . . . 120 A3
Bedford Gardens Ho
W8 . . . . . . 31 C1 113 C1
Bedford Gdns
W8 . . . . . . 31 C1 113 C1
Bedford Hill SW12 . 73 C1
Bedford Ho
Acton W4 . . . . 38 A2
7 Stockwell SW4 . . 62 A3
BEDFORD PARK . . 38 A3

Beechwood Rd E8 . . 16 B2
Bedford Park Cnr 5
W4 . . . . 38 A2
Bedford Park Mans 4
W4 . . . . 37 C2
Bedford Pas SW6 . 154 B2
Bedford Pl WC1 . . 106 A4
Bedford Rd
Acton W4 . . . . 38 A3
Stockwell SW2,
SW4 . . . . 62 A3
Bedford Row
WC1 . . . . 107 A3
Bedford Sq WC1 . . 105 C3
Bedford St WC2 . . 120 B3
Bedford Way WC1 . 93 C1
Bedgebury Gdns
SW19 . . . . 70 A2
Bedlam Mews
SE11 . . . . 149 B4
Bedlow CI NW8 . . . 89 C1
Bedser Ct SE11 . . . 163 A4
Bedwell Ho 18
SW9 . . . . 173 B1
Beech Ave W3 . . . . . 29 A1
Beech Cl
Deptford SE8 . . . . . 51 B4
Putney SW15 . . . . . 68 C4
Beech Ct
1 Child's Hill NW2 . . 1 B2
Marylebone W1 . . . 102 C2
Notting Hill W2 . . . 31 C4
7 Rotherhithe
SE16 . . . . 33 A1
Beechdale Rd
SW2 . . . . 62 B1
Beechdene 4
SE15 . . . . 50 A2
Beeches Rd SW17 . 72 B1
Beeches The 1
N19 . . . . 5 A3
Beechey Ho 30 E1 . . 32 A1
Beech Gdns W5 . . . 36 A3
Beech Ho
1 Maitland Pk
NW3 . . . . 12 B2
2 Rotherhithe
SE16 . . . . 40 B4
5 Stoke Newington
N16 . . . . 6 C2
Beechmore Rd
SW11 . . . . 169 A3
Beech St EC2 . . . . 109 A4
Beech Tree Cl N1 . 14 C1
Beechwood Ave
TW9 . . . . 44 C2
Beechwood Ct
Chiswick W4 . . . . . 45 C4
Stamford Hill N16 . . . 7 A4
Beechwood Gr
W3 . . . . 29 A2
Beechwood Ho 28
E2 . . . . 24 C3

Beechworth Cl
NW3 . . . . 1 C2
Beecroft La SE4 . . . 66 A2
Beecroft Mews
SE4 . . . . 66 A2
Beecroft Rd SE4 . . 66 A2
Beehive Cl E8 . . . . 16 B1
Beehive Pl SW9 . . . 62 C4
Beeston Cl 5 E8 . . 16 C3
Beeston Pl SW1 . . 132 B2
Beeston's Ho SE15 . 65 A4
Beethoven St W10 . 23 A2
Begbie Ho SW9 . . . 173 A2
Begonia Wlk W12 . . 29 B3
Beira St SW12 . . . . 73 A4
Beis Chinuch Lebonos
Girls Sch N4 . . . . . . 6 B4
Beis Hamedrash Elyon
NW11 . . . . 1 A4
Beis Malka Girls Sch
N16 . . . . 7 B3
Beis Rochel d'Satmar
Girls Sch 1 N16 . . . 7 A4
Bekesbourne St 17
E14 . . . . 33 A3
Beldanes Ho NW10 . . 8 C1
Belenoyd Ct SW16 . 74 B1
Belfast Rd N16 . . . . 7 B2
Belford Ho 7 E8 . . 24 B4
Belford Ho 7 E8 . . 24 B4
Belfort Rd SE15 . . . 50 B1
Belfry Cl 33 SE16 . . 40 A1
Belgrade Ho N16 . . 16 A4
Belgrade Rd N16 . . 16 A4
Belgrave Cl 1 W3 . . 37 B4
Belgrave Ct
3 Acton Green
W4 . . . . 37 B1
22 Limehouse E14 . 33 B2
Nine Elms SW8 . . . 160 C1
Belgrave Gdns
Kilburn NW8 . . . . . 78 C3
St John's Wood
NW8 . . . . 78 C3
Belgrave Mans
NW8 . . . . 78 C3
Belgrave Mews N
SW1 . . . . 131 B3
Belgrave Mews S
SW1 . . . . 131 C2
Belgrave Mews W
SW1 . . . . 131 B2
Belgrave Pl SW1 . . 131 C1
Belgrave Rd
Barnes SW13 . . . . . 46 B3
Westminster SW1 . 146 C3
Belgrave Sq SW1 . 131 B2
Belgrave St E1 . . . 32 C3
Belgrave Yd SW1 . 132 A1
Belgravia Ct SW1 . 132 A2
BELGRAVIA 146 A4
Belgravia Ho 11
SW11 . . . . 60 B1
Belgrove St WC1 . . 94 B4
Belham Wlk 18
SE5 . . . . 48 C2
Belinda Rd 8
SW9 . . . . 63 A4
Belitha Villas N1 . . 14 C1
Bellamy Cl
13 Millwall E14 . . . 41 C4
West Kensington
SW5 . . . . 141 A1
Bellamy's Ct 16
SE16 . . . . 32 C1

Bellamy St SW12 . . 73 A4
Bellasis Ave SW2 . . 74 A2
Bell Ct SE13 . . . . . . 51 C4
Bell Dr SW18 . . . . . 70 A4
Bellefields Rd
SW9 . . . . 62 B4
Bellenden Prim Sch
SE15 . . . . 49 C1
Bellenden Rd SE15 . 49 C2
Bellenden Rd Ret Pk
SE15 . . . . 49 C2
Bellenden Road Bsns
Ctr SE15 . . . . 49 B1
Bellerbys Coll SE8 . 51 C4
Belleville Prim Sch
SW11 . . . . 60 B2
Belle Vue Gdns
SW9 . . . . 172 B1
Bellevue Pl E1 . . . . 25 B1
Bellevue Rd
Barnes SW13 . . . . . 46 C1
Upper Tooting
SW17 . . . . 72 B3
Bellew St SW17 . . . 71 B1
Bell Flats 41 NW2 . . 8 C2
Bellflower Ct SE13 . 67 A3
Bellgate Mews
NW5 . . . . 4 A1
Bellgrave Lo 9
W4 . . . . 37 A1
Bell Ho
Greenwich SE10 . . . 52 B4
Streatham SW2 . . . 74 C4
3 Wapping E1 . . . 32 A1
Bell Ind Est 8 W4 . 37 B2
Bell Inn Yd EC3 . . 109 C1
Bell La
Newham E16 . . . . . 35 C1
Spitalfields E1 . . . 110 C3
Bell Language Sch
W1 . . . . 92 C1
Bell La
E3 . . . . 33 C4
Bellmaker Ct 13
E3 . . . . 33 C4
Bell Moor NW3 . . . . 2 B1
Bello Cl SE24 . . . . . 75 A3
Bellot Gdns 1
SE10 . . . . 43 A1
Bellot St SE10 . . . . 43 A1
Bell Wharf La
EC4 . . . . 123 A4
Bellwood Rd SE15 . 65 C3
Bell Yard Mews
SE1 . . . . 138 B3
Bell Yd WC2 . . . . . 107 B1
Belmont Cl SW4 . . 61 B4
Belmont Ct
Highbury N5 . . . . . 15 B4
5 Stamford Hill N16 . 7 A3
Belmont Gr
Chiswick W4 . . . . . 37 C2
Lewisham SE13 . . . 67 C4
Belmont Hall Ct
SE13 . . . . 67 C4
Belmont Hill SE13 . 67 C4
Belmont Mews
SW19 . . . . 69 C2
Belmont Prim Sch 10
W4 . . . . 37 C2
Belmont Rd
Clapham SW4 . . . . . 61 B4
London W4 . . . . 37 C2

Belmont Terr W4 ....37 C2
Belmore Ho N7 ....13 C3
Belmore La N7 ....13 C3
Belmore St SW8 ..171 B4
Beloe Cl SW15 ....56 C3
Belper Ct 11 E5 ....17 C4
Belsham St E9 ....17 B2
Belsize Ave NW3 ..12 A3
Belsize Court Garages
 1 NW3 ....11 C3
Belsize Cres NW3 ..11 C3
Belsize Ct NW3 ....11 C3
Belsize Gr NW3 ....12 A2
Belsize La NW3 ....11 C3
Belsize Mews
 NW3 ....11 C2
Belsize Park Gdns
 NW3 ....12 A2
Belsize Park Mews 1
 NW3 ....11 C2
Belsize Pk Sta
 NW3 ....12 A3
Belsize Pk NW3 ....11 C2
Belsize Pl NW3 ....11 C3
Belsize Rd NW6 ..78 B4
Belsize Sq NW3 ....11 C2
Belsize Terr NW3 ..11 C2
Beltane Dr SW19 ..69 C1
Belthorn Cres
 SW12 ....73 B4
Belton Rd NW2 ....8 C2
Belton Way E3 ....33 C4
Beltran Rd SW6 ..166 A1
Belvedere Bldgs
 SE1 ....136 B3
Belvedere Ct
 Brondesbury NW2 ...9 C2
 7 Clapham Pk
   SW4 ....61 C1
 Putney SW15 ....57 B3
 33 Shoreditch N1 ..24 A4
Belvedere Htss
 NW6 ....90 A2
Belvedere Mews
 SE15 ....65 B4
Belvedere Pl
 Brixton SW2 ....62 B3
 Lambeth SE1 ..136 B3
Belvedere Rd SE1 121 A1
Belvedere The
 SW10 ....167 A3
Belvoir Lo SE22 ...76 C4
Belvoir Rd SE22 ...76 C4
Bembridge Cl
 NW6 ....10 A1
Bembridge Ho
 9 Deptford SE8 ...41 B2
 Wandsworth SW18 ..59 A1
Bemerton St N1 ...84 C4
Bemish Rd SW15 ..57 C4
Benabo Ct 6 E8 ..16 C3
Benbow Ho 8 ....39 A3
Benbow Ho 12
 SE8 ....51 C4
Benbow Rd W6 ....39 A3
Benbow St SE8 ....51 C4
Bence Ho 15 SE8 ..41 A2
Bendall Mews
 NW1 ....102 B4
Bendemeer Rd
 SW15 ....57 C4
Benden Ho SE13 ..67 B2
Bendon Valley
 SW18 ....71 A4

Benedict Rd SW9...62 B4
Benenden Ho
 SE17 ....152 B2
Ben Ezra Ct SE17 151 A3
Benfleet Ct 6 E8...24 B4
Bengal Ct EC3 ....109 C1
Bengal Ho E1 ....32 C4
Bengeworth Rd
 SE5 ....63 B4
Benham Ho SW10 156 B2
Benham's Pl 11
 NW3 ....11 B4
Benhill Rd SE5 ....48 C2
Benington Ct N4 ...6 B2
Benjamin Cl E8 ....24 C4
Benjamin Franklin
 House SW1 ....120 A2
Benjamin Ho 2
 W3 ....28 A1
Benjamin Mews
 SW12 ....73 B4
Benjamin St EC1 ..108 A4
Ben Jonson Ct 10
 N1 ....24 A3
Ben Jonson Prim Sch
 2 ....25 A4
Ben Jonson Rd E1 33 A4
Benledi Rd E14 ....34 C3
Bennelong Cl W12..30 A3
Bennerley Rd
 SW11 ....60 B2
Bennet's Hill EC4. 122 B4
Bennett Ct
 Hampstead NW6 ...11 A2
 Lower Holloway N7 ..5 B1
 7 South Acton W3 ..37 A4
Bennett St EC3...52 A2
Bennett Ho
 2 Streatham
   SW4 ....73 C4
 Westminster SW1 147 C4
Bennett St
 Chiswick W4 ....38 A1
 St James SW1 ..118 C2
Benn Ho E2 .....24 C2 99 B3
Benn St E9 ....18 A2
Benns Wlk 8 TW9..54 A3
Bensbury Cl SW15..69 B4
Ben Smith Way 27
 SE16 ....139 C2
Benson Ct
 South Lambeth
   SW8 ....172 A4
 1 Tufnell Pk N19 ..13 B4
Benson Ho
 Lambeth SE1 ....121 C1
 Shoreditch
 E2 ....24 B1 98 C2
Benson Quay E1...32 B2
Benthal Ct N16 ....7 C1
Benthal Prim Sch
 N16 ....7 C1
Bentham Ct 11 N1..15 B1
Bentham Ho SE1 137 B2
Bentham Rd E9 ...17 C2
Bentinck Cl NW8 ..80 B1
Bentinck Ho 4
 W12 ....30 A2
Bentinck Mans
 W1 ....103 C2
Bentinck Mews
 W1 ....103 C2
Bentinck St W1 ...103 C2
Bentley Cl SW19 ..70 C1

Bentley Ct SE13 ...67 B3
Bentley Dr NW2 ...10 B1
Bentley Ho
 6 Bow SE5 ....26 C1
 4 Camberwell SE5 49 A3
Bentley Rd N1 .....16 A2
Bentworth Ct 1
 E2 ....24 C1 99 B2
Bentworth Prim Sch
 W12 ....30 A3
Bentworth Rd
 W12 ....30 A3
Benwell Rd N7 ....14 C3
Benwick Cl SE16...40 A2
Benworth St E3 ...26 B2
Benyon Ho EC1 ....95 C4
Benyon Rd N1 ....87 C4
Benyon Wharf 81
 E8 ....24 A4
Beormund Sch
 SE1 ....137 C3
Bequerel Ct SE10 ..43 B3
Berberis Ho 17 E3 27 C2
Berber Pl 2 E14 ...33 C2
Berber Rd SW11 ...60 B2
Berebinder Ho 21
 E3 ....26 B3
Berenger Twr
 SW10 ....157 B2
Berenger Wlk
 SW10 ....157 B2
Berens Rd NW10 ..22 C2
Beresford Ct E9 ...18 A3
Beresford Ho
 Dulwich SE21 ....76 A1
 18 Stockwell SW4 62 A3
Beresford Lo N4 ..15 C3
Beresford Rd N5 ..15 C3
Beresford Terr 3
 N5 ....15 B3
Bere St E1 ....32 C2
Berestede Rd 4
 W6 ....38 B1
Bergen Ho 1 SE5 ..48 B1
Bergen Sq SE16 ...41 A3
Berger Prim Sch 50
 E9 ....17 C2
Berger Rd E9 ....17 C2
Berghem Mews
 W14 ....39 C3
Bergholt Cres N16..7 A4
Bergholt Mews 4
 NW1 ....13 C1
Berglen Ct E14 ....33 A2
Bering Sq E14 ....41 C1
Berisford Mews
 SW18 ....59 B1
Berkeley Ct
 1 Golders Green
   NW11 ....1 B4
 Marylebone NW1 .. 91 A1
 Willesden NW10...8 A4
Berkeley Gdns
 W8 ....31 C1 113 C1
Berkeley Ho
 17 Bow E3 ....26 C2
 4 Deptford SE8....41 B1
Berkeley Mews
 W1 ....103 A1
Berkeley Rd N15 ..36 C2
Berkeley Sq W1 ..118 B3
Berkeley St W1 ...118 B2
Berkeley The NW11..2 A4
Berkeley Wlk 1 N7..5 B2
Berkley Gr NW1 ...12 C1
Berkley Rd NW1 ...12 C1

Berkshire Ho
 WC2 ....106 A2
Berkshire Rd E9...18 B2
Bermans Way NW10..8 B4
BERMONDSEY 40 A4
Bermondsey Leather
 Mkt SE1 ....138 A3
Bermondsey Sq
 SE1 ....138 B2
Bermondsey St
 SE1 ....138 B3
Bermondsey Sta
 SE16 ....40 A3
Bermondsey Trad Est
 SE16 ....40 B1
Bermondsey Wall E
 SE16 ....40 A4
Bermondsey Wall W
 SE1, SE16 ....139 B4
Bernard Angell Ho 4
 SE10 ....52 C4
Bernard Cassidy St 2
 E16 ....35 B4
Bernard Ho E1 ....110 C3
Bernard Shaw Ct 5
 NW1 ....13 B1
Bernard Shaw Ho 2
 NW10 ....20 C4
Bernard St WC1 ...94 B1
Bernay's Gr SW9 ..62 B3
Berners Ho N1 ....85 B2
Berners Mews
 W1 ....105 A3
Berners Pl W1 ....105 A2
Berners Rd N1 ....86 A3
Berners St W1 ....105 A2
Berner Terr 27 E1 111 C1
Bernhard Baron Ho 35
 E1 ....111 C1
Bernhardt Cres
 NW8 ....90 A2
Bernie Grant Ho 40
 E9 ....17 B1
Bernwood Ho 6
 N4 ....6 C4
Berridge Mews
 NW6 ....10 C3
Berriman Rd N7 ...5 B1
Berry Cotts 2 E14 33 A3
Berryfield Rd
 SE17 ....150 B2
Berry Ho
 10 Battersea
   SW11 ....169 A2
 28 Bethnal Green
   E1 ....25 A1
Berrymead Gdns
 W3 ....37 B4
Berrymede Inf Sch
 W3 ....37 A4
Berrymede Jun Sch
 W3 ....37 A4
Berrymede Rd W4 37 C3
Berry Pl EC1 ....96 B3
Berry St EC1 ....96 B1
Berry Way W5 ....36 A3
Bertha Neubergh Ho
 1 SE5 ....48 B2
Berthon St SE8 ...51 C4
Bertie Rd NW10 ...8 C2
Bertram St N19 ...4 A2
Bertrand Ho 1
 SW16 ....74 A1
Bertrand St SE13 ..67 A4
Bertrum House Sch
 SW17 ....72 C2

Berwick St W1 ....105 A1
Berwick Street Mkt
 W1 ....105 A1
Berwyn Ho 3 N16..7 B3
Berwyn Rd
 Mortlake SW14,
   TW10 ....55 A3
 Streatham SE24 ...75 A3
Beryl Rd W6 ....39 C1
Besant Cl NW2 ....1 A1
Besant Ct N1 ....15 C3
Besant Ho NW8 ...78 C3
Besant Pl SE22 ....64 B3
Besant Rd NW2 ...10 A4
Besant Wlk N7 ....5 B2
Besford Ho 21 E2..24 C3
Bessant Dr TW9 ...45 A2
Bessborough Gdns
 SW1 ....147 C2
Bessborough Pl
 SW1 ....147 C1
Bessborough Rd
 SW15 ....68 C3
Bessborough St
 SW1 ....147 B2
Bessemer Ct 7
 NW1 ....13 B1
Bessemer Grange
 Prim Sch SE5 ....64 A3
Bessemer Park Ind
 Est 3 SE24....63 A3
Bessemer Rd SE5 ..48 B1
Bessingham Wlk
 SE4 ....65 C3
Besson St SE14 ...50 C2
Bessy St E2 ....25 B2
Bestwood St SE8 ..40 C2
Beswick Mews 1
 NW6 ....11 A2
Beta Pl 20 SW4....62 B3
Betchworth Ho 8
 N7 ....13 C3
Bethlehem Ho 13
 E14 ....33 B2
BETHNAL GREEN ..25 A2
Bethnal Green Rd
 E2 ....24 C2 99 B3
 Shoreditch E1,
 E2 ....24 B1 99 A2
Bethnal Green Sta
 Bethnal Green E2..25 A1
 Shoreditch E1 ....24 B1 99 A2
Bethnal Green Tech
 Coll 63 E2 ..24 B2 99 A3
Bethune Rd
 North Acton
   NW10 ....20 C1
 Stamford Hill N16..7 A4
Bethwin Rd SE5 ...48 B3
Betsham Ho SE1 ..137 B4
Betterton Ho
 WC2 ....106 B1
Betterton St WC2 106 B1
Bettridge Rd SW6 165 A1
Betts Ho E1 ....32 A2
Betts St E1 ....32 A2
Betty Layward Prim
 Sch 1 N16 ....6 C1
Betty May Gray Ho 2
 E14 ....42 B2
Bevan St N1 ....87 A3
Bev Callender Cl 4
 SW8 ....61 A4

Bevenden St N1 . . . . . . 97 C4
Beveridge Rd 🚺
  NW10 . . . . 8 A1
Beverley Cl
  Barnes SW13 . . . . 46 C1
  🚺 Wandsworth
  SW11 . . . . 59 C3
Beverley Cotts
  SW15 . . . . 68 A1
Beverley Ct
  🚺 Acton Green
  W4 . . . . 37 B1
  🚺 Acton W12 . . . . . . 38 A4
  Brockley SE4 . . . . 66 B4
  Islington N5 . . . . 15 A2
Beverley Gdns
  Barnes SW13 . . . . 56 B4
  Hendon NW11 . . . . 1 A4
Beverley Ho 🚺
  TW10 . . . . 54 A2
Beverley Path 🚺
  SW13 . . . . 46 B1
Beverley Rd
  Barnes SW13 . . . . 56 B4
  Chiswick W4 . . . . 38 B1
Beversbrook Rd
  N19 . . . . 4 C1
Beverstone Rd
  SW2 . . . . 62 B2
Beverston Mews
  NW1 . . . . 102 C3
Bevin Cl SE16 . . . . 33 A1
Bevin Ct WC1 . . . . 95 A4
  Bevington Prim Sch
  🚺 W10 . . . . 31 A4
Bevington Rd W10 . . . 31 A4
Bevington St
  SE16 . . . . 139 C3
Bevin Ho
  🚺 Bethnal Green
  E2 . . . . 25 B2
  🚺 Bow E3 . . . . 26 C2
Bevin Sq SW17 . . . . . . 72 B1
Bevin Way WC1 . . . . . . 95 B4
Bevis Marks EC3 . . . . 110 B2
Bew Ct SE21 . . . . 76 C4
Bewdley Ho N4 . . . . 6 B4
Bewdley St N1 . . . . . . 14 C1
Bewick Mews
  SE15 . . . . 50 A3
Bewick St SW8 . . . . . 170 B1
Bewley Ct SW2 . . . . . . 62 B1
Bewley Ho 🚺 E1 . . . . . 32 A2
Bewley St E1 . . . . 32 A2
Bexhill Rd
  Catford SE4 . . . . 66 B1
  Mortlake SW14 . . . . . . 55 B4
Bexley Ho SE4 . . . . 66 A3
BFI Imax (Cinema)
  SE1 . . . . 121 B1
BFI Southbank
  SE1 . . . . 121 A2
Bianca Rd 🚺
  SE15 . . . . 49 C4
Bicester Rd TW9 . . . . . 55 A4
Bickenhall Mans
  W1 . . . . 103 A4
Bickenhall St W1 . . . 103 A4
Bickerton Rd N19 . . . . . 4 B2
Bicknell Ho 🚺 E1 . . . 111 C1
Bicknell Rd SE5 . . . . . . 63 B4
Bicknor Ho 🚺 E5 . . . . . 17 A3
Bidborough St N1,
  WC1 . . . . 94 A3
Biddenham Ho 🚺
  SE16 . . . . 40 C2

Bidder St E16 . . . . 35 A4
Biddesden Ho
  SW3 . . . . 144 C3
Biddestone Rd N7 . . . 14 B4
Biddulph Mans
  W9 . . . . 88 B3
Biddulph Rd W9 . . . . . 88 B3
Bidwell St SE15 . . . . . 50 A2
Big Ben SW1 . . . . 134 B3
Biggerstaff Rd E15 . . 27 B4
Biggerstaff St N4 . . . . . 5 C2
Bigg's Row SW15 . . . . 57 C4
Biggs Sq E9 . . . . 18 B2
  Bigland Green Prim
  Sch 🚺 E1 . . . . 32 A3
Bigland St E1 . . . . 32 A3
Bilberry Ho 🚺 E3 . . . 33 C4
Billie Holiday Ct
  NW10 . . . . 20 C3
Billingford Ct SE4 . . . 65 C3
Billing Ho 🚺 E1 . . . . . 32 C3
Billingley NW1 . . . . . . 82 C3
Billing Pl SW10 . . . . . 156 B2
Billing Rd SW10 . . . . 156 B2
Billingsgate Mkt
  E14 . . . . 34 B1
Billing St SW10 . . . . 156 B2
Billington Ho 🚺
  SW8 . . . . 171 C3
Billington Rd SE14 . . 50 C3
Billiter Sq EC3 . . . . . . 110 B1
Billiter St EC3 . . . . . . 110 B1
Bilton Ct SE14 . . . . . . 42 B2
Bilton Ho SW8 . . . . . 171 B3
Bilton Twrs W1 . . . . . 103 A1
Bina Gdns SW5 . . . . . 142 C3
Binbrook Ho 🚺
  W10 . . . . 30 B4
Binden Rd W12 . . . . . . 38 B3
Binfield Ct SE5 . . . . . . 48 B1
Binfield Rd SW4 . . . . 172 B3
Bingfield St N1 . . . . . . 84 C4
Bingham Pl W1 . . . . . 103 B4
Bingham St N1 . . . . . . 15 C2
Binley Ho SW15 . . . . . 56 B1
Binney St W1 . . . . 103 C1
Binnie Ct SE10 . . . . . . 52 A3
Binnie Ho SE1 . . . . . . 136 C1
Binns Rd W4 . . . . 38 A1
Binns Terr 🚺 W4 . . . . 38 A1
Binstead Ho SW18 . . . 59 A1
Binyon Ho 🚺 N16 . . . 16 A4
Birbeck Ho 🚺 N19 . . . 4 C3
Bircham Path SE4 . . . 65 C3
Birch Cl
  Newham E16 . . . . 35 A4
  Peckham SE15 . . . . . . 49 C1
  Upper Holloway N19 . . 4 B2
Birchdown Ho 🚺
  E3 . . . . 27 A2
Birches The SE5 . . . . . 49 A1
Birchfield Ho 🚺 E14 . . . 33 C2
Birchfield St E14 . . . . 33 C2
Birchgrove Ho
  TW9 . . . . 45 A3
Birch Ho
  New Cross Gate
  SE14 . . . . 51 B2
  🚺 Tulse Hill SW2 . . . 62 C1
Birchington Ct 🚺
  NW6 . . . . 78 A4
Birchington Ho 🚺
  E5 . . . . 17 A3
Birchington Rd
  NW6 . . . . 23 C4

Birchin La EC3 . . . . . . 109 C1
Birchlands Ave
  SW12 . . . . 72 B4
Birchmere Lo 🔟
  SE16 . . . . 40 A1
Birchmere Row
  SE3 . . . . 53 B1
Birchmore Wlk N5 . . . 6 B1
Birch Vale Ct NW8 . . 89 C2
Birchwood Dr NW3 . . . 2 A1
Birdcage Wlk
  SW1 . . . . 133 B3
Birdhurst Rd
  SW18 . . . . 59 B2
Bird In Bush Rd
  SE15 . . . . 49 C3
Bird In Hand Yd 🔟
  NW3 . . . . 11 B4
Birdsall Ho 🚺 SE5 . . 64 A4
Birdsfield La 🔟
  E3 . . . . 26 B4
Bird St W1 . . . . 103 C1
Birdwood Ave 🚺
  SE13 . . . . 67 C1
Birkbeck Ave 🚺 W3 . 28 B2
Birkbeck Coll W1 . . . 105 B2
Birkbeck Ct W3 . . . . . . 28 C1
Birkbeck Gr 🚺 W3 . . 37 C4
Birkbeck Hill SE21 . . 75 A3
Birkbeck Mews 🚺
  E8 . . . . 16 B3
Birkbeck Pl SE21 . . . . 75 B2
Birkbeck Rd
  Acton W3 . . . . 28 C1
  Dalston E8 . . . . 16 B3
Birkbeck St E2 . . . . . . 25 A2
  Birkbeck Univ of
  London WC1 . . . . 93 B2
Birkdale Cl 🔟
  SE16 . . . . 40 A1
Birkenhead Ho 🚺
  N7 . . . . 14 C3
Birkenhead St
  WC1 . . . . 94 B4
Birkwood Cl SW12 . . 73 C4
Birley Lo NW8 . . . . 79 C2
Birley St SW11 . . . . . 169 B1
Birnam Rd N4 . . . . 5 B2
Birrell Ho 🚺 SW9 . . . 172 C1
Birse Cres NW10 . . . . . 8 A4
Birtwhistle Ho 🚺
  E3 . . . . 26 B4
Biscay Ho 🔟 E1 . . . . . 25 C1
Biscay Rd W6 . . . . 39 C1
Biscoe Way SE13 . . . . 67 C4
Biscott Ho 🚺 E3 . . . . 27 A1
Bisham Gdns N6 . . . . . 3 C3
Bishop Challoner
  Collegiate Sch 🚺
  E1 . . . . 32 B3
Bishop Ct 🔟 SW2 . . 62 C1
Bishop Duppa's
  Almshouses 🚺
  TW10 . . . . 54 A2
Bishop King's Rd
  W14 . . . . 140 B4
Bishop's Ave SW6 . . 164 A2
Bishop's Bridge Rd
  W2 . . . . 100 C2
Bishops Cl W4 . . . . 37 B1
Bishops Cl N19 . . . . 4 B1
Bishops Ct
  🔟 Bayswater
  W2 . . . . 100 B2
  Richmond TW9 . . . . . . 54 A4

Bishop's Ct
  Holborn EC4 . . . . 108 A2
  Holborn WC2 . . . . . . 107 B2
Bishopsdale Ho 🚺
  NW6 . . . . 23 C4
Bishopsgate EC2 . . . 110 A2
Bishopsgate Arc
  E1 . . . . 110 B3
Bishopsgate
  Churchyard EC2 . . . 110 A2
  Bishopsgate Inst
  EC2 . . . . 110 B3
Bishops Ho SW8 . . . 162 B1
Bishop's Mans
  SW6 . . . . 47 C1
Bishops Mead SE5 . . 48 B3
Bishop's Park Rd
  SW6 . . . . 47 C1
Bishops Rd SW6 . . . 164 C4
Bishops Sq E1 . . . . . . 110 B4
Bishop St N1 . . . . 86 C4
Bishop's Terr
  SE11 . . . . 149 C4
Bishopstone Ho 🚺
  SW11 . . . . 169 B2
Bishop's Way E2 . . . . 25 B3
Bishopswood Rd
  N6 . . . . 3 A4
Bishop Wilfred Wood
  Cl SE15 . . . . 49 C1
Bisley Ho SW19 . . . . . 69 C2
Bissextile Ho SE13 . . 52 A1
Bisson Rd E15 . . . . . . 27 B3
Bittern Ct 🚺 SE8 . . . 51 C4
Bittern Ho SE1 . . . . . 136 C3
Bittern St SE1 . . . . . . 136 C3
Blackall St
  EC2 . . . . 24 A1 98 A2
Blackburn Ct 🚺
  SW2 . . . . 62 C1
Blackburne's Mews
  W1 . . . . 117 B3
Blackdown Ho E8 . . . 16 C4
Blackett St SW15 . . . . 57 C4
Blackfriars Bridge
  EC4 . . . . 122 A3
Blackfriars Ct
  EC4 . . . . 122 A4
Black Friars La
  EC4 . . . . 108 A1
Blackfriars Pas
  EC4 . . . . 122 A4
Blackfriars Pier
  EC4 . . . . 122 A4
Blackfriars Rd
  SE1 . . . . 122 A1
Blackfriars Underpass
  EC4 . . . . 121 C4
Blackheath SE3 . . . . . 53 A2
Blackheath Ave
  SE3 . . . . 53 A3
Blackheath Bsns Est
  SE10 . . . . 52 B2
Blackheath Gr SE3 . . 53 B1
Blackheath High Jun
  Sch SE3 . . . . 53 B1
Blackheath High Sch
  SE3 . . . . 53 C3
Blackheath Hill
  SE10 . . . . 52 B2
Blackheath Prep Sch
  SE3 . . . . 53 C2
Blackheath Rd
  SE10 . . . . 52 A2

Blackheath Rise
  SE13 . . . . 52 B1
BLACKHEATH
  VALE 53 B1
Blackheath Vale
  SE3 . . . . 53 A1
Blackheath Village
  SE3 . . . . 53 B1
Black Horse Ct
  SE1 . . . . 137 C2
Blackhorse Rd
  SE8 . . . . 51 A4
Blacklands Terr
  SW3 . . . . 145 A3
Black Lion La 🚺 W6 . 38 C2
Black Lion Mews 🚺
  W6 . . . . 38 C2
Blackmore Ho
  Islington N1 . . . . 85 A3
  🚹 Wandsworth
  SW18 . . . . 59 A2
Blackmore Twr 🚺
  W3 . . . . 37 B3
Blackpool Rd SE15 . . 50 A1
Black Prince Rd SE1,
  SE11 . . . . 149 A3
Black Roof Ho 🚺
  SE5 . . . . 48 C2
Black's Rd W6 . . . . 39 B2
Blackstock Ho 🚺
  N5 . . . . 6 A1
Blackstock Mews
  N4 . . . . 6 A1
Blackstock Rd N4,
  N5 . . . . 6 A1
Blackstone Ho
  Dulwich SE21 . . . . . . 76 A1
  Pimlico SW1 . . . . 146 C1
Blackstone Rd NW2 . 9 B4
Black Swan Yd
  SE1 . . . . 138 A4
Blackthorn Ct
  🔟 Camberwell
  SE15 . . . . 49 B3
  🚺 Leyton E15 . . . . . . 19 C4
Blackthorn St E3 . . . . 26 C1
Blacktree Mews 🔟
  SW9 . . . . 62 C4
BLACKWALL 34 C2
Blackwall Sta E14 . . 34 B2
Blackwall Trad Est
  E14 . . . . 34 C4
Blackwall Tunnel E14,
  SE10 . . . . 34 C1
Blackwall Tunnel App
  SE10 . . . . 43 A4
Blackwall Tunnel
  Northern Approach
  E14, SE10 . . . . 27 B1
Blackwall Way
  E14 . . . . 34 B2
Blackwater St
  NW8 . . . . 101 C4
Blackwater St
  SE22 . . . . 64 B2
Blackwell Cl 🔟 E5 . . 17 C4
Blackwell Ho 🚹
  SW4 . . . . 61 C1
Blackwood Ho 🔟
  E1 . . . . 25 A1
Blackwood St
  SE17 . . . . 151 B2
Blade Mews SW15 . . 58 B3
Bladen Ho 🚺 E1 . . . . 32 C3

Blades Ct
4 Hammersmith
W6 . . . . 39 A1
Putney SW15 . . . . 58 B3
Blades Ho 12
SE11 . . . . 162 C3
Blades Lo 16 SW2 . 62 C3
Blagdon Rd SE13 . . . . 67 A1
Blagrove Rd 1
W10 . . . . 31 B4
Blair Cl N1 . . . . 15 C3
Blair Ct NW8 . . . . 79 B4
Blairderry Rd SW2 . 74 A2
Blairgowrie Ct 13
E14 . . . . 34 C3
Blair Ho SW9 . . . . . . 172 C3
Blair St E14 . . . . 34 C3
Blake Coll W1 . . . . . . 104 C4
Blake Ct
8 Bermondsey
SE16 . . . . 40 A1
Kilburn NW6 . . . . 23 C2
Blake Gdns SW6 . . 166 A4
Blake Ho
2 Deptford SE8 . . . . 51 C4
Isle Of Dogs E14 . . . . 42 A4
1 Kentish Town
N19 . . . . 13 C3
Lambeth SE1 . . . . . . 135 B2
5 Stoke Newington
N16 . . . . 16 A4
Blake Mews 15
TW9 . . . . 44 C2
Blakemore Rd
SW16 . . . . 74 A1
Blakeney Cl
5 Camden Town
NW1 . . . . 13 C1
3 Dalston E8 . . . . . . 16 C3
Blakenham Ct
W12 . . . . 29 C1
Blaker Rd E15 . . . . . . 27 B4
Blakes Cl W10 . . . . . . 30 B4
Blake's Rd SE15 . . . . 49 A3
Blanca Ho 18 N1 . . 24 A3
Blanchard Way E8 . . 16 C2
Blanch Cl SE15 . . . . . 50 B3
Blanchedowne
SE5 . . . . 63 C3
Blandfield Rd
SW12 . . . . 72 C4
Blandford Ct
Brondesbury Pk
NW6 . . . . 10 A1
6 De Beauvoir Town
N1 . . . . 16 A1
Blandford Ho
SW8 . . . . 162 C2
Blandford Rd W4 . . 38 A3
Blandford Sq NW1 . 90 B1
Blandford St W1 . . 103 B3
Bland Ho SE11 . . . . . 149 A2
Blantyre St SW10 . 157 B2
Blantyre Twr
SW10 . . . . 157 B2
Blantyre Wlk
SW10 . . . . 157 B2
Blashford Ho 3 N1 . 12 B1
Blasker Wlk 8
E14 . . . . 42 A1
Blaxland Ho 12
W12 . . . . 30 A2
Blazer Ct NW8 . . . . . 89 C3

Blechynden Ho 17
W10 . . . . 30 C3
Blechynden St
W10 . . . . 30 C2
Bleeding Heart Yd
EC1 . . . . 107 C3
Blemundsbury
WC1 . . . . 106 C4
Blendworth Point 4
SW15 . . . . 69 A3
Blenheim 26 SW19 . 69 C3
Blenheim Cres
Notting Hill W11 . . . . 31 A3
Notting Hill
W11 . . . . 31 A2 112 B4
Blenheim Ct
Barnsbury N7 . . . . . . 14 A2
Richmond TW9 . . . . . 54 B4
17 Rotherhithe
SE16 . . . . 32 C1
Upper Holloway N19 . . 5 A2
Blenheim Gdns
Clapham Pk SW2 . . . . 62 B1
Dollis Hill NW2 . . . . . . 9 B3
Kilburn NW6 . . . . 23 C4
Blenheim Gr SE15 . 49 C1
Blenheim Pas NW8 78 C2
Blenheim Rd
Acton W4 . . . . 38 A3
St John's Wood
NW8 . . . . 79 A2
Blenheim St W1 . . 104 A1
Blenheim Terr
NW8 . . . . 78 C2
Blenkarne Rd
SW11 . . . . 60 B1
Blessed Sacrament
RC Prim Sch N1 . . 84 C3
Blessington Cl
SE13 . . . . 67 C4
Blessington Rd
SE13 . . . . 67 C3
Bletchley Ct N1 . . . . 87 B1
Bletchley St N1 . . . . 87 A1
Bletsoe Wlk N1 . . . . 87 A2
Blick Ho 6 SE16 . . 40 B3
Blincoe Cl SW19 . . . 69 C2
Blissett St SE10 . . . . 52 B2
Bliss Mews 14
W10 . . . . 23 A2
Blisworth Ho 12
E2 . . . . 24 C4
Blithfield St W8 . . . 128 A1
Bloemfontein Ave
W12 . . . . 30 A1
Bloemfontein Rd
W12 . . . . 30 A2
Blomfield Ct
Battersea SW11 . . . . 167 C4
Paddington W9 . . . . . 89 A2
Blomfield Ho 4
E14 . . . . 34 A2
Blomfield Mans 3
W12 . . . . 30 B1
Blomfield Rd W9 . . 100 C4
Blomfield St EC2 . . 109 C3
Blomfield Villas
W9 . . . . 100 C4
Blondel St SW11 . . 169 B2
Blondin St E3 . . . . . . 26 C3
Bloomburg St
SW1 . . . . 147 A3
Bloomfield Ho 19
E1 . . . . 111 B3
Bloomfield Pl W1 . 118 B4

Bloomfield Terr
SW1 . . . . 145 C2
Bloom Gr SE27 . . . . . 75 A1
Bloom Park Rd
SW6 . . . . 154 C1
BLOOMSBURY 106 A4
Bloomsbury Ct
WC1 . . . . 106 B3
Bloomsbury Ho 10
SW4 . . . . 61 C1
**Bloomsbury
International
Language Sch**
London WC1 . . . . 59 B2
St Giles WC1 . . . . 106 B3
Bloomsbury Pl
WC1 . . . . 106 B3
Bloomsbury Sq
WC1 . . . . 106 B3
Bloomsbury St
WC1 . . . . 105 C3
Bloomsbury Way
WC1 . . . . 106 B3
Blore Cl SW8 . . . . . . 171 B3
Blore Ct W1 . . . . 119 B4
Blore Ho SW10 . . . . 156 B2
Blossom Cl W5 . . . . . 36 A4
Blossom Pl
E1 . . . . 24 A1 98 B1
Blossom St
E1 . . . . 24 A1 98 B1
Blount St E14 . . . . . . 33 A3
Blucher Rd SE5 . . . . 48 B3
Blue Anchor Alley 1
SW9 . . . . 54 A3
Blue Anchor La
SE16 . . . . 40 A2
Blue Anchor Yd
E1 . . . . 125 B4
Blue Ball Yd SW1 . 118 C1
Bluebell Cl 10 E9 . . 25 B4
Blue Gate Fields Jun
& Inf Schs E1 . . . . . . 32 B2
Bluegate Mews E1 . 32 A2
Blue Lion Pl SE1 . . 138 A2
Blueprint Apartments
SW12 . . . . 73 A4
Blundell Cl E8 . . . . . 16 C4
Blundell St N7 . . . . . 14 A2
Blurton Rd E5 . . . . . . 17 C4
Blyth Cl 1 E14 . . . . . 42 C2
Blythe Ho 3 SE11 . 163 C4
Blythe Ms 1
W14 . . . . 126 A1
Blythendale Ho 2
E2 . . . . 24 C3
Blythe Rd W14 . . . . 126 A1
Blyth's Wharf E14 . 33 A2
Blythwood Rd N4 . . 5 A4
BMI Fitzroy Square
Hospl W1 . . . . 92 C1
**Bnois Jerusalem Girls
Sch**
N16 . . . . 11 C4
Boades Mews 3
NW3 . . . . 11 C4
Boadicea St N1 . . . . 84 C3
Boardwalk Pl E14 . . 34 B1
Boarley Ho SE17 . . 152 A3
Boathouse Ctr The
W10 . . . . 22 C1
Boathouse Wlk 22
SE15 . . . . 49 B3
Boat Lifter Way 19
SE16 . . . . 41 A2
Bobbin Cl SW4 . . . . . 61 B4

Bob Marley Way 10
SE24 . . . . 62 C3
Bobov Foundation
Sch 4 N16 . . . . 7 B4
Bocking St E8 . . . . . . 25 A4
Boddicott Cl SW19 . 70 A2
Boddington Gdns
W3 . . . . 36 C4
Boddington Ho 2
SE14 . . . . 50 B2
Bodeney Ho 10
SE5 . . . . 49 A2
Bode Ho 4 E1 . . . . 111 B4
Bodington Ct 2
W12 . . . . 39 C4
Bodley Manor Way
SE24 . . . . 74 C4
Bodmin St SW18 . . . 70 C3
Bodney Rd E5, E8 . . 17 A3
Bogart Ct 13 E14 . . 33 C2
Bohemia Pl 1 E8 . . 17 A2
Bohn Rd E1 . . . . 33 A4
Boileau Rd SW13 . . 47 A4
Boilerhouse 11
SE1 . . . . 124 C1
Boisseau Ho 31 E1 . 32 B4
Boldero Pl NW8 . . . . 90 A1
Boldero St SW8 . . . 162 A1
Boleyn Rd N16 . . . . . 16 A3
Bolina Rd SE16 . . . . 40 B1
Bolingbroke Gr
SW11 . . . . 60 B1
Bolingbroke Rd
W14 . . . . 39 C3
Bolingbroke Wlk
SW11 . . . . 168 A4
Bollo Bridge Rd
W3 . . . . 37 B3
Bollo Ct 2 W3 . . . . . 37 B3
Bollo La W3 . . . . 37 A4
Bolney Gate SW7 . . 130 A3
Bolney St SW8 . . . . 162 C1
Bolsover St W1 . . . . 92 B1
Bolt Ct EC4 . . . . 107 C1
Bolton Cres SE5 . . 48 A3
Bolton Ct SW11 . . . 169 C3
Bolton Gdns
Kensal Rise
NW10 . . . . 22 C3
South Kensington
SW5 . . . . 142 B2
Bolton Gdns Mews
SW10 . . . . 142 C2
Bolton Ho 8 SE10 . 43 A1
Bolton Pl SW5 . . . . 142 C2
Bolton Rd
Chiswick W4 . . . . 45 B3
Harlesden NW10 . . . . 21 A4
Kilburn NW8 . . . . 78 B3
Boltons Ct SW5 . . . 142 B2
Bolton St W1 . . . . . 118 B2
Boltons The
SW10 . . . . 142 C2
Bolton Studios
SW10 . . . . 143 A1
Bolton Wlk N7 . . . . . 5 B2
Bombay Ct 8
SE16 . . . . 40 B4
Bombay St SE16 . . . 40 A2
Bomore Rd
W11 . . . . 31 A2 112 A4
Bonar Rd SE15 . . . . . 49 C3
Bonchurch Rd
W10 . . . . 31 A4
Bond Ct EC4 . . . . . . 109 B1
Bond Ho 6 NW6 . . 23 B3

Bonding Yard Wlk
SE16 . . . . 41 A3
Bond St W4 . . . . 37 C2
Bond Street Sta
W1 . . . . 103 C1
Bondway SW8 . . . . 162 B4
Bonfield Rd SE13 . . 67 B3
Bonham Ho
W11 . . . . 31 B1 112 C2
Bonham Rd SW2 . . . 62 B2
Bonheur Rd W4 . . . . 37 C4
Bonhill St EC2 . . . . . 97 C1
Bonington Ho N1 . . 84 C1
Bonita Mews SE15 . 65 C4
Bonner Ho 3
SW15 . . . . 56 C2
Bonner Prim Sch 30
E2 . . . . 25 B2
Bonner Rd E2 . . . . . . 25 B3
Bonner St E2 . . . . . . 25 B3
Bonneville Gdns
SW4 . . . . 61 B1
Bonneville Prim Sch
SW4 . . . . 61 B1
Bonnington Sq
SW8 . . . . 162 C4
Bonny St NW1 . . . . . 13 B1
Bonsor Ho SW8 . . . 171 A4
Bonsor St SE5 . . . . . 49 A3
Bonthron Ho
SW15 . . . . 47 B1
Booker Cl 18 E14 . . 33 B4
Boord St SE10 . . . . . 43 A3
Boothby Rd N19 . . . 4 C2
Booth Cl 10 E9 . . . . 25 A4
Booth Ho 2 SW2 . . 74 C4
Booth La EC4 . . . . . . 122 C4
Booth's Pl W1 . . . . . 105 A3
Boot St N1 . . . . 24 A2 98 A3
Bordon Wlk 5
SW15 . . . . 68 C4
Boreas Wlk N1 . . . . 86 B1
Boreham Ave E16 . . 35 C3
Boreman Ho 11
SE10 . . . . 52 B4
Borland Rd SE15 . . . 65 B3
Borneo St SW15 . . . 57 B4
Borough High St
SE1 . . . . 123 B2
Borough Mkt SE1 . . 123 B2
Borough Rd SE1 . . . 136 C2
Borough Sq SE1 . . . 136 C3
Borough Sta SE1 . . 137 A3
BOROUGH THE 136 C4
Borrett Cl SE17 . . . 150 C1
Borrodaile Rd
SW18 . . . . 59 A1
Borrowdale NW1 . . . 92 C3
Borthwick St SE8 . . 41 C1
Boscastle Rd NW5 . 4 A1
Boscobel Ho 6
E8 . . . . 17 A2
Boscobel Pl SW1 . . 145 C4
Boscobel St NW8 . . 89 C1
Boscombe Cl E5 . . . 18 A3
Boscombe Rd
W12 . . . . 38 C4
Boss Ho SE1 . . . . . . 138 C4
Boss St SE1 . . . . 138 C4
Boston Gdns W4 . . . 46 A4
Boston Ho
24 Camberwell
SE5 . . . . 48 B1
Earl's Ct SW5 . . . . . . 142 B3
Lisson Gr NW1 . . . . . 90 C2
Boston Pl NW1 . . . . . 90 C1

Bosun Cl E14 .....41 C4
Boswell Ct
  Bloomsbury WC1 .. **106** B4
  9 Hammersmith
  W14 ....39 C3
Boswell Ho WC1 .. **106** B4
Boswell St WC1 .... **106** B4
Bosworth Ho 4
  W10 ....23 A1
Bosworth Rd W10 ..23 A1
Bothwell Cl E16 ....35 B4
Bothwell St **6** W6 ..47 C4
Botolph Alley EC3 **124** A4
Botolph La EC3 ... **124** A4
Bott's Mews W2 ....31 C3
Boughton Ho SE1 **137** B4
Boulcott St E1 ......32 C3
Boulevard The
  Chelsea SW6 .... **167** A3
  4 Upper Tooting
  SW17 ....72 C2
Boulogne Ho SE1 **138** C2
Boulter Ho 4
  SE14 ....72 C2
Boulton Ho W4 .....36 A1
Boundaries Mans 3
  SW12 ....72 C3
Boundaries Rd
  SW12 ....72 C3
Boundary Ho
  Balham SW12 .....73 A3
  1 Camberwell SE5 ..48 B3
  15 Notting Hill W11 ..30 C1
Boundary La SE17 ..48 B4
Boundary Pas
  E2 ....98 C2
Boundary Rd NW8 .79 A4
Boundary Road Est
  NW8 ....78 C3
Boundary Row
  SE1 .... **136** A4
Boundary St
  E2 ....24 B1 98 C2
Bourchier St W1 .. **119** B4
Bourdon Pl W1 .... **118** B3
Bourdon St W1 .... **118** B3
Bourke Cl
  London SW4 ....62 A1
  Willesden NW10 ...8 A1
Bourlet Cl W1 ..... **104** C3
Bourne Cl SW4 ....45 B4
Bourne Ho **5** SW4 .45 B4
Bourne Mews W1 . **103** C1
Bournemouth Cl
  SE15 ....49 C1
Bournemouth Rd
  SE15 ....49 C1
Bourne Pl W4 ......37 C1
Bourne St SW1 ...145 B3
Bourne Terr W2 ... **100** B4
Bousfield Prim Sch
  SW10 .... **142** C2
Bousfield Rd SE14 **50** C1
Boutcher CE Prim Sch
  SE1 .... **152** C4
Boutflower Rd
  SW11 ....60 A3
Bouverie Mews N16 .7 A2
Bouverie Pl W2 ... **101** C2
Bouverie Rd N16 ....7 A2
Bouverie St EC4 .. **107** C1
Bovingdon Cl 4
  N19 ....4 B2
Bovingdon Rd
  SW6 .... **166** B3
BOW 26 B3

Bowater Cl SW2 ....62 A1
Bowater Ho EC1 ....97 A1
Bow Brook The 20
  E2 ....25 C3
Bow Church Sta
  E3 ....26 C2
Bow Common La
  E3 ....26 B1
Bowden Ho **22** E3 ..27 A2
Bowden St SE11 .. **149** C1
Bowditch SE8 .....41 B1
Bowen Ct **2** N5 ....15 A4
Bowen Dr SE21 ....76 A1
Bowen St E14 ......34 A3
Bower Ave SE3 ....53 A3
Bowerdean St
  SW6 .... **166** A2
Bower Ho SE14 ....50 C2
Bowerman Ave
  SE14 ....51 A4
Bowerman Ct 1
  N19 ....4 C2
Bower St E1 ....32 C3
Bowfell Rd W6 .....47 B4
Bowhill Cl SW9 ... **163** C2
Bow Ho 1 E3 ......26 C2
Bowie Cl SW4 .....73 C4
Bow La EC2, EC4 . **109** A1
Bowland Ho N4 .....6 B4
Bowland Rd SW4 ..61 C3
Bowland Yd SW1 . **131** A3
Bowl Ct EC2 ..24 A1 98 B1
Bowles Rd **1** SE1 ..49 C4
Bowley Ho 6
  SE16 .... **139** B2
Bowling Green Cl
  SW19 ....69 A4
Bowling Green Ho
  SW10 .... **157** B2
Bowling Green La
  EC1 ....95 C2
Bowling Green Pl
  SE1 .... **137** B4
Bowling Green St
  SE11 .... **163** B4
Bowling Green Wlk
  N1 ....24 A2 98 A4
Bowman Ave E16 ..35 B2
Bowman Mews
  St George in I East
  E1 ....125 C4
  Wandsworth SW18 ..70 B3
Bowman's Mews
  N7 ....5 A1
Bowman's Pl N7 ....5 A1
Bowmore Wlk
  NW1 ....13 C1
Bowness Cl **5** E8 ..16 B2
Bowness Ho SE15 ..50 B3
Bowood Rd SW11 ..60 C2
Bow Rd E3 ....26 C2
Bow Road Sta E3 ..26 C2
Bowry Ho **14** E14 ..33 B4
Bow Sec Sch **15** 26 C2
Bowsprit Point 1
  E14 ....41 C3
Bow St WC2 ...... **106** B1
Bowstead Ct
  SW11 .... **167** C3
Bow Triangle Bsns Ctr
  17 E3 ....26 C1

Bradenham **11**
  SE17 ....48 C4
Bradenham Cl
  SE17 ....48 C4
Braden St W9 ......88 A1
Bradfield Ct **14**
  NW1 ....13 A1
Bradfield Ho 15
  SW8 .... **171** B2
Bradford Ho 4
  W14 ....39 C3
Bradford Rd W3 ...38 A4
Bradgate Rd SE6 ..67 A1
Brading Rd SW2 ...74 B4
Brading Terr W12 ..38 C3
Bradiston Rd W9 ..23 B2
Bradley Cl N7 ......14 B2
Bradley Ho
  Bermondsey SE16 ..40 A2
  1 Bromley E3 .....27 A2
Bradley Mews
  SW12 ....72 B3
Bradley's Cl N1 ....85 C2
Bradlord Rd SW21 .76 A1
Bradmead SW8 ....170 C4
Bradmore Park Rd
  W6 ....39 A2
Brad St SE1 ...... **121** C1
Bradstock Ho E9 ..18 A1
Bradstock Rd E9 ..17 C2
Bradwell Ho 8
  NW6 ....78 A3
Bradwell St **1** E1 ..25 C2
Brady Ho
  London SW4 ....61 C2
  South Lambeth
  SW8 .... **171** A4
Brady St E1 ....25 A1
Braefoot Ct SW15 ..57 C2
Braemar SW15 .....57 C1
Braemar Ave SW18,
  SW19 ....70 C2
Braemar Mans
  W8 .... **128** B1
Braes St **1** N1 .....15 A1
Braganza St SE17 **150** A1
Braham St E1 ..... **111** A1
Brahma Kumaris
  World Spiritual Univ
  NW10 ....8 C1
Braid Ave W3 ......29 A3
Braid Ho SE10 .....52 B2
Braidwood St SE1 **124** A1
Brailsford Rd SW2 .62 C1
Braintree Ho 6
  E1 ....25 B1
Braintree St E2 ....25 B2
Braithwaite Ho
  EC1 ....97 B2
Braithwaite Twr
  W2 .... **101** B4
Bramah Gn SW9 . **173** C4
Bramall Cl E15 .....19 C3
Bramber WC1 ......94 A3
Bramber Ct TW8 ...36 A2
Bramber Rd W14 . **154** C4
Brambledown
  N4 ....5 A4
Bramble Gdns
  W12 ....29 B2
Bramble Ho **10** E3 .33 C4
Brambling Ct 25
  SE8 ....51 B4
Bramcote Gr SE16 .40 B1

Bramcote Rd
  SW15 ....57 A3
Bramerton NW6 ....9 C1
Bramerton St
  SW3 .... **158** A4
Bramfield Ct N4 ....6 B2
Bramfield Rd
  SW11 ....60 B2
Bramford Rd
  SW18 ....59 B3
Bramham Gdns
  SW5 .... **142** B3
Bramham Ho SE22 .64 A3
Bramlands Cl
  SW11 ....60 A4
Bramley Cres
  SW8 .... **161** C2
Bramley Ct SE13 ..67 C2
Bramley Ho
  11 North Kensington
  W10 ....30 C3
  Roehampton SW15 ..56 B1
Bramley Rd W10 ...30 C3
Brampton WC1 ... **106** C3
Bramshaw Rd E9 ..17 C2
Bramshill Gdns
  NW5 ....4 A1
Bramshill Rd
  NW10 ....21 B3
Bramshurst NW8 ..78 B3
Bramston Rd
  Harlesden NW10 ....21 C3
  Wandsworth SW17 .71 B1
Bramwell Ho
  Borough The SE1 . **137** A1
  Chelsea SW1 .... **160** C4
Bramwell Mews
  N1 ....85 A4
Brancaster Ho
  22 Globe Town
  E1 ....25 C2
  Islington N5 ......15 A3
Brancaster Rd
  SE16 ....74 A1
Branch Hill NW3 ....2 B1
Branch Pl N1 ..... **87** C4
Branch Rd E14 .....33 A2
Branch St SE15 ....49 A3
Brand Cl N4 ....6 A3
Branden Lo **3** W4 .37 B1
Brandlehow Prim Sch
  SW15 ....58 B3
Brandlehow Rd
  SW15 ....58 B3
Brandon Mews
  Barbican EC2 .... **109** B4
  Walworth SE17 .. **151** A3
Brandon Rd N7 ....14 A1
Brandon St SE17 . **151** A3
Brandrams Wharf
  SE16 ....40 B4
Brandreth Rd
  SW17 ....73 A2
Brand St SE10 .....52 B3
Brangton Rd SE11 **149** A1
Brangwyn Ct W14 **126** A1
Branksea St SW6 . **154** A1
Branksome Ho
  SW8 .... **162** C2
Bransby Ct **4** N16 .16 A4
Branscombe NW1 . **83** A3

Branscombe St
SE13 ....67 A4
Bransdale Ct NW6..23 C4
Branstone Ct **9**
TW9 ....44 B2
Branstone Rd NW9..44 B2
Branston Ho N7....14 C3
Brantwood Ho **9**
SE5 ....48 B3
Brantwood Rd
SE24 ....63 B2
Brasenose Dr
SW13 ....47 B4
Brashley Road Cvn
Site NW10........21 A2
Brassey Ho **1** E14..42 A2
Brassey Rd NW6....10 B2
Brassey Sq SW11..60 C4
Brassie Ave W3....29 A3
Brass Talley Alley **31**
SE16 ....40 C4
Brathay NW1 **83** A1
Brathway Rd
SW18 ....70 C4
Bratley St **11**
E1............24 C1 **99** B1
Bravington Pl W9..23 B1
Bravington Rd W9..23 B2
Brawne Ho **12**
SE17 ....48 A4
Braxfield Rd SE4..66 B3
Bray NW3 ....12 A1
Brayard's Rd SE15..50 A1
Braybrook St W12..29 B3
Brayburne Ave
SW4 ....171 A1
Bray Cres SE16....40 C4
Braydon Rd N16....7 C3
Bray Dr E16........35 B2
Brayfield Terr N1..14 C1
Brayford Sq **12** E1..32 B3
Bray Pl SW3......144 C3
Bread St EC2, EC4 **109** A1
Breakspeare SE21..76 B1
Breakspears Mews
SE4 ....51 C1
Breakspears Rd
SE4 ....66 C4
Breakwell Ct **16**
W10 ....23 A1
Breamore Cl
SW15 ....68 C3
Breamore Ho **21**
SE15 ....49 C3
Bream's Bldgs
EC4 ....107 B2
Bream St E3......18 C1
Breasley Cl SW15..57 A3
Brechin Cl SW7 **143** A3
Brecknock Prim Sch
10 N7 ....13 C2
Brecknock Rd N19..13 C3
Brecon Ho
Stamford Hill N16...7 B3
Wandsworth SW18 ..70 C4
Brecon Rd W6....154 B3
Bredel Ho **1** E14..33 C4
Bredgar SE13......67 A2
Bredgar Rd N19....4 B2
Bredinghurst SE22..76 C4
Bredinghurst Sch
SE15 ....65 C3
Bredin Ho SW10 **156** B2
Breer St SW6......59 A4

Breezer's Ct **22**
E1............125 C3
Breezer's Hill E1 **125** C3
Brehon Ho NW1....82 C3
Bremans Row **1**
SW18 ....71 B2
Bremner Rd SW7 **129** A2
Brenchley Gardens SE15,
SE22, SE23 ......65 C1
Brenda Rd SW17..72 B2
Brendon Ave NW10..8 A4
Brendon Ho W1 **103** B4
Brendon St W1 **102** B2
Brenley Ho SE1 **137** B4
Brennands Ct **14**
N19............4 B1
Brent Adult Comm
Education Service
Coll **5** NW10....20 C4
Brent Ct **5** W12..38 A3
Brentford Fountain L
Ctr W4 ....37 A1
Brent Ho **18** E9....17 B2
Brenthouse Rd E9 ..17 B2
Brenthurst Rd
NW10 ....8 B2
Brent Mus NW10..9 A2
Brent New Ent Ctr
NW10 ....8 B2
Brenton Ct E9....18 A3
Brenton St E14....33 A3
Brent Rd E16......35 C4
Brent Trad Est
NW10 ....8 A3
Brentwick Gdns
TW8 ....36 A2
Brereton Ho **9**
SW2 ....74 C4
Bressenden Pl
SW1 ....132 C2
Breton Ho
Bermondsey SE1 ..138 C2
St Luke's EC2....97 A1
Brett Cl N16......7 A2
Brett Cres NW10..20 C4
Brett Ho SE17....151 C1
Brett Ho **3** SW15..69 C4
Brett House Cl **2**
SW15 ....69 C4
Brettinghurst **8**
SE1 ....153 B1
Bretton Ho N19....5 A3
Brett Pas **23** E8..17 A3
Brett Rd E8......17 A3
Brewers Bldgs EC1..96 A4
Brewers Ct **2**..100 C2
Brewer's Sq SW1 **133** B2
Brewers Hall Gdns
EC2 ....109 A3
Brewer St W1 ..119 A4
Brewery Ind Est The
N1............87 A1
Brewery Rd N7....14 A2
Brewery Sq
Bermondsey SE1 ..124 C1
Clerkenwell EC1....96 B2
Brewhouse La
Putney SW15....58 A4
Wapping E1......32 A1
Brewhouse Wlk
SE16 ....33 A1
Brewhouse Yd EC1 **96** A2
Brewster Gdns
W10 ....30 B4
Brewster Ho
Bermondsey SE1 **153** A4

Brewster Ho continued
Poplar E14 ....33 B2
Briant Ho SE1 **135** A1
Briant St SE14....50 C3
Briar Ct
7 Bow E3........26 C3
10 Dalston E8....16 B1
Briar Wlk
Putney SW15....57 A3
West Kilburn W10..23 A1
Briarwood Rd
SW4 ....61 C2
Briary Cl NW3....12 A1
Briary Ct **10** E16..35 B3
Brickbarn Cl
SW10 ....157 A2
Brick Ct EC4....107 B1
Brick Farm Cl
TW9 ....45 A2
Brick La
Shoreditch
E2............24 B2 **99** A3
Spitalfields
E1............24 B1 **99** A1
Brick Lane Mkt E2. **99** A2
Bricklayers Arms
SE1 ....137 C1
Brick St W1 ....118 A1
Brickworth Ho **26**
SW9 ....173 C4
Brideale Cl SE15..49 B4
Bride Ct EC4....108 A1
Bride La EC4....108 A1
Bridel Mews N1 ..86 A3
Bride St N7......14 B2
Bridewain St SE1 **138** C2
Bridewell Pl
Holborn EC4....108 A1
20 Wapping E1....32 A1
Bridford Mews
W1 ....104 B4
Bridge Acad The
E2............24 B4
Bridge App NW3 ..12 C1
Bridge Ave W6....39 B1
Bridge Avenue Mans
1 W6............39 B1
Bridge Ct **13** W10..30 C3
Bridge Ho
8 Blackwall E14..34 C2
St John's Wood NW8 ..11 A1
Bridge Field Ho **7**
W2............100 A2
Bridge Gdns N16..15 C4
Bridge Ho
Brockley SE4....66 B3
1 Camden Town
NW1 ....12 C1
Homerton E9 ....18 B1
Bridge House Quay
E14............34 B1
Bridge La SW11 **168** B3
Bridgeman Ho **19**
E9............17 B1
Bridgeman Rd N1..14 B1
Bridgeman St NW8 **80** A1
Bridge Meadows
SE14 ....50 C4

Bridgend Rd SW18 .59 B3
Bridgen Ho **1** E1..32 A3
Bridge Pk **7**
SW18 ....58 C2
Bridge Pl SW1 ..146 B4
Bridgeport Pl **4**
E1............125 C2
Bridge Rd
Stratford Marsh
E15............27 C4
Willesden NW10..8 A2
Bridge Sch The
Clerkenwell EC1....96 A2
Kentish Town N7 ..13 A3
Bridges Cl SW11 **167** B1
Bridges Ho **15** SE5 ..48 C3
Bridge St
Chiswick W4....37 C2
Westminster SW1 **134** B3
Bridge Terr E15....19 C1
Bridgeview **2** W6 ..39 B1
Bridgewater Rd
E15............27 B4
Bridgewater Sq
EC2 ....108 C4
Bridgewater St
EC2 ....108 C4
Bridgeway St NW1 **83** A1
Bridge Wharf **18**
E2............25 C3
Bridge Yd SE1....123 C2
Bridgford St SW17,
SW18 ....71 B1
Bridgman Rd W4 ..37 B3
Bridgnorth Ho **14**
SE15 ....49 C4
Bridgwater Ho
W2............100 C2
Bridle La W1 ....119 A4
Bridlington Ho
SW18 ....59 B3
Bridport SE17 ..151 A1
Bridport Ho N1....87 C3
Bridport Pl N1....87 C3
Bridstow Pl W2...31 C3
Brief St SE5......48 A2
Brierfield NW1....82 C3
Brierley Rd
Leyton E11 ......19 C4
Upper Tooting
SW12 ....73 B2
Brierly Gdns E2..25 B3
Brigade St SE3....53 B1
Briggford Cl **5** E5 ..7 C2
Briggs Ho **2**
E2............24 B2 **99** A4
Brightling Rd SE4 ..66 B1
Brightlingsea Pl **5**
E14............33 B2
Brightman Rd
SW18 ....71 C3
Brighton Bldgs
SE1 ....138 A1
Brighton Ct SW15 ..58 B1
Brighton Gr SE14 ..51 A2
Brighton Ho **7**
SE5............48 C2
Brighton Rd N16 ..16 A4
Brighton Terr SW9 ..62 B3
Brightside Rd
SE13 ....67 C1
Bright St E14......34 A4
Brightwell Ct N7 ..14 A3
Brightwells **1**
SW6 ....166 A2
Brig Mews SE8....51 C4

Brigstock Ho SE5...48 B1
Brill Pl NW1 ....83 C1
Brimsdown Ho E3 ..27 B1
Brindley Ho
37 Notting Hill
W2............31 C4
2 Streatham
SW12 ....74 A4
Brindley St SE14..51 B2
Brine Ho **11** E3....26 A3
Brinklow Ho W2..100 A3
Brinkworth Way
E9............18 B2
Brinsley Ho **17** E1 ..32 B3
Brinsley St **9** E1..32 A3
Brinton Wlk SE1 **122** A1
Brion Pl E14......34 B4
Brisbane Ho **3**
W12............30 A2
Brisbane St SE5...48 C3
Briset St EC1....96 A1
Briset Way N7....5 B2
Bristol Gdns
Putney SW15....69 B4
Westbourne Green
W9............88 B1
Bristol Ho SE11..135 B1
Bristol Mews W9..88 B1
Bristowe Ct **24**
SW2 ....62 C1
Britannia Building
N1............84 B1
Britannia Cl SW4..61 C3
Britannia Gate **1**
E16............35 C1
Britannia Junc
NW1 ....82 B4
Britannia L Ctr N1..24 A4
Britannia Rd
23 Millwall E14....41 C2
Walham Green
SW6 ....156 A1
Britannia Row N1..86 C4
Britannia St WC1 ..94 C4
Britannia Way
NW10 ....20 A1
Britannia Wlk N1 **97** B4
British Coll of
Osteopathic
Medicine NW3 ..11 B2
British Dental
Association Mus
W1............104 A3
British Gr W4....38 B1
British Grove Pas **2**
W4............38 B1
British Grove S **3**
W4............38 B1
British Library The
WC1............93 C4
British Mus WC1.. **106** A3
British Optical
Association Mus
SW1 ....120 A2
British St E3......26 B2
British Wharf Ind Est
SE14 ....50 C4
Britley Ho **15** E14..33 B3
Brittage Rd **11**
NW10 ....8 A1
Brittany Ho SW15..57 B3
Brittany Point
SE11 ....149 B3
Britten Cl NW11..2 A3
Britten Ho SW3 **144** B2
Britten St SW3 **144** A2

Britton St EC1 . . . . . . 96 A1
BRIXTON 62 C4
Brixton Day Coll ⑥
　SW9 . . . . 62 A4
Brixton Hill SW2 . . . . 62 B2
Brixton Hill ◻
　SW2 . . . . 62 B2
Brixton Hill Pl
　SW2 . . . . 74 A4
Brixton Mkt SW9 . . . 62 C3
Brixton Rd SW9 . . 173 B2
Brixton Rec Ctr
　SW9 . . . . 62 C4
Brixton Sta SW9 . . . 62 C3
Brixton Station Rd
　SW2 . . . . 62 B2
Brixton Water La
　SW2 . . . . 62 B2
Broadbent Cl N6 . . . . 4 A3
Broadbent St W1 . 118 A4
Broadbridge Cl
　SE3 . . . . 53 C3
Broad Common Est
　N16 . . . . 7 C3
Broad Ct WC2 . . . 106 B1
Broadfield NW6 . . . 11 A2
Broadfield La
　NW1 . . . . 14 A1
Broadfield Way
　NW10 . . . . 8 B3
Broadford Ho ⑫
　E1 . . . . 26 A1
BROADGATE 110 A4
Broadgate EC2 . . . 110 A4
Broadgate Circ
　EC2 . . . . 110 A3
Broadgates Ct
　SE11 . . . . 149 C1
Broadgates Rd
　SW18 . . . . 71 C3
Broadgate Twr The
　EC2 . . . . 98 B1
Broadhinton Rd
　SW4 . . . . 61 B4
Broadhurst Cl
　Hampstead NW6 . . . 11 B2
　⑨ Richmond TW10 . . 54 B2
Broadhurst Gdns
　NW6 . . . . 11 A2
Broadhurst Mans
　NW6 . . . . 11 A2
Broad La EC2 . . . . 110 A4
Broadlands N6 . . . . . 3 C4
Broadlands Ave
　SW16 . . . . 74 A2
Broadlands Cl
　Highgate N6 . . . . . . 3 C4
　Streatham SW16 . . . 74 A2
Broadlands Ct
　TW9 . . . . 44 C3
Broadlands Lo N6 . . . 3 B4
Broadlands Mans ②
　SW16 . . . . 74 A2
Broadlands Rd N6 . . . 3 B4
Broadley St NW8 . 102 A4
Broadley Terr
　NW1 . . . . 90 B1
Broadmayne SE17 151 B2
Broadmead W14 . . 140 A3
Broadoak Ct ⑧
　SW9 . . . . 62 C4
Broadoak Ho ⑪
　NW6 . . . . 78 B3
Broad St Ave EC2 . 110 A3
Broad Sanctuary
　SW1 . . . . 134 A3

Broadstone Ho
　SW8 . . . . 162 C1
Broadstone Pl
　W1 . . . . 103 B3
Broad Street Pl
　EC2 . . . . 109 C3
Broadwalk Ho
　SW7 . . . . 128 C3
Broadwalk La NW11 . 1 B4
Broadwall SE1 . . . 121 C2
Broadway
　Stratford E15 . . . . . 19 C1
　Westminster SW1 . 133 B2
Broadway Arc ③
　W6 . . . . 39 B2
Broadway Ho ②
　E8 . . . . 25 A4
Broadway Mans
　SW6 . . . . 155 C1
Broadway Market
　E8 . . . . 25 A4
Broadway Market
　Mews ㉑ E8 . . . . 24 C4
Broadway Mews E5 . 7 B4
Broadway Mkt E8 . . 25 A4
Broadway Ret Pk
　W9 . . . . 9 C4
Broadway Sh Ctr ⑥
　W6 . . . . 39 B2
Broadway The
　Barnes SW13 . . . . . 46 A1
　South Acton W3 . . . 36 C4
Broadway Wlk ④
　E14 . . . . 41 C3
Broadwick St W1 . 105 A1
Broad Wlk
　Mayfair W1 . . . . . 117 B2
　Regent's Pk NW1 . . 81 C1
　Richmond TW9 . . . . 44 C3
Broad Wlk The
　W8 . . . . 114 B1
Broadwood Terr
　W14 . . . . 141 A4
Broad Yd EC1 . . . . . 96 A1
Brocas Cl NW3 . . . . 12 A1
Brockbridge Ho
　SW15 . . . . 56 B1
Brocket Ho ⑩
　SW8 . . . . 171 B2
Brockham Dr SW2 74 B4
Brockham Ho
　Camden Town
　NW1 . . . . 83 A3
　⑧ Streatham SW2 . 74 B4
Brockham St SE1 . 137 A2
Brockhurst Ho N4 . . 6 C4
Brockill Cres SE4 . 66 A3
Brocklebank Rd
　SW18 . . . . 71 B4
Brocklebank Road Ind
　Est SE7 . . . . 43 C2
Brocklehurst St
　SE14 . . . . 50 C3
Brockley Cross
　SE4 . . . . 66 B3
Brockley Cross Bsns
　Ctr SE4 . . . . 66 A4
Brockley Gdns SE4 . 51 B1
Brockley Gr SE4 . . 66 B2
Brockley Hall Rd
　SE4 . . . . 66 A2
Brockley Ho SE17 152 A2
Brockley Mews
　SE4 . . . . 66 A2

Brockley Prim Sch
　SE4 . . . . 66 B2
Brockley Rd SE4 . . 66 B2
Brockley Sta SE4 . . 66 A4
Brockley Way SE4 . 66 A3
Breckmer Ho ⑤
　E8 . . . . 32 A1
Brock Pl E3 . . . . . . 27 A1
Brock St SE15 . . . . 65 B4
Brockweir ㉘ E2 . . 25 B3
Brockwell Ho ⑤
　SE11 . . . . 163 A4
Brockwell Lido
　SE24 . . . . 63 A1
Brockwell Park
　SE24 . . . . 63 A1
Brockwell Park Gdns
　SE24 . . . . 75 A4
Brockwell Park Row
　SW2 . . . . 62 C1
Broderick Ho
　SE21 . . . . 76 A1
Brodia Rd N16 . . . . . 7 A1
Brodick Ho ⑰ E3 . . 26 B3
Brodie Ho SE1 . . . 153 A2
Brodie St SE1 . . . . 153 A2
Brodlove La E1 . . . . 32 C2
Brodrick Rd SW17 . 72 A2
Brody Ho E1 . . . . . 110 C3
Broken Wharf
　EC4 . . . . 122 C4
Brokesley St E3 . . . 26 B2
Broke Wlk
　Hackney E8 . . . . . . 24 B4
　⓫ Hackney E8 . . . . 24 C4
Bromar Rd SE5 . . . . 64 A4
Bromehead St ⑧
　E1 . . . . 32 B3
Bromell's Rd SW4 . 61 B3
Bromfelde Rd
　SW4 . . . . 171 C1
Bromfield Ct ㉒
　SE16 . . . . 139 C2
Bromfield St N1 . . . 85 C2
Bromleigh Ho
　SE1 . . . . 138 C2
BROMLEY E3 . . . . . 27 A2
Bromley-by-Bow Sta
　E3 . . . . 98 A4
Bromley Hall Rd
　E14 . . . . 34 B4
Bromley High St E3 . 27 A2
Bromley Pl W1 . . . 104 C4
Bromley St E1 . . . . 32 C3
BROMPTON 130 A1
Brompton Arc
　SW1 . . . . 131 A3
Brompton Oratory
　SW3 . . . . 130 A1
Brompton Park Cres
　SW6 . . . . 156 A3
Brompton Pl SW3 130 B2
Brompton Rd
　SW3 . . . . 130 A1
Brompton Sq
　SW3 . . . . 130 A2
Bromstone Ho ⑲
　SW9 . . . . 173 B3
Bromwich Ave N6 . . 3 C2
Bromwich Ho ⑧
　TW10 . . . . 54 A1
Bromyard Ave W3 . 29 A2

Bromyard Ho
　Acton W3 . . . . 29 A1
　③ Peckham SE15 . . 50 A3
Brockley Rd SE4 . . 66 B2
Bron Ct NW6 . . . . . 23 C4
BRONDESBURY . . . 10 A2
Brondesbury Coll for
　Boys ⑤ NW6 . . . . 10 A1
Brondesbury Ct
　NW2 . . . . 9 C2
Brondesbury Mews ⑪
　NW6 . . . . 10 C1
BRONDESBURY
PARK 22 C4
Brondesbury Park Sta
　NW6 . . . . 23 A4
Brondesbury Pk
　NW6 . . . . 9 C1
Brondesbury Rd
　NW6 . . . . 23 C3
Brondesbury Sta
　NW6 . . . . 10 B1
Brondesbury Villas
　NW6 . . . . 23 C3
Bronsart Rd SW6 . 154 A1
Bronte Ct W14 . . . . 39 C3
Bronte Ho
　Kilburn NW6 . . . . . 23 C2
　⑥ Stoke Newington
　N16 . . . . 16 A3
Bronti Cl SE17 . . . 151 A2
Bronwen Ct NW8 . . 89 B3
Bronze St SE8 . . . . 51 C3
Brookbank Rd
　SE13 . . . . 67 A4
Brook Cl SW17 . . . . 72 C2
Brook Com Prim Sch
　E8 . . . . 16 C3
Brook Ct SW14 . . . 56 A4
Brookdale Rd SE6 . 67 A1
Brook Dr SE11 . . . 150 A4
Brooke Ct W10 . . . 23 A3
Brooke Ho ④
　SE14 . . . . 51 A2
Brooke Rd E5,N16 . . 7 C1
Brooke Ct EC1 . . . 107 B4
Brooke's Mkt EC1 107 C4
Brooke St EC1 . . . 107 B3
Brookfield
　Dartmouth Pk N6 . . 3 C1
　⓫ Finsbury Pk N4 . . 5 B2
Brookfield Ho ㉓
　E2 . . . . 25 A3
Brookfield Pk NW5 . 4 A1
Brookfield Prim Sch
　N19 . . . . 4 A2
Brookfield Rd
　Acton W4 . . . . 37 C4
　Homerton E9 . . . . . 18 A2
Brookgate N16 . . . . . 6 C2
Brook Gate W1 . . . 117 A3
Brook Gdns SW13 . 56 B4
Brook Gn W6 . . . . . 39 C2
BROOK GREEN . . . 39 C2
Brook Green Flats ⑪
　W14 . . . . 39 C3
Brook Ho
　③ Clapham Pk
　SW4 . . . . 61 B2
　Ealing W3 . . . . 36 C4
　④ Hammersmith
　W6 . . . . 39 B2
　Marylebone WC1 . 105 B4
Brook Hos NW1 . . . 83 A1
Brooklands Ave
　SW18 . . . . 71 A2

Brooklands Court
　Apartments ⑧
　NW6 . . . . 10 B1
Brooklands Ct ②
　NW6 . . . . 10 B1
Brooklyn Ct W12 . . 30 B1
Brookmarsh Ind Est
　SE10 . . . . 52 A3
Brook Mews N
　W2 . . . . 115 A4
Brookmill Rd SE8 . . 51 C2
Brooksbank Ho ⑦
　E9 . . . . 17 B2
Brooksbank St ⑧
　E9 . . . . 17 B2
Brooksby Ho ⑨
　N1 . . . . 14 C1
Brooksby Mews
　N1 . . . . 14 C1
Brooksby St N1 . . . 14 C1
Brooksby's Wlk E9 . 17 C3
Brooks Ct
　Bayswater W2 . . . 115 C4
　Mayfair W1 . . . . . 118 C4
Brooks Ho ⑥ SW2 . 74 C3
Brookside Rd N19 . . 4 B2
Brooks La W4 . . . . 44 C4
Brook's Mews W1 . 118 A4
Brook St W4 . . . . . 36 C1
Brook St
　Bayswater W2 . . . 115 C4
　Mayfair W1 . . . . . 118 C4
Brookstone Ct
　SE15 . . . . 65 A3
Brooksville Ave
　NW6 . . . . 23 A4
Brookville Rd
　SW6 . . . . 154 C1
Brookwood Ave
　SW13 . . . . 46 B1
Brookwood Ho
　SE1 . . . . 136 B3
Brookwood Rd
　SW18 . . . . 70 C3
Broome Ct ③
　TW9 . . . . 44 C2
Broome Ho ⑦ E5 . . 17 A3
Broome Way SE5 . . 48 C3
Broom Farm SW6 165 C2
Broomfield ⑦
　NW1 . . . . 12 C1
Broomfield Ho
　SE17 . . . . 152 B3
Broomfield House Sch
　TW9 . . . . 44 B2
Broomfield Rd
　TW9 . . . . 44 B2
Broomfield St E14 . 34 A4
Broomgrove Rd
　SW9 . . . . 173 A1
Broomhill Ct ⑦
　SW18 . . . . 58 C2
Broomhouse La
　SW6 . . . . 58 C4
Broomhouse Rd
　SW6 . . . . 165 B2
Broomsleigh St
　NW6 . . . . 10 B3
Broomwood Hall
　(Lower Sch) ⑥
　SW12 . . . . 60 D1
Broomwood Hall Sch
　(Lower Sch)
　SW16 . . . . 73 C1

Broomwood Hall Sch (Upper Sch) 3
SW12 ....72 C4
Broomwood Rd
SW11 ....60 C2
Brougham Rd
Acton W3 ....28 B3
Hackney E8 ......24 C4
Brougham St
SW11 ....169 A2
Brough Cl SW8 ....162 B1
Broughton Dr 10
SW9 ....63 A3
Broughton Rd
SW6 ....166 B2
Broughton Road App
2 SW6 ......166 A2
Broughton St
SW8 ....170 A2
Brouncker Rd W3 ..37 B4
Browne Ho 13 SE8 ..51 C3
Brownfield St E14 ..34 B3
Brownflete Ho
SE4 ....66 A3
Brown Hart Gdns
W1 ....117 C4
Browning Cl W9 ....89 A1
Browning Ct W14 ..154 C4
Browning Ho
7 London SE1 ....
Shepherd's Bush
W12 ....30 B3
10 Stoke Newington
N16 ....16 A4
Browning Mews
W1 ....103 C3
Browning St SE17 ..151 A3
Brownlow Ho 10
SE16 ....139 B3
Brownlow Mews
WC1 ....95 A1
Brownlow Rd
Hackney E8 ......24 C4
Willesden NW10 ....8 A1
Brownlow St WC1 ..107 A3
Brown's Bldgs
EC3 ....110 B1
Brown St W1 ......102 C2
Brownswood Rd N4 ..6 B2
Broxash Rd SW11 ..60 C1
Broxbourne Ho 1
E3 ....27 A1
Broxholme Ho
SW6 ....166 A4
Broxholm Rd SE27,
SW16 ....74 C1
Broxwood Way
NW8 ....80 B3
Bruce Cl W10 ......30 C4
Bruce Glasier Ho 13
N19 ....
Bruce Ho
4 Clapham Pk
SW4 ....61 C1
3 North Kensington
W10 ....30 C4
Putney SW15 ......57 A2
Bruce Rd E3 ......27 A2
Bruckner St W10 ..23 B2
Bruges Pl NW1 ......13 B1
Brune Ho E1 ......110 C3
Brunei Gall W1 .... 105 C4
Brunel Ct 6 SW13 ..46 B1
Brunel Est W2 ......31 C4

Brunel Ho
Chelsea SW10 ....157 C2
4 Gospel Oak
NW5 ....13 A4
Millwall E14 ......42 A1
New Cross SE8 ....51 B3
2 Streatham SW2 ..74 A4
Brunel Mews
NW10 ....22 C2
Brunel Mus SE16 ..40 B4
Brunel Rd
Acton W3 ....29 A4
Wapping SE16 ......32 B1
Brunel St E16 ......35 B3
Brune St E1 ......110 C3
Brunlees Ho SE1 ..137 A1
Bruno Ct 8 E8 ......16 C2
Brunswick Ct
Bermondsey SE1 ..138 B4
Finsbury EC1 ......96 A3
Westminster SW1 ..147 C3
Brunswick Gdns
W8 ....31 C1 113 C1
Brunswick Ho
4 Haggerston E2 ..24 B3
Lisson Gr NW1 ....90 C2
Brunswick Mews
W1 ....103 A2
Brunswick Park Prim
Sch 22 SE5 ......48 C3
Brunswick Pk SE5 ..49 A2
Brunswick Pl N1 ..97 C3
Brunswick Quay
SE16 ....40 C3
Brunswick Rd E14 ..34 B3
Brunswick Sh Ctr
WC1 ....94 B2
Brunswick Sq WC1 ..94 B2
Brunswick Villas 2
SE5 ....49 A2
Brunton Pl E14 ....33 A3
Brushfield St E1 ..110 C4
Brussels Rd SW11 ..59 C3
Bruton La W1 ......118 B3
Bruton Pl W1 ......118 B3
Bruton St W1 ......118 B3
Brutus Ct SE11 ....150 A3
Bryan Ave NW10 ....9 A1
Bryan Ho 1 SW1 ..102 C2
Bryan Ho SE16 ....41 B4
Bryan Rd SE16 ....41 B4
Bryanston Ct W1 ..102 C2
Bryanston Ho
SE15 ....49 B2
Bryanston Mans
W1 ....102 C4
Bryanston Mews E
W1 ....102 C3
Bryanston Mews W
W1 ....102 C2
Bryanston Pl W1 ..102 C3
Bryanston Sq W1 ..102 C3
Bryanston St W1 ..103 A1
Bryant Ct
Acton W3 ....28 C1
Haggerston E2 ....24 B3
Bryantwood Rd N5,
N7 ....14 C3
Bryce Ho 28 SE14 ..50 C4
Brydale Ho 2
SE16 ....40 C2
Brydges Pl WC2 ..120 A3
Brydges Rd E15 ....19 C3
Brydon Wlk N1 ....84 B4
Bryer Ct EC2 ......108 C4
Bryett Rd N7 ......5 A1

Bryher Ho W4 ......37 B1
Brymay Cl E3 ......26 C3
Brymon Ct W1 ....103 A3
Brynmaer Ho
SW11 ....169 A3
Brynmaer Rd
SW11 ....169 A3
Bryony Rd W12 ....29 C2
Bryony Rd W12 ....
BT Twr W1 ....104 C4
Buccleuch Ho E5 ..7 C4
Buchan Ct 10
SE16 ....40 C2
Buchan Gdns
NW10 ....22 A3
Buchan Ho
Dulwich SE21 ......76 A1
South Acton W3 ..37 A4
Buchan Rd SE15 ..65 B4
Bucharest Rd
SW18 ....71 B4
Buckfast St
E2 ....24 C2 99 C3
Buck Hill Wlk W2 ..115 C3
Buckhold Rd
SW18 ....58 C1
Buckhurst Ho 10
N7 ....13 C3
Buckhurst St E1 ..25 A1
Buckingham Ave
SW1 ....120 B3
Buckingham Gate
SW1 ....133 A2
Buckingham Ho
Finsbury Pk N4 ....6 B3
Richmond TW10 ..54 C2
Buckingham Mans
NW6 ....11 A3
Buckingham Mews
Harlesden NW10 ..21 B3
7 Kingsland N1 ....16 A2
Westminster SW1 ..132 C2
Buckingham Pal
SW1 ....132 C2
Buckingham Palace
Rd SW1 ....146 B4
Buckingham Pl
SW1 ....132 C2
Buckingham Rd
Harlesden NW10 ..21 B3
Kingsland N1 ......16 A2
Buckingham St
WC2 ....120 B3
Buckingham Yd
NW10 ....21 B3
Buckland Cres
NW3 ....11 C2
Buckland Ct 6 N1 ..24 A3
Buckland Ho 3
SW1 ....
Buckland St N1 ....87 C1
Buckland Wlk 2
W3 ....37 B4
Buckler's Alley
SW6 ....155 A2
Bucklersbury EC2,
EC4 ....109 B1
Buckle St
8 Whitechapel
E1 ....111 B2
Whitechapel E1 ..111 A2
Buckley Ct 5
NW6 ....10 B1
Buckley Rd NW6 ..10 B1
Buckmaster Cl 1
SW9 ....62 C4

Buckmaster Ho 1
N7 ....14 B4
Buckmaster Rd
SW11 ....60 B2
Bucknall St WC1, ..106 A2
Bucknell Cl 2 SW2 ..62 B3
Buckner Rd SW2 ..62 B3
Buckridge Bldg
EC1 ....107 B4
Buckshead Ho 19
W2 ....31 C4
Buck St NW1 ......13 A1
Buckstone Cl SE23 ..65 B1
Buckters Rents
SE16 ....33 A1
Buckthorne Rd
SE4 ....66 A2
Budge Row EC4 ..109 B1
Budge's Wlk W2 ..115 A2
Budleigh Ho 18
SE15 ....49 C3
Buer Rd SW6 ......164 B1
Bugsby's Way
SE10 ....43 B2
Buick Ho 4 E3 ....26 C1
Building Crafts Coll
The E15 ....19 C1
Bulbarrow NW8 ....78 B3
Bulinga St SW1 ..147 C3
Bullace Row SE5 ..48 C2
Bullards Pl 1 E2 ..25 C2
Bulleid Way SW1 ..146 B3
Bullen Ho 13 E1 ..25 A1
Bullen St SW11 ..168 B2
Buller Cl SE15 ....49 C3
Buller Rd NW10 ..22 C2
Bullfinch Ct 4
SE21 ....75 C2
Bullingham Mans
W8 ....127 C4
Bull Inn Ct WC2 ..120 B3
Bullivant St 9 E14 ..34 B2
Bulls Alley SW14 ..45 C1
Bulls Gdns 3 SW3 ..144 B4
Bulls Head Pas
EC3 ....110 A1
Bull Yd SE15 ......49 C2
Bulmer Mews
W11 ....31 C1 113 B2
Bulow Ct 3 SW6 ..166 B2
Bulstrode Pl W1 ..103 C3
Bulstrode St W1 ..103 C2
Bulwer St W12 ....30 B1
Bunbury Ho SE15 ..49 C3
Bunhill Row EC1 ..97 B1
Bunhouse Pl SW1 ..145 C2
Bunkers Hill NW11 ..2 B4
Bunning Way N7 ..14 A4
Bunning Way N7 ....
Bunsen Ho 2 E3 ..26 A3
Bunsen St 3 E3 ....26 A3
Bunyan Ct EC2 ....108 C4
Buonaparte Mews
SW1 ....147 B2
Burbage Cl SE1 ..137 B1
Burbage Ho
18 Deptford SE14 ..50 C4
Shoreditch N1 ....87 C3
Burbage Rd SE21,
SE24 ....75 C4
Burbage Sch 34
N1 ....24 A3
Burcham St E14 ..34 B3
Burchell Ho SE11 ..149 A2
Burchell Rd SE15 ..50 A2

Burcher Gale Gr 5
SE15 ....49 B3
Burcote Rd SW18 ..71 C4
Burden Ho SW8 ..162 A1
Burdenshott Ave
TW10 ....55 A3
Burder Cl N1 ......16 A2
Burder Rd N1 ......16 A2
**Burdett Coutts &
Townshend CE Prim**
Sch SW1 ....147 C3
Burdett Mews 4
W2 ....100 A2
Burdett Rd
Richmond TW9 ....54 B4
Tower Hamlets E3 ..33 B4
Burdett St SE1 ....135 C2
Burford Ct SE8 ....51 C4
Burford Ho
1 Brentford
TW8 ....36 A1
5 South Lambeth
SW9 ....173 A1
Burford Rd
Brentford TW8 ....36 A1
5 Stratford Marsh
E15 ....27 C4
Burford Wlk SW6 ..156 B1
Burgate Ct 9
SW9 ....62 C4
Burges Gr SW13 ..47 A3
Burgess Bsns Pk
SE5 ....48 C3
Burgess Hill NW2 ..10 C4
Burgess Ho 5 SE5 ..48 B3
Burgess Park Mans
NW6 ....10 C4
Burgess St E14 ....33 C4
Burge St SE1 ......137 C1
**Burgh House &
Hampstead Mus**
NW3 ....11 C4
Burghley Hall Cl
SW19 ....70 A3
Burghley Ho SW19 ..70 A1
Burghley Rd NW5 ..13 A4
Burghley Twr W3 ..29 B2
Burgh St N1 ......86 B2
Burgon St EC4 ....108 B1
Burgos Gr SE10 ..52 A2
Burgoyne Rd SW9 ..62 B4
Burhan Uddin Ho
E1 ....24 B1 98 C1
Burke Ho 3 SW11 ..59 B3
Burke Cl SW15 ....56 A3
Burke Ho 1 SW1 ..59 C3
Burke St E16 ......35 B4
Burland Rd SW11 ..60 B2
Burleigh Ho SW10 ..39 B2
Burleigh Ho
Chelsea SW3 ....157 C3
5 North Kensington
W10 ....30 C4
Burleigh Pl SW15 ..57 C2
Burleigh St WC2 ..120 C4
Burley Ho E1 ......32 C3
Burlington Arc
W1 ....118 C3
Burlington Ave
TW9 ....44 C2
Burlington Cl W9 ..23 C1
Burlington Ct
Chiswick W4 ......45 B3
Highgate N6 ......3 C3

Burlington Danes
 Acad W12 . . . . 30 A3
Burlington Gdns
 Acton Green W4 . . . . . 37 B1
 Acton W3 . . . . 28 B1
 4 Fulham SW6 . . . . 164 B1
 Marylebone W1 . . . . . 104 B1
Burlington Ho
 NW3 . . . . 11 C3
Burlington La W4 . . . . 45 C3
Burlington Lodge
 SW6 . . . . 164 B1
Burlington Mews
 Acton W3 . . . . 28 B3
 2 Putney SW15 . . . . 58 B2
Burlington Pl
 SW6 . . . . 164 B1
Burlington Rd
 Acton Green W4 . . . . . 37 B1
 Fulham SW6 . . . . 164 B1
Burma Rd N16 . . . . . . 15 C4
Burmarsh **6** NW5 . . . 12 C2
Burmester Ho
 SW17 . . . . 71 B1
Burmester Rd
 SW17 . . . . 71 B1
Burnaby Cres W4 . . . . 45 B4
Burnaby Ct **8**
 SE16 . . . . 139 C3
Burnaby Gdns W4 . . . 45 B4
Burnaby St SW10 . . . 157 A1
Burnand Ho **3**
 W14 . . . . 39 C3
Burnbury Rd SW12 . . . 73 B3
Burne Jones Ho
 W14 . . . . 140 B3
Burnell Ho **10**
 SW2 . . . . 74 C3
Burnell Wlk SE1 . . . . 153 A2
Burness Cl N7 . . . . . . 14 B2
Burne St NW1 . . . . . . 102 A4
Burnett Cl E9 . . . . 17 B3
Burnett Ct SW11 . . . . 168 A3
Burnett Ho **6**
 SE13 . . . . 52 B1
Burney St SE10 . . . . . 52 B3
Burnfoot Ave
 SW6 . . . . 164 B3
Burnham NW3 . . . . . . 12 A1
Burnham Cl SE1 . . . . 153 A3
Burnham Ct W2 . . . . 114 B4
Burnham Est **8**
 E2 . . . . 25 B2
Burnham St E2 . . . . . 25 B2
Burnhill Ho EC1 . . . . . 96 C3
Burnley Rd
 London SW9 . . . . . . 172 C2
 Willesden NW10 . . . . . 8 C3
Burnsall St SW3 . . . . 144 B2
Burns Ho
 18 Bethnal Green
 E2 . . . . 25 B2
 1 Islington N7 . . . . . 14 B2
 Kennington SE17 . . . . 150 B1
 11 Stoke Newington
 N16 . . . . 16 A4
Burn's Ho NW10 . . . . . 21 A4
Burnside Cl SE16 . . . . 32 C1
Burns Rd SW11 . . . . 168 C2
Burn's Rd NW10 . . . . . 21 B4
Burnthwaite Rd
 SW6 . . . . 155 A1
Burntwood Cl
 SW18 . . . . 72 A3
Burntwood Ct
 SW17 . . . . 71 B1

Burntwood Grange Rd
 SW18 . . . . 72 A3
Burntwood La
 SW17 . . . . 71 C2
Burntwood Sch
 SW17 . . . . 71 C2
Buross St **9** E1 . . . . . 32 A3
Burrage Ct **17**
 SE16 . . . . 40 C2
Burrard Ho **11** E2 . . . . 25 B3
Burrard Rd NW6 . . . . 10 C4
Burr Cl E1 . . . . 125 B2
Burrell St SE1 . . . . . 122 A2
Burrell's Wharf Sq
 E14 . . . . 42 A1
Burrhill Ct SE16 . . . . . 40 C3
Burrow Ho **10**
 SW9 . . . . 173 A1
Burrow Rd SE22 . . . . 64 A3
Burrows Mews
 SE1 . . . . 136 A4
Burrows Rd NW10 . . . 22 B2
Burrow Wlk SE21 . . . . 75 B4
Burr Rd SW18 . . . . . . 70 C4
Bursar St SE1 . . . . . 124 A1
Burslem St E1 . . . . . 111 C1
Burstock Rd SW15 . . . 58 A3
Burston Rd SW15 . . . . 57 C2
Burtley Cl N4 . . . . 6 B3
Burton Bank N1 . . . . . 15 C1
Burton Ct SW3 . . . . . 145 A2
Burton Gr SE17 . . . . . 151 B1
Burton Ho
 5 Bermondsey
 SE16 . . . . 40 A4
 8 Brixton SE5 . . . . . 48 A3
Burton Lo **6**
 SW15 . . . . 58 B2
Burton Mews
 SW1 . . . . 145 C3
Burton Pl WC1 . . . . . . 93 C3
Burton Rd
 7 Brixton SW9 . . . . 173 B2
 Brixton SW9 . . . . 48 A1
 Brixton Ct SE15 . . . . . 19 C1
 Burton St WC1 . . . . . . 93 C2
Burtonwood Ho N4 . . . 6 C4
Burtt Ho **6**
 N1 . . . . 24 A2 98 A4
Burwash Ho SE1 . . . . 137 C3
Burwell Cl **17** E1 . . . . 32 A3
Burwell Wlk **14** E3 . . . 26 C1
Burwood Ho **11**
 SW9 . . . . 63 A3
Burwood Pl W2 . . . . . 102 B2
Bury Cl SE16 . . . . 32 C1
Bury Ct EC3 . . . . 110 B2
Buryfield Ct **23**
 SE8 . . . . 40 C2
Bury Pl WC1 . . . . 106 B3
Bury St
 St James SW1 . . . . . 119 A2
 Whitechapel EC3 . . . . 110 B2
Bury Wlk SW3 . . . . . 144 A2
Busbridge Ho **24**
 E14 . . . . 33 C4
Busby Mews **5**
 NW1 . . . . 13 C2
Busby Pl NW5 . . . . . . 13 C2
Bushbaby Cl **1** SE1 . . 138 A1
Bushberry Rd E9 . . . . 18 A2
Bush Cotts **12**
 SW18 . . . . 58 C2
Bush Ct **7** W12 . . . . . 39 C4
Bushell Cl SW2 . . . . . 74 B2

Bushell St **18** E1 . . . 125 C2
Bushey Down
 SW12 . . . . 73 A2
Bushey Hall SE5 . . . . 48 B2
Bushey Hill Rd
 SE5 . . . . 49 B2
Bushfield Ho N5 . . . . . 15 B3
Bush Ind Est
 N19 . . . . 20 C1
Bush La EC4 . . . . 123 B4
Bushnell Rd SW17 . . . 73 A1
Bush Rd
 Bermondsey SE8 . . . . 40 C2
 Hackney E8 . . . . 25 A4
 Richmond TW9 . . . . . . 44 B4
Bushwood Dr SE1 . . . 153 A3
Bushwood Rd
 TW9 . . . . 44 C4
Business Design Ctr
 N1 . . . . 85 C3
Buspace Studios **3**
 W10 . . . . 23 A1
Butcher Row E1 . . . . . 32 C3
Butchers Rd E16 . . . . 35 C3
Bute Gdns W6 . . . . . . 39 C2
Bute House Prep Sch
 W6 . . . . 39 C2
Bute St SW7 . . . . 143 B4
Bute Wlk **18** N1 . . . . 15 C2
Butfield Ho **6** E9 . . . . 17 B2
Butler Ho
 32 Bethnal Green
 E2 . . . . 25 B2
 5 Brixton SW9 . . . . 48 A2
 11 Poplar E14 . . . . . 33 B3
Butler Pl SW1 . . . . . 133 B2
Butler Rd NW10 . . . . . 8 B1
Butler St **6** E2 . . . . . 25 B2
Butlers & Colonial
 Wharf **11** SE1 . . . . 139 A4
Butler St **33** E2 . . . . . 25 B2
Butler's Wharf W
 SE1 . . . . 124 C1
Butley Ct **8** E3 . . . . . 26 A3
Butterfield Cl **1**
 SE16 . . . . 40 A4
Butterfly Wlk **2**
 SE5 . . . . 48 C2
Buttermere **4** NW1 . . 92 B4
Buttermere Cl
 Bermondsey SE1 . . . . 152 C3
 Leyton E11 . . . . 19 C4
Buttermere Ct
 NW8 . . . . 79 B4
Buttermere Dr
 SW15 . . . . 58 A2
Buttermere Ho **13**
 E3 . . . . 26 B2
Buttermere Wlk **9**
 E8 . . . . 16 B2
Butterwick W6 . . . . . . 39 B2
Butterworth Ct
 SW16 . . . . 74 A1
Buttesland St N1 . . . . 97 C4
Buxhall Cres E9 . . . . . 18 B2
Buxted Rd
 Camberwell SE22 . . . . 64 A3
 Dalston E8 . . . . 16 B1
Buxton Ct N1 . . . . 97 A4
Buxton Gdns W3 . . . . 28 A2
Buxton Ho **3**
 SW11 . . . . 59 C3
Buxton Mews
 SW4 . . . . 171 C2
Buxton Rd
 Mortlake SW14 . . . . . . 56 A4
 Upper Holloway N19 . . . 4 C3

Buxton Rd *continued*
 Willesden NW2 . . . . . . 9 A2
Buxton St
 E1 . . . . 24 B1 99 A1
Byam Shaw Sch of Art
 8 N19 . . . . 4 C2
Byam St SW6 . . . . . . 166 C1
Byards Ct SE16 . . . . . 40 C3
Byas Ho **6** E3 . . . . . . 26 B2
Byefield Cl SE16 . . . . . 41 A4
Byelands Cl **12**
 SE16 . . . . 32 C1
Bye The W3 . . . . 29 A3
Byeway The SW14 . . . 55 B4
Byfeld Gdns SW13 . . . 46 C2
Bygrove Prim Sch **2**
 E14 . . . . 34 A3
Bygrove St E14 . . . . . 34 A3
Byng Pl WC1 . . . . 93 B1
Byng St E14 . . . . 41 C4
Byrne Ho **11** SW2 . . . 62 B2
Byrne Rd SW12 . . . . . 73 A2
Byron Ct **24**
 Chelsea SW3 . . . . . . 144 B3
 Dulwich SE21 . . . . . . 76 C3
 8 Hampstead
 NW6 . . . . 11 B1
 Paddington W9 . . . . . 23 C1
 St Pancras WC1 . . . . . 94 C2
Byron Mews
 Hampstead NW3 . . . . . 12 A4
 2 Maida Vale W9 . . . 23 C1
Byron St E14 . . . . 34 B3
Bythorn St **9** SW9 . . . 62 B3
Byward St EC3 . . . . . 124 B3
Bywater Pl SE16 . . . . 33 A1
Bywater St SW3 . . . . 144 C2
Bywell Pl W1 . . . . . . 104 C3
Byworth Wlk N19 . . . . . 5 A3

C

Cabbell St NW1 . . . . 102 A3
Cabinet Off SW1 . . . . 134 A4
Cabinet War Rooms &
 Churchill Mus
 SW1 . . . . 133 C4
Cable Ho WC1 . . . . . . 95 B4
Cable Pl SE10 . . . . . . 52 B2
Cable St E1 . . . . 32 A2
Cabot Ct SE16 . . . . . . 40 C3
Cabot Sq E14 . . . . . . 33 C1
Cabul Rd SW11 . . . . 168 B1
Cactus Cl SE5 . . . . . . 49 A1
Cactus Wlk W12 . . . . 29 B3
Cadbury Way **1**
 SE16 . . . . 153 B4
Caddington Rd
 NW2 . . . . 1 A1
Cadell Cl E2 . . . . 24 B3
Cadell Ho **9** E2 . . . . . 24 B3
Cade Rd SE10 . . . . . . 52 C2
Cader Rd SW18 . . . . . 59 B1
Cadet Dr SE1 . . . . . . 153 A2
Cade Tyler Ho **10**
 SE10 . . . . 52 B2
Cadiz St SE17 . . . . . . 151 A1
Cadman Cl **9** SW9 . . . 48 A3
Cadmore Ho **4**
 N1 . . . . 15 A1
Cadmus Cl **1**
 SW4 . . . . 61 C4
Cadmus Ct **6**
 SW9 . . . . 173 B4

Cadnam Lo E14 . . . . . 42 C3
Cadnam Point **15**
 SW15 . . . . 69 A3
Cadogan Cl E9 . . . . . . 18 B1
Cadogan Ct SW3 . . . . 144 C3
Cadogan Ct Gdns
 SW1 . . . . 145 A4
Cadogan Gate
 SW1 . . . . 145 A4
Cadogan Gdns
 SW3 . . . . 145 A3
Cadogan Hall
 SW1 . . . . 145 A4
Cadogan La SW1 . . . . 131 B1
Cadogan Pier
 SW3 . . . . 158 B3
Cadogan Pl SW1 . . . . 131 A1
Cadogan Sq SW1 . . . . 131 A1
Cadogan St SW3 . . . . 144 C3
Cadogan Terr E9 . . . . 18 B1
Caedmon Rd N7 . . . . . 14 B4
Caernarvon Ho
 W2 . . . . 100 C2
Caesar Ct **8** E2 . . . . . 25 C3
Cahill St EC1 . . . . 97 A1
Cahir St E14 . . . . 42 A2
Caine Ho W3 . . . . 37 A4
Caird St W10 . . . . 23 B2
Cairns Ho **8** N7 . . . . . 14 B4
Cairns Rd SW11 . . . . . 60 A2
Caister Ho N7 . . . . . . 14 B2
Caister Ho **10**
 SW12 . . . . 73 A4
Caistor Mews
 SW12 . . . . 73 A4
Caistor Rd SW12 . . . . 73 A4
Caithness Ho N1 . . . . 84 C4
Caithness Rd W14 . . . 39 C3
Calabria Rd N5 . . . . . 15 A3
Calais Gate SE5 . . . . . 48 A2
Calais St SE5 . . . . 48 A2
Calbourne Rd
 SW12 . . . . 72 C4
Calcraft Ho **10** E2 . . . 25 B3
Caldecot Ct SE5 . . . . . 48 B1
Caldecot Rd SE5 . . . . 48 B1
Calder Ct SE16 . . . . . 33 B1
Calderon Ho NW8 . . . 80 A2
Calderon Pl **20**
 W10 . . . . 30 B4
Caldew St SE5 . . . . . . 48 C3
Caldwell St SW9 . . . . 163 A1
Caldy Wlk **18** N1 . . . . 15 B2
Caleb St SE1 . . . . 137 A4
Caledonia Ho **16**
 E14 . . . . 33 A3
Caledonian Market
 SE1 . . . . 138 B2
Caledonian Rd
 Islington N1 . . . . 84 C3
 Lower Holloway N7 . . . 14 B2
Caledonian Road &
 Barnsbury Sta
 N7 . . . . 14 B1
Caledonian Road Sta
 N7 . . . . 14 B2
Caledonian Sq **6**
 NW1 . . . . 13 C2
Caledonia St N1 . . . . . 84 B1

Cale St SW3..... **144** A2
Caletock Way
SE10..............43 B1
Calgarth NW1.....83 A1
Calgary Ct **20** SE16 .40 B4
Caliban Twr **1** N1. .24 A3
Calico Ho **4** SW11 .59 B4
Calico Row **5**
SW11..............59 B4
Calidore Cl SW11 .59 B4
California Bldg **2**
SE13............52 B1
Callaby Terr **11**
N1...............15 C2
Callahan Cotts **8**
E1...............32 B4
Callan Sch The
W1............ **105** A2
Callcott St W8 .....31 C1 **113** B2
Callcott Rd NW6 . .10 B1
Callcott St
W8 ....31 C1 **113** B2
Callendar Rd
SW7........... **129** B2
Callingham Cl **13**
E14............33 B4
Callingham Ho **1**
SW4..............62 A4
Callow St SW3 .. **157** B4
Calmington Rd
SE5..............49 A4
Calshot Ho N1....84 C2
Calshot St N1.....84 C1
Calstock Ho N1 ...87 A4
Calstock Rd SE13 .149 C2
Calthorpe St WC1 .95 A2
Calton Ave SE21...64 A1
Calver **13** NW5 ....13 A4
Calverley Gr N19 ...4 C3
Calvert Ave
E2 ....24 B2 **98** C3
Calvert Ct
1 Richmond N19.....4 B3
3 Richmond TW9 . .54 B3
Calvert Ho **9** W12 .30 A2
Calverton SE5 .....49 A4
Calvert Rd SE10 ...43 B1
Calvert's Bldgs
SE1........... **123** B1
Calvert St NW1 ...81 B4
Calvin St E1 ..24 B1 **98** C1
Calypso Cres **6**
SE15..............49 B3
Calypso Way N1 **8**,
SE16............41 B2
Cambalt Ho **3**
SW15............57 C2
Cambalt Rd SW15 .57 C2
Cambay Ho **7** E1 ..26 A1
Camber Ho **7**
SE15..............50 B4
Camberley Ho
NW1.............82 B1
CAMBERWELL....48 B2
Camberwell Bsns Ctr
SE5............48 C3
Camberwell Church St
SE5.............48 C2
Camberwell Coll of
Arts
18 Camberwell
SE5...........49 A2
25 Camberwell
SE15............49 B3

Camberwell Glebe
SE5..............49 A2
Camberwell Gn
SE5..............48 C2
Camberwell Gr
SE5..............49 A1
Camberwell Green
SE5..............48 B2
Camberwell New Rd
SW9.............48 A3
Camberwell Rd
SE5..............48 B3
Camberwell Station
Rd SE5...........48 B2
Camberwell Trad Est
SE5..............48 B2
Camborne Rd
SW18...........70 C4
Cambourne Mews **9**
W11............31 A3
Cambray Ho **14**
E14............33 A4
Cambria Lo **3**
SW15............58 B2
Cambrian Cl SE27 . .75 A1
Cambrian Rd
TW10.............54 B1
Cambria Rd SE5 ...63 B4
Cambria St SW6. . **156** B1
Cambridge Ave
NW6.............23 C3
Cambridge Cir
WC2........... **105** C1
Cambridge Cotts
TW9..............44 C4
Cambridge Cres **20**
E2...............25 A3
Cambridge Gate
NW1.............92 A2
Cambridge Gate
Mews NW1...... **92** B2
Cambridge Gdns
NW6.............23 C3
North Kensington
W10.............31 A3
Cambridge Gr W6 . .39 A2
Cambridge Heath Rd
E1, E2............25 A3
Cambridge Heath Sta
E2...............25 A3
Cambridge Ho
SW6..............58 A4
Cambridge Mans
SW11............60 A4
Cambridge Pas **9**
E9...............17 B1
Cambridge Pl **18** W8 **128** B3
Cambridge Rd
Barnes SW13......46 B1
Battersea SW11... **168** C3
Kilburn NW6......23 C2
Kilburn NW6......23 C3
Richmond TW9 ....44 C3
Cambridge Rd N
W4..............37 A1
Cambridge Rd S **3**
W4..............37 A1

Cambridge Sch **15**
W6..............39 A2
Cambridge Sq
W2........... **102** A2
Cambridge St
SW1........... **146** C2
Cambridge Terr
NW1............ **92** A3
Cambridge Terr Mews
NW1............ **92** B3
Cambus Rd E16 ...35 C4
Cam Ct **2** SE15 ....49 B4
Camden Coll of
English **8** NW1 . .12 C1
Camden Gdns
NW1............ **82** C4
Camden High St
NW1............ **82** C3
Camden Ho **6**
SE8..............41 B1
Camdenhurst St
E14............33 A3
Camden Lock Mkt
NW1............13 A1
Camden Lock Pl
NW1............13 A1
Camden Mews
NW1............13 C2
Camden Mkt NW1 . **82** B4
Camden Park Rd
NW1............13 C2
Camden Pas N1 ...86 A3
Camden Rd NW1 . . **82** B4
Camden Road Sta
NW1............13 B1
Camden Row SE3 . .53 A1
Camden Sch for Girls
The NW5......... .13 B2
Camden Sq NW1 ...13 C2
Camden St NW1 ...83 A3
Camden Studios
NW1............83 A3
Camden Terr **17**
NW1............13 C2
CAMDEN TOWN . .13 A1
Camden Town Sta
NW1............82 B4
Camden Wlk N1...86 A3
Cameford Ct **20**
SW2..............74 A4
Camelford NW1 ...83 A3
Camelford Ct **15**
W11............31 A3
Camelford Ho
SE1........... **148** B1
Camelford Wlk **13**
W11............31 A3
Camellia Ho SE8. . .51 B3
Camellia St SW8 . **162** A1
Camelot Ho **18**
NW1............13 C2
Camelot Prim Sch
SE15..............50 B4
Camera Pl SW10. . **157** B4
Camera Press Gall
E1............ **138** C4
Cameret Ct **3**
W11............31 A1
Cameron Ct **3**
SW19............70 A3
Cameron Ho
Camberwell SE5...48 B3
St John's Wood
NW8............ **80** A2
Cameron House Sch
SW10........... **157** C4

Cameron Pl SW16 . .74 C2
Camerton Cl **8** E8 . .16 B2
Camilla Rd SE16 ...40 A2
Camlet St
E2 ....24 B1 **98** C2
Camley St Natural Pk
NW1............ **83** C3
Camley St NW1 . . . **83** C3
Camomile St EC3 . **110** B2
Campaign Ct W9 ...23 B1
Campana Rd SW6 **165** C4
Campbell Ct
Dulwich SE21.....76 C3
South Kensington
SW7........... **128** C1
Campbell Gordon Way
NW2..............9 A4
Campbell Ho
Paddington W2.....89 B1
Pimlico SW1.... **146** C1
30 Shepherd's Bush
W12............30 A2
Campbell Rd E3....26 C2
Campbell Wlk N1. . .84 B4
Campdale Rd N7 ....4 C1
Campden Gr W8. ...127 C4
Campden Hill W8 . **127** B3
Campden Hill Ct
W8............ **127** C4
Campden Hill Gate
W8............ **127** B3
Campden Hill Mans
W8............ **31** C1 **113** B2
Campden Hill Pl
W14 ....31 B1 **113** A2
Campden Hill Rd
W8............ **127** B4
Campden Hill Sq
W14 ....31 B1 **113** A2
Campden Ho **4**
NW1............11 C1
Campden Hos
W8............ **31** C1 **113** B1
Campden House Cl
W8............ **127** C4
Campden St
W8............ **31** C1 **113** B1
Campen Cl SW19 . .70 A2
Camperdown St
E1............ **111** A1
Campion Ho **19**
N16............16 A3
Campion Rd SW15 .57 B2
Campion St SE14 . .50 C3
Camphill Pl SE13 . .67 B2
Camphill Rd SE13 . .67 B2
Campton Hill Twrs
W8............ **31** C1 **113** B2
Cam Rd E15........27 C4
Camsey Ho **8**
SW2..............62 B2
Canada Cres W3 . . . .20 B1
Canada Gdns SE13 . .67 B2
Canada Rd W3 . . . . .28 B4
Canada Sq E14....34 A1
Canada St SE16...40 C4
Canada Water Sta
SE16............40 C3
Canada Way W12 . .30 A2
Canal App SE8 ....51 A4
Canal Bldg N1.... **86** C2
Canal Bridge SE15 . .49 C4
Canal Bvd **7** NW1 . .13 C2

Canal Cl
Mile End E1........26 A1
North Kensington
W10.............22 C1
Canal Gr SE15 .....50 A4
Canal Head Public Sq
1 SE15........... **49** C2
Canal Path **22** E2 . .24 B4
Canalside Studios **20**
N1...............24 A4
Canal St SE5......48 C4
Canal Way W10...22 C1
Canal Wlk N1.... **87** C4
CANARY WHARF . .34 A1
Canary Wharf Pier
E14............33 B1
Canary Wharf Sta
E14............34 A1
Canary Wharf Sta
(DLR) E14........33 C1
Canberra Prim Sch
W12.............30 A2
Canbury Mews
SE26............76 C1
Cancell Rd SW9 . . **173** C4
Candahar Rd
SW11........... **168** B1
Candida Ct **1**
NW1............13 A1
Candishe Ho SE1 . **138** C4
Candle Gr SE15....65 A4
Candlemakers **5**
SW11............59 C4
Candover St W1 . . **104** C3
Candy St E3.......26 B4
Canfield Gdns
NW6..............11 A1
Canfield Pl NW6 . . .11 B2
Canford Rd SW11 . .60 C2
Canham Rd W3....28 A4
Cann Ho W14.... **126** B1
Canning Cross
SE5..............49 A1
Canning Ho **28**
W12.............30 A2
Canning Pas W8. . **128** C2
Canning Pl W8 . . . **128** C2
Canning Pl Mews
W8............ **128** C2
Canning Rd N5....15 A4
Cannington **14**
NW5..............12 C2
CANNING TOWN . .35 B3
Canning Town
E16............35 A3
Canning Town Sta
E16............35 A3
Cannock Ho N4 ....6 C4
Cannon Dr **21** E14 . .33 C2
Cannon Hill NW6 . .10 C3
Cannon Ho SE11. . **149** A3
Cannon La NW3 ....2 C1
Cannon Pl NW3 ....2 C1
Cannon St EC4 ... **123** A4
Cannon Street Rd
E1...............32 A3
Cannon Street Sta
EC4............ **123** B4
Cannon Wharf Bsns
Ctr **12** SE8.......41 A2
Canon Barnett Prim
Sch E1.......... **111** A2
Canon Beck Rd
SE16............40 B4
CANONBURY....15 B2

Canonbury Bsns Ctr
N1. . . . . **87** A4
Canonbury Cres
N1. . . . . 15 B1
Canonbury Ct **21**
N1. . . . . 15 A1
Canonbury Gr N1. . . 15 A1
Canonbury Hts **6**
N1. . . . . 15 A1
Canonbury La N1. . 15 A1
Canonbury Pk N
N1. . . . . 15 B2
Canonbury Pk S
N1. . . . . 15 A2
Canonbury Pl N1. . 15 A2
Canonbury Prim Sch
4 N1. . . . . 15 A2
Canonbury Rd N1 . . 15 A1
Canonbury Sq N1 . . 15 B1
Canonbury St N1 . . . 15 B1
Canonbury Sta N1,
N5. . . . . 15 A2
Canonbury Villas
N1. . . . . 15 A1
Canonbury Yd E **28**
N1. . . . . 15 B2
Canon Murnane Rd
SE1. . . . . **138** C1
Canon Row SW1. . . **134** A4
Canon CI N2. . . . . 2 C4
Canon St N1. . . . . . . **86** C3
Canrobert St E2. . . . 25 A2
Cantelowes Rd
NW1. . . . . 13 C2
Canterbury SE13. . . 67 B2
Canterbury CI **6**
SE5. . . . . 48 B1
Canterbury Cres
SW9. . . . . 62 C4
Canterbury
Acton W3. . . . . 29 A1
Kilburn NW6. . . . . . . 23 C3
Canterbury Gr SE27,
SW16. . . . . 75 B2
Canterbury Ho
6 Bromley E3. . . . . . 27 A2
Lambeth SE1. . . . . . **135** C3
Canterbury Ind Pk **6**
SE15. . . . . 50 B4
Canterbury Mans
NW6. . . . . 11 A2
Canterbury Pl
SE17. . . . . **150** B3
Canterbury Rd
NW6. . . . . 23 C3
Canterbury Terr
NW6. . . . . 23 C3
Cantium Ret Pk
SE1. . . . . 49 C4
Canton St E14. . . . . 33 C3
Cantrell Rd E3 . . . . . 26 C1
Canute Ct SW16. . . . 74 C1
Canute Gdns SE16. . 40 C2
Canvey St SE1. . . . **122** C2
Cape Henry Ct **13**
E14. . . . . 34 C2
Capel Ho E9. . . . . . 17 B1
Capel Lo
5 Richmond
TW9. . . . . 44 B2
12 Streatham SW2 . . 74 B4
Capener's CI SW1 **131** B3
Capern Rd SW18 . . . 71 B3
Capio Nightingale
Hospl NW1. . . . . . **102** B4

Capital City Acad
NW10. . . . . 22 A4
Capital East Apts **7**
E16. . . . . 35 C2
Capital Interchange
Way TW8. . . . . 36 C1
Capital Sh Ctrs
SW1. . . . . **133** B3
Capital Wharf **14**
E1. . . . . **125** C1
Capland Ho NW8. . **89** C2
Capland St NW8. . . **89** C2
Caple Ho SW10. . . **157** A2
Caple Rd NW10. . . 21 B3
Capper St WC1. . . . 93 A1
Capstan Ho E14 . . 42 B2
Capstan Rd SE8 . . . 41 A2
Capstan Sq E14 . . . 42 B4
Capstan Way SE16. 33 A1
Capulet Mews **1**
E16. . . . . 35 C1
Caradoc CI W2. . . . 31 C3
Caradoc St SE10. . . 43 A1
Cara Ho **10** N1 . . . 14 C1
Caranday Villas **5**
W11. . . . . 30 C1
Caravel CI E14. . . . . 41 C3
Caravel Mews **16**
SE8. . . . . 51 C4
Carberry Rd SE19 . . 75 C1
Carbery Ave W3 . . . 36 B4
Carbis Rd E14 . . . . 33 B3
Carbroke Ho **9**
E9. . . . . 25 B4
Carburton St W1 . . 92 B1
Cardale St **1** E14 . . 42 B3
Carden Rd SE15. . . 65 A4
Cardiff Ho **9** SE15 . . 49 C4
Cardigan Rd
Barnes SW13. . . . . 46 C1
Bow E3. . . . . 26 C3
Richmond TW10. . . 54 A1
Cardigan St SE11. 149 B2
Cardigan Wlk **18**
N1. . . . . 15 B1
Cardinal Bourne St
SE1. . . . . **137** C1
Cardinal Cap Alley
SE1. . . . . **122** C3
Cardinal Hinsley CI
NW10. . . . . 21 C3
Cardinal Hinsley
Mathematics &
Computing Coll
NW10. . . . . 21 C4
Cardinal PI SW15. 57 C3
Cardinal PI SW1. . **132** C1
Cardinal Pole RC Sch
London E9. . . . . . . 17 C1
London E9. . . . . . . 18 A3
Cardinals Way N19 . . 4 C3
Cardinal Vaughan
Meml Sch The
W14. . . . . **126** A4
Cardinal Wlk SW1 **132** C1
Cardine Mews
SE15. . . . . 50 A3
Cardington St
NW1. . . . . 93 A3
Cardozo Rd N7. . . . 14 A3
Cardross St W6. . . . 39 A3
Cardwell Rd **6** N7 . . 14 A4
Career Ct **11** SE16 . . 40 C4
Carew CI N7. . . . . 5 B2
Carew Ct **15** SE14. . 50 C4
Carew Ho SW16. . . . 74 C1

Carew St SE5. . . . . . 48 B1
Carey PI **20** SE5. . . 48 B1
Carey Gdns SW8. . **171** B3
Carey La EC2. . . . . **108** C2
Carey St WC2. . . . **107** A1
Carfax PI SW4 . . . . 61 C3
Carfree CI **8** N1. . . 14 C1
Cargill Rd SW18. . . 71 B3
Carinthia Ct **7**
SE8. . . . . 41 A2
Carisbrooke Ct
Acton W3. . . . . 37 B4
1 Streatham
SW16. . . . . 74 B1
Carisbrooke Gdns
SE15. . . . . 49 B3
Carisbrooke Ho
11 Richmond
TW10. . . . . 54 C2
Carker's La
Crouch End N19. . . . 4 C4
Gospel Oak NW5. . . 13 A3
Carleton Gdns
N19. . . . . 13 B3
Carleton Rd N7. . . 13 C3
Carlile CI E3. . . . . . 26 B3
Carlile Ho SE1. . . **137** C1
Carlingford Rd
NW3. . . . . 11 C4
Carlisle Ave
Acton W3. . . . . 29 A3
Whitechapel EC3. . **110** C1
Carlisle La SE1. . . **135** A2
Carlisle PI SW1. . . **132** C1
Carlisle Rd
Finsbury Pk N4. . . . . 5 C4
Kilburn NW6. . . . . . 23 A4
Carlisle St W1. . . . **105** B1
Carlos PI W1. . . . . **118** A3
Carlow St NW1. . . . **82** C2
Carlson Ct SW15 . . 58 B3
Carlton Cl
Brixton SW9. . . . . . 48 A2
Hampstead NW3 . . . 1 C2
8 Willesden NW2. . 9 B2
Carlton Dr SW15 . . . 58 A2
Carlton Gdns
SW1. . . . . **119** B1
Carlton Gr SE15 . . . 50 A2
Carlton Hill NW8. . . 79 A1
Carlton Ho
8 Kilburn NW6. . . 23 B3
Kilburn NW6. . . . . . 23 C3
Marylebone W1 . . **103** A2
Carlton House Terr
SW1. . . . . **119** C2
Carlton Lo N4. . . . . . 5 C4
Carlton Mans
Brixton SW9. . . . . . 62 C3
Cricklewood NW2 . . . 9 C3
Kensington W14 . . **126** B4
Maida Vale W9. . . . **88** B4
7 South Hampstead
NW6. . . . . 10 C1
Stamford Hill N16. . . . 7 B4
Carlton Prim Sch
NW5. . . . . 12 C3
Carlton Rd
Acton W4. . . . . 37 C4
Finsbury Pk N4. . . . . 5 C4
Mortlake SW14 . . . 55 B3
Carlton Sq E1. . . . . 25 C1
Carlton St SW1. . . **119** B3

Carltons The **6**
SW15. . . . . 58 A2
Carlton Tower PI
SW1. . . . . **131** A2
Carlton Vale NW6. . 23 C3
Carlton Vale Inf Sch
18 NW6. . . . . 23 B2
Carlyle Ho
4 Camberwell
SE5. . . . . 48 B3
Chelsea SW3 . . . . **157** C4
12 Stoke Newington
N16. . . . . 7 A1
Carlyle Mans
SW3. . . . . **158** A3
Carlyle Mews **24**
E1. . . . . 25 C1
Carlyle PI SW15 . . . 57 C3
Carlyle Rd **6**
NW10. . . . . 20 C4
Carlyle's Ho The **5**
SW3. . . . . **158** A3
Carlyle Sq SW3 . . . **143** C1
Carmalt Gdns
SW15. . . . . 57 B3
Carmarthen Ho **6**
SW15. . . . . 69 B4
Carmarthen PI
SE1. . . . . **138** A4
Carmel Ct W8 . . . **128** A4
Carmelite St EC4. . **121** C4
Carmel Lo SW6. . . **155** B4
Carmen St E14 . . . 34 A3
Carmichael Cl **8**
SW11. . . . . 59 C4
Carmichael Ct **5**
SW13. . . . . 46 B1
Carmichael Ho **6**
E14. . . . . 34 B2
Carmichael Mews
SW18. . . . . 71 C4
Carminia Rd SW17. . 73 A2
Carnaby St W1. . . **104** C1
Carnac St SE21,
SE27. . . . . 75 C1
Carna Ct TW9. . . . . 54 A4
Carnegie Ho NW3 . . 2 C1
Carnegie PI SW19 . 69 C1
Carnegie St N1. . . **85** A3
Carnicot Ho **9**
SE15. . . . . 50 A2
Carnoustie Dr N1. . 14 B1
Carnwath Ho SW6. . 59 A4
Carnwath Rd SW6. . 59 A4
Caroline Cl
Bayswater W2 . . . **114** B3
Streatham SW16. . . 74 B1
Caroline Gdns
E2. . . . . 24 A2 **98** B4
Caroline Ho
Bayswater W2 . . . **114** B3
20 Hammersmith
W6. . . . . 39 B1
Caroline Martyn Ho **8**
N19. . . . . 4 C4
Caroline PI
Bayswater W2 . . . **114** B3
Clapham SW4. . . . **169** C1
Caroline PI Mews
W2. . . . . **114** B3
Caroline St E1. . . . . 32 C3
Caroline Terr
SW1. . . . . **145** B3
Caroline Wlk SW6 **154** A3
Carol St NW1. . . . . **82** C4
Caronia Ct **4**
SE16. . . . . 41 A2

Carpenter Ho
11 Tower Hamlets
E14. . . . . 33 C4
5 Tufnell Pk N19. . . 13 C4
Carpenters Ct
NW1. . . . . **82** C4
Carpenter's PI
SW4. . . . . 61 C3
Carpenters Prim Sch
E15. . . . . 27 B4
Carradale Ho **2**
E14. . . . . 34 B3
Carrara CI **18** SW9. . 63 A3
Carrara Wharf
SW6. . . . . 58 A4
Carriage Dr E
SW11. . . . . **159** C2
Carriage Drive E
SW11. . . . . **159** C2
Carriage Drive N SW11,
SW8. . . . . **159** C3
Carriage Dr N
Battersea SW8,
SW11. . . . . **158** C2
Battersea SW8,
SW11. . . . . **159** C3
Carriage Dr S
SW11. . . . . **169** B4
Carriage Drive S
SW11. . . . . **159** C2
Carriage Drive W SW11,
SW8. . . . . **159** C3
Carriage Dr W
SW11. . . . . **158** C1
Carrick Ho
Islington N7 . . . . . 14 B2
Kennington SE11 . . **150** A2
Carrick Mews SE8 . . 51 C4
Carrington Ct
SW11. . . . . 60 A3
Carrington Ho
W1. . . . . **118** A1
Carrington Lo **3**
TW10. . . . . 54 A2
Carrington Rd
TW10. . . . . 54 C3
Carrington St W1 . **118** A1
Carrol CI NW5. . . . 13 A4
Carroll Ct
Acton W3. . . . . 37 A3
4 Shacklewell E5 . . . 7 C2
Carroll Ho W2. . . . **115** B4
Carron CI E14 . . . . 34 A3
Carroun Rd SW8. . **162** C2
Carr St **3** E14. . . . 33 A3
Carslake Rd SW15. . 57 B1
Carson Rd
Dulwich SE21. . . . . **75** C2
Newham E16. . . . . . 35 C4
Carter Ct EC4 . . . **108** B1
Carteret Ho **3**
W12. . . . . **30** A2
Carteret St SW1. . . **133** B3
Carteret Way SE8. . **40** C2
Carter Ho
11 London SW2. . . . **62** C2
Spitalfields E1 . . . . **110** C3
Carter PI SE17. . . . **151** A1
Carter St SE17. . . . **150** C1
Carter's Yd SW18. . . **58** C2
Carthew Rd W6 . . . . **39** A3
Carthew Villas W6. . **39** A3
Carthusian St EC1. **108** C4
Cartier Circ E14 . . . **34** B1
Carting La WC2. . . **120** B3

Cartmel NW1 . . . . . . **92** C4
Carton Ho
4 Bermondsey
SE16 . . . . **139** B2
17 Shepherd's Bush
W11 . . . . .30 C2
Cartoon Mus The
WC1 . . . . **106** A3
Cartwright Gdns
NW1 . . . . .94 A3
Cartwright Ho
SE1 . . . . **137** A1
Cartwright St E1 . . **125** A3
Cartwright Way
SW13 . . . . .47 A3
Carvel Ho E14 . . . . . .42 B1
Carver Cl SW4 . . . . . .37 B3
Carver Rd SE24 . . . . .63 B1
Carville Cres TW8 . .36 A2
Caryl Ho SW19 . . . . . .69 C3
Carysfort Rd N16 . . . .15 C4
Casby Ho 7 SE16 **139** B2
Casella Rd SE14 . . . . .50 C3
Casey Cl NW8 . . . . . . .90 B3
Casino Ave SE24 . . . .63 C2
Caspian Ho E1 . . . . . .32 C4
Caspian St SE5 . . . . . .48 C3
Cassandra Ct 7
NW2 . . . . .9 B2
Cass Bsns Sch EC1 **97** B1
Cassell Ho 21
SW9 . . . . **172** B2
Casserley Ho W4 . . . .37 C3
Cass Ho 2 E9 . . . . . .17 C2
Cassidy Rd SW6 . . **155** B1
Cassilis Rd E14 . . . . . .41 C4
Cassinghurst SE24 . .63 C2
Cassland Rd E9 . . . . . .17 C2
Casson Ho 1 E1 . . **111** B4
Casson St E1 . . . . . . **111** B3
Castalia Sq 6 E14 . .42 B4
Castellain Mans
W9 . . . . .88 A2
Castellain Rd W9 . . . .88 B2
Castell Ho 11 SE8 . .51 C3
Castello Ave SW15 .57 B2
Castelnau SW13 . . . . .47 A3
Castelnau Gdns
SW13 . . . . .47 A4
Castelnau Mans
SW13 . . . . .47 A4
Castelnau Row
SW13 . . . . .47 A4
Casterbridge
Kilburn NW6 . . . . . . .78 B4
3 Notting Hill W11 . .31 C3
Casterton St E8 . . . .17 A2
Castleacre W2 . . . . **102** A1
Castle Baynard St
EC4 . . . . **122** C4
Castlebrook Cl
SE11 . . . . **150** A4
Castle Cl
12 Acton W3 . . . . . .37 B4
Homerton E9 . . . . . . .18 A3
South Acton W3 . . . . .37 A4
Wimbledon SW19 . . . .69 C1
Castlecombe Dr
SW19 . . . . .69 C4
Castle Ct EC3 . . . . **109** C1
Castleden Ho
NW6 . . . . .11 C1
Castleford Ct NW8 . **89** C2

Castlefrank Ho 20
N1 . . . . . .24 A2 98 B4
Castlegate TW9 . . . .54 B4
Castlehaven Rd
NW1 . . . . .13 A1
Castle Ho
Newington SE1 . . . . **150** C4
South Lambeth
SW8 . . . . **162** B2
Castle Ind Est
SE17 . . . . **150** C4
Castle La SW1 . . . **132** C2
Castlemaine 8
SW11 . . . . **169** A2
Castlemaine St 2
E1 . . . . .32 A4
Castle Mead SE5 . . .48 B3
Castle Mews NW1 . .13 A2
Castle Pl
8 Acton W4 . . . . . . .38 A2
Camden Town NW1 . .13 A2
Castle Rd NW1 . . . . . .13 A2
Castlereagh St
W1 . . . . **102** C2
Castleton Ho 6
E14 . . . . .42 B2
Castletown Rd
W14 . . . . **140** B1
Castleview Cl N4 . . . .6 B4
Castle Way SW19 . . .69 C1
Castlewood Ho
WC1 . . . . **105** C2
Castle Yd
Highgate N6 . . . . .3 C4
Lambeth SE1 . . . . . **122** B2
Castor La E14 . . . . **120** C1
Catalpa Ct SE13 . . . .67 C1
Caterham Rd SE13 . .67 C4
Catesby Ho 3 E9 . .25 B4
Catesby St SE17 . . **151** C3
Cathay Ho SE16 . . . .40 A4
Cathay St 12 SE16 .40 A4
Cathcart Hill N19 . . . .4 B1
Cathcart Rd SW10 **156** C4
Cathcart St NW5 . . **13** A2
Cathedral Ct EC4 . **108** B1
Cathedral Lo EC1 . **108** C4
Cathedral of St
Saviour & St Mary
Overie Prim Sch
SE1 . . . . **137** A4
Cathedral St SE1 . . **123** B2
Cathedral Wlk
SW1 . . . . **132** C2
Catherall Rd N5,
N16 . . . . .6 B1
Catherine Baird Ct 3
SW12 . . . . .73 A4
Catherine Dr TW9 . .54 A3
Catherine Gr SE10 . .52 A2
Catherine Griffiths Ct
EC1 . . . . .95 C2
Catherine Ho 18
N1 . . . . .24 A4
Catherine Pl SW1 . **132** C2
Catherine St WC2 . **120** C4
Catherine Wheel Alley
E1 . . . . **110** B3
Catherine Wheel Yd
SW1 . . . . **118** C1
Catherwood Ct N1 . **87** B1
Cathles Rd SW12 . . . .61 A1
Cathnor Rd W12 . . . .39 A4
Catlin St SE16 . . . . **40** A1
Catman Ho N4 . . . . . .5 B3
Cato Rd SW4 . . . . . . .61 C3

Cator St
Camberwell SE15 . . . .49 B3
Camberwell SE15 . . . .49 B4
Cato St W1 . . . . . . **102** B2
Catton St WC1 . . . . **106** C3
Caughley Ho
SE11 . . . . **135** C1
Caulfield Ct 15
NW1 . . . . .13 B1
Caulfield Rd SE15 . .50 A1
Causeway The
SW18 . . . . .59 A2
Causton Cotts 3
E14 . . . . .33 A3
Causton Ho SE5 . . . .48 B3
Causton Rd N6 . . . . . .4 A4
Causton St SW1 . . **147** C2
Cautley Ave SW4 . . .61 B2
Cavalry Gdns
SW15 . . . . .58 B2
Cavaye Ho SW10 . . **157** A4
Cavaye Pl SW10 . . **143** A1
Cavell Ct 5 N19 . . . . .4 B2
Cavell Ho 8 N1 . . . . .24 A4
Cavell St E1 . . . . .32 A4
Cavendish Ave
NW8 . . . . **79** C1
Cavendish Cl
Brondesbury NW6 . . . .10 B2
3 Putney SW15 . . . . .58 A2
St John's Wood
NW8 . . . . **79** C1
Cavendish Coll
WC1 . . . . **105** B4
Cavendish Ct EC2 . **110** B2
Cavendish Gdns
SW4 . . . . .61 B1
Cavendish Ho
South Lambeth
SW8 . . . . **172** A4
St John's Wood
NW8 . . . . **79** C1
Cavendish Jun & Inf
Sch W4 . . . . .46 A3
Cavendish Mans
2 Clapham Pk
SW4 . . . . .61 B1
Hackney E5 . . . . .17 B3
Holborn EC1 . . . . . . **95** B1
8 West Hampstead
NW6 . . . . .10 C3
Cavendish Mews N
W1 . . . . **104** B3
Cavendish Mews S
W1 . . . . **104** B3
Cavendish Par
SW12 . . . . .61 A1
Cavendish Pl
Balham SW4 . . . . . . .61 A1
Brondesbury NW2 . . . .9 C2
Marylebone W1 . . . **104** B2
Cavendish Rd
Brondesbury NW6 . . . .10 B2
Chiswick W4 . . . . . . .45 B2
Clapham Pk SW12 . . .61 B2
Cavendish Sch 22
SE16 . . . . .40 B2
Cavendish Sch The
NW1 . . . . .82 B4
Cavendish Sq W1 . **104** B2
Cavendish St N1 . . . **87** B1
Cavendish Terr 11
E3 . . . . .26 B2
Cavendish The
NW11 . . . . .2 A4

Caversham Ho 7
SE15 . . . . .49 C4
Caversham Rd
NW5 . . . . .13 B2
Caversham St
SW3 . . . . **158** C4
Caverswall St W12 . .30 B3
Cavour Ho SE17 . . **150** B2
Cawdor Gr E3 . . . . . .26 C2
Caxton Hall SW1 . **133** B2
Caxton Gr E3 . . . . . . .27 A2
Caxton Rd W12 . . . . .39 C4
Caxton St N E16 . . . .35 B3
Caxton St SW1 . . . **133** B2
Caxton Wlk WC2 . . **105** C1
Cayford Ho 1
NW3 . . . . .12 B3
Cayley Prim Sch 2
E14 . . . . .33 A3
Caygill Pl EC1 . . . . **97** B3
Cayton St EC1 . . . . **97** B3
Cazenove Mans 1
N16 . . . . .7 C2
Cazenove Rd N16 . . .7 C2
Cecil Ct
Chelsea SW10 . . . **156** C4
South Hampstead
NW6 . . . . .11 A1
St James WC2 . . . **120** A3
Cecilia Rd E8 . . . . . .16 C3
Cecil Mans 2
SW17 . . . . .72 C2
Cecil Rd
Acton W3 . . . . .28 B4
Harlesden NW10 . . . . .21 A4
Cecil Rhodes Ho
NW1 . . . . **83** B2
Cedar Cl
Old Ford E3 . . . . .26 B4
West Norwood
SE21 . . . . .75 B2
Cedar Ct
Islington N1 . . . . .15 B1
Marylebone W1 . . . **102** B2
Mortlake SW14 . . . . . .55 B3
Wimbledon SW19 . . . .69 C3
Cedar Gr W5 . . . . . . .36 A3
Cedar Ho
6 Cubitt Town
E14 . . . . .42 B4
Kensington W8 . . . . **128** A2
New Cross Gate
SE14 . . . . .50 C2
6 Richmond TW9 . . . .45 A2
10 Rotherhithe
SE16 . . . . .40 C4
Cedar Lo
Brondesbury NW2 . . .10 B2
Fulham SW6 . . . . . . .47 C2
Cedarne Rd SW6 . **156** A1
Cedars Cl SE13 . . . . .67 C4
Cedars Ct SW15 . . . .56 C1
Cedars Ho 2 SW2 . .62 B3
Cedars Mews SW4 . .61 A3
Cedars Rd
Barnes SW13 . . . . . . .46 C1
Clapham SW4 . . . . . . .61 A3
Cedars The E9 . . . . . .17 C1
Cedar Terr TW9 . . . . .54 A3
Cedar Way NW1 . . . . .83 B4
Cedra Ct N16 . . . . . . .7 C3
Cedric Chambers
NW8 . . . . **89** B2
Celandine Cl E3,
E14 . . . . .33 C4
Celandine Dr E8 . . . . .16 B1

Celbridge Mews
W2 . . . . **100** B3
Celestial Gdns
SE13 . . . . .67 C3
Celia Blairman Ho
E1 . . . . **110** C4
Celia Ct 7 TW9 . . . .44 B2
Celia Ho 10 N1 . . . . .24 A3
Celia Rd N19 . . . . . . .13 B4
Celtic St E14 . . . . . . .34 A4
Cenacle Cl NW3 . . . . .1 C1
Cenotaph SW1 . . . **134** A4
Centaur Ct 3
TW8 . . . . .36 A1
Centaur St SE1 . . . **135** A2
Central Ave SW11 **159** A1
Central Bsns Ctr
NW10 . . . . .8 A3
Central Foundation
Boys' Sch
EC2 . . . . **97** C2
Central Foundation
Lower Girls Sch The
10 E3 . . . . .26 B2
Central Foundation
Upper Girls Sch The
E3 . . . . .26 B2
Central Ho E15 . . . . .27 B3
Central Middlesex
Hospl NW10 . . . . . . .20 B2
Central Par W3 . . . . .37 A4
Central St Martins
Coll EC1 . . . . **95** C1
Central St Martins
College of Art &
Design N1 . . . . . **84** A3
Central St Martins
Coll of Art & Design
WC1 . . . . **105** C1
Central St Martins
Coll of Art & Design
(The London Inst)
WC1 . . . . **106** C3
Central Sch of Ballet
EC1 . . . . **95** C1
Central Sch of Speech
& Drama NW3 . . . **11** C1
Central St EC1 . . . . **96** C3
Central Way NW10 . .20 B2
Centre Acad 2
SW11 . . . . .59 C3
Centre Ave W3 . . . . .28 C1
Centre Bldg SE17 **151** A4
Centre Hts 5
NW3 . . . . .11 C1
Centre Point 1
SE1 . . . . **153** B2
Centre Point Ho
WC2 . . . . **105** C2
Centre St E2 . . . . . . .25 A3
Centurion Bldg
SW8 . . . . **160** A3
Centurion Cl N7 . . . . .14 B1
Centurion La E3 . . . .26 B3
Century Ho SE13 . . . .52 A1
Cephas Ave E1 . . . . .25 B1
Cephas Ho 9 E1 . . . .25 B1
Cephas St E1 . . . . . . .25 B1
Cerise Rd SE15 . . . . .49 C2
Cerney Mews W2 . **115** B4
Cervantes Ct 3
W2 . . . . **100** B1
Cester St E2 . . . . . . .24 C4
Ceylon Rd
6 Hammersmith
W14 . . . . .39 C3
Kensington W14 . . . **126** A1

Chabot Dr SE15.....65 A4
Chadacre Ho 10
  SW9.....63 A3
Chadbourn St E14..34 A4
Chadston Ho 17
  N1.....15 A1
Chadswell WC1.....94 B3
Chadwell St EC1.....95 C4
Chadwick Ct SW15..68 B4
Chadwick Rd
  Harlesden NW10..21 B4
  Peckham SE15.....49 B1
Chadwick St SW1. 133 B1
Chadworth Ho
  Finsbury EC1.....96 C3
  Finsbury Pk N4.....65 B3
Chagford Ho
  36 Bromley E3.....27 A2
  Marylebone NW1.....90 C1
Chagford St NW1.. 91 A1
Chalbury Ho 8
  SW9.....62 B3
Chalbury Wlk N1.. 85 B2
Chalcot Cres NW1. 81 A4
Chalcot Gdns NW3 .12 B2
Chalcot Mews
  SW16.....74 A1
Chalcot Rd NW1.. 81 B4
Chalcot Sch 21
  NW1.....13 A1
Chalcot Sq NW1.. 12 C1
Chaldon Rd SW6. 154 B2
Chale Rd SW2.....62 A1
Chalfont Ct NW1.. 91 A1
Chalford Ho 2
  SE16.....40 A3
Chalford 7 NW3. 11 B2
Chalford Ct 19
  SW15.....57 C1
Chalkers Cnr TW9.. 55 A4
Chalk Farm Sta
  NW3.....12 C1
Chalk Hill Rd W6...39 C2
Chalkwell Ho 10
  E1.....32 C3
Challenge Cl
  NW10.....21 A4
Challenger Ho 7
  E14.....33 A2
Challice Way SW2. 74 B3
Challoner Cres
  W14..... 140 C1
Challoner Mans
  W14..... 140 C1
Challoner St W14 140 C1
Chalmers Ho 15
  SW11.....59 B4
Chalmer's Wlk 14
  SE17.....48 A4
Chalner Ho SW2...74 C3
Chaloner Ct SE1.. 137 B4
Chalsey Lodge
  SE4.....66 B3
Chalsey Rd SE4.....66 B3
Chalton St NW1.. 83 B1
Chamberlain Cotts
  SE5.....48 C2
Chamberlain Ho 8
  E1.....32 B2
Chamberlain St 7
  NW1.....12 B1
Chamberlayne Mans
  3 NW10.....22 C2
Chamberlayne Rd
  NW10.....22 B4
Chambers La NW10..9 B1

Chambers Rd N7 ..14 A4
Chambers St
  SE16.....139 C3
Chamber St E1.... 125 A4
Chambon Pl 7
  W6.....38 C2
Chambord Ho 22
  E2.....24 B2 99 A3
Chambord St
  E2.....24 B2 99 A3
Champion Gr SE5..63 C4
Champion Hill SE5 .63 C4
Champion Pk SE5 .48 C1
Champlain Ho 20
  W12.....30 A2
Chancel Ct W1 .. 119 B4
Chancellor Gr
  SE21.....75 B1
Chancellor Ho
  South Kensington
  SW7.....129 A2
  26 Wapping E1.....32 A1
Chancellor Pas
  E14.....33 C1
Chancellors' Ct
  WC1.....106 C3
Chancellors Rd
  W6.....39 B1
Chancellors St W6..39 B1
Chancellors Wharf 2
  W6.....39 B1
Chancel St SE1.. 122 A1
Chancery Bldgs 14
  E1.....32 B2
Chancery Ho W2 107 B3
Chancery La EC4.. 107 B2
Chancery Lane Sta
  WC1.....107 B3
Chancery Mews
  SW17.....72 A2
Chance St
  E2.....24 B1 98 C2
Chandler Ave E16 .35 C4
Chandlers Mews
  E14.....41 C4
Chandler St E1.....32 A1
Chandlers Way 11
  SE24.....74 C4
Chandler Way
  SE15.....49 B3
Chandlery Ho 20
  E1.....111 B1
Chandos Pl WC2.. 120 A3
Chandos Rd
  Cricklewood NW2.....9 B3
  Old Oak Comm
  NW10.....21 A1
  Stratford New Town
  E15.....19 C3
Chandos St W1.. 104 B3
Change Alley EC3 109 C1
Channel Gate Rd
  NW10.....21 A2
Channel Ho E14 ..33 A4
Channel Sea Bsns Ctr
  E15.....27 C4
Channelsea Rd
  E15.....27 C4
Channing Jun Sch
  N6.....3 C1
Channing Sch N6 ....4 A3
Chantrey Rd SW9..62 B4
Chantry Cl W9.....23 B1
Chantry Cres NW10..8 B2
Chantry Ct SW6 ..58 A4

Chantry Sq W8 ... 128 A1
Chantry St N1.....86 B3
Chant Sq E15.....19 C1
Chant St E15.....19 C1
Chapel Cl NW10.....8 B2
Chapel Ct SE1.... 137 B4
Chapel House St
  E14.....42 A2
Chapel Mkt N1.....85 B2
Chapel Pl
  Islington N1.....85 C2
  Marylebone W1 .. 104 A1
  12 Shoreditch
  EC2.....24 A2 98 A3
Chapel Side W2 .. 114 A3
Chapel St
  Paddington NW1 .. 102 A3
  Westminster SW1 . 131 C3
Chaplin Cl SE1 ... 136 A4
Chaplin Ho 6
  SW9.....62 C3
Chaplin Rd NW2.....8 C2
Chaplow Cl SW6.. 166 C2
Chapman Ho
  28 Stepney E1.....32 A3
  2 West Norwood
  SE27.....75 A1
Chapman Rd E9 ..18 B2
Chapmans Park Ind
  Est NW10.....8 B2
Chapman Sq
  SW19.....69 C2
Chapman St E1.....32 A2
Chapone Pl W1 .. 105 B1
Chapter Cl W4.....37 B3
Chapter House &
  Jewel Twr SW1. 134 A2
Chapter Rd
  Kennington SE17 .. 150 B1
  Willesden NW2.....8 C3
Chapter St SW1 .. 147 B3
Chara Pl W4.....45 C4
Charcot Ho SW15..56 B1
Charcroft Ct 11
  W14.....39 C4
Chard Ho 7 N7.....5 B2
Chardin Ho 30
  SW9.....173 C4
Chardin Rd 11 W4..38 A2
Chardmore Rd N16 ..7 C3
Charecroft Way
  W12.....39 C4
Charfield Ct W9 ..88 B1
Charford Rd E16...35 C4
Chargrove Cl 24
  SE16.....40 C4
Charing Cross
  SW1.....120 A2
Charing Cross Hospl
  W6.....39 C1
Charing Cross Sta
  WC2.....120 B2
Charing Cross Sta
  SE1.....135 C4
Chariot Cl 3 E3.....26 C4
Charlbert Ct NW8 .80 A2
Charlbert St NW8 .80 A2
Charles Allen Ho
  EC1.....95 B4
Charles Auffray Ho 20
  E1.....32 B4
Charles Barry Cl
  SW4.....61 B4

Charles Burton Ct
  E5.....18 A2
Charles Coveney Rd
  4 SE15.....49 B2
Charles Darwin Ho 3
  E2.....25 A2
Charles Dickens Ho 1
  E2.....25 A2
Charles Dickens Mus
  The WC1.....95 A1
Charles Dickens Prim
  Sch SE1.....136 C3
Charles Edward
  Brooke Sch 31
  SW9.....48 A2
Charles Edward
  Brooke Sch (Dennen
  Site) 10 SE5 .....48 A2
Charles Flemwell
  Mews 7 E16.....35 C1
Charles Haller St 21
  SW2.....74 C4
Charles Harrod Ct
  SW13.....47 B4
Charles Hobson Ho 4
  8 NW10.....8 A1
Charles Hocking Ho
  3 W3.....37 B4
Charles II Pl SW3 144 C1
Charles II St SW1. 119 B2
Charles La NW8 .. 80 A2
Charles Lamb Ct
  N1.....86 B2
Charles Mackenzie Ho
  16 SE16.....153 C4
Charles Pl NW1 ... 93 A3
Charles Rowan Ho
  WC1.....95 B3
Charles Sq N1.....97 C3
Charles St
  Barnes SW13.....46 A1
  Mayfair W1.....118 A2
Charleston St
  SE17.....151 A3
Charles Townsend Ho
  EC1.....96 A2
Charles Utton Ct
  E8.....16 C4
Charlesworth Ho 6
  E14.....33 C3
Charleville Ct
  W14.....140 C1
Charleville Mans
  W14.....140 C1
Charleville Rd
  W14.....140 C1
Charlotte Ct 10
  W6.....38 C2
Charlotte Ho 6
  W6.....39 B1
Charlotte Mews
  Marylebone W1 .. 105 A4
  North Kensington
  W10.....30 C3
  West Kensington
  W14.....140 A4
Charlotte Pl
  Marylebone W1 .. 105 A3
  Westminster SW1 . 146 C3
Charlotte Rd
  Barnes SW13.....46 B1
  Shoreditch
  EC2.....24 A1 98 A2

Charlotte Row
  SW4.....61 B4
Charlotte Sharman
  Prim Sch SE11 .. 136 A1
Charlotte Sq 6
  TW10.....54 B1
Charlotte Terr N1 . 85 A3
Charlotte Turner Prim
  Sch SE8.....51 C4
Charlton Ct
  26 Hackney E2.....24 B4
  8 Kentish Town
  N7.....13 C3
Charlton Ho
  6 Brentford
  TW8.....44 A4
  Somers Town NW1 . 93 B4
Charlton King's Rd
  NW5.....13 C3
Charlton Pl N1.... 86 A2
Charlton Rd NW10..21 A4
Charlton Way SE10,
  SE3.....53 A2
Charlwood Ho
  Richmond TW9.....45 A3
  1 Streatham SW2 . 74 B3
  Westminster SW1 . 147 B3
Charlwood Pl
  SW1.....147 A3
Charlwood Rd
  SW15.....57 C3
Charlwood St
  SW1.....147 A2
Charlwood Terr 5
  SW15.....57 C3
Charman Ho
  18 London SW2.....62 C1
  South Lambeth
  SW8.....162 A2
Charmian Ho 19
  N1.....24 A3
Charmouth Ct
  TW10.....54 B2
Charmouth Ho
  SW8.....162 C2
Charnock Ho 22
  W12.....30 A2
Charnwood Gdns
  E14.....41 C2
Charrington Ho 42
  E1.....25 B1
Charrington St
  NW1.....83 B2
Charter Bldgs 14
  SE10.....52 A2
Charter Ct
  Finsbury Pk N5.....5 C3
  Marylebone W1 .. 102 B3
Charter Ho WC2 .. 106 B1
Charterhouse Bldgs
  EC1.....96 C1
Charterhouse Mews
  EC1.....108 B4
Charterhouse Rd
  E8.....16 C3
Charterhouse Sq
  EC1.....108 B4
Charterhouse Square
  Sch The EC1.....108 B4
Charterhouse St
  EC1.....108 A3
Charterhouse Works
  SW18.....59 B3

Charteris Rd
Finsbury Pk N4 . . . . 5 C3
Kilburn NW6 . . . . 23 B4
Charteris Sp Ctr
NW6 . . . . 23 C4
Charter Sch SE24 . . . . 63 C2
Chartes Ho SE1 . . . 138 B2
Chartfield Ave
SW15 . . . . 57 B2
Chartfield Sq
SW15 . . . . 57 C2
Chartham Ct 18
SW9 . . . . 172 B1
Chartham Gr SE27 . . 75 A1
Chartham Ho SE1 137 C2
Chart House The 5
E14 . . . . 42 A1
Chartridge SE17 . . . 48 C4
Chart St N1 . . . . . . 97 C4
Chartwell 25
SW19 . . . . 69 C3
Chase Ct SW3 . . . . 130 C1
Chase Ctr The
NW10 . . . . 20 C2
Chaseley Ct W4 . . . 37 A1
Chaseley St E14 . . . 33 A3
Chasemore Ho
SW6 . . . . 154 B2
Chase Rd NW10 . . . 20 C1
Chase Road Trad Est
NW10 . . . . 20 C1
Chase The SW4 . . . . . 61 A4
Chater Ho 6 E2 . . . 25 C2
Chatfield Rd SW11 . 59 B4
Chatham St NW1 . . 60 B2
Chatham Ho 7
SE5 . . . . 49 A1
Chatham PI E9 . . . . 17 B2
Chatham Rd SW11 . 60 B2
Chatham St SE17 151 C4
Chatsworth Ct
Brondesbury NW2 . . . . 9 C2
Clapton E5 . . . . 17 C4
Earl's Ct W8 . . . . . . 141 B4
Chatsworth Est E5 . 17 C4
Chatsworth Gdns
W3 . . . . 28 A1
Chatsworth Lo 8
W4 . . . . 37 C1
Chatsworth Rd
Brondesbury NW2 . . . . 9 C2
Chiswick W4 . . . . 45 B4
Clapton E5 . . . . 17 C4
Chatsworth Way
SE27 . . . . 75 B1
Chattenden Ho
N4 . . . . 6 C4
Chatterton Ct TW9 . 44 B1
Chatterton Rd N4 . . 6 A1
Chatto Rd SW11 . . . 60 B2
Chaucer Ave TW9 . . 44 C1
Chaucer Ct N16 . . . 16 A4
Chaucer Dr SE1 . . . 153 A3
Chaucer Ho SW1 . . 146 C1
Chaucer Rd
Acton W3 . . . . 28 B1
Herne Hill SE24 . . . . . 63 A2
Chauldon Rd E5 . . . . 97 C3
Cheadle Ct NW8 . . . . 89 C2
Cheadle Ho 17
E14 . . . . 33 B3
Cheam St 6 SE15 . . 65 A4
Cheapside EC2 . . . 109 A1
Chearsley SE17 . . . 151 A4

Cheddington Ho 9
E2 . . . . 24 C4
Chedworth CI E16 . . 35 B3
Chedworth Ho 2
E5 . . . . 7 C2
Cheesemans Terr
W14 . . . . 140 C1
Chelmer Rd E9 . . . . 17 C3
Chelmsford CI W6 . 47 C4
Chelmsford Ho 1
N7 . . . . 14 B4
Chelmsford Sq
NW10 . . . . 22 B4
CHELSEA 144 B1
Chelsea Antiques Mkt
SW3 . . . . 144 B1
Chelsea Barracks
SW1 . . . . 145 C2
Chelsea Bridge
SW1 . . . . 160 A4
Chelsea Bridge Rd
SW1 . . . . 145 C2
Chelsea CI NW10 . . 20 C4
Chelsea Cloisters
SW3 . . . . 144 B3
Chelsea Coll of Art &
Design SW1 . . . . . . 148 A2
Chelsea Cres
Brondesbury NW2 . . . 10 B2
SW10 . . . . 167 A3
Chelsea Ct SW3 . . 159 B4
Chelsea Emb
SW3 . . . . 158 C3
Chelsea Est SW3 . 158 A3
Chelsea Farm Ho
SW10 . . . . 157 C3
Chelsea Gate
SW1 . . . . 145 C1
Chelsea Gdns
SW1 . . . . 145 C1
Chelsea Harbour
Design Ctr
SW10 . . . . 167 A4
Chelsea Harbour Dr
SW10 . . . . 167 A4
Chelsea Harbour Pier
SW10 . . . . 167 B3
Chelsea Ind Coll
SW6 . . . . 156 A1
Chelsea Lo SW3 . . 158 A3
Chelsea Manor Ct
SW3 . . . . 158 B4
Chelsea Manor Gdns
SW3 . . . . 144 B1
Chelsea Manor St
SW3 . . . . 144 B1
**Chelsea Manor
Studios** SW3 . . . . 144 B1
Chelsea Mus SW3 156 B2
Chelsea Park Gdns
SW3 . . . . 157 B3
Chelsea Physic Gdn
SW1 . . . . 158 C4
Chelsea Reach Twr
SW10 . . . . 157 B2
Chelsea Sp Ctr
SW3 . . . . 144 B1
Chelsea Sq SW3 . 143 C1
Chelsea Twrs
SW3 . . . . 158 B4
Chelsea &
Westminster Hospl
SW10 . . . . 157 A3
Chelsfield Ho
SE17 . . . . 152 A3

Chelsfield Point 3
E9 . . . . 17 C1
Chelsham Ho 1
SW4 . . . . 61 C4
Chelsham Rd SW4 . 61 C4
Cheltenham PI
10 Acton W3 . . . . . . 28 A1
Acton W3 . . . . 37 B4
3 South Acton W3 . . 37 A4
Cheltenham Rd
SE15 . . . . 65 B2
Cheltenham Terr
SW3 . . . . 145 A2
Chelverton Ct
SW15 . . . . 57 C3
Chelverton Rd
SW15 . . . . 57 C3
Chelwood Ho 4
W2 . . . . 101 C1
Chelwood NW5 . . . 12 C3
Chelwood Gdns
TW9 . . . . 44 C1
Chelwood Ho W2 . . 101 C1
Chenies Ho W2 . . . 114 A4
Chenies Mews
WC1 . . . . 93 B1
Chenies PI NW1 . . 83 C2
Chenies St WC1 . . 105 B4
Chenies The NW1 . 83 C2
Cheniston Gdns
W8 . . . . 128 A3
Chepstow CI SW15 . 58 A2
Chepstow Cres
W11 . . . . 31 C2 113 B4
Chepstow Ct
W11 . . . . 31 C2 113 B4
Chepstow PI
W2 . . . . 31 C2 113 C4
Chepstow Rd W2 . . 31 C3
Chepstow Villas
W11 . . . . 31 C2 113 B4
Chequers Ct EC1 . . 97 B1
Chequers Ho NW8 . 90 A2
Chequer St EC1 . . . 97 A1
Cherbury Ct N1 . . . 87 C1
Cherbury St N1 . . . 87 C1
Cheriton Ho 9 E5 . 17 A3
Cheriton Sq SW17 . 72 C2
Cherry Ct 7 W3 . . . 29 A1
Cherry Ct
Acton W3 . . . . 29 A1
6 Rotherhithe
SE16 . . . . 33 A1
Cherry Garden Ho 7
SE16 . . . . 40 A4
Cherry Garden Sch 4
SE16 . . . . 153 C4
Cherry Garden St
SE16 . . . . 40 A4
Cherry Laurel Wlk
SW2 . . . . 62 B1
Cherry Tree CI 8
E9 . . . . 25 B4
Cherry Tree Ct
1 Camden Town
NW1 . . . . 13 B1
11 Peckham SE15 . . 50 A2
Cherry Tree Dr
SW16 . . . . 74 A1
Cherrytree Ho 6
W10 . . . . 22 C2
Cherry Tree Ho
SE14 . . . . 51 B1
Cherry Trees Sch The
2 E3 . . . . 26 C2

Cherry Tree Terr
SE1 . . . . 138 B4
Cherry Tree Wlk
EC1 . . . . 97 A1
Cherrywood CI E3 . 26 A2
Cherrywood Dr
SW15 . . . . 57 C2
Chertsey Ct SW14 . 55 A4
Chertsey Ho 37
E2 . . . . 24 B2 98 C3
Cherwell Ho NW8 . 89 C1
Cheryls CI SW6 . . . 166 B4
Chesham CI SW1 . 131 B1
Chesham St SW18 . 71 C4
Chesham Flats
W1 . . . . 117 C4
Chesham Ho SW1 . 131 B1
Chesham Mews
SW1 . . . . 131 B2
Chesham PI SW1 . 131 B1
Chesham St SW1 . 131 B1
Cheshire St
E2 . . . . 24 B1 99 A2
Chesholm Rd N16 . . 7 A1
Cheshunt Ho 9
NW6 . . . . 78 A3
Chesil Ct
17 Bethnal Green
E2 . . . . 25 B3
Chelsea SW3 . . . . . . 158 B4
Chesilton Rd SW6 . 164 C4
Chesney Ct W9 . . . 23 C1
Chesney Ho SE13 . . 67 C3
Chesney St SW11 . 169 B3
Chessington Ho 10
SW8 . . . . 171 B2
Chesson Rd W14 . . 155 A4
Chessum Ho E8 . . . 16 C2
Chester Ave TW10 . 54 B1
Chester CI
Barnes SW13 . . . . . . 57 A4
Knightsbridge
SW1 . . . . 132 A3
1 Richmond TW10 . 54 B1
Chester Close S
NW1 . . . . 92 B4
Chester Cres E8 . . . 16 B3
Chester Ct
Bermondsey SE8 . . . . 40 C1
4 Camberwell SE5 . . 48 C3
Gospel Oak NW5 . . . . 12 C4
Regent's Pk NW1 . . . 92 B3
Chesterfield Ct
SE13 . . . . 67 B4
Chesterfield Gdns
Greenwich SE10 . . . . 52 C3
Mayfair W1 . . . . 118 A2
Chesterfield Gr
SE22 . . . . 64 B2
Chesterfield Hill
W1 . . . . 118 A3
Chesterfield Rd
W4 . . . . 45 B4
Chesterfield St
W1 . . . . 118 A2
Chesterfield Way
SE15 . . . . 50 B3
Chesterford Gdns
NW3 . . . . 11 A4
Chester Gate NW1 . 92 B3

Chester Ho
Dartmouth Pk N19 . . . 4 A2
1 Deptford SE8 . . . . 51 B4
Chesterman Ct
W4 . . . . 46 A3
Chester Mews
SW1 . . . . 132 A2
Chester PI NW1 . . . 92 A4
Chester Rd
Dartmouth Pk N19 . . . 4 A2
Regent's Pk NW1 . . . 92 A4
Chester Row SW1 . 145 C4
Chester Sq SW1 . . 146 A4
Chester Sq Mews
SW1 . . . . 132 A2
Chester St
Bethnal Green
E2 . . . . 24 C1 99 C2
Westminster SW1 . . 131 C2
Chester Terr NW1 . 92 A4
Chesterton CI
SW18 . . . . 58 C2
Chesterton Ct W3 . 37 A3
Chesterton Ho
20 Battersea
SW11 . . . . 59 C4
8 Kensal Town
W10 . . . . 31 A4
Chesterton Prim Sch
SW11 . . . . 169 B3
Chesterton Rd
W10 . . . . 31 A4
Chesterton Sq
W8 . . . . 141 B3
Chester Way SE11 149 C3
Chestnut Alley
SW6 . . . . 155 A3
Chestnut Ave 11
SW14 . . . . 55 C4
Chestnut CI
New Cross Gate
SE14 . . . . 51 B2
1 Stoke Newington
N16 . . . . 6 C2
Chestnut Ct SW6 . 155 A4
Chestnut Gr SW12 . 72 C3
Chestnut Grove Sch
6 SW12 . . . . 72 C3
Chestnut Ho
1 Acton W4 . . . . 38 A2
Brockley SE4 . . . . 66 B4
7 Maitland Pk
NW3 . . . . 12 B2
West Norwood
SE27 . . . . 75 B1
Chestnuts The 8
N5 . . . . 15 A4
Chettle CI SE1 . . . . 137 B2
Chetwode Ho NW8 . 90 A2
Chetwode Rd
SW17 . . . . 72 B1
Chetwynd Rd NW5 . 4 A1
Cheval Ct SW15 . . . 57 A3
Cheval PI SW7 . . . 130 B2
Cheval St E14 . . . . 41 C3
Chevening Rd
Cubitt Town SE10 . . . 43 B1
Kilburn NW6 . . . . 23 A3
Cheverell Ho 25
E2 . . . . 24 C3
Cheverton Rd N19 . 4 C3
Chevet St E9 . . . . . 18 A3
Chevington NW2 . . 10 B2
Cheviot Ct 16 SE14 . 50 B3

Cheviot Gate NW2 . . . 1 A2
Cheviot Gdns NW2 . . . 1 A2
Cheviot Ho N16 . . . . 7 B3
Chevron Cl E16 . . . . 35 C3
Cheylesmore Ho
SW1 . . . . 146 A2
Cheyne Cl SW3 . . . 158 C4
Cheyne Gdns
SW3 . . . . 158 B3
Cheyne Mews
SW3 . . . . 158 B3
Cheyne Pl SW3 . . . 158 C3
Cheyne Wlk SW10 157 B2
Cheyney Ho 2 E9 . . 17 C2
Chichele Mans
NW2 . . . . 9 C3
Chichele Rd NW2 . . . 9 C3
Chicheley St SE1 135 A4
Chichester Ct 2
NW1 . . . . 13 B1
Chichester Ho
NW6 . . . . 23 C3
Chichester Rd
Bayswater W2 . . . 100 B4
Kilburn NW6 . . . . . 23 C3
Chichester Rents
WC2 . . . . 107 B2
Chichester St
SW1 . . . . 147 A1
Chichester Way
E14 . . . . 42 C2
Chicksand Ho 14
E1 . . . . 111 B4
Chicksand St E1 . . 111 A3
Chicksand Street
E1 . . . . 111 B3
Chiddingstone
SE13 . . . . 67 B2
Chiddingstone St
SW6 . . . . 165 C3
Chigwell Ct 1 E9 . . 18 A2
Chigwell Hill E1 . . . . 32 A2
Chiham Ho 5
SE15 . . . . 50 B4
Chilcombe Ho 6
SW15 . . . . 68 C4
Chilcot Cl 3 E14 . . . 34 A3
Childebert Rd
SW17 . . . . 73 A2
Childeric Prim Sch
SE14 . . . . 51 A3
Childeric Rd SE14 . 51 A3
Childerley St
SW6 . . . . 164 A4
Childers St SE8 . . . . 51 B4
Child La SE10 . . . . 43 B3
Childrens House
Upper Sch N1 . . . 16 A2
CHILD'S HILL 1 C2
Child's Hill Sch
NW2 . . . . 1 A1
Child's Mews
SW5 . . . . 141 C3
Child's Pl SW5 . . . 141 C3
Child's St SW5 . . . 141 C3
Child's Wlk SW5 . 141 C3
Chilham Ct 13
SW9 . . . . 62 C4
Chilham Ho SE1 . . . 137 C2
Chillingdon Dr
SW11 . . . . 59 C3
Chillingworth Rd
N7 . . . . 14 C3
Chiltern Ct
16 Deptford SE14 . . 50 B3

Chiltern Ct continued
Marylebone NW1 . . . 91 A1
Chiltern Ho
Camberwell SE17 . . 48 C4
4 Kensal Town
W10 . . . . 31 A4
5 Stamford Hill N16 . . 7 B3
Chiltern Rd E3 . . . . 26 C1
Chiltern St W1 . . . 103 B4
Chilton Gr SE8 . . . . 41 A2
Chilton Rd TW9 . . . . 54 C4
Chilton St
E2 . . . . 24 B1 99 A2
Chilver St SE10 . . . . 43 B1
Chilworth 8
SW19 . . . . 69 C3
Chilworth Mews
W2 . . . . 101 B1
Chilworth St W2 . . 101 A1
Chimney Ct 28 E1 . . 32 A1
China Ct 1 E1 . . . . 32 A1
China Hall Mews 16
SE16 . . . . 40 B3
China Mews 17
SW2 . . . . 74 B4
Chindit Ho 11 N16 . . 15 C4
China WC2 . . . . . . 106 A1
Chinnocks Wharf
E14 . . . . 33 A2
Chipka St E14 . . . . 42 B4
Chipley St SE14 . . . 51 A4
Chippendale Ho
SW1 . . . . 146 B1
Chippenham Gdns
NW6 . . . . 23 C2
Chippenham Mews
W9 . . . . 23 C1
Chippenham Rd
W9 . . . . 23 C2
Chip St SW4 . . . . . . 61 C3
Chipstead Ho 4
SW2 . . . . 74 B3
Chipstead St SW6 165 C2
Chisenhale Prim Sch
E3 . . . . 26 A3
Chisenhale Rd E3 . 26 A3
Chisholm Ct 1
W6 . . . . 38 C1
Chisholm Rd 13
TW10 . . . . 54 B1
Chisledon Wlk E9 . 18 B2
Chislehurst Rd
TW10 . . . . 54 A2
Chislet 1 NW5 . . . . 12 C2
Chiswell St
Barbican EC1 . . . . 109 B4
Camberwell SE5 . . . 48 C3
CHISWICK 38 B1
Chiswick & Bedford
Park Prep Sch 4
W4 . . . . 38 A2
Chiswick Common Rd
W4 . . . . 38 A2
Chiswick Green
Studios 1 W4 . . . . 37 B2
Chiswick High Rd
W4 . . . . 38 A2
Chiswick High Road
(North Circular Rd)
W4 . . . . 36 C1
Chiswick La W4 . . . 38 A1
Chiswick La S W4 . 46 B4

Chiswick Mall W4 . . 38 B1
Chiswick Park Sta
W4 . . . . 37 B2
Chiswick Pier W4 . 46 B3
Chiswick Pk W4 . . . 37 C2
Chiswick Plaza
W4 . . . . 45 B4
Chiswick Quay W4 . . 45 B2
Chiswick Rdbt W4 . . 36 C1
Chiswick Sq W4 . . . 46 A4
Chiswick Sta W4 . . 45 B3
Chiswick Staithe
W4 . . . . 45 B2
Chiswick Terr 6
W4 . . . . 37 B2
Chiswick Village
W4 . . . . 45 A4
Chiswick Wharf
W4 . . . . 46 B4
Chitty St W1 . . . . 105 A4
Chivalry Rd SW11 . . 60 A2
Chivelston 27
SW19 . . . . 69 C3
Chobham Gdns
SW19 . . . . 69 C2
Chobham Rd E15 . . 19 C3
Cholmeley Cres N6 . . 4 A4
Cholmeley Lo N6 . . . 4 A3
Cholmeley Pk N6 . . . 4 A4
Cholmley Gdns
NW6 . . . . 10 C3
Cholmondeley Ave
NW10 . . . . 21 C3
Chopin's Ct 16 E1 . . 32 A1
Chopwell Cl E15 . . 19 C1
Choumert Gr SE15 . 49 C1
Choumert Mews
SE15 . . . . 49 C1
Choumert Rd SE15 . 49 B1
Choumert Sq 4
SE15 . . . . 49 C1
Chow Sq 2 E8 . . . . 16 B3
Chrisp Ho SE10 . . . 53 A4
Chrisp St E14 . . . . . 34 A3
Christ Church
TW9 . . . . 54 A4
Christ Church Ave
NW6 . . . . 10 A1
Christ Church
Bentinck CE Prim
Sch NW1 . . . . . . 102 B4
Christ Church
Brondesbury CE Jun
& Inf Sch NW6 . . . 10 B1
Christchurch CE
Prim Sch
Battersea SW11 . . . 60 A4
Cubitt Town SW11 . 43 A1
Christ Church CE
Prim Sch,
Hampstead NW3 . . . 2 C1
Christchurch CE Sch
E1 . . . . 111 A3
Christ Church Ct
1 Brondesbury Pk
NW6 . . . . 10 A1
Harlesden NW10 . . . 21 A4
Christchurch Hill
NW3 . . . . 11 C4
Christchurch Pas
NW3 . . . . 2 B1

Christchurch Rd
Mortlake SW14 . . . . 55 B2
Streatham SW2 . . . . 74 C3
Christ Church Sch
NW1 . . . . 92 B4
Christchurch Sq 2
E9 . . . . 25 B4
Christchurch St
SW3 . . . . 158 C4
Christ Church
Streatham CE Prim
Sch 18 SW2 . . . . . 74 C3
Christchurch Terr
SW3 . . . . 158 C4
Christchurch Way
SE10 . . . . 43 A1
Christian Ct SE16 . . 33 B1
Christian St 1 E1 . . 111 C1
Christie
Maitland Pk NW3 . . 12 A3
2 Upper Holloway
N19 . . . . 5 A2
Christie Ho 2
SE10 . . . . 43 B1
Christie Rd E9 . . . . 18 A2
Christina Sq N4 . . . . 6 A3
Christina St
EC2 . . . . 24 A1 98 A2
Christopher Boone's
Almshouses
SE13 . . . . 67 C3
Christopher Cl
SE16 . . . . 40 C4
Christopher France
Ho 6 E1 . . . . 25 C1
Christopher Hatton
Prim Sch EC1 . . . . 95 B1
Christopher Lo 2
N6 . . . . 4 C4
Christopher Pl
NW1 . . . . 93 C3
Christopher St EC2 97 C1
Christ's Sch TW10 . 54 C2
Christ the King RC
Prim Sch 7 N4 . . . 5 B2
Christ the King Sixth
Form Coll SE13 . . . 67 A4
Chryssell Rd SW9 113 C1
Chubworthy St 5
SE14 . . . . 51 A4
Chudleigh Rd
Hampstead NW6 . . . 9 C1
London SE4 . . . . . . 66 C2
Chudleigh St E1 . . 32 C3
Chumleigh Gdns
SE5 . . . . 49 A4
Chumleigh St SE5 . 49 A4
Church App SE21 . . 75 C1
Church Ave
Camden Town
NW1 . . . . 13 A2
Mortlake SW14 . . . . 55 C4
Church Cl W8 . . . 128 A4
Church Cres E9 . . . 17 C1
Churchcroft Cl
SW12 . . . . 72 C4
Church Ct
Holborn EC4 . . . . . 107 C1
Rotherhithe SE16 . . 41 B4
Churchdale Cl 1

Churchfield Ho
W2 . . . . 89 B1
Churchfields Mews 5
SW6 . . . . 165 A1
Churchfield Rd
W3 . . . . 28 B1
Churchfield Rd W3 . 52 B1
Church Garth 4
N19 . . . . 4 C2
Church Gate SW6 58 A4
Church Gn 4
SW9 . . . . 173 C2
Church Gr SE13 . . . 67 A2
Church Ho EC1 . . . 96 B2
Churchill Cl
Finsbury Pk N4 . . . . 5 C4
Peckham SE15 . . . . 49 C1
Willesden NW2 . . . . 9 A3
Churchill Gardens
Prim Sch SW1 . . . 147 A1
Churchill Gdns
SW1 . . . . 160 C4
Churchill Gdns Rd
SW1 . . . . 160 C4
Churchill Pl E14 . . . 34 A1
Churchill Rd
Gospel Oak NW5 . . 13 A4
Willesden NW2 . . . . 9 B2
Churchill Wlk E9 . . 17 B3
Church Mead SE5 . 48 B3
Churchmead Rd
NW10 . . . . 8 C2
Church Path W4 . . 37 B3
Church Pl SW1 . . . 119 A3
Church Rd
Acton W3 . . . . 37 B4
Barnes SW13 . . . . . 46 C2
2 Canonbury N1 . . 15 B2
Richmond TW10,
TW9 . . . . 54 A2
Willesden NW10 . . . 8 A1
Church Row NW3 . . 11 B4
Church St
Chiswick W4 . . . . . 46 B4
Lisson Gr NW8 . . . 90 A1
Church St Est
NW8 . . . . 89 C1
Church Studios 18
NW1 . . . . 13 C2
Churchward Ho
Camberwell SE17 . . 48 A4
West Kensington
SW5 . . . . 141 A1
Churchway NW1 . . 93 C4
Church Wlk
Barnes SW13 . . . . . 46 C2
Canonbury N16 . . . . 15 C4
Child's Hill NW2 . . . 1 C1
Churchyard Row
SE11 . . . . 150 B4
Churnfield 2 N4 . . . . 5 C2
Churston Cl 18
SW2 . . . . 74 C3
Churston Mans
WC1 . . . . 95 A1
Churton Pl
Brentford W4 . . . . . 45 A4
Pimlico SW1 . . . . . 147 A3
Churton St SW1 . . 147 A3
Chute Ho W9 173 B1
Chuter Ede Ho
SW6 . . . . 155 A2
Cicada Rd SW18 . . 59 B2

Cicely Ho NW8 .... **79** C1
Cicely Rd SE15 .... **49** C2
Cinema Mus The
SE11 .... **150** A3
Cinnabar Wharf
Central ⑬ E1 .. **125** C2
Cinnabar Wharf East
⑮ E1 .... **125** C2
Cinnabar Wharf West
⑰ E1 .... **125** C2
Cinnamon Cl ⑤
SE15 .... **49** B3
Cinnamon Row ⑧
SW11 .... **59** B4
Cinnamon St E1 .. **32** A1
Cinnamon Wharf
SE1 .... **139** A4
Circle Ho ⑭ E14 .. **34** C3
Circle The SE1 .... **139** A4
Circus Ho NW1 ... **102** C4
Circus Lo NW8 .... **89** B4
Circus Mews W1 .. **102** C4
Circus Pl EC2 .... **109** C3
Circus Rd NW8 .... **79** B1
Circus St SE10 .... **52** B3
Cirencester St
W2 .... **100** A4
Cissbury Ho ⑥
SE26 .... **76** C1
Citadel Pl SE11 .. **148** C2
Citizen Ho N7 .... **14** C4
Citizen Rd N7 .... **14** C4
Citron Terr ④
SE15 .... **65** A4
Citrus Ho ⑭ SE8 .. **41** B1
City Banking Coll
SE1 .... **137** C2
City Bsns Coll EC1 .. **96** B3
City Bsns Coll ㉝
SE16 .... **40** B4
City Central Est
EC1 .... **96** C3
City Coll N1 ...... **97** B4
City Coll of London
The WC1 .... **107** A3
City Forum EC1 ... **96** C4
City Garden Row
N1 .... **86** B1
City Gate E1 ...... **25** B1
City & Guilds of
London Art Sch The
SE11 .... **149** C1
City & Hackney Ctr for
Mental Health
(Hospl) E9 .... **18** A3
City Hall SE1 .... **124** B1
City Harbour E14 ... **42** A3
City & Islington 6th
Form Coll EC1 ... **96** A4
City & Islington Coll
(Ctr for Applied
Sciences) EC1 .... **96** A4
City & Islington Coll
(Ctr for Bsns, Arts &
Technology) ⑧
N7 .... **14** A4
City & Islington Coll
(Ctr for Health,
Social & Child Care)
⑦ N7 .... **14** B4
City & Islington Coll
(Ctr for Lifelong
Learning) ⑨ N4 ... **6** A2
City Law Sch The
EC1 .... **107** A3

City Lights The
SE11 .... **149** C1
CITY OF
LONDON **122** B4
City of London Acad-
Islington N1 ..... **86** C3
City of London Acad
The SE1 .... **153** C2
City of London
Information Ctr
EC4 .... **108** B1
City of London Sch
EC4 .... **122** C4
City of London Sch for
Girls EC2 .... **109** A4
City of London
Coll W2 .... **101** B4
City of Westminster
Coll, Cosway Street
Ctr NW1 .... **102** B3
City of Westminster
Coll, Maida Vale Ctr
① W9 .... **88** A3
City of Westminster
Coll, Queens Park
Ctr ⑩ W9 .... **23** C2
City Rd EC1 .... **97** A4
City Thameslink Sta
EC4 .... **108** A1
City University EC1 .. **96** A3
City Wlk SE1 ..... **138** C3
Civil Service Coll
SW1 .... **146** C3
Clabon Mews
SW1 .... **144** C4
Clack St SE16 .... **40** B4
Claire Ct NW2 .... **10** A2
Claire Pl E14 ..... **41** C3
Clancarty Rd SW6 .. **165** C1
Clandon St SE8 ... **51** C1
Clanfield Ho ⑫
SW15 .... **68** C3
Clanricarde Gdns
W2 .... **31** C2 **113** C3
CLAPHAM **61** A4
Clapham Common
SW4 .... **61** A3
Clapham Common
North Side SW4 .. **60** C3
Clapham Common
South Side SW4 .. **61** B2
Clapham Common Sta
SW4 .... **61** B3
Clapham Common
West Side
Clapham SW4,
SW11 .... **60** B3
Clapham SW11 .... **60** C2
Clapham Computer &
Secretarial Coll ①
SW11 .... **60** B2
Clapham Court Terr
② SW4 .... **62** A2
Clapham Cres
SW4 .... **61** C3
Clapham Ct ⑧
SW4 .... **62** A2
Clapham High St
SW4 .... **61** C3
Clapham High Street
Sta SW4 .... **61** C4
Clapham Junction Est
SW11 .... **60** A4
Clapham Junction Sta
SW11 .... **60** A3

Clapham L Ctr
SW4 .... **61** C4
Clapham Manor St ①
SW4 .... **61** B4
Clapham Manor Prim
Sch ⑧ SW4 ...... **61** B4
Clapham Manor St
SW4 .... **61** B4
Clapham Mans
SW4 .... **61** A1
Clapham North Bsns
Ctr ⑩ SW4 ...... **61** C3
Clapham North Sta
SW4 .... **62** A4
CLAPHAM PARK ... **61** C2
Clapham Park Rd
SW4 .... **61** C3
Clapham Park Terr ④
SW2 .... **62** A2
Clapham Rd SW9 .. **163** A2
Clapham South Sta
SW4 .... **61** A1
Clapton Comm E5 .. **7** C4
Clapton Girls Tec Coll
E5 .... **17** B3
Clapton Pas E5 ... **17** B3
Clapton Sq E5 .... **17** B3
Clapton Terr E5 ... **7** C3
Clapton Way E5 ... **16** C4
Clara Grant Ho ⑩
E14 .... **42** B3
Clara Grant Prim Sch
The ⑯ E3 .... **26** C1
Clare Ct WC1 ..... **94** B3
Claredale Ho ⑧
E2 .... **25** A3
Claredale St E2 ... **24** C3
Clare Ho
Bermondsey SE1 .. **153** A2
⑥ Old Ford E3 ... **26** B4
Clare La N1 ...... **15** B1
Clare Lawn Ave
SW14 .... **55** C2
Clare Mews SW6 .. **156** A1
Clare Mkt WC2 ... **107** A1
Claremont ①
SW15 .... **58** A2
Claremont Cl
Finsbury N1 ...... **85** C1
④ Streatham SW2 .. **74** B3
Claremont Ct ①
W9 .... **23** B2
Claremont Gr ⑭ W4 .. **46** A3
Claremont Rd
Highgate N6 ...... **4** A4
West Kilburn W9 .. **23** B2
Claremont Sq N1 .. **85** B1
Claremont St SE10 .. **52** A4
Clarence Ave SW4 .. **61** C1
Clarence Cres
SW4 .... **61** C1
Clarence Ct ⑩
W6 .... **39** A2
Clarence Gate
NW1 .... **91** A2
Clarence Gate Gdns
NW1 .... **91** A1
Clarence Gdns
NW1 .... **92** B3
Clarence Ho SE17 .. **48** B4
Clarence Ho NW1 .. **119** A1
Clarence La SW15 .. **56** B1
Clarence Mews
Balham SW12 .... **73** A4

Clarence Mews
continued
Hackney E5 ...... **17** A3
① Rotherhithe
SE16 .... **32** C1
Clarence Pl ㉕ E5 .. **17** A3
Clarence Rd
Brentford W4 .... **36** C1
Brondesbury NW6 .. **10** B1
Greenwich SE8 ... **52** A4
Lower Clapton E5 .. **17** A4
Richmond TW9 ... **44** C2
Clarence St ⑤
TW9 .... **54** A3
Clarence Terr
NW1 .... **91** A2
Clarence Way
NW1 .... **13** A1
Clarence Wlk ⑨
SW4 .... **172** A2
Clarendon Cl
Bayswater W2 .... **116** A4
㊲ Hackney E9 .... **17** B1
Clarendon Cross
W11 .... **31** A2 **112** B3
Clarendon Ct
Paddington W9 ... **89** A2
⑧ Richmond TW9 .. **44** C2
Willesden NW2 ... **9** B1
Clarendon Dr
SW15 .... **57** B3
Clarendon Flats
W1 .... **103** C1
Clarendon Gdns
W9 .... **89** A1
Clarendon Gr NW1 .. **93** B4
Clarendon Ho
NW1 .... **83** A1
Clarendon Mews
W2 .... **116** A4
Clarendon Pl W2 .. **116** A4
Clarendon Rd
W11 .... **31** A2 **112** B4
Clarendon Rise
SE13 .... **67** B3
Clarendon St
SW1 .... **146** B2
Clarendon Terr
W9 .... **89** A2
Clarendon Wlk ⑪
W11 .... **31** A3
Clare Pl SW15 .... **68** B4
Clare Rd
New Cross Gate
SE14 .... **51** B2
Willesden NW10 .. **8** C1
Clare St E2 ...... **25** A3
Clareville Ct ⑦ SW7 .. **143** A3
Clareville Gr SW7 .. **143** A3
Clareville Grove Mews
SW7 .... **143** A3
Clareville St SW7 .. **143** A3
Clarewood Ct W1 .. **102** C3
Clarewood Wlk
SW9 .... **62** C3
Clarges Ho W1 ... **118** B2
Clarges Mews
W1 .... **118** A2
Clarges St W1 .... **118** B2
Clariat St SW3 ... **57** C4
Claribel Rd SW9 .. **48** A1
Claridge Ct SW6 .. **164** C3
Clarissa Ho ⑦ E14 .. **34** A3
Clarissa St E8 ... **24** B4
Clarke Ho ② SW4 .. **61** B4
Clarke Path N16 ... **7** C3

Clarkes Mews W1 .. **103** C4
Clark Ho SW10 ... **156** C2
Clark Lawrence Ct ⑩
SW11 .... **59** C4
Clarkson Rd E16 ... **35** B3
Clarkson Row
NW1 .... **82** C1
Clark's Pl EC2 .... **110** A2
Clark St E1 ...... **32** A4
Classic Mans ㉝
E9 .... **17** B1
Classinghall Ho ⑭
SW15 .... **57** C1
Claude Rd SE15 .. **50** A1
Claude St E14 .... **41** C2
Claudia Jones Way
SW2 .... **62** A1
Claudia Pl SW19 .. **70** A3
Clavell St ⑧ SE10 .. **52** B4
Claverdale Rd
SW2 .... **74** C4
Clavering Ave
SW13 .... **47** A4
Clavering Ho SE13 .. **67** C3
Claverton St SW1 .. **147** A1
Clave St E1 ...... **32** B1
Claxton Gr
W6 .... **39** C1 **140** A1
Claybank Gr SE13 .. **67** A4
Claybrook Rd W6 .. **154** A3
Claydon SE17 .... **150** C4
Clayhall Ct ⑳ E3 .. **26** B3
Claylands Pl SW8 .. **163** B2
Claylands Rd
SW8 .... **163** A3
Claypole Rd E15 .. **27** B3
Claponds Ave
TW9 .... **36** A2
Claponds Hospl
W5 .... **36** A2
Claponds La TW8 .. **36** A1
Clays Ct N16 ...... **7** B3
Clay St W1 ...... **103** A3
Clayton Cres N1 .. **84** C3
Clayton Ct N16 ... **7** C4
Clayton Ho ㉒ E9 .. **17** B1
Clayton Mews
SE10 .... **52** C2
Clayton Rd SE15 .. **49** C2
Clayton St SE11 .. **163** B4
Clearbrook Way ⑬
E1 .... **32** B3
Clear Water Ho ⑨
TW10 .... **54** A2
Clearwater Terr ④
W11 .... **39** C4
Clearwell Dr W9 .. **88** B1
Cleaver Ho ⑥
NW3 .... **12** B1
Cleaver Sq SE11 .. **149** C1
Cleaver St SE11 .. **149** C1
Cleeve Ho ⑮
E2 .... **24** A2 **98** B3
Cleeve Way SW15 .. **68** B4
Cleeve Workshops ⑭
E2 .... **24** A2 **98** B3
Clegg St ⑱ E1 .... **32** A1
Cleland Ho ⑰ E2 .. **25** B3
Clematis St W12 .. **29** C2
Clem Atlee Par
SW6 .... **155** A3
Clem Attlee Ct
SW6 .... **155** A3
Clemence St E14 .. **33** B4

Clement Attlee Ho
NW10 . . . . 8 B1
Clement Ave SW4 . . 61 C3
Clement Cl
Acton W4 . . . . 37 C2
Hampstead NW6 . . . . . 9 B1
Clement Danes Ho 2
W12 . . . . 30 A3
Clement Ho
14 Deptford SE8 . . . . 41 A2
17 North Kensington
W10 . . . . 22 B1
Clements Ave 1
E16 . . . . 35 C2
Clements Inn
WC2 . . . . 107 A1
Clements Inn Pas
WC2 . . . . 107 A1
Clement's La EC2,
EC4 . . . . 123 C4
Clement's Rd SE16 . . 40 A3
Clemson Ho 9 E8 . . 24 B4
Clennam St SE1 . . . 137 A4
Clenston Mews
W1 . . . . 102 C2
Clent Ho 4 N16 . . . . 7 B3
Cleopatra's Needle
WC2 . . . . 120 C3
Clephane Rd 13
N1 . . . . 15 B2
Clephane Rd N N1 . . 15 B2
Clephane Rd S N1 . . 15 C2
Clere Pl EC2 . . . . . . 97 C2
Clere St EC2 . . . . . . 97 C2
CLERKENWELL 96 A1
Clerkenwell Gn
EC1 . . . . 96 A1
Clerkenwell Parochial
CE Prim Sch EC1 . 95 C1
Clerkenwell Rd
EC1 . . . . 96 A1
Clermont Rd E9 . . . 25 B4
Clevedon Ct
Battersea SW11 . . . 168 A4
Dulwich SE21 . . . . . . 75 C1
Clevedon Mans
NW5 . . . . 12 C4
Cleve Ho NW6 . . . . . 11 A1
Cleveland Ave W4 . . 38 B2
Cleveland Ct W1 . . . 93 A1
Cleveland Gdns
Barnes SW13 . . . . . . 46 B1
Paddington W2 . . . 100 C1
Cleveland Gr 38
E1 . . . . 25 B1
Cleveland Mans
8 Brixton SW9 . . . 163 B1
4 Brondesbury
NW6 . . . . 10 B1
Paddington W9 . . . . 23 C1
Cleveland Mews
W1 . . . . 104 C4
Cleveland Pl SW1 . 119 A2
Cleveland Rd
Barnes SW13 . . . . . . 46 B1
Islington N1 . . . . 15 C1
14 South Acton W4 . 37 B3
Cleveland Row
SW1 . . . . 119 A1
Cleveland Sq W2 . 100 C1
Cleveland St W1 . . . 92 C1
Cleveland Terr
W2 . . . . 101 A2
Cleveland Way E1 . . 25 B1
Clevedon Cl N16 . . . 7 B1

Cleve Rd NW6 . . . . . 11 A1
Cleverly Cotts
W12 . . . . 29 B1
Cleverly Est W12 . . 29 C2
Cley Ho SE4 . . . . . . 65 C3
Clifden Mews E5 . . . 17 C3
Clifden Rd E5 . . . . . 17 C3
Cliff Ct 14 NW1 . . . . 13 C2
Cliffe Ho 8 SE10 . . 43 B1
Clifford Ave
Mortlake SW14 . . . . 45 B1
Mortlake SW14,
TW9 . . . . 55 A4
Clifford Ct
Bayswater W2 . . . . 100 A3
Wandsworth SW18 . . 71 C4
Willesden NW10 . . . . 8 A4
Clifford Dr SW9 . . . 63 A3
Clifford Gdns
NW10 . . . . 22 B3
Clifford Haigh Ho
SW6 . . . . 47 C3
Clifford Ho W14 . . . 140 C3
Clifford's Inn Pas
EC4 . . . . 107 B1
Clifford St W1 . . . . 118 C3
Clifford Way NW10 . . 8 B4
Cliff Rd NW1 . . . . . . 13 C2
Cliff Road Studios 13
NW1 . . . . 13 C2
Cliffsend Ho 23
SW9 . . . . 173 C3
Cliff Terr SE8 . . . . . 51 C1
Cliffview Rd SE13 . . 66 C4
Cliff Villas NW1 . . . . 13 C2
Cliff Wlk E16 . . . . . . 35 B4
Clifton Ave W12 . . . 29 B1
Clifton Cres SE15 . . 50 A3
Clifton Ct
Finsbury Pk N4 . . . . . 5 C4
Paddington NW8 . . . 89 B2
Peckham SE15 . . . . . 50 A3
Putney SW15 . . . . . . 57 C2
Clifton Gate
SW10 . . . . 156 C4
Clifton Gdns
Chiswick W4 . . . . . . 37 C2
Paddington W9 . . . . 88 C1
Clifton Hill NW8 . . . 78 C3
Clifton Ho
E2 . . . . 24 B1 98 C2
Clifton Mans 4
SW9 . . . . 62 C3
Clifton Pl
Paddington W2 . . . 101 C1
Rotherhithe SE16 . . 40 B4
Clifton Rd
Harlesden NW10 . . . 21 C3
Newham E16 . . . . . . 35 A4
Paddington W9 . . . . 89 A2
Shacklewell E16 . . . 16 A4
Clifton St
EC2 . . . . 24 A1 98 A1
Clifton Terr N4 . . . . . 5 C2
Clifton Villas W9 . . 100 C4
Clifton Way SE15 . . 50 B3
Climsland Ho SE1 . 121 C2
Clinch Ct 11 E16 . . 35 C4
Cline Ho SW15 . . . . 57 A3
Clink Prison Mus The
SE1 . . . . 123 B2
Clink St SE1 . . . . . . 123 B2
Clinton Rd E3 . . . . . 26 A2

Clipper Appts 12
SE10 . . . . 52 B4
Clipper Cl 3 SE16 . . 40 C4
Clipper Ho E14 . . . . 42 B1
Clipper Way SE13 . . 67 B3
Clipstone Ho 10
SW5 . . . . 56 C2
Clipstone Mews
W1 . . . . 104 C4
Clipstone St W1 . . 104 C4
Clissold Cres N16 . . 15 C4
Clissold Ct N4 . . . . . 6 B2
Clissold Ho 4 N16 . . 6 C2
Clissold Rd N16 . . . 6 C1
Clitheroe Rd SW9 . 172 B1
Clive Ct W9 . . . . 89 A2
Cliveden Ho SW1 . . 145 B4
Cliveden Pl SW1 . . 145 B4
Clive Ho
18 Clapham SW8 . . 171 B2
Greenwich SE10 . . . . 52 B4
Clive Rd SE21,
SE27 . . . . 75 C1
Cloak La EC4 . . . . . 123 B4
Clochar Ct NW10 . . 21 B4
Clock Ho N16 . . . . . . 7 B4
Clockhouse Cl
SW19 . . . . 69 B2
Clockhouse Pl
SW15 . . . . 58 A1
Clockhouse The
SW19 . . . . 69 A1
Clockmakers' Mus
EC2 . . . . 109 A2
Clock Tower Mews
N1 . . . . 87 A3
Clock Tower Pl 1
N7 . . . . 14 A2
Clock View Cres 2
N7 . . . . 14 A2
Cloister Rd
Acton W3 . . . . 28 B4
Child's Hill NW2 . . . . 1 B2
Cloisters Ct N6 . . . . 4 A3
Cloisters The 22
SW9 . . . . 173 C3
Clonbrock Rd N16 . 16 A4
Cloncurry St SW14 . 55 A2
Clone Ct 4 W12 . . . 38 A3
Clonmel Rd SW6 . . 165 A4
Clonmore St SW18 . 70 B3
Clorane Gdns NW3 . 1 C1
Close The
Lewisham SE3 . . . . . 52 C1
Mortlake SW14 . . . . 55 C4
Cloth Ct EC1 . . . . . . 108 B3
Cloth Fair EC1 . . . . 108 B3
Clothier St EC3 . . . 110 B2
Cloth St EC1 . . . . . 108 C4
Cloudesdale Rd
SW17 . . . . 73 A2
Cloudesley Mans
N1 . . . . 85 C3
Cloudesley Pl N1 . . 85 C3
Cloudesley Rd N1 . . 85 C3
Cloudesley Sq N1 . . 85 C3
Cloudesley St N1 . . 85 C3
Clove Cres E14 . . . . 34 C2
Clovelly Ct NW2 . . . 9 B3
Clovelly Ho W2 . . . 100 C2
Clovelly Rd W4 . . . . 37 C4
Clovelly Way E1 . . . 32 B3
Clover Mews SW3 . 159 A4
Clowes Ho 3 SW4 . 62 A3
Cloysters Gn E1 . . . 125 B2
Club Row E2 . . 24 B1 98 C2

Clunbury St N1 . . . . 87 C1
Clunie Ho SW1 . . . 131 A2
Cluny Mews SW5 . . 141 B3
Cluny Pl SE1 . . . . . 138 A2
Cluse Ct N1 . . . . . . 86 C2
Clutton St E14 . . . . 34 A4
Clyde Ct NW1 . . . . . 83 C2
Clyde Flats SW6 . . 154 C2
Clydesdale Gdns
TW10 . . . . 55 A3
Clydesdale Ho 4
W11 . . . . 31 B3
Clydesdale Rd
W11 . . . . 31 B3
Clyde St SE8 . . . . . 51 B4
Clynes Ho 3 E2 . . . 25 C2
Clyro Ct N4 . . . . 5 B3
Clyston St SW8 . . . 171 A3
Coach & Horses Yd
W1 . . . . 118 C4
Coach House La
Highbury N5 . . . . . . 15 A4
Wimbledon SW19 . . . 69 C1
Coach House Mews
SE23 . . . . 65 C1
Coach House Yd 5
NW3 . . . . 11 C4
Coachmaker Mews 4
SW9 . . . . 62 A4
Coalbrook Mans 3
SW12 . . . . 73 A3
Coaldale Wlk SE21 . 75 B4
Coalecroft Rd
SW15 . . . . 57 B2
Coalport Ho SE11 . 149 B4
Coatbridge Ho 8
N1 . . . . 14 B1
Coates Ave SW18 . . 60 A1
Coates Ct SW3 . . . 12 A3
Coate St E2 . . . . . . 24 C3
Coates Wlk TW8 . . 36 A1
Cobbett St SW8 . . 163 A1
Cobbett St SW8 . . . 1 C1
Cobble La N1 . . . . . 15 A1
Cobble Mews N4,
N5 . . . . 6 B1
Cobbold Ct SW1 . . 147 B4
Cobbold Ind Est
NW10 . . . . 8 B3
Cobbold Mews
W12 . . . . 38 B4
Cobbold Rd
Bedford Pk W12 . . . . 38 B4
Willesden NW10 . . . . 8 B2
Cobb's Hall 1
SW6 . . . . 47 C4
Cobb St E1 . . . . 110 C3
Cobden Bldgs WC1 . 94 C4
Cobden Ho
11 Bethnal Green
E2 . . . . 24 C2 99 C4
Regent's Pk NW1 . . 82 C2
Cobham Cl SW11 . . 60 A1
Cobham Mews 3
NW1 . . . . 13 C1
Coborn Mews 9
E3 . . . . 26 B2
Coborn Rd E3 . . . . . 26 B2
Coborn St E3 . . . . . 26 B2
Cobourg Prim Sch
SE5 . . . . 49 B4
Cobourg Rd SE5 . . 49 B4
Cobourg St NW1 . . 93 A3
Coburg Cl SW1 . . . 147 A4
Coburg Cres SW2 . 74 C3
Coburg Dwellings 11
E1 . . . . 32 B2

Cochrane Cl NW8 . . 79 C1
Cochrane Ho 15
E14 . . . . 41 C4
Cochrane Mews
NW8 . . . . 79 C1
Cochrane St NW8 . . 79 C1
Coci Ho W14 . . . . . 141 A3
Cockburn Ho
SW1 . . . . 147 C1
Cock Hill E1 . . . . . . 110 B3
Cock La EC1 . . . . . 108 A3
Cockpit Yd WC1 . . . 107 A4
Cockspur Ct SW1 . 119 C2
Cockspur St SW1 . 119 C2
Coda Ctr The
SW6 . . . . 164 B4
Code St E1 . . 24 B1 99 A1
Codicote Ho 2
SE8 . . . . 40 C2
Codicote Terr N4 . . 6 B2
Codrington Ct 3
SE16 . . . . 33 A1
Codrington Ho 7
E1 . . . . 25 A1
Codrington Mews
W11 . . . . 31 A3
Cody Rd E16 . . . . . . 27 C1
Coffey St SE8 . . . . . 51 C3
Coin St SE1 . . . . . . 121 B2
Coity Rd NW5 . . . . . 12 C2
Cokers La SE21 . . . 75 C3
Coke St E1 . . . . 111 C2
Colas Mews 7
NW6 . . . . 23 C4
Colbeck Mews
SW5 . . . . 142 B3
Colberg Pl N16 . . . . 7 B4
Colbert 1 SE5 . . . . 49 B2
Colborne Ho 9
E14 . . . . 33 C2
Colchester Ho 17
SW8 . . . . 171 B2
Colchester St E1 . . 111 A2
Coldbath Sq EC1 . . 95 B2
Coldbath St SE13 . . 52 A1
Cold Blow La SE14 . 50 C4
Coldharbour E14 . . 34 B1
Coldharbour Ind Est
SE5 . . . . 48 B1
Coldharbour La
SW9 . . . . 63 A4
Coldharbour Pl
SE5 . . . . 48 B1
Coldstream Gdns
SW18 . . . . 58 B1
Colebeck Mews
N1 . . . . 15 A2
Colebert Ave E1 . . . 25 B1
Colebert Ho 21 E1 . 25 B1
Colebrook Cl
SW19 . . . . 69 C4
Colebrook Ct
SW3 . . . . 144 B3
Colebrooke Pl N1 . . 86 B3
Colebrooke Row
Islington N1 . . . . . . 84 B4
Islington N1 . . . . . . 86 A2
Islington N1 . . . . . . 86 B3
Colebrook Ho 1
E14 . . . . 34 A3
Coleby Path 21
SE5 . . . . 48 C3

Colechurch Ho **9**
SE1 . . . . **153** B1
Colefax Bldg **12**
E1 . . . . **111** C2
Coleford Rd SW18 . .**59** B2
Colegrave Rd E15 . .**19** C3
Colegrave Sch
E15 . . . .**19** C3
Colegrove Rd
SE15 . . . .**49** B4
Coleherne Ct
SW10 . . . .**142** A1
Coleherne Mans
SW5 . . . .**142** B2
Coleherne Mews
SW10 . . . .**142** A1
Coleherne Rd
SW10 . . . .**142** A1
Colehill Gdns
SW6 . . . .**164** A3
Colehill La SW6 . . .**164** B3
Cole Ho SE1 . . . . . .**135** C3
Coleman Ct SW18 . .**70** C4
Coleman Fields
N1 . . . .**87** A4
Coleman Mans N19 . .**5** A4
Coleman Rd SE5 . . .**49** A3
Coleman St EC2 . . .**109** B2
Coleman Street Bldgs
EC2 . . . .**109** B2
Colenso Rd E5 . . . . .**17** B4
Coleraine Rd SE3 . .**53** B4
Coleridge Cl SW8 .**170** B1
Coleridge Ct W14 . .**39** C3
Coleridge Gdns
NW6 . . . .**11** B1
Coleridge Ho
Pimlico SW1 . . . . . .**147** A1
Walworth SE17 . . . .**151** A2
Coleridge Prim Sch
N8 . . . .**4** C4
Coleridge Rd
N7 . . . .**5** C2
Coleridge Sq
SW10 . . . .**156** C2
Coles Ct SW11 . . . .**167** C3
Coleshill Flats
SW1 . . . .**145** C3
Cole St SE1 . . . . . .**137** A3
Colestown St **4**
SW11 . . . .**168** B2
Colet Gdns W14 . . .**39** C2
Colet Ho SE17 . . . .**150** B1
Colette Ct **5** SE16 .**40** C4
Coley St WC1 . . . . . .**95** A1
Colfe & Hatchcliffe's
Glebe SE4 . . . .**67** A2
Colgate Ho E3 . . . . .**52** A1
Colin Blanchard Ho
SE4 . . . .**51** C1
Colin Ct SW16 . . . . .**73** C2
Colinette Rd SW15 .**57** B3
Colin Rd NW10 . . . . .**8** C2
Colinsdale N1 . . . . .**86** A3
Colin Winter Ho **43**
E1 . . . .**25** B1
Coliston Pas SW18 .**70** C4
Coliston Rd SW18 . .**70** C4
Collamore Ave
SW18 . . . .**72** A3
Collard Pl NW1 . . . .**13** A1
Collcutt Lo SW4 . . .**62** A3
College App SE10 . .**52** B4
College Cl E5 . . . . . .**17** B3

College Cres NW3 . .**11** C2
College Cross N1 . . .**14** C1
College Ct
Chelsea SW3 . . . . .**145** A1
5 Hammersmith
W6 . . . .**39** B1
Hampstead NW3 . . .**11** C2
College Gdns
Dulwich SE21 . . . . . .**76** A3
Upper Tooting
SW17 . . . .**72** A2
College Gr **11** NW1 .**83** B4
College Green Ct
SW9 . . . .**63** A4
College Hill EC4 . . .**123** A4
College La NW5 . . . .**13** A4
College Mews **6**
SW18 . . . .**59** A2
COLLEGE PARK . .**22** A2
College Park Cl
SE13 . . . .**67** C3
College Park Sch **20**
W2 . . . .**100** A1
College Pl
Camden Town
NW1 . . . .**83** A3
Chelsea SW10 . . . .**156** C2
College Rd
Dulwich SE19,
SE21 . . . .**76** A2
Kensal Green
NW10 . . . .**22** B3
College St **4** EC4 .**123** A4
College Terr E3 . . . .**26** B2
Collent Ho **9** E9 . . .**17** B2
Collent St E9 . . . . . .**17** B2
Collerston Ho
SE10 . . . .**43** B1
Collette Ho **1** N16 . .**7** B3
Collett Rd SE16 . . .**139** C2
Colley Ho **7** N7 . . . .**13** C3
Collier St N1 . . . .**84** C1
Collingbourne Rd
W12 . . . .**30** A1
Collingham Gdns
SW5 . . . .**142** B3
Collingham Pl
SW5 . . . .**142** B4
Collingham Rd
SW5 . . . .**142** B3
Collingham Tutors
Coll SW5 . . . .**142** B3
Collington St SE10 .**42** C1
Collingwood Ho
27 Bethnal Green
E1 . . . .**25** A1
Marylebone W1 . . .**104** C4
Collingwood St **1**
E1 . . . .**25** A1
Collins Ct E8 . . . . . .**16** C2
Collins Ho
5 Cubitt Town
E14 . . . .**42** B3
4 Poplar E14 . . . . .**34** B2
Collinson Ct **5**
SE1 . . . .**136** C3
Collinson Ho **14**
SE15 . . . .**49** C3
Collinson St SE1 . .**136** C3
Collinson Wlk
SE1 . . . .**136** C3
Collins Rd N5, N16 .**15** B4
Collins Sq SE3 . . . . .**53** B1
Collins St SE3 . . . . .**53** A1
Collins Yd N1 . . . . . .**86** A3
Collison Pl N16 . . . . .**7** A3
Coll of Arms EC4 . .**122** C4

Coll of Central
London The
EC2 . . . .**24** A1 **98** A2
Coll of Law The
(Bloomsbury)
EC1 . . . .**105** B4
Coll of Law The
(Moorgate) EC1 . . .**97** B1
Coll of NW London **15**
NW6 . . . .**23** C4
Coll of NW London
(Willesden Centre)
NW10 . . . .**8** B3
Coll of Optometrists
The SW1 . . . .**120** A2
Coll Sharp **41**
E2 . . . .**24** B2 **98** C3
Coll's Rd SE15 . . . . .**50** B2
Collyer Pl SE15 . . . .**49** C2
Colmans Wharf **7**
E14 . . . .**34** A4
Colmar Cl **3** E1 . . .**25** C1
Colmore Mews
SE15 . . . .**50** A2
Colnbrook St SE1 .**136** A2
Colne Ho NW8 . . . . .**89** C1
Colne Rd E5 . . . .**18** A4
Cologne Rd SW11 . .**59** C3
Colombo St SE1 . . .**122** A1
Colomb St SE10 . . . .**43** A1
Colonades The **4**
SE5 . . . .**48** B3
Colonial Dr W4 . . . .**37** B2
Colonnade WC1 . . . .**94** B1
Colonnade Ho SE3 . .**53** B1
Colonnades The **6**
E8 . . . .**17** A2
Colonnade The **12**
SE8 . . . .**51** B4
Colorado Bldg **9**
SE13 . . . .**52** A2
Colosseum Terr
NW1 . . . .**92** B2
Colour Ho SE1 . . . .**138** C3
Colstead Ho **22** E1 .**32** A3
Colston Rd SW14 . . .**55** B3
Colthurst Cres N4 . . .**6** B2
Coltman Ho SE10 . . .**52** B4
Coltman St E14 . . . . .**33** A4
Columba Ho SE14 . .**51** B2
Columbas Dr NW3 . . .**2** C3
Columbia Ho **18**
E3 . . . .**26** C2
Columbia Point **7**
SE16 . . . .**40** B3
Columbia Prim Sch **5**
E2 . . . .**24** B2 **99** A4
Columbia Rd
1 Hackney E2 . . . . .**24** C3
Shoreditch
E2 . . . .**24** B2 **98** C4
Columbia Road
Flower Mkt
E2 . . . .**24** B2 **99** A4
Colverson Ho **6**
E1 . . . .**32** B4
Colvestone Cres
E8 . . . .**16** B3
Colvestone Prim Sch
E8 . . . .**16** B3
Colville Gdns W11 . .**31** B3
Colville Ho
32 Bethnal Green
E2 . . . .**25** B3
Notting Hill W11 . . . .**31** B3

Colville Mews
W11 . . . .**31** B3
Colville Pl W1 . . . .**105** A3
Colville Prim Sch **6**
W11 . . . .**31** B3
Colville Rd
Notting Hill W11 . . . .**31** B3
South Acton W3 . . . .**37** A3
Colville Sq W11 . . . .**31** B3
Colville Terr W11 . . .**31** B3
Colwall Ho **18**
SW9 . . . .**173** A1
Colwell Rd SE22 . . . .**64** B2
Colwick Cl N6 . . . . . .**4** C4
Colwith Rd W6 . . . . .**47** B4
Colworth Gr SE17 . .**151** A3
Colwyn Ho SE1 . . . .**135** B1
Colyton Rd SE22 . . . .**65** A2
Combe Ave SE3 . . . .**53** B3
Combe Ho
3 Paddington W2 . .**31** C4
SW18 . . . .**70** A3
Mortlake SW14 . . . .**45** B1
Combedale Rd
SE10 . . . .**43** C1
Combemartin Rd
SW18 . . . .**70** A3
Combe Mews **4**
SE3 . . . .**53** B3
Comber Gr SE5 . . . .**48** B3
Comber Grove Prim
Sch **34** SE5 . . . .**48** B3
Comber Ho SE5 . . . .**48** B3
Combermere Rd
SW9 . . . .**62** B4
Combe The **1** NW1 .**92** B3
Com Coll Hackney
The **21** E8 . . . .**25** A4
Comeragh Mews
W14 . . . .**140** B1
Comeragh Rd
W14 . . . .**140** B1
Comerford Rd SE4 . .**66** B3
Comet Pl SE8 . . . . . .**51** C3
Comet St SE8 . . . . . .**51** C3
Comfort St **5**
SE15 . . . .**49** A4
Comins Ho SW4 . . . .**61** B2
Commercial Rd
Stepney E1 . . . .**32** B3
Whitechapel E1 . . .**111** C2
Commercial St
E1 . . . .**110** C4
Commercial Way
Peckham SE15 . . . .**49** C3
Wembley NW10 . . . .**20** A3
Commerell Pl
SE10 . . . .**43** B1
Commerell St
SE10 . . . .**43** A1
Commodity Quay
E1 . . . .**125** A3
Commodore Ct
SE8 . . . .**51** C2
Commodore Ho **7**
E14 . . . .**34** B2
Commodore St E1 . .**26** A1
Commondale
SW15 . . . .**57** B4
Common Rd SW13 . .**56** C4
Common View
SW15 . . . .**57** B4
Commonwealth Ave
42 W12 . . . .**30** A2
Commonwealth Ho
WC1 . . . .**106** B2
Community La N7 . . .**13** C3

Community Rd
E15 . . . .**19** C3
Comodore Ho
SW18 . . . .**59** B3
Companla Bldg **12**
E1 . . . .**32** C2
Compass Ct SE1 . . .**124** C1
Compass Ho
Bayswater W2 . . . .**100** A1
London SE8 . . . .**52** A2
Compass Point **10**
E14 . . . .**33** C2
Compayne Gdns
NW6 . . . .**11** A1
Compton Ave
Islington N1 . . . .**15** A2
London N6 . . . .**3** A4
Compton Cl
Camberwell SE15 . . .**49** B3
Regent's Pk NW1 . . .**92** B3
Compton Cres W4 . .**45** B4
Compton Ho
SW11 . . . .**168** A4
Compton Pas EC1 . .**96** B2
Compton Pl WC1 . . .**94** A2
Compton Rd
Islington N1 . . . .**15** A2
Kensal Green
NW10 . . . .**22** C2
Compton St EC1 . . . .**96** B2
Compton Terr N1 . . .**15** A2
Comus Ho SE17 . . .**152** A3
Comus Pl SE17 . . . .**152** A3
Comyn Rd SW11 . . . .**60** A3
Comyns Cl E16 . . . . .**35** B4
Conant Ho SE11 . . . .**48** A4
Conant Mews **1**
E1 . . . .**125** B4
Concanon Rd SW2,
SW4 . . . .**62** B3
Concert Hall App
SE1 . . . .**121** A1
Concord Bsns Ctr
W3 . . . .**28** A4
Concorde Way
SE16 . . . .**40** C2
Concordia Wharf **10**
E14 . . . .**34** B1
Concord Rd W3 . . . . .**28** A4
Condell Rd SW8 . . .**171** A3
Conder St E14 . . . . .**33** A4
Condray Pl SW11 . .**158** A1
Conduit Ct WC2 . . .**120** A4
Conduit Ho SE10 . . .**52** C2
Conduit Mews
W2 . . . .**101** B1
Conduit Pas W2 . . .**101** B1
Conduit Pl W2 . . . .**101** B1
Conduit St W1 . . . .**118** C4
Conewood St N5 . . . .**6** A1
Coney Acre SE21 . . .**75** B3
Coney Way SW8 . . .**163** A3
Congers Ho SE8 . . . .**51** C3
Congress Ho WC1 .**105** C2
Congreve Ho
N16 . . . .**19** C3
Congreve St SE17 . .**152** A3
Conifer Ct **23**
SW19 . . . .**69** C3
Conifer Gdns
SW16 . . . .**74** B1
Conifer Ho SE4 . . . .**66** B3
Coniger Rd SW6 . . .**165** B2
Coningham Ct
SW10 . . . .**157** A2

Coningham Mews
W12 . . . . 29 C1
Coningham Rd
W12 . . . . 39 A4
Coningsby Rd N4 . . . . . . 6 A4
Conington Rd
SE13 . . . . 52 B1
Conisbrough NW1 . . 82 C3
Coniston NW1 . . . . 92 C4
Coniston Cl
Barnes SW13 . . . . 46 B3
Chiswick W4 . . . . 45 A3
Coniston Ct
Marylebone W2 . . . 102 B1
 6 Rotherhithe
SE16 . . . . 40 C4
Conistone Way N7 . . 14 A1
Coniston Ho
 1 Bow E3 . . . . 26 B2
 18 Camberwell SE5 . 48 B3
Coniston Wlk E9 . . . . 17 B3
Conlan St W10 . . . . 23 A1
Conley Rd NW10 . . . . . 8 A2
Conley St SE10 . . . . . . 43 A1
Connaught Ave
SW14 . . . . 55 B3
Connaught Cl W2 . 102 B1
Connaught Ho
College Pk NW10 . . . 22 A2
Mayfair W1 . . . . 118 A3
Connaught House Sch
W2 . . . . 103 B2
Connaught Lo N4 . . . 5 C4
Connaught Mans
Battersea SW11 . . . 168 B3
 2 Brixton SW9 . . . . 62 C3
 13 Canonbury N16 . 15 C4
Fulham SW6 . . . . 164 A4
Connaught Pl W2 . 102 C1
Connaught Rd
Finsbury Pk N4 . . . . . . 5 C4
Harlesden NW10 . . . 21 A3
 5 Richmond TW10 . 54 B2
Connaught Sq
W2 . . . . 102 C1
Connaught St W2 . 102 B1
Connaught Works
E3 . . . . 26 A4
Connell Ct 6
SE14 . . . . 50 C4
Connor Ct SW11 . . . 170 A4
Connor St E9 . . . . 25 C4
Conrad Ho
 8 Limehouse
SE16 . . . . 33 A2
South Lambeth
SW8 . . . . 162 A2
 12 Stoke Newington
N16 . . . . 16 A3
Conrad Twr W3 . . . . . 37 A3
Consort Ho W2 . . . 114 B3
Consort Lo NW8 . . . 80 C3
Consort Rd SE15 . . . 50 A1
Cons St SE1 . . . . 135 C4
Constable Ct 11
SE16 . . . . 40 A1
Constable Ho
 25 Millwall E14 . . . . 41 C4
Primrose Hill NW3 . . 12 B1
Constable Wlk
SE21 . . . . 76 A1
Constant Ho 28
E14 . . . . 34 A2
Constantine Ho
SW2 . . . . 75 A3

Constantine Rd
NW3 . . . . 12 A4
Constitution Hill
W1 . . . . 132 B4
Consul Ho 5 E3 . . . . 26 C1
Content St SE17 . . . 151 B3
Convent Gdns
W11 . . . . 31 B3
Convent of Jesus &
Mary Language Coll
NW10 . . . . 21 B4
Convent of Jesus &
Mary RC Inf Sch 9
NW2 . . . . 9 B2
Conway Gr W3 . . . . . . 28 C4
Conway Ho
Chelsea SW3 . . . . 145 A1
 1 Millwall E14 . . . . 42 A2
 5 Streatham SW2 . 74 A3
Conway Mews W1 . . 92 C1
Conway St W1 . . . . . . 92 C1
Conybeare NW3 . . . . 12 A1
Conyer St 21 E3 . . . . 26 A3
Cookham Cres
SE16 . . . . 40 C4
Cookham Ho
E2 . . . . 24 B1 98 C2
Cook's Rd
Camberwell SE17 . . . 48 A4
Stratford Marsh
E15 . . . . 27 A3
Coomassie Rd W9 . . 23 B1
Coombe Ho 19 N7 . . 13 C3
Coombe Rd W4 . . . . . 38 A1
Coomber Ho SW6 . . 59 A4
Coombs St N1 . . . . . . 86 B1
Coomer Mews
SW6 . . . . 155 A3
Coomer Pl SW6 . . . 155 A3
Cooper Cl SE1 . . . . . 135 C3
Cooper Ho NW8 . . . . 89 B1
Cooper Rd NW10 . . . . 8 C3
Coopersale Rd E9 . . 17 C3
Coopers Cl E1 . . . . . . 25 B1
Coopers La NW1 . . . 83 C1
Coopers Lo SE1 . . . 138 C4
Cooper's Rd SE1 . . 153 A2
Cooper's Row
EC3 . . . . 124 C4
Coopers St E3 10 E16 35 B4
Coopers Yd N1 . . . . . 15 A1
Copeland Dr E14 . . . 41 C2
Copeland Ho
SE11 . . . . 135 A1
Copeland Rd SE15 . . 50 A1
Copenhagen Gdns
W4 . . . . 37 C4
Copenhagen Ho
N1 . . . . 85 B3
Copenhagen Pl
E14 . . . . 33 B3
Copenhagen Prim Sch
N1 . . . . 84 C3
Copenhagen St N1 84 C3
Cope Pl W8 . . . . 127 B1
Cope St SE16 . . . . 40 C2
Copford Wlk N1 . . . . 86 C4
Copleston Rd SE15 . 64 B4
Copley Cl 16 SE17 . . 48 A4
Copley St E1 . . . . 32 C4

Coppedhall 2
SE21 . . . . 75 C2
Copperas St SE8 . . . 52 A4
Copper Beech N6 . . 3 C4
Copperbeech Cl
NW3 . . . . 11 C3
Copperfield Ho 17
SE1 . . . . 139 B3
Copperfield Rd E3 . 33 A4
Copperfields Ct
W3 . . . . 36 C4
Copperfield St
SE1 . . . . 136 C4
Copper Mews 19
W4 . . . . 37 B3
Copper Row SE1 . . . 124 C1
Coppice Dr SW15 . . . 57 A1
Coppin Ho SW2 . . . . 75 A3
Coppock Cl SW11 . . 168 A1
Copse Ct SW15 . . . . . 58 A2
Copthall Ave EC2 . 109 C2
Copthall Bldgs
EC2 . . . . 109 C2
Copthall Cl EC2 . . . 109 B2
Copthorne Ave
SW12 . . . . 73 C3
Coptic St WC1 . . . . . 106 A3
Copton Cl E3 . . . . 33 C4
Coral Apts 6 E16 . . 35 C2
Coral Ho 5 E1 . . . . . 26 A1
Coral Row 1
SW11 . . . . 59 B4
Coral St SE1 . . . . 135 C3
Coram Ho
Bloomsbury WC1 . . . 94 A2
 5 Chiswick W4 . . . 38 A1
Coram Mans WC1 . . 94 A1
Coram St WC1 . . . . . 94 A1
Corbden Ct SE15 . . . 49 B2
Corbet Ct EC3 . . . . . 109 C1
Corbet Ho N1 . . . . . . 85 B3
Corbet Pl E1 . . . . 110 C4
Corbett Ho SW10 . . 156 C4
Corbett's La SE16 . . 40 B2
Corbetts Pas 8
SE16 . . . . 40 B2
Corbidge Ct SE8 . . . 52 A4
Corbiere Ho 5 N1 . . 24 A4
Corbin Ho 7 E3 . . . . 27 A2
Corbridge Cres E2 . 25 A3
Corbyn St N4, N19 . . 5 A3
Corby Rd NW10 . . . . . 20 C3
Corby Way E13 . . . . . 27 C1
Cordelia Cl SE24 . . . 63 A3
Cordelia Ho 20 N1 . 24 A3
Cordelia St E14 . . . . 34 A3
Cording St E14 . . . . . 34 A4
Cordwainers Ct 18
E9 . . . . 17 B1
Corfe Ho SE8 . . . . . . 162 C2
Corfe Lodge 15
SE21 . . . . 75 C2
Corfield St E2 . . . . . . 25 A2
Corfton Rd W5 . . . . . 36 A2
Coriander Ave E14 . . 34 C3
Coriander Ct SE1 . . 139 A4
Corinne Rd N19 . . . . 13 B4
Cork St Mews W1 . 118 C3
Cork Sq E1 . . . . 32 A1
Cork St W1 . . . . 118 C3
Corlett St NW1 . . . . . 102 A4
Cormont Rd SE5 . . . 48 A2
Cormorant Ct
 26 Deptford SE8 . . 51 B4
 13 Dulwich SE21 . . 75 C2

Corbury Ho 5
SE8 . . . . 51 B4
Cornelia St N7 . . . . . 14 B2
Cornell Bldg 1
E1 . . . . 111 B2
Corner Fielde
SW2 . . . . 74 B3
Corner Gn SE3 . . . . . 53 C1
Corner House St
WC2 . . . . 120 A2
Cornerstone Ct 13
E1 . . . . 24 C1 99 C1
Cornerways SW15 . . 56 C3
Corney Rd W4 . . . . . . 46 A4
Corney Reach Way
W4 . . . . 46 A3
Cornflower Terr
SE22 . . . . 65 A1
Cornford Gr SW12 . 73 A2
Cornhill EC3 . . . . 109 C1
Cornick Ho 7
SE16 . . . . 40 A3
Cornish Ho
Brentford TW8 . . . . . . 36 B1
 7 Camberwell
SE17 . . . . 48 A4
Cornmill La SE13 . . . 67 B4
Cornmow Dr NW10 . 8 C3
Cornwall Ave E2 . . . 25 B2
Cornwall Cres
W11 . . . . 31 A3
Cornwall Flats
SE1 . . . . 135 C4
Cornwall Gdns
Kensington SW7 . . . 128 B1
Willesden NW10 . . . . 9 A2
Cornwall Gdns Wlk
SW7 . . . . 128 B1
Cornwall Gr W4 . . . . 38 A1
Cornwall Ho
Marylebone NW1 . . . 91 A1
 3 Putney SW15 . . . 69 B4
Cornwallis Ct
SW8 . . . . 172 A4
Cornwallis Ho 24
W12 . . . . 30 A2
Cornwallis Rd N19 . 5 A2
Cornwallis Sq
 3 Finsbury Park
N4 . . . . 5 C2
London N19 . . . . 5 A2
Cornwall Mans
Chelsea SW10 . . . . . 157 A2
Marylebone NW1 . . . 91 A1
Cornwall Mews S
SW7 . . . . 128 C1
Cornwall Mews W
SW7 . . . . 128 B1
Cornwall Rd
Finsbury Pk N4 . . . . . . 5 C4
Lambeth SE1 . . . . . . 135 C4
Cornwall Sq SE11 . 150 A2
Cornwall St 4 E1 . . . 32 A2
Cornwall Terr
NW1 . . . . 91 A1
Cornwall Terrace
Mews NW1 . . . . 91 A1
Cornwood Dr E1 . . . 32 B3
Coronation Ave 4
N16 . . . . 16 B4
Coronation Ct 19
W10 . . . . 30 B4
Coronet St
N1 . . . . 24 A2 98 A3
Corporation Row
EC1 . . . . 95 C2

Corporation St N7 . 14 A3
Corpus Christi RC
Prim Sch 10 SW2 . . 62 B2
Corrance Rd SW2,
SW4 . . . . 62 A3
Corringham Ct
NW11 . . . . 1 C4
Corringham Ho 11
E1 . . . . 32 C3
Corringham Rd
NW11 . . . . 1 C4
Corringway NW11 . . 2 A4
Corry Dr SW9 . . . . . . 63 A3
Corry Ho 2 E14 . . . . 34 A2
Corsham St N1 . . . . . 97 C3
Corsica St N5 . . . . . . 15 A2
Corsley Way E9 . . . . 18 B2
Cortayne Rd SW6 . 165 A2
Cortis Rd SW15 . . . . 57 A1
Cortis Terr SW15 . . . 57 A1
Corunna Rd SW8 . . 171 A4
Corunna Terr
SW8 . . . . 170 C4
Corvette Sq 5
SE10 . . . . 52 C4
Coryton Path 7 W9 . 23 B1
Cosbycote Ave
SE24 . . . . 63 B2
Cosgrove Ho 11
E2 . . . . 24 C4
Cosmo Pl WC1 . . . . 106 B4
Cosmur Cl W12 . . . . 38 B3
Cossall Wlk SE15 . . 50 A2
Cossar Mews 6
SW2 . . . . 62 C2
Cosser St SE1 . . . . . 135 B2
Costa St SE15 . . . . . . 49 C1
Coston Wlk 4
SE4 . . . . 65 C3
Cosway Mans
NW1 . . . . 102 B4
Cosway St NW1 . . . 102 B4
Cotall St E14 . . . . 33 C4
Cotes Ho NW8 . . . . . 90 A1
Cotham St SE17 . . . 151 A3
Cotherstone Rd
SW2 . . . . 74 B3
Cotleigh Rd NW6 . . 10 C1
Cotman Cl SW15 . . . 57 C2
Cotman Ho NW8 . . . 80 A2
Cotrill Gdns E8 . . . . 17 A2
Cotswold Ct EC1 . . . 96 C2
Cotswold Gate NW2 . 1 A3
Cotswold Ho N16 . . 7 B3
Cotswold Mews
SW11 . . . . 167 C3
Cottage Gn SE5 . . . . 48 C3
Cottage Gr SW9 . . . 62 A4
Cottage Pl SW3 . . . 130 A1
Cottage St E14 . . . . . 34 A2
Cottages The SE1 . 134 C1
Cottage Wlk 2 N16 . 7 B1
Cottenham Ho 5
N19 . . . . 5 A2
Cottesbrook St 9
SE14 . . . . 51 A3
Cottesloe Ho NW8 . 90 A2
Cottesloe Mews
SE1 . . . . 135 C2
Cottesmore Ct
W8 . . . . 128 B2
Cottesmore Gdns
W8 . . . . 128 B2

Cottingham Rd
SW8 .... **163** A2
Cottington St
SE11 .... **150** A2
Cotton Av W3 ..... **28** C3
Cotton Ho
Bedford Pk W12 ..... **38** B4
18 Streatham
SW12 .... **74** A4
Cotton Row SW11 ..**59** B4
Cotton's Gdns
E2 .... **24** A2 **98** B4
Cottons La SE1 .... **123** C2
Cotton St E14 ...... **34** B2
Cottrell Ct SE10 .... **43** B2
Couchman Ho **8**
SW4 .... **61** B1
Coulgate St SE4 ... **66** A4
Coulsdon Ho **5**
SW2 .... **74** A3
Coulson St SW3 .. **144** C2
Coulter Rd W6 ..... **39** A3
Coults Cres SW5 .... **3** C1
Councillor St SE5 ... **48** B3
Counters Ct W14 . **126** B2
Counter St SE1 ... **124** A1
Countess Rd NW5 .. **13** B3
Countisbury Ho
SE26 .... **76** C1
County Gr SE5 ..... **48** B2
County Ho
22 Herne Hill
SE24 .... **63** A3
3 South Lambeth
SW9 .... **173** B4
County St SE1 .... **137** A1
Courier Ho **17**
SW2 .... **74** C4
Courland Gr SW8 **171** C3
Courland St SW8 **171** C3
Courland Ho **7**
E2 .... **24** C3
Courtauld Inst of Art
WC2 .... **120** C4
Courtauld Rd N19 .. **5** A3
Courtenay Ave N6 .. **3** A4
Courtenay Sq
SE11 .... **149** B1
Courtenay St
SE11 .... **149** B2
Courtfield Gdns
SW5 .... **142** B3
Courtfield Ho EC1 **107** B4
Courtfield Mews
SW7 .... **142** B3
Courtfield Rd
SW7 .... **142** C3
Courthill Rd SE13 .. **67** B3
Courthope Ho
11 Rotherhithe
SE16 .... **40** B3
South Lambeth
SW8 .... **162** A1
Courthope Rd
NW3 .... **12** B4
Court La SE21 ...... **76** B4
Courtlands SW10 .. **54** C2
Courtlands Ave
TW9 .... **45** A1
Court Lane Gdns
SE21 .... **76** A4
Court Mans **8**
W6 .... **38** C2

Courtmead Cl
SE24 .... **63** B1
Courtnell St W2 .... **31** C3
Courtney Ct N7 .... **14** C3
Courtney Ho W14 . **126** B2
Courtney Rd N7 ... **14** C3
Courtrai Rd SE23 .. **66** A1
Court Royal SW15 . **58** A2
Court St E3 **11** **32** A4
Courtville Ho **12**
W10 .... **23** A2
Court Way W3 ...... **28** B4
Courtyard The
Fulham W6 .... **164** A3
Islington N1 .... **14** B1
18 Wandsworth
SW18 .... **59** C3
Cousin La EC4 .... **123** B3
Couzens Ho **8** E3 .. **33** B4
Coval Gdns SW14 .. **55** A3
Coval La SW14 ...... **55** A3
Coval Pas SW14 .... **55** B3
Coval Rd SW14 ..... **55** B3
Covell Ct **16** SE8 .. **51** C3
Covent Garden Sta
WC2 .... **106** B1
Coventry Cl NW6 ... **23** C4
Coventry Rd E1 .... **25** A1
Coventry St W1 ... **119** B3
Coverdale Rd
Brondesbury
NW2 .... **10** A2
Hammersmith W12 . **39** A4
Hampstead NW6 .... **9** C1
Coverham Ho **8**
SE4 .... **65** C3
Coverley Cl E1 .... **111** C4
Coverley Point
SE11 .... **148** C3
Cowcross St EC1 . **108** A4
Cowdenbeath Path
N1 .... **84** C4
Cowdray Hall Royal
Coll of Nursing
W1 .... **104** A2
Cowdray Ho **22**
SE22 .... **64** A4
Cowdry Rd E9 ...... **18** B2
Cowley Rd
Brixton SW9 .... **173** C4
East Acton W3 ..... **29** B1
Mortlake SW14 ..... **56** A4
Cowley St SW1 ... **134** A1
Cowling Cl
W11 .... **31** A1 **112** C2
Cowper Ho
Pimlico SW1 .... **147** C1
Walworth SE17 ... **151** A2
Cowper Rd
Acton W3 .... **28** C1
Stoke Newington
N16 .... **16** A4
Cowper's Ct EC3 . **109** C1
Cowper Terr W10 .. **30** C4
Cowthorpe Rd
SW8 .... **171** C4
Cox Ho W6 .... **154** A4
Coxson Way SE1 . **138** C3
Coysh Ct **5** SW15 . **58** A2
Crabtree Cl E2 ..... **24** B3
Crabtree Hall SW6 . **47** B3
Crabtree La SW6 .. **47** C3
Craddock St NW5 . **12** C2
Cragie Ho SE1 .... **153** A3
Craigleith SW15 .... **57** C1

Craignair Rd SW2 . **74** C4
Craig's Ct SW1 ... **120** A2
Craik Ct NW6 ...... **23** B3
Crail Row SE17 ... **151** C3
Cramer St W1 .... **103** C3
Crammond Cl W6 **154** A3
Crampton Prim Sch
SE17 .... **150** B2
Crampton St SE17 **150** C2
Cranbrook Alley
WC2 .... **119** C2
Cranbourne Ct
SW11 .... **158** B2
Cranbourne Rd
E15 .... **19** B4
Cranbourn Pas **5**
SE16 .... **40** A4
Cranbourn St
WC2 .... **119** C4
Cranbrook NW1 .... **83** A3
Cranbrook Ho **5**
E5 .... **17** A3
Cranbrook Rd
Chiswick W4 .... **38** A1
St Johns SE8 .... **51** C2
Cranbrook St E2 ... **25** C3
Cranbury Rd SW6 **166** B3
Crandale Ho **8** E5 . **17** A3
Crandley Ct SE8 ... **41** A2
Crane Ave W3 ...... **28** B2
Crane Ct
Acton W12 .... **38** A4
Holborn EC4 ...... **107** C1
Crane Gr N7 .... **14** C2
Crane Ho
2 Bow E3 .... **26** A3
15 Peckham SE15 ... **49** B2
Crane Mead SE16 .. **40** C2
Crane St
Greenwich SE10 .... **42** C1
6 Peckham SE15 ... **49** B2
Cranfield Ct NW1 . **102** B3
Cranfield Ho WC1 **106** B4
Cranfield Rd SE4 ... **66** B4
Cranford Cotts **1**
E1 .... **32** C2
Cranford Lo SW19 . **69** C2
Cranford St E1 ..... **32** C2
Cranhurst Rd NW2 . **9** B3
Cranleigh
W11 .... **31** B1 **112** C2
Cranleigh Ct
Richmond TW9 ..... **54** C4
8 Stamford Hill N16 . **7** A3
Cranleigh Hos
NW1 .... **83** A1
Cranleigh Mews
SW11 .... **168** C1
Cranleigh St NW1 . **83** A1
Cranley Gdns
SW7 .... **143** B2
Cranley Mews
SW7 .... **143** A2
Cranley Pl SW7 ... **143** B3
Cranmer Ct SW3 . **144** B3
Cranmer Ho
SW11 .... **168** A4
Cranmer Rd SW9 . **163** C2
Cranswick Rd
SE16 .... **40** A1
Cranwell Cl E3 ..... **27** A1
Cranwich Rd N16 .. **7** A4
Cranwood Ct EC1 .. **97** C3
Cranwood St EC1 .. **97** C3

Cranworth Gdns
SW9 .... **173** B4
Cranworth Ho **6**
N7 .... **14** B4
Craster Rd SW2 ... **74** B4
Craston Ho **2** SE5 . **49** A1
Craven Cl N16 .... **7** C4
Craven Cottage
(Fulham FC)
SW6 .... **47** C2
Craven Ct NW10 ... **21** A4
Craven Hill W2 ... **115** A4
Craven Hill Gdns
W2 .... **114** C4
Craven Hill Mews
W2 .... **115** A4
Craven Ho **2**
SW14 .... **55** C4
Craven Lo
Bayswater W2 ... **115** A4
6 Hammersmith
W6 .... **47** C2
Craven Mews **6**
SW11 .... **60** C4
Craven Park Mews
NW10 .... **21** A4
Craven Park Rd
NW10 .... **21** A4
Craven Pk NW10 ... **21** A4
Craven Pas **2**
WC2 .... **120** A2
Craven Pk NW10 ... **21** A4
Craven Rd
Paddington W2 ... **101** A1
Stonebridge NW10 . **20** C4
Craven St WC2 ... **120** A2
Craven Terr W2 ... **115** A4
Craven Wlk E5, N16 . **7** C4
Crawford Bldgs
NW1 .... **102** B3
Crawford Mews
W1 .... **102** C3
Crawford Pas EC1 . **95** C1
Crawford Pl W1 ... **102** B3
Crawford Place
Dwellings NW1 ... **102** B3
Crawford Point **4**
E16 .... **35** B3
Crawford Prim Sch
SE5 .... **48** B2
Crawford Rd SE5 .. **48** B1
Crawford St W1 ... **102** C3
Crawshay Ct SW9 **173** C4
Crawshay Ho **13**
N16 .... **15** C4
Crawthew Gr SE22 . **64** B3
Crayford Ho
Bermondsey SE1 . **137** C3
8 Lower Holloway
N7 .... **14** A4
Crayford Rd N7 ... **14** A4
Crayle Ho EC1 ...... **96** B2
Crealock St SW18 . **59** A1
Creasy Est SE1 ... **138** A1
Crebor St SE22 ... **64** C1
Credenhill Ho **2**
SE15 .... **50** A3
Crediton Hill NW6 . **11** A3
Crediton Rd NW10 . **22** C4
Credon Rd SE16 ... **40** A1
Creechurch La
EC3 .... **110** B1
Creechurch Pl
EC3 .... **110** B1
Creed Ct **5** EC4 .... **108** B1
Creed Ho SE15 ..... **65** A4
Creed La EC4 ...... **108** B1
Creek Ho W14 .... **126** B2
Creek Rd SE10, SE8 . **52** A4

Creek Road Ind Est
SE8 .... **52** A4
Creekside SE8 ...... **52** A4
Creekside Foyer
SE8 .... **52** A4
Crefeld Cl W6 .... **154** A3
Creighton Cl W12 . **30** A2
Creighton Rd NW6 . **22** C3
Cremer Bsns Ctr **3**
E2 .... **24** B3
Cremer St **8** E2 .... **24** B3
Cremer St E2 .... **24** B3
Cremorne Rd
SW10 .... **157** B2
Creon Ct **3** SW9 . **173** B4
Crescent Ct E3 ... **124** C4
Crescent Arc **1**
SE10 .... **52** B4
Crescent Court Bsns
Ctr **18** E16 .... **27** C1
Crescent Ct SW4 ... **61** C2
Crescent Gdns
SW19 .... **70** C1
Crescent Gr SW4 .. **61** B3
Crescent Ho SE13 . **52** A1
Crescent La SW4 .. **61** C2
Crescent Mans
Islington N5 .... **15** A3
Notting Hill
W11 .... **31** A2 **112** B4
Crescent Pl SW3 . **144** B4
Crescent Row EC1 . **96** C1
Crescent St N1 ..... **14** B1
Crescent Stables
SW15 .... **58** A2
Crescent The
Acton W3 .... **29** A3
Barnes SW13 .... **46** C1
Wimbledon SW19 .. **70** C1
Crescent Way SE4 . **66** C4
Crescent Wood Rd
SE21, SE26 .... **76** C1
Cresford Rd SW6 . **166** A3
Cressage Ho **9**
TW8 .... **44** A4
Cressall Ho **14** E14 . **41** C3
Cresset Ho E9 ...... **17** B2
Cresset Rd E9 ...... **17** B2
Cresset St SW4 .... **61** C4
Cressfield Cl NW5 . **12** C3
Cressida Rd N19 .... **4** C3
Cressingham Rd
SE13 .... **67** B4
Cressington Cl **4**
N16 .... **16** A3
Cresswell Gdns
SW5 .... **142** C2
Cresswell Pl
SW10 .... **143** A2
Cressy Ct
Hammersmith W6 .. **39** A3
6 Stepney E1 .... **32** B4
Cressy Ho **7** E1 .... **32** B4
Cressy Hos SW13 . **57** A4
Cressy Pl E1 .... **32** B4
Cressy Rd NW3 .... **12** B4
Cresta Ho
7 Bow E3 .... **26** C1
Hampstead NW6 .. **11** C1
Crestfield St N1,
WC1 .... **94** B4
Crestview NW5 ..... **4** A1
Crestway SW15 .... **57** A1
Creswick Ct W3 ... **28** A2
Creswick Rd W3 ... **28** A2

Creswick Wlk **7**
E3 . . . . .26 C2

Crewdson Rd
SW9 . . . . **163** B1

Crewe PI NW10 . . . . .21 B2

Crewkerne Ct
SW11 . . . . **167** C4

Crews St E14 . . . . .41 C2

Crewys Rd
Child's Hill NW2 . . . . . .1 B2
London SE15 . . . . .50 A1

Crichton St SW8 . . **170** C2

Cricketers Mews **4**
SW18 . . . . .59 A2

Cricketfield Rd E5 . . .17 A4

Cricklade Ave
SW2 . . . . .74 B2

CRICKLEWOOD 9 B4

Cricklewood
Broadway NW2 . . . . .9 C4

Cricklewood La
NW2 . . . . .1 B1

Cricklewood Sta
NW2 . . . . .9 C4

Crieff Rd SW18 . . . . .59 B1

Criffel Ave SW2 . . . . .73 C3

Crimscott St E1 . . . **138** B1

Crimsworth Rd
SW8 . . . . **161** C1

Crinan St N1 . . . . . . .84 B2

Cringle St SW8 . . . **160** C2

Cripplegate St
EC1 . . . . **109** A4

Crispe Ho N1 . . . . . . .85 A3

Crispian CI NW10 . . . .8 A4

Crispin CI SE17 . . . . **152** A3

Crispin PI E1 . . . . . . **110** C4

Crispin St E1 . . . . . **110** C3

Crisp Rd W6 . . . . . . .39 B1

Cristowe Rd SW6 . . **165** A1

Criterion Mews
N19 . . . . .4 C2

Crockerton Rd
SW17 . . . . .72 B2

Croft CI SW18 . . . . . .67 B1

Croftdown Rd NW5 . .4 A1

Crofters Ct **5** SE8 . .41 A2

Crofters Way NW1 . .83 B4

Croft Ho
Putney SW15 . . . . . . .58 A1
11 West Kilburn
W10 . . . . .23 A2

Crofton Ave W4 . . . .45 C3

Crofton Gate Way
SE4 . . . . .66 A2

Crofton Park Rd
SE4 . . . . .66 B1

Crofton Park Sta
SE4 . . . . .66 A2

Crofton Rd SE5 . . . . .49 A1

Crofton Ter
Homerton E5 . . . . . . .18 A3
Richmond TW9 . . . . .54 B3

Crofts Ho **21** E2 . . .24 C3

Crofts St E1 . . . . . . **125** B3

Croft St SE8 . . . . . . .41 A2

Croft The NW10 . . . .21 B3

Crogsland Rd
NW1 . . . . .12 C1

Cromartie Rd N19 . . .4 C4

Cromarty Ho **8**
E1 . . . . .33 A4

Crombie Mews **5**
SW11 . . . . **168** B2

Cromdale Ct N16 . . . .7 B4

Cromer Ct
Streatham SW16 . . . .74 A1
Wandsworth SW18 . .58 B1

Crome Rd NW10 . . . . .8 A2

Cromer St WC1 . . . . .94 B3

Cromer Terr E8 . . . . .16 C3

Cromer Villas Rd
SW18 . . . . .58 B1

Cromford Path **4**
E5 . . . . .17 C4

Cromford Rd
SW18 . . . . .58 C2

Crompton Ct SW3 **144** A4

Crompton Ho
Borough The SE1 . . **137** A1
Paddington W2 . . . . .89 B1
South Lambeth
SW8 . . . . **171** A3

Crompton St W2 . . . .89 B1

Cromwell Ave
Hammersmith W6 . . .39 A2
Highgate N6 . . . . .4 A3

Cromwell CI
Acton W3 . . . . .28 B1
4 Gunnersbury
W4 . . . . .37 A1

Cromwell Cres
SW5 . . . . **141** B4

Cromwell Ctr
NW10 . . . . .20 C2

Cromwell Gdns
SW7 . . . . **129** C1

Cromwell Gr W6 . . . .39 B3

Cromwell Ho
Battersea SW11 . . . **169** C3
Putney SW15 . . . . . .56 C3

Cromwell Hospl
(BUPA) SW5 . . . . . **142** A4

Cromwell Lo **9**
E1 . . . . **25** A1

Cromwell Mans
SW5 . . . . **141** C4

Cromwell Mews
SW7 . . . . **143** C4

Cromwell PI
8 Acton W3 . . . . . .28 B1
Barbican EC1 . . . . . **109** A4
Highgate N6 . . . . .4 A3
Mortlake SW14 . . . . .55 B4
South Kensington
SW7 . . . . **143** C4

Cromwell Rd
Brixton SW9 . . . . . . .48 A2
South Kensington
SW7 . . . . **143** A4

Cromwell Twr
EC2 . . . . **109** A4

Crondace Rd SW6 **165** C3

Crondall Ct **7** N1 . . .24 A3

Crondall Ho SW15 . .68 C3

Crondall PI **16** N1 . .24 A3

Crondall St N1 . . . . . .24 A3

Crone Ct **5** NW6 . . .23 B3

Cronin St SE15 . . . . .49 B3

Crooked Billet Yd **18**
E2 . . . . .24 A3

Crookham Rd
SW6 . . . . **164** C3

Croom's Hill SE10 . .52 C3

Croom's Hill Gr
SE10 . . . . .52 B3

Cropley Ct N1 . . . . . .87 B2

Cropley St N1 . . . . . .87 B2

Cropthorne Ct W9 . .89 A3

Crosby Ct SE1 . . . . **137** B4

Crosby Ho **10** E14 . .42 B3

Crosby Row SE1 . . **137** B4

Crosby Sq EC3 . . . **110** A2

Crosby Wlk
3 Dalston E8 . . . . .16 C2
Streatham SE24 . . . .74 C4

Crosfield Ct **3**
W10 . . . . .30 C3

Crosfield Ho
W11 . . . . **31** A2 **112** A3

Crosland PI **5**
SW11 . . . . .60 C4

Crossbow Ho **15**
N1 . . . . .24 A4

Cross CI SE15 . . . . . .50 A1

Cross Ct SE5 . . . . . . .63 C4

Crossfield Rd
NW3 . . . . .11 C2

Crossfield St SE8 . . .51 C3

Crossford St SW9 . **172** C1

Crossharbour Sta
E14 . . . . .42 A3

Cross Keys CI W1 . **103** C3

Cross La EC3 . . . . . **124** A3

Crosslet St SE17 . . **151** C4

Crosslet Vale SE10 . .52 A2

Crossley St N7 . . . . .14 C2

Crossman Hos **10**
SW12 . . . . .74 A4

Crossmount Ho **3**
SE5 . . . . .48 B3

Cross Rd SE5 . . . . . . .49 A1

Cross St
Islington N1 . . . . .86 B4
Mortlake SW13 . . . . .56 A4

Crossthwaite Ave SE5,
SE24 . . . . .63 C3

Crosstrees Ho **7**
E14 . . . . .41 C3

Crosswall EC3 . . . . **124** C4

Crossway N16 . . . . . .16 A3

Crossway Ct SE4 . . .51 A1

Crossways Acad
SE4 . . . . .51 A1

Croston St E8 . . . . . .24 C4

Crouch End Hill N8 . .4 C4

Crouch Hall Ct N19 . .5 A3

Crouch Hill N4, N8,
N19 . . . . .5 A4

Crouch Hill Sta N4 . .5 B4

Crouchmans CI SE21,
SE26 . . . . .76 B1

Crowder St E1 . . . **32** A2

Crowfield Ho N5 . . . .15 B4

Crowfoot CI E9 . . . . .18 B3

Crowhurst CI
SW9 . . . . **173** C2

Crowhurst Ho **21**
SW9 . . . . **173** C2

Crowland Ho NW8 . .78 C3

Crowland Terr N1 . . .15 C1

Crowline Wlk **1**
N1 . . . . .15 B2

Crown CI
Bow E3 . . . . .26 C4
Hampstead NW6 . . . .11 A2

Crown Close Bsns Ctr
E3 . . . . .26 C4

Crown Ct
City of London
EC4 . . . . **109** A1
4 Putney SW15 . . .57 B3
St Giles WC2 . . . . . **106** B1

Crown Ct continued
St John's Wood
NW8 . . . . .90 B3

Crowndale Ct NW1 .83 B2

Crowndale Rd
NW1 . . . . .83 A2

Crowne Ho SE1 . . . **123** A1

Crownfield Rd E15 . .19 C4

Crowngate Ho **33**
E3 . . . . .26 B3

Crownhill Rd
NW10 . . . . .21 B4

Crownleigh Ct
SW2 . . . . .62 C2

Crown Lo SW3 . . . **144** B3

Crown Mews **9**
E1 . . . . .32 C4

Crown Office Row
EC4 . . . . **121** B4

Crown Pas SW1 . . . **119** A1

Crown PI
Broadgate EC2 . . . . **110** A4
Kentish Town NW5 . .13 A2

Crown Reach
SW1 . . . . **147** C1

Crown St
Acton W3 . . . . .28 A1
Camberwell SE5 . . . .48 B3

Crownstone Ct **11**
SW2 . . . . .62 C2

Crownstone Rd
SW2 . . . . .62 C2

Crown Terr TW9 . . . .54 B3

Crows Rd E3, E15 . . .27 C2

Crowther Ave
TW8 . . . . .36 A2

Crowther CI SW6 . . **155** A3

Crowthorne CI
SW18 . . . . .70 B3

Crowthorne Rd
W10 . . . . .30 C3

Croxley Rd W9 . . . . .23 B2

Croxted CI SE21 . . . .75 B4

Croxted Rd SE21,
SE24 . . . . .75 C3

Croxteth Ho **11**
SW8 . . . . **171** B2

Croydon Ho SE1 . . **135** C4

Crozier Ho SW8 . . **162** C1

Crozier Terr E9 . . . . .17 C3

Crucifix La SE1 . . . **138** A4

Cruden Ho
15 Bow E3 . . . . . .26 B3
2 Camberwell
SE17 . . . . .48 A4

Cruden St N1 . . . . . . .86 B3

Cruikshank St
WC1 . . . . .95 B4

Cruikshank Ho
NW8 . . . . .80 B2

Crusader Ho E1 . . . .96 A1

Crusoe Mews N16 . . .6 C2

Crutched Friars
EC3 . . . . **124** B4

Crystal Palace Rd
SE22 . . . . .64 C2

Crystal Wharf N1 . . .86 B1

Cuba St E14 . . . . .41 C4

Cubitt Bldg SW1 **146** A1

Cubitt Ho **4** SW4 . .61 B1

Cubitt St WC1 . . . . . .95 A3

Cubitt Terr SW4 . . . .61 B4

CUBITT TOWN 42 B2

Cubitt Town Jun & Inf
Sch E14 . . . . .42 B3

Cuddington SE17 . . **151** A4

Cudworth Ho
SW8 . . . . **171** A3

Cudworth St E1 . . . .25 A1

Cuffley Ho **3** W10 . .30 B4

Cuff Point **12**
E2 . . . . **24** B2 **98** C4

Culand Ho SE17 . . **152** A3

Culford Gdns
SW3 . . . . **145** A3

Culford Gr N1 . . . . . .16 A2

Culford Mans
SW3 . . . . **145** A3

Culford Mews N1 . .16 A2

Culford Rd
Kingsland N1 . . . . . .16 A2
Shoreditch N1 . . . . . .24 A4

Culham Ho
21 Paddington
W2 . . . . .31 C4
33 Shoreditch
E2 . . . . **24** B2 **98** C3

Cullen Ho W9 . . . . . .23 B3

Cullen Way NW10 . .20 B1

Culling Rd SE16 . . . .40 B3

Cullingworth Rd
NW10 . . . . .9 A3

Culloden CI **17**
SE16 . . . . **153** C1

Culloden Prim Sch **15**
E14 . . . . .34 B3

Cullum St EC3 . . . . **124** A4

Culmore Rd SE15 . . .50 B3

Culmstock Rd
SW11 . . . . .60 C2

Culpepper Ct
SE11 . . . . **149** B4

Culross Bldgs
NW1 . . . . .84 A2

Culross St W1 . . . . **117** B3

Culver Ct SW18 . . . .59 A1

Culverden Rd
SW12 . . . . .73 B2

Culverhouse WC1 **106** C3

Culverhouse Gdns
SW16 . . . . .74 B1

Culverin Ct **1** N7 . .14 B3

Culvert Ct SW11 . . **169** B2

Culvert PI SW11 . . **169** B2

Culvert Rd SW11 . **169** A2

Culworth Ho NW8 . .80 A2

Culworth St NW8 . . .80 A1

Cumber Ho SW18 . . .70 C3

Cumberland Ave
NW10 . . . . .20 A2

Cumberland Bsns Pk
NW10 . . . . .20 A2

Cumberland CI E8 . .16 B2

Cumberland Cres
W14 . . . . **140** B4

Cumberland Ct
W1 . . . . **103** A1

Cumberland Gate
W1 . . . . **117** A4

Cumberland Gdns
WC1 . . . . .95 B4

Cumberland Ho
Paddington W9 . . . . .88 C1
1 Putney SW15 . . .69 B4

Cumberland Mans
Marylebone W1 . . . **102** C2
7 West Hampstead
NW6 . . . . .10 C3

Cumberland Market
NW1 . . . . .92 B4

Cumberland Mills Sq
E14 . . . . 42 C1
Cumberland Park Ind
Est NW10 . . . . 21 C2
Cumberland Pk
W3 . . . . 28 B2
Cumberland Rd
NW1 . . . . 92 A4
Cumberland Rd
Acton W3 . . . . 28 B2
Barnes SW13 . . . . 46 C2
Richmond TW9 . . . . . . 44 C2
Cumberland St
SW1 . . . . 146 B2
Cumberland Terr
NW1 . . . . 82 A1
Cumberland Terrace
Mews NW1 . . . . 82 A1
Cumberland Villas
W3 . . . . 28 B2
Cumberland Wharf
SE16 . . . . 40 B4
Cumbrian Gdns
NW2 . . . . 1 A2
Cuming Mus SE17 150 C3
Cumming St N1 . . . 85 A1
Cumnor Cl 23
SW9 . . . . 173 A2
Cunard Pl EC3 . . . 110 B1
Cunard Rd NW10 . . 20 C2
Cunard Wlk 3
SE16 . . . . 41 A2
Cundy St SW1 . . . 145 C3
Cunningham Ct
W2 . . . . 89 B1
Cunningham Ho 10
SE5 . . . . 48 C3
Cunningham Pl
NW8 . . . . 89 B2
Cunnington St W4 . 37 B2
Cupar Rd SW11 . 169 C4
Cureton St SW1 . 147 C3
Curlew Ho
Brockley SE4 . . . . . . 66 A3
7 Peckham SE15 . . 49 B2
Curlew St SE1 . . . 139 A4
Curness St SE13 . . 67 B3
Curran Ho SW3 . 144 A3
Curricle St W3 . . . 29 A1
Currie Ho 13
SW12 . . . . 73 C4
Cursitor St EC4 . 107 B2
Curtain Pl
EC2 . . . . 24 A1 98 B2
Curtain Rd
EC2 . . . . 24 A1 98 B2
Curtis Dr W3 . . . . . 28 C3
Curtis Ho SE17 . 151 B2
Curtis St SE1 . . . 152 C4
Curtis Way SE1 . 152 C4
Curve Bldg The
SE4 . . . . 66 B2
Curve The W12 . . . 29 C1
Curwen Gall W1 . 105 B3
Curwen Rd W12 . . . 38 C4
Curzon Cres NW10 . 8 A1
Curzon Gate W1 . 117 C1
Curzon Sq W1 . . . 117 C1
Curzon St W1 . . . 118 A2
Custance Ho N1 . . 87 B1
Custance St N1 . . . 97 B4
Custom House

Custom House Reach
SE16 . . . . 41 B3
Cutbush Ho N7 . . . 13 C3
Cutcombe Rd SE5 . 48 B1
Cuthbert Harrowing
Ho EC1 . . . . 96 C1
Cuthbert Ho W2 . . 101 B4
Cuthbert St W2 . . . 89 B1
Cuthill Wlk SE5 . . 48 C2
Cutlers Gdns EC2 . 110 B2
Cutlers Gdns Arc
EC2 . . . . 110 B2
Cutlers Sq E14 . . . 41 C2
Cutler St EC2 . . . 110 B2
Cut The SE1 . . . 135 C4
Cutty Sark SE10 . . 52 B4
Cutty Sark Ho 17
E14 . . . . 42 A2
Cutty Sark Sta
SE10 . . . . 52 B4
Cuxton Ho SE17 . 152 B2
Cyclops Mews 12
E14 . . . . 41 C2
Cygnet Ho NW8 . . . 78 C4
Cygnet House N 9
E14 . . . . 34 A3
Cygnet House S 10
E14 . . . . 34 A3
Cygnet St
E1 . . . . 24 B1 99 A2
Cygnus Bsns Ctr
NW10 . . . . 8 B2
Cynthia St N1 . . . 85 A1
Cyntra Pl 8 E8 . . 17 A1
Cypress Cl 9 E5 . . 7 C2
Cypress Ct SE11 . 19 C4
Cypress Gdns SE4 . 66 A2
Cypress Ho SE14 . 50 C2
Cypress Pl W1 . . . 93 A1
Cyprus Pl 22 E2 . 25 B3
Cyprus St E2 . . . . 25 B3
Cyrena Rd SE22 . 64 B2
Cyril Jackson Prim
Sch (North Bldg) 24
E14 . . . . 33 B2
Cyril Jackson Prim
Sch (South Bldg) 24
SW6 . . . . 165 C3
Cyril Thatcher Ho
SW6 . . . . 165 C3
Cyrus Ho EC1 . . . . 96 B2
Cyrus St EC1 . . . . 96 B2
Czar St SE8 . . . . . 51 C4

D

Dabb's La EC1 . . . 95 C1
Dabin Cres SE10 . . 52 B2
Dacca St SE8 . . . . 51 B4
Dace Rd E3 . . . . . . 26 C4
Dacre Ho SW3 . . 157 C3
Dacre St SW1 . . . 133 B2
Daffodil St W12 . . 29 B2
Dafforne Rd SW17 . 72 C1
Dagmar Ct E14 . . 42 B3
Dagmar Gdns
NW10 . . . . 22 C3
Dagmar Pas N1 . . 86 B4
Dagmar Rd
Camberwell SE5 . . . 49 A2
Finsbury Pk N4 . . . . 5 C4
Dagmar Terr N1 . . 86 B4
Dagnall St SW11 . 169 B3
Dagnan Rd SW12 . 73 A4

Dagobert Ho 27
E1 . . . . 32 B4
Daimler Ho 8 E3 . 26 C1
Dainton Ho 22 W2 . 31 C4
Daintry Way E9 . . . 18 B2
Dairy Ho NW10 . . . 21 C4
Dairyman Ct 11 . . . 51 A1
Daisy Dormer Ct 11
SW9 . . . . 173 B4
Daisy La SW6 . . . . 58 C4
Dakin Pl 6 E1 . . . 33 A4
Dakota bldg 6
SE13 . . . . 52 A2
Dalberg Rd SW2 . 62 C2
Dalbury Ho 6
SW9 . . . . 62 B3
Dalby Rd SW18 . . 59 B3
Dalby St NW5 . . . 13 A2
Dalebury Rd SW17 . 72 B2
Dale Croft N4 . . . . 6 B1
Dalehead Ho NW1 . 82 C1
Daleham Gdns
NW3 . . . . 11 C2
Daleham Mews
NW3 . . . . 11 C2
Dale Ho
Camberwell SE17 . . 48 A4
Gospel Oak NW5 . . 12 C3
Dale Row W11 . . . 31 A3
Dale St W4 . . . . 38 A1
Daley Ho 6 W12 . 30 A3
Daley St E9 . . . . . . 17 C2
Daley Thompson Way
7 SW8 . . . . 61 A4
Dalgarno Gdns
W10 . . . . 30 B4
Dalgarno Way
W10 . . . . 22 B1
Daling Way E3 . . . 26 A3
Dalkeith Ct SW1 . 147 C3
Dalkeith Ho 6
SW9 . . . . 48 A2
Dalkeith Rd SE21 . 75 B4
Dalling Rd W6 . . . 39 A2
Dallington Sch
EC1 . . . . 96 B2
Dallington St EC1 . 96 B2
Dalmeny Ave N7 . . 13 C4
Dalmeny Avenue Est
8 N7 . . . . 13 C4
Dalmeny Ct 8
SW4 . . . . 172 A2
Dalmeny Rd N7 . . 13 C4
Dalmore Rd SE21 . 75 B2
Dalrymple Rd SE4 . 66 A3
Dalston Jct E8 . . . 16 B2
Dalston Junction Sta
E8 . . . . 16 B2
Dalston Kingsland Sta
E8 . . . . 16 B3
Dalston La E8 . . . . 16 C3
Dalton Ho
7 Balham SW12 . . . 73 A4
10 Bow E3 . . . . 26 A3
15 Deptford SE14 . 50 C4
Dalton St SE27 . . 75 A1

Dalwood St SE5 . . . 49 A2
Dalyell Rd SW9 . . 62 B4
Damascene Wlk
SE21 . . . . 75 B3
Damer Ho 9
TW10 . . . . 54 B1
Damer Terr SW10 . 157 A1
Dame St N1 . . . . . . 86 C2
Damien Ct 12 E1 . 32 A3
Damien St E1 . . . . 32 A3
Damory Ho 1
SE16 . . . . 40 B2
Dan Bryant Ho 5
SW12 . . . . 73 B4
Danbury St N1 . . . 86 B2
Danby Ho
23 Hackney E9 . . . 17 B1
8 West Kilburn
W9 . . . . 23 B2
Dancer Rd
Fulham SW6 . . . . . 164 C3
Richmond TW9 . . . . 54 C4
Dandridge Cl SE10 . 43 B1
Dandridge Ho E1 . 110 C4
Danebury
W10 . . . . 30 B4
Danebury Ave
SW15 . . . . 56 B1
Danecroft Rd SE24 . 63 C2
Dane Ho 15 SE5 . 48 B1
Danehurst St
SW6 . . . . 164 A4
Danemere St
SW15 . . . . 57 B4
Dane Pl E3 . . . . 26 B3
Danes Ct NW8 . . . 80 C3
Danesdale Rd E9 . 18 A2
Danesfield SE5 . . . 49 A4
Danes Ho W10 . . . 30 B4
Dane St WC1 . . . 106 C3
Daneville Rd SE5 . 48 C2
Daniel Bolt Cl E14 . 34 A4
Daniel Ct W3 . . . . 29 A2
Daniel Gdns SE15 . 49 B3
Daniell Ho N1 . . . 87 C2
Daniel's Rd SE15 . 65 B4
Dan Leno Wlk
SW6 . . . . 156 A1
Dansey Pl W1 . . . 119 B4
Dante Pl SE11 . . . 150 B3
Dante Rd SE11 . . . 150 A4
Danube Ct 13 SE15 . 49 B3
Danvers Ho 13 E1 . 111 C1
Danvers St SW3 . 157 C3
Da Palma Ct SW6 . 155 B3
Daphne St SW18 . 59 B1
Daplyn St 3 E1 . 111 B4
D'arblay St W1 . . . 105 A1
Darcy Ho E8 . . . . . 25 A4
Darell Prim Sch
TW9 . . . . 54 C4
Darell Rd TW9 . . . 54 C4
Daren Ct N7 . . . . . . 14 A4
Darenth Rd N16 . . 7 B3
Darfield NW1 . . . . 82 C3
Darfield Rd SE4 . 66 B2
Darfield Way W10 . 30 C3
Darfur St SW15 . 57 C4
Darien Ho
10 London SW11 . 59 C4
11 Stepney E1 . . . 32 C4
Darien Rd SW11 . 59 C4
Daring Ho 25 E3 . 26 A3
Darlan Rd SW6 . 155 A1

Darley Ho SE11 . . 148 C1
Darley Rd SW11 . . 60 B1
Darling Ho SE4 . . 66 C4
Darling Row E1 . . 25 A1
Darlington Ho
SW8 . . . . 161 C1
Darnall Ho 4
SE10 . . . . 52 B2
Darnay Ho 3
SE16 . . . . 139 B2
Darnell Ho 9
SE10 . . . . 52 B3
Darnley Ho 7 E14 . 33 A3
Darnley Rd E9 . . . 17 B2
Darnley Terr 12
W11 . . . . 30 C1
Darrell Rd SE22 . 64 C2
Darren Cl N4 . . . . . 5 B4
Darsley Dr SW8 . 172 A4
Dartford Ho SE1 . 153 A4
Dartford St SE17 . 48 B4
Dartington NW1 . 83 A3
Dartington Ho
Bayswater W2 . . . 100 A4
7 London SW8 . . 162 D1
Dartle Ct 2 SE16 . 139 C3
Dartmoor Wlk 18
E14 . . . . 41 C2
Dartmouth Cl W11 . 31 C3
Dartmouth Ct
SE10 . . . . 52 B2
Dartmouth Gr
SE10 . . . . 52 B2
Dartmouth Hill
SE10 . . . . 52 B2
Dartmouth Ho
Dartmouth Pk N19 . 4 A2
Lewisham SE10 . . . 52 B1
DARTMOUTH
PARK 4 A1
Dartmouth Park Ave
NW5 . . . . 4 A1
Dartmouth Park Hill
N19 . . . . 4 A2
Dartmouth Park Rd
NW5 . . . . 4 A1
Dartmouth Pl W4 . 46 A4
Dartmouth Rd NW2 . 9 C2
Dartmouth Row
SE10 . . . . 52 B2
Dartmouth St
SW1 . . . . 133 C2
Dartmouth Terr
SE10 . . . . 52 C2
Darton Ct W3 . . . . 28 B1
Dartrey Twr
SW10 . . . . 157 B2
Dartrey Wlk
SW10 . . . . 157 A2
Dart St W10 . . . . . . 23 B2
Darville Rd N16 . . 7 B1
Darwen Pl E2 . . . . 25 A4
Darwin Ct NW1 . . 81 C4
Darwin Ctr SW7 . 129 B1
Darwin Ho 6
SE13 . . . . 52 B1
Darwin St SE17 . 151 C4
Daryngton Ho
SW8 . . . . 162 A1
Dashwood Ho
SE21 . . . . 76 B1
Data Point Bsns Ctr
E16 . . . . 27 C1
Datchelor Pl 14
SE5 . . . . 48 C2
Datchet Ho NW1 . 92 B4

Datchett Ho 40
E2 . . . . 24 B2 98 C3
Datchwood Ct N4 . . . 6 B1
Datchworth Ho
N1 . . . . 15 A1
Date St SE17 . . . 151 B1
Daubeney Prim Sch
E5 . . . . 18 A4
Daubeney Rd E5 . . . . 18 A4
Daubeney Twr 2
SE8 . . . . 41 B1
Dault Rd SW18 . . . . 59 B1
Dauney Ho SE1 . . 136 A3
Dave Adams Ho 3
E3 . . . . 26 B3
Davenant Ho 20
E1 . . . . 111 C3
Davenant St E1 . . . 111 C3
Davenport Ho
SE11 . . . . 135 B1
Davenport Mews 3
W12 . . . . 30 A1
Davenport Rd SE6 . 67 B1
Daventry St NW1 . 102 A4
Dave Porter Hts
SW19 . . . . 70 A4
Daver Ct SW3 . . . 144 B1
Davern Cl SE10 . . . 43 B2
Davey Cl N7 . . . . . . 14 B2
Davey Rd E9 . . . . . . 18 C1
Davey's Ct WC2 . . 120 A4
Davey St SE15 . . . . 49 B4
David Devine Ho 7
E8 . . . . 16 C3
David Game Coll
SW7 . . . . 143 B3
Davidge Ho SE1 . . 135 C3
Davidge St SE1 . . . 136 B3
David Hewitt Ho 3
E3 . . . . 34 A4
David Ho
8 Putney SW15 . . 56 C2
South Lambeth
SW8 . . . . 162 A2
David Mews W1 . . 103 A4
Davidson Gdns
SW8 . . . . 162 A2
Davidson Ho 7
N19 . . . . 13 B4
David St E15 . . . . . 19 C3
Davies Laing & Dick
Coll W1 . . . . 103 C2
Davies Mews W1 . 118 A4
Davies St W1 . . . . 118 A4
Davina Ho
Brondesbury NW2 . 10 B2
14 Hackney E5 . . . . 17 A3
Da Vinci Ct 12
SE16 . . . . 40 A1
Davis Ho 35 W12 . . 30 A2
Davis Rd W3 . . . . . 38 B4
Davisville Rd W12 . 38 C4
Dawbe Ho SE17 . . 151 B3
Dawes Ho SE17 . . 151 C3
Dawes Rd SW6 . . . 154 C2
Dawes St SE17 . . . 151 C2
Dawlish Ave SW18 . 71 A2
Dawlish Rd NW2 . . 9 C2
Dawnay Gdns
SW18 . . . . 71 C2
Dawnay Rd SW17,
SW18 . . . . 71 C2
Dawson Cres E15 . . 27 C4
Dawson Ho
28 Bethnal Green
E2 . . . . 25 B2

Dawson Ho continued
5 Camberwell SE5 . . 49 A2
Dawson Pl
W2 . . . . . . 31 C2 113 C4
Dawson Rd NW2 . . . 9 B4
Dawson St E2 . . . . 24 B3
Day Ho 2 SE5 . . . . 48 B3
Daylesford Ave
SW15 . . . . 56 C3
Daynor Ho 4
NW6 . . . . 23 C4
Daysbrook Rd
SW2 . . . . 74 B3
Dayton Gr SE15 . . . 50 B2
Deacon Ho SE11 . 149 A3
Deacon Mews N1 . 15 C1
Deacon Rd NW2 . . . 8 C2
Deacon Way SE17 151 A4
Deal Ho
Deptford SE15 . . . . 50 C4
Walworth SE17 . . . 152 B2
Deal Porters Way
SE16 . . . . 40 C3
Deal St E1 . . . . . 111 B4
Dealtry Rd SW15 . . 57 B3
Deal Wlk 3 SW9 . 163 C1
Dean Bradley St
SW1 . . . . 134 A1
Dean Cl
Hackney E9 . . . . . . 17 B3
Rotherhithe SE16 . . 32 C1
Dean Coll of London
4 N7 . . . . 5 B1
Dean Ct
Acton W3 . . . . 28 B3
South Lambeth
SW8 . . . . 162 A1
Deanery Mews
W1 . . . . 117 C2
Deanery St W1 . . . 117 C2
Dean Farrar St
SW1 . . . . 133 C2
Deanhill Ct 2
SW14 . . . . 55 A3
Deanhill Rd SW14 . 55 A3
Dean Ho
London N4 . . . . 6 B4
New Cross SE14 . . . 51 B3
Stamford Hill N16 . . 7 B3
18 Stepney E1 . . . . 32 B3
Dean Rd NW2 . . . . . 9 B2
Dean Ryle St SW1 148 A4
Dean's Bldgs
SE17 . . . . 151 C3
Deans Ct EC4 . . . 108 B1
Dean's Gateway 9
SE10 . . . . 52 C3
Deanshanger Ho 21
SE8 . . . . 40 C2
Dean St W1 . . . . . 105 B1
Dean Stanley St
SW1 . . . . 134 A1
Dean's Yd SW1 . . 133 C2
Dean Trench St
SW1 . . . . 134 A1
Dearmer Ho 6
SW2 . . . . 74 C4
Deason St E15 . . . . 27 B4
Deauville Ct
13 London SW4 . . . 61 B1
4 Rotherhithe
SE16 . . . . 40 C4

Deauville Mans 13
SW4 . . . . 61 B1
De Barowe Mews
4 Highbury N5 . . . 15 A4
1 London N5 . . . . 15 A4
Debdale Ho 20 E2 . 24 C4
De Beauvoir Cres
N1 . . . . 24 A4
De Beauvoir Ct 1
N1 . . . . 15 C1
De Beauvoir Pl 5
N1 . . . . 16 A2
De Beauvoir Prim Sch
15 N1 . . . . 16 A2
De Beauvoir Rd
N1 . . . . 16 A1
De Beauvoir Sq
N1 . . . . 16 A1
DE BEAUVOIR
TOWN 16 A1
Debenham Ct E8 . . 24 C4
Debnams Rd SE16 . 40 B2
Decima St 1 . . . . 138 A2
Deck Cl SE16 . . . . 32 C1
De Crespigny Pk
SE5 . . . . 48 C1
Deeley Rd SW8 . . 171 B4
Deepdale N4 . . . . . . 5 B4
Deepdene Gdns
SW2 . . . . 74 B4
Deepdene Ho N16 . . 6 C3
Deepdene Lo 7
SW2 . . . . 74 B4
Deepdene Mans
SW6 . . . . 164 C4
Deepdene Rd SE5,
SE24 . . . . 63 C3
Deerbrook Rd SE24,
SW2 . . . . 75 A3
Dee Rd TW9 . . . . . 54 B3
Deerdale Rd SE24 . 63 B3
Deerhurst Ho 6
SE15 . . . . 49 C4
Deerhurst Rd NW2 . 9 C2
Deer Lo SW6 . . . . . 58 A4
Deeside Rd SW17 . 71 C1
Dee St E14 . . . . . . 34 B3
Defoe Ave TW9 . . . 44 C3
Defoe Ho
Barbican EC2 . . . 108 C4
5 Stoke Newington
N16 . . . . 7 A1
Defoe Pl EC2 . . . . 108 C4
Defoe Rd
Rotherhithe
SE16 . . . . 41 B4
Stoke Newington
N16 . . . . 7 A1
De Gama Pl 3
E14 . . . . 41 C1
Dekker Ho 19 SE5 . 48 C3
Dekker Rd SE21 . . 64 A1
Delafield Ho 22
E1 . . . . 111 C1
Delaford Rd SE16 . 40 A1
Delaford St SW6 . . 154 B3
Delamere Ho 4 N4 . . 6 C4
Delamere Rd W5 . . 36 A4
Delamere St W2 . . 100 C3
Delamere Terr
W2 . . . . 100 B4
Delancey Pas NW1 82 B3
Delancey St NW1 . 82 B3
Delancey Studios
NW1 . . . . 82 B3
Delany Ho SE10 . . . 52 B4
Delarch Ho SE1 . . 136 A3
De Laune St SE17 150 A1

Delaware Rd W9 . . 88 A2
Delawyk Cres
SE24 . . . . 63 C1
Delft Way 2 SE22 . 64 A2
Delhi St N1 . . . . . . 84 B3
Delia St SW18 . . . . 71 A4
Delius Gr E15 . . . . 27 B3
Dellafield N4 . . . . . 5 C2
Dell Cl E15 . . . . . . 27 C4
Dellow Ho 6 E1 . . 32 A2
Dellow St E1 . . . . . 32 A2
Dell's Mews SW1 . 147 A3
Deloraine Ho SE8 . 51 C2
Deloraine St SE8 . . 51 C2
Delorme St W6 . . . 47 C4
Delta Bldg 8 E14 . 34 B3
Delta Ho N1 . . . . . 97 B4
Delta Pk SW18 . . . 59 A3
Delta Point 5
E2 . . . . 24 C2 99 B4
Delta St 4
E2 . . . . 24 C2 99 B4
Delverton Ho
SE17 . . . . 150 B2
Delverton Rd
SE17 . . . . 150 B2
Delvino Rd SW6 . . 165 C3
De Montfort Ct 1
SW16 . . . . 74 A1
De Montfort Rd
SW16 . . . . 74 A2
De Morgan Rd
SW6 . . . . 59 A4
Dempster Rd
SW18 . . . . 59 B2
Denbigh Cl
W11 . . . . 31 B2 113 A4
Denbigh Gdns
TW10 . . . . 54 B2
Denbigh Ho
Knightsbridge
SW1 . . . . 131 A2
7 Notting Hill W11 . 31 B3
Notting Hill
W11 . . . . 31 B2 113 A4
Denbigh Mews
SW1 . . . . 146 C3
Denbigh Pl SW1 . 146 C2
Denbigh Rd
W11 . . . . 31 B2 113 A4
Denbigh St SW1 . 147 A2
Denbigh Terr
W11 . . . . 31 B2 113 A4
Denbury Ho 48 E3 . 27 A2
Denby Ct SE11 . . . 149 A4
Dence Ho 18
E2 . . . . 24 C2 99 B4
Denchworth Ho 14
SW9 . . . . 173 B1
Dene Cl SE4 . . . . . 66 A3
Denehurst Gdns
Acton W3 . . . . 28 A1
Richmond TW10 . . . 54 C3
Dene Mans 1
NW6 . . . . 10 C2
Denesmead SE24 . . 63 B2
Denewood Rd N6 . . 3 C4
Dengie Wlk N1 . . . 86 C4
Denham Ho 32
W12 . . . . 30 A2
Denham St SE10 . . 43 C1
Denholme Rd W9 . 23 B2
Denland Ho SW8 . 163 A1
Denman Ho 1 N16 . 7 A2
Denman Rd SE15 . . 49 B1
Denman St W1 . . . 119 B3

Denmark Gr N1 . . . 85 B2
Denmark Hill SE5 . . 48 C1
Denmark Hill Sta
SE5 . . . . 48 C1
Denmark Mans 14
SE5 . . . . 48 B1
Denmark Pl
2 Bromley E3 . . . . 26 C2
Soho WC2 . . . . . . 105 C2
Denmark Rd
Camberwell SE5 . . . 48 B1
Kilburn NW6 . . . . . 23 B3
Denmark St WC2 . 105 C2
Denmead Ho
SW15 . . . . 56 B1
Denne Terr E8 . . . . 24 B4
Dennett's Gr SE14 . 50 C1
Dennett's Rd SE14 . 50 B2
Denning Cl NW8 . . 89 A3
Denning Mews
SW12 . . . . 60 C1
Denning Point E1 . 111 A2
Denning Rd NW3 . . 11 C4
Dennington Park
Mansions 12
NW6 . . . . 10 C3
Dennington Park Rd
NW6 . . . . 10 C2
Dennis Ct SE10 . . . 52 B2
Dennis Ho 4 E3 . . 26 B3
Dennison Point
E15 . . . . 19 B1
Dennis Severs' House
E1 . . . . 110 B4
Dennis Way SW4 . . 61 C4
Denny Cres SE11 . . 149 C2
Denny St SE11 . . . 149 C2
Densham Ho NW8 . 79 C1
Denstone Ho 5
SE15 . . . . 49 C4
Dent Ho SE17 . . . 152 A3
Denton NW1 . . . . . 12 C2
Denton Ho N1 . . . . 15 A1
Denton St SW18 . . 59 A1
Dents Rd SW11 . . . 60 B1
Denver Rd N16 . . . . 7 A4
Denyer Ho 1
NW5 . . . . 13 A4
Denyer St SW3 . . . 144 B4
Denys Bldg EC1 . . 107 B4
Deodar Rd SW15 . . 58 A3
Depot App NW2 . . . 9 C4
Depot Rd W12 . . . . 30 B2
Depot St SE5 . . . . . 48 C4
DEPTFORD 50 C3
Deptford Bridge
SE8 . . . . 51 C2
Deptford Bridge Sta
SE8 . . . . 51 C2
Deptford Broadway
SE8, SE14 . . . . 51 C2
Deptford Church St
SE8 . . . . 51 C3
Deptford Ferry Rd 24
E14 . . . . 41 C2
Deptford Gn SE8 . . 51 C3
Deptford Green Sch
SE14 . . . . 51 B3
Deptford Green Sch
(Annex) 3 SE14 . . 51 A3
Deptford High St
SE8 . . . . 51 C3

Deptford Park Prim
Sch ☑ SE8...........41 A1
Deptford Sta SE8 ....51 C3
Deptford Trad Est
SE8...................51 A4
Deptford Wharf
SE8...................41 B2
De Quincey Mews ☑
E16...................35 C1
Derby Ct ☑ E5.......17 C4
Derby Gate SW1...134 A4
Derby St SE11 .....149 B4
Derby Rd
Mortlake SW14.....55 A3
South Hackney E9 ..25 C4
Dereham St
E2..........24 C2 99 C3
Derby St W1 ......117 C1
Dereham Ho ☑
SE4...................65 C3
Dereham PI
EC2..........24 A1 98 B2
Derek Walcott CI
SE24.................63 A2
Dericote St E8 .....25 A4
Dering St W1 ......104 B1
Dermody Gdns
SE13.................67 C2
Dermody Rd SE13 ..67 C2
Deronda Rd SE24,
SW2.................75 A3
Derrick Ho ☑
SW2.................74 C3
Derrycombe Ho ☑
W2...................31 C4
Derry St W8 ......128 B3
Dersingham Rd
NW2 ....1 A1
Derwent Ct W1 ....92 C3
Derwent Ho ☑
☑ Hammersmith
W6...................38 C2
☑ Rotherhithe
SE16.................40 C4
Derwent Gr SE22 ...64 B3
Derwent Ho
South Kensington
SW7...............143 A4
Tower Hamlets E3 ..26 B1
Derwent St SE10 ....43 A1
Derwentwater Mans
☑ W3.................28 B1
Derwentwater Prim
Sch W3...............28 B1
Derwentwater Rd
W3...................28 B1
Desborough CI
W2..................100 B4
Desborough Ho
W14 ....155 A4
Desenfans Rd
SE21.................64 A1
Design Mus SE1 ...139 A4
Desmond St SE14 ..51 A4
Despard Ho SW2 ...74 C2
Despard Rd N19 .....4 B3
Desvignes Dr SE13 .67 C1
Dethick Ct E3 ......26 A4
Detling Ho SE17 ...152 A3
Devas St E3 ....27 A1
Deventer Cres ☑
SE22.................64 A2
De Vere Cotts W8 .128 C2
De Vere Gdns W8 .128 C3

Deverell St 137 B1
De Vere Mews
W8 ....128 C2
Devereux Ct WC2 .107 B1
Devereux Ho ☑
SW15.................56 C2
Devereux La SW13 .47 A3
Devereux Rd
SW11.................60 B1
Devitt Ho ☑ E14 ...34 A2
Devizes St N1 ......87 C3
Devonhurst PI ☑
W4...................37 C1
Devonia Rd N1 .....86 B2
Devon Mans SE1 ..138 B4
Devonport W2 ....102 A2
Devonport Ho
Greenwich SE10.....52 B4
☑ Paddington W2 ..31 C4
Devonport Rd
W12 ....39 A4
Devonport St E1 ....32 C3
Devonshire CI
W1 ....104 A4
Devonshire Ct
☑ Balham SW12 ...73 A4
☑ Richmond TW9 ..44 C2
Devonshire Dr
SE10.................52 A2
Devonshire Gdns
W4...................45 B3
Devonshire Gr
SE15.................50 A4
Devonshire Hall ☑
E9 ....17 B2
Devonshire Ho
Brondesbury NW6 ..10 B2
Newington SE17 ...150 B3
☑ Paddington W2 ..31 C4
☑ Putney SW15 ....69 B4
Westminster SW1 .147 C2
Devonshire House
Prep Sch NW3.......11 B3
Devonshire Mews ☑
W4...................38 A1
Devonshire Mews N
W1 ....104 A4
Devonshire Mews S
W1 ....104 A4
Devonshire Mews W
W1 ....103 C4
Devonshire PI
Child's Hill NW2.....1 C1
☑ Kensington W8 .128 A1
Marylebone W1 ...103 C4
Devonshire Place
Mews W1 ....103 C4
Devonshire Rd
Chiswick W4........38 A1
Marylebone W1 ...104 A4
Devonshire Row
EC2 ....110 B3
Devonshire Row
Mews W1 ....92 B1
Devonshire Sq
EC2 ....110 B2
Devonshire St
Chiswick W4........38 A1
Marylebone W1 ...104 A4
Devonshire Terr
W2 ....101 A1
Devons Rd E3 ......27 A1
Devons Road Sta
E3....................27 A1
Devon St SE15 .....50 A4
De Walden Ho
NW8 ....80 A2

De Walden St W1 .103 C3
Dewar St SE15.....64 C4
Dewberry St E14 ...34 B4
Dewey Rd N1.......85 B2
Dewhurst Rd W14 .39 C3
Dewsbury Ct ☑
W4....................37 B2
Dewsbury Rd NW10 .8 C3
Dewsbury Terr
NW1 ....82 B4
D'eynsford Rd SE5 ..48 C2
Dhonau Ho SE16 ..153 A4
Diadem Ct W1 ....105 B2
Dial Wlk The W8 ..128 B4
Diamond Est
SW17 ....72 A1
Diamond Ho ☑
E3....................26 A3
Diamond Terr
SE10.................52 B2
Diana CI ☑ SE8 ....51 B4
Diana Ho
Barnes SW13.......46 B2
☑ Brixton SW2 .....62 B2
Diana, Princess of
Wales Meml
Fountain W2 .....129 C4
Diana, Princess of
Wales Meml Wlk
W2 ....114 C3
Dibden Ho ☑ SE5 ..49 A3
Dibden St N1 ....86 C4
Dibdin Ho W9 ......78 A1
Dicey Ave NW2 .....9 B4
Dickens Ct EC1 ....96 A4
Dickens Ho
Bloomsbury WC1 ...94 A2
Kennington SE17 ..150 B1
Kilburn NW6 ....23 C2
☑ Paddington W2 ..89 C2
Dickenson Rd N8....5 A4
Dickens Sq SE1 ...137 A2
Dickens St SW8 ...170 B2
Dickinson Ho ☑
E2..........24 C2 99 B3
Dicksee Ho NW8 ...89 B1
Dick Shepherd Ct ☑
SW2 ....62 C1
Dickson Ho ☑ E1 ..32 A3
Didbin Ho N7.......14 B2
Digby Bsns Ctr E9 ..17 C2
Digby Cres N4 ......6 B2
Digby Mans W6 ....39 B1
Digby Rd E9 ....17 C2
Digby St E2 ....25 B2
Diggon St E1 ....32 C4
Dighton Ct SE17 ...48 B4
Dighton Rd SW18 ..59 B3
Dignum St N1 ......85 B2
Digswell St N7 .....14 C2
Dilke St SW3 ......159 A4
Dilston Gr SE16 ....40 B2
Dilton Gdns SW15 ..69 A3
Dimes PI ☑ W6 .....39 A2
Dimson Cres ☑ E3 ..26 C2
Dinerman Ct NW8 ..79 A4
Dingle Gdns E14 ...33 C2
Dingley La SW16 ...73 C2
Dingley PI EC1 .....97 A3
Dingley Rd EC1 ....96 C3
Dingwall Rd SW18 .71 B4
Dinmont Ho ☑ E2 ..24 C3
Dinmont St ☑ E2 ..25 A3
Dinmore Ho ☑ E9 ..25 B4

Dinnington Ho ☑
E1....................25 A1
Dinsdale Rd SE3 ...53 B4
Dinsmore Rd
SW12 ....73 A4
Dinton Ho NW8 ....90 A2
Dinwiddy Ho N1 ...84 C1
Dionis Ho SW6 ...165 B2
Disbrowe Rd W6 ..154 B3
Discovery Bsns Pk ☑
SE16.................139 C1
Discovery Dock E
E14...................42 A4
Discovery Ho ☑
E14...................34 B2
Disney PI SE1 .....137 A4
Disney St SE1 .....137 A4
Disraeli CI ☑ W4 ...37 C2
Disraeli Gdns
SW15.................58 B3
Disraeli Rd
Acton NW10 ....20 C3
Putney SW15 ....58 A3
Diss St E2....24 B2 98 C4
Distaff La EC4 .....122 C4
Distillery La W6 ....39 B1
Distillery Rd W6 ...39 B1
Distillery Wlk ☑
TW8 ....44 A4
Distin St SE11 .....149 B3
Ditchburn St E14 ..34 B2
Ditton Ho ☑ E5 ....17 A3
Divis Way SW15 ...57 A1
Dixon Clark Ct N1 ..15 A2
Dixon Ho ☑ NW10 .30 C3
Dixon Rd SE14 ....51 A2
Dixon's Alley ☑
SE16.................40 A4
Dixon Way ☑ NW10 .8 A1
Dobree Ave NW10 ..9 A1
Dobson CI NW6 ....11 C1
Dobson Ho ☑
SE14.................50 C4
Doby Ct EC4 ....123 A4
Dockers Tanner Rd ☑
E14...................41 C2
Dockhead SE1 ....139 A3
Dockhead Wharf
SE1 ....139 A4
Dock Hill Ave
SE16.................40 C4
Docklands Ct ☑
E14...................33 B3
Docklands Visitor Ctr
E14...................42 B4
Dockley Rd SE16 ..139 B1
Dockley Road Ind Est
☑ SE16 ....139 B1
Dock Offices ☑
SE16.................40 B3
Dock Rd E16........35 B2
Dock St E1 ....125 B4
Doctor Spurstowe
Almshouses ☑
E8....................17 A2
Docura Ho N7.......5 B2
Docwras Bldgs N1 .16 A2
Dodbrooke Rd
SE27.................75 A1
Dodd Ho ☑ SE16 ..40 A2
Doddington Gr
SE17 ....150 B1
Doddington PI ☑
SE17.................48 A4
Dodson St SE1 ....135 C3
Dod St E14 ....33 C3

Dog & Duck Yd
WC1 ....106 A3
Dog Kennel Hill
SE22.................64 A4
Dog Kennel Hill Sch
☑ SE22 ....64 A4
Dolben Ct SW1 ...147 C3
Dolben St SE1 .....122 B1
Dolby Rd SW6 ....164 C1
Doleman Ho ☑
SE10.................52 A2
Dolland Ho SE11 ..149 A1
Dolland St SE11 ...149 A1
Dollar Bay E14 .....42 B4
DOLLIS HILL 9 A4
Dollis Hill Sta NW2 .8 C3
Dolman Rd W4 .....37 C2
Dolman St SW4 ....62 B3
Dolphin CI ☑
SE16.................40 C4
Dolphin Ct N7 .....13 C4
Dolphin La E14 ....34 A2
Dolphin Sch SW11 .60 B2
Dolphin Sq SW1 ..147 A1
Dolphin Twr ☑
SE8...................51 B4
Dombey Ho
☑ Bermondsey
SE1 ....139 B3
☑ Shepherd's Bush
W11 ....30 C1
Dombey St WC1 ..106 C4
Domelton Ho
SW18.................59 A1
Domett CI SE5 ....63 C3
Domfe PI E5 ....17 B4
Domingo St EC1 ...96 C1
Dominion St EC2 ..109 C4
Donaghue Cotts ☑
E14...................33 A4
Donaldson Rd
NW6 ....23 B4
Donegal Ho ☑ E1 ..25 B1
Donegal St N1 .....85 A1
Doneraile Ho
SW1 ....146 A1
Doneraile St SW6 ..47 C2
Dongola Rd E1 .....33 C4
Don Gratton Ho ☑
E1....................111 B3
Donkey Alley SE22 .64 C1
Donkin Ho ☑
SE16.................40 A2
Donne Ct SE24 ....63 B1
Donne Ho
☑ Canonbury
N16...................15 C4
☑ Deptford SE14...50 C4
☑ Poplar E14 ......33 C3
Donnelly Ct SW6 ..154 B2
Donne PI SW3 ....144 B4
Donnington Ct
☑ Camden Town
NW1 ....13 A1
☑ Willesden NW10 ..9 A1
Donnington Ho ☑
SW8 ....171 B2
Donnington Prim Sch
NW10.................22 A4
Donnington Rd
NW10.................22 A4
Donovan Ct SW7 ..143 B1
Donovan Ho ☑ E1 ..32 B2
Don Phelan CI
SE5...................48 C2

Doon St SE1 . . . . 121 B2
Doradus Ct 20
SW19 . . . . 69 C3
Dora Ho
11 Shepherd's Bush
W11 . . . . 30 C2
1 Tower Hamlets
E14 . . . . 33 B3
Dorando Cl W12 . . . . . 30 A2
Doran Wlk
Stratford E15 . . . . 19 B1
Stratford Marsh
E15 . . . . 27 B4
Dora St E14 . . . . 33 B3
Dorcas Ct 8
SW18 . . . . 59 C3
Dorchester Ct
1 De Beauvoir Town
N1 . . . . 16 A1
Herne Hill SE24 . . . . . 63 B2
Knightsbridge
SW1 . . . . 131 A1
5 Streatham
SW16 . . . . 74 A2
Dorchester Dr
SE24 . . . . 63 B2
Dorchester Gr W4 . . . 38 B1
Dorchester Ho
TW9 . . . . 45 A3
Dordrecht Rd W3 . . . 29 A1
Doria Rd SW6 . . . . . . 165 A2
Doric Ho 7 E2 . . . . . . 25 C3
Doric Way NW1 . . . . . 93 B4
Doris Emmerton Ct
SW18 . . . . 59 B3
Dorking Cl SE8 . . . . . . 51 B4
Dorking Ho 1 SE1 . . 137 C2
Dorland Ct SW15 . . . . 58 B1
Dorlcote Rd SW18 . . . 72 A4
Dorleston Ct N1 . . . . . 87 C4
Dorman Way NW8 . . . 79 B4
Dormay St SW18 . . . . 59 A2
Dormstone Ho
SE17 . . . . 152 A3
Dornberg Cl SE3 . . . . 53 C3
Dorncliffe Rd
SW6 . . . . 164 B2
Dorney NW3 . . . . 12 A1
Dorney Ct SW6 . . . . . 58 A4
Dornfell St NW6 . . . . . 10 B3
Dornoch Ho 28 E3 . . 26 B3
Dornton Rd SW12,
SW17 . . . . 73 B2
Dorothy Charrington
Ho 11 SE22 . . . . 64 C3
Dorothy Rd SW11 . . . . 60 B4
Dorrell Pl 8 SW9 . . . 62 C4
Dorrien Wlk SW16 . . 73 C2
Dorrington Point 20
E3 . . . . 27 A2
Dorrington St
EC1 . . . . 107 B4
Dorrit Ho 2 W11 . . . 30 C1
Dorrit St SE1 . . . . 137 A4
Dorset Bldgs EC4 . . 108 A1
Dorset Cl NW1 . . . . . 102 C4
Dorset Ct 3 N1 . . . . 16 A1
Dorset Mans 2
W6 . . . . 47 C4
Dorset Mews
SW1 . . . . 132 A2
Dorset Pl E15 . . . . 19 C2
Dorset Rd SW8 . . . . . 162 C2
Dorset Rise EC4 . . . . 108 A1
Dorset Sq NW1 . . . . . 90 C1
Dorset St W1 . . . . 103 A3

Dorton Cl 6 SE15 . . . 49 A3
Dorville Cres W6 . . . . 39 A3
Doughty Ct 11 E1 . . . 32 A1
Doughty Mews
WC1 . . . . 94 C1
Doughty St WC1 . . . . 94 C1
Douglas Bldgs
SE1 . . . . 137 A4
Douglas Ct 1
NW6 . . . . 10 C1
Douglas Gracey Ho 7
SW18 . . . . 70 A4
Douglas Ho
Putney SW15 . . . . 57 C1
Westminster SW1 . . 147 B3
Douglas Johnstone
Ho SW6 . . . . 154 C3
Douglas Mews NW2 . 1 A1
Douglas Path E14 . . . 42 B1
Douglas Rd
Islington N1 . . . . 15 B1
Kilburn NW6 . . . . 23 B4
6 Newham E16 . . . . . 35 C4
Douglas Rd N N1 . . . 15 B2
Douglas Rd S N1 . . . 15 B2
Douglas St SW1 . . . . 147 B3
Douglas Waite Ho
NW6 . . . . 11 B1
Douglas Way SE8 . . . 51 B3
Doulton Ho SE11 . . . 149 A4
Doulton Mews 4
NW6 . . . . 11 A2
Dounesforth Gdns
SW18 . . . . 71 A3
Douro Pl W8 . . . . 128 B2
Douro St E3 . . . . 26 C3
Douthwaite Sq 11
E1 . . . . 125 C2
Dovecote Gdns 6
SW14 . . . . 55 C4
Dove Ct EC2 . . . . 109 B1
Dovedale Cotts 8
SW11 . . . . 168 C2
Dovedale Ho N16 . . . 6 C4
Dovedale Rd SE22 . . 65 A1
Dovehouse St
SW3 . . . . 144 A1
Dove Mews SW7 . . . 143 A2
Dovercourt Rd
SE22 . . . . 64 B1
Dover Ct
Clerkenwell EC1 . . . . 96 A2
17 Greenwich SE10 . 52 A2
Dove Rd N1 . . . . 15 C2
Doverfield Rd
SW2 . . . . 74 A4
Dover Flats SE1 . . . . 152 B3
Dover Ho
Brixton SW9 . . . . 48 A2
11 Deptford SE15 . . . 50 B4
Dover House Rd
SW15 . . . . 57 A2
Dover Mans 16
SW9 . . . . 62 C4
Dover Row E2 . . . . . . 24 C3
Dover Park Dr
SW15 . . . . 57 A1
Dover St W1 . . . . 118 C2
Dover Terr TW9 . . . . . 44 C1
Dover Yd W1 . . . . 118 C2
Doves Yd N1 . . . . 85 B3
Doveton St 4 E1 . . . 25 B1
Doveton St 8 E1 . . . 25 B1
Dove Wlk SW1 . . . . . 145 B2
Dovey Cl 4 N1 . . . . . 14 C1

Dowdeny Cl 12
NW5 . . . . 13 B3
Dowdeswell Cl
SW15 . . . . 56 A3
Dowding Ho N6 . . . . . 3 C4
Dowell Ho SE21 . . . . 76 B1
Dowes Ho 1
SW16 . . . . 74 A1
Dowgate Hill EC4 . . 123 B4
Dowland St W10 . . . . 23 A2
Dowlas St SE5 . . . . . . 49 A3
Dowlen Ct 14 E14 . . 41 C4
Dowler Ho 32 E1 . . 111 C1
Downbarton Ho 11
SW9 . . . . 173 B4
Downbury Mews 13
SW18 . . . . 58 C2
Downend Ct 1
SE15 . . . . 49 A4
Downer's Cotts
SW4 . . . . 61 B3
Downey Ho 6 E1 . . . 25 C1
Downfield Cl W9 . . . . 88 A1
Downham Ct 1
N1 . . . . 15 C1
Downham Rd N1 . . . . 15 C1
Downing Ho
2 North Kensington
W10 . . . . 30 C3
4 Putney SW15 . . . . 56 C2
Downing St SW1 . . . 134 A4
Down Pl W6 . . . . 39 A1
Down St Mews
W1 . . . . 118 A1
Downs Ct 18 E8 . . . . 17 A3
Downsell Prim Sch
E15 . . . . 19 C4
Downsell Rd E15 . . . . 19 C4
Downshire Hill
NW3 . . . . 11 C4
Downside 2
SW15 . . . . 58 A2
Downside Cres
NW3 . . . . 12 A3
Downs La 5 E5 . . . . . 17 A4
Downs Park Rd E5,
E8 . . . . 16 C3
Downs Rd E5, N16 . . 16 C4
Down St W1 . . . . 118 A1
Downsview Sch
E5 . . . . 17 A4
Downton Ave SW2 . . 74 B2
Downtown Rd
SE16 . . . . 41 A4
Dowrey St N1 . . . . 85 B4
Dowson Cl SE5 . . . . . 63 C3
Dowson Ct SE13 . . . . 67 C4
Dowson Ho 8 E1 . . . 32 C3
Doyce St SE1 . . . . . . 136 C4
Doyle Gdns NW10 . . 22 A4
Doyle Ho W3 . . . . 37 A4
D'Oyley St SW1 . . . . 145 B4
Doynton St N19 . . . . 4 A2
Draco St SE17 . . . . . . 48 B4
Dragon Ct WC2 . . . . 106 B2
Dragon Rd SE15 . . . . 49 A4
Dragon Yd WC1 . . . . 106 B2
Dragoon Rd SE8 . . . . 41 B1
Dragor Rd NW10 . . . 20 B1
Drake Cl 30 SE16 . . . 40 C4
Drake Croft N16 . . . . 6 C2
Drake Ct 5 W12 . . . . 39 A4
Drakefell Rd SE4,
SE14 . . . . 65 C4
Drakefield Rd
SW17 . . . . 72 C1

Drake Ho
2 Limehouse
E14 . . . . 33 A2
20 Stepney E1 . . . . . . 32 B4
Drakeley Ct N5 . . . . . 15 A4
Drake Rd SE4 . . . . . . 66 C4
Drakes Ctyd NW6 . . 10 B1
Drake St WC1 . . . . . . 106 C3
Drama Ctr London
EC1 . . . . 95 C1
Draper Ho SE1 . . . . . 150 B4
Draper Pl N1 . . . . 86 B4
Drapers Almhouses 5
E3 . . . . 26 C2
Drapers Gdns
EC2 . . . . 109 C2
Draper's Rd E15 . . . . 19 C4
Drapers Way 8
SE16 . . . . 153 C4
Drappers Way 8
SE16 . . . . 153 C4
Draycott Ave SW3 . . 144 B3
Draycott Cl SE5 . . . . 48 C3
Draycott Cl SW11 . . 168 A4
Draycott Ho SW3 . . 144 C3
Draycott Pl SW3 . . . 144 C3
Draycott Terr
SW3 . . . . 145 A3
Drayford Cl W9 . . . . . 23 B1
Dray Gdns SW2 . . . . 62 B2
Draymans Ct 4
SW9 . . . . 62 B4
Draymans Mews
SE15 . . . . 49 B1
Drayson Mews
W8 . . . . 127 C3
Drayton Ct SW10 . . 143 A1
Drayton Gdns
SW10 . . . . 143 A1
Drayton Ho 14 SE5 . 48 C3
Drayton Park Mews 12
N5 . . . . 14 C3
Drayton Park Prim
Sch 13 N5 . . . . 14 C3
Drayton Park Sta
N5 . . . . 14 C3
Drayton Pk N5, N7 . . 14 C4
Drayton Rd NW10 . . 21 B4
DRCA Business Ctr
SW11 . . . . 169 C3
Dreadnought St
SE10 . . . . 43 A3
Dresden Cl NW6 . . . . 11 A2
Dresden Ho
5 Clapham
SW11 . . . . 169 B2
Lambeth SE11 . . . . . 149 A4
Dresden Rd N19 . . . . 4 C3
Dressington Ave
SE4 . . . . 66 C1
Drewett Ho 51 E1 . . 111 C1
Drew Ho 5 SW16 . . 74 A1
Drewstead La
SW16 . . . . 73 C2
Drewstead Rd
SW16 . . . . 73 C2
Driffield Rd E3 . . . . . 26 A3
Driftway Ho 12 E3 . . 26 B3
Drinkwater Ho 11
SE5 . . . . 48 C3
Drive Mans 1
SW6 . . . . 164 B2
Drive The
Acton W3 . . . . 28 B3
Harlesden NW10 . . . 21 B4
Hendon NW11 . . . . . 1 A4
Islington N7 . . . . 14 B2

Dr Johnson Ave
SW17 . . . . 73 A1
Dr Johnson's House
EC4 . . . . 107 C1
Droitwich Cl SE26 . . 76 C1
Dromore Rd SW15 . . 58 A1
Dron Ho E1 . . . . 32 B4
Droop St W10 . . . . . . 23 A1
Drovers Ct SE13 . . . . 67 B4
Drovers Pl SE15 . . . . 50 A3
Drovers Way N7 . . . . 14 C3
Druce Rd SE21 . . . . . 64 A1
Druid St SE1 . . . . 138 C3
Drummer Lo N7 . . . . 5 B1
Drummond Cres
NW1 . . . . 93 B4
Drummond Gate
SW1 . . . . 147 C2
Drummond Ho 13
E2 . . . . 24 C3
Drummond Rd
SE16 . . . . 40 A3
Drummonds Pl
TW9 . . . . 54 A3
Drummond St
NW1 . . . . 92 C2
Drury Ho SW8 . . . . . 170 C4
Drury La WC2 . . . . . 106 B1
Dryad St SW15 . . . . . 57 C4
Dryburgh Ho SW1 . 146 B2
Dryburgh Mans
SW15 . . . . 57 B4
Dryburgh Rd
SW15 . . . . 57 B4
Dryden Bldg 10
E1 . . . . 111 B2
Dryden Ct SW4 . . . . . 61 C2
Dryden Ct SE11 . . . . 149 C3
Dryden Ho
6 Camberwell
SE5 . . . . 49 A2
16 Stoke Newington
N16 . . . . 7 A1
Dryden St WC2 . . . . 106 B1
Dryfield Wlk
SE8 . . . . 51 C4
Drysdale Flats 3
E8 . . . . 16 B3
Drysdale Ho 18
E2 . . . . 24 A2 98 B4
Drysdale Pl
N1 . . . . 24 A2 98 B4
Drysdale St
N1 . . . . 24 A2 98 B4
Dublin Ave E8 . . . . . . 24 C4
Ducal St 25
E2 . . . . 24 B2 99 A3
Ducane Cl 6 W12 . . 30 B3
Du Cane Ct SW12 . . 72 C3
Du Cane Rd W12 . . . 29 C3
Ducavel Ho SW2 . . . 74 B3
Duchess Mews
W1 . . . . 104 B3
Duchess of Bedford
Ho W8 . . . . 127 B4
Duchess of Bedford's
Wlk W8 . . . . 127 B3
Duchess St W1 . . . . 104 B3
Duchy St SE1 . . . . . . 121 C2
Ducie Ho 2 SW15 . . 57 B2
Ducie St SW4 . . . . . . 62 B3
Duckett St E1 . . . . . . 33 A4
Duck La W1 . . . . 105 B1
Du Cros Rd W3 . . . . . 29 A1

DUDDEN HILL....... 8 C3
Dudden Hill La
NW10.............. 8 B3
Dudley Ct
Marylebone W1..... **102** C1
St Giles WC2....... **106** A2
Dudley Ho
� Brixton SW9... **173** B2
Paddington W2..... **101** B3
Dudley Rd
Kilburn NW6....... 23 B3
Richmond TW9..... 44 B1
Dudley St W2..... **101** B3
Dudmaston Mews
SW3.............. **143** C2
Duffell Ho SE11... **149** A1
Dufferin Ave EC1... **97** B1
Dufferin Ct EC1.... **97** B1
Dufferin St EC1.... **97** A1
Duffield Ho N4..... 6 B4
Duff Miller Coll
SW7.............. **129** A1
Duff St E14........ 34 A3
Dufour's Pl W1.... **105** A1
Dugard Way SE11 **150** A3
Dugdale Ho N7.. **13** C3
SW2.............. 62 C1
Dudley St W2..... **101** B3

Duke Humphrey Rd
SE3............... 53 A1
Duke of Wellington Pl
SW1, W1....... **131** C4
Duke of York's Sq
SW3............. **145** A3
Duke of York St
SW1............. **119** A2
Duke Rd W4....... 37 C1
Duke St Hill SE1 **123** C2
Duke St St James's
SW1............. **119** A2
Duke's Ave W4..... 37 C1
Dukes Ct
Dulwich SE22...... 76 C3
East Dulwich SE22.. 65 A2
Lewisham SE13..... 52 B1
Mortlake SW14..... 45 C1
Dukes Gate 🔳 W4.. 37 B2
Dukes Head Yd N6.. 4 A3
Duke Shore Wharf
E14.............. 33 B2
Dukes La W8.... **128** A4
Duke's Mews W1 **103** C2
Dukes Pl EC3.... **110** B1
Dukes Point N6... 4 A3
Duke's Rd WC1.... 93 C3
Duke St W1...... **103** C1
Duke Street Mans
W1.............. **103** C1
Duke's Yd W1.... **117** C4
Dulas St N4....... 5 B3
Dulford St
W11....... 31 A2 **112** A4
Dulka Rd SW11..... 60 B2
Dulverton NW1.... 83 A3
Dulverton Mans
WC1............. **95** A1
DULWICH......... 76 A2
Dulwich Coll SE21.. 76 A2
Dulwich Coll Prep Sch
SE21............. 76 A1
Dulwich Com Hospl
SE22............. 64 A3

Dulwich Comm
SE21............. 76 A3
Dulwich Hamlet Jun
Sch SE21......... 63 C1
Dulwich Lawn Cl
SE22............. 64 B2
Dulwich L Ctr
SE22............. 64 C3
Dulwich Mead
SE24............. 63 B1
Dulwich Mews
🔳 East Dulwich
SE22............. 64 B3
East Dulwich SE22.. 64 B3
Dulwich Oaks The
SE21............. 76 B1
Dulwich Picture Gall
SE21............. 76 A4
Dulwich Rd SE24... 63 A1
DULWICH
VILLAGE....... 76 A4
Dulwich Village
SE21............. 64 A1
Dulwich Village CE Inf
Sch SE21......... 64 A1
Dumain Ct SE11.. **150** A3
Du Maurier Ho 🔳
NW3............. 12 B3
Dumbarton Ct 🔳
SW2............. 74 A4
Dumbarton Rd
SW2............. 62 A1
Dumont Rd N16.... 7 A1
Dumphreys Ho 🔳
SW4............. 73 C4
Dumpton Pl NW1.. **12** C1
Dunbar St SE27..... 75 B1
Dunbar Wharf 🔳
E14.............. 33 B2
Dunboyne Rd NW3 **12** B3
Dunbridge Ho
SW15............ 56 B1
Dunbridge St
Bethnal Green
E2......... 24 C1 **99** C2
Bethnal Green E2.... 25 A1
Duncan Ct 🔳 E14.. 34 B4
Duncan Gr W3..... 29 A3
Duncan Ho 🔳
NW3............. 12 B1
Duncannon Ho
SW1............. **147** C1
Duncannon St
WC2............. **120** A3
Duncan Rd
Hackney E8........ 25 A4
Richmond TW9..... 54 A3
Duncan St N1..... 86 A2
Duncan Terr N1... 86 A2
Dunch St 🔳 E1.... 32 A3
Duncombe Ho 🔳
SW19............ 69 C3
Duncombe Prim Sch
N19.............. 5 A3
Duncombe Rd N19.. 4 C3
Duncrievie Rd
SE13............. 67 C1
Dundalk Ho 🔳 E1.. 32 B3
Dundalk Rd SE4... 66 A4
Dundas Ho 🔳 E2.. 25 B3
Dundas Rd SE15... 50 B1
Dundee Ct 🔳 E1... 32 A1
Dundee Ho W9.... **88** C4
Dundee St E1..... 32 A1
Dundee Wharf
E14.............. 33 B2

Dundonald Rd
NW10............ 22 C4
Dundry Ho 🔳
SE26............. 76 C1
Dunelm Gr SE27... 75 B1
Dunelm St E1..... 32 C3
Dunford Rd N7..... 14 B4
Dungarvan Ave
SW15............ 56 C3
Dungeness Ho
SW18............ 59 B3
Dunhill Point 🔳
SW15............ 69 A3
Dunkeld Ho 🔳
E14.............. 34 C3
Dunlace Rd E5.... 17 C4
Dunlin Ct 🔳 SE21. 75 C2
Dunlin Ho 🔳 SE16. 40 C2
Dunloe Ct 🔳 E2... 24 B3
Dunloe St E2..... 24 B3
Dunlop Pl SE16... **139** A1
Dunmore Point 🔳
E2............... 24 B2 **98** C3
Dunmore Rd NW6.. 23 A4
Dunmow Ho SE11 **149** A2
Dunmow Rd E15... 19 C4
Dunmow Wlk N1... 86 C4
Dunnage Cres
SE16............. 41 A2
Dunne Mews 🔳
NW5............. 13 B3
Dunnet Ho 🔳 E3.. 26 B3
Dunnico Ho SE17. **152** A2
Dunnock Ct 🔳
SE21............. 75 C2
Dun's Pas WC1... **106** B2
Dunn St E8....... 16 B3
Dunollie Pl NW5... 13 B3
Dunollie Rd NW5.. 13 B3
Dunoon Ho N1.... 84 C3
Dunraven Ho 🔳
TW9............. 44 B2
Dunraven Rd W12. 29 C1
Dunraven Sch
SW16............ 74 B1
Dunraven St W1.. **117** A4
Dunrobin Ct NW3.. 11 A3
Dunsany Rd W14.. 39 C3
Dunsfold Ho 🔳
SW2............. 74 B4
Dunsford Way
SW15............ 57 A1
Dunsmure Rd N16.. 7 A3
Dunstable Ct 🔳
SE3............... 53 C3
Dunstable Mews
W1.............. **103** C4
Dunstable Rd TW10,
TW9............. 54 A3
Dunstall Ho 🔳
SE15............. 49 C2
Dunstan Ho SE4... 51 B1
Dunstan Hos 🔳
E1............... 32 B4
Dunstan Rd NW11. 1 C3
Dunstan's Gr SE22. 65 A1
Dunstan's Rd SE22 64 C1
Dunster Ct EC3.. **124** B4
Dunster Gdns
NW6............. 10 B1
Dunsterville Way
SE1............. **137** C3
Dunston Rd
Clapham SW11.... **169** C1
Hackney E8........ 24 B4
Dunston St E8.... 24 B4

Dunton Ho 🔳
SW16............ 74 A1
Dunton Rd SE1... **152** C3
Duntshill Rd SW18. 71 A3
Dunworth Mews
W11............. 31 B3
Duplex Ride SW1 **131** A3
Durand Gdns
SW9............. **173** A3
Durand Prim Sch
SW9............. **173** A4
Durant St E2... 24 C2 **99** B4
Durban Ho 28 🔳
W12............. 30 A2
Durdans Ho 🔳
NW1............. **13** B3
Durfey Pl SE5..... 48 C3
Durford Cres
SW15............ 69 A3
Durham Ct
Brockley SE4....... 66 C4
🔳 Kilburn NW6..... 23 C3
Durham Ho
🔳 Dartmouth Pk
NW5............. 4 B1
Lisson Gr NW8..... 90 B3
Durham House St
WC2............. 120 B3
Durham Pl SW3.. **144** C1
Durham Rd N4, N7.. 5 B2
Durham Row E1... 33 A4
Durham St SE11.. **162** C4
Durham Terr W2.. **100** A2
Durley Rd N16..... 7 A4
Durlock Ho 🔳
SW9............. **173** B4
Durlston Rd E5.... 7 C2
Durnford St 🔳
SE10............. 52 B4
Durnsford Ave SW18,
SW19............ 70 C2
Durnsford Rd SW18,
SW19............ 70 C2
Durrell Rd SW6.. **164** C3
Durrels Ho W14.. **141** A4
Durrington Rd E5.. 18 A4
Durrington Twr 🔳
SW8............. **171** A2
Durrisdeer Ho
NW2............. 10 B4
Durston NW5..... 12 C3
Durward St E1.... 32 A4
Durweston Mews
W1.............. **103** A4
Durweston St
W1.............. **103** A3
Dutch Yd SW18... 58 C2
Dutton Ho SW2... 75 A3
Dutton St SE10... 52 B2
Dwight Ct 🔳 SW6. 164 B2
Dycer Ho 🔳 E9... 17 C2
Dye House La E3.. 26 C4
Dyer Ho SE4...... 51 A1
Dyer's Bldgs EC1 **107** B3
Dyer's La SW15... 57 A3
Dykes Ct 🔳 SW2.. 74 B3
Dylan Rd 🔳 SE24. 63 A3
Dylways SE5...... 63 C3
Dymchurch Ho 🔳
E5............... 17 A3
Dymes Path SW19. 69 C2
Dymock St SW6... 59 A4
Dyne Rd NW6..... 10 B1
Dynevor Rd
Richmond TW10.... 54 A2
Shacklewell N16... 7 A1

Dyott St
Soho WC1......... **105** C2
St Giles WC1, WC2 **106** A2
Dysart St
EC2.......... 24 A1 **98** A1
Dyson Ho 🔳 SE10 **43** B1

E

Eade Rd N4....... 6 B4
Eagle Cl SE16..... 40 B1
Eagle Ct
🔟 Dulwich SE21... 75 C2
Holborn EC1....... **108** A4
Eagle Dwellings
EC1.............. **97** A4
Eagle Ho
🔳 Bethnal Green
E1............... 25 A1
Finsbury Pk N7.... 5 B1
Eagle Hts 🔟 SW11. 60 A4
Eagle Lo NW11.... 1 B4
Eagle Mans N16... 16 B3
Eagle Mews N1... 16 A2
Eagle Pl
South Kensington
SW7............. **143** A2
St James SW1..... **119** A3
Eagle St WC1..... **106** C3
Eagle Wharf SE1. **124** C1
Eagle Wharf Rd
N1............... 87 A2
Eagle Works
E1............ 24 B1 **99** A1
Eagling Cl E3..... 26 C2
Ealing, Hammersmith
& West London Coll
W14............. **140** A2
Eamann Casey Ho 🔳
SW9............. **173** C3
Eamont Ct NW8... 80 B2
Eamont St NW8... 80 B2
Eardley Cres SW5 **141** C1
Earldom Rd SW15. 57 B3
Earle Ho SW1.... **147** C3
Earlham St WC2.. **106** A1
Earl Ho NW1...... 90 B1
Earlom Ho WC1... 95 B3
Earl Rd SW14..... 55 B3
EARL'S COURT... **141** C3
Earls Court Ex Ctr
SW5............. **141** B1
Earl's Court Gdns
SW5............. **142** A3
Earls Court Rd SW5,
W8.............. **141** C4
Earl's Court Sq
SW5............. **142** A2
Earls Court Sta
SW5............. **141** C3
Earlsferry Way N1.. 14 A1
EARLSFIELD...... 71 B3
Earlsfield Prim Sch
SW18............ 71 B3
Earlsfield Rd
SW18............ 71 B4
Earlsfield Sta
SW18............ 71 B3
Earlsmead Rd
NW10............ 22 B2
Earl St EC2...... **110** A4
Earls Terr W8.... **127** A1
Earlsthorpe Mews 🔳
SW12............ 60 C1
Earlstoke St EC1.. **96** A4

Earlston Gr E9 . . . . .25 A4
Earls Wlk W8 . . . . **127** B1
Earlswood Cl **10**
SE10 . . . . .43 A1
Earlswood Ho **2**
SW2 . . . . .74 B3
Earlswood St SE10 . .43 A1
Earnshaw Ho SW1 . . .82 B4
Earnshaw St WC1,
WC2 . . . .**105** C2
Earsby St W14 . . . . . .**140** B4
Earth Galleries
SW7 . . . .**129** C1
Eashing Point **5**
SW15 . . . . .69 A3
Easleys Mews W1 . .**103** C2
EAST ACTON 29 A1
East Acton Arc
W3 . . . . .29 B3
East Acton Ct W3 . . .29 B3
East Acton La W3 . . .29 A2
East Acton Prim Sch
W3 . . . . .29 B3
East Acton Sta
W12 . . . . .29 B3
East Arbour St E1 . .32 C3
East Bank N16 . . . . . .7 A4
East Block **5** E1 . . . .32 C2
Eastbourne Ave
W3 . . . . .28 C3
Eastbourne Gdns
SW14 . . . . .55 B4
Eastbourne Mews
W2 . . . .**101** A2
Eastbourne Ho W4 . .45 B4
Eastbourne Terr
W2 . . . .**101** A2
Eastbury Gr W4 . . . . .38 A1
Eastbury Terr E1 . . . .25 C1
Eastcastle St W1 . .**105** A2
Eastcheap EC3 . . . . .**124** A4
East Churchfield Rd
W3 . . . . .28 C1
Eastcote St SW9 . . .**172** C1
East Cross Route
Bow E3 . . . . .26 C4
Hackney Wick E9 . . .18 B3
Eastdown Ho E8 . . . .16 C4
Eastdown Pk SE13 . .67 C3
East Dulwich Gr
SE22 . . . . .64 A2
East Dulwich Rd SE15,
SE22 . . . . .64 C2
East Dulwich Sta
SE22 . . . . .64 B4
East End Computing &
Bsns Coll **10** E1 . . .32 A3
Eastern Rd SE4 . . . . .66 C3
East Ferry Rd E14 . . .42 A2
Eastfields Ave
SW18 . . . . .58 C3
Eastfields Rd W3 . . .28 B4
Eastfield St E14 . . . .33 A4
East Harding St
EC4 . . . .**107** C2
East Heath Rd NW3 . . .2 C1
East Hill SW18 . . . . . .59 B2
East India Bldgs **9**
E14 . . . . .33 C2
East India Ct **7**
SE16 . . . . .40 B4
East India Dock Basin
E14 . . . . .35 A2

East India Dock Rd
E14 . . . . .34 A2
East India Dock Road
Tunnel **16** E14 . . . .34 C3
East India Sta E14 . .34 C2
East La **5** SE16 . . . .**139** B3
Eastlake Ho NW8 . . .89 C1
Eastlake Rd SE5 . . . .48 B1
Eastlands Cres
SE21 . . . . .64 B1
Eastleigh Wlk **5**
SW15 . . . . .68 C4
Eastman Dental Hospl
WC1 . . . . .94 C2
Eastman Ho **4**
SW4 . . . . .61 B1
Eastman Rd W3 . . . . .37 C4
Eastmearn Rd SE21,
SE27 . . . . .75 B2
East Mount St E1 . . .32 A4
Eastney St SE10 . . . .42 C1
Easton Ho **4** SE27 . .75 A1
Easton St WC1 . . . . . .95 B2
East Parkside
SE10 . . . . .43 B4
East Pas EC1 . . . . . .**108** C4
East Plaza E14 . . . . . .34 A1
East Point **4** SE1 . .**153** B2
East Poultry Ave
EC1 . . . .**108** A3
East Putney Sta
SW15 . . . . .58 A2
East Rd
Chelsea SW1 . . . . . .**145** B1
Shoreditch N1 . . . . . .97 C4
East Row W10 . . . . . .23 A1
East St SE17 . . . . . .**151** B2
East Row SW8 . . . . .**162** A1
EAST SHEEN 55 C3
East Sheen Ave
SW14 . . . . .55 C3
East Sheen Prim Sch
SW14 . . . . .56 A3
East Smithfield
E1 . . . .**125** A3
East St SE17 . . . . . .**151** B2
East Surrey Gr
SE15 . . . . .49 B3
East Tenter St E1 . .**111** A1
Eastvale W3 . . . . .29 B1
East View NW3 . . . . . .2 C2
Eastway E3, E9 . . . . .26 A4
Eastwell Ho SE1 . . .**137** C2
Eastwick Ct **2**
SW19 . . . . .69 C2
Eastwood Cl **2**
N7 . . . . .14 C3
Eaton Cl SW1 . . . . . .**145** B3
Eaton Dr SW9 . . . . . .63 A3
Eaton Gate SW1 . . .**145** B4
Eaton Ho
Battersea SW11 . . . .**167** C3
23 Limehouse E14 . .33 B2
Eaton House Sch
SW1 . . . .**145** B4
Eaton House The
Manor Sch SW4 . . . .61 A3
Eaton La SW1 . . . . . .**132** B1
Eaton Mans SW1 . . .**145** B3
Eaton Mews N
SW1 . . . .**131** C1
Eaton Mews S
SW1 . . . .**145** C4
Eaton Mews W
SW1 . . . .**145** C4
Eaton Pl SW1 . . . . . .**131** C1
Eaton Row SW1 . . . .**132** C1

Eaton Sq SW1 . . . . . .**131** C1
Eaton Sq Pre-Prep
Sch SW1 . . . .**146** A4
Eaton Sq Prep Sch
SW1 . . . .**146** C2
Eaton Terr
Belgravia SW1 . . . . .**145** C4
Bow E3 . . . . .26 A2
Eaton Terr Mews
SW1 . . . .**145** B4
Eatonville Rd
SW17 . . . . .72 B2
Eatonville Villas
SW17 . . . . .72 B2
Ebbisham Dr SW8 .**162** C3
Ebbsfleet Rd NW2 . .10 A4
Ebenezer Ho
SE11 . . . .**150** A3
Ebenezer Mussel Ho
2 E2 . . . . .25 B3
Ebenezer St N1 . . . . .97 B4
Ebley Cl SE15 . . . . . .49 B4
Ebner St SW18 . . . . .59 A2
Ebony Ct NW10 . . . . . .8 B2
Ebony Ho
27 Bethnal Green
E2 . . . . .24 C2 **99** B3
3 West Hampstead
NW3 . . . . .11 A2
Ebor Cots SW15 . . . .68 A1
Ebor St E1,
E2 . . . . .24 B1 **98** C2
Eburne Rd N7 . . . . . . .5 A1
Ebury Bridge Rd
SW1 . . . .**145** C1
Ebury Mews
Belgravia SW1 . . . . .**146** A4
West Norwood
SE27 . . . . .75 A1
Ebury Mews E
SW1 . . . .**132** A1
Ebury Sq SW1 . . . . .**145** C3
Ebury St SW1 . . . . . .**146** A4
Ecclesbourne Rd
N1 . . . . .15 B1
Eccles Cl SE11 . . . . .**149** A1
Eccles Rd SW11 . . . .60 B3
Eccleston Ho **1**
SW2 . . . . .62 C1
Eccleston Mews
SW1 . . . .**131** C1
Eccleston Pl SW1 . .**146** A4
Eccleston Sq
SW1 . . . .**146** B3
Eccleston Sq Mews
SW1 . . . .**146** C3
Eccleston St SW1 . .**146** A4
Eckford St N1 . . . . . .85 B2
Eckstein Rd SW11 . .60 A3
Edans Ct W12 . . . . . .38 B4
Edbrooke Rd W9 . . . .23 C1
Eddisbury Ho **7**
SE26 . . . . .76 C1
Eddiscombe Rd
SW6 . . . .**165** A2
Eddison Ct N19 . . . . . .5 A2
Eddystone Rd SE4 . .66 A2
Eddystone Twr
SE8 . . . . .41 A1
Edenbridge Cl **29**
SE16 . . . . .40 A1
Edenbridge Rd E9 . .17 C1
Eden Cl
Child's Hill NW3 . . . . .1 C2
Kensington W8 . . . .**127** C2
Edendale W3 . . . . . . .28 A2

Eden Gr
Islington N7 . . . . . . .14 B3
Willesden NW10 . . . . .9 A2
Edenham Way
W10 . . . . .31 B4
Eden High Sch **9**
W6 . . . . .38 C1
Eden Ho
18 Battersea
SW11 . . . . .60 A4
Lisson Gr NW8 . . . . .90 A1
Edenhurst Ave
SW6 . . . . .58 B4
Eden Lodge NW6 . . . .9 C1
Eden Mews SW17 . .71 B1
Edensmuir Ct SE3 . .53 C3
Edensor Gdns W4 . .46 A3
Edensor Rd W4 . . . . .46 A3
Edenvale St SW6 . .**166** C1
Eden Way E3 . . . . . . .26 B4
Edgar Ho
Homerton E9 . . . . . . .18 A3
South Lambeth
SW8 . . . .**162** A2
Edgar Kail Way
SE22 . . . . .64 A3
Edgarley Terr
SW6 . . . .**164** A3
Edgar Rd E3 . . . . . . .27 A2
Edgar Wallace Cl **4**
SE15 . . . . .49 A3
Edgcott Ho **2**
W10 . . . . .30 B4
Edgecombe Ho
4 London SE5 . . . .49 A1
Putney SW19 . . . . . . .70 A4
Edgecote Cl **7**
W3 . . . . .28 B1
Edgehill Ho **4**
SW9 . . . . .48 A1
Edgeley La SW4 . . . .61 C4
Edgeley Rd SW4 . . . .61 C4
Edgel St SW18 . . . . . .59 A3
Edge St
W8 . . . . .31 C1 **113** C2
Edgeworth Ho
NW8 . . . . .78 C4
Edgson Ho SW1 . . .**146** A2
Edgware Acad
WC2 . . . .**106** B1
Edgware Rd W1, W2,
NW1, NW8 . . . .**102** A3
Edgware Road Sta
(Bakerloo) NW1 . . .**102** A3
Edgware Road Sta
(Met, Distr, Circle)
NW1 . . . .**102** B3

Ear–Edw 209

Edithna St SW9 . . . . .62 A4
Edith Neville Cotts
NW1 . . . . .93 B4
Edith Neville Prim Sch
NW1 . . . . .83 B1
Edith Ramsay Ho **2**
E1 . . . . .33 A4
Edith Rd
Stratford New Town
E15 . . . . .19 C3
West Kensington
W14 . . . .**140** B3
Edith Row SW6 . . . .**166** B4
Edith St E2 . . . . .24 C3
Edith Summerskill Ho
SW6 . . . .**154** A2
Edith Terr SW10 . . .**156** C2
Edith Villas W14 . . .**140** C2
Edith Yd SW10 . . . . .**157** A2
Edmeston Cl E9 . . . .18 A2
Edmond Ct SE14 . . . .50 B2
Edmonton Ct **5**
SE16 . . . . .40 B3
Edmund Halley Way
SE10 . . . . .43 A4
Edmund Ho
Kensington SE17 . .**150** B1
New Cross Gate
SE14 . . . . .51 B2
Edmundsbury Ct Est
18 SW9 . . . . .62 B3
Edmund St SE5 . . . . .48 C3
Edmund Waller Prim
Sch SE14 . . . . .50 C1
Ednam Ho SE15 . . . .49 C4
Edna St SW11 . . . . .**168** A3
Edred Ho E9 . . . . . . .18 A4
Edrich Ho SW4 . . . .**172** A3
Edric Ho SW1 . . . . .**147** C4
Edric Rd SE14 . . . . . .50 C3
Edridge Ho **8**
SE27 . . . . .75 A1
Edward Alleyn Ho
SE21 . . . . .64 A1
Edward Ct **2** E16 . . .35 C4
Edward Dodd Ct
N1 . . . . .97 C4
Edward Edward's Ho
SE1 . . . .**122** A1
Edwardes Pl W8 . . .**127** A1
Edwardes Sq W8 . .**127** A1
Edward Friend Ho **6**
N16 . . . . .7 A1
Edward Ho
Paddington W2 . . . . .89 B1
Vauxhall SE11 . . . .**149** A2
Edward Kennedy Ho
18 W10 . . . . .23 A1
Edward Mann Cl **13**
E1 . . . . .32 C3
Edward Mews
NW1 . . . . .82 B1
Edward Pl SE8 . . . . .51 B4
Edward Robinson Ho
3 SE14 . . . . .50 C3
Edward's Cotts **11**
N1 . . . . .15 A1
Edward's La N16 . . . .7 A2
Edwards Mews
Islington N1 . . . . . . .14 C1
Marylebone W1 . . . .**103** B1
Edward Sq
Islington N1 . . . . . . .84 C3

Edward Sq *continued*
 1 Rotherhithe
  SE16 . . . . 33 A1
Edward St SE14 . . . . 51 B3
Edward VII Mans
  NW10 . . . . 22 C2
Edward Wilson Prim
  Sch 2 W2 . . . . . 100 A4
Edwin's Mead E9 . . . 18 A4
Edwin St
  Bethnal Green E1 . . . 25 B1
  Newham E16 . . . . 35 C4
Edwy Ho E9 . . . . 18 B4
Edwyn Ho SW18 . . . 59 A1
Effie PI SW6 . . . . . 155 C1
Effie Rd SW6 . . . . . 155 C1
Effingham Ho 27
  SW8 . . . . 171 B1
Effra Ct SW2 . . . . . . 62 B2
Effra Mans SW2 . . . . 62 C2
Effra Par SW2 . . . . . 62 C2
Effra Rd SW2 . . . . . . 62 C2
Effra Road Ret Pk
  SW2 . . . . 62 C2
EF International
  Language Sch
  SE1 . . . . 121 C1
Egbert Ho E9 . . . . . . 18 A3
Egbert St NW1 . . . . . 81 B4
Egbury Ho SW15 . . . 56 B1
Egerton Cres
  SW3 . . . . 144 B4
Egerton Ct 5
  TW10 . . . . 54 A2
Egerton Dr SE10 . . . 52 A2
Egerton Gdns
  Knightsbridge
  SW3 . . . . 130 A1
  Willesden NW10 . . . . 22 B4
Egerton Gdns Mews
  SW3 . . . . 130 B1
Egerton Ho W4 . . . . 45 B4
Egerton PI SW3 . . . 130 B1
Egerton Rd N16 . . . . . 7 B4
Egerton Terr SW3 . . 130 B1
Egham Cl SW19 . . . . 70 A2
Eglantine Rd
  SW18 . . . . 59 B2
Eglington Ct SE17 . . 48 B4
Egliston Mews
  SW15 . . . . 57 B4
Egmont St SE14 . . . 50 C3
Egremont Ho SE13 . . 52 A1
Egremont Rd SE27 . . 74 C1
Egret Ho 10 SE16 . . . 40 C2
Eider Ct 28 SE8 . . . . 51 B4
Elaine Ct 13 NW3 . . 12 B2
Elaine Gr NW5 . . . . . 12 C3
Elaine Ho N4 . . . . 5 A3
Elam Cl SE5 . . . . 48 A1
Elam St SE5 . . . . 48 A1
Elan Ct E1 . . . . 32 A4
Eland Rd SW11 . . . . . 60 B4
Elba PI SE17 . . . . . . 151 A4
Elbe St SW6 . . . . . . 166 C2
Elborough St
  SW18 . . . . 70 C3
Elbury Dr E16 . . . . . 35 C3
Elcho St SW11 . . . . 158 B1
Elcot Ave SE15 . . . . 50 A3
Elderberry Rd W5 . . 36 A4

Elderfield Ho 4
  E14 . . . . 33 C2
Elderfield Rd E5 . . . . 17 B4
Elder St E1 . . 24 B1 98 C1
Elder Wlk
  Islington N1 . . . . 86 B4
  2 Lewisham SE13 . . 67 B4
Eldon Ct NW6 . . . . . 23 C4
Eldon Gr NW3 . . . . . 11 C3
Eldon Ho SW9 . . . . . 63 A4
Eldon Rd W8 . . . . . . 128 B1
Eldon St EC2 . . . . . 109 C3
Eldon Way NW10 . . . 20 A3
Eldridge Ct SE16 . . 139 B1
Eleanor Cl SE16 . . . . 40 C4
Eleanor Ct 12 E2 . . . 24 C4
Eleanor Gr SW13 . . . 56 A4
Eleanor Ho
  16 Hammersmith
  W6 . . . . 39 B1
  1 Kentish Town
  NW5 . . . . 13 B3
Eleanor Palmer Prim
  Sch 18 NW5 . . . . . . 13 B4
Eleanor Rathbone Ho
  1 N6 . . . . 4 C4
Eleanor Rd E8 . . . . . 17 A1
Eleanor St E3 . . . . . 26 C2
Electra Ct 6 NW2 . . . 9 B2
Electric Ave SW9 . . . 62 C3
Electric Ho 13 E3 . . . 26 C2
Electric La 2
  SW9 . . . . 62 C3
Electric Mans 1
  SW9 . . . . 62 C3
Elephant & Castle
  Newington SE1 . . . 136 B1
  Newington SE1 . . . 150 B4
Elephant & Castle Sh
  Ctr SE1 . . . . 150 C4
Elephant & Castle Sta
  Lambeth SE1 . . . . . 136 B1
  Newington SE17 . . 150 C4
Elephant La SE16 . . . 40 B4
Elephant Rd SE17 . . 150 C4
Elfindale Rd SE24 . . 63 B2
Elfort Rd N5 . . . . . . 14 C4
Elf Row E1 . . . . 32 B2
Elgar Ave W5 . . . . . . 36 A4
Elgar Cl SE8 . . . . 51 C3
Elgar Ct W14 . . . . . 126 A1
Elgar Ho
  Pimlico SW1 . . . . . 146 B1
  South Hampstead
  NW6 . . . . 11 B1
Elgar St SE16 . . . . . . 41 A3
Elgin Ave
  Hammersmith
  W12 . . . . 39 A3
  Westbourne Green
  W9 . . . . 88 B4
Elgin Cl W12 . . . . . . 39 A4
Elgin Cres
  W11 . . . . 31 A2 112 B4
Elgin Ct W9 . . . . 88 A2
Elgin Ho 8 E14 . . . . 34 A3
Elgin Mans W9 . . . . . 88 A3
Elgin Mews N1 . . . . 31 A3
Elgin Mews N W9 . . 88 B4
Elgin Mews S W9 . . . 88 B4
Elgood Cl
  W11 . . . . 31 A1 112 A1
Elgood Ho NW8 . . . . 79 C1
Elham Ho 15 E5 . . . . 17 A3
Elia Mews N1 . . . . . . 86 A1
Elias PI SW8 . . . . . . 163 B3

Elia St N1 . . . . 86 A1
Elim Est SE1 . . . . . 138 A2
Elim St SE1 . . . . . . 138 A2
Eliot Cotts SE3 . . . . 53 A1
Eliot Ct SW18 . . . . . 59 A1
Eliot Gdns SW15 . . . 56 C3
Eliot Hill SE13 . . . . . 52 B1
Eliot Ho 10 TW10 . . 54 A1
Eliot Mews NW8 . . . 78 C1
Eliot PI SE3 . . . . 52 C1
Eliot Vale SE3 . . . . . 52 C1
Elizabeth Ave
  Islington N1 . . . . 15 C1
  Shoreditch N1 . . . . . 87 A4
Elizabeth Barnes Ct 5
  SW6 . . . . 166 B2
Elizabeth Blount Ct 4
  E14 . . . . 33 A3
Elizabeth Cl
  Paddington W9 . . . . . 89 A1
  12 Poplar E14 . . . . . 34 A3
Elizabeth Cooper Lo
  SW12 . . . . 60 C1
Elizabeth Cotts 5
  TW9 . . . . 44 C2
Elizabeth Ct
  Chelsea SW10 . . . . 157 C3
  East Dulwich SE22 . . 64 C3
  Marylebone NW8 . . . 90 B2
  Westminster SW1 . . 133 C1
Elizabeth Finn Ho 1
  W12 . . . . 38 C3
Elizabeth Garrett
  Anderson Hospl
  NW1 . . . . 93 A1
Elizabeth Garrett
  Anderson Language
  Coll N1 . . . . 85 A1
Elizabeth Gdns
  W3 . . . . 29 B1
Elizabeth Ho
  15 Hammersmith
  W6 . . . . 39 B1
  Lambeth SE11 . . . . 149 C3
Elizabeth Ind Est
  SE14 . . . . 50 C4
Elizabeth Kenny Ho
  N1 . . . . 15 B2
Elizabeth Mews
  28 Hackney E2 . . . . 24 C3
  Maitland Pk NW3 . . . 12 B2
Elizabeth Selby Inf
  Sch 31 E2 . . 24 C2 99 C4
Elizabeth Sq 13
  SE16 . . . . 33 A2
Elizabeth St SW1 . . 145 C4
Elkington Point
  SE11 . . . . 149 B3
Elkstone Rd W10 . . . 31 B4
Ellacombe Ho 1
  SW2 . . . . 74 C4
Ellacombe Ho W6 . . 47 C4
Ella Mews NW3 . . . . 12 B4
Elland Ho 10 E14 . . . 33 B3
Elland Rd SE15 . . . . 65 B3
Ella Rd N4, N8 . . . . . . 5 A4
Ellenborough Ho 5
  W12 . . . . 30 A2
Ellenborough Pl
  SW15 . . . . 56 C3
Ellen St E1 . . . . 111 C1
Ellen Wilkinson Ho
  7 Globe Town
  E2 . . . . 25 C2

Ellen Wilkinson Ho
  continued
  West Brompton
  SW6 . . . . 155 A3
Ellerby St SW6 . . . . 47 C2
Ellerdale Cl 15
  NW3 . . . . 11 B4
Ellerdale Rd NW3 . . 11 B3
Ellerdale St SE13 . . . 67 A4
Ellerker Gdns
  TW10 . . . . 54 A1
Ellerslie Gdns
  NW10 . . . . 21 C4
Ellerslie Ind Est
  SW2 . . . . 62 A2
Ellerslie Rd W12 . . . 30 A1
Ellerton St SW3 . . . . 37 A4
Ellerton Rd
  Barnes SW13 . . . . . 46 C2
  Wandsworth SW17,
  SW18 . . . . 71 C3
Ellery Cl 5 NW10 . . 21 B3
Ellery Ho SE17 . . . . 151 C3
Ellery St SE15 . . . . . 50 A1
Ellesmere Ct W4 . . . 45 C4
Ellesmere Rd
  Bow E3 . . . . 26 A3
  Chiswick W4 . . . . . . 45 C4
  Willesden NW10 . . . . 8 C3
Ellesmere St E14 . . . 34 A3
Ellingfort Rd E8 . . . . 17 A1
Ellingham Rd
  Leyton E15 . . . . 19 C4
  Shepherd's Bush
  W12 . . . . 38 C4
Ellington Ho SE1 . . 137 A1
Ellington St N7 . . . . 14 C2
Elliott Rd
  Acton W4 . . . . 38 A2
  Brixton SW9 . . . . . . 48 A2
Elliott Sch SW15 . . . 57 B1
Elliott's PI N1 . . . . . 86 B3
Elliott Sq NW3 . . . . . 12 A1
Elliott's Row SE11 . 150 B4
Ellis Cl NW10 . . . . . . 9 B2
Ellisfield Dr SW15 . . 68 C4
Ellis Franklin Ct
  NW8 . . . . 78 C2
Ellis Ho SE17 . . . . . 151 B2
Ellis Ho 3 SE13 . . . 52 B1
Ellison Rd SW13 . . . 46 B1
Ellis St SW1 . . . . . . 145 B4
Ellsworth St E2 . . . . 25 A2
Ellwood Ct 1 W9 . . . 88 B1
Elmar Ct SW6 . . . . . 164 B2
Elm Bank Gdns
  SW13 . . . . 46 A1
Elm Bank Mans
  SW13 . . . . 46 A1
Elmbourne Rd
  SW17 . . . . 73 A1
Elmbridge Wlk E8 . . 16 C1
Elm Cl N19 . . . . 4 B2
Elmcourt Rd SE21,
  SE27 . . . . 75 A2
Elm Cres W5 . . . . . . 36 A4
Elmcroft N6 . . . . 4 B4
Elmcroft Ave NW11 . 1 B4
Elmcroft Cres
  NW11 . . . . 1 A4
Elmcroft St E5 . . . . . 17 B4
Elm Ct
  Brixton SW9 . . . . . 173 B4
  Lewisham SE13 . . . . 67 C4
  42 Notting Hill W2 . . 31 C4
  Strand EC4 . . . . . . 121 B4

Elm Ct Sch SE27 . . . 74 B4
Elmer Ho NW1 . . . 102 A4
Elmfield Ho
  6 Canonbury N5 . . . 15 B3
  Paddington W9 . . . . 23 C1
Elmfield Mans 5
  SW17 . . . . 72 C2
Elmfield Rd SW17 . . 73 A2
Elmfield Way W9 . . . 31 C4
Elm Friars Wlk
  NW1 . . . . 13 C1
Elm Gn W3 . . . . 29 A3
Elm Gr
  Cricklewood NW2 . . . 9 C4
  Peckham SE15 . . . . 49 C1
Elmgreen Sch The
  SE27 . . . . 75 A2
Elm Grove Rd
  Barnes SW13 . . . . . 46 C1
  Ealing W5 . . . . 36 A4
Elm Ho 6 E14 . . . . . 42 B4
Elmhurst Mans
  SW4 . . . . 61 C4
Elmhurst St SW4 . . . 61 C4
Elmhurst Villas
  SE15 . . . . 65 B3
Elmington Rd SE5 . . 48 C3
Elmira St SE13 . . . . . 67 A4
Elmore Ho SW9 . . . . 48 A1
Elmore St N1 . . . . . . 15 C1
Elm Park Gdns
  SW10 . . . . 143 B1
Elm Park Ho
  SW10 . . . . 143 B1
Elm Park La SW3 . . 143 B1
Elm Park Mans
  SW10 . . . . 157 A4
Elm Park Rd SW3 . . 157 B4
Elm Pk SW2 . . . . 74 B4
Elm PI SW7 . . . . . . 143 B2
Elm Quay SW8 . . . . 161 B3
Elm Rd SW14 . . . . . . 55 B3
Elm Row NW3 . . . . . 2 B1
Elms Cres SW4 . . . . 61 C1
Elmshaw Rd SW15 . . 56 C2
Elmslie Point 2
  E3 . . . . 33 B4
Elms Mews W2 . . . 115 B4
Elms Rd SW4 . . . . . . 61 B2
Elm St WC1 . . . . 95 A1
Elms The
  Barnes SW13 . . . . . 56 B4
  8 Harlesden
  NW10 . . . . 21 A3
Elmstone Rd SW6 . . 165 B4
Elm Tree Cl NW8 . . . 89 B4
Elm Tree Ct NW8 . . . 89 B4
Elm Tree Ct
  5 Camberwell
  SE5 . . . . 48 B2
  St John's Wood
  NW8 . . . . 89 B4
Elm Way NW10 . . . . . 8 A4
Elm Wlk NW3 . . . . . . 1 C2
Elmwood Ct
  SW11 . . . . 170 A4
Elm Wood Prim Sch
  SE27 . . . . 75 C1
Elmwood Rd
  Chiswick W4 . . . . . . 45 B4
  Herne Hill SE24 . . . . 63 C2
Elmworth Gr SE21 . . 75 C2

Elnathan Mews W9 ... 88 B1
Elphinstone St N5 ... 15 A4
Elrington Rd E8 ... 16 C2
Elsa St E1 ... 33 A4
Elsdale Ho 14 E9 ... 17 B2
Elsdale St E9 ... 17 B1
Elsden Mews E2 ... 25 B3
Elsenham St SW18, SW19 ... 70 B2
Elsfield NW5 ... 13 A3
Elsham Rd W14 ... 126 A3
Elsham Terr W14 ... 126 A3
Elsie Lane Ct W2 ... 100 A3
Elsiemaud Rd SE4 ... 66 B2
Elsie Rd SE22 ... 64 B3
Elsinore Gdns NW2 ... 1 A1
Elsinore Ho
12 Camberwell
SE5 ... 48 B1
Islington N1 ... 85 B3
Elsinore Way TW9 ... 55 A4
Elsley Rd SW11 ... 60 C4
Elsley Sch 3
SW17 ... 72 C2
Elspeth Rd SW11 ... 60 B3
Elstead Ho 9 SW2 ... 74 B4
Elsted St SE17 ... 151 C3
Elstow Grange NW6 ... 9 C1
Elswick Rd SE13 ... 52 A1
Elswick St SW6 ... 166 C2
Elsworthy Rd NW3 ... 80 A4
Elsworthy Rise
NW3 ... 12 A1
Elsworthy Terr
NW3 ... 12 A1
Elsynge Rd SW18 ... 59 C2
Elsynge Road Mans
SW18 ... 59 C2
Elthiron Rd SW6 ... 165 C3
Elthorne Rd N19 ... 4 C2
Elthruda Rd SE13 ... 67 C1
Elton Ho 3 E3 ... 26 B4
Elton Pl N16 ... 16 A3
Elton St 11 N16 ... 16 A3
Eltringham St
SW18 ... 59 B3
Elvaston Mews
SW7 ... 129 A2
Elvaston Pl SW7 ... 129 A1
Elveden Ho 17
SW9 ... 63 A3
Elver Gdns 3
E2 ... 24 C2 99 C4
Elverson Rd SE8 ... 52 A1
Elverson Rd Sta
SE8 ... 52 A1
Elverton St SW1 ... 147 B4
Elvin Ho 2 E9 ... 17 B2
Elvis Rd NW2 ... 9 B2
Elwin St E2 ... 24 C2 99 B4
Elwood Ho N5 ... 6 A1
Elwood St N4, N5 ... 6 A1
Elworth Ho SW8 ... 163 A1
Ely Cotts SW8 ... 162 C1
Ely Court Flats
SW8 ... 164 A3
Ely Ct
Holborn EC1 ... 107 C3
3 Maida Vale
NW6 ... 23 C3
Ely Ho 22 SE15 ... 49 C3
Ely Pl EC1 ... 107 C3
Elysium Gate 7
SW6 ... 164 C2
Elysium Pl SW6 ... 164 C1

Elysium St SW6 ... 164 C1
Elystan Ct SW15 ... 57 A2
Elystan Pl SW3 ... 144 C2
Elystan St SW3 ... 144 B3
Elystan Wlk N1 ... 85 B3
Emanuel Ave W3 ... 28 B3
Emanuel Ct W3 ... 28 C3
Emanuel Sch
SW11 ... 60 A2
Embankment
SW15 ... 47 C1
Embankment Gdns
SW3 ... 159 A4
Embankment Pier
WC2 ... 120 B2
Embankment Pl
WC2 ... 120 B2
Embankment Sta
WC2 ... 120 B2
Embassy Ct NW8 ... 79 C1
Embassy Ho 2
NW6 ... 10 C1
Emba St SE16 ... 139 C3
Ember Ct 2 W12 ... 38 A3
Emberton SE5 ... 49 A4
Emberton Ct EC1 ... 96 A3
Embleton Rd SE13 ... 67 A3
Emden St SW6 ... 166 B4
Emerald Rd NW10 ... 20 C4
Emerald St WC1 ... 106 C4
Emerson Ho N16 ... 16 A3
Emerson St SE1 ... 122 C2
Emery Hill St
SW1 ... 133 A1
Emery St SE1 ... 135 C2
Emily St 1 E16 ... 35 B3
Emirates Airway
SE10 ... 35 B1
Emirates Greenwich
Peninsula SE10 ... 43 A4
Emirates Royal Dock
E16 ... 35 C2
Emirates Stad
(Arsenal FC) N7 ... 14 C4
Emlyn Gdns 3
W12 ... 38 A3
Emlyn Rd W12 ... 38 B3
Emmanuel CE Prim
Sch NW6 ... 10 C3
Emmanuel Ho
Dulwich SE21 ... 75 C1
Lambeth SE11 ... 149 B3
Emmanuel Rd
SW12 ... 73 C3
Emma St E2 ... 25 A3
Emminster NW6 ... 78 A4
Emmott Cl E1 ... 26 A1
Emperor's Gate
SW7 ... 142 C4
Empingham Ho 20
SE8 ... 40 C2
Empire Ho SW3 ... 130 A1
Empire Sq N19 ... 5 A1
Empire Wharf E3 ... 26 A4
Empire Wharf Rd
E14 ... 42 C2
Empress Mews 25
SE5 ... 48 B1
Empress Pl SW5 ... 141 B1
Empress St SE17 ... 48 B4
Empress State
Building SW6 ... 141 B1
Empson St E3 ... 27 A1
Emsworth St SW2 ... 74 B2
Emu Rd SW8 ... 170 A1
Enard Ho 28 E3 ... 26 B3

Enbrook St W10 ... 23 A2
Enclave Ct EC1 ... 96 B2
Endell St WC2 ... 106 A1
Enderby St SE10 ... 43 A1
Endlesham Ct 2
SW12 ... 72 C4
Endlesham Rd
SW12 ... 72 C4
Endsleigh Gdns
WC1 ... 93 B2
Endsleigh Mans 4
SW16 ... 74 A1
Endsleigh Pl WC1 ... 93 C2
Endsleigh St WC1 ... 93 C2
Endwell Rd SE4 ... 51 A1
Endymion Rd
Harringay N4 ... 6 A4
Tulse Hill SW2 ... 62 B1
Energen Cl NW10 ... 8 A2
Enfield Cloisters 7
N1 ... 24 A2 98 A4
Enfield Ho 8
SW9 ... 172 B2
Enfield Rd
De Beauvoir Town E8,
N1 ... 16 A1
South Acton W3 ... 37 A4
Enford St W1 ... 102 C4
Engadine St SW18 ... 70 C3
Engate St SE13 ... 67 B3
England's La NW3 ... 12 B2
Englefield NW1 ... 92 C3
Englefield Rd N1 ... 16 A1
Englewood Rd
SW12 ... 61 B1
English Gardening
Sch The SW3 ... 158 C4
English Grounds
SE1 ... 124 A1
English Martyrs RC
Prim Sch
Walworth SE17 ... 151 C3
Whitechapel E1 ... 111 A1
English St E3 ... 26 B1
Enid St SE16 ... 139 A2
Enid Stacy Ho 11
N19 ... 5 A4
Enmore Ct SW14 ... 55 C2
Enmore Gdns
SW14 ... 55 C2
Enmore Rd SW15 ... 57 B2
Ennerdale Ho 3
N4 ... 6 C4
Ennerdale Rd TW9 ... 44 B1
Ennersdale Rd
SE13 ... 67 C2
Ennis Ho 16 E14 ... 34 A3
Ennismore Ave
W4 ... 38 B2
Ennismore Gdns
SW7 ... 130 A2
Ennismore Gdns
Mews SW7 ... 130 A2
Ennismore Mews
SW7 ... 130 A2
Ennismore St
SW7 ... 130 A2
Ennis Rd N4 ... 5 C3
Ensbury Ho SW8 ... 162 C2
Ensign Ct 12 E1 ... 125 C3
Ensign Ho 11 E14 ... 41 C4
Ensign St E1 ... 125 B4
Ensor Mews SW7 ... 143 B2
Enterprise Ho 38
E9 ... 17 B1

Enterprise Way
College Pk NW10 ... 21 C2
Wandsworth SW18 ... 58 C3
Enterprize Way
SE8 ... 41 B2
Epirus Mews SW6 ... 155 B2
Epirus Rd SW6 ... 155 A2
Epping Cl E14 ... 41 C2
Epping Ho 5 E5 ... 7 C2
Epping Pl N1 ... 14 C2
Epple Rd SW6 ... 165 A4
Epstein Ct N1 ... 86 B3
Epworth St EC2 ... 97 C1
Equity Sq 20
E2 ... 24 B2 99 A3
Erasmus St SW1 ... 147 C3
Erconwald St W12 ... 29 B3
Eresby Ho SW7 ... 130 B3
Eresby Pl NW6 ... 10 C1
Erica Ct SW4 ... 172 B3
Erica Ho SE4 ... 66 B4
Erica St W12 ... 29 C2
Ericcson Cl SW18 ... 58 C2
Eric Fletcher Ct 15
N1 ... 15 B1
Eric Macdonald Ho
SW6 ... 165 C3
Eric Rd NW10 ... 8 B2
Ericson Ho
London SE13 ... 67 C3
Stamford Hill N16 ... 7 B3
Eric St E3 ... 26 B1
Eric Wilkins Ho 14
SE1 ... 153 B1
Eridge Ho SE22 ... 64 B4
Eridge House Sch 13
SW6 ... 164 C3
Eridge Rd W4 ... 37 C3
Erin Ct NW2 ... 9 B2
Erlanger Rd SE14 ... 50 C1
Ermine Rd SE13 ... 67 A3
Ernest Bevin Coll
SW17 ... 72 A2
Ernest Gdns W4 ... 45 A4
Ernest Simmonds Ho
SE14 ... 50 B1
Ernshaw Pl SW15 ... 58 A2
Eros (Shaftesbury
Meml Fountain)
W1 ... 119 B3
Erpingham Rd
SW15 ... 57 B4
Errington Rd W9 ... 23 B1
Errol St EC1 ... 97 A1
Erskine Ho SW1 ... 146 C1
Erskine Rd NW3 ... 12 B1
Escuan Lo N5 ... 15 B3
Esher Gdns SW19 ... 69 C2
Esher Ho 8 SW8 ... 171 C2
Eskdale NW1 ... 82 C1
Esk Ho E3 ... 26 B1
Esme Ho SW15 ... 56 B3
Esmeralda Rd
SE1 ... 153 C3
Esmond Ct SE17 ... 128 B2
Esmond Gdns W4 ... 37 C2
Esmond Rd
Acton W4 ... 37 C3
Kilburn NW6 ... 23 B4
Esmond St SW15 ... 58 A3
Esparto St SW18 ... 71 A4
Espirit Ct E1 ... 110 C3
Espirit Ho 6
SW15 ... 58 A2

Essendine Mans
W9 ... 23 C2
Essendine Prim Sch
11 W9 ... 23 C2
Essendine Rd W9 ... 23 C2
Essex Ct
Barnes SW13 ... 46 B1
Hammersmith W6 ... 39 B3
Holborn EC4 ... 107 B1
Essex Ho 2 E14 ... 34 A3
Essex Park Mews
W3 ... 29 A1
Essex Pl W4 ... 37 B2
Essex Place Sq 5
W4 ... 37 C2
Essex Rd
Acton W3 ... 28 B2
Chiswick W4 ... 37 C2
Islington N1 ... 86 B4
Willesden NW10 ... 8 A1
Essex Road Sta N1 ... 15 B1
Essex Villas W8 ... 127 B3
Essian St E1 ... 33 A4
Essington SW15 ... 58 A1
Estcourt Rd SW6 ... 154 C2
Estella Ho 11 W11 ... 30 C2
Estelle Rd NW3 ... 12 B4
Esterbrooke St
SW1 ... 147 B3
Este Rd SW11 ... 60 A4
Estoria Cl 22 SW2 ... 74 C4
Etal Ho N1 ... 15 A1
Etchingham Rd
E15 ... 19 B4
Eternit Wlk SW6 ... 47 C2
Ethelbert Ho E9 ... 18 A4
Ethelbert St SW12 ... 73 A3
Ethelburga St
SW11 ... 168 B4
Ethelburga Twr
SW11 ... 168 B4
Ethel Rankin Ct 8
SW6 ... 164 C2
Ethel St SE17 ... 151 A3
Ethelworth Ct 4
SW2 ... 74 C3
Etherow St SE22 ... 76 C4
Ethnard Rd SE15 ... 50 A4
Eton Ave NW3 ... 12 A1
Eton Cl SW18 ... 71 A4
Eton College Rd
NW3 ... 12 B2
Eton Ct NW3 ... 11 C1
Eton Garages 11
NW3 ... 12 A2
Eton Hall NW3 ... 12 B2
Eton Ho
Hackney E9 ... 18 B2
Highbury N5 ... 15 A4
Eton Pl NW1 ... 12 C1
Eton Rd NW3 ... 12 B2
Eton Rise NW3 ... 12 B2
Eton St TW10 ... 54 A2
Eton Villas NW3 ... 12 B2
Etta St SE8 ... 51 A4
Ettrick St E14 ... 34 B3
Eugene Cotter Ho
SE17 ... 151 C3
Eugenia Rd SE16 ... 40 B2
Euro Cl NW10 ... 8 C2

Eurolink Bsns Ctr
SW2 . . . . 62 C2
Europa Pl EC1 . . . . . . 96 C3
European Coll 46
E1 . . . . 111 B2
Eustace Bldg
SW8 . . . . 160 A3
Eustace Ho SE11 . . 148 C4
Eustace Rd SW6 . . 155 B2
Euston Rd NW1 . . . . 93 A2
Euston Sq NW1 . . . . 93 B3
Euston Square Sta
WC1 . . . . 93 A2
Euston St NW1 . . . . . 93 B3
Euston Sta NW1 . . . . 93 B3
Euston Underpass
NW1 . . . . 92 C2
Evan Cook Cl SE15 . 50 B2
Evandale Rd SW9 . 173 C2
Evangelist Rd
NW5 . . . . 13 A4
Evans Cl E8 . . . . 16 B2
Evans Ho
34 Shepherd's Bush
W12 . . . . 30 A2
South Lambeth
SW8 . . . . 161 C1
Evelina Childrens'
Hospl NW1 34 134 C2
Evelina Mans 9
SE5 . . . . 48 C3
Eveline Lowe Prim
Sch 28 SE1 . . . . . 153 C1
Evelyn Ct
Marylebone W1 . . 102 C1
Shacklewell E8 . . . . 16 C4
Shoreditch N1 . . . . . 87 B1
Evelyn Denington Ct
2 N1 . . . . 15 A1
Evelyn Fox Ct W10 . 30 B4
Evelyn Gdns
Richmond TW9 . . . . 54 A3
South Kensington
SW7 . . . . 143 B1
Evelyn Grace Acad
SE24 . . . . 63 A3
Evelyn Ho
Bedford Pk W12 . . . . 38 B4
3 Brixton SW2 . . . . 62 B2
18 Spitalfields E1 . 111 B3
Evelyn Rd
Acton W4 . . . . 37 C3
Richmond TW9 . . . . 54 A3
Evelyn St
Greenwich SE10 . . . . 52 B4
SE8 . . . . 41 A1
Evelyn Terr TW9 . . . . 54 A4
Evelyn Wlk N1 . . . . . 87 B1
Evelyn Yd W1 . . . . 105 B2
Evenwood Cl
SW15 . . . . 58 A2
Everard Ho 33 E1 . 111 C2
Everatt Cl SW18 . . . 58 B2
Everdon Rd SW13 . . 46 C4
Everest Pl E14 . . . . . 34 B4
Everett Ho
Islington N7 . . . . 14 C4
Walworth SE17 . . . 151 B2
Evergreen Sq 3
E8 . . . . 16 B1
Everilda St N1 . . . . . 85 A3
Evering Rd E5, N16 . 7 C1
Everington St W6 . . 47 C4

Everitt Rd NW10 . . . 20 C2
Everleigh St N4 . . . . 5 B3
Eversfield Rd TW9 . . 44 B1
Evershed Ho 1 . . . 111 A2
Evershed Wlk W4 . . 37 C2
Eversholt St NW1 . . 93 B4
Evershot Rd N4 . . . . 5 B3
Eversleigh Rd
SW11 . . . . 169 B1
Eversley Ho 15
E2 . . . . 24 C2 99 B3
Everthorpe Rd
SE15 . . . . 64 B4
Evesham Ho
1 Bethnal Green
E2 . . . . 25 B3
Pimlico SW1 . . . . . 146 B2
St John's Wood
NW8 . . . . 78 C3
Evesham St W11 . . . 30 C2
Evesham Way
SW11 . . . . 60 C4
Evesham Wlk
Brixton SW9 . . . . . 173 B2
Camberwell SE5 . . . 48 C1
Ewald Rd SW6 . . . 164 C1
Ewart Pl 13 E3 . . . . 26 B3
Ewe Cl N7 . . . . 14 A2
Ewen Cres SW2 . . . . 74 C4
Ewen Henderson Ct
10 SE14 . . . . 51 A3
Ewen Ho N1 . . . . . . 84 C3
Ewer St SE1 . . . . . . 122 C1
Ewhurst SW15 . . . . . 57 C1
Ewhurst Cl E1 . . . . . 32 B4
Ewhurst Rd SE4 . . . . 66 B1
Exbury Ho
Hackney E9 . . . . 17 B2
4 London SW9 . . . . 62 B3
Excel Ct WC2 . . . . . 119 C3
Excelsior Gdns
SE13 . . . . 52 B1
Excelsior Ind Est
SE16 . . . . 50 B4
Exchange Arc
EC2 . . . . 110 B4
Exchange Ct WC2 . 120 B3
Exchange Mans 2
NW11 . . . . 1 B4
Exchange Pl EC2 . 110 A4
Exeter Ct NW6 . . . . . 23 C3
Exeter Ho
Paddington W2 . . . 100 C2
11 Peckham SE15 . . 49 C4
Putney SW15 . . . . . . 57 B1
Exeter Mans NW2 . . 10 A2
Exeter Mews
Fulham SW6 . . . . . 155 B2
12 Hampstead
NW6 . . . . 11 A2
Exeter Rd
Brondesbury
NW2 . . . . 10 A2
Newham E16 . . . . . . 35 C4
Exeter St WC2 . . . . 120 C4
Exeter Way 2
SE14 . . . . 51 B3
Exford Ct SW11 . . . 167 C4
Exhibition Cl W12 . . 30 B2
Exhibition Rd
SW7 . . . . 129 C2
Exmoor Ho 29 E3 . . 26 A3

Exmoor St W10 . . . . . 30 C4
Exmouth Ho
Clerkenwell EC1 . . . 95 C2
6 Millwall E14 . . . . 42 A2
Exmouth Market
EC1 . . . . 95 C2
Exmouth Mews
NW1 . . . . 93 A3
Exmouth Pl E8 . . . . . 17 A1
Exmouth St E1 . . . . . 32 B3
Exonbury NW8 . . . . . 78 B3
Exon St SE17 . . . . . 152 A3
Explorers Ct 5
E14 . . . . 34 C2
Express Wharf 10
E14 . . . . 41 C4
Exton St SE1 . . . . . 121 B1
Eynella Rd SE21 . . . 76 B4
Eynham Rd W12 . . . 30 B3
Eynsford Coll V1 . 105 B2
Eynsford Ho
Borough The SE1 . 137 B4
12 Deptford SE15 . . 50 B4
Walworth SE17 . . . 152 A3
Eyot Gdns W6 . . . . . 38 B1
Eyot Gn W4 . . . . 38 B1
Eyre Ct NW8 . . . . . . 79 B2
Eyre St Hill EC1 . . . . 95 B1
Eythorne Rd SW9 . 173 C3
Ezra St E2 . . . 24 B2 99 A4

F

Faber Rd SW6 . . . 155 A2
Fabyan Rd TW9 . . . . 44 C3
Fairacres SW15 . . . . 56 C3
Fairbairn Gn 1
SW9 . . . . 48 A2
Fairbriar Residence
SW7 . . . . 143 A4
Fairbridge Rd N19 . . 4 C2
Fairburn Ct SW15 . . 58 A2
Fairburn Ho
9 Stamford Hill
N16 . . . . 7 A3
West Kensington
SW5 . . . . 141 A1
Fairby Ho SE1 . . . . 153 A4
Faircharm Trad Est
SE8 . . . . 52 A3
Fairchild Cl 6
SW11 . . . . 167 C1
Fairchild Ho
13 Hackney E9 . . . . 17 B1
Pimlico SW1 . . . . . 147 A3
5 Shoreditch
N1 . . . . 24 A2 98 A4
Fairchild Pl
EC2 . . . . 24 A1 98 B1
Fairchild St
EC2 . . . . 24 A1 98 B1
Fairclough St E1 . . 111 C1
Faircourt TW3 . . . . 12 B2
Faircroft N16 . . . . . . 6 C3
Fairdale Gdns
SW15 . . . . 57 A3
Fairdene Ct N7 . . . . . 14 A3
Fairfax Ho
3 Brixton SW9 . . . 173 C1
Putney SW15 . . . . . . 56 C2
Fairfax Mews
SW15 . . . . 57 B3
Fairfax Pl
Kensington W14 . . 126 B1

Fairfax Pl continued
South Hampstead
NW6 . . . . 11 B1
Fairfax Rd
Acton W4 . . . . 38 A3
South Hampstead
NW6 . . . . 11 B1
Fairfield
Camden Town
NW1 . . . . 82 C3
4 Stepney E1 . . . . 32 B4
Fairfield Ct
Harlesden NW10 . . . 21 C4
1 London SW18 . . . 59 A2
Fairfield Dr SW18 . . 59 A2
Fairfield Rd E3 . . . . 26 C3
Fairfield St SW18 . . 59 A2
Fairfoot Rd E3 . . . . 26 C1
Fairford Ho SE11 . 149 C3
Fairhazel Gdns
NW6 . . . . 11 B1
Fairheathe SW15 . . . 57 C1
Fairholme Rd
W14 . . . . 140 B1
Fairholt Cl N16 . . . . . 7 A3
Fairholt Rd N16 . . . . 6 C3
Fairholt St SW7 . . . 130 B2
Fairhurst 4 NW6 . . 11 B2
Fairlawn Ave W4 . . . 37 B2
Fairlawn Ct 5 W4 . . 37 B2
Fairlawn Gr W4 . . . . 37 B2
Fairlawn Mans
SE14 . . . . 50 C2
Fairlawns SW15 . . . . 57 C2
Fairlead Ho 6
E14 . . . . 41 C3
Fairley House Sch
SW1 . . . . 147 C2
Fairlie Ct
2 Bromley E3 . . . . 27 A2
1 Tufnell Pk N7 . . . 13 C4
Fairlight Ave
NW10 . . . . 21 A3
Fairlight Ct 4
NW10 . . . . 21 A3
Fairlop Pl NW8 . . . . 89 C3
Fairmead Ho E9 . . . . 18 A4
Fairmead Rd N7,
N19 . . . . 5 A1
Fairmont Ave E14 . . 34 C1
Fairmount Rd
SW2 . . . . 62 B1
Fair St SE1 . . . . . . 138 C4
Fairstead Wlk N1 . . 86 C4
Fairthorn Rd SE7,
SE10 . . . . 43 C1
Fairview Ho 14
SW2 . . . . 74 B4
Fairview Pl SW2 . . . 74 B4
Fairwall Ho 9
SE5 . . . . 49 A2
Fairway Cl NW11 . . . 2 B4
Fairway Ct 13
SE16 . . . . 40 C4
Fairway The W3 . . . . 29 A3
Fairweather Ho
N7 . . . . 14 A4
Faith Ct NW2 . . . . . . 9 A2
Faithfull Ho N5 . . . . 15 B3
Fakruddin St
E1 . . . . 24 C1 99 C1
Falconberg Ct
W1 . . . . 105 C2

Falconberg Mews
W1 . . . . 105 C2
Falconbrook Prim Sch
28 SW11 . . . . 59 C4
Falcon Cl
Chiswick W4 . . . . . . 45 B4
Lambeth SE1 . . . . . 122 B2
Falcon Ct
2 Dulwich SE21 . . 75 C2
Holborn EC4 . . . . . 107 B1
Islington N1 . . . . . . 86 B1
Falconer Wlk 12 N7 . 5 B2
Falcon Gr SW11 . . . 60 A4
Falcon Ho 11 SE15 . 49 B2
Falcon La SW11 . . . 60 A4
Falcon Lo
11 Paddington
W9 . . . . 31 C4
West Hampstead
NW3 . . . . 11 A4
Falcon Pk Ind Est
NW10 . . . . 8 A3
Falcon Point SE1 . 122 B3
Falcon Rd SW11 . . . 60 A4
Falcons Pre Prep
school The 1
W4 . . . . 45 A4
Falcons Prep Sch for
Boys The TW9 . . . . 54 A3
Falcon Terr SW11 . . 60 A4
Falcon Way E14 . . . 42 A2
Falconwood Ct
SE3 . . . . 53 B1
Falkener Ct SW11 . 169 C3
Falkirk Ct 11 SE16 . 32 C1
Falkirk Ho W9 . . . . . 88 B4
Falkirk St N1 . . . . . . 24 A3
Falkland Ho
Kensington W8 . . . 128 A1
4 London W14 . . . 140 C2
Falkland Pl 2
NW5 . . . . 13 B3
Falkland Rd NW5 . . 13 B3
Falkner House Sch
SW7 . . . . 143 A2
Fallodon Ho
6 London SW8 . . 171 C2
Paddington W11 . . . 31 B4
Fallow Ct 32 SE16 . 153 C1
Fallowfield N4 . . . . . 5 B2
Falmouth Ho
Bayswater W2 . . . 116 A4
Kennington SE11 . . 149 C2
Falmouth Rd SE1 . 137 A1
Falmouth St E15 . . . 19 C3
Falstaff Ct SE11 . . 150 A3
Falstaff Ho 13 N1 . . 24 A3
Fane St W14 . . . . . 155 A4
Fan Mus The SE10 . 52 B3
Fann St EC1 . . . . . . 97 A1
Fanshaw St
N1 . . . . 24 A2 98 A4
Fanthorpe St
SW15 . . . . 57 B4
Faraday Cl N7 . . . . . 14 B2
Faraday Ho
6 Balham SW12 . . 73 A4
10 Gospel Oak
NW5 . . . . 13 A4
Kensal Town W10 . . 23 A1
6 Poplar E14 . . . . 33 B2
Faraday Lo SE10 . . . 43 B3
Faraday Rd
Acton W3 . . . . 28 B2
Kensal Town W10 . . 31 A4

Fareham Ho 13
SW15 . . . . 68 C3
Fareham St W1 . . . . . 105 B2
Farjeon Ho NW6 . . . . 11 C1
Farleigh Pl N16 . . . . . 16 B4
Farleigh Rd N16 . . . . 16 B4
Farley Ct
Kensington W14 . . . . 126 C2
Marylebone NW1 . . . . 91 B1
Farlington Pl
SW15 . . . . 69 A4
Farlow Rd SW15 . . . . 57 C4
Farlton Rd SW18 . . . 71 A4
Farm Ave NW2 . . . . . . 1 B1
Farm Cl SW6 . . . . . . 155 C2
Farmdale Rd SE10 . . 43 C1
Farmer Ho 4
SE16 . . . . 40 A3
Farmers Mkt W8 . . . 113 C2
Farmers Rd SE5 . . . . 48 A3
Farmer St
W8 . . . . 31 C1 113 B2
Farm La SW6 . . . . . 155 C2
Farm Lane Trad Ctr
SW6 . . . . 155 C3
Farmleigh Ho
SW9 . . . . 63 A2
Farm Pl
W8 . . . . 31 C1 113 B2
Farm Rd NW10 . . . . . 20 C4
Farm St W1 . . . . 118 A3
Farnaby Ho 2
W10 . . . . 23 B2
Farnborough Ho 1
SW15 . . . . 68 C3
Farncombe St
SE16 . . . . 139 C3
Farndale Ho 3
NW6 . . . . 78 A4
Farnell Mews
SW5 . . . . 142 B2
Farnell Pl W3 . . . . . . 28 A2
Farnfield Ho 12
SW2 . . . . 62 B2
Farnham Ct 2 N16 . . 7 A3
Farnham Ho
Borough The SE1 . . . 122 C1
Marylebone NW1 . . . . 90 B1
Farnham Pl SE1 . . . . 122 B1
Farnham Royal
SE11 . . . . 149 A1
Farnhurst Ho 7
SW11 . . . . 169 B2
Farningham Ho 9
N4 . . . . 6 C4
Farnsworth Ct
SE10 . . . . 43 B3
Farnworth Ho 5
E14 . . . . 42 C2
Faroe Rd W14 . . . . . . 39 C3
Farquhar Rd SW19 . . 70 C1
Farrance St E14 . . . . 33 C3
Farrant Ho 14
SW11 . . . . 169 B2
Farrell Ho 1
E1 . . . . 32 B3
Farrer Ho SE8 . . . . . 51 C3
Farriers Mews
SE15 . . . . 65 B4
Farrier St NW1 . . . . . 13 B1
Farrier Wlk SW10 . . 156 C4
Farringdon La EC1 . . 95 C1
Farringdon Rd EC1 . . 95 C1
Farringdon
EC4 . . . . 108 A2

Farringdon Sta
EC1 . . . . 108 A4
Farrins Rents
SE16 . . . . 33 A1
Farrow La SE14 . . . . 50 B3
Farrow Pl SE16 . . . . 41 A3
Farthingale Wlk
E15 . . . . 19 C1
Farthing Alley 8
SE1 . . . . 139 B3
Farthing Fields 5
E1 . . . . 32 A1
Fashion Retail Acad
The W1 . . . . 105 B2
Fashion St E1 . . . . . 111 A3
Fashion & Textile Mus
SE1 . . . . 138 A4
Fassett Rd E8 . . . . . . 16 C2
Fassett Sq E8 . . . . . . 16 C2
Fauconberg Ct
W4 . . . . 45 B4
Fauconberg Rd
W4 . . . . 45 B4
Faulkner Ho SW15 . . 47 B1
Faulkner's Alley
EC1 . . . . 108 A4
Faulkner St SE14 . . . 50 B2
Faunce Ho 1
SE17 . . . . 48 A4
Faunce St SE17 . . . . 150 A1
Favart Rd SW6 . . . . 165 C3
Faversham Ho
Camden Town
NW1 . . . . 83 A3
Walworth SE17 . . . . . 152 A1
Fawcett Cl SW11 . . 167 C1
Fawcett Est E5 . . . . . 7 C3
Fawcett Ho 5
SW9 . . . . 172 B2
Fawcett Rd NW10 . . . 8 B1
Fawcett St SW10 . . . 156 C4
Fawe Park Rd
SW15 . . . . 58 B3
Fawe St E14 . . . . 34 A4
Fawkham Ho SE1 . . 153 A3
Fawley Ct SE27 . . . . 75 A2
Fawley Lo 2 E14 . . . 42 C2
Fawley Rd NW6 . . . . 11 A3
Fawnbrake Ave
SE24 . . . . 63 B2
Fayetville Ho 26
N19 . . . . 5 A4
Faygate Rd SW2 . . . 74 B2
Fazerley Ct 10 W2 . . 31 C4
Fearnley Ho SE5 . . . 49 A1
Fearon St SE10 . . . . 43 C1
Feathers Pl SE10 . . . 52 C4
Featherstone St
EC1 . . . . 97 B2
Featley Rd SW9 . . . . 63 A4
Felbridge Ho 21
SE22 . . . . 64 A4
Felday Rd SE13 . . . . 67 A1
Felden St SW6 . . . . 164 C3
Feldman Cl N16 . . . . 7 C3
Feldman Markets 4
W6 . . . . 39 A2
Felix St 5 E2 . . . . . . 25 A3
Felixstowe Rd
NW10 . . . . 22 A2
Fellbrigg Rd SE22 . . 64 B2
Fellbrigg St 21 E1 . . 25 A1
Fell Ho 11 N19 . . . . . 4 B1
Fellows Ct E2 . . . . . 24 B3
Fellows Rd NW3 . . . 12 A1

Fells Haugh 6
W3 . . . . 28 B3
Felltram Way SE7 . . 43 C1
Felmersham Cl 2
SW4 . . . . 61 C3
Felsberg Rd SW2 . . . 74 A4
Felsham Ho 5
SW15 . . . . 57 C4
Felsham Mews 4
SW15 . . . . 57 C4
Felsham Rd SW15 . . 57 C4
Felstead St E9 . . . . . 18 B2
Felstead Wharf
E14 . . . . 42 B1
Felton Ho N1 . . . . . . 87 C3
Felton St N1 . . . . 87 C3
Fenchurch Ave
EC3 . . . . 110 A1
Fenchurch Bldgs
EC3 . . . . 110 B1
Fenchurch Pl EC3 . . 124 B4
Fenchurch St EC3 . . 124 B4
Fenchurch Street Sta
EC3 . . . . 124 B4
Fen Ct EC3 . . . . 124 A4
Fendall St SE1 . . . . . 138 B1
Fender Ct 5 SW4 . . . 172 A3
Fenelon Pl W14 . . . . 141 A3
Fenham Rd SE15 . . . 50 A3
Fenner Cl SE16 . . . . 40 A2
Fenner Ho 25 E1 . . . 32 A1
Fenner Sq 7
SW11 . . . . 59 C4
Fenning St SE1 . . . . 138 A4
Fenn St E9 . . . . 17 B3
Fen St E16 . . . . 35 B2
Fenstanton 3 N4 . . . 5 B3
Fenstanton Prim Sch
20 SW2 . . . . 74 C3
Fentiman Rd SW8 . 162 C2
Fenton Cl
16 Dalston E8 . . . . . 16 B2
South Lambeth
SW9 . . . . 172 C1
Fenton Ho SE14 . . . . 51 A3
Fenton House NW3 . . 2 B1
Fentons SE3 . . . . 53 B3
Fenton St E1 . . . . . . 32 A3
Fenwick Gr SE15 . . . 64 C4
Fenwick Pl SW9 . . . . 62 A4
Fenwick Rd SE15 . . . 64 C4
Ferdinand Ho 1
NW1 . . . . 13 A1
Ferdinand Pl NW1 . . 12 C1
Ferdinand St NW1 . . 12 C1
Ferguson Dr W3 . . . . 28 C3
Ferguson Ho SE10 . . 52 B2
Ferguson's Cl E14 . . 41 C2
Fergus Rd N5 . . . . . . 15 A3
Fermain Ct E N1 . . . 24 A4
Fermain Ct N N1 . . . 24 A4
Fermain Ct W N1 . . . 24 A4
Fermoy Rd W9 . . . . . 23 B1
Fernbank Mews
SW12 . . . . 61 B1
Fern Cl 3 N1 . . . . . . 24 A3
Fencliff Rd E8 . . . . . 16 C3
Ferncroft Ave
NW3 . . . . 10 C4
Fern Ct SE14 . . . . . . 50 C1
Ferndale Com Sp Ctr
SW9 . . . . 62 B3
Ferndale Ct 3
SE3 . . . . 53 B3
Ferndale Ho N16 . . . 6 C3

Ferndale Rd SW4,
SW9 . . . . 62 B3
Ferndene Rd SE24 . . 63 B3
Ferndown Lo 17
E14 . . . . 42 B3
Fernhead Rd W9 . . . 23 B2
Fernhill Ho E5 . . . . . . 7 C2
Fernholme Rd
SE15 . . . . 65 C2
Fernhurst Rd
SW6 . . . . 164 B4
Fernie Ho SE22 . . . . 64 B4
Fernlea Rd SW12 . . . 73 A3
Fernleigh Cl W9 . . . 23 B2
Fernsbury St WC1 . . 95 B3
Fernshaw Mans
SW10 . . . . 156 C3
Fernshaw Rd
SW10 . . . . 156 C3
Fernside NW11 . . . . . . 1 C3
Fernside Rd SW12 . . 72 C4
Fern St E3 . . . . 26 C1
Ferntower Rd N5 . . . 15 C3
Fern Wlk 18 SE16 . . 153 C1
Fernwood SW19 . . . . 70 B3
Ferrey Mews 19
SW9 . . . . 173 B1
Ferriby Cl N1 . . . . . . 14 C1
Ferrier Ind Est
SW18 . . . . 59 A3
Ferrier Point 6
E16 . . . . 35 C4
Ferrier St SW18 . . . . 59 A3
Ferrings 21 SE21 . . . 76 A1
Ferris Rd SE22 . . . . . 64 C3
Ferrybridge Ho
SE11 . . . . 135 A1
Ferry La
Barnes SW13 . . . . . . 46 B4
Brentford TW8 . . . . . 44 A4
Richmond TW9 . . . . . 44 C4
Ferry Rd SW13 . . . . . 46 C2
Ferry Sq 1 TW8 . . . . 44 A4
Ferry St E14 . . . . 42 B1
Festing Rd SW15 . . . 57 C4
Festival Ct 5 E8 . . . 16 B1
Festival Pier SE1 . . . 120 C2
Fetter La EC4 . . . . . 107 C2
Fettes Ho NW8 . . . . . 79 C1
Ffinch St SE8 . . . . . . 51 C3
Field Ct
Hampstead NW3 . . . 11 B3
Holborn WC1 . . . . . . 107 A3
Lower Holloway N7 . . 14 A3
Wimbledon SW19 . . . 70 C1
Fieldgate Mans 28
E1 . . . . 111 C3
Fieldgate St E1 . . . . 111 C3
Field Ho NW10 . . . . . 22 C2
Fieldhouse Rd
SW12 . . . . 73 B3
Fielding Ho
Chiswick W4 . . . . 46 A4
6 Kilburn NW6 . . . . 23 C2
St John's Wood
NW8 . . . . 78 C4
Fielding Mews
SW13 . . . . 47 A4
Fielding Rd
Acton W4 . . . . 38 A3
Hammersmith W14 . . 39 C3
Fielding St SE17 . . . . 48 B4
Field Lo NW10 . . . . . . 8 B2
Field Rd W6 . . . . 154 A4
Fields Est E8 . . . . 16 C1
Field St WC1 . . . . 94 C4

Fieldsway Ho N5 . . . 14 C3
Fieldview SW17,
SW18 . . . . 71 C3
Fieldview Ct 2
N5 . . . . 15 A3
Fieldway Cres N5,
N7 . . . . 14 C3
Fieldwick Ho 14
E9 . . . . 17 C2
Fife Rd
Mortlake SW14 . . . . . 55 B2
Newham E16 . . . . 35 C4
Fife Terr N1 . . . . 85 A2
Fifth Ave W10 . . . . . . 23 A2
Fig Tree Cl NW10 . . . 21 A4
Filey Ave N16 . . . . 7 C3
Filey Ho SW18 . . . . . 59 B3
Filigree Ct SE16 . . . . 33 B1
Filmer Ho SW6 . . . . 164 B4
Filmer Mews
SW6 . . . . 164 B4
Filmer Rd SW6 . . . . 154 C1
Filton Ct 14 SE14 . . 50 B3
Finborough Rd
SW10 . . . . 156 B4
Finchdean Ho
SW15 . . . . 68 B4
Finch Ho 1 SE8 . . . . 52 A3
Finch La EC2, EC3 . . 109 C1
Finchley Pl NW8 . . . . 79 B2
Finch Mews 3
SE15 . . . . 49 B2
Finch's Ct 10 E14 . . 34 A2
Findhorn St 8
E14 . . . . 34 B3
Findon Cl SW18 . . . . 58 C1
Findon Rd W12 . . . . 38 C4
Fineran Ct 18
SW11 . . . . 59 C3
Fingal St SE10 . . . . . 43 B1
Fingest Ho NW8 . . . . 90 A2
Finland Rd SE4 . . . . 66 A4
Finland St SE16 . . . . 41 A3
Finlay St SW6 . . . . . 47 C2
Finmere Ho 11 N4 . . 6 B4
Finnemore Ho N1 . . 86 C4
Finn Ho N1 . . . . 97 C4
Finnis St E2 . . . . 25 A1
FINSBURY 95 C4
Finsbury Ave EC2 . . 109 C3
Finsbury Cir EC2 . . . 109 C3
Finsbury Ct EC2 . . . 109 B4
Finsbury L Ctr EC1 . . 96 C3
Finsbury Market
EC2 . . . . 110 A4
Finsbury Mkt
EC2 . . . . . 24 A1 98 A1
FINSBURY PARK . . 5 B3
Finsbury Park Rd N4,
N5 . . . . 6 A2
Finsbury Park Sta
N4 . . . . 5 C2
Finsbury Pavement
EC2 . . . . 109 C4

Finsbury Sq EC2 . . . . **109** C4
Finsbury St EC2 . . . . **109** B4
Finsen Rd SE5 . . . . **63** B4
Finstock Rd W10 . . . . **30** C3
Finton House Sch
SW17 . . . . **72** B2
Finucane Ct TW9 . . . . **54** B4
Finwhale Ho E14 . . . . **42** A3
Fiona Ct 2 NW6 . . . . . **23** B3
Firbank Rd SE15 . . . . . **50** A1
Fircroft N1 . . . . **86** B4
Fircroft Prim Sch
SW17 . . . . **72** B1
Fircroft Rd SW17 . . . . **72** B1
Fire Brigade Pier
SE1 . . . . **148** B4
Firecrest Dr NW3 . . . . **2** A1
Firle Ho 9 W10 . . . . . **30** B4
Fir Lo SW15 . . . . **57** A3
Firmston Ho 9
SW14 . . . . **55** C4
Firs Ave SW14 . . . . . . **55** B3
Firsby Rd N16 . . . . **7** C3
First Ave
East Acton W3 . . . . . **29** B1
Mortlake SW14 . . . . . **56** A4
West Kilburn W10 . . . **23** B1
First St SW3 . . . . **144** B4
Firth Gdns SW6 . . . . **164** A3
Fir Tree Ho 10
SE14 . . . . **50** B3
Fir Trees Cl SE16 . . . . **33** A1
Fisher Ho
Islington N1 . . . . **85** B3
9 Shadwell E1 . . . . **32** B2
2 Tufnell Pk N19 . . . **4** B1
Fishermans Dr
SE16 . . . . **40** C4
Fisherman's Wlk
E14 . . . . **33** C1
Fishers Cl SW16 . . . . **73** C1
Fishers Ct SE14 . . . . . **50** C2
Fisher's La W4 . . . . . . **37** C2
Fisher St
Holborn WC1 . . . . . **106** C3
Newham E16 . . . . **35** C4
Fisherton St NW8 . . . **89** C2
Fisherton Street Est
NW8 . . . . **89** C1
Fishlock Ct 6
SW4 . . . . **172** A2
Fish St Hill EC3 . . . . **123** C3
Fitch Ct SW2 . . . . **62** C2
Fitzalan St SE11 . . . . **149** B4
Fitzclarence Ho
W11 . . . . **126** A4
Fitz-George Ave
W14 . . . . **140** A3
Fitzgerald Ave
SW14 . . . . **56** A4
Fitzgerald Ho
15 Brixton SW9 . . . . **173** B1
14 Poplar E14 . . . . . . **34** A3
Fitzgerald Rd
SW14 . . . . **55** C4
Fitzhardinge Ho
W1 . . . . **103** B2
Fitzhardinge St
W1 . . . . **103** B2
Fitzherbert Ho 11
TW10 . . . . **54** B1
Fitzhugh Gr SW18 . . . **59** C1
Fitzjames Ave
W14 . . . . **140** B3

Fitzjohn's Ave
NW3 . . . . **11** C3
Fitzjohns Mans
NW3 . . . . **11** B2
Fitzjohns Prim Sch 4
NW3 . . . . **11** C3
Fitzmaurice Ho 17
SE16 . . . . **40** A2
Fitzmaurice Pl
W1 . . . . **118** B2
Fitzneal St W12 . . . . . **29** B3
FITZROVIA **104** A4
Fitzroy Cl N6 . . . . **3** B3
Fitzroy Cres W4 . . . . . **45** C3
Fitzroy Ct W1 . . . . **93** A1
Fitzroy Ho
Bermondsey SE1 . . . **153** A2
12 Tower Hamlets
E14 . . . . **33** B3
Fitzroy Mews W1 . . . . **92** C1
Fitzroy Pk N6 . . . . **3** B3
Fitzroy Rd NW1 . . . . . **81** B4
Fitzroy Sq W1 . . . . **92** C1
Fitzroy St W1 . . . . **92** C1
Fitzroy Yd NW1 . . . . . **81** B4
Fitzwarren Gdns
N19 . . . . **4** B3
Fitzwilliam Ave
TW9 . . . . **44** B1
Fitzwilliam Mews
E16 . . . . **35** C1
Fitzwilliam Rd
SW4 . . . . **61** B4
Fives Ct SE11 . . . . . . **136** A1
Fiveways Rd SW9 . . . **173** C1
Flamborough Ho 12
SE15 . . . . **49** C2
Flamborough St
E14 . . . . **33** A3
Flamingo Ct 2
SE8 . . . . **51** C3
Flamsteed Ct 13
SE13 . . . . **52** A2
Flamsteed Ho
SE10 . . . . **52** C3
Flanchford Rd
W12 . . . . **38** B3
Flanders Ho N16 . . . . **7** A1
Flanders Mans 11
W4 . . . . **38** B2
Flanders Rd W4 . . . . . **38** A2
Flanders Way E9 . . . . **17** C2
Flank St 9 E1 . . . . . . **125** B4
Flansham Ho 2
E14 . . . . **33** B3
Flask Cotts 4
NW3 . . . . **11** C4
Flask Wlk NW3 . . . . . **11** C4
Flatiron Sq SE1 . . . . **123** A1
Flatiron Yd SE1 . . . . **123** A1
Flavell Mews SE10 . . **43** A1
Flaxman Ct W1 . . . . **105** B1
Flaxman Ho
4 Chiswick W4 . . . . **38** A1
Newington SE1 . . . . **136** B2
Flaxman Rd SE5 . . . . **48** A1
Flaxman Sp Ctr
SE5 . . . . **48** B1
Flaxman Terr WC1 . . . **93** C3
Flecker Ho 6 SE5 . . . **48** C3
Fleece Wlk N7 . . . . . . **14** A2
Fleet Ct 1 W12 . . . . . **38** A3
Fleetfield WC1 . . . . . . **94** B4
Fleet Ho
6 Brixton SW2 . . . . **62** C2
4 Limehouse E14 . . **33** A2

Fleet Pl EC4 . . . . **108** A2
Fleet Prim Sch 15
NW3 . . . . **12** B3
Fleet Rd NW3 . . . . **12** B3
Fleet Sq WC1 . . . . **95** A3
Fleet St EC4 . . . . **107** C1
Fleet Street Hill 10
E1 . . . . **24** C1 **99** B1
Fleetway WC1 . . . . . . **94** B4
Fleet Wood Rd N16 . . **7** B2
Fleetwood Rd
NW10 . . . . **8** C3
Fleetwood St N16 . . . **7** A2
Fleming Cl 8 W9 . . . . **23** C1
Fleming Ct W2 . . . . . **101** B4
Fleming Ho
14 Bermondsey
SE16 . . . . **139** B3
Finsbury Pk N4 . . . . . **6** B3
Fleming Rd SE17 . . . . **48** A4
Fletcher Bldgs
WC2 . . . . **106** B1
Fletcher Ct 9
NW5 . . . . **13** A4
Fletcher Ho 16
N16 . . . . **16** A4
Fletcher Path 7
SE8 . . . . **51** C3
Fletcher Rd W4 . . . . . **37** B3
Fletcher St 8 E1 . . . **125** C4
Fleur De Lis St
E1 . . . . **24** B1 **98** C1
Fleur Gates 7
SW19 . . . . **69** C4
Flinders Ho 28 E1 . . . **32** A1
Flinton St SE17 . . . . **152** B2
Flint St SE17 . . . . . . **151** C3
Flitcroft St WC2 . . . . **105** C1
Flitton Ho 1 N1 . . . . . **15** A1
Flock Mill Pl
SW18 . . . . **71** A3
Flodden Rd SE5 . . . . . **48** B2
Flood St SW3 . . . . . . **158** B4
Flood Wlk SW3 . . . . **158** B4
Flora Gardens Prim
Sch 17 W6 . . . . **39** A2
Flora Gdns 2 W6 . . . **39** A2
Floral St WC2 . . . . . . **120** A4
Florence Ct W9 . . . . . **89** A3
Florence Gdns W4 . . **45** B4
Florence Ho
20 Bermondsey
SE16 . . . . **40** A1
2 Brixton SW2 . . . . . **62** B2
11 Shepherd's Bush
W11 . . . . **30** C2
7 Wandsworth
SW18 . . . . **59** C3
Florence Mans
SW6 . . . . **164** C4
Florence Nightingale
Ho 14 N1 . . . . **15** B2
Florence Nightingale
Mus SE1 . . . . **135** A3
Florence Rd
Acton W4 . . . . **37** C3
Finsbury Pk N4 . . . . . **6** A4
New Cross Gate
SE14 . . . . **51** B2
Florence St N1 . . . . . **15** A1
Florence Terr
Kingston u T
SW15 . . . . **68** A1
New Cross Gate
SE14 . . . . **51** B2

Florence Way
SW12 . . . . **72** B3
Flores Ho 13 E1 . . . . **32** C4
Florfield Rd E8 . . . . . . **17** A2
Florian SE5 . . . . **49** A2
Florian Rd SW15 . . . . **58** A3
Florida St
E2 . . . . **24** C2 **99** C3
Florida State Univ
W1 . . . . **105** C3
Florin Ct SE1 . . . . . . **138** C3
Floris Pl 7 SW4 . . . . . **61** B4
Florys Ct 7 SW19 . . . **70** A3
Floss St SW15 . . . . . . **47** B1
Flower & Dean Wlk
E1 . . . . **111** A3
Flowersmead
SW17 . . . . **72** C2
Flowers Mews 1
N19 . . . . **4** B2
Flower Wlk The
SW7 . . . . **129** A4
Floyer Cl TW10 . . . . . **54** B2
Flynn Ct 10 E14 . . . . . **33** C2
Foley Ho 10 E1 . . . . . **32** B3
Foley St W1 . . . . **104** C3
Folgate St E1 . . . . . . **110** C4
Foliot Ho N1 . . . . **84** C2
Foliot St W12 . . . . **29** B3
Follett Ho SW10 . . . . **157** B2
Follett St E14 . . . . **34** B3
Folly Wall E14 . . . . . . **42** B4
Fonda Ct 14 E14 . . . . **33** C2
Fontarabia Rd
SW11 . . . . **60** C3
Fontenelle SE5 . . . . . **49** A2
Fontenoy Ho
SE11 . . . . **150** A3
Fontenoy Rd SW12,
SW17 . . . . **73** B2
Fonthill Ho
Kensington W14 . . . **126** B2
Pimlico SW1 . . . . . . **146** B2
Fonthill Mews N4 . . . **5** B2
Fonthill Rd N4 . . . . **5** C2
Fontley Way SW15 . . **68** C4
Footpath The
SW15 . . . . **56** C2
Forber Ho 23 E2 . . . . **25** B2
Forbes Ho 2 W4 . . . . **36** C1
Forbes St E1 . . . . **111** C1
Forburg Rd N16 . . . . . **7** C3
Ford Cl 12 E3 . . . . **26** A3
Fordcombe 13
NW5 . . . . **12** C2
Fordham Ho 11
SE14 . . . . **51** A3
Fordham St 11
E1 . . . . **111** C2
Fordingley Rd W9 . . . **23** B2
Ford Rd E3 . . . . **26** B3
Fords Park Rd E16 . . **35** C3
Ford Sq E1 . . . . **32** A4
Ford St
Bow E3 . . . . **26** A3
Canning Town E16 . . **35** B3
Fordwych Rd NW2 . . **10** A3
Fordwych Rd NW2 . . **10** A3
Fordyce Rd SE13 . . . . **67** B2
Forecastle Ct E14 . . . **41** C4
Foreign &
Commonwealth
Office SW1 . . . . **134** A4
Foreland Ho
W11 . . . . **31** A2 **112** A4
Foreshore SE8 . . . . . . **41** B2
Fore St EC2 . . . . **109** A3

Forest Cl NW6 . . . . . . **10** A1
Forester Rd SE15 . . . . **65** A4
Forest Gr E8 . . . . **16** B2
Forest Hill Rd
SE22 . . . . **65** A1
Forest Rd
Dalston E8 . . . . **16** B2
Richmond TW9 . . . . . **44** C3
Fore Street Ave
EC2 . . . . **109** B3
Forest Way 19 N7 . . . . **14** A3
Forfar Rd SW11 . . . . **169** C4
Forge Pl NW1 . . . . **12** C2
Forman Ho SE4 . . . . . **66** C3
Formby Ct 9 N7 . . . . . **14** C3
Formosa Ho 1 E1 . . . **26** A1
Formosa St W9 . . . . . **88** B1
Formunt Cl E16 . . . . . **35** B4
Forrest Ct N7 . . . . **14** C2
Forrest Ho SW15 . . . . **47** B1
Forset Ct W1 . . . . . . **102** B2
Forset St W1 . . . . **102** B2
Forster Rd SW2 . . . . . **74** A4
Forston St N1 . . . . **87** A2
Forsyth Gdns SE17 . . **48** A4
Forsyth Ho
14 Hackney E9 . . . . . **17** B1
Pimlico SW1 . . . . . . **147** A3
Forsythia Ho SE4 . . . **66** A4
Fortescue Ave 1
E8 . . . . **17** A1
Fortess Gr NW5 . . . . . **13** B3
Fortess Rd NW5 . . . . . **13** B3
Fortess Wlk NW5 . . . . **13** A3
Fortess Wlk NW5 . . . . **13** A3
Forthbridge Rd
SW11 . . . . **60** C3
Fortior Ho NW10 . . . . **26** B3
Forties The 2
NW5 . . . . **13** B3
Fortior Ct N6 . . . . **4** B4
Fortnam Rd N19 . . . . . **4** C2
Fort Rd SE1 . . . . **153** A3
Fortrose Cl E14 . . . . . **34** C3
Fortrose Gdns SW12,
SW2 . . . . **74** A3
Fort St E1 . . . . **110** B3
Fortuna Cl N7 . . . . **14** B2
Fortune Ct 8 E8 . . . . . **16** B1
Fortune Gate Rd
NW10 . . . . **21** A4
Fortune Green Rd
NW6 . . . . **10** C4
Fortune Ho
Lambeth SE11 . . . . . **149** B3
St Luke's EC1 . . . . . . **97** A1
Fortune Way
NW10 . . . . **21** C2
Forty Acre La E16 . . . **35** C4
Forum Cl 7 E3 . . . . . . **26** C4
Forward Bsns Ctr The
3 E16 . . . . **27** C1
Fosbrooke Ho
SW8 . . . . **162** A1
Fosbury Ho 7
SW9 . . . . **62** B3
Fosbury Mews
W2 . . . . **114** B3
Foscote Mews W9 . . . **31** C4
Foskett Rd SW6 . . . . **165** A1
Fossil Rd SE13 . . . . . . **66** C4
Foster Ct
6 Camden Town
NW1 . . . . **13** B1
Canning Town E16 . . **35** B2
Foster Ho SE14 . . . . . **51** B2

Foster La EC2 .... 108 C2
Foster Rd
Acton W3 .... 29 A2
Chiswick W4 .... 37 C1
Foubert's PI W1 .. 104 C1
Foulden Rd N16 .... 16 B4
Foulden Terr N16 ... 16 B4
Foulis Terr SW7 .. 143 C2
Foulser Rd SW17 .. 72 C1
Foundary Ho [6]
E14 .... 34 A4
Founders Ct EC2 . 109 B2
Founders Ho NW1 147 B2
Foundling Ct WC1 . 94 B2
Foundling Muse The
WC1 .... 94 B2
Foundry Cl SE16 ... 33 A1
Foundry Mews
NW1 .... 93 A2
Foundry PI
Stepney E1 .... 32 B4
Wandsworth SW18 ..71 A4
Fountain & Colonnade
Sh Ctr SW1 .... 146 B4
Fountain Ct
Belgravia SW1 ... 146 A3
[14] Shepherd's Bush
W11 .... 39 C4
Strand EC4 .... 121 B4
Fountain Green Sq [4]
SE16 .... 139 C3
Fountain Ho
[33] Bermondsey
SE16 .... 139 C3
[3] Brondesbury Pk
NW6 .... 10 A1
Mayfair W1 .... 117 B2
Fountain Mews
[1] Highbury N5 .... 15 B4
Maitland Pk NW3 ...12 B2
Fountain PI SW9 . 173 C3
Fountayne Rd N16 ..7 C2
Fount St SW8 .... 161 C1
Fournier St E1 .... 111 A4
Fourscore Mans
E8 .... 16 C1
Four Seasons Cl
E3 .... 26 C3
Fourth Ave W10 .... 23 A2
Fovant Ct [5] SW8 . 170 C1
Fowey Cl E1 .... 32 A1
Fowey Ho SE11 .... 149 B2
Fowler Cl SW11 ... 59 C4
Fowler Ho
[5] Camberwell
SE5 .... 49 A1
Islington N1 .... 86 B4
South Lambeth
SW8 .... 171 C3
Fowler Rd N1 .... 86 B4
Fownes St SW11 .... 60 B4
Fox and Knot St
EC1 .... 108 B4
Foxberry Ct SE4 .... 66 B3
Foxberry Rd SE4 .... 66 A4
Foxborough Gdns
SE4 .... 66 C2
Foxbourne Rd
SW17 .... 72 C2
Fox Cl
Bethnal Green E1 .. 25 B1
Newham E16 .... 35 C4
Foxcombe Rd [6]
SW15 .... 68 C3
Foxcote SE5 .... 152 B1
Foxcroft WC1 .... 85 A1

Fox Ct EC1 .... 107 B3
Foxfield NW1 .... 82 B3
Foxglove St W12 ... 29 B2
Foxham Rd N19 .... 4 C1
Fox Ho [2] SW11 ... 59 C3
Foxley Cl E8 .... 16 C3
Foxley Ho [4] E3 .. 27 A2
Foxley Rd SW9 .... 48 A3
Foxley Sq [3] SW9 . 48 A2
Foxmore St SW11 . 168 C3
Fox Prim Sch
W8 .... 31 C1 113 B1
Fox Rd E16 .... 35 B4
Fox's Yd E2 .... 24 B1 99 A2
Foxwell Mews SE4 .. 66 A4
Foxwell St SE4 .... 66 A4
Foyle Rd SE3 .... 53 B4
Fradel Lo N16 .... 6 C3
Framfield Rd N5 ... 15 A3
Frampton NW1 .... 13 C1
Frampton Ct [3]
W3 .... 37 B4
Frampton Ho NW8 . 89 C1
Frampton Park Rd
E9 .... 17 B1
Frampton St NW8 . 89 C1
Francemary Rd
SE4 .... 66 C2
Franche Court Rd
SW17 .... 71 B1
Francis Chichester
Way SW11 .... 169 C3
Francis Cl [6] E14 .. 42 C2
Francis Ct [12] SE14.50 C4
Francis Ho
Harlesden NW10 .. 21 B4
[11] Shoreditch N1 .. 24 A4
Walham Green
SW10 .... 156 B2
Francis Holland Sch
Belgravia SW1 ... 145 C3
Marylebone NW1 .. 90 C2
Francis Snary Lo [11]
SW18 .... 58 C2
Francis St [11] SW1 147 A4
Francis Terr N19 ... 4 B1
Francis Terrace Mews
[18] N19 .... 4 B1
Francis Wlk N1 .... 84 C4
Franconia Rd SW4 ..61 C2
Frank Barnes Sch [13]
NW3 .... 11 C1
Frank Beswick Ho
SW6 .... 155 A3
Frank Dixon Cl
SE21 .... 76 A3
Frank Dixon Way
SE21 .... 76 A3
Frankfurt Rd SE24 . 63 B2
Frankham Ho [3]
SE8 .... 51 C3
Frankham St SE8 .. 51 C3
Frank Ho SW8 .... 162 A2
Frankland Cl SE16 . 40 A2
Frankland Ho [4]
SW12 .... 73 A4
Frankland Rd
SW7 .... 129 B1
Franklin Bldg [5]
E14 .... 41 C4
Franklin Cl
Greenwich SE13 ... 52 A2
West Norwood
SE27 .... 75 A1
Franklin Ho
New Cross SE4 .... 51 A1

Franklin Ho continued
[28] Wapping E1 .... 32 A1
Franklin PI SE13 ... 52 A2
Franklin Sq SW5 . 141 A1
Franklin's Row
SW3 .... 145 A2
Franklin St [5] E3 .. 27 A2
Franklyn Rd NW10.. 8 B2
Frank Soskice Ho
SW6 .... 155 A3
Frank Whymark Ho [4]
SE16 .... 40 B4
Frans Hals Ct E14 . 42 C3
Fraserburgh Ho [29]
E3 .... 26 B3
Fraser Ct SW11 ... 168 A4
Fraser Ho
Brentford TW8 .... 36 B1
[40] Clapham SW8 . 171 B1
Fraser Regnart Ct [12]
NW5 .... 12 B3
Fraser St W4 .... 38 A1
Frazier St SE1 .... 135 B3
Frean St SE16 .... 139 B2
Frearson Ho WC1 .. 95 A4
Freda Corbett Cl [10]
SE15 .... 49 C3
Frederica St [4]
N7 .... 14 B1
Frederick Blg N1 .. 16 A2
Frederick Charrington
Ho [4] E1 .... 25 B1
Frederick Cl W2 .. 116 C4
Frederick Cres
SW9 .... 48 A3
Frederick Ct SW6 . 58 A4
Frederick's PI
EC2 .... 109 B1
Frederick Sq [11]
SE16 .... 33 A2
Frederick's Row
EC1 .... 96 A4
Frederick St WC1 . 94 C3
Frederick Terr [8] E8.16 B1
Frederic Mews
SW1 .... 131 B3
Freedom St SW11 169 A2
Freegrove Rd N7 ...14 A3
Freeling Ho NW8 .. 79 B4
Freeling St [7] N1 .. 14 B1
Freeman Ho [6]
SW2 .... 74 A4
Freemantle St
SE17 .... 152 A2
Freemens Ho [1]
SW9 .... 62 B3
Freke Rd SW11 .... 60 C4
Fremantle Ho [14]
E1 .... 25 A1
Fremont St E9 .... 25 B4
French Inst The
SW7 .... 143 B4
French PI
E1 .... 24 A1 98 B2
Frendsbury Rd
SE4 .... 66 A3
Frensham Ct N5 ... 15 B3
Frensham Dr
SW15 .... 68 C2
Frensham St SE15 .. 49 C4
Frere St [6] SW11 . 168 B2
Freshfield Ave E8 .. 16 B1
Freshfield Cl SE13 . 67 C3
Freshford St SW17,
SW18 .... 71 B1

Freston Rd W10,
W11 .... 30 C2
Freswick Ho [6]
SE8 .... 41 A2
Freud Mus The
NW3 .... 11 B2
Frewell Bldg EC1 . 107 B4
Frewin Rd SW18 ... 71 C3
Friar Mews SE27 ... 75 A1
Friars Ave
Putney SW15 .... 58 A2
Roehampton SW15.. 68 B1
Friars Cl SE1 .... 122 B1
Friars Gdns W3 .... 28 C3
Friars Mead E14 ... 42 B3
Friars Place La
W3 .... 28 C2
Friars Prim
Foundation Sch
SE1 .... 136 B3
Friars Stile Pl [9]
TW10 .... 54 A1
Friars Stile Rd
TW10 .... 54 A1
Friar St EC4 .... 108 B1
Friars Way W3 .... 28 C3
Friary Park Ct [2]
W3 .... 28 B3
Friary Rd
Acton W3 .... 28 C3
Peckham SE15 .... 49 C3
Friday Grove Mews [1]
SW12 .... 73 B4
Friday St EC4 .... 122 C4
Frideswide Pl
NW5 .... 13 B3
Friendly PI [16]
SE13 .... 52 A2
Friendly St SE8 .... 51 C1
Friendly Street Mews
SE8 .... 51 C1
Friendship Way
E15 .... 27 B4
Friend St EC1 .... 96 A4
Friern Rd SE22 .... 64 C1
Frigate Ho [9] E14 . 42 B2
Frigate Mews SE8 . 51 C4
Frimley Cl SW19 ... 70 A2
Frimley Way E1 .... 25 C1
Frinstead Ho [1]
W10 .... 30 C2
Friston St SW6 .... 166 A1
Frith Ho
Bethnal Green
E2 .... 24 C2 99 B3
Paddington NW8 .. 89 C1
Frith Rd E11 .... 19 C4
Frith St W1 .... 105 B1
Frithville Ct [2]
W12 .... 30 B1
Frithville Gdns
W12 .... 30 B1
Frobisher Ct
[1] Greenwich
SE10 .... 52 C4
[3] Shepherd's Bush
W12 .... 39 B4
Frobisher Ho [27]
E1 .... 32 A1
Frobisher Pas E14 . 33 C1
Frobisher PI SE14 . 50 B2
Frobisher St SE10 . 53 A4
Frogley Rd SE22 ... 64 B3
Frogmore SW18 ... 58 C2
Frogmore Est
NW10 .... 20 B2

Frogmore Ind Est
N5 .... 15 B4
Frognal NW3 .... 11 B3
Frognal Cl NW3 .... 11 B3
Frognal Ct NW3 .... 11 B2
Frognal Gdns NW3 . 11 B4
Frognal La NW3 .... 11 A3
Frognal Par NW3 ... 11 B2
Frognal Rise NW3 .. 11 B4
Frognal Way NW3 .. 11 B4
Frome Ho SE15 .... 65 B3
Frome St N1 .... 86 C2
Fromow's Cnr [14]
W4 .... 37 B1
Frontenac NW10 .... 9 A1
Frostic Wlk E1 .... 111 A3
Froude St SW8 .... 170 B1
Frye Ct [3] E3 .... 26 B2
Frying Pan Alley
E1 .... 110 C3
Fry Rd NW10 .... 21 B4
Fulbeck Ho N7 .... 14 B2
Fulbourne St E1 .... 32 A4
Fulcher Ct [3] SE8 . 51 B4
Fulcher Ho
[3] Deptford SE8 .. 41 B1
[10] Shoreditch N1 .. 24 A4
Fulford Mans [3]
N19 .... 5 A1
Fulford St SE16 .... 40 A4
FULHAM 47 C1
Fulham Broadway
SW6 .... 155 C1
Fulham Broadway Sh
Ctr SW6 .... 155 C1
Fulham Broadway Sta
SW6 .... 155 C2
Fulham Bsns
Exchange SW6 .. 167 A3
Fulham Cross Girls
Sec Sch SW6 .... 154 A1
Fulham Ct SW6 .... 165 B4
Fulham High St
SW6 .... 164 B1
Fulham Pal SW6 .. 164 A1
Fulham Palace Rd SW6,
W6 .... 47 C4
Fulham Park Gdns
SW6 .... 164 C2
Fulham Park Rd
SW6 .... 164 C2
Fulham Prep Sch
[6] Fulham SW6 .. 164 B1
Fulham W14 .... 154 B4
Fulham Prim Sch
SW6 .... 155 B3
Fulham Rd
Chelsea SW10 .... 157 A4
Fulham SW6 .... 165 A4
Fuller Cl [4]
E2 .... 24 C1 99 B2
Fullers Ho [5]
SW18 .... 58 C2
Fullerton Rd SW18 . 59 B2
Fullwood's Mews
N1 .... 97 C4
Fulmar Ct [5] SE21 . 75 C2
Fulmar Ho
[12] Bermondsey
SE16 .... 40 C2
Marylebone NW8 .. 90 B1
Fulmead St SW6 .. 166 B3
Fulneck [1] E1 .... 32 B4

Fulthorp SE3 . . . . . **53** C1
Fulton Mews W2 . . **114** C4
Fulwood Pl WC1 . . **107** A3
Fulwood Wlk
SW19 . . . . **70** A3
Furber St W6 . . . . . . **39** A3
Furley Ho **7** SE15 . . **49** C3
Furley Rd SE15 . . . . **49** C3
Furlong Rd N7 . . . . . **14** C2
Furmage St SW18 . . **71** A4
Furness Ho **1**
SW14 . . . . **55** A3
Furness La **4**
SW14 . . . . **55** A3
Furness Prim Sch
NW10 . . . . **21** C3
Furness Rd
Harlesden NW10 . . . **21** C3
Sands End SW6 . . . . **166** B2
Furnival St EC4 . . . **107** B2
Furrow La E9 . . . . . . **17** B3
Fursecroft W1 . . . . **102** C2
Furze St E3 . . . . **33** C4
Fusion Ct SW15 . . . . **68** A1
Futters Ct **1**
NW10 . . . . **21** A3
Fyfield N4 . . . . **5** C2
Fyfield Rd **5** SW9 . . **62** C4
Fynes St SW1 . . . . **147** B4

G

Gable Ho **12** W4 . . . . **38** A2
Gables Cl SE5 . . . . . **49** A2
Gables The
3 Clapham SW4 . . **61** B4
Hampstead NW3 . . . **2** C2
Gabriel Ho SE11 . . **148** C4
Gabrielle Ct NW3 . . **11** C2
Gabriel Mews NW2 . . **1** B2
Gabriel's Wharf
SE1 . . . . **121** B2
Gaddesden Ho EC1 **97** C3
Gadsden Ho
6 Homerton E9 . . **17** C2
8 Kensal Town
W10 . . . . **23** A1
Gagarin Ho SW11 . . **59** C4
Gage Rd E16 . . . . . . **35** A4
Gage St WC1 . . . . **106** B4
Gainford Ho **18** E2 . . **25** A2
Gainford St N1 . . . . **85** B4
Gainsborough Ct
6 Bermondsey
SE16 . . . . **40** A1
Dulwich SE21 . . . . . **76** A2
Shepherd's Bush
W12 . . . . **39** B4
Gainsborough Gdns
Golders Green
NW11 . . . . **1** B4
Hampstead NW3 . . . **2** C1
Gainsborough Ho
Finsbury Pk N4 . . . . **5** B3
3 Hampstead
NW3 . . . . **11** B4
5 Limehouse E14 . . **33** A2
Westminster SW1 . **147** C3
Gainsborough Prim
Sch E9 . . . . **18** B3
Gainsborough Rd
Bedford Pk W4 . . . . **38** B2
Richmond TW9 . . . . **54** B4

Gainsborough St **3**
E9 . . . . **18** B2
Gainsborough Studios
N1 . . . . **87** B3
Gainsford St SE1 . **139** A4
Gairloch Ho **2**
NW1 . . . . **13** C1
Gairloch Rd SE5 . . . . **49** A1
Gaisford St NW5 . . . **13** B2
Gaitskell Ct SW11 . **168** A2
Gaitskell Ho SE17 . . **48** C4
Gaitskell Way SW1 **136** C4
Galata Rd SW13 . . . **46** C3
Galatea Sq SE15 . . . **65** A4
Galaxy Bldg **8**
E14 . . . . **41** C2
Galaxy Ho EC2 . . . . **97** C2
Galbraith St E14 . . . **42** B3
Galen Ho **10** SW2 . . **62** B2
Galena Ho **4** W6 . . . **39** A2
Galena Rd W6 . . . . . **39** A2
Galen Pl WC1 . . . . **106** B3
Galesbury Rd
SW18 . . . . **59** B1
Gales Gdns E2 . . . . . **25** A2
Gale St E3 . . . . **33** C4
Galgate Cl **4**
SW19 . . . . **70** A3
Galleon Cl SE16 . . . . **40** C4
Galleon Ho **8** E14 . . **42** B2
Galleries of Modern
London EC1 . . . . . **108** C3
Gallery Ct SW10 . . **156** C3
Gallery St SE21 . . . . **75** C3
Galleywall Rd
SE16 . . . . **40** A2
Galleywall Road Trad
Est **3** SE16 . . . . . . **40** A2
Galleywood Ho **1**
W10 . . . . **30** B4
Gallia Rd N5 . . . . **15** A3
Galloway Rd W12 . . **29** C1
Galpin's Rd CR4 . . . **40** A4
Galsworthy Ave
E14 . . . . **33** A4
Galsworthy Ct W3 . . **37** A3
Galsworthy Ho **2**
NW2 . . . . **10** A4
Galsworthy Rd
NW2 . . . . **10** A4
Galton St W10 . . . . . **23** A2
Galveston Ho **2**
E1 . . . . **26** A1
Galveston Rd
SW15 . . . . **58** B2
Galway Cl **20** SE16 . . **40** A1
Galway Ho
Finsbury EC1 . . . . . . **97** A3
1 Stepney E1 . . . . **32** C4
Galway St EC1 . . . . . **97** A3
Gambetta St **3**
SW8 . . . . **170** B1
Gambia St SE1 . . . **122** B1
Gambier Ho EC1 . . . **97** A3
Gamlen Rd SW15 . . . **57** C3
Gandolfi St **6**
SE15 . . . . **49** A4
Ganley Ct **18** SW11 **59** C4
Gannet Ct **6** SE21 . . **75** C2
Gannet Ho SE15 . . . . **49** B2
Ganton St W1 . . . . **105** A1
Garand Ct **7** N7 . . . . **14** B3
Garbett Ho **2**
SE17 . . . . **48** A4
Garbutt Pl W1 . . . . **103** C3
Garden Cl SW15 . . . . **69** A4

Garden Ct
4 Richmond
TW9 . . . . **44** B2
12 South Acton W4 **37** B3
St John's Wood
NW8 . . . . **89** B4
Strand EC4 . . . . . . **121** B4
Garden Flats
SW12 . . . . **61** A1
Garden Ho **12**
SW9 . . . . **172** B2
Garden House Sch
SW3 . . . . **145** A2
Garden La SW2 . . . . **74** B3
Garden Mews
W2 . . . . **31** C2 **113** C3
Garden Mus SE1 . . **134** C1
Garden Pl **28** E2 . . . . **24** B4
Garden Rd
Richmond TW9 . . . . **54** C4
St John's Wood
NW8 . . . . **89** A4
Garden Row SE1 . . **136** A2
Garden Royal **10**
SW15 . . . . **57** C1
Garden St E1 . . . . **32** C4
Gardens The
East Dulwich
SE22 . . . . **64** C3
Stamford Hill N16 . . . **7** B4
Garden Terr
Knightsbridge
SW7 . . . . **130** B3
Pimlico SW1 . . . . . **147** B2
Garden Wlk
EC2 . . . . **24** A1 **98** A2
Gardiner Ave NW2 . . **9** C2
Gardiner Ct NW10 . . **20** C4
Gardiner Ho
SW11 . . . . **168** A4
Gardner Ct
Finsbury EC1 . . . . . . **96** A4
Islington N5 . . . . **15** B3
Gardners La EC4 . . **122** C4
Gardnor Mans **14**
NW3 . . . . **11** B4
Gard St EC1 . . . . **96** B4
Gareth Ct SW16 . . . **73** C1
Garfield Ho W2 . . . **102** C1
Garfield Mews **7**
SW11 . . . . **60** C4
Garfield Rd SW11 . . . **60** C4
Garford St E14 . . . . . **33** C2
Garland Ct **12** E14 . . **33** C2
Garland Ho N16 . . . . . **6** C1
Garlands Ho NW8 . . . **78** B2
Garlick Hill EC4 . . . **123** A4
Garlinge Ho **1**
SW9 . . . . **173** B4
Garlinge Rd NW2 . . **10** B2
Garnault Mews
EC1 . . . . **95** C3
Garnault Pl EC1 . . . . **95** C3
Garner St **2** E2 . . . . **24** C3
Garnet Rd NW10 . . . . **8** A2
Garnet St E1 . . . . **32** B2
Garnett Ho **5**
NW3 . . . . **12** B3
Garnett Rd NW3 . . . **12** B3
Garnham Cl **2** N16 . . **7** B2
Garnham St **1** N16 . . **7** B2
Garnies Cl SE15 . . . . **49** B3
Garrad's Rd SW16 . . **73** C1
Garrard Wlk NW10 . . **8** A2
Garratt Ho **8** N16 . . . **7** A3
Garratt La SW18 . . . **71** A3

Garratt Park Sec
Specl Sch **6**
SW18 . . . . **71** B2
Garraway Ct SW13 . . **47** B3
Garraway Ho SE21 . . **76** B1
Garrett Cl W3 . . . . . . **28** C4
Garrett Ho **8** W12 . . **30** A3
Garrick Cl SW18 . . . . **59** B3
Garrick Ho
Chiswick W4 . . . . . . **46** A4
Mayfair W1 . . . . . **118** A1
Garrick Rd TW9 . . . . **44** C1
Garrick St WC2 . . . **120** A4
Garrick Yd WC2 . . . **120** A4
Garsdale Terr
SW5 . . . . **141** A2
Garsington Mews
SE4 . . . . **66** B4
Garson Ho W2 . . . **115** B4
Garston Ho **5** N1 . . . **15** A1
Garter Way SE16 . . . **40** C4
Garth Ct W4 . . . . **45** C4
Garth Ho NW2 . . . . . . **1** B2
Garth Rd
Child's Hill NW2 . . . . . **1** B2
Chiswick W4 . . . . . . **45** B3
Gartmoor Gdns
SW19 . . . . **70** B3
Garton Ho **5** N6 . . . . . **4** C4
Garton Pl SW18 . . . . **59** B1
Gartons Way
SW11 . . . . **59** B4
Garway Rd W2 . . . **100** A1
Gascoigne Pl **17**
E2 . . . . . . **24** B2 **98** C3
Gascony Ave NW6 . . **10** C1
Gascoyne Ho **2**
E9 . . . . **17** C1
Gascoyne Rd E9 . . . . **17** C1
Gaselee St E14 . . . . . **34** B2
Gasholder Pl
SE11 . . . . **149** A1
Gaskarth Rd SW12 . . **61** A1
Gaskell St SW4 . . . **172** A2
Gaskin Ho N16 . . . . . . **6** C1
Gaskin St N1 . . . . **86** A4
Gaspar Cl SW7 . . . **142** B4
Gaspar Mews
SW5 . . . . **142** B4
Gasson Ho **24**
SE14 . . . . **50** C4
Gastein Rd W6 . . . . . **47** C4
Gastigny Ho EC1 . . . **97** A3
Gaston Bell Cl
TW9 . . . . **54** B4
Gaston Gate **5** SW8 **172** C4
Gataker Ho **5**
SE16 . . . . **40** A3
Gataker St **6**
SE16 . . . . **40** A3
Gatcliff Cl SW1 . . . **145** C1
Gatcombe Ho **20**
SE22 . . . . **64** A4
Gatcombe Rd
8 Newham E16 . . . **35** C1
Tufnell Pk N19 . . . . . **4** C1
Gatefield Ct SE15 . . . **64** C4
Gateforth St NW8 . . **90** A1
Gate Hill Ct
W11 . . . . **31** B1 **113** A2
Gatehouse Sch **28**
E2 . . . . **25** C3
Gatehouse Sq
SE1 . . . . **123** A2
Gateley Ho **6** SE4 . . **65** C3

Gateley Rd SW9 . . . . **62** B4
Gate Mews SW7 . . **130** B3
Gatesborough St
EC2 . . . . . . **24** A1 **98** A2
Gates Ct SE17 . . . . **150** C2
Gatesden WC1 . . . . . **94** B3
Gateside Rd SW17 . . **72** B1
Gate St WC2 . . . . . **106** C2
Gateway SE17 . . . . . **48** B4
Gateway Arc N1 . . . . **86** A2
Gateway Ho SW12 . . **60** C1
Gateway Ind Est
NW10 . . . . **21** C1
Gateway Mews **4**
E8 . . . . **16** B3
Gateway Prim Sch
NW8 . . . . **89** C2
Gateways The
SW3 . . . . **144** B3
Gateway Trad Est
NW10 . . . . **21** C2
Gathorne St **18** E2 . . **25** C3
Gatliff Rd SW1 . . . **146** A1
Gatonby St SE15 . . . **49** B2
Gatwick Ho **8** E14 . . **33** B3
Gatwick Rd SW18 . . **70** B4
Gauden Cl SW4 . . . . **61** C4
Gauden Rd SW4 . . . **61** C4
Gaugin Ct **13** SE16 . . **40** A1
Gaunt St SE1 . . . . . **136** B2
Gautrey Rd SE15 . . . **50** B1
Gavel St SE17 . . . . **151** C4
Gaverick Mews **3**
E14 . . . . **41** C2
Gaviller Pl **8** E5 . . . . **17** A4
Gawber St E2 . . . . . . **25** B2
Gawthorne Ct E3 . . . **26** C3
Gay Cl NW2 . . . . **9** A3
Gaydon Ho W2 . . . **100** A4
Gayfere St SW1 . . . **134** A1
Gayford Rd W12 . . . **38** B4
Gay Ho N16 . . . . **16** A3
Gayhurst SE17 . . . . . **48** C4
Gayhurst Ho NW8 . . **90** B2
Gayhurst Prim Sch
E8 . . . . **16** C1
Gayhurst Rd E8 . . . . **16** C1
Gaymead NW8 . . . . . **78** B3
Gay Rd E15 . . . . **27** C3
Gaysley Ho SE11 . . **149** B3
Gay St SW15 . . . . . . **57** C4
Gayton Cres NW3 . . **11** C4
Gayton Ho E3 . . . . . . **26** C1
Gayton Rd NW3 . . . . **11** C4
Gayville Rd SW11 . . . **60** B1
Gaywood Cl SW2 . . . **74** C3
Gaywood St SE1 . . **136** B1
Gaza St SE17 . . . . . **150** A1
Gaze Ho **11** E14 . . . . **34** C3
Gean Ct **3** E11 . . . . . **19** C4
Geary Ho N7 . . . . **14** B3
Geary Rd NW10 . . . . . **8** C3
Geary St N7 . . . . **14** B3
Gedling Ho SE22 . . . **64** B4
Gedling Pl SE1 . . . **139** A2
Gees Ct W1 . . . . . . **103** C1
Gee St EC1 . . . . **96** C2
Geffrye Ct N1 . . . . . . **24** A3
Geffrye Mus **2** E2 . . **24** A3
Geffrye St E2 . . . . . . **24** B3
Geldart Rd SE15 . . . **50** A3
Geldeston Rd E5 . . . . **7** C2
Gellatly Rd SE14 . . . **50** C1
Gemini Bsns Ctr
E16 . . . . **27** C1
Gemini Ho **11** E3 . . . **26** C4

Gems Hampshire Sch (Main Sch) SW7 . 144 A1
Gems Hampshire Sch (The Early Years) SW7 . . . . 143 A3
General Wolfe Rd SE10 . . . . 52 C2
Genesis Bsns Pk NW10 . . . . 20 A3
Geneva Ct
 1 Putney SW15 . . 57 C2
 Stoke Newington N16 . . . . 6 C3
Geneva Dr SW9 . . 62 C3
Genoa Ave SW15 . . 57 A2
Genoa Ho E1 . . . . . 25 C1
Geoffrey Cl SE5 . . 48 B1
Geoffrey Ct SE4 . . 66 B4
Geoffrey Ho SE1 . 137 C2
Geoffrey Jones Ct NW10 . . . . 21 C4
Geoffrey Rd SE4 . . 66 B4
George Beard Rd **11** SE8 . . . . 41 B2
George Belt Ho **8** E2 . . . . 25 C2
George Ct WC2 . . 120 B3
George Downing Est N16 . . . . 7 B2
George Eliot Ho SW1 . . . . 147 A3
George Eliot Jun & Inf Schs NW8 . . . . . . 79 B4
George Elliot Ho SE17 . . . . 150 C2
George Elliston Ho **13** SE1 . . . . 153 B1
George Eyre Ho NW8 . . . . 79 C1
George Green's Sch E14 . . . . 42 B1
George Inn Yd SE1 . . . . 123 B1
George La SE13 . . 67 B1
George Lansbury Ho
 7 Bow E3 . . . . . 26 B2
 8 Willesden NW10 . 8 A1
George Lashwood Ct **12** SW9 . . . . 62 B3
George Leybourne Ho **18** E1 . . . . 125 C4
George Lindgren Ho SW6 . . . . 155 A2
George Loveless Ho **4** E2 . . . . 24 B2 99 A4
George Mathers Rd SE11 . . . . 150 A4
George Mews
 27 Brixton SW9 . 173 B1
 NW1 . . . . 92 C3
George Peabody Ct NW1 . . . . 102 A4
George Row SE16 139 B3
George's Rd N7 . . 14 B3
George's Sq SW6 155 A4
George St
 6 Canning Town E16 . . . . 35 B3
 Marylebone W1 . 103 A2
George Tingle Ho SE1 . . . . 139 A2
George Vale Ho **58** E2 . . . . 24 C3

George Walter Ho **11** SE16 . . . . 40 B2
George Wyver Cl SW18 . . . . 70 A4
George Yd
 City of London EC3 . . . . 109 C1
 Mayfair W1 . . . . 117 C4
Georgiana St NW1 . 83 A4
Georgian Ct **12** E9 . 25 B4
Georgina Gdns **10** E2 . . . . 24 B2 99 A4
Geraldine Rd
 Brentford W4 . . . 44 C4
 Wandsworth SW18 . 59 B2
Geraldine St SE11 136 A1
Gerald Mews SW1 . . . . 145 C4
Gerald Rd SW1 . . 145 C4
Gerard Ct NW2 . . . 9 C3
Gerard Rd SW13 . . 46 B2
Gerards Cl SE16 . . 40 B1
Gernigan Ho SW18 . . . . 59 C1
Gernon Rd E3 . . . 26 A3
Gerrard Ho **5** SE14 . . . . 50 C3
Gerrard Pl W1 . . 119 C4
Gerrard Rd N1 . . . 86 B2
Gerrard St W1 . . 119 C4
Gerridge Ct SE1 . 135 C2
Gerridge St SE1 . 135 C2
Gerry Raffles Sq E15 . . . . 19 C2
Gertrude St SW10 157 A3
Gervase St SE15 . . 50 A3
Getters Talmud Torah **3** N16 . . . . 6 C4
Ghent Way E8 . . . 16 B2
Gherkin The (30 St Mary Axe) EC2 . 110 B2
Giant Arches Rd **5** SE24 . . . . 63 B1
Gibbings Ho **5** SE1 136 B3
Gibbins Rd E15 . . 19 B1
Gibbon Ho NW8 . . 89 C1
Gibbon Rd
 Acton W3 . . . . . 29 A2
 Nunhead SE15 . . . 50 B1
Gibbons Rd NW10 . 8 A2
Gibbon's Rents SE1 . . . . 124 A1
Gibbon Wlk SW15 . 56 C3
Gibbs Gn W14 . . 141 A2
Gibbs Green Rd W14 . . . . 140 C2
Gibbs Green Specl Sch W14 . . . . . 141 A2
Gibbs Ho **5** SW12 . 73 A4
Gibraltar Ho NW10 . . . . 21 A3
Gibraltar Wlk **28** E2 . . . . 24 B2 99 A4
Gibson Cl E1 . . . . 25 B1
Gibson Gdns N16 . . 7 B2
Gibson Rd SE11 . . 149 A3
Gibson Sq N1 . . . 85 C4
Gibson St SE10 . . 43 A1
Gideon Rd SW11 . . 60 C4
Giesbach Rd N19 . . 4 C2
Giffen Square Mkt SE8 . . . . 51 C3
Giffin St SE8 . . . 51 C3
Gifford Ho
 5 Clapham SW4 . . 61 C3
 Greenwich SE10 . . 42 C1

Gifford Ho continued
 Pimlico SW1 . . . 146 C1
Gifford Rd NW10 . . 8 A1
Gifford St N1 . . . . 14 A1
Gilbert Ho
 Barbican EC2 . . . 109 A3
 Deptford SE8 . . . . 51 C4
 5 Globe Town E2 . 25 C2
 Pimlico SW1 . . . 146 B1
 South Lambeth SW8 . . . . 162 A2
Gilbert Pl WC1 . . 106 A3
Gilbert Sheldon Ho W2 . . . . 101 C4
Gilbertson Ho **11** E14 . . . . 41 C3
Gilbert St W1 . . . 103 C1
Gilbeys Yd NW1 . . 12 C1
Gilby Ho **6** E9 . . . 17 C2
Gilda Cres N16 . . . 7 C3
Gildea St W1 . . . 104 B3
Gilden Cres NW5 . . 12 C3
Giles Ho
 6 Bermondsey SE16 . . . . 139 B2
 Notting Hill W11 . . 31 C3
Gilesmead SE5 . . . 48 C2
Gilkes Cres SE21 . . 64 A1
Gilkes Pl SE21 . . . 64 A1
Gillam Ho **9** SE16 . 40 B2
Gill Ave E16 . . . . 35 C3
Gillender St E3 . . . 27 B1
Gillespie Prim Sch N5 . . . . 6 A1
Gillespie Rd N5, N4 . 6 A1
Gillett Pl **27** E8, N16 . 16 A3
Gillett St E8, N16 . . 16 A3
Gillfoot NW1 . . . . 82 C1
Gillian St SE13 . . . 67 A2
Gillies St NW5 . . . 12 C3
Gilling Ct **5** NW3 . 12 A2
Gillingham Ho SW1 . . . . 146 C4
Gillingham Mews SW1 . . . . 146 C4
Gillingham Rd NW2 . 1 A1
Gillingham Row SW1 . . . . 146 C4
Gillingham St SW1 . . . . 146 C4
Gillison Wlk **19** SE16 . . . . 139 C2
Gillman Ho **22** E2 . 24 C3
Gillray Ho SW10 . 157 B3
Gill St E14 . . . . . 33 B2
Gilmore Ho SW4 . . 60 B3
Gilmore Rd SE13 . . 67 C3
Gilpin Ave SW14 . . 55 C3
Gilpin Cl W2 . . . 101 A4
Gilpin Rd E5 . . . . 18 A4
Gilpin Sq **11** E9 . . 18 A2
Gilray Ho W2 . . . 115 B4
Gilstead Rd SW6 . 166 B2
Gilston Rd SW10 . 143 A1
Giltspur St EC1 . . 108 B2
Gilwell Ct **7** E5 . . 17 A4
Gipsy Cnr W3 . . . 28 C4
Gipsy La SW15 . . . 57 A4
Giraud St E14 . . . 34 A3
Girdlers Rd W14 . . 39 C2
Girdlestone Wlk N19 . . . . 4 B2
Girdwood Rd SW18, SW19 . . . . 70 A4
Girling Ho **9** N1 . . 24 A4
Gironde Rd SW6 . 155 A1

Girton Ho SW15 . . 57 C1
Girton Villas **6** W10 . . . . 30 C3
Gisburn Ho **23** SE15 . . . . 49 C3
Gissing Wlk N1 . . 14 C1
Glade The W12 . . . 39 A4
Glading Terr N16 . . 7 B1
Gladsmuir Rd N19 . . 4 B3
Gladstone Ct
 Westminster SW1 . . . . 147 C3
 Willesden NW2 . . . 9 A3
Gladstone Ho **16** E14 . . . . 33 C3
Gladstone Park Sch NW10 . . . . 9 A3
Gladstone Rd W4 . . 37 C3
Gladstone St SE1 . 136 A2
Gladstone Terr SW8 . . . . 170 B4
Gladwin Ho NW1 . . 83 A1
Gladwyn Rd SW15 . 57 C4
Gladys Rd NW6 . . . 10 C1
Glaisher St SE8 . . . 52 A4
Glamis Ct W3 . . . 37 A4
Glamis Est **3** E1 . . 32 C2
Glamis Pl E1 . . . . 32 B2
Glamis Rd E1 . . . . 32 B2
Glanville Ho **4** SW12 . . . . 73 B4
Glanville Rd SW2 . . 62 A2
Glasbury Ho **5** SW2 . . . . 62 B3
Glaserton Rd N16 . . 7 A4
Glasgow Ho W9 . . 78 B1
Glasgow Terr SW1 . . . . 146 C1
Glasshill St SE1 . . 136 B4
Glasshouse Fields E1 . . . . 32 C2
Glasshouse St W1 . . . . 119 A3
Glasshouse The SE13 . . . . 67 B3
Glasshouse Wlk SE11 . . . . 148 C2
Glasshouse Yd EC1 . 96 C1
Glass St **4** E2 . . . 25 A1
Glastonbury Ct **12** SE14 . . . . 50 B3
Glastonbury Ho SW1 . . . . 146 A2
Glastonbury Pl **22** E1 . . . . 32 B3
Glastonbury St NW6 . . . . 10 B3
Glaucus St E3 . . . 34 A4
Glazbury Rd W14 . 140 B2
Glazebrook Cl SE21 . . . . 75 C2
Glebe Cl **1** W4 . . . 38 A1
Glebe Ho **3** SE16 . 40 A3
Glebelands Cl SE5 . 64 A4
Glebe Pl SW3 . . . 158 A4
Glebe Rd
 Barnes SW13 . . . 46 C1
 Dalston E8 . . . . . 16 B1
 Willesden NW10 . . . 8 C2
Glebe St W4 . . . . 38 A1
Gledhow Gdns SW5 . . . . 142 C3
Gledstanes Rd W14 . . . . 140 B1
Glegg Pl **3** SW15 . 57 C3
Glenaffric Ave E14 . 42 C2

Glen Albyn Rd SW19 . . . . 69 C2
Glenalmond Ho **7** SW15 . . . . 57 C1
Glenarm Rd E5 . . . 17 C4
Glenbrook Prim Sch SW4 . . . . 61 C1
Glenbrook Rd NW6 . . . . 10 C3
Glenburnie Rd SW17 . . . . 72 B1
Glencoe Mans **6** SW9 . . . . 163 B1
Glendall St SW9 . . 62 B3
Glendarvon St SW15 . . . . 57 C4
Glendower Gdns **10** SW14 . . . . 55 C4
Glendower Pl SW7 . . . . 143 B4
Glendower Prep Sch SW7 . . . . 143 B4
Glendown Ho **2** E8 . . . . 16 C3
Glendun Ct W3 . . . 29 A2
Glendun Rd W3 . . . 29 A2
Gleneagles Cl **21** SE16 . . . . 40 A1
Glenelg Rd SW2 . . 62 A2
Glenfield Rd SW12 . 73 B3
Glenfinlas Way SE5 . . . . 48 A3
Glenforth St SE10 . 43 B1
Glengall Gr E14 . . 42 B3
Glengall Pass **2** NW6 . . . . 23 C4
Glengall Rd
 Camberwell SE15 . . 49 B4
 Kilburn NW6 . . . . 23 B4
Glengall Terr SE15 . 49 B4
Glengarnock Ave E14 . . . . 42 B2
Glengarry Rd SE22 . 64 B2
Glenhurst Ave NW5 . . . . 12 C4
Glenilla Rd NW3 . . 12 A2
Glenister Rd SE10 . 43 B1
Glenkerry Ho **1** E14 . . . . 34 B3
Glenloch Rd NW3 . 12 A2
Glenluce Rd SE3 . . 53 C4
Glenmore SW15 . . 57 C1
Glenmore Ho **6** TW10 . . . . 54 A1
Glenmore Rd NW3 . 12 A2
Glennie Ct SE21 . . 76 C3
Glennie Ho SE10 . . 52 B2
Glennie Rd SE27, SW16 . . . . 74 C1
Glenridding NW1 . . 83 A1
Glenrosa St SW6 . 166 C2
Glenroy St W12 . . 30 B3
Glensdale Rd SE4 . . 66 B4
Glenshaw Mans **7** SW9 . . . . 163 B1
Glentanner Way SW17 . . . . 71 C1
Glentham Gdns SW13 . . . . 47 A4

Glentham Rd
SW13 . . . . .47 A4
Glenthorne Mews
W6 . . . . .39 A2
Glenthorne Rd W6.39 A2
Glenthorpe SW15. . .56 C3
Glentworth St
NW1 . . . . .91 A1
Glenville Gr SE8. . .51 B3
Glenville Mews
SW18 . . . . .70 C4
Glenworth Ave
E14 . . . . .42 C2
Gliddon Rd W14. .140 A2
Globe Acad SE1 . .137 C1
Globe Pond Rd
SE16 . . . . .33 A1
Globe Prim Sch **37**
E2 . . . . .25 B2
Globe Rd E1, E2. . .25 B1
Globe St SE1 . . . . .137 B3
Globe Terr **8** E2. . .25 B2
Globe Theatre The
SE1. . . . . .122 C3
GLOBE TOWN. . . .25 C2
Globe View EC4. . .122 C4
Globe Yd W1 . . . . .104 A1
Gloucester W14 . .141 A3
Gloucester Ave
NW1 . . . . .81 C4
Gloucester Cir
SE10. . . . . .52 B3
Gloucester Cres
NW1 . . . . .82 A4
Gloucester Ct
Borough The SE1 . .137 A2
City of London EC3. .124 B3
Dulwich SE22. . . . . .76 C3
Golders Green NW11. .1 B4
Richmond TW9. . . . .44 C3
Gloucester Dr N4. . . .6 A2
Gloucester Gate
NW1 . . . . .82 A2
Gloucester Gate Mews
NW1 . . . . .82 A2
Gloucester Gdns
Golders Green
NW11. . . . . .1 B4
Paddington W2. . . .100 C2
Gloucester Ho
Kilburn NW6. . . . . . .23 C3
Richmond TW10. . . .54 C2
Gloucester Mews
W2 . . . . .101 A1
Gloucester Mews W
W2 . . . . .101 A1
Gloucester Pk
SW7 . . . . .142 C4
Gloucester Pl W1 .103 A4
Gloucester Pl Mews
W1 . . . . .103 A3
Gloucester Prim Sch
SE15 . . . . .49 A3
Gloucester Rd
Acton W3 . . . . .37 B4
Richmond TW9. . . . .44 C3
South Kensington
SW7 . . . . .142 C4
Gloucester Road Sta
SW7 . . . . .142 C4
Gloucester Sq
6 Hackney E2. . . .24 C4
Paddington W2. . . .102 A1

Gloucester St
SW1 . . . . .146 C2
Gloucester Terr
W2 . . . . .101 A1
Gloucester Way
EC1. . . . . .95 C3
Gloucester Wlk
W8 . . . . .127 C4
Glover Ho
London SE15. . . . . .65 A3
2 South Hampstead
NW6. . . . . .11 B1
Glycena Rd SW11. .60 B4
Glyn Ct SE27 . . . . .74 C1
Glynde Mews
SW3 . . . . .130 B1
Glynde Reach W2. .94 B3
Glynde St SE4 . . . . .66 B1
Glynfield Rd NW10. . .8 A1
Glyn Mans W14. . .140 B4
Glyn Rd E5. . . . . . .17 C4
Glyn St SE11 . . . . .148 C1
Goater's Alley
SW6 . . . . .155 A1
Goat Wharf TW8. . .44 A4
Godalming Rd E14 .34 A4
Goddard Ho SW19 .69 C2
Goddard Pl N19 . . . .4 B1
Godfrey Ho EC1 . . . .97 B3
Godfrey St
Chelsea SW3 . . . . .144 B2
Mill Meads E15. . . . .27 B3
Godley Rd SW18. . .71 C3
Godliman St EC4 . .122 C4
Godman Rd SE15 . .50 A1
Godolphin Ho
Primrose Hill
NW3 . . . . .12 A1
7 Streatham SW2 . .74 C3
Godolphin & Latymer
Sch **10** W6. . . . . . .39 A2
Godolphin Pl W3 . .28 C2
Godolphin Rd
W12 . . . . .39 A4
Godson St N1 . . . . .85 B2
Godstone Ct **1** N16 .7 A3
Godstone Ho SE1 .137 C2
Godwin Cl N1 . . . . .87 A2
Godwin Ct NW1 . . .83 A2
Godwin Ho
6 Haggerston E2 . .24 B3
Kilburn NW6. . . . . . .78 A2
Goffers Ho SE3. . . .53 A1
Goffers Rd SE3,
SE13. . . . . .53 A1
Goffton Ho **4**
SW9 . . . . .173 A1
Golborne Gdns
5 Kensal Town
W10 . . . . .23 B1
West Kilburn W10 . .23 B1
Golborne Mews **9**
W10 . . . . .31 A4
Golborne Rd W10. .31 A4
Golden Cross Mews
2 W11. . . . . .31 B3
Golden Hinde The
SE1 . . . . .123 B2
Golden Hind Pl **5**
SE8 . . . . .41 B2
Golden La EC1. . . . .97 A1
Golden Lane Campus
EC1. . . . . .97 A1
Golden Lane L Ctr
EC1. . . . . .96 C1

Golden Plover Cl
E16. . . . . .35 C3
Golden Sq W1. . . .119 A4
Golders Ct NW11 . . .1 B4
Golders Gdns NW11 .1 B4
GOLDERS GREEN . .1 C4
Golders Green Coll
NW11. . . . . .1 C3
Golders Green Cres
NW11. . . . . .1 C3
Golders Green Rd
NW11. . . . . .1 B4
Golders Green Sta
NW11. . . . . .1 C4
Golders Hill Sch
NW11. . . . . .1 C4
Golderslea NW11. . .1 C3
Golders Park Cl
NW11. . . . . .1 C3
Golders Way NW11 .1 B4
Goldhawk Ind Est
W6 . . . . .39 A3
Goldhawk Mews **2**
W12 . . . . .39 A4
Goldhawk Road Sta
W12 . . . . .39 B4
Goldhurst Terr
NW6. . . . . .11 B1
Goldie Ho N19. . . . .4 C4
Golding St E1 . . . .111 C1
Goldington Cres
NW1 . . . . .83 B2
Goldington Ct
NW1 . . . . .83 B3
Goldington St
NW1 . . . . .83 B2
Goldman Cl
E2. . . . . .99 B2
Goldney Rd W9. . . .23 C1
Goldsboro Rd
SW8 . . . . .161 C1
Goldsborough Ho
SW8 . . . . .171 C3
Goldsmith Ave W3 .28 C2
Goldsmith Cl
WC1. . . . . .106 B2
Goldsmith Rd
Acton W3 . . . . .28 C2
Peckham SE15 . . . . .49 C2
Goldsmiths Bldgs
W3 . . . . .28 C1
Goldsmith's Row
E2. . . . . .24 C3
Goldsmith's Sq **17**
E2. . . . . .24 C3
Goldsmiths Coll, Univ
of London SE14 . . .51 A2
Goldsmith's Pl **8**
NW6. . . . . .78 A3
Goldthorpe NW1 . .82 C3
Goldwell Ho
SE22 . . . . .64 A3
Goldwin Cl SE14. . .50 B2
Goldwing Cl E16. . .35 C3
Gomm Rd SE16. . . .40 B3
Gondar Gdns NW6. .10 B3
Gondar Mans NW6 .10 B3
Gonson St SE8 . . . .52 A4
Gonston Cl SW19 . .70 A2
Gonville Ho **8**
SW15. . . . . .57 C1
Gonville St SW6 . . .58 A4
Gooch Ho EC1. . . .107 B4

Goodall Ho **10** SE4 .65 C3
Goodenough Coll
WC1. . . . . .94 C2
Goodfaith Ho **18**
E14 . . . . .34 A2
Goodge Pl W1. . . .105 A3
Goodge St W1. . . .105 A3
Goodge Street Sta
W1 . . . . .105 B4
Goodhall St NW10 .21 B2
Good Hart Pl E14. . .33 A2
Goodhope Ho **17**
E14 . . . . .34 A2
Goodinge Cl N7 . . .14 A2
Goodinge Rd N7 . . .14 A2
Goodman Cres
SW2 . . . . .73 C2
Goodman's Stile **17**
E1 . . . . .111 B2
Goodman's Yd E1,
EC3. . . . . .124 C4
Goodrich Com Prim
Sch SE22. . . . . . . .64 C1
Goodrich Ct **9**
W10 . . . . .30 C3
Goodrich Ho
26 Bethnal Green
E2. . . . . .25 B3
Stamford Hill N16. . .7 A4
Goodrich Rd SE22. .64 C1
Good Shepherd RC
Prim Sch The
W12 . . . . .38 B4
Goodson Rd NW10. .8 A1
Goodspeed Ho **20**
E14 . . . . .34 A2
Goodsway NW1 . . .84 A2
Goodway Gdns
E14 . . . . .34 C3
Goodwill Ho **22**
E14 . . . . .34 A2
Goodwin Cl SE16 .139 A1
Goodwin Ho **2**
SE15 . . . . .65 A4
Goodwin Rd W12 . .38 C4
Goodwins Ct **1** WC2 .120 A4
Goodwin St N4. . . . .5 C2
Goodwood Ct W1. .104 B4
Goodwood Ho **3**
W4 . . . . .37 B1
Goodwood Mans **3**
SW9 . . . . .62 C4
Goodwood Rd
SE14. . . . . .51 A3
Goose Green Prim
Sch SE22. . . . . . . .64 B3
Goose Green Trad Est
SE22 . . . . .64 C3
Gophir La EC4. . . .123 B4
Gopsall St N1 . . . . .87 C3
Gordon Ave SW14 .56 A3
Gordonbrock Prim
Sch SE4. . . . . .66 C2
Gordonbrock Rd
SE4. . . . . .66 C2
Gordon Ct **3** W12 . .30 B3
Gordondale Rd SW18,
SW19 . . . . .70 C2
Gordon Gr SE5 . . . .48 A1
Gordon Ho **2** E1 . . .32 B2
Gordon Hospl
SW1. . . . . .147 B3
Gordon House Rd
NW5 . . . . .12 C4
Gordon Lo N16. . . . .6 C3
Gordon Mans WC1 .93 B1

Gordon Pl W8 . . . .127 C4
Gordon Rd
Chiswick W4. . . . . . .45 A4
Leyton E15 . . . . . . .19 B4
Peckham SE15 . . . . .50 A1
Richmond TW9. . . . .44 B1
Gordon Sq WC1 . . .93 C2
Gordon St WC1 . . . .93 B2
Gorefield Ho NW6. .23 C3
Gorefield Pl NW6. .23 C3
Gore Rd E9. . . . . . .25 B4
Gore St SW7 . . . . .129 A2
Gorham Ho **12**
SW4 . . . . .60 C3
Gorham Pl
W11 . . . .31 A2 112 A3
Goring St EC3 . . . .110 B2
Gorleston St W14. .140 B4
Gorse Cl E16. . . . . .35 C3
Gorsefield Ho **6**
E14 . . . . .33 C2
Gorst Rd
London SW11. . . . . .60 B1
North Acton NW10. . .20 C1
Gorsuch Pl **1**
E2. . . . . .24 B2 98 C4
Gorsuch St
E2. . . . . .24 B2 98 C4
Gosberton Rd
SW12 . . . . .72 C3
Gosfield St W1 . . . .104 C3
Gosford Ho **25** E3. .26 B3
Goslett Yd WC2. . .105 C2
Gosling Ho **2** E1 . . .32 A2
Gosling Way SW9. .173 B4
Gospatric Home Ho
SW14 . . . . .56 A4
GOSPEL OAK 12 C4
Gospel Oak Prim Sch
NW5 . . . . .12 C4
Gospel Oak Sta
NW5 . . . . .12 C4
Gosport Ho **9**
SW15 . . . . .68 C3
Gosset St E2 . . . . . .24 C2 99 B4
Gosterwood St
SE8 . . . . .51 A4
Goswell Pl EC1. . . . .96 B3
Goswell Rd EC1. . . .96 B4
Gothic Ct **17** SE5 . . .48 B3
Gottfried Mews
NW5 . . . . .13 B4
Gough Ho N1 . . . . .86 B4
Gough Sq EC4. . . .107 C2
Gough St WC1 . . . .95 A1
Gough Wlk **14** E14 .33 C3
Goulden Ho SW11 .168 A2
Gouldman Ho **33**
E1. . . . . .25 B1
Gould Terr **22** E8 . . .17 A3
Goulston St E1 . . .110 C2
Goulton Rd E5 . . . .17 A4
Govan St E2. . . . . . .24 C4
Gover Ct **3** SW4 . .172 B2
Gowan Ave SW6. . .164 A4
Gowan Ho **22**
E2. . . . . .24 B2 99 A3
Gowan Rd NW10. . . .9 A2
Gower Cl SW4. . . . .61 B1
Gower Ct WC1. . . . .93 B2
Gower Ho SE17. . . .151 A2
Gower Mews
WC1 . . . . .105 C4
Gower Pl NW1,
WC1 . . . . .93 B2

Gower Sch The 4
N7.............14 A2
Gower St WC1.....93 B1
Gower's Wlk E1...111 B1
Gowlett Rd SE15...64 C4
Gowrie Rd SW11...60 C4
Gracechurch St EC2,
EC4............123 C4
Gracefield Gdns
SW16...........74 A1
Gracefield 2 E1...32 B4
Grace Ho SE11....163 A4
Grace Jones Cl E8..16 C2
Grace Pl E3.......27 A2
Graces Mews SE5...49 A1
Grace's Mews SE5...49 A1
Grace St E3.......27 A2
Graemesdyke Ave
SW14...........55 A3
Grafton Cres NW1..13 A2
Grafton Ct 10 E8...16 C3
Grafton Ho
10 Bow E3.......26 C2
2 Deptford SE8...41 B1
Grafton Mans SW4..61 B3
Grafton Mews W1...92 C1
Grafton 6 NW1....93 C3
Grafton Prim Sch 5
N7.............5 A1
Grafton Rd
Acton W3.......28 B2
Gospel Oak NW5...13 A3
Grafton Sq SW4...61 B4
Grafton St SW1...118 B3
Grafton Way W1...93 A1
Grafton Yd NW5...13 A2
Graham Ct 5
SE14...........50 C4
Graham Ho
1 Balham SW12...73 A4
5 Tufnell Pk N19..13 C3
Graham Mans 2
E8.............17 A2
Acton W4.......37 C3
Dalston E8.......16 C3
Graham St N1......86 B1
Graham Terr SW1..145 C3
Graham Twr W3....37 A3
Grainger Ct 2
SE5.............48 B3
Grampian Gdns
NW2............1 A3
Grampians The 10
W14...........140 C3
Granard Ave SW15..57 A2
Granard Ho 9 E9...17 C2
Granard Prim Sch
SW15............57 B1
Granard Rd SW11,
SW12...........72 B4
Granary Rd E1....25 A1
Granary Sq
Islington N1.....14 C2
N1.............84 A3
Granary St NW1....83 B3
Granary The SE8...51 C3
Granby PI SE1....135 B3
Granby St
Bethnal Green
E2........24 C1 99 B2
Shoreditch
E2........24 B1 99 A2
Granby Terr NW1...82 C1

Grand Ave EC1....108 B4
Grandfield Ct W4...45 C4
Grandison Rd
SW11...........60 B2
Grand Junction Wharf
N1.............86 C1
Grand Par SW14...55 B3
Grand Union Cl
W9.............31 B4
Grand Union Cres
E8.............24 C4
Grand Union Ind Est
NW10...........20 A3
Grand Univ Vale Ind Est
SE1............122 B1
Granfield St
SW11...........167 C3
Grangecourt Rd
N16............7 A3
Grange Ct
Peckham SE15....49 B1
Strand WC2.....107 A1
Grange Gdns NW3...2 A1
Grange Gr N1.....15 B2
Grange Ho
Bermondsey SE1..138 C1
Willesden NW10...9 A1
Grange La SE21....76 B2
Grangemill
NW5............13 A4
GRANGE MILLS....73 B3
Grange Mills
SW12...........73 B3
Grange Prim Sch
SE1............138 A1
Grange Rd
Barnes SW13.....46 C2
Bermondsey SE1..138 C1
Gunnersbury W4...37 A1
Willesden NW10...9 A1
Grange St N1......87 C3
Grange The
7 Gunnersbury
W4.............37 A1
Hammersmith W12..39 A3
10 Maitland Pk
NW3............12 B2
South Acton W3...37 A4
West Kensington
W14...........140 C3
Grangeway NW6...10 C1
Grange Wlk SE1...138 C1
Grange Yd SE1....138 C1
Granite Apts E15...19 C2
Grannary The 10
SE16............40 B4
Gransden Ave E8...17 A1
Gransden Ho 1
SE8.............41 A1
Gransden Rd W12...38 B4
Grantbridge St N1..86 B2
Grantham Ct 9
SE16............40 C4
Grantham Ho 12
SE15............49 C4
Grantham Pl W1...118 A1
Grantham Rd
Chiswick W4......46 A3
South Lambeth
SW9...........172 B1
Grant Ho
38 Clapham SW8..171 B1

Grant Ho continued
Clerkenwell EC1...108 B4
Grantley Ho
2 Deptford SE14..50 C4
5 Putney SW15...69 C3
Grantley St E1.....25 C1
Grant Mus of Zoology
WC1............93 B1
Grant Rd SW11....60 A4
Grant St N1......85 B2
Grantully Rd W9...88 A3
Granville 8
2 Deptford SE14..51 A3
Shacklewell N1....87 C4
Granville Ct SE14...51 B3
Granville Ho 16
E14............33 C3
Granville Ind Est
NW2............1 B2
Granville Mans 8
W12............39 B4
Granville Pk SE13..67 C4
Granville Pl
Marylebone W1...103 B1
Walham Green
SW6...........156 A1
Granville Point
NW2............1 B2
Granville Rd
Child's Hill NW2...1 B2
Kilburn NW6.....23 C3
Wandsworth SW18..70 B4
Granville Sq
5 Camberwell
SE15............49 A3
Finsbury WC1....95 A3
Granville St WC1..95 A3
Grape St WC2....106 A2
Grasgarth Cl W3...28 B2
Grasmere NW1....92 B3
Grasmere Ave W3..28 C2
Grasmere Ct
SW13...........46 C4
Grasmere Ho 20
N16............15 C4
Grasmere Point 2
SE15............50 B3
Grasmere Prim Sch
N16............15 C4
Grateley Ho 10
SW15...........69 A3
Gratton Rd W14..126 A1
Graveley Ho 7
SE8.............41 A2
Gravel La E1.....110 C2
Gravesend Rd
W12............29 C2
Grayfriars Pas
EC1............108 B2
Gray Ho SE17....151 A2
Grayland Ct WC1...94 C3
Grayling Rd N16...6 C2
Grayling Sq
E2........24 C2 99 C4
Grayshott Rd
SW11...........60 C4
Gray's Inn WC1...107 A4
Gray's Inn Pl WC1.107 A3
Gray's Inn Rd WC1.95 A2
Gray's Inn Sq
WC1...........107 B4
Grayson Ho EC1...97 A3
Gray St SE1......135 C3
Grayswood Point 13
SW15............68 C3
Gray's Yd W1....103 C2

Grazebrook Rd N16..6 C2
Great Arthur Ho
EC1............96 C1
Great Bell Alley
EC2............109 B2
Great Castle St
W1............104 C2
Great Central St
NW1...........102 C4
Great Chapel St
W1............105 B2
Great Chart St
SW11............59 B3
Great Chertsey Rd
SW14, W4.......45 C2
Great Church La
W6.............39 C1
Great College St
SW1...........134 A2
Great Croft WC1...94 B3
Great Cross Ave
SE3.............53 A1
Great Cumberland
Mews W1.......102 C1
Great Cumberland Pl
W1............103 A1
Great Dover St
SE1............137 B2
Great Eastern Bldgs
10 E8...........17 A2
Great Eastern Ent Ctr
E14.............41 C1
Great Eastern Pier
E14.............41 C1
Great Eastern Rd
E15.............19 C2
Great Eastern St
EC2.......24 A1 98 A2
Great Eastern Wharf
SW11...........158 B1
Great Field 7
NW5............13 B3
Greatfield Cl
London SE6.....66 C3
4 Tufnell Pk N19..13 B4
Great George St
SW1...........134 A3
Great Guildford Bsns
Sq SE1.........122 C1
Great Guildford St
SE1............122 C1
Gresham Wlk 3
SW15............68 C3
Great James St
WC1...........106 B4
Great Marlborough St
W1............104 C1
Great Maze Pond
SE1............137 C4
Great Newport St
WC2...........120 A4
Greatorex Ho 15
E1.............111 B4
Greatorex St E1..111 B4
Great Ormond St
Hospl for Children
WC1............94 C1
Great Ormond St
WC1............94 C1
Great Percy St
WC1............95 B4
Great Peter St
SW1...........133 C1
Great Portland St
W1............104 B3

Great Portland Street
Sta W1..........92 B1
Great Pulteney St
W1............119 A4
Great Queen St
WC2...........106 B2
Great Russell Mans
WC1...........106 A3
Great Russell St
WC1...........106 A3
Great St Helen's
EC3............110 A2
Great St Thomas
Apostle EC4....123 A4
Great Scotland Yd
SW1...........120 A2
Great Smith St
SW1...........133 C2
Great Spilmans
SE22............64 A2
Great Suffolk St
SE1............122 B1
Great Sutton St
EC1............96 B1
Great Swan Alley
EC2............109 B2
Great Titchfield St
W1............104 C3
Great Tower St
EC3............124 A4
Great Trinity La
EC4............123 A4
Great Turnstile
WC2...........107 A3
Great Western Rd W2,
W9............31 B4
Great West Rd W4,
W6.............45 C4
Great West Road
Cedars Rd W4....45 B4
Great West Road
Hogarth La W4....46 A4
Great Winchester St
EC2............109 C2
Great Windmill St
W1............119 B4
Great Yd SE1....138 B4
Greaves Cotts 10
E14.............33 A4
Greaves Twr
SW10..........157 A2
Grebe Ct 18 E14...42 B4
Greek Ct W1.....105 C1
Greek Sch of London
W3.............28 A2
Greek St W1.....105 C1
Greenacre Ct E8...16 C3
Greenacre Sq 26
SE16............40 C4
Green Arbour Ct
EC1............108 A2
Greenaway Gdns
NW3............11 A4
Greenaway Ho
Finsbury WC1....95 B3
St John's Wood
NW8............78 C4
Green Bank E1....32 A1
Greenberry St
NW8............80 A1
Greencoat Ho 1
SW1............2 B4
Greencoat Pl
SW1...........147 A4

Greencoat Row
SW1 . . . . **133** A1
Greencourt Ho
E1 . . . . **25** C1
Greencroft Gdns
NW6 . . . .**11** B1
Green Ct 2 NW10 . . **8** A4
Green Dale SE22 . . .**64** A2
Greendale Cl SE22. .**64** A2
Green Dragon Ct
SE1 . . . . **123** B1
Green Dragon Ho
WC1 . . . . **106** B2
Green Dragon La
TW8 . . . . **36** B1
Green Dragon Prim
Sch TW8 . . . .**44** A4
Green Dragon Yd **24**
E1 . . . . **111** B3
Greene Ct 20 SE14 . .**50** C4
Greene Ho SE1 . . . . **137** B1
Greenend Rd W4 . . .**38** A4
Greener Ho 3
SW4 . . . . **61** C4
Greenfell Mans
SE8 . . . . **52** A4
Greenfield Gdns
NW2 . . . . **1** A1
Greenfield Ho 28
SW19 . . . .**69** C3
Greenfield Rd E1 . . **111** C2
Greenham Cl SE1 . . **135** B3
Greenham Ho 6
E9 . . . .**25** B4
Greenheath Bsns Ctr
3 E2 . . . . **25** A1
Greenhill NW3 . . . . **11** C4
Greenhill Pk
NW10 . . . . **21** A4
Greenhill Rd
NW10 . . . . **21** A4
Greenhill's Rents
EC1 . . . . **108** A4
Greenhills Terr 16
N1 . . . . **15** C2
Green Ho The 5
SW19 . . . .**70** A3
Green Hundred Rd
SE15 . . . .**49** C4
Greening Ho SE13 . . **67** C3
Greenland Ho
Bermondsey SE8 . . . **40** C1
4 Mile End E1 . . . . **26** A1
Greenland Mews
SE8 . . . . **40** C1
Greenland Pier
SE8 . . . . **41** B3
Greenland Pl NW1 . .**82** B4
Greenland Quay
SE16 . . . . **40** C2
Greenland Rd NW1 . **82** C4
Greenland St NW1 . .**82** B4
Green Lanes N4, N8,
N15 . . . . **6** A4
Greenleaf Cl 8
SW2 . . . .**74** C4
Green Link Wlk
TW9 . . . . **45** A2
Greenman St N1 . . . **86** C4
Greenmead Prim Sch
SW15 . . . .**57** A2
Greenock Rd 11
W3 . . . . **37** B3

Green Park SW1,
W1 . . . . **132** B4
Green Park Sta
W1 . . . . **118** C2
Greenroof Way
SE10 . . . . **43** B3
Greens Ct W1 . . . . . **119** B4
Green's Ct
W11 . . . . . . **31** B1 **112** C1
Greenside Prim Sch
W12 . . . .**38** C4
Greenside Rd W12. .**38** C4
Green St W1 . . . . . . **117** B4
Greenstead Gdns
SW15 . . . .**57** A2
Greenstreet Hill
SE4 . . . . **65** C4
Greensward Ho
SW6 . . . . **166** C2
Green Terr EC1 . . . . **95** C3
Green The W3 . . . . . **29** A1
Greenview Cl W3 . . .**29** A1
Greenview Ct
East Dulwich
SE22 . . . .**64** C3
Wandsworth SW18 . . **72** A4
Greenway Cl N4 . . . . **6** B2
Greenwell St W1 . . . **92** B1
GREENWICH **43** C3
Greenwich Acad
SE10 . . . . **52** A2
Greenwich Bsns Ctr
SE10 . . . . **52** A3
Greenwich Bsns Pk
SE10 . . . . **52** B3
Greenwich Church St
SE10 . . . . **52** B4
Greenwich Coll 17
SE10 . . . . **52** B3
Greenwich Ct 11
E1 . . . .**32** A3
Greenwich High Rd
SE10 . . . . **52** A3
Greenwich Ho SE13 . **67** C1
Greenwich Ind Est
SE10 . . . . **52** A3
Greenwich Mkt 2
SE10 . . . . **52** B4
Greenwich Park
SE10 . . . . **53** A4
Greenwich Park St
SE10 . . . . **52** C4
Greenwich Pier
SE10 . . . . **42** B1
Greenwich Quay
SE8 . . . . **52** A4
Greenwich South St
SE10 . . . . **52** B2
Greenwich Sta
SE10 . . . . **52** A3
Greenwich View Pl
E14 . . . . **42** A3
Green Wlk SE1 . . . . **138** A1
Greenwood 8
SW19 . . . .**69** C3
Green Wood NW5 . . **13** B3
Greenwood Ho
Finsbury WC1 . . . . . .**95** B3
2 Nunhead SE4 . . . **65** C3
Greenwood Pl
NW5 . . . . **13** A3
Greenwood Rd E8 . . **16** C2
Greenwood Terr
NW10 . . . . **20** C3
Green Yd WC1 . . . . . **95** A2

Greet Ho SE1 . . . . . **135** C3
Greet St SE1 . . . . . . **121** C1
Gregor Mews SE3 . . .**53** C3
Gregory Pl W8 . . . . **128** A4
Greig Terr SE17 . . . .**48** A4
Grenada Ho 18 E14 . .**33** B2
Grenade St E14 . . . . .**33** B2
Grena Gdns TW9 . . . **54** B3
Grena Rd TW10,
TW9 . . . . **54** B3
Grenard Cl SE15 . . . .**49** C3
Grendon Ho
22 Hackney E9 . . . . . **17** B1
Pentonville N1 . . . . . **84** C1
Grendon St NW8 . . . **90** A2
Grenfell Ho SE5 . . . . **48** B3
Grenfell Rd W11 . . . .**30** C2
Grenfell Twr 5
W11 . . . . **30** C2
Grenfell Wlk 4
W11 . . . . **30** C2
Grenier Apartments
11 SE15 . . . .**50** A3
Grenville Ho
28 Bow E3 . . . . **26** A3
4 Deptford SE8 . . . . **51** C4
Grenville Lo N6 . . . . . **4** B4
Grenville Mans
WC1 . . . . **94** A2
Grenville Mews
SW7 . . . . **142** C3
Grenville Pl SW7 . . **142** C4
Grenville Rd N19 . . . .**5** A3
Grenville St WC1 . . . **94** B1
Gresham Almshouses
3 SW9 . . . . **62** C4
Gresham Coll EC1 . . **107** C3
Gresham Gdns
NW11 . . . .**1** A3
Gresham Pl 2 N19 . . .**4** C2
Gresham Rd SW9 . . . **62** C4
Gresham St EC2 . . . **109** A2
Gresham Way
SW19 . . . .**70** C1
Gresham Way Est
SW19 . . . .**71** A1
Gresley St N1 . . . . . **171** C4
Gresley Rd N19 . . . . . **4** B4
Gressenhall Rd
SW18 . . . .**70** B4
Gresse St W1 . . . . . **105** B2
Greswell St SW6 . . . .**47** C2
Greta Ho SE3 . . . . . . **53** B4
Gretton Ho 2 E2 . . . .**25** B2
Greville Hall NW6 . . **78** B2
Greville Ho
Knightsbridge
SW1 . . . . **131** B2
Putney SW15 . . . . . . **57** C4
Greville Lo 6 W2 . . **100** A2
Greville Mews 6
NW6 . . . . **78** A3
Greville Pl W9 . . . . . **78** B2
Greville Rd
Kilburn NW6 . . . . . . **78** B2
Richmond TW10 . . . . **54** B1
Greville St EC1 . . . . **107** C3
Grey Coat Hospital
The (Sch) SW1 . . . . **147** B3
SW1 . . . . **133** B1
Greycoat Pl SW1 . . **133** B1
Greycoat St SW1 . . **133** B1
Grey Eagle St
E1 . . . . **24** B1 **99** A1

Greyfriars 18 SE26 . .**76** C1
Greyfriars Ho SE3 . . .**53** B4
Grey Ho 27 W12 . . . .**30** A2
Greyhound Ct
WC2 . . . . **121** B4
Greyhound Rd
College Pk NW10 . . . **22** A2
Fulham W6 . . . . **154** A4
Greyladies Gdns
SE10 . . . . **52** B2
Greystoke Ho SE15 . .**49** C4
Greystoke Pl EC4 . . **107** C2
Grey Turner Ho
W12 . . . . **29** C3
Grice Ct N1 . . . . **15** B2
Grierson Rd SE23 . . .**66** A1
Griffin Cl NW10 . . . . . **9** A3
Griffin Ct
3 Brentford
TW8 . . . . **44** A4
Chiswick W4 . . . . . . **38** B1
Shepherd's Bush
W12 . . . . **30** A1
Griffin Gate 1
SW15 . . . .**57** C4
Griffon Ho 3
SW11 . . . . **168** A4
Grigg's Pl SE1 . . . . . **138** B1
Grimaldi Ho N1 . . . . **84** C2
Grimsby St
Bethnal Green
E2 . . . . **24** C1 **99** A2
Shoreditch
E2 . . . . **24** B1 **99** A2
Grimsel Path SE5 . . .**48** A3
Grimshaw Cl N6 . . . . .**3** C4
Grimston Rd SW6 . . **164** C1
Grimthorpe Ho
EC1 . . . . **96** A2
Grimwade Cl SE15 . .**65** B4
Grindall Ho 20 E1 . . .**25** A1
Grindal St SE1 . . . . . **135** B3
Grindley Ho 3 E3 . . .**33** B4
Grinling Gibbons Prim
Sch **22** SE8 . . . . . . **51** B4
Grinling Pl SE8 . . . . . **51** C4
Grinstead Rd SE8 . . .**41** A1
Grisedale NW1 . . . . . **92** C4
Grittleton Rd W9 . . . .**23** C1
Groombridge Rd
E9 . . . . **17** C1
Groom Cres SW18 . . **71** C4
Groom Ho SE11 . . . **149** A3
Groom Pl SW1 . . . . **131** C2
Grosse Way SW15 . .**57** A1
Grosvenor Ave
Canonbury N5 . . . . . **15** B3
Mortlake SW14 . . . . .**56** A4
Richmond TW10 . . . . **54** A2
Grosvenor Bridge
SW1 . . . . **160** B3
Grosvenor Cotts
SW1 . . . . **145** B4
Grosvenor Court Mans
W2 . . . . **102** C1
Grosvenor Cres
SW1 . . . . **131** C3
Grosvenor Cres Mews
SW1 . . . . **131** B3
Grosvenor Ct
Brondesbury Pk
NW6 . . . . **22** C4
Gunnersbury W4 . . . **37** A1
22 Poplar E14 . . . . . **33** B3
Putney SW15 . . . . . . **58** A2

Grosvenor Gdns
Cricklewood NW2 . . . .**9** B3
Mortlake SW14 . . . . .**56** A4
Westminster SW1 . . **132** B1
Grosvenor Gdns Mews
E SW1 . . . . **132** B2
Grosvenor Gdns Mews
N SW1 . . . . **132** B1
Grosvenor Gdns Mews
S SW1 . . . . **132** B1
Grosvenor Hill
W1 . . . . **118** A4
Grosvenor Hill Ct
W1 . . . . **118** A4
Grosvenor Park
SE5 . . . . **48** B3
Grosvenor Pier
SW1 . . . . **161** B4
Grosvenor Pk SE5 . . **48** B3
Grosvenor Pl
SW1 . . . . **132** A3
Grosvenor Rd
Acton Green W4 . . . . **37** B1
Pimlico SW1 . . . . . . **161** A4
Richmond TW9 . . . . . **54** A3
Grosvenor Residences
4 W14 . . . . **39** C3
Grosvenor Sq W1 . . **117** C4
Grosvenor St W1 . . **118** A4
Grosvenor Terr
SE5 . . . . **48** B4
Grosvenor The
NW11 . . . .**2** A4
Grosvenor Wharf Rd
E14 . . . . **42** C2
Grote's Bldgs SE3 . . .**53** A1
Grote's Pl SE3 . . . . . .**53** A1
Groton Rd SW18 . . . .**71** A2
Grotto Ct SE1 . . . . . **136** C4
Grotto Pas W1 . . . . **103** B4
Grove Crescent Rd
E15 . . . . **19** C2
Grove Ct
Camberwell SE5 . . . .**49** A1
Clapham SW4 . . . . . .**61** B4
South Kensington
SW10 . . . . **143** A1
St John's Wood
NW8 . . . . **89** B4
Grovedale Rd N19 . . .**4** C2
Grove Dwellings
E1 . . . . **32** B4
Grove End Gdns
NW8 . . . . **79** A1
Grove End Ho NW8 . **89** B3
Grove End Rd NW8 . **89** B3
Grove Gdns NW8 . . . **90** B3
Grove Hall Ct
Bow E3 . . . . **26** C3
St John's Wood
NW8 . . . . **89** B4
Grove Hill Rd SE5 . . .**64** A4
Grove Ho
Blackheath SE3 . . . . .**53** B1
Chelsea SW3 . . . . . . **158** B4
Grove La SE5 . . . . . . **64** A4
Groveland Ct EC4 . . **109** A1
Grovelands Cl SE5 . .**49** A1
Grove Lane Terr
SE5 . . . . **48** C1
Groveley Ho 4 N4 . . . .**6** B4
Grove Lo SW4 . . . . . .**61** B3

Grove Mans
London SW4 . . . . 60 B3
2 Shepherd's Bush
W6 . . . . 39 B4
3 Stamford Hill N16 . . 7 C3
Grove Mews W6 . . . . . . 39 B4
GROVE PARK W4 . . . . 45 B2
Grove Park Bridge
W4 . . . . 45 B3
Grove Park Gdns
W4 . . . . 45 B3
Grove Park Mews
W4 . . . . 45 B3
Grove Park Prim Sch
W4 . . . . 45 B3
Grove Park Rd W4 . . . . 45 A3
Grove Park Terr
W4 . . . . 45 A4
Grove Pk SE5 . . . . 49 A1
Grove Pl
Acton W3 . . . . 28 B1
Balham SW12 . . . . 61 A1
Hampstead NW3 . . . . . . 2 C1
Grover Ct SE13 . . . . 52 A1
Grove Rd
Acton W3 . . . . 28 B1
Barnes SW13 . . . . 46 B1
Bow E3 . . . . 26 C3
Richmond TW10 . . . . . . 54 B1
Willesden NW2 . . . . 9 B2
Grover Ho
4 London SW4 . . . . . . 61 B2
Vauxhall SE11 . . . . . . 149 A1
Groveside Ct
SW11 . . . . 167 B2
Grove St SE8 . . . . 41 B1
Grove Terr NW5 . . . . . . 13 A4
Grove Terrace Mews
NW5 . . . . 4 A1
Grove The
Dulwich SE21 . . . . 76 C3
Hendon NW11 . . . . 1 A4
Highgate N6 . . . . 3 C3
Stroud Green N4 . . . . . . 5 B4
Grove Vale SE22 . . . . . . 64 B3
Groveway SW9 . . . . . . 173 A3
Grovewood **9**
W3 . . . . 44 C2
Grovewood Ho
NW2 . . . . 1 B2
Grummant Rd
SE15 . . . . 49 B2
Grundy St E14 . . . . 34 A3
Guardian Angels RC
Prim Sch **5** E3 . . . . . . 26 A2
Guards Mus The
SW1 . . . . 133 B3
Gubyon Ave SE24 . . . . . 63 A2
Gudden Dr E5 . . . . 17 A4
Guerin Sq E3 . . . . 26 B2
Guernsey Gr SE24 . . . . 75 B4
Guernsey Ho **10**
N1 . . . . 15 B2
Guernsey Rd **11**
N1 . . . . 15 B2
Guildford Gr SE10 . . . . 52 A2
Guildford Ho **23**
SE5 . . . . 48 B1
Guildford Rd SW8 . . . 172 B4
Guildhall Art Gall
EC2 . . . . 109 A2
Guildhall Ho EC2 . . . . 109 B2
14 Bethnal Green
E2 . . . . 24 C3
Guildhall Sch Music &
Drama EC2 . . . . 109 A2
Guildhall Yd EC2 . . . . 109 A2

Guildhouse St
SW1 . . . . 146 C3
Guilford Pl WC1 . . . . . . 94 C1
Guilford St WC1 . . . . . . 94 B1
Guillemot Ct **28**
SE8 . . . . 51 B4
Guinness Cl E9 . . . . . . 18 A1
Guinness Ct
Chelsea SW3 . . . . 144 C3
Finsbury EC1 . . . . 97 A3
Primrose Hill NW8 . . . . 80 B3
Whitechapel E1 . . . . . . 111 A1
Guinness Sq SE1 . . . . 152 A4
Guinness Trust Bldgs
Bermondsey SE1 . . . . 138 C4
7 Bethnal Green
E2 . . . . 24 C3
Chelsea SW3 . . . . 144 C3
Hammersmith W6 . . . . . 39 B1
Kennington SE11 . . . . . 150 A2
Guion Rd SW6 . . . . . . 165 A2
Gujarat Ho **1** N16 . . . . 7 A1
Gulland Wlk **21** N1 . . 15 B2
Gullane Ho **22** E3 . . . 26 B3
Gulliver St SE16 . . . . . 41 B3
Gulston Wlk SW3 . . . . 145 A3
Gunmakers La E3 . . . . 26 A4
GUNNERSBURY 37 A2
Gunnersbury Avenue
(North Circular Rd)
W3 . . . . 36 C3
Gunnersbury Cl **8**
W4 . . . . 37 A1
Gunnersbury Cres
W3 . . . . 36 C4
Gunnersbury Ct **8**
W3 . . . . 37 A4
Gunnersbury Dr
W5 . . . . 36 B4
Gunnersbury Gdns
W3 . . . . 36 C4
Gunnersbury La
W3 . . . . 36 C4
Gunnersbury Mews **6**
W4 . . . . 37 A1
Gunnersbury Park
W3 . . . . 36 C3
Gunnersbury Park
Mus W3 . . . . 36 C3
Gunnersbury Sta
W4 . . . . 37 A1
Gunnersbury Triangle
Nat Res W12 . . . . 37 B2
Gunners Rd SW18 . . . 71 C2
Gunpowder Sq
EC4 . . . . 107 C2
Gun St E1 . . . . 110 C3
Gunstor Rd N16 . . . . . 16 A4
Gunter Gr SW6 . . . . . 156 C2
Gunterstone Rd
W14 . . . . 140 B2
Gunthorpe St E1 . . . . 111 A2
Gunwhale Cl SE16 . . . 32 C1
Gun Wharf
Old Ford E3 . . . . 26 A4
Wapping E1 . . . . 32 B1
Gurdon Ho **7** E14 . . . 33 C3
Gurdon Rd SE7 . . . . . . 43 C1
Gurney Ho
3 Bayswater
W2 . . . . 100 A3
Gurney Rd SW6 . . . . . . 59 B4
Guthrie Ct SW1 . . . . . 135 C3
Guthrie St SW3 . . . . . 144 A2

Gutter La EC2 . . . . . . 108 C2
Guyscliff Rd SE13 . . . . 67 B2
Guy's Hospl SE1 . . . . 137 C4
Guy St SE1 . . . . 137 C4
Gwalior Rd SW15 . . . . 57 C4
Gwendolen Ave
SW15 . . . . 57 C2
Gwendolen Cl
SW15 . . . . 57 C2
Gwendwr Rd W14 . . . 140 B2
Gwent Ct **15** SE16 . . 32 C1
Gwilym Maries Ho **11**
E2 . . . . 25 A2
Gwyn Cl SW6 . . . . 156 C1
Gwynne Cl W4 . . . . . . 46 B4
Gwynne Ho
Finsbury WC1 . . . . 95 B3
1 Streatham SW2 . . 74 B3
Whitechapel E1 . . . . . . 32 A4
Gwynne Pl WC1 . . . . . . 95 A3
Gwynne Rd SW11 . . . 167 C2
Gye Ho **2** SW4 . . . . . 62 A3
Gylcote Cl SE5 . . . . . . 63 C3

H

Haarlem Rd **12**
W14 . . . . 39 C3
Haberdasher Pl **4**
N1 . . . . 97 A4 98 A4
Haberdashers' Aske's
Hatcham Coll
SE4 . . . . 51 A1
Haberdasher St
N1 . . . . 97 C4
Hackford Rd SW9 . . . 173 A4
Hackford Wlk
SW9 . . . . 173 B3
HACKNEY 17 A2
Hackney Central Sta
E8 . . . . 17 A2
Hackney Com Coll **33**
N1 . . . . 24 A2 98 B4
Hackney Downs Sta
E8 . . . . 17 A3
Hackney Empire
E8 . . . . 17 A2
Hackney Free &
Parochial CE Sec
Sch **13** E9 . . . . 17 B2
Hackney Gr E8 . . . . . . 17 A2
Hackney Rd E2 . . . . . . 24 C3
HACKNEY WICK 18 C2
Hackney Wick E9 . . . . 18 B2
Hackney Wick Sta
E9 . . . . 18 C2
Hackworth Point **20**
E3 . . . . 27 A2
Hacon Sq **12** E8 . . . . 17 A1
Haddo Ho
Gospel Oak NW5 . . . . . 12 A4
Greenwich SE10 . . . . . . 52 A4
Haddon Ct **3** W3 . . . 29 B2
Haddo St SE10 . . . . . . 52 B4
Haden Ct N4 . . . . 5 C2
Hadfield Ho **3**
E1 . . . . 111 C1
Hadleigh Cl **17** E1 . . 25 B1
Hadleigh Ho **18** E1 . . 25 B1
Hadleigh St E2 . . . . . . 25 B2
Hadley Ct N16 . . . . 7 C3
Hadley Gdns W4 . . . . . 37 C1
Hadley St NW1 . . . . . . 13 A2
Hadlow Ho **17** SE17 . 152 B2
Hadrian Cl **5** E3 . . . . 26 C4

Hadrian Ct SE4 . . . . . . 66 C4
Hadrian Est **33** E2 . . . 24 C3
Hadrian St SE10 . . . . . 43 A1
Hadstock Ho NW1 . . . . 93 C4
Hadyn Park Ct **13**
W12 . . . . 38 C4
Hadyn Park Rd
W12 . . . . 38 C4
Hafer Rd SW11 . . . . . . 60 B3
Hafton Rd SE6 . . . . . . 67 A1
HAGGERSTON 24 B3
Haggerston Rd E8 . . . . 24 B4
Haggerston Sch **15**
E2 . . . . 24 B3
Haggerston Sta
E2 . . . . 24 B4
Haggerston Studios
30 E8 . . . . 24 B4
Hague Prim Sch **9**
E2 . . . . 25 A1
Hague St **30**
E2 . . . . 24 C2 99 C3
Haig Ho **4** E2 . . . . . . 24 C3
Hailsham Ave SW2 . . . 74 B2
Hainford Cl SE4 . . . . . . 65 C3
Haining Cl **8** W4 . . . . 36 C1
Hainton Cl E1 . . . . 32 A3
Halcomb St N1 . . . . . . 24 A4
Halcrow St E1 . . . . 32 A4
Haldane Pl SW18 . . . . 71 A3
Haldane Rd SW6 . . . . 155 A3
Haldon Rd SW18 . . . . 58 B1
Hale Ho SW1 . . . . 147 C2
Hales Ho **3** SW12 . . 73 A4
Hales Prior N1 . . . . . . 84 C1
Hales St SE8 . . . . 51 C3
Hale St E14 . . . . 34 A2
Halesworth Rd
SE13 . . . . 67 A4
Half Moon Cres
N1 . . . . 85 A2
Half Moon La SE24 . . . 63 B1
Halfmoon Pas E1 . . . . 111 A1
Half Moon St W1 . . . . 118 B1
Halford Ho **9**
SW15 . . . . 57 C2
Halford Rd
Richmond TW10 . . . . . . 54 A2
West Brompton
SW6 . . . . 155 B3
Haliday Ho N1 . . . . 15 C2
Haliday Wlk **4** N1 . . . 15 C2
Halidon Cl E9 . . . . 17 B3
Haliwell Ho **10**
NW6 . . . . 78 A3
Halkett Ho **11** E2 . . . 25 B4
Halkin Arc SW1 . . . . . 131 A2
Halkin Mews SW1 . . . 131 B2
Halkin Pl SW1 . . . . . . 131 B2
Halkin St SW1 . . . . . . 131 C3
Hallam Ct W1 . . . . . . 104 B4
Hallam Ho
17 Brixton SW9 . . . 173 B4
Pimlico SW1 . . . . 147 A1
Hallam Mews W1 . . . 104 B4
Hallam Rd SW13 . . . . 57 A4
Hallam St W1 . . . . 104 B4
Halley Gdns SE13 . . . . 67 C3
Halley Ho
16 Bethnal Green
E2 . . . . 24 C3
8 Cubitt Town
SE10 . . . . 43 B1
Halley Prim Sch
E14 . . . . 33 A4
Halley St E14 . . . . 33 A4

Hallfield Jun & Inf
Schs **3** W2 . . . . 100 B1
Hall Gate NW8 . . . . . . 89 A4
Halliday Ho **8** E1 . . . 111 C1
Halliford St N1 . . . . 15 C1
Halling Ho **6** SE1 . . . 137 C3
Hallings Wharf
Studios **2** E15 . . . . . 27 C4
Halliwell Ct **4**
SE22 . . . . 64 C2
Halliwell Rd SW2 . . . . 62 B1
Hall Oak Wlk NW6 . . . 10 B2
Hall Pl W2 . . . . 89 B1
Hall Rd
Leyton E15 . . . . 19 C4
St John's Wood
NW8 . . . . 89 A4
Hall Sch The NW3 . . . 11 C2
Hall Sch Wimbledon
SW15 . . . . 68 C1
Hall St EC1 . . . . 96 B4
Hallsville Prim Sch
E16 . . . . 35 C3
Hallsville Rd E16 . . . . . 35 B3
Hall Twr W2 . . . . 101 C4
Halpin Pl SE17 . . . . . . 151 C3
Halsbury Ho **4** N7 . . 14 B4
Halsbury Rd W12 . . . . 30 A1
Halsey St SW3 . . . . . . 144 C4
Halsmere Rd SE5 . . . . 48 A2
Halstead Ct N1 . . . . . . 87 C1
Halston Cl SW11 . . . . . 60 B1
Halstow **12** NW5 . . . 12 C2
Halstow Prim Sch **5**
SE10 . . . . 43 C1
Halstow Rd
Greenwich SE3,
SE10 . . . . 43 C1
Kensal Green
NW10 . . . . 22 C2
Halton Cross St
N1 . . . . 86 B4
Halton Ho **22** N1 . . . 15 A1
Halton Mans N1 . . . . . 15 A1
Halton Pl N1 . . . . 86 C4
Halton Rd N1 . . . . 86 B4
Halyard Ho E14 . . . . . . 42 B3
Hambalt Rd SW4 . . . . 61 B2
Hambledon SE17 . . . . 48 C4
Hambledon Chase
N4 . . . . 5 A4
Hambledon Ho E5 . . . 17 A4
Hambledon Pl
SE21 . . . . 76 B3
Hambledon Rd
SW18 . . . . 70 B4
Hamble St SW6 . . . . . 59 A4
Hambley Ho **5**
SE16 . . . . 40 A2
Hamblyn Ho **7** N1 . . . 7 B4
Hambridge Way
SW2 . . . . 74 C4
Hambrook Ct **12**
NW5 . . . . 13 A4
Hamers Ho **18**
SW2 . . . . 74 C4
Hamilton Cl
Rotherhithe SE16 . . . . 41 A4
St John's Wood
NW8 . . . . 89 B3
Hamilton Ct W9 . . . . . 88 C4

Hamilton Gdns
NW8 .... **89** A4
Hamilton Hall
NW8 .... **78** C1
Hamilton Ho
2 Bow E3 .... **26** B2
Chiswick W4 ...... **46** A4
Kensington W8 .... **128** A4
1 Poplar E14 .... **33** B2
Putney SW15 ...... **56** C2
10 Richmond TW9 .. **44** C2
St John's Wood
NW8 .... **89** B4
Hamilton La N5 ... **15** A4
Hamilton Lo **17** E14 .. **41** E1
Hamilton Mews
W1 .... **132** A4
Hamilton Pk N5 ... **15** A4
Hamilton Pk W N5 **15** A4
Hamilton Pl W1 .. **117** C1
Hamilton Rd
Acton W4 .... **38** A4
Hendon NW11 ..... **1** A4
Willesden NW10 .. **8** C3
Hamilton Sq SE1 . **137** C4
Hamilton St SE8 .. **51** C4
Hamilton Terr
NW8 .... **89** A4
Hamlet Ct
1 Hammersmith
W6 .... **38** C2
Kensington SE11 .. **150** A2
Hamlet Gdns W6 .. **38** C2
Hamlet Ind Ctr E9 .. **18** C1
Hamlet Sq NW2 ... **1** A1
Hamlets Way E3 .. **26** B1
Hamlet The SE5 ... **63** C4
Hamlet Way SE1 . **137** C4
Hammelton Gn **2**
SW9 .... **48** A2
Hammersley Ho **8**
SE14 .... **50** B3
HAMMERSMITH .. **39** B2
Hammersmith Bridge
Rd W6, SW13 ..... **39** B1
Hammersmith
Broadway
Hammersmith W6 .. **39** B1
5 Hammersmith
W6 .... **39** B2
Hammersmith Flyover
W6 .... **39** B3
Hammersmith Gr
W6 .... **39** B3
Hammersmith Hospl
W12 .... **30** A3
Hammersmith Rd
Hammersmith W6 .. **39** C2
Kensington W14 .. **140** B4
Hammersmith Sta
W6 .... **39** C2
Hammersmith Terr **6**
W6 .... **38** C1
Hammett St EC3 . **124** C4
Hammond Ho
10 Deptford SE14 .. **50** B3
Millwall E14 ...... **42** A3
Hammond Lo **6**
W9 .... **31** C4
Hammond St NW5 . **13** B2
Hampden Cl NW1 .. **24** A3
Hampden Cl NW1 . **83** C2
Hampden Gurney CE
Prim Sch W1 ..... **102** B2

Hampden Gurney St
W1 .... **102** B1
Hampden Rd N19 .. **4** C2
Hampshire Ct **6**
SW13 .... **46** B1
Hampshire Hog La
1 Hammersmith
W6 .... **39** A1
11 Hammersmith
W6 .... **39** A2
Hampshire St
NW5 .... **13** C2
Hampson Way
SW8 .... **172** C4
HAMPSTEAD **11** B2
Hampstead Coll of
Fine Arts &
Humanities **12**
NW3 .... **12** A2
Hampstead Com Mkt
NW3 .... **11** C4
Hampstead Gate
NW3 .... **11** B3
Hampstead Gn
NW3 .... **12** A3
Hampstead Gr NW3 . **2** B1
Hampstead Heath
NW3 .... **2** C2
Hampstead Heath Pre
Prep Sch NW3 .... **12** B4
Hampstead Heath Sta
NW3 .... **12** A4
Hampstead High Sch
3 NW3 .... **11** C4
Hampstead High St
NW3 .... **11** C4
Hampstead Hill Gdns
NW3 .... **12** A4
Hampstead Hill Sch
1 NW3 .... **11** C4
Hampstead La N6 .. **3** A4
Hampstead Parochial
CE Prim Sch **30**
NW3 .... **11** B4
Hampstead Rd
NW1 .... **92** C4
Hampstead Sch
NW2 .... **10** A4
Hampstead Sq **1**
NW3 .... **2** B1
Hampstead Sta
NW3 .... **11** C4
Hampstead Theatre
NW3 .... **11** C1
Hampstead West **4**
NW6 .... **10** C2
Hampstead Wlk **1**
E3 .... **26** B4
Hampton Cl NW6 . **23** C2
Hampton Ct
1 Islington N1 .... **15** A2
19 Rotherhithe
SE16 .... **32** C1
Hampton St SE1 . **150** B3
Hamstead Gates **11**
NW5 .... **13** A2
Ham Yd W1 .... **119** B4
Hana Mews E5 .... **17** A4
Hanbury Ho
8 Bethnal Green
E1 .... **111** B4
South Lambeth
SW8 .... **162** B3
Hanbury Mews N1 . **87** A3
Hanbury St E1 .... **111** A4

Hancock Nunn Ho **1**
NW3 .... **12** B1
Hancock Rd E3 .... **27** B2
Handa Wlk **3** N1 .. **15** B2
Hand Ct WC1 ..... **107** A3
Handel House
Museum **11** W1 .. **118** B4
Handel Mans
Barnes SW13 ..... **47** B3
Bloomsbury WC1 .. **94** B2
Handel St WC1 ... **94** B2
Handforth Rd
SW9 .... **163** B2
Handley Rd E9 .... **25** B4
Hands Wlk E16 ... **35** C3
Hanford Cl SW18 . **70** C3
Hankey Pl SE1 ... **137** C3
Hanley Ct N4 ..... **5** B3
Hanley Gdns N4 .. **5** B3
Hanley Rd N4, N19 .. **5** A3
Hanmer Wlk N7 ... **5** B2
Hannah Mary Way **17**
SE1 .... **153** C3
Hannay La N8 .... **4** C4
Hannay Wlk SW16 . **73** C2
Hannell Rd SW6 .. **154** B2
Hannen Ho SE5 ... **48** C1
Hannen Rd SE27 . **75** A1
Hannibal Rd E1 .. **32** B4
Hannington Rd
SW4 .... **61** A4
Hanover Ave E16 .. **35** C1
Hanover Cl TW9 .. **44** C3
Hanover Ct
Shepherd's Bush
W12 .... **29** C1
Stamford Hill N16 . **7** B4
Hanover Gate Mans
NW1 .... **90** B2
Hanover Gdns
SE11 .... **163** B3
Harrow NW8 ...... **80** A1
Hanover Mans **1**
SW2 .... **62** C2
Hanover Pk SE15 . **49** C2
Hanover Pl
16 Bow E3 .... **26** B2
St Giles WC2 .... **106** B1
Hanover Prim Sch
N1 .... **86** C2
Hanover Rd NW10 . **22** B4
Hanover Sq W1 .. **104** B1
Hanover Stps W2 . **102** B1
Hanover Terr NW1 . **90** C3
Hanover Terrace
Mews NW1 .... **90** B3
Hanover West Ind Est
NW10 .... **20** C2
Hanover Yd N1 ... **86** C2
Hansard Mews
W14 .... **39** C4
Hanscomb Mews
SW4 .... **61** B3
Hans Cres SW1 .. **130** C2
Hansler Ct **14**
SW19 .... **70** A3
Hansler Rd SE22 . **64** B2
Hanson Cl
Balham SW12 ..... **73** A4
Mortlake SW14 ... **55** B4
Hanson Ho **2** E1 . **125** C4
Hanson St W1 .... **104** C4
Hans Pl SW1 ..... **130** C2
Hans Rd SW3 .... **130** C2
Hans St SW1 ..... **131** A1

Hanway Ho **25**
SW9 .... **173** C4
Hanway Pl W1 ... **105** B2
Hanway St W1 ... **105** B2
Hanworth Ho SE5 . **48** A3
Harben Rd NW6 .. **11** B1
Harberson Rd
SW12 .... **73** A3
Harberton Rd N19 . **4** A3
Harbet Rd W2 ... **101** C3
Harbinger Prim Sch
11 E14 .... **42** A2
Harbinger Rd E14 . **42** A2
Harbin Ho **5** SW2 . **74** C3
Harbledown Ho
SE1 .... **137** B3
Harbledown Rd
SW6 .... **165** B4
Harbord Cl
Camberwell SE15 .. **49** A3
London SE5 ...... **48** C1
Harbord Ho **5**
SE16 .... **40** C2
Harbord St SW6 .. **47** C2
Harbour Ave
SW10 .... **167** A3
Harbour Exchange Sq
E14 .... **42** A4
Harbour Rd SE5 .. **63** B4
Harbridge Ave
SW15 .... **68** C4
Harbut Rd SW11 .. **59** C3
Harcombe Rd N16 .. **7** A1
Harcourt Ho
7 Clapham SW8 .. **171** B2
Marylebone W1 .. **104** A2
4 Willesden NW10 .. **9** A2
Harcourt Rd SE4 .. **66** B4
Harcourt St W1 .. **102** B3
Harcourt Terr
SW10 .... **142** B1
Hardcastle Ho
3 New Cross Gate
SE14 .... **51** A2
8 Peckham SE15 .. **49** C2
Hardel Rise SW2 . **75** A3
Hardel Wlk SW2 .. **74** C4
Harden Ho SE5 ... **49** A1
Harders Rd SE15 .. **50** A1
Hardess St SE24 .. **63** B4
Hardham Ho **5**
SW2 .... **62** C1
Harding Cl SE17 . **48** B4
Harding Ho
SW13 .... **47** A4
Hardinge Rd E11 . **32** B3
Hardinge St E1 .. **32** B3
Hardington **2**
NW1 .... **12** C1
Hardwicke Ho **14**
E3 .... **27** A2
Hardwicke Mews
WC1 .... **95** A3
Hardwick Ho
14 London SW8 .. **171** B2
Marylebone NW8 . **90** B2
Hardwick St EC1 . **95** C3
Hardwick's Way
SW18 .... **58** C2
Hardwidge St SE1 **138** A4
Hardy Ave **4** E16 . **35** C1
Hardy Cl SE16 ... **40** C4
Hardy Cotts **2**
SE10 .... **52** C4

Hardy Ct SE3 ..... **53** B4
Hardy Rd SE3 .... **53** B4
Hare and Billet Rd
SE3 .... **52** C1
Harecourt Rd N1 . **15** B2
Hare Ct EC4 ..... **107** B1
Haredale Ho **24**
SE16 .... **139** B3
Haredale Rd SE24 . **63** B3
Harefield Mews
SE4 .... **66** B4
Harefield Rd SE4 . **66** B4
Hare Marsh
E2 .... **24** C1 **99** B2
Hare Pl EC4 ..... **107** C1
Hare Row E2 ..... **25** A3
Hare Wlk N1 ..... **24** A3
Harewood Ave
NW1 .... **90** B1
Harewood Pl W1 . **104** B1
Harewood Row
NW1 .... **102** B3
Harfield Gdns **1**
SE5 .... **64** A4
Harfleur Ct SE11 . **150** A3
Harford Ho
Camberwell SE5 .. **48** B4
Notting Hill W11 . **31** B4
Harford Mews **6**
N19 .... **4** C1
Harford St E1 .... **26** A1
Hargrave Mans **3**
N19 .... **4** C2
Hargrave Park Prim
Sch **14** N19 ..... **4** B2
Hargrave Pk N19 .. **4** B2
Hargrave Pl N7 .. **13** C3
Hargrave Rd N19 .. **4** B2
Hargreaves Ho **14**
W12 .... **30** A2
Hargwyne St SW9 . **62** B4
Harkness Ho **20**
E1 .... **111** C1
Harlech Twr **5**
W3 .... **37** B4
Harlescott Rd
SE15 .... **65** C3
HARLESDEN **21** B4
Harlesden Gdns
NW10 .... **21** B4
Harlesden Plaza **2**
NW10 .... **21** B3
Harlesden Prim Sch
NW10 .... **21** A3
Harlesden Rd
NW10 .... **21** C4
Harlesden Sta
NW10 .... **20** C3
Harleyford Ct
SW8 .... **162** C4
Harleyford Manor **3**
W3 .... **28** B1
Harleyford Rd
SE11 .... **162** C4
Harleyford St
SE11 .... **163** B3
Harley Gdns
SW10 .... **143** A1
Harley Gr E3 ..... **26** B2
Harley Ho NW1 ... **91** C1
Harley Pl W1 .... **104** A3
Harley Rd
Hampstead NW3 .. **11** C1
Harlesden NW10 .. **21** A3
Harley St W1 .... **104** A3

Harley Villas
NW10 ... 21 A3
Harling Ct 3
SW11 ... 168 C2
Harlowe Ho 13 E8 ... 24 B4
Harlynwood 19
SE5 ... 48 B3
Harman Cl
10 Bermondsey
SE1 ... 153 B1
Cricklewood NW2 ... 1 A1
Harman Dr NW2 ... 10 A4
Harmood Gr NW1 ... 13 A1
Harmood Ho 7 SE8 ... 41 B2
Harmood St NW1 ... 13 A1
Harmsworth St
SE17 ... 150 B2
Harnage Ho TW8 ... 36 A1
Harney Ct SE14 ... 51 A2
Harold Ct 14 SE16 ... 40 C4
Harold Est SE1 ... 138 B1
Harold Ho 16 E2 ... 25 C3
Harold Laski Ho
EC1 ... 96 B3
Harold Maddison Ho
SE17 ... 150 B2
Harold Wilson Ho
SW6 ... 155 A3
Harp Alley EC4 ... 108 A2
Harpenden Rd SE27,
SW16 ... 75 A2
Harpenmead Point
NW2 ... 1 B2
Harper Ho 3 SW9 ... 63 A4
Harper Mews
SW17 ... 71 B1
Harper Rd SE1 ... 137 A2
Harp La EC3 ... 124 A3
Harpley Sq E1 ... 25 C1
Harpsden St
SW11 ... 169 B3
Harpur Mews
WC1 ... 106 C4
Harpur St WC1 ... 106 C4
Harrier Ho 8
SW11 ... 60 A4
Harriet Cl E8 ... 24 C4
Harriet Ho SW6 ... 156 B1
Harriet St SW1 ... 131 A3
Harriet Tubman Cl 21
SW2 ... 74 C4
Harriet Wlk SW1 ... 131 A3
Harrington Ct
South Kensington
SW7 ... 143 C4
9 West Kilburn
W9 ... 23 B2
Harrington Gdns
SW7 ... 142 C3
Harrington Ho
Regent's Pk NW1 ... 92 C4
Westminster SW1 ... 147 C2
Harrington Sq
NW1 ... 82 C1
Harrington St NW1 ... 92 C3
Harriott Cl SE10 ... 43 B2
Harriott Ho 11 E1 ... 32 B3
Harris Acad at
Peckham SE15 ... 49 B2

Harris Acad
Bermondsey
SE1 ... 153 A4
Harris Girl's Acad
SE15 ... 65 B2
Harris Ho
11 Bow E3 ... 26 C2
7 Brixton SW9 ... 62 C4
Harrison Ho SE17 ... 151 B2
Harrison Rd NW10 ... 20 C4
Harrisons Ct 1
SE14 ... 50 C4
Harrison St WC1 ... 94 B3
Harris St SE5 ... 48 C3
Harrodian Sch The
SW13 ... 46 B3
Harrogate Ct 2
SE26 ... 76 C1
Harrold Ho 1
NW3 ... 11 B1
Harroway Rd
SW11 ... 167 C2
Harrowby St W1 ... 102 B2
Harrowgate Ho 22
E9 ... 17 C2
Harrowgate Rd E9 ... 18 A1
Harrow La E14 ... 34 B2
Harrow Pl E1 ... 110 B2
Harrow Rd
Little Venice W2,
Westbourne Green W2,
W9 ... 23 C1
Harrow St NW1 ... 102 A3
Harry Gosling Prim
Sch E1 ... 111 C1
Harry Hinkins Ho
SE17 ... 151 A1
Harry Lambourn Ho
15 SE15 ... 50 A3
Hartfield Terr E3 ... 26 C3
Hartham Cl N7 ... 14 A3
Hartham Rd N7 ... 14 A3
Hart Ho SW2 ... 74 C3
Hartington Ct
Chiswick W4 ... 45 A3
South Lambeth
SW8 ... 172 A4
Hartington Rd
Chiswick W4 ... 45 B2
4 South Lambeth
SW8 ... 162 A1
Hartismere Rd
SW6 ... 155 A2
Hartlake Rd E9 ... 18 A2
Hartland NW1 ... 83 A3
Hartland Rd
Camden Town
NW1 ... 13 A1
Kilburn NW6 ... 23 B4
Hartley Ho
Bermondsey SE1 ... 153 A4
Putney SW15 ... 56 C2
Hartley St E2 ... 25 B2
Hartnoll Ho 4 N7 ... 14 C3
Hartnoll St N7 ... 14 B3
Harton Lodge 7
SE8 ... 51 C2
Harton St SE8 ... 51 C2
Hartopp Ct 20 N16 ... 7 A1
Hartopp Point
SW6 ... 154 B2
Hartshorn Alley
EC3 ... 110 B1
Hart's La SE14 ... 51 A2
Hart St EC3 ... 124 B4

Hartswood Ho 9
SW2 ... 74 A3
Hartswood Rd
W12 ... 38 B3
Hartwell Cl 12
SW2 ... 74 B3
Hartwell Ct 2 SE22 ... 64 C3
Hartwell St E8 ... 16 B2
Harvard Ho 6
Camberwell
SE17 ... 48 A4
Putney SW15 ... 57 C1
Harvard Mans 18
SW11 ... 169 C3
Harvard Rd
18 Acton Green
W4 ... 37 B1
Gunnersbury W4 ... 37 A1
Lewisham SE13 ... 67 B2
Harvey Ct SW11 ... 168 B4
Harvey Ho
10 Bethnal Green
E1 ... 25 A1
Brentford TW8 ... 36 A1
Pimlico SW1 ... 147 C1
Shoreditch N1 ... 87 C3
Harvey Lodge 10 W9 ... 31 C4
Harvey Point 7
E16 ... 35 C4
Harvey Rd 18 SE5 ... 48 C2
Harvey St N1 ... 87 C3
Harvington Wlk
E8 ... 16 C1
Harvist Rd NW6 ... 23 A3
Harwood Ct
Putney SW15 ... 57 B3
Shoreditch N1 ... 87 C3
Harwood Point
SE16 ... 41 B4
Harwood Rd SW6 ... 156 A1
Harwood Terr
SW6 ... 166 A4
Hascombe Ho 11
SW15 ... 69 A3
Hascombe Terr 2
SE5 ... 48 C1
Haselrigge Rd
SW4 ... 61 C3
Hasker St SW3 ... 144 B4
Haslam Cl N1 ... 14 C1
Haslam Ho 12 N1 ... 15 B1
Haslam St SE15 ... 49 B2
Haslemere Ave
SW18 ... 71 A2
Haslemere Ct 5
N16 ... 7 A3
Haslemere Ind Est
SW18 ... 71 A2
Haslemere Rd N8 ... 5 A4
Hassard St E2 ... 24 B3
Hassett Rd E9 ... 18 A2
Hassop Rd NW2 ... 9 C4
Hastings Cl 17
SE15 ... 49 C3
Hastings Ho 18
W12 ... 30 A2
Hastings Hos SW1 ... 94 A3
Hastings St WC1 ... 94 A3
Hatcham Mews Bsns
Ctr SE14 ... 50 C2
Hatcham Park Mews
SE14 ... 50 C2
Hatcham Park Rd
SE14 ... 50 C2

Hatcham Rd SE15 ... 50 B4
Hatchard Rd N19 ... 5 A2
Hatchers Mews
SE1 ... 138 B2
Hatcliffe Almshouses
8 SE10 ... 43 A1
Hatcliffe St SE10 ... 43 B1
Hatfield Cl SE14 ... 50 C3
Hatfield Ct SE3 ... 53 C3
Hatfield Ho EC1 ... 96 C1
Hatfield Rd W4 ... 37 C4
Hatfields SE1 ... 121 C2
Hathaway Ho 3
N1 ... 24 A2 98 A4
Hatherley Ct 6
W2 ... 100 A2
Hatherley Gr W2 ... 100 A2
Hatherley Rd TW9 ... 44 B2
Hatherley St SW1 ... 147 A3
Hathersage Ct N1 ... 15 C3
Hathersley Ho 3
SW2 ... 74 C4
Hathorne Cl 3
SE15 ... 50 A1
Hathway Ho 3
SE15 ... 50 B1
Hathway St 3
SE15 ... 50 B1
Hatley Rd N4, N7 ... 5 B2
Hat & Mitre Ct EC1 ... 96 B1
Hatstone Ct 2
NW3 ... 11 B3
Hatteraick St 6
SE16 ... 40 B4
Hatton Gdn EC1 ... 107 C4
Hatton Ho E1 ... 125 C4
Hatton Pl EC1 ... 107 C4
Hatton Row NW8 ... 89 C1
Hatton St NW8 ... 89 C1
Hatton Wall EC1 ... 107 C4
Haunch of Venison Yd
W1 ... 104 A1
Hauteville Court Gdns
2 W6 ... 38 B3
Havana Rd SW18 ... 70 C2
Havannah St E14 ... 41 C4
Havelock Cl 13
W12 ... 30 A2
Havelock Ct 8
SE15 ... 50 A3
Havelock St N1 ... 84 B4
Havelock Terr
SW8 ... 160 B1
Haven Cl SW19 ... 69 C1
Havenpool NW8 ... 78 B3
Haven St 18 NW1 ... 13 A1
Haven The TW9 ... 54 C4
Havercourt 3
NW3 ... 12 A2
Haverfield Gdns
TW9 ... 44 C3
Haverfield Rd E3 ... 26 A2
Haverhill Rd SW12 ... 73 B3
Havering 6 NW1 ... 13 A1
Havering Ho N4 ... 6 B4
Havering St E1 ... 32 C3
Haversham Lo NW2 ... 9 C3
Haversham Pl N6 ... 3 B2
Haverstock Hill
NW3 ... 12 B2
Haverstock Rd
NW5 ... 12 C3
Haverstock Sch 22
NW1 ... 12 C2
Haverstock St N1 ... 86 B1

Har–Hay 223

Havil St SE5 ... 49 A2
Havisham Ho 25
SE16 ... 139 B3
Hawarden Gr SE24 ... 75 B4
Hawberry Lo N7 ... 14 A2
Hawes St N1 ... 15 A1
Hawgood St E3 ... 33 C4
Hawke Ho 20 E1 ... 25 C1
Hawke Pl 29 SE16 ... 40 C4
Hawkesbury Rd
SW15 ... 57 A2
Hawkesdown House
Sch W2 ... 31 C1 113 C1
Hawkesworth Ho 5
SW4 ... 61 B1
Hawke Twr 4
SE14 ... 51 A4
Hawkins Ho 7 SW1 ... 60 A4
Hawkins Ho 3
SE8 ... 51 C4
Hawkins Rd NW10 ... 8 A1
Hawkley Gdns
SE27 ... 75 A2
Hawkridge 19
NW5 ... 12 C2
Hawkshaw Cl 23
SW2 ... 74 A4
Hawkshead NW1 ... 92 C4
Hawkshead Rd
Acton W4 ... 38 A4
Willesden NW10 ... 8 B1
Hawkslade Rd
SE15 ... 65 C2
Hawksley Rd N16 ... 7 A1
Hawks Mews 10
SE10 ... 52 B3
Hawksmoor Mews
E1 ... 32 A2
Hawksmoor Pl 2
E2 ... 24 C1 99 B2
Hawksmoor St 3
W6 ... 47 C4
Hawkstone Rd
SE16 ... 40 B2
Hawkwell Wlk N1 ... 87 A4
Hawley Cres NW1 ... 13 A1
Hawley Inf Sch 28
NW1 ... 13 A1
Hawley Mews 4
NW1 ... 13 A1
Hawley Rd 3
NW1 ... 13 A1
Hawley St NW1 ... 13 A1
Haworth Ho 7
SW2 ... 62 C1
Hawstead Rd SE6 ... 67 A4
Hawthorn Ct
Putney SW15 ... 57 A4
Richmond TW9 ... 45 A2
Hawthorne Ave E3 ... 26 B4
Hawthorne Cl N1 ... 16 A2
Hawthorne Ho
SW1 ... 147 A1
Hawthorn Rd NW10 ... 51 B2
Hawthorn Wlk
W10 ... 23 A1
Hawtrey Rd NW3 ... 12 A1
Haycroft Gdns
NW10 ... 22 A4
Haycroft Mans
NW10 ... 21 C4
Haycroft Rd SW2 ... 62 A2
Hay Currie St E14 ... 34 A3

Hayday Rd E16 . . . . . 35 C4
Hayden Piper Ho
SW3 . . . . 158 C4
Hayden's Pl W11 . . . . 31 B3
Haydon St E1, EC3 124 C4
Haydon Way SW11 . . 59 C3
Haydon Wlk E1 . . . . . 111 A1
Hayes Ct
23 Camberwell
SE5 . . . . 48 B3
Streatham SW12 . . . 74 A3
Hayes Gr SE15,
SE22 . . . . 64 B3
Hayes Pl NW1 . . . . . 90 B1
Hayfield Pas E1 . . . . 25 B1
Hayfield Yd 18 E1 . . . 25 B1
Hay Hill W1 . . . . . . 118 B3
Hayhurst N1 . . . . . . 86 B4
Hayles Bldgs
SE11 . . . . 150 B4
Hayles St SE11 . . . . 150 A4
Hayling Cl 20 N16 . . 16 A3
Haymans Point
SE11 . . . . 148 C2
Haymarket SW1 . . . 119 B3
Haymerle Ho 6
SE15 . . . . 49 C3
Haymerle Rd SE15 . . 49 C4
Haymerle Sch 13
SE15 . . . . 49 C4
Hayne Ho
W11 . . . . . . 31 A1 112 A2
Haynes Ho 8 E9 . . . 17 C2
Hayne St EC1 . . . . . 108 B4
Hay's Galleria SE1 124 A2
Hay's La SE1 . . . . . 124 A2
Hay's Mews W1 . . . 118 A2
Hay St E2 . . . . 24 C4
Hayter Ho W12 . . . . 29 C2
Hayter Rd SW2 . . . . 62 B2
Haythorn Ho
SW11 . . . . 167 C3
Hayton Cl 11 E8 . . . . 16 B2
Hayward Ct 14
SW4 . . . . 172 B2
Hayward Gallery
SE1 . . . . 121 A2
Hayward Gdns
SW15 . . . . 57 B1
Hayward Ho N1 . . . . 85 B2
Haywards Pl EC1 . . . 96 A2
Hayward's Pl EC1 . . 96 A2
Haywood Lo 23
N7 . . . . 13 C3
Hazelbourne Rd
SW12 . . . . 61 A1
Hazel Cl
Peckham SE15 . . . . 49 C1
Upper Holloway N19 . . 4 B2
Hazel Ct 8 SE16 . . . 33 A1
Hazeldon Rd SE4 . . . 66 A2
Hazel Ho
London SE4 . . . . . . 66 B4
12 Maitland Pk
NW3 . . . . 12 B2
Hazellville Rd N19 . . 4 C3
Hazelmere Ct 10
SW2 . . . . 74 B3
Hazelmere Rd
NW6 . . . . 23 B4
Hazel Rd NW10 . . . . 22 B2
Hazel Way SE1 . . . . 152 C4
Hazelwood Cl SW5 . . 36 A4

Hazelwood Ho 11
SE8 . . . . 41 A2
Hazelwood Mans
SW6 . . . . 164 C4
Hazlebury Rd
SW6 . . . . 166 B2
Hazledene Rd W4 . . 45 B4
Hazlewell Rd
SW15 . . . . 57 B2
Hazlewood Cres
W10 . . . . 23 A1
Hazlewood Twr
W10 . . . . 23 B1
Hazlitt Mews
W14 . . . . 126 A1
Hazlitt Rd W14 . . . . 126 A1
Headbourne Ho
SE1 . . . . 137 C2
Headcorn 18 NW5 . . 12 C2
Headfort Pl SW1 . . . 131 C3
Headlam Rd SW4 . . . 73 C4
Headlam St E1 . . . . . 25 A1
Heads Mews W11 . . . 31 C3
Heald St SE8, SE14 . . 51 C2
Healey St NW1 . . . . 13 A2
Healy Ho 22 E3 . . . . 26 C1
Heanor Ct 4 E5 . . . . 17 C4
Hearne Rd W4 . . . . . 44 C4
Hearn's Bldgs
SE17 . . . . 151 C3
Hearnshaw St 1
E14 . . . . 33 A3
Hearn St
EC2 . . . . . . 24 A1 98 B1
Hearnville Rd
SW12 . . . . 72 C3
Heart Hospl The
W1 . . . . 103 C3
Heart Radio W11 . . . 30 C2
Heathbrook Prim Sch
11 SW4 . . . . 170 C1
Heath Brow NW3 . . . 2 B1
Heath Cl NW11 . . . . . 2 A4
Heathcote Point 23
E9 . . . . 17 C2
Heathcote St WC1 . . 94 C3
Heathcroft NW11 . . . 2 A3
Heath Ct
2 Hampstead
NW3 . . . . 11 B2
Stoke Newington
N16 . . . . 6 C3
Heath Dr NW3 . . . . . 11 A4
Heather Cl SW8 . . . . 61 A4
Heather Rd E14 . . . . 34 B3
Heather Ho 11 E14 . 34 B3
Heatherley Ct N16 . . 7 C1
Heatherley Sch of
Fine Art SW10 . . . 156 C1
Heather Lo N16 . . . . 7 A3
Heather Wlk W10 . . . 23 A1
Heathfield Ave
SW18 . . . . 71 C4
Heathfield Ct
1 Bow E3 . . . . 26 C3
5 Chiswick W4 . . . . 37 C1
Wandsworth SW18 . . 71 C4
Heathfield Gdns
Acton Green W4 . . . 37 B1
Blackheath SE3 . . . . 53 A1
Wandsworth SW18 . . 71 C4
Heathfield Ho SE3 . . 53 A1

Heathfield House Sch
15 W4 . . . . 37 B1
Heathfield Pk NW2 . . 9 B2
Heathfield Rd
South Acton W3 . . . 37 A4
Wandsworth SW18 . . 59 C1
Heathfield Sq
SW18 . . . . 71 C4
Heathfield Terr
W4 . . . . 37 C1
Heathgate Pl NW3 . 12 B4
Heath House Prep Sch
1 SE8 . . . . 53 B1
Heath Hurst Rd
NW3 . . . . 12 A4
Heath La SE3 . . . . . . 52 C1
Heathland Rd N16 . . 7 A3
Heath Mans
5 Hampstead
NW3 . . . . 11 B4
Putney SW15 . . . . . 57 C4
Heathman's Rd
SW6 . . . . 165 A3
Heath Mead SW19 . . 69 C1
Heathmere Prim Sch
SW15 . . . . 68 C3
Heath Park Gdns
NW3 . . . . 2 A1
Heathpool Ct 8
E1 . . . . 25 A1
Heath Rd SW8 . . . . 170 B1
Heath Rise SW15 . . . 57 C1
Heath Royal SW15 . . 57 C1
Heathshott 8
TW10 . . . . 54 A1
Heathside NW3 . . . . 11 C4
Heathside Prep Sch
55 NW3 . . . . 11 B4
Heath St NW3 . . . . . 2 B1
Heathstan Rd W12 . . 29 C3
Heath View NW5 . . . 12 C4
Heathview
SW19 . . . . 69 C2
Heathview Gdns
SW15 . . . . 69 B4
Heath Villas NW3 . . . 2 C1
Heathville Rd N4,
N19 . . . . 5 A4
Heathwall St
SW11 . . . . 60 B4
Heathway SE3 . . . . . 53 C3
Heathway Ct NW3 . . . 1 C2
Heathwood Ct
SW12 . . . . 73 B3
Heaton Ho
Chelsea SW10 . . . . 157 A4
6 Peckham SE15 . . 50 A1
Heaton Rd SE15 . . . 50 A1
Heaven Tree Cl
N1 . . . . 15 B3
Heaver Rd 23
SW11 . . . . 59 C4
Hebden Ct 24 E2 . . . 24 B4
Hebdon Rd SW17 . . . 72 A1
Heber Prim Sch
SE22 . . . . 64 B1
Heber Rd
Cricklewood NW2 . . . 9 C4
East Dulwich SE22 . . 64 B1
Hebron Rd W6 . . . . . 39 A3
Heckfield Pl SW6 . . 155 B1
Heckford Ho E14 . . . 34 A3
Heckford St E1 . . . . 32 C2
Hector Ct
1 London SW9 . . . 173 B4
Putney SW15 . . . . . 57 C2

Hector Ho 14 E2 . . . 25 A3
Heddington Gr N7 . . 14 B3
Heddon St W1 . . . . 118 C4
Hedger's Gr E9 . . . . 18 A2
Hedger St SE11 . . . 150 A4
Hedingham Cl 6
N1 . . . . 15 B1
Hedley Ct SW15 . . . 57 C1
Hedley Ho E14 . . . . 42 B3
Hedley Row N5,
N16 . . . . 15 C3
Hedsor Ho
E2 . . . . . . 24 B1 98 C2
Heidegger Cres
SW13 . . . . 47 A3
Heights The NW3 . . 11 B4
Heiron St SE17 . . . . 48 A4
Helby Rd SW4 . . . . . 61 C1
Heldar Ct SE1 . . . . . 137 C3
Helena Pl 8 E9 . . . . 25 B4
Helena Rd NW10 . . . 9 A3
Helena Sq 12 SE16 . 33 A2
Helen Gladstone Ho
SE1 . . . . 136 A4
Helen Ho 9 E2 . . . . 25 A3
Helen Mackay Ho 10
E14 . . . . 34 C3
Helen Peele Cotts 10
SE16 . . . . 40 B3
Helenslea Ave
NW11 . . . . 1 C3
Helen's Pl E2 . . . . . 25 B2
Helen Taylor Ho 5
SE16 . . . . 153 B4
Helix Ct 17 W11 . . . 30 C1
Helix Gdns SW2 . . . 62 B1
Helix Rd SW2 . . . . . 62 B1
Helix The SW19 . . . 69 C2
Hellings St E1 . . . . 125 C1
Helmet Row EC1 . . . 97 A2
Helmsdale Ho
NW6 . . . . 78 A1
Helmsley Pl E8 . . . . 17 A1
Helmsley St 8 E8 . . 17 A1
Helperby Rd NW10 . . 8 A1
Helsby Ct NW8 . . . . 89 B2
Helsinki Sq SE16 . . . 41 A3
Helston NW1 . . . . . . 83 A2
Helston Ho SE11 . . . 149 C2
Hemans St SW8 . . . 161 C1
Hemans St SW8 . . . 161 C1
Hemberton Rd
SW9 . . . . 62 A4
Hemingford Rd N1 . . 85 A4
Hemlock Rd W12 . . . 29 B2
Hemming St
E1 . . . . . . 24 C1 99 C1
Hemmingway Cl
NW5 . . . . 12 C4
Hemp Wlk SE17 . . . 151 C4
Hemstal Rd NW6 . . . 10 C1
Hemsworth Ct N1 . . 24 A3
Hemsworth St N1 . . 24 A3
Hemus Pl SW3 . . . . 144 B1
Henchman St W12 . . 29 B3
Henderson Ct
8 Deptford SE14 . . 50 C4
Hampstead NW3 . . . 11 C3
Wandsworth SW18 . . 72 A4
Henderson Dr
NW8 . . . . 89 B2
Henderson Rd
SW18 . . . . 72 A4

Hendham Rd
SW17 . . . . 72 B2
Hendre Ho SE1 . . . 152 B3
Hendre Rd SE1 . . . 152 B3
Hendrick Ave
SW12 . . . . 72 B4
Heneage La EC3 . . . 110 B1
Heneage Pl EC3 . . . 110 B1
Heneage St E1 . . . . 111 A4
Henfield Cl N19 . . . . 4 B3
Hengrave Rd SE23 . . 65 B1
Henley Ct
Brondesbury NW2 . . 9 C2
Peckham SE15 . . . . 64 C4
Henley Dr SE1 . . . . 153 A4
Henley Ho
E2 . . . . 24 B1 99 A2
Henley Prior N1 . . . 84 C1
Henley Rd NW10 . . . 22 B4
Henniker Mews
SW3 . . . . 157 B3
Henniker Rd E15 . . . 19 C3
Henning St SW11 . . 168 A3
Henrietta Cl SE8 . . . 51 C4
Henrietta Ho 11
W6 . . . . 39 B1
Henrietta Mews
WC1 . . . . 94 B2
Henrietta Pl W1 . . . 104 A2
Henrietta St
Strand WC2 . . . . . 120 B4
Stratford New Town
E15 . . . . 19 B3
Henriques St E1 . . . 111 C1
Henry Cavendish Prim
Sch SW12 . . . . 73 B3
Henry Compton Sch
SW6 . . . . 47 C2
Henry Dent Cl SE5 . . 63 C4
Henry Dickens Ct
W11 . . . . . . 31 A1 112 A2
Henry Fawcett Prim
Sch SE11 . . . . 163 B4
Henry Ho
Lambeth SE1 . . . . . 121 C1
South Lambeth
SW8 . . . . 162 A2
St John's Wood
NW8 . . . . 80 A2
Henry Jackson Ho 4
SW15 . . . . 57 C4
Henry Jackson Rd
SW15 . . . . 57 C4
Henry Rd N4 . . . . . . 6 B3
Henryson Rd SE4 . . 66 C2
Henry Wise Ho
SW1 . . . . 147 A3
Henshall Point 19
E3 . . . . 27 A2
Henshall St N1 . . . . 15 C2
Henshaw St SE17 . . 151 B4
Hensley Point 28
E9 . . . . 17 C2
Henslow Ho 12
SE15 . . . . 49 C3
Henson Ave NW2 . . . 9 B3
Henson Ct 3 N5 . . . 15 B4
Henstridge Pl
NW8 . . . . 80 A3
Henty Cl SW11 . . . . 168 B4
Henty Wlk SW15 . . . 57 A2
Hepburn Mews
SW11 . . . . 60 B2

Hepplestone Cl
SW15 . . . . 57 A1
Hepscott Rd E9 . . . 18 C1
Hepworth Ct
Chelsea SW1 . . . 146 A1
Islington N1 . . . . . 86 A4
Hera Ct 15 E14 . . . 41 C2
Heralds Pl SE11 . . 150 A4
Herald St 5 E2 . . . . 25 A1
Herbal Hill EC1 . . . 95 C1
Herbert Chapman Ct
N5 . . . . 15 A4
Herbert Cres SW1 131 A2
Herbert Gdns
Chiswick W4 . . . . 45 A4
Willesden Green
NW10 . . . . 22 A3
Herbert Ho E1 . . . 110 C2
Herbert Mews 15
SW2 . . . . 62 C1
Herbert Morrison
Prim Sch SW8 . . . 162 A1
Herbert St NW5 . . . 12 C2
Herbrand Est WC1 . 94 A2
Herbrand St WC1 . . 94 A2
Hercules Ct 7
SE14 . . . . 51 A4
Hercules Pl N7 . . . . 5 A1
Hercules Rd SE1 . . 135 A1
Hercules St N7 . . . . 5 A1
Hereford Bldgs
SW3 . . . . 157 C4
Hereford Ho
5 Brixton SW2 . . . 62 C3
23 Camberwell SE5 . 48 B1
Knightsbridge
SW3 . . . . 130 B2
Walham Green
SW10 . . . . 156 B2
Hereford Mans 10
W2 . . . . 31 C3
Hereford Mews 11
W2 . . . . 31 C3
Hereford Rd
Acton W3 . . . . . . 28 B2
Bayswater
W2 . . . . 31 C2 113 C4
Hereford Retreat 5
SE15 . . . . 49 C3
Hereford Sq SW7 . 143 A3
Hereford St
E2 . . . . . . 24 C1 99 B2
Hereward House Sch
NW3 . . . . 11 C2
Heritage Cl SW9 . . 63 A4
Heritage Ct SE8 . . . 40 C1
Heritage Ho 22
SW19 . . . . 70 A3
Hermes Cl 5 W9 . . 23 C1
Hermes Ct 4
SW9 . . . . 173 B4
Hermes St N1 . . . . 85 B1
Hermitage Ct
2 Child's Hill NW2 . 1 C1
13 Wapping E1 . . . 125 C1
Hermitage Gdns
NW2 . . . . 1 C1
Hermitage La NW2 . 1 C1
Hermitage Prim Sch
15 E1 . . . . 125 C2
Hermitage Row 9
E8 . . . . 16 C3
Hermitage St W2 . 101 B3

Hermitage The
Barnes SW13 . . . . 46 B2
Richmond TW10 . . . 54 A2
Hermitage Villas
SW6 . . . . 155 B4
Hermitage Wall
E1 . . . . 125 C1
Hermit Pl NW6 . . . . 78 A3
Hermit St EC1 . . . . 96 A4
Herndon Rd SW18 . 59 B2
HERNE HILL 63 B2
Herne Hill SE24 . . . 63 B2
Herne Hill Ho
SE24 . . . . 63 A1
Herne Hill Mans
SE24 . . . . 63 B1
Herne Hill Rd
SE24 . . . . 63 B3
Herne Hill Sch
SE24 . . . . 63 B2
Herne Hill Sta
SE24 . . . . 63 A1
Herne Hill Velodrome
SE24 . . . . 63 A2
Herne Pl SE24 . . . . 63 A2
Heron Cl NW10 . . . . 8 A2
Heron Ct
16 Cubitt Town
E14 . . . . 42 B3
7 Dulwich SE21 . . 75 C2
Herondale Ave
SW18 . . . . 72 A3
Heron Dr N4 . . . . . . 6 B2
Herongate N1 . . . . 87 A4
Heron Ho
Battersea SW11 . . 168 B4
Peckham SE15 . . . 49 B2
St John's Wood
NW8 . . . . 80 A1
Heron Pl
Marylebone W1 . . 103 C2
Rotherhithe SE16 . . 33 A1
Heron Quays E14 . . 33 C1
Heron Quays Sta
E14 . . . . 33 C1
Heron Rd SE24 . . . . 63 B3
Heron Trad Est
W3 . . . . 28 A4
Herrick Ho
18 Camberwell
SE5 . . . . 48 C3
17 Canonbury N16 . 15 C4
Herrick Rd N5 . . . . 6 B1
Herrick St SW1 . . . 147 C3
Herries St W10 . . . . 23 A3
Hersant Cl NW10 . . 21 C4
Herschell's Mews
SE5 . . . . 63 B4
Hersham Cl SW15 . 68 C4
Hershell Ct 1
SW14 . . . . 55 A3
Hertford Ave
SW14 . . . . 56 A3
Hertford Ct 10
SW11 . . . . 60 A4
Hertford Lo 10
SW19 . . . . 70 A3
Hertford Pl W1 . . . . 93 A1
Hertford Rd N1 . . . . 24 A4
Hertford St W1 . . . 118 A1
Hertmitage The 5
SE13 . . . . 52 B1
Hertslet Rd N7 . . . . 5 B1
Hertsmere Rd E14 . 33 C2
Hesewall Ct 4
SW4 . . . . 171 A1

Hesketh Pl
W11 . . . . 31 A2 112 A3
Heslop Ct 1
SW12 . . . . 72 C3
Heslop Rd SW12 . . 72 B3
Hesper Mews
SW5 . . . . 142 A3
Hesperus Cres
E14 . . . . 42 A2
Hessel Rd W13 . . . . 34 A3
Hessel St E1 . . . . . 32 A3
Hestercombe Ave
SW6 . . . . 164 B3
Hester Rd SW11 . . 158 A1
Hester Terr TW9 . . . 54 C4
Hestia Ho SE1 . . . 138 A3
Heston Ho
Gunnersbury W4 . . 37 A1
5 St Johns SE8 . . 51 C2
Heston St SE14 . . . 51 B2
Hetherington Rd SW2,
SW4 . . . . 62 A1
Hethpool Ho W2 . . 89 B1
Hetley Rd W12 . . . . 39 A4
Hetty Rees Ct 6
N19 . . . . 5 A4
Hevelius Cl SE10 . . 43 B1
Hever Ho SE15 . . . 50 C4
Heversham Ho
SE15 . . . . 50 B4
Heward Ct SE13 . . . 52 B1
Hewer Ho 6 SW4 . . 61 B2
Hewer St W10 . . . . 30 C4
Hewett Ho SW15 . . 47 B1
Hewett St
EC2 . . . . 24 A1 98 B1
Hewison St E3 . . . . 26 B3
Hewlett Rd E3 . . . . 26 A3
Hewling Ho 1
N16 . . . . 16 A3
Hexagon The N6 . . . 3 B3
Hexham Rd SE27 . . 75 B2
Hexton Ct N4 . . . . . 6 B2
Heybridge 9 NW1 . 13 A2
Heydon Ho 3
SE14 . . . . 50 B2
Heyford Ave SW8 . 162 B2
Heyford Terr SW8 . 162 B2
Heygate St SE17 . . 151 A4
Heylyn Sq E3 . . . . . 26 B2
Heysham La NW3 . . 2 A1
Heythorp St SW18 . 70 B2
Heythrop Coll W8 128 A2
Heywood Ho
6 Deptford SE14 . . 50 C4
5 Tulse Hill SW2 . . 62 C1
Heyworth Rd E5 . . . 17 A4
Hibbert Ho 15 E14 . 41 C3
Hibbert St SW11 . . 59 C4
Hichisson Rd SE15 . 65 B2
Hicken Rd SW2 . . . 62 B2
Hickes Ho 6 NW6 . . 11 C1
Hickey's Almshouses
7 TW9 . . . . 54 B3
Hickin Cl SE24 . . . 42 B3
Hickin St 2 E14 . . . 42 B3
Hickleton Ho N1 . . 83 A3
Hickling Ho 10
SE16 . . . . 40 A3
Hickmore Wlk
SW4 . . . . 61 B4
Hicks Cl SW11 . . . 60 A4
Hicks St SE8 . . . . . 41 A1
Hide Pl SW1 . . . . . 147 B3
Hide Twr SW1 . . . 147 B3
Hieover SE21 . . . . . 75 B2
Higgins Ho 7 N1 . . 24 A4

Higginson Ho 2
NW3 . . . . 12 B1
Higgs Ind Est 9
SE24 . . . . 63 A4
High Bridge Wharf
SE10 . . . . 42 C1
Highburty Mans 24
N1 . . . . 15 A1
HIGHBURY 15 A1
Highbury Cnr N5 . . 15 A2
Highbury Corner
N5 . . . . 15 A2
Highbury Cres N5 . 15 A2
Highbury Fields Sch
4 N5 . . . . 15 A2
Highbury Gr N5 . . . 15 A2
Highbury Grange
N5 . . . . 15 B4
Highbury Grove Ct
N5 . . . . 15 A2
Highbury Grove Sch
7 N5 . . . . 15 B3
Highbury Hill N5 . . 15 A3
Highbury & Islington
Sta N1 . . . . 15 A2
Highbury New Pk
N5 . . . . 15 B4
Highbury Pk N5 . . . 15 A4
Highbury Pl N5 . . . 15 A2
Highbury Pool N5 . 15 A2
Highbury Quadrant
N5 . . . . 6 B1
Highbury Quadrant
Prim Sch N5 . . . . 15 B4
Highbury Station Rd
N1 . . . . 14 C2
Highbury Terrace
Mews N5 . . . . . . 15 A3
Highcliffe Dr
SW15 . . . . 56 B1
Highcroft Rd N19 . . . 5 A4
Highcross Way 4
SW15 . . . . 68 C3
Highdown Rd
SW15 . . . . 57 A1
Highfield Ave NW11 . 1 A4
Highfield Cl SE13 . . 67 C1
Highfield Mews
NW6 . . . . 11 A1
Highfield Rd W3 . . . 28 B4
Highfields Gr N6 . . . 3 B3
HIGHGATE 3 C4
Highgate Archway
N6 . . . . 4 B3
Highgate Ave N6 . . . 4 A4
Highgate Cemetery
N19 . . . . 4 A2
Highgate Cl N6 . . . . 3 C4
Highgate High St
N6 . . . . 4 A3
Highgate Hill N19 . . 4 B3
Highgate Ho 11
SE26 . . . . 76 C1
Highgate Pre-Prep &
Jun Sch N6 . . . . . 3 C4
Highgate Rd NW5 . 13 A4
Highgate Sch N6 . . . 3 C4
Highgate West Hill
Highgate N6 . . . . . 3 C3
London N6 . . . . . . 3 C2
Highgrove Point 2
NW3 . . . . 11 B4

High Holborn
WC1 . . . . 106 C3
High Holborn Ho
WC1 . . . . 107 A3
Highlands Ave W3 . 28 B2
Highlands Cl N4 . . . 5 A4
Highlands Heath
SW15 . . . . 69 B4
Highlever Rd W10 . 30 B4
High London 8 N6 . 4 C4
Highmore Rd SE3 . . 53 A3
High Mount 1 N4 . . 5 A4
High Park Ave
TW9 . . . . 44 C2
High Park Rd TW9 . 44 C2
High Par The
SW16 . . . . 74 A1
High Point N6 . . . . . 3 C4
High Rd NW10 . . . . 21 C4
Highshore Rd
SE15 . . . . 49 B1
Highshore Sch 12
SE15 . . . . 49 B2
High St
Acton W3 . . . . . . 28 A1
Brentford TW8 . . . 44 A4
Stratford Marsh
E15 . . . . 27 B4
High Street Harlesden
NW10 . . . . 21 B3
High Street
Kensington Sta
W8 . . . . 128 A3
High The SW16 . . . 74 A1
High Timber St
EC4 . . . . 122 C4
High Trees SW2 . . . 74 C3
Hightrees Ho
SW12 . . . . 60 C1
Highview N6 . . . . . . 4 A4
Highview Ct 2
N6 . . . . 4 A4
High View Prim Sch
5 SW11 . . . . 59 C3
Highway Bsns Pk The
7 E1 . . . . 32 C2
Highway The E1 . . . 32 B2
Highway Trad Ctr The
7 E1 . . . . 32 C2
Highwood Cl SE22 . 76 C3
Highwood Rd N19 . . 5 A1
Highworth St
NW1 . . . . 102 B4
Hilary Cl SW6 . . . . 156 A2
Hilary Rd W12 . . . . 29 B2
Hilborough Ct 1
E8 . . . . 24 B4
Hilborough Rd 1
E8 . . . . 16 B1
Hilda Terr 2
SW9 . . . . 173 C2
Hilditch Ho 7
TW10 . . . . 54 B1
Hildreth St 6
SW12 . . . . 73 A3
Hildreth Street Mews
2 SW12 . . . . 73 A3
Hildyard Rd SW6 . 155 C4
Hiley Rd NW10 . . . 22 B2
Hilgrove Rd NW6 . . 11 B1
Hillary Ct 13 W12 . 39 B4
Hillbeck Cl
Deptford SE15 . . . 50 B3

Hillbeck Cl continued
Deptford SE15 . . . . 50 B4
Hillbrow 7 TW10 . . . . 54 A1
Hillbury Rd SW17 . . . . 73 A1
Hillcourt Rd SE22 . . . . 65 A1
Hillcrest
Camberwell SE24 . . . . . . 63 C3
Highgate N6 . . . . 3 C4
Notting Hill
W11 . . . . 31 B2 112 C3
Hillcrest Ct NW2 . . . . 10 A3
Hillcrest Rd W3 . . . . . 28 A1
Hill Ct
Hampstead NW3 . . . . . . 12 A4
Putney SW15 . . . . 57 C2
Hilldrop Cres N7 . . . . 13 C3
Hilldrop La N7 . . . . . . 13 C3
Hilldrop Rd N7 . . . . . . 13 C3
Hillersdon Ave
SW13 . . . . 46 C1
Hillersdon Ho
SW1 . . . . 146 A2
Hillery Cl SE17 . . . . . 151 C3
Hill Farm Rd W10 . . . 30 C4
Hillfield Ct NW3 . . . . 12 A3
Hillfield Ho N5 . . . . . . 15 B3
Hillfield Mans
NW3 . . . . 12 A3
Hillfield Rd NW6 . . . . 10 C3
Hillgate Pl
Balham SW12 . . . . 73 A4
Kensington
W8 . . . . 31 C1 113 B2
Hillgate St
W8 . . . . 31 C1 113 B2
Hill House
International Jun
Sch SW1 . . . . 131 A1
Hilliard Ho 15 E14 . . . 32 A1
Hilliard's Ct E1 . . . . . 32 B1
Hillier Ho 1 NW1 . . . 13 C1
Hillier Rd SW11 . . . . . 60 B1
Hillingdon St SE17 . . 48 A4
Hill Lo SW11 . . . . 59 C3
Hillman Dr 12
NW10 . . . . 22 B1
Hillman St E8 . . . . 17 A2
Hillmarton Rd N7 . . . 14 A3
Hillmead Dr SW9 . . . 63 A3
Hill Mead Prim Sch EE
SW9 . . . . 63 A3
Hillmore Ct SE13 . . . . 67 C4
Hill Rd NW8 . . . . 79 A1
Hillrise Mans N19 . . . 5 A4
Hillrise Rd N19 . . . . . . 5 A4
Hillsboro Rd SE22 . . . 64 A2
Hillsborough Ct 13
NW6 . . . . 78 A3
Hillside
Greenwich SE10 . . . . . . 52 C3
Stonebridge NW10 . . . . 20 C4
Hillside Cl NW8 . . . . . 78 B2
Hillside Gdns SW2 . . 74 C2
Hillside Rd SW2 . . . . . 74 C2
Hillsleigh Rd
W14 . . . . 31 B1 113 A2
Hills Pl W1 . . . . 104 C1
Hill St W1 . . . . 118 A2
Hillstone Ct 3 E3 . . . 27 A1
Hilltop Ct
12 London SW18 . . . . 59 C3
South Hampstead
NW8 . . . . 11 B1

Hilltop Ho 7 N6 . . . . 4 C4
Hilltop Rd NW6 . . . . . 10 C1
Hill View NW1 . . . . . . 81 A4
Hillway N6 . . . . 3 C2
Hill Wood Ho NW1 . . 83 B1
Hilsea Point 7
SW15 . . . . 69 A3
Hilsea St E5 . . . . 17 B4
Hilton Docklands Pier
SE16 . . . . 33 B1
Hilton Ho
Lower Holloway
N7 . . . . 14 A4
9 Nunhead SE4 . . . . . 65 C3
Hilversum Cres 10
SE22 . . . . 64 A2
Hinckley Rd SE15 . . . 64 C3
Hind Ct EC4 . . . . 107 C1
Hinde Mews N1 . . . . 103 C2
Hinde St W1 . . . . 103 C2
Hind Gr E14 . . . . 33 C3
Hindhead Point 6
SW15 . . . . 69 A3
Hind Ho
13 Deptford SE14 . . . 50 C4
Islington N7 . . . . 14 C4
Hindle Ho E8 . . . . 16 B3
Hindley Ho N7 . . . . 5 B1
Hindlip Ho SW8 . . . . 171 B3
Hindmans Rd
SE22 . . . . 64 C2
Hindmarsh Cl E1 . . . 125 C4
Hindrey Rd E5 . . . . . . 17 A3
Hinstock NW6 . . . . . . 78 A4
Hinton Rd SE24 . . . . . 63 A4
Hippodrome Mews
W11 . . . . 31 A2 112 A3
Hippodrome Pl
W11 . . . . 31 A2 112 A3
Hirst Ct SW1 . . . . . . 146 A1
Hitchin Sq E3 . . . . 26 A3
Hither Gr 15 SE16 . . . 40 B3
Hitherfield Prim Sch
SW16 . . . . 74 C2
Hitherfield Rd SW16,
SW27 . . . . 74 C1
Hither Green La
SE13 . . . . 67 C1
Hither Green Prim
Sch SE13 . . . . 67 C1
Hitherlands SW12 . . . 73 A2
HM Prison
Wormwood Scrubs
W12 . . . . 29 C3
HMS Belfast SE1 . . . 124 B2
Hoadly Rd SW16 . . . . 73 C2
Hobart Pl SW1 . . . . . 132 A2
Hobbes Wlk SW15 . . . 57 A2
Hobb's Ct SE1 . . . . . 139 A4
Hobbs' Pl N1 . . . . 24 A4
Hobday St E14 . . . . . . 34 A3
Hobhouse Ct SW1 . . 119 C3
Hobsons Pl 7 E1 . . . 111 B4
Hobury St SW10 . . . 157 B3
Hocker St 9
E2 . . . . 24 B2 98 C3
Hockett Cl SE8 . . . . . . 41 B2
Hockley Ho 9 E9 . . . . 17 B2
Hockliffe Ho 5
W10 . . . . 30 B4

Hockney Ct 1
SE16 . . . . 40 A1
Hockworth Ho 7
N16 . . . . 7 A3
Hocroft Ave NW2 . . . . 1 B1
Hocroft Ct NW2 . . . . . 1 B1
Hocroft Rd NW2 . . . . . 1 B1
Hocroft Wlk NW2 . . . . 1 B1
Hodford Lo NW11 . . . . 1 C2
Hodford Rd NW11 . . . . 1 C2
Hodister Cl 26 SE5 . . 48 B3
Hodnet Gr SE16 . . . . . 40 B2
Hoffman Sq N1 . . . . . 97 C4
Hofland Rd W14 . . . . 126 A2
Hogan Mews 2 W2 . 101 B4
Hogan Way E5 . . . . 7 C2
Hogarth Bsns Pk
W4 . . . . 46 A4
Hogarth Ct
1 Camden Town
NW1 . . . . 13 B1
City of London EC3 . . . 124 B4
24 Whitechapel E1 . . . 111 C1
Hogarth Ind Est
NW10 . . . . 21 C1
Hogarth La W4 . . . . . . 46 A4
Hogarth Pl SW5 . . . . 142 A3
Hogarth Rd SW5 . . . . 142 A3
Hogarth Roundabout
W4 . . . . 46 A4
Hogarth's House
W4 . . . . 46 A4
Holbeach Mews 1
SW12 . . . . 73 A3
Holbeck Row SE15 . . 49 C3
Holbein Ho SW1 . . . . 145 B2
Holbein Mews
SW1 . . . . 145 B2
Holbein Pl SW1 . . . . 145 B3
Holberton Gdns
NW10 . . . . 22 A2
HOLBORN 107 C3
Holborn EC1 . . . . 107 C3
Holborn Cir EC1 . . . . 107 C3
Holborn Ho 1
W12 . . . . 30 A3
Holborn Pl WC1 . . . . 106 C3
Holborn Sta WC1 . . . . 106 C3
Holborn Viaduct
EC1 . . . . 108 A3
Holbrook Cl N19 . . . . . 4 A3
Holbrooke Ct N7 . . . . 14 A4
Holbrook Ho
Acton W3 . . . . 28 C4
5 Streatham SW2 . . . 74 B3
Holcombe Ho
SW9 . . . . 62 A4
Holcombe Pl SE4 . . . . 66 A4
Holcombe St W6 . . . . 39 A2
Holcroft Ct W1 . . . . . 104 C4
Holcroft Ho
Battersea SW11 . . . . . . 59 C4
Lewisham SE10 . . . . . . 52 B2
Holcroft Rd E9 . . . . . . 17 B1
Holdenby Rd SE4 . . . . 66 A2
Holden Ho
12 Deptford SE8 . . . . 51 C3
Islington N1 . . . . 86 C3
Holden Point E15 . . . 19 C2
Holden St SW11 . . . . 169 B1
Holderness Ho
SE5 . . . . 64 A4

Holdsworth Ho 5
SW2 . . . . 74 C4
Holford Ho
6 Bermondsey
SE16 . . . . 40 A2
Finsbury WC1 . . . . 95 A4
Holford Pl WC1 . . . . . 95 A4
Holford Rd NW3 . . . . . 2 B1
Holford St WC1 . . . . . 95 B4
Holford Yd WC1 . . . . . 85 B1
Holgate Ave SW11 . . . 59 C4
Holland Gdns
Brentford TW8 . . . . 44 A4
Kensington W14 . . . . . 126 B2
Holland Gr SW9 . . . . 163 C1
Holland Park
W11 . . . . 31 B1 112 C1
Holland Park Ave
W11 . . . . 31 A1 112 B1
Holland Park Ct
W14 . . . . 126 B4
Holland Park Gdns
W14 . . . . 126 A4
Holland Park Mews
W11 . . . . 31 B1 112 C1
Holland Park Pre Prep
Sch W14 . . . . 126 C1
Holland Park Rd
W14 . . . . 127 A1
Holland Park Rdbt
W12 . . . . 39 C4
Holland Park Sch
W8 . . . . 127 A4
Holland Park Sta
W11 . . . . 31 B1 112 C1
Holland Pas N1 . . . . . 86 C4
Holland Pl W8 . . . . . . 128 A4
Holland Rd
West Kensington
W14 . . . . 126 B1
Willesden Green
NW10 . . . . 22 A3
Holland Rise Ho
SW9 . . . . 163 A1
Holland St
Kensington W8 . . . . . . 127 C4
Lambeth SE1 . . . . 122 B2
Holland Villas Rd
W14 . . . . 126 B1
Holland Wlk
Kensington W14 . . . . . 127 A4
Upper Holloway N19 . . 4 C3
Hollar Rd N16 . . . . 7 B1
Holles Ho 8 SW9 . . . 173 B2
Holles St W1 . . . . 104 B2
Holley Rd W3 . . . . 38 A4
Holliday Sq 6
SW11 . . . . 59 C4
Hollies The SW12 . . . 73 B2
Hollies Way 1
SW12 . . . . 72 C4
Hollingbourne Rd
SE24 . . . . 63 B2
Hollins Ho N7 . . . . 14 A4
Hollisfield WC1 . . . . . 94 B3
Holloway Rd
Lower Holloway
N7 . . . . 14 B4
Upper Holloway N19 . . 4 C3
Holloway Road Sta
N7 . . . . 14 B3
Upper Holloway N7 . . 13 C3
Holly Berry La 8
NW3 . . . . 11 B4

Hollybush Gdns
E2 . . . . 25 A2
Holly Bush Hill 2
NW3 . . . . 11 B4
Hollybush Ho 23
E2 . . . . 25 A2
Holly Bush Steps 2
NW3 . . . . 11 B4
Holly Bush Vale 10
NW3 . . . . 11 B4
Holly Cl NW10 . . . . 8 A1
Hollycroft Ave NW3 . . 1 C1
Hollydale Prim Sch 7
SE15 . . . . 50 B1
Hollydale Rd SE15 . . . 50 B1
Hollydene
Hither Green
SE13 . . . . 67 C1
5 Peckham SE15 . . . . 50 A2
Hollyhedge Ho 7
SE13 . . . . 52 C1
Holly Hill NW3 . . . . . . 11 B4
Holly Lo SW13 . . . . . . 56 B4
Holly Lodge SW13 . . . 57 C3
Holly Lodge Gdns
N6 . . . . 3 C3
Holly Lodge Mans
N6 . . . . 3 C3
Holly Mews SW10 . . 143 A1
Holly Mount NW3 . . . 11 B4
Hollymount Ct 9
SE10 . . . . 52 B2
Holly Park Rd N4 . . . . . 5 B4
Holly Pk N4 . . . . 5 B4
Holly Pl NW3 . . . . 11 B4
Holly Rd 6 W4 . . . . . . 37 C2
Holly St E8 . . . . 16 B1
Holly Terr N6 . . . . 3 C3
Hollytree Cl SW19 . . . 69 C3
Holly Tree Ho SE4 . . . 66 B4
Holly Village N6 . . . . . 4 A2
Holly Wlk NW3 . . . . . . 11 B4
Hollywood Lofts
E1 . . . . 24 B1 98 C1
Hollywood Mews
SW10 . . . . 156 C4
Hollywood Rd
SW10 . . . . 156 C4
Holman Ho 2 E2 . . . . 25 C2
Holman Hunt Ho
W14 . . . . 140 A1
Holman Rd SW11 . . . 167 B1
Holmbrook NW1 . . . . 83 A1
Holmbury Ct SW17 . . 72 B1
Holmbury Ho SW9 . . . 63 A2
Holmbush Rd
SW15 . . . . 58 A1
Holmcote Gdns
N5 . . . . 15 B3
Holmdale Rd NW6 . . . 10 C3
Holmdene Ave
SE24 . . . . 63 B2
Holmead Rd SW6 . . . 156 B1
Holmefield Ct 4
NW3 . . . . 12 A2
Holmefield Ho
W10 . . . . 23 A1
Holmes Cl SE22 . . . . . 64 C3
Holmes Ho
18 South Acton
W4 . . . . 37 B3

Holmes Ct continued
18 South Lambeth
SW4 . . . . **172** A2
Holmesdale Ave
SW14 . . . . 55 A3
Holmesdale Ho 12
NW6 . . . . 23 C2
Holmesdale Rd
Highgate N6 . . . . 4 A4
Richmond TW9 . . . . 44 B2
Holmesley Rd
SE23 . . . . 66 A1
Holmes Pl SW10 . . **157** A4
Holmes Rd NW5 . . . . 13 A3
Holmes Terr SE1 . . **135** B4
Holmewood Gdns
SW2 . . . . 74 B4
Holmewood Rd
SW2 . . . . 74 B4
Holmhurst SE13 . . . . 67 C1
Holmleigh Prim Sch
N16 . . . . 7 A3
Holmleigh Rd N16 . . . 7 A3
Holm Oak Cl SW15 . 58 B1
Holmsbury Ho 6
N7 . . . . 13 C3
Holmsdale Ho 24
E14 . . . . 34 A2
Holmside Ct SW12 . 60 C1
Holmside Rd
SW12 . . . . 60 C1
Holmsley Ho SW15 . 68 B4
Holm Wlk SE3 . . . . . 53 C1
Holmwood Ct 8
N16 . . . . 7 B4
Holocaust Meml Gdn
W2 . . . . **131** A4
Holroyd Rd SW15 . . 57 B2
Holsgrove Ct E9 . . . . 18 A2
Holst Mans SW13 . . 47 B3
Holsworthy Ho 26
E3 . . . . 27 A2
Holsworthy Sq
WC1 . . . . 95 A1
Holt Ct SE10 . . . . . . 52 B4
Holt Ho SW2 . . . . . . 62 C1
Holton St E1 . . . . . . 25 C1
Holwood Pl 7
SW4 . . . . 61 C3
Holybourne Ave
SW15 . . . . 68 C4
Holy Cross Prim Sch
SW6 . . . . **165** B4
Holy Ghost RC Prim
Sch 23 SW12 . . . . 72 C4
Holyhead Cl E3 . . . . . 26 C2
Holyoake Ct SE16 . . 41 B4
Holyoak Rd SE11 . . **150** B3
Holyport Rd SW6 . . 47 C3
Holyrood Ho N4 . . . . 6 B3
Holyrood Mews
6 Greenwich
SE7 . . . . 43 C1
10 Newham E16 . . . . 35 C1
Holyrood St SE1 . . **124** A1
Holy Trinity CE Prim
Sch
Belgravia SW1 . . . . **145** B4
Dalston E8 . . . . 16 B2
10 Hampstead
NW3 . . . . 11 B2
Richmond TW10 . . . 54 C3
Streatham SW2 . . . . 74 B4

Holy Trinity & Saint
Silas CE Prim Sch 22
NW1 . . . . 13 A1
Holywell Cl
33 Bermondsey
SE16 . . . . 40 A1
2 Greenwich SE3 . . 53 A4
Holywell La
EC2 . . . . 24 A1 98 B2
Holywell Row
EC2 . . . . 24 A1 98 A1
Homan Ho 6 SW4 . 73 C4
Homecross Ho 7
W4 . . . . 37 C2
Homefield Rd W4 . . . 38 B1
Homefield St 14
N1 . . . . 24 A3
Homeleigh Ct 8
SW16 . . . . 74 A1
Homeleigh Rd
SE15 . . . . 65 C2
Homemead SW12 . . 73 A2
Home Office SW1 **133** C1
Home Park Rd
SW19 . . . . 70 B1
Home Rd SW11 . . . **168** A2
Homer Dr E14 . . . . . 41 C2
Homer Rd E9 . . . . . . 18 A2
Homer Row W1 . . . **102** B3
Homer St W1 . . . . . **102** B3
HOMERTON 17 C1
Homerton Gr E9 . . . 17 C3
Homerton High St
E9 . . . . 17 C2
Homerton Rd E9 . . . 18 B3
Homerton Row E9 . . 17 B3
Homerton Terr E9 . . 17 B2
Homerton University
Hospl E9 . . . . 17 C3
Homestall Rd SE22 . 65 B2
Homestead Rd
SW6 . . . . **155** A1
Homewoods 2
SW12 . . . . 73 B4
Homildon Ho 10
SE26 . . . . 76 C1
Honduras St EC1 . . . 96 C2
Honeybourne Rd
NW6 . . . . 11 A3
Honeybrook Rd SW12,
SW4 . . . . 73 B4
Honeyfield N4 . . . . . . 5 C2
Honey La EC2 . . . . . **109** A1
Honey Lane Ho
SW10 . . . . **156** B4
Honeyman Cl NW6 . . 9 C1
Honeywell Jun & Inf
Schs 5 SW11 . . . . 60 B1
Honeywell Rd
SW11 . . . . 60 C2
Honeywood Ho 6
SE15 . . . . 49 C2
Honeywood Rd
NW10 . . . . 21 B3
Honiton Gdns 1
SE15 . . . . 50 B1
Honiton Ho 29 SE5 . 48 B1
Honiton Rd NW6 . . **23** B3
HONOR OAK 65 B2
Honor Oak Park Sta
SE23 . . . . 65 C1
Honor Oak Pk
SE23 . . . . 65 C1
Honor Oak Rise
SE23 . . . . 65 B1

Honwell Ho 24 W2 . 31 C4
Hood Ave SW14 . . . 55 B2
Hood Ct N7 . . . . 5 B1
Hood Ho 17 SE5 . . . 48 C3
Hooke Cl SE10 . . . . . 52 B2
Hooke Ho 22 E3 . . . 26 A3
Hookham Ct SW8 . **171** B4
Hooks Cl SE15 . . . . . 50 A2
Hooper Ho 9
SW18 . . . . 58 B2
Hooper Rd E16 . . . . 35 C3
Hooper's Ct SW1 . **130** C3
Hooper's Mews 4
W3 . . . . 28 B1
Hooper St E1 . . . . . **111** B1
Hoop La NW11 . . . . . 1 C4
Hope Cl 7
2 Brentford
TW8 . . . . 36 A1
Canonbury N1 . . . . 15 B2
Hope Gdns 10 W3 . 37 A4
Hope St SW11 . . . . . 59 C4
Hopetown St E1 . . **111** A3
Hopewell St SE5 . . . 48 C3
Hop Gdns WC2 . . . **120** A3
Hopgood St 6
W12 . . . . 30 B1
Hopkins Ho 17
E14 . . . . 33 C3
Hopkinson Ho 1
SW11 . . . . **169** B2
Hopkinson's Pl
NW1 . . . . 81 B4
Hopkins St W1 . . . **105** B1
Hopping La N1 . . . . . 15 A2
Hop St SE10 . . . . . . 43 B2
Hopton Ho 5
SW9 . . . . 48 A1
Hopton's Gdns
SE1 . . . . **122** B2
Hopton St SE1 . . . **122** B2
Hopwood Cl SW17 . 71 B1
Hopwood Rd SE17 . 48 C4
Hopwood Wlk E8 . . 16 C1
Horatio Ho 13 E2 . . 24 B3
Horatio Ho 9 E14 . . 34 B1
Horatio St 11 E2 . . 24 B3
Horbury Cres
W11 . . . . 31 C2 **113** B3
Horbury Mews
W11 . . . . 31 B2 **113** A3
Horder Rd SW6 . . . **164** B3
Hordle Prom E 4
SE15 . . . . 49 B3
Hordle Prom N 4
SE15 . . . . 49 B3
Hordle Prom S 7
SE15 . . . . 49 B3
Horizon Bldg 22
E14 . . . . 33 C2
Horizon Ind Est
SE15 . . . . 50 A4
Horizon Sch N16 . . . 16 A4
Horle Wlk SE5 . . . . . 48 A1
Hormead Rd W9 . . . 23 B1
Hornbeam Cl 1
SE11 . . . . **149** B4
Hornbeam Ho 2
NW3 . . . . 12 B2
Hornbeam Sq 6
E3 . . . . 26 B4
Hornblower Cl 2
SE16 . . . . 41 A2
Hornby Cl NW3 . . . . 11 C1

Hornby Ho 6
SE11 . . . . **163** C4
Horndean Cl 3
SW15 . . . . 68 C3
Horner Hos 18 N1 . . 24 A4
Horne Way SW15 . . 47 B1
Horn La
Acton W3 . . . . 28 B3
Greenwich SE10 . . 43 C2
Horn Link Way
SE10 . . . . 43 C2
Hornby House Sch 7
SW12 . . . . 72 C3
Hornsey La N6 . . . . . 4 B4
Hornsey Lane Gdns
N6 . . . . 4 B4
Hornsey Rd N19, N7, N8 . 5 B2
Hornsey Rise Gdns
N19 . . . . 5 A4
Hornsey St N7 . . . . 14 B3
Hornshay St SE15 . 50 B4
Hornton Ct W8 . . . **127** C3
Hornton Pl W8 . . . **127** C3
Hornton St W8 . . . **127** C4
Horrocks Ho
SW15 . . . . 57 A2
Horse & Dolphin Yd
W1 . . . . **119** C4
Horseferry Pl SE10 . 52 B4
Horseferry Rd
Limehouse E14 . . . . 33 A2
Westminster SW1 . **147** C4
Horseferry Rd Est
SW1 . . . . **133** C1
Horse Guards Ave
SW1 . . . . **120** A1
Horse Guards Par
SW1 . . . . **119** C1
Horse Guards Rd
SW1 . . . . **133** C4
Horsell Rd N5 . . . . . 14 C3
Horselydown La
SE1 . . . . **124** C1
Horselydown Mans
SE1 . . . . **138** C4
Horsemongers Mews
SE1 . . . . **137** A3
Horsendon Ho 11
N7 . . . . 13 C3
Horseshoe Cl E14 . 42 B1
Horse Yd N1 . . . . . . 86 B4
Horsfield Ho 15
N1 . . . . 15 B1
Horsford Rd SW2 . . 62 B2
Horsley Ct SW1 . . **147** C3
Horsley Ho 18 SE4 . 65 C3
Horsley St 3 SE17 . 48 C4
Horsman Ho SE5 . . 48 B4
Horsman St SE5 . . . 48 B4
Horsmonden Rd
SE4 . . . . 66 B1
Horston Ho 6 N4 . . . 6 B4
Hortensia Ho
SW10 . . . . **156** C2
Hortensia Rd
SW10 . . . . **156** C2
Horticultural Pl 6
W4 . . . . 37 C1
Horton Ave NW2 . . . 10 A4
Horton Ho
13 Deptford SE15 . 50 B4
South Lambeth
SW8 . . . . **162** C2
West Kensington
W14 . . . . **140** A1
Horton Rd E8 . . . . . . 17 A2

Horton St SE13 . . . . 67 A4
Horwood Ho
24 Bethnal Green
E2 . . . . 25 A2
Marylebone NW8 . . . 90 B2
Hosack Rd SW12,
SW17 . . . . 72 C2
Hosier La EC1 . . . . **108** B3
Hoskins St SE10 . . . 42 C1
Hospl for Tropical
Diseases NW1 . . . 93 A1
Hospl of St John & St
Elizabeth NW8 . . . 79 B1
Hotham Prim Sch
SW15 . . . . 57 C3
Hotham Rd SW15 . . 57 B4
Hotbefore 16
E8 . . . . 16 B2
Hotham Sq SW9 . . 42 A4
Houghton Cl 10
E8 . . . . 16 B2
Houghton Sq SW9 . 62 A4
Houghton St WC2 . **107** A1
Houndsditch EC3 . **110** B2
Household Cavalry
Mus SW1 . . . . . **120** A2
Houseman Way 20
SE5 . . . . 48 C3
House Mill The E3 . . 27 B2
Houses of Parliament
SW1 . . . . **134** B2
Hoveden Rd NW2 . . 10 A3
Howard Bldg
SW8 . . . . **160** A3
Howard Cl
Acton W3 . . . . 28 A3
Cricklewood NW2 . . 10 A4
Howard Ct
Lewisham SE10 . . . 52 B2
Peckham SE15 . . . . 64 C4
Howard Ho
6 Brixton SW9 . . . . 62 C4
14 Deptford SE8 . . . 51 B4
Fitzrovia W1 . . . . . 92 B1
Howard Mews N5 . . 15 A4
Howard Rd
Canonbury N16 . . . 15 C4
Cricklewood NW2 . . 9 C4
Howard's La SW15 . 57 B3
Howbury Rd SE15 . . 65 B4
Howcroft Ho 3
E3 . . . . 26 B2
Howden St SE15 . . . 64 C4
Howell Ho 5 N7 . . . 13 C3
Howell Wlk SE1 . . **150** B3
Howgate Rd SW14 . 55 C4
Howick Pl SW1 . . . **133** A1
Howie St SW11 . . . **158** A1
Howitt Cl
6 Maitland Pk
NW3 . . . . 12 A2
Stoke Newington
N16 . . . . 16 A4
Howitt Rd NW3 . . . . 12 A2
Howland Ho 6
SW16 . . . . 74 A1
Howland Mews E
W1 . . . . **105** A4
Howland St W1 . . . **105** A4
Howland Way
SE16 . . . . 41 A4
Howletts Rd SE24 . . 63 B1
Howley Pl W2 . . . . **101** A4

Howsman Rd
SW13 . . . . .46 C4
Howson Rd SE4 . . . . .66 A3
Howson Terr
TW10 . . . . .54 A1
How's St E2 . . . . .24 B3
HOXTON 24 A3
Hoxton Mkt **10**
N1 . . . . .24 A2 98 A3
Hoxton Point
EC1 . . . . .24 A2 98 A3
Hoxton Sq
N1 . . . . .24 A2 98 A3
Hoxton St N1 . . . . . .24 A3
Hoxton Sta E2 . . . . . .24 B3
Hoylake Rd W3 . . . . .29 A3
Hoyland Cl **4**
SE15 . . . . .50 A3
Hoy St E16 . . . . .35 A3
Hub Buildings The **4**
SW12 . . . . .73 A3
Hub E15 E15 . . . . . . .27 A3
Huberd Ho SE1 . . . .137 C2
Hubert Gr SW9 . . . . .62 A4
Hubert Ho NW8 . . . . .90 A1
Hub The NW1 . . . . . .81 A1
Hucknall Ct NW8 . . . .89 B2
Huddart St **8** E3 . . .33 B4
Huddleston Cl E2 . . .25 B3
Huddlestone Rd
NW2 . . . . .9 A2
Huddleston Rd N7 . .13 B4
Hudson Cl **15** W12 . .30 A2
Hudson Ct **1** E14 . .41 C1
Hudson Ho
Chelsea SW10 . . . .156 C2
5 Notting Hill W11 .31 A3
Hudson's Pl SW1 . . .146 C4
Huggin Ct EC4 . . . . .123 A4
Huggin Hill EC4 . . . .123 A4
Huggins Ho **6** E3 . . .26 C2
Huggins Pl SW2 . . . .74 B3
Hughan Rd E15 . . . . .19 C3
Hugh Astor Ct
SE1 . . . . .136 B2
Hugh Dalton Ave
SW6 . . . . .154 C3
Hughenden Ho
NW8 . . . . .90 A2
Hughendon Terr
E15 . . . . .19 B4
Hughes Ho
28 Bethnal Green
E2 . . . . .25 B2
Camberwell SE5 . . . .48 B2
18 Deptford SE8 . . .51 C4
Newington SE17 . . .150 B3
Hughes Mans
E1 . . . . .24 C1 99 C1
Hughes Terr **8**
E16 . . . . .35 B4
Hugh Gaitskell Cl
SW6 . . . . .154 C3
Hugh Gaitskell Ho
Stoke Newington
N16 . . . . .7 B2
Willesden NW10 . . . . .8 B1
Hugh Mews SW1 . . .146 B3
Hugh Morgan Ho **5**
SW4 . . . . .61 C4
Hugh Myddelton Prim
Sch EC1 . . . . .95 C3

Hugh Platt Ho **29**
E2 . . . . .25 A3
Hugh St SW1 . . . . . .146 B3
Hugo Ho SW1 . . . . .131 A2
Hugon Rd SW6 . . . . .59 A4
Hugo Rd N19 . . . . . . .13 B4
Huguenot Ct **1**
E1 . . . . .111 B4
Huguenot Pl
London SW18 . . . . . .59 B2
Spitalfields E1 . . . . .111 A4
Huguenot Sq SE15 . .65 A4
Hullbridge Mews
N1 . . . . .87 B4
Hull Cl SE16 . . . . .32 C1
Hull St EC1 . . . . .96 C3
Hulme Pl SE1 . . . . . .137 A3
Humber Dr W10 . . . .22 C1
Humber Rd SE3 . . . . .53 B4
Humberton Cl E9 . . . .18 A3
Humbolt Rd W6 . . . .154 A3
Hume Ct N1 . . . . .15 A1
Hume Ho **10** W11 . . .30 C1
Humphrey Ct
SW11 . . . . .167 C3
Humphrey St SE1 . . .152 C2
Humphry Ho **10**
SW15 . . . . .57 C2
Hungerford Bridge
WC2 . . . . .120 C2
Hungerford Ho
SW1 . . . . .161 A4
Hungerford La
WC2 . . . . .120 B2
Hungerford Prim Sch
16 N7 . . . . .13 C2
Hungerford Rd
12 Camden Town
N7 . . . . .13 C2
Lower Holloway N7 . .14 A3
Hungerford St **21**
E1 . . . . .32 A3
Hunsdon Rd SE14 . . .50 C3
Hunslett St **20** E2 . .25 B3
Hunstanton Ho
NW1 . . . . .102 B4
Hunt Cl W11 . . . . .30 C1
Hunter Cl
Borough The SE1 . . .137 C1
Upper Tooting
SW12 . . . . .72 C3
Huntercombe-
Roehampton Hospl
The SW15 . . . . .68 C4
Hunter Ct
8 London SE5 . . . . .63 C3
37 Streatham SW2 .74 C4
Hunter Ho
Bloomsbury WC1 . . . .94 B2
Lambeth SE1 . . . . . .136 B3
South Lambeth
SW8 . . . . .161 C1
15 Tufnell Pk N19 . . .4 B1
West Brompton
SW5 . . . . .141 C1
Hunterian Mus
WC2 . . . . .107 A2
Hunter Lo **9** W9 . . . .31 C4
Hunter St WC1 . . . . . .94 B3
Huntingdon Ct
SW14 . . . . .55 B4
Huntingdon Gdns
W4 . . . . .45 B3
Huntingdon Ho
SW5 . . . . .141 C4

Huntingdon St
Canning Town
E16 . . . . .35 B3
Islington N1 . . . . .14 B1
Huntingfield Rd
SW15 . . . . .56 C2
Huntingford Ho
SW15 . . . . .47 B1
Huntington Ho N2 . . .9 B2
Huntley St WC1 . . . . .93 B1
Hunton St E1 . . . . . . .111 B4
Hunts Cl SE3 . . . . . . .53 C1
Hunt's Ct WC2 . . . . .119 C3
Huntshaw Ho **37**
E3 . . . . .27 A2
Huntsman St
SE17 . . . . .152 A3
Huntspill St SW17 . . .71 B1
Hunts Slip Rd
SE21 . . . . .76 A1
Huntsworth Mews
NW1 . . . . .90 C1
Hurdwick Ho NW1 . . .82 C2
Hurdwick Pl NW1 . . .82 C2
Hurleston Ho **11**
SE8 . . . . .41 B1
Hurley Cres SE16 . . .40 C4
Hurley Ho
Lambeth SE11 . . . . .149 C3
34 Shoreditch
E2 . . . . .24 B2 98 C3
Hurley Lo SE22 . . . . .65 B1
Hurlingham Bsns Pk
SW6 . . . . .58 C4
Hurlingham & Chelsea
Sec Sch SW6 . . . . . .58 C4
Hurlingham Court
Mans SW6 . . . . .165 B1
Hurlingham Ct
SW6 . . . . .58 B4
Hurlingham Gdns
SW6 . . . . .58 B4
Hurlingham Rd
SW6 . . . . .165 A1
Hurlingham Sch
SW15 . . . . .58 B3
Hurlingham Sq
SW6 . . . . .59 A4
Hurlock Ho **1** N5 . . . .6 A1
Hurlock St N5 . . . . . . .6 A1
Huron Rd SW17 . . . . .72 C1
Huron Univ WC1 . . .106 A4
Hurstbourne Ho
SW15 . . . . .56 B1
Hurstdene Gdns
N15 . . . . .7 A4
Hurst Ho WC1 . . . . . .85 A1
Hurst St SE24 . . . . . .63 A1
Hurstway Wlk **2**
W11 . . . . .30 C2
Husbourne Ho **8**
SE8 . . . . .41 A2
Huson Cl NW3 . . . . . .12 A1
Hutching's St E14 . . .41 C4
Hutching's Wharf **11**
E14 . . . . .41 C4
Hutchins Cl E15 . . . . .19 B1
Hutchins Ho **3**
SW4 . . . . .73 C4
Hutchinson Ho **5**
SE14 . . . . .50 B3
Hutton Ct **4** N4 . . . . .5 B3
Hutton Ho **10**
E2 . . . . .24 C2 99 B3
Hutton St EC4 . . . . .107 C1

Huxbear St SE4 . . . . .66 B2
Huxley Ho
4 London SW9 . . .172 C2
Paddington NW8 . . . .89 C1
Huxley St W10 . . . . . .23 A2
Hyacinth Rd SW15 . .68 C3
Hyde Farm Mews
SW12 . . . . .73 C3
Hyde La SW11 . . . . .168 A4
Hyde Park **4** 116 C1
Hyde Park Cnr
SW1 . . . . .131 C4
Hyde Park Corner Sta
SW1 . . . . .131 C4
Hyde Park Cres
W2 . . . . .102 A1
Hyde Park Gate Mews
SW7 . . . . .129 A3
Hyde Park Gdns
W2 . . . . .115 C4
Hyde Park Gdns Mews
W2 . . . . .116 A4
Hyde Park Mans
NW1 . . . . .102 B3
Hyde Park Pl W2 . . .116 B4
Hyde Park Sq W2 . . .102 A1
Hyde Park Square
Mews W2 . . . . .102 A1
Hyde Park St W2 . . .102 A1
Hyde Park Twrs
W2 . . . . .114 C3
Hyde Rd
Richmond TW10 . . . .54 B2
Shoreditch N1 . . . . . .24 A4
Hyde's Pl **12** N1 . . . .15 A1
Hyde St SE8 . . . . . . .51 C4
Hydethorpe Rd
SW12 . . . . .73 B3
Hyde Vale SE10 . . . . .52 B3
Hylda Ct NW5 . . . . . . .3 C1
Hyndman Ho **4**
N19 . . . . .13 C4
Hyndman St SE15 . . .50 A4
Hyperion Ho
3 Bow E3 . . . . .26 A3
Streatham SW2 . . . . .74 B4
Hyson Rd SE16 . . . . .40 A1
Hythe Ho **14** SE16 . .40 B4
Hythe Rd NW10 . . . . .21 C1
Hythe Road Ind Est
NW10 . . . . .21 C1

Ian Hamilton Ho
NW1 . . . . .93 B4
Ian Mikardo Sch **3**
E3 . . . . .27 A2
Ibberton Ho
Kensington W14 . . . .126 B1
South Lambeth
SW8 . . . . .162 C2
Ibbotson Ave E16 . . .35 B3
Ibbott St **2** E1 . . . . .25 B1
Iberia Ho **2** N19 . . . .4 C4
Ibis Ct SE8 . . . . .51 B4
Ibis La W4 . . . . .45 B2
Ibsley Gdns SW15 . .68 C3
Ibstock Place Sch
SW15 . . . . .56 A1
Icarus Ho **2** E3 . . . . .26 B2
Iceland Rd E3 . . . . . . .26 C4
Iceland Wharf
SE16 . . . . .41 A2
Iceni Ct **23** E3 . . . . . .26 B4

Ice Wharf NW1 . . . . . .84 B2
Idaho Bldg **7**
SE13 . . . . .52 A2
Ida St E14 . . . . .34 B3
Identity & Passport
Office SW1 . . . . . . .146 B3
Idmiston Rd SE21,
SE27 . . . . .75 B2
Idol La EC3 . . . . .124 A3
Idonia St SE8 . . . . . . .51 C3
Iffley Ho **2**
E2 . . . . .24 B2 98 C3
Iffley Rd W6 . . . . .39 A3
Ifield Ho SE17 . . . . .152 B2
Ifield Rd SW10 . . . . .156 B4
Ifor Evans Pl E1 . . . .25 C1
Ightham Ho SE17 . . .152 A3
Ikon Ho **21** E1 . . . . . .32 B2
Ilbert St W10 . . . . . . .23 A2
Ilchester Gdns
W2 . . . . .114 A4
Ilchester Mans
W8 . . . . .127 B2
Ilchester Pl W14 . . . .127 A2
Ildersly Gr SE21 . . . .75 C2
Ilderton Prim Sch **16**
SE16 . . . . .40 B1
Ilderton Rd SE15,
SE16 . . . . .50 B4
Ilex Rd NW10 . . . . . . .8 B2
Ilford Ho **14** N1 . . . .15 C2
Ilfracombe Flats
SE1 . . . . .137 A4
Iliffe St SE17 . . . . . . .150 B2
Iliffe Yd SE17 . . . . . .150 B2
Ilkeston Ct **7** E5 . . .17 C4
Ilminster Gdns
SW11 . . . . .60 A3
Ilsley Ct **8** SW8 . . .170 C1
Imber St N1 . . . . .87 B3
Imperial Ave **5**
N16 . . . . .16 A4
Imperial Cl NW2 . . . . .9 A3
Imperial College
London (Charing
Cross) W6 . . . . .39 C1
Imperial College
London (Chelsea &
Westminster)
SW10 . . . . .157 A3
Imperial College
London
(Hammersmith)
W12 . . . . .30 A3
Imperial College
London (Royal
Brompton) SW3 . . . .144 A2
Imperial College
London (South
Kensington)
SW7 . . . . .129 B2
Imperial College
London (St Mary's)
W2 . . . . .101 C2
Imperial College Rd
SW7 . . . . .129 B2
Imperial Cres
SW6 . . . . .167 A1
Imperial Ct NW8 . . . .80 B2
Imperial Ho
1 Bow E3 . . . . .26 A2
2 Poplar E14 . . . . . .33 B2
Strand WC2 . . . . . . .106 C1
Imperial Rd SW6 . . .166 B3
Imperial Sq SW6 . . .166 B4
Imperial St E3 . . . . . .27 B2

Imperial Twrs 3
NW3 . . . . 11 B2
Imperial War Mus SE1,
SE11 . . . . 135 C1
Imperial Wharf Sta
SW10 . . . . 167 A3
Imre Cl W12 . . . . 30 A1
Inchbald Sch of
Design (Garden
Design) SW1 . . . 146 B3
Inchbald Sch of
Design (Interior
Design) SW1 . . . 145 B4
Independent Pl E8 . 16 A3
Indescon Ct E14 . . . 42 A4
India St EC3 . . . . . . 110 C1
India Way W12 . . . . 30 A2
Indigo Mews N16 . . . 6 C1
Indus Ct 16 SE15 . . 49 B3
Ingate Pl SW8 . . . 170 B3
Ingelow Ho 16 . . . 128 A4
Ingersoll Rd W12 . . 30 A1
Ingestre Pl W1 . . . 105 A1
Ingestre Rd NW5 . . 13 A4
Ingham Rd NW6 . . . 10 C4
Inglebert St EC1 . . 95 B4
Ingleborough St
SW9 . . . . 173 B2
Ingleby Rd N7 . . . . . 5 A1
Inglefield Sq 12
E1 . . . . 32 A1
Ingle Ho 3 SW12 . . 73 C3
Inglesham Wlk E9 . 18 B2
Ingleside Gr 12 SE3 . 53 B4
Inglethorpe Ho 6
E5 . . . . 7 C2
Inglethorpe St
SW6 . . . . 47 C2
Ingleton St SW9 . . 173 B2
Inglewood Cl E14 . . 41 C2
Inglewood Mans 10
NW6 . . . . 10 C3
Inglewood Rd
NW6 . . . . 10 C3
Inglis Ho 1 SW15 . 57 B2
Inglis St SE5 . . . . . 48 A2
Ingram Ave NW11 . . 2 B4
Ingram Cl SE11 . . 149 A4
Ingram Ho 1 . . . . . 26 A4
Ingram Lo 8 SW4 . 61 C1
Ingrave St SW11 . . 60 A4
Ingrebourne Ho
NW8 . . . . 101 C4
Ingress St 4 W4 . . 38 A1
Inigo Pl WC2 . . . . 120 A4
Inkerman Rd NW5 . 13 A2
Inkerman Terr
W8 . . . . 127 C1
Inkster Ho 8
SW11 . . . . 60 A4
Inman Rd
Harlesden NW10 . . 21 A4
Wandsworth SW18 . 71 B4
Inner Circ NW1 . . . 91 B4
Inner Park Rd
SW19 . . . . 69 C2
Inner Temple EC4 . 121 B4
Inner Temple La
EC4 . . . . 107 B1
Innes Gdns SW15 . . 57 A1
Innisfree Ho NW2 . . 9 C2
Innis Ho SE17 . . . 152 A2
Insley Ho 15 E3 . . . 27 A2

Institute of Cancer
Research The
SW7 . . . . 143 A2
Institute Pl 1 E8 . . 17 A3
Inst of Child Health
WC1 . . . . 94 C1
Inst of Neurology
Bloomsbury WC1 . . 106 B4
St Pancras WC1 . . . 94 B1
Int Coll of
Accountancy The
SW17 . . . . 72 B1
Interchange The
NW5 . . . . 13 A3
International Com Sch
W1 . . . . 91 C1
International House
Language Sch
WC2 . . . . 106 B2
International Sch of
London W3 . . . . . . 36 C2
Inver Ct
11 Bayswater
W2 . . . . 100 B1
4 Hammersmith
W6 . . . . 38 C3
Inverforth Cl NW3 . . 2 B3
Inverforth Ho NW3 . 2 B3
Invergarry Ho
NW6 . . . . 78 A1
Invermead Cl W6 . . 38 C2
Inverness Gdns
W8 . . . . 114 A1
Inverness Mews
W2 . . . . 114 B4
Inverness Pl W2 . . 114 B4
Inverness St NW1 . 82 B4
Inverness Terr
W2 . . . . 114 B4
Inverton Rd SE15 . . 65 C3
Invicta Cl 1 E3 . . . 33 C4
Invicta Plaza SE1 . 122 A2
Invicta Prim Sch
SE3 . . . . 53 C3
Invicta Rd SE3, SE7 . 53 C4
Inville Rd SE17 . . . 151 C1
Inwen Ct SE8 . . . . 41 A1
Inwood Ct 1 N1 . . . 15 B1
Inwood Ho 19
E14 . . . . 64 A4
Ionian Bldg 22 E14 . 33 A2
Ionian Ho 22 E1 . . 25 C1
Ipsden Bldgs SE1 . 136 A3
Ipswich Ho SE4 . . . 65 C2
Iqra Int Sch SW9 . . 62 C4
Irby Ho SW2 . . . . . 62 C1
Ireland Yd EC4 . . . 108 B1
Irene Rd SW6 . . . . 165 C3
Ireton Ho 22 SW9 . 173 C1
Ireton St 3 E3 . . . 26 C1
Iris Ct 3 SE15 . . . 50 A1
Iroko Ho 9 NW3 . . 11 A2
Iron Bridge Cl
NW10 . . . . 8 A3
Iron Bridge Ho
NW3 . . . . 12 B1
Irongate Ho EC3 . . 110 B2
Iron Mill Pl SW18 . . 59 A1
Iron Mill Rd SW18 . 59 A1
Ironmonger La
EC2 . . . . 109 B1

Ironmonger Pas
EC1 . . . . 97 A3
Ironmonger Row
EC1 . . . . 97 A3
Ironmonger Row
Baths EC1 . . . . . . 97 A3
Ironmongers Pl
E14 . . . . 41 C2
Ironmonger's Pl 2
E14 . . . . 41 C2
Ironside Cl SE16 . . 40 C4
Ironside Ho E9 . . . 18 A4
Ironworks 1 E3 . . . 26 C4
Irvine Cl N1 . . . . . 93 A1
Irvine Ho N7 . . . . 14 B2
Irving Gr SW9 . . . 172 C1
Irving Ho SE17 . . . 150 A1
Irving Mews N1 . . . 15 B2
Irving Rd W14 . . . . 39 C3
Irving St WC2 . . . . 119 C3
Irwell Est 51 SE16 . 40 B4
Irwin Gdns NW10 . 22 A4
Isabella Ct 8
W10 . . . . 54 B1
Isabella Ho
16 Hammersmith
W6 . . . . 39 B1
Kensington SE11 . . 150 A2
Isabella Mews 11
E8 . . . . 16 C3
Isabella Rd E9 . . . 17 B3
Isabel St SW9 . . . 173 A4
Isambard Mews
E14 . . . . 42 B3
Isambard Pl SE16 . 32 B1
Iseldon Ct N14 . . . 14 A4
Isel Way 4 SE22 . . 64 A2
Isis Cl SW15 . . . . . 57 B3
Isis Ct W4 . . . . . . 45 A3
Isis Ho NW8 . . . . . 89 C1
Isis St SW18 . . . . . 71 B2
Island Row E14 . . . 33 A3
Islay Wlk 17 N1 . . . 15 B2
Isleden Ho N1 . . . 86 C4
Isledon Rd N4, N7 . . 5 C1
ISLE OF DOGS 42 B2
ISLINGTON 14 C2
Islington Arts & Media
Sch 6 N4 . . . . 5 B3
Islington Bsns Ctr
N1 . . . . 87 A4
Islington Est 1 N1 . 86 C4
Islington Gn N1 . . . 86 A3
Islington High St
N1 . . . . 86 A2
Islington Mus WC1 . 96 A3
Islington Park Mews
1 N1 . . . . 15 A1
Islington Park St
N1 . . . . 14 C1
Islington Tennis Ctr
N7 . . . . 14 A2
Islip St NW5 . . . . . 13 B3
Isokon Flats 3
NW3 . . . . 12 B3

Issac Way SE1 . . . 137 A4
Italia Conti Acad of
Theatre Arts EC1 . 96 C1
Ivanhoe Ho
11 Balham SW12 . . 73 A4
24 Bow E3 . . . . . . 26 A3
Ivanhoe Rd SE5 . . 64 B4
Ivatt Pl W14 . . . . 141 A1
Iveagh Cl E9 . . . . . 25 C4
Iveagh Ct EC3 . . . 110 C1
Iveagh Ho
2 Brixton SW9 . . . 48 A1
Chelsea SW10 . . . 157 A2
Ivebury Ct 8 W10 . 30 B3
Iveley Rd SW4 . . . 170 C1
Iver Ct N1 . . . . . . 15 B2
Iverna Ct W8 . . . . 127 C2
Iverna Gdns W8 . . 127 C2
Iverson Rd NW6 . . 10 C2
Ives Rd E16 . . . . . 35 A4
Ives St SW3 . . . . . 144 B4
Ivimey St E2 . . . . 24 C2 99 C4
Ivinghoe Ho 14 N7 . 13 C3
Ivor Ct NW1 . . . . . 90 C2
Ivories The N1 . . . . 15 B1
Ivor Mayor Lo
SW12 . . . . 60 C1
Ivor Pl NW1 . . . . . 90 C1
Ivor St NW1 . . . . . 13 B1
Ivory Ho
9 London SW11 . . 59 B4
St George in E1
E1 . . . . 125 A2
Ivory Sq 15 SW18 . 59 B4
Ivybridge Ho 18 . . . 64 A4
Ivybridge La WC2 . 120 B3
Ivy Church La SE1,
SE17 . . . . 152 C2
Ivy Cotts E14 . . . . 34 A2
Ivy Cres W4 . . . . . 37 B2
Ivy Ct 18 SE16 . . . 153 C1
Ivy Rd
Brockley SE4 . . . . 66 C3
Cricklewood NW2 . 9 B4
Newham E16 . . . . 35 C3
Ivy St N1 . . . . 24 A3
Ixworth Pl SW3 . . 144 A3

Jacaranda Gr E8 . . 16 B1
Jackman Ho 22 E1 . 32 A1
Jackman St E8 . . . 25 A4
Jackson Cl E9 . . . . 17 C1
Jackson Ho 13
SW11 . . . . 59 C4
Jackson Rd N7 . . . 14 B4
Jackson's La N6 . . . 4 A4
Jack Taylor Sch
NW8 . . . . 78 C4
Jack Tizard Sch
W12 . . . . 30 A1
Jack Walker Ct
N5 . . . . 15 A4
Jacobin Lo N7 . . . . 14 A3
Jacob Mans 13 E1 . 32 A3
Jacobson Ct
SW11 . . . . 168 B3
Jacobson Ho E1 . . 110 C2

Jacob St SE1 . . . . 139 B4
Jacob's Well Mews
W1 . . . . 103 C2
Jacotts Ho W10 . . . 22 B1
Jacqueline Ho 8
E1 . . . . 32 C4
Jaeger Ho SW11 . . 168 C3
Jago Wlk SE5 . . . . 48 C3
Jamahirya Sch
SW3 . . . . 158 A4
Jamaica Rd
Bermondsey SE1 . . 139 A3
Bermondsey SE16 . 40 A3
Jamaica St E1 . . . . 32 B4
James Allen's Girls'
Sch 12 SE22 . . . . 64 A2
James Allen's Pre-
Prep Sch SE21 . . . 63 C1
James Allen's Prep
Sch 13 SE22 . . . . 64 A2
James Anderson Ct 20
E2 . . . . 24 A3
James Ave NW2 . . . 9 B3
James Brine Ho 6
E2 . . . . 24 B2 99 A4
James Campbell Ho
2 E2 . . . . 25 B3
James Collins Ct
W9 . . . . 23 B1
James Docherty Ho 4
E2 . . . . 25 B3
James Hammett Ho
2 E2 . . . . 24 B3
James Ho
16 Mile End E1 . . . 26 A1
35 Rotherhithe
SE16 . . . . 40 C4
James Joyce Wlk 7
SE24 . . . . 63 A3
James Leicester Hall
of Residence N7 . . 14 A2
James Lind Ho 6
SE8 . . . . 41 B2
James Middleton Ho
20 E2 . . . . 25 A2
Jameson Ct 6 E2 . . 25 B3
Jameson Ho SE11 . 148 C2
Jameson Pl 11 W3 . 37 B4
Jameson St
W8 . . . . . . 31 C1 113 C2
Jamuna Cl E14 . . . 33 A4

Jane St E1 . . . . 32 A3
Janet St E14 . . . . 41 C3
Janeway Pl **2**
SE16 . . . . 40 A4
Janeway St SE16 . 139 C3
Jansen Ho **5**
SW15 . . . . 56 C2
Jansen Wlk SW11 . 59 C3
Japan Cres N4 . . . . . 5 A3
Jardine Rd E1 . . . . . . 32 C2
Jarman Ho
Bermondsey SE16 . . . 40 C2
10 Stepney E1 . . . . . 25 B1
Jarrett Cl SW2 . . . . . 75 A3
Jarrow Rd SE16 . . . . 40 A2
Jarrow Way E9 . . . . 18 A4
Jarvis Ho **3** SE15 . . 49 C2
Jarvis Rd SE22 . . . . . 64 A3
Jasmin SE1 . . . . . 125 A1
Jasmin Sq **10** E3 . . 26 B4
Jasmin Ho SE4 . . . . 66 B3
Jasmin Lo **17** SE16 . 40 A1
Jason Ct
2 London SW1 . . . . 173 B4
Marylebone W1 . . 103 C2
Jasper Wlk N1 . . . . . 97 B4
Java Wharf SE1 . . 139 A4
Jay Ho SW15 . . . . . . 47 B1
Jay Mews SW7 . . . 129 A3
Jean Darling Ho
SW10 . . . . 157 B3
Jean Pardies Ho **2**
E1 . . . . 32 B4
Jebb Ave SW2 . . . . . 62 A1
Jebb St E3 . . . . 26 C3
Jedburgh St SW11 . 60 C3
Jeddo Mews W12 . 38 B4
Jeddo Rd W12 . . . . 38 B4
Jefferson Bldg **3**
E14 . . . . 41 C4
Jeffrey's Ct **2**
SW4 . . . . 172 A2
Jeffrey's Pl NW1 . . 13 B1
Jeffrey's Rd SW4 . 172 A2
Jeffrey's St NW1 . . 13 B1
Jeff Wooller Coll
WC1 . . . . 106 B3
Jeger Ave **2** E2 . . . 24 B4
Jelf Rd SW2 . . . . 62 C2
Jellicoe Ho
5 Bethnal Green
E2 . . . . 24 C3
Fitzrovia NW1 . . . . . 92 B1
1 Putney SW15 . . 57 C2
Jemotts Ct **9**
SE14 . . . . 50 C4
Jenkins Ho SW8 . 171 B4
Jenkinson Ho **12**
E2 . . . . 25 C2
Jenner Ave W3 . . . . 28 C4
Jenner Ho **3** SE3 . . 53 A4
Jenner Rd SW13 . . 47 A4
Jenner Rd N16 . . . . 7 B1
Jennifer Ho SE13 . 67 C2
Jennings Ho SE10 . 42 C1
Jennings Rd SE22 . 64 B1
Jensen Ho **10** E3 . . 26 C1
Jephson Ct **17**
SW4 . . . . 172 B1
Jephson Ho **6**
SE17 . . . . 48 A4
Jephson St SE5 . . . 48 C2
Jephtha Rd SW18 . 58 C1
Jerdan Pl SW6 . . . 155 B2

Jeremiah St **11**
E14 . . . . 34 A3
Jeremy Bentham Ho
8 E2 . . . . 24 C2 99 C3
Jermyn St SW1 . . 119 A2
Jerningham Ct
SE14 . . . . 51 A2
Jerningham Rd
SE14 . . . . 51 A2
Jerome Cres NW8 . 90 A2
Jerome Ho NW1 . 102 B4
Jerome St
1 E1 . . . . . 24 B1 98 C1
Jerome Twr **3**
W3 . . . . 37 A4
Jerrard St **3** SE13 . 67 A4
Jerrold Lo SW15 . . 57 B4
Jerrold St **1** N1 . . 24 A3
Jersey Ho N1 . . . . . 15 B2
Jersey Rd N1 . . . . . 15 B2
Jersey St E2 . . . . . . 25 A2
Jerusalem Pas
EC1 . . . . 96 A1
Jervis Bay Ho **9**
E14 . . . . 34 C3
Jervis Ct
2 Greenwich
SE10 . . . . 52 B2
Marylebone W1 . . 104 B1
Jessel Ho
St Pancras WC1 . . 94 A3
Westminster SW1 . 147 C4
Jessica Rd SW18 . . 59 B2
Jessie Blythe La **4**
N19 . . . . 5 A4
Jessie Duffett Ho **11**
SE5 . . . . 48 B3
Jesson Ho SE17 . 151 B3
Jessop Ct N1 . . . . . 86 B1
Jessop Ho **9** W4 . . 37 C2
Jessop Sq E14 . . . . 33 C1
Jeston Ho **10** SE27 . 75 A1
Jethou Ho **11** N1 . . 15 B2
Jevons Ho NW8 . 11 C1
Jewell Ho **3**
SW12 . . . . 73 B4
Jewish Mus NW1 . 82 B3
Jewry St EC3 . . . . 110 C1
Jews Row SW18 . . 59 B3
Jeymer Ave NW2 . . 9 B3
Jeypore Rd SW18 . 59 B1
Jim Griffiths Ho
SW6 . . . . 155 A3
Jim Veal Dr **3**
N17 . . . . 14 A2
Joanna Ho **7** W6 . 39 B1
Joan St SE1 . . . . . 122 A1
Jocelin Ho N1 . . . . 85 A3
Jocelyn Rd TW9 . . 54 A4
Jocelyn St SE15 . . 49 C2
Jockey's Fields
WC1 . . . . 107 A4
Jodane St SE8 . . . . 41 B2
Jodrell Rd E3 . . . . 18 B1
Johanna Prim Sch
SE1 . . . . 135 B3
Johanna St SE1 . . 135 B3
John Adam St
WC2 . . . . 120 B3
John Aird Ct W2 . 101 A4
John Archer Way
SW18 . . . . 59 C1
John Ashby Cl
SW2 . . . . 62 A1
John Ball Prim Sch
SE3 . . . . 53 A1

John Barker Ct
NW6 . . . . 10 A1
John Betts' Ho
W12 . . . . 38 C3
John Betts Prim Sch
W6 . . . . 39 A3
John Bond Ho **2**
E3 . . . . 26 B3
John Brent Ho **5**
SE8 . . . . 40 C2
John Buck Ho
NW10 . . . . 21 B4
John Burns Prim Sch
11 SW11 . . . . . 169 C1
John Campbell Rd **2**
N16 . . . . 16 A3
John Carpenter St
EC4 . . . . 122 A4
John Cartwright Ho
7 E2 . . . . 25 A2
John Clynes Ct
SW15 . . . . 57 A3
John Conwey Ho **23**
SW2 . . . . 62 C1
John Dee Ho **3**
SW14 . . . . 55 C4
John Donne Prim Sch
15 SE15 . . . . . . 50 A2
John Dwight Ho
W6 . . . . 39 A1
John Fearon Wlk **5**
W10 . . . . 23 A2
John Felton Rd **18**
SE16 . . . . 139 B3
John Fielden Ho **10**
E2 . . . . 25 A2
John Fisher St E1 125 B4
John Harris Ho
SE15 . . . . 64 C4
John Harrison Way
SE10 . . . . 43 B3
John Islip St SW1 148 A3
John Keall Ho **3**
SW15 . . . . 57 C4
John Keble CE Prim
Sch NW10 . . . . . . 21 B4
John Kennedy Ct **1**
N1 . . . . 15 C2
John Kennedy Ho **9**
SE16 . . . . 40 C2
John Kennedy Lo **2**
N1 . . . . 15 C2
John King Ct **5**
N19 . . . . 4 C2
John Kirk Ho
21 Battersea
SW11 . . . . 59 C4
3 Streatham
SW16 . . . . 74 A1
John Knight Lo
SW6 . . . . 155 C2
John McDonald Ho **3**
E14 . . . . 42 B3
John McKenna Wlk **17**
SE16 . . . . 139 C2
John Maurice Cl
SE17 . . . . 151 B4
John Nettleford Ho **14**
E2 . . . . 25 A2
John Orwell Sports
Ctr E1 . . . . 32 A1
John Parker Sq **7**
SW11 . . . . 59 C4

John Parry Ct **28**
N1 . . . . 24 A3
John Paul II Sch **3**
SW19 . . . . 69 C4
John Penn Ho SE8 . 51 B3
John Penn St
SE13 . . . . 52 A2
John Perryn Prim Sch
W3 . . . . 29 A3
John Prince's St
W1 . . . . 104 B2
John Pritchard Ho **1**
E1 . . . . 24 C1 99 C1
John Ratcliffe Ho **6**
NW6 . . . . 23 C2
John Rennie Wlk **1**
E1 . . . . 32 B1
John Roan Sch
SE3 . . . . 53 A3
John Roll Way
SE16 . . . . 139 C2
John Ruskin Prim Sch
SE5 . . . . 48 B4
John Ruskin St
SE5 . . . . 48 B4
John Scurr Ho **18**
E14 . . . . 33 B3
John Scurr Prim Sch
48 E1 . . . . 25 B1
John Silkin La SE8 . 40 C1
John's Mews WC1 . 95 A1
John Smith Ave
SW6 . . . . 154 C2
John Smith Mews
E14 . . . . 34 C2
Johnson Cl E8 . . . . 24 C4
Johnson Ct **10**
SW18 . . . . 59 C3
Johnson Ho
Belgravia SW1 . . 145 C3
22 Bethnal Green
E2 . . . . . . 24 C2 99 C3
Somers Town NW1 . 83 A1
South Lambeth
SW8 . . . . 161 C1
Johnson Lo **12** W9 . 31 C4
Johnson Rd NW10 . 20 C4
Johnsons Ct EC4 . 107 C1
Johnson's Pl SW1 . 146 C1
Johnson St E1 . . . . 32 B3
Johnsons Way
NW10 . . . . 20 A1
John Spencer Sq
N1 . . . . 15 A2
John's Pl E1 . . . . . 32 A3
John St WC1 . . . . . 95 A1
John Stainer Prim
Sch SE4 . . . . 66 A4
Johnston Ho **9**
SW9 . . . . 173 A3
Johnstone Ho
SE13 . . . . 67 C4
John Strachey Ho
SW6 . . . . 155 A3
John Trundle Ct
EC4 . . . . 108 C4
John Tucker Ho **8**
E14 . . . . 41 C3
John Wesley's House
& Mus of Methodism
EC1 . . . . 97 C2
John Wheatley Ho
14 London N19 . . 4 C4
West Brompton
SW6 . . . . 155 A3
John Williams Cl
SE14 . . . . 50 C4

Joiners Arms Yd **1**
SE5 . . . . 48 C2
Joiner St SE1 . . . . 123 C1
Joiners Yd N1 . . . . 84 B1
Jolles Ho **9** E3 . . . . 27 A2
Jonathan Ct **9**
W4 . . . . 38 A2
Jonathan St SE11 148 C2
Jones Ho
4 South Bromley
E14 . . . . 34 C3
Stamford Hill N16 . . 7 A3
Jones St W1 . . . . . 118 A3
Jones Wlk **6**
TW10 . . . . 54 B1
Jonson Ho
Borough The SE1 137 C1
16 Canonbury N16 15 C4
Jordan Ct SW15 . . 57 C3
Jordan Ho
12 London SE4 . . 65 C3
Shoreditch N1 . . . . 87 C3
Jordans Ho NW8 . 90 A1
Joscoyne Ho **5**
E1 . . . . 32 A3
Joseph Ave W3 . . . 28 C3
Joseph Conrad Ho
SW1 . . . . 147 A3
Joseph Ct N16 . . . . 7 A4
Joseph Hardcastle Cl
SE14 . . . . 50 C3
Josephine Ave
SW2 . . . . 62 B2
Joseph Irwin Ho **11**
E14 . . . . 33 B2
Joseph Powell Cl **1**
SW12 . . . . 61 B1
Joseph Priestley Ho
17 E2 . . . . 25 A2
Joseph St E3 . . . . . 26 B1
Joseph Trotter Cl
EC1 . . . . 95 C3
Joshua St E14 . . . . 34 B3
Joslings Cl W12 . . 29 C2
Josseline Ct **5** E3 . 26 A3
Joubert Mans
SW3 . . . . 144 B2
Joubert St SW11 . 169 A2
Jowett **27**
SW9 . . . . 172 B1
Jowett St SE15 . . . 49 B3
Jubet Ho **6** SW18 . 58 C2
Jubilee Bldgs NW8 79 B2
Jubilee Cl
NW10 . . . . 21 B3
Jubilee Cres E14 . . 42 B3
Jubilee Ct N1 . . . . 84 B4
Jubilee Hall Mkt
WC2 . . . . 120 B4
Jubilee Ho SE11 . 149 C3
Jubilee Ho NW2 . . 10 B2
Jubilee JMI Sch
N16 . . . . 7 C3
Jubilee Mans **10**
E1 . . . . 32 B3
Jubilee Pl SW3 . . 144 B2
Jubilee Primary
SW2 . . . . 62 C1
Jubilee St E1 . . . . . 32 B4
Jubilee The **2**
SE10 . . . . 52 A3
Jubilee Yd SE1 . . 138 C4
Judd St WC1 . . . . . 94 A3
Jude St E16 . . . . . . 35 B3
Judges' Wlk NW3 . 2 B1
Juer St SW11 . . . . 158 B1

Julian Ave W3 . . . . 28 A2
Julian Ct SW13 . . . . . . 46 B2
Julian Pl E14 . . . . 42 A1
Julia St NW5 . . . . 12 C3
Juliet Ho 🔟 N1 . . . . . . 24 A3
Julius Ct 🔢 E8 . . . . 24 C4
Julius Ho E14 . . . . . . 34 C3
Julius Nyerere Cl
N1 . . . . 84 C3
Junction App
Battersea SW11 . . . . 60 A4
Lewisham SE13 . . . . . 67 B4
Junction Mews
W2 . . . . 102 A2
Junction Pl W2 . . . . . 101 C2
Junction Rd N19 . . . . . 4 B1
Juniper Cres NW1 . . . 12 C1
Juniper Ct N16 . . . . . . 6 C2
Juniper Dr SW18 . . . . 59 B3
Juniper Ho
🟡 Peckham SE14,
SE15 . . . . 50 B3
🚇 Richmond TW9 . . . 45 A2
Juniper St E1 . . . . 32 B2
Juno Ct 🔟 SW9 . . . . 163 B1
Juno Ho 🔢 E3 . . . . . . 26 C4
Jura Way SE14 . . . . . . 50 C4
Juno Way Ind Est
SE14 . . . . 50 C4
Jupiter Ct 🔟
SW9 . . . . 163 B1
Jupiter Way N7 . . . . . 14 B2
Jupp Rd E15 . . . . 19 C1
Jupp Rd W E15 . . . . . 27 C4
Jura Ho SE16 . . . . 41 A2
Jurston Ct SE1 . . . . . 135 C3
Justice Wlk SW3 . . . . 158 A3
Justines Pl E2 . . . . 25 C2
Jutland Cl N19 . . . . 5 A3
Jutland Ho 🟡 E5 . . . . 48 B1
Juxon St SE11 . . . . . 149 A4

K

Kambala Rd SW11 . . . 59 C4
Kara Way NW2 . . . . . . 9 C4
Karen Ct
🟡 Camberwell
SE5 . . . . 64 A4
Forest Hill SE23 . . . . 66 A1
Karen Ho 🟡 N16 . . . 16 B4
Kasmin Ct NW10 . . . . 8 C1
Kassala Rd SW11 . . . 169 A3
Katherine Cl 🟡
SE16 . . . . 32 C1
Katherine Ho 🔢
W10 . . . . 23 A1
Katherine St
W11 . . . . 31 A1 112 A2
Kathleen Ave W3 . . . . 28 B4
Kathleen Rd SW11 . . 60 B4
Kay Rd SW9 . . . . 172 C1
Kay St E2 . . . . 24 C3
Kean Ho 🟡 SE17 . . . . 48 A4
Kean St WC2 . . . . . . 106 C1
Keates Est N16 . . . . . . 7 B2
Keates Cl
Bermondsey SE1 . . . 152 C3
Hampstead NW3 . . . . 12 A4
Keats Gr NW3 . . . . . . 12 A4
Keats Ho
🔢 Bethnal Green
E2 . . . . 25 B2
🔢 Camberwell SE5 . . 48 B3
Chelsea SW1 . . . . . . 161 A4

Keats House (Mus)
NW3 . . . . 12 A4
Keats Pl EC2 . . . . . . 109 B3
Keble Ho 🟡 SW15 . . . 57 C1
Keble Pl SW13 . . . . . . 47 A4
Kedelston Ct E5 . . . . 18 A4
Kedge Ho 🔟 E14 . . . 41 C3
Kedleston Wlk 🟡
E2 . . . . 25 A2
Keel Cl SE16 . . . . 32 C1
Keel Ct 🔢 E14 . . . . . 34 C2
Keeley St WC2 . . . . . 106 C1
Keeling Ho 🟡 E2 . . . . 25 A3
Keelson Ho 🟡 E14 . . 41 C3
Keen's Yd N1 . . . . 15 A2
Keeper Wharf E1 . . . 32 C2
Keeper Wharf 🔟
E1 . . . . 32 C2
Keep The SE3 . . . . . . 53 C1
Keeton's Rd SE16 . . . 40 A3
Keevil Dr SW19 . . . . . 70 A4
Keighley Cl N7 . . . . . . 14 A4
Keildon Rd SW11 . . . 60 B3
Keir Hardie Ho
Fulham W6 . . . . 47 C4
🟡 Upper Holloway
N19 . . . . 4 C4
Willesden NW10 . . . . . 8 B1
Keir Hardie Prim Sch
E16 . . . . 35 C4
Keith Connor Cl 🟡
SW8 . . . . 61 A4
Keith Gr W12 . . . . 29 C1
Keith Ho NW6 . . . . . . 78 A1
Kelby Ho N7 . . . . 14 B2
Kelfield Ct 🔟 W10 . . 30 C3
Kelfield Gdns W10 . . 30 C3
Kelfield Mews
W10 . . . . 30 C3
Kellett Ho N1 . . . . 87 C3
Kellett Rd SW2 . . . . . 62 C3
Kellow Ho SE1 . . . . 137 B4
Kell St SE1 . . . . 136 B2
Kelly Ave SE15 . . . . . 49 B2
Kelly Ct 🔟 E14 . . . . . 33 C2
Kelly Mews 🟡 W9 . . 23 B1
Kelly St NW1 . . . . 13 A2
Kelman Cl SW4 . . . . 171 C1
Kelmore Gr SE22 . . . 64 C3
Kelmscott Gdns
W12 . . . . 38 C3
Kelmscott House
W6 . . . . 39 A1
Kelmscott Rd
SW11 . . . . 60 B2
Kelross Rd N5 . . . . . . 15 B4
Kelsall Mews TW9 . . 45 A2
Kelsey St E2 . . . . 24 C1 99 C2
Kelshall Ct N4 . . . . . . 6 B2
Kelson Ho E14 . . . . . . 42 B3
Kelso Pl W8 . . . . 128 B2
Kelvedon Ho SW8 . . 172 B4
Kelvedon Rd SW6 . . 155 A1
Kelvin Ct
Chiswick W4 . . . . 45 B3
Notting Hill
W11 . . . . 31 C2 113 B3
Kelvin Rd
Bow E3 . . . . 26 A3
Kilburn NW6 . . . . 23 B4
Kenley Wlk
W11 . . . . 31 A2 112 A3
Kenmont Gdns
NW10 . . . . 22 B2
Kenmont Prim Sch
NW10 . . . . 22 B2
Kenmore Cl TW9 . . . 44 C3

Kemey's St E9 . . . . 18 A3
Kemp Ct SW8 . . . . . 162 A1
Kempe Ho SE1 . . . . 137 C1
Kempe Rd NW6 . . . . . 22 C3
Kemp Ho
Finsbury EC1 . . . . . . 97 B3
🟡 Globe Town E2 . . 25 C3
Kempis Way 🟡
SE22 . . . . 64 A2
Kemplay Rd NW3 . . . 11 C4
Kemp's Ct W1 . . . . . 105 B1
Kemps Dr E14 . . . . . . 33 C2
Kempsford Gdns
Lambeth SE11 . . . . . 149 C3
Newington SE11 . . . 150 A3
Kemps Gdns SE13 . . 67 B2
Kempson Rd SW6 . . 155 C1
Kempthorne Rd
SE8 . . . . 41 B2
Kempton Ct E1 . . . . . 32 A4
Kempton Ho 🟡
N1 . . . . 24 A4
Kemsing Ho SE1 . . . 137 C3
Kemsing Rd SE10 . . . 43 C1
Kemsley SE13 . . . . . . 67 A2
Kenbrook Ho
Kensington W14 . . . 127 A1
🟡 Kentish Town
NW5 . . . . 13 B3
Kenbury Gdns 🔟
SE5 . . . . 48 B1
Kenbury Mans 🔟
SE5 . . . . 48 B1
Kenbury St SE5 . . . . . 48 B1
Kenchester Cl
SW8 . . . . 162 B1
Kendal NW1 . . . . 92 B4
Kendal Ave W3 . . . . . 28 A4
Kendal Cl SE5 . . . . . . 48 A3
Kendal Ct NW2 . . . . . 10 A3
Kendal Ho
🔢 Hackney E9 . . . . . 17 B1
Islington N1 . . . . 85 A2
Kendall Ct 🔢 SE22 . . 64 C2
Kendall Pl W1 . . . . . 103 B3
Kendal Pl SW15 . . . . 58 B2
Kendal Rd NW10 . . . . . 8 C4
Kendal St W2 . . . . . . 102 B1
Kendal Stps W2 . . . . 102 B1
Kender Prim Sch
SE14 . . . . 50 B2
Kender St SE14 . . . . . 50 B2
Kendoa Rd 🔟
SW4 . . . . 61 C3
Kendon Ho E15 . . . . . 19 C1
Kendrick Ct 🔢
SE15 . . . . 50 A2
Kendrick Mews
SW7 . . . . 143 B3
Kendrick Pl SW7 . . . 143 B3
Kenilford Rd
SW12 . . . . 73 A4
Kenilworth Ct
SW6 . . . . 58 A4
Kenilworth Rd
Bow E3 . . . . 26 A3
Kilburn NW6 . . . . 23 B4

Kenmure Ct NW6 . . . 10 C1
Kenmure Rd E8 . . . . . 17 A3
Kenmure Yd E8 . . . . . 17 A3
Kennacraig Cl 🟡
E16 . . . . 35 C1
Kennard Ho 🔢
SW11 . . . . 169 C3
Kennard Rd E15 . . . . 19 C1
Kennard St 🟡
SW11 . . . . 169 B3
Kennedy Cox Ho 🟡
E16 . . . . 35 B4
Kennedy Ho SE11 . . 148 C2
Kennedy Wlk
SE17 . . . . 151 C3
Kennet Cl SW11 . . . . 59 C3
Kennet Ct 🔢 W2 . . . 31 C4
Kenneth Campbell Ho
NW8 . . . . 89 C2
Kenneth Cres NW2 . . 9 A3
Kennet Ho NW8 . . . . 89 C1
Kenneth Ct SE11 . . . 149 C4
Kennet Rd W9 . . . . . . 23 B1
Kennet St E1 . . . . . . 125 C2
Kennett Wharf La
EC4 . . . . 123 A4
Kenning 🟡 N1 . . . . . . 24 A4
Kenning St 🔢
SE16 . . . . 40 B4
Kennings Way
SE11 . . . . 149 C2
KENNINGTON 149 B1
Kennington Ent Ctr
SE17 . . . . 150 A1
Kennington La
SE11 . . . . 149 A1
Kennington Oval
SE11 . . . . 163 A3
Kennington Palace Ct
SE11 . . . . 149 B1
Kennington Park Gdns
SE17 . . . . 48 A4
Kennington Park Ho
SE11 . . . . 149 C1
Kennington Park Pl
SE11 . . . . 48 A4
Kennington Park Rd
SE11 . . . . 150 A1
Kennington Rd
SE11 . . . . 149 B3
Kennington Sta
SE11 . . . . 150 A2
Kennoldes SE21 . . . 75 C2
Kenrick Pl W1 . . . . . 103 B3
KENSAL GREEN . . 22 B2
Kensal Green Cemy
(All Souls) NW10 . . . 22 B2
Kensal Ho W10 . . . . . 22 B1
Kensal Rd W10 . . . . . 23 A1
KENSAL RISE 22 B3
Kensal Rise Prim Sch
NW6 . . . . 22 C3
Kensal Rise Sta
NW10 . . . . 22 C3
KENSAL TOWN . . . 23 A1
KENSINGTON . . . 127 C3
Kensington Acad
SW6 . . . . 156 A1
Kensington & Chelsea
Coll
Chelsea SW10 . . . 156 C2

Kensington & Chelsea
Coll continued
🔢 Kensal Town
W10 . . . . 31 A4
Kensington Church Ct
W8 . . . . 128 A3
Kensington Church St
W8 . . . . 31 C1 113 C1
Kensington Church
Wlk W8 . . . . 128 A3
Kensington Court
Mans W8 . . . . 128 B2
Kensington Court
Mews W8 . . . . 128 B2
Kensington Court Pl
W8 . . . . 128 B2
Kensington Ct
W8 . . . . 128 B3
Kensington Ct Gdns
W8 . . . . 128 B2
Kensington Gardens
W2 . . . . 115 A1
Kensington Gate
W8 . . . . 128 C2
Kensington Gdns Sq
W2 . . . . 100 A1
Kensington Gore
SW7 . . . . 129 B3
Kensington Hall Gdns
W14 . . . . 140 C2
Kensington High St
W8 . . . . 127 C2
Kensington Ho 🔢
NW5 . . . . 13 B3
Kensington Hts
W8 . . . . 31 C1 113 B1
Kensington L Ctr
W11 . . . . 31 A2 112 A4
Kensington Mall
W8 . . . . 31 C1 113 C2
Kensington Mans
SW5 . . . . 141 C2
Kensington Olympia
Sta W14 . . . . 126 A2
Kensington Pal
W8 . . . . 114 B1
Kensington Palace
Gdns W8 . . . . 114 A2
Kensington Park Gdns
W11 . . . . 31 B2 113 A3
Kensington Park
Mews W11 . . . . 31 B3
Kensington Park Rd
W11 . . . . 31 B2 113 A4
Kensington Pl
W8 . . . . 31 C1 113 B2
Kensington Prep Sch
SW6 . . . . 165 A4
Kensington Rd
SW7 . . . . 129 A3
Kensington Sq
W8 . . . . 128 A3
Kensington Village
W14 . . . . 141 A3
Kensington W
W14 . . . . 140 A4
Kenworth Ho EC1 . . . 97 C3
Kent Ct 🔢 E2 . . . . . . 24 B3
Kent Ho
Camberwell SE1 . . . 153 A1
🔢 Chiswick W4 . . . . 38 A1
Marylebone W1 . . . 104 C2
Pimlico SW1 . . . . . . 147 B1
Richmond TW10 . . . . 54 C2

Kentish Bldgs
SE1 . . . . 123 B1
KENTISH TOWN . . . 13 B2
Kentish Town CE Prim
Sch 1 NW5 . . . . . . 13 B3
Kentish Town City
Farm NW5 . . . . 12 C3
Kentish Town Rd
NW1 . . . . 13 A2
Kentish Town Sp Ctr
NW1 . . . . 13 A2
Kentish Town Sta
NW5 . . . . 13 A3
Kentish Town West
Sta NW5 . . . . 13 A2
Kent Lo 9 SW19 . . . 69 C3
Kentmere Ho SE15 . . 50 B4
Kenton Ct W14 . . . . 126 C1
Kenton Ho
20 Globe Town E1 . . 25 B1
Highbury N5 . . . . . . 5 C1
Kenton St E9 . . . . . . 17 C2
Kenton St WC1 . . . . 94 A2
Kent Pas NW1 . . . . . 90 C2
Kent Pk Ind Est
SE15 . . . . 50 A4
Kent Rd
Richmond TW9 . . . . 44 C3
South Acton W4 . . . . 37 B3
Kent St E2 . . . . 24 B3
Kent Terr NW1 . . . . . 90 B3
Kentwell Cl SE4 . . . . 66 A3
Kentwode Gn
SE13 . . . . 46 C3
Kent Yard SW7 . . . . 130 B3
Kenway Rd SW5 . . . 142 A3
Ken Wilson Ho 19
E2 . . . . 24 C3
Kenwood Cl NW3 . . . 2 C3
Kenwood Ho 15
SW9 . . . . 63 A3
Kenwood Ho NW3 . . 3 A3
Kenworthy Rd E9 . . . 18 A2
Kenwrick Ho N1 . . . . 85 A3
Kenwyn Rd SW4 . . . 61 C3
Kenyon Ho 31 SE5 . . 48 B3
Kenyon St SW6 . . . . 47 C2
Kepler Ho 9 SE10 . . 43 B1
Kepler Rd SW2,
SW4 . . . . 62 A3
Keppel Ho
Brompton SW3 . . . . 144 A3
5 Deptford SE8 . . . . 41 B1
Keppel Row SE1 . . . 122 C1
Keppel St WC1 . . . . 105 C4
Kerbela St
E2 . . . . 24 C1 99 B2
Kerbey St E14 . . . . . 34 A3
Kerfield Cres SE5 . . 48 C2
Kerfield Pl SE5 . . . . 48 C2
Kerridge Ct 10 N1 . . 16 A2
Kerrier Ho SW10 . . . 157 A1
Kerrington Ct 7
W12 . . . . 39 B4
Kerrison Rd
Battersea SW11 . . . . 60 A4
Mill Meads E15 . . . . 27 C4
Kerry N7 . . . . 14 A2
Kerry Ho 5 E1 . . . . . 32 B3
Kerry Path SE8 . . . . 51 B4
Kerry Rd SE8 . . . . . 51 B4
Kerscott Ho 30 E3 . . 27 A2
Kersfield Ho SW15 . . 57 C1
Kersfield Rd SW15 . . 57 C1

Kershaw Cl SW18 . . . 59 C1
Kershaw Ho 7
SE27 . . . . 75 A1
Kersley Mews
SW11 . . . . 168 C3
Kersley Rd N16 . . . . 7 A1
Kersley St SW11 . . . 168 C2
Kerwick Cl 1 N7 . . . 14 B1
Keslake Mans
NW10 . . . . 22 C3
Keslake Rd NW6 . . . 22 C3
Keston Ho 17 SE17 . . 152 B2
Keston Rd SE15 . . . . 64 C4
Kestrel Ave SE24 . . . 63 B2
Kestrel Ho
4 Battersea
SW11 . . . . 60 A4
Finsbury EC1 . . . . . . 96 C4
Kestrel Pl SE14 . . . . 51 A4
Keswick Broadway 1
SW15 . . . . 58 B2
Keswick Ct 2
SW15 . . . . 58 A2
Keswick Ho 8
SE5 . . . . 48 B2
Keswick Hts 4
SW15 . . . . 58 A2
Keswick Lo 6 SE8 . . 16 B2
Keswick Rd SW15 . . 58 A2
Kett Gdns SW2 . . . . 62 B2
Kettleby Ho NW9 . . . 63 A4
Ketton Ho 11 W10 . . 22 B1
Kevan Ho SE5 . . . . . 48 B3
KEW 44 C4
Kew Bridge TW8 . . . 36 B1
Kew Bridge Ct 4
W4 . . . . 36 C1
Kew Bridge
Distribution Ctr
TW8 . . . . 36 B1
Kew Bridge Rd
TW8 . . . . 36 B1
Kew Bridge Sta
TW8 . . . . 36 B1
Kew Bridge Steam
Mus TW8 . . . . 36 B1
Kew Coll TW9 . . . . . 44 B2
Kew Foot Rd TW9 . . 54 A4
Kew Gardens Rd
TW9 . . . . 44 C2
Kew Gardens Sta
TW9 . . . . 44 C2
Kew Gn TW9 . . . . . . 44 B4
Kew Green TW9 . . . . 44 C4
Kew Green Prep Sch
TW9 . . . . 44 B4
Kew Lo 11 TW9 . . . . 44 B2
Kew Pal TW9 . . . . . . 44 A3
Kew Pier TW9 . . . . . 44 C4
Kew Rd TW9 . . . . . . 44 C4
Kew Ret Pk TW9 . . . 45 A2
Kew Riverside Prim
Sch TW9 . . . . 45 A1
Key Cl E1 . . . . 25 A1
Keyes Ct SE22 . . . . . 64 C2
Keyes Rd NW2 . . . . . 9 C3
Keyham Ho 5 W2 . . . 31 C4
Key Ho 5 SE11 . . . . 163 B4
Keymer Rd SW2 . . . . 74 B2
Keynsham Ho 2
N4 . . . . 6 B4
Keystone Cres N1 . . 84 B1
Keyworth Cl E5 . . . . 18 A4
Keyworth Pl SE1 . . . 136 B2

Keyworth Prim Sch
SE17 . . . . 150 A2
Keyworth St SE1 . . . 136 B2
Kezia St SE8 . . . . . . 41 A1
Khyber Rd SW11 . . . 168 A1
Kia Ora Th (the Surrey
Cnty Crkt Club)
SE11 . . . . 163 A4
Kibworth St SW8 . . . 162 C1
Kidbrooke Gdns
SE3 . . . . 53 C2
Kidderpore Ave
NW3 . . . . 10 C4
Kidderpore Gdns
NW3 . . . . 10 C4
Kiffen St EC2 . . . . . 97 C2
Kilbrennan Ho 8
E14 . . . . 34 B3
KILBURN 23 C4
Kilburn Bridge 14
NW6 . . . . 23 C4
Kilburn Gate NW6 . . 78 A2
Kilburn High Rd
NW6 . . . . 78 A3
Kilburn High Road Sta
NW6 . . . . 78 A3
Kilburn Ho 11 W9 . . 23 B2
Kilburn La W10 . . . . 23 A3
Kilburn Park Rd
NW6 . . . . 23 C2
Kilburn Park Sch 10
NW6 . . . . 23 C3
Kilburn Park Sta
NW6 . . . . 23 C3
Kilburn Pl NW6 . . . . 23 C4
Kilburn Priory
NW6 . . . . 78 A3
Kilburn Sq NW6 . . . . 23 C4
Kilburn Vale NW2 . . 10 B2
Kilburn Vale Est 13
NW6 . . . . 78 A3
Kilby Ct SE10 . . . . . 43 B3
Kildare Ct W2 . . . . . 31 C3
Kildare Gdns W2 . . . 31 C3
Kildare Rd E16 . . . . 35 C4
Kildare Terr W2 . . . . 31 C3
Kildare Wlk E14 . . . 33 C2
Kildoran Rd SW2 . . . 62 A2
Kilgour Rd SE23 . . . 66 A1
Kilkie St SW6 . . . . . 166 C1
Killarney Rd SW18 . . 59 B1
Killick St N1 . . . . . . 84 C1
Killieser Ave SW2 . . 74 A2
Killip Cl E16 . . . . . . 35 B3
Killoran Ho 9 E14 . . 42 B3
Killowen Rd E9 . . . . 17 C2
Killyon Rd SW8 . . . . 171 B1
Kilmaine Rd SW6 . . . 154 B1
Kilmarsh Rd W6 . . . 39 B2
Kilmore Ho 7 E14 . . 34 A3
Kilmuir Ho SW1 . . . . 145 C3
Kilner Ho 3 SE11 . . 163 B4
Kilner St E14 . . . . . . 33 C4
Kiln Pl NW5 . . . . . . 12 C3
Kilpatrick Ct N16 . . . 7 B3
Kilpeck Ho 3 N4 . . . 6 B4
Kilravock St W10 . . . 23 A2
Kilronan 5 W3 . . . . 28 C3
Kimbell Gdns
SW6 . . . . 164 A3

Kimber Ctr The
SW18 . . . . 70 C4
Kimberley Ave
SE15 . . . . 65 B4
Kimberley Ct NW6 . . 23 A4
Kimberley Ho 7
E14 . . . . 42 B3
Kimberley Rd
Kilburn NW6 . . . . . . 23 A4
Stockwell SW9 . . . . . 62 A4
Kimber Rd SW18 . . . 71 A4
Kimble Ho
Lisson Gr NW8 . . . . 90 B2
1 Lower Holloway
N7 . . . . 14 A3
Kimbolton Row
SW3 . . . . 144 A3
Kimpton Ct 13 SE5 . . 48 C2
Kimpton Ho SW15 . . 68 C4
Kimpton Rd SE5 . . . 48 C2
Kinburn St SE16 . . . 40 C4
Kincaid Rd SE15 . . . 50 A3
Kincardine Gdns
W9 . . . . 23 C1
Kindell Ho 2
SW14 . . . . 55 C4
Kinder Ho N1 . . . . . 87 C2
Kindersley Ho 38
E1 . . . . 111 C1
Kinder St 10 E1 . . . . 32 A3
Kinefold Ho N7 . . . . 14 A2
Kinfauns Rd SW2 . . . 74 C2
King Alfred Sch
SE1 . . . . 2 A3
King Arthur Cl
SE15 . . . . 50 B3
King Charles Ct 16
SE17 . . . . 48 A4
King Charles Ho
SW6 . . . . 156 B2
King Charles St
SW1 . . . . 134 A4
King Charles Terr 11
E1 . . . . 32 A2
King Charles Wlk 6
SW19 . . . . 70 A3
King David La L1 . . . 32 B2
King Edward Mans 12
E8 . . . . 24 C4
Kingdom Ho 8
E14 . . . . 34 C2
Kingdon Cl W10 . . . 30 C3
King Edward Mans 17
SW13 . . . . 46 C2
King Edwards Mans
SW6 . . . . 155 B1
King Edward's Rd
E9 . . . . 25 B4
King Edward St
EC1 . . . . 108 C2
King Edward The
Third Mews 11
SE16 . . . . 40 A4
King Edward VII Hospl
for Officers W1 . . . 103 C4
King Edward Wlk
SE1 . . . . 135 C2
King Fahed Acad
W3 . . . . 29 B2
Kingfield St E14 . . . . 42 B2
Kingfisher Ct
1 Battersea
SW11 . . . . 60 A4
17 Cubitt Town E14 . . 42 B4

Kingfisher Ct *continued*
Putney SW19 . . . . . . 70 A2
Kingfisher Ho
16 Battersea
SW11 . . . . 59 B4
Peckham SE15 . . . . . 49 B2
West Kensington
W14 . . . . 126 C2
Kingfisher Mews
SE13 . . . . 67 A2
Kingfisher Sq 19
SE8 . . . . 51 B4
King Frederik IX Twr
SE16 . . . . 41 B3
King George Sq
TW10 . . . . 54 B1
King George St
SE10 . . . . 52 B3
Kingham Cl
3 Shepherd's Bush
W11 . . . . 39 C4
Wandsworth SW18 . . 71 B4
Kingham Ind Est
NW10 . . . . 20 C2
King Henry's Rd
NW3 . . . . 12 A1
King Henry's Reach
W6 . . . . 47 B4
King Henry St N16 . . 16 A3
King Henry's Wlk
N1 . . . . 16 A2
King Henry's Yd 5
N16 . . . . 16 A3
King Henry Terr 11
E1 . . . . 32 A2
Kinghorn St EC1 . . . 108 C3
King James Ct
SE1 . . . . 136 B3
King James St
SE1 . . . . 136 B3
King John Ct
EC2 . . . . 24 A1 98 B2
King John St E1 . . . . 32 C4
Kinglake St SE17 . . . 152 B2
Kingly Ct W1 . . . . . . 119 A4
Kingly St W1 . . . . . . 118 C4
King & Queen St
SE17 . . . . 151 A2
King's Arms Ct 1 . . . 111 B3
King's Arms Yd
EC2 . . . . 109 B2
Kings Ave SW4 . . . . 62 A1
Kings Avenue Sch
SW4 . . . . 62 A2
King's Bench St
SE1 . . . . 136 B4
King's Bench Wlk
EC4 . . . . 107 C1
King's Boulevard
NW1 . . . . 84 A1
Kingsbridge N16 . . . 6 C3
Kingsbridge Ave
W3 . . . . 36 B4
Kingsbridge Ct
E14 . . . . 41 C2
Kingsbridge Rd
W10 . . . . 30 B3
Kingsbury Rd N1 . . . 16 A2
Kingsbury Terr N1 . . 16 A2
Kingsclere Cl
SW15 . . . . 68 C4
Kingscliffe Gdns
SW19 . . . . 70 B3
King's Coll SE24 . . . 63 C1

Kings College Ct NW3 ... 12 A1
King's College Hospl SE5 ... 48 C1
Kings College Rd NW3 ... 11 C1
King's Coll London (Denmark Hill Campus) SE5 ... 48 B1
King's Coll London School of Medicine SE1 ... 123 C1
King's Coll London (Strand Campus) WC2 ... 121 A4
King's Coll London (St Thomas' Campus) SE1 ... 134 C1
King's Coll London (Waterloo Campus) SE1 ... 121 B1
Kingscote NW11 ... 1 B3
Kingscote Rd W4 ... 37 C3
Kingscote St EC4 ... 122 A4
King's Court N SW3 ... 144 A1
Kingscourt Rd SW16 ... 74 A1
King's Court S SW3 ... 144 A1
Kingscroft SW4 ... 62 A1
Kingscroft Rd NW2 ... 10 B2
KING'S CROSS ... 84 C2
King's Cross WC1 ... 94 B4
King's Cross Bridge WC1 ... 94 B4
King's Cross Rd WC1 ... 95 A3
King's Cross, St Pancras N1 ... 94 A4
King's Cross Sta N1 ... 84 B1
Kings Ct
  [6] Barnsbury N7 ... 14 B1
  Chiswick W6 ... 38 C2
  East Dulwich SE22 ... 64 C3
  Primrose Hill NW8 ... 80 C3
  [15] Putney SW15 ... 68 C4
Kingsdale Gdns W11 ... 30 C1
Kingsdale Sch SE21 ... 76 A1
Kingsdown Ave W3 ... 29 A2
Kingsdown Cl
  [26] Deptford SE16 ... 40 A1
  [8] Notting Hill W11 ... 31 A3
Kingsdown Ct SW11 ... 60 A4
Kingsdown Ho [1] E8 ... 16 C3
Kingsdown Rd [4] N19 ... 5 A2
Kings Farm Ave TW10 ... 54 C3
Kingsfield Ho [18] N16 ... 7 A1
Kingsford St NW5 ... 12 B3
Kingsgate Est N1 ... 16 A2
Kingsgate Ho [20] SW9 ... 173 C4
Kingsgate Par SW1 ... 133 A1

Kingsgate Prim Sch NW6 ... 10 C1
Kingsgate Rd NW6 ... 10 C1
King's Gdns NW6 ... 10 C1
King's Gr
  Peckham SE15 ... 50 A2
  Peckham SE15 ... 50 A3
Kingshall Mews SE13 ... 67 B4
King's Head Yd SE1 ... 123 B1
Kingshill SE17 ... 151 A4
Kings Ho
  [19] Limehouse E14 ... 33 B2
  South Lambeth SW8 ... 162 B2
Kingshold Rd E9 ... 17 B1
King's House Sch TW10 ... 54 B2
King's House Sch (Jun) TW10 ... 54 B2
King's Keep [6] SW15 ... 57 C2
KINGSLAND ... 88 A4
Kingsland NW8 ... 80 B3
Kingsland Gn [1] [8] N1 ... 16 A2
Kingsland High St E8 ... 16 B3
Kingsland Pas [2] E8 ... 16 A2
Kingsland Rd E2 ... 24 A3
Kingsland Sh Ctr [12] E8 ... 16 B3
Kingsley Cl [11] SW15 ... 57 A2
Kingsley Ct [12] NW2 ... 9 A2
Kingsley Flats SE1 ... 152 B3
Kingsley Ho
  Chelsea SW3 ... 157 C3
  [3] Clapham SW4 ... 171 C2
Kingsley Mews
  Kensington W8 ... 128 B1
  [18] St George in t East E1 ... 32 A2
Kingsley PI N6 ... 3 C4
Kingsley Rd NW6 ... 23 B4
Kingsley St SW11 ... 60 B4
Kings Mall Sh Ctr W6 ... 39 B2
King's Mans SW3 ... 158 A3
Kingsmead TW10 ... 54 B1
Kingsmead Ho E9 ... 18 A4
Kingsmead Prim Sch E9 ...
Kingsmead Rd SW2 ... 74 C2
King's Mead Way E5 ...
Kingsmere Cl [13] SW15 ... 57 C4
Kingsmere PI N16 ... 6 C3
Kingsmere Rd SW19 ... 69 C2
King's Mews
  [1] Clapham Pk SW4 ... 61 C2
  Gray's Inn WC1 ... 95 A1
Kingsmill NW8 ... 79 C2
Kingsmill Terr NW8 ... 79 C2

Kingsnorth Ho [12] W10 ... 30 C3
King Solomon Acad NW1 ... 102 A4
King's Par
  [1] Hammersmith W12 ... 38 C3
  Willesden NW10 ... 22 B4
Kings PI W4 ... 37 B2
Kings PI N1 ... 84 B2
King's PI SE1 ... 136 C3
King Sq EC1 ... 96 C3
King's Quay SW10 ... 167 A4
Kings Rd
  Richmond TW10, TW9 ... 54 B2
  Willesden NW10 ... 9 A1
King's Rd
  Chelsea SW3 ... 144 B1
  Chelsea SW10 ... 157 B3
  Mortlake SW14 ... 55 A4
Kings Ride Gate TW10 ... 54 C3
Kingsridge SW19 ... 70 A2
King's Scholars' Pas SW1 ... 146 C4
King St
  Acton W3 ... 28 B1
  Hammersmith W6 ... 38 C2
  St James SW1 ... 119 A2
  Strand WC2 ... 120 A4
  Whitechapel EC2 ... 109 A1
King Stairs Cl SE16 ... 40 A4
King's Terr NW1 ... 82 C3
Kingston Ho [4] NW6 ... 10 A1
Kingston Ho E SW7 ... 130 A3
Kingston Ho N SW7 ... 130 A3
Kingston Ho S SW7 ... 130 A3
Kingston Ho SW15, SW19 ... 69 A3
Kingston Univ (Roehampton Vale) SW15 ... 68 B1
Kingston Vale SW15 ... 68 B1
Kingstown St NW1 ... 81 B4
King Street Cloisters [8] W6 ... 39 A2
King Street Coll W12 ... 39 B2
Kingswater PI SW11 ... 158 A1
Kingsway
  Mortlake SW14, TW9 ... 55 A4
  St Giles WC2 ... 106 C2
Kingsway Coll [1] NW5 ... 13 A2
Kingsway Mans WC1 ... 106 C4
Kingsway PI EC1 ... 96 A2
Kingswear Rd NW5 ... 4 A1
Kings Well [25] NW3 ... 11 B4
Kings Wlk Sh Mall SW3 ... 144 C2
Kingswood [31] E2 ... 25 B3
Kingswood Ave NW6 ... 23 A3
Kingswood Cl SW8 ... 162 B1

Kingswood Ct
  Hither Green SE13 ... 67 C1
  [7] Richmond TW10 ... 54 B2
Kings Wood Ct [4] NW6 ... 10 C1
Kingswood Rd
  South Acton W4 ... 37 B3
  Streatham SW2 ... 74 A4
Kingswood Terr W4 ... 37 B3
Kings Yd E15 ... 19 A3
Kington Ho [18] NW6 ... 78 B3
Kingward Ho E1 ... 111 B4
Kingweston Ct NW2 ... 1 A1
King William La [3] SE10 ... 43 A1
King William St EC4 ... 123 C4
King William Wlk SE10 ... 52 B4
Kingwood Ho [5] SW8 ... 154 A1
Kinloch St N7 ... 5 B1
Kinnaird Ave W4 ... 45 B3
Kinnear Rd W12 ... 38 B4
Kinnerton PI N SW1 ... 131 A3
Kinnerton PI S SW1 ... 131 A3
Kinnerton St SW1 ... 131 B3
Kinnerton Yd SW1 ... 131 B3
Kinnoul Mans [10] E5 ... 17 A4
Kinnoul Rd W6 ... 154 A4
Kinross Ho N1 ... 84 C4
Kinsale Rd SE15 ... 64 C4
Kinsham Ho [5] E2 ... 99 C2
Kintore Way SE1 ... 152 C4
Kintyre Ct [17] SW2 ... 74 A4
Kintyre Ho [6] E14 ... 34 B1
Kinver Ho N4 ... 6 C4
Kipling Ho [20] SE5 ... 48 B3
Kipling St SE1 ... 137 C4
Kipling Twr [3] W3 ... 37 B3
Kirby Est SE16 ... 40 A3
Kirby Gr SE1 ... 138 A4
Kirby St EC1 ... 107 C4
Kirkeby Bldg EC1 ... 107 B4
Kirkland Wlk [4] E8 ... 16 B2
Kirkley Ho [16] N16 ... 7 A3
Kirkman Ho W1 ... 105 B3
Kirkman PI W1 ... 105 B3
Kirkmichael Rd E14 ... 34 B3
Kirkside Rd SE3 ... 53 C4
Kirk St WC1 ... 94 A1
Kirkstall Gdns SW2 ... 74 A3
Kirkstall Ho SW1 ... 146 A2
Kirkstall Rd SW2 ... 74 A3
Kirkstead Ct E5 ... 18 A4
Kirkstone NW1 ... 92 C4
Kirkwall PI E2 ... 25 B2
Kirkwood Rd SE15 ... 50 A1
Kirtley Ho SW8 ... 171 A4
Kirtley Rd SW2 ... 74 C4
Kirton Cl W4 ... 37 C2
Kirton Gdns [2] E2 ... 24 B2 99 A3
Kirwin Way SE5 ... 48 A3
Kitcat Terr E3 ... 26 C2

Kite Ho [5] SW11 ... 60 A4
Kite PI [9] E2 ... 24 C2 99 C4
Kitson Rd
  Barnes SW13 ... 46 C2
  Camberwell SE5 ... 48 B3
Kittiwake Ct [26] SE8 ... 51 B4
Kitto Rd SE14 ... 50 C1
Kiver Rd N19 ... 5 A2
Klea Ave SW4 ... 61 B1
Kleffens Ct [2] SE3 ... 53 B3
Kleine Wharf [8] N1 ... 24 A4
Knapp Cl NW10 ... 8 A2
Knapp Rd E3 ... 26 C1
Knaresborough Dr SW18 ... 71 A3
Knaresborough Ho [4] N4 ... 6 B4
Knaresborough PI SW5 ... 142 A4
Knatchbull Rd
  Brixton SE5 ... 48 A2
  Stonebridge NW10 ... 20 C4
Knebworth Ho
  South Lambeth SW8 ... 171 C3
  [2] Stoke Newington N16 ... 16 A4
Knebworth Rd [8] N16 ... 16 A4
Kneller Ho [9] SW8 ... 171 C3
Kneller Rd SE4 ... 66 A3
Knighten St E1 ... 32 A1
Knighthead Point [26] E14 ... 41 C4
Knight Ho SE17 ... 152 A3
Knightleas Ct NW2 ... 9 B2
Knightrider Ct EC4 ... 122 C4
Knightrider St EC4 ... 122 C4
Knights Arc SW1 ... 130 C3
Knight's Ave W5 ... 36 A4
KNIGHTSBRIDGE ... 130 A2
Knightsbridge SW1, SW7 ... 130 C3
Knightsbridge Ct SW1 ... 131 A3
Knightsbridge Gn SW1 ... 130 C3
Knightsbridge Sch SW11 ... 130 C1
Knightsbridge Sta ...
Knightsbridge Under Sch SW7 ... 143 A3
Knights Cl E9 ... 17 B3
Knights Ho
  Bermondsey SE1 ... 138 C4
  South Lambeth SW8 ... 162 B1
  West Kensington SW5 ... 140 C2
Knights Rd E16 ... 43 C4
Knight's Wlk SE11 ... 150 A3
Knightswood Ct N6 ... 4 C4
Knivet Rd SW6 ... 155 B3
Knoll Ho NW8 ... 78 C2
Knoll Rd SW18 ... 59 B2

Knolly's Cl SE27,
SW16 . . . . 74 C1
Knolly's Rd
SW16 . . . . 74 C1
Knot Ho SE1 . . . . 124 C1
Knottisford St E2 . . . . . 25 B2
Knowlden Ho 5
E1 . . . . 32 B2
Knowle Cl SW9 . . . . 62 C4
Knowledge Point Sch
6 N7 . . . . 14 B2
Knowles Hill Cres
SE13 . . . . 67 C2
Knowles Ho
Wandsworth
SW18 . . . . 59 A1
Willesden Green
NW10 . . . . 21 C4
Knowles Wlk SW4 . . . . . 61 B4
Knowlton Ho 32
SW9 . . . . 173 C4
Knowsley Rd
SW11 . . . . 168 C1
Knox Ct 16 SW4 . . . . . 172 B2
Knox Ho SW15 . . . . 47 B1
Knox St W1 . . . . 102 C4
Knoyle Ho W14 . . . . . . 126 B2
Knoyle St SE14 . . . . 51 A4
Kobi Nazrul Prim Sch
13 E1 . . . . 111 C2
Kossuth St SE10 . . . . . . 43 A1
Kotree Way 18
SE1 . . . . 153 C4
Kramer Mews
SW5 . . . . 142 A1
Kreedman Wlk 8
E8 . . . . 16 C3
Kreisel Wlk TW9 . . . . . . 44 B4
Kylemore Ct 4
W12 . . . . 38 C4
Kylemore Rd NW6 . . . . . 10 C1
Kylestrome Ho
SW1 . . . . 145 C3
Kynance Mews
SW7 . . . . 128 B1
Kynance Pl SW7 . . . . . 128 C1
Kynaston Ho 7
SW2 . . . . 74 B3
Kynaston Rd N16 . . . . . . 7 A1
Kyrle Rd SW11 . . . . 60 C1
Kyverdale Rd N16 . . . . . . 7 B4

L

Laburnham Ct NW2 . . 1 B2
Laburnum Cl 5
SE15 . . . . 50 B3
Laburnum Ct 28
E2 . . . . 24 B4
Laburnum Ho
New Cross SE4 . . . . 51 B1
16 Stoke Newington
N16 . . . . 6 C2
Laburnum St E2 . . . . . . 24 B4
Lacey Ho 7 SE13 . . . . . 67 B1
Lacey Mews 9 E3 . . . . . 26 C3
Lacine Ct 12 SE16 . . . . . 40 C4
Lackington St
EC2 . . . . 109 C4
Lackland Ho 11 SE1 . . 153 A2
Lacland Ho SW10 . . . . 157 B2
Lacon Rd SE22 . . . . 64 C3
Lacy Rd SW15 . . . . 57 C3

Ladbroke Cres
W11 . . . . 31 A3
Ladbroke Gdns
W11 . . . . 31 B2 112 C4
Ladbroke Gr
Kensal Town W10 . . . . 31 A4
Notting Hill
W11 . . . . 31 B2 112 C4
Ladbroke Grove Ho
W11 . . . . 31 B2 112 C4
Ladbroke Grove Sta
W10 . . . . 31 A4
Ladbroke Ho 11 . . . . 111 A3
Ladbroke Mews
W11 . . . . 112 B1
Ladbroke Rd
W11 . . . . 31 B1 112 C2
Ladbroke Sq
W11 . . . . 31 B2 113 A3
Ladbroke Terr
W11 . . . . 31 B1 113 A2
Ladbroke Wlk
W11 . . . . 31 B1 113 A2
Ladlands SE22 . . . . 76 C4
Ladybower Ct 6
E5 . . . . 17 C4
Ladycroft Rd SE13 . . . . 67 A4
Lady Elizabeth Ho
SW14 . . . . 55 B4
Ladyfern Ho 19 E3 . . . . 33 C4
Lady Florence Ctyd 18
SE8 . . . . 51 C3
Lady Margaret Rd
NW5 . . . . 13 B3
Lady Margaret Sch
SW6 . . . . 165 B3
Lady Somerset Rd
NW5 . . . . 13 A4
LADYWELL 66 C1
Ladywell Arena
SE13 . . . . 67 A1
Ladywell Cl SE4 . . . . . . 66 C3
Ladywell Hts SE4 . . . . . 66 B1
Ladywell Rd SE13 . . . . . 67 A2
Ladywell Sta SE13 . . . . 67 A2
Ladywell Water Twr
SE4 . . . . 66 C2
Lafitte Ho 22 N19 . . . . . 4 C4
Lafone Ho 11 SW2 . . . . 74 A4
Lafone St SE1 . . . . 138 C4
Lagado Mews
SE16 . . . . 32 C1
Lagonda Ho 10 E3 . . . . 26 C1
Lagonier Ho EC1 . . . . . 97 A3
Laindon Ho 6 N16 . . . . . 7 B3
Laing Ho SE5 . . . . 48 B3
Lainson St SW18 . . . . . 70 C4
Lairdale Cl SE21 . . . . . . 75 B4
Lairs Cl N7 . . . . 14 A2
Laitwood Rd SW12 . . . . 73 A3
Lakanal 5 SE5 . . . . 49 A2
Lake Ho SE1 . . . . 136 C3
Laker Ct SW4 . . . . 172 B2
Laker Pl SW15 . . . . 58 A1
Lakeside Ct N4 . . . . 6 B3
Lakeside Rd W14 . . . . . 39 C3
Lakis Cl NW3 . . . . 11 B4
Laleham Ho
E2 . . . . 24 B1 98 C2
Lalor St SW6 . . . . 164 B2
Lambard Ho 4
SE10 . . . . 52 B3

Lamb Ct 16 E14 . . . . . 33 A2
Lamberhurst Ho 14
SE15 . . . . 50 B4
Lambert Ave TW9 . . . . . 55 A4
Lambert Ho
16 Brixton SW9 . . . . . 173 B1
11 Crouch End N19 . . . . 4 C4
Lambert Rd SW2 . . . . . . 62 B2
Lambert St N1 . . . . 14 C1
LAMBETH 134 C3
Lambeth Acad
SW4 . . . . 61 B2
Lambeth Coll (Brixton
Ctr) SW2 . . . . 62 B2
Lambeth Coll
(Clapham Ctr)
SW4 . . . . 61 B2
Lambeth Coll
(Vauxhall Ctr)
SW8 . . . . 171 B4
Lambeth Ct 8
SE18 . . . . 58 C2
Lambeth High St
SE1 . . . . 148 C4
Lambeth Hill EC4 . . . . . 122 C4
Lambeth Hospl
SE11 . . . . 62 B4
Lambeth North Sta
SE1 . . . . 135 B2
Lambeth Pal SE1 . . . . . 134 C1
Lambeth Palace Rd
SE1 . . . . 134 C2
Lambeth Pier SE1 . . . . 134 B1
Lambeth Rd
SE1 . . . . 135 C1
Lambeth Twrs
SE11 . . . . 135 C1
Lambeth Wlk
SE11 . . . . 149 A4
Lambfold Ho N7 . . . . . . 14 A2
Lamb Ho
28 Camberwell
SE5 . . . . 48 B3
17 Camberwell SE5 . . . 48 C2
Greenwich SE10 . . . . . 52 B4
Lamb La E8 . . . . 17 A1
Lamb St SE8 . . . . 51 C4
Lamb St E1 . . . . 110 C4
Lamble St NW5 . . . . 12 C4
Lamb's Bldgs EC1 . . . . . 97 B1
Lamb's Conduit Pas
WC1 . . . . 106 C4
Lamb's Conduit St
WC1 . . . . 94 C1
Lamb's Mews N1 . . . . . . 86 A3
Lamb's Pas EC1 . . . . . . 97 B1
Lamb St E1 . . . . 110 C4
Lambton Ct 2 N19 . . . . . 5 A3
Lambton Mews 4
N19 . . . . 5 A3
Lambton Pl
W11 . . . . 31 B2 113 A4
Lambton Rd N19 . . . . . . 5 A3
Lamb Wlk SE1 . . . . 138 A3

Lamerton Lo 10
TW9 . . . . 44 B2
Lamerton St 8
SE8 . . . . 51 C4
Lamington St 3
W6 . . . . 39 A2
Lamlash St SE11 . . . . . 150 A4
Lamley Ho SE10 . . . . . . 52 A3
Lammas Rd E9 . . . . 17 C1
Lammermoor Rd
SW12 . . . . 73 A4
Lamont Rd SW10 . . . . . 157 B3
Lamont Rd Pas
SW10 . . . . 157 B3
Lampard Gr N16 . . . . . . 7 B3
Lampern Sq 9
E2 . . . . 24 C2 99 C4
Lampeter Sq W6 . . . . . 154 A3
Lamplighter Cl 3
E1 . . . . 25 B1
Lampson Ho 6
N19 . . . . 13 B4
Lanark Ho 19 SE1 . . . . 153 A1
Lanark Mans
Paddington W9 . . . . . . 89 A2
5 Shepherd's Bush
W12 . . . . 39 B4
Lanark Mews NW8 . . . . 89 A3
Lanark Pl W9 . . . . 89 A2
Lanark Rd W9 . . . . 88 C3
Lanark Sq E14 . . . . 42 A3
Lanbury Rd SE15 . . . . . 65 C3
Lancashire Ct W1 . . . . 118 B4
Lancaster Ave SE21,
SE27 . . . . 75 B2
Lancaster Cl
10 De Beauvoir Town
N1 . . . . 16 A1
Kensington W2 . . . . . . 114 A3
Lancaster Cotts 7
TW10 . . . . 54 A1
Lancaster Ct
Bayswater W2 . . . . . . 115 A4
Parsons Green
SW6 . . . . 155 A1
West Norwood
SE27 . . . . 75 A2
Lancaster Dr
Canary Wharf E14 . . . . 34 B1
Maitland Pk NW3 . . . . . 12 A2
Lancaster Gate
W2 . . . . 115 A4
Lancaster Gate Sta
W2 . . . . 115 B4
Lancaster Gr NW3 . . . . 12 A2
Lancaster Hall 11
E16 . . . . 35 C1
Lancaster Ho
SW15 . . . . 47 B1
Lancaster Lo 2
W11 . . . . 31 A3
Lancaster Mews
Bayswater W2 . . . . . . 115 A4
2 Richmond TW10 . . . . 54 A1
3 Wandsworth
SW18 . . . . 59 A2
Lancaster Pk
TW10 . . . . 54 A2
Lancaster Pl WC2 . . . . 120 C3
Lancaster Rd
Dudden Hill NW10 . . . . 8 C3
Finsbury Pk N4 . . . . 5 C4

Lancaster Rd continued
Notting Hill W11 . . . . . 31 A3
Lancaster St SE1 . . . . . 136 B3
Lancaster Stables 10
NW3 . . . . 12 A2
Lancaster Terr
W2 . . . . 115 B4
Lancaster Wlk
W2 . . . . 115 A2
Lancefield Ho
SE15 . . . . 65 A4
Lancefield St W10 . . . . 23 B2
Lancell St N16 . . . . 7 A2
Lancelot Pl SW7 . . . . . 130 C3
Lancer Sq W8 . . . . 128 A4
Lanchester Ct W2 . . . . 102 C1
Lanchester Way
SE14 . . . . 50 C2
Lancing St NW1 . . . . . . 93 B3
Lancresse Ct N1 . . . . . . 24 A4
Landale Ct SE10 . . . . . . 52 B2
Landale Ho 13
SE16 . . . . 40 B3
Landcroft Rd SE22 . . . . 64 B1
Landells Rd SE22 . . . . . 64 C1
Landford Rd SW15 . . . . 57 B4
Landleys Field 21
N7 . . . . 13 C3
Landmann Ho 18
SE16 . . . . 40 A2
Landmann Way
SE14 . . . . 40 C1
Landmark Hts E5 . . . . . 18 A4
Landon Pl SW1 . . . . . . 130 C2
Landons Cl E14 . . . . . . 34 B1
Landon Wlk 18
E14 . . . . 34 A2
Landor Ct N16 . . . . 16 A3
Landor Ho 7 SE5 . . . . . 48 C3
Landor Rd SW9 . . . . . . 62 A4
Landor Wlk 17
W12 . . . . 38 C4
Landrake NW1 . . . . 83 A3
Landridge Rd
SW6 . . . . 164 C2
Landseer Ct 10 N19 . . . . 5 A2
Landseer Ho
Battersea SW11 . . . . . 169 C3
Paddington NW8 . . . . . 89 C2
Westminster SW1 . . . . 147 C3
Landseer Rd N19 . . . . . . 5 A2
Landulph Ho
SE11 . . . . 149 C2
Landward Ct W1 . . . . . 102 B2
Lane Cl SW11 . . . . 72 B4
Lanercost Cl SW2 . . . . . 74 C2
Lanercost Rd SW2 . . . . 74 C2
Lane The NW8 . . . . 78 C1
Laneway SW15 . . . . 57 A2
Laney Bldg EC1 . . . . . . 107 B4
Lanfranc Rd E3 . . . . 26 A3
Lanfrey Pl W14 . . . . . . 140 C1
Langbourne Ave N6 . . . . 3 C2
Langbourne Ho 4
SW2 . . . . 62 C2
Langbourne Mans
N6 . . . . 3 C2
Langbourne Pl
E14 . . . . 42 A1
Langbourne Prim Sch
SE21 . . . . 76 A1
Langdale NW1 . . . . 92 C4
Langdale Cl
Camberwell SE17 . . . . 48 B4
Mortlake SW14 . . . . . . 55 A3

Langdale Ho SW1 . . 146 C1
Langdale Rd SE10 . . 52 B3
Langdale St 25 E1 . . 32 A3
Langdon Ct
  Finsbury EC1 . . . . . 86 B1
  Harlesden NW10 . . . 21 A4
Langdon Ho 3
  E14 . . . . 34 B3
Langdon Park Rd
  N6 . . . . 4 B4
Langdon Park Sch
  E14 . . . . 34 B3
Langdon Park Sta
  E14 . . . . 34 B3
Langdon Pk L Ctr
  E14 . . . . 34 B3
Langdon Pk Sta
  E3 . . . . 34 B4
Langdon Rd SW6 . . . 155 B4
Langdon Way 19
  SE1 . . . . 153 C3
Langford Cl
  Shacklewell E8 . . . . 16 C3
  St John's Wood
  NW8 . . . . 79 A2
Langford Cl 3 . . . . . 79 A2
Langford Gn SE5 . . . 64 A4
Langford Ho 5
  SE8 . . . . 51 C4
Langford Pl NW8 . . . 79 A2
Langford Prim Sch
  SW6 . . . . 166 B2
Langford Rd 4
  SW6 . . . . 166 B2
Langham Ct 4
  SW15 . . . . 57 C2
Langham Ho SW4 . . . 61 B2
Langham Mans
  SW5 . . . . 142 A1
Langham Pl
  Chiswick W4 . . . . . . 46 A4
  Fitzrovia W1 . . . . . . 104 B3
Langham St W1 . . . . 104 B3
Lang Ho
  South Lambeth
  SW8 . . . . 162 A1
  Tufnell Pk N19 . . . . . 4 B1
Langholm Cl
  SW12 . . . . 73 C4
Langhorne Ct 10
  NW8 . . . . 11 C1
Langhurst Ho 10
  SW11 . . . . 169 B2
Langland Gdns
  NW3 . . . . 11 A3
Langland Ho 10
  SE5 . . . . 48 C3
Langland Mans
  NW3 . . . . 11 A3
Langler Rd NW10 . . . 22 B3
Langley Ct
  South Lambeth
  SW8 . . . . 172 A4
  Strand WC2 . . . . . . 120 A4
Langley Dr W3 . . . . . 37 A4
Langley Ho
  11 Lower Clapton
  E5 . . . . 17 A3
  38 Paddington W2 . . 31 C4
Langley La SW8 . . . . 162 B4
Langley Mans
  SW8 . . . . 162 B4
Langley St WC2 . . . . 106 A1
Langmead Ho 5
  E3 . . . . 27 A2

Langmore Ho 30
  E1 . . . . 111 C1
Langport Ho 1
  SW9 . . . . 48 A1
Langridge 18 NW5 . . 12 C2
Langroyd Rd SW17 . . 72 B2
Langside Ave
  SW15 . . . . 56 C3
Lang St E1 . . . . 25 B1
Langston Hughes Cl
  5 SE24 . . . . 63 A3
Langthorn Ct EC2 . . 109 C2
Langthorne Lo 30
  SW16 . . . . 74 A1
Langthorne St
  SW6 . . . . 47 C3
Langton Cl WC1 . . . . 95 A2
Langton Ct SW15 . . . 58 B1
Langton Ho SE11 . . . 149 A4
Langton Pl SW18 . . . 70 C3
Langton Rd SW9 . . . 48 A3
Langton St SW10 . . . 157 A3
Langton Way SE3 . . . 53 C3
Langtry Pl SW6 . . . . 155 C4
Langtry Rd NW8 . . . . 78 A3
Langtry Wlk NW8 . . . 78 C4
Lanhill Rd W9 . . . . . 23 C1
Lanier Rd SE13 . . . . 67 C1
Lanner Ho 2
  SW11 . . . . 60 A4
Lannoy Point
  SW6 . . . . 154 B2
Lanrick Rd E14 . . . . . 35 A3
Lansbury Gdns 1
  E14 . . . . 34 C3
Lansbury Lawrence
  Prim Sch 4 E14 . . . 34 A3
Lanscombe Wlk
  SW8 . . . . 162 A1
Lansdell Ho 9
  SW2 . . . . 114 A3
Lansdowne Cres
  W11 . . . . 31 A2 112 B3
Lansdowne Dr E8 . . . 16 C1
Lansdowne Gdns
  SW8 . . . . 172 A4
Lansdowne Gr
  NW10 . . . . 8 A4
Lansdowne Hill
  SE27 . . . . 75 A1
Lansdowne Ho
  W11 . . . . 31 B1 112 C2
Lansdowne Mews
  W11 . . . . 31 B1 112 C2
Lansdowne Pl
  SE1 . . . . 137 C2
Lansdowne Rd
  W11 . . . . 31 A2 112 B3
Lansdowne Rise
  W11 . . . . 31 A2 112 B3
Lansdowne Row
  W1 . . . . 118 B2
Lansdowne Sch 2
  SW9 . . . . 62 B4
Lansdowne Terr
  WC1 . . . . 94 B1
Lansdowne Way SW4,
  SW8 . . . . 172 B3
Lansdowne Wlk
  W11 . . . . 31 B1 112 C2
Lansdowne Wood Cl
  5 SE27 . . . . 75 A1
Lansdown Ho 28
  SE5 . . . . 48 B1

Lantern Cl SW15 . . . 56 C3
Lantern Ho E14 . . . . 41 C4
Lanterns Ct E14 . . . . 41 C3
Lant Ho SE1 . . . . . . 136 C3
Lantry Ct 1 W3 . . . . 28 A1
Lant St SE1 . . . . . . 137 A4
Lanvanor Rd SE15 . . 50 B1
Lanyard Ho 4 SE8 . . 41 B2
Lapford Cl W9 . . . . . 23 B1
Lapsang SE1 . . . . . 125 A1
Lapwing Twr 31
  SE8 . . . . 51 B4
Lapworth Ct W2 . . . 100 B4
Lara Cl SE13 . . . . . . 67 B1
Larch Ave W3 . . . . . 29 A1
Larch Cl
  11 Balham SW12 . . . 73 A2
  18 Deptford SE8 . . . . 51 B4
  10 Upper Holloway
  N19 . . . . 4 B2
Larch Ct 33 W9 . . . . 31 C4
Larches Ave SW14 . . 55 C3
Larchfield Ho 2
  N5 . . . . 15 B3
Larch Ho 20 SE16 . . . 40 B4
Larchmore Ct N19 . . . 5 A2
Larch Rd NW2 . . . . . . 9 B4
Larcom St SE17 . . . . 151 A3
Larden Rd W3 . . . . . 38 A4
La Retraite RC Girls
  Sch SW12 . . . . 73 B4
Larissa St SE17 . . . . 151 C3
Larix Ct NW10 . . . . . 21 C4
Larkfield Rd TW9 . . . 54 A3
Larkhall Rise SW4 . . 171 B1
Larkhall Rise
  SW4 . . . . 171 B1
Lark Row E2 . . . . . . 25 B4
Larmenier & Sacred
  Heart RC Prim Sch
  4 W6 . . . . 39 C2
Larnaca Ho SE1 . . . . 138 C2
Larnach Rd W6 . . . . . 47 C4
Larpent Ave SW15 . . 57 B2
La Saint Union RC Sec
  Sch NW5 . . . . 3 C1
Lascelles Ho 1 NW1 . 90 B1
Lassell St SE10 . . . . 42 C1
Lasseter Pl SE3 . . . . 53 B4
Latchmere Rd
  SW11 . . . . 168 C1
Latchmere St 5
  SW11 . . . . 168 C2
Latham Ho E1 . . . . . . 32 C3
Latimer SE17 . . . . . 152 A1
Latimer Ho
  11 Homerton E9 . . . . 17 C2
  Notting Hill
  W11 . . . . 31 B2 113 A3
Latimer Ind Est 1
  NW10 . . . . 30 B3
Latimer Pl W10 . . . . 30 B3
Latimer Rd W10 . . . . 30 B3
Latimer Road Sta
  W10 . . . . 30 C2
Latona Rd SE15 . . . . 49 C4
Lattimer Pl W4 . . . . . 46 A4
Latvia Ct SE17 . . . . 151 A1
Latymer Ct W6 . . . . . 39 C2
Latymer Upper Sch 14
  W6 . . . . 38 C2
Lauderdale Mans
  W9 . . . . 88 B3
Lauderdale Rd W9 . . 88 B3

Lauderdale Twr
  EC2 . . . . 108 C4
Laud St SE11 . . . . . 148 C2
Laughton Ho 11
  SW2 . . . . 62 C1
Launcelot St SE1 . . . 135 B3
Launceston Pl
  W8 . . . . 128 B1
Launch St E14 . . . . . 42 B3
Laundress La N16 . . . 7 C1
Laundry La 11 N1 . . . 15 B1
Laundry Rd W6 . . . . 154 A3
Laura Pl E5 . . . . 17 B4
Laurel Bank Gdns 3
  SW6 . . . . 165 A2
Laurel Cl
  6 Fulham N19 . . . . . . 4 B2
Laurel Ct
  Dalston E8 . . . . 16 B1
  2 Putney SW15 . . . . 57 C2
  9 Rotherhithe
  SE16 . . . . 33 A1
Laurel Ho
  6 Deptford SE8 . . . . 51 B4
  5 Hamstead NW3 . . . 11 A2
Laurel Rd SW13 . . . . 46 C1
Laurel St E8 . . . . . . 16 B2
Laurence Mews 12
  W12 . . . . 38 C4
Laurence Pountney
  Hill EC4 . . . . 123 C4
Laurence Pountney La
  EC4 . . . . 123 C4
Laurie Gr SE14 . . . . 51 A2
Laurie Ho
  Newington SE1 . . . . 136 B1
  Notting Hill
  W8 . . . . 31 C1 113 B1
Laurier Rd NW5 . . . . . 4 A1
Lauriston Ho 6
  E9 . . . . 17 C2
Lauriston Lo NW6 . . . 10 B2
Lauriston Prim Sch 1
  E9 . . . . 25 C4
Lauriston Rd E9 . . . . 17 C1
Lausanne Rd SE15 . . 50 B2
Lavell St N16 . . . . . . 15 C4
Lavender Cl SW3 . . . 157 C3
Lavender Ct SW4 . . . 172 B3
Lavender Gdns
  SW11 . . . . 60 B3
Lavender Gr E8 . . . . . 16 C1
Lavender Hill
  SW11 . . . . 60 C4
Lavender Ho
  6 Richmond
  TW9 . . . . 45 A2
  14 Rotherhithe
  SE16 . . . . 32 C1
Lavender Rd
  Battersea SW11 . . . . 59 C4
  Rotherhithe SE16 . . . 33 A1
Lavender Sweep
  SW11 . . . . 60 B3
Lavender Terr 12
  SW11 . . . . 60 A4
Lavender Wlk
  SW11 . . . . 60 B3
Lavendon Ho NW8 . . 90 B2
Lavengro Rd SE27 . . . 75 B2
Lavenham Rd
  SW18 . . . . 70 C3
Lavers Rd N16 . . . . . . 7 A1
Laverstoke Gdns
  SW15 . . . . 68 C4
Laverton Mews
  SW5 . . . . 142 B3

Laverton Pl SW5 . . . 142 B3
Lavina Gr N1 . . . . . . 84 C2
Lavington Cl E9 . . . . 18 B2
Lavington St SE1 . . . 122 B1
  Liddle Jun Sch 8
  E2 . . . . 24 C2 99 C4
Lawford Rd
  Chiswick W4 . . . . . . 45 B3
  De Beauvoir Town
  N1 . . . . 16 A1
  Kentish Town NW5 . . 13 B2
Lawfords Wharf 18
  NW1 . . . . 13 B1
Lawless Ho 6 E14 . . . 34 B2
Lawless St E14 . . . . . 34 A2
Lawley St E5 . . . . . . 17 B4
Lawman Ct 2
  TW9 . . . . 44 B2
Lawn Cres TW9 . . . . 44 C1
Lawnfield Ct NW6 . . . 9 C1
Lawn House Cl
  E14 . . . . 42 B4
Lawn La SW8 . . . . . 162 C4
Lawn Rd NW3 . . . . . 12 B3
Lawns The N16 . . . . . 6 C3
Lawrence Ave
  NW10 . . . . 20 C4
Lawrence Bldgs 1
  N16 . . . . 7 B1
Lawrence Cl
  Bow E3 . . . . 26 C3
  6 Shepherd's Bush
  W12 . . . . 30 A2
Lawrence Ct
  4 South Acton
  W3 . . . . 37 B3
  Stoke Newington N16 . 7 B1
Lawrence Ho
  20 Camden Town
  NW1 . . . . 13 A1
  Westminster SW1 . . 147 C3
Lawrence La EC2 . . . 109 A2
Lawrence Mans
  SW3 . . . . 158 A3
Lawrence Pl N1 . . . . 84 B4
Lawrence St
  Canning Town
  E16 . . . . 35 B4
  Chelsea SW3 . . . . . 158 A3
Lawrence Trad Est
  SE10 . . . . 43 A2
Lawrence Univ
  SW7 . . . . 143 A3
Lawson Cl SW19 . . . . 69 C1
Lawson Ct 1 N4 . . . . 5 B3
Lawson Ho 17
  W12 . . . . 30 A2
Law St SE1 . . . . 137 C2
Lawton Rd E3 . . . . . . 26 A2
Laxfield Ct E8 . . . . . 24 C4
Laxley Cl SE5 . . . . . . 48 A3
Laxton Path 1
  SE4 . . . . 65 C3
Laxton Pl NW1 . . . . . 92 B2
Layard Rd SE16 . . . . 40 A2
Layard Sq SE16 . . . . 40 A2
Laybourne Ho 18
  E14 . . . . 41 C4
Laycock Prim Sch 11
  N1 . . . . 15 A2
Laycock St N1 . . . . . 14 C2
Layfield Ho 1
  SE10 . . . . 43 C1
Laystall Ct EC1 . . . . 95 B1

Laystall St EC1 . . . . . . **95** B1
Layton Pl TW9 . . . . 44 C2
Lazar Wlk 图 N7. . . . . . . 5 B2
Leabank Sq E9 . . . . 18 C2
Leabourne Rd N16 . . 7 C4
Leacroft Ave SW12 . . 72 B4
Lea Ct 图 W12 . . . . 38 A4
Leadenhall Building
The EC3 . . . . **110** A1
Leadenhall Mkt
EC3 . . . . **110** A1
Leadenhall Pl
EC3 . . . . **110** A1
Leadenhall St
EC3 . . . . **110** A1
Leadenham Ct 图
E3 . . . . **26** C1
Lea Ho NW8 . . . . **90** A1
Leahurst Rd SE13 . . **67** C2
Lea Int E9 . . . . 18 C3
Leake St
Lambeth SE1 . . . . . **135** B3
South Bank SE1 . . . **135** A4
Leamington Ct
图 Forest Hill
SE26 . . . . .76 C1
North Acton W3 . . . . .28 C4
Leamington Ho 图
W11 . . . . .31 B4
Leamington Pk
W3 . . . . .28 C4
Leamington Rd Villas
W11 . . . . .31 B4
Leamore St W6 . . . . . .39 B2
Leamouth Rd E14 . . 34 C3
Leander Ct
图 Hackney E9 . . . . .17 B1
St Johns SE8 . . . . . . .51 C2
Leander Rd SW2 . . 62 C1
Leary Ho SE11 . . . . . 149 A1
Lea Sq 图 E3 . . . . .26 B4
Leatherdale St
图 Bethnal Green
E1 . . . . .25 C1
图 Globe Town E1 . .25 C2
Leatherhead Cl N16 . 7 B3
Leather La Mkt
EC1 . . . . **107** C4
Leathermarket Ct
SE1 . . . . **138** A3
Leathermarket St
SE1 . . . . **138** A3
Leather Rd SE16 . . . .40 C2
Leathwaite Rd
SW11 . . . . .60 B2
Leathwell Rd SE8 . . 52 A1
Lebanon Gdns
SW18 . . . . .58 C1
Lebanon Rd SW18 . .58 C2
Lebus Ho NW8 . . . . . .80 A1
Lechmere Rd NW2 . . .9 A2
Leckford Rd SW18 . .71 B3
Leckhampton Pl 图
SW2 . . . . .74 C4
Lecky Ho NW2 . . . . 9 A4
Lecky St SW7 . . . . . . 143 B2
L'École des Petits Scholars
SW6 . . . . 166 A2
Leconfield Ave SW13,
SW15 . . . . .56 B4
Leconfield Ho SE5 . .64 A4
Leconfield Rd N5 . . .15 C4
Lector Ct EC1 . . . . **95** C1

Leda Ct 图 SW9 . . **163** B1
Ledam Bldg EC1 . . **107** B4
Ledbury Mews N
W11 . . . . **31** C3
Ledbury Mews W
W11 . . . . 32 113 B4
Ledbury Rd W11 . . . .31 C3
Ledbury St SE15 . . . 49 C3
Ledo Ho 图 N16 . . . . . 15 C4
Lee Conservancy Rd
E9 . . . . .18 B3
Lee Ct SE13 . . . . .67 C3
Leeds Ct EC1 . . . . . . .96 A2
Lee Ho 图 N19 . . . . . .13 C3
Leeland Way NW10 . . 8 B4
Leerdam Dr E14 . . . .42 B3
Lees Ct W1 . . . . **117** B4
Lees Ho SE17. . . . . . **151** C1
Leeson Rd 图
SE24 . . . . .62 C3
Lees Pl W1 . . . . **117** B4
Lee St E8 . . . . .24 B4
Leet Ct N16 . . . . .15 C4
Leeve Ho 图 W9 . . . .23 B2
Leeward Ct 图 E1 . . 125 C2
Leeway SE8 . . . . .41 B1
Lefevre Wlk E3 . . . . .26 C4
Leffern Rd W12. . . . . .38 C4
Left Ho 图 NW6 . . . . .10 A1
Lefroy Ho 图 SE1 . . 136 C3
Lefroy Rd W12 . . . . . .38 B4
Legard Rd N5 . . . . 6 A1
Leggatt Rd E15 . . . . .27 B3
Legge St SE13 . . . . . .67 B2
Leghorn Rd NW10 . .21 C3
Legion Cl N1 . . . . .14 C1
Legion Terr E3 . . . . . .26 C4
Leicester Ct
图 Paddington
W2 . . . . .31 C4
图 St James WC2 . . **119** C4
Leicester Ho
图 Brixton SW9 . . .63 A4
图 Putney SW15 . . .69 B4
Leicester Pl WC2 . . 119 C4
Leicester Sq WC2 . . 119 C3
Leicester Square Sta
WC2 . . . . 119 C4
Leicester St WC2 . . 119 C4
Leigham Ave
SW16 . . . . .74 A1
Leigham Cl 图
SW16 . . . . .74 B1
Leigham Court Rd
SW16 . . . . .74 A1
Leigham Hall 图
SW16 . . . . .74 A1
Leigham Hall Par 图
SW16 . . . . .74 A1
Leigham Vale SE27,
SW16, SW2 . . . . .74 C2
Leigh Ct 图 SW2 . . . .62 C2
Leighfield Ho 图 N4 . . 6 B4
Leigh Gdns NW10 . .22 B3
Leigh Ho 图 SW15 . .56 C2
Leigh Orchard Cl
SW16 . . . . .74 B1
Leigh Pl EC1 . . . . . . 107 B4
Leigh Rd N5 . . . . .15 A4
Leigh St WC1 . . . . . . .94 A3
Leighton Cres
NW5 . . . . .13 B3

Leighton Gdns
NW10 . . . . .22 B3
Leighton Gr NW5 . . .13 B3
Leighton House Mus
W14 . . . . **127** B2
Leighton Pl NW5 . . .13 B3
Leighton Rd NW5. . .13 B3
Leinster Ave SW14 . .55 B3
Leinster Ct NW10 . . 21 C2
Leinster Gdns
W2 . . . . **114** C4
Leinster Mews
W2 . . . . **114** C4
Leinster Pl W2 . . . . **100** C1
Leinster Sq W2 . . . . **100** A1
Leinster Terr W2 . . . **114** C4
Leithcote Gdns
SW16 . . . . .74 B1
Leithcote Path
SW16 . . . . .74 B1
Leith Ho
图 Kentish Town
N7 . . . . .13 C3
图 Streatham SW2 . .74 B4
Leith Mans W9 . . . . .88 A3
Leith Yd 图 NW6 . . .23 C4
Lelitia Cl E8 . . . . .24 C4
Leman St E1 . . . . 111 B1
Lemmon Rd SE10. . . .53 A4
Le Moal Ho 图 E1 . . .32 B4
Lemsford Ct N4 . . . . . 6 B2
Lena Gardens Prim
Sch W6 . . . . .39 B3
Lena Gdns W6 . . . . . .39 B3
Lendal Terr 图
SW4 . . . . .61 C4
Len Freeman Pl
SW6 . . . . 154 C3
Lenham 图 NW5 . . . .12 C2
Lenham Ho SE1 . . . 137 C3
Lennon Rd NW2 . . . . . 9 B2
Lennox Gdns
Knightsbridge
SW1 . . . . 130 C1
Willesden NW10 . . . 8 B4
Lennox Gdns Mews
SW1 . . . . 144 C4
Lennox Ho 图 E9 . . . 17 B2
Lennox Rd N4, N7 . . . 5 C2
Lenthall Ho 图
SW1 . . . . 147 A1
Lenthall Rd E8 . . . . . .16 C1
Lenthorp Rd SE10 . . 43 B2
Lenton Rise TW9 . . . .54 A4
Len Williams Ct
NW6 . . . . .23 C3
Leonard Ct
Bloomsbury WC1 . . . 94 A2
Kensington W8 . . . **127** B2
Leonard Day Ho 图
N5 . . . . .13 B3
Leonard Pl 图 N16 . .16 A4
Leonard St EC2 . . . . . 97 C2
Leonora Ho W9 . . . . .88 C2
Leontine Cl SE15 . . .49 C3
Leopards Ct EC1 . . . 107 B4
Leopold Bldgs 图
E2 . . . . 24 82 98 B4
Leopold Mews E9 . . 25 B4
Leopold Prim Sch
NW10 . . . . 8 A1
Leopold Rd NW10 . . 8 A1
Leopold St E3 . . . . . . .33 B4
Leopold Wlk SE11 . . 148 C1
Leo St SE15 . . . . .50 A3
Leppoc Rd SW4 . . . . .61 C2
Leroy St SE1 . . . . 152 A4
Lerry Cl W14 . . . . 155 A4
Lerwick Ho SW18. . . .59 B3

Lesley Ct SW1 . . . . . 133 B1
Leslie Prince Ct 图
SE5 . . . . .48 C3
Leslie Rd E11 . . . . .19 C4
Lessar Ave SW4 . . . . .61 B1
Lessar Ct SW4 . . . . . .61 B1
Lester Ct 图 E3 . . . . .27 A2
Leswin Pl N16 . . . . 7 B1
Leswin Rd N16 . . . . . . 7 B1
Letchford Gdns
NW10 . . . . .21 C2
Letchford Mews
NW10 . . . . .21 C2
Letchmore Ho 图
W10 . . . . .22 B1
Lethaby Ho 图
SW4 . . . . .62 B3
Lethbridge Cl
SE13 . . . . .52 B1
Letterstone Rd
SW6 . . . . 154 C1
Lettice St SW6 . . . . 165 A3
Lett Rd E15 . . . . .19 C1
Lettsom St SE5 . . . . .49 A1
Levana Cl SW19 . . . . .70 A3
Levant Ho 图 E1 . . . .25 C1
Leventurst Way SW4,
SW9 . . . . .62 A3
Leven Rd E14 . . . . . . .34 C3
Lever Ct 图 E9 . . . . . .17 C2
Leverett St SW3 . . . 144 B4
Leverington Pl N1 . . .97 C3
Leverton Pl NW5 . . .13 B3
Leverton St NW5 . . .13 B3
Levison Way 图
N19 . . . . 4 C3
Levita Ho NW1 . . . . . .93 C4
Levyne Ct EC1 . . . . . .95 C2
Lewesdon Cl 图
SW19 . . . . .69 C3
Lewes Ho
Bermondsey SE1 . . . 138 B4
Peckham SE15 . . . . .49 C4
Leweston Pl N16 . . . . 7 B4
Lewey Ho E3 . . . . .26 B1
Lewin Rd SW14 . . . . .55 C4
Lewis Ct 图 SE16 . . .40 A1
Lewis Gr SE13 . . . . . .67 B4
LEWISHAM 67 B3
Lewisham Bridge
Prim Sch 图
SE13 . . . . .67 A4
Lewisham Hill
SE13 . . . . .52 B1
Lewisham Hospl
SE13 . . . . .67 A2
Lewisham Pk SE13 . .67 B2
Lewisham Rd SE13 . .52 B1
Lewisham Sh Ctr
SE13 . . . . .67 B4
Lewisham Sta SW1 . 133 C3

Lewisham Way SE4,
SE14 . . . . .51 B2
Lewis Pl E8 . . . . .16 C3
Lewis Silkin Ho 图
SE15 . . . . .50 B4
Lewis St NW1 . . . . . . .13 A2
Lexden Rd W3 . . . . . .28 A1
Lexfield Ho N5 . . . . . .15 B4
Lexham Gardens
Mews W8 . . . . 128 B1
Lexham Gdns W8 . . 142 A4
Lexham Mews
W8 . . . . 141 C4
Lexham Wlk W8. . . 128 B1
Lexington St W1 . . . 119 A4
Lexton Gdns SW12 . .73 C3
Leybourne Pk TW9 . .44 C2
Leybourne Ho 图
SE15 . . . . .50 B4
Leybourne Rd 图
NW1 . . . . .13 A1
Leybourne St 图
NW1 . . . . .13 A1
Leyden Mans 图
N19 . . . . 5 A4
Leyden St E1 . . . . 110 C3
Leydon Cl
Rotherhithe SE16. . . .32 C1
SE16 . . . . .32 C1
Ley Ho SE1 . . . . 136 C3
Leyland Ho 图 E14. . .34 A2
Leylands SW18 . . . . . .58 B1
Leylang Rd SE14 . . . .50 C3
Leys Ct 图 SW9 . . . . 173 B1
Leysdown 图 NW5 . .12 C2
Leysdown Ho 图
SE17 . . . . 152 B2
Leysfield Rd W12. . . .38 C4
Leythe Rd W3 . . . . . .37 B4
LEYTON 19 C4
Leyton Mill Ret Pk
E10 . . . . .19 B4
Leyton Mills E10 . . . .19 B4
Leyton Rd E15 . . . . . .19 C2
Liardet St SE14 . . . . .51 A4
Liberia Rd N5 . . . . . . .15 A2
Liberty Mews
SW12 . . . . .61 A1
Liberty St SW9 . . . . 173 A4
Libra Rd 图 E3 . . . . . .26 B3
Library Mans 图
W12 . . . . .39 B4
Library Par NW10. . . .21 A4
Library Pl E1 . . . . .32 A2
Library St SE1 . . . . . 136 B3
Lichfield Ct TW9. . . . .54 A3
Lichfield Gdns TW10,
TW9 . . . . .54 A2
Lichfield Ho 图
SE5 . . . . .48 B1
Lichfield Rd
Mile End E3 . . . . . . .26 A2
Richmond TW9 . . . . .44 B2
West Hampstead
NW2 . . . . .10 A4
Lichfield Terr 图
TW9 . . . . .54 A2
Lickey Ho W14 . . . . . 155 A4
Lidcote Gdns 图
SW9 . . . . 173 A1
Liddell Gdns
NW10 . . . . .22 B3
Liddell Rd NW6. . . . . .10 C2
Lidfield Rd N16 . . . . .15 C4
Lidgate Rd 22
SE15 . . . . .49 B3

Lidiard Rd SW18 . . . . 71 B2
Lidlington Pl NW1 . . . 83 A1
Lido The W2 . . . . 116 A1
Lidyard Rd N19 . . . . 4 B3
Liffey Ct NW10 . . . . 8 C1
Liffords Pl SW13 . . . . . . 46 B1
Liford St SW15 . . . . 57 C3
Lighter Cl E16 . . . . . . 41 A2
Lighterman Mews **15**
E1 . . . . 25 C2
Lighterman's Rd
E14 . . . . 42 A4
Lighterman's Wlk
SW18 . . . . 58 C3
Light Horse Ct
SW1 . . . . 145 B1
Ligonier St
E2 . . . . 24 B1 98 C2
Lilac Ho SE4 . . . . 66 B4
Lilac Pl SE11 . . . . . . 148 C3
Lilac St W12 . . . . 29 C2
Lilestone Est NW8 . . 89 C1
Lilestone Ho NW8 . . 89 C2
Lilestone St NW8 . . . 90 A2
Liford Ho P1 SE5 . . . . 48 B1
Liford Rd SE15 . . . . . 48 A1
Lilian Baylis Ho
N1 . . . . 15 B2
Lilian Baylis Tech Sch
SE11 . . . . 149 A1
Lilley Cl E1 . . . . 125 C1
Lillian Ave W3 . . . . . . 36 C4
Lillian Cl N16 . . . . 7 A1
Lillian Rd SW13 . . . . . 47 A4
Lillie Ho N5 . . . . 14 C3
Lillie Rd SW6 . . . . . . 154 C3
Lillie Road Mans
SW6 . . . . 154 B3
Lillieshall Rd SW4 . . 61 B4
Lillie Yd SW6 . . . . . . 155 B4
Lillingston Ho N7 . . . 14 C4
Lily Cl W14 . . . . 39 C2
Lily Pl EC1 . . . . 107 C4
Lilyville Rd SW6 . . . 164 C3
Limborough Ho **5**
E14 . . . . 33 C4
Limburg Rd SW11 . . . 60 A3
Limeburner La
EC4 . . . . 108 A2
Lime Cl E1 . . . . 125 C2
Lime Gr W12 . . . . 39 B4
Limeharbour E14 . . . 42 A4
Lime Ho **10** W12 . . . . . 45 A2
LIMEHOUSE 33 A2
Limehouse Cswy
E14 . . . . 33 B2
Limehouse Ct **5**
E14 . . . . 33 C3
Lime House Ct **23**
E14 . . . . 33 B3
Limehouse Cut **4**
E14 . . . . 34 A4
Limehouse Fields Est
14 E14 . . . . 33 A4
Limehouse Link
(Tunnel) E14 . . . . . . 33 B2
Limehouse Sta
E14 . . . . 33 A2
Limekiln Wharf **21**
E14 . . . . 33 B2
Limerick Cl SW12 . . . 73 B4
Limerick Ct **1**
SW12 . . . . 73 B4
Limerston St
SW10 . . . . 157 A3

Lime St Pas EC3 . . . 124 A4
Limes Ave
Barnes SW13 . . . . . . 46 B1
Golders Green NW11 . . 1 A4
Limes Field Rd
SW14 . . . . 56 C4
Limesford Rd
SE15 . . . . 65 C3
Limes Gdns SW18 . . 58 C1
Limes Gr SE13 . . . . . 67 B3
Limes The
Camberwell SE5 . . . . 64 A4
Kensington
W2 . . . . . 31 C2 113 C3
Limes Wlk SE15 . . . . 65 B3
Limetree Cl SW2 . . . 74 B3
Lime Tree Ct **14**
E3 . . . . 33 C4
Limpsfield Ave
SW19 . . . . 69 C2
Limscott Ho **18** E3 . . 27 A2
Linacre Cl SE15 . . . . 65 A4
Linacre Ct W6 . . . . . . 39 C1
Linacre Rd NW2 . . . . . 9 A2
Linale Ho N1 . . . . 87 B1
Linberry Wlk **8**
SE8 . . . . 41 B2
Lincoln Ave SW19 . . 69 C1
Lincoln Ct N16 . . . . 6 C4
Lincoln Ho
Bloomsbury WC1 . . 107 A3
Dartmouth Pk
NW5 . . . . 4 B1
2 Islington N1 . . . . . 15 B1
Knightsbridge
SW1 . . . . 130 C3
Lincoln Mews
NW6 . . . . 23 B4
Lincoln's Inn WC2 . 107 A2
Lincoln's Inn Fields
WC2 . . . . 107 A2
Lincoln St SW3 . . . . 144 C3
Lindale SW19 . . . . . . 70 A2
Lindal Rd SE4 . . . . . . 66 B2
Linden Ave NW10 . . . 22 C3
Linden Ct
3 Battersea
SW11 . . . . 59 C3
7 Shepherd's Bush
W12 . . . . 30 B1
Linden Gdns
Chiswick W4 . . . . 37 C1
Notting Hill
W2 . . . . . 31 C2 113 C3
Linden Gr SE15 . . . . . 65 B4
Linden Ho **10** SE8 . . . 51 B4
Linden Lodge Sch
SW19 . . . . 70 A3
Linden Mews
Kensington
W2 . . . . . 31 C2 113 C3
Stoke Newington
N1 . . . . 15 C3
Lindens The W4 . . . . 45 B2
Lindfield Gdns
NW3 . . . . 11 B3
Lindfield Hts NW3 . . 11 B3
Lindfield St E14 . . . . 33 C3
Lindisfarne Way
E9 . . . . 18 A4
Lindley Ho
15 Peckham SE15 . . 49 C3
9 Stepney E1 . . . . . 32 B4

Lindley Pl TW9 . . . . . 44 C2
Lindley St E1 . . . . 32 B4
Lindop Ho **8** E1 . . . . 26 A1
Lindore Rd SW11 . . . 60 B3
Lindo St SE15 . . . . . . 50 B1
Lindrop St SW6 . . . 166 C2
Lindsay Ct SW11 . . . 167 C3
Lindsay Sq SW1 . . . 147 C2
Lindsell St **6**
SE10 . . . . 52 B2
Lindsey Ho SW10 . . 157 C2
Lindsey Mews **18**
N1 . . . . 15 B1
Lindsey St EC1 . . . . 108 B4
Lind St SE8 . . . . 52 A1
Linfield WC1 . . . . 94 C3
Linford Christie
Stadium The
W12 . . . . 30 A4
Linford Ho **17** E2 . . 24 C4
Linford St SW8 . . . . 170 C4
Linford Street Bsns
Est SW8 . . . . 170 C4
Lingard Ho **1** E14 . . 42 B3
Lingards Rd SE13 . . . 67 B3
Lingfield Ho
5 Acton Green
W4 . . . . 37 B1
Lambeth SE1 . . . . . . 136 B3
Lingham St SW9 . . . 172 C1
Ling Rd E16 . . . . 35 C4
Ling's Coppice
SE21 . . . . 75 C2
Lingwell Rd SW17 . . 72 A1
Lingwood Rd E5 . . . . . 7 C4
Linhope St NW1 . . . . 90 C1
Linkenholt Mans **3**
W6 . . . . 38 B2
Link St E9 . . . . 17 B3
Links Yd
10 Spitalfields
E1 . . . . 111 B4
4 Spitalfields
E1 . . . . 111 A4
Link The W3 . . . . 28 A3
Linkway N4 . . . . 6 B4
Linkwood Wlk
NW1 . . . . 13 C1
Linnell Ho
Spitalfields E1 . . . . 110 C4
St John's Wood
NW8 . . . . 78 C4
Linnell Rd SE5 . . . . . 49 A1
Linnet Mews
SW12 . . . . 72 C4
Linom Rd SW4 . . . . . 62 A3
Linscott Rd E5 . . . . . 17 B4
Linsey St
Bermondsey
SE16 . . . . 153 B4
Bermondsey SE16 . 139 C1
Linslade Ho
10 Hackney E2 . . . . 24 C4
Marylebone NW8 . . . 90 B2
Linstead St **1**
NW6 . . . . 10 C1
Linstead Way SW18 .
SW19 . . . . 70 A4
Lintaine Cl W6 . . . . . 154 B3
Linthorpe Rd N16 . . . . 7 A4
Linton Ho
Lower Holloway
N7 . . . . 14 B4
2 Tower Hamlets
E3 . . . . 33 C4
Linton St N1 . . . . 87 A3
Linver Rd SW6 . . . . . 165 B2

Linwood Cl SE5 . . . . 49 B1
Lion Cl SE4 . . . . 66 C1
Lionel Ho **6** W10 . . . 31 A4
Lionel Mans **12**
W14 . . . . 39 C3
Lionel Mews **13**
W10 . . . . 31 A4
Lionel Road N
TW8 . . . . 36 A2
Lionel Road Prim Sch
TW8 . . . . 36 A2
Lionel Road S
TW8 . . . . 36 B1
Lion Gate Gdns
TW9 . . . . 54 B4
Lion Gate Mews
SW18 . . . . 70 C4
Lion House Sch
SW15 . . . . 57 C3
Lion Mills **35** E2 . . . 24 C3
Lion Yd SW4 . . . . 61 C3
Lipton Rd **9** E1 . . . . 32 C3
Lisburne Rd NW3 . . . 12 B4
Lisford St SE15 . . . . . 49 B2
Lisgar Terr W14 . . . 140 C4
Liskeard Gdns SE3 . . 53 C2
Liskeard Ho SE11 . . 149 C2
Lisle Ct NW2 . . . . 1 A1
Lisle St WC2 . . . . . . 119 C4
Lismore Cir NW5 . . . 12 C3
Lismore Wlk **4**
N1 . . . . 15 B2
Lissenden Gdns
NW5 . . . . 12 C4
Lissenden Mans
NW5 . . . . 12 C4
Lisson Cotts NW1 . . 102 B4
Lisson Gr NW1,
NW8 . . . . 90 A2
LISSON GROVE 90 B1
Lisson Ho NW1 . . . . 102 A4
Lisson St NW1 . . . . . 102 A4
Lister Ct N16 . . . . 7 A2
Lister Ct W3 . . . . 28 C4
Lister Ho
Greenwich SE3 . . . . . 53 A4
Marylebone W1 . . . 104 A2
Spitalfields E1 . . . . 111 C4
Lister Hospl SW1 . . 146 A1
Lister Mews N7 . . . . . 14 B4
Liston Rd SW4 . . . . . 61 B4
Listowel Cl **2**
SW9 . . . . 163 C2
Listria Lo N16 . . . . 7 B2
Listria Pk N16 . . . . 7 B2
Litcham Ho **22** E1 . . 25 C2
Litchfield Gdns
NW10 . . . . 8 C2
Litchfield St WC2 . . 119 C4
Lithos Rd NW3 . . . . . 11 B2
Little Albany St
NW1 . . . . 92 B2
Little Argyll St
W1 . . . . 104 C1
Little Boltons The
SW10 . . . . 142 B1
Little Britain EC1 . . 108 C3
Littlebury Rd SW4 . . 61 C4
Little Chelsea Ho
SW10 . . . . 157 A3
Little Chester St
SW1 . . . . 132 A2
Little Cloisters
SW1 . . . . 134 A2
Little College St
SW1 . . . . 134 A2

Little Combe Cl **13**
SW15 . . . . 57 C1
Littlecote Cl SW19 . . 70 A4
Little Cottage Pl
SE10 . . . . 52 A3
Little Deans Yd
SW1 . . . . 134 A2
Little Dimocks
SW12 . . . . 73 A2
Little Dorrit Ct
SE1 . . . . 137 A4
Little Edward St
NW1 . . . . 92 B4
Little Essex St
WC2 . . . . 121 B4
Littlefield Cl N19 . . . 13 B4
Little George St
SW1 . . . . 134 A3
Little Green St
NW5 . . . . 13 A4
Little Marlborough St
W1 . . . . 104 C1
Little Newport St
WC2 . . . . 119 C4
Little New St EC4 . . 107 C2
Little Portland St
W1 . . . . 104 C2
Little Russell St
WC1 . . . . 106 A3
Little St James's St
SW1 . . . . 118 C1
Little St Leonards
SW14 . . . . 55 B4
Little Sanctuary
SW1 . . . . 134 A3
Little Smith St
SW1 . . . . 133 C2
Little Somerset St
E1 . . . . 110 C1
Little Titchfield St
W1 . . . . 104 C3
Littleton St SW18 . . . 71 B2
Little Trinity La
EC4 . . . . 123 A4
Little Turnstile
WC1 . . . . 106 C3
LITTLE VENICE 101 A4
Little Venice W9 . . . 100 C4
Littlewood SE13 . . . . 67 B1
Livermere Ct **3**
E8 . . . . 24 B4
Livermere Rd E8 . . . . 24 B4
Liverpool Gr SE17 . . 151 B1
Liverpool Ho N7 . . . . 14 C2
Liverpool Rd
Islington N1 . . . . 85 C3
Islington N1, N7 . . . . 14 C1
Newham E16 . . . . 35 A4
Liverpool St EC2 . . 110 A3
Liverpool Street Sta
EC2 . . . . 110 A3
Livesey Pl SE15 . . . . 49 C4
Livingstone Ho **16**
SE5 . . . . 48 B3
Livingstone Lo **13**
W9 . . . . 31 C4
Livingstone Pl E14 . . 42 B1
Livingstone Rd
5 Battersea
SW11 . . . . 59 C4
Mill Meads E15 . . . . . 27 B4
Livity Sch The
SW2 . . . . 62 A2
Livonia St W1 . . . . . 105 A1

Lizard St EC1........ 97 A3
Llandovery Ho 1
E14.................. 42 B4
Llanelly Rd NW2..... 1 B2
Llanvanor Rd NW2... 1 B2
Llewellyn Ho 10
N19.................... 4 B1
Llewellyn St SE16 139 C3
L'Ile aux Enfants
NW5................. 12 C3
Lloyd Baker St
WC1.................. 95 B3
Lloyd Ct
Ladywell SE13...... 67 A2
6 West Norwood
SE27................ 75 A1
Lloyd Ho N16........ 6 C1
Lloyd's Ave EC3 .. 110 B1
Lloyd's Bldg EC3 .. 110 A1
Lloyd's PI SE3...... 53 A1
Lloyd Sq WC1....... 95 B4
Lloyd's Row EC1... 96 A3
Lloyd St WC1....... 95 B4
Lloyd Villas SE4.... 51 C1
Lloyd Williamson Sch
17 W10.............. 31 A4
Loampit Hill SE13 .. 52 A1
Loampit Vale SE13 .. 67 B4
Loanda CI 17 E8... 24 B4
Loats Rd SW2....... 62 A2
Locarno Rd 6 W3.. 28 B1
Lochaline St W6.... 47 B4
Lochbie 9 N4........ 5 A4
Lochinvar St SW12 .73 A4
Lochmore Ho
SW1................ 145 C3
Lochnagar St E14 .. 34 B4
Lockbridge Ct 8
W9.................. 31 C4
Locke Ho
Nine Elms SW8.... 170 C4
Stamford Hill N16.... 7 B3
Lockesfield PI E14.. 42 A1
Lockgate Ct E5..... 18 B3
Lockhart CI N7..... 14 B2
Lockhart St E3...... 26 B1
Lockhurst St E5.... 17 C4
Lockington Rd
SW8................ 170 B4
Lockmead Rd
SE13................ 67 B4
Lock Mews 9
NW1................ 13 C2
Lockside 17 E14... 33 A2
Locksley St E14.... 33 B4
Lock View Ct 9
E14.................. 33 A2
Lockwood Ho 10
SE11................ 163 B3
Lockwood Sq
SE16................ 40 A3
Lockyer Est SE1 .. 137 C3
Lockyer Ho
7 Greenwich
SE10................ 43 B1
10 Putney SW15.. 57 C4
South Lambeth
SW8................ 162 A2
Lockyer St SE1 ... 137 C3
Locton Gn 4 E3.... 26 B4
Loddiges Ho 5 E9 .17 B1
Loddiges Rd E9 ... 17 B1
Lodenham Ho NW8.. 89 C1
Loder St SE15...... 50 B3

Lodge Ave SW14....56 A4
Lodge Rd NW8..... 90 A3
Lodge The 9 W4... 38 A3
Lodore St E14...... 34 B3
Lodsworth Ho
SW11................ 169 B3
Loftie St SE16 .... 139 C3
Lofting Ho 8 N1... 14 C1
Lofting Rd N1...... 14 C1
Lofts on the Park 24
E9.................... 17 C2
Loftus Rd W12...... 30 A1
Loftus Rd (Queens
Park Rangers FC)
W12.................. 30 A1
Logan Mews W8.. 141 B4
Logan PI W8 ..... 141 B4
Loggetts SE21..... 76 A2
Lohmann Ho 5
SE11................ 163 B3
Lolesworth CI E1 111 A3
Lollard St SE11.... 149 B3
Lollards Twr SE1... 134 C1
Loman St SE1 .... 136 B4
Lomas Dr 10 E8... 16 B1
Lomas St E1 ...... 111 C4
Lombard Ct
14 Acton W3 ...... 28 A1
City of London EC3 123 C4
Lombard La EC4... 107 C1
Lombard Rd
SW11................ 167 B2
Lombard St EC3.. 109 C1
Lombardy PI W2... 114 B3
Lomley Ho 10 SW2 .62 C1
Lomond Gr SE5.... 48 C3
Lomond Ho 10
SE5.................. 48 C2
Loncroft Rd SE5.. 49 A4
Londesborough Ho 1
N16.................. 16 A4
Londesborough Rd
N16.................. 16 A4
London Acad for
Higher Education
The E15.............. 27 C4
London Acad of
Computing &
Electronics SW17..72 B1
London Bridge EC4,
SE1................. 123 C3
London Bridge City
Pier
SE1................. 124 A2
SE1................. 124 A2
London Bridge
Experience The
SE1................. 123 C2
London Bridge Hospl
SE1................. 123 C3
London Bridge Sta
SE1................. 123 C1
London Bridge Wlk
SE1................. 123 C2
London Britannia Coll
N1.................... 97 B4
London Business Sch
NW1.................. 90 C2
London Canal Mus
N1...................... 84 B2
London Central
Mosque NW8...... 90 B3
London Chest Hospl
E2..................... 25 B3

London Christian Sch
SE16.................. 40 B3
London City Sh Ctr
EC1.................. 97 A1
London Clinic (Hospl)
NW1.................. 91 C1
London Coll of
Advanced Studies
SE1................. 123 B1
London Coll of Beauty
Therapy W1 ..... 105 A1
London Coll of Bsns &
Computer Studies 12
SW4.................. 61 C3
London Coll of
Communication (Sch
of Printing &
Publishing)
SE11................ 136 B3
London Coll of
Economics &
Science NW10..... 20 B1
London Coll of
Fashion (Curtain Rd)
EC2................. 110 A4
London Coll of
Fashion (Golden La)
EC1.................. 96 C1
London Coll of
Fashion (John
Prince's) W1 .... 104 A1
London Coll of
Fashion (Lime
Grove) 15 W6..... 39 B4
London Coll of
Fashion (Mare St)
E8..................... 17 B1
London Coll of
International
Business Studies
WC1................ 106 B3
London Ct 3
SW18.................. 58 C2
London City Hall
SE1................. 134 C4
London Dungeon The
SE1................. 123 C2
London Electronics
Coll SW5 .... 142 A2
London Eye
(Millennium Wheel)
SE1................. 134 C4
London Fields East
Side E8............... 17 A1
London Fields Prim
Sch 18 E8........... 25 A4
London Fields Sta
E8..................... 17 A1
**London Fields West
Side** E8.............16 C1
London Film Mus
SE1................. 134 C4
London Fire Brigade
Mus SE1 .... 138 A3
London Glassblowing
Workshop SE1 ... 138 A3
London Ho 16 W6 .. 38 C2
London Ho TW9 ... 54 B4
London Ho NW8... 80 B2
London Hospital
Dental Inst 18 E1.. 32 A4
London Independent
Hospl The E1 ..... 32 C4
London International
Film Sch WC2 ... 106 A1

London Irish Rifles
Mus SW9.......... 48 B2
London La E8 ..... 17 A1
London Meridian Coll
2 N7................. 5 B1
London Metrocity Coll
13 E3................. 26 C2
London Metropolitan
Univ
Islington N7 ...... 14 C4
Whitechapel E1 .. 110 C1
London Metropolitan
Univ (Central Ho)
E1................... 111 B2
London Metropolitan
Univ (Commercial
Rd) 25 E1.......... 111 B2
London Metropolitan
Univ (Ladbrook Rd)
8 N5................ 15 A3
London Metropolitan
Univ (Moorgate)
EC2................. 109 C3
London Metropolitan
Univ (Tower Hill)
EC3................. 124 C4
London Metropolitan
Univ (Spring Ho) 1
N7..................... 14 C2
London Mews W2 101 C2
London Nautical Sch
SE1................. 121 C2
London Oratory Sch
The SW6 .... 155 C2
London Oratory Sch
SW7................ 130 A1
London Rd SE1 .. 136 B2
London Sch of
Economics &
Political Science
WC2................ 107 A1
London South Bank
Univ SE1 .... 136 B2
London St
City of London
EC3................. 124 B4
Paddington W2... 101 B1
London Stile 5
W4..................... 36 C1
London Stock
Exchange EC2... 108 C2
London Terr 1 E2 .. 24 C3
London Transport
Mus WC2........ 120 B4
London Trocadero
W1................... 119 B3
London Wall EC2.. 109 C3
London Wall Bldgs
EC2................. 109 C3
London Wetland Ctr
SW13................ 47 A3
London Wharf 4
E2.................... 25 A4
London Zoo NW1.. 81 B3
Long Acre WC2... 106 B1
Longbeach Rd
SW11................ 60 B4
Longberrys NW2 ... 1 B1
Longbridge Way
SE13................ 67 B2
Longcliffe Ho
SW18................ 59 A2
Long Dr W3.......... 29 A3
Longfellow Way
SE1................. 153 A3
Longfield Dr SW14 .55 A2

Longfield Est SE1 153 A3
Longfield St SW18.. 70 C4
Longford Ct
1 Bedford Pk
W12.................. 38 A4
2 Clapton Pk E5.. 17 C4
Longford Ho 3 E1 .. 32 B3
Longford St NW1.. 92 B2
Longford Wlk 9
SW2.................. 74 C4
Longhope CI SE15.. 49 B4
Longhurst Ho 8
W9.................... 23 B2
Long La
Bermondsey SE1 . 137 C3
Holborn EC1...... 108 B4
Longland Ct
Bermondsey SE1 . 153 B2
Hackney E9......... 18 A3
Longlands Ct
W11............... 31 B2 113 A4
Longleat Ho SW1 147 B2
Longleigh Ho 8
SE5.................. 49 A2
Longlents Ho 5
NW10................ 21 A4
Longley Ho 5 N19 .13 B4
Longley St SE1 ... 153 B4
Longman Ho
9 Globe Town
E2.................... 25 C3
10 Shoreditch E8 .. 24 B4
Long Meadow 20
N7..................... 14 C3
Longmoor Point 14
SW15................ 69 A3
Longmore St SW1 146 C3
Longnor Rd E1..... 25 C2
Long Pond Rd SE3 .53 A2
Long Rd SW4....... 61 B3
Longridge Ho SE1 137 A1
Longridge Rd
SW5................ 141 C3
Longs Ct 2 TW9 ... 54 B3
Long's Ct W1..... 119 C3
Longshore SE8 ..... 41 B2
Long St E2 ..24 B2 98 C4
Longstaff Cres
SW18................ 70 C4
Longstaff Rd
SW18................ 58 C1
Longstone Ave
NW10................ 21 B4
Longthorne Ho 18
E3.................... 26 B2
Longthorpe Ct 9
W6.................... 38 C2
Longville Rd SE11 150 B4
Long Wlk SE1 ... 138 B2
Longwood Dr
SW15................ 56 C1
Long Yd WC1..... 94 C1
Lonsdale Ho
6 Stoke Newington
N4...................... 6 B4
Lonsdale Mews
Notting Hill W11... 31 B3
4 Richmond TW9 .. 44 C2
Lonsdale PI N1 ... 14 C1
Lonsdale Rd
Barnes SW13..... 46 B3
Chiswick W4...... 38 B2
Kilburn NW6...... 23 C4
Notting Hill W11... 31 B3

Lonsdale Sq
Islington N1 . . . . 14 C1
Islington N1 . . . . 85 C4
Lopez Ho 4 SW9 . . . . 62 A4
Loraine Ct
Chiswick W4 . . . . 45 A4
Islington N7 . . . . 14 B4
Lord David Pitt Ho 3
SE24 . . . . 62 C3
Lorden Wlk 13
E2 . . . . 24 C2 99 B3
Lord Hills Rd W2 . . 100 B4
Lord Holland La 5
SW9 . . . . 173 C2
Lord Napier Pl W6 . 38 C1
Lord North St
SW1 . . . . 134 A1
Lord Roberts Mews
SW6 . . . . 156 A1
Lords Cl SE21 . . . . . 75 B2
Lord's Cricket Mus
NW8 . . . . 89 C3
Lordship Gr N16 . . . . 6 C2
Lordship Ho 3 N16 . . 6 C2
Lordship La SE22 . . 64 B1
Lordship Park Mews
N16 . . . . 6 B2
Lordship Pl N16 . . . . 6 C2
Lordship Pl SW3 . 158 A3
Lordship Rd N16 . . . . 6 C2
Lordship Terr N16 . . 6 C2
Lord's Indoor Cricket
Sch NW8 . . . . 90 A4
Lord's (MCC &
Middlesex Cty
Cricket Ground)
NW8 . . . . 89 C4
Lord's View NW8 . . . 89 C3
Loreburn Ho 2
N7 . . . . 14 B4
Lorenzo St N1,
WC1 . . . . 94 C4
Loris Rd W6 . . . . 39 B3
Lorn Ct SW9 . . . . . . 173 B2
Lorne Cl NW8 . . . . . . 90 B3
Lorne Gdns 5
W11 . . . . 39 C4
Lorne Ho
Hornsey N4 . . . . 5 B4
7 Tower Hamlets
E1 . . . . 33 A4
Lorne Rd
Finsbury Pk N4 . . . . . 5 B3
3 Richmond TW10 . . 54 B2
Lorn Rd SW9 . . . . . 173 B2
Lorraine Ct 10
NW1 . . . . 13 A1
Lorrimore Rd
SE17 . . . . 48 A4
Lorrimore Sq SE17 . 48 A4
Lorton Ho 9 NW6 . . 23 C4
Lostock Ho 10
SW8 . . . . 171 B2
Lothair Rd S N4 . . . . 6 A4
Lothbury EC2 . . . . . 109 B2
Lothian Rd SW9 . . . 48 A2
Lothrop St W10 . . . . 23 A2
Lots Rd SW10 . . . . 157 A1
Loudoun Rd NW8 . . 79 A3
Loughborough Ct 7
SW9 . . . . 63 A4
Loughborough
Junction Sta
SW9 . . . . 63 A4

Loughborough Pk
SW9 . . . . 63 A3
Loughborough Prim
Sch SW9 . . . . 48 A1
Loughborough Rd SE5,
SW9 . . . . 48 A1
Loughborough St
SE11 . . . . 149 A1
Lough Rd N7 . . . . . . 14 B2
Louisa Cl E9 . . . . . . 25 C4
Louisa Gdns E1 . . . . 25 C1
Louisa Ho SW15 . . . 56 B3
Louisa St E1 . . . . . . 25 C1
Louise Bennett Cl 9
SE24 . . . . 63 A3
Louise De Marillac Ho
12 E1 . . . . 32 B4
Louise White Ho 1
N19 . . . . 4 C3
Louisville Rd
SW17 . . . . 72 C1
Louvaine Rd SW11 . 59 C3
Lovat La EC3 . . . . . . 124 A3
Lovatt Ct SW12 . . . . 73 A3
Loveday Ho 2
SW2 . . . . 74 C3
Lovegrove St SE1 . . 49 C4
Lovegrove Wlk
E14 . . . . 34 B1
Love La EC2 . . . . . 109 A2
Lovelace Ho 12 E8 . 24 B4
Lovelace Rd SE21 . . 75 B3
Lovelinch Cl SE15 . 50 B4
Lovell Ho E8 . . . . . . 24 C4
Lovell Pl SE16 . . . . 41 A3
Loveridge Mews
NW6 . . . . 10 B2
Loveridge Rd NW6 . 10 B2
Lover's Wlk W1 . . . 117 B1
Lovette Ho 4 E3 . . . 26 C2
Lovetts Pl SW18 . . . 59 A3
Love Wlk SE5 . . . . . 48 C1
Low Cross Wood La
SE21 . . . . 76 B1
Lowden Rd SE24 . . . 63 B3
Lowder Ho 6 E1 . . . 32 A1
Lowe Ave E16 . . . . . 35 C4
Lowell Ho 10 SE5 . . 48 B3
Lowell St E14 . . . . . 33 A3
Lower Addison Gdns
W14 . . . . 126 A3
Lower Belgrave St
SW1 . . . . 132 A1
Lower Clapton Rd
E5 . . . . 17 B4
Lower Clarendon Wlk
9 W11 . . . . 31 A3
Lower Comm S
SW15 . . . . 57 A4
Lower Grosvenor Pl
SW1 . . . . 132 B2
Lower Grove Rd
TW10 . . . . 54 B2
Lower James St
W1 . . . . 119 A4
Lower John St
W1 . . . . 119 A4
Lower Lea Crossing
E14, E16 . . . . 35 A2
Lower Mall W6 . . . . 39 A1
Lower Marsh SE1 . 135 B3
Lower Merton Rise
NW3 . . . . 12 A1

Lower Mortlake Rd
TW9 . . . . 54 B4
Lower Pk
Acton W3 . . . . 20 B1
8 Putney SW15 . . . . . 57 C2
LOWER PLACE 20 B3
Lower Place Bsns Ctr
NW10 . . . . 20 B3
Lower Rd SE16 . . . . 40 B4
Lower Richmond Rd
Mortlake SW14,
TW9 . . . . 55 A4
Putney SW15 . . . . 57 B4
Lower Robert St
WC2 . . . . 120 B3
Lower Sloane St
SW1 . . . . 145 B2
Lower Terr NW3 . . . . 2 B1
Lower Thames St
EC3 . . . . 124 A3
Lowerwood Ct
W11 . . . . 31 A3
Loweswater Ho 2 E3 36 B1
Lowfield Rd
Dagenham W3 . . . . . 28 B3
Hampstead NW6 . . . . 10 C1
Lowlands NW3 . . . . 12 A2
Lowman Rd N7 . . . . 14 B4
Lowndes Cl SW1 . . 131 C1
Lowndes Ct
Knightsbridge
SW1 . . . . 131 A2
Marylebone W1 . . . . 104 C1
Lowndes Ho E 131 B2
Lowndes Lo SW1 . 131 A2
Lowndes Pl SW1 . . 131 B1
Lowndes Sq SW1 . 131 A3
Lowndes St SW1 . . 131 A2
Lowood Ho 10 E1 . . 32 B2
Lowood St E1 . . . . . 32 A2
Lowry Ct 3 SE16 . . . 40 A1
Lowther Ho
Pimlico SW1 . . . . . . 147 A1
11 Shoreditch E8 . . . 24 B4
Lowther Prim Sch
SW13 . . . . 46 C4
Lowther Rd
Barnes SW13 . . . . . . 46 C2
Islington N7 . . . . 14 C3
Lowth Rd SE5 . . . . . 48 B1
Loxford Ho SW1 . . 145 C3
Loxham St WC1 . . . 94 B3
Loxley Rd SW18 . . . 71 C3
LTC Coll London
W1 . . . . 104 C2
Lubavitch Boys Prim
Sch 6 E5 . . . . 7 B4
Lubavitch Girls Prim
Sch 8 N16 . . . . 7 A4
Lubavitch House Sch
(Jun Boys) 8 E5 . . 7 B4
Lubbock Ho 21
E14 . . . . 34 A2
Lubbock St SE14 . . . 50 B3
Lucan Ho N1 . . . . . . 87 C3
Lucan Pl SW3 . . . . 144 B3
Lucas Ct SW11 . . . 169 C3
Lucas Ho
2 Clapham SW8 . . . 171 A2
Walham Green
SW10 . . . . 156 B2
Lucas St SE4, SE8 . 51 C2
Lucas Vale Prim Sch
10 SE8 . . . . 51 C2
Lucerne Mews
W8 . . . . . . 31 C1 113 C2
Lucerne Rd N5 . . . . 15 A4

Lucey Rd SE16 . . . 139 B1
Lucey Way SE16 . . 153 C4
Lucien Rd SW18 . . . 71 A2
Lucraft Ho 12 SW2 . 74 A4
Lucy Ashe Ho
SE17 . . . . 150 B3
Lucy Brown Ho
SE1 . . . . 123 A1
Lucy Cres W3 . . . . . 20 B1
Ludgate Broadway
EC4 . . . . 108 B1
Ludgate Cir EC4 . . 108 A1
Ludgate Hill EC4 . . 108 B1
Ludgate Ho EC4 . . 108 A1
Ludgate Sq EC4 . . 108 B1
Ludham NW5 . . . . . 12 B3
Ludlow Ct W3 . . . . . 37 B4
Ludlow St EC1 . . . . 96 C2
Ludovick Wlk
SW15 . . . . 56 A3
Ludwell Ho W14 . . 126 B2
Ludwick Mews
SE14 . . . . 51 A3
Lugard Ho 2 W12 . 30 A1
Lugard Rd SE15 . . . 50 A2
Luke Ho 67 E1 . . . . 32 A3
Luke St EC2 . . 24 A1 98 A2
Lukin St E1 . . . . 32 B3
Lullingstone Ho 4
SE15 . . . . 50 B4
Lullingstone La
SE13 . . . . 67 C1
Lulot Gdns N19 . . . . 4 A2
Lulworth
Camden Town
NW1 . . . . 13 C1
Walworth SE17 . . . 151 B2
Lumiere Ct 7
SW17 . . . . 72 C2
Lumina Bldg 1
E14 . . . . 34 B1
Lumley Ct WC2 . . . 120 B3
Lumley Flats SW1 . 145 B2
Lumley St W1 . . . . 103 C1
Lumsdon NW8 . . . . . 78 B4
Lunan Ho 10 E3 . . . 26 B3
Lund Point E15 . . . . 27 B4
Luntley Pl E1 . . . . . 111 B3
Lupin Cl SW2 . . . . . 75 A2
Lupino Ct SE11 . . . 149 A4
Lupin Point SE1 . . 139 A3
Lupton St NW5 . . . . 13 B4
Lupus St SW1 . . . . 147 A1
Luralda Gdns E14 . . 42 C1
Lurgan Ave W6 . . . . 47 C4
Lurline Gdns
SW11 . . . . 169 C4
Luscombe Ho
SW18 . . . . 58 B2
Luscombe Way
SW8 . . . . 162 A2
Lusher Ho SW15 . . . 57 C1
Lushington Rd
NW10 . . . . 22 A3
Lushington Terr 11
E8 . . . . 16 C3
Luton Pl SE10 . . . . . 52 B3
Luton St NW8 . . . . . 89 C1
Luttrell Ave SW15 . 57 A2
Lutyens Ho SW1 . . 146 C1
Luxborough Ho
W1 . . . . 103 B4
Luxborough St
W1 . . . . 103 B4

Luxborough Twr
W1 . . . . 103 B4
Luxemburg Gdns
W6 . . . . 39 C2
Luxford St SE16 . . . 40 C2
Luxmore St SE4 . . . 51 B2
Luxor St SE5 . . . . . 63 B4
Lyall Mews SW1 . . 131 B1
Lyall Mews W
SW1 . . . . 131 B1
Lyall St SW1 . . . . . 131 B1
Lyal Rd E3 . . . . 26 A3
Lycett Ho 10 SW2 . 74 A4
Lycett Pl 6 W12 . . . 38 C4
Lycott Gr SE22 . . . . 64 B2
Lydden Gr SW18 . . . 71 A4
Lydden Rd SW18 . . 71 A4
Lyford Rd NW1 . . . . 83 A3
Lyford Cl 22 N16 . . 16 A3
Lyford Rd
Brondesbury NW2 . . . 9 C2
Paddington W9 . . . . . 23 B1
Lydgate Ho 8
N16 . . . . 16 A3
Lydhurst Ave SW2 . 74 B2
Lydney Cl
Camberwell SE15 . . . 49 A3
Putney SW19 . . . . . . 70 A2
Lydon Rd SW4 . . . . 61 B4
Lydwell Ho 29
SW8 . . . . 171 B1
Lyford Rd SW18 . . . 72 A3
Lygon Ho 6 N6 . . . . 4 C4
Lygon Ho 9
E2 . . . . 24 C2 99 B4
Lygon Pl SW1 . . . . 132 A1
Lyham Cl SW2 . . . . 62 A1
Lyham Rd SW2 . . . . 62 A1
Lyle St PW15 . . . . . 57 C1
Lyly Ho SE1 . . . . . . 137 C1
Lyme Gr E9 . . . . 17 B1
Lyme Grove Ho 2
E9 . . . . 17 B1
Lyme St NW1 . . . . . 82 C4
Lyminge Gdns SW17,
SW18 . . . . 72 A3
Lymington Mans
NW6 . . . . 11 A2
Lymington Rd
NW6 . . . . 11 A2
Lympstone Gdns
SE15 . . . . 49 C3
Lynbrook Gr SE15 . 49 B3
Lynch Wlk 2 SE8 . . 51 B4
Lyncott Cres SW4 . 61 A3
Lyncourt SE3 . . . . . 52 C1
Lyncroft Gdns
NW6 . . . . 10 C3
Lyncroft Mans 4
NW6 . . . . 10 C3
Lyndale NW2 . . . . . . 1 B1
Lyndale Ave NW2 . . . 1 B1
Lyndale Cl SE3 . . . . 53 B4
Lynde Ho 2 SW4 . . 61 C4
Lynden Gate SW15 . 69 A4
Lyndhurst Gdns
NW3 . . . . 11 B3
Lyndhurst Gr SE5,
SE15 . . . . 49 B1
Lyndhurst Ho 2
SW15 . . . . 68 C4
Lyndhurst House Prep
Sch NW3 . . . . 11 B3

Lyndhurst Lo **3**
E14 . . . . 42 C2
Lyndhurst Rd NW3 . 11 C3
Lyndhurst Sch SE5 .48 C1
Lyndhurst Sq SE15. .49 B2
Lyndhurst Terr
NW3 . . . . .11 C3
Lyndhurst Way
SE15. . . . . .49 B1
Lyneham Wlk E5 . . .18 A3
Lynette Ave SW4 . . .61 B1
Lynford French Ho
SE17. . . . . .150 C2
Lyngham Ct E4 N4. . .5 A4
Lynhurst Ct NW8. . .79 B3
Lynmouth Rd N16. . . .7 B3
Lynne Ct NW6 . . . . . .11 A1
Lynnett Ct E9 . . . . . .18 A3
Lynn Ho SE15 . . . . . .49 C4
Lynn Rd SW12. . . . . .73 A4
Lynton Cl NW10 . . . . .8 B3
Lynton Ct **3** W3 . . . .28 B3
Lynton Est SE1 . . . .153 B3
Lynton Ho **2** W2 . .100 B1
Lynton Lo N5. . . . . . .15 A3
Lynton Mans SE1 . .135 B2
Lynton Rd
  Acton W3 . . . . .28 A2
  Bermondsey SE1 . . .152 A3
  Paddington NW6 . . . .23 B3
Lynton Terr **4** W3 . .28 B3
Lynx Terr SW19. . . . .70 C1
Lyon Ho NW8. . . . . . .90 A1
Lyons Pl NW8 . . . . . .89 B1
Lyon St N1 . . . . .14 B1
Lyons Wlk W14 . . . .140 A4
Lyric Rd SW13. . . . . .46 B2
Lysander Gr N19 . . . .4 C3
Lysander Ho **10**
E2 . . . . .25 A3
Lysander Mews N19 .4 B3
Lysia Ct SW6 . . . . . .47 C3
Lysias Rd SW12. . . . .61 A1
Lysia St SW6 . . . . . . .47 C3
Lysons Wlk SW15. . .56 C2
Lytham St SE17. . . .151 B1
Lyttelton Ct **6** W12 . .38 C4
Lyttleton Ho **10** N19 . . .4 B1
Lytton Ct WC1 . . . . .106 B3
Lytton Gr SW15. . . . .58 A1

M

Mabel Thornton Ho **12**
N16. . . . . .15 C4
Mabledon Pl NW1,
  WC1 . . . . .93 C3
Mablethorpe Rd
SW6 . . . . .154 A1
Mabley St E9 . . . . . .18 A3
MacArthur Ho **4**
SW2 . . . . .74 A4
Macartney Ho
SE10 . . . . .52 C3
Macaulay CE Prim
  Sch SW4 . . . . .61 A3
Macaulay Ct SW4. . .61 A4
Macaulay Ho
  2 Kensal Town
  W10 . . . . .31 A4

Macaulay Ho continued
  10 Stoke Newington
  N16. . . . . .7 A1
Macaulay Rd SW4. . .61 A4
Macaulay Sq SW4 . .61 A3
McAuley Cl SE1 . . . .135 B2
Macauley Mews
SE13 . . . . .52 B1
McAusland Ho **5**
E3 . . . . .26 A3
Macbeth Ho **4** N1 . .24 A3
Macbeth St W6 . . . . .39 A1
McBride Ho **6** E3. . .26 B3
McCall Cl SW4 . . . .172 A2
McCall Ho N7 . . . . . . .14 A4
McCarthy Ct
SW11 . . . . .168 B3
Macclesfield Rd
EC1. . . . . .96 C4
Macclesfield St
W1 . . . . .119 C4
McCoid Way SE1 . . .136 C3
Mcconnell Ho
SW8 . . . . .171 B3
McCrone Mews **3**
NW3 . . . . .11 C2
McCullum Rd E3 . . .26 B4
McDermott Cl
SW11 . . . . .60 A4
McDermott Rd
SE15 . . . . .64 C4
Macdonald Ho **2**
SW11 . . . . .169 B2
McDougall Ct
TW9 . . . . .44 C1
Mcdougall Ho
E2 . . . . .24 C2 99 B3
McDowall Cl E16 . . .35 B4
McDowall Rd SE5 . .48 B2
Macduff Rd SW11 . .169 C4
Mace Cl E1 . . . . .32 A1
Mace St E2 . . . . .25 C3
McEwan Way E15. . .27 C4
Macey Ho
  Battersea SW11 . . . .168 A3
  10 Greenwich SE10 . .52 B4
Macfarlane Rd
W12 . . . . .30 B1
MacFarren Ho **3**
W10 . . . . .23 A2
MacFarren Pl NW1 . .91 C1
McGlashon Ho **19**
E1 . . . . .24 C1 99 B1
McGregor Ct **3**
N1 . . . . .24 A2 98 B4
MacGregor Ho **2**
SW12 . . . . .73 C3
McGregor Rd W11. . .31 B4
Machell Rd SE15 . . .65 B4
McIndoe Ct N1 . . . . .87 B4
McIntosh Ho **11**
SE16 . . . . .40 B2
McIntyre Ct **10**
SW4 . . . . .172 B2
Mackay Ho **33**
W12 . . . . .30 A2
Mackay Rd SW4 . . . .61 A4
McKenna Ho **3**
E3 . . . . .26 B3
Mackennal St NW8 .80 B2
Mackenzie Cl **7**
W12 . . . . .30 A2
Mackenzie Rd N7. . .14 B2

Mackenzie Wlk
E14 . . . . .33 C1
McKerrell Rd SE15. .49 C2
Mackeson Rd NW3 .12 B4
Mackie Ho **16**
SW2 . . . . .74 C4
Mackie Rd SW2 . . . .74 C4
McKiernan Ct **2**
SW11 . . . . .168 A2
McKinnon Wood Ho
16 E2 . . . . . . .24 C2 99 B3
Mackintosh La E9 . .17 C3
Macklin St WC2 . . .106 B2
Mackonochie Ho
EC1. . . . . .107 B4
Mackrow Wlk **11**
E14 . . . . .34 B2
Macks Rd SE16 . . . .153 C4
Mackworth Ho
NW1 . . . . .92 C4
Mackworth St
NW1 . . . . .92 C4
Mac Laren Mews
SW15 . . . . .57 B3
Maclean Ho **4**
SW17 . . . . .71 C3
Macleod Ct SE21 . . .76 C3
McLeod's Mews
SW7 . . . . .142 B4
Macleod St SE17 . .151 A1
Maclise Rd W14. . . .126 A1
McManus Ho **2**
SW11 . . . . .59 B4
Mcmillan Ho SE4 . .66 A4
Macmillan Ho
  Cricklewood NW2. . . .9 A4
  Lisson Gr NW8. . . . . .90 B3
McMillan St SE8 . . .51 C4
Mcmorran Ho **4**
N7 . . . . .14 A4
Macnamara Ho
SW10 . . . . .157 B2
Mcneil Ho SE5. . . . . .49 A1
McNicol Dr NW10 . .20 B3
Maconochies Rd **2**
E14 . . . . .42 A1
Macquarie Way
E14 . . . . .42 A2
Macready Ho W1. . .102 B3
Macready Pl **2**
N7 . . . . .14 A4
Macroom Ho W9 . . .23 B2
Macroom Rd W9 . . .23 B2
Mac's Pl EC4 . . . . . .107 C2
Madame Tussaud's
NW1 . . . . .91 B1
Madani Girls Sch **3**
E1 . . . . .111 C2
Maddams St E3 . . . .27 A1
Maddocks Ho **3**
E1 . . . . .32 A2
Maddock Way
SE17. . . . . .48 A4
Maddox St W1 . . . .118 C4
Madinah Rd
  7 Dalston E8 . . . . .16 C2
  London E8. . . . . .16 C3
Madison Ho E3 . . . .27 B2
Madras Pl N7 . . . . . .14 C2
Madron St SE17 . . .152 B2
Mafeking Ave
E6 . . . . .35 A4
Magdala Ave N19. . . .4 B2
Magdalene Cl **7**
SE15 . . . . .50 A1

Magdalene Ho **7**
SW15 . . . . .57 C1
Magdalen Pas E1 . .125 A4
Magdalen Rd
SW18 . . . . .71 C3
Magdalen St SE1 . .124 A1
Magee St SE11 . . . .163 B4
Magellan Ho **10**
E1 . . . . .25 C1
Magellan Pl **23**
E14 . . . . .41 C2
Magnin Cl **3** E8. . . .24 C4
Magnolia Ct
  Richmond TW9 . . . . .45 A2
  Wandsworth SW11 . .60 B1
Magnolia Ho **3**
SE8 . . . . .51 B4
Magnolia Pl SW4 . . .62 A2
Magnolia Rd W4 . . .45 A4
Magnolia Wharf
W4 . . . . .45 A4
Magpie Ho **7** E3. . .26 B4
Magpie Pl SE14. . . .51 A4
Magri Wlk **21** E1 . .32 B4
Maguire St SE1 . . . .139 A4
Mahatma Gandhi Ind
  Est **1** SE24. . . . . .63 A3
Mahogany Cl SE16. .33 A1
Mahoney Ho SE14 . .51 B2
Maida Ave W2 . . . . . .89 A1
MAIDA VALE 88 A4
Maida Vale W9 . . . . .88 C3
Maida Vale Sta
W9 . . . . .88 B4
Maiden La
  Borough The SE1 . . .123 A2
  Camden Town NW1 . .13 C1
  Strand WC2 . . . . . . .120 B4
Maidenstone Hill
SE10 . . . . .52 B2
Maidstone Bldgs
SE1 . . . . .123 B1
Maidstone Ho **3**
E14 . . . . .34 A3
Mail Coach Yd **23**
E2 . . . . .24 A2 98 B4
Main Yd E9. . . . . .18 C2
Maismore St SE15 . .49 C4
Maitland Cl **3**
SE10 . . . . .52 A3
Maitland Ct **2** W2 .115 B4
Maitland Ho
  Chelsea SW1 . . . . . .160 C4
  South Hackney
  E2 . . . . .25 B3
MAITLAND PARK . . .12 B2
Maitland Park Rd
NW3 . . . . .12 B2
Maitland Park Villas
NW3 . . . . .12 B2
Maitland Pl E5 . . . . .17 B4
Majestic Ct N4 . . . . . .6 A3
Major Cl SW9 . . . . . .63 A4
Majorie Mews **6**
E1 . . . . .32 C3
Major Rd SE16 . . . .139 C3
Makepeace Ave
N6. . . . . .3 C2
Makepeace Mans
N6. . . . . .3 C2
Makins St SW3 . . . .144 B3
Malabar Ct **8**
W12 . . . . .30 A2
Malabar St E14. . . . .41 C4
Malam Ct SE11 . . . .149 B3
Malam Gdns **3**
E14 . . . . .34 A2

Malay Ho **2** E1 . . . .32 B1
Malbrook Rd
SW15 . . . . .57 A3
Malcolm Ho **10** N1 .24 A3
Malcolm PI E2 . . . . . .25 B1
Malcolm Rd E1 . . . . .25 B1
Malcolmson Ho
SW1 . . . . .147 C1
Malden Cres NW1 . .12 C2
Malden Pl NW5. . . . .12 C3
Malden Rd NW5 . . . .12 C2
Maldon Cl
  Camberwell SE5. . . . .64 A4
  Shoreditch N1. . . . . .87 A4
  Stratford New Town
  E15. . . . . .19 C3
Maldon Rd W3. . . . . .28 B2
Malet PI WC1 . . . . . .93 B1
Malet St WC1 . . . . .105 C4
Maley Ave SE27. . . . .75 A2
Malfort Rd SE5 . . . . .64 A4
Malins Ct SW12 . . . .60 C1
Mallams Mews **1**
SW9 . . . . .63 A4
Mallard Cl
  1 Hackney E9. . . . .18 B2
  Kilburn NW6. . . . . . .23 C4
Mallard Ho
  8 Camberwell
  SE15 . . . . .49 B2
  St John's Wood
  NW8 . . . . .80 A1
Mallard Point **8**
E3 . . . . .26 C2
Mallet Ho **11**
SW15 . . . . .56 C2
Mallet Rd SE13 . . . .67 C1
Mall Galleries
SW1 . . . . .119 C2
Malling SE13 . . . . . .67 A2
Mallinson Rd
SW11 . . . . .60 B2
Mallinson Sp Ctr
N6. . . . . .3 A4
Mallon Gdns E1 . . .111 A3
Mallord St SW3 . . . .157 C4
Mallory Cl SE4 . . . . .66 A3
Mallory Ct SE4 . . . . .66 A3
Mallory Ho NW8 . . .90 B2
Mallow Ct SE13. . . . .52 B1
Mallow St EC1. . . . . .97 B2
Mallow Ho E14 . . . . .34 A4
Mall Studios **5**
NW3 . . . . .12 B3
Mall The
  Mortlake SW14 . . . . .55 B2
  St James SW1 . . . .119 B1
Malmesbury **30** E2 .25 B3
Malmesbury Prim Sch
22 E3 . . . . .26 B2
Malmesbury Rd
  3 Bow E3 . . . . . . .26 B3
  Newham E16 . . . . . .35 A4
Malmesbury Terr
E16 . . . . .35 B4
Malmsey Ho SE11 . .149 A2
Malmsmead Ho
E9 . . . . .18 A3
Malorees Jun & Inf
  Schs NW6. . . . . .9 C1
Malpas Rd
  Hackney E8. . . . . . . .17 A2
  New Cross SE4 . . . . .51 B1
Malta St EC1 . . . . . .96 B2
Maltby St SE1 . . . .138 C2
Malthouse Dr W4. . .46 B4

Malthouse Pas
SW13 . . . . 46 A1
Malting Ho E14 . . . . . 33 B2
Maltings W4 . . . . 36 C1
Maltings Cl SW13 . . . 46 A1
Maltings Lo W44 . . . . 46 A3
Maltings Pl
Bermondsey SE1 . . **138** B4
Parsons Green
SW6 . . . . 166 B3
Malt Mill SE1 . . . . . 124 C1
Malton Mews **1**
W10 . . . . 31 A3
Malton Rd W10 . . . . 31 A3
Maltravers St
WC2 . . . . 121 B4
Malt St SE1 . . . . . . 49 C4
Malva Cl SW18 . . . . 59 A2
Malvern Cl W10 . . . 31 B4
Malvern Ct
15 Shepherd's Bush
W12 . . . . 38 C4
South Kensington
SW7 . . . . 143 C4
Malvern Gdns
London N16 . . . . 7 B3
SE17 . . . . 151 A1
Malvern Mews
NW6 . . . . 23 C2
Malvern Pl NW6 . . . 23 B2
Malvern Rd
Dalston E8 . . . . 16 C1
Maida Vale NW6 . . . 23 C2
Upper Holloway N19 . 4 C3
Malvern Terr N1 . . . . 85 B4
Malwood Rd SW12 . 61 A1
Malyons Rd SE13 . . 67 A2
Malyons Terr SE13 . 67 A2
Managers St **5**
E14 . . . . 34 B1
Manaton Cl SE15 . . 50 A1
Manbre Rd W6 . . . . 47 B4
Manchester Dr
W10 . . . . 23 A1
Manchester Gr
E14 . . . . 42 B1
Manchester Ho
SE17 . . . . 151 A2
Manchester Mans
N19 . . . . 4 C4
Manchester Mews
W1 . . . . 103 B3
Manchester Rd
E14 . . . . 42 B3
Manchester Sq
W1 . . . . 103 C2
Manchester St
W1 . . . . 103 B3
Manchuria Rd
SW11 . . . . 60 C1
Manciple St SE1 . . 137 C2
Mandalay Ho **5**
N16 . . . . 15 C4
Mandalay Rd SW4 . 61 B2
Mandarin Ct **6**
SE8 . . . . 51 C4
Mandela Cl **38**
W12 . . . . 30 A2
Mandela Ho **18**
E2 . . . . 24 B2 **98** C4
Mandela Rd E16 . . . 35 C3
Mandela St
Camden Town
NW1 . . . . 83 A4
Kennington SW9 . . 163 B1

Mandela Way SE1 152 B4
Manderville Ho
SE1 . . . . 153 A2
Mandeville Cl **5**
SE3 . . . . 53 B3
Mandeville Ct
NW3 . . . . 11 A3
Mandeville Ctyd
SW11 . . . . 169 B3
Mandeville Ho **8**
SW4 . . . . 61 B2
Mandeville Pl W1 103 C2
Mandrake Rd
SW17 . . . . 72 B1
Mandrell Rd SW2 . . 62 A2
Manette St W1 . . . 105 C1
Manfred Ct **7**
SW15 . . . . 58 B2
Manfred Rd SW15 . 58 B2
Manger Rd N7 . . . . 14 A2
Manilla St E14 . . . . 41 C4
Manitoba Ct **29**
SE16 . . . . 40 B4
Manley Ct N16 . . . . . 7 B1
Manley Ho SE11 . . 149 B2
Manley St NW1 . . . 81 B4
Manneby Prior N1 . 85 A1
Mannering Ho **16**
SW2 . . . . 62 B2
Manningford Cl
EC1 . . . . 96 A4
Manning Ho **8**
W11 . . . . 31 A3
Manning Pl TW10 . 54 B1
Manningtree Cl
SW19 . . . . 70 A3
Manningtree St **2**
E1 . . . . 111 B2
Manny Shinwell Ho
SW6 . . . . 155 A3
Manor Ave SE4 . . . 51 B1
Manor Circus TW9 54 C4
Manor Ct
2 Brixton SW2 . . . . 62 B2
Camberwell SE15 . . 49 B2
Gunnersbury W3 . . . 36 C2
Parsons Green
SW6 . . . . 166 B3
Streatham SW16 . . 74 A1
Manorfield Cl **3**
N19 . . . . 13 B4
Manorfield Prim Sch
8 E14 . . . . 34 A4
Manor Gdns
5 Chiswick W4 . . . 38 A1
Clapham SW4 . . . 171 A1
Gunnersbury W3 . . . 36 C2
Richmond TW10,
TW9 . . . . 54 B3
Upper Holloway N7 . 5 A1
Manor Gr
Deptford SE15 . . . . 50 B4
Richmond TW9 . . . 54 C4
Manor Gt SW15 . . . 58 A2
Manor Ho NW1 . . . 102 B4
Manor House Ct
W9 . . . . 88 C1
Manor House Dr
NW6 . . . . 9 C1
Manor House Sta
N4 . . . . 6 A3
Manor Lo NW2 . . . . 9 C2

Manor Mews
New Cross SE4 . . . . 51 B1
Paddington NW6 . . . 23 C3
Manor Oak Mans
SE22 . . . . 65 A1
Manor Par N16 . . . . 7 B2
Manor Park Par
SE13 . . . . 67 C3
Manor Park Rd
NW10 . . . . 21 B4
Manor Pk TW9 . . . . 54 B3
Manor Pl SE17 . . . 150 C2
Manor Rd
Richmond TW10,
TW9 . . . . 54 B3
Stamford Hill N16 . . . 7 A3
Manor Specl Sch
SW3 . . . . 158 A4
Manor The N1 . . . . 15 B1
Manor Way W3 . . . 36 C2
Manresa Rd SW3 144 A1
Mansel Ct SW11 . . 168 B3
Mansell Ho SW8 . . 171 A4
Mansell Rd W3 . . . 37 C4
Mansell St E1 . . . . 111 A1
Mansell Rd N16 . . . 7 B1
Mansfield Ct **27**
E2 . . . . 24 B4
Mansfield Ho
SW15 . . . . 57 C1
Mansfield Mews
W1 . . . . 104 A3
Mansfield Pl **28**
NW3 . . . . 11 B4
Mansfield Rd
Acton W3 . . . . 20 A1
Maitland Pk NW3 . . 12 B4
Mansfield St W1 . . 104 A3
Mansfield Ct SW9 . 173 C4
Mansion Gdns NW3 . 2 A1
Mansion House EC4 109 B1
Mansion House St
EC2 . . . . 109 B1
Mansion House Sta
EC4 . . . . 123 A4
Mansions The
NW6 . . . . 10 B3
Manson Mews
SW7 . . . . 143 B3
Manson Pl SW7 . . 143 B3
Manston Ho **1**
W14 . . . . 126 B1
Mantell Ho SW4 . . 61 B2
Mantle Rd SE4 . . . 66 A4
Manton Ho N16 . . . 6 C2
Mantua St **23**
SW11 . . . . 59 C4
Mantus Cl E1 . . . . . 25 B1
Mantus Rd E1 . . . . 25 B1
Manville Gdns
SW17 . . . . 73 A1
Manville Rd SW17 . 73 A1
Manwood Rd SE4 . 66 B1
Many Gates SW12 73 A2
Mapesbury Ct
NW2 . . . . 10 A3
Mapesbury Rd
NW2 . . . . 10 A2
Mapeshill Pl NW2 . . 9 B2
Mapes Ho **7** NW6 10 A1

Mape St E2 . . . . . . 25 A1
Maple Ave W3 . . . . 29 A1
Maple Cl SW4 . . . . 61 C1
Maple Ct **3** NW2 . . 9 C4
Mapledene Est E8 . 16 C1
Mapledene Rd E8 . 16 C1
Maple Ho
11 Maitland Pk
NW3 . . . . 12 B2
5 New Cross SE8 . 51 B3
4 Richmond TW9 . 45 A2
SE16 . . . . 40 C4
Maple Lo SW15 . . . 58 A1
Maple Mews NW6 . 78 A2
Maple Pl W1 . . . . . 93 A1
Maples Pl E1 . . . . . 32 A4
Maple St
5 Bethnal Green
E2 . . . . 25 A3
Fitzrovia W1 . . . . . . 93 A1
Maplestead Rd
SW2 . . . . 74 B4
Mapleton Cres
SW18 . . . . 59 A1
Mapleton Rd
SW18 . . . . 59 A1
Maple Wlk W10 . . . 22 C1
Maplin St E3 . . . . . 26 B2
Marada Ho NW6 . . 10 A1
Marais W4 . . . . 45 B3
Marban Rd W9 . . . . 23 B2
Marble Arch W1 . 117 A4
Marble Arch Sta
W1 . . . . 103 A1
Marble Cl W3 . . . . . 28 A1
Marbleford Ct **4**
N6 . . . . 4 C4
Marble Ho W9 . . . . 23 B1
Marcella Rd SW9 . 173 B1
Marchant Ho **13**
SW2 . . . . 62 B2
Marchant St SE14 . 51 A4
Marchbank Rd
W14 . . . . 155 A4
Marchmont St
WC1 . . . . 94 A2
Marchwood Cl **9**
SE5 . . . . 49 A3
Marcia Rd SE1 . . . 152 B3
Marcilly Rd SW18 . 59 C2
Marcol Ho W1 . . . 104 B2
Marcon Ct **22** E8 . 17 A3
Marcon Pl E8 . . . . 17 A3
Marco Rd W6 . . . . 39 B3
Marcus Ct TW8 . . . 44 A3
Marcus Garvey Mews
SE22 . . . . 65 A2
Marcus Garvey Way
8 SE24 . . . . . . 62 C3
Marcus Ho **14**
SE15 . . . . 49 B2
Marcus St SW18 . . 59 A1
Marcus Terr SW18 . 59 A1
Marden Ho **6** E8 . 17 A3
Marden Sq SE16 . . 40 A3
Mardyke Ho SE17 151 C4
Maresfield Gdns
NW3 . . . . 11 B2
Mare St E8 . . . . . . 17 A1
Margaret Bondfield
Ho
6 Bow E3 . . . . . 26 A3

Margaret Bondfield
Ho continued
22 Kentish Town
N7 . . . . 13 C3
Margaret Ct W1 . . 104 C2
Margaret Herbison Ho
SW6 . . . . 155 A3
Margaret Ho **16**
W6 . . . . 39 B1
Margaret Ingram Cl
SW6 . . . . 154 C3
Margaret Mcmillan
Ho **10** N19 . . . . . . 4 C4
Margaret Rd N16 . . 7 B3
Margaret Rutherford
Pl **8** SW12 . . . . 73 B3
Margaret St W1 . . 104 C2
Margaretta Terr
SW3 . . . . 158 B4
Margaret White Ho
NW1 . . . . 93 B4
Margate Rd SW2 . . 62 A2
Margery Fry Ct N7 . 5 A1
Margery St WC1 . . 95 B3
Margravine Gdns
Hammersmith W6 . 39 C1
West Kensington
W14 . . . . 140 A2
Margravine Rd
W6 . . . . 154 A4
Marham Gdns
SW18 . . . . 72 A3
Maria Cl **13** SE1 . 153 C4
Maria Fidelis Convent
Sch (Lower) NW1 93 A3
Maria Fidelis Convent
Sch (Upper) NW1 93 A4
Marian Ct E9 . . . . . 17 B3
Marian Pl E2 . . . . . 25 A3
Marian Sq E2 . . . . . 25 A3
Marian St **2** E2 . . 25 A3
Marian Way NW10 . 8 B1
Maria Terr E1 . . . . . 25 C1
Maribor **15** SE10 . 52 B3
Marie Curie SE5 . . 49 A2
Marie Lloyd Ct **13**
SW9 . . . . 62 C3
Marie Lloyd Gdns **1**
N19 . . . . 5 A4
Marie Lloyd Ho N1 87 B1
Marie Stopes Ct **3**
N19 . . . . 5 A4
Marigold St SE16 . 40 A4
Marina Ct **3** E3 . . 26 C2
Marina Point **4**
E14 . . . . 42 A3
Marinefield Rd
SW6 . . . . 166 B2
Marinel Ho **25** SE5 48 B3
Mariners Mews
E14 . . . . 42 C2
Marine St SE16 . . 139 B2
Marine Twr **29**
SE8 . . . . 51 B4
Marion Richardson
Prim Sch **17** E1 . 32 C3
Marischal Rd SE13 67 C4
Maritime Greenwich
Coll **13** SE8 . . . . 51 C3
Maritime Ho **5**
SW4 . . . . 61 B4
Maritime Quay **5**
E14 . . . . 41 C1
Maritime St E3 . . . . 26 B1

Marius Mans 3
SW17 . . . . .72 C2
Marius Rd SW17. . .72 C2
Marjorie Gr SW11 . .60 B3
Market Ct W1 . . . .104 C2
Market La W12 . . . .39 B4
Market Mews W1 118 A1
Market Pl
3 Acton W3 . . . . . .28 B1
1 Bermondsey
SE16 . . . . .40 A2
Marylebone W1 . . .104 C2
Market Rd
Barnsbury N7. . . . . .14 A2
Richmond TW9 . . . . .54 C4
Market Sq E14 . . . .34 A3
Market St E1. . . . .110 C4
Market Studios 14
W12 . . . . .39 B4
Market Way E14. . .34 A3
Market Yd Mews
SE1 . . . . .138 C2
Markham Pl SW3 144 C2
Markham Sq SW3 144 C2
Markham St SW3. 144 B2
Mark Ho 3 E2. . . . .25 C2
Mark La EC3. . . . .124 B4
Markland Ho W10 . .30 C2
Mark Mans 38 C4
Marksbury Ave
TW9 . . . . .54 C4
Mark Sq EC2 .24 A1 98 A2
Mark St EC2 . .24 A1 98 A2
Markstone Ho
SE1 . . . . .136 A3
Markyate Ho 6
W10 . . . . .22 B1
Marland Ho SW1 .131 A2
Marlborough
11 Putney SW19 . . .69 C3
St John's Wood W9 . .88 C4
Marlborough Ave 3
E8 . . . . .24 C4
Marlborough Cl
SE17 . . . . .150 B3
Marlborough Cres
W4 . . . . .38 A3
Marlborough Ct
Kensington W8. . . .141 B4
Marylebone W1 . . .104 C1
Marlborough Flats
SW3 . . . . .144 B4
Marlborough Gr
SE1 . . . . .153 B1
Marlborough Hill
NW8 . . . . .79 A3
Marlborough Ho
Marylebone NW1. . .92 B2
Richmond TW10 . . . .54 C2
Stoke Newington N4 . .6 B3
Marlborough Ho
SW1 . . . . .119 A1
Marlborough Lo
SW19 . . . . .69 C1
Marlborough Lo
38 Stepney E1 . . . . .25 B1
St John's Wood
NW8 . . . . .78 C2
Marlborough Mans 5
NW6 . . . . .10 C3
Marlborough Mews 16
SW2 . . . . .62 B3
Marlborough Pl
NW8 . . . . .79 A2

Marlborough Prim
Sch SW3 . . . . . . .144 B3
Marlborough Rd
Acton Green W4. . . .37 B1
Richmond TW10 . . . .54 B1
St James SW1 . . . .119 A1
Upper Holloway N19 . .5 A2
Marlborough St
SW3 . . . . .144 B3
Marlborough Trad Est
TW9 . . . . .45 A2
Marlborough Yd
N19 . . . . .4 C2
Marlbury NW8. . . . .78 B3
Marley Ho 14 W11. .30 C2
Marley Wlk NW2 . . .9 B3
Marlins Ho SW15 . .58 A2
Marloes Rd W8 . . .128 A1
Marlow Ct NW6 . . . .9 C1
Marlow Ho
Bermondsey SE1 . . .138 C2
16 Kensington W2. .100 B1
44 Spitalfields
E2 . . . . . .24 B2 98 C3
Marlow Studio
Workshops 43
E2 . . . . . .24 B2 98 C3
Marlow Way SE16 . .40 C4
Marl Rd SW18 . . . .59 B3
Marlstone Ho 92 B3
Marlton St SE10 . . .43 B1
Marmara Apts 4
E16 . . . . .35 C2
Marmion Ho 13
SW12 . . . . .73 A4
Marmion Mews 4
SW11 . . . . .60 C4
Marmont Rd SW11. .60 C3
Marmora Ho SE15 . .49 C3
Marmora Rd E1. . . .33 A4
Marmora St SE22 . .65 B1
Marner Prim Sch 6
E3 . . . . .27 A1
Marne St W10 . . . . .23 A2
Marney Rd SW11 . . .60 C3
Marnfield Cres
SW2 . . . . .74 B3
Marnham Ave
NW2 . . . . .10 A4
Marnock Ho SE17 151 B2
Marnock Rd SE4. . .66 B2
Maroon St E14 . . . .33 A4
Marquess Rd N1 . . .15 C2
Marquis Ct N4. . . . .5 B3
Marquis Rd
Finsbury Pk N4. . . . .5 C4
Kentish Town NW1. . .13 C2
Marrick Cl SW15 . . .56 C3
Marrick Ho 8
NW6 . . . . .78 B3
Marriott Rd N4. . . . .5 B3
Marryat Ct 12 W6. .39 A2
Marryat Ho SW1. . .146 C1
Marryat Sq SW6. . .164 A4
Marsala Rd SE13 . .67 A3
Marsalis Ho 3 E3 . .26 C2
Marsden Rd SE15 . .64 B4
Marsden St NW5 . . .12 C2
Marshall Ho

Marshall Ct SW4 . .172 B3
Marshall Ho
Paddington NW6 . . . .23 B3
Shoreditch N1. . . . . .87 C2
Walworth SE17. . . .151 B2
Marshall Rd E10. . . .19 A4
Marshall St L Ctr
W1 . . . . .105 A1
Marshall's Pl
SE16 . . . . .139 A1
Marshall St W1 . . .105 A1
Marshalsea Rd
SE1 . . . . .137 A4
Marsham St
18 Putney SW19 . . .69 C3
Westminster SW1 . .147 C4
Marsham St SW1 . .147 C4
Marsh Ct E8. . . . . .16 C2
Marshfield St E14 . .42 B3
Marsh Gate Bsns Ctr
E15 . . . . .27 B3
Marshgate Sch
TW10 . . . . .54 B2
Marsh Hill E9 . . . . .18 A3
Marsh Ho
Nine Elms SW8. . . .171 A4
Pimlico SW1. . . . . .147 C1
Marsh St E14. . . . . .42 A2
Marsh Wall E14 . . . .42 A4
Marshwood Ho 10
NW6 . . . . .23 C4
Marsland Cl SE17. .150 B1
Marsom Ho 5 N1. . .87 B1
Marston 8 SE17 . . .151 A4
Marston Cl NW6. . . .11 B1
Marston Ho 2
SW9 . . . . .173 C1
Marsworth Ho 8
E2 . . . . .24 C4
Martaban Rd N16. . . .7 B2
Martello St E8. . . . .17 A1
Martello Terr E8. . . .17 A1
Martell Rd SE21 . . .75 C1
Martel Pl E8 . . . . . .16 B2
Martha's Bldgs
EC1. . . . . .97 B2
Martha St E1 . . . . .32 B3
Martin Ct 15 E14 . . .42 B4
Martindale SW14 . . .55 B2
Martindale Ave 2
E16 . . . . .35 C2
Martindale Ho 23
E14 . . . . .34 A2
Martineau Rd
SW1 . . . . .73 A4
Martineau Mews
N5. . . . . .15 A4
Martineau Rd N5. . .15 A4
Martin Ho
Newington SE1 . . . .137 A1
South Lambeth
SW8 . . . . .162 A2
Martin La EC4. . . .123 C4
Martlett Ct WC2 . .106 B1
Bartlett Ct NW3. . . .11 A4
Martley Ho SW8 . .171 A4
Martock Ct 10
SE15 . . . . .50 A2
Marton Rd 2 N16. . . .7 A1
Marvel Ho 5 SE5. . .48 C3
Marville Rd SW6 . .154 C1
Marvin St 8 E8 . . . .17 A2
Marwell Ct SE3. . . .52 C1

Mary Adelaide Cl
SW15 . . . . .68 A1
Mary Adelaide Ho
W2 . . . . .101 C4
Mary Ann Bldgs
SE8 . . . . .51 C4
Mary Datchelor Cl
SE5. . . . . .48 C2
Mary Dine Ct
SW8 . . . . .163 A1
Mary Gn NW8 . . . . .78 B4
Mary Ho
8 Hammersmith
W6 . . . . .39 B1
6 Stockwell SW9 . .172 C1
Mary James Ho 22
E2 . . . . .24 C3
Mary Jones Ho 20
E14 . . . . .33 C2
Maryland Rd
Paddington W9 . . . .23 C1
Stratford New Town
E15 . . . . .19 C3
Marylands Rd W9 . .88 A1
Maryland St E15 . . .19 C3
Mary Lawrenson Pl 3
SE3 . . . . .53 C3
MARYLEBONE . . .104 B2
Marylebone Flyover
NW1. . . . . .102 A3
Marylebone High St
W1 . . . . .103 C4
Marylebone La
W1 . . . . .103 C2
Marylebone Mews
W1 . . . . .104 A3
Marylebone Pas
W1 . . . . .105 A2
Marylebone Rd
NW1. . . . . .103 A4
Marylebone St
W1 . . . . .103 C3
Marylebone Sta
NW1 . . . . .90 C1
Marylee Way
SE11 . . . . .149 A3
Mary McArthur Ho 12
N19 . . . . .4 C4
Mary Macarthur Ho
16 Globe Town
E2 . . . . .25 C2
14 W14 . . . . .154 A4
Maryon Mews
NW3 . . . . .12 A4
Mary Pl W11 . .31 A2 112 A3
Mary's Cl NW6 . . . .90 B2
Mary Secole Cl 2
E8 . . . . .24 B4
Mary Smith Ct
SW5 . . . . .141 C3
Mary St
5 Canning Town
E16 . . . . .35 B4
Shoreditch N1. . . . . .87 A3
Mary Terr NW1 . . . .82 C3
Mary Wharrie Ho 4
NW3 . . . . .12 B1
Masbro' Rd W14. . . .39 C3
Mascotte Rd 2
SW15 . . . . .57 C3
Mascotts Cl NW2 . . .1 A1
Masefield Ho 4
NW6 . . . . .23 C2
Mashie Rd W3. . . . .29 A3
Maskall Cl SW2. . . .74 C3

Maskell Rd SW17 . .71 B1
Maskelyne Cl
SW11 . . . . .168 B4
Mason Cl
Bermondsey
SE16 . . . . .153 C2
Newham E16 . . . . .35 C2
Mason Ho
16 Bermondsey
SE16 . . . . .153 C2
18 Hackney E9. . . . .17 B1
Mason's Arms Mews
W1 . . . . .118 A2
Mason's Ct EC2 . .109 B2
Mason's Pl EC1. . . .96 C4
Mason St SE17 . . . .151 C4
Mason Yd
Finsbury EC1 . . . . . .96 B4
St James SW1 . . . .119 A2
Massie Rd E8 . . . . .16 C2
Massinger St SE1,
SE17 . . . . .152 A3
Massingham St E1 .25 C1
Mast Ct 17 SE16 . . .41 A2
Masterman Ho 8
SE5. . . . . .48 C3
Masters Dr SE16 . . .40 A1
Masters Lo 24 E1. . .32 B3
Master's St 18 E1. . .32 C4
Mast House Terr
E14. . . . . .41 C2
Masthouse Terrace
Pier SE8 . . . . .41 C1
Mastin Ho SW18. . .70 C3
Mast L Ctr The
SE16. . . . . .41 C4
Mastmaker Rd
E14. . . . . .41 C4
Matara Mews
SE17. . . . . .150 C1
Matching Ct 14 E3. .26 C2
Matham Gr SE22 . . .64 B3
Matheson Lang Ho
SE1 . . . . .135 B3
Matheson Rd
W14 . . . . .140 C3
Mathews Yd WC2 .106 A1
Mathieson Ct SE1 .136 B3
Mathison Ho
SW10 . . . . .156 C2
Matilda Gdns 10
E3 . . . . .26 C3
Matilda Ho E1. . . .125 B2
Matilda St N1 . . . . .85 A4
Matlock Cl SE24. . . .63 B3
Matlock Ct
7 Herne Hill SE5. . . .63 C3
St John's Wood
NW8 . . . . .78 C2
Matlock St E14. . . . .33 A3
Maton Ho SW6 . . . .154 C2
Matson Ho
9 Bermondsey
SE16 . . . . .40 A3
16 Homerton E9. . . .17 C2
Matthew Cl W10. . . .22 C1
Matthew Parker St
SW1 . . . . .133 C3
Matthews Ct N5 . . .15 B4
Matthews Ho 3
E14 . . . . .33 C4
Matthews St
SW11 . . . . .168 C2
Matthias Ct 12
TW10 . . . . .54 A1

Matthias Ho 2	
N16	16 A3
Matthias Rd N16	16 A3
Mattingly Way 5	
SE15	49 B3
Maude Ho 3 E2	24 C3
Maude Rd SE5	49 B2
Maudslay Ho TW8	36 A1
Maudsley Hospl	
SE5	48 C1
Maud St E16	35 B4
Maud Wilkes Cl 10	
NW5	13 B3
Maugham Ct 5	
W3	37 B3
Mauleverer Rd	
SW2	62 A2
Maundeby Wlk	
NW10	8 A2
Maunsel St SW1	147 B4
Maurer Ct SE10	43 B3
Maury Rd N16	7 C1
Maverton Rd	
SE23	26 C4
Mavor Ho N1	85 A3
Mawbey Ho 3 SE1	153 A1
Mawbey Pl SE1	153 A1
Mawbey Rd SE1	153 A1
Mawbey St SW8	162 A1
Mawdley Ho SE1	135 C3
Mawson Ct N1	87 C3
Mawson Ho EC1	107 B4
Mawson La W4	46 B4
Maxden Ct SE15	64 C4
Maxted Rd SE15	64 B4
Maxwell Ct SE21	76 C3
Maxwell Rd SW6	156 B1
Maya Cl SE15	50 A1
Mayall Rd SE24	63 A2
Maybury Ct SW1	103 C3
Maybury Gdns	
NW10	9 A2
Maybury Mews N6	4 B4
Maydew Ho SE16	40 B2
Maydwell Ho 6	
E14	33 C4
MAYFAIR	118 A3
Mayfair Pl W1	118 B2
Mayfield Ave W4	38 A2
Mayfield Cl	
Clapham Pk SW4	61 C2
Dalston E8	16 B2
Mayfield Ho	
8 Bethnal Green	
E2	25 A3
Stamford Hill N16	7 A4
Mayfield Mans	
SW15	58 B2
Mayfield Rd	
Acton W3	37 A4
Bedford Pk W12	38 A4
Dalston E8	16 B1
Mayflower Cl SE16	40 C2
Mayflower Prim Sch	
22 E14	34 A3
Mayflower Rd	
SW9	62 A4
Mayflower St 1	
SE16	40 B4

Mayford NW1	83 A2
Mayford Cl SW12	72 B4
Mayford Rd SW12	72 C4
Maygood Ho N1	85 B2
Maygood St N1	85 B2
Maygrove Rd NW6	10 B2
Mayhew Ct 5 SE5	63 C3
Maylands Ho SW3	144 B3
Maylie Ho 4 SE16	40 A4
Maynard Cl SW6	156 B1
Maynard Ho E1	26 A2
Maynards Quay E1	32 B2
Mayne Ct 8	16 C4
Mayo Ho 10 E1	32 B4
Mayola Rd E5	17 B4
Mayo Rd NW10	8 A3
May's Buildings Mews 8	
SE10	52 C3
Mays Ct WC2	120 A3
Mays Ct SE10	52 C3
Maysoule Rd	
SW11	59 C3
May St W14	141 A1
Mayston Mews 3	
E8	43 C1
Maythorne Cotts	
SE13	67 C1
Mayton St N7	5 B1
May Tree Ho SE4	66 B4
Maytree Wlk SW2	74 C2
Mayward Ho 7	
SE5	49 A2
Maze Hill SE10,	
SE3	53 A4
Maze Hill Lodge 7	
SE10	53 A4
Maze Hill Sta SE10	53 A4
Mazenod Ave	
NW6	10 C1
Maze Rd TW9	44 C3
Mead Cl 13	
NW1	12 C1
Meadcroft Rd	
SE17	48 A4
Meade Cl W4	45 A4
Meader Ct SE14	50 C3
Mead Ho	
W11	31 B1 112 C2
Mead Lo W4	37 C4
Meadowbank	
NW3	12 B1
Meadow Bank 8	
SW15	58 B2
Meadowbank Cl	
SW6	47 B3
Meadow Cl E9	18 B3
Meadowcroft 8	
SE4	66 A4
Meadow Mews	
SW8	162 C3
Meadow Pl	
Chiswick W4	46 A3
South Lambeth	
SW8	162 B2
Meadow Rd SW8	162 C2
Meadow Row SE1	136 C1
Mead Pl E9	17 B2
Mead Row SE1	135 B2
Meadway The SE3	53 C1
Meakin Est SE1	138 A2
Meakin Ho N7	14 B3
Meard St W1	105 B1
Meath Cres E1, E2	25 C2
Meath Ho SE24	63 A1
Meath St SW11	170 A4

Mecklenburgh Pl	
WC1	94 C2
Mecklenburgh Sq	
WC1	94 C2
Mecklenburgh St	
WC1	94 C2
Medburn St NW1	83 B2
Medcroft Gdns	
SW14	55 B3
Medfield St SW15	69 A4
Medhurst Cl 8 E3	26 A3
Median Rd E5	17 B3
Medina Ct N7	5 C1
Medina Gr N7	5 C1
Medina Ho SE15	65 B3
Medina Rd N7	5 C1
Medlar St SE5	48 B2
Medley Rd NW6	10 C2
Medora Rd SW2	74 B4
Medresco Ho NW3	11 C3
Medusa Rd SE6,	
SE13	67 A1
Medway Bldgs E3	26 A3
Medway Ct WC1	94 A3
Medway Ho	
Bermondsey SE1	137 C3
Paddington NW8	89 B3
Stoke Newington	
N16	15 C4
Medway Mews 21	
E3	26 A3
Medway Rd E3	26 A3
Medway St SW1	133 C1
Medwin St SW4	62 B3
Meecham Ct 1	
SW11	168 A2
Meeson St E5	18 A4
Meeting House Alley	
7 E1	32 A1
Meeting House La	
SE15	50 A3
Mehetabel Rd E9	17 B3
Melba Way SE13	52 A2
Melbourne Ct	
Hackney E5	17 C4
Paddington W9	89 A2
Melbourne Gr	
SE22	64 B3
Melbourne Ho	
W8	31 C1 113 B1
Melbourne Mews	
SW9	173 B3
Melbourne Pl	
WC2	95 C2
Melbourne Sq 21	
SW9	173 B3
Melbray Mews 11	
SW6	164 C1
Melbreak Ho 11	
SE22	64 A4
Melbury Ct W8	127 A2
Melbury Dr SE5	49 A3
Melbury Ho	
SW8	162 C2
Melbury Rd W14	127 A2
Melchester 5	
W11	31 B3
Melchester Ho 1	
N19	4 C1
Melcombe Ct	
NW1	102 C4
Melcombe Ho	
SW8	162 C1
Melcombe Pl	
NW1	102 C4
Melcombe Prim Sch	
6 W6	47 C4

Melcombe St NW1	91 A1
Meldon Cl SW6	166 B3
Melford Ct	
Bermondsey SE1	138 B2
Dulwich SE22	76 C4
Melford Rd SE21,	
SE22	76 C3
Melgund Rd N5	14 C3
Melina Ct	
Putney SW15	56 C4
St John's Wood	
NW8	89 B3
Melina Pl NW8	89 B3
Melina Rd W12	39 A4
Melior Pl SE1	138 A4
Melior St SE1	138 A4
Melisa Ct N6	4 C4
Mellington Ct 2	
N16	16 A4
Mellis Ave N5	5 A1
Mellish Ho 8 E1	32 A3
Mellish St E14	41 C3
Mellitus St W12	29 B3
Mell St 6 SE10	43 A1
Melody La N5	15 A3
Melody Rd SW18	59 B2
Melon Pl W8	127 C4
Melon Rd SE15	49 C2
Melrose Ave	
Cricklewood NW2	9 B3
Wimbledon SW19	70 C1
Melrose Ct SW18	58 B1
Melrose Gdns W6	39 B3
Melrose Ho	
Maida Vale NW6	23 C2
Pimlico SW1	146 B2
Melrose Rd	
Barnes SW13	46 B1
Wandsworth SW18	58 B1
Melrose Terr W6	39 B3
Melton Ct SW7	143 C3
Melton Ho E5	17 A4
Melton St NW1	93 A3
Melville Court Flats 8	
W12	39 A4
Melville Ct	
4 Brentford W4	36 C1
Rotherhithe SE8	41 A2
Melville Ho SE10	52 B2
Melville Pl 4 N1	15 B1
Melville Rd SW13	46 C2
Melville Villas Rd	
W3	28 C1
Melvin Ct 11 TW9	44 C2
Melwood Ho 2	
E1	32 A3
Melyn Cl N7	13 C3
Memel Ct EC1	96 C1
Memel St EC1	96 C1
Menai Pl 2 E3	26 C3
Menard Ct EC1	97 A3
Mendham Ho SE1	138 A2
Mendip Ct	
12 Battersea	
SW11	59 B4
Deptford SE14	50 B4
Mendip Dr NW2	1 A2
Mendip Ho 2	
NW11	1 A2
Mendip Hos 12 E2	25 B2
Mendip Rd SW11	59 B4
Mendora Rd SW6	154 C2
Menelik Rd NW2	10 B4
Menorah Prim Sch	
NW11	1 A4

Menotti St 8	
E2	24 C1 99 C2
Menteath Ho 9	
E14	33 C3
Mentmore Terr E8	17 A1
Mentone Ct SW8	172 B4
Meon Rd W3	37 B4
Mepham St SE1	121 B1
Merbury Cl SE13	67 C2
Mercator Pl 4	
E14	41 C1
Mercator Rd SE13	67 C3
Merceron Ho	
E2	25 B2
Merceron St E1	25 A1
Mercers Cl SE10	43 B2
Mercer's Cotts 8	
E1	33 A3
Mercers Mews N7	13 C4
Mercers Pl W6	39 C2
Mercers Rd N19	4 C1
Mercer St WC2	106 A1
Merchant Ct E1	32 B1
Merchants Ho	
SE10	42 C1
Merchant Sq W2	101 B3
Merchant St E3	26 B2
Merchant Taylors' Hall	
EC3	109 C1
Merchon Ho N7	13 B4
Mercia Gr SE13	67 B3
Mercia Ho 9 SE5	48 B1
Mercie Ct SE22	76 C3
Mercier Rd SW15	58 A2
Mercury Ct	
8 Brixton SW9	173 B4
10 Millwall E14	41 C2
Mercury Ho 6 E3	26 C4
Mercury Way SE14	50 C4
Mercy Terr SE13	67 A2
Mere Cl SW15,	
SW19	69 C4
Meredith Ave NW2	9 B3
Meredith Ho 17	
N16	16 A3
Meredith Mews	
SE4	66 B3
Meredith St EC1	96 A3
Meredith Twr W3	37 A3
Meredyth Rd	
SW13	46 C1
Meretone Cl SE4	66 A3
Mereton Mans 8	
SE8	51 C2
Merewood Ho 3	
SE15	50 B4
Merganser Ct 17	
SE8	51 B4
Meridan Ct SE13	67 C3
Meriden Ct SW3	144 A1
Meriden Ho 22 N1	24 A4
Meridian Courtyard	
SE10	52 C3
Meridian Ho SE10	43 A2
Meridian Pl E14	42 B4
Meridian Prim Sch 6	
SE10	52 C4
Meridian Sq E15	19 C1
Merivale Rd SW15	58 A3
Merlin Ho	
7 Chiswick W4	37 C1
West Hampstead	
NW3	11 A4

Merlin Sch The 🔟
SW15 . . . . .58 A2
Merlins Ct EC1 . . . . .95 B3
Merlin St EC1 . . . . . .95 B3
Mermaid Ct
Bermondsey SE1 . . 137 B4
Rotherhithe SE16 . . .33 B1
Mermaid Ho 🞰
E14 . . . . .34 B2
Mermaid Twr 🞰
SE8 . . . . .51 B4
Meroe Ct N16 . . . . . .7 A2
Merredene St
SW2 . . . . .62 B1
Merriam Ave 🞰
E9 . . . . .18 B2
Merricks Ct 🞰
SW14 . . . . .55 A3
Merrick Sq SE1 . . . 137 B2
Merrington Rd
SW6 . . . . 155 C4
Merritt Rd SE4 . . . . .66 B2
Merrivale N14 . . . . .83 A3
Merrow St SE17 . . . 151 B1
Merrow Wlk SE17 151 C2
Merryfield SE3 . . . . .53 B1
Merryweather Ct 🔞
N19 . . . . .4 B1
Mersey Ho 🔟 N7 . .14 C3
Merstone Ho
SW18 . . . . .59 A1
Merthyr Terr
SW13 . . . . .47 A4
Merton Ave W4 . . . .38 B2
Merton Ho SW18 . . .70 C3
Merton La N6 . . . . . .3 B2
Merton Rd SW18 . . .70 C4
Merton Rise NW3 . .12 A1
Merton Road Ind Est
SW18 . . . . .70 C4
Merttins Rd SE15 . . .65 C2
Mervan Rd SW2 . . . .62 C3
Messaline Ave W3 . .28 B3
Messina Ave NW6 . .10 C1
Messiter Ho N1 . . . .85 A3
Metcalfe Ho 🞰
SW8 . . . . 171 B2
Met Collection (Mus)
SW6 . . . . 141 B1
Meteor St SW11 . . . .60 C3
Methley Ho 🞰 N7 . . .5 B2
Methley St SE11 . . . 149 C1
Methodist Central
Hall SW1 . . . . 133 C3
Methwold Rd W10 . .30 C4
Metropolis
Apartments 🞰
SW12 . . . . .73 A3
Metropolitan Benefit
Societies
Almshouses 🞰
N1 . . . . .16 A3
Metropolitan Bsns Ctr
🞰 N1 . . . . .16 A2
Metropolitan Cl 🞰
E14 . . . . .33 C4
Mews St E1 . . . . . . 125 B2
Mews The
Shoreditch N1 . . . . .87 A4
🞰 Upper Holloway
N19 . . . . .4 C3
Mexborough NW1 . .82 C3
Mexfield Rd SW15 . .58 B2

Meyer Ho 🞰
SW12 . . . . .73 A4
Meymott St SE1 . . . 122 A1
Meynell Cres E9 . . . .17 C1
Meynell Gdns E9 . . .17 C1
Meynell Rd E9 . . . . .17 C1
Meyrick Ho 🞰 E14 . .33 C4
Meyrick Rd
Battersea SW11 . . . . .60 A4
Willesden NW10 . . . .9 A1
Miah Terr 🞰 E1 . . . 125 C1
Micawber Ct N1 . . . .97 A4
Micawber Ho 🞰
SE16 . . . . 139 C3
Micawber St N1 . . . .97 A4
Michael Cliffe Ho
EC1 . . . . .95 C3
Michael Faraday Ho
SE17 . . . . 151 C1
Michael Faraday Prim
Sch SE17 . . . . 151 C1
Michael Manley Ind
Est 🞰 SW8 . . . . 171 A2
Michael Rd SW6 . . . 166 B4
Michael Tippett Sch
The SE24 . . . . .63 B3
Michelangelo Ct 🞰
SE16 . . . . .40 A1
Michels Almshouses
🞰 TW10 . . . . .54 A2
Michelsdale Dr 🞰
TW9 . . . . .54 A3
Michelson Ho
SE11 . . . . 149 A3
Michel's Row 🞰
TW9 . . . . .54 A3
Micklethwaite La
SW6 . . . . 155 C3
Mickleton Ho 🞰
W2 . . . . .31 C4
Middlefield NW8 . . .79 B4
Middle Row Prim Sch
🞰 W10 . . . . .23 A1
Middlesex Ct 🞰
W4 . . . . .38 B2
Middlesex Ho W1 . 105 A4
Middlesex Pas
EC1 . . . . 108 B3
Middlesex Pl 🞰
E9 . . . . .17 B2
Middlesex St E1 . . . 110 C2
Middlesex Univ
(Archway Campus)
N19 . . . . .4 B2
Middle St EC1 . . . . 108 C4
Middle Temple
EC4 . . . . 121 B4
Middle Temple La
EC4 . . . . 121 B4
Middleton Dr SE16 .40 C4
Middleton Gr N7 . . .14 A3
Middleton Ho
Dalston E8 . . . . .16 B1
Newington SE1 . . . 137 B1
Middleton Mews
N7 . . . . .14 A3
Middleton Pl W1 . . 104 C3
Middleton Rd
Dalston E8 . . . . .16 B1
Golders Green NW11 . .1 C4

Middleton Way
SE13 . . . . .67 C3
Middle Yd SE1 . . . . 124 A2
Midford Pl W1 . . . . .93 A1
Midhope Ho WC1 . . .94 B3
Midhope St WC1 . . .94 B3
Midhurst Ct N8 . . . . .5 A4
Midhurst Ho 🞰
E14 . . . . .33 B3
Midhurst Way E5 . . .16 C4
Midland Pl E14 . . . . .42 B1
Midland Rd NW1 . . .94 A4
Midland Terr
NW10 . . . . .21 A1
Midlothian Ho NW2 . .9 A4
Midlothian Rd E3 . . .26 B1
Midmoor Rd SW12 . .73 B3
Midship Cl SE16 . . . .32 C1
Midship Point E14 . .41 C4
Midstrath Rd NW10 . .8 A4
Midway Ho EC1 . . . .96 B4
Milborne Gr
SW10 . . . . 143 A1
Milborne Ho 🔟 E9 .17 B2
Milborne St E9 . . . . .17 B2
Milbrook Ct NW3 . . .2 B3
Milcote St SE1 . . . . 136 B3
Mildmay Ave N1 . . . .15 C2
Mildmay Gr N N1 . . .15 C3
Mildmay Gr S N1 . . .15 C3
Mildmay Ho 🞰
SW15 . . . . .57 B2
Mildmay Mission
Hospl E2 . . .24 B2 98 C3
Mildmay Pk N1 . . . . .15 C2
Mildmay Rd N1 . . . . .16 A3
Mildmay St N1 . . . . .15 C2
MILE END 26 A1
Mile End Hospl E2 . .25 C2
Mile End Park L Ctr &
Stad E3 . . . . .33 B4
Mile End Pl E1 . . . . .25 C1
Mile End Rd E1, E3, E5,
E1, E3 . . . . .25 C1
Mile End Sta E3 . . . .26 B3
Miles Bldgs NW1 . . 102 A4
Miles Coverdale Prim
Sch W12 . . . . .39 B4
Miles Ct E1 . . . . .32 A3
Miles Ho 🞰 SE10 . . .43 A1
Miles Lo E15 . . . . . . .19 C3
Miles Pl NW8 . . . . . 101 C4
Miles St SW8 . . . . . 162 B3
Milestone Green
SW14 . . . . .55 C3
Milfoil St W12 . . . . .29 C2
Milford Ct 🞰 N16 . . .7 A3
Milford La WC2 . . . 121 B4
Milford Mews
SW16 . . . . .74 B1
Milk St EC2 . . . . . . 109 A2
Milkwell Yd 🞰
SE5 . . . . .48 B2
Milkwood Rd SE24 . .63 A3
Milk Yd E1 . . . . .32 B2
Millais Rd E11 . . . . .19 C4
Milland Ho 🞰
SW15 . . . . .68 C3
Millard Cl 🞰 N16 . . .16 A3
Millard Rd SE8 . . . . .41 B1
Millbank SW1 . . . . 148 A3
Millbank Millennium
Pier SW1 . . . . 148 B3
Millbank Prim Sch
SW1 . . . . 147 C3

Millbrooke Ct 🞰
SW15 . . . . .58 A2
Millbrook Ho 🞰
SE15 . . . . .49 C4
Millbrook Pl NW1 . .82 C2
Millbrook Rd SW9 . .63 A4
Millender Wlk
SE16 . . . . .40 B2
Millennium Bridge SE1,
EC4 . . . . 122 C3
Millennium City Acad
W1 . . . . 104 B3
Millennium Dr
E14 . . . . .42 C2
Millennium Harbour
E14 . . . . .41 C4
Millennium Pl 🞰
E2 . . . . .25 A3
Millennium Prim Sch
The SE10 . . . . .43 B3
Millennium Sq
SE1 . . . . 139 A4
Millennium Way
SE10 . . . . .43 A3
Miller Ho 🞰 SW2 . . .74 A4
Miller's Ave E8,
N16 . . . . .16 B3
Miller's Ct 🞰 W4 . . .38 B1
Miller's Terr 🞰 E8 . .16 B3
Miller's Terr 🞰 E8 . .16 B3
Miller's Way W6 . . . .39 B4
Millers Wharf Ho
E1 . . . . 125 B1
Miller Wlk SE1 . . . . 121 C1
Millfield N4 . . . . .5 C2
Millfield La N6 . . . . . .3 B2
Millfield Pl N6 . . . . . .3 C2
Millfields Com Sch
E5 . . . . .17 B4
Millgrove St 🞰
SW11 . . . . 169 B2
Millharbour E14 . . . .42 A4
Mill Hill SW13 . . . . .56 C4
Mill Hill Gr 🟪 W3 . .28 A1
Mill Hill Rd
Barnes SW13 . . . . . . .46 C1
South Acton W3 . . . . .37 A4
Mill Hill Terr 🟪
W3 . . . . .28 A1
Mill Ho SE13 . . . . . .67 B4
Milligan St E14 . . . . .33 B2
Milliners Ho SW18 . .58 C3
Millington Ho N16 . . .6 C1
Mill La NW6 . . . . . . .10 B3
Millman Ct WC1 . . . .94 C1
Millman Mews
WC1 . . . . .94 C1
Millman Pl WC1 . . . .95 A1
Millman St WC1 . . . .94 C1
Millmark Gr SE14 . . .51 A1
MILL MEADS 27 C2
Millner Ct SE4 . . . . .51 B1
Mill Pl E14 . . . . .33 A3
Mill Pond Cl SW8 . . 161 C1
Millpond Est SE16 . .40 A4
Mill Row N1 . . . . . . .24 A4
Mills Ct EC2 . . . . . . .24 A2 98 B3
Mills Gr 🟪 E14 . . . . .34 B4
Mills Ho SW8 . . . . . 171 A4
Millshott Cl SW6 . . .47 B2
Mills Row 🞰 W4 . . . .37 C2
Mill St
Bermondsey SE1 . . 139 A4
Mayfair W1 . . . . . . 118 C4
Millstone Cl E15 . . . .19 C2

Millstream Ho 🔢
SE16 . . . . .40 A4
Millstream Rd
SE1 . . . . 138 C3
Mill Trad Est The
NW10 . . . . .20 B2
MILLWALL 41 C3
Millwall Dock Rd
E14 . . . . .41 C3
Millwood St 🔟
W10 . . . . .31 A4
Mill Yd E1 . . . . 125 B4
Milman Rd NW6 . . . .23 A3
Milman's Ho
SW10 . . . . 157 B3
Milman's St SW10 157 B3
Milner Bldg N16 . . . .6 C1
Milner Ho 🞰
SW11 . . . . .59 C4
Milner Pl N1 . . . . . . .85 C4
Milner Sq N1 . . . . . .15 A1
Milner St SW3 . . . . 144 C4
Milnthorpe Rd W4 . .45 C4
Milo Rd SE22 . . . . . .64 B1
Milrood Ho 🞰 E1 . . .32 C4
Milroy Wlk SE1 . . . 122 A2
Milson Rd W14 . . . 126 A2
Milsted Ho 🞰 E5 . . .17 A3
Milton Ave
Becontree NW10 . . . .20 C4
Crouch End N6 . . . . . .4 B4
Stonebridge NW10 . . .20 B4
Milton Cl SE1 . . . . . 152 C3
Milton Court Rd
SE14 . . . . .51 A4
Milton Ct
Fulham SW6 . . . . . . .58 A4
St Luke's EC2 . . . . . 109 B4
🞰 Wandsworth
SW18 . . . . .58 C2
Milton Gr N16 . . . . .16 A4
Milton Ho
🔟 Bethnal Green
E2 . . . . .25 B2
🞰 Camberwell SE5 . .48 C3
Milton House Mans
E8 . . . . .16 B4
Milton Pk N6 . . . . . . .4 B4
Milton Pl 🞰 N7 . . . .14 C3
Milton Rd
Acton W3 . . . . .28 C1
Crouch End N6 . . . . . .4 B4
Mortlake SW14 . . . . .55 C4
Tulse Hill SE24 . . . . . .63 A2
Milton St EC1, EC2 109 B4
Milverton NW5 . . . . .12 C3
Milverton Rd NW6 . . .9 B1
Milverton St SE11 . 149 C1
Milward St E1 . . . . .32 A4
Mimosa St SW6 . . . 164 C3
Mimosa St SW6 . . . 165 A3
Mina Rd SE17 . . . . . 152 B2
Minchin Ho 🔟
E14 . . . . .33 C3
Mincing La EC3 . . . 124 A4
Minera Mews
SW1 . . . . 145 C4
Minerva Cl SW9 . . . 163 C2
Minerva St E2 . . . . .25 A3
Minerva St 🞰 E2 . . .25 A3
Minerva Wlk EC1 . . 108 C2
Minet Ave NW10 . . .21 A3
Minet Gdns NW10 . .21 A3
Minet Ho 🞰 E1 . . . 111 B1
Minet Rd SE5, SW9 . .48 A1

Minford Gdns
 W14 .... 39 C4
Mingard Wlk N7.... 5 B1
Ming St E14 .... 33 C2
Minnow Wlk SE17 152 B3
Minories EC3.... 124 C4
Minshull St SW8.. 171 B3
Minson Rd E9.... 25 C4
Minstead Gdns
 SW15.... 68 B4
Minster Ct EC3.. 124 B4
Minster Rd NW2.. 10 A3
Mint Bsns Pk [12]
 E16.... 35 C4
Mintern St N1.... 87 C2
Minton Ho SE11.. 149 B4
Minton Mews [3]
 NW6.... 11 A2
Mint St SE1.... 137 A4
Mirabel Rd SW6.. 155 A2
Miranda Cl [11] E1.. 32 B4
Miranda Ho [17] N1.. 24 A3
Miranda Rd N19.... 4 B3
Missenden SE17.. 151 C1
Missenden Ho
 NW8.... 90 A2
Mission Pl SE15.. 49 C2
Mission Sq [13]
 TW8.... 44 A4
Mission The
 [13] Bermondsey
  SE16.... 40 A4
 [14] Poplar E14 .. 33 B3
Misterton Ct
 SW11.... 167 C4
Mistral SE5.... 49 A2
Mitali Pas [2] E1.. 111 B1
Mitcham Ho [9]
 SE5.... 48 B2
Mitchell Brook Prim
 Sch NW10.... 8 A2
Mitchell St EC1.. 97 A2
Mitchison Rd N1.. 15 C2
Mitford Rd N19.... 5 A2
Mitre Bridge Ind Pk
 W10.... 22 A1
Mitre Rd SE1.... 135 C4
Mitre Sq EC3.... 110 B1
Mitre St EC3.... 110 B1
Mitre Way W10.... 30 A4
Mizzen Ct E14.... 41 C4
Moatfield NW6.... 10 A1
Moat Pl
 Acton W3.... 28 A3
 Stockwell SW9.... 62 B4
Moat Sch The [7]
 SW6.... 164 A2
Moberly Rd SW4.. 73 C4
Mobey Ct SW4.... 172 A3
Mocatta Ho [9] E1.. 25 A1
Modbury Gdns
 NW5.... 12 C2
Modder Pl SW15.. 57 C3
Model Cotts SW13.. 56 B4
Modling Ho [8] E2.. 25 C3
Melwyn Hughes Sch
 N7.... 13 C3
Moffat Ho [24] SE5.. 48 B3

Mohawk Ho [3] E3.. 26 A3
Moira Ct SW17.... 72 C2
Moira Ho [3] SW9.. 173 B4
Molasses Ho [1]
 SW11.... 59 B4
Molasses Row [2]
 SW11.... 59 B4
Mole Ct [2] W12.... 38 A4
Mole Ho NW8.... 89 C1
Molesey Ho
 E2.... 24 B1 98 C2
Molesford Rd
 SW6.... 165 B3
Molesworth Ho [9]
 SE17.... 48 A4
Molesworth St
 SE13.... 67 B4
Molly Huggins Cl
 SW12.... 73 B4
Molton Ho N1.... 85 A3
Molyneux Ho W1.. 102 B2
Molyneux St W1.. 102 B3
Mona Rd SE15.... 50 B1
Mona St E16.... 35 B4
Monck's Row
 SW18.... 58 B1
Monck St SW1.... 133 C1
Monckton Ct W14 126 C2
Monclar Rd SE5.... 63 C3
Moncorvo Cl SW7 130 A3
Moncrieff St SE15.. 49 C1
Mondragon Ho
 SW8.... 172 B4
Monet Ct [15] SE16.. 40 A1
Moneyer Ho N1.... 97 B4
Monica Shaw Ct
 NW1.... 83 C1
Monier Rd E3.... 18 C1
Monkbretton Ho
 E2.... 24 C2 99 B3
Monk Ct W12.... 29 C1
Monk Dr E16.... 35 C2
Monkridge [3] N8.... 4 C4
Monksfield N4.... 5 C2
Monkswell Ho
 [2] Bermondsey
  SE16.... 40 A4
 [3] Shepherd's Bush
  W12.... 30 A2
Monkton Ho
 [5] Bermondsey
  SE16.... 40 A4
 [6] Hackney E5.... 17 A3
Monkton St SE11.. 149 C4
Monkwell Sq EC2 109 A3
Monmouth Ho
 [4] Camden Town
  NW5.... 13 A2
 Wandsworth SW18 58 C1
Monmouth Pl W2 100 A1
Monmouth Rd W2.. 31 C3
Monmouth St
 WC2.... 106 A1
Monnery Rd N19.... 4 B1
Monnow Rd SE1.. 153 B3
Monroe Dr SW14.. 55 A2
Monroe Ho
 [10] Crouch End N19 .. 4 C4
 Lisson Gr NW8.... 90 B3
Monro Ho
 [3] Hampstead
  NW3.... 11 B4
 Putney SW15.... 57 A2
Monro Way E5.... 16 C4
Monsal Ct E5.... 18 A4
Monsell Ct N4.... 6 A1

Monsell Rd N4, N5... 6 A1
Monson Rd
 Deptford SE14.... 50 C3
 Willesden Green
  NW10.... 22 A3
Montagu Ct W1.... 103 A3
Montague Ave
 SE4.... 66 C3
Montague Cl SE1.. 123 B2
Montague Pl WC1 105 C4
Montague Rd
 Richmond TW10.... 54 A1
 Shacklewell E8.... 16 C3
Montague Sq SE15.. 50 B3
Montague St
 Bloomsbury WC1 .. 106 A4
 City of London EC1 108 C3
Montagu Mans
 W1.... 103 A3
Montagu Mews N
 W1.... 103 A3
Montagu Mews S
 W1.... 103 A2
Montagu Mews W
 W1.... 103 A2
Montagu Pl W1.... 103 A3
Montagu Row W1 103 A3
Montagu Sq W1.... 103 A3
Montagu St W1.... 103 A2
Montaigne Cl
 SW1.... 147 C3
Montana Bldg [4]
 SE13.... 52 A2
Montana Rd SW17.. 72 C1
Montcalm Ho E14.. 41 C3
Montclare St
 E2.... 24 B1 98 C2
Monteagle Ct [1]
 N1.... 24 A3
Monteagle Way
 Nunhead SE15.... 65 A4
 Shacklewell E5.... 7 C1
Montefiore Ct [2]
 N16.... 7 B3
Montefiore St [3]
 SW8.... 170 B1
Montego Cl [3]
 SW2.... 62 C3
Montem Prim Sch [3]
 N7.... 5 B1
Montem St N4.... 5 B3
Monterey Studios
 W10.... 23 A3
Montesquieu Terr [3]
 E16.... 35 B3
Montfort Ho
 [4] Bethnal Green
  E2.... 25 B2
 Cubitt Town E14.... 42 B3
Montfort Pl SW19.. 69 C3
Montgomery Ct
 W4.... 45 B4
Montgomery Ho [5]
 SW14.... 55 C4
Montgomery Lo [28]
 E1.... 25 B1
Montgomery Rd
 W4.... 37 B2
Montgomery St
 E14.... 34 A1
Montholme Rd
 SW11.... 60 B1
Monthope Rd [17]
 E1.... 111 B3

Montolieu Gdns
 SW15.... 57 A2
Montpelier Gr
 NW5.... 13 B3
Montpelier Mews
 SW7.... 130 B2
Montpelier Pl
 [1] Knightsbridge
  SW7.... 130 B2
 [2] Stepney E1.... 32 B3
Montpelier Rd
 SE15.... 50 A2
Montpelier Rise
 NW11.... 1 A4
Montpelier Row
 SE3.... 53 B1
Montpelier Sq
 SW7.... 130 B3
Montpelier St
 SW7.... 130 B2
Montpelier Terr
 SW7.... 130 B3
Montpelier Vale
 SE3.... 53 B1
Montpelier Way
 NW11.... 1 A4
Montpelier Wlk
 SW7.... 130 B2
Montreal Pl WC2.. 120 C4
Montrell Rd SW2.. 74 A3
Montrose Ave
 NW6.... 23 A3
Montrose Ct SW7 129 C3
Montrose Ho
 [1] Belgravia SW1.. 131 C3
 Millwall E14.... 41 C3
Montrose Pl SW1.. 131 C3
Montrose Villas [5]
 W6.... 38 C1
Montserrat Rd
 SW15.... 58 A3
Monument Gdns
 SE13.... 67 B2
Monument St EC3 123 C4
Monument Sta
 EC3.... 123 C4
Monza Bldg The
 E1.... 32 B2
Monza St E1.... 32 B2
Moodkee St SE16.. 40 B3
Moody Rd SE15.... 49 B2
Moody St E1.... 25 C2
Moon St N1.... 86 A4
Moorcroft Rd
 SW16.... 74 A1
Moore Ct SW14.... 55 B4
Moore Ct N1.... 86 A3
Moore Ho
 [18] Bethnal Green
  E2.... 25 B2
 [5] Greenwich SE10 .. 43 B1
 [7] Shadwell E1.... 32 B2
 Wandsworth SW17 .. 71 C1
Moore Park Ct
 SW6.... 156 B2
Moore Park Rd
 SW6.... 156 A1
Moorfields EC2.... 109 B3
Moorfields Eye Hospl
 EC1.... 97 B3
Moorfields Highwalk
 EC2.... 109 B3
Moorgate EC2.... 109 B3
Moorgate Pl EC2.. 109 B2

Moorgate Sta
 EC2.... 109 B3
Moorgreen Ho EC1 96 A4
Moorhouse EC2 .. 109 B3
Moorhouse Rd
 W2.... 31 C3
Moor La EC2.... 109 B3
Moorland Rd SW9 63 A3
Moor Pl EC2.... 109 B3
Moor St W1.... 105 C1
Morant Ho SW9.. 172 C2
Morant St E14.... 33 C2
Mora Prim Sch
 NW2.... 9 B4
Mora Rd NW2.... 9 B4
Mora St EC1.... 97 A3
Morat St SW9.... 173 A4
Moravian Cl SW3 157 C3
Moravian Pl
 SW10.... 157 C3
Moravian St [10] E2.. 25 B2
Moray Ho [9] E1.... 26 A1
Moray Mews N4, N7.. 5 B2
Moray Rd N4, N7.... 5 B2
Mordaunt Ho
 [1] Becontree
  NW10.... 20 C4
 [2] Clapham SW8.. 171 B1
Mordaunt Rd
 NW10.... 20 C4
Mordaunt St SW9 62 B4
Morden Hill SE13.. 52 B1
Morden Ho [10]
 SW2.... 62 C1
Morden La SE13.. 52 B2
Morden Mount Prim
 Sch [11] SE13.... 52 A1
Morden Rd SE3.... 53 C1
Morden Road Mews
 SE3.... 53 C1
Morden St SE13.... 52 A2
Morden Wharf Rd
 SE10.... 43 A3
Mordern Ho NW1.. 90 B1
Morecambe Cl [3]
 E1.... 32 C4
Morecambe St
 SE17.... 151 A2
More Cl
 [1] Canning Town
  E16.... 35 B3
 [2] West Kensington
  W14.... 140 A3
Moredown Ho [3]
 E8.... 16 C3
More House Sch
 SW1.... 131 A1
Moreland Ct [3]
 NW2.... 1 C1
Moreland Prim Sch
 EC1.... 96 B4
Moreland St EC1.. 96 B4
Morella Rd SW11,
 SW12.... 72 B4
Morell Ho [5] SW9.. 173 A1
More London Pl
 SE1.... 124 A1
Moresby Wlk [6]
 SW8.... 170 B1
More's Gdn SW3 157 C3
Moreton Ho SE16.. 40 A3
Moreton Pl SW1.. 147 A2
Moreton St SW1.. 147 B2

Moreton Terr
SW1 . . . . **147** A2
Moreton Terr Mews N
SW1 . . . . **147** A2
Moreton Terr Mews S
SW1 . . . . **147** A2
Moreton Twr 🔢
W3 . . . . .28 A1
Morgan Ct 🟦
SW11 . . . . **167** C2
Morgan Ho
Nine Elms SW8 . . . **171** A4
Pimlico SW1 . . . . . **147** A3
Morgan St
Islington N7 . . . . . . .14 C3
Notting Hill W10 . . . .31 A4
Morgans La SE1 . . . **124** A1
Morgan St
Canning Town
E16 . . . . .35 A4
Globe Town E3 . . . . .25 C2
Morgan's Wlk
SW11 . . . . **158** A1
Moriatry Cl N7 . . . . . .14 A4
Morie St SW18 . . . . .59 A2
Morkyns Wlk SE21 . .76 A1
Morland Cl NW11 . . . . .2 A3
Morland Ct W12 . . . . .39 A4
Morland Est SE8 . . . .16 C1
Morland Ho
Kilburn NW6 . . . . . . .23 C4
Notting Hill W11 . . . .31 A3
Somers Town NW1 . .83 A1
Westminster SW1 . .148 A4
Morland Mews N1 . .14 C1
Morley Coll SE1 . . .135 C2
Morley Ct SE13 . . . .67 B3
Morley Ho
Stoke Newington
N16 . . . . .7 C2
Streatham SW2 . . . .74 A4
W1 . . . . .104 C3
Morley Rd SE13 . . . .67 B3
Morna Rd SE5 . . . . .48 B1
Morning La E9 . . . . .17 B2
Morningside Prim Sch
🔢 17 B2
Mornington Ave
W14 . . . . .140 C3
Mornington Avenue
Mans W14 . . . . . .140 C3
Mornington Cres
Camden Town
NW1 . . . . .82 C2
NW1 . . . . .82 C2
Mornington Crescent
Sta NW1 . . . . .82 C2
Mornington Ct
NW1 . . . . .82 C2
Mornington Gr E3 . .26 C2
Mornington Mews 🟦
SE5 . . . . .48 B2
Mornington Pl
🔢 New Cross
SE8 . . . . .51 B3
Regent's Pk NW1 . . .82 C2
Mornington Rd SE14,
SE8 . . . . .51 B3
Mornington St
NW1 . . . . .82 B2
Mornington Terr
NW1 . . . . .82 B2
Morocco St SE1 . . .138 A3

Morpeth Gr E9 . . . . .25 C4
Morpeth Rd E9 . . . . .25 C4
Morpeth Sch E2 . . . .25 C2
Morpeth St E2 . . . . .25 C2
Morpeth Terr
SW1 . . . . .146 A1
Morrel Ct 🔢 E2 . . . .24 C3
Morris Blitz Ct 🟦
N16 . . . . .16 A4
Morris Ct 🟦 SE5 . . .63 C3
Morris Gdns SW18 . .70 C4
Morris Ho
🔢 Bethnal Green
E2 . . . . .25 B2
Lisson Gr NW8 . . . . .90 A1
🔟 Stockwell SW4 . .62 A3
🔟 Tufnell Pk N19 . .13 B4
Morrish Rd SW2 . . . .74 A4
Morrison Bldgs 🟦
E1 . . . . .111 B2
Morrison Ho SW2 . . .74 C3
Morrison St SW11 . .60 C4
Morris Pl N4 . . . . . . .5 C2
Morris Rd E14 . . . . .34 A4
Morriss Ho 🟦
SE16 . . . . .40 A4
Morshead Mans
W9 . . . . .23 C2
Morshead Rd W9 . . .23 C2
Mortain Ho 🟦
SE16 . . . . .40 A2
Morten Cl SW4 . . . . .61 C1
Mortimer Cl
🔢 Child's Hill NW2 . .1 B1
Streatham SW16 . . .73 C2
Mortimer Cres
NW6 . . . . .78 B3
Mortimer Ct NW8 . . .79 A1
Mortimer Est NW6 . .78 B3
Mortimer Ho
🔢 Shepherd's Bush
W11 . . . . .30 C1
West Kensington
W14 . . . . .140 B3
Mortimer Lo 🔢
SW19 . . . . .70 A3
Mortimer Market
WC1 . . . . .93 A1
Mortimer Pl NW6 . . .78 A3
Mortimer Rd
De Beauvoir Town
N1 . . . . .16 A1
Kensal Green
NW10 . . . . .22 B2
Mortimer Sq W11 . . .30 C2
Mortimer St W1 . . .105 A3
Mortimer Terr
NW5 . . . . .13 A4
MORTLAKE 55 C4
Mortlake High St
SW14 . . . . .55 C4
Mortlake Ho 🔢
W4 . . . . .37 B2
Mortlake Rd SW14,
TW9 . . . . .44 C2
Mortlake Sta
SW14 . . . . .55 B4
Mortlake Terr
TW9 . . . . .44 C2
Mortlock Cl SE15 . . .50 A2
Morton Cl 🟦 E1 . . . .32 B3
Morton Ho SE17 . . . .48 A4
Morton Mews
SW5 . . . . .142 A3
Morton Pl SE1 . . . .135 B1

Morton Rd N1 . . . . . .15 B1
Morval Rd SW2 . . . . .62 C2
Morven Rd SW17 . . .72 B1
Morville Ho SW18 . . .59 C1
Morville St E3 . . . . . .26 C3
Morwell St WC1 . . .105 C3
Moscow Pl W2 . . . .114 A4
Moscow Rd W2 . . . .114 A4
Mosedale NW1 . . . . .92 B3
Mosey Row SE10 . . .43 B2
Mosque Tower 🟦
E1 . . . . .111 C3
Mossbourne Com
Acad E8 . . . . .16 C3
Mossbury Rd
SW11 . . . . .60 A4
Moss Cl E1 . . . . . . .111 C4
Mossford St E3 . . . . .26 B1
Mossington Gdns
SE16 . . . . .40 B2
Mossop St SW3 . . .144 B4
Mostyn Gdns
NW10 . . . . .22 C3
Mostyn Gr E3 . . . . . .26 C3
Mostyn Lo N5 . . . . . .15 B4
Mostyn Rd SW9 . . .173 C3
Motcomb St SW1 . .131 B2
Mothers Sq The 🔟
E5 . . . . .17 A4
Motley Ave
EC2 . . . . .24 A1 98 A2
Motley St SW8 . . . .170 C2
Moules Ct SE5 . . . . .48 B3
Moulins Rd E9 . . . . .17 B1
Moulsford Ho
🔢 Lower Holloway
N7 . . . . .14 A3
🟦 Paddington W2 . .31 C4
Mounsey Ho 🟦
W10 . . . . .23 A2
Mount Adon Pk SE21,
SE22 . . . . .76 C4
Montague Pl 🟦
E14 . . . . .34 B2
Mountain Ho
SE11 . . . . .148 C2
Mount Angelus Rd
SW15 . . . . .68 B4
Mount Ararat Rd
TW10 . . . . .54 A2
Mountbatten Ho N6 .3 C4
Mountbatten Mews
SW18 . . . . .71 B3
Mount Carmel 🟦
N7 . . . . .14 B3
Mount Carmel RC
Tech Coll for Girls
🟦 N19 . . . . .4 C3
Mountearl Gdns SW16,
SW2 . . . . .74 B1
Mount Ephraim La
SW16 . . . . .73 C1
Mount Ephraim Rd
SW16 . . . . .73 C1
Mountfield NW2 . . . . .1 B2
Mountfield Ct
SE13 . . . . .67 C1
Mount Ford St E1 . .111 B2
Mountfort Cres
N1 . . . . .14 C1
Mountfort Terr 🔢
N1 . . . . .14 C1
Mountgrove Rd N5 . .6 B1
Mountjoy Ho EC2 . .108 C3
Mount Lodge SW4 . .61 D3
Mount Mills EC1 . . . .96 B3

Mount Nod Rd SW16,
SW2 . . . . .74 B1
Mount Pl 🔢 W3 . . . .28 A1
Mount Pleasant
WC1 . . . . .95 B1
Mount Pleasant Cres
N4 . . . . .5 B4
Mount Pleasant Rd
Lewisham SE13 . . . .67 B1
Willesden NW10 . . . .22 B4
Mount Pleasant Villas
N4 . . . . .5 B4
Mount Rd SW18,
SW19 . . . . .71 A2
Mount Row W1 . . . .118 A3
Mounts Pond Rd SE3,
SE13 . . . . .52 C1
Mount Sq The 🟦
NW3 . . . . .2 B1
Mount St W1 . . . . .117 C3
Mount Terr E1 . . . . .32 A4
Mount The
Hampstead NW3 . . . . .2 B1
Kensington
W8 . . . . .31 C1 113 B1
Mount Tyndal NW3 . .2 C3
Mount Vernon
NW3 . . . . .11 B4
Mountview 🟦
SW16 . . . . .74 B1
Mountview Cl NW11 .2 B3
Mount Villas SE27 . .75 A1
Mourne Ho NW3 . . . .11 C2
Mowatt Cl N19 . . . . . .4 C3
Mowbray Rd NW6 . .10 A1
Mowlem Prim Sch 🟦
E2 . . . . .25 B3
Mowlem St E2 . . . . .25 A3
Mowll St SW9 . . . . .163 B1
Moxon St W1 . . . . .103 B3
Moye Cl 🟦 E2 . . . . .24 C3
Moylan Rd W6 . . . .154 B3
Moyle Ho SW1 . . . .161 A4
Moyne Ho 🔢 SW9 . .63 A3
Mozart St W10 . . . . .23 B2
Mudchute Pk & Farm
🟦 42 B2
Mudchute Sta E14 . .42 B2
Mudie Ho 🟦 SW2 . .74 A4
Mudlarks Blvd 🟦
SE10 . . . . .43 B3
Muirdown Ave
SW14 . . . . .55 C3
Muir Dr SW18 . . . . . .60 A1
Muirfield W3 . . . . . . .29 A3
Muirfield Cl 🟦
SE16 . . . . .40 A1
Muirfield Cres
E14 . . . . .42 A3
Muir Rd E5 . . . . .7 C1
Mulberry Bsns Ctr
SE16 . . . . .40 C4
Mulberry Cl
Chelsea SW3 . . . . .157 C3
East Dulwich SE22 . .64 C1
Hampstead NW3 . . . .11 C4
Mulberry Ct
Finsbury EC1 . . . . . .96 B3
Islington N5 . . . . . . .15 A3
🔢 Leyton E11 . . . . .19 C4
🔟 Paddington W9 . .23 B2
Mulberry Ho
🔢 Bethnal Green
E2 . . . . .25 B2
🟦 Deptford SE8 . . . .51 B4

Mulberry House Sch
NW2 . . . . .10 A3
Mulberry Mews
SE14 . . . . .51 B2
Mulberry Pl W6 . . . .38 C1
Mulberry Rd E8 . . . .16 B1
Mulberry Sch for Girls
🔢 Stepney E1 . . . . .32 A3
🟦 St George in the East
E1 . . . . .32 A2
Mulberry St 🔢
E1 . . . . .111 B2
Mulberry Wlk
SW3 . . . . .157 C4
Mulgrave Rd
West Kensington
W14 . . . . .154 C4
Mulkern Rd N19 . . . . .4 C3
Mullard Ho WC1 . . .105 B4
Mullens Ho 🔢
SW15 . . . . .57 B2
Mullen Twr EC1 . . . .95 B1
Muller Rd SW4 . . . . .61 C1
Mullet Gdns 🔢
E2 . . . . .24 C2 99 C4
Mulletsfield WC1 . . .94 B3
Mull Ho 🟦 E3 . . . . . .26 B3
Mullins Path
SW14 . . . . .55 C4
Mulready St NW8 . . .90 A1
Multi Way W3 . . . . . .38 A4
Multon Ho E9 . . . . . .17 B1
Multon Rd SW18 . . .71 C4
Mulvaney Way
SE1 . . . . .137 C3
Mumford Rd SE24 . .63 A2
Muncaster Rd
SW11 . . . . .60 C2
Mundania Ct SE22 . .65 A1
Mundania Rd SE22 . .65 B1
Munday Ho SE1 . . .137 B1
Munday Rd E16 . . . . .35 C2
Munden Ho 🟦 E3 . . .27 A2
Munden St W14 . . .140 A4
Mund St W14 . . . . .141 A1
Mundy Ho 🟦 W10 . .23 A2
Mundy St
N1 . . . . .24 A2 98 B4
Munro Ho
Bermondsey SE1 . . .137 C3
Lambeth SE1 . . . . .135 B3
Munro Mews W10 . .31 A4
Munster Ct SW6 . . .164 C2
Munster Rd SW6 . . .154 B2
Munster Residences
SW6 . . . . .154 B2
Munster Sq NW1 . . .92 B2
Munton Rd SE1,
SE17 . . . . .151 A4
Murchison Ho 🔢
W10 . . . . .31 A4
Murdoch Ho 🟦
SE16 . . . . .40 B3
Murdock Cl E16 . . . .35 B3
Murdock St SE15 . . .50 A4
Murfett Cl SW19 . . . .70 A2
Muriel St N1 . . . . . . .85 A4
Murphy Ho SE1 . . . .136 B2
Murphy St SE1 . . . .135 B3
Murray Gr N1 . . . . . .87 B1
Murray Mews
NW1 . . . . .13 C1
Murray St NW1 . . . .13 C1
Murray Terr NW3 . . .11 C4
Musard Rd W6 . . . .154 B4

Musbury St E1 . . . . . .32 B3
Muscal W6 . . . . .154 A4
Muscatel Pl SE5 . . . .49 A2
Muschamp Rd
SE15 . . . . .64 B4
Muscott Ho 12 E2 . .24 C4
Muscovy St EC3 . . . .124 B4
Museum & Galleries
of Modern London
EC2 . . . . .108 C3
Museum Ho 7 . . . . .25 B2
Museum La SE7 . . . .129 B1
Museum Mans
WC1 . . . . .106 A3
Museum of Brands,
Packaging &
Advertising W11 . . .31 B3
Museum of Childhood
(V&A) E2 . . . . .25 B2
Museum of
Instruments
SW7 . . . . .129 B2
Museum of London
EC2 . . . . .108 C3
Museum of London
Docklands E14 . . . .33 C2
Museum of the Order
of St John EC1 . . . .96 A1
Museum of the Royal
Pharmaceutical
Society SE1 . . . . . .148 C4
Museum St WC1 . . .106 A2
Museum Way W3 . . .36 C4
Musgrave Cres
SW6 . . . . .165 C4
Musgrave Ct
SW11 . . . . .168 A4
Musgrove Ho 1
E9 . . . . .17 C2
Musgrove Rd SE14 . .51 A2
Musical Mus The
TW8 . . . . .44 B4
Musjid Rd 7
SW11 . . . . .167 C1
Mustow Pl 7
SW6 . . . . .165 A2
Mutrix Rd NW6 . . . .23 C4
Mutton Pl NW1 . . . .12 C2
Myatt Garden Prim
Sch SE4 . . . . .51 B1
Myatt Ho SE5 . . . . . .48 A1
Myatt Rd SW9 . . . . .48 A2
Myatts Field Ct
SE5 . . . . .48 C2
Mycenae Rd SE3 . . .53 C4
Myddelton Pas
EC1 . . . . .95 C4
Myddelton Sq EC1 . .95 C4
Myddelton St EC1 . . .95 C3
Myddleton Ave N4 . . .6 B2
Myers Ho 5 . . . . . . .48 B3
Myers La SE14 . . . . .50 C4
Mylius Cl SE14 . . . .50 B2
Mylne Cl W6 . . . . . .38 C1
Mylne St EC1 . . . . . .85 C1
Mynterne Ct 16
SW19 . . . . .69 C3
Myrdle Ct 14 E1 . . .111 C2
Myrdle St E1 . . . . . .111 C2
Myron Pl SE13 . . . . .67 B4
Myrtle Ho SE14 . . . .50 C2
Myrtle Rd W3 . . . . . .28 B1
Myrtle Wlk 20 N1 . . .24 A3
Mysore Rd SW11 . . .60 B3
Mytton Rd SE21 . . . .75 C1
Mytton Ho SW8 . . .162 C1

N

N1 Sh Ctr N1 . . . . . . .85 C2
Nags Head N7 . . . . . .14 B4
Nags Head Ct EC1 . .97 A1
Nags Head Sh Ctr The
N7 . . . . .14 B4
Nainby Ho SE11 . . .149 B3
Nairne Gr SE5,
SE24 . . . . .48 A1
Nairn St E14 . . . . . . .34 B4
Naldera Gdns SE3 . .53 C4
Nalton Ho 4 NW6 . .11 B1
Namco Sta SE1 . . . .134 C4
Nankin St E14 . . . . . .33 C3
Nansen Rd SW11 . . .60 C4
Nant Ct NW2 . . . . .1 B2
Nant Ho NW2 . . . . .1 B2
Nantes Cl SW18 . . . .59 B3
Nant Rd NW2 . . . . .1 B2
Nant St E2 . . . . .25 A2
Naoroji St WC1 . . . . .95 B3
Napier Ave
Deptford E14 . . . . . .41 C1
Fulham SW6 . . . . . . .58 B4
Napier Cl
New Cross SE14,
SE8 . . . . .51 B3
West Kensington
W14 . . . . .126 C2
Napier Ct
Fulham SW6 . . . . . . .58 B4
Shoreditch N1 . . . . . .87 B2
Napier Gr N1 . . . . . . .87 A2
Napier Ho SE17 . . . .48 A4
Napier PI W14 . . . .126 C1
Napier Rd
College Pk NW10 . . .22 A2
Kensington W14 . . .126 C1
Napier Terr N1 . . . . .15 A1
Narbonne Ave
SW4 . . . . .61 B2
Narborough St
SW6 . . . . .166 A1
Narcissus Rd NW6 . .10 C3
Narford Rd E5 . . . . . . .7 C2
Narrow St
6 Acton W3 . . . . . . .28 A1
Limehouse E14 . . . . .33 A2
Nascot St W12 . . . . .30 B3
Naseby Cl NW6 . . . . .11 B1
Nashe Ho SE1 . . . .137 B1
Nash Ho
5 Millwall E14 . . . . .41 C3
Pimlico SW1 . . . . . .146 B1
Nash Rd SE4 . . . . . . .66 A2
Nash St NW1 . . . . . . .92 B4
Nasmyth St W6 . . . . .39 A3
Nassau Rd SW13 . . .46 B2
Nassau St W1 . . . . .104 C3
Nassington Rd
NW3 . . . . .12 B4
Nathan Ho SE11 . . .149 C3
Nathaniel Cl E1 . . . .111 A3
National Archives The
TW9 . . . . .45 A3
National Army Mus
SW3 . . . . .159 A4
National Gallery
W1 . . . . .119 C3
National Hospl for
Neurology and
Neurosurgery
WC1 . . . . .94 B1

National Maritime
Mus SE10 . . . . .52 C4
National Portrait
Gallery W1 . . . . .119 C3
National Tennis Ctr
SW15 . . . . .56 A2
National Theatre
SE1 . . . . .121 A2
Natural History Mus
SW7 . . . . .129 B1
Nautilus Bldg The
EC1 . . . . .96 A4
Naval Row E14 . . . . .34 B2
Navarino Gr E8 . . . .16 C2
Navarino Mans 16 C2
Navarino Rd E8 . . . .16 C2
Navarre St
E2 . . . . . . .24 B1 98 C2
Navenby Wlk 13
E3 . . . . .26 C1
Navy St SW4 . . . . . . .61 C4
Naxos Bldg 1 E14 . . .41 C4
Naylor Bldg W 4
E1 . . . . .111 B2
Naylor Ho
33 Clapham SW8 . .171 B1
4 Walworth SE17 . . .151 C2
West Kilburn
W10 . . . . .23 B2
Naylor Rd SE15 . . . .50 A3
Nayor Bldg E 6
E1 . . . . .111 B2
Nazareth Cl SE15 . . .50 A1
Nazrul St E2 . .24 B2 98 C4
Nealden St SW9 . . . .62 B4
Neal St WC2 . . . . . .106 A1
Neal's Yd WC2 . . . . .106 A1
Neasden Cl NW10 . . .8 A3
Neasden Junc
NW10 . . . . .8 A3
Neasden La NW10 . . .8 A3
Neasden La N
NW10 . . . . .8 A4
Neasden Sta NW10 . .8 A3
Neathouse Pl
SW1 . . . . .146 C4
Nebraska Bldg 11
SE13 . . . . .52 A2
Nebraska St SE1 . . .137 B3
Neckinger SE16 . . . .139 A2
Neckinger Est
SE16 . . . . .139 A2
Neckinger St SE1 . .139 A2
Nectarine Way
SE13 . . . . .52 A1
Nedahall Ct 4
NW4 . . . . .1 B4
Needham Ho
SE11 . . . . .149 B3
Needham Rd W11 . .31 C3
Needleman St
SE16 . . . . .40 C4
Needwood Ho N4 . . .6 B3
Neilson-Terry Ct 4
SW9 . . . . .62 B3
Neil Wates Cres 17
SW2 . . . . .74 C3
Nella Rd W6 . . . . . . .47 C4
Nelldale Rd SE16 . . .40 B2
Nell Gwynn Ho
SW3 . . . . .144 B3
Nelson Cl 2 NW6 . . .23 C2
Nelson Ct SE16 . . . . .33 B1
Nelson Docks
SE16 . . . . .33 B1
Nelson Gdns
E2 . . . . .24 C2 99 C4
Nelson Pas EC1 . . . .97 A4

Nelson Pl N1 . . . . . . .86 B1
Nelson Rd SE10 . . . .52 B4
Nelson's Monument
WC2 . . . . .120 A2
Nelson Sq SE1 . . . .136 A4
Nelsons Row SW4 . .61 C3
Nelson St
Canning Town
E16 . . . . .35 B2
Stepney E1 . . . . .32 A3
Nelsons Yd NW1 . . .82 C2
Nelson Terr N1 . . . . .86 B1
Nemoure Rd W3 . . .28 B2
Nepaul Rd 17
SW11 . . . . .60 A4
Nepean St SW15 . . . .68 C4
Neptune Ct 14 E14 . .41 C2
Neptune Ho
2 Rotherhithe
SE16 . . . . .40 B3
14 Stoke Newington
N16 . . . . .16 A3
Neptune St SE16 . . . .40 B3
Nesham Ho 10 N1 . .24 A4
Nesham St E1 . . . . .125 B2
Ness St 9 SE16 . . . .139 B2
Nestor Ho 12 E2 . . .25 A3
Netheravon Rd
W4 . . . . .38 B1
Netheravon Rd S
W4 . . . . .38 B1
Netherby Ho 22
SW8 . . . . .171 B1
Nethercombe Ho 1
SE3 . . . . .53 C4
Nethercott Ho 27
E3 . . . . .27 A2
Netherfield Rd
SW17 . . . . .72 C1
Netherford Rd
SW4 . . . . .171 A1
Netherhall Gdns
NW3 . . . . .11 B3
Netherhall Way
NW3 . . . . .11 B3
Netherleigh Cl N6 . . .4 A3
Netherton Gr
SW10 . . . . .157 A3
Netherwood Rd
W14 . . . . .39 C4
Netherwood St
NW6 . . . . .10 C2
Netley 6 SE5 . . . . . .49 A2
Netley Prim Sch
NW1 . . . . .92 C3
Netley Rd TW8 . . . . .44 A4
Netley St NW1 . . . . . .92 C3
Nettlecombe NW1 . .13 C1
Nettleden Ho
SW3 . . . . .144 B3
Nettlefold Pl SE27 . .75 A1
Nettleton Rd SE14 . .50 C2
Nevada St SE10 . . . .52 B4
Nevena Ct 3 SW2 . .62 C2
Nevern Mans
SW5 . . . . .141 B2
Nevern Pl SW5 . . . .141 C3
Nevern Rd SW5 . . . .141 B3
Nevern Sq SW5 . . . .141 C3
Nevil Ho 7 SW9 . . .48 A1
Nevill Ct SW10 . . . .156 C2
Nevill Rd
Acton W3 . . . . .37 B4
Paddington NW6 . . . .23 B3

Mus–New 247

Neville Cl continued
Peckham SE15 . . . . .49 C2
Somers Town NW1 . .83 C1
Neville Ct SW12 . . . .73 B4
Neville Gill Cl
SW18 . . . . .59 A1
Neville Ho N4 . . . . . . .6 A4
Neville Rd NW6 . . . .23 B3
Neville St SW7 . . . .143 B2
Neville Terr SW7 . . .143 B2
Nevill Rd N16 . . . . . . .7 A1
Nevinson Cl SW18 . .59 C1
Nevis Rd SW17 . . . . .72 C2
Nevitt Ho N1 . . . . . . .87 C1
Newall Ho SE1 . . . .137 A2
Newark Cres
NW10 . . . . .20 C2
Newark Ho 3
SW9 . . . . .48 A1
Newark St E1 . . . . . .32 A4
New Atlas Wharf
E14 . . . . .41 C3
New Bentham Ct 10
N1 . . . . .15 B1
Newbery Ho N1 . . . .15 B1
Newbold Cotts 4
E1 . . . . .32 B3
Newbolt Ho SE17 . .151 B2
New Bond St W1 . . .118 B4
New Bridge St
EC4 . . . . .108 A1
New Broad St
EC2 . . . . .110 A3
New Bsns Ctr The
NW10 . . . . .21 B2
Newburgh Rd W3 . .28 B1
Newburgh St W1 . . .105 A1
New Burlington Mews
W1 . . . . .118 C4
New Burlington Pl
W1 . . . . .118 C4
New Burlington St
W1 . . . . .118 C4
Newburn Ho SE11 . .149 A2
Newburn St SE11 . .149 A2
Newbury Ct E5 . . . . .18 A3
Newbury Ho
Brixton SW9 . . . . . . .48 A1
14 Kensington W2 . .100 B1
Newbury Mews
NW5 . . . . .12 C2
Newbury St EC1 . . . .108 C4
New Butt La SE8 . . .51 C3
Newby PI E14 . . . . . .92 C4
Newby St SW8 . . . . . .61 A4
New Caledonian Mkt
SE1 . . . . .138 B2
New Caledonian
Wharf SE16 . . . . . . .41 B3
New Campden Ct 9
NW3 . . . . .11 B4
Newcastle Cl EC4 . .108 A2
Newcastle Ct EC4 . .123 A4
Newcastle Ho W1 . .103 B4
Newcastle Pl W2 . . .101 C4
Newcastle Row
EC1 . . . . .95 C1
New Cavendish St
W1 . . . . .104 A3
New Change EC4 . . .108 C1
New Charles St
EC1 . . . . .96 B4

New Church Rd
32 Camberwell
SE5 . . . . 48 B3
Camberwell SE5 . . 48 C4
New College Ct 6
NW3 . . . . 11 B2
New College Mews 17
N1 . . . . 14 C1
New College Par 1
NW3 . . . . 11 B1
Newcombe Ho N5 . 15 B3
Newcombe St
W8 . . . . . . 31 C1 113 C2
Newcomen Ho 5
NW5 . . . . 13 A4
Newcomen St
SW11 . . . . 59 C4
Newcomen St
SE1 . . . . 137 B4
New Compton St
WC2 . . . . 106 A1
New Concordia Wharf
SE1 . . . . 139 A4
Newcourt Ho 28
E2 . . . . 25 A2
Newcourt St NW8 . 80 A1
New Covent Garden
Flower Market
SW8 . . . . 162 A3
New Covent Garden
Fruit & Vegetable
Mkt SW8 . . . . . 161 B1
New Crane Pl E1 . 32 B1
New Crescent Yd 1
NW10 . . . . 21 B3
NEW CROSS 51 B2
New Cross SE14 . . 51 B3
NEW CROSS
GATE 50 C2
New Cross Gate
SE14 . . . . 50 C2
New Cross Gate Sta
SE14 . . . . 51 A3
New Cross Rd
SE14 . . . . 51 A2
New Cross Sta
SE14 . . . . 51 B3
New Ct
City of London
EC4 . . . . 107 B1
20 Hampstead
NW3 . . . . 11 B4
Stoke Newington
N16 . . . . 6 C3
New Den (Millwall
FC) The SE16 . . . 40 B1
Newdigate Ho 5
E14 . . . . 33 B3
Newell St E14 . . 33 B3
New End NW3 . . . 2 B1
New End Prim Sch 53
NW3 . . . . 11 B4
New End Sq NW3 . 11 C4
Newent Cl SE15 . . 49 A3
New Fetter La
EC4 . . . . 107 C2
Newfield Prim Sch
NW10 . . . . 8 B1
Newgate St EC1 . 108 B2
New Globe Wlk
SE1 . . . . 122 C2
New Goulston St
E1 . . . . 110 C2

Newham Sixth Form
Coll (Stratford Ctr)
7 E15 . . . . 19 C1
Newham's Row
SE1 . . . . 138 B3
Newhaven La 3
E16 . . . . 35 C4
New Hope Christian
Sch **8** SE22 . . . . 64 B3
NEWINGTON . . . 150 B4
**Newington Barrow
Way** N7 . . . . . . 5 B1
Newington Butts SE1,
SE11 . . . . 150 B3
Newington Cswy
SE1 . . . . 136 C2
Newington Gn
N16 . . . . 15 C3
**Newington Green
Mans** N16 . . . . . 15 C3
Newington Green
Prim Sch **1** N16 . 15 C3
Newington Green Rd
N1 . . . . 15 C3
Newington Ind Est
SE17 . . . . 150 C3
New Inn Broadway
EC2 . . . . 24 A1 98 B2
New Inn Sq
EC2 . . . . 24 A1 98 B2
New Inn St
EC2 . . . . 24 A1 98 B2
New Inn Yd
EC2 . . . . 24 A1 98 B2
New James Ct
SE15 . . . . 65 A4
New Kent Rd SE1 151 A4
New King's Prim Sch
12 SW6 . . . . . 165 A2
New King's Rd
SW6 . . . . 165 C3
New King St SE8 . 51 C4
Newland Ct EC1 . . 97 B2
Newland Ho 17
SE14 . . . . 50 C4
Newlands NW1 . . . 92 C4
Newlands Quay E1 . 32 B2
New London St
EC3 . . . . 124 B4
Newlyn NW1 . . . . 83 A3
Newman Pas W1 . 105 A3
Newman's Ct EC3 109 C1
Newman's Row
WC2 . . . . 107 A3
Newman Ho E3 . . 27 B1
Newmount NW3 . . 11 C3
New Mount St E15 . 19 C1
Newnes Path
SW15 . . . . 57 A3
Newnham Ho 3
SW15 . . . . 57 C1
Newnham Terr
SE1 . . . . 135 B2
New North Com Sch
N1 . . . . 86 C4
New North Pl
EC2 . . . . 24 A1 98 B2
New North Rd N1 . 87 B3
**New North Road
Bridge** N1 . . . . . 87 B2
New North St
WC1 . . . . 106 C4
New Oxford St
WC1 . . . . 106 A2

New Palace Yd
SW1 . . . . 134 A3
New Park Ct 28
SW2 . . . . 74 A4
New Park Par 14
SW2 . . . . 74 A4
New Place Sq
SE16 . . . . 40 A3
Newport Ave E14 . 34 C2
Newport Ct WC2 . 119 C4
Newport Pl WC2 . 119 C4
Newport Rd SW13 . 46 C2
Newport St SE11 . 149 A4
New Priory Ct 9
NW6 . . . . 10 C1
**New Providence
Wharf** E14 . . . . . 34 C1
Newquay Ho SE11 149 B2
New Quebec St
W1 . . . . 103 A1
New Rd E1 . . . . . 32 A4
New River Ct N5 . 15 C4
New River Way N4 . 6 C4
New Row WC2 . . 120 A4
New Scotland Yard
SW1 . . . . 133 B2
**New Shepherd's Bush
Mkt 6** W12 . . . . 39 B4
New Spring Gdns Wlk
SE11 . . . . 148 B1
New Sq WC2 . . . 107 A2
New Square Pas
SE2 . . . . 107 B2
New St EC2 . . . . 110 B3
Newstead Ho N1 . . 85 C2
Newton Ave W3 . . 37 B4
Newton Gr W4 . . . 38 A2
Newton Ho
21 Clapham SW8 . 171 B2
Paddington NW8 . . 78 B4
1 Stepney E1 . . . 32 A2
Newton Point 1
E16 . . . . 35 B3
Newton Prep Sch
SW8 . . . . 170 B4
Newton Rd
Acton W3 . . . . . 37 B4
Kensington W2 . . 100 A1
Stratford New Town
E15 . . . . 19 C3
Newton St WC2 . . 106 B2
Newton's Yd 14
SW18 . . . . 58 C2
New Tower Bldgs 21
E1 . . . . 32 A1
Newtown Ct
Battersea SW11 . 170 A3
Clapham SW4 . . . 61 A2
New Union Cl E14 . 42 B3
New Union St
EC2 . . . . 109 B3
New Wharf Rd N1 . 84 B2
Niagara Cl N1 . . . 87 A2
Niagara Ct 6
SE16 . . . . 40 B3
Nicholas Ct
Chiswick W4 . . . . 46 A3
Golders Green NW11 1 C4
Nicholas Ho 2
SW15 . . . . 56 C2
Nicholas La EC2,
EC4 . . . . 123 C4

Nicholas Pas EC3 123 C4
Nicholas Rd
Bethnal Green E1 . . 25 B1
20 Shepherd's Bush
W11 . . . . 30 C2
Nicholay Rd N19 . . 4 C3
Nicholl Ho N4 . . . 6 B3
Nichol St E2 . . . . 24 B4
Nichols Cl N4 . . . 5 C2
Nichols Ct E2 . . . 24 B3
Nicholson Ho
SE17 . . . . 151 B2
Nicholson St SE1 . 122 A1
Nickleby Ho
18 Bermondsey
SE1 . . . . 139 B3
17 Shepherd's Bush
W11 . . . . 30 C1
Nickols Wlk SW18 . 59 A3
Nicoll Ct NW10 . . 21 A4
Nicoll Rd NW10 . . 21 A4
Nicosia Rd SW18 . 72 A4
Nigel Bldg EC1 . 107 B4
Nigel Playfair Ave
W6 . . . . 39 A1
Nigel Rd
Deptford SE15 . . . 64 C4
16 Peckham VW . 48 A4
Nightingale Cl
14 Cubitt Town
E14 . . . . 42 B3
Finsbury Pk N4 . . . 5 C4
Nightingale Gr
SE13 . . . . 67 C2
Nightingale Ho
21 Hoxton E1 . . . 24 A4
North Kensington
W12 . . . . 30 B3
7 St George in t East
E1 . . . . 125 B2
Nightingale La SW11,
SW12 . . . . 60 C1
Nightingale Lo 5
W9 . . . . 31 C4
Nightingale Mans 4
SW12 . . . . 60 C1
Nightingale Mews
1 Bow E3 . . . . . 26 A3
Newington SE11 . 150 A4
Nightingale Pl
SW10 . . . . 157 A4
Nightingale Prim Sch
E5 . . . . 16 C4
Nightingale Rd
22 Canonbury N1 . 15 B2
Dagenham NW10 . . 21 B3
Nightingale Sch
SW17 . . . . 72 A2
Nightingale Wlk SW18,
SW12 . . . . 72 A4
Nile Cl N16 . . . . . 7 B1
Nile Ho N1 . . . . . 97 B4
Nile St N1 . . . . . 97 B4
Nile Terr SE1,
SE15 . . . . 153 A1
Nimegen Way 1
SE22 . . . . 64 A2
Nimrod Pas 4 N1 . 16 A2
NINE ELMS 160 C4
Nine Elms La
SW8 . . . . 161 B3
Nisbet Ho E9 . . . . 17 C3
Niton Rd TW9 . . . 54 C4
Niton St SW6 . . . 47 C3
Nobel Ho 8 SE5 . 48 B1

Noble Ct E1 . . . . 32 A2
Noble St EC2 . . . 108 C2
Noel Coward Ho
SW1 . . . . 147 A3
Noel Ho 3 NW3 . . 11 C1
Noel Rd
Acton W3 . . . . . 28 A3
Islington N1 . . . . 86 B2
Noel St W1 . . . . 105 A1
Noko NW10 . . . . 22 C2
Nolan Way E5 . . . 16 C4
Noll Ho N7 . . . . . 5 B2
Norbiton Rd E14 . . 33 B3
Norbroke St W12 . 29 B2
Norburn St W10 . . 31 A4
Norcombe Ho 2
N19 . . . . 4 C1
Norcott Rd N16 . . 7 C1
Norcroft Gdns
SE22 . . . . 76 C4
Norden Ho 22 E2 . 25 A2
Nore Ct NW10 . . . 8 C1
Norfolk Cres W2 . 102 B2
Norfolk Ho
City of London
EC4 . . . . 122 C4
Greenwich SE3 . . . 53 A4
8 Putney SW15 . . 69 B4
Richmond TW10 . . 54 C2
Shacklewell E8 . . . 16 B4
St Johns SE8 . . . . 51 C2
Westminster SW1 . 147 C4
Norfolk House Rd
SW16 . . . . 74 A1
Norfolk Mans
Battersea SW11 . 169 A3
10 Wandsworth
SW18 . . . . 58 C2
Norfolk Mews 12
W10 . . . . 31 A4
Norfolk Pl W2 . . . 101 C2
Norfolk Rd
St John's Wood
NW8 . . . . 79 C3
Willesden NW10 . . . 8 A1
Norfolk Row SE1,
SE11 . . . . 148 C4
Norfolk Sq W2 . . 101 C2
Norfolk Sq Mews
W2 . . . . 101 C1
Norgrove St SW12 . 72 C4
Norland Ho 13
W11 . . . . 30 C1
Norland Pl
W11 . . . . . 31 A1 112 B1
Norland Place Sch
W11 . . . . . 31 A1 112 A1
Norland Rd 16
W11 . . . . 30 C1
Norland Sq
W11 . . . . . 31 A1 112 B1
Norley Vale SW15 . 68 C3
Norman Butler Ho 1
W10 . . . . 23 A1
Normanby Cl
SW15 . . . . 58 B2
Normanby Rd NW10 8 B3
Norman Ct
Dulwich SE22 . . . 76 C4
Finsbury Pk N4 . . . 5 C4
Willesden NW10 . . 22 A3
Normand Croft Com
Sch W14 . . . . . 155 A4
Normand Mews
W14 . . . . 154 B4
Normand Rd W14 154 C4

Normandy Ho 🔟
E14 . . . . .42 B4
Normandy Rd
SW9 . . . . .173 B3
Norman Gr E3 . . . . . .26 A3
Norman Ho SW8 162 A2
Normanhurst Rd
SW2 . . . . .74 B2
Norman Rd SE10 . . .52 A3
Norman St EC1 . . . . .97 A3
Normanton Ave SW18,
SW19 . . . . .70 C2
Normanton Ho 🔟
SW4 . . . . .61 B1
Norman Way W3 . . .28 A3
Norris Ho
🔟 Hoxton N1 . . . . .24 A4
🔟 South Hackney
E9 . . . . .25 B4
Norris St SW1 . . . . .119 B3
Norroy Rd SW15 . . .57 C3
Norse Ho 🔟 SE5 . . .48 B3
Norstead Pl SW15 . .68 C2
NORTH ACTON 20 C2
North Acton Rd
NW10 . . . . .20 C2
North Acton Sta
W3 . . . . .28 C4
Northampton Gr
N1 . . . . .15 C3
Northampton Pk
N1 . . . . .15 C2
Northampton Rd
EC1 . . . . .95 C2
Northampton Sq
EC1 . . . . .96 A3
Northampton St
N1 . . . . .15 B1
North Audley St
W1 . . . . .117 B4
North Ave 🔟 W4 . . .38 A1
Northaw Ho 🔟
W10 . . . . .22 B1
North Bank NW8 . . .90 A3
North Block 🔟 E1 . .32 B2
Northbourne Ho 🔟
E5 . . . . .17 A3
Northbourne Rd
SW4 . . . . .61 C2
North Bridge House
Sch 🔟 NW3 . . . . . .11 B2
North Bridge House
Senior Sch NW1 . .82 A3
Northbrook CE Sch
SE12 . . . . .97 B2
Northburgh St EC1 .96 B2
North Carriage Dr
W2 . . . . .116 B4
Northchurch
SE17 . . . . .151 C2
Northchurch Ho 🔟
E2 . . . . .24 C4
Northchurch Rd
N1 . . . . .15 C1
Northchurch Terr
N1 . . . . .16 A1
North Circular Rd NW2,
NW10 . . . . .8 A3
North Colonnade The
E14 . . . . .34 A1
Northcote Lodge Sch
SW11 . . . . .60 B1
Northcote Rd
Wandsworth
SW11 . . . . .60 B2
Willesden NW10 . . . .8 A1

Northcourt W1 . . .105 A4
North Cres
Marylebone WC1 . .105 A4
Newham E16 . . . . . .27 C1
Northcroft Ct 🔟
W12 . . . . .38 C4
North Cross Rd
SE22 . . . . .64 C2
North Ct SW1 . . . . .134 A1
Northdown St N1 . . .84 C1
North Dulwich Sta
SE21 . . . . .63 C2
North End NW3 . . . . .2 B2
North End Ave NW3 .2 B2
North End Cres
W14 . . . . .140 C3
North End Ho
W14 . . . . .140 B3
North End Par
W14 . . . . .140 B3
North End Rd
Golders Green
NW11 . . . . .2 A3
West Kensington
W14 . . . . .141 A1
North End Way
NW3 . . . . .2 B2
Northern Hts N8 . . . .4 C4
Northesk Ho 🔟
E1 . . . . .25 A1
North Eyot Gdns 🔟
W6 . . . . .38 B1
Northey St E14 . . . . .33 A2
Northfield Hall N6 . . .3 C4
Northfield Ho 🔟
SE15 . . . . .49 C4
Northfield Rd N16 . . .7 A4
Northfields SW18 . . .58 C3
Northfields Prospect
SW18 . . . . .58 A3
Northfleet Ho
SE1 . . . . .137 B4
North Flower Wlk
W2 . . . . .115 B3
North Gate NW8 . . . .80 A1
Northgate Ct 🔟
SW9 . . . . .62 C4
North Gower St
NW1 . . . . .93 A3
North Gr N6 . . . . .3 C4
North Greenwich Pier
SE10 . . . . .35 B1
North Greenwich Sta
SE10 . . . . .43 A4
North Hill Ct N6 . . . . .3 C4
North Ho 🔟 SE8 . . .41 B1
Northiam WC1 . . . . .94 B3
Northiam St E9 . . . . .25 A4
Northington St
WC1 . . . . .95 A1
NORTH
KENSINGTON 30 C4
Northlands St SE5 . .48 B1
Northleigh Ho 🔟
E3 . . . . .27 A2
North Lo SW4 . . . . . .61 B1
North Lodge Cl
SW15 . . . . .57 C2
North London Science
Ctr 🔟 N1 . . . . . . .14 C1
North Mews WC1 . . .95 A1
Northolme Rd N5 . . .15 B4
North Pas SW18 . . .58 C2

Northpoint Sq 🔟
N1 . . . . .13 C2
North Pole Rd
W10 . . . . .30 B4
Northport St N1 . . . . .87 C3
North Rd
Barnsbury N7 . . . . . .14 A2
Brentford TW8 . . . . .44 A4
Highgate N6 . . . . .3 C4
Richmond TW9 . . . . .44 C1
North Ride W2 . . . .116 A3
North Rise W2 . . . .102 B1
North Row W1 . . . .117 B4
NORTH SHEEN 44 C1
North Sheen Sta
TW10 . . . . .54 C3
North Side
Wandsworth Comm
SW18 . . . . .59 C2
North St SW4 . . . . . .61 B4
Northstead Rd
SW2 . . . . .74 C2
North Tenter St
E1 . . . . .111 A1
North Terr SW3 . . .130 A1
Northumberland Alley
EC3 . . . . .110 B1
Northumberland Ave
WC2 . . . . .120 A2
Northumberland Ho
NW5 . . . . .13 B2
Northumberland Mans
E5 . . . . .17 B4
Northumberland Pl
🔟 W6 . . . . .38 C2
North Verbena Gdns
🔟 W6 . . . . .38 C1
Northview 🔟 N7 . . . .5 A1
Northview Cres
NW10 . . . . .8 B4
Northview Prim Sch
NW10 . . . . .8 B4
North Villas NW1 . . .13 C2
Northway Rd SE5 . . .63 B4
Northways Par 🔟
NW3 . . . . .11 C1
North West London
Jewish Day Sch
NW6 . . . . .10 A1
Northwest Pl 🔟 N1 .85 C2
North Wharf Rd
W2 . . . . .101 B3
Northwick Cl NW8 . . .89 B2
Northwick Ho
NW8 . . . . .89 A2
Northwick Terr
NW8 . . . . .89 B2
North Wlk W2 . . . .114 C3
Northwold Prim Sch
E5 . . . . .7 C2
Northwood Rd E5,
N16 . . . . .7 C2
North Wood Lo
NW3 . . . . .11 A4
Northwood Rd N6 . . .4 A4
North Worple Way
SW14 . . . . .55 C4
Norton Folgate
E1 . . . . .110 B4

Norton Ho
🔟 Globe Town
E2 . . . . .25 C2
🔟 Stepney E1 . . . .32 A3
🔟 Stockwell SW9 .173 A1
Norval Gn 🔟 SW9 . .173 C2
Norvic Ho 🔟 SE5 . . .48 B1
Norway Gate SE16 . .41 A3
Norway Pl E14 . . . . .33 B3
Norway St SE10 . . . .52 A4
Norwich Ho 🔟
E14 . . . . .34 A3
Norwich St EC4 . . .107 B2
Norwood Cl NW2 . . . .1 A1
Norwood Ho 🔟
E14 . . . . .34 A2
Norwood NHS Ctr
SE27 . . . . .75 A1
Norwood Rd SE24,
SE27 . . . . .75 A3
Notley St SE5 . . . . . .48 C3
Notre Dame RC Girls
Sch SE1 . . . . .136 B1
Notting Barn Rd
W10 . . . . .22 C1
Nottingdale Sq
W11 . . . . .31 A1 112 A2
Nottingham Ct
WC2 . . . . .106 A1
Nottingham Ho
🔟 Camberwell
SE5 . . . . .48 B1
Stoke Newington N4 . .6 B3
Nottingham Pl
W1 . . . . .103 B4
Nottingham Rd
SW17 . . . . .72 B3
Nottingham St
W1 . . . . .103 B4
Nottingham Terr
NW1 . . . . .91 B1
NOTTING HILL 112 C3
Notting Hill Gate
W11 . . . . .31 C1 113 B2
Notting Hill Gate Sta
W11 . . . . .31 C1 113 B2
Notting Hill Prep Sch
🔟 W11 . . . . .31 B2
Nottingwood Ho
W11 . . . . .31 A2 112 A4
Nova Bldg 🔟 E14 . .41 C2
Nova Ct E 🔟 E14 . .34 B1
Nova Ct W 🔟 E14 . .34 B1
Novello St SW6 . . .165 B4
Nowell Rd SW13 . . .46 C4
Noyna Rd SW17 . . . .72 B1
Nucleus NW10 . . . . .20 B2
Nuding Cl SE13 . . . .66 C4
Nuffield Lo 🔟 W9 . . .31 C4
Nugent Ct 🔟 N19 . . .5 A3
Nugent Rd N19 . . . . .5 A3
Nugent Terr NW8 . . .79 A1
Nun Ct EC2 . . . . . .109 B2
NUNHEAD 65 B3
Nunhead Cres
SE15 . . . . .65 A4
Nunhead Gn SE15 . .65 A4
Nunhead Gr SE15 . .65 B4
Nunhead La SE15 . .65 A4
Nunhead Sta SE15 . .50 B1
Nursery Cl
New Cross SE4 . . . . .51 B1
Putney SW15 . . . . . .57 C3
Nursery La
North Kensington
W10 . . . . .30 B4

Nursery La continued
Shoreditch E2 . . . . . .24 B4
Nursery Rd
Hackney E9 . . . . .17 B2
Stockwell SW9 . . . . . .62 B3
Nursery Row
SE17 . . . . .151 B3
Nutbourne St W10 . .23 A2
Nutbrook St SE15 . . .64 C4
Nutcroft Rd SE15 . . .50 A3
Nutfield Rd
East Dulwich
SE22 . . . . .64 B3
Leyton E15 . . . . .19 B4
Nutford Pl W1 . . . .102 C2
Nuthurst Ave SW2 . .74 B2
Nutley Terr NW3 . . . .11 C2
Nutmeg La E14 . . . . .34 C3
Nuttall St N1 . . . . . . .24 A3
Nutt St SE15 . . . . . . .49 B3
Nye Bevan Ho
SW6 . . . . .154 C2
Nye's Wharf SE1,
SE15 . . . . .49 B4
Nylands Ave TW9 . . .44 C1
Nynehead St SE14 . .51 A3
Nyton Cl N19 . . . . . . .5 A3

O

O2 Ctr NW6 . . . . . . .11 B2
O2 Millennium Dome
The SE10 . . . . .35 A1
Oakbank Gr SE24 . . .63 B3
Oakbury Rd SW6 . .166 B1
Oakcourt 🔟 SE15 . . .49 B3
Oak Cres E16 . . . . . .35 A4
Oakcroft Ct SE3 . . . .53 C2
Oakcroft Rd SE13 . . .52 C1
Oakdale Ct N19 . . . . .5 A2
Oakdale Rd SE15 . . .65 B4
Oakdene 🔟 SE15 . . .50 A2
Oakdene Ho 🔟 N16 . .7 A3
Oakden St SE11 . . .149 C4
Oakeford Ho W14 . .126 B1
Oakend Ho 🔟 N4 . . . .6 C4
Oakeshott Ave N6 . . .3 C2
Oakey La SE1 . . . . .135 B2
Oakfield
Clapham Pk SW4 . . .62 A1
Finsbury Pk N8 . . . . . .5 A4
Oakfield Prep Sch
SE21 . . . . .75 C3
Oakfield Rd
Finsbury Pk N4 . . . . . .5 C4
Wimbledon SW19 . . .69 C1
Oakfield St SW10 156 C4
Oakford Rd NW5 . . .13 B4
Oak Gr NW2 . . . . . . .10 A4
Oakham Ho 🔟
W10 . . . . .22 B1
Oakhill Ave NW3 . . . .11 A4
Oakhill Ct
Honor Oak SE23 . . . .65 B1
Putney SW15 . . . . . .58 B2
Oak Hill Lo NW3 . . . .11 A4
Oak Hill Park Mews
NW3 . . . . .11 B4
Oak Hill Pk NW3 . . . .11 A4
Oakhill Pl SW15 . . . .58 C2
Oakhill Rd SW15 . . . .58 B2
Oak Hill Way NW3 . .11 B4

Oak Ho
🔞 Cubitt Town
E14 . . . . .42 B4
🔟 Maitland Pk
NW3 . . . . .12 B2
🔟 Richmond TW9 . . .45 A2
🔟 Stoke Newington
N16 . . . . .6 C2
Oakhurst Gr SE22 . . . .64 C3
Oakington Rd W9 . . .23 C1
Oakington Way N8 . .5 A4
Oak La E14 . . . . .33 B2
Oaklands Ct
Dagenham NW10 . . . .21 A4
🔝 Shepherd's Bush
W12 . . . . .30 A1
Oaklands Gr W12 . . . .29 C1
Oaklands Ho SE4 . . . .66 B4
Oaklands Mews 🔟
NW2 . . . . .9 C4
Oaklands Pas NW2 . .9 C4
Oaklands Pl 🔝
SW4 . . . . .61 C3
Oaklands Rd
Cricklewood NW2 . . . .9 C4
Mortlake SW14 . . . . .55 B4
Oaklands Sec Sch S11
E2 . . . . .25 A2
Oakley Cres EC1 . . .86 B1
Oakley Dr SE13 . . . .67 C1
Oakley Gdns SW3 . .158 A4
Oakley Ho SW1 . . . .145 A4
Oakley Pl SE1 . . . . .152 C1
Oakley Rd N1 . . . . . .15 C1
Oakley Sq NW1 . . . .83 A2
Oakley St SW3 . . . .158 A4
Oakley Wlk W6 . . . . .47 C4
Oak Lodge 🔟
SE21 . . . . .75 C2
Oak Lodge Sch
SW12 . . . . .72 C4
Oakman Ho 🔟
SW19 . . . . .69 C3
Oakmead Rd
SW12 . . . . .73 A3
Oak Park Gdns
SW19 . . . . .69 C3
Oak Park Mews
N16 . . . . .7 B1
Oakshaw Rd SW18 . .71 A4
Oakshott Ct NW1 . . .83 B1
Oaks Ho Ctr The
W3 . . . . .28 B1
Oaks The
Brondesbury Pk
NW6 . . . . .9 C1
Willesden NW10 . . . . . .9 A4
Oak Tree Ct
Acton W3 . . . . .28 A2
🔝 Clapham Pk
SW4 . . . . .62 A2
Oak Tree Ho W9 . . . .88 A2
Oak Tree Rd NW8 . . .90 A3
Oakview Lo NW11 . . .1 B4
Oak Village NW5 . . . .12 C4
Oak Way W3 . . . . . . .29 A1
Oakwell Ho 🔟
SW8 . . . . .171 B1
Oakwood Cl SE13 . .67 C1
Oakwood Ct W14 . . .126 C2
Oakwood La W14 . . .126 C2
Oakworth Rd W10 . . .30 C4
Oast Ct 🔞 E14 . . . . .33 B2
Oast Lo W4 . . . . .46 A3

Oat La EC2 . . . . . . .109 A2
Oatlands Ct 🔝
SW19 . . . . .69 C3
Oatwell Ho SW3 . . .144 B3
Oban Ho E14 . . . . . . .34 C3
Oban St E14 . . . . . . .34 C3
Oberon Ho 🔝 N1 . . .24 A3
Oberstein Rd 🔞
SW11 . . . . .59 C3
Oborne Cl SE24 . . . .63 A2
O'Brian Ho 🔟 E1 . . .25 C2
Observatory Gdns
W8 . . . . .127 C4
Observatory Mews
E14 . . . . .42 C2
Observatory Rd
Kensington SW7 . . . .129 B1
Mortlake SW14 . . . . .55 B3
Occupation Rd
SE17 . . . . .150 C2
Ocean St E1 . . . . . . .32 C4
Ocean Wharf E14 . . .41 C4
Ockbrook 🔝 E1 . . . .32 B4
Ockendon Rd N1 . . . .15 C2
Ockley Rd SW16 . . . .74 A1
Octagon Arc E2 . . . .110 A3
Octagon The NW3 . . .11 B4
Octavia Ho W10 . . . .23 A1
Octavia Mews 🔟
W9 . . . . .23 B1
Octavia St SW11 . . .168 B3
Octavius St SE8 . . . .51 C3
Odell Wlk SE13 . . . .67 B4
Odeon Ct
Dagenham NW10 . . . .21 A4
🔝 Newham E16 . . . . .35 C4
Odessa Rd NW10 . . . .21 C3
Odessa St SE16 . . . .41 B3
Odette Duval Ho 🔞
E1 . . . . .32 B4
Odger St SW11 . . . . .169 A2
Odhams Wlk WC2 . . .106 B1
Odin Ho 🔝 SE5 . . . . .48 B1
O'Donnell Ct WC1 . . .94 B2
O'Driscoll Ho 🔝
W12 . . . . .30 A3
Offa's Mead E9 . . . . .18 A4
Offenbach Ho 🔞
E2 . . . . .25 C3
Offerton Rd SW4 . . . .61 B4
Offham Ho SE17 . . . .152 A3
Offley Ho 🔟 E9 . . . . .17 C2
Offley Rd SW9 . . . . .163 B2
Offord Rd N1 . . . . . . .14 B1
Offord St N1 . . . . . . .14 B1
Ogilvie Ho 🔝 E1 . . . .32 C3
Oglander Rd SE15 . . .64 B4
Ogle St W1 . . . . .104 C4
O'Gorman Ho
SW10 . . . . .157 A2
Ohio Bldg 🔞 SE13 . .52 A2
Oil Mill La W6 . . . . . .38 C1
Okehampton Rd
NW10 . . . . .22 C4
Okeover Manor
SW4 . . . . .61 A3
Olaf St W11 . . . . .30 C2
Old Bailey EC4 . . . .108 B1
**Old Bailey (Central
Criminal Court)**
EC4 . . . . .108 B2
Old Barrack Yd
SW1 . . . . .131 B3
Old Bellgate Wharf
E14 . . . . .41 C3

Old Bethnal Green Rd
E2 . . . . .25 A2
Old Billingsgate Wlk
EC3 . . . . .124 A3
Old Bldgs WC2 . . . .107 B2
Old Bond St W1 . . . .118 C3
Old Brewery Mews
NW3 . . . . .11 C4
Old Broad St EC2 . . .109 C2
Old Brompton Rd SW5,
SW7 . . . . .143 A3
Old Burlington St
W1 . . . . .118 C3
Oldbury Ct E9 . . . . . .18 A3
Oldbury Pl W1 . . . . .103 C4
Old Castle St E1 . . . .111 A2
Old Cavendish St
W1 . . . . .104 A1
Old Change Ct
EC4 . . . . .108 C1
Old Chiswick Yd
W4 . . . . .46 A4
Old Church Rd E1 . . .32 C3
Old Church St
SW3 . . . . .143 C1
Old Compton St
W1 . . . . .105 B1
Old Court Ho W8 . . . .128 A3
Old Court Pl W8 . . . .128 A3
Old Covent Gdn
WC2 . . . . .120 B4
Old Dairy Mews
🔝 Balham SW12 . . . .72 C3
🔞 Camden Town
NW5 . . . . .13 A2
Old Deer Park Gdns
TW9 . . . . .54 A4
Old Devonshire Rd
SW12 . . . . .73 A4
Old Dock Cl TW9 . . . .44 C4
Oldfield Gr SE16 . . . .40 C2
Oldfield Ho 🔟 W4 . . .38 A1
Oldfield Mews N6 . . . .4 B4
Old Forge Mews
W12 . . . . .39 A4
Old Forge Rd N19 . . . .4 C2
Old Gloucester St
WC1 . . . . .106 B4
Oldham Terr W3 . . . . .28 B1
Oldhill St N16 . . . . . . .7 C3
Old Hospital Cl SW12,
SW17 . . . . .72 B3
Olding Ho 🔝
SW12 . . . . .73 B4
Old Jamaica Bsns Est
🔞 SE16 . . . . .139 B1
Old Jamaica Rd
SE16 . . . . .139 B2
Old James St SE15 . .65 A4
Old Jewry EC2 . . . . .109 B1

Old Kent Rd
Deptford SE1,
SE15 . . . . .50 A4
Walworth SE1 . . . . . .152 B2
Old Laundry The 🔞
SW18 . . . . .59 C3
Old Manor Ct NW8 . . .79 A2
Old Manor Yd
SW5 . . . . .142 A3
Old Market Sq 🔟
E2 . . . . .24 B2 B2
Old Marylebone Rd
NW1 . . . . .102 B3
Old Mitre Ct EC4 . . . .107 C1
Old Montague St
E1 . . . . .111 B3
Old Nichol St
E2 . . . . .24 B1 B1 98 C2
Old North St WC1 . . .106 C4
**OLD OAK
COMMON** 21 B2
Old Oak Common La
W3 . . . . .21 B2
Old Oak Prim Sch
W12 . . . . .29 B3
Old Oak Rd W3 . . . . .29 B2
Old Orch The NW3 . . .12 B4
Old Palace Prim Sch
🔞 E3 . . . . .27 A2
Old Paradise St
SE11 . . . . .148 C4
Old Park Ave
SW12 . . . . .60 C1
Old Park La W1 . . . .118 A1
Old Pearson St
SE10 . . . . .52 A3
Old Pye St SW1 . . . .133 B2
Old Pye Street Est
SW1 . . . . .133 B1
Old Quebec St
W1 . . . . .103 A1
Old Queen St
SW1 . . . . .133 C3
Oldridge Rd SW12 . . .73 A4
Old Royal Free Pl
N1 . . . . .85 C3
Old Royal Free Sq
N1 . . . . .85 C3
Old School Sq 🔞
E14 . . . . .33 C3
Old School The
WC1 . . . . .107 A4
Old Seacoal La
EC4 . . . . .108 A2
Old South Lambeth Rd
SW8 . . . . .162 B2
Old Spitalfields Mkt
E1 . . . . .110 C4
Old Sq WC2 . . . . . . .107 B2
Old St EC1 . . . . .97 C2
Old Stable Mews
N5 . . . . .6 B1
Old Street Sta EC1 . . .97 C2
Old Sun Wharf
E14 . . . . .33 A2
Old Swan Wharf
SW11 . . . . .167 C4
Old Theatre Ct
SE1 . . . . .123 A2
Old Town SW4 . . . . . .61 B4
Old Vicarage Sch 🔟
TW10 . . . . .54 A1
Old Woolwich Rd
SE10 . . . . .42 C1
Old York Rd SW18 . . .59 A2

O'Leary Sq E1 . . . . . .32 B4
Olga Prim Sch 🔞
E3 . . . . .26 A3
Olga St 🔞 E3 . . . . . . .26 A3
Oliphant St W10 . . . .23 A2
Olive Blythe Ho 🔞
W10 . . . . .23 A1
Oliver Bsns Pk
NW10 . . . . .20 B3
Oliver Cl W4 . . . . .45 A4
Olive Rd NW2 . . . . .9 B4
Oliver Goldsmith Prim
Sch SE5 . . . . .49 B2
Oliver Ho
🔞 Bermondsey
SE16 . . . . .139 B3
Notting Hill
W11 . . . . .31 A2 112 A3
South Lambeth
SW8 . . . . .162 A2
Oliver House Prep
Sch 🔞 SW4 . . . . .61 A1
Oliver Mews SE15 . . .49 C1
Oliver's Yd EC1 . . . . .97 C2
Olive Tree Ho 🔝
SE15 . . . . .50 B4
Olive Tree Sch The
SE13 . . . . .67 A1
Olivette St 🔟
SW15 . . . . .57 C3
Olive Waite Ho
NW6 . . . . .11 A1
Ollerton Gn E3 . . . . . .26 B4
Ollgar Cl W12 . . . . . . .29 B1
Olliffe St E14 . . . . . . .42 B3
Olmar St SE1 . . . . . . .49 C4
Olney Ho NW8 . . . . . .90 B2
Olney Rd SE17 . . . . . .48 B4
Olympia Ex Ctr
W14 . . . . .126 B1
Olympian Ct 🔞
E14 . . . . .41 C2
Olympia Way
W14 . . . . .126 B1
Olympia Yd W2 . . . . .114 B3
Olympic Ho 🔟
W10 . . . . .30 B3
Olympic Park E15 . . . .19 A4
Olympic Stadium
E15 . . . . .19 A1
Olympus Sq E5 . . . . . .7 C1
Oman Ave NW2 . . . . . . .9 B4
Oman Ct NW4 . . . . . . .9 A4
Ombersley Ho N4 . . . .6 B4
Omeara St SE1 . . . . .123 A1
Omega Cl E14 . . . . . . .42 A3
Omega Ho SW10 . . . .157 A2
Omega Pl N1 . . . . . . .84 B1
Omega St SE14 . . . . .51 C2
Omega Works E3 . . . .18 C1
Ommaney Rd SE14 . . .51 A2
Omnibus Bsns Ctr
N7 . . . . .14 A3
Ondine Rd SE15 . . . . .64 B4
Onedin Point 🔟
E1 . . . . .125 C3
Onega Gate SE16 . . . .41 A3
O'Neill Ho NW8 . . . . .79 C1
One New Change 🔞
Ctr EC4 . . . . .108 C1
One Tree Cl SE23 . . . .65 B1
Ongar Ho 🔝 N1 . . . . .15 C2
Ongar Rd SW6 . . . . .155 C4
Onslow Ave TW10 . . . .54 A2
Onslow Avenue Mans
🔟 TW10 . . . . .54 A2

Onslow Cl W9 . . . . **23** B2
Onslow Ct SW10 . . **143** A1
Onslow Gdns
SW7 . . . . **143** B2
Onslow Lo **20** SW2 . . **74** C4
Onslow Mews E
SW7 . . . . **143** B3
Onslow Mews W
SW7 . . . . **143** B3
Onslow Rd TW10 . . . **54** A1
Onslow Sq SW7 . . . . **143** C3
Onslow St EC1 . . . . . . **95** C1
Ontario St SE1 . . . . . **136** B2
Ontario Way E14 . . . . **33** C2
Opal St SE11 . . . . **150** A2
**Open Air Theatre,
Regent's Pk Royal** . **91** B3
Openview SW17,
SW18 . . . . **71** C2
Opera Ct 7 N19 . . . . . **4** C1
**Operating Theatre
Mus & Herb Garret
The** SE1 . . . . **123** C1
Ophelia Gdns NW2 . . . **1** A1
Ophir Terr SE15 . . . . . **49** C2
Opie Ho NW8 . . . . **80** B2
Oppenheim Rd
SE13 . . . . **52** B1
Oppidan Apartments
NW6 . . . . **78** C4
Oppidans Rd NW3 . . **12** B1
Orange Pl SE16 . . . . . **40** B3
Orangery Gallery The
W8 . . . . **114** C3
Orange St WC2 . . . . **119** C3
Orange Yd WC2 . . . . **105** C1
Oransay Rd **21** N1 . . . **15** B2
Oratory La SW3 . . . . **143** C2
Oratory RC Prim Sch
SW3 . . . . **144** A2
Orbain Rd SW6 . . . . . **154** B1
Orbel St SW11 . . . . . **168** A3
Orb St SE17 . . . . **151** B3
Orchard Cl
Honor Oak SE23 . . . **65** B1
21 Islington N1 . . . . **15** B1
Kensal Town W10 . . **31** A4
Orchard Ct
Barnes SW13 . . . . . **56** B4
Marylebone W1 . . . **103** B2
Orchard Dr SE3 . . . . **53** A1
Orchard Hill SE13 . . **52** A2
Orchard Ho
Camberwell SE5 . . . **48** B2
11 Rotherhithe
SE16 . . . . **40** B3
Shepherd's Bush
W12 . . . . **29** C1
Orchard House Sch 15
W4 . . . . **37** A2
Orchard Mead Ho
NW11 . . . . **1** C2
Orchard Mews N1 . . **15** C1
Orchard Pl E14 . . . . . **35** A2
Orchard Prim Sch 17
E9 . . . . **17** B1
Orchard Rd
Highgate N6 . . . . **4** A4
Richmond TW9 . . . . **54** C4
Orchard Rise
TW10 . . . . **55** B3
Orchardson Ho
NW8 . . . . **89** C1
Orchardson St
NW8 . . . . **89** C1
Orchard Sq W14 . . . **140** C1

Orchard St W1 . . . **103** C2
Orchard The
Acton Green W4 . . . **37** C2
Lewisham SE13 . . . . **52** C1
Orchid Cl SE13 . . . . . **67** C2
Orchid St W12 . . . . . **29** C2
Orde Hall St WC1 **106** C4
Orde Ho **10** N16 . . . . **15** C4
Ordell Ct **33** E3 . . . . **26** B3
Ordell Rd E3 . . . . **26** B3
Ordnance Cres
SE10 . . . . **42** C4
Ordnance Hill
NW8 . . . . **79** C3
Ordnance Mews
NW8 . . . . **79** C2
Ordnance Rd E16 . . **35** B4
Oregano Dr E14 . . . . **34** C3
Oregon Bldg 5
SE13 . . . . **52** A2
Orestes Mews 1
NW6 . . . . **10** C3
Orford Ct SE27 . . . . . **75** A2
Oriana Ho **3** E14 . . . **33** B2
Oriel Ct NW3 . . . . . . **11** B4
Oriel Dr SW13 . . . . . **47** B4
Oriel Rd
Hackney E9 . . . . **18** A2
Homerton E9 . . . . . **17** C2
Orient St SE11 . . . . . **150** A4
Orion Bsns Ctr
SE14 . . . . **40** C1
Orion Ho **20** E1 . . . . **25** A1
Orion Point 1
E14 . . . . **41** C2
Orkney Ho N1 . . . . . . **84** C4
Orkney St SW11 . . **169** B2
Orlando Rd SW4 . . . . **61** B4
Orleston Mews N7 . . **14** C2
Orleston Rd N7 . . . . . **14** C2
Orlop St SE10 . . . . . . **43** A1
Orme Ct W2 . . . . **114** A3
Orme Ct Mews
W2 . . . . **114** A3
Orme Ho **8** E8 . . . . . **24** B4
Orme La W2 . . . . **114** A3
Ormeley Rd SW12 . . **73** A3
Ormerod Ho **3**
SW9 . . . . **62** A4
Orme Sq W2 . . . . . . **114** A3
Ormiston Gr W12 . . **30** A1
Ormiston Rd SE10 . . **43** C1
Ormond Cl WC1 . . **106** B4
Ormond Ct SW15 . . **57** B3
Ormonde Gate
SW3 . . . . **145** A1
Ormonde Mans
WC1 . . . . **106** B4
Ormonde Pl SW1 . . **145** C3
Ormonde Rd SW14 . **55** A4
Ormonde Terr
NW8 . . . . **80** C3
Ormond Ho **7** N16 . . **6** C2
Ormond Mans
WC1 . . . . **94** C1
Ormond Mews
WC1 . . . . **94** B1
Ormond Rd N4, N19 . . **5** A3
Ormond Yd SW1 . . **119** A2
Ormrod Ct W11 . . . . **31** B3
Ormsby Lo **7** W4 . . . **38** A3
Ormsby Pl N16 . . . . . . **7** B1
Ormsby St E2 . . . . . . **24** B3
Ornside St SE15 . . . . **50** B4
Ornan NW3 . . . . **12** A3
Orpen Ho SW5 . . . . **141** C3

Orpen Wlk N16 . . . . . . **7** A1
Orpheus Ho 25 N19 . . **4** C4
Orpheus Ho 6
Orpheus St SE5 . . . . **48** C2
Orsett Mews W2 . . . **100** C2
Orsett St SE11 . . . . . **149** B2
Orsett Terr W2 . . . . **100** C2
Orsman Rd N1 . . . . . . **24** A4
Orton St E1 . . . . **125** B1
Orville Rd SW11 . . . . **167** C2
Orwell Ct
Hackney E8 . . . . **24** C4
Highbury N5 . . . . . . **15** B4
Orwell Ho W12 . . . . . **29** C2
Osbaldeston Rd
N16 . . . . **7** C2
Osbert St SW1 . . . . **147** B3
Osborn Cl E8 . . . . . . **24** C4
Osborne Rd
Finsbury Pk N4 . . . . . **5** C3
Hackney E9 . . . . **18** B2
South Acton W3 . . . **37** A4
Willesden NW2 . . . . . **9** A2
Osborn St E1 . . . . . **111** A4
Osbourne Ho
TW10 . . . . **54** C2
Oscar Faber Pl 8
N1 . . . . **16** A1
Oscar St SE8 . . . . . . **51** C1
Oseney Cres NW5 . . **13** C2
Osier Ct E1 . . . . **25** C1
Osier La SE10 . . . . . . **43** B3
Osier St E1 . . . . **25** B1
Osiers Rd SW18 . . . . **58** C3
Oslac Rd SE6 . . . . . . **67** A1
Oslo Ct NW8 . . . . **80** A1
Oslo Ho **2** SE5 . . . . . **48** B1
Oslo Sq SE16 . . . . . . **41** A3
Oslow Cl W10 . . . . . . **23** B2
Osman Prim Sch 1
E1 . . . . **111** C4
Osman Rd W6 . . . . . . **39** B3
Osmington Ho
SW8 . . . . **163** A1
Osmund St W12 . . . . **29** B4
Osnaburgh St NW1 . . **92** B2
Osnaburgh Terr
NW1 . . . . **92** B2
Osprey Ct SW3 . . . . **141** A4
Osprey Ho
Camberwell SE15 . . **49** B2
3 Limehouse E14 . . **33** A2
Ospringe Ho SE1 . . **121** C1
Ospringe Rd NW5 . . **13** B4
Osram Ct W6 . . . . . . **39** B3
Osric Path 1 N1 . . . . **24** A3
Ossian Mews N4 . . . . **5** B4
Ossian Rd N4 . . . . **5** B4
Ossington Bldgs
W1 . . . . **103** B3
Ossington Cl
W2 . . . . **31** C2 **113** C3
Ossington St W2 . . . **114** A3
Ossory Rd SE1 . . . . **153** A1
Ossulston St NW1 . . **83** C1
Ostade Rd SW2 . . . . **74** B4
Osten Mews SW7 . . **128** B1
Osterley Ho 5
E14 . . . . **34** A3
Osterley Rd N16 . . . . **16** A4
Oswald Bldg SW8 . . **160** A3
Oswald's Mead E9 . . **18** A4
Oswald Rd SW12,
SW17 . . . . **72** B1
Oswell Ho **3** E1 . . . . **32** A1
Oswin St SE11 . . . . . **150** B4
Oswyth Rd SE5 . . . . **49** A1

Otford Cres SE4 . . . . **66** B1
Otford Ho
Bermondsey SE1 . . **137** C3
6 Deptford SE15 . . **50** B4
Otha Ho **13** SW9 . . . **172** B2
Othello Cl SE11 . . . . **150** A2
Otis St E3 . . . . **27** B2
Otley Ho N5 . . . . **6** A1
Ottaway Ct E5 . . . . . . **7** C1
Ottaway St E5 . . . . . . **7** C1
Otterburn Ho 12
SE5 . . . . **48** B3
Otter Cl E15 . . . . **27** B4
Otto St SE17 . . . . **48** A4
**Our Lady of Dolours
RC Prim Sch 5**
W2 . . . . **100** A4
**Our Lady of Lourdes
RC Prim Sch**
1 Lewisham
SE13 . . . . **67** C4
London NW10 . . . . **20** B4
**Our Lady of Victories
RC Prim Sch**
1 Putney SW15 . . . **57** C3
South Kensington
SW7 . . . . **143** A3
**Our Lady Queen of
Heaven RC Prim Sch**
10 SW19 . . . . **69** C4
Our Lady RC Prim Sch
Camden Town
NW1 . . . . **83** A4
2 Poplar E14 . . . . **33** B3
**Our Lady & St Joseph
RC Prim Sch 14**
N1 . . . . **16** A2
**Our Lady's Convent
RC High Sch 3**
N15 . . . . **7** A4
Ouseley Rd SW12 . . **72** B3
Outer Circ NW1 . . . **81** A1
Outgate Rd NW10 . . **8** B1
Outram Pl N1 . . . . . . **84** B4
Outwich St EC3 . . . **110** B2
Outwood Ho **3**
SW2 . . . . **74** B4
Oval Mans SE11 . . . **163** A4
Oval Pl SW8 . . . . **163** A2
Oval Rd NW1 . . . . . . **82** A4
Oval Sta SE11 . . . . . **163** B3
Oval The **25** A3
Oval Way SE11 . . . . **149** A1
Overbury Ho **3**
E5 . . . . **17** C4
Overbury St E5 . . . . . **17** C4
Overcliff Rd SE13 . . **66** C4
Overhill Rd SE21,
SE22 . . . . **76** C4
Overlea Rd E5 . . . . . . **7** C4
Oversley Ho 17
W2 . . . . **31** C4
Overstone Ho 16
E14 . . . . **33** C3
Overstone Rd W6 . . **39** B2
Overstrand Mans
SW11 . . . . **169** B3
Overton Ho SW15 . . **68** B4
Overton Rd SW9 . . **173** C1
Overy Ho SE1 . . . . . . **136** A3
Ovex Cl E14 . . . . **42** B4
Ovington Ct SW3 . . **130** B1
Ovington Gdns
SW3 . . . . **130** B1
Ovington Mews
SW3 . . . . **130** B1

Ovington Sq SW3 . . **130** B1
Ovington St SW3 . . **144** B4
Owen Ho **11** N19 . . . . **13** A4
Owen's Ct EC1 . . . . . **96** A4
Owen's Row EC1 . . . **96** A4
Owen St EC1 . . . . **86** A1
Owgan Cl SE5 . . . . . . **48** C3
Oxberry Ave SW6 . . **164** B2
Oxbridge Ct 8
W4 . . . . **37** A1
Oxendon St SW1,
W1 . . . . **119** B3
Oxenford St SE15 . . . **64** B4
Oxenham Ho 22
SE8 . . . . **51** C4
Oxenholme NW1 . . . **83** A1
Oxestalls Rd SE8 . . **41** A1
**Oxford & Cambridge
Mans** NW1 . . . . . **102** B3
Oxford Cir W1 . . . . . **104** C1
Oxford Circus Ave
W1 . . . . **104** C1
Oxford Circus Sta
W1 . . . . **104** C1
Oxford Ct
City of London
EC4 . . . . **123** B4
Gunnersbury W4 . . **37** A1
18 Paddington W2 . **31** C4
Oxford Dr SE1 . . . . . **124** A1
**Oxford Gardens Prim
Sch 19**
W10 . . . . **30** C3
Oxford Gate W6 . . . . **39** C2
Oxford Gdns
Brentford W4 . . . . . **44** C4
North Kensington
W10 . . . . **30** C3
Oxford Ho N4 . . . . **5** C3
Oxford Rd
Finsbury Pk N4 . . . . . **5** C3
Paddington NW6 . . **23** C3
Putney SW15 . . . . . **58** A3
Stratford E15 . . . . . **19** C2
Oxford Rd N W4 . . . **37** A1
Oxford Rd S W4 . . . . **37** A1
Oxford Sq W2 . . . . . **102** B1
Oxford St W1 . . . . . . **104** B1
Oxley Cl SE1 . . . . . . **153** A2
Oxonian St SE22 . . . **64** B3
OXO Tower SE1 . . . . **121** C3
Oxo Tower Wharf
SE1 . . . . **121** C3
Oxted Ct N16 . . . . **7** A3
Oyster Row E1 . . . . . **32** B3
Ozolins Way E16 . . . . **35** C3

P

Pablo Neruda Cl 4
SE24 . . . . **63** A3
Pace Pl E1 . . . . **32** A3
Pacific Ho **15** E1 . . . . **25** C1
Pacific Rd E16 . . . . . . **35** C3
Pacific Wharf
SE16 . . . . **32** C1
Packenham Ho
24 Crouch End N19 . . **4** C4
21 Spitalfields
E2 . . . . **24** B2 **99** A4
Packington Sq N1 . . **86** C4
Packington St N1 . . **86** B3
Padbury SE17 . . . . . **152** B1

Padbury Ct
E2 . . . . 24 B2 99 A3
Padbury Ho NW8 . . . . 90 B2
Paddenswick Ct 2
W6 . . . . .39 A3

Paddenswick Rd
W6 . . . . .38 C3
PADDINGTON 100 C3
Paddington Acad 7
W9 . . . . .23 C1
Paddington Gn
W2 . . . . 101 B4
Paddington Green
  Prim Sch NW8 . . . . 89 B1
Paddington St
W1 . . . . 103 B4
Paddington Sta
W2 . . . . 101 B2
Paddock Cl SE3 . . . .53 C1
Paddock Prim Sch
SW11 . . . . .60 C3
Paddock Sch
SW15 . . . . .56 B3
Paddock Way 11
SW15 . . . . .69 B4
Padfield Rd SE5 . . . .63 B4
Padstone Ho 50
E3 . . . . .27 A2
Padstow Ho 12
E14 . . . . .33 B2
Pagden St SW8 . . . .170 B4
Pageant Cres SE16 .33 B1
Pageantmaster Ct
EC4 . . . . 108 A1
Page Ho SE10 . . . . . .52 B4
Page St SW1 . . . . . .147 C4
Page's Wlk SE1 . . . .138 B1
Page's Yd W4 . . . . . .46 A4
Paget Ho 22 E2 . . . .25 B3
Paget Rd N16 . . . . . . .6 C3
Paget St EC1 . . . . . . .96 A4
Pagham Ho 6
W10 . . . . .22 B1
Pagnell St SE14 . . . .51 B3
Pagoda Ave TW9 . . .54 B4
Pagoda Gdns SE3 . .52 C1
Pagoda Gr SE27 . . . .75 B2
Paine Ct SE3 . . . . . . .53 B4
Painsthorpe Rd 3
N16 . . . . .7 A1
Painswick Ct 1
SE15 . . . . .49 B3
Painters Mews
SE16 . . . . 153 C4
Pakeman Ho SE1 . .136 B4
Pakeman Prim Sch
N7 . . . . .5 B1
Pakeman St N7 . . . . .5 B1
Pakenham Cl
SW12 . . . . .72 C3
Pakenham St WC1 . .95 A2
Palace Ave W8 . . . .128 B4
Palace Cl 4 E9 . . . .18 B2
Palace Ct
  Hampstead NW3 . . . .11 A3
  Kensington W2 . . . .114 A3
  Streatham SW2 . . . .74 C2
Palace Garden Mews
W8 . . . . 31 C1 113 C2
Palace Gate W8 . . . .128 C3
Palace Gdns Mews
W8 . . . . 114 B1
Palace Gn W8 . . . . . 114 A1
Palace Mans W14 . .140 B4

Palace Mews
  Belgravia SW1 . . . .145 C3
  Fulham SW6 . . . . . .155 A2
Palace Pl SW1 . . . . .132 C2
Palace Rd SE27, SW16,
  SW2 . . . . .74 C2
Palace St SW1 . . . . .132 C2
Palatine Ave N16 . . .16 A4
Palatine Rd N16 . . . .16 A4
Palazzo Apartments
11 N1 . . . . .16 A1
Palemead Cl SW6 . . .47 C2
Palermo Rd NW10 . . .21 C3
Palewell Common Dr
SW14 . . . . .55 C2
Palewell Pk SW14 . .55 C3
Palfrey Pl SW8 . .163 A2
Palgrave Gdns
NW1 . . . . .90 B2
Palgrave Ho
7 Camberwell
  SE5 . . . . .48 B3
4 Maitland Pk
  NW3 . . . . .12 B3
Palgrave Rd W12 . . .38 B3
Palissy St 5 8
E2 . . . . 24 B2 98 C3
Pallant Ho SE1 . . . .137 C1
Pallester Ct NW11 . .1 A3
Palliser Ct 4 . . . . .140 A1
Palliser Ho
3 Greenwich
  SE10 . . . . .52 C4
8 Stepney E1 . . . . .25 C1
Palliser Rd W14 . . . .140 A1
Pallister Terr
SW15 . . . . .68 B2
Pall Mall SW1 . . . . .119 B1
Pall Mall E SW1 . . . .119 C2
Pall Mall Pl SW1 . . .119 A1
Palm Ct
18 Camberwell
  SE15 . . . . .49 B3
  Stoke Newington
  N16 . . . . .6 C2
Palmer Ho
6 Deptford SE14 . . .50 C3
8 Kentish Town
  NW5 . . . . .13 B4
5 Tufnell Pk N19 . . . .4 B1
Palmer Pl N7 . . . . . . .14 C3
Palmers Rd
  Globe Town E2 . . . . .25 C3
  Mortlake SW14 . . . . .55 B4
Palmer St SW1 . . . .133 B2
Palmerston Ct 22
E3 . . . . .25 C3
Palmerston Ho
  Battersea SW11 . . .169 C3
  Kensington
  W8 . . . . . .31 C1 113 B1
Palmerston Rd
  Acton Green W3 . . . .37 B3
  Brondesbury NW6 . . .10 B1
  Hampstead NW6 . . . .10 C1
  Mortlake SW14 . . . . .55 B3
Palmerston Way
SW8 . . . . .160 B1
Palm Gr W5 . . . . .36 A3
Palm Tree Ho 2
SE14 . . . . .50 C3
Pamela Ct NW10 . . . .8 C1
Pamela Ho 44 E8 . . .24 B4
Pamlion Ct N4 . . . . . .5 A4
Panama Ho 6 E1 . . .32 C4
Pancras La EC2 . . . .109 B1

Pancras Rd NW1 . . .83 C2
Pancras Way 3 E3 .26 C3
Pandian Way 4
NW5 . . . . .13 C3
Pandora Rd NW6 . . .10 C2
Pangbourne NW1 . . .92 C3
Pangbourne Ave
W10 . . . . .30 B4
Pangbourne Ho 4
N7 . . . . .14 A3
Pankhurst Cl 2
SE14 . . . . .50 C3
Pankhurst Ho 2
NW10 . . . . .30 B3
Panmure Cl N5 . . . . .15 A4
Pan Peninsula Sq
E14 . . . . .42 A4
Pansy Gdns W12 . . .29 C2
Panther Dr NW10 . . . .8 A3
Panyer Alley EC2 . .108 C2
Paper Mill Wharf
E14 . . . . .33 A2
Papworth Gdns
N7 . . . . .14 B3
Papworth Way
SW2 . . . . .74 C4
Parade Mans 4
SE5 . . . . .48 B1
Parade Mews SE27,
  SW2 . . . . .75 A2
Parade The SW11 . .159 A2
Paradise Pas N7 . . .14 C3
Paradise Rd
  Richmond TW10 . . . .54 A2
  South Lambeth
  SW4 . . . . .172 A2
Paradise Row 2 E2 .25 A2
Paradise St SE16 . .40 A4
Paradise Wlk
SW3 . . . . .159 A4
Paragon Christian
  Acad E5 . . . . .17 C4
Paragon Cl E16 . . . .35 C3
Paragon Ho SE3 . . . .53 B1
Paragon Mews
SE1 . . . . .151 C4
Paragon Pl SE3 . . . .53 B1
Paragon Rd E9 . . . . .17 B2
Paragon The
  Kidbrooke SE3 . . . . .53 C1
  Walworth SE17 . . . . .151 C1
Paramount Bldg
EC1 . . . . .96 A2
Paramount Ct
WC1 . . . . .93 A1
Parbury Rd SE23 . . .66 A1
Pardoner St SE1 . .137 C2
Pardon St EC1 . . . . .96 B2
Parfett Cl NW11 . . . .2 B3
Parfitt Cl NW11 . . . .111 C2
Parfrey St W6 . . . . . .47 B4
Paris Gdn SE1 . . . . .122 A2
Paris Ho 22 E2 . . . .25 A3
Park Ave
  Golders Green
  NW11 . . . . .2 A3
  Mortlake SW14 . . . . .55 C3
  Willesden NW10 . . . . .9 B2
Park Ave N NW10 . . .9 A3
Park Cl
  Kensington W14 . . . .127 A2
  Knightsbridge
  SW1 . . . . .130 C3
19 South Hackney
  E9 . . . . .25 B4
Park Cres W1 . . . . . .92 A1

Park Crescent Mews E
W1 . . . . .92 B1
Park Crescent Mews
W W1 . . . . .92 A1
Park Dr
  Acton W3 . . . . .36 C3
  Golders Green NW11 . .2 A3
  Mortlake SW14 . . . . .55 C3
Park Dwellings 7
NW3 . . . . .12 B3
Park End NW3 . . . . . .12 A4
Parker Ct
  Shoreditch N1 . . . . .87 A4
  South Lambeth
  SW11 . . . . .172 A3
Parke Rd SW13 . . . .46 C2
Parker Mews
WC2 . . . . .106 B2
Parkers Row 19
SE1 . . . . .139 B3
Parker's Row SE1 . .139 A3
Parker St WC2 . . . . .106 B2
Parkfield Ave
SW14 . . . . .56 A3
Parkfield Ct SE14 . . .51 B2
Parkfield Ind Est
SW11 . . . . .169 C2
Parkfield Rd
  New Cross SE14 . . . .51 B2
  Willesden NW10 . . . . .9 A1
Parkfields SW15 . . . .57 B3
Parkfield St N1 . . . . .85 C2
Park Flats N6 . . . . . .3 A4
Parkgate Gdns
SW14 . . . . .55 C2
Parkgate House Sch
SW11 . . . . .59 C3
Parkgate Mews N6 . .4 B4
Parkgate Rd
  SW11 . . . . .158 B1
  Willesden NW10 . . . . .8 A4
Park Hall SE10 . . . . .52 C4
Park Hall Rd SE21 . .75 C1
Park Hall Road Trad
  Est SE21 . . . . .75 C1
Parkham St SW11 . .168 A3
Park Heights Ct 2
E14 . . . . .33 B3
Park Hill
  Clapham Pk SW4 . . . .61 C2
  Richmond TW10 . . . .54 B1
Park Hill Ct SW17 . . .72 B1
Parkhill Rd NW3 . . . .12 B3
Park Hill Wlk 10
NW3 . . . . .12 B3
Park Ho
8 Camberwell
  SE5 . . . . .48 C2
22 Hackney E9 . . . . . .6 A2
33 Hackney E9 . . . . . .17 B1
Parkholme Rd E8 . . .16 C2
Parkhouse St SE5 . .48 C3
Parkhurst Ct N7 . . . .14 A4
Parkhurst Rd N7 . . . .14 A4
Parkinson Dr
  Finsbury N1 . . . . .97 B3
  Shoreditch EC1 . . . . .97 C4

Parkinson Ho 6
E9 . . . . .17 B1
Park La
  Mayfair W1 . . . . . . .117 B3
  Mill Meads E15 . . . . .27 C4
Parkland Ct W14 . . .126 A4
Parkland Gdns 12
SW19 . . . . .69 C3
Parklands
  East Dulwich
  SE22 . . . . .65 A2
  Highgate N6 . . . . .4 A4
Parklands Cl SW14 . .55 B2
Park Lea Ct N16 . . . . .7 A4
Parklife Oxford St
W1 . . . . .103 B1
Park Lo
11 South Hampstead
  NW8 . . . . .11 C1
10 Wapping E1 . . . . . .32 A1
  Willesden NW2 . . . . . .9 B4
Park Lofts 5 SW4 . .62 A3
Park Lorne NW8 . . . .90 B3
Park Mans
  Battersea SW11 . . . .168 C3
  Bedford Pk W6 . . . . .38 B3
  Fulham SW6 . . . . . .164 B3
  Knightsbridge
  SW1 . . . . .130 C3
  St John's Wood
  NW8 . . . . .80 A1
  Vauxhall SW8 . . . . .162 B4
Parkmead SW15 . . . .57 A1
Park Mews
  Greenwich SE10 . . . .43 B1
  Kensal Rise W10 . . . .23 A3
Park Par
  Acton W3 . . . . .36 C3
  Dagenham NW10 . . . .21 B3
Park Piazza 3
SE13 . . . . .67 C1
Park Pl
  Canary Wharf E14 . . .33 C1
  Gunnersbury W3 . . . .36 C2
  Shoreditch N1 . . . . . .87 C4
  St James SW1 . . . . .118 C2
Park Place Dr W3 . . .36 C2
Park Place Ho 8
SE10 . . . . .52 C4
Park Place Villas
W2 . . . . .101 A4
Park Rd
  Chiswick W4 . . . . . . .45 C4
  Dagenham NW10 . . . .21 A4
  Lisson Gr NW1,
  NW8 . . . . .90 B2
  Richmond TW10 . . . .54 B1
Park Rd E W3 . . . . . .37 B4
Park Rd N
  Chiswick W4 . . . . . . .37 C1
  South Acton W3 . . . .37 A4
Park Road E 11
W3 . . . . .37 A4
Park Row SE10 . . . . .52 C4
PARK ROYAL 20 A2
Park Royal NW10 . . .20 B1
Park Royal Bsns Ctr
  NW10 . . . . .20 B1
Park Royal Metro Ctr
  NW10 . . . . .20 A1
Park Royal Rd NW10,
  W3 . . . . .20 B1
Park S SW11 . . . . . .169 B3
Park St James
  NW8 . . . . .80 C3

Park Sheen **3**
SW14 . . . . .55 A3
Parkshot TW9 . . . . . . .54 A3
Parkside
East Acton W3 . . . . . . .29 A1
Greenwich SE3. . . . . . .53 B3
Park Side NW2 . . . . .9 A4
Parkside Bsns Est
SE8 . . . . .51 A4
Parkside Cres N7 . . . . . .5 C1
Parkside Est E9 . . . . . .25 C4
Parkside (Private)
Hospl SW19 . . . . .69 C1
Parkside St SW11 . . . .169 B3
Park Sq E NW1 . . . . . .92 B2
Park Square Mews
NW1 . . . . .92 A1
Park Sq W NW1 . . . . . .92 A1
Park St
Borough The SE1 . . . .123 A2
Mayfair W1 . . . . .117 B3
Parkstead Rd
SW15 . . . . .56 C2
Parkstone Rd **5**
SE15 . . . . .49 C1
Park Stps W2 . . . . . . .116 B4
Park The NW11 . . . . . . .1 C4
Parkthorne Rd
SW12 . . . . .73 C4
Park Twrs W1 . . . . . . .118 A1
Park View
Dagenham W3 . . . . . . .28 B4
Highbury N5 . . . . .15 B4
Willesden NW2 . . . . . . .9 B4
Parkview Ct SW6 . . . . .164 B1
Park View Ct
SW18 . . . . .58 C1
Park View Ho
SE24 . . . . .63 A1
Park View Mans N4 . . . .6 A4
Park View Mews **2**
SW9 . . . . .172 C2
Park View Rd NW10 . . . .8 B4
Park Village E
NW1 . . . . .82 B1
Park Village W
NW1 . . . . .82 A2
Parkville Rd SW6 . . . .154 C1
Park Vista SE10 . . . . . .52 C4
Park Walk Prim Sch
SW10 . . . . .157 B3
Parkwat Cres E15 . . . . .19 B3
Parkway NW1 . . . . . . .82 A2
Park Way W3 . . . . .36 C2
Parkway Ho SW14 . . . .55 C3
Park West W2 . . . . . . .102 B2
Park West Pl W1,
W2 . . . . .102 B2
Park Wlk
Chelsea SW10 . . . . . .157 B4
Highgate N6 . . . . .3 C4
Parkwood NW8 . . . . . .80 C3
Parkwood Prim Sch
1 N4 . . . . .6 A2
Parliament Ct
NW3 . . . . .12 A4
Parliament Hill
NW3 . . . . .12 A4
Parliament Hill Mans
NW5 . . . . .12 C4
Parliament Hill Sch
NW5 . . . . .12 C4
Parliament Mews
SW14 . . . . .45 B1
Parliament Sq
SW1 . . . . .134 A3

Parliament St
SW1 . . . . .134 A4
Parliament View
Apartments
SE11 . . . . .148 C4
Parma Cres SW11 . . . .60 B3
Parminter Ind Est **24**
E2 . . . . .25 B3
Parmiter St **25**
E2 . . . . .25 A3
Parmoor Ct EC1 . . . . . .96 C2
Parnell Cl W12 . . . . . . .39 A3
Parnell Ho WC1 . . . . . .105 C2
Parnell Rd E3 . . . . .26 B4
Parnham St E14 . . . . . .33 A3
Parolles Rd N19 . . . . . .4 B3
Parr Ct N1 . . . . .87 B2
Parrington Ho **1**
SW4 . . . . .61 C1
Parr Ho W4 . . . . .38 B2
Parry Ho **32** E1 . . . . . .32 A1
Parry Rd W10 . . . . .23 A2
Parry St SW8 . . . . .162 B4
Parsifal Coll **1**
NW3 . . . . .10 C4
Parsifal Ho NW3 . . . . .10 C4
Parsifal Rd NW6 . . . . .10 C3
Parsonage St E14 . . . . .42 B2
Parsons Gn SW6 . . . . .165 B3
PARSONS
GREEN 165 B4
Parsons Green La
SW6 . . . . .165 B4
Parsons Green Sta
SW6 . . . . .165 B3
Parsons Ho
Paddington W2 . . . . . .89 B1
2 Streatham
SW12 . . . . .74 A4
Parsons Lo NW6 . . . . .11 A1
Parthenia Rd
SW6 . . . . .165 C3
Partington Cl N19 . . . . .4 C3
Parton Lo **14** E8 . . . . . .16 B2
Partridge Ct EC1 . . . . .96 A2
Partridge Ho **22**
E3 . . . . .26 B3
Pascall Ho SE17 . . . . . .48 B4
Pascal St SW8 . . . . . . .161 C2
Pascoe Rd SE13 . . . . . .67 C2
Pasley Cl SE17 . . . . . .150 C1
Passfield Dr E14 . . . . . .34 A4
Passfields W14 . . . . . .140 C1
Passing Alley EC1 . . . . .96 B1
Passmore St SW1 . . . .145 B2
Pastor St SE1,
SE11 . . . . .150 B4
Patcham Terr
SW8 . . . . .170 A4
Patent Ho E14 . . . . . . .34 A4
Paternoster La
EC4 . . . . .108 B2
Paternoster Sq
EC4 . . . . .108 B2
Pater St W8 . . . . .127 B1
Patience Rd
SW11 . . . . .168 A1
Patience Villas
SE13 . . . . .67 C4
Patio Cl SW4 . . . . .61 C1
Patmore Ho **9**
N16 . . . . .16 A3
Patmore St SW8 . . . . .171 A4
Patmos Rd SW9 . . . . . .48 A2
Paton Cl E3 . . . . .26 C2
Paton Ho **3** SW9 . . . .172 C2

Paton St EC1 . . . . .96 C3
Patrick Coman Ho
EC1 . . . . .96 A3
Patrick Connolly Gdns
41 E3 . . . . .27 A2
Patriot Sq E2 . . . . .25 A3
Patrol Pl SE6 . . . . .67 A1
Pat Shaw Ho **2**
E1 . . . . .25 C1
Patshull Pl NW5 . . . . . .13 B2
Patshull Rd NW5 . . . . .13 B2
Patten Ho N4 . . . . .6 B3
Patten Rd SW18 . . . . . .72 A4
Patterdale NW1 . . . . . .92 B3
Patterdale Rd
SE15 . . . . .50 B3
Pattina Wlk SE16 . . . . .33 A1
Pattison Point **10**
E16 . . . . .35 C4
Pattison Ho
Borough The SE1 . . . .137 A4
1 Stepney E1 . . . . . . .32 C3
Pattison Rd NW2 . . . . . .1 C1
Pat Williams Ho
SE27 . . . . .75 B1
Paul Daisley Ct **2**
NW6 . . . . .10 A1
Paulet Rd SE5 . . . . .48 A2
Pauline Ho **15** W10 . . .23 A1
Pauline Ho **15** E1 . . . .111 C4
Paul Julius Cl E14 . . . . .34 C2
Paul St EC2 . . . .24 A1 98 A2
Paultons Sq SW3 . . . .157 C4
Paultons Sq SW3 . . . .157 C3
Paultons St SW3 . . . . .157 C3
Pauntley Ho **7** N19 . . . .4 B3
Pauntley St **4** N19 . . . .4 B3
Pavan Ct **22** E2 . . . . . .25 B2
Paveley Dr SW11 . . . .158 A1
Paveley Ho N1 . . . . .84 C1
Paveley St NW8 . . . . . .90 B2
Pavement The
Brentford W5 . . . . .36 A4
Clapham SW4 . . . . . . .61 B3
Pavilion Ct
3 Hampstead
NW3 . . . . .11 B4
Hampstead NW3 . . . . .11 C3
3 Paddington
NW6 . . . . .23 C2
Pavilion Mans **10**
SW9 . . . . .62 B3
Pavilion Rd SW1 . . . . .131 A1
Pavilion Sq SW17 . . . . .72 B1
Pavilion St SW1 . . . . .131 A1
Pavilion Terr **6**
W12 . . . . .30 B3
Pavillion Ct SW1 . . . . .160 A4
Pavitt Ct NW10 . . . . .8 B1
Paxton Cl TW9 . . . . . . .44 B1
Paxton Ho SE17 . . . . .151 A2
Paxton Rd W4 . . . . . . .46 A4
Paxton Terr SW1 . . . . .160 B4
Paymal Ho **8** E1 . . . . . .32 B4
Payne Ho N1 . . . . .85 A3
Payne Rd E3 . . . . .27 A3
Paynesfield Ave
SW14 . . . . .55 C4
Payne St SE8 . . . . .51 B4
Paynes Wlk W6 . . . . . .154 A3
Peabody Ave SW1 . . . .146 B1
Peabody Bldgs
6 Camberwell
SE5 . . . . .48 C2
Walworth SE17 . . . . . .151 B3
Peabody Cl SW1 . . . . .160 B4

Peabody Ct
9 Camberwell
SE5 . . . . .48 C2
St Luke's EC1 . . . . .97 A1
Peabody Est
18 Bethnal Green
E2 . . . . .25 A3
Borough The SE1 . . . .122 C1
Fulham SW6 . . . . .155 A4
17 Hammersmith
W6 . . . . .39 B1
Holborn EC1 . . . . .95 C1
Lambeth SE1 . . . . . . .121 C1
North Kensington
W10 . . . . .30 B4
4 Ratcliff E1 . . . . .32 C2
37 St George in East
E1 . . . . .125 B4
St Luke's EC1 . . . . .97 A1
Strand WC2 . . . . .106 C1
Streatham SE24 . . . . . .75 B4
Westminster SW1 . . . .147 A4
Peabody Hill SE21 . . . .75 B3
Peabody Sq SE1 . . . . .136 A3
Peabody Twr EC1 . . . . .97 A1
Peabody Yd N1 . . . . . . .86 C4
Peach Rd W10 . . . . . . .23 A2
Peachum Rd SE3 . . . . .53 B4
Peach Walk Mews **24**
E3 . . . . .25 C3
Peacock St SE17 . . . . .150 B3
Peacock Yd SE17 . . . . .150 B3
Peak Ho N4 . . . . .6 B3
Pearce Ho
Camden Town N19 . . . .4 B1
7 Streatham SW2 . . . .74 A4
Westminster SW1 . . . .147 C3
Pear Cl SE14 . . . . .51 A3
Pear Ct **21** SE15 . . . . . .49 B3
Peardon St SW8 . . . . .170 B1
Pearfield Ho **1**
N5 . . . . .15 B3
Pearl St E1 . . . . .32 A1
Pearman Ho **3**
SE1 . . . . .52 B1
Pearman St SE1 . . . . .135 C3
Pear Pl SE1 . . . . .135 B4
Pearscroft Ct
SW6 . . . . .166 B3
Pearscroft Rd
SW6 . . . . .166 B3
Pearse St E3 SE15 . . . .49 A4
Pearson Cl E5 SE15 . . .48 B2
Pearson Ho SW15 . . . .47 B1
Pearson's Ave SE8,
SE14 . . . . .51 C2
Pearson St E2 . . . . .24 B3
Peartree Ave
SW17 . . . . .71 B1
Pear Tree Cl **2** E2 . . . .24 B4
Pear Tree Ct
Holborn EC1 . . . . .95 C1
Putney SW15 . . . . .57 A3
Pear Tree Ho SE4 . . . . .66 B3
Peartree La E1 . . . . .32 B2
Peartree St EC1 . . . . . .96 C2
Peartree Way
SE10 . . . . .43 C2
Peary Pl E2 . . . . .25 B2
Peckarmans Wood
SE21, SE26 . . . . .76 C1
Peckett Sq **3** N5 . . . . .15 A4
Peckford Pl SW9 . . . . .173 C1
PECKHAM 49 C2

Peckham Gr SE15 . . . .49 A3	

Peckham High St
SE15 . . . . .49 C2
Peckham Hill St
SE15 . . . . .49 C3
Peckham Park Prim
Sch **90** SE15 . . . . .49 C3
Peckham Park Rd
SE15 . . . . .49 C3
Peckham Rd SE5 . . . . .49 A2
Peckham Rye
East Dulwich
SE22 . . . . .64 C3
Peckham SE15,
SE22 . . . . .65 A3
Peckwater Ho **2**
NW5 . . . . .13 C2
Peckwater St NW5 . . . .13 B3
Pedlars Wlk N7 . . . . . . .14 A3
Pedley St E1 . .24 B1 99 A1
Pedro St E5 . . . . .17 C4
Pedworth Gdns **4**
SE16 . . . . .40 B2
Peel Gr E2 . . . . .25 B3
Peel Pass
W8 . . . . .31 C1 113 B1
Peel Prec NW6 . . . . . . .23 C3
Peel St W8 . .31 C1 113 B1
Peerless St EC1 . . . . . .97 B3
Pegasus Cl N16 . . . . . .15 C4
Pegasus Ct
31 Acton W3 . . . . . . .28 B3
Brentford TW8 . . . . . . .36 B1
College Pk W10 . . . . . .22 A2
Pegasus Ho **1** E1 . . . .25 C1
Pegwell Ho **19** E5 . . . . .17 A3
Pekin St E14 . . . . .33 C3
Pekoe SE1 . . . . .125 A1
Peldon Ct TW10 . . . . . .54 B2
Pelham Cl SE5 . . . . . . .64 A4
Pelham Cres SW7 . . . .144 A3
Pelham Ct SW3 . . . . . .144 A3
Pelham Ho W14 . . . . .140 C3
Pelham Pl SW7 . . . . . .144 A3
Pelham St SW7 . . . . . .143 C3
Pelican Ho **8** SE8 . . . . .41 B2
Pelican Pas **3** E1 . . . . .25 B1
Pelier St SE17 . . . . . . .48 B4
Pella Ho SE11 . . . . . . .149 A2
Pellant Rd SW6 . . . . . .154 B2
Pellatt Rd SE22 . . . . . .64 B2
Pellerin Rd N16 . . . . . . .16 A3
Pellew Ho **15** E1 . . . . . .25 A1
Pelling St E14 . . . . .33 C3
Pelter St **24** E2 . . . . .98 C4
Pelton Rd SE10 . . . . . . .43 A1
Pember Rd NW10 . . . . .22 C2
Pemberton Ct **18**
E1 . . . . .25 C2
Pemberton Gdns
N19 . . . . .4 B1
Pemberton Pl **2**
E8 . . . . .17 A1
Pemberton Row
EC4 . . . . .107 C2
Pemberton Terr
N19 . . . . .4 B1
Pembridge Cres
W11 . . . . .31 C2 113 B4
Pembridge Gdns
W2 . . . . .31 C2 113 B3

Pembroke Hall Prep
Sch for Girls
W2 . . . . 31 C2 113 C3
Pembroke Mews
W11 . . . . .31 C2 113 B4
Pembroke Pl
Notting Hill
W11 . . . . 31 C2 113 C4
1 Wandsworth
SW15 . . . . .58 C2
Pembroke Rd
W11 . . . . .31 C2 113 B3
Pembroke Sq
W11 . . . . .31 C2 113 C3
Pembroke Villas
W11 . . . . .31 C2 113 B4
Pembroke W14 . . . 141 A3
Pembroke Ave N1. 84 B4
Pembroke Bldgs
NW10 . . . . .21 C2
Pembroke Cl
SW1 . . . . .131 C3
Pembroke Gdns
W8 . . . . .141 A4
Pembroke Gdns Cl
W8 . . . . .127 B1
Pembroke Ho
Acton W3 . . . . 37 B4
Chelsea SW1 . . . . 131 B1
5 Clapham Pk
. . . . .62 A2
7 Kensington W2 100 B1
Putney SW15 . . . . . 56 C2
Pembroke Lo **2**
SW16 . . . . .74 B1
Pembroke Mews
8 Bow E3 . . . . . . 26 A2
Kensington W8 . . 127 B1
Pembroke Pl W8 . 127 B1
Pembroke Rd W8 . 141 B4
Pembroke Sq W8 . 127 B1
Pembroke St N1 . . 84 B4
Pembroke Studios
W8 . . . . .127 A1
Pembroke Terr
NW8 . . . . .79 B3
Pembroke Villas
W8 . . . . .141 B4
Pembroke Wlk
W8 . . . . .141 B4
Pembury Cl E5 . . . .17 A3
Pembury Ho SE5 . . 49 A1
Pembury Pl **15** E5,
E8 . . . . .17 A3
Pembury Rd E5 . . . .17 A3
Pemell Cl **30** E1 . . 25 B1
Pemell Ho **81** E1 . . 25 B1
Penally Pl N1 . . . . .87 C4
Penang St E1 . . . . .32 A1
Penarth Ctr The
SE15 . . . . .50 B4
Penarth St SE15 . . 50 B4
Pencombe Mews
W11 . . . . .31 B2 113 A4
Pencraig Way
SE15 . . . . .50 A4
Penda's Mead E9. .18 A4
Pendennis Ho **15**
SE8 . . . . .41 A2
Penderyn Way N7 . 13 C4
Pendle Ho **13**
SE26 . . . . .76 C1
Pendley Ho **18** E2 .24 C4
Pendrell Ho WC2 . 105 C1

Pendrell Rd SE4 . . .51 A1
Penelope Ho **20**
SW9 . . . . .173 B3
Penfield Lo **7** W9 .31 C4
Penfields Ho N7 . . .14 A2
Penfold Pl NW1 . . 102 A4
Penfold St NW8 . . 89 C1
Penford St SE5 . . . .48 A1
Penhurst Mews
SW6 . . . . .164 C4
Peninsula Ct E14 . .42 A3
Peninsula Ret Pk
TW9 . . . . .43 C2
Peninsular Park Rd
SE7 . . . . .43 C2
Penmayne Ho
SE11 . . . . .149 C2
Pennack Rd SE15 . .49 B4
Penn Almshouses **1**
SE10 . . . . .52 B2
Pennant Mews
W8 . . . . .142 A4
Pennard Mans **5**
W12 . . . . .39 B4
Pennard Rd W12 . . 39 B4
Pennefather Ho
N1 . . . . .15 C2
Penner Cl SW19 . . .70 A2
Pennethorne Cl
E9 . . . . .25 B4
Pennethorne Ho
SW11 . . . . .59 C4
Pennethorne Rd
SE15 . . . . .50 A3
Penn Ho NW8 . . . . 90 A1
Pennine La NW2 . . .1 A2
Pennine Mans NW2 .1 A2
Pennine Par NW2 . .1 A2
Pennington Ct
1 Rotherhithe
SE16 . . . . .33 A1
23 St George in East
E1 . . . . .125 C3
Pennington St E1 .32 A2
Penn Rd N7 . . . . . 14 A4
Penn St N1 . . . . . . 87 C3
Penny Ct SW10 . . 157 A4
Pennyfields E14 . . .33 C2
Pennyford Ct NW8. 89 B2
Penny Mews
SW12 . . . . .73 A4
Pennymore Wlk
W9 . . . . .23 B1
Penny Rd NW10 . . .20 A2
Penpoll Rd E8 . . . . .17 A2
Penrhyn Cres
SW14 . . . . .55 B3
Penrith Cl SW15 . . .58 A2
Penrith Pl SE27 . . .75 A2
Penrose Gr **1**
SE17 . . . . .150 C1
Penrose Ho SE17 . 150 C1
Penrose St SE17. . 150 C1
Penryn Ho SE11 . . 150 A2
Penryn St NW1 . . . 83 B2
Pensbury Pl SW8 . 171 A2
Pensbury St SW8 . 171 A2
Pensford Ave TW9 . 44 C1
Penshurst **2** NW5. .12 C2
Penshurst Ho **1**
SE15 . . . . .50 B4
Penshurst Rd E9 . .17 C1
Pentland Cl NW11 . .1 A2
Pentland Gdns
SW18 . . . . .59 B1

Pentland Ho
17 Camden Town
NW5 . . . . .12 C2
3 Stamford Hill N16. .7 B3
Pentland Rd **1**
NW6 . . . . .23 C2
Pentland St SW18 .59 B1
Pentlow St SW15 . .57 B4
Pentney Rd SW12. .73 B3
Penton Gr N1 . . . . .85 B1
Penton Ho N1 . . . . .85 B1
Penton Pl SE17. . . 150 B2
Penton Rise WC1 . .95 A4
Penton St N1 . . . . .85 B1
Pentonville Rd
N1 . . . . .84 C1
Pentridge St SE15 .49 B3
Penwith Rd SW18 . .71 A2
Penwood Ho
SW15 . . . . .56 B1
Penywern Rd
SW5 . . . . .141 C2
Penzance Ho
SE11 . . . . .149 C2
Penzance Pl
W11 . . . . .31 A1 112 B2
Penzance St
W11 . . . . .31 A1 112 A2
Peony Gdns W12 . .29 C2
Peperfield WC1. . . 94 C3
Pepler Ho **10** W10 .23 A1
Pepler Mews SE1 . 152 C1
Peploe Rd NW6 . . .22 C3
Peppermead Sq
SE13 . . . . .66 C2
Pepper St
Borough The SE1 . 136 C4
Millwall E14 . . . . .42 A3
Peppie Cl N16 . . . . .7 A2
Pepys Cres **2** E16 .35 C1
Pepys Ent Ctr **13**
SE8 . . . . .41 B2
Pepys Ho
14 Bethnal Green
E2 . . . . .25 B2
Clapham Pk SW4 . .61 C2
Pepys Rd SE14 . . . .50 C1
Pepys St EC3 . . . . 124 B4
Perceval Ave NW3. .12 A3
Percheron Ct **3**
SW9 . . . . .62 B4
Perch St E8 . . . . . . 16 B4
Percival Rd SW14. .55 B3
Percival St EC1 . . . .96 B3
Percy Laurie Ho **6**
SW15 . . . . .57 C3
Percy Mews W1 . . 105 B3
Percy Pas W1 . . . . 105 B3
Percy Rd
Newham E16 . . . . . .35 A4
Shepherd's Bush
W12 . . . . .38 C4
Percy St W1 . . . . . 105 B3
Peregrine Ho
4 Battersea
SW11 . . . . .60 A4
Finsbury EC1 . . . . . 96 B4
Perham Rd W14 . . 140 B1
Perifield SE21 . . . . .75 B3
Perkins Ho **15** E14. .33 B4
Perkins Rents
SW1 . . . . .133 B1
Perkins Sq SE1 . . . 123 A2
Perley Ho **9** E3. . . .33 B4

Perotti Ho SW6 . . . .59 A4
Perran Rd SE24,
SW2 . . . . .75 A2
Perren St NW5 . . . .13 A2
Perrers Rd W6 . . . . 39 A2
Perring Est E3 . . . . 33 C4
Perrins Ct **8** NW3 . .11 B4
Perrin's La NW3 . . .11 B4
Perrin's Wlk NW3 . .11 B4
Perronet Ho SE1 . . 136 B1
Perry Ave W3 . . . . .28 C3
Perry Ct **6** E14 . . . .41 C1
Perry Ho **21** SW2 . .74 A4
Perrymead St
SW6 . . . . .166 A3
Perryn Ho W3 . . . . .29 A2
Perryn Rd
Acton W3 . . . . 28 C2
1 Bermondsey
SE16 . . . . .40 A3
Perry's Pl W1 . . . . 105 B2
Perrywood Ho **17**
E5 . . . . .17 A3
Perseverance Works
17 E2 . . . . .24 A2 98 B4
Perth Cl **5** SE5 . . . .63 C3
Perth Ho N1 . . . . . .14 B1
Perth Rd N4 . . . . . . .5 C3
Petchey Acad The
E8 . . . . .16 B3
Peter Ave NW10 . . . .9 A1
Peter Best Ho **1**
E1 . . . . .32 A3
Peterboat Cl SE10 .43 A2
Peterborough Ct
EC4 . . . . .107 C1
Peterborough Mews
SW6 . . . . .165 B2
Peterborough Rd
SW6 . . . . .58 C4
Peterborough Villas
SW6 . . . . .166 A4
Peter Butler Ho **9**
SE1 . . . . .139 B3
Peterchurch Ho
SE15 . . . . .50 A4
Petergate SW11. . .59 B3
Peter Harrison
Planetarium
SE10 . . . . .52 C3
Peter Heathfield Ho
4 E15 . . . . .27 C4
Peter Hills Ho **6**
SE16 . . . . .153 B4
Peter Hills Sch **8**
SE16 . . . . .32 C1
Peter Ho SW8 . . . . 162 A2
Peter James Ent Ctr
NW10 . . . . .20 B2
Peterley Bsns Ctr **2**
E2 . . . . .25 A3
Peter Scott Visitor
Centre SW13 . . . .47 A2
Peters Ct **2** W2 . . 100 B2
Peter's Cl SW9 . . . .62 B1
Petersfield Rd W3 .37 B4
Petersfield Rise
SW15 . . . . .69 A3
Petersham Ho **1**
SW7 . . . . .143 B4
Petersham La
SW7 . . . . .128 C2
Petersham Mews
SW7 . . . . .129 A1
Petersham Pl
SW7 . . . . .129 A2

Peter's La EC1 . . . .108 B4
Peter St W1 . . . . . .119 B4
Peterstow Cl
SW19 . . . . .70 A2
Petherton Ct
NW10 . . . . .22 C4
Petherton Ho N4 . . .6 B3
Petherton Rd N5 . .15 B3
Petiver Cl **8** E9 . . .17 B1
Petley Rd W6 . . . . .47 C3
Peto Pl NW1 . . . . . .92 B2
Peto St N E16 . . . . .35 B3
Petrel Ct **8** SE21. . .75 C2
Petrie Cl NW2 . . . . .10 A2
Petrie Mus of
Egyptian
Archaeology
WC1 . . . . .93 B1
Petros Gdns **1**
NW3 . . . . .11 B2
Petticoat Lane Mkt
EC2 . . . . .110 C3
Petticoat Sq E1 . . 110 C2
Petticoat Twr E1. . 110 C2
Pettiward Cl SW15 .57 B3
Petty France SW1 133 B2
Petty Wales EC3 . . 124 B3
Petworth Ho **18**
SE22 . . . . .64 A4
Petworth St
SW11 . . . . .168 B4
Petyt Pl SW3 . . . . 158 A3
Petyward SW3. . . . 144 B3
Pevensey Ct
4 South Acton
W3 . . . . .37 A4
West Norwood
SW16 . . . . .74 C1
Pevensey Ho **5**
E1 . . . . .33 A4
Peveril Ho SE1 . . . 137 C1
Pewsham Ho N4 . . .6 B3
Peyton Pl SE10 . . . .52 B3
Pharamond NW2 . . .9 C2
Phelps Ho **11**
SW15 . . . . .57 C4
Phelp St SE17 . . . . .48 C4
Phene St SW3 . . . . 158 B4
Philadelphia Ct
SW10 . . . . .157 A1
Philbeach Gdns
SW5 . . . . .141 B2
Phil Brown Pl **3**
SW8 . . . . .61 A4
Philchurch Pl **58**
E1 . . . . .111 C1
Philia Ho **4** NW1. .13 B1
Philip Blairman Ho
E1 . . . . .24 B1 98 C1
Philip Ct W2 . . . . . 101 B4
Philip Ho **52** NW6. .78 A3
Philip Turner Est **28**
E9 . . . . .17 B1
Philip Wlk SE15 . . .64 C4
Phillimore Ct **1**
W8 . . . . .127 C3
Phillimore Gardens Cl
W8 . . . . .127 B2
Phillimore Gdns
Kensington W8. . . 127 C3
Willesden NW10. . .22 B4
Phillimore Pl W8 . 127 B3
Phillimore Terr
W8 . . . . .127 C2
Phillimore Wlk
W8 . . . . .127 C2
Phillip Ho E1. . . . . 111 A3

Phillipp St N1....24 A4
Philpot La EC3.. 124 A4
Philpot Sq SE6...59 A4
Philpot St E1....32 A3
Philson Mans 13
E1...............32 B3
Phipps Ho SE12..36 C3
Phipp St
EC2....24 A1 98 A2
Phoebeth Rd SE4..66 C2
Phoenix Bsns Ctr 22
E3...............33 C4
Phoenix Cl 18 E8..24 C4
Phoenix Ct
4 Brentford
TW8............36 A1
2 Deptford SE14..51 A4
Millwall E14.....41 C2
Phoenix High Sch
W12............29 C2
Phoenix Ho SW1 145 B4
Phoenix Lodge Mans
1 W6...........39 B2
Phoenix Pl WC1 .. 95 A2
Phoenix Rd NW1 .. 93 B4
Phoenix Sch The 15
NW3............11 B2
Phoenix Sec & Prim
Sch 28 E3......26 B2
Phoenix St WC2 .. 105 C1
Phoenix Wharf
SE1............139 A3
Phyllis Hodges Ho
NW1............83 B1
Physic Pl SW3 ... 158 C4
Piccadilly W1....118 C2
Piccadilly Cir W1. 119 B3
Piccadilly Arc
SW1............118 C2
Piccadilly Circus Sta
SW1............119 B3
Piccadilly Ct 5
N7.............14 B2
Piccadilly Pl W1.. 119 A3
Pickard St EC1 ... 96 B4
Pickering Cl E9....17 C1
Pickering Ho
18 Kensington
W2.............100 B1
Stoke Newington N4 ..6 C4
Pickering Mews 9
W2.............100 B1
Pickering Pl SW1 119 A1
Pickering St N1 .. 86 B4
Pickets St SW12 ..73 A4
Pickfords Wharf
N1.............86 C1
Pickwick Ho
21 Bermondsey
SE16...........139 B3
9 Shepherd's Bush
W11............30 C1
Pickwick Rd SE21 ..76 A4
Pickwick St SE1 .. 136 C3
Pickworth Cl SW8 162 B1
Picton Ho 1 SW4 ..74 A4
Picton Pl W1.....103 C1
Picton St SE5 .... 48 C3
Picture Ho 6
SW16...........74 A2
Pied Bull Ct WC1 . 106 B3
Pied Bull Yd WC1 106 B3
Pier Head E1.....32 A1
Pierhead Wharf 37
E1.............32 A1
Pier Ho SW3 .... 158 B3

Piermont Rd SE22..65 A2
Pierpoint Bldg 4
E14............28 A2
Pierrepoint Rd
W3.............28 A2
Pierrepoint Row
N1.............86 A2
Pier St E14.......42 B2
Pier Terr SW18...59 B3
Piggott Ho 2 E2..25 C3
Pigott St E14.....33 C3
Pilgrimage St
SE1............137 B3
Pilgrim Ho SE1 .. 137 C1
Pilgrims Cloisters 1
SE5............49 A3
Pilgrims Ct SE3...53 C2
Pilgrim's La NW3 .. 11 C4
Pilgrims Mews 12
E14............34 C2
Pilgrim's Pl 6
NW3............11 C4
Pilgrim St EC4 ... 108 A1
Pilgrims Way N19 ..4 C3
Pilgrims Way Prim
Sch 22 SE15....50 B4
Pilkington Rd 4
SE15...........50 A1
Pilot Ind Ctr NW10..21 A1
Pilsden Cl SW19 ..69 C3
Pilton Pl SE17 ... 151 A2
Pimlico Sta SW1. 147 B2
PIMLICO.........146 C1
Pimlico Acad
SW1............147 A1
Pimlico Rd SW1 .. 145 C2
Pimlico Wlk 1
N1.............24 A2 98 A4
Pinchin St E1 .... 125 C4
Pincombe Ho
SE17...........151 B2
Pincott Pl SE4....65 C4
Pindar St EC2 ... 110 A4
Pindock Mews W9. 88 B1
Pine Apple Ct
SW1............132 C2
Pine Ave E15.....19 C3
Pine Cl 11 N19 ... 4 B2
Pinedene 2 SE15 ..50 A2
Pinefield Cl E14...33 C2
Pine Gr N4, N19....5 B2
Pine Ho
Bow E3.........26 A4
21 Rotherhithe
SE16...........40 B4
Pinehurst Ct 6
W11............31 B3
Pinelands Cl 7
SE3............53 B3
Pine Lo SW15....58 A1
Pine Rd NW2.....9 C4
Pines Ct E14.....41 A2
Pine St EC1......95 B2
Pine Tree Ho SE14..50 C3
Pine Tree Way 1
SE13...........67 A4
Pinewood Ct SW4 ..61 C1
Pinkham Mans
W4.............36 C1
Pinnacle Ho E14 .. 42 B3
Pinnacle Ho EC3 . 124 A3
Pinnacle The EC2 110 A1
Pinnacle The 7
N1.............15 C2
Pinner Ct NW8 ... 89 B2
Pinner Ho 30 SE5..48 B1

Pintail Ct SE8 .... 51 B4
Pinter Ho SW9 .. 172 B1
Pioneer Cl
10 Bow Comm
E14............34 A4
London W12.....30 A3
Pioneer St SE15 .. 49 C2
Pioneer Way W12..30 B3
Piper Cl N7......14 B3
Pipers Ho SE10...42 C1
Pippin Ho 17 W10..30 C2
Pirate Castle The
NW1............82 A4
Pirbright Rd SW18..70 C3
Pitcairn Ho 1 E9..17 B1
Pitfield Ho N5....15 B3
Pitfield St N1....24 A3
Pitman Ho 3 SE8..51 C2
Pitman St SE5....48 B3
Pitmaston Ho 2
SE13...........52 B1
Pitsea Pl E1......32 C3
Pitsea St E1......32 C3
Pitt Ho 4 SW11...59 C3
Pitt's Head Mews
W1.............117 C1
Pitt St W8...... 127 C4
Pixley St E14.....33 B3
Planetree Ct W6..39 C2
Plane Tree Ho
SE8............51 A4
Plantain Pl SE1 .. 137 B4
Plantation La EC3 124 A4
Plantation The
SE3............53 C1
Platehouse The 3
E14............42 A1
Platina St EC2 ... 97 C2
Plato Pl 1 SW6 .. 165 A2
Plato Rd SW2....62 A3
Platt's La NW3 ... 1 C1
Platt St NW1 .... 83 B2
Plaxdale Ho SE17 152 A3
Playfair St W6....39 B1
Playfield Cres
SE22...........64 B2
Playford Rd
Finsbury Pk N4 ...5 B2
Finsbury Pk N4 ...5 C2
Playhouse Yd EC4 108 A1
Playon (Canary Wharf
Indoor Sports)
E14............34 B1
Plaza Sh Ctr W1. 105 A2
Pleasance Rd
SW15...........57 A2
Pleasance The
SW15...........57 A3
Pleasant Pl N1....15 A1
Pleasant Row NW1..82 B3
Plender Ct NW1 .. 83 A3
Plender St NW1 .. 83 A3
Pleshey Rd N7....13 C4
Plevna St E14....42 B3
Pleydell Ave W6..38 B2
Pleydell Ct EC4 .. 107 C1
Pleydell St EC4 .. 107 C1
Plimsoll Cl E14...34 A3
Plimsoll Rd N4....5 C2
Plough Ct EC3 ... 123 C4
Plough La SE22...64 B1
Ploughmans Cl
NW1............83 B4
Plough Mews 15
SW11...........59 C3
Plough Pl EC4 ... 107 C2

Plough Rd SW11 .. 59 C3
Plough St 16 E1 .. 111 B2
Plough Terr SW11..59 C3
Plough Way SE16..41 A2
Plough Yd
EC2....24 A1 98 B1
Plover Ho 4 SW9 163 B2
Plover Way SE16 .. 41 A3
Plowman Ho
SW19...........69 C2
Plumbers Row E1 111 C2
Plumbridge 7
SE10...........52 B2
Plume Ho SE10...52 A4
Plummer Ct SE13..67 A1
Plummer Rd SW4 ..73 C4
Plumtree Ct EC4 . 108 A2
Plymouth Ho 2
SE10...........52 A4
Plymouth Rd E16..35 C4
Plymouth Wharf
E14............42 C2
Plympton Ave
NW6............10 B1
Plympton Pl NW1. 90 A1
Plympton Rd NW6..10 B1
Plympton St NW8. 90 A1
Pocklington Ct
SW15...........68 C3
Pocklington Lo 6
W12............38 C3
Pocock St SE1 ... 136 B4
Podmore Rd SW18..59 B3
Poets Cnr SW1 .. 134 A2
Poets Mews 3
SE24...........63 A2
Poet's Rd N5.....15 C3
Point Cl SE10.....52 B2
Pointer Sch The
SE3............53 C3
Pointers Cl E14...42 A1
Point Hill SE10...52 B2
Point Ho SE10....52 B2
Point Pleasant
SW18...........58 C3
Point Wharf La
TW8............44 A3
Poland Ho 3 E15 . 27 C4
Poland St W1 ... 105 A1
Polesworth Ho 16
W2.............31 C4
Polish Inst & Sikorski
Mus SW7........129 C3
Polish Univ Abroad 11
W6.............38 C2
Pollard Cl
Islington N7 .... 14 B4
Newham E16 .... 35 C2
Pollard Ho N1 ... 84 C1
Pollard Row
E2.....24 C2 99 C4
Pollard St
E2.....24 C2 99 C4
Pollen St W1 .... 104 B1
Pollitt Dr NW8 ... 89 C2
Pollock Ho W10...23 A1
Pollock's Toy Mus
W1.............105 A4
Polperro Mans 3
NW6............10 C3
Polperro Mews
SE11...........150 A4
Polygon Rd NW1 .. 83 B1
Polygon The
1 Clapham SW4 ..61 B3

Phi–Pop 255

Polygon The continued
St John's Wood
NW8............79 C4
Pomell Way E1 .. 111 A2
Pomeroy Ct W11 .. 31 A3
Pomeroy Ho 4 E2. 25 C3
Pomeroy St SE14 .. 50 B2
Pomfret Rd SE5 .. 63 A4
Pomoja La N19 ... 5 A2
Pomona Ho 10
SE8............41 A2
Pond Cl SE3 .... 53 C1
Pond Cotts SE21 .. 76 A3
Ponder St 8 N7...14 B1
Pondfield Ho 4
N5.............15 B3
Pond Ho SW3 ... 144 A3
Pond Mead SE21 . 63 C1
Pond Pl SW3 .... 144 A3
Pond Rd SE3 .... 53 B1
Pond Sq N6......3 C3
Pond St NW3.....12 A3
Ponler St E1......32 A3
Ponsard Rd NW10..22 A2
Ponsford St E9 ...17 B2
Ponsonby Ho 13
E2.............25 B3
Ponsonby Pl SW1 147 C2
Ponsonby Rd
SW15...........69 A4
Ponsonby Terr
SW1............147 C2
Ponton Rd SW2 .. 74 C3
Ponton Rd SW8 . 161 C3
Pont St Mews
SW1............130 C1
Pont St SW1 .... 131 A1
Pontypool Pl SE1 136 A4
Poole Ct N1......16 A1
Poole Ho SE11 ... 135 A1
Poole Rd E9......17 C2
Pooles Bldgs EC1. 95 B1
Pooles La SW10 .. 156 C1
Pooles Park Prim Sch
18 N4..........5 B2
Pooles Pk N4.....5 C2
Poole St N1......87 B3
Pooley Ho E1.....25 C2
Pool Ho NW8 .... 101 C4
Poolmans St SE16..40 C4
Poonah St E1.....32 B3
Pope Ho
2 Bermondsey
SE16...........40 A2
3 Camberwell SE5..48 C3
Pope John Prim Sch
W12............30 A2
Pope's Head Alley
EC3............109 C1
Pope's La W5.....36 A3
Pope's Rd SW9...62 C4
Pope St SE1 .... 138 B3
Popham Ct N16...7 A1
Popham Gdns
TW9............55 A4
Popham Rd N1 .. 86 C4
Popham St
Islington N1 .... 86 B4
Shoreditch N1 .. 86 C4
POPLAR.........33 C3
Poplar Bath St 11
E14............34 A2
Poplar Bsns Pk
E14............34 B2

Poplar Cl E9 . . . .**18** B3
Poplar Ct **4** SW16. .**74** B1
Poplar Gr W6 . . . .**39** B4
Poplar High St
E14 . . . .**34** A2
Poplar Ho
Brockley SE4 . . . . . .**66** B3
15 Rotherhithe
SE16 . . . .**40** C4
Poplar Mews **4**
W12 . . . .**30** B1
Poplar Pl W2 . . . . .**114** B4
Poplar Rd SE24. . . . .**63** B3
Poplar Sta E14 . . . . .**34** A2
Poplars The NW5 . . .**13** B3
Poplar WIk SE24. . . .**63** B3
Poppins Ct EC4. . . .**108** A1
Porchester Ct **2** **100** B1
Porchester Gate
W2 . . . .**114** C3
Porchester Gdn Mews
W2 . . . .**100** B1
Porchester Gdns
W2 . . . .**114** B4
Porchester Ho **3**
E1 . . . .**32** A3
Porchester Mews
W2 . . . .**100** B2
Porchester Pl W2 **102** B1
Porchester Rd
W2 . . . .**100** B2
Porchester Sq
W2 . . . .**100** B2
Porchester Terr
W2 . . . .**114** C4
Porchester Terr N
W2 . . . .**100** B2
Porden Rd SW2 . . . . .**62** B3
Porland Ct SE1 . . . .**137** B2
Porlock Ho **5**
SE26 . . . .**76** C1
Porlock St SE1 . . . .**137** C4
Porson Ct SE13. . . . .**67** A4
Portal Cl SE27. . . . . .**74** C1
Portal Way W3 . . . . .**28** C4
Portbury Ct **17**
SE15 . . . .**49** C2
Portchester Cl
SE24 . . . .**63** C3
Portelet Ct **1** NL . . .**24** A4
Portelet Rd E1 . . . . .**25** C2
Porten Hos W14 . . .**126** A1
Porten Rd W14 . . . .**126** A1
Porter Sq N19. . . . . . .**5** A3
Porter St
Borough The SE1 .**123** A2
Marylebone W1 . . .**103** A4
Porteus Rd W2 . . . .**101** A4
Portfleet Pl **34** N1 . .**24** A4
Portgate Cl W9 . . . . .**23** B1
Port Ho **6** SW11 . . .**59** B4
Port House The **6**
E14 . . . .**42** A1
Portia Way E3 . . . . . .**26** B1
Porticos The SW3 **157** B3
Portinscale Rd
SW15 . . . .**58** B2
Portishead Ho **29**
W2 . . . .**31** C4
Portland Ave N16. . . .**7** B4
Portland Ct
7 De Beauvoir Town
N1 . . . .**16** A1
1 Deptford SE14. . . .**51** A4

Portland Gr SW8 . .**172** C4
Portland Ho **18**
SW2 . . . .**74** C3
Portland Hospl for
Women & Children
The W1 . . . .**92** B1
Portland Mews
W1 . . . .**105** A1
Portland Pl W1 . . . .**104** B3
Portland Place Sch
W1 . . . .**104** B4
Portland Rd
Notting Hill
W11 . . . .**31** A1 **112** B2
Notting Hill
W11 . . . .**31** A2 **112** A3
Portland Rise N4. . . . .**6** B3
Portland Sq E1 . . . . .**32** A1
Portland St SE17 . .**151** B1
Portland Village
W6 . . . .**39** B3
Portman Ave
SW14 . . . .**55** C4
Portman Cl W1 . . . .**103** B2
Portman Gate
NW1 . . . .**90** B1
Portman Hts **1**
NW3 . . . .**1** C1
Portman Mews S
W1 . . . .**103** B1
Portman Pl E2 . . . . . .**25** B2
Portman Sq W1 . . . .**103** B2
Portman St W1 . . . .**103** B1
Portman The NW11 . .**1** C4
Portman Twrs
NW1 . . . .**103** A2
Portnall Rd W9. . . . . .**23** B2
Portobello Ct Est
W11 . . . .**31** B1
Portobello Mews
W11 . . . .**31** C2 **113** B3
Portobello Rd
W11 . . . .**31** B2 **113** A4
Portobello Road Mkt
W10 . . . .**31** A4
Portpool La EC1. . . .**107** B4
Portree St E14 . . . . . .**34** C3
Port Royal Pl **3**
N16 . . . .**16** A3
Portsea Hall **4**
W2 . . . .**102** B1
Portsea Ho **3**
SW15 . . . .**69** A3
Portsea Mews
W2 . . . .**102** B1
Portsea Pl W2. . . . . .**102** B1
Portslade Rd SW8 .**170** C2
Portsmouth Rd
SW15 . . . .**57** B1
Portsmouth St
WC2 . . . .**107** A1
Portsoken St E1. . . . .**24** C4 ... **124** C4
Portswood Pl
SW15 . . . .**56** B1
Portugal St WC2. . .**107** A1
Poseidon Ct **9**
E14 . . . .**41** C2
Post Office Way
SW8 . . . .**161** B2
Potier St SE1 . . . . . .**137** C1
Potterne Cl **5**
SW19 . . . .**69** C4
Potters Cl **5** SE15 . .**49** A3
Potters Fields
SE1 . . . .**124** B1

Potters Lo E14 . . . . .**42** B1
Potters Rd SW6 . . .**166** C1
Pottery La
W11 . . . .**31** A1 **112** B2
Pottery Rd TW8. . . . .**44** A4
Pottery St SE16. . . . .**40** A4
Pott St E2. . . . .**25** A2
Poullett Ho SW2 . . .**75** A3
Poulton Cl E8 . . . .**17** A2
Poultry EC2 . . . .**109** B1
Pound La NW10 . . . . . .**8** C2
Pountney Rd
SW11 . . . .**60** C4
Povey Ho
Tulse Hill SW2 . . . . .**62** C1
17 Walworth SE17 .**152** A3
Powell's Wlk W4 . . . .**46** B4
Powergate Bsns Pk
NW10 . . . .**20** C1
Power Ho **3** TW9. . . .**44** C2
Power Ho The W4 . . .**38** B2
Power Rd W4 . . . .**36** C2
Powerscroft Rd
E5 . . . .**17** B4
Powis Gdns
Golders Green
NW11 . . . .**1** B4
Notting Hill W11 . . . .**31** B3
Powis Ho WC2 . . . .**106** B2
Powis Mews W11. . . .**31** B3
Powis Pl WC1 . . . . . .**94** B1
Powis Rd E3 . . . .**27** A2
Powis Sq W11. . . . . . .**31** B3
Powis Terr W11. . . . . .**31** B3
Powlesland Ct **21**
E14 . . . .**33** A3
Pownall Rd E8 . . . . . .**24** C4
Powlett Ho N1. . . . . . .**13** A2
Powlett Pl NW1 . . . . .**13** A1
Pownall Rd E8 . . . . . .**24** C4
Powrie Ho **4**
SW11 . . . .**167** C2
Poynder Ct **3** N7 . . .**14** A3
Poynders Ct **9**
SW4 . . . .**61** B1
Poynders Gdns
SW4 . . . .**73** B4
Poynings Rd N19 . . . .**4** B1
Poynter Ho
Paddington NW8 . . .**89** B2
10 Shepherd's Bush
W11 . . . .**30** C1
Poyntz Rd SW11. . . .**168** C1
Poyser St E2 . . . .**25** A3
Praed Mews W2 . . . .**101** C2
Praed St W2 . . . .**101** C2
Prague Pl SW2 . . . . . .**62** A2
Prah Rd N4 . . . .**5** C2
Prairie St SW8 . . . . .**170** A1
Pratt Mews NW1. . . .**82** C3
Pratt St NW1 . . . .**82** C4
Pratt Wlk SE1,
SE11. . . . .**149** A4
Preachers Ct EC1. . . .**96** B1
Prebend Gdns W4,
W6 . . . .**38** B2
Prebend Mans **4**
W4 . . . .**38** B2
Prebend St N1 . . . . . .**86** C4
Precinct The
Islington N1 . . . .**86** B3
Islington N5. . . . .**15** A3
Premier Corner
NW6 . . . .**23** B2
Premier Ho **28** N1 . .**15** A1

Premier Park Rd
NW10 . . . .**20** A3
Premier Pk NW10 . . .**20** A3
Premier Pl **17** E14 . .**33** C2
Prendergast Ho **2**
SW4 . . . .**73** C4
Prendergast Ladywell
Fields Coll SE4 . . . . .**66** C1
Prendergast Sch
SE4 . . . .
Prescot St E1 . . . . . .**125** A4
Prescott Ho **13**
SE17 . . . .**48** A4
Prescott Pl SW4 . . . .**61** C3
Presentation Mews
SW2 . . . .**74** B3
President Dr E1 . . . . .**32** A1
President Ho EC1. . . .**96** B3
President St EC1. . . . .**96** C4
Prestage Way **13**
E14 . . . .**34** B2
Prested Rd SW11. . . .**60** A3
Preston Gdns NW10 . .**8** A2
Preston Ho
Bermondsey SE1 . . .**138** C2
Walworth SE1 . . . . .**152** A4
Preston Pl
Richmond TW10 . . . .**54** A2
Willesden NW2 . . . . . .**8** C2
Preston's Rd E14 . . . .**34** B1
Prestwich Terr
SW4 . . . .**61** C2
Prestwood Ho **3**
SE16 . . . .**40** A3
Prestwood St N1 . . . .**87** A1
Priam Ho **2** E2 . . . . .**25** A3
Price Cl SW17 . . . . . .**72** B1
Price Ho N1 . . . .**86** C3
Prices Ct SW11 . . . . .**59** C4
Price's St SE1 . . . . . .**122** B2
Price's Yd N1 . . . .**85** A3
Prichard Ct
Battersea SW11 . . . .**167** C3
Islington N7 . . . .**14** B3
Prideaux Ho WC1 . . .**95** A4
Prideaux Pl
Acton W3 . . . .**28** C2
St Pancras WC1 . . . . .**95** A4
Prideaux Rd SW9. . . .**62** A4
Pride Ct N1 . . . .**85** C2
Priestley Cl N16 . . . . .**7** B4
Priestley Ho
2 Camden Town
NW5 . . . .**13** A2
St Luke's EC1 . . . .**97** A2
Priestman Point **27**
E3 . . . .**27** A2
Priests Bridge
SW14 . . . .**56** A4
Priest's Ct EC2 . . . .**108** C2
Prima Rd SW9 . . . . .**163** B2
Primrose Cl **6** E3 . . .**26** C3
Primrose Ct
2 Child's Hill NW2 . . . .**1** C1
Primrose Hill NW8 . . .**80** C3
11 Streatham
SW12 . . . .**73** C4
Primrose Gdns
NW3 . . . .**12** A2
PRIMROSE HILL **12** B1
Primrose Hill EC4 . .**107** C1
Primrose Hill Ct
NW3 . . . .**12** B1
Primrose Hill Rd NW1,
NW3 . . . .**12** B1

Primrose Hill Sch
NW1 . . . .**81** C4
Primrose Hill Studios
NW1 . . . .**81** B4
Primrose Ho
7 Peckham SE15 . . . .**49** C2
1 Richmond TW9 . . . .**44** B2
Primrose Mans
SW11 . . . .**169** B4
Primrose Mews **9**
NW1 . . . .**12** B1
Primrose Sq E9 . . . . .**25** B4
Primrose St EC2. . . .**110** B4
Primrose Wlk **6**
SE14 . . . .**51** A3
Primula St W12 . . . . .**29** C3
Prince Albert Ct
NW8 . . . .**80** C3
Prince Albert Rd
NW8 . . . .**80** C3
Prince Arthur Ct **11**
NW3 . . . .**11** B4
Prince Arthur Mews
17 NW3 . . . .**11** B4
Prince Arthur Rd
NW3 . . . .**11** B3
Prince Charles Rd
SE3 . . . .**53** B2
Prince Consort Ho
SE1 . . . .**148** B2
Prince Consort Rd
SW7 . . . .**129** B2
Princedale Rd
W11 . . . .**31** A1 **112** B2
Prince Edward Mans
W2 . . . .**100** B1
Prince Edward Rd
E9 . . . .**18** B2
Prince George Rd
N16 . . . .**16** A4
Princelet St E1 . . . .**111** A4
Prince of Orange La
3 SE10 . . . .**52** B3
Prince of Wales Dr
SW11 . . . .**169** B4
Prince of Wales Mans
Battersea SW11. . . .**169** C4
Clapham SW4 . . . . . .**61** A2
Prince of Wales Pas
NW1 . . . .**92** C3
Prince of Wales Rd
Blackheath Vale
SE3 . . . .**53** B2
Camden Town NW5 . .**12** C2
Prince of Wales Terr
Chiswick W4. . . . .**38** A1
Kensington W8 . . . .**128** B3
Prince Regent Ct **2**
SE16 . . . .**33** A1
Prince Regent Mews
NW1 . . . .**92** C3
Princes Arc SW1 . . .**119** A2
Princes Ave W3 . . . . .**36** C3
Princes Cir WC2. . . .**106** A2
Princes Cl N4 . . . .**6** A3
Princes Coll WC1 . .**106** A2
Princes Court Bsns
Ctr **14** E1. . . . .**32** A2
Princes Ct
Brondesbury
NW2 . . . .**10** A3
Hampstead NW3 . . . .**11** C4
Stepney E1 . . . .**32** A2
Prince's Ct SE16 . . . .**41** B3
Princes Gate SW7 . .**129** C3

Prince's Gate
SW7 . . . . **130** A3
Princes Gate Ct
SW7 . . . . **129** C3
Princes Gate Mews
SW7 . . . . **129** C2
Princes Gdns
SW7 . . . . **129** C2
Princes Ho
W11 . . . . **31** C2 **113** B3
Prince's Mews
1 Hammersmith
W6 . . . . **39** A1
Kensington W2 . . . **114** A4
Princes Pl
Notting Hill
W11 . . . . . . **31** A1 **112** A2
St James SW1 . . . . **119** A2
Princes Rd
Kew TW9 . . . . **44** B2
Richmond TW10 . . . . **54** B2
Prince's Rd SW14 . . **55** C4
Princes Rise SE13 . . **52** B1
Princes Riverside Rd
7 SE16 . . . . **32** C1
Princess Alexandra
School of Nursing
The **8** E1 . . . . **32** A4
Princess Alice Ho 1
W10 . . . . **22** B1
Princess Beatrice Ho
SW10 . . . . **142** A1
Princess Cres N4 . . . **6** A2
Princess Ct
Hampstead NW6 . . . **11** A1
Kensington W2 . . . **114** B4
Marylebone W1 . . . **102** C3
Princess Frederica CE
Jun & Inf Sch
NW10 . . . . **22** B3
Princess Grace Hospl
The W1 . . . . **91** B1
Princess Louise Cl
W2 . . . . **101** C4
Princess Mary Ho
SW1 . . . . **147** C3
Princess May Prim
Sch 2 N16 . . . . **16** B4
Princess May Rd
N16 . . . . **16** A4
Princess Mews
NW3 . . . . **11** C2
Prince's Sq W2 . . . **114** A4
Princess Rd
Camden Town
NW1 . . . . **81** C4
Paddington NW6 . . . **23** C3
Princess St SE1 . . . **136** B1
Princes St W1 . . . . **104** B1
Prince's St
City of London
EC2 . . . . **109** B1
Richmond TW10,
TW9 . . . . **54** A2
Prince St SE8 . . . . . **51** B4
Princes Way
Acton W3 . . . . **36** C3
Putney SW15,
SW19 . . . . **70** A3
Princes Yd
W11 . . . . . . **31** A1 **112** B1
Princethorpe Ho
W2 . . . . **100** A4
Princeton Ct 12
SW15 . . . . **57** C4

Princeton Mans
WC1 . . . . **106** C3
Princeton St WC1 . **106** C4
Principal Sq E9 . . . . . **17** C3
Printers Mews E3 . . . **26** A4
Printer St EC4 . . . . **107** C2
Printing House Yd 16
E2 . . . . **24** A2 **98** B3
Print Village Ind Est
SE15 . . . . **49** B1
Prior Bolton St N1 . **15** A2
Prioress Ho 2 E3 . . . **27** A2
Prioress Rd SE27 . . . **75** A1
Prioress St SE1 . . . **137** C1
Priors Lo 4 TW10 . . **54** A1
Prior St SE10 . . . . . . **52** B3
Prior Weston Prim
Sch EC1 . . . . **97** B2
Priory Ave W4 . . . . . . **38** A3
Priory Ct
City of London
EC4 . . . . **108** B1
Homerton E9 . . . . . . **17** C3
Nunhead SE15 . . . . . **65** B3
Roehampton SW15 . . **56** B3
South Lambeth
SW8 . . . . **171** C4
Priory Gdns
Barnes SW13 . . . . . . **56** B4
6 Chiswick W4 . . . . **38** A2
Priory Gn N1 . . . . . . **84** C2
Priory Gr SW8 . . . . **172** A3
Priory Ho
Clerkenwell EC1 . . . . **96** A2
Pimlico SW1 . . . . . **147** B2
Spitalfields E1 . . . . **110** C4
Priory Hospl Grange
Roehampton
SW15 . . . . **68** A4
Priory Hts N1 . . . . . **85** A2
Priory La SW15 . . . . **56** B2
Priory Lo 7 W4 . . . . **36** C1
Priory Mans
1 Maitland Pk
NW3 . . . . **12** B2
South Kensington
SW10 . . . . **143** A1
Priory Park Rd
Bedford Pk W4 . . . . **37** C3
Hampstead NW6 . . . **11** A1
Richmond TW9 . . . . **44** C3
Priory St 6 E3 . . . . . **27** A2
Priory Terr NW6 . . . . **78** A4
Priory The SE1 . . . **136** A3
Priory Wlk SW10 . . **143** A1
Pritchard Ho 38
E2 . . . . **24** C3
Pritchard's Rd E2 . . . **24** C3
Priter Rd SE16 . . . . **139** C1
Priter Road Hostel 14
SE16 . . . . **139** C1
Probert Rd SW2 . . . . **62** C2
Probyn Ho SW1 . . . **147** C4
Probyn Rd SW2 . . . . **75** A2
Procter Ho 12 SE5 . . . **48** C3
Procter St WC1 . . . **106** C3
Proctor Ho 5
SE1 . . . . **153** B1
Prome Ho 3 N16 . . . **15** C4
Promenade Approach
Rd W4 . . . . **46** A3
Promenade The
W4 . . . . **46** A2

Prospect Cotts
SW18 . . . . **58** C3
Prospect Ho
1 Dalston E8 . . . . . **16** B2
Islington N1 . . . . . . **85** B1
Newington SE11 . . . **136** B1
14 North Kensington
W10 . . . . **30** C3
Prospect House Sch
11 SW15 . . . . **69** C4
Prospect Pl
5 Child's Hill NW2 . . **1** B1
2 Chiswick W4 . . . . **37** C1
6 Deptford SE8 . . . . **51** B4
12 Hampstead
NW3 . . . . **11** B4
7 Lower Holloway
N7 . . . . **14** A4
Wapping E1 . . . . **32** B1
Prospect Quay
SW18 . . . . **58** C3
Prospect Rd NW2 . . . . **1** C1
Prospect St SE16 . . . **40** A4
Prospect Wharf
E1 . . . . **32** B2
Prospero Rd N19 . . . . **4** C3
Prothero Rd SW6 . . **154** C2
Proud Ho 10 E1 . . . . . **32** A3
Prout Gr NW10 . . . . . **8** B4
Provence St N1 . . . . **86** C2
Providence Cl E9 . . . . **25** C4
Providence Ct
Islington N1 . . . . . . **86** A3
Mayfair W1 . . . . . . **117** C4
Providence Pl N1 . . . **86** A3
Providence Row
N1 . . . . **84** C1
Providence Row Bldg 11
E1 . . . . **32** B2
Providence Sq 39
SE1 . . . . **139** B4
Providence Yd 1
E2 . . . . **24** C2 **99** B4
Provost Ct NW3 . . . . **12** B2
Provost Rd NW3 . . . . **12** B1
Provost St N1 . . . . . . **97** B3
Prowse Pl NW1 . . . . . **13** B1
Prudent Pas 6 EC2 . **109** A1
Prusom's Island 8
E1 . . . . **32** A1
Prusom St E1 . . . . . . **32** A1
Pryors The NW3 . . . . . **2** C1
Pudding La EC3 . . . **123** C4
Pudding Mill La
E15 . . . . **27** A4
Pudding Mill Lane Sta
E15 . . . . **27** A4
Puddle Dock EC4 . . **122** B4
Pugin Ct N1 . . . . **14** C1
Pulborough Rd
SW18 . . . . **70** B4
Pulham Ho SW8 . . . **162** C1
Pullman Ct SW2 . . . . **74** B3
Pullman Gdns
SW15 . . . . **57** B1
Pulross Rd SW9 . . . . **62** B4
Pulteney Cl 20 E3 . . . **26** B4
Pulteney Terr N1 . . . . **85** A4
Pulton Ho SE4 . . . . . **66** A3
Pulton Pl SW6 . . . . **155** B1
Puma Ct E1 . . . . . . **110** C4
Pump Ct EC4 . . . . . **107** B1
Pump House Cl
SE16 . . . . **40** B4

Pumphouse
Educational Mus The
SE16 . . . . **33** A1
Pump House Gall
SW11 . . . . **159** B1
Pumping Ho 3
E14 . . . . **34** C2
Pumping Station Rd
W4 . . . . **46** A4
Pump La SE14 . . . . . . **50** B3
Punderson's Gdns
E2 . . . . **25** A2
Purbeck Ho SW8 . . . **162** C1
Purbrook Est SE1 . . **138** B3
Purbrook Ho 2
SW15 . . . . **69** A3
Purbrook St SE1 . . . **138** B2
Purcell Cres SW6 . . **154** A2
Purcell Ho SW10 . . . **157** B3
Purcell Mews 2
NW10 . . . . **8** A1
Purcell St N1 . . . . . . **24** A3
Purchase St SW11 . . **167** C2
Purday Ho 4 W10 . . . **23** B2
Purdon Ho 11
SE15 . . . . **49** C2
Purdy St E3 . . . . **27** A1
Purley Ave NW2 . . . . . **1** A2
Purley Pl N1 . . . . . . **15** A1
Purser Ho 3 SW2 . . . **62** C1
Pursers Cross Rd
SW6 . . . . **165** A4
Purves Rd NW10 . . . . **22** B3
Pusey Ho 20 E14 . . . **33** C3
Puteaux Ho 6 E2 . . . **25** C3
PUTNEY **57** B3
Putney Bridge App
SW6 . . . . **58** A4
Putney Bridge Rd
SW15 . . . . **58** B3
Putney Bridge Sta
SW6 . . . . **58** B4
Putney Comm
SW15 . . . . **57** B4
Putney Exchange
Shopping Ctr
SW15 . . . . **57** C3
PUTNEY HEATH **57** B1
Putney Heath
SW15 . . . . **57** C2
Putney Heath La
SW15 . . . . **57** C2
Putney High Sch
SW15 . . . . **57** C2
Putney High St
SW15 . . . . **58** A3
Putney Hill
12 Putney SW15 . . . **69** B4
Putney SW15 . . . . . . **57** C2
Putney L Ctr SW15 . . **57** C3
Putney Park Ave
SW15 . . . . **56** C3
Putney Park La
SW15 . . . . **57** A2
Putney Park Sch
SW15 . . . . **56** C2
Putney Pier SW15 . . . **58** A4
Putney School of Art
& Design SW15 . . . . **58** A3
Putney Sta SW15 . . . **58** A3
PUTNEY VALE **68** C1
Putney Wharf Twr
SW15 . . . . **58** A4
Pykewell Lo 18
E8 . . . . **16** C3
Pylon Trad Est
E16 . . . . **34** C4

Pymers Mead
SE21 . . . . **75** B3
Pynfolds SE16 . . . . . **40** A4
Pynnersmead
SE24 . . . . **63** B2
Pyrford Ho 12
SW9 . . . . **63** A3
Pyrland Rd
Richmond TW10 . . . . **54** B1
Stoke Newington
N5 . . . . **15** C3
Pyrmont Gr SE27 . . . **75** A1
Pyrmont Rd W4 . . . . . **44** C4
Pytchley Rd SE22 . . . **64** A4

Q

Quadrangle Cl
SE1 . . . . **152** A4
Quadrangle The
Chelsea SW10 . . . . . **167** A4
Fulham SW6 . . . . . . **154** A1
Herne Hill SE24 . . . . **63** B3
8 North Kensington
W12 . . . . **30** B3
Paddington W2 . . . **102** A2
Quadrant Arc W1 . . **119** A3
Quadrant Bsns Ctr
NW6 . . . . **23** A4
Quadrant Gr NW5 . . . **12** B3
Quadrant The
4 Kensal Green
W10 . . . . **22** C2
Richmond TW9 . . . . **54** A3
Quaker Ct SE1 . . . . . **97** A2
Quaker St
E1 . . . . **24** B1 **98** C1
Quality Ct WC2 . . . **107** B2
Quantock Ho N16 . . . . **7** B3
Quantock Mews 2
SE15 . . . . **49** C1
Quarrendon St
SW6 . . . . **165** C2
Quarry Rd SW18 . . . . **59** B1
Quarterdeck The
E14 . . . . **41** C4
Quayside Ct 8
SE16 . . . . **32** C1
Quebec & Crown
Wharves E14 . . . . . . **33** B3
Quebec Ind Est
SE16 . . . . **41** A3
Quebec Mews
W1 . . . . **103** A1
Quebec Way SE16 . . . **41** A4
Quebec Wharf 32
E8 . . . . **24** A4
Quedgeley Ct 3
SE15 . . . . **49** B4
Queen Alexandra
Mans WC1 . . . . **94** A3
Queen Anne Mews
W1 . . . . **104** B3
Queen Anne Rd
E9 . . . . **17** C2
Queen Anne's Gate
SW1 . . . . **133** B3
Queen Anne's Gdns
Bedford Pk W4 . . . . **38** A3
Ealing W5 . . . . **36** A4
Queen Anne's Gr
Bedford Pk W4 . . . . **38** A3
Ealing W5 . . . . **36** A4

Queen Anne St
W1 . . . . **104** A3
Queen Anne Terr 9
E1 . . . . .32 A2
Queen Caroline St
W6 . . . . .39 B1
Queen Charlotte's &
Chelsea Hospl
W12 . . . . .29 C3
Queen Ct WC1 . . . .94 B1
Queen Elizabeth Ct 5
N1 . . . . .15 C2
Queen Elizabeth Hall
& Purcell Room
SE1 . . . . **121** A2
Queen Elizabeth Ho
SW12 . . . . .72 C4
Queen Elizabeth II
Con Ctr SW1 . . . **133** C3
Queen Elizabeth II
Jubilee Sch 5
W9 . . . . .23 B1
Queen Elizabeth's Cl
N16 . . . . .6 C2
Queen Elizabeth's Coll
15 SE10 . . . . .52 B3
Queen Elizabeth St
SE1 . . . . **138** C4
Queen Elizabeth's Wlk
N16 . . . . .6 C2
Queen Elizabeth Wlk
SW13 . . . . .47 A2
Queenhithe EC4 . . **123** A4
Queen Margaret Flats
22 E2 . . . . .25 A2
Queen Margarets Ct
N1 . . . . .16 A3
Queen Margaret's Gr
N1 . . . . .16 A4
Queen Mary's Gdns
NW1 . . . .**91** B3
Queen Mary's Univ
Hospl SW15 . . . . .56 C1
Queen Mary, Univ of
London E1 . . . . . . .26 A1
Queen Mother Sp Ctr
SW1 . . . . **146** C2
Queen of Denmark Ct
SE16 . . . . .41 B3
Queen St Pl EC4 . . **123** A4
Queensberry Mews W
SW7 . . . . **143** B4
Queensberry Pl
SW7 . . . . **143** B4
Queensberry Way
SW7 . . . . **143** B4
Queensborough Mews
W2 . . . . **114** A4
Queensborough Pas
W2 . . . . **114** A4
Queensborough Terr
W2 . . . . **114** B4
Queensbridge Ct 1
E2 . . . . .24 B3
Queensbridge Inf Sch
11 E8 . . . . .16 B1
Queensbridge Rd
Dalston E8 . . . . . . .16 B1
Shoreditch E2, E8 . . .24 B4
Queensbury St
N1 . . . . .15 B1
Queen's CE Prim Sch
The TW9 . . . . . . .44 C3
Queen's Cir SW11 **160** A1

Queen's Club Gdns
W14 . . . . **154** B4
Queen's Club The
W14 . . . . **140** B1
Queen's Coll W1 . **104** A3
Queen's Coll Prep Sch
W1 . . . . **104** A4
Queens Cres TW10 .54 B2
Queen's Cres NW5 . .12 C2
Queens Ct
Battersea SW11 . . . **170** A4
Camberwell SE5 . . . .49 A1
4 Limehouse E14 . . .33 B2
Queen's Ct
Barnes SW13 . . . . . .56 C4
Kensington W2 . . . **114** B3
3 Richmond TW10 . .54 B1
St John's Wood
NW8 . . . . .79 B2
Queensdale W11 . . .30 C1
Queensdale Cres
W11 . . . . .30 C1
Queensdale Pl
W11 . . . . .31 A1 **112** A1
Queensdale Rd
Notting Hill W11 . . . .30 C1
Notting Hill
W11 . . . . .31 A1 **112** A1
Queensdale Wlk
W11 . . . . .31 A1 **112** A1
Queensdown Rd
E5 . . . . .17 A4
Queen's Dr N4 . . . . .6 A2
Queen's Elm Par
SW3 . . . . **143** C2
Queen's Elm Sq
SW3 . . . . **143** C1
Queen's Gallery
SW1 . . . . **132** B3
Queen's Gate
SW7 . . . . **129** A1
Queensgate Gdns
SW15 . . . . .57 A3
Queen's Gate Gdns
SW7 . . . . **129** A1
Queensgate Ho 34
E3 . . . . .26 B3
Queen's Gate Jun Sch
SW7 . . . . **143** B4
Queen's Gate Mews
SW7 . . . . **129** A1
Queensgate Pl 10
NW6 . . . . .10 C1
Queen's Gate Pl
SW7 . . . . **129** A1
Queen's Gate Pl Mews
SW7 . . . . **129** A1
Queen's Gate Terr
SW7 . . . . **129** A1
Queen's Gate Villas
E9 . . . . **118** A4
Queens Gdns W2 . **114** C4
Queen's Gr NW8 . . . .79 C3
Queen's Yd W1 . . . .93 A1
Queen's Head Pas
EC2 . . . . **108** C2
Queen's Head St
N1 . . . . .86 B3
Queen's Head Yd
SE1 . . . . **123** B1
Queens Ho 1
SE17 . . . . .48 C4
Queen's House The
SE10 . . . . .52 C4
Queensland Rd
N7 . . . . .14 C4

Queens Manor Sch
SW6 . . . . .47 C3
Queens Mans
NW6 . . . . .11 A3
Queen's Mans W6 . .39 C2
Queensmead NW8 . .79 C4
Queensmere Cl
SW19 . . . . .69 C2
Queensmere Ct
SW13 . . . . .46 C4
Queensmere Rd
SW19 . . . . .69 C2
Queen's Mews
W2 . . . . **114** A4
Queensmill Rd
SW6 . . . . **165** C1
Queensmill Sch
SW6 . . . . **165** C1
Queens Par 3 NW2 . .9 B2
Queens Park Com Sch
NW6 . . . . .22 C4
Queens Park Ct 5
W10 . . . . .22 C2
Queen's Park Prim
Sch 20 W10 . . . . .23 A1
Queen's Park Sta
NW6 . . . . .23 B3
Queen Sq WC1 . . . **106** B4
Queen's Quay EC4 **123** A4
Queen's Rd
Mortlake SW14 . . . . .55 C4
New Cross Gate SE14,
SE15 . . . . .50 B2
Richmond TW10 . . . .54 B1
Queen's Ride
SW13 . . . . .57 A4
Queen's Rise
TW10 . . . . .54 B1
Queen's Road Sta
SE15 . . . . .50 B2
Queen's Row SE17 . .48 C4
Queen St
City of London
EC4 . . . . **123** A4
Mayfair W1, SW1 . . **118** A2
Queens Terr NW8 . . .79 B2
Queenstown Mews
SW8 . . . . **170** A3
Queenstown Rd
SW8 . . . . **170** A4
Queenstown Road
(Battersea) Sta
SW8 . . . . **170** B4
Queensville Rd SW12,
SW4 . . . . .73 C4
Queensway W2 . . . **114** B4
Queensway 9
SW4 . . . . .73 C4
Queens Wlk W5 . . . .36 A3
Queen's Wlk SW1 . **118** C1
Queenswood Ct 7
SW4 . . . . .62 A2
Radipole Rd SW6 . **164** C4
Queens Yd E9 . . . . .18 C2
Queen's Yd W1 . . . .93 A1
Queen Victoria Meml
SW1 . . . . **132** C4
Queen Victoria St
EC4 . . . . **122** C4
Queen Victoria Terr
12 E1 . . . . .32 A2
Quelch Ho 2 N19 . .13 C3
Quemerford Rd
N7 . . . . .14 B3
Quendon Ho 9
W10 . . . . .22 B1
Quenington Ct 5
SE15 . . . . .49 B4

Quenington Mans
SW6 . . . . **164** C4
Quennel Ho 7
SW12 . . . . .73 B4
Querrin St SW6 . . . **166** C1
Quested Ct 27 E8 . . .17 A3
Quex Mews NW6 . . .23 C4
Quex Rd NW6 . . . . .23 C4
Quick St N1 . . . . . . .86 B1
Quick Street Mews
N1 . . . . .86 B1
Quickswood NW3 . . .12 A1
Quill La SW15 . . . . .57 C3
Quill St N4 . . . . .5 C1
Quilp St SE1 . . . . . **136** C4
Quilter St
E2 . . . . . . .24 C2 **99** B4
Quilting Ct 28
SE16 . . . . .40 C4
Quince Rd SE13 . . . .67 A4
Quintin Ct W4 . . . . .45 B3
Quintin Kynaston Sch
NW8 . . . . .79 B3
Quintock Ho 2
TW9 . . . . .44 C2
Quinton Ho SW8 . . **162** A2
Quinton St SW18 . . .71 B2
Quixley St E14 . . . . .34 C2
Quorn Rd SE22 . . . .64 A4

R

Rabbit Row
W8 . . . . . . .31 C1 **113** C2
Raby St E14 . . . . . **33** A3
Racine 18 SE5 . . . . .49 A2
Racton Rd SW6 . . **155** B3
Radbourne Ct E5 . . .17 C4
Radbourne Rd
SW12 . . . . .73 C3
Radcliff Bldg EC1 . **107** B4
Radcliffe Ave
NW10 . . . . .21 C3
Radcliffe Coll
Marylebone W1 . . . **104** C1
Soho W1 . . . . **105** B1
Radcliffe Ho 10
SE16 . . . . .40 A2
Radcliffe Path 5
SW8 . . . . **170** B1
Radcliffe Rd SE1 . . **138** B2
Radcliffe Sq SW15 . .57 C1
Radcot St SE11 . . . **149** C1
Raddington Rd
W10 . . . . .31 A4
Radfield Ho 25
NW6 . . . . .78 A3
Radford Ho
7 Bow Comm
E14 . . . . .34 A4
Islington N7 . . . . . . .14 B3
Radford Rd SE13 . . .67 B1
Radland Rd E16 . . . .35 C3
Radlett Pl NW8 . . . . .80 A4
Radley Ct 23 SE16 . .40 C4
Radley Ho NW1 . . . . .90 C2
Radley Lo 9
SW19 . . . . .69 C3
Radley Mews W8 . . **127** C1
Radley Terr 1
E16 . . . . .35 B4
Radnor Lo W2 . . . **101** C1
Radnor Mews W2 . **101** C1
Radnor Pl W2 . . . . **102** A1

Radnor Rd
Kensal Rise NW6 . . . .23 A4
Peckham SE15 . . . . .49 C3
Radnor St EC1 . . . . .97 A3
Radnor Terr W14 . . **140** C4
Radnor Way NW10 . .20 A1
Radnor Wlk
Chelsea SW3 . . . . **144** C1
2 Millwall E14 . . . . .41 C2
Radstock St
SW11 . . . . **158** A1
Radway Ho 30 W2 . .31 C4
Radwell Ho SW2 . . . .62 C2
Raebarn Ct 6
SW16 . . . . .74 A1
Raeburn St SW2 . . . .62 A3
Ragged School Mus
E3 . . . . .33 A4
Raglan Ct SW9 . . . . .62 C4
Raglan St NW5 . . . .13 A2
Ragley Cl W3 . . . . . .37 B4
Rahere Ho EC1 . . . . .96 C4
Railey Mews NW5 . .13 B3
Railton Rd SE24 . . . .63 A2
Railway App SE1 . . **123** C2
Railway Cotts W6 . . .39 B4
Railway Gr SE14 . . . .51 B3
Railway Rise SE22 . .64 A3
Railway Side
SW13 . . . . .56 A4
Railway St N1 . . . . . **84** B1
Railway Terr SE13 . . .67 A2
Rainbow Ave E14 . . .42 A1
Rainbow Ct 3
SE14 . . . . .51 A4
Rainbow Montessori
Sch NW6 . . . . .11 A1
Rainbow Quay
SE16 . . . . .41 A3
Rainbow Sch 15
SW17 . . . . .71 B2
Rainbow St SE5 . . . .49 A3
Raines Ct N16 . . . . . .7 B2
Raine's Foundation
Lower Sch 32 E2 . . .25 A2
Raine's Foundation
Sch 22 E2 . . . . . . .25 B3
Raine St E1 . . . . . . .32 A1
Rainford Ho 9 N7 . . .5 B2
Rainham Cl SW11 . . .60 A1
Rainham Ho NW1 . . .83 A3
Rainham Rd NW10 . .22 B2
Rainhill Way E3 . . . .26 C2
Rainsborough Ave
SE8 . . . . .41 A2
Rainsford Ct
NW10 . . . . .20 A3
Rainsford Ho 14
SW2 . . . . .62 B2
Rainsford Rd
NW10 . . . . .20 A3
Rainsford St W2 . . **102** A2
Rainton Rd SE7 . . . .43 C1
Rainville Rd W6 . . . .47 B4
Raleigh Ct
Hammersmith
W6 . . . . .39 A4
2 Rotherhithe
SE16 . . . . .32 C1
Raleigh Gdns SW2 . .62 B1
Isle of Dogs E14 . . . .42 A4
Raleigh Mews N1 . . .86 B3
Raleigh Rd TW9 . . . .54 B4

Raleigh St N1 . . . . 86 B3
Ralph Ct 8 W2 . . . . . 100 B2
Ralston St SW3 . . . . 144 C1
Ramar Ho 12 E1 . . . 111 B4
Ramilles Cl SW2 . . . . . 62 A1
Ramilles Ho 11 W1 . . 105 A1
Ramilles Pl W1 . . . . 104 C1
Ramilles Rd W4 . . . . 37 C3
Ramillies St W1 . . . . 104 C1
Rampart St E1 . . . . . . 32 A3
Rampayne St
  SW1 . . . . 147 B2
Ramsay Ho NW8 . . . . 90 A2
Ramsay Rd W3 . . . . . . 37 B4
Ramsdean Ho 11
  SW15 . . . . 69 A3
Ramsden Rd SW12 . . 72 C4
Ramsey Ct
  Putney SW15 . . . . . . 57 B1
  8 Upper Holloway
  N19 . . . . 4 C2
Ramsey Ho
  8 Battersea
  SW11 . . . . 59 C3
  10 Kennington
  SW9 . . . . 163 C1
Ramsey St
  E2 . . . . 24 C1 99 C2
Ramsey Wlk N1 . . . . . 15 C2
Ramsfort Ho 14
  SE16 . . . . 40 A2
Ramsgate St E8 . . . . 16 B2
Ram St SW18 . . . . . . 59 A2
Randal Cremer JMI
  Sch 18 E2 . . . . 24 B3
Randall Cl SW11 . . . 168 A4
Randall Pl SE10 . . . . 52 B3
Randall Row SE11 . . 148 C3
Randell's Rd N1 . . . . . 84 C4
Randolf Ct
  Paddington NW6 . . . . 78 A1
  St John's Wood
  NW8 . . . . 78 C2
Randolph Ave W9 . . . 88 C3
Randolph Cres W9 . . 88 C2
Randolph Gdns
  NW6 . . . . 78 A1
Randolph Mews
  W9 . . . . 89 A1
Randolph Rd W9 . . . . 89 A1
Randolph St NW1 . . . 13 B1
Ranelagh Ave
  Barnes SW13 . . . . . 46 C4
  Fulham SW6 . . . . . . 58 B4
Ranelagh Gardens
  Mans SW6 . . . . 58 A4
Ranelagh Gardens
  (site of Chelsea
  Flower Show)
  SW1 . . . . 145 C1
Ranelagh Gdns
  8 Bedford Pk
  W6 . . . . 38 B3
  Chiswick W4 . . . . . . 45 B3
  Fulham SW6 . . . . . . 58 B4
Ranelagh Gr SW1 . . 145 C2
Ranelagh Ho SW3 . . 144 C2
Ranelagh Mans
  SW6 . . . . 165 A2
Ranelagh Rd
  Dagenham NW10 . . . 21 A3
  Pimlico SW1 . . . . . 147 A1
Rangdon St EC3 . . . 110 C1

Ranger's House (The
  Wernher Collection)
  SE10 . . . . 52 C2
Rangers Sq SE10 . . . 52 C2
Rangoon Ho 5
  N16 . . . . 15 C4
Rankine Ho SE1 . . . 136 C1
Ranmere St SW12 . . 73 A3
Rann Ho 1 SW14 . . . 55 C4
Rannoch Rd W6 . . . . . 47 C4
Ransomes Dock Bsns
  Ctr SW11 . . . . 158 B1
Ransomes Mews
  SW11 . . . . 158 B2
Ranston St NW1 . . . 102 A4
Ranulf Rd NW2 . . . . . 10 B4
Ranwell Cl 18 E3 . . . 26 B4
Ranwell Ho 17 E3 . . . 26 B4
Raphael Ct 9
  SE16 . . . . 40 A1
Raphael St SW7 . . . 130 C3
Rapley Ho 14
  E2 . . . . 24 C2 99 B3
Rashleigh Ct 8
  SW8 . . . . 61 A4
Rashleigh Ho WC1 . . 94 A3
Rastell Ave SW12 . . . 73 C3
Ratcliffe Cross St
  E1 . . . . 32 C3
Ratcliffe Ho 10
  E14 . . . . 33 A3
Ratcliffe La 10
  E14 . . . . 33 A3
Ratcliffe Orch 9
  E14 . . . . 33 A3
Rathbone Ho
  5 Canning Town
  E16 . . . . 35 B3
  Kilburn NW6 . . . . . . 23 C4
Rathbone Mkt 3
  E16 . . . . 35 B3
Rathbone Pl W1 . . . 105 B2
Rathbone St
  Canning Town
  E16 . . . . 35 B3
  Fitzrovia W1 . . . . . 105 A3
Rathgar Rd SW9 . . . 63 A4
Rathmell Dr SW4 . . . 61 C1
Rattray Rd SW2 . . . . 62 C2
Raul Rd SE15 . . . . . . 49 C2
Raveley St NW5 . . . . 13 B4
Ravenet Ct
  Battersea SW11 . . . 170 A3
  Clapham SW4 . . . . . 61 A2
Ravenet St SW11 . . . 170 A3
Ravenfield Rd
  SW17 . . . . 72 B1
Raven Ho 16 SE16 . . 40 C2
Ravenna Rd SW15 . . 57 C2
Raven Row E1 . . . . . . 32 A4
Ravensbourne Ho
  NW8 . . . . 102 A4
Ravensbourne Mans
  5 SE8 . . . . 51 C4
Ravensbourne Pl
  SE13 . . . . 52 A1
Ravensbury Rd
  SW18 . . . . 71 A2
Ravensbury Terr
  SW18 . . . . 71 A2
Ravenscar NW1 . . . . 82 C3
Ravenscourt 1 N16 . 7 C1
Ravenscourt Ave
  W6 . . . . 38 C2

Ravenscourt Gdns
  W6 . . . . 38 C2
Ravenscourt Ho 18
  W6 . . . . 39 A2
Ravenscourt Park
  Mans 1 W6 . . . . 39 A3
Ravenscourt Park
  Prep Sch W6 . . . . . . 38 C2
Ravenscourt Park Sta
  W6 . . . . 38 C2
Ravenscourt Pl
  W6 . . . . 39 A2
Ravenscourt Rd
  W6 . . . . 39 A2
Ravenscourt Sq
  W6 . . . . 38 C3
Ravenscourt Theatre
  Sch 20 W6 . . . . 39 A2
Ravenscroft Ave
  NW11 . . . . 1 B4
  E16 . . . . 35 C4
Ravenscroft Cl 4
  E16 . . . . 35 C4
Ravenscroft Ct
  NW11 . . . . 1 B4
Ravenscroft Point 9
  E9 . . . . 17 C2
Ravenscroft Rd
  Acton W4 . . . . 37 B2
  Newham E16 . . . . . . 35 C4
Ravenscroft St
  E2 . . . . 24 B2 99 A4
Ravensdon St
  SE11 . . . . 149 C1
Ravenshaw St
  NW6 . . . . 10 B3
Ravenslea Rd SW11,
  SW12 . . . . 72 B4
Ravensmede Way
  W4 . . . . 38 B2
Ravenstone SE17 . . 152 B1
Ravenstone Prim Sch
  SW12 . . . . 72 C2
Ravenstone St
  SW12 . . . . 72 C3
Ravenswood Rd
  SW12 . . . . 73 A4
Ravensworth Rd
  NW10 . . . . 22 A2
Raven Wharf SE1 . . 138 C4
Ravey St
  EC2 . . . . 24 A1 98 A2
Rav Pinter Cl N16 . . 7 A4
Rawlings St SW3 . . . 144 C4
Rawlinson Ho
  SE13 . . . . 67 C3
Rawlinson Point 5
  E16 . . . . 35 B4
Rawreth Wlk N1 . . . . 87 A4
Rawson Ct SW11 . . . 169 C3
Rawson St SW11 . . . 170 A3
Rawstone Pl EC1 . . . 96 A4
Rawstone St EC1 . . . 96 A4
Rayburne Ct W14 . . 126 A2
Raydon St N19 . . . . . 4 A2
Ray Ho
  7 North Kensington
  W10 . . . . 30 C3
  Shoreditch N1 . . . . . 87 C3
Raymede Twr 2
  W10 . . . . 30 C4
Raymond Bldgs
  WC1 . . . . 107 A4

Raymouth Rd
  SE16 . . . . 40 A2
Raynald Ho 15
  SW16 . . . . 74 A1
Rayne Ct SE1 . . . . . 138 C4
Rayne Ho
  1 Balham SW12 . . . 60 C1
  Paddington W9 . . . . 88 A2
Rayner Ct 10 W12 . . 39 B4
Rayner's Rd SW15 . . 58 A2
Raynes Ho 2 . . . . . . 102 A2
Raynham Ho 1
  E1 . . . . 25 C1
Raynham Rd W6 . . . . 39 A2
Raynor Pl
  23 Canonbury N1 . . 15 B1
  N1 . . . . 87 A4
Ray St EC1 . . . . 95 C1
Ray Wlk N7 . . . . 5 B2
Reachview Ct 17
  NW1 . . . . 13 B1
Reade Ct 3 W3 . . . . . 37 B3
Reade Wlk 5
  NW10 . . . . 8 A1
Read Ho 4 SE11 . . . 163 B4
Reading Ho
  Paddington W2 . . . 100 C1
  Peckham SE15 . . . . 49 C4
Reading La E8 . . . . . 17 A2
Reapers Cl 1 NW1 . . 83 B4
Reardon Ho 5 E1 . . . 32 A1
Reardon Path 31
  E1 . . . . 32 A1
Reardon St E1 . . . . . 32 A1
Reaston St SE14 . . . . 50 C3
Reay Prim Sch
  SW9 . . . . 163 A1
Reckitt Rd W4 . . . . . 38 A1
Record St SE16 . . . . . 40 C1
Rector St N1 . . . . 86 C3
Rectory Gdns 6
  SW4 . . . . 61 B4
Rectory Gr SW4 . . . . 61 B4
Rectory Rd
  Barnes SW13 . . . . . 46 C1
  1 London W3 . . . . . 28 B1
  Shacklewell N16 . . . 7 B1
Rectory Road Sta
  N16 . . . . 7 B1
Rectory Sq E1 . . . . . 32 C4
Reculver Ho 2
  SE15 . . . . 50 B4
Reculver Rd SE16 . . . 40 C1
Red Anchor Cl
  SW3 . . . . 158 A3
Redan Pl W2 . . . . . . 100 A1
Redan St W14 . . . . . 39 C3
Redan Terr SE5 . . . . 48 A1
Redbourne Ho 7
  E14 . . . . 33 B3
Redbourn Ho 10
  W10 . . . . 22 B1
Redbridge Gdns
  SE5 . . . . 49 A3
Redburn St SW3 . . . 158 C4
Redcar St SE5 . . . . . . 48 B3
Redcastle Cl E1 . . . . 32 B2
Redchurch St
  E2 . . . . 24 B1 98 C2
Redcliffe Cl 5 SW5 . 142 A1
Redcliffe Gdns
  Chiswick W4 . . . . . . 45 A3
  Fulham SW10 . . . . . 156 B4
Redcliffe Mews
  SW10 . . . . 142 B1

Redcliffe Pl SW10 . . 156 C3
Redcliffe Rd
  SW10 . . . . 157 A4
Redcliffe Sch
  SW10 . . . . 156 C3
Redcliffe Sq
  SW10 . . . . 142 B1
Redcliffe St SW10 . . 156 B4
Redclyf Ho 15 E1 . . . 25 B1
Redcroft 5 NW6 . . . . 10 C2
Red Cross Cotts
  SE1 . . . . 137 A4
Redcross Way
  SE1 . . . . 123 A1
Reddins Rd SE15 . . . 49 C4
Rede Pl
  W2 . . . . 31 C2 113 C4
Redesdale St
  SW3 . . . . 158 C4
Redfern Rd NW10 . . . 8 A1
Redfield La SW5 . . . 142 A4
Redfield Mews
  SW5 . . . . 141 C4
Redfiff Est SE16 . . . . 41 B3
Redford Wlk N1 . . . . 86 C4
Redgate Terr
  SW15 . . . . 57 C1
Redgrave Rd
  SW15 . . . . 57 C4
Redhill Ct SW2 . . . . . 74 C2
Redhill St NW1 . . . . . 92 B4
Red House Ho 20 . . . 15 B1
Redington Gdns
  NW3 . . . . 11 A4
Redington Ho N1 . . . 85 A2
Redington Rd
  NW3 . . . . 11 A4
Redlands Prim Sch 55
  E1 . . . . 32 B4
Redlands Way
  SW2 . . . . 74 B4
Red Lion Cl 9
  SE17 . . . . 48 C4
Red Lion Ct EC4 . . . 107 C1
Red Lion Row
  SE17 . . . . 48 B4
Red Lion Sq WC1 . . 106 C3
Red Lion St WC1 . . . 106 C3
Red Lion Yd W1 . . . 117 C2
Redlynch Ct W14 . . 126 B3
Redlynch Ho 27
  SW9 . . . . 173 C4
Redman Bldg EC1 . . 107 B4
Redman Ho SE1 . . . 137 A3
Redman's Rd E1 . . . 32 B4
Redmayne Ho 15
  SW9 . . . . 173 A2
Redmead La E1 . . . 125 B1
Redmill Ho 24 E1 . . . 25 A1
Redmond Ho N1 . . . 85 A3
Redmore Rd W6 . . . . 39 A2
Red Pl W1 . . . . 117 B4
Red Post Hill SE21,
  SE24 . . . . 63 C2
Redriff Prim Sch
  SE16 . . . . 41 A4
Redriff Rd SE16 . . . . 41 A3
Red Rover SW13 . . . 56 C4
Redrup Ho 21
  SE14 . . . . 50 C4
Redruth Rd E9 . . . . . 25 B4
Red Sq The N16 . . . . 6 C1
Redstart Cl SE14 . . . 51 A3

Redvers St
E2 . . . . .24 A2 98 B4
Redwald Rd E5 . . . .17 C4
Redwood Cl
4 Bow E3 . . . . . .26 C3
Rotherhithe SE16 . . .33 A1
Redwood Ct
Brondesbury
NW6 . . . . .10 A1
Crouch End N19 . . . .4 C4
Redwood Mews 2
SW4 . . . . .61 A4
Redwoods SW15. . .68 C3
Reece Mews SW7 143 B4
Reed Cl E16 . . . . . .35 C4
Reedham St SE15. . .64 C4
Reed Ho SW15 . . . .56 C1
Reedholm Villas
N16 . . . . .15 C4
Reed Pl
Battersea SW11 . . . .60 A3
Clapham SW4 . . . . .61 C3
Reed's Pl NW1 . . . .13 B1
Reedworth St
SE11 . . . . .149 C3
Reef Ho E14 . . . . . .42 B3
Rees St N1 . . . . . . .87 A3
Reeves Ho
Lambeth SE1 . . . . .135 B3
Mayfair W1 . . . . . .117 C3
Reeves Mews W1 117 C3
Reeves Rd E3 . . . . .27 A1
Reflection Ho 5
E2 . . . . .24 C1 99 B2
Reform St SW11. . .169 A2
Regal Cl E1 . . . . . .111 C4
Regal La NW1 . . . . .81 C3
Regal Pl
8 Tower Hamlets
E3 . . . . .26 B2
Walham Green
SW6 . . . . .156 B1
Regan Way N1 . . . . .24 A3
Regatta Point TW8 .44 B4
Regency Ct
9 Bow E3 . . . . . . .26 B3
14 South Hackney
E9 . . . . .25 B4
Regency Ho NW1. . .92 B2
Regency Lo NW3 . . .11 C1
Regency Mews
Camberwell SW9 . . .48 A3
1 Willesden NW10 . .8 C2
Regency Pl SW1 . .147 C4
Regency St SW1 . .147 C3
Regency Terr
SW7 . . . . .143 B2
Regency Wlk 8
TW10 . . . . .54 A2
Regeneration Rd
SE16 . . . . .40 C1
Regent Ct
Lisson Gr NW8. . . . .90 A3
1 Stamford Hill N16. .7 B4
Regent Ho W14 . . .140 A4
Regent Pl W11 . . . .119 A4
Regent Rd SE24 . . .63 A2
Regents Bridge Gdns
SW8 . . . . .162 B2
Regents Canal Ho 19
E14 . . . . .33 B3
Regent's Coll NW1 91 B2
Regents Ct E8 . . . . .24 C4

Regents Gate Ho 20
E14 . . . . .33 A2
Regents Lo 9
SW2 . . . . .74 B3
Regents Mews
NW8 . . . . .79 A2
REGENT'S PARK . . .92 A4
Regent's Park
NW1 . . . . .81 B1
Regent's Park
Barracks NW1 . . . .82 C4
Regent's Park Rd
Camden Town
NW1 . . . . .81 B4
Primrose Hill NW3 . .12 C1
Regent's Park Sta
NW1 . . . . .92 A1
Regent's Park Terr
NW1 . . . . .82 A4
Regent's Pl SE3 . . . .53 C1
Regents Plaza 2
NW6 . . . . .78 A2
Regent Sq
22 Bromley E3 . . . . .27 A2
St Pancras WC1 . . . .94 B3
Regent's Row E8 . . .24 C4
Regent St
Brentford W4 . . . . . .36 C1
7 Kensal Green
NW10 . . . . .22 C2
Mayfair W1 . . . . . .118 C4
Regents Wharf
3 Hackney E2 . . . . .25 A4
Islington N1 . . . . . .84 C2
Reginald Pl 6
SE8 . . . . .51 C3
Reginald Rd SE8. . . .51 C3
Reginald Sq SE8. . . .51 C3
Regina Point SE16. .40 B3
Regina Rd N4 . . . . . .5 B3
Regis Ct NW1 . . . .102 C4
Regis Pl 17 SW2. . . .62 B3
Regis Rd NW5 . . . . .13 A3
Regnart Bldgs
NW1 . . . . .93 A3
Reid Ct SW14. . . . . .45 B1
Reighton Rd E5 . . . . .7 C2
Reizel Cl N16. . . . . . .7 B3
Relay Rd W12 . . . . . .30 B1
Relf Rd SE15 . . . . . .64 C4
Reliance Sq
E2 . . . . .24 A1 98 B2
Relton Ct W3. . . . . .36 C4
Relton Mews
SW7 . . . . .130 B2
Rembrandt Cl E14 . .42 C3
Rembrandt Ct
SE16 . . . . .40 A1
Rembrandt Cl SW1 .145 B3
Remington St N1. . . .86 B1
Remnant St WC2 . .106 C2
Remsted Ho 7
NW6 . . . . .78 A3
Remus Rd E3. . . . . .18 C1
Renaissance Wlk 4
SE10 . . . . .43 B3
Renbold Ho 5
SE10 . . . . .52 B2
Rendlesham Ho 3 E5,
N16 . . . . .7 C1
Rendlesham Rd E5 . . .7 C1
Renforth St SE16 . . .40 B4
Renfrew Ho NW6 . . .78 A1
Renfrew Rd SE11 . .150 A3
Rennell Ho 18 E9. . .17 C2
Rennell St SE13 . . . .67 B4

Rennie Cotts 29
E1 . . . . .25 B1
Rennie Ct SE1 . . . .122 A2
Rennie Ho SE1 . . . .136 C1
Rennie St SE1 . . . .122 A2
Renoir Ct 7 SE16 . . .40 A1
Renton Cl SW2 . . . . .62 B1
Rephidim St SE1 . .138 A1
Replingham Rd
SW18 . . . . .70 C3
Reporton Rd SW6 . .154 B1
Repton Ct N1 . . . . . .87 A4
Repton St E14 . . . . .33 A3
Reservoir Rd SE4 . . .51 A1
Reservoir Studios 14
E1 . . . . .32 C3
Resolution Way 14
SE8 . . . . .51 C3
Restell Cl SE3 . . . . .53 A4
Reston Pl SW7 . . . .128 C3
Restoration Sq
SW11 . . . . .167 C3
Retcar Pl N19 . . . . . .4 A2
Retford St E2. . . . . .24 A3
Retreat Ho 5 E9 . . . .17 B2
Retreat Pl E9. . . . . . .17 B2
Retreat The SW14 . .56 A4
Reunion Row E1 . . . .32 A2
Reveley Sq SE16 . . . .41 A4
Revelon Rd SE4 . . . .66 A4
Revelstoke Rd SW18,
SW19 . . . . .71 C2
Reverdy Rd SE1 . . . .153 B3
Rewell St SW6 . . . .156 C1
Rex Pl W1 . . . . .117 C2
Reynard Cl SE4 . . . . .66 A4
Reynard Pl SE14. . . .51 A4
Reynolds Ho
Finsbury Pk N4 . . . . .5 A3
1 South Hackney
E2 . . . . .25 B3
St John's Wood
NW8 . . . . .79 C1
Westminster SW1 . .147 C3
Reynolds Pl 12
4 Acton Green SW4 . .37 B3
Richmond TW10 . . . .54 B1
Reynolds Rd
Acton Green W4 . . . .37 B3
Nunhead SE15 . . . . .65 B3
Reynolds Sp Ctr
W3 . . . . .29 A2
Rffra Rd Ret Pk
SW2 . . . . .62 C2
Rheidol Mews N1 . . .86 C2
Rheidol Terr N1 . . . . .86 C2
Rhizotron & Xstrata
Treetop Walkway
TW9 . . . . .44 A2
Rhoda St E2 . . . . . . .24 B1 99 A2
Rhodes Ho
Shepherd's Bush
W12 . . . . .30 A1
Shoreditch N1. . . . . .97 B4
Rhodesia Rd SW9 . .172 B1
Rhodes St N7 . . . . . .14 B3
Rhodeswell Rd
E14 . . . . .33 B3
Rhondda Gr E3 . . . . .26 B2
Rhyl Prim Sch 21
NW5 . . . . .12 C2
Rhyl St NW5. . . . . . .12 C2
Ribblesdale Ho 11
NW6 . . . . .23 C4
Ribbon Dance Mews
SE5 . . . . .48 C2

Ribstone Ho 12 E9. .17 C2
Ricardo St E14 . . . . .34 A3
Riceyman Ho WC1. . .95 B3
Richard Anderson Ct
1 SE14 . . . . .50 C3
Richard Atkins Prim
Sch 22 SW2 . . . . . .74 A4
Richard Burbidge
Mans SW13 . . . . . .47 B4
Richard Cloudesley
Sch (Prim Dept)
EC1 . . . . .97 A1
Richard Cloudesley
Sch (Secondary
Dept) EC1. . . . . . . .96 C1
Richard Cobden Prim
Sch NW1 . . . . .83 B2
Richard Fox Ho N4 . .6 B1
Richard Ho 9
SE16 . . . . .40 B2
Richard Knight Ho
SW6 . . . . .165 C4
Richard Neale Ho 2
E1 . . . . .32 A2
Richardson Cl 10
E8 . . . . .24 B4
Richardson Ct 20
SW4 . . . . .172 B2
Richardson Ho 1
E14 . . . . .33 C4
Richardson's Mews
W1 . . . . .92 C1
Richard's Pl SW3 . .144 B4
Richard St 21 E1 . . .32 A3
Richbell Cl SW6 . . .106 B4
Richbell Pl WC1 . . .106 C4
Richborne Terr
SW8 . . . . .163 A2
Richborough Ho
15 Deptford SE15. . .50 B4
14 Hackney E5. . . . .17 A4
Richborough Rd
NW2 . . . . .10 A4
Richbourne Ct
W1 . . . . .102 B2
Richford Gate W6 . .39 B3
Richford St W6 . . . . .39 B3
Rich Ind Est SE15 . .50 A4
Rich La SW5 . . . . . .142 A2
Richland Ho 4
SE15 . . . . .49 C2
Richman Ho 10
SE8 . . . . .41 B1
Rich Mix E1. . . . . . . .99 A2
RICHMOND 54 B3
Richmond Ave
Islington N1 . . . . . .85 A4
Willesden NW10 . . . .9 B2
Richmond Bldgs
W1 . . . . .105 B1
Richmond Circus
TW9 . . . . .54 A3
Richmond Coll
W8 . . . . .128 B2
Richmond Cres N1 . .85 A4
Richmond Ct
SW1 . . . . .131 A3
Richmond Gr N1 . . . .15 A1
Richmond Healthcare
Hamlet Hospl
TW9 . . . . .54 A4
RICHMOND HILL . . .54 A1
Richmond Hill
TW10 . . . . .54 A1
Richmond Hill Ct 5
TW10 . . . . .54 A1

Richmond Ho
12 Forest Hill
SE26 . . . . .76 C1
Regent's Pk NW1 . . .82 B1
Walworth SE17. . . .151 B2
Richmond
International Bsns
Ctr 2 TW9 . . . . . . .54 B3
Richmond Mans
Earl's Ct SW5 . . . . .142 A2
Putney SW15 . . . . . .58 A4
Richmond Mews
W1 . . . . .105 B1
Richmond Park Rd
SW14 . . . . .55 C3
Richmond Rd
Dalston E8 . . . . .16 C1
Ealing W5 . . . . .36 A4
Richmond Sta
TW9 . . . . .54 A3
Richmond Terr
SW1 . . . . .134 A4
Richmond Way W12,
W14 . . . . .39 C4
Rich St E14. . . . . . . .33 B2
Rickard St SW2 . . . .74 C3
Rickett St SW6 . . . .155 C4
Rickman Ho 28 E2. . .25 B1
Rickman St 27 E1 . . .25 B1
Rick Roberts Way
E15 . . . . .27 C3
Rickthorne Rd 7
N19 . . . . .5 A2
Riddell Ct SE1 . . . . .152 C2
Ridgdale St E3 . . . . .27 A3
Ridge Hill NW11. . . . .1 A3
Ridge Rd NW2 . . . . . .1 B1
Ridgeway 11
TW10 . . . . .54 A1
Ridgeway Dr W3 . . . .37 A3
Ridgeway Gdns N6 . .4 B4
Ridgeway The
Acton W3 . . . . .36 C3
Golders Green NW11. .1 B3
Ridgewell Cl N1 . . . . .87 A4
Ridgmount Gdns
WC1 . . . . .93 B1
Ridgmount Pl
WC1 . . . . .105 B4
Ridgmount Rd
SW18 . . . . .59 A2
Ridgmount St
WC1 . . . . .105 B4
Ridgway Rd SW9 . . .63 A4
Riding House St
W1 . . . . .104 C3
Ridings Cl N6 . . . . . . .4 B4
Riding The NW11 . . . .1 B4
Ridley Ho 8
SW11 . . . . .60 A4
Ridley Rd
Dalston E8 . . . . .16 B3
Willesden Green
NW10 . . . . .21 C3
Ridley Road Mkt
E8 . . . . .16 B3
Riffel Rd NW2 . . . . . .9 B3
Rifle Ct SE11 . . . . . .163 C4
Rifle Pl W11 . . . . . . .30 C1
Rifle St E14 . . . . .34 A4
Riga Ho 12 E1 . . . . . .32 C4
Rigault Rd SW6 . . . .164 B1
Rigden St E14 . . . . . .34 A3
Rigeley Rd NW10 . . .21 C2
Rigge Pl SW4 . . . . . .61 C3
Rigg Ho 2 SW4 . . . .74 A4

Rignold Ho **6** SE5..49 A1

Riley Ho
  9 Bow E3 ....26 C1
  Chelsea SW10 ....**157** B3
  1 Streatham SW4 ..73 C4
Riley Rd SE1 ....**138** C2
Riley St SW10 ....49 A3
Rill Ho **15** SE5 .....49 A3
Rimini Ct SW12 ......72 B3
Rinaldo Rd SW12 ..73 A4
Ringcroft St N7 ....14 C2
Ringford Ho SW18 ..58 B2
Ringford Rd SW18 ..58 C1
Ring Ho **16** E1 ......32 B2
Ringmer Ave SW6 **164** B3
Ringmer Gdns **3**
  N19 ....5 A2
Ringmer Ho **15**
  SE22 ....64 A4
Ring Rd W12 ....30 B1
Ringsfield Ho
  SE17 ....**151** A1
Ringwood Gdns
  17 Millwall E14 ....41 C2
  Roehampton SW15 ..68 B3
Ripley Gdns SW14 ..55 C4
Ripley Ho
  Mortlake SW14 ....56 A4
  Nine Elms SW11 ..**160** C4
Ripley's Believe It or
  Not! SW1 ....**119** B3
Riplington Ct
  SW15 ....69 A4
Ripplevale Gr N1 ..14 B1
Risborough SE17 ..**150** C4
Risborough Ho
  NW8 ....**90** B2
Risborough St
  SE1 ....**136** B4
Risdon Ho **30** SE16 ..40 B4
Risdon St **27** SE16 ..40 B4
Riseholme Ct E9 ...18 B2
Riseholme Ho **14**
  SE22 ....64 A4
Riseldine Rd SE23 ..66 A1
Risinghill St N1 ....85 B2
Rising Sun Ct EC1 **108** B3
Risley Ho **7** E9 .....17 C2
Rita Rd SW8 ....**162** C2
Ritchie Ho
  Crouch End N19 ....4 C4
  8 Rotherhithe
    SE16 ....40 B3
  1 South Bromley
    E14 ....34 C3
Ritchie St N1 ....85 C2
Ritherdon Rd
  SW17 ....73 A2
Ritson Ho N1 ......84 C3
Ritson Rd E8 ....16 C2
Rivaz Pl E9 ....17 B2
Riven Ct **10** W2 ..**100** B1
Riverains The
  SW11 ....**167** B3
River Barge Cl E14 ..42 B4
Rivercourt Rd W6 ..39 A1
River Ct SE1 ....**122** A3
Riverdale Dr SW18 ..71 A3
Riverfleet WC1 ....**94** C4
Riverford Ho **28**
  W2 ....31 C4
River Ho SW13 .....46 A1
River House
  Montessori Sch
  E14 ....42 A4
Rivermead Ct SW6 .58 B4

Rivermead Ho E9 ..18 A3
River Pl N1 ....15 B1
River Plate Ho
  EC2 ....**109** C3
Riversdale Prim Sch
  N5 ....70 C1
Riversdale Rd N5....6 B1
Riversdene N5 ......6 B1
Rivers Ho **10** TW8 ..36 C1
Riverside
  Battersea SW11 ..**158** B2
  1 Rotherhithe
    SE16 ....40 B4
  St Pancras WC1 ....94 B4
Riverside Bsns Ctr
  SW18 ....71 A3
Riverside Ct SW8 **161** C4
Riverside Dr W4....46 A2
Riverside Gdns
  W6 ....39 A1
Riverside Health &
  Racquets Club
  Chiswick The
  W4 ....46 A2
Riverside Ho **16**
  N1 ....15 B1
Riverside Mans **4**
  E1 ....32 B1
Riverside Prim Sch **5**
  SE16 ....**139** C3
Riverside Rd
  Mill Meads E15.....27 B3
  Wandsworth SW17,
    SW19 ....71 B1
Riverside Wlk Mkt
  WC2 ....**121** A2
Riverside Workshops
  SE1 ....**123** A2
River St EC1 ....95 B4
River Terr
  London W6 ....39 B1
  St James SW1 ....**120** C3
Riverton Cl W9 .....23 B2
Riverview Gdns
  SW13 ....47 A4
Riverview Gr W4 ..45 A4
Riverview Rd W4 ..45 A4
River Way SE10 ....43 B3
Rivet Ho SE1 ......**153** A2
Rivington Ct
  NW10 ....21 C4
Rivington Pl
  EC2 ....24 **82** 98 B3
Rivington St
  EC2 ....24 **82** 98 A3
Rivington Wlk **4**
  E8 ....24 C4
Rixon St N7 ....5 C1
Roach Rd E3 ....18 C1
Roads Pl N19 ....5 A2
Roan St SE10 ......52 B4
Robert Adam St
  W1 ....**103** B2
Roberta St
  E2 ....24 C2 **99** C4
Robert Bell Ho **2**
  SE16 ....**153** B4
Robert Blair Prim Sch
  N7 ....14 A2
Robert Browning Prim
  Sch SE17 ....**151** B2
Robert Cl **9** W9 ...89 A1
Robert Dashwood
  Way SE17 ....**150** C3
Robert Gentry Ho
  W14 ....**140** B1

Robert Jones Ho **3**
  SE16 ....**153** B4
Robert Keen Cl **18**
  SE15 ....49 C2
Robert Lowe Cl
  SE14 ....50 C3
Robert Owen Ho
  Fulham SW6 ....47 C2
  6 Spitalfields
    E2 ....24 **82** 99 A4
Robert Owen Lo **4**
  E5 ....17 A4
Roberts Ct
  Islington N1 ....86 B3
  Willesden NW10....8 A1
Roberts Ho **5**
  SE27 ....75 A1
Roberts Mews
  SW1 ....**131** B1
Robertson Ho **11**
  SE10 ....52 B3
Robertson St
  SW8 ....**170** B1
Robert's Pl EC1....**95** C2
Robert St
  Regent's Pk NW1 ..**92** B3
  Strand WC2 ....**120** B3
Robert Sutton Ho **20**
  E1 ....32 B3
Robeson St **9** E3 ..33 B4
Robin Ct **15** E14 ..42 A3
Robin Gr
  Dartmouth Pk N6 ...3 C2
  Highgate N6 ....3 C2
Robin Ho **4** NW8 ..80 A1
Robin Hood Gdns **4**
  E14 ....34 B2
Robin Hood La
  E14 ....34 B2
Robinscroft Mews **5**
  SE10 ....52 A2
Robins Ct TW10 ..54 A1
Robin's Ct SW4 ....62 A1
Robinsfield Inf Sch
  NW8 ....80 A2
Robinson Ct
  Islington N1 ....86 B4
  3 Richmond TW9 ..54 B3
Robinson Ho
  4 North Kensington
    W10 ....30 C3
  12 Tower Hamlets
    E14 ....33 C4
Robinson Rd E2 ...25 B3
Robinson St SW3 **158** C4
Robinswood Mews **8**
  N5 ....15 A3
Robsart St SW9 ..**173** B2
Robson Ave NW10 ..8 C1
Robson Rd SE21,....
Roby Ho EC1 ....**96** C2
Rochdale Way **4**
  SE8 ....51 C3
Roche Ho **15** E14 ..33 B2
Rochelle Cl SW11 ..59 C3
Rochelle Ct E1 .....32 B3
Rochelle St **31**
  E2 ....24 **82** 98 C3
Rochemont Wlk **2**
  E8 ....24 C4
Roche Sch The **16**
  SW18 ....58 C2

Rochester Ct
  1 Bethnal Green
    E2 ....25 A1
  2 Camden Town
    NW1 ....13 B1
Rochester Ho
  Bermondsey SE1 ..**137** C3
  14 Deptford SE15...50 B4
Rochester Mews
  NW1 ....13 B1
Rochester Pl NW1 ..13 B2
Rochester Rd NW1 ..13 B2
Rochester Row
  SW1 ....**147** A4
Rochester Sq NW1 ..13 B1
Rochester St SW1 **133** B1
Rochester Terr
  NW1 ....13 B2
Rochester Wlk
  SE1 ....**123** B2
Rochford Wlk **8**
  E8 ....16 C1
Rochfort Ho **4**
  SE8 ....41 B1
Rock Ave **13** SW14 ..55 C4
Rockell's Pl SE22 ..65 A1
Rockfield Ho SE10 ..52 B4
Rock Grove Way
  SE16 ....**153** C4
Rockhall Rd NW2 ...9 C4
Rockingham Cl
  SW15 ....56 B3
Rockingham St
  SE1 ....**136** C1
Rockland Rd
  SW15 ....58 A3
Rockley Ct **13** W14 ..39 C4
Rockley Rd W14 ..39 C4
Rocks La SW13 ....56 C4
Rock St N4 ....5 C2
Rockstraw Ho **5**
  NW3 ....12 B1
Rockwood Ct N16 ...7 C4
Rocliffe St N1 .....86 B1
Rocque Ho SW6 ..**154** C2
Rodborough Rd
  NW11 ....1 C3
Rodenhurst Ct
  SW4 ....61 C2
Rodenhurst Rd
  SW4 ....61 C1
Roden St N7 ....5 B1
Roderick Ho **3**
  SE16 ....40 B2
Roderick Rd NW3 ..12 B4
Rodgers Ho **2**
  SW4 ....73 C4
Rodin Ct N1 ....86 A3
Roding Ct **6** W12 ..38 A4
Roding Ho N1 ....85 B3
Roding Mews E1 ..**125** C2
Roding Rd E5 ......18 A3
Rodmarton St W1 **103** A3
Rodmell WC1 ....94 B3
Rodmere St SE10 ..43 A1
Rodney Ct NW8 ....89 A2
Rodney Ho
  4 Cubitt Town
    E14 ....42 A2
  Islington N1 ....85 A1
  Notting Hill
    W11 ....31 C2 **113** B4
Rodney Pl SE17....**151** A4
Rodney Rd SE17...**151** B3
Rodney St N1 ....85 A1
Rodway Rd SW15 ..68 C4

Rig–Rom **261**

Rodwell Rd SE22 ..64 B1
Roedean Cres
  SW15 ....56 A2
ROEHAMPTON 68 A2
Roehampton Church
  Sch SW15 ....69 A4
Roehampton Cl
  SW15 ....56 C3
Roehampton Ct
  SW13 ....56 C3
Roehampton Gate
  SW15 ....56 A1
Roehampton High St
  SW15 ....68 C4
Roehampton La
  Putney SW15 ......56 C1
  Roehampton SW15..69 A3
Roehampton Vale
  SW15 ....68 B2
Roffey St E14 ......42 B4
Rogate Ho E5 ......7 C1
Roger Dowley Ct **8**
  E2 ....25 B3
Roger's Almshouses
  3 SW9 ....62 B3
Rogers Ct **11** E14 ..33 C2
Rogers Est **23** E2 ..25 B2
Rogers Ho SW1 ...**147** C4
Rogers Rd E16 .....35 B3
Roger St WC1 ......95 A1
Rokeby Ho
  9 Balham SW12 ..73 A4
  Bloomsbury WC1 ..**94** C1
Rokeby Rd SE4 ....51 B1
Rokeby Sch E15 ..19 C1
Rokeland Ho SE4 ..66 A3
Roland Gdns SW7 **143** A2
Roland Ho SW7 ...**143** A2
Roland Mews **1**
  E1 ....32 C4
Roland Way
  South Kensington
    SW7 ....**143** A2
  Walworth SE17 ...**151** C1
Rollins St SE15 ...50 B4
Rollit Ho N7 ....14 C3
Rollit St N7 ....14 C3
Rollo Ct SW11 ....**170** A3
Rolls Bldgs EC4 ..**107** C2
Rollscourt Ave
  SE24 ....63 B2
Rolls Pas EC4 ....**107** B2
Rolls Rd SE1 ......**153** A2
Rolt St SE8 ....51 A4
Roman Cl W3 ......37 A4
Roman Ct **4** N7 ..14 B2
Romanfield Rd
  SW2 ....74 B4
Roman Rd
  Chiswick W4 ......38 B2
  Globe Town E2, E3 ..25 C3
  25 Old Ford E3 ....26 B4
Roman Road Mkt **1**
  E3 ....26 B3
Roman Way
  Barnsbury N7 .....14 B2
  4 Deptford SE15...50 B3
Roma Read Cl
  SW15 ....69 A4
Romayne Ho SW4 ..61 C4
Romberg Rd SW17 ..72 C1
Romborough Gdns
  SE13 ....67 B2

Romborough Way
SE13 . . . . 67 B2
Romer Ho **9** SW2 . .62 B2
Romero Cl SW9 . . . . . . 62 B4
Romeyn Rd SW16 . . . . 74 B1
Romford Ho N1 . . . . 15 C2
Romford St E1 . . . . . . 32 A4
Romilly Rd N4 . . . . 6 A2
Romilly St W1 . . . . . 119 C4
Romily Ct **2** SW6 . 164 B2
Romney Cl
  7 Deptford SE14 . . 50 B3
  North End NW11 . . . 2 B3
Romney Ct
  9 Hammersmith
  W12 . . . . 39 B4
  9 Hampstead
  NW3 . . . . 12 A2
Romney Ho **2**
  E14 . . . . 34 C2
Romney Mews
  W1 . . . . 103 B4
Romney Rd SE10 . . 52 C4
Romney St SW1 . . . 134 A1
Romola Rd SE24,
  SW2 . . . . 75 A3
Ronald Ross Prim Sch
  6 SW19 . . . . 70 A4
Ronaldshay N4 . . . . . . 5 C3
Ronalds Rd N5 . . . . 14 C3
Ronald St E1 . . . . 32 B3
Rona Rd NW3 . . . . . . 12 C4
Rona Wlk **20** N1 . . 15 C2
Rondu Rd NW2 . . . . 10 A3
Rood La EC3 . . . . . . 124 A4
Rookery Rd SW4 . . 61 B3
Rooke Way SE10 . . 43 B1
Rookwood Rd N16 . . 7 C4
Roosevelt Ct **15**
  SW19 . . . . 70 A3
Rootes Dr W10 . . 30 C4
Ropemaker Rd
  E14 . . . . 41 A3
Ropemaker's Fields **7**
  E14 . . . . 33 B2
Ropemaker St
  EC2 . . . . 109 B4
Roper La SE1 . . . . . 138 B3
Roper's Orch SW3 158 B3
Ropers Wlk
  SE24 . . . . 74 C4
Ropery St E3 . . . . 26 B1
Rope St SE16 . . . . . . 41 A3
Ropewalk Gdns **1**
  E1 . . . . 111 C2
Ropley St E **6** E2 . . . 24 C3
Rosa Alba Mews
  N5 . . . . 15 B4
Rosalind Ho **25** N1 . .24 A3
Rosaline Rd SW6 . 154 B1
Rosaline Terr
  SW6 . . . . 154 B1
Rosa Parks Ho **8**
  SW9 . . . . 172 C1
Rosary Ct **17** E1 . . 32 C4
Rosary Gdns SW7 143 A3
Rosary RC Prim Sch
  NW3 . . . . 12 A3
Rosaville Rd SW6 154 C1
Rosbury SW15 . . . . 58 A1
Roscastle Rd SE4 . . 66 A2
Roscoe St EC1 . . . . 97 A1
Roscommon Ho **2**
  NW3 . . . . 11 C3

Rose Alley
  Borough The SE1 . . 123 A2
  Broadgate EC2 . . . 110 B3
Rosebank
  2 Dagenham W3 . .28 C3
  Fulham SW6 . . . . . . 47 B3
Rosebank Gdns
  Bow E3 . . . . 26 B3
  2 Dagenham W3 . .28 C3
Rosebank Way
  W3 . . . . 28 C3
Rosebank Wlk
  NW1 . . . . 13 C1
Rosebay Ho **20** E3 . .33 C4
Roseberry Pl E8 . . . . 16 B2
Roseberry St SE16 . .40 A2
Rosebery Ave EC1 . 95 C3
Rosebery Ct
  Holborn EC1 . . . . . . 95 B2
  Mayfair W1 . . . . . . 118 A2
Rosebery Ho **21**
  E2 . . . . 25 B3
Rosebery Sq EC1 . . 95 B1
Rosebery Sq EC1 . . 95 B1
Rosebery Rd SW6 166 B3
Rose Bush Ct NW3 . .12 B3
Rosecroft Ave NW3 . . 1 C1
Rose & Crown Ct
  EC2 . . . . 108 C2
Rose & Crown Yd
  SW1 . . . . 119 A1
Rose Ct
  1 Dalston E8 . . . 16 B1
  Islington N1 . . . . 86 A3
  Spitalfields E1 . . . 111 A3
Rosedale Ct N5 . . . . 15 A4
Rosedale Ho N16 . . . . 6 C3
Rosedale Rd TW9 . . 54 A3
Rosedale Terr W6 . . 39 A3
Rosedene NW6 . . . . 22 C4
Rosedene Ave
  SW16 . . . . 74 B1
Rosedew Rd W6 . . 47 C4
Rosefield Gdns
  E14 . . . . 33 C2
Roseford Ct **18**
  W12 . . . . 39 C4
Rosegate Ho **32**
  E3 . . . . 26 B3
Rosehart Mews **6**
  W11 . . . . 31 C3
Rosehill Rd SW18 . . 59 B2
Rose Joan Mews
  NW6 . . . . 10 C4
Roseland Ho SW6 . . 58 A4
Rosemary Ave N1 . . 15 A4
Rosemary Branch
  Bridge **1** 87 C4
Rosemary Ct **38**
  SE8 . . . . 51 B4
Rosemary Dr **16**
  E14 . . . . 34 C3
Rosemary Gdns
  SW14 . . . . 55 B4
Rosemary Ho
  Shoreditch N1 . . . . 87 C3
  Willesden NW10 . . 22 C4
Rosemary La
  SW14 . . . . 55 B4
Rosemary Rd
  Camberwell SE15 . . 49 B3
  Wandsworth SW17 . . 71 B1
Rosemary St N1 . . . 87 C4
Rosemary Works Sch
  N1 . . . . 87 C3

Rosemead Prep Sch
  SE27 . . . . 75 B2
Rosemont Mans **11**
  NW3 . . . . 11 A2
Rosemont Rd
  Acton W3 . . . . 28 A2
  Richmond TW10 . . 54 A1
  South Hampstead
  NW3 . . . . 11 B2
Rosemoor St SW3 144 C3
Rosemount Ct **2**
  W3 . . . . 28 A1
Rosemount Lo W3 . .28 A1
Rosenau Cres
  SW11 . . . . 168 C3
Rosenau Rd SW11 168 C4
Rosendale Prim Sch
  SE24 . . . . 75 B2
Rosendale Rd SE21,
  SE24 . . . . 75 B3
Roseneath Rd
  SW11 . . . . 60 C1
Rosenthal Ho SE6 . . 67 A1
Rosenthal Rd SE6 . . 67 B1
Rosenthorpe Rd
  SE15 . . . . 65 C2
Roserton St E14 . . 42 B4
Rose Sq SW7 . . . . . 143 C2
Rose St
  Holborn EC4 . . . . . 108 B2
  Strand WC2 . . . . . 120 A4
Rose Theatre SE1 122 C2
Rosethorn Cl
  SW12 . . . . 73 C4
Rosetta Cl SW8 . . . 162 B1
Roseway SE21 . . . . 63 C1
Rosewood Ct **2**
  E11 . . . . 19 C4
Rosewood Gdns
  SE13 . . . . 52 B1
Rosewood Ho **9**
  NW3 . . . . 11 A2
Rosewood Sq W12 . .29 C3
Rosher Cl E15 . . . . . 19 C1
Rosina St E9 . . . . . . 17 C2
Roskell Rd SW15 . . 57 C4
Roslin Ho **2** E1 . . . 32 C2
Roslin Rd W3 . . . . . 37 A3
Rosmead Rd
  W11 . . . . . . 31 A2 112 B4
Rosoman Pl EC1 . . . 95 C2
Rosoman St EC1 . . . 95 C3
Ross Ct
  1 Hackney E5 . . . . .17 A4
  6 Putney SW15 . . . .69 C4
Rossdale Rd SW15 . .57 B3
Rosse Gdns SE13 . . 67 C1
Rossendale Way
  NW1 . . . . 83 A4
Rossetti Ct WC1 . . 105 B4
Rossetti Gdns Mans
  SW3 . . . . 158 C4
Rossetti Ho SW1 . . 147 C3
Rossetti Mews
  NW8 . . . . 79 C3
Rossetti Rd SE16 . . 40 A1
Rossetti Studios
  SW3 . . . . 158 B4
Ross Ho **18** E1 . . . . . 32 A1
Rossington St E5 . . . 7 C2
Rossiter Rd SW12 . . 73 A3
Rosslyn Ave SW13 . .56 B4
Rosslyn Ct NW3 . . . 12 A3
Rosslyn Hill NW3 . . 11 C3
Rosslyn Ho **8**
  TW9 . . . . 44 B2

Rosslyn Mans
  8 Hampstead
  NW3 . . . . 11 B2
  South Hampstead
  NW6 . . . . 11 B2
Rosslyn Mews **7**
  NW3 . . . . 11 C4
Rosslyn Park Mews
  NW3 . . . . 11 C3
Rossmore Ct NW1 . . 90 C2
Rossmore Rd NW1 . . 90 B2
Rostrevor Mans
  SW6 . . . . 164 C4
Rostrevor Mews
  SW6 . . . . 164 C3
Rostrevor Rd
  SW6 . . . . 164 C4
Rotary La **12** SE27 . .75 A1
Rotary St SE1 . . . . 136 B2
Rothay NW1 . . . . . . 92 B4
Rothbury Rd E9 . . . 18 C1
Rotheley Ho **30** E9 . .17 B1
Rotherfield Ct
  De Beauvoir Town
  N1 . . . . 15 C1
  Shoreditch N1 . . . . 87 B4
Rotherfield Prim Sch
  N1 . . . . 87 A4
Rotherfield St
  Islington N1 . . . . 15 B1
  Shoreditch N1 . . . . 87 B4
Rotherham Wlk
  SE1 . . . . 122 A1
ROTHERHITHE 40 C3
Rotherhithe Bsns Est
  6 SE16 . . . . 40 B2
Rotherhithe New Rd
  SE16 . . . . 40 A1
Rotherhithe Old Rd
  SE16 . . . . 40 C2
Rotherhithe Prim Sch
  24 SE16 . . . . 40 C2
Rotherhithe St
  SE16 . . . . 40 B4
Rotherhithe Sta
  SE16 . . . . 40 B4
Rotherhithe Tunnel
  SE16 . . . . 32 C1
Rother Ho SE15 . . . 65 A3
Rotherwick Rd
  NW11 . . . . 1 C4
Rotherwood Rd
  SW15 . . . . 57 C4
Rothery St N1 . . . . . 86 B4
Rothesay Ave SW14,
  TW10 . . . . 55 A3
Rothesay Ct **13**
  SE11 . . . . 163 B3
Rothley Ct NW8 . . . 89 B2
Rothsay St SE1 . . . 138 A1
Rothsay Wlk **19**
  E14 . . . . 41 C2
Rothschild Rd W4 . .37 B3
Rothwell St
  1 Hampstead
  NW1 . . . . 81 A4
  Primrose Hill NW1 . . 81 A4
Roth Wlk N7 . . . . 5 B2
Rotten Row SW1 . . 130 C4
Rotterdam Dr E14 . .42 B3
Rouel Rd
  Bermondsey
  SE16 . . . . 153 B4
  Bermondsey SE16 . .139 B1
Roundacre SW19 . . 69 C2
Roundel Cl SE4 . . . . 66 B3

Roundhouse Theatre
  NW1 . . . . 12 C1
Roundwood Rd
  NW10 . . . . 8 B1
Rounton Rd E3 . . . 26 C1
Roupell Rd SW2 . . 74 B3
Roupell St SE1 . . . 121 C1
Rousden St NW1 . . 13 B1
Routh Rd SW18 . . . 72 A4
Rover Ho **6** N1 . . . . 24 A4
Rowallan Rd SW6 . 154 A1
Rowan Cl W5 . . . . . . 36 A4
Rowan Ct
  19 Camberwell
  SE15 . . . . 49 B3
  Wandsworth SW11 . . 60 B1
Rowan Ho
  5 Bow E3 . . . . 26 B4
  Dagenham NW10 . .21 B1
  5 Maitland Pk
  NW3 . . . . 12 B2
Rowan Rd W6 . . . . 39 C2
Rowan Terr W6 . . . . 39 C2
Rowan Wlk
  7 Dartmouth Pk
  N19 . . . . 4 B2
  Kensal Town W10 . .23 A1
Rowberry Cl SW6 . . 47 B3
Rowcross St SE1 . . 153 A2
Rowditch La
  SW11 . . . . 169 B2
Rowdon Ave NW10 . . 9 A1
Rowe Ho E9 . . . . . . 17 B2
Rowe La E9 . . . . 17 B3
Rowena Cres
  SW11 . . . . 168 B1
Rowfant Rd SW12,
  SW17 . . . . 72 C2
Rowhill Mans **1**
  E5 . . . . 17 A4
Rowhill Rd E5 . . . . . 17 A4
Rowington Cl W2 . 100 A4
Rowland Hill Ho
  SE1 . . . . 136 A4
Rowland Hill St
  NW3 . . . . 12 A3
Rowley Gdns N4 . . . . 6 B4
Rowley Ho SE8 . . . 51 C4
Rowley Ind Pk W3 . .37 A3
Rowley Way NW8 . . 78 C4
Rowntree Cl NW6 . . 10 C2
Rowse Cl E15 . . . . . 27 B4
Rowstock Gdns
  N7 . . . . 13 C3
Roxby Pl SW6 . . . . 155 C4
Roxford Ho **2** E3 . .27 A1
Roxley Rd SE13 . . . 67 A1
Roxwell **10** NW1 . . 13 A2
Roxwell Rd W12 . . . 38 C4
Royal Academy of
  Dramatic Art
  WC1 . . . . 105 B4
Royal Acad of Arts
  W1 . . . . 118 C3
Royal Acad of Dance
  SW11 . . . . 167 C3
Royal Acad of Music
  NW1 . . . . 91 C1
Royal Albert Hall
  SW7 . . . . 129 B3
Royal Arc W1 . . . . 118 C3
Royal Armouries The
  E1 . . . . 124 C3
Royal Ave SW3 . . . 144 C2

Royal Avenue Ho
SW3 . . . . **144** C2
Royal Ballet Upper
Sch WC2 . . . . . **106** B1
Royal Brompton Hospl
Chelsea SW3 . . . . **143** B2
Chelsea SW3 . . . . **144** A2
Royal Cir SE27 . . . . **75** A1
Royal Cl
Deptford SE8 . . . . **51** B4
Putney SW15 . . . . . **69** C2
Stamford Hill N16 . . . . **7** A3
Royal College of
Physicians Liby
NW1 . . . . **92** B2
Royal College St
NW1 . . . . **83** A4
Royal Coll of
Anaesthetists
WC1 . . . . **106** C3
Royal Coll of Art
SW7 . . . . **129** B3
Royal Coll of Art
Sculpture Sch
SW11 . . . . **158** A1
Royal Coll of
Midwives W1 . . . . **104** A3
Royal Coll of Music
SW7 . . . . **129** B2
Royal Coll of
Obstetricians &
Gynaecologists
NW1 . . . . **90** C3
Royal Coll of
Ophthalmologists
NW1 . . . . **91** B1
Royal Coll of
Paediatrics & Child
Health W1 . . . . . **107** A4
Royal Coll of
Pathologists
SW1 . . . . **119** B1
Royal Coll of
Physicians NW1 . . **92** B2
Royal Coll of
Radiologists W1 . . **104** B4
Royal Coll of Science
SW7 . . . . **129** B2
Royal Coll of Speech
Language Therapists
SE1 . . . . **123** B1
Royal Coll of
Surgeons WC2 . . . **107** A2
Royal Coll of
Veterinary Surgeons
SW1 . . . . **134** A1
Royal Courts of
Justice WC2 . . . . . **107** B1
Royal Cres
W11 . . . . . **31** A1 **112** A4
Royal Crescent Mews
W11 . . . . **30** C1
Royal Ct
City of London
EC3 . . . . **109** C1
Rotherhithe SE16 . . . **41** B3
Royal Duchess Mews
16 SW12 . . . . **73** A4
Royal Exchange
EC3 . . . . **109** C1
Royal Exchange Bldgs
EC3 . . . . **109** C1
Royal Festival Hall
SE1 . . . . **121** A1
Royal Free Hospl
NW3 . . . . **12** A3

Royal Fusiliers Mus
E1 . . . . **124** C3
Royal Geographical
Society SW7 . . . . . **129** C3
Royal Hill SE10 . . . . **52** B3
Royal Hill Ct 2
SE10 . . . . **52** B3
Royal Horticultural
Society (Lawrence
Hall & Conf Ctr)
SW1 . . . . **133** B1
Royal Horticultural
Society (Lindley
Hall) SW1 . . . . . . **147** B4
Royal Hospital
Chelsea The
SW3 . . . . **145** B1
Royal Hospital Rd
SW3 . . . . **145** B1
Royal Hospl for Neuro-
Disability The
SW15 . . . . **58** A1
Royal Hospl Mus
SW3 . . . . **145** A1
Royal Institute of
British Architects
W1 . . . . **104** B4
Royal Institution Mus
The SW1 . . . . **118** C3
Royal Langford
Apartments 3
NW6 . . . . **78** A2
Royal London Est The
NW10 . . . . **20** C3
Royal London Hospl
for Integrated
Medicine W1 . . . . **106** B4
Royal London Hospl
Mus E1 . . . . **32** A4
Royal London Hospl
(Whitechapel) The
E1 . . . . **32** A4
Royal Marsden Hospl
SW3 . . . . **143** C2
Royal Mews The
SW1 . . . . **132** B2
Royal Mint Pl 6
E1 . . . . **125** A4
Royal Mint St E1 . . . **125** A4
Royal National
Orthopaedic Hospl
W1 . . . . **92** B1
Royal National TNE
Hospl The WC1 . . . **94** C4
Royal Naval Pl
SE14 . . . . **51** B3
Royal Oak Ct 8
N1 . . . . **24** A2 **98** A4
Royal Oak Pl SE22 . . **65** A1
Royal Oak Rd 5
E8 . . . . **17** A2
Royal Oak Sta W2 . . **100** B3
Royal Oak Yd SE1 . . **138** A3
Royal Observatory
The SE10 . . . . **52** C3
Royal Opera Arc
SW1 . . . . **119** B2
Royal Orchard Cl
SW18 . . . . **70** A4
Royal Par
Blackheath Vale
SE3 . . . . **53** B1
Fulham SW6 . . . . . . **154** A2
12 Richmond TW9 . . . . **44** C2
Royal Pl 1 SE10 . . . . **52** B3
Royal Rd SE17 . . . . . **48** A4

Royal Sch Hampstead
The **8** NW3 . . . . **11** C4
Royal St SE1 . . . . . **135** A2
Royalty Ho W1 . . . . **105** B1
Royalty Mews W1 . . **105** B1
Royalty Studios
W11 . . . . **31** A3
Royal United Services
Mus SW1 . . . . **120** A1
Royal Veterinary Coll
NW1 . . . . **83** B3
Royal Victoria Sta
E16 . . . . **35** C2
Roy Ridley Ho 5
SW4 . . . . **61** C4
Roy Sq E14 . . . . **33** A2
Royston Cl
New Cross SE4 . . . . . **51** B1
3 Richmond TW9 . . . **44** B2
Royston Ho 14
SE15 . . . . **49** C4
Royston Rd TW10 . . . **54** A2
Royston St 8 E2 . . . **25** B3
Rozel Cl 3 N1 . . . . . **24** A4
Rozel Rd SW4 . . . . . **61** B4
Ruby St SE15 . . . . . . **50** A4
Ruby Triangle
SE15 . . . . **50** A4
Ruckholt Rd E9,
E10 . . . . **18** C4
Rucklidge Ave
NW10 . . . . **21** C3
Rudall Cres NW3 . . . **11** C4
Rudbeck Ho 11
SE15 . . . . **49** C3
Ruddington Cl E5 . . . **18** A4
Rudge Ho 1
SE16 . . . . **139** C2
Rudgwick Terr
NW8 . . . . **80** B3
Rudhall Ho 4
SW2 . . . . **62** C1
Rudloe Rd SW12 . . . **73** B4
Rudolf Pl SW8 . . . . **162** B3
Rudolph Rd NW6 . . . **23** C3
Rudstone Ho 10
E3 . . . . **27** A2
Rudyard Ct SE1 . . . **137** C3
Rufford St N1 . . . . . . **84** B4
Rufford Street Mews
N1 . . . . **14** A1
Rufford Twr 5
W3 . . . . **28** A1
Rufus Bsns Ctr
SW18 . . . . **71** A2
Rufus Ho SE1 . . . . . **139** A2
Rufus St N1 . . **24** A2 **98** A3
Rugby Mans W14 . . **140** B4
Rugby Rd W4 . . . . . . **38** A4
Rugby St WC1 . . . . **94** C1
Rugg St E14 . . . . **33** C2
Rugless Ho 2 E14 . . **42** B4
Rugmere 4 NW1 . . . **12** C1
Rumball Ho 14
SE5 . . . . **49** A3
Rumbold Rd SW6 . . **156** B1
Rum Cl E1 . . . . **32** B2
Rumford Ho SE1 . . . **136** C1
Rumsey Rd SW9 . . . . **62** B3
Runacres Ct SE17 . . **150** C1
Runcorn Pl
W11 . . . . . **31** A2 **112** A4

Rundell Twr SW8 . . . **172** C4
Running Horse Yd 12
TW8 . . . . **44** A4
Runnymede Ct
SW15 . . . . **68** C3
Runnymede Ho
Hackney E9 . . . . **18** A4
Richmond TW10 . . . . **54** C2
Rupack St 3 SE16 . . **40** B4
Rupert Ct W1 . . . . . **119** B4
Rupert Gdns SW9 . . . **48** A1
Rupert Ho
SE11 . . . . **149** C3
8 Upper Holloway
N19 . . . . **4** C1
Rupert Rd
Bedford Pk W4 . . . . . **38** A3
Paddington NW6 . . . **23** B3
Upper Holloway N19 . . **4** C2
Rupert St W1 . . . . . **119** B4
Rusbridge Cl E8 . . . . **16** C3
Ruscoe Rd E16 . . . . . **35** B3
Rusham Rd SW12 . . . **72** B4
Rushbrook Ho 20
SW8 . . . . **171** B2
Rushby Ct SW4 . . . . **172** A3
Rush Common Mews
18 SW2 . . . . **74** B4
Rushcroft Rd SW2,
SW9 . . . . **62** C3
Rushcutters Ct 18
SE16 . . . . **41** A2
Rushey Mead SE4 . . . **66** C2
Rushford Rd SE4 . . . . **66** B1
Rush Hill Mews 3
SW11 . . . . **60** C4
Rush Hill Rd SW11 . . **60** C4
Rushlake Ho 3
SW11 . . . . **169** B2
Rushmead 6 E2 . . . . **25** A2
Rushmere Ho 2
SW15 . . . . **68** C3
Rushmore Cres 9
E5 . . . . **17** C4
Rushmore Ho
9 Kentish Town
N7 . . . . **13** C3
W14 . . . . **126** B1
Rushmore Prim Sch
12 E5 . . . . **17** C4
Rushmore Rd
Clapton Pk E5 . . . . . **17** C4
Hackney E5 . . . . **18** A4
Rusholme Rd
SW15 . . . . **58** A1
Rushton Ho 26
SW8 . . . . **171** B1
Rushton St N1 . . . . . **87** C2
Rushworth St SE1 . . **136** B3
Ruskin Ave TW9 . . . . **44** C3
Ruskin Ct SE5 . . . . . **63** C4
Ruskin Ho SW1 . . . **147** C3
Ruskin Park Ho
SE5 . . . . **63** C4
Ruskin Wlk SE24 . . . **63** B2
Rusper Ct SW9 . . . . **172** B1
Russell Cl W4 . . . . . . **46** B4
Russell Ct
Battersea SW11 . . . . **169** C3
5 Bloomsbury N1 . . **94** A1
9 Peckham SE15 . . . **50** A1
St James SW1 . . . . . **119** A1
Russell Gdns W14 . . **126** A2
Russell Gdns Mews
W14 . . . . **126** A2

Russell Gr 33 . . . . . **173** C4
Russell Ho
2 Poplar E14 . . . . . . **33** C3
SW1 . . . . **146** C2
Russell Kerr Cl
W4 . . . . **45** B3
Russell Lo SE1 . . . . . **137** B2
Russell Mans
WC1 . . . . **106** B4
Russell Pickering Ho
2 SW4 . . . . **62** A4
Russell Pl
Hampstead NW3 . . . . **12** A3
Rotherhithe SE16 . . . **41** A3
Russell Rd W14 . . . **126** B1
Russell Sq WC1 . . . . **94** A1
Russell Square Ho
WC1 . . . . **94** A1
Russell Square Mans
WC1 . . . . **106** B4
Russell Square Sta
WC1 . . . . **94** A1
Russell St WC2 . . . . **120** B4
Russell's Wharf 2
W9 . . . . **23** B1
Russell Wlk 4
TW10 . . . . **54** B1
Russell Yd SW15 . . . . **58** A3
Russet Cres N7 . . . . . **14** B3
Russett Way SE13 . . . **52** A1
Russia Dock Rd
SE16 . . . . **33** A1
Russia La E2 . . . . **25** B3
Russia Row EC2 . . . **109** A1
Rusthall Ave W4 . . . . **37** C3
Rusthall Mans 3
W4 . . . . **37** C2
Ruston Mews W11 . . **31** A3
Ruston St E3 . . . . **26** B4
Rust Sq SE5 . . . . **48** C3
Ruth Ct 10 E3 . . . . . . **26** A3
Rutherford Ho 12
E1 . . . . **25** A1
Rutherford St
SW1 . . . . **147** B4
Ruth Ho W10 . . . . . . **23** A1
Ruthin Rd SE3 . . . . . . **53** C4
Ruthven St E9 . . . . . . **25** C4
Rutland Cl SW14 . . . . **55** B4
Rutland Ct
Herne Hill SE5 . . . . . . **63** C3
SW7 . . . . **130** B3
Rutland Gate
SW7 . . . . **130** B3
Rutland Gate Mews
SW7 . . . . **130** A3
Rutland Gdns
SW7 . . . . **130** B3
Rutland Gdns Mews
SW7 . . . . **130** B3
Rutland Gr W6 . . . . . **39** A1
Rutland Ho
10 Putney SW15 . . . **69** B4
W8 . . . . **128** A1
Rutland Mews 21
NW8 . . . . **78** B3
Rutland Mews E
SW7 . . . . **130** B2
Rutland Mews S
SW7 . . . . **130** A2
Rutland Mews W
SW7 . . . . **130** A2

Rutland Park Gdns **1**
NW2 . . . . .9 B2
Rutland Park Mans **2**
NW2 . . . . .9 B2
Rutland Pk NW2 . . . . . . .9 B2
Rutland Pl EC1 . . . . . . .108 B4
Rutland Rd E9 . . . . .25 C4
Rutland St SW7 . . . . . .130 B2
Rutland Studios
NW10 . . . . .21 C2
Rutley Cl SE11 . . . . .48 A4
Rutt's Terr SE14 . . . . . . .50 C2
Ruvigny Gdns
SW15 . . . . .57 C4
Ruvigny Mans **7**
SW15 . . . . .57 C4
Rycott Path SE22 . . . . . .76 C4
Rycuiff Sq SE3 . . . . .53 B1
Rydal Ho **25** SW8 . . . .171 B1
Rydal Water NW1 . . . . . .92 C3
Ryde Ho **1** NW6 . . . . . .23 C4
Ryde Vale Rd
SW12 . . . . .73 B2
Rydon St N1 . . . . .87 A4
Rydston Cl **2** N7 . . . . .14 B1
Ryecotes Mead
SE21 . . . . .76 A3
Ryecroft Rd SE13 . . . . . .67 B2
Ryecroft St SW6 . . . . . .166 A3
Ryedale SE22 . . . . .65 A1
Ryefield Path **7**
SW15 . . . . .68 C3
Ryegates **2** SE15 . . . . .50 A1
Rye Hill Pk SE15 . . . . . . .65 B3
Rye Ho **11** SE16 . . . . . .40 B4
Rye La SE15 . . . . .49 C1
Rye Lane Mkt
SE15 . . . . .49 C1
Rye Oak Sch **7**
SE15 . . . . .65 A4
Rye Wlk SW15 . . . . .57 C2
Ryfold Rd SW19 . . . . . . .70 C1
Ryland Rd NW5 . . . . . . .13 A2
Rylett Cres W12 . . . . . . .38 B3
Rylett Rd W12 . . . . .38 B3
Rylston Rd SW6 . . . . . .154 C3
Rymer St SE24 . . . . .63 A1
Rysbrack St SW1 . . . . . .130 C2

S

Saatchi Gallery
SW3 . . . . .145 A2
Sabbarton St **8**
E16 . . . . .35 B3
Sabella Ct E3 . . . . .26 B3
Sabine Rd SW11 . . . . . . .60 C4
Sable St N1 . . . . .15 A1
Sacketts Ho **24**
SW9 . . . . .173 C4
Sackville Ho **18**
SW16 . . . . .74 A1
Sackville St W1 . . . . . . .119 A3
Sacred Heart High
Sch **9** W6 . . . . .39 B2

Sacred Heart Prim
Sch, Battersea
SW11 . . . . .168 B1
Sacred Heart RC Prim
Sch SW15 . . . . .56 C2
Sacred Heart RC Sec
Sch SE5 . . . . .48 B2
Sacred Heart Sch
N7 . . . . .14 B3
Saddlers Mews
SW8 . . . . .172 B4
Sadler Ho
17 Bromley E3 . . . . . .27 A2
EC1 . . . . .96 A4
Saffron Ave E14 . . . . . . .34 C2
Saffron Cl **11** N1 . . . . .15 C2
Saffron Hill EC1 . . . . . .107 C4
Saffron Ho **9**
TW9 . . . . .45 A2
Saffron St EC1 . . . . .107 C4
Saffron Wharf
SE1 . . . . .139 A4
Sage Mews SE22 . . . . . .64 B2
Sage St E1 . . . . .32 B2
Sage Way WC1 . . . . .94 C3
Sailacre Ho **10**
SE10 . . . . .43 B1
Sail Ct **10** E14 . . . . . . .34 C2
Sailmakers Ct
SW6 . . . . .59 B4
Sail Loft SE11 . . . . .149 A4
Sainfoin Rd SW17 . . . . . .72 C2
St Agnes Cl E9 . . . . .25 B4
St Agnes Pl SE11 . . . . . .48 A4
St Agnes RC Prim Sch
2 E3 . . . . .27 A2
London NW2 . . . . .1 A1
St Aidan's Prim Sch
N4 . . . . .5 C2
St Aidan's Rd SE22 . . . . .65 A2
St Albans Ave W4 . . . . . .37 C3
St Alban's CE Prim
Sch EC1 . . . . .108 B4
St Alban's Cl NW11 . . . . . .1 C3
St Alban's Gr W8 . . . . . .128 B2
St Albans La NW11 . . . . . .1 C3
St Albans Mans
W8 . . . . .128 B2
St Alban's Pl N1 . . . . . . .86 A3
St Alban's Rd
Dagenham NW10 . . . . . .21 A4
Dartmouth Pk NW5 . . . . . .4 A1
St Albans St SW1 . . . . . .119 B3
St Albans Studios
W8 . . . . .128 B2
St Albans Terr
W6 . . . . .154 A4
St Alban's Villas
NW5 . . . . .3 C1
St Alfege Pas SE10 . . . . .52 B4
St Alfege with St
Peter's CE Prim Sch
SE10 . . . . .52 B4
St Aloysius Convent
NW1 . . . . .93 B4
St Aloysius RC Coll **9**
N19 . . . . .4 B3
St Aloysius RC Inf Sch
NW1 . . . . .93 B4
St Aloysius RC Jun
Sch NW1 . . . . .83 B1
St Alphage Gdn
EC2 . . . . .109 A3
St Alphage Highwalk
EC2 . . . . .109 A3

St Alphonsus Rd
SW4 . . . . .61 C3
St Andrew & St
Francis CE Prim Sch
8 NW2 . . . . .8 C2
St Andrew's
(Barnsbury) Prim
Sch N1 . . . . .85 A4
St Andrews Chambers
W1 . . . . .105 A2
St Andrews Cl **28**
SE16 . . . . .40 A1
St Andrews Ct W4 . . . . . .45 B2
St Andrew's Ct **2**
SW18 . . . . .71 B2
St Andrew's Gr N16 . . . . .6 C3
St Andrew's Greek
Sch NW1 . . . . .13 A1
St Andrew's Hill
EC4 . . . . .108 B1
St Andrews Ho **1**
SE16 . . . . .40 A3
St Andrews Mans **9**
E5 . . . . .17 A4
St Andrew's Mans
W1 . . . . .103 B3
St Andrews Mews
Greenwich SE3 . . . . .53 C3
5 Streatham
SW12 . . . . .73 C3
St Andrew's Mews
N16 . . . . .7 A3
St Andrew's Pl
NW1 . . . . .92 B2
St Andrew's Prim Sch
SW9 . . . . .172 B1
St Andrew's Rd
W14 . . . . .154 B4
Willesden NW2 . . . . .9 A2
St Andrew's Sq
W11 . . . . .31 A3
St Andrew St EC4 . . . . . .107 C3
St Andrew's Way
E3 . . . . .27 B1
St Andrew's Wharf
SE1 . . . . .139 A4
St Anne RC Prim Sch
10 E1 . . . . .24 C1 99 B1
St Anne's CE Prim Sch
6 SW18 . . . . .59 A2
St Anne's Cl N6 . . . . .3 C1
St Anne's Ct
Kensal Rise NW6 . . . . . . .23 A4
W1 . . . . .105 B1
St Anne's Flats
NW1 . . . . .93 B4
St Anne's Pas E14 . . . . . .33 B3
St Anne's Rd **1**
SE11 . . . . .162 C4
St Anne's Row E14 . . . . .33 B3
St Anne St E14 . . . . .33 B3
St Anne's Trad Est **23**
E14 . . . . .33 B3
St Ann's Cres
SW18 . . . . .59 B1
St Ann's Gdns
NW5 . . . . .12 C2
St Ann's Hill SW18 . . . . .59 B1
St Ann's Ho WC1 . . . . . . .95 B3
St Ann's La SW1 . . . . . . .133 C1
St Ann's Park Rd
SW18 . . . . .59 B1
St Anns Rd
Barnes SW13 . . . . .46 B2

St Anns Rd continued
Shepherd's Bush
W11 . . . . .30 C2
St Ann's St SW1 . . . . . . .133 C2
St Ann's Terr NW8 . . . . . .79 C2
St Ann's Villas
W11 . . . . .112 A1
St Anselm's Pl
W1 . . . . .118 A4
St Anselm's RC Prim
Sch SW17 . . . . .72 C1
St Anthonys Cl **8**
SW17 . . . . .72 A2
St Anthony's Cl
6 E1 . . . . .125 B2
5 Hackney Wick
E9 . . . . .18 B2
St Anthony's Ct
2 Balham SW12 . . . . .60 C1
Upper Tooting
SW17 . . . . .72 C2
St Anthony's Flats
NW1 . . . . .83 B1
St Anthony's RC Prim
Sch SE22 . . . . .64 C1
St Asaph Ct SE4 . . . . . . .65 C4
St Asaph Rd SE4 . . . . . . .65 C4
St Aubins Ct N1 . . . . .87 C4
St Augustine's CE
High Sch **5**
NW6 . . . . .23 C3
St Augustine's Ho
NW1 . . . . .93 B4
St Augustine's Prim
Sch **8** NW6 . . . . .78 A2
St Augustine's RC
Prim Sch W6 . . . . .154 B3
St Augustine's Rd
NW1 . . . . .13 C1
St Austell Rd SE13 . . . . . .52 C1
St Barnabas CE Prim
Sch SW1 . . . . .145 C2
St Barnabas Cl **11**
SE22 . . . . .64 C2
St Barnabas & St
Philip CE Prim Sch
W8 . . . . .127 B1
St Barnabas St
SW1 . . . . .145 C2
St Barnabas Terr
E9 . . . . .17 C3
St Barnabas Villas
SW8 . . . . .172 B4
St Bartholomew's
Hospl EC1 . . . . .108 B3
St Bede's RC Inf Sch
SW12 . . . . .73 C3
St Benets Cl **6**
SW17 . . . . .72 A2
St Benet's Pl EC3 . . . . . .123 C4
St Bernadette RC Jun
Sch **3** SW12 . . . . .73 B4
St Bernard Ho **8**
E14 . . . . .42 B3
St Botolph St E1,
EC3 . . . . .110 C2
St Brelades Ct N1 . . . . . .87 C4
St Bride's EC4 . . . . .108 A1
St Bride's Ave
EC4 . . . . .108 A1
St Bride's Pas
EC4 . . . . .108 A1

St Bride St EC4 . . . . . . .108 A2
St Catherines Cl **7**
SW17 . . . . .72 A2
St Catherine's Ct **8**
W4 . . . . .38 A3
St Catherine's Dr
SE14 . . . . .50 C1
St Catherines Mews
SW3 . . . . .144 C4
St Cecilia's CE Sch
SW18 . . . . .70 B3
St Chad's Pl WC1 . . . . . .94 C4
St Chad's St WC1 . . . . . .94 B4
St Charles' Hospl
W10 . . . . .30 C4
St Charles Pl W10 . . . . . .31 A4
St Charles RC Prim
Sch **2** W10 . . . . .30 C4
St Charles RC Sixth
Form Coll **3**
W10 . . . . .30 C4
St Charles Sq W10 . . . . .30 C4
St Christina's RC Prep
Sch NW8 . . . . .80 B2
St Christophers Ct **18**
N19 . . . . .4 C2
St Christopher's Ho
NW1 . . . . .83 B1
St Christopher's Pl
W1 . . . . .103 C2
St Christopher's Sch
5 NW3 . . . . .11 C3
St Clair Ho **17** E3 . . . .26 B2
St Clare St EC3 . . . . . . .110 C1
St Clement Danes CE
Prim Sch WC2 . . . . . . .106 C1
St Clement & St
James CE Prim Sch
W11 . . . . .31 A1 112 A2
St Clements Ct
Barnsbury N7 . . . . .14 B2
7 SE14 . . . . .50 C4
8 Shepherd's Bush
W11 . . . . .30 C2
St Clement's Ct
EC3 . . . . .123 C4
St Clement's Ct
E1 . . . . .110 C3
St Clement's La
WC2 . . . . .107 A1
St Clements Mans **3**
SW6 . . . . .47 C4
St Clements St N7 . . . . . .14 C1
St Columb's Ho **11**
W10 . . . . .31 A4
St Crispins Cl
NW3 . . . . .12 A4
St Cross St EC1 . . . . . . .107 C4
St Cuthbert's Rd
NW2 . . . . .10 B2
St Cuthbert with St
Matthias CE Prim
Sch SW5 . . . . .142 A2
St Davids Cl **27**
SE16 . . . . .40 A1
St David's Sq E14 . . . . . .42 A1
St Dionis Rd SW6 . . . . .165 A2
St Dominic RC Prim
Sch **14** NW5 . . . . .12 B3
St Dominics RC Prim
Sch E9 . . . . .18 A2
St Donatt's Rd
London SE14 . . . . .51 B2
New Cross Gate
SE4 . . . . .51 B1

St Dunstan Ave W3 .... 28 C2
St Dunstan Gdns W3 .... 28 C2
St Dunstan's Alley EC3 .... 124 A3
St Dunstan's Ct EC4 .... 107 C1
St Dunstan's Hill EC3 .... 124 A3
St Dunstan's La EC3 .... 124 A3
St Dunstan's Rd W6 .... 39 C1
St Edmunds Cl 8 SW17 .... 72 A2
St Edmund's Cl NW8 .... 80 C3
St Edmund's Dr NW8 .... 80 C3
St Edmunds RC Prim Sch E14 .... 41 C2
St Edmund's Sq SW13 .... 47 B4
St Edmund's Terr NW8 .... 80 C3
St Edward's RC Prim Sch NW1 .... 90 B1
St Elizabeth RC Prim Sch 8 E2 .... 25 B2
St Elizabeth's RC Prim Sch TW10 .... 54 B1
St Elmo Rd W12 .... 38 B4
St Elmos Rd SE24 .... 75 A4
St Ermin's Hill SW1 .... 133 B2
St Ervan's Rd W10 .. 31 B4
St Eugene de Mazenod RC Prim Sch 2 NW6 .... 10 C1
St Faith's CE Prim Sch 1 SW18 .... 59 B2
St Faith's Rd SE24 .. 75 A4
St Francesca Cabrini RC Prim Sch SE23 .... 65 B1
St Francis' Ho NW1 .... 83 B1
St Francis of Assisi Prim Sch 10 W11 .. 30 C2
St Francis Pl SW12 .... 61 A1
St Francis RC Prim Sch 3 SE15 .... 49 C3
St Francis Rd SE22 .... 64 A3
St Francis Xavier Coll SW12 .... 61 A1
St Frideswides Mews 5 E14 .... 34 B3
St Gabriel's CE Prim Sch SW1 .... 146 C1
St Gabriels Cl 8 E14 .... 34 A4
St Gabriel's Rd NW2 .... 9 C3
St George SW11 .... 169 C3
ST GEORGE IN THE EAST 32 A2
St George's Ave N7 .... 13 C4
St George's Bldgs SE11 .... 136 A1
St George's Cath NW1 .... 92 B4

St George's Cath RC Prim Sch SE1 .... 136 A2
St George's CE Prim Sch
  18 SE5 .... 49 A3
  SW8 .... 161 A1
St George's Circ SE1 .... 136 A2
St Georges Cl SW8 .... 171 A4
St Georges Ct SW15 .... 58 B3
St George's Ct Brompton SW3 .. 144 A4
  Kensington SW7 .. 128 C1
  Newington SE1 .... 136 A1
St George's Dr SW1 .... 146 C2
St George's Field W2 .... 102 B1
St George's Gr SW17 .... 71 C1
St Georges Hanover Sq Sch W1 .... 117 C3
St George's Ho NW1 .... 83 A1
St George's La EC3 .... 124 A4
St Georges Mews 11 NW1 .... 12 B1
St George's Mews
  2 Rotherhithe SE8 .... 41 B2
  SE1 .... 135 C2
St Georges Pl N7 .. 13 C4
St George's Pools E1 .... 32 A2
St George's RC Cath Sch W9 .... 78 B1
St George's RC Sec Sch W9 .... 78 B1
St George's Rd Newington SE1 .... 136 A1
  Richmond TW9 .... 54 B4
St George's Residences 4 SW2 .... 62 C2
St George's Sq 1 EC4 .... 108 A2
  E14 .... 33 A2
St George's Sq Rotherhithe SE8 .. 41 B2
  SW1 .... 147 B1
St George's Square Mews SW1 .... 147 B1
St George St W1 .... 118 B4
St Georges Terr Hampstead NW1 .... 12 B1
  NW1 .... 81 A4
St George's Way SE15 .... 49 A4
St George the Martyr CE Prim Sch WC1 .... 95 A1
St George's Wharf SW8 .... 162 A4
St George's Wharf Pier SW8 .... 162 A4
St Gerards Cl SW4 .. 61 B2
St German's Pl SE3 .... 53 C2
St Gildas' RC Jun Sch 18 N8 .... 5 A4

ST GILES 106 A2
St Giles Cir WC1 .... 105 C2
St Giles Coll WC1 .. 106 B4
St Giles Ct WC2 .... 106 A2
St Giles High St WC2 .... 105 C2
St Giles Ho SW16 .. 74 A1
St Giles Pas WC2 .. 105 C1
St Giles Rd SE5 .... 49 A2
St Giles Terr EC1 .. 109 A3
St Giles Twr 5 SE5 .... 49 A2
St Gilles Ho 15 E2 .. 25 C3
St Helena Rd W11 .. 95 B3
St Helena Rd SE16 .. 40 C2
St Helena St WC1 .. 95 B3
St Helens Gdns W10 .... 30 C3
St Helen's Pl EC3 .. 110 A2
St Helen's RC Prim Sch E14 .... 33 C3
St Helier Ct 4 N1 .. 24 A4
St Hilda's Cl 2 SW17 .... 72 A2
St Hilda's Cl NW6 .... 9 C1
St Hilda's Rd SW13 .... 47 A4
St Hilda's Wharf E1 .... 32 B1
St Hubert's Ho 2 E14 .... 41 C3
St Hughes Cl 4 SW17 .... 72 A2
St Ives Ct NW2 .... 10 A2
ST JAMES 119 B2
St James Ct
  28 Bethnal Green E2 .... 25 A2
  2 Brentford W4 .. 36 C1
St James' Ct Bedford Pk W4 .... 37 C3
  SW1 .... 133 A2
St James Ho N7 .... 13 C3
St James Independent Schs W14 .... 140 B4
St James Ind Mews 18 SE1 .... 153 C1
St James' Mans NW6 .... 10 C1
St James Mews E14 .... 42 B3
St James's SE14 .... 51 A2
St James & St Michael's CE Prim Sch W2 .... 115 A4
St James's App EC2 .... 24 A1 98 A2
St James's Ave 2 E2 .. 25 B3
St James's CE Prim Sch SE14 .... 51 A2
St James School Flats 5 N7 .... 14 B2
St James's Cl NW8 .... 80 C3
  Upper Tooting SW17 .... 72 B2
St James's Cloisters 2 SE22 .... 64 B3
St James's Cres SW9 .... 62 C4
St James's Dr Balham SW12, SW17 .... 72 B4
  Upper Tooting SW17 .... 72 B2

St James's Gdns W11 .... 31 A1 112 A2
St James's Gr SW11 .... 169 A2
St James's Market SW1 .... 119 B3
St James's Pal SW1 .... 119 A1
St James's Park Sta SW1 .... 133 B2
St James's Pas EC3 .... 110 B1
St James's Pk SW1 .... 133 B4
St James's Pl SW1 .... 118 C1
St James's Rd Bermondsey SE1, SE16 .... 153 C4
  Peckham SE1 .... 49 C4
St James's Sq SW1 .... 119 A2
St James's St SW1 .... 118 C2
St James Terr NW8 .... 80 C4
  2 Upper Tooting SW12 .... 72 C3
St James's Terrace Mews NW8 .... 80 C3
St James The Great RC Prim Sch 7 SE15 .... 49 B2
St James Wlk EC1 .. 96 A2
St Joan of Arc RC Prim Sch N5 .. 15 B4
St John of Jerusalem CE Prim Sch 9 E9 .... 17 B1
ST JOHN'S 51 C1
St John & St James CE Prim Sch 1 E9 .... 17 B3
St John's Angell Town CE Prim Sch SW9 .... 173 B1
St John's Ave Dagenham NW10 .. 21 B4
  Putney SW15 .... 57 C2
St John's CE Prim Sch 15 E2 .... 25 B3
St John's CE Walham Green Prim Sch SW6 .... 164 B4
St John's Church Rd E9 .... 17 B3
St John's Cl SW6 .. 155 B2
St John's Concert Hall SW1 .... 134 A1
St John's Cres SW9 .... 62 C4
St Johns Ct 6 E1 .... 32 A1
St John's Ct Finsbury Pk N4 .. 6 A2
  Hammersmith W6 .. 39 A2
  Lewisham SE13 .... 52 B1
  5 South Hampstead NW3 .... 11 B2
Saint John's St EC1 .... 96 B3
St John's Dr SW18 .. 71 A3
St John's Est SE1 .. 138 C3
St John's Gdns W11 .... 31 B2 112 C3
St John's Gr
  3 Barnes SW13 .... 46 B1

St John's Gr continued
1 Richmond TW9 .... 54 A3
Upper Holloway N19 .. 4 B2
St John's Highbury Vale CE Prim Sch N5 .... 6 A1
St John's Hill SW11 .... 59 C3
St John's Hill Gr SW11 .... 59 C3
St Johns Ho 5 SE17 .... 48 C4
St John's Ho 1 E14 .... 42 B2
St John's La EC1 .. 108 B4
St John's Lodge 3 SE8 .... 51 C2
St John's Mans 5 .17 B3
St John's Park Mans N19 .... 4 B4
St John's Path EC1 .. 96 A1
St John's Pk SE3 .... 53 C3
St John's Pl EC1 .... 96 A1
St John's RC Prim Sch SE16 .... 41 A4
St John's Rd Battersea SW11 .... 60 A3
  Canning Town E16 .. 35 C3
  Richmond TW9 .... 54 A3
St John's & St Clements CE Jun & Inf Sch 5 SE15 .. 64 C1
St John's Sq EC1 .. 96 A1
St Johns Sta SE8 .. 51 C1
St John's St EC1 .. 96 A2
St John's Terr W10 .... 22 C1
St John's Therapy Ctr SW11 .... 59 C3
St John's Upper Holloway CE Prim Sch 7 N19 .... 4 C2
St John's Vale SE8 .. 51 C1
St John's Villas Upper Holloway N19 .... 4 C2
  W8 .... 128 B1
St John's Walworth CE Prim Sch SE17 .... 151 A3
ST JOHN'S WOOD .79 B1
St John's Wood Ct NW8 .... 89 C3
St John's Wood High St NW8 .... 80 A1
St John's Wood Park NW8 .... 79 B4
St John's Wood Pre-Prep Sch NW8 .. 90 A4
St John's Wood Rd NW8 .... 89 C3
St John's Wood Sta NW8 .... 79 B2
St John's Wood Terr NW8 .... 80 A2
St John the Baptist VA CE Prim Sch N1 .... 87 C1
St John the Divine CE Jun & Inf Sch SE5 .... 48 A3
St John the Evangelist RC Prim Sch N1.. 86 A2

St Joseph's Cl
W10 . . . .**31** A4
St Josephs Ct 3
NW10 . . . .**21** B3
St Joseph's Flats
NW1 . . . . **93** B4
St Joseph's Ho
W6 . . . .**39** C2
St Joseph's Hospice E9,
E8 . . . .**25** A4
St Joseph's RC Inf &
Jun Schs 36 SE5. . .**48** B3
St Joseph's RC Prim
Sch
Chelsea SW3 . . . . .**144** C3
10 Deptford SE8. . . .**51** C3
11 Greenwich SE10 . .**43** A1
Paddington W9. . . . .**88** C3
Rotherhithe SE16 . . .**40** B3
St Giles WC2. . . . .**106** B2
Upper Holloway N19 . .**4** A3
16 Wandsworth
SW18 . . . .**58** C2
8 Willesden NW10. . .**8** A1
St Joseph's Vale
SW8 . . . .**170** B4
St Joseph's Vale
SE3 . . . .**67** C4
St Jude & St Paul's CE
Prim Sch N1 . . . . .**16** A2
St Jude's CE Prim Sch
4 London SE24 . . . .**63** A2
SE1 . . . .**136** A1
St Judes Ho 6
W10 . . . .**23** B2
St Jude's Rd E2 . . . .**25** A3
St Jude St N16 . . . . .**16** A3
St Julian's Rd
NW6 . . . .**23** C4
St Katharine's Ho
N1 . . . .**85** B2
St Katharine's Prec
NW1 . . . .**82** A2
St Katharine's Way
E1 . . . .**125** A2
St Katharine's Pier
E1 . . . .**125** A2
St Katharine's Row
EC3 . . . .**110** B1
St Katherine's Wlk 1
W11 . . . .**30** C1
St Kilda's Rd N16 . . .**7** A3
St Laurence's Cl
NW6 . . . .**22** C4
St Lawrence Ct N1 **87** C4
St Lawrence Ho
SE1 . . . .**138** C2
St Lawrence St
E14 . . . .**34** B1
St Lawrence Terr
W10 . . . .**31** A4
St Lawrence Way
SW9 . . . .**173** C2
St Leonards Ct
SW14 . . . .**55** B4
St Leonard's Ct N1 **97** C4
St Leonard's Hospl
N1 . . . .**24** A3
St Leonards Rd
SW14 . . . .**55** B4
St Leonard's Rd
Becontree NW10 . . .**20** C1
South Bromley E14. . .**34** B4

St Leonard's Sq
NW5 . . . .**12** C2
St Leonard's St E3 .**27** A2
St Leonard's Terr
SW3 . . . .**145** A1
St Loo Ave SW3 . . .**158** A3
St Loo Ct SW3 . . . .**158** C4
St Luke Prim CE SE1
13 E16 . . . .**35** B3
ST LUKE'S **97** A2
St Luke's Ave SW4 .**61** C3
St Luke's CE Prim Sch
7 Cubitt Town
E14 . . . .**42** C2
Paddington W9. . . . .**23** B2
Shoreditch EC1 . . . . .**97** A3
St Luke's Cl EC1 . . .**97** A2
St Luke's Ct W11 . . .**31** B3
St Luke's Mews
W11 . . . .**31** B3
St Luke's Rd W11 . . .**31** B4
St Luke's Sq E16 . . .**35** B3
St Luke's St SW3 . .**144** B2
St Margaret's Cres
Putney SW15 . . . . . .**57** A2
St Margaret's Ct
SE1 . . . .**123** B1
St Margaret's La
W8 . . . .**128** A1
St Margarets Lo
W3 . . . .**37** A4
St Margaret's Rd
Brockley SE4. . . . . .**66** B3
Kensal Green
NW10 . . . .**22** B2
St Margaret's Sch
NW3 . . . .**11** A4
St Margaret St
SW1 . . . .**134** A3
St Mark's CE Prim Sch
SE11 . . . .**163** A4
St Marks Cl 5
SE10 . . . .**52** B3
St Mark's Cres
NW1 . . . .**81** C4
St Marks Gate E9. . .**18** B1
St Mark's Gr
SW10 . . . .**156** B2
St Marks Ho 6
SE17 . . . .**48** C4
St Mark's Mans 14
N4 . . . .**5** B2
St Mark's Pl W11 . . .**31** A3
St Mark's Prim Sch **11**
N19 . . . .**5** A2
St Marks Rd
15 North Kensington
NW10 . . . .**30** C3
North Kensington
NW10 . . . .**30** C4
St Mark's Rd W11 . .**31** A3
St Mark's Rise E8 . .**16** B3
St Mark's Sq NW1 . .**81** B3
St Mark St E1 . . . . .**111** A1
St Martin-in-the-
Fields High Sch **21**
SW2 . . . .**74** C3
St Martin's
Almshouses NW1. .**82** C4
St Mark's Cl NW1 . .**82** C4
St Martins Ct N1 . . .**24** A4
St Martin's Ct
WC2 . . . .**120** A4
West Norwood
SE27 . . . .**75** A2

St Martin's La
WC2 . . . .**120** A3
St Martin's Le Grand
EC1 . . . .**108** C2
St Martin's Pl
WC2 . . . .**120** A3
St Martin's Rd
SW9 . . . .**172** C2
St Martin's St
WC2 . . . .**119** C3
St Martin's Way
SW17 . . . .**71** B1
St Mary Abbots CE
Prim Sch W8 . . . . .**128** A3
St Mary Abbot's Ct
W14 . . . .**126** C1
St Mary Abbot's Pl
W8 . . . .**127** A1
St Mary Abbots Terr
W14 . . . .**127** A1
St Mary at Hill
EC3 . . . .**124** A3
St Mary Axe EC3. .**110** B2
St Marychurch St
SE16 . . . .**40** B4
St Mary Graces Ct
E1 . . . .**125** A3
St Marylebone CE Sch
The W1 . . . .**103** C4
St Mary le Bow
Church EC2 . . . . . .**109** A1
St Mary-le-Park Ct
SW11 . . . .**158** B1
St Mary Magdalene
Acad N7 . . . .**14** C2
St Mary Magdalene
CE Prim Sch
9 Paddington
W2 . . . .**100** A4
10 Peckham SE15 . .**50** A1
St Mary Magdalen's
RC Prim Sch
Brockley SE4. . . . . .**66** A3
14 Mortlake SW14. . .**55** C4
St Mary Magdalen's
RC Jun Sch **1**
SW14 . . . .**9** A2
St Mary Newington Cl
SE17 . . . .**152** B2
St Mary of the Angels
RC Prim Sch **12**
W2 . . . .**31** C3
St Mary RC Prim Sch
6 W10 . . . .**23** A2
St Mary & St Michael
Prim Sch **7** E1 . . .**32** B3
St Mary & St Pancras
CE Prim Sch
NW1 . . . .**83** B1
St Mary's Bryanston
Square CE Sch
W1 . . . .**102** C4
St Mary's CE Prim Sch
Islington N1. . . . . . .**86** B4
London SE13. . . . . .**67** A2
18 Putney SW15 . . .**57** C4
Willesden NW10. . . . .**9** A2
St Mary's Ct W6 . . .**38** B3
St Mary's Flats
NW1 . . . .**93** B4
St Mary's Gate
W8 . . . .**128** A1
St Mary's Gdns
SE11 . . . .**149** C4

St Mary's Gr
Barnes SW13 . . . . . .**57** A4
Chiswick W4 . . . .**45** A4
Islington N1 . . . .**15** A2
Richmond TW10,
TW9 . . . .**54** B3
St Mary's Ho N1 . . .**86** B4
St Mary's Hospl
W2 . . . .**101** C2
St Mary's Hospl
Medical Sch W2 . .**101** C2
St Mary's Kilburn CE
Prim Sch 16
NW6 . . . .**23** C4
St Mary's Mans
Dagenham NW10. . . .**21** A4
Paddington W2. . . .**101** B4
St Mary's Mews
St Mary's Path N1. . .**86** B4
St Mary's Pl W8 . . .**128** A1
St Mary's RC Prim Sch
Chiswick W4 . . . .**45** A4
10 Clapham Pk
SW4 . . . .**61** B2
Clapham SW8. . . . .**170** A4
Hammersmith W14 . .**39** C3
Paddington NW6 . . . .**23** C3
St Mary's Rd
Golders Green
NW11 . . . .**1** A4
Harlesden NW10 . . . .**21** A4
Nunhead SE15 . . . . . .**50** B1
St Mary's Sch
Hampstead NW3 . . .**11** C3
St Mary's Sq W2. . .**101** B4
St Mary's Stoke
Newington CE Prim
Sch **8** N16. . . . .**7** A2
St Mary's Terr
W2 . . . .**101** B4
St Mary's Twr EC1 . .**97** A1
St Mary's Wlk
SE11 . . . .**149** C4
St Matthews CE Sch
SW1 . . . .**133** C2
St Matthews Ct
SE1 . . . .**136** C1
St Matthew's Ho 8
SE17 . . . .**48** C4
St Matthew's Lo
NW1 . . . .**83** A2
St Matthew's Rd
SW2 . . . .**62** B2
St Matthew's Row
E2 . . . .**24** C1 **99** B2
St Matthew St
SW1 . . . .**133** B1
St Matthias CE Prim
Sch E2. . . . . . .**24** B1 **99** A2
St Matthias's CE Prim
Sch 3 N16. . . . . . .**16** A4
St Mauritius Ho
SE13 . . . .**67** B2
St Maur Rd SW6 . .**165** A3
St Michael & All
Angels CE Acad **32**
SE5 . . . .**48** A3
St Michael's Alley
EC3 . . . .**109** C1
St Michael's Cath Coll
30 SE16 . . . .**139** B3
St Michael's CE Prim
Sch
Camden Town
NW1 . . . .**82** C4

St Michael's CE Prim
Sch continued
Highgate N6. . . . .**3** C4
Wandsworth SW18 . .**70** B4
St Michaels Ct 2
E14 . . . .**34** B4
St Michael's Ct
NW11 . . . .**1** B4
St Michael's Flats
NW1 . . . .**83** B1
St Michael's Gdns
W10 . . . .**31** A4
St Michael's Rd
Cricklewood NW2. . . .**9** B4
Stockwell SW9 . . . .**172** C2
St Michael's St
W2 . . . .**102** A2
St Michael Steiner
Sch The **10** SW18 .**58** C2
St Mildred's Ct
EC2 . . . .**109** B1
St Monica's RC Prim
Sch **24** N1. . . .**24** A2 **98** A4
St Nicholas' Flats
NW1 . . . .**83** B1
St Nicholas Ho
SE8 . . . .**51** C4
St Nicholas Mans
SW17 . . . .**72** B2
St Nicholas St SE8 .**51** C2
St Norbert Gn SE4. .**66** A3
St Norbert Rd SE4. .**66** A3
St Olaf's Rd SW6 . .**154** B1
St Olaves Ct W2 . .**114** A3
St Olave's Ct EC2. .**109** B1
St Olave's Est SE1 .**138** B4
St Olave's Gdns
SE11 . . . .**149** B4
St Olave's Mans
SE11 . . . .**149** B4
St Olav's Sq 32
SE16 . . . .**40** B4
St Osmund's RC Prim
Sch SW13 . . . .**46** B2
St Oswald's Pl
SE11 . . . .**148** C1
St Oswulf St SW1 .**147** C3
St Owen Ho SE1 . .**138** B2
ST PANCRAS **94** B4
St Pancras
Almshouses 13
NW5 . . . .**12** B3
St Pancras
Commercial Ctr
NW1 . . . .**83** A4
St Pancras Hospl
NW1 . . . .**83** B3
St Pancras
International Sta
WC1 . . . .**94** A4
St Pancras Way
NW1 . . . .**83** B4
St Patrick's Coll
W11 . . . .**105** B2
St Patrick's RC Prim
Sch NW5 . . . .**13** A3
St Paul's Ave
Rotherhithe SE16 . . .**32** C1
Willesden NW2. . . . . .**9** B2
St Paul's Cath
EC4 . . . .**108** C1
St Paul's Cath Sch
EC4 . . . .**108** C1
St Paul's CE Prim Sch
22 Hammersmith
W6 . . . .**39** B1

St Paul's CE Prim Sch
continued
Hampstead NW3 . . . . **12** B1
SE17 . . . . **150** C2
St Paul's Church Yd
EC4 . . . . **108** C1
St Pauls Cl W5 . . . . . **36** B3
St Pauls Cres NW1 . **13** C1
St Paul's Ct
Clapham SW4 . . . . . . **61** C3
6 Upper Holloway
N19 . . . . **4** C2
St Paul's Dr E15 . . . **19** C3
St Paul's Girls' Sch 1
W6 . . . . **39** C2
St Pauls Mews
NW1 . . . . **13** C1
St Paul's Pl N1 . . . . . **15** C2
St Pauls Rd N1W . . . **54** B4
St Paul's Rd N1 . . . . **15** B2
St Paul's Sch
SW13 . . . . **38** C1
St Paul's Sta EC2 . . . **108** C2
St Paul Steiner Sch
22 N1 . . . . **15** C1
St Paul St N1 . . . . . . **87** A3
St Paul's Terr
SE17 . . . . **48** B4
St Pauls View WC1 . . **95** B3
St Paul's Way E3 . . . **33** C4
St Paul's Way Com
Sch 25 E3 . . . . **33** C4
St Paul's with St
Michael's Prim Sch
24 E8 . . . . **24** C4
St Paul with St Luke
CE Prim Sch 18
E3 . . . . **33** B4
St Peter & St Paul RC
Prim Sch EC1 . . . . **96** B2
St Peter's Alley
EC3 . . . . **109** C1
St Peter's Ave 37
E2 . . . . **24** C3
St Petersburgh Mews
W2 . . . . **114** A4
St Petersburgh Pl
W2 . . . . **114** A3
St Peter's CE Prim
Sch
18 Chiswick W6 . . . **38** C1
6 E1 . . . . **32** B1
6 Paddington W9 . . **23** C1
SE17 . . . . **151** B1
SW1 . . . . **132** B1
St Peter's Church Ct
N1 . . . . **86** B3
St Peters Cl 1
SW17 . . . . **72** A2
St Peter's Cl E2 . . . . **24** C3
St Peters Ct
New Cross SE4 . . . . . **51** B4
28 Stepney E1 . . . . . **25** B1
St Peter's Gdns
SE27 . . . . **74** C1
St Peter's Gr W6 . . . **38** C2
St Peters Ho W1 . . . . **94** B3
St Peter's Ho
4 SE17 . . . . **48** C4
Stamford Hill N16 . . . **7** A4
St Peter's Pl W9 . . . . **88** A1
St Peter's Rd W6 . . . **38** C1
St Peter's Sq
Chiswick W6 . . . . **38** B1
Hackney E2 . . . . **24** C3
St Peter's St N1 . . . . **86** B3

St Peter's Street
Mews N1 . . . . **86** B2
St Peter's Terr
SW6 . . . . **154** B1
St Peter's Villas 5
W6 . . . . **38** C2
St Peter's Way N1 . **16** A1
St Peter's Wharf 7
W6 . . . . **38** C1
St Philip Ho WC1 . . . **95** B3
St Philip Sq 1
SW8 . . . . **170** B1
St Philip's Rd E8 . . **16** C2
St Philip's Sch
SW7 . . . . **143** A3
St Philip St SW8 . . **170** A1
St Philip's Way N1 . **87** A3
St Quintin Ho
SW18 . . . . **59** C1
St Quintin Ave
W10 . . . . **30** C4
St Quintin Gdns 21
W10 . . . . **30** B4
St Regis Hts NW3 . . **2** A1
St Richard's Ho
NW1 . . . . **93** B4
St Rule St SW8 . . . **170** C1
St Saviours SW4 . . . **61** A3
St Saviour's CE Prim
Sch
9 Bow Comm
E14 . . . . **34** A4
Camberwell SE24 . . . **63** B4
SE13 . . . . **67** B3
St Saviours Ho 30
SE1 . . . . **139** B3
St Saviour's RC Prim
Sch SE13 . . . . **67** B3
St Saviour's Rd
SW2 . . . . **62** B2
St Saviour's Wharf
SE1 . . . . **139** A4
St Scholastica's RC
Prim Sch E5 . . . . . **7** C1
St Silas Pl NW5 . . . **12** C2
St Simon's Ave
SW15 . . . . **57** B2
St Stephen's Ave
W12 . . . . **39** A4
St Stephen's CE Prim
Sch
Paddington W2 . . . . . **31** C4
17 Shepherd's Bush
W12 . . . . **39** B4
8 St Johns SE8 . . . . **51** C1
SW8 . . . . **162** C2
St Stephen's Cl
Maitland Pk NW5 . . . **12** B3
NW8 . . . . **80** B3
St Stephen's Cres
W2 . . . . **31** C3
St Stephen's Gdns
Notting Hill W2 . . . . . **31** C3
41 Putney SW15 . . **58** B2
St Stephens Ho 9
SE17 . . . . **48** C4
St Stephen's Mews 34
W2 . . . . **31** C4
St Stephen's Rd
E3 . . . . **26** B3
St Stephen's Row
EC4 . . . . **109** B1

St Stephen's Terr
SW8 . . . . **162** C1
St Stephen's Wlk
SW7 . . . . **142** C4
St Swithin's La
EC4 . . . . **123** B4
St Swithun's Rd
SE13 . . . . **67** C1
St Theresas Ct E9 . . **18** B4
St Thomas' CE Prim
Sch 26 W10 . . . . . . **23** A1
St Thomas Ct 14
NW1 . . . . **13** B1
St Thomas Ho 1
E1 . . . . **32** C3
St Thomas More
Language Coll
SW3 . . . . **144** C3
St Thomas of
Canterbury RC Prim
Sch SW6 . . . . **154** C2
St Thomas Rd E16 . . **35** C3
St Thomas' Rd W4 . . **45** B4
St Thomas's Gdns
NW5 . . . . **12** C2
St Thomas's Hospl
SE1 . . . . **134** C2
St Thomas's Ho 20
E9 . . . . **17** B1
St Thomas's Rd
Dagenham NW10 . . . **21** A4
Highbury N4, N5 . . . . **5** C1
St Thomas's Sq E9 . **17** B1
St Thomas St SE1 . . **123** C1
St Thomas's Way
SW6 . . . . **155** A2
St Thomas the
Apostle Coll
SE15 . . . . **50** B2
St Ursula's Convent
Sch SE10 . . . . **52** C2
St Vincent De Paul Ho
24 E1 . . . . **32** B4
St Vincent De Paul RC
Prim Sch SW1 . . . **132** C2
St Vincent Ho
SE1 . . . . **138** C2
St Vincent's RC Prim
Sch
Acton W3 . . . . **28** A2
Marylebone W1 . . . . **103** B3
3 St Vincent St W1 . **103** C3
Salamanca Pl SE1 **148** C3
Salamanca St SE1,
SE11 . . . . **148** C3
Salcombe Gdns
SW4 . . . . **61** A3
Salcombe Lo NW5 . . **12** C4
N16 . . . . **16** A3
Salcombe Villas 18
TW10 . . . . **54** A2
Salcot N4 . . . . **5** B2
Salcott Rd SW11 . . . **60** B2
Salehurst Rd SE4 . . **66** B1
Salem Ho 18 E9 . . . . **17** C2
Salem Rd W2 . . . . . **114** B4
Sale Pl W2 . . . . **102** A2
Salesian Coll
SW11 . . . . **168** A3
Sale St E2 . . . . **24** C1
Salford Ho 5 E14 . . **42** B2
Salford Rd SW12,
SW2 . . . . **73** C3
Salisbury Cl SE17 . **151** B4

Salisbury Ct
15 Bermondsey
SE16 . . . . **139** C1
Chiswick W4 . . . . **38** A2
EC4 . . . . **108** A1
Hackney E9 . . . . **18** A3
Salisbury Ho
2 Islington N1 . . . . . **15** A2
Islington N1 . . . . **86** A4
3 Poplar E14 . . . . . . **34** A3
Westminster SW1 . . **147** C2
Wimbledon SW19 . . . **69** C1
Salisbury Mews
SW6 . . . . **154** C1
Salisbury Pl
Camberwell SW9 . . . **48** A3
Marylebone W1 . . . . **102** C4
Salisbury Rd TW9 . . **54** A3
Salisbury Sq EC4 . . **107** C1
Salisbury St
10 Acton W3 . . . . . . **37** B4
NW8 . . . . **90** A1
Salisbury Terr
SE15 . . . . **65** B4
Salisbury Wlk N19 . . **4** B2
Salmon La E14 . . . . **33** A3
Salmon St 15 E14 . . **33** B3
Saltcoats Rd W4 . . . **38** A4
Saltdene N4 . . . . **5** B3
Salter Rd
Rotherhithe SE16 . . . **32** C1
SE16 . . . . **33** A1
Salters' Hall Ct
EC4 . . . . **123** B4
Salters Rd W10 . . . . **22** C1
Salter St
College Pk NW10 . . . **21** C2
14 Poplar E14 . . . . . **33** C2
Salterton Rd N7 . . . **5** B1
Saltoun Rd SW2,
SW9 . . . . **62** C3
Saltram Cres W9 . . . **23** C2
Saltwell St E14 . . . . **33** C2
Saltwood Gr SE17 . **151** B1
Saltwood Ho 16
SE15 . . . . **50** B4
Salusbury Prim Sch
NW6 . . . . **23** B4
Salusbury Rd NW6 . **23** B4
Salutation Rd
SE10 . . . . **43** A2
Salvin Rd SW15 . . . . **57** C4
Salway Rd E15 . . . . . **19** C2
Salween Ho 2
N16 . . . . **15** C4
Sambrook Ho 25
E1 . . . . **32** B4
Samels Ct W6 . . . . . **38** C1
Samford Ho N1 . . . . **85** B3
Samford St NW8 . . . **90** A1
Sam Manners Ho 5
SE10 . . . . **43** A1
Sam March Ho 5
E14 . . . . **34** C3
Sampson St E1 . . . **125** C1
Samuel Cl
SE14 . . . . **50** C4
Shoreditch E8 . . . . . . **24** B4
Samuel Ct
N1 . . . . **24** A2
Samuel Ho 18 E8 . . **24** B4
Samuel Jones Ind Est
7 SE15 . . . . **49** A3
Samuel Lewis Bldgs
N1 . . . . **14** C2

Samuel Lewis Trust
Dwellings
6 Camberwell
SE5 . . . . **48** B2
Chelsea SW3 . . . . . . **144** A3
Walham Green
SW6 . . . . **155** C2
West Kensington
W14 . . . . **140** B4
Samuel Rhodes Sch
N1 . . . . **85** B4
Samuel Richardson
Ho W14 . . . . **140** C3
Samuel's Cl 2 W6 . . **39** B2
Samuel St SE11 . . . . **49** B3
Sancroft Ct SW11 . **168** B4
Sancroft Ho SE11 . **149** B2
Sancroft St SE11 . . **149** B2
Sanctuary Mews 15
E8 . . . . **16** B2
Sanctuary St SE1 . . **137** A4
Sanctuary The
22 Wapping E1 . . . **32** A1
Westminster SW1 . . **133** C2
Sandale Cl N16 . . . . . **6** C1
Sandall Ho 7 E3 . . . . **26** A3
Sandall Rd NW5 . . . . **13** B2
Sandalwood Cl 11
E1 . . . . **26** A1
Sandalwood Ho 8
NW3 . . . . **11** A2
Sandbourne
4 Kensington
W11 . . . . **31** C3
14 Paddington NW8 . **78** B4
Sandbourne Rd
SE4 . . . . **51** A1
Sandbrook Rd N16 . . **7** A1
Sandby Ho
6 Camberwell
SE5 . . . . **49** A2
6 Kilburn NW6 . . . . **23** C4
Sandell St SE1 . . . . **135** B4
Sanderling Ct 20
SE8 . . . . **51** B4
Sanders Ho WC1 . . . **95** B4
Sanderson Cl NW5 . . **13** A4
Sanderson Ho 7
SE8 . . . . **41** B1
Sanderstead Ave
NW2 . . . . **1** A2
Sanderstead Cl
SW12 . . . . **73** B4
Sanders Way 3
N19 . . . . **4** C3
Sandfield WC1 . . . . . **94** B3
Sandford Ct N16 . . . . **7** A3
Sandford Row
SE17 . . . . **151** C2
Sandford St SW6 . . **156** B1
Sandgate Ho 19
E5 . . . . **17** A4
Sandgate La SW17,
SW18 . . . . **72** A4
Sandgate St SE15 . . **50** A4
Sandgate Trad Est
SE15 . . . . **50** A4
Sandham Ct SW4 . . **172** B3
Sandhills The
SW10 . . . . **157** A4
Sandhurst Ct SW2 . **62** A3
Sandhurst Ho 12
E1 . . . . **32** B4

Sandilands Rd
SW6 . . . . 166 A3
Sandison St SE15 . . . 64 C4
Sandland St WC1 . 107 A3
Sandmere Rd SW4 . 62 A3
Sandon Ho 6
SW2 . . . . 74 A4
Sandown Ho 2
W4 . . . . 37 B1
Sandpiper Cl SE16 . 41 B4
Sandpiper Ct
18 Cubitt Town
E14 . . . . 42 B3
1 SE8 . . . . 51 C3
Sandridge St 3
N19 . . . . 4 B2
Sandringham Cl 1
SW19 . . . . 69 C3
Sandringham Ct
Marylebone W1 . . 105 A1
Putney SW15 . . . . . 57 C1
18 Rotherhithe
SE16 . . . . 32 C1
St John's Wood W9 . 89 A3
Sandringham Flats
WC2 . . . . 119 C4
Sandringham Ho
Richmond TW10 . . . . 54 C2
W14 . . . . 140 A4
Sandringham Rd
Dalston E8 . . . . 16 B3
Golders Green NW11 . . 1 A4
Willesden NW2 . . . . . 9 A2
Sandrock Rd SE13 . 66 C4
SANDS END 59 B4
Sands End La
SW6 . . . . 166 B4
Sandstone TW9 . . . . 44 C3
Sandstone PI NW19 . . 4 A2
Sandways 5 TW9 . . 44 C2
Sandwell Cres 2
NW6 . . . . 10 C2
Sandwell Mans 3
NW6 . . . . 10 C2
Sandwich Ho
18 Rotherhithe
SE16 . . . . 40 B4
WC1 . . . . 94 A3
Sandwich St WC1 . 94 A3
Sandycombe Ctr
TW9 . . . . 44 C1
Sandycombe Rd
TW9 . . . . 44 C1
Sandy Lo N6 . . . . 4 B4
Sandy Rd NW3 . . . . . . 2 A2
Sandy's Row E1 . . . 110 B3
Sanford La 3 N16 . . 7 B2
Sanford St SE14, . . .
SE8 . . . . 51 A4
Sanford Terr N16 . . 7 B1
Sanford Wlk
SE14 . . . . 51 A4
4 Stoke Newington
N16 . . . . 7 B2
Sangora Rd 17
SW11 . . . . 59 C3
San Ho 29 E9 . . . . 17 C2
Sankey Ho 22 E2 . . 25 B3
Sansom St
Camberwell SE5 . . . 48 C2
SE5 . . . . 48 C3
Sans Wlk EC1 . . . . 96 A2
Santley Ho SE1 . . 135 C3

Santley St SW4 . . . . 62 B3
Santos Rd SW18 . . . . 58 C2
Sapcote Trad Ctr
NW10 . . . . 8 C3
Saperton Wlk
SE11 . . . . 149 A4
Sapperton Ct EC1 . 96 C2
Sapphire Ct 3
E1 . . . . 125 B4
Saracen's Head Yd
EC2 . . . . 110 B1
Saracen St E14 . . . 33 C3
Sarah Ho
Roehampton
SW15 . . . . 56 B3
4 Stepney E1 . . . 32 A3
Sarah Swift Ho 8
SE1 . . . . 137 C4
Sara Lane Ct 31
N1 . . . . 24 A3
Saratoga Rd E5 . . . 17 B4
Sardinia Ho WC2 . 106 C1
Sardinia St WC2 . . 106 C2
Sarjant Path SW19 . 69 C2
Sark Ho 9 N1 . . . . 15 B2
Sarnesfield Ho
SE15 . . . . 50 A4
Sarratt Ho 6 W10 . 30 B4
Sarre Rd NW2 . . . . 10 B3
Sarsden Bldgs
W1 . . . . 103 C1
Sarsfeld Rd SW12,
Sartor Rd SE15 . . . 65 C3
Sarum Hall Sch
NW3 . . . . 12 A1
Sarum Ho
W11 . . . . 31 B2 113 A3
Sassoon Ho SE15 . 50 B1
Satchwell Rd 17
E2 . . . . 24 C2 99 B3
Saturn Ho 4 E3 . . 26 C4
Saul Ct 5 SE15 . . . 49 B4
Saunders Cl 14
E14 . . . . 33 B2
Saunders Ho 11
SW2 . . . . 74 C4
Saunders Ness Rd
E14 . . . . 42 C1
Saunders St SE11 . 149 B4
Savage Gdns EC3 . 124 B4
Savana N16 . . . . 7 A1
Savannah Cl 4
SE15 . . . . 49 B3
Savernake Ho N4 . . 6 C4
Savernake Rd
NW3 . . . . 12 B4
Saville Rd W4 . . . . 37 C3
Saville Row 4 W1 . 118 C4
Savill Ho 2 SW4 . . 61 C1
Savona Ct SW8 . . . 160 C1
Savoy Circus W3 . . 29 B2
Savoy Ct
Earl's Ct SW5 . . . 141 C4
Strand WC2 . . . . 120 C3
Savoy Hill WC2 . . 120 C3
Savoy Mews SW9 . 62 A4
Savoy Pier WC2 . . 120 C3
Savoy Pl WC2 . . . 120 C3
Savoy Row WC2 . . 120 C3
Savoy Stps WC2 . . 120 C3
Savoy Way WC2 . . 120 C3
Sawkins Ct SW19 . 70 A2
Sawley Rd W12 . . . 29 C1

Sawmill Yd E3 . . . . . 26 A4
Sawyer St SE1 . . . 136 C4
Saxby Rd SW2 . . . . 74 A4
Saxonbury Ct
16 Kentish Town
N7 . . . . 13 C3
2 Lower Holloway
N7 . . . . 14 A3
Saxoncroft Ho
SW16 . . . . 73 C1
Saxon Dr W3 . . . . 28 A4
Saxonfield Cl SW2 . 74 B4
Saxon Hall W2 . . . 114 A3
Saxon Ho 4 SW4 . . 61 C3
Saxon Rd E3 . . . . 26 B3
Saxton Cl SE13 . . . 67 C4
Sayer Ho SE4 . . . . 66 A3
Sayes Court St
SE8 . . . . 51 B4
Sayes Ct SE8 . . . . 51 B4
Scafell NW1 . . . . . 92 C4
Scala St W1 . . . . . 105 A4
Scampston Mews 5
W10 . . . . 30 C3
Scandrett St 38
E1 . . . . 32 A1
Scarba Wlk N1 . . . 15 C2
Scarborough Rd N4 5 C3
Scarborough St
E1 . . . . 111 A1
Scarlette Manor Wlk
10 SE24 . . . . 74 C4
Scarsbrook Ho 2
SW2 . . . . 62 C1
Scarsdale Pl W8 . . 128 A2
Scarsdale Villas
W8 . . . . 127 C1
Scarth Rd SW13 . . 56 B4
Scawen Rd SE8 . . . 41 A1
Scawfell St E2 . . . . 24 B3
Sceptre Ho 10 E1 . 25 B1
Sceptre Rd E2 . . . . 25 B2
Schiller International
Univ SE1 . . . . 121 B1
Schofield Wlk SE3 . 53 C3
Scholars Ct 5 N19 . 4 C3
Scholars Rd SW12 . 73 B3
Scholefield Rd N19 . 4 C2
Scholey Ho SW11 . 60 A4
Schomberg Ho
SW1 . . . . 147 C4
Schonfeld Sq N16 . 6 C3
School App 21
E2 . . . . 24 A2 98 B4
Schoolbank Rd
SE10 . . . . 43 B2
School Bell Cloisters
17 E3 . . . . 26 A3
Schoolbell Mews 18
E3 . . . . 26 A3
School Flats SW8 . 172 A3
School Ho SE1 . . . 152 A4
Schoolhouse La
E1 . . . . 32 C2
School Rd NW10 . . 20 C1
School Sq SE10 . . . 43 B3
Schooner Cl
Cubitt Town E14 . . 42 C3
1 Rotherhithe
SE16 . . . . 40 C4
Schubert Rd SW15 . 58 B2

Science Mus SW7 129 B1
Sclater St
E1 . . . . 24 B1 99 A2
Scoles Cres SW2 . . 74 C3
Scoresby St SE1 . . 122 A1
Scorton Ho 2 N1 . 24 A3
Scotch Ho SW1 . . 130 C3
Scoter Ct 28 SE8 . . 51 B4
Scotia Bldg 10 E1 . 32 C2
Scotia Ct 3 SE16 . 40 B3
Scotia Rd 2 SW2 . 74 C4
Scotland Pl SW1 . 120 A1
Scotney Ho E9 . . . 17 B2
Scotson Ho SE11 . 149 B3
Scotswood St EC1 . 95 C2
Scott Ave SW15,
SW18 . . . . 58 A1
Scott Ct
Acton W4 . . . . 37 B3
4 Clapham SW11 . 170 B1
17 Stoke Newington
N16 . . . . 7 A1
Scott Ellis Gdns
NW8 . . . . 89 B3
Scott Ho
2 Barnsbury N7 . . 14 B2
Islington N1 . . . . . 87 B4
Lisson Gr NW8 . . . 90 A1
17 Millwall E14 . . 41 C4
Scott Lidgett Cres
SE16 . . . . 139 C3
Scotts Ct 6 W12 . . 39 A4
Scott's Rd W12 . . . 39 A4
Scott's Sufferance
Wharf SE1 . . . . . 139 A3
Scott St E1 . . . . . 25 A1
Scott's Yd EC4 . . . 123 B4
Scouling Ho 2
E14 . . . . 33 B3
Scoulding Rd E16 . 35 C3
Scouler St 3 E14 . 34 C2
Scout App NW10 . . 8 A4
Scout La SW4 . . . . 61 B4
Scovell Cres SE1 . . 136 C3
Scovell Rd SE1 . . . 136 C3
Scriven Ct 2 E8 . . 24 B4
Scriven St E8 . . . . 24 B4
Scroby St SE6 . . . 67 C4
Scrope Bldg EC1 . 107 B4
Scrubs La NW10 W10,
W12 . . . . 22 A2
Scrutton Cl SW12 . 73 C4
Scrutton St
EC2 . . . . . 24 A1 98 A1
Scutari Rd SE22 . . 65 B2
Scylla Rd SE15 . . . 65 A4
Seabright St 22
E2 . . . . 25 A2
Seacole Cl W3 . . . 28 C4
Seacon Twr 8
E14 . . . . 41 C4
Seaford Ho 13
SE16 . . . . 40 B4
Seaford St WC1, . . 94 B3
Seaforth Cres N5 . . 15 B3
Seaforth Lo 2
SW13 . . . . 46 B1
Seaforth Pl SW1 . . 133 A2
Seagrave Lo SW6 . 155 C4
Seagrave Rd SW6 . 155 C4
Seagrove Cl E1 . . . 32 C4
Seagull La E16 . . . 35 C2
Seal Ho SE1 . . . . 137 C2
SEA LIFE London
Aquarium SE1 . . 134 C3
Seal St E8. . . . . 16 B4

Searle Pl N4 . . . . 5 B3
Searles Cl SW11 . . 158 B1
Searles Rd SE1 . . . 151 C4
Searson Ho SE17 . 150 B3
Sears St SE5 . . . . 48 C3
Seasalter Ho 10
SW9 . . . . 173 B4
Seaton Cl SW15 . . 69 A4
Seaton Point E15 . . 76 B4
Seavington Ho 3
SE5 . . . . 64 A4
Sebastian Ho 22
N1 . . . . 24 A3
Sebastian St EC1 . 96 B3
Sebbon St N1 . . . . 15 A1
Sebright Ho 22 E2 . 25 A3
Sebright Pas 29
E2 . . . . 24 C3 . . . . .
Sebright Sch 21
E2 . . . . 24 C3
Secker Ho SW9 . . 48 A1
Secker St SE1 . . . 121 B1
Second Ave
East Acton W3 . . . 29 B1
Kensal Town W10 . . 23 A1
Mortlake SW14 . . . 56 A4
Sedan Way 3 SE17 . 152 A2
Sedding St SW1 . . 145 B4
Seddon Ho EC2 . . 108 C4
Seddon St WC1 . . 95 A3
Sedgeford Rd
W12 . . . . 29 B1
Sedgewick Ho
SW19 . . . . 69 C2
Sedgley Ho N4 . . . . 5 B2
Sedgmoor Pl SE5 . 49 A3
Sedgwick St E9 . . 17 C3
Sedleigh Rd SW18 . 58 B1
Sedlescombe Rd
SW6 . . . . 155 B4
Sedley Ho SE11 . . 149 A2
Sedley Pl W1 . . . . 104 A1
Seething La EC3 . . 124 B4
Sefton St SW15 . . 57 B4
Sekforde St EC1 . . 96 A2
Selbie Ave NW10 . . 8 B3
Selborne 2 SW11 . 60 C4
Selborne Ho 1 SE1 137 B3
Selborne Rd 4
SE5 . . . . 48 C1
Selby Ho 10 SW4 . 61 B1
Selby Sq 1 W10 . . 23 A2
Selby St E1 . . 24 C1 99 C1
Selden Ho 2 SE15 . 50 B1
Selden Rd SE15 . . 50 B1
Seldon Ho
New Elms SW8 . . . 160 C1
Pimlico SW1 . . . . 146 C1
Selhurst Cl SW19 . 69 C3
Selina Ho NW8 . . . 89 C2
Selkirk Ho
N1 . . . . 84 C4
6 Stoke Newington
N16 . . . . 7 A1
Sellons Ave NW10 . 21 A4
Selma Ho 7 W12 . . 30 A3
Selman Ho 33 E9 . 18 A2
Selsdon Way E14 . . 42 A3
Selsea Pl N16 . . . . 16 A3
Selsey St E14 . . . . 33 C4
Selway Ho SW9 . . 172 B4
Selwood Ho 1 N4 . 6 C4
Selwood Pl SW7. . 143 B2
Selwood Terr
SW7 . . . . 143 B2

Selworthy Ho
SW11 . . . . 167 C4
Selwyn Ave TW9 . . . . 54 A4
Selwyn Ct 8
TW10 . . . . 54 B2
Selwyn Ho 8
SW15 . . . . 57 C1
Selwyn Rd
Bow E3 . . . . 26 B3
Willesden NW10 . . . . . 8 A1
Semley Gate E9 . . . . 18 B2
Semley Ho SW1 . . . . 146 A3
Semley Pl SW1 . . . . . 146 A3
Senate St SE15 . . . . . 50 B1
Senators Lo 31 E3 . . 26 A3
Sendall Ct 12
SW11 . . . . 59 C4
Senior St W2 . . . . . . 100 A4
Senrab St E1 . . . . 32 C3
Seraph Ct EC1 . . . . . . 96 C4
Serenaders Rd 20
SW9 . . . . 173 B1
Sergeant Ind Est The
SW18 . . . . 59 A1
Serica Ct 14 SE10 . . 52 B3
Serjeants' Inn
EC4 . . . . 107 C1
Serlby Ct W14 . . . . . 126 C2
Serle St WC2 . . . . . . 107 A2
Sermon La EC4 . . . . 108 C1
Serpentine Ct 10
SE16 . . . . 40 C4
Serpentine Gallery
W2 . . . . 129 C4
Serpentine Rd
W2 . . . . 116 C3
Serpentine The
W2 . . . . 116 B3
Service Route No 1
E15 . . . . 19 C1
Service Route No 2 11
E15 . . . . 19 C1
Service Route No 3 12
E15 . . . . 19 C1
Servite Ho SE13 . . . . 52 A2
Servite RC Prim Sch
SW10 . . . . 156 C4
Setchell Rd SE1 . . . . 152 C4
Setchell Way SE1 . . . 152 C4
Seth St 28 SE16 . . . . 40 B4
Settlers Ct 11 E14 . . 34 C2
Settles St E1 . . . . . . 111 C2
Settrington Rd
SW6 . . . . 166 A1
Seven Dials WC2 . . . 106 A1
Seven Islands L Ctr
SE16 . . . . 40 B3
Seven Mills Prim Sch
27 E14 . . . . 41 C4
Sevenoaks Rd SE4 . . 66 B1
Seven Sisters Rd
Finsbury Pk N4 . . . . . . 6 A2
Stoke Newington N7, N4,
N15 . . . . 6 B4
Seven Stars Cnr
W12 . . . . 38 C3
Seven Stars Yd
E1 . . . . 111 A4
Severnake Cl E14 . . . 41 C2
Severn Ave 2
W10 . . . . 23 A2
Severn Way NW10 . . 8 B3
Severus Rd SW11 . . . 60 A3
Seville Ho 10 E1 . . . 125 C1
Seville Mews N1 . . . . 16 A1
Seville St SW1 . . . . . 131 A3

Sevington St W9 . . . . 88 A1
Seward St EC1 . . . . . . 96 C3
Sewardstone Rd
E2 . . . . 25 B3
Sewell Ho 7 N16 . . . . 16 A3
Sextant Ave E14 . . . . 42 C2
Sexton Ct 7 E14 . . . . 34 C2
Sexton's Ho 5
SE13 . . . . 52 B4
Seymour Ct
Putney SW15 . . . . 57 A3
Upper Clapton N16 . . . 7 C3
Seymour Gdns
SE4 . . . . 66 A4
Seymour Ho
Bloomsbury WC1 . . . . 94 A2
1 Clapham SW8 . . . . 171 A2
Somers Town NW1 . . . 93 C3
Seymour Mews
W1 . . . . 103 B2
Seymour Pl W1 . . . . . 102 C2
Seymour Rd
Acton W4 . . . . 37 B2
Wandsworth SW18 . . . 58 B1
Wimbledon SW19 . . . . 69 C1
Seymour St W1 . . . . 103 A1
Seymour Wlk
SW10 . . . . 156 C4
Seyssel St E14 . . . . . 42 B2
Shaa Rd W3 . . . . 28 C2
Shabana Ct 3
W12 . . . . 30 A1
Shackleton Ct
1 Dulwich SE21 . . . . . 75 C2
4 Isle of Dogs E14 . . 41 C1
4 Shepherd's Bush
W12 . . . . 39 A4
Shackleton Ho 5
E1 . . . . 32 B1
SHACKLEWELL 16 B4
Shacklewell Ho 3
E8 . . . . 16 B4
Shacklewell La E8 . . 16 B3
Shacklewell Prim Sch
6 E8 . . . . 16 B3
Shacklewell Rd
N16 . . . . 16 B4
Shacklewell Row
E8 . . . . 16 B4
Shacklewell St 20
E2 . . . . 24 B2 99 A3
Shad Thames SE1 . . 139 A4
SHADWELL 32 B2
Shadwell Gdns E1 . . 32 B2
Shadwell Pier head
E1 . . . . 32 B2
Shadwell Pl 1 E1 . . . 32 B2
Shadwell Sta E1 . . . . 32 A2
Shaftesbury Ave
W1 . . . . 119 C4
Shaftesbury Ct
Borough The SE1 . . . . 137 B2
1 Herne Hill SE5 . . . . 63 C3
Shoreditch N1 . . . . . . 87 C3
Streatham SW16 . . . . 73 C1
Shaftesbury Ctr
NW10 . . . . 22 C1
Shaftesbury Gdns
NW10 . . . . 21 A1
Shaftesbury Ho
1 Canning Town
E16 . . . . 35 B3
2 Stoke Newington
N16 . . . . 7 A1
W2 . . . . 114 B4

Shaftesbury Lo 9
E14 . . . . 34 A3
Shaftesbury Mews
2 Clapham Pk
SW4 . . . . 61 B2
W8 . . . . 127 C1
Shaftesbury Park
Chambers 1
SW11 . . . . 60 C4
Shaftesbury Rd
Finsbury Pk N4,
N19 . . . . 5 A3
Richmond TW9 . . . . . 54 A4
Shaftesbury St N1 . . 87 B1
Shafteswood Ct
SW17 . . . . 72 B1
Shafto Mews
SW1 . . . . 131 A1
Shafton Rd E9 . . . . . . 25 C4
Shaftsbury Park Prim
Sch 15 SW11 . . . . . . 169 B1
Shafts Ct EC3 . . . . . 110 A1
Shahjalal Ho 10
E2 . . . . 24 C3
Shakespeare Ave 7
NW10 . . . . 20 C4
Shakespeare Ho 3
E9 . . . . 17 B1
Shakespeare Rd
Acton W3 . . . . 28 B1
Brixton SE24 . . . . 63 A3
Stonebridge NW10 . . . 20 C4
Shakespeare's Globe
Theatre (site of)
SE1 . . . . 123 A2
Shakespeare Twr
EC2 . . . . 109 A4
Shakspeare Mews 7
N16 . . . . 16 A4
Shakspeare Wlk
N16 . . . . 16 A4
Shalbourne Sq E9 . . 18 B2
Shalcomb St
SW10 . . . . 157 A3
Shalden Ho SW15 . . . 56 B1
Shalfleet Dr W10 . . . . 30 C2
Shalford Ho SE1 . . . . 137 C2
Shalford Ct N1 . . . . . . 86 A2
Shalford Ho SE1 . . . . 137 C2
Shalimar Gdns W3 . . 28 B2
Shalimar Lo W3 . . . . . 28 B2
Shalimar Rd W3 . . . . 28 B2
Shalstone Rd SW14,
TW9 . . . . 55 A4
Shamrock St SW4 . . . 61 C4
Shandon Ct SE4 . . . . 51 A1
Shandon Rd SW4 . . . 61 B1
Shand St SE1 . . . . . 138 B4
Shandy St E1 . . . . . . 25 C1
Shan Ho WC1 . . . . . . 94 C1
Shannon Ct
11 Peckham SE15 . . . 49 B3
Stoke Newington
N16 . . . . 7 A1
Willesden NW10 . . . . . 8 A4
Shannon Gr SW9 . . . 62 B3
Shannon Pl NW8 . . . 80 B2
Shanti Ct SW18 . . . . 70 C3
Shapla Prim Sch 30
E1 . . . . 125 C3
Shardcroft Ave
SE24 . . . . 63 A2
Shardeloes Rd
SE14 . . . . 51 B1
Shard's Sq SE15 . . . . 49 C4
Shard The SE1 . . . . . 123 C1

Sharebourne Ho
SW2 . . . . 62 C2
Sharman Ho 13
E14 . . . . 34 B3
Sharnbrook Ho
W6 . . . . 155 B4
Sharon Gdns E9 . . . . 25 B4
Sharon Rd W4 . . . . . . 37 C1
Sharp Ho SW8 . . . . . . 61 A4
Sharples Hall St 8
NW1 . . . . 12 B1
Sharpness Ct 2
SE15 . . . . 49 B3
Sharratt St SE15 . . . . 50 B4
Sharsted St SE17 . . 150 A1
Sharwood WC1 . . . . . 85 A1
Shaver's Pl SW1 . . . 119 B3
Shawbury Ct SE22 . . 64 B2
Shawbury Rd SE22 . . 64 B2
Shaw Cres 5 E14 . . . 33 A3
Shaw Ct
3 Acton Green
W3 . . . . 37 B3
11 Battersea SW11 . . 59 C4
Upper Holloway N19 . . 5 A2
Shawfield St SW3 . . 144 B1
Shawford Ct 5
SW15 . . . . 68 C4
Shaw Rd SE22 . . . . . . 64 A3
Shearling Way N7 . . . 14 A2
Shearsmith Ho 15
E1 . . . . 125 C4
Shearwater Ct 24
SE8 . . . . 51 B4
Sheba Pl E1 . . . . 24 B1 99 A1
Sheen Common Dr
SW14,TW10 . . . . 54 C2
Sheen Court Rd
TW10 . . . . 54 C3
Sheen Ct TW10 . . . . . 54 C3
Sheendale Rd
TW9 . . . . 54 B3
Sheen Gate Gdns
SW14 . . . . 55 B3
Sheengate Mans
SW14 . . . . 55 B3
Sheen Gr N1 . . . . 85 B4
Sheen La SW14 . . . . . 55 B3
Sheen Mount Prim
Sch SW14 . . . . 55 A2
Sheen Pk TW10,
TW9 . . . . 54 A3
Sheen Rd TW10,
TW9 . . . . 54 B3
Sheen Wood
SW14 . . . . 55 B2
Sheepcote La
SW11 . . . . 169 A1
Sheep La E8 . . . . 25 A4
Sheffield Ho 5
SE15 . . . . 49 B2
Sheffield Sq 2 E3 . . . 26 B2
Sheffield St WC2 . . . 106 C1
Sheffield Terr
W8 . . . . 31 C1 113 C4
Shelbourne Ho 20
N19 . . . . 4 C4
Shelburne Ct
SW15 . . . . 57 C2
Shelburne Rd N7 . . . 14 B4
Shelbury Rd SE22 . . . 65 A2
Sheldon Ct SW8 . . . 162 A1
Sheldon Ho 9 E9 . . . 17 C2
Sheldon Pl E2 . . . . . . 25 A3
Sheldon Rd NW2 . . . . 9 C4
Sheldon Sq W2 . . . . 101 A3

Sheldrake Ho 15
SE16 . . . . 40 C2
Sheldrake Pl W8 . . . 127 B4
Shelduck Ct 37
SE8 . . . . 51 B4
Shelford Ho N1 . . . . . 6 C1
Shelgate Rd SW11 . . 60 B2
Shell Ctr SE1 . . . . . . 121 A1
Shelley Cl SE15 . . . . . 50 A1
Shelley Ct
Finsbury Pk N4 . . . . . . 5 B3
SW3 . . . . 159 A4
Shelley Ho
41 Bethnal Green
E2 . . . . 25 B2
Chelsea SW1 . . . . . . 160 C4
9 Stoke Newington
N16 . . . . 16 A4
Walworth SE17 . . . . . 151 A2
Shelley Rd NW10 . . . 20 C4
Shellgrove Rd 31
N16 . . . . 16 A3
Shellness Rd E5 . . . . 17 A3
Shell Rd SE13 . . . . . . 67 A4
Shellwood Rd
SW11 . . . . 168 C1
Shelmerdine Cl
E3 . . . . 33 C4
Shelton St WC2 . . . . 106 A1
Shene Bldg EC1 . . . 107 B4
Shene Sch SW14 . . . 56 A3
Shenfield St N1 . . . . . 24 A3
Shenley Rd SE5 . . . . 49 A2
Shepard Ho
SW11 . . . . 59 C4
Sheperdess Pl N1 . . 97 A4
Shepherd Cl W1 . . . 117 B4
Sheperdess Wlk
N1 . . . . 87 A1
Shepherd Ho
Barnsbury N7 . . . . . . 14 A2
10 Poplar E14 . . . . . . 34 A3
Shepherd Mkt
W1 . . . . 118 A1
SHEPHERD'S
BUSH 30 A1
Shepherd's Bush Gn
W12 . . . . 39 B4
Shepherd's Bush
Market W12 . . . . 39 B4
Shepherd's Bush Mkt
Sta W12 . . . . 30 B1
Shepherd's Bush
Overground Sta
W12 . . . . 39 C4
Shepherd's Bush Pl
W12 . . . . 39 C4
Shepherd's Bush Rd
W6 . . . . 39 B3
Shepherd's Bush Sta
W12 . . . . 39 C4
Shepherds Ct 8
W12 . . . . 39 C4
Shepherd's La E9 . . . 17 C2
Shepherds Path 9
W12 . . . . 30 A2
Shepherd St W1 . . . 118 A1
Shepherd's Wlk
NW3 . . . . 11 C4
Sheppard Dr SE16 . . 40 A1
Sheppard Ho
31 Hackney E2 . . . . . 24 C3
2 Streatham SW2 . . . 74 C3
Shepperton Rd N1 . . 87 B4
Sheppey Ho 18 E5 . . 17 A4

Shepton Ct SW11 .. **167** C4
Shepton Hos **11**
E2 .... **25** B2
Sherard Ct N19 .... **5** A1
Sherard Ho **24** E9 .. **17** B1
Sheraton Ho SW1 **160** B4
Sheraton St W1 ... **105** B1
Sherborne Ho
Pimlico SW1 .... **146** B2
South Lambeth
SW8 .... **162** C1
Sherborne La EC4 **123** C4
Sherborne St N1 .. **87** B4
Sherbourne Ct
SW5 .... **142** A4
Sherbrooke Ho **3**
E2 .... **25** B3
Sherbrooke Rd
SW6 .... **154** B1
Sherbrooke Terr
SW6 .... **154** B1
Shere Ho SE1 ..... **137** B2
Sherfield Gdns
SW15 .... **56** B1
Sheridan Bldgs
WC2 .... **106** B1
Sheridan Ct
Earl's Ct SW5 ... **142** A3
South Hampstead
NW6 .... **11** B1
South Lambeth
SW9 .... **173** A3
Sheridan Ho
SE11 .... **149** C3
7 Stoke Newington
N16 .... **7** A1
Sheridan Pl SW13 ..**56** B4
Sheridan St **31** E1 ..**32** A3
Sheringdale Prim Sch
SW18 .... **70** B3
Sheringham Ho
NW1 .... **79** C4
Sheringham Ho
NW1 .... **102** B4
Sheringham Mews **4**
SW18 .... **71** B2
Sheringham Rd
N7 .... **14** C2
Sherlock Ct NW8 ..**79** C4
Sherlock Holmes Mus
NW1 .... **91** A1
Sherlock Mews
W1 .... **103** B4
Sherren Ho **3** E1 ..**25** B1
Sherrick Green Rd
NW10 .... **9** A3
Sherriff Ct NW6 ...**10** C2
Sherriff Rd NW6....**10** C2
Sherrin Rd E10 ....**19** A4
Sherston Ct
Finsbury WC1 ....**95** B3
Newington SE1 ..**150** B4
Sherwin Ho **1**
SE11 .... **163** B4
Sherwin Rd SE14 ..**50** C2
Sherwood NW6....**10** A1
Sherwood Cl
SW13 .... **57** A4
Sherwood Ct
1 Battersea
SW11 .... **59** B4
St Johns SE13 ....**52** A1
W1 .... **102** C3
Sherwood Gdns
Bermondsey SE16 ..**40** A1

Sherwood Gdns
continued
Millwall E14 ...... **41** C2
Sherwood Ho N4 ...**6** B4
Sherwood St W1 **119** A4
Shetland Rd E3....**26** B3
Shillaker Ct W3 ...**29** B1
Shillibeer Pl W1..**102** B3
Shillingford Ho **40**
E3 .... **27** A2
Shillingford St **23**
N1 .... **15** A1
Shillingstone Ho
W14 .... **126** B1
Shinfield St W12 ..**30** B3
Shipka Rd SW12...**73** A3
Ship La SW14 .....**45** B1
Shiplake Ho **45**
E2 .... **24** B2 **98** C3
Shipley Ho **31**
SW8 .... **171** B1
Ship & Mermaid Row
SE1 .... **138** A4
Ship St SE8 ....**51** C2
Ship Tavern Pas
EC3 .... **124** A4
Shipton Ho
1 Camden Town
NW5 .... **12** C2
14 Haggerston E2 ..**24** B3
Shipton St
E2 .... **24** B2 **99** A4
Shipwright Rd
SE16 .... **41** A4
Shirbutt St E14....**34** A2
Shire Pl SW18 ....**71** B4
Shirland Mews
W9 .... **23** B2
Shirland Rd W9 ...**23** C1
Shirley Gr SW11 ..**60** C4
Shirley Ho **5** SE5 ..**48** C3
Shirley Rd W4 ....**37** C4
Shirley St E16....**35** B3
Shirlock Rd NW3 ..**12** B4
Shoe La EC4 .... **107** C2
Shooters Hill Rd SE3,
SE10 .... **53** A2
Shoot-Up Hill
NW2 .... **10** A2
Shopstop SW11 ...**60** A3
Shore Bsns Ctr **8**
E9 .... **17** B1
SHOREDITCH **87** C1
Shoreditch Ct **2**
E8 .... **16** B1
Shoreditch High St
E1 .... **24** B1
Shoreditch High St
Sta E2 .... **24** B1
Shoreditch Ho N1 ..**97** C3
Shoreham Cl
SW18 .... **59** A2
Shore Ho SW8 ....**61** A4
Shore Mews **30** E9 ..**17** B1
Shore Pl E9 ....**17** B1
Shore Rd E9 ....**17** B1
Shorncliffe Rd
SE1 .... **152** C2
Shorrolds Rd
SW6 .... **155** A2
Shortcroft Mead Ct
NW10 .... **8** C3
Shorter St EC3 .. **125** A4
Shortlands W6 ....**39** C2

Short Rd W4 ......**46** A4
Shorts Gdns WC2 **106** A1
Short St SE1 .... **135** C4
Shottendane Rd
SW6 .... **165** B4
Shottfield Ave
SW14 .... **56** A3
Shottsford **1** W11 ..**31** C3
Shoulder of Mutton
Alley **10** E14 ......**33** A2
Shouldham St
W1 .... **102** B3
Shreveport Ho **22**
N19 .... **5** A4
Shrewsbury Ave
SW14 .... **55** C3
Shrewsbury Cres
NW10 .... **20** C4
Shrewsbury Ho
Chelsea SW3 .. **158** A3
Kennington SE11 ..**163** A3
Shrewsbury Mews **33**
W2 .... **31** C4
Shrewsbury Rd
W2 .... **31** C3
W10 .... **22** B1
Shropshire Ho
WC1 .... **93** A1
Shroton St NW1 ..**102** B4
Shrubbery Cl N1 ..**87** A3
Shrubland Rd E8 ..**24** C4
Shrubs Ho SW1 .. **147** C3
Shurland Gdns
SE15 .... **49** B3
Shuters Sq W14 .. **140** C1
Shuttle St
E1 .... **24** C1 **99** B1
Shuttleworth Rd
SW11 .... **168** A2
Sibella Rd SW4.. **171** C1
Sicilian Ave WC1 .. **106** B3
Siddings Mews N7.. **14** C4
Siddons Ct WC2 .. **106** C1
Siddons Ho **8**
NW3 .... **12** B3
Siddons La NW1 .. **91** A1
Sidford Ho SE1 ..**135** A1
Sidford Pl SE1 .. **135** A1
Sidgwick Ho **20**
SW9 .... **172** B1
Sidings Mews N7 ...**14** C4
Sidlaw Ho N16 ....**7** B3
Sidmouth Ho
18 Camberwell
SE15 .... **49** C3
Marylebone W1 ..**102** B2
26 Streatham SW2 ..**74** C4
Sidmouth Mews
WC1 .... **94** C3
Sidmouth Par NW2 ..**9** B1
Sidmouth Rd NW2 ..**9** B1
Sidmouth St WC1 ..**94** C3
Sidney Boyd Ct
NW6 .... **10** C1
Sidney Godley (VC)
Ho **31** E2 ....**25** B2
Sidney Gr EC1 ....**86** A1
Sidney Ho **4** E2 ..**25** B3
Sidney Miller Ct **8**
W3 .... **28** A1
Sidney Rd SW9 .. **173** A1
Sidney Sq E1 .....**32** B4
Sidney St E1 ......**32** B4
Sidworth St **8** E8 ..**17** A1
Siebert Rd SE3 ....**53** C4

Siege Ho **14** E1.... **32** A3
Sigdon Rd E8 ......**16** C3
Signal Ho
9 London E8........**17** A1
E1 .... **17** A1
Signmakers Yd
NW1 .... **82** B3
Silbury Ho **6**
SE26 .... **76** C1
Silbury St N1 ......**97** B4
Silchester Rd W10..**30** C3
Silesia Bldgs E8....**17** A1
Silex St SE1 .... **136** B3
Silkin Mews **27**
SE15 .... **49** C3
Silk Mews SE11 .. **149** C1
Silk Mills Path
SE13 .... **67** B4
Silk Mills Sq E9 ...**18** B2
Silk St **2** EC2 .. **109** A4
Sillitoe Ho N1 ....**87** C3
Silsoe Ho NW1 ...**82** B1
Silverbirch Wlk **1**
NW3 .... **12** C2
Silverburn Ho **3**
SW9 .... **173** B4
Silver Cl SE14 ....**51** A3
Silver Cres W4 ....**37** A2
Silver Ct N19 ......**4** B1
Silverdale NW1 ...**92** C4
Silverdale Ct EC1 ..**96** B2
Silvermere Rd SE6 ..**67** A1
Silver Pl W1 .... **119** A4
Silver Rd
Shepherd's Bush
W12 .... **30** C2
St Johns SE13 ....**67** A4
Silverthorn **17**
NW6 .... **78** B3
Silverthorne Rd
SW8 .... **170** B1
Silverton Rd W6...**47** C4
Silvertown Way
E16 .... **35** B3
Silver Wlk SE16 ...**33** B1
Silvester Ho
27 Bethnal Green
E2 .... **25** B2
1 Notting Hill W11 ..**31** B3
8 Stepney E1 ......**32** A3
Silvester Rd SE22..**64** B2
Silvester St SE1 .. **137** B3
Silwex Ho
E1 .... **24** B1 **98** C1
Silwood St SE16 ...**40** B1
Simla Ho N1 .... **137** C3
Simmonds Ct
SW5 .... **142** A3
Simmons Ho
20 Bethnal Green
E2 .... **25** B2
Finsbury Pk N7 ..**5** B2
Simms Ct SW6 ....**58** A4
Simms Rd SE1 .. **153** C3
Simon Cl
W11 ...... **31** B2 **113** A4
Simon Ct W9 ......**23** C2
Simon Lo **31** SW19 ..**69** C3
Simon Marks Jewish
Prim Sch **8** N16 ..**7** B2
Simons Wlk E15 ...**19** C3
Simpson Dr W3 ....**28** C3
Simpson Ho
Lisson Gr NW8 ....**90** A3
Vauxhall SE11 .. **148** C1
Simpson's Rd E14..**34** A2

Simpson St SW11 **168** A1
Sinclair Ct N5......**15** B2
Sinclair Gdns W14..**39** C4
Sinclair Ho **1**
W12 .... **73** C3
Sinclair Mans **13**
W12 .... **39** C4
Sinclair Pl SE4 ....**66** C1
Sinclair Rd W14 .. **126** A2
Sinclairs Ho **18** E3..**26** B3
Singer St EC2 .....**97** C3
Sion Ho SE13 .....**67** B3
Sion-Manning RC Sch
for Girls
B Kensal Town
W10 .... **31** A4
6 North Kensington
W10 .... **30** C4
Sir Abraham Dawes
Cotts SW15.......**58** A3
Sir Alexander Cl
W3 .... **29** B1
Sir Alexander Rd
W3 .... **29** B1
Sirdar Rd
W11 ...... **31** A2 **112** A3
Sir Francis Drake
Prim Sch **1** SE8..**41** A1
Sirinham Point
SW8 .... **163** A3
Sirius Bldg **13** E1 ..**32** C2
Sir James Barrie Prim
Sch SW8 ...... **171** A3
Sir John Cass's
Foundation &
Redcoat CE Sec Sch
10 E1 .... **32** C4
Sir John Cass's
Foundation Prim
Sch EC3 .... **110** B3
Sir John Kirk Cl **33**
SE5 .... **48** B3
Sir John Lillie Prim
Sch SW6 ...... **154** B3
Sir John Soane's Mus
WC2 .... **106** C2
Sir Oswald Stoll
Foundation The
SW6 .... **156** A2
Sir Thomas Abney
Prim Sch N16 .....**6** C3
Sir Thomas More Est
SW3 .... **157** C3
Sir William Burrough
Prim Sch **27** E14..**33** B3
Sir William Powell's
Almshos SW6 ....**58** A4
Sise La EC4 ...... **109** B1
Siskin Ho **14** SE16 ..**40** C2
Sispara Gdns
SW18 .... **58** B1
Sissinghurst Ho **17**
SE15 .... **50** B4
Sister Mabel's Way **15**
SE15 .... **49** C3
Sisters Ave SW11..**60** B3
Sisters of St
Marcellina Sch **34**
NW3 .... **11** B4
Sistova Rd SW12 ..**73** A3
Sisulu Pl SW9 .....**62** C4
Site of Changing of
the Guard SW1 .. **132** C3
Sivill Ho **9**
E2 .... **24** B2 **99** A4

Siward Rd SW17 .... 71 B1
Six Bridges Ind Est 16
SE1 .... 153 C1
Sixth Ave W10 ..... 23 A2
Skardu Rd NW2 ..... 10 A3
Skeena Hill SW18,
SW19 .... 70 A4
Skeggs Ho 5 E14 .. 42 B3
Skegness Ho 3
N7 .... 14 B1
Skelbrook St
SW18 .... 71 B2
Skelgill Rd SW15 .. 58 B3
Skelton Cl 7 E8 ... 16 B2
Skelton Ho N16 .... 16 A3
Skelwith Rd W6 .... 47 B4
Skenfrith Ho SE15 . 50 A4
Sketchley Gdns
SE16 .... 40 C1
Skiffington Cl
SW2 .... 74 C3
Skinner Pl SW1 ... 145 B3
Skinners Company
Sch (Upper) 10
N16 .... 7 B4
Skinners La EC4 .. 123 A4
Skinner St EC1 .... 95 C2
Skipsea Ho SW18 .. 59 C1
Skipton Ho SE4 .... 66 A3
Skipwith Bldg
EC1 .... 107 B4
Skipworth Rd E9 ... 25 B4
Skua Cl 33 SE8 .... 51 B4
Skyline Cl SE1 .... 138 C1
Skyline Plaza Bldg 19
E1 .... 111 C2
Skylines E14 ...... 42 B4
Slade Ct NW2 ...... 10 A3
Sladen Pl 26 E5 ... 17 A4
Slagrove Pl SE13 .. 67 A2
Slaidburn St
SW10 .... 157 A3
Slaithwaite Rd
SE13 .... 67 B3
Slaney Ct NW10 .... 9 B1
Slaney Pl 1 N7 ... 14 C3
Sleaford Ho 18 SE3 26 C1
Sleaford Ind Est
SW8 .... 161 A1
Sleaford St SW8 .. 161 A1
Sleat Ho 11 E3 ... 26 B3
Slievemore Cl 8
SW4 .... 61 C4
Sligo Ho 8 E1 .... 25 C1
Slingsby Pl WC2 .. 120 A4
Slippers Pl SE16 .. 40 A3
Slipway Ho 1 E14 . 42 A1
Sloane Ave SW3 ... 144 B3
Sloane Avenue Mans
SW3 .... 144 B3
Sloane Ct E SW3 .. 145 B2
Sloane Ct W SW3 .. 145 B2
Sloane Gate Mans
SW1 .... 145 B4
Sloane Gdns SW1 .. 145 B3
Sloane Ho 7 E9 ... 17 B1
Sloane Sq SW1 .... 145 A3
Sloane Square Sta
SW1 .... 145 B3
Sloane St SW1 .... 131 A1
Sloane Terr SW1 .. 145 B4
Sloane Terr Mans
SW1 .... 145 B4
Sly St E1 .... 111 C1
Smallbrook Mews
W2 .... 101 B1

Smalley Cl N16 .... 7 B1
Smart's Pl WC1,
WC2 .... 106 B2
Smart St E2 .... 25 C2
Smeaton Ct SE1 .. 136 C1
Smeaton Rd SW18 .. 70 C4
Smeaton St E1 .... 32 A1
Smedley St SW4 .. 171 C2
Smeed Rd E3 ...... 18 C1
Smiles Pl SE13 .... 52 B1
Smith Cl SE16 ..... 32 C1
Smithfield Mkt
EC1 .... 108 B3
Smithfield St EC1 . 108 A3
Smith's Ct W1 .... 119 B4
Smith Sq SW1 .... 134 A1
Smith St SW3 .... 144 C1
Smith's Yd SW18 .. 71 B2
Smith Terr SW3 .. 144 C1
Smithwood Cl
SW19 .... 70 A3
Smithy St E1 ...... 32 B4
Smithy Street Sch 34
E1 .... 32 B4
Smugglers Way
SW18 .... 59 A3
Smyrk's Rd SE17 .. 152 A1
Smyrna Mans 8
NW6 .... 10 C1
Smyrna Rd NW6 ... 10 C1
Smythe St E14 .... 34 A2
Snarsgate St W10 . 30 B4
Sneath Ave NW11 .. 1 B4
Sneyd Rd NW2 ..... 9 B3
Snowberry Cl E11 . 19 C4
Snowbury Rd 6
SW6 .... 166 B1
Snowden St
EC2 .... 24 A1 98 A1
Snowe Ho SE27 .... 75 A1
Snow Hill EC1 .... 108 A3
Snowman Ho NW6 .. 78 B4
Snowsfields SE1 .. 137 C4
Snowsfields Prim Sch
SE1 .... 138 A4
Soames St SE15 ... 64 B4
Soane Ct 12 NW1 . 13 B1
Soane Ho SE17 ... 151 C1
Soaphouse La
TW8 .... 44 A3
Sobell L Ctr N7 ... 5 B1
SOHO 105 B1
Soho W1 .... 105 B2
Soho Parish CE Prim
Sch SW1 .... 119 B4
Soho Sq W1 ...... 105 B2
Soho St W1 .... 105 B2
Sojourner-Truth Cl 11
E8 .... 17 A2
Solander Gdns
E1 13 Shadwell E1 .. 32 B2
Stepney E1 .... 32 A2
Soldene Ct N7 .... 14 B2
Solebay St E1 .... 26 A1
Solent Ho 6 E1 ... 33 A4
Solent Rd NW6 .... 10 C3
Soley Mews WC1 .. 95 B4
Solidarity Ho 6
NW10 .... 9 A1
Solna Ave SW15 .. 57 B2
Solomon's Pas
SE15 .... 65 A3
Solon New Rd
SW4 .... 62 A3
Solon Rd SW2 ..... 62 A3
Solway Ho 12 E1 .. 25 C1

Solway Rd SE22 ... 64 C3
Somali Rd NW2 .... 10 B3
Somborne Ho 11
SW15 .... 68 C4
Sombrook Ho
SE11 .... 149 B3
Somer Ct SW6 .... 155 B3
Somerfield Rd N4 . 6 A2
Somerfield St
SE16 .... 40 C1
Somerford Gr N16 . 16 B4
Somerford Grove Est
N16 .... 16 B4
Somerford St E1 .. 25 A1
Somerford Way
SE16 .... 41 A4
Somerleyton Rd
SW9 .... 62 C3
Somers Cl NW1 ... 83 B2
Somers Cres 2 W2 102 A1
Somerset Gdns
Highgate N6 .... 3 C4
St Johns SE13 .... 52 A2
Somerset Ho
WC2 .... 121 A4
Somerset Ho
SW19 .... 70 A1
Somerset Lo
SW15 .... 57 A3
Somerset Rd
Bedford Pk W4 .... 37 C3
Wimbledon SW19 .. 70 C1
Somerset Sq W14 126 C3
Somers Pl SW2 ... 74 B4
Somers Rd SW2 ... 62 B1
SOMERS TOWN 93 C4
Somers Town Est
NW1 .... 83 A1
Somerton Ave
TW9 .... 55 A4
Somerton Rd
Cricklewood NW2 ... 1 A1
Nunhead SE15 .... 65 A3
Somerville Ave
SW13 .... 47 B4
Somerville Cl
SW9 .... 173 A2
Somerville Ho 10
SW15 .... 57 C1
Somerville Point
SE16 .... 41 B4
Sonderburg Rd 13
N7 .... 5 B2
Sondes St SE17 .. 48 C4
Sonia Gdns NW10 . 8 B4
Sonning Ho 27
E2 .... 24 B2 98 C3
Sophia Cl N7 ..... 14 B2
Sophia Ho 10 W6 . 39 B1
Sophia Sq 16 SE16 33 A2
Soseki Mus SW4 .. 61 A4
Sotheby Rd N5 ... 15 B4
Sotheran Cl E8 ... 24 C4
Sotheron Pl SW6 . 156 B1
Soudan Rd SW11 . 168 C3
Souldern Rd 10
W14 .... 39 C3
SOUTH ACTON 37 B4
South Acton Sta W3,
W4 .... 37 B3

South Africa Rd
W12 .... 30 A2
Southall Pl SE1 .. 137 B3
Southam Ho 9
W10 .... 23 A1
Southampton Bldgs
WC2 .... 107 B3
Southampton Pl
WC1 .... 106 B3
Southampton Rd
NW5 .... 12 B3
Southampton Row
WC1 .... 106 B4
Southampton St
WC2 .... 120 B4
Southampton Way
SE5 .... 49 A3
South Audley St
W1 .... 117 C2
South Ave TW9 ... 44 C1
SOUTH BANK 120 C1
South Bank Bsns Ctr
SW8 .... 161 C3
Southbank
International Sch 14
SW11 .... 11 B2
Southbank
International Sch
(Westminster
Campus) W1 .... 104 A4
Southbank Int Sch
W11 .... 31 C2 113 B3
South Bank Univ
SW8 .... 171 C4
South Bank University
(Erlang House)
SE1 .... 136 A3
South Bermondsey
Sta SE16 .... 40 B1
South Black Lion La
7 W6 .... 38 C1
South Bldg SW1 .. 133 A2
South Block 20 E1 32 B2
South Bolton Gdns
SW10 .... 142 B2
Southborough Ho
SE17 .... 152 B2
Southborough Rd
E9 .... 25 B4
South Building
SE10 .... 52 C3
Southbury NW8 ... 79 A4
South Camden Com
Sch NW1 .... 83 B2
South Carriage Dr SW1,
SW7 .... 130 C4
South Chelsea Coll 22
SW9 .... 62 B3
South Colonnade The
E14 .... 34 A1
South Cres
Newham E16 ...... 27 C1
WC1 .... 105 B3
Southcroft 8
NW10 .... 20 C4
South Ct SW15 ... 57 C1
Southdean Gdns
SW19 .... 70 B2

Southdown N7 .... 14 A2
South Eastern Univ 3
N7 .... 5 B1
South Eaton Pl
SW1 .... 145 C4
South Edwardes Sq
W8 .... 127 B1
South End W8 .... 128 B2
South End Cl NW3 12 A4
South End Gn
NW3 .... 12 A4
South End Rd
NW3 .... 12 A4
South End Row
W8 .... 128 B2
Southerngate Way
SE14 .... 51 A3
Southern Gr E3 .. 26 B1
Southern Row
W10 .... 23 A1
Southern St N1 ... 84 C2
Southern Way
SE10 .... 43 B3
Southernwood Ret Pk
SE1 .... 153 A2
Southerton Rd W6 39 B2
Southey Ho SE17 . 151 A2
Southey Mews
E16 .... 35 C1
Southey Rd SW9 . 173 B4
Southfield Lo W4 . 37 C4
Southfield Prim Sch
W4 .... 38 A4
Southfield Rd W4 . 37 C4
SOUTHFIELDS 71 A3
Southfields Com Coll
SW18 .... 70 C3
Southfields Rd
SW18 .... 58 C1
Southfields Sta
SW18 .... 71 A4
Southgate Ct N1 .. 15 C1
Southgate Gr N1 . 15 C1
Southgate Rd N1 . 87 C4
South Gr N6 .... 3 C3
South Grove Ho N6 . 3 C3
SOUTH HACKNEY . 25 B4
SOUTH
HAMPSTEAD 11 B3
South Hampstead
High Sch 11
NW3 .... 11 C2
South Hampstead Sta
NW8 .... 11 B1
South Hill Pk NW3 12 A4
South Hill Pk Gdns
NW3 .... 12 A4
Southill St E14 ... 34 A3
South Island Pl
SW9 .... 163 B1
SOUTH
KENSINGTON 143 A3
South Kensington Sta
SW7 .... 143 C4
South Kensington
Station Arc SW7 143 C4
SOUTH
LAMBETH 172 B3
South Lambeth Pl
SW8 .... 162 B4
South Lambeth Rd
SW8 .... 162 B2
Southlands Dr
SW19 .... 69 C2

South Lo NW8 .... **89** B4
South London Gall
SE5 ....**49** A2
South London
Montessori Sch
SW11 ....**168** A3
Southmead Prim Sch
🔟 SW19 ....**70** A3
Southmead Rd
SW19 ....**70** A3
South Molton La
W1 ....**104** A1
South Molton Rd
E16 ....**35** C3
South Molton St
W1 ....**104** A1
Southmoor Way
E9 ....**18** B3
Southolm St
SW11 ....**170** B3
South Par W4 ......**37** C2
South Parade
SW3 ....**143** C2
South Park Mews
SW6 ....**59** A4
South Pl EC2 ......**109** C3
South Pl Mews
EC2 ....**109** C3
South Quay Plaza
E14 ....**42** A4
South Quay Sta
E14 ....**42** A4
South Rise W2 ....**116** B4
South Row SE3 ....**53** B1
South Sea St SE16 .**41** B3
Southside N7 ......**13** C4
South Side W6 ....**38** B3
Southside Ind Est
SW8 ....**170** C4
Southside Quarter 🔟
SW11 ....**168** C2
Southside Sh Ctr
SW18 ....**59** A1
South Sq WC1 ....**107** B3
South St W1 ......**117** C2
South Tenter St
E1 ....**111** A1
South Terr SW7 ...**144** A4
South Thames Coll
(Putney Ctr) 🔟
SW15 ....**57** C2
South Thames Coll
(Roehampton Ctr)
SW15 ....**56** C1
South Thames Coll
(Wandsworth Ctr) 🔟
SW18 ....**59** A2
Southvale Rd SE3 .**53** A1
Southview Ave
NW10 ....**8** B3
South Villas NW1 ..**13** C2
Southville
London SW8 ......**171** C3
South Lambeth
SW8 ....**172** A3
SOUTHWARK **40** B2
Southwark Bridge SE1,
EC4 ....**123** A3
Southwark Bridge Rd
SE1 ....**123** A1
Southwark Cath
SE1 ....**123** B2
Southwark Coll
SE1 ....**136** A4

Southwark Coll
(Blackfriars Ctr)
SE1 ....**122** A1
Southwark Coll
(Camberwell Ctr)
SE5 ....**49** A3
Southwark Coll
(Grange Ctr)
SE1 ....**138** B1
Southwark Coll
(Surrey Docks Ctr)
🔟 SE16 ....**40** A3
Southwark Park Est
🔟 SE16 ....**40** A2
Southwark Park Prim
Sch 🔟 SE16 ......**40** A2
Southwark Park Rd
SE16 ....**153** B4
Southwark Pk Sports
Complex SE16 ....**40** B2
Southwark Sta
SE1 ....**122** C1
Southwater Cl 🔟
E14 ....**33** B3
Southway N20 ......**2** A4
Southwell Gdns
SW7 ....**142** C3
Southwell Ho
🔟 Bermondsey
SE16 ....**40** A2
🔟 Stoke Newington
N16 ....**16** A3
Southwell Rd SE5 .**63** B4
South Wharf Rd
W2 ....**101** C2
Southwick Mews
W2 ....**101** C2
Southwick Pl W2 .**102** A1
Southwick St W2 ..**102** A2
Southwick Yd W2 .**102** A1
Southwold Mans
W9 ....**23** C2
Southwold Prim Sch
E5 ....**17** B3
Southwood Ave N6 ..**4** A4
Southwood Ct EC1 ..**96** A3
Southwood Ho
W11 ....31 A2 **112** A4
Southwood Hts N6 ..**4** A4
Southwood La N6 ...**3** C4
Southwood Lawn Rd
N6 ....**4** A4
Southwood Park
N6 ....**3** C4
Southwood Smith Ho
4 E2 ....**25** A2
Southwood Smith St
N1 ....**86** A3
South Worple Ave
SW14 ....**56** A4
Southwyck Ho
SW9 ....**62** D3
South Yd EC1 ....**109** B4
Sovereign Cl E1 ...**32** A2
Sovereign Cres
SE16 ....**33** A2
Sovereign Ct
🔟 Richmond
TW9 ....**54** B3
🔟 Stepney E1 ....**32** A2
Sovereign Ho 🔟
E1 ....**25** A1
Sovereign Mews 🔟
E2 ....**24** B3
Sovereign Pk
NW10 ....**20** A1

Space Bsns Pk
NW10 ....**20** A2
Spa Ct 🔟 SE16 ...**139** B1
Spafield St EC1 ....**95** B2
Spalding Ho SE4 ..**66** A3
Spanby Rd E3 ......**26** C1
Spaniards Cl NW11 ..**2** C3
Spaniards End NW3 ..**2** C3
Spaniards Rd NW3 ..**2** B2
Spanish Bilingual Sch
W10 ....**31** A4
Spanish Pl W1 ....**103** C2
Spanish Rd SW18 .**59** B2
Spa Rd SE16 ......**139** A1
Sparke Terr 🔟
E16 ....**35** B3
Sparkford Ho
SW11 ....**167** C4
Sparks Cl W3 ......**28** C3
Sparsholt Rd N19 ..**5** B3
Sparta St SE10 ....**52** B2
Spa Sch SE1 ......**153** B4
Spa View SE16 ....**74** B1
Spear Mews SW5 .**141** C3
Spears Rd N19 ....**5** A3
Spectrum Ho NW5 .**12** C4
Spedan Cl NW3 ....**2** B1
Speechly Mews
E8 ....**16** B3
Speed Ho EC2 ....**109** B4
Speedwell St 🔟
SE8 ....**51** C3
Speedy Pl WC1 ....**94** A3
Speldhurst Rd
Bedford Pk W4 ....**37** C3
Homerton E9 ......**17** C1
Spellbrook Wlk N1 .**87** A4
Spelman Ho 🔟
E1 ....**111** B3
Spelman St E1 ....**111** B4
Spence Cl SE16 ....**41** B4
Spencer Gdns
SW14 ....**55** B2
Spencer Ho
🔟 Clapham SW8 ..**171** B1
🔟 Putney SW19 ...**69** C3
Vale of Health NW3 ..**2** C1
Wimbledon SW19 ..**69** C1
Spencer House Mus
SW1 ....**118** C1
Spencer Mews
Fulham W6 ......**154** A4
South Lambeth
SW9 ....**172** C3
Spencer Park Ct
SW18 ....**59** C2
Spencer Pk SW18 .**59** C2
Spencer Pl
🔟 Islington N1 ....**15** A1
SW1 ....**133** A1
Spencer Rd
Acton W3 ....**28** B1
Chiswick W4 ......**45** B3
Wandsworth SW18 .**59** C2
Spencer Rise NW5 ..**4** A1
Spencer St EC1 ....**96** A3
Spencer Way 🔟
E1 ....**32** A3
Spencer Wlk
🔟 Hampstead
NW3 ....**11** B4
Putney SW15 ......**57** C3
Spencer Yd SE3 ...**53** B1

Spenlow Ho 🔟
SE16 ....**139** C2
Spenser Gr N16 ...**16** A4
Spenser Mews
SE21 ....**75** C3
Spenser Rd SE24 ..**63** A2
Spenser St SW1 ..**133** A2
Spens Ho 🔟
WC1 ....**94** C1
Spensley Wlk N16 ..**6** C1
Spert St E14 ......**33** A2
Spey St E14 ....**34** B4
Spezia Rd NW10 ..**21** C3
Spice Ct
🔟 Battersea
SW11 ....**59** B4
St George in t East
E1 ....**125** C2
Spice Quay Htss
SE1 ....**125** A1
Spicer Cl SE5, SW9 .**48** A1
Spicer Ho
E2 ....24 C2 **99** B3
Spindrift Ave E14 ..**42** A2
Spinnaker Ho 🔟
E14 ....**41** C4
Spinney The
Barnes SW13 ......**47** A4
Streatham SW16 ..**73** C1
Spire Ct 🔟 TW10 ..**54** A1
Spire Ho W2 ......**115** A4
Spirit Quay E1 ....**32** A1
SPITALFIELDS **111** A4
Spital Sq E1 ......**110** B4
Spital St E1 ......**111** B4
Spital Yd E1 ......**110** B4
Splendour Wlk
SE16 ....**40** B1
Spode Ho SE11 ...**135** B1
Spode Wlk NW3 ...**11** A3
Sporle Ct 🔟 SW11 .**59** C4
Sprewell SW15 ....**58** A1
Spriggs Ho 🔟 N1 ..**15** A1
Sprimont Pl SW3 .**144** C2
Springall St 🔟
SE15 ....**50** A3
Springalls Wharf 🔟
SE16 ....**139** B3
Springbank Wlk
NW1 ....**13** C1
Spring Cott 🔟
W12 ....**38** C4
Spring Ct NW2 ....**10** B2
Springdale Rd
N16 ....**15** C4
Springett Ho 🔟
SW2 ....**62** B2
Springfield Ct
🔟 Dagenham W3 ..**28** B3
🔟 Hampstead NW3 ..**12** A1
Springfield Ho
Acton W3 ....**28** B1
🔟 Camberwell SE5 .**49** A1
🔟 Dalston E8 ......**16** B2
Springfield La
NW6 ....**78** A3
Springfield Rd
NW8 ....**79** A3
Springfield University
Hospl SW17 ......**72** A1
Springfield Wlk
NW6 ....**78** A3
Spring Gdns
Islington N5 ......**15** B3
SW1 ....**120** A2
Spring Gr W4 ......**44** C4

Spring Grove Rd
TW10 ....**54** B2
Spring Hill E5 ......**7** C4
Springhill Cl SE5 ..**63** C4
Spring Ho WC1 ....**95** B3
Spring Mews W1 ..**103** A4
Springpark Dr N4 ..**6** B3
Spring Pl NW5 ....**13** A3
Springrice Rd
SE13 ....**67** C1
Spring St W2 ......**101** B1
Spring Terr TW10 .**54** A2
Springtide Cl 🔟
SE15 ....**49** C2
Springvale Ave
TW8 ....**36** A1
Springvale Terr 🔟
W14 ....**39** C3
Springwater WC1 .**106** C3
Springwell Ave
NW10 ....**21** B4
Spring Wlk E1 ....**111** C4
Springwood Cl 🔟
E3 ....**26** C3
Spruce Ct W5 ......**36** A3
Spruce Ho 🔟
SE16 ....**40** C4
Sprules Rd SE4 ...**51** A1
Spurgeon St SE1 .**137** B2
Spurling Rd SE22 .**64** B3
Spur Rd SE1 ......**135** B4
Spurstowe Rd E8 .**17** A2
Spurstowe Terr
E8 ....**17** A3
Square Rigger Row 🔟
SW11 ....**59** B4
Square The
Hammersmith W6 .**39** B1
SW6 ....**58** A4
Squarey St SW17 ..**71** B1
Squire Gdns NW8 .**89** B3
Squires Ct 🔟
SW4 ....172 B3
Squire's Mount
NW3 ....**2** C1
Squirrels The
SE13 ....**67** C4
Squirries St
E2 ....24 C2 **99** C3
Stable Ho 🔟 SE16 .**40** B4
Stables Way SE11 .**149** B2
Stable Way W10 ...**30** B3
Stable Yd Rd
SW1 ....**133** A4
Stacey St
Highbury N7 ....**5** C1
Soho WC2 ....**105** C1
Stack Ho SW1 ....**145** C3
Stackhouse St
SW1 ....**130** C2
Stacy Path 🔟 SE5 .**49** A3
Stadium St SW10 .**157** A1
Stafford Cl NW6 ..**23** C2
Stafford Cripps Ho
🔟 Bethnal Green
E2 ....**25** B2
SW6 ....**155** A3
Stafford Ct
Kensington W8 ....**127** C2
South Lambeth
SW8 ....**172** A3
Stafford Ho SE1 ..**153** A2
Stafford Mans
🔟 Hammersmith
W14 ....**39** C3
🔟 Stockwell SW4 .**62** A3
SW11 ....**158** C1

Stafford Pl SW1 . . 132 C2
Stafford Rd
  Bow E3 . . . . .26 B1
  Maida Vale NW6 . . . .23 C2
Staffordshire St
  Peckham SE15 . . . . .49 C2
  Peckham SE15 . . . . .50 A2
Stafford St W1 . . . . 118 C2
Stafford Terr W8 . . 127 B2
Stag La SW15 . . . . . .68 B2
Stagshaw Ho 17
  SE22 . . . . .64 A4
Stainer St 123 C1
Staining La EC2 . . . 109 A2
Stainsby St 25
  E2 . . . . .25 B2
Stainsby Rd E14 . . . .33 C3
Stalbridge Flats
  W1 . . . . 103 C1
Stalbridge Ho
  NW1 . . . . .82 C1
Stalbridge St
  NW1 . . . . 102 B3
Stalham St SE16 . . . .40 A3
Stambourne Ho
  SW8 . . . . 172 B4
Stamford Bridge
  Stadium (Chelsea
  FC) SW6 . . . . 156 A2
Stamford Brook Ave
  W6 . . . . .38 B3
Stamford Brook Gdns
  1 W6 . . . . .38 B3
Stamford Brook Mans
  2 W6 . . . . .38 B3
Stamford Brook Rd
  W6 . . . . .38 B3
Stamford Brook Sta
  W6 . . . . .38 B3
Stamford Cl 2
  NW3 . . . . .2 B1
Stamford Cotts
  SW10 . . . . 156 B2
Stamford Ct W6 . . . .38 C2
Stamford Gr E 1
  N16 . . . . .7 C3
Stamford Gr W 4
  N16 . . . . .7 C3
STAMFORD HILL 7 A3
Stamford Hill N16 . . .7 B3
Stamford Hill Mans 1
  N16 . . . . .7 B3
Stamford Hill Sta
  N16 . . . . .7 A4
Stamford Lo 2 N16 . .7 B4
Stamford Mans 2
  N16 . . . . .7 C3
Stamford Rd N 16 A2
Stamford St SE1 . . . 121 C2
Stamp Pl E2 . . 24 B2 99 A4
Stanard Cl N16 . . . . .7 A4
Stanborough Ho 4
  E3 . . . . .27 A1
Stanborough Pas
  E8 . . . . .16 B2
Stanbridge Mans
  SW15 . . . . .57 B4
Stanbridge Rd
  SW15 . . . . .57 B4
Stanbrook Ct W1 . . 118 C2
Stanbury Ct 4
  NW3 . . . . .12 B2
Stanbury Rd
  Nunhead SE15 . . . . .50 B1
  Peckham SE15 . . . . .50 A1

Standard Pl 13
  EC2 . . . . .24 A2 98 B3
Standard Rd
  NW10 . . . . .20 C1
Standen Rd SW18 . . .70 C4
Standish Ho 6
  W6 . . . . .38 C2
Standish Rd W6 . . . .38 C2
Stanesgate Ho 20
  SE15 . . . . .49 C3
Stanfield Ho NW8 . . .89 C2
Stanfield Rd 14 E3 . .26 A3
Stanford Ct
  Kensington W8 . . . 128 B1
  Walham Green
  SW6 . . . . 156 B2
Stanford Pl SE1 . . . 152 A3
Stanford Rd W8 . . . 128 B2
Stanford St SW1 . . . 147 B3
Stangate SE1 . . . . . 135 A2
Stanhope Cl 28
  SE16 . . . . .40 C4
Stanhope Gate
  W1 . . . . 117 C2
Stanhope Gdns
  SW7 . . . . 143 A4
Stanhope Ho
  4 Putney SW15 . . .57 B2
  SE8 . . . . .51 B3
Stanhope Mews E
  SW7 . . . . 143 A4
Stanhope Mews S
  SW7 . . . . 143 A3
Stanhope Mews W
  SW7 . . . . 143 A4
Stanhope Par NW1 . .92 C4
Stanhope Pl W2 . . . 102 C1
Stanhope Rd N6 . . . . .4 B4
Stanhope Row
  W1 . . . . 118 A1
Stanhope St NW1 . . .92 C3
Stanhope Terr
  W2 . . . . 115 B4
Stanier Cl SW5 . . . . 141 A1
Stanlake Mews 7
  W12 . . . . .30 B1
Stanlake Rd W12 . . .30 B1
Stanlake Villas 8
  W12 . . . . .30 B1
Stanley Cohen Ho
  EC1 . . . . .96 C1
Stanley Cres
  W11 . . . . . . .31 B2 112 C4
Stanley Gdns
  Bedford Pk W3 . . . . .38 A4
  Cricklewood NW2 . . . .9 B3
  W11 . . . . . . .31 B2 112 C4
Stanley Gr SW11 . . . 169 C1
Stanley Ho
  3 Clapham SW8 . . 171 B1
  22 Poplar E14 . . . . .33 C3
Stanley Holloway Ct
  E16 . . . . .35 C3
Stanley Mans
  SW10 . . . . 157 A4
  Upper Tooting
  SW17 . . . . .72 B2
Stanley Rd
  Acton Green W3 . . . .37 B3
  Mill Meads E15 . . . . .27 C4
  Mortlake SW14 . . . . .55 A3
Stanley St SE14, ...
  SE8 . . . . .51 B3
Stanley Studios
  SW10 . . . . 157 A4

Stanley Terr 8 N19 . .5 A2
Stanliff Ho 8 E14 . . .41 C3
Stanmer St SW11 . . 168 B2
Stanmore Gdns
  TW9 . . . . .54 B4
Stanmore Ho 21
  SW8 . . . . 171 C2
Stanmore Rd TW9 . . .54 B4
Stanmore St N1 . . . .84 C4
Stannard Cotts 27
  E1 . . . . .25 B1
Stannard Mews
  E8 . . . . .16 C2
Stannard Rd E8 . . . .16 C2
Stannary Pl SE11 . . 149 C1
Stannary St SE11 . . 149 C1
Stansbury Sq 3
  W10 . . . . .23 A2
Stansfeld Ho SE1 . . 153 A3
Stansfield Rd SW9 . .62 B4
Stanstead Ho 3 E3 . .27 B1
Stansted Express
  Terminal EC2 . . . . 110 A4
Stanswood Gdns
  SE5 . . . . .49 A3
Stanton Ct N16 . . . . .6 C4
Stanton Ho 8
  SE10 . . . . .52 B4
Stanton Rd SW13 . . .46 B1
Stanway Ct 28 N1 . . .24 A3
Stanway St N1 . . . . .24 A3
Stanwick Rd W14 . . 140 C3
Stanworth St SE1 . . 139 A3
Stapleford Cl 3
  SW2 . . . . .71 A4
Stapleford Cl
  SW19 . . . . .70 A4
Staplehurst Ct 1
  SW11 . . . . .60 B1
Staplehurst Ho 18
  E5 . . . . .17 A3
Staple Inn WC2 . . . 107 B3
Staple Inn Bldgs
  WC2 . . . . 107 B3
Staples Cl SE16 . . . .33 A1
Staple St SE1 . . . . . 137 C3
Stapleton Hall N4 . . .5 B4
Stapleton Hall Rd
  N4 . . . . .5 B4
Stapleton Ho 10
  E2 . . . . .25 A2
Stapleton Rd
  SW17 . . . . .72 C1
Starboard Way
  E14 . . . . .41 C3
Starcross St NW1 . . .93 A3
StarDome NW1 . . . . .91 B1
Starfield Rd W12 . . .38 C4
Star & Garter Mans 8
  SW15 . . . . .57 C4
Star Lane Sta E16 . . .35 B4
Starliner Ct N7 . . . . .14 C2
Starling Ho NW8 . . . .80 A2
Star Pl E1 . . . . 125 A3
Star Rd W14 . . . . . . 140 C1
Star St W2 . . . . 102 A2
Star Works NW10 . . .21 C2
Star Yd WC2 . . . . . 107 B2
Statham Ct N7 . . . . . .5 A1
Statham Gr N16 . . . . .6 C1
Statham Ho SW8 . . . 170 C4
Station App
  Dagenham NW10 . . .21 B2
  Fulham SW6 . . . . . .58 A4

Station App continued
  Richmond TW9 . . . . .44 C2
Station Approach Rd
  W4 . . . . .45 B3
Station Approach
  Road SE1 . . . . 135 B4
Station Ave
  5 Brixton SW9 . . . .63 A4
  8 Richmond TW9 . . .44 C2
Station Cres SE3 . . . .43 C1
Station Ct 5 SE15 . . .50 B1
Stationers Hall Ct
  EC4 . . . . 108 B1
Station Gdns W4 . . . .45 B3
Station Mews Terr 4
  SE3 . . . . .43 B1
Station Par
  Cricklewood NW2 . . . .9 B2
  Richmond TW9 . . . . .44 C2
  4 Upper Tooting
  SW12 . . . . .72 C3
Station Pas SE15 . . . .50 B2
Station Pl N4 . . . . . . .5 C2
Station Rd
  Barnes SW13 . . . . . .46 B1
  Camden Town N19 . . .4 B1
  Harlesden NW10 . . . .21 B3
  Lewisham SE13 . . . . .67 B4
Station Rise 2 SE27 . .75 A2
Station St E15 . . . . . .19 C1
Station Terr
  Camberwell SE5 . . . .48 B2
  Kensal Rise NW10 . . .22 C3
Staunton Ho SE17 . . 152 A3
Staunton St SE8 . . . .51 B4
Staveley NW1 . . . . . .92 C4
Staveley Cl
  Hackney E9 . . . . . . .17 B3
  Lower Holloway N7 . .14 A4
  New Cross Gate
  SE15 . . . . .50 B2
  8 Peckham SE15 . . .50 A2
Staveley Gdns W4 . . .45 C2
Staveley Rd W4 . . . . .45 C3
Staveley Rd W4 . . . . .46 A2
Stavers Ho 8 E3 . . . .26 B3
Staverton Rd NW2 . . .9 B1
Stave Yard Rd
  SE16 . . . . .33 A1
Stavordale Lo
  W14 . . . . 127 A2
Stavordale Rd N5 . . .15 A4
Stayner's Rd E1 . . . .25 C1
Steadman Ct EC1 . . .97 A2
Stead St SE17 . . . . . 151 B3
Stebbing Ho 8
  W11 . . . . .30 C1
Stebondale St E14 . . .42 B2
Stebon Prim Sch 28
  E14 . . . . .33 C4
Stedham Pl WC1 . . . 106 A2
Steedman St
  SE17 . . . . 150 C3
Steele Rd
  Acton Green W4 . . . .37 B3
  Becontree NW10 . . . .20 B3
Steele's Mews N
  NW3 . . . . .12 B2
Steele's Mews S
  NW3 . . . . .12 B2
Steele's Rd NW3 . . . .12 B2
Steel's La 22 E1 . . . .32 B3
Steen Way 7
  SE22 . . . . .64 A2
Steep Hill SW16 . . . .73 C1

Steeple Cl SW6 . . . 164 B1
Steeple Ct 16 E1 . . . .25 A1
Steeple Wlk N1 . . . . .87 A4
Steerforth St
  SW18 . . . . .71 B2
Steers Way SE16 . . . .41 A4
Stefan Ho NW1 . . . . .95 A4
Stellman Cl E5 . . . . . .7 C1
Stephan Cl E8 . . . . . .24 C4
Stephen Ct 18
  SW19 . . . . .69 C3
Stephendale Rd
  SW6 . . . . 166 C2
Stephen Fox Ho 7
  W4 . . . . .38 A1
Stephen Hawking Sch
  E14 . . . . .33 A3
Stephen Mews
  W1 . . . . 105 B3
Stephen Pl SW4 . . . .61 B4
Stephen Saunders Ct
  SW11 . . . . .60 A2
Stephens Ct SE4 . . . .66 A4
Stephenson Ho
  3 Gospel Oak
  NW5 . . . . .13 A4
  8 Maitland Pk
  NW3 . . . . .12 B3
  Newington SE1 . . . . 136 C2
Stephenson St
  Dagenham NW10 . . .21 B2
  Newham E16 . . . . . .35 A4
Stephenson Way
  NW1 . . . . .93 A2
Stephen St W1 . . . . 105 B3
STEPNEY 32 C4
Stepney City E1 . . . .32 B4
Stepney City Farm
  E1 . . . . .32 C4
Stepney E1 . . . . .32 C4
Stepney Cswy E1 . . . .32 C3
Stepney Gn E1 . . . . .32 C4
Stepney Greencoat CE
  Prim Sch The 22
  E14 . . . . .33 B3
Stepney Green 4
  E1 . . . . .32 C4
Stepney Green Maths
  & Computing Coll 11
  E1 . . . . .32 C4
Stepney Green Sta
  E1 . . . . .25 C1
Stepney High St
  E1 . . . . .32 C4
Stepney Way E1 . . . .32 B4
Sterling Cl NW10 . . . .8 C1
Sterling Gdns
  SE14 . . . . .51 A4
Sterling Pl W5 . . . . . .36 A2
Sterling St SW7 . . . 130 B2
Sterndale Rd W14 . . .39 C3
Sterne St W12 . . . . .39 C4
Sternhall La SE15 . . .64 C4
Sternhold Ave SW12, . .
  SW2 . . . . .73 C2
Sterry St SE1 . . . . . 137 B3
Steve Biko Ct W10 . .22 C1
Steve Biko Rd N7 . . . .5 C1
Stevedore St 3
  E1 . . . . .32 A1
Stevenage Rd
  SW6 . . . . .47 C2
Stevens Ave E9 . . . . .17 B2

Stevenson Cres SE16....40 A1
Stevenson Ho
1 Battersea SW11....168 C1
6 Clapham Pk SW2....62 A2
NW8....78 C4
Stevens St SE1....138 B2
Steventon Rd W12....29 B2
Stewart Headlam Prim Sch SE2 E1....25 A1
Stewart Ho SE1....138 A1
Stewart Rd E15....11 C4
Stewart's Gr SW3....144 A2
Stewart's Rd SW8....170 C4
Stewart St E14....42 B4
Stew La EC4....122 C4
Steyne Ho
15 Acton W3....28 A1
11 Acton W3....28 B1
Steyne Rd W3....28 A1
Stifford Ho E1....32 B4
Stile Hall Gdns W4....36 C1
Stile Hall Par **6** W4....36 C1
Stileman Ho **3** E3....33 B4
Stillingfleet Rd SW13....46 C4
Stillington St SW1....147 A4
Stillness Jun & Inf Schs SE23....66 A1
Stillness Rd SE23....66 B1
Stirling Ct
Clerkenwell EC1....96 A2
Strand WC2....106 C1
Stirling Mans NW6....11 B2
Stirling Rd
South Acton W3....37 A3
Stockwell SW9....172 B1
Stoatley Ho **10** SW15....68 C3
Stockbeck Ho**1** E1....83 A1
Stockfield Rd SW16....74 B1
Stockholm Ho E1....125 C4
Stockholm Rd SE16....40 B1
Stockholm Way E1....125 B2
Stockhurst Cl SW15....47 C1
Stockleigh Hall NW8....80 B2
Stock Orchard Cres N7....14 B3
Stock Orchard St N7....14 B3
Stocks Ct **6** E1....33 C2
Stocks Pl **16** E14....33 B2
Stockton Ho **16** E2....25 A2
STOCKWELL....62 A4
Stockwell Ave SW9....62 B4
Stockwell Gdns SW9....172 C3
Stockwell Gn SW9....172 C1
Stockwell La SW9....172 C1
Stockwell Park Cres SW9....173 A2

Stockwell Park High Sch SW9....172 C3
Stockwell Park Rd SW9....173 A3
Stockwell Park Wlk SW9....173 A2
Stockwell Prim Sch **6** SW9....62 B4
Stockwell St SE10....52 B4
Stockwell Sta SW4....172 B2
Stockwell Terr SW9....172 C3
Stoddart Ho SW8....163 A3
Stodmarsh Ho **28** SW9....173 C4
Stofield Cl **4** SW19....70 A4
Stokenchurch St SW6....166 A3
STOKE NEWINGTON....7 A2
Stoke Newington Church St N16....7 A2
Stoke Newington Comm N16....7 B2
Stoke Newington High St N16....7 B1
Stoke Newington Rd N16....16 B4
Stoke Newington Sch N16....6 C1
Stoke Newington Sta N16....7 B2
Stoke Pl NW10....21 B2
Stokesley St W12....29 B3
Standon Pk SE23....66 A1
Stone Bldgs WC2....107 A3
STONEBRIDGE....20 B4
Stonebridge Ctr **8** NW10....20 C4
Stonebridge Prim Sch NW10....20 C4
Stone Cl SW4....171 A1
Stonecutter St EC4....108 A2
Stonefield N4....5 B2
Stonefield Mans N1....85 B3
Stonefield St N1....85 C4
Stonehall Ho **55** SE5....55 C2
Stonehill Rd
Brentford W4....36 C1
Mortlake SW14....55 C2
Stonehills Ct SE21....76 A1
Stonehill's Mans **3** SW16....74 A2
Stonehouse N1....83 A3
Stonehouse Ct EC2....110 B2
Stonehouse Ho **27** W2....31 C4
Stoneleigh Lo **13** TW9....44 B2
Stoneleigh Mews **15** E3....26 A3
Stoneleigh Pl W11....30 C2
Stoneleigh St W11....30 C2
Stoneleigh Terr N19....4 A2
Stonell's Rd SW11....60 B2
Stonenest St N4....5 B3
Stones End St SE1....136 C3
Stoneyard La E14....34 A2

Stoney La EC3....110 B2
Stoney St SE1....123 B2
Stonhouse St SW4....61 C3
Stonor Rd W14....140 C3
Stopes St SE15....49 B3
Stopford Rd SE17....150 B1
Stopher Ho SE1....136 B3
Storace Ho **6** SW2....62 A3
Storers Quay E14....42 C2
Store St
Bloomsbury WC1....105 B4
Stratford New Town E15....19 C3
Storey Ct NW8....89 B3
Storey Ho **13** E14....34 A2
Storey's Gate SW1....133 C3
Stories Rd SE5....64 A4
Storks Rd SE16....139 C1
Stormont House Sch E5....17 A4
Stormont Rd
Clapham SW11....60 C3
Highgate N6....3 B4
Storrington WC1....94 B3
Story St N1....14 B1
Stothard Ho **2** E1....25 B1
Stothard Pl E2....110 B4
Stothard St **1** E1....25 B1
Stott Cl SW18....59 C1
Stoughton Cl
Roehampton SW15....68 C3
SE11....149 A3
Stourcliffe Cl W1....102 C2
Stourcliffe St W1....102 C2
Stourhead Cl **6** SW19....69 C4
Stour Rd E3....18 C1
Stowage SE8....52 A4
Stowe Ho **11** N16....7 A1
Stowe Rd W12....39 A4
Stracey Rd NW10....20 C4
Stradbroke Rd N5....15 B4
Stradella Rd SE24....63 B1
Straffan Lo **3** NW3....12 A2
Strafford Ho **9** SE8....41 B1
Strafford Rd W3....37 B4
Strafford St E14....41 C4
Strahan Rd E3....26 A2
Straightsmouth SE10....52 B3
Strale Ho **11** N1....24 A4
STRAND....120 C4
Strand
Strand WC2....120 C4
Strand WC2....107 A1
Strand Dr TW9....45 A3
Strand La WC2....121 A4
STRAND ON THE GREEN....44 C4
Strand-on-the-Green W4....44 C4
Strand-on-the-Green Schs **5** W4....44 C4
Strang Ho N1....86 C3
Strangways Terr W14....126 C1
Stranraer Way N1....14 A1
Strasburg Rd SW11....170 A3
STRATFORD....19 B2

Stratford Bus Sta E15....19 C1
Stratford Coll (Newham 6th Form Coll) E15....19 C1
Stratford Gr SW15....57 C3
Stratford High St E15....27 C4
Stratford International Sta E15....19 B2
STRATFORD MARSH....27 A4
STRATFORD NEW TOWN....19 B3
Stratford Pl W1....104 A1
Stratford Rd W8....127 C1
Stratford Sh Ctr E15....19 C1
Stratford Sta E15....19 C1
Stratford Studios W8....128 A1
Stratford Villas NW1....13 C1
Stratford Workshops E15....19 C1
Strathan Cl SW18....58 A1
Strathblaine Rd SW11....59 C3
Strathdon Dr SW17....71 C1
Strathearn Ho W2....116 A4
Strathearn Pl W2....116 A4
Stratheden Par SE3....53 C3
Stratheden Rd SE3....53 C3
Strathleven Rd SW2....62 A2
Strathmore Ct NW8....90 A4
Strathmore Gdns W8....31 C1 113 C2
Strathmore Rd SW19....70 C1
Strathnairn St SE1....153 C3
Strathray Gdns NW3....12 A2
Strath Terr SW11....60 A3
Strathville Rd SW18....71 A2
Stratton Ct **4** N1....16 A1
Stratton St W1....118 B2
Strauss Rd W4....37 C4
Streamline Mews SE22....76 C3
Streatham Cl SW16....74 A2
Streatham & Clapham High Sch SW16....73 C1
Streatham Ct SW16....74 A1
STREATHAM HILL....74 A3
Streatham Hill SW2....74 A3
Streatham Hill & Clapham High Sch **14** SW2....74 A4
Streatham Hill Sta SW2....74 A4
Streatham Pl SW2....74 A4

Streatham St WC1....106 A2
Streathbourne Rd SW17....72 C1
Streatham Wells Prim Sch SW2....74 C2
Streatleigh Par **4** SW16....74 A2
Streatley Pl
27 Hampstead NW3....11 B4
Hampstead NW3....2 C1
Streatley Rd NW6....10 B1
Streimer Rd E15....27 B3
Strelley Way W3....29 A2
Stretton Mans **16** SE8....51 C4
Strickland Ct SE15....64 C4
Strickland Ho **28** E2....99 A3
Strickland Row SW18....71 C4
Strickland St SE8....51 C2
Stringer Hos **19** N1....24 A4
Strode Ho **3** SW2....74 C3
Strode Rd
SW6....154 A2
Willesden NW10....8 C2
Strome Ho NW6....78 A1
Stronsa Rd W12....38 B4
Strood Ho SE1....137 C3
Stroud Cres SW15....68 C3
Stroud Green Prim Sch N4....5 C3
Stroud Green Rd N4....5 C3
Stroudley Ho SW8....171 A4
Stroudley Wlk **3** E3....27 A2
Stroud Rd SW19....70 C1
Strout's Pl **2** E2....24 B2 98 C4
Strudwick Ct SW4....172 B3
Strutton Ground SW1....133 B1
Strype St E1....110 C3
Stuart Ave W5....36 A4
Stuart Ho
Hammersmith W6....39 B3
1 Homerton E9....17 C1
5 Stockwell SW4....62 A3
W14....140 A4
Stuart Mill Ho N1....84 C1
Stuart Rd
Acton W3....28 B1
Maida Vale NW6....23 C2
Nunhead SE15....65 B3
Wimbledon SW19....70 C1
Stubbs Dr SE16....40 A1
Stubbs Ho
Finsbury Pk N4....5 B3
1 Globe Town E2....25 C2
Stucley Pl **19** NW1....13 A1
Studdridge St SW6....165 C2
Studd St N1....86 A4
Studholme Ct NW3....10 C4
Studholme St SE15....50 A3
Studio Pl SW1....131 A3
Studios NW8....78 C2
Studios The
4 Clapham SW4....61 B3

Studios The *continued*
SW8 . . . . **171** C3
Studland St E17 . . . **151** B2
Studland Ho E14 . . . **33** A3
Studland St W6 . . . . **39** A2
Studley Cl E5 . . . . . . **18** A3
Studley Ct E14 . . . **34** C2
Studley Rd SW4 . . . **172** B2
Stukeley St WC2 . . . **106** B2
Stunell Ho E
SE14 . . . . **50** C4
Sturdee Ho E2 . . . . . **24** C3
Sturdy Ho E2E3 . . . . **26** A3
Sturdy Rd SE15 . . . . **50** A1
Sturgeon Rd SE17 . . **150** C1
Sturge St SE1 . . . . . **136** B4
Sturmer Way N7 . . . . **14** B3
Sturminster Ho
SW8 . . . . **163** A1
Sturry St E14 . . . . . . **34** A3
Sturt St N1 . . . . **87** A1
Stutfield St E1 . . . . **111** C1
Stuttle Ho E
E1 . . . . **24** C1 **99** B1
Styles Gdns SW9 . . . **63** A4
Styles Ho SE1 . . . . **122** A1
Stylus Apartments E
E1 . . . . **25** C2
Sudbourne Prim Sch
E SW2 . . . . **62** B2
Sudbourne Rd
SW2 . . . . **62** B2
Sudbrooke Rd
SW12 . . . . **60** C1
Sudbury Ct SW8 . . . **171** C4
Sudbury Ho SW18 . . . **59** A2
Sudeley St N1 . . . . . **86** B1
Sudlow Rd SW18 . . . **58** C2
Sudrey St SE1 . . . . **136** B3
Suffield Ho SE17 . . . **150** B2
Suffolk Ho E NW5 . . . . **4** B1
Suffolk Pl SW1 . . . . **119** C2
Suffolk Rd
Barnes SW13 . . . . . **46** C3
Willesden NW10 . . . . **8** A1
Suffolk St SW1 . . . . **119** C2
Sugar House La
E15 . . . . **27** B3
Sugar Loaf Wlk G
E2 . . . . **25** B2
Sugden Rd SW11 . . . **60** C3
Sulby Ho SE4 . . . . . . **66** A3
Sulgrave Gdns E
W6 . . . . **39** B4
Sulgrave Rd W6 . . . . **39** B4
Sulina Rd SW2 . . . . . **74** A4
Sulivan Ct SW6 . . . **165** B1
Sulivan Ent Ctr
SW6 . . . . **58** C4
Sulivan Prim Sch
E SW6 . . . . **165** B1
Sulivan Rd SW6 . . . **165** B1
Sulkin Ho E E1 . . . . **22** C2
Sullivan Cl SW11 . . . **60** A4
Sullivan Ct
Stamford Hill N16 . . . . **7** B3
SW5 . . . . **141** C4
Sullivan Ho
Chelsea SW1 . . . . **160** B4
Vauxhall SE11 . . . . **149** A3
Sullivan Rd SE11 . . . **149** C4
Sultan St SE5 . . . . . . **48** B3
Sumatra Rd NW6 . . . **10** C2
Sumburgh Rd
SW12 . . . . **60** C1

Summercourt Rd
E1 . . . . **32** B3
Summerfield Ave
NW6 . . . . **23** A3
Summer Ho SE13 . . . **67** C3
Summerhouse Rd
N16 . . . . **7** A2
Summerlands Ave
W3 . . . . **28** B2
Summerley St
SW18 . . . . **71** A2
Summers St EC1 . . . **95** B1
SUMMERSTOWN . . . **71** B1
Summit Ct NW2 . . . . **10** A3
Summit Est N16 . . . . . **7** C4
Sumner Ave SE15 . . . **49** B2
Sumner Bldgs
SE1 . . . . **122** C2
Sumner Ct SW8 . . . **172** A4
Sumner Ho E E3 . . . . **34** A4
Sumner Place Mews
SW7 . . . . **143** B3
Sumner Rd SE15 . . . **49** B3
Sumner St SE1 . . . . **122** C2
Sumpter Cl NW3 . . . **11** B2
Sun Alley E TW9 . . . . **54** A3
Sun Alliance Ho
WC2 . . . . **107** B2
Sunbeam Cres
W10 . . . . **22** B1
Sunbeam Rd
NW10 . . . . **20** C1
Sunbury Ave
SW14 . . . . **55** C3
Sunbury Ho E
E2 . . . . **24** B2 **98** C3
Sunbury La SW11 . . . **167** C4
Sunbury Workshops
E E2 . . . . **24** B2 **98** C3
Sun Ct EC3 . . . . **109** C1
Sunderland Ct
SE22 . . . . **76** C4
Sunderland Ho E
W2 . . . . **31** C4
Sunderland Terr
W2 . . . . **100** A2
Sundew Ave W12 . . . **29** C2
Sundra Wlk E E1 . . . **25** C1
Sundridge Ho G
E9 . . . . **17** C1
Sunley Ho E1 . . . . . **111** A3
Sunlight Sq E2E2 . . . **25** A2
Sunningdale Cl E
SE16 . . . . **40** A1
Sunningdale Gdns
W8 . . . . **127** C1
Sunninghill Ct E
W3 . . . . **37** B4
Sunninghill Rd
SE13 . . . . **52** A1
Sunnyhill Cl E5 . . . . **18** A4
Sunnymead Rd
SW15 . . . . **57** A2
Sunnyside E NW2 . . . **1** B1
Sunnyside Ho E
NW2 . . . . **1** B1
Sunnyside Rd N19 . . . . **4** C4
Sun Pas E SE16 . . . **139** B2
Sunray Ave SE5,
SE24 . . . . **63** C3
Sun Rd W14 . . . . . . **140** C1

Sun St Pas EC2 . . . **110** A3
Sunset Rd SE5 . . . . . **63** C3
Sun St EC2 . . . . . . **109** C4
Sunwell Cl SE15 . . . . **50** A2
Surcot Ho E
SW4 . . . . **171** C1
Surma Cl E1 . . . **24** C1 **99** C1
Surrendale Pl W9 . . . **23** C1
Surrey Canal Rd SE14,
SE8 . . . . **50** C4
Surrey Cres E
W4 . . . . **36** C1
Surrey Docks Farm
SE16 . . . . **41** B4
Surrey Docks
Watersports Ctr
SE8 . . . . **41** B2
Surrey Gr E SW11 . . **152** A1
Surrey Ho E SE16 . . . **32** C1
Surrey La SW11 . . . **168** B3
Surrey Quays Rd
SE16 . . . . **40** C4
Surrey Quays Sh Ctr
SE16 . . . . **40** C3
Surrey Quays Sta
SE16 . . . . **40** C2
Surrey Rd SE15 . . . . **65** C2
Surrey Row E SE1 . . **136** B4
Surrey Sq SE17 . . . **152** A2
Surrey Square Jun
Sch SE17 . . . . . . **152** A2
Surrey St WC2 . . . . **121** A4
Surrey Terr SE17 . . . **152** B2
Surrey Water Rd
SE16 . . . . **32** C1
Surrey Wharf SE1 . . **49** C4
Surridge Ct E
SW9 . . . . **172** B2
Surr St N7 . . . . **14** A3
Susan Constant Ct E
E14 . . . . **34** C2
Susannah St E14 . . . **34** B3
Sussex Cl N19 . . . . . . **5** A2
Sussex Ct
Barnes SW13 . . . . . **46** B1
Greenwich SE10 . . . . **52** B4
Paddington W2 . . . **101** B1
Sussex Gdns W2 . . . **101** C1
Sussex Ho
Hampstead NW3 . . . **12** A2
Richmond TW9 . . . . . **44** B1
Sussex House Sch
SW3 . . . . **144** C4
Sussex Lo W2 . . . . **101** C1
Sussex Mans
South Kensington
SW7 . . . . **143** B3
Strand WC2 . . . . . **120** B4
Sussex Mews E
W2 . . . . **101** C1
Sussex Mews W
W2 . . . . **115** C4
Sussex Pl
E Hammersmith
W6 . . . . **39** B1
Lisson Gr NW1 . . . . . **90** C2
Paddington W2 . . . **101** C1
Sussex Sq W2 . . . . **115** C4
Sussex St SW1 . . . . **146** B2
Sussex Way
Upper Holloway N7 . . . **5** B1
Upper Holloway N7,
N19 . . . . **5** A2
Upper Holloway N19 . . . **4** C3

Sutherland Ave
W9 . . . . **88** C2
Sutherland Ct
E Paddington
W9 . . . . **23** C1
Stoke Newington
N16 . . . . **7** A1
Sutherland Gdns
SW14 . . . . **56** A4
Sutherland Gr SW18,
SW19 . . . . **70** B4
Sutherland Ho
Kensington W8 . . . **128** A1
E Putney SW15 . . . . **69** B4
E South Hampstead
NW6 . . . . **11** C1
Sutherland Pl W2 . . . **31** C3
Sutherland Rd W4 . . . **46** A4
Sutherland Row
SW1 . . . . **146** B2
Sutherland Sq
SE17 . . . . **150** C1
Sutherland St
SW1 . . . . **146** B2
Sutherland Wlk
SE17 . . . . **151** A1
Sutterton St N7 . . . . **14** B2
Sutton Court Mans
W4 . . . . **45** B4
Sutton Court Rd
W4 . . . . **45** B4
Sutton Ct
Chiswick W4 . . . . . . **45** B4
E Hackney E5 . . . . . **17** A4
Sutton Est The E
W10 . . . . **30** B4
Sutton Est E9 . . . . . **17** B3
Sutton La EC1 . . . . . **96** B1
Sutton La N SW4 . . . **37** B1
Sutton La S SW4 . . . **45** B4
Sutton Row W1 . . . **105** C2
Sutton Sq E9 . . . . . . **17** B3
Sutton St E1 . . . . . . **32** B3
Suttons Way EC1 . . . **97** A1
Sutton Way W10 . . . **30** B4
Sutton Wlk SE1 . . . **121** A1
Swaby Rd SW17,
SW18 . . . . **71** B2
Swaffield Prim Sch
SW18 . . . . **71** B4
Swaffield Rd
SW18 . . . . **71** B4
Swain's La N6 . . . . . . **4** A2
Swainson Rd N7 . . . . **14** C4
Swain St NW8 . . . . . **90** A2
Swallow Cl SE14 . . . **50** C2
Swallow Ct E W9 . . . **31** C4
Swallowfield NW1 . . . **92** B3
Swallow Ho NW8 . . . **80** A2
Swallow Pl
E Poplar E14 . . . . . **33** B3
W1 . . . . **104** B1
Swallow St W1 . . . . **119** A3
Swanage Ct E N1 . . . **16** A1
Swanage Ho SW8 . . **162** C1
Swanage Rd SW18 . . **59** B1
Swanbourne SE17 . . **150** C3
Swanbourne Ho
NW8 . . . . **90** A2
Swan Bsns Ctr E
W4 . . . . **37** C2
Swan Ct
Chelsea SW3 . . . . **144** B1

SW6 . . . . **155** B1
Poplar E14 . . . . **33** B3
Swan Ctr SW17 . . . . **71** B1
Swandon Way
SW18 . . . . **59** A3
Swanfield St E
E2 . . . . **24** B2 **99** A3
Swan Ho N1 . . . . **15** C1
Swan La EC4 . . . . . **123** C3
Swan Lane Pier
EC4 . . . . **123** B3
Swanlea Sch E1 . . . . **25** A1
Swanley Ho SE17 . . . **152** B2
Swan Mead SE1 . . . **138** A1
Swan Mews
Stockwell SW9 . . . . **172** C2
SW6 . . . . **165** B4
Swanmore Ct
SW18 . . . . **59** B1
Swanne Ho E
SE10 . . . . **125** B3
Swan Pas E E1 . . . **125** B3
Swan Pl SW13 . . . . . **46** B1
Swan Rd SE16 . . . . . **40** B4
Swanscombe Ho E
W11 . . . . **30** C1
Swanscombe Point E
E16 . . . . **35** B4
Swanscombe Rd
E Chiswick W4 . . . . . **38** A1
Shepherd's Bush
W11 . . . . **30** C1
Swan St SE1 . . . . . **137** A3
Swanton Gdns
SW19 . . . . **69** C3
Swanwick Cl
SW15 . . . . **68** B4
Swan Wlk SW3 . . . . **158** C4
Swan Yd N1 . . . . **15** A2
Swaton Rd E3 . . . . . . **26** C1
Swaythling Ho
SW15 . . . . **56** B1
Swedenborg Gdns
E1 . . . . **32** A2
Sweden Gate SE16 . . **41** A2
Swedish Quays
SE16 . . . . **41** A3
Swedish Sch The
SW13 . . . . **46** C4
Sweeney Cres
SE1 . . . . **139** A3
Sweyn Pl SE3 . . . . . . **53** C1
Swift Ho
E Stepney E1 . . . . . **32** B3
E Stoke Newington
N16 . . . . **7** A1
E SW9 . . . . **163** C2
Swift St SW6 . . . . . **164** C4
Swinbrook Rd
W10 . . . . **31** A4
Swinburne Ct E
SE5 . . . . **63** C3
Swinburne Ho E
E2 . . . . **25** B2
Swinburne Rd
SW15 . . . . **56** C3
Swindon St W12 . . . . **30** B1
Swinford Gdns
SW9 . . . . **63** A4
Swingfield Ho E
E9 . . . . **25** B4
Swinley Ho NW1 . . . . **92** B4

276   Swi–Tem

Swinnerton St E9...18 A3
Swinton Ho 21
  E2...24 C2 **99** B3
Swinton Pl N1...**94** C4
Swinton St WC1...**94** C4
Swiss Cottage
  NW3...11 C1
Swiss Cottage L Ctr
  NW3...11 C1
Swiss Cottage Sch
  14 South Hampstead
  ...11 C1
  St John's Wood
  NW8...**79** C4
Swiss Cottage Sta
  NW3...11 C1
Swiss Terr 7
  NW3...11 C1
Switch Ho 4 E14...34 C2
Sybil Phoenix Cl
  SE8...40 C1
Sybil Thorndike
  Casson Ho SW5...**141** C1
Sybil Thorndike Ho 12
  N1...15 B2
Sycamore Ave E3...26 B4
Sycamore Cl W3...29 A1
Sycamore Ct
  Kilburn NW6...23 C4
  Tufnell Pk N19...4 C1
Sycamore Gdns W6,
  W12...39 A3
Sycamore Gr SE6...67 B1
Sycamore Ho
  16 Maitland Pk
  NW3...12 B2
  17 Rotherhithe
  SE16...40 C4
  11 Shepherd's Bush
  W6...39 A4
  2 Stoke Newington
  N16...6 C2
Sycamore Lo
  SW15...57 A4
Sycamore Mews 4
  SW4...61 B4
Sycamore St EC1...**96** C1
Sycamore Wlk 1
  W10...23 A1
Sydcote SE21...75 B3
Sydenham Hill SE21,
  SE22, SE23, SE26,
  SE19...76 C1
Sydenham Hill Sta
  SE21...76 B1
Sydenham Hill Wood
  Nature Reserve
  SE26...76 C2
Sydner Mews N16...16 B4
Sydner Rd N16...16 B4
Sydney Cl SW3...**143** C3
Sydney Ho 4 W4...38 A2
Sydney Mews
  SW3...**143** C3
Sydney Pl SW7...**144** A3
Sydney Rd TW10,
  TW9...54 A3
Sydney St SW3...**144** A2
Sylva Cotts 3 SE8...51 C2
Sylva Ct 3 SW15...69 C4
Sylvan Ct 1 NW6...**78** A4
Sylvan Gr
  Hampstead NW2...9 C2

Sylvan Gr continued
  SE15...50 A4
Sylvester Ho 7
  E8...17 A2
Sylvester Path 8
  E8...17 A2
Sylvester Rd E8...17 A2
Sylvia Ct N1...**87** B1
Sylvia Pankhurst Ho
  10 E2...25 C2
Sylvia Young Theatre
  Sch NW1...**90** B1
Symes Mews NW1...**82** C2
Symington Ho
  SE1...**137** B1
Symington Mews
  ...17 C3
Symister Mews
  N1...24 A2 **98** A3
  15 Shoreditch
  N1...24 A2 **98** A3
Symons St SW3...**145** A3
Symphony Mews 15
  W10...23 A2
Syracuse Univ
  W11...31 B2 **112** C5
Syringa Ho SE4...66 B4

T

Tabard Ct 6 E14...34 B3
Tabard Ho SW1...**137** C2
Tabard Sq SE1...**137** B3
Tabard St SE1...**137** B2
Tabernacle St EC2...**97** C2
Tableer Ave SW4...61 C2
Tabley Rd N7...14 A4
Tabor Rd W6...39 A3
Tachbrook Est
  SW1...**147** C1
Tachbrook Mews
  SW1...**146** C4
Tachbrook St
  SW1...**147** A3
Tack Mews SE4...66 C4
Tadema Ho NW8...**89** C1
Tadema Rd SW10...**157** A1
Tadmor St W12...30 C1
Tadworth Ho SE1...**136** A3
Taeping St E14...42 A2
Taffrail Ho 2 E14...42 A1
Taft Way 44 E3...27 A2
Tailworth St 18
  E1...**111** B3
Tait Ct
  10 Old Ford E3...26 B4
  SW8...**171** C4
Tait Ho
  SE1...**121** C1
  2 Tufnell Pk N19...13 B4
Takhar Mews
  SW11...**168** B1
Talacre Com Sp Ctr
  NW5...13 A2
Talacre Rd NW5...12 C2
Talbot Ct EC3...**123** C4
Talbot Grove Ho 10
  W11...31 A3
Talbot Ho
  Highbury N7...5 C1
  Poplar E14...34 A3
Talbot Pl SE3...53 A1
Talbot Rd
  Camberwell SE22...64 A3

Talbot Rd continued
  Notting Hill W2...31 C3
  Notting Hill W11...31 B3
Talbot Sq W2...**101** B1
Talbot Wlk
  Notting Hill W11...31 A3
  Willesden NW10...8 A2
Talbot Yd SE1...**123** B1
Talcott Path 2
  SW2...74 C3
Talfourd Pl SE15...49 B2
Talfourd Rd SE15...49 B2
Talgarth Rd
  Hammersmith W6...39 B1
  W14...**140** B2
Talia Ho E14...42 B3
Talleyrand Ho SE5...48 B1
Tallis St EC4...**121** C4
Talma Rd SW2...62 C3
Talmud Torah
  Machzikei Hadass
  Sch E5...7 C4
Talmud Torah Tiferes
  Shlomo 1 NW11...1 A2
Talmud-Torah Yetev-
  Lev 4 N16...7 C3
Talwin St E3...27 A2
Tamar Cl 2 E3...26 B4
Tamar Ho
  10 Cubitt Town
  E14...42 B4
  SE11...**149** C2
Tamarind Ct 8
  W3...28 B3
Tamarind Ho 4
  SE15...49 C3
Tamarind Yd 5
  E1...**125** C2
Tamarisk Sq W12...29 B2
Tamworth N7...14 A2
Tamworth St SW6 **155** B3
Tangier Rd TW10...55 A4
Tangley Gr SW15...68 B4
Tangmere WC1...**94** C3
Tanhurst Ho 27
  SW2...74 A4
Tankerton St WC1...**94** B3
Tanner Ho SE1...**138** B3
Tanner's Hill SE8...51 C2
Tanners Mews
  SE8...51 B2
Tanner St SE1...**138** B3
Tanners Yd 23 E2...25 A3
Tannery Ho 21 E1...**111** B4
Tannington Terr N5...5 C1
Tansley Cl N7...13 C3
Tanswell St SE1...**135** B3
Tantallon Rd
  SW12...72 C3
Tant Ave E16...35 B3
Tanza Rd NW3...12 B4
Tapley Ho 1 SE1...**139** B3
Tapp St E1...25 A1
Taranto Ho 14 E1...32 C4
Tarbert Rd SE22...64 A2
Tarbert Wlk E1...32 B2
Tarling Rd E16...35 B3
Tarling St E1...32 B3
Tarnbrook Ct
  SW1...**145** B3

Tarn St SE1...**136** C1
Tarns The NW1...**92** C4
Tarplett Ho 22
  SE14...50 C4
Tarragon Cl SE14...51 A3
Tarranbrae NW6...10 A1
Tarrant Ho E2...25 B2
Tarrant Pl W1...**102** C3
Tarrant Ho W14...**126** A2
Tarriff Cres SE8...41 B2
Tarrington Cl
  SW16...73 C1
Tartan Ho 12 E14...34 B3
Tarver Rd SE17...**150** B2
Tarves Way SE10...52 A3
Tasker Ho 4 E14...33 B4
Tasker Lo W8...**127** B4
Tasker Rd NW3...12 B3
Tasman Ct 8 E14...42 A2
Tasman Ho 1 E1...32 A1
Tasman Rd SW9...62 A4
Tasso Rd W6...**154** A4
Tasso Yd W6...**154** A3
Tatchbury Ho
  SW15...56 B1
Tate Britain SW1...**148** A3
Tate Ho 10 E2...25 C3
Tate Modern EC4...**122** B2
Tatham Pl NW8...**79** C2
Tatnell Rd SE23...66 A1
Tatton Cres E5, N16...7 B4
Tatum St SE17...**151** C3
Tauheed Cl N4...6 B2
Taunton Ho W2...**100** C1
Taunton Mews
  NW1...**90** C1
Taunton Pl NW1...**90** C2
Taverne Cl SE1...**137** A1
Taverner Ho N5...33 A3
Taverners Cl
  W11...31 A1 **112** A1
Taverner Sq 4 N5...15 B4
Tavern La SW9...**173** C2
Tavistock Cl N16...16 A3
Tavistock Cres
  Notting Hill W11...31 B4
Tavistock Ho 3
Tavistock Mews 3
  W11...31 B3
Tavistock Pl WC1...**94** A2
Tavistock Rd
  Dagenham NW10...21 B3
  Notting Hill W11...31 B4
Tavistock Sq WC1...**93** C2
Tavistock St WC2...**120** B4
Tavistock Twr
  SE16...41 A3
Taviton St WC1...**93** B2
Tavy Cl SE11...**149** C2
Tawhid Boys Sch
  ...7 B2
Tawny Way SE16...40 C2
Taybridge Rd
  SW11...60 C3
Tay Ho 10 E3...26 B3
Tayler Ct NW8...**79** B4
Taylor Ave TW9...45 A1
Taylor Cl SE8...51 B4
Taylor Ho 10 SW2...74 C3
Taylor's Gn W3...29 A3
Taylor's La NW10...8 A1
Tayport Cl N1...14 A1

Tayside Ct 6 SE5...63 C3
Teak Cl SE16...33 A1
Tealby Cl N7...14 B2
Teal Cl 30 SE8...51 B4
Teale St 1 SE2...24 C3
Teather St 12 SE5...49 A3
Tebbs Ho 4 SW2...74 C4
Tedman Ct SE13...67 B3
Ted Roberts Ho 20
  E2...25 A3
Tedworth Gdns
  SW3...**144** C1
Tedworth Sq SW3 **144** C1
Teesdale Cl E2...25 A3
Teesdale St E2...25 A3
Teesdale Yd 34 E2...25 A3
Tee The W3...29 A3
Teignmouth Cl 6
  SW4...61 C3
Teignmouth Rd
  NW2...9 C2
Telegraph Hill NW3...2 A1
Telegraph Pl E14...42 A2
Telegraph Rd
  SW15...69 B4
Telegraph St EC2...**109** B2
Telephone Pl
  SW6...**155** A4
Telfer Cl 4 W3...37 B4
Telfer Ho EC1...**96** B3
Telferscot Prim Sch
  5 SW12...73 A3
Telferscot Rd
  SW12...73 C3
Telford Ave SW12,
  SW2...74 A3
Telford Avenue Mans
  8 SW2...74 A3
Telford Ho
  W10...31 A4
  SE1...31 A4
Telford Parade Mans
  8 SW2...74 A3
Telford Rd W10...31 A4
Telford Terr SW1...**160** C4
Telford Way W3...29 A4
Tell Gr SE22...64 B3
Telscombe Ho
  SW11...**169** B3
Temair Ho 1 SE10...52 B3
Temeraire Pl 8 TW8...36 B1
Temeraire St SE16...40 B4
Temperley Rd
  SW12...72 C4
Templar Ho NW2...10 B2
Templar St SE5...48 A1
Temple Ave EC4...**121** C4
Temple Bar EC4...**108** B1
Temple Bar EC4...**108** B1
Templecombe Rd
  E9...25 B4
Temple Ct
  Stepney E1...32 C4
  SW8...**162** A1
Temple Dwellings 7
  E2...25 A3
Temple Gr Hatcham
  SE14...50 C1
Temple Ho
  13 Battersea
  SW11...60 A4
  4 Tufnell Pk N7...4 B1
Temple La EC4...**107** C1

Templemead Cl
W3 . . . . 29 A3
Templemead Ho
E9 . . . . 18 A4
TEMPLE MILLS 19 A3
Temple Mills La
London E10, E15 . . . . 19 A4
Stratford E15 . . . . . . 19 A4
Temple Mills Rd
E9 . . . . 18 C4
Temple Pl WC2 . . . . 121 A4
Temple Rd
Acton Green W4 . . . . 37 B3
Richmond TW9 . . . . 54 B4
Temple Sheen
SW14 . . . . 55 B3
Temple Sheen Rd
SW14 . . . . 55 B3
Temple St E2 . . . . . . 25 A3
Temple Sta WC2 . . . 121 B4
Templeton Cl 26
N16 . . . . 16 A3
Templeton Pl
SW5 . . . . 141 C3
Temple West Mews
SE11 . . . . 136 A3
Templewood Ave
NW3 . . . . 2 A1
Templewood Gdns
NW3 . . . . 2 A1
Templewood Point
NW2 . . . . 1 B2
Tenbury Ct SW12 . . . 73 C3
Tenby Ho
Islington N7 . . . . 14 B2
W2 . . . . 100 C1
Tench St E1 . . . . 32 A1
Tenda Rd SE16 . . . . . 40 A2
Tendring Ho SW2 . . . 62 C1
Tenham Ave SW2 . . . 73 C2
Tenison Ct W1 . . . . 118 C4
Tenison Way SE1 . . 121 B1
Tenniel Cl W2 . . . . . 114 B4
Tennis St SE1 . . . . . 137 B4
Tennyson Ho
SE17 . . . . 151 A2
Tennyson Rd NW6 . . 23 B4
Tennyson St SW8 . . 170 A1
Tensing Ho N1 . . . . . 15 A2
Tenterden Ho
SE17 . . . . 152 B2
Tenterden St W1 . . 104 B1
Tenter Ground E1 . . 110 C3
Tent St E1 . . . . 25 A1
Tequila Wharf E14 . . 33 A3
Terborch Way 6
SE22 . . . . 64 A2
Tercelet Terr NW3 . . 11 B4
Teredo St SE16 . . . . 40 C3
Terling Ho 9 W10 . . 30 B4
Terling Wlk N1 . . . . . 86 C4
Terminus Pl SW1 . . 132 B1
Tern Ho 9 SE15 . . . . 50 B4
Terrace Gdns
SW13 . . . . 46 B1
Terrace La TW10 . . . 54 A1
Terrace Rd E9 . . . . . 17 B1
Terrace The
Barnes SW13,
SW14 . . . . 46 A1
EC4 . . . . 107 C1
Kilburn NW6 . . . . 10 A1
10 Rotherhithe SE8 . . 41 B2
Terrano Ho 1
TW9 . . . . 45 A2
Terrapin Ct SW17 . . . 73 A1

Terrapin Rd SW17 . . . 73 A1
Terrick St W12 . . . . . 30 A3
Territorial Ho
SE11 . . . . 149 C3
Terry Ho SW2 . . . . . . 74 C3
Tersha St TW9 . . . . . 54 B3
Tessa Sanderson Pl 6
SW8 . . . . 61 A4
Testerton Wlk 8
W11 . . . . 30 C2
Tetcott Rd SW10 . . . 156 C1
Tevesham La
SE8 . . . . 172 B4
Teviot St E14 . . . . . . 34 B4
Teyham Ct 2
SW11 . . . . 60 B1
Thackeray Ct
Chelsea SW3 . . . . . . 144 C2
West Kensington
W14 . . . . 126 A1
Thackeray Ho
College Pk NW10 . . . . 21 C2
SW17 . . . . 72 A2
Thackeray Mews 6
E8 . . . . 16 C2
Thackeray Rd
SW8 . . . . 170 B1
Thackeray's
Almshouses SE6 . . . 67 A1
Thackeray St W8 . . 128 B2
Thalia Cl SE10 . . . . . 52 C4
Tham Cl 10 SE24 . . . 63 A4
Thame Rd SE16 . . . . 40 C4
Thames Ave
SW10 . . . . 167 A4
Thames Bank
SW14 . . . . 45 B1
Thames Christian Coll
23 SW11 . . . . 59 C4
Thames Circ E14 . . . 41 C2
Thames Cres W4 . . . 46 A3
Thames Ct 10
SE15 . . . . 49 B3
Thames Hts SE1 . . . 138 C4
Thameside Ctr
TW8 . . . . 44 B4
Thames Link Ho 7
TW9 . . . . 54 A3
Thames Pl SW15 . . . 57 C4
Thames Quay
Millwall E14 . . . . 42 A4
SW10 . . . . 167 A3
Thames Rd W4 . . . . . 45 A4
Thames Reach W6 . . 47 B4
Thames Row TW9 . . . 44 B4
Thames St SE10 . . . . 52 A4
Thames Village
W4 . . . . 45 B2
Thames Wlk
SW11 . . . . 158 A2
Thane Mans N7 . . . . . 5 B1
Thanet Ho
WC1 . . . . 94 A3
1 West Norwood
SE27 . . . . 75 A1
Thanet Lo NW2 . . . . . 10 A2
Thanet St WC1 . . . . . 94 A3
Thane Villas N7 . . . . . 5 B1
Thane Works N7 . . . . . 5 B1
Thavies Inn EC4 . . . 107 C2
Thaxted Ct N1 . . . . . . 87 C1
Thaxted Ho SE16 . . . 40 B2
Thaxton Rd W14 . . . 155 A4
Thayer St W1 . . . . . 103 C2
Theatre Royal E10 . . 19 C3
Theatre Sq E15 . . . . 19 C2

Theatre St SW11 . . . . 60 B4
Theberton St N1 . . . . 86 A4
Theed St SE1 . . . . . . 121 C1
Thelbridge Ho 28
E3 . . . . 27 A2
Theobalds Ct N4 . . . . 6 B2
Theobald's Rd
WC1 . . . . 106 C4
Theobald St SE1 . . . 137 B1
Theodore Ct SE13 . . 67 C1
Theodore Ho 1
SW15 . . . . 56 C2
Theodore Rd SE13 . . 67 C1
Therapia Rd SE22 . . . 65 B1
Theresa Rd W6 . . . . . 38 C2
Therfield Ct N4 . . . . . . 6 B2
Thermopylae Gate
E14 . . . . 42 A2
Theseus Ho 2
E14 . . . . 34 C3
Theseus Wlk N1 . . . . 86 B1
Thessaly Ho SW8 . . 160 C1
Thessaly Rd SW8 . . 171 A4
Thetford Ho SE1 . . . 138 C2
Thetis Terr TW9 . . . . 44 C4
Third Ave
East Acton W3 . . . . . 29 B1
West Kilburn W10 . . . 23 A2
Thirleby Rd SW1 . . . 133 A1
Thirlmere NW1 . . . . . 92 B4
Thirlmere Ho 10
N16 . . . . 7 A1
Thirsk Rd SW11 . . . . 60 C3
Thistle Gr SW7 . . . . 143 A1
Thistle Ho 10 E14 . . . 34 B3
Thistlewood Cl 3
N7 . . . . 5 B2
Thistly Ct SE8 . . . . . 52 A4
Thomas Baines Rd
SW11 . . . . 59 C4
Thomas Burt Ho 9
E2 . . . . 25 A2
Thomas Buxton Jun &
Inf Sch 17
E1 . . . . 24 C1 99 C1
Thomas Crowell Ct 28
N16 . . . . 16 A3
Thomas Doyle St
SE1 . . . . 136 B2
Thomas Fairchild
Com Sch N1 . . . . 87 A2
Thomas Ho
3 Hackney E9 . . . . . 17 B2
4 Stockwell SW4 . . . 62 A3
Thomas Hollywood Ho
1 E2 . . . . 25 B3
Thomas Jones Prim
Sch 18 W11 . . . . 31 A3
Thomas London Ind
Day Sch W8 . . . . . . 128 B2
Thomas Milner Ho 8
SE15 . . . . 49 C3
Thomas More Ho
EC2 . . . . 108 C3
Thomas More Sq
E1 . . . . 125 B3
Thomas More St
E1 . . . . 125 B2
Thomas Neal's Ctr
WC1 . . . . 106 A1
Thomas North Terr 4
E16 . . . . 35 B4
Thomas Pl W8 . . . . . 128 A1
Thomas Rd E14 . . . . . 33 C4
Thomas Road Ind Est
2 E14 . . . . 33 C3

Thomas's Prep Sch
Clapham SW11 . . . . . 60 B2
Thomas's Prep Schs
SW11 . . . . 167 C3
Thompson Ave
Richmond TW9 . . . . . 54 C4
6 SE5 . . . . 48 B3
Thompson Ho
14 Kensal Town
W10 . . . . 23 A1
SE14 . . . . 50 C4
Thompson Rd
SE22 . . . . 64 B1
Thomson Ct 4 E8 . . 16 C2
Thomson Ho
Pimlico SW1 . . . . . . 147 C1
Walworth SE17 . . . . 152 A3
Thorburn Ho SW1 . . 131 B3
Thorburn Sq SE1 . . 153 B3
Thoresby Ho N16 . . . . 6 C1
Thoresby St N1 . . . . . 97 A4
Thornaby Ho 15
E2 . . . . 25 A2
Thornbill Ho 1
SE15 . . . . 49 C3
Thornbury Cl N16 . . . 16 A3
Thornbury Ct
W11 . . . . 31 C2 113 B4
Thornbury Ho N6 . . . . 4 B3
Thornbury Rd
SW2 . . . . 62 A1
Thornbury Sq N6 . . . . 4 B3
Thorncliffe Ct
SW2 . . . . 62 A1
Thorncliffe Rd
SW2 . . . . 62 A1
Thorncombe Rd
SE22 . . . . 64 A2
Thorncroft St
SW8 . . . . 162 A1
Thorndale Ho 10
N16 . . . . 7 A3
Thorndean St
SW18 . . . . 71 B2
Thorndike Cl
SW10 . . . . 156 C2
Thorndike Ho
SW1 . . . . 147 B2
Thorndike Rd 21
N1 . . . . 15 C2
Thorndike St
SW1 . . . . 147 B3
Thorne Cl E16 . . . . . 35 C3
Thorne Ho
34 Bethnal Green
E2 . . . . 25 B2
4 Cubitt Town E14 . . 42 B3
Thorne Pas 7
SW13 . . . . 46 B1
Thorne Rd SW8 . . . . 162 B1
Thorness Ct SW18 . . 59 B1
Thorne St SW13,
SW14 . . . . 56 A4
Thornewill Ho 8
E1 . . . . 32 B2
Thorney Cres
SW11 . . . . 157 C1
Thorneycroft Ho 11
W4 . . . . 38 A1
Thorney Ct W8 . . . . 128 C3
Thorney Hedge Rd
W4 . . . . 37 A2
Thorney St SW1 . . . 148 A4
Thornfield Ho 5
E14 . . . . 33 C2

Tem–Thr 277

Thornfield Rd
W12 . . . . 39 A4
Thornford Rd
SE13 . . . . 67 B2
Thorngate Rd W9 . . . 23 C1
Thornham Gr E15 . . . 19 C3
Thorn Ham Ho
SE1 . . . . 137 C2
Thornham St SE10 . . 52 A4
Thornhaugh St
WC1 . . . . 93 C1
Thornhill Bridge
Wharf N1 . . . . 84 C3
Thornhill Cres N1 . . . 14 B1
Thornhill Gr N1 . . . . . 14 C1
12 Chiswick W4 . . . . 38 A1
Islington N1 . . . . 14 C1
Thornhill Mews
SW15 . . . . 58 B3
Thornhill Prim Sch 4
N1 . . . . 14 C1
Thornhill Rd N1 . . . . . 85 B4
Thornhill Sq N1 . . . . . 14 B1
Thornicroft Ho 12
SW9 . . . . 173 A1
Thorney Pl 2
SE10 . . . . 43 A1
Thornsett Rd
SW18 . . . . 71 A3
Thornton Ave
Chiswick W4 . . . . 38 A2
Streatham SW2 . . . . 73 C3
Thornton Ct N7 . . . . . 14 A3
Thornton Gdns
SW12 . . . . 73 C3
Thornton Ho
SE17 . . . . 152 A3
Thornton Pl W1 . . . 103 A4
Thornton Rd
Mortlake SW14 . . . . . 55 C4
Streatham SW12,
SW2 . . . . 73 C3
Thornton St SW9 . . 173 B2
Thornville St SE8 . . . 51 C2
Thornwood Gdns
W8 . . . . 127 B4
Thornwood Lo
W8 . . . . 127 B4
Thornycroft Ct
TW9 . . . . 44 B1
Thorold Ho
SE1 . . . . 136 C4
8 Streatham SW2 . . 74 A4
Thorparch Rd
SW8 . . . . 161 C1
Thorpebank Rd
W12 . . . . 29 C1
Thorpe Cl W10 . . . . . 31 A3
Thorpedale Rd N4 . . . 5 B3
Thorpe Ho N1 . . . . . . 85 A3
Thorverton Rd NW2 . . 1 A1
Thoydon Rd E3 . . . . . 26 A3
Thrale St SE1 . . . . . 123 A1
Thrasher Cl 20 E8 . . 24 B4
Thrawl St E1 . . . . . . 111 A3
Thrayle Ho 2
SW9 . . . . 62 B4
Threadgold Ho 8
N1 . . . . 15 C2
Threadneedle St EC2,
EC3 . . . . 109 C1
Three Colts La E2 . . 25 A1
Three Colt St E14 . . 33 B2

Three Cups Yd
WC1 . . . . **107** A3
Three Kings Yd
W1 . . . . **118** A4
Three Mill La E3 . . . . **27** B2
Three Nun Ct EC2 **109** A2
Three Oak La SE1 **138** C4
Threshers Pl
W11 . . . . . **31** A2 **112** A4
Thring Ho ② SW7 **172** C2
Throgmorton Ave
EC2 . . . . **109** C2
Throgmorton St
EC2 . . . . **109** C2
Thrush St SE17 . . **150** C2
Thurland Ho ③
SE16 . . . . **40** A2
Thurland Rd SE16 **139** B2
Thurlby Ave
SW12 . . . . **60** C1
Thurleigh Ct SW12 **60** C1
Thurleigh Rd
SW12 . . . . **60** C1
Thurloe Cl SW7 . . **144** A4
Thurloe Ct SW3 . . **144** A3
Thurloe Pl SW7 . . **143** C4
Thurloe Place Mews
SW7 . . . . **143** C4
Thurloe Sq SW7 . . **144** A4
Thurloe St SW7 . . **143** C4
Thurlow Hill SE21 . **75** B2
Thurlow Ho **17**
SW16 . . . . **74** A1
Thurlow Park Rd SE21,
SE24 . . . . **75** B2
Thurlow Rd NW3 . . **11** C3
Thurlow St SE17 . . **152** A1
Thurlow Terr NW5 . **12** C3
Thurlow Twrs
SE27 . . . . **74** C1
Thurlow Wlk
SE17 . . . . **152** A1
Thurnscoe NW1 . . **82** C3
Thursley Gdns
SW19 . . . . **69** C2
Thursley Ho **10**
SW2 . . . . **74** B4
Thurso Ho NW6 . . . **78** A1
Thurston Ind Est
SE13 . . . . **67** A4
Thurston Rd SE8,
SE13 . . . . **52** A1
Thurtle Rd E2 . . . . **24** B3
Tibbatt's Rd E3 . . . **27** A1
Tibberton Sq N1 . . **86** C4
Tibbets Cl SW19 . . **69** C3
Tibbet's Corner
SW19 . . . . **69** C4
Tibbet's Ride
SW19 . . . . **69** C4
Tiber Cl **10** E3 . . . . **26** C4
Tiber Gdns N1 . . . . **84** B3
Tickford Ho NW8 . . **90** A3
Tidal Basin Rd E16 . **35** B2
Tidbury Ct SW8 . . **160** C1
Tidemill Prim Sch **20**
SE8 . . . . **51** C3
Tideswell **10** NW5 . **13** A4
Tideswell Rd
SW15 . . . . **57** B3
Tideway Ct **9**
SE16 . . . . **32** C1
Tideway Ho E14 . . . **41** C4

Tideway Ind Est
SW8 . . . . **161** A3
Tideway Wharf
SW13 . . . . **46** A1
Tideway Yd SW13 . . **46** A1
Tidey St E3 . . . . . . **33** C4
Tidworth Ho **8**
SE22 . . . . **64** A4
Tidworth Rd E3 . . . **26** C1
Tierney Rd SW2 . . . **74** A3
Tierney Terr SW2 . . **74** A3
Tiffany Hts SW11 . . **93** C3
Tiger Ho **17** **17** A4
Tiger Way E5 . . . . . **17** A4
Tilbury Cl **14** SE15 . **49** B3
Tilbury Ho **4**
SE14 . . . . **50** C4
Tildesley Rd SW15 . **57** B1
Tilehurst NW1 . . . . **92** B3
Tilehurst Rd SW17,
SW18 . . . . **71** C3
Tile Kiln La N6 . . . . . **4** B3
Tilford Gdns SW19 . **69** C3
Tilford Ho **8** SW2 . . **74** B4
Tilia Rd E5 . . . . **17** A4
Tilia Wlk **3** SW9 . . **63** A3
Tiller Ho **26** N1 . . . . **24** A4
Tiller L. Ctr E14 . . . **41** C3
Tiller Rd E14 . . . . . **41** C3
Tillet Sq SE16 . . . . **41** A4
Tillet Way **5**
E2 . . . . **24** C2 **99** B4
Tilling Ho **5** SE15 . **65** A4
Tillman Ho **5**
SW2 . . . . **74** B3
Tillman St E1 . . . . . **32** A3
Tilloch St **5** N1 . . . **14** B1
Tillotson Ct SW8 . . **161** C1
Tilney Ct EC1 . . . . . **97** A2
Tilney Gdns **12** N1 . **15** C2
Tilney St W1 . . . . . **117** C2
Tilson Ct **2** SE15 . . **49** A3
Tilson Gdns SW2,
SW4 . . . . **74** A4
Tilson Ho SW2 . . . . **74** A4
Tilton St SW6 . . . . **154** B3
Tiltwood The W3 . . **28** B2
Timberland Cl **18**
SE15 . . . . **49** C3
Timberland Rd E1 . . **32** A3
Timber Mill Way
SW4 . . . . **61** C4
Timber Pond Rd
SE16 . . . . **40** C4
Timber St EC1 . . . . . **96** C2
Times Sq E8 . . . . . **16** B3
Timothy Cl **1**
SW4 . . . . **61** B2
Timsbury Wlk **3**
SW15 . . . . **68** C3
Tina Ct SW16 . . . . . **74** C1
Tindal St SW9 . . . . **48** A2
Tinniswood Cl N5 . . **14** C3
Tinsley Rd E1 . . . . . **32** B4
Tintagel Cres SE22 . **64** B3
Tintagel Ct EC1 . . . **96** A2
Tintern Ct SW15 . . **58** A2
Tintern Ho
Belgravia SW1 . . **146** A3
Regent's Pk NW1 . . **82** B1
Tintern St SW4 . . . . **62** A3
Tinworth St SE11 . . **148** B2
Tipthorpe Rd
SW11 . . . . **60** C4
Tiptree **7** NW1 . . . **13** A1

Tisbury Ct W1 . . . . **119** B4
Tisdall Pl SE17 . . . **151** C3
Tissington Ct **4**
SE16 . . . . **40** C2
Titan Bsns Est **3**
SE8 . . . . **51** C3
Titan Ct TW8 . . . . . **36** B1
Titchborne Row
W2 . . . . **102** B1
Titchfield Rd NW8 . **80** C4
Titchwell Rd
SW18 . . . . **71** C3
Tite St SW3 . . . . . **158** C4
Titmuss St W12 . . . **39** B4
Tiverton Rd NW6,
NW10 . . . . **22** C4
Tiverton St SE1 . . **136** C2
Tivoli Ct SE16 . . . . . **33** B1
Tobago St **12** E14 . . **41** C4
Toby La E1 . . . . **26** A1
Todber Ho W14 . . . **126** A2
Todds Wlk N7 . . . . . **5** B2
Tokenhouse Yd
EC2 . . . . **109** B2
Token Yd SW15 . . . . **58** A3
Toland Sq SW15 . . . **56** C2
Tolchurch **21** W11 . . **31** C3
Toldos Sch N16 . . . . **7** A3
Tolhurst Dr **4**
W10 . . . . **23** A2
Tollbridge **9** E14 . . **34** B3
Tollet St E1 . . . . . . **25** C1
Tollgate Dr SE21 . . **76** A2
Tollgate Ho **6**
NW6 . . . . **78** A2
Tollhouse Way N19 . . **4** B2
Tollington Ct N4 . . . . **5** B2
Tollington Ho **4**
N19 . . . . **5** A1
Tollington Pk N4 . . . **5** B2
Tollington Pl N4 . . . . **5** B2
Tollington Rd N7 . . . **14** B4
Tollington Way N7 . . **5** A1
Tolmers Sq NW1 . . . **93** A2
Tolpaide Ho SE11 . **149** B3
Tolpuddle St N1 . . . **85** B2
Tolsford Rd E5 . . . . **17** A3
Tom Groves Cl
E15 . . . . **19** C3
Tom Hood Cl E15 . . **19** C3
Tom Jenkinson Rd **5**
E16 . . . . **35** C1
Tomkyns Ho SE11 . **149** B3
Tomline Ho **3** SE1 . **122** C1
Tomlin's Gr E3 . . . . **26** C2
Tomlinson Cl
2 Gunnersbury
W4 . . . . **37** A1
Spitalfields
E1 . . . . **111** A3
Tomlins Terr E14 . . **33** A3
Tomlins Wlk **4** N7 . . **5** B2
Tompion Ho **3** EC1 . **96** B2
Tompion St EC1 . . . **96** B3
Tom Smith Cl
SE10 . . . . **53** A4
Tomson Ho SE1 . . **138** C2
Tom Williams Ho
SW6 . . . . **154** C3
Tonbridge Hos
WC1 . . . . **94** A3
Tonbridge St WC1 . . **94** A3
Toneborough **18**
NW8 . . . . **78** B3
Tonsley Hill SW18 . **59** A2

Tonsley Pl SW18 . . **59** A2
Tonsley Rd SW18 . . **59** A2
Tonsley St SW18 . . **59** A2
Took's Ct EC4 . . . . **107** B2
Tooley St SE1 . . . . **124** A1
Tooting Bec Sta
SW17 . . . . **72** C1
Topham Ho **8**
SE10 . . . . **52** B3
Topham St EC1 . . . . **95** B2
Topiary Sq TW9 . . . **54** B4
Topmast Point **25**
E14 . . . . **41** C4
Torah Vodaas
NW11 . . . . **1** B3
Tora Temimah Prim
Sch NW2 . . . . **9** C2
Torbay Ct **13** NW1 . **13** A1
Torbay Mans NW6 . . **23** B4
Torbay Rd NW6 . . . **10** B1
Torbay St **15** NW1 . **13** A1
Tor Ct W8 . . . . . . **127** C4
Tor Gdns W8 . . . . **127** B4
Tornay Ho
Hackney E9 . . . . . . **17** B1
N1 . . . . **84** C2
Torquay St W2 . . . **100** A3
Torrence Ho **6** N19 . **4** B2
Torrens Ct SE5 . . . . **63** C4
Torrens Rd SW2 . . . **62** B2
Torrens St EC1 . . . . **86** A1
Torres Sq E14 . . . . **41** C1
Torriano Ave NW5 . . **13** C3
Torriano Cotts
NW5 . . . . **13** B3
Torriano Jun & Inf
Schs **2** NW5 . . . . **13** C3
Torriano Mews
NW5 . . . . **13** B3
Torridge Gdns
SE15 . . . . **65** B3
Torridon Ho NW6 . . **78** A1
Torrington Pl
Bloomsbury WC1 . **105** B4
St George in East
E1 . . . . **125** C2
Torrington Sq
WC1 . . . . **93** C1
Tortington Ho **1**
SE15 . . . . **50** A3
Torwood Rd SW15 . **56** C2
Tothill Ho SW1 . . . **147** C4
Tothill St SW1 . . . **133** C3
Totland Ho SW18 . . **59** A1
Totnes Terr E1 . . . . **32** C3
Tottenhall **4** NW1 . **12** C1
Tottenham Court Rd
W1 . . . . **105** A4
Tottenham Court
Road Sta W1 . . . **105** C2
Tottenham Mews
W1 . . . . **105** A4
Tottenham Rd N1 . . **16** A2
Tottenham St W1 . . **105** A4
Totteridge Ho
SW11 . . . . **167** C2
Touchard Ho N1 . . . **97** C3
Toulmin St SE1 . . . **136** C3
Toulon St SE5 . . . . **48** B3
Toulouse Ct **2**
SE16 . . . . **40** A1
Tounson Ct SW1 . . **147** C3
Tournay Rd SW6 . . **155** A2
Toussaint Wlk **18**
SE16 . . . . **139** C2
Tovy Ho **6** SE1 . . . **153** B1

Towcester Rd E3 . . **27** B1
Tower 42 EC2 . . . . **110** C2
Tower Bldgs **22**
E1 . . . . **32** A1
Tower Br App E1,
EC3 . . . . **124** C3
Tower Bridge EC3,
SE1, EC4, ... **124** C3
Tower Bridge Bsns
Complex SE16 . . . . **40** A2
Tower Bridge Bsns Sq
SE16 . . . . **40** A2
Tower Bridge Ex
E1 . . . . **124** C3
Tower Bridge Piazza
SE1 . . . . **124** C1
Tower Bridge Prim
Sch SE1 . . . . **138** C4
Tower Bridge Rd
SE1 . . . . **138** A3
Tower Bridge Sq
SE1 . . . . **138** C4
Tower Cl NW3 . . . . **11** C3
Tower Ct
Brockley SE4 . . . . **66** A3
Stamford Hill E5 . . . **7** B4
St John's Wood
NW8 . . . . **80** B2
Towergate SE1 . . . **152** A4
Towergate Ho **35**
E3 . . . . **26** B3
Tower Gateway Sta
EC3 . . . . **124** C4
TOWER HAMLETS . . **33** B4
Tower Hamlets Coll
12 Poplar E14 . . . **34** A3
22 Poplar E14 . . . **34** A2
18 Stepney E1 . . . **32** C3
Tower Hill EC3 . . . **125** A3
Tower Hill Sta
EC3 . . . . **124** C3
Tower House Sch
SW14 . . . . **55** B3
Tower Mans SE1 . . **138** C1
Tower Mews E5 . . . **18** A3
Tower Millennium
Pier EC3 . . . . **124** B2
Tower Mill Rd
7 Camberwell
SE15 . . . . **49** A4
1 SE15 . . . . **49** A4
Tower of London The
EC3 . . . . **124** B3
Tower Pl E EC3 . . . **124** B3
Tower Pl W EC3 . . . **124** B3
Tower Rd NW10 . . . . **8** C1
Tower Rise TW9 . . . **54** A4
Tower Royal EC4 . . **123** B4
Towers Pl TW10 . . . **54** A2
Towers The
Dartmouth Pk NW5 . **4** A1
1 Richmond TW9 . **54** B3
Tower Terr SE4 . . . **66** A3
Towerview SE13 . . . **66** C2
Tower Wharf SE1 . **138** C4
Tower Wlk SE1 . . . **152** A4
Towncourt Path N4 . **6** B3
Townhall Ave **3**
W4 . . . . **37** C1
Town Hall Rd
SW11 . . . . **60** B4
Town Hos EC1 . . . . **96** B1
Townley Rd SE22 . . **64** A2
Townley St SE17 . . **151** B2

Townmead Bsns Ctr
SW6 . . . . .59 B4
Townmead Rd
Richmond TW9 . . . . .45 A1
Sands End SW6 . .166 C1
Townsend Ho 14
SE1 . . . . .153 C3
Townsend Ind Est
NW10 . . . . .20 B3
Townsend Mews 3
SW18 . . . . .71 B2
Townsend Prim Sch
SE17 . . . . .152 A1
Townsend Rd NW8 .80 C2
SE17 . . . . .152 A1
Townsend St SE1, .
Townsend Yd N6 . . .4 A3
Townshend Ct
NW8 . . . . .80 B2
Townshend Est
NW8 . . . . .80 A2
Townshend Rd
Primrose Hill NW8 . .80 B3
Richmond TW9 . . . . .54 B3
Townshend Terr
TW9 . . . . .54 C3
Towns Ho 3 SW4 . .61 C4
Towpath Wlk E9 . . .18 B3
Towton Rd SE27 . . .75 B2
Toxteth Ho N4 . . . . .6 B4
Toynbee St E1 . . .110 C3
Toynbee Studios
E1 . . . . .111 A3
Tracey Ave NW2 . . . .9 C3
Tracy Ho 13 E3 . . . .26 B2
Tradescant Ho 18
E9 . . . . .17 B1
Tradescant Rd
SW8 . . . . .162 B1
Trade Twr 3
SW11 . . . . .59 B4
Trade Winds Ct 1
E1 . . . . .125 C2
Trading Estate Rd
NW10 . . . . .20 B1
Traemore Ct
SW16 . . . . .74 C1
Trafalgar Ave
SE15 . . . . .49 B4
Trafalgar Cl 1
SE16 . . . . .41 A2
Trafalgar Gdns
Stepney E1 . . . . . . .32 C4
W8 . . . . .128 B2
Trafalgar Gr SE10 . .52 C4
Trafalgar Ho
SE17 . . . . .151 A2
Trafalgar Mews
E9 . . . . .18 B2
Trafalgar Point 2
N1 . . . . .15 C1
Trafalgar Rd SE10 . .43 A1
Trafalgar Sq SW1 .119 C2
Trafalgar St SE17 .151 C2
Trafalgar Way E14 . .34 B1
Trafford Ho N1 . . . .87 C2
Tragail SW15 . . . . . .58 A2
Trahorn Cl E1 . . . . .25 A1
Traitors Gate EC3 .124 C2
Tralee Ct 31 SE16 . .40 A1
Tramway Ave E15 . .19 C1
Trance Way W4 . . . .36 C3
Tranmere Ho 7
N7 . . . . .14 C3
Tranmere Rd SW17,
SW18 . . . . .71 B2

Tranquil Pas SE3 . . .53 B1
Tranquil Vale SE3 . . .53 A1
Transept St NW1 .102 B3
Transom Cl SE16 . . .41 A2
Transom Sq E14 . . . .42 A1
Tranton Rd SE16 . . .40 A3
Trappes Ho 2
SE16 . . . . .40 A2
Travers Ho 3
SE10 . . . . .52 C4
Travers Rd N7 . . . . . .5 C1
Travis Ho SE10 . . . . .52 B2
Treadgold Ho 7
W11 . . . . .30 C2
Treadgold St W11 . .30 C2
Treadway St E2 . . . .25 A3
Treasury Bldgs
SW1 . . . . .134 A4
Treaty St N1 . . . . . .84 C3
Trebeck St W1 . . . .118 A1
Treborough Ho
W1 . . . . .103 B4
Trebovir Rd SW5 .141 C3
Treby St E3 . . . . . . .26 B1
Trecastle Way 2
N7 . . . . .13 C4
Tredegar Mews 10
E3 . . . . .26 B2
Tredegar Rd E3 . . . .26 B3
Tredegar Sq E3 . . . .26 B2
Tredegar Terr E3 . . .26 B2
Trederwen Rd E8 . .24 C4
Treen Ave SW13 . . .56 B4
Trees The N16 . . . . . .6 C4
Trefil Wlk N7 . . . . . .14 A4
Trefoil Rd SW18 . . .59 B2
Tregarvon Rd
SW11 . . . . .60 C3
Trego Rd E9 . . . . . .18 C1
Tregothnan Rd
SW9 . . . . .62 A4
Tregunter Rd
SW10 . . . . .142 C1
Treherne Ct SW9 . . .48 A2
Trehern Rd 3
SW14 . . . . .55 C4
Trehurst St E5 . . . . .18 A3
Trelawney Est E9 . .17 B2
Trelawney Ho
SE1 . . . . .136 C4
Trelawn Rd SW2 . . .62 C2
Trellis Sq 1 E3 . . . .26 B2
Tremadoc Rd SW4 . .61 C3
Tremaine Cl SE4 . . .51 C1
Trematon Ho
SE11 . . . . .149 C2
Tremlett Gr N19 . . . .4 B1
Tremlett Mews 7
N19 . . . . .4 B1
Trenchard St SE10 . .42 C1
Trenchold St
SW8 . . . . .162 A3
Trendell Ho 3
E14 . . . . .33 C3
Trenmar Gdns
NW10 . . . . .22 A2
Trentham St SW18 . .70 C3
Trent Ho SE15 . . . . .65 B3
Trent Rd SW2 . . . . .62 B2
Treport St SW18 . . .71 A4
Tresco Ho SE11 . . .149 B2
Tresco Rd SE15 . . . .65 A3
Tresham Cres
NW8 . . . . .90 A2
Tresham Wlk E9 . . .17 B3

Tresidder Ho 10
SW4 . . . . .73 C4
Tressel Cl 20 N1 . . .15 A1
Tressillian Cres
SE4 . . . . .66 C4
Tressillian Rd SE4 . .66 C3
Trevanion Rd
W14 . . . . .140 B2
Trevelyan Gdns
NW10 . . . . .22 B4
Trevelyan Ho
16 Globe Town
E2 . . . . .25 C2
SE5 . . . . .48 A3
Treveris St SE1 . . .122 B1
Treverton St W10 . .22 C1
Treverton Twr 1
W10 . . . . .30 C4
Treves Ho
E1 . . . . .24 C1 99 C1
Treville St SW15 . . .69 A4
Trevithick Ho 1
SE16 . . . . .40 A2
Trevithick St SE8 . . .51 C4
Trevor Pl SW7 . . . .130 B3
Trevor Roberts Sch
NW8 . . . . .11 C1
Trevor Sq SW7 . . .130 B3
Trevor St SW7 . . . .130 B3
Trevose Ho SE11 . .149 A2
Trewint St SW18 . . .71 B2
Triangle Est The
SE11 . . . . .149 B1
Triangle Ho SE1 . .138 C4
Triangle Pl SW4 . . .61 C3
Triangle Rd 7 E8 . .25 A4
Triangle The
Crouch End N19 . . . .4 C4
EC1 . . . . .96 B2
10 Hackney E8 . . . .25 A4
Trident Ho 10 E14 . .34 B3
Trident St SE16 . . . .40 C2
Trieste Ct SW12 . . .72 B3
Trig La EC4 . . . . . .122 C4
Trigon Rd SW8 . . .163 A2
Trillington Ho
W12 . . . . .29 C1
Trimdon NW1 . . . . .83 A3
Trimmer Wlk 11
TW8 . . . . .44 A4
Trim St SE8 . . . . . . .51 B4
Trinder Gdns N19 . . .5 A3
Trinder Rd N4, N19 . .5 A3
Trinidad Ho 17
E14 . . . . .33 B2
Trinidad St E14 . . . .33 B2
Trinity Church Rd
SW13 . . . . .47 A4
Trinity Church Sq
SE1 . . . . .137 A2
Trinity Cl
3 Clapham SW4 . . .61 B3
Lewisham SE13 . . . .67 C3
Trinity Coll London
SE1 . . . . .148 B1
Trinity Coll of Music
SE10 . . . . .52 C4
Trinity Cotts TW9 . .54 B4
Trinity Cres SW17 . .72 C2
Trinity Ct
Finsbury WC1 . . . . .94 C2

Trinity Ct continued
2 Hoxton N1 . . . . . .24 A4
Rotherhithe SE16 . . .41 A4
Willesden NW2 . . . . .9 B3
Trinity Gdns
E16 . . . . .35 B4
Stockwell SW2,
SW9 . . . . .62 B3
Trinity Gn 1 E1 . . . .32 B4
Trinity Gr 7 SE10 . .52 B2
Trinity Ho SE1 . . . .137 A2
Trinity Homes 14
SW2 . . . . .62 B3
Trinity Mews
SW18 . . . . .70 C4
Trinity Pl EC3 . . . .124 C3
Trinity Rd
Wandsworth SW17,
SW18 . . . . .72 A4
Trinity Rise SE24,
SW2 . . . . .75 A4
Trinity St Mary's Prim
Sch 3 SW12 . . . . .72 C3
Trinity Sq EC3 . . . .124 B4
Trinity St
3 Newham E16 . . . .35 C4
SE1 . . . . .137 B2
Trinity Way W3 . . . .29 B2
Trio Pl SE1 . . . . . . .137 A2
Tristan Ct 34 SE8 . .51 B4
Triton Ct EC2 . . . . .97 C1
Triton Ho 2 E14 . . .42 A2
Tritton Rd SE21, ...
SE27 . . . . .75 C1
Trocette Mans
SE1 . . . . .138 B2
Trojan Ct NW6 . . . .10 A1
Trojan Ind Est
NW10 . . . . .8 B2
Troon Cl 36 SE16 . .40 A1
Troon Ho 9 E14 . . . .33 A3
Troon St E1 . . . . . . .33 A3
Tropical Ct 2
W10 . . . . .22 C2
Trossachs Rd
SE22 . . . . .64 A2
Trothy Rd SE1 . . . .153 C3
Trotman Ho 1
SE14 . . . . .50 B2
Trott St SW11 . . . .168 A3
Trotwood Ho 3
SE16 . . . . .40 A4
Troubridge Ct 12
W4 . . . . .37 B1
Troutbeck NW1 . . . .92 B3
Troutbeck Rd
SE14 . . . . .51 A2
Trouville Rd SW4 . . .61 B1
Trowbridge Est 6
E15 . . . . .19 B2
Trowbridge Rd E9 . .18 B2
Trower Ho 5 E9 . . .18 A2
Troy Ct 8 W8 . . . . .127 B2
Troyes Ho NW3 . . . .12 B3
Troy Town SE15 . . . .64 C4
Troy Town Flats
SE15 . . . . .64 C4
Truman's Rd 24
N16 . . . . .16 A3
Trump St EC2 . . . .109 A1
Trundle St SE1 . . . .136 C4
Trundleys Rd SE8 . .51 A4
Trundley's Rd SE8 . .40 C1
Trundley's Terr
SE8 . . . . .40 C2

Truro Ho 29 W2 . . .31 C4
Truro St NW5 . . . . .12 C2
Truslove Rd SE27 . .74 C4
Trussley Rd W6 . . . .39 B3
Tryon Cres E9 . . . . .25 B4
Tryon St SW3 . . . .144 C2
Tubbs Rd NW10 . . .21 B3
Tudor Cl
Crouch End N6 . . . . .4 B4
Hampstead NW3 . . .12 A2
Tulse Hill SW2 . . . . .62 B1
Tudor Ct
Kingsland N1 . . . . . .16 A2
5 Rotherhithe
SE16 . . . . .32 C1
South Acton W5 . . . .36 C4
Tudor Gdns SW14 . .45 A3
Tudor Gr E9 . . . . . . .17 B1
Tudor Ho
Brook Green W14 . . .39 C2
24 Hackney E9 . . . .17 B1
Tudor Mews 2
NW10 . . . . .8 C2
Tudor Rd E9 . . . . . .25 A4
Tudor St EC4 . . . . .121 C4
Tudor Way W3 . . . . .36 C4
Tufnell Ct 13 E3 . . .26 B4
Tufnell Mans 7
N7 . . . . .5 A1
Tufnell Park Mans 2
N7 . . . . .5 A1
Tufnell Park Prim Sch
N7 . . . . .13 C4
Tufnell Park Rd N19,
N19 . . . . .13 B4
Tufnell Park Sta
N19 . . . . .13 B4
Tufton Ct SW1 . . . .134 A1
Tufton St SW1 . . . .134 A1
Tuke Sch SE15 . . . .50 A2
Tullis Ho 12 E9 . . . .17 B1
Tulse Hill SW2 . . . . .74 C4
Tulse Hill SW27 . . . .75 A2
Tulse Hill Sta
SE27 . . . . .75 A2
Tulse Ho SW2 . . . . .62 C1
Tulsemere Rd SE21, ...
SE27 . . . . .75 B2
Tunbridge Ct 1
SE26 . . . . .76 C1
Tunbridge Ho EC1 . .96 A4
Tunis Rd W12 . . . . .30 A1
Tunley Gn 12 E14 . .33 B4
Tunley Rd
Dagenham NW10 . . .21 A4
Upper Tooting SW12,
SW17 . . . . .72 C2
Tunley Rd
Dagenham NW10 . . .21 A4
Tunnel Ave SE10 . . .43 A4
Tunnel Rd SE16 . . . .40 B4
Tunstall Ct 14
TW9 . . . . .44 B2
Tunstall Rd SW9 . . .62 B3
Tunstall Wlk 10
TW8 . . . . .44 A4
Tunworth Cres
SW15 . . . . .56 B1
Tun Yd SW8 . . . . . .61 A4

Tupman Ho **26**
SE16 .... **139** B3
Turberville Ho **1**
SW9 .... 62 B4
Turenne Cl SW18 ...59 B3
Turin St E2 ....24 C2 **99** B3
Turk's Head Yd
EC1 .... **108** A4
Turks Row SW3 **145** A2
Turle Rd N4 .... 5 B2
Turlewray Cl N4 ...5 B3
Turnagain La EC4 **108** A2
Turnberry Cl **24**
SE16 .... 40 A1
Turnberry Quay **1**
E14 .... 42 A3
Turnbull Ho N1 ...86 B4
Turnchapel Mews **1**
SW4 .... 61 A4
Turner Cl **7** SW9 ..48 A2
Turner Ct
9 Herne Hill SE5...63 C3
24 Rotherhithe
SE16 .... 40 B4
Turner Ho
Finsbury Pk N4 ...5 B3
2 Millwall E14 ...41 C4
St John's Wood
NW8 .... 80 A2
Strand WC2 ..... **120** B3
Westminster SW1 . **147** C3
Turner Lo **10**
SW19 .... 69 C3
Turner Pl SW11 ...60 A2
Turners Ct E15 ....19 B4
Turner's Rd E3 ....33 B4
Turner St
Canning Town
E16 .... 35 B3
Stepney E1 .... 32 A4
Turnerville Rd
W14 .... **154** C4
Turney Rd SE21 ...75 C4
Turney Sch SE21...75 B4
Turnham Green Sta
W4 .... 38 A2
Turnham Green Terr
W4 .... 38 A2
Turnham Ho SE4 ..66 A3
Turnham Prim Sch **1**
SE4 .... 66 A3
Turnmill Ho SE4...66 B4
Turnmill St **8**
SW2 .... 62 C2
Turnmill St EC1 . **108** A4
Turnour Ho **31**
E1 .... 32 A3
Turnpike Cl SE8 ...51 B3
Turnpike Ho EC1 .96 B3
Turnpin La **3**
SE10 .... 52 B4
Turpentine La
SW1 .... **146** B1
Turpin Ho SW11 . **170** A4
Turpin Way N19 ... 4 C3
Turquand St SE17 **151** A3
Turret Gr SW4 ....61 B4
Turville Ho NW8 ..90 A2
Turville St
E2 ....24 B1 **98** C2
Tuscan Ho **38** E2 ..25 B2
Tuskar St SE10 ....43 A1
Tuttle Ho SW1 ... **147** C1
Tweed Ho E14 .....27 B1

Tweezer's Alley
WC2 .... **121** B4
Twelvetrees Bsns Pk
E16 .... 27 C1
Twelvetrees Cres
E3 .... 27 B1
Twig Folly Cl **21**
E2 .... 25 C3
Twilley St SW18 ...71 A4
Twine Ct E1 .... 32 B2
Twinings Mus
WC2 .... **107** B1
Twisden Rd NW5 ...13 A4
Twycross Mews
SE10 .... 43 A2
Twyford CE High Sch
W3 .... 28 A1
Twyford Ho N5 .....6 A1
Twyford Sp Ctr
W3 .... 28 A1
Twyford St N1 ....84 C4
Twynholm Mans
SW6 .... **154** A2
Tyburn Tree (site of)
W2 .... **116** C4
Tyburn Way N1 ... **117** A4
Tyer's Est SE1 .... **138** A4
Tyers Gate SE1 ... **138** A3
Tyers St SE11 .... **148** C2
Tyers Terr SE11 . **149** A1
Tyler Cl E2 ....24 B3
Tyler Ho SE3 ......52 C1
Tyler St
Greenwich SE10...43 A1
SE10 .... 53 A4
Tylney Ho **10** E1 ..32 A3
Tymperley Ct
SW19 .... 70 A3
Tyndale La N1 ....15 A1
Tyndale Mans ...15 A1
Tyndale Terr **13**
N1 .... 15 A1
Tyneham Cl **9**
SW11 .... 60 C4
Tyneham Rd SW11.60 C4
Tynemouth St
SW6 .... **166** C2
Tyne St E1 .... **111** A2
Tynsdale Rd NW10..8 A2
Tynte Ct E9 .... 18 A3
Tynwald Ho **14**
SE26 .... 76 C1
Type St E2 .... 25 C3
Tyrawley Rd SW6 **166** A4
Tyrells Ct **3** SE15 ..65 A4
Tyrrell Ho SW1 .. **161** A4
Tyrrell Rd SE22 ...64 C3
Tyrwhitt Rd SE4 ..66 C4
Tysoe St EC1 ......95 C3
Tyssen Com Prim Sch
N16 .... 7 C3
Tyssen Rd N16 .....7 B1
Tyssen St
Dalston E8 ....16 B2
Hoxton N1 ....24 A3
Tyson Ho E9 ....18 A1
Tytherton **22** E2 ..25 B3
Tytherton Rd N19...4 C1

U
Uamvar St E14 ....34 A4
Udall St SW1 ..... **147** A3
Udimore Ho **11**
W10 .... 30 B4

Uffington Rd
NW10 .... 22 A4
Ufford St SE1 .... **135** C4
Ufton Gr N1 ....15 C1
Ufton Rd N1 ......16 A1
Uhura Sq **19** N16 ...7 A1
Ujima Ct N19 ......5 A3
Ullin St E14 ....34 B4
Ullswater SW15 ...57 C1
Ullswater Ho SE15..50 B4
Ullswater Rd
Barnes SW13 .....46 C3
West Norwood SE27,
SE16 .... 75 A2
Ulster Pl NW1 .... **92** A1
Ulster Terr NW1 .. **92** A2
Ulundi Rd SE3 ....53 A4
Ulva Rd SW15 .....57 C3
Ulverscroft Rd
SE22 .... 64 C2
Ulverstone Rd
SE27 .... 75 A2
Ulysses Rd NW6 ...10 B3
Umberston St E1 ..32 A3
Umbria St SW15 ...56 C1
Una Ho **7** NW5 ...13 A2
Undercliff SE10 ...52 B2
Undercliff Rd
SE13 .... 67 A4
Underhill Ho **7**
E14 .... 33 C4
Underhill Pas NW1 **82** B4
Underhill St NW1.. **82** B3
Undershaft EC3 .. **110** A1
Underwood Ho
W6 .... 39 A3
Underwood Rd
E1 ....24 C1 **99** C1
Underwood Row
N1 .... 97 A4
Underwood St N1 .97 A4
Undine Rd E14 ....42 A2
Unicorn Bldg **14**
E1 .... 32 C2
Unicorn Sch TW9...44 B2
Union Cl E11 ......19 C4
Union Ct
42 Paddington
W2 .... 31 C4
2 Richmond TW10 .54 A2
South Lambeth
SW4 .... **172** A1
Whitechapel EC2 . **110** A2
Union Dr E1 ....26 A1
Union Gr SW8 ... **171** C2
Union Mews **22**
SW9 .... **172** A1
Union Pk **13** SE10..43 B1
Union Rd SW8 ... **171** C1
Union Sq N1 ...... **87** A3
Union St
Mill Meads E15 ...27 C4
SE1 .... **122** C1
Union Wharf N1 .. **87** A2
Union Wlk
E2 ....24 A2 **98** B4
Union Yd W1 .... **104** B1
United International
Coll W1 .... **104** B3
Unity Cl NW10 ....8 C2
Unity Mews NW1 . **83** B2
Univ Coll Jun Sch **31**
NW3 .... 11 B2
Univ Coll London
Bloomsbury WC1 . **93** B2
Bloomsbury WC1 . **94** B2

Univ Coll London
(Windeyer Inst)
W1 .... **105** A4
Univ Coll London
(Wolfson Ho)
NW1 .... **93** A3
University Coll Hospl
W1 .... **93** A2
University Coll Sch
NW3 .... 11 B3
University Mans
SW15 .... 57 C4
University St WC1 . **93** A1
Univ of California
WC1 .... **105** A3
Univ of East London
(Duncan Ho) **7**
E15 .... 27 C4
Univ of Greenwich
SE10 .... 52 C4
Univ of London
WC1 .... **93** C1
Univ of London
(King's Coll Hall)
SE5 .... 63 C4
Univ of London
(Queen Mary &
Westfield Coll)
E1 .... 26 A1
Univ of Notre Dame
SW1 .... **119** C3
Univ of Notre Dame
SW1 .... **119** C3
Univ of Roehampton
(Digby Stuart Coll)
SW15 .... 56 C2
Univ of Roehampton
(Froebel Coll)
SW15 .... 56 B1
Univ of Roehampton
(Southlands Coll)
SW15 .... 56 C2
Univ of Roehampton
(Whitelands Coll)
SW15 .... 68 C4
Univ of Westminster
(Cavendish Campus)
W1 .... **104** C4
Univ of Westminster
(Marylebone
Campus) W1 .... **103** B4
Univ of Westminster
(Regent Campus)
W1 .... **104** C3
Univ of Westminster
(Regent Campus,
Univ HQ) W1 ... **104** B2
Univ of Westminster
(Wigram House
Halls of Residence)
SW1 .... **133** A1
Unwin Cl SE15 ....49 C4
Unwin Rd SW7 ... **129** C2
Ubrook Mews
W2 .... **101** A1
Upcerne Rd SW10 **157** A1
Upcott Ho
13 Bromley E3 ....27 A2
4 Hackney E9 .... **17** B1
Upgrove Manor Way
17 SE24 ....75 A4
Upham Park Rd
W4 .... 38 A2
Upnall Ho SE17 ...64 C1
Upnall Ho **18** SE15..50 B4

Upnor Way SE17.. **152** B2
Upper Addison Gdns
W14 .... **126** A4
Upper Bank St
E14 .... 34 A1
Upper Bardsey Wlk **1**
N1 .... 15 B2
Upper Belgrave St
SW1 .... **131** C2
Upper Berkeley St
W1 .... **103** A1
Upper Brockley Rd
SE4 .... 51 B1
Upper Brook St
W1 .... **117** B4
Upper Caldy Wlk **18**
N1 .... 15 B2
Upper Camelford Wlk
1 W10 ....31 A4
Upper Cheyne Row
SW3 .... **158** A4
Upper Clarendon Wlk
12 W11 ....31 A3
Upper Dengie Wlk
N1 .... 86 C4
Upper Grosvenor St
W1 .... **117** B3
Upper Ground
SE1 .... **121** B2
Upper Gulland Wlk **22**
N1 .... 15 B2
Upper Hampstead Wlk
26 NW3 ....11 B4
Upper Handa Wlk **2**
N1 .... 15 B2
Upper Harley St
NW1 .... **91** C1
Upper Hawkwell Wlk
N1 .... 87 A4
UPPER HOLLOWAY .4 C2
Upper Holloway Sta
N19 .... 4 C2
Upper James St
W1 .... **119** A4
Upper John St
W1 .... **119** A4
Upper Lismore Wlk **8**
N1 .... 15 B2
Upper Mall W6 ....39 A1
Upper Marsh SE1 . **135** A2
Upper Montague St
W1 .... **102** C3
Upper North St E3,
E14 .... 33 C4
Upper Park Rd
NW3 .... 12 B3
Upper Phillimore
Gdns W8 .... **127** B3
Upper Ramsey Wlk **19**
N1 .... 15 C2
Upper Rawreth Wlk
N1 .... 87 A4
Upper Richmond Rd
SW15 .... 57 B3
Upper Richmond Rd
W TW10, SW14,
SW15 .... 55 B3
Upper St Martin's La
WC2 .... **120** A4
Upper St N1 ...... **86** A3
Upper Tachbrook St
SW1 .... **147** A4
Upper Talbot Wlk **7**
W10 .... 31 A3
Upper Terr NW3 ...2 B1

Upper Thames St
EC4 . . . . 123 A4
Upper Tollington Pk
N4. . . . . 5 C3
UPPER TOOTING . . . 72 B1
Upper Tooting Park
Mans **1** SW17. . . 72 C2
Upper Tooting Pk
SW17. . . . . 72 B2
Upper Tooting Rd
SW17. . . . . 72 B1
Upper Tulse Hill
SW2 . . . . 74 B3
Upper Wimpole St
W1 . . . . 103 C4
Upstall St SE5. . . . 48 A2
Upton Cl NW2 . . . . . 1 A1
Urban Mews N4. . . . 6 A4
Urlwin St SE5 . . . . 48 A4
Urlwin Wlk SW9. . . 48 A2
Urmston Dr SW19 . . 70 A3
Urmston Ho **4**
E14 . . . . 42 B2
Ursula Mews N4. . . . 6 A3
Ursula St SW11. . . 168 A3
Urswick Rd E5, E9 . 17 B2
Usborne Mews
SW8 . . . . 163 A2
Usher Rd E3. . . . . . 26 B3
Usk Rd SW11. . . . . 59 B3
Usk St E2 . . . . 25 C2
Utah Bldg **3** SE13. 52 A2
Utopia Ho **3** NW2. . 8 C2
Utopia Village
NW1 . . . . 81 B4
Uverdale Rd
SW10 . . . . 157 A1
Uxbridge Rd W12. . 30 A1
Uxbridge St
W8 . . . . . . 31 C1 **113 B2**

V

Vadnie Bish Ho
NW5 . . . . 13 B2
Vaine Ho **4** E9 . . . . 18 A2
Vale Cl W9 . . . . . . 88 C3
Vale Ct
East Acton W3 . . . 29 B1
St John's Wood W9 . 88 C3
Vale End SE22 . . . . 64 A3
Vale Est The SW3 . . 29 A1
Vale Gr
Acton W3 . . . . . . 28 C1
Stoke Newington N4 . 6 B4
Valens Ho **1** SW2 . . 74 C3
Valentia Pl SW9 . . . 62 C3
Valentine Ho
1 Clapham Pk
SW4 . . . . 61 B1
28 Old Ford E3 . . . 26 B4
Valentine Pl SE1 . . 136 A4
Valentine Rd E9 . . . 17 C2
Valentine Row
SE1 . . . . 136 A3
VALE OF HEALTH . . . 2 C1
Vale of Health NW3 . 2 C1
Vale Rise NW11 . . . . 1 B3
Vale Row N5 . . . . . . 6 A1
Vale Royal N7 . . . . 14 A1
Vale Sch The
SW7 . . . . 128 C1

Vale The
Cricklewood NW11 . . 1 A2
East Acton W3 . . . 29 A1
Valetta Rd W3 . . . . 38 C4
Valette Ho E9 . . . . 17 B2
Valette St E9 . . . . 17 A2
Valiant Ho
6 Cubitt Town
E14 . . . . 42 B4
SW11 . . . . 167 C3
Vallance Rd
E1, E2 . . . . . 24 C1 **99 C1**
Valliere Rd NW10. . 21 C2
Val McKenzie Ave
N7. . . . . 5 C1
Valmar Rd SE5 . . . 48 B2
Valmar Trad Est
SE5. . . . . 48 B2
Valois Ho SE1 . . . 138 C2
Valonia Gdns
SW18 . . . . 58 B1
Vanbern Ho NW5. . . 12 C2
Vanbrugh Ct SE11 . 149 C3
Vanbrugh Fields
SE3 . . . . 53 B3
Vanbrugh Hill SE10,
SE3 . . . . 53 B4
Vanbrugh Ho **8**
E9 . . . . 17 B1
Vanbrugh Park Rd
SE3 . . . . 53 B3
Vanbrugh Park Rd W
SE3 . . . . 53 B3
Vanbrugh Pk SE3 . . 53 B3
Vanbrugh Rd W4 . . 37 C3
Vanbrugh Terr
SE3 . . . . 53 B2
Vanburgh Ho E1. . 110 C4
Vancover Ho **33**
E1. . . . . 32 A1
Vanderbilt Rd
SW18 . . . . 71 B3
Vanderbilt Villas **1**
W12. . . . . 39 C4
Vandon Ct SW1 . . 133 A2
Vandon Pas SW1 . 133 A2
Vandon St SW1 . . 133 A2
Vandyke Cl SW15. . 57 C1
Vandy St
EC2. . . . . 24 A1 **98 A1**
Vane Cl NW3 . . . . . 11 C4
Vane St SW1 . . . . 147 A4
Vange Ho **10** W10. . 30 B4
Van Gogh Ct E14 . . 42 C3
Vanguard Bldg **3**
E14 . . . . 41 C4
Vanguard Ho **11**
E8 . . . . 17 A1
Vanguard St SE8 . . 51 C2
Vanneck Sq SW15. . 56 C2
Vanner Point **17**
E9 . . . . 17 C2
Vansittart St **7**
SE14 . . . . 51 A3
Vanston Pl SW6 . . 155 C2
Vantage Mews **7**
E14 . . . . 34 B1
Vantage Pl W8 . . . 127 C1
Vantrey Ho SE11. . 149 B3
Varcoe Rd SE16 . . . 40 B1
Vardens Rd SW11. . 59 C3
Varden St E1. . . . . 32 A3
Vardon Cl W3 . . . . 28 C3
Vardon Ho SE10 . . . 52 B2
Varey Ho E1. . . . . . 26 A2

Varley Ho **5** NW6 . . 23 C4
Varma Ct SE3 . . . . 53 C2
Varna Rd SW6 . . . 154 C1
Varndell St NW1. . . 92 C4
Varnishers Yard
N1 . . . . 84 B1
Varsity Row SW14 . 45 B1
Vascroft Est NW10 . 20 A1
Vassall Ho **3** E3. . . 26 A2
Vassall Rd SW9 . . 163 C1
Vat Ho SW8 . . . . 162 B2
Vauban Est SE16. . 139 A1
Vauban St SE16 . . 139 A1
Vaudeville Ct N4 . . . 5 C2
Vaughan Ave W6 . . 38 B2
Vaughan Est **8**
E2. . . . . . . 24 B2 **98 C4**
Vaughan Ho SE1 . . 136 A4
Vaughan Rd SE5 . . 63 B4
Vaughan St SE16 . . 41 B4
Vaughan Way E1 . 125 C2
Vaughan Williams Cl
SE8 . . . . 51 C3
VAUXHALL. 148 B1
Vauxhall Bridge Rd
SW1 . . . . 147 A3
Vauxhall City Farm
SE11 . . . . 148 C1
Vauxhall Cross SE1,
SW8 . . . . 148 B1
Vauxhall Gr SW8 . 162 C4
Vauxhall Prim Sch
SE11 . . . . 149 A2
Vauxhall St SE11 . 149 A2
Vauxhall Sta SE11 148 B1
Vauxhall Wlk
SE11 . . . . 148 C2
Vawdrey Cl E1. . . . 25 B1
Vaynor Ho N7 . . . . 14 A4
Vectis Ct SW18 . . . 59 A1
Veda Rd SE13 . . . . 66 C3
Velde Way **2**
SE22 . . . . 64 A2
Vellacott Ho **3**
W12 . . . . 30 A3
Velletri Ho **17** E2 . . 25 C3
Venables St NW8 . 101 C4
Vencourt Pl W6 . . . 38 C2
Venetian Rd SE5. . . 48 B1
Venice Ct **5** SE5 . . 48 B3
Venn Ho N1 . . . . . 85 A3
Ventnor Rd SE14. . . 50 C3
Ventura Ho **12**
SW2 . . . . 62 A3
Venue St E14 . . . . 34 B4
Venus Ho
7 Millwall E14 . . . 41 C2
8 Old Ford E3. . . . 26 C4
Vera Ct **4** W2 . . . 100 A2
Vera Rd SW6 . . . . 164 B4
Verbena Gdns **4**
W6 . . . . 38 C1
Verdun Rd SW13. . . 46 C4
Vere Bank SW19 . . 70 B3
Vereker Rd W14 . . 140 B1
Vere St W1 . . . . . 104 A1
Verity Cl W11. . . . . 31 A3
Verity Ho **20** E3 . . . 26 B2
Vermeer Ct E14 . . . 42 C3
Vermont Rd SW18 . 59 A1
Verne Ct **9** W3. . . . 37 B3
Verneer Gdns
SE15 . . . . 65 B3
Verney Ho
Lisson Gr NW8 . . . 90 A2

Verney Ho continued
South Kensington
SW10 . . . . 156 C4
Verney Way SE16. . 40 A1
Vernon Ct NW2. . . . 1 B1
Vernon Ho SE11 . . 149 A1
Vernon Mews
W14 . . . . 140 B3
Vernon Pl WC1 . . . 106 B3
Vernon Rd
Bow E3 . . . . 26 B3
Mortlake SW14 . . . 55 C4
Vernon Rise WC1 . . 95 A4
Vernon Sq WC1 . . . 95 A4
Vernon St W14 . . . 140 B3
Vernon Yd
W11 . . . . . 31 B2 **112 C4**
Verona Ct
Chiswick W4. . . . . 38 A1
10 SE14 . . . . 50 C4
Veronica Ho
Brockley SE4 . . . . 66 B4
48 Bromley E3. . . . 27 A2
Veronica Rd SW17 . 73 A2
Verran Rd SW12 . . 73 A4
Verulam Bldgs
WC1 . . . . 107 A4
Verulam Ho **1**
W6 . . . . 39 B4
Verulam St EC1 . . 107 B4
Vervain Ho **2**
SE15 . . . . 49 C3
Verwood Ho SW8 . 163 A1
Verwood Lo **1**
E14 . . . . 42 C2
Vesage Ct EC1. . . 107 C3
Vesey Path **11** E14 . 34 A3
Vespan Rd W12. . . 38 C4
Vesta Ct SE1 . . . . 138 A3
Vesta Ho **9** E3. . . . 26 C4
Vesta Rd SE4, SE14. 51 A1
Vestry Mews **9**
SE5 . . . . 49 A2
Vestry Rd SE5 . . . 49 A2
Vestry St N1. . . . . 97 B4
Viaduct Pl **2** E2. . . 25 A2
Viaduct St E2 . . . . 25 A2
Vian St SE13. . . . . 67 A4
Vibart Gdns SW2 . . 74 B4
Vibart Wlk N1 . . . . 84 B4
Vicarage Ave SE3 . . 53 C3
Vicarage Cres
SW11 . . . . 167 B3
Vicarage Ct
7 Putney SW15 . . . 57 C2
W8 . . . . 128 A4
Vicarage Dr SW14 . 55 C2
Vicarage Gate
W8 . . . . 114 A1
Vicarage Gdns
Mortlake SW14 . . . 55 C2
W8 . . . . . . 31 C1 **113 C1**
Vicarage Gr SE5 . . 48 C2
Vicarage Rd SW14 . 55 C2
Vicarage Wlk
SW11 . . . . 167 C4
Vicar's Cl E9 . . . . . 25 B4
Vicars Hill SE13 . . . 67 A3
Vicar's Rd NW5. . . 12 C3
Viceroy Ct NW8. . . 80 B2
Viceroy Rd SW8 . . 172 A4
Vic Johnson Ho **21**
E3 . . . . 26 B4
Vickery Ct EC1. . . . 97 A2

Vickery Ho **13**
SW4 . . . . 62 A3
Vickery's Wharf **3**
E14 . . . . 33 C3
Victor Cazalet Ho
N1 . . . . 86 A4
Victoria & Albert Mus
SW7 . . . . 129 C1
Victoria Arc SW1 . 132 B1
Victoria Ave EC2. . 110 B3
Victoria Bldgs **13**
E8 . . . . 25 A4
Victoria Chambers
EC2 . . . . . . 24 A1 **98 A2**
Victoria Coach Sta
SW1 . . . . 146 A3
Victoria Coll WC2. 107 B2
Victoria Cotts
7 Richmond
TW9 . . . . 44 C2
8 Spitalfields E1. . 111 B4
Victoria Ct
5 Clapham Pk
SW4 . . . . 61 C1
South Acton W3 . . 36 C4
8 St George in t East
E1 . . . . 125 B3
Victoria Dr SW19 . . 69 C3
Victoria Emb
WC2 . . . . 121 B3
Victoria Gdns
W11 . . . . . 31 C1 **113 B2**
W8 . . . . 128 C2
Victoria Gr Mews
W2 . . . . 114 A3
Victoria Hall **16**
E16 . . . . 35 C1
Victoria Ho
6 Clapham Pk
SW4 . . . . 61 C1
9 Shepherd's Bush
W12 . . . . 38 C4
SW1 . . . . 146 A3
Victoria Ind Est
W3 . . . . 29 A4
Victoria Mans
6 Islington N7 . . . 14 C3
Willesden NW10. . . 9 A1
Victoria Mews
Kilburn NW6. . . . . 23 C4
Wandsworth SW18 . 71 B3
Victoria Mills **1**
E15 . . . . 27 C4
Victorian Gr N16 . . 7 A1
Victorian Rd N16 . . 7 B1
Victoria Park Ct **11**
E9 . . . . 17 B1
Victoria Park Ind Ctr
E9 . . . . 18 B1
Victoria Park Lofts
E9 . . . . 25 C4
Victoria Park Rd
E9 . . . . 17 C1
Victoria Park Sq
E2 . . . . 25 B2
Victoria Pas NW8. . 89 B2
Victoria Place Sh Ctr
SW1 . . . . 146 B4
Victoria Rd
Finsbury Pk N4. . . 5 B3
Kensington W8. . . 128 C2
Kilburn NW6. . . . . 23 B4
Mortlake SW14 . . . 55 C4
North Acton NW10 . 21 A1

Victoria Rise SW4 . . . . **61** A4
Victoria Sq SW1 . . . . **132** B2
Victoria St SW1 . . . . **133** A1
Victoria Sta SW1 . . . . **146** B4
Victoria Terr
Dagenham NW10 . . . . **21** A1
Finsbury Pk N4 . . . . . . **5** C3
Victoria
(Underground)
SW1 . . . . **132** B1
Victoria Villas
TW9 . . . . **54** B3
Victoria Wharf
E14 . . . . **33** A2
Victoria Yd **5** E1 . . . . **111** C1
Victoria Rd NW10 . . . . **22** A2
Victory Pl
6 Limehouse
E14 . . . . **33** A2
SE17 . . . . **151** B4
Victory Prim Sch
SE17 . . . . **151** A4
Victory Way SE16 . . **41** A4
Victory Wlk SE8 . . . . **51** C2
Video Ct N4 . . . . **5** A4
View Cl N6 . . . . **3** B4
Viewfield Rd
SW18 . . . . **58** B1
Viewpoint 3 N5 . . . . **15** A3
Vigo St W1 . . . . **118** C3
Viking Cl **18** E3 . . . . **26** A3
Viking Ho **3** SE5 . . . **48** B1
Village Cl NW3 . . . . . **11** C3
Village Mount 19
NW3 . . . . **11** B4
Village Sch The
NW3 . . . . **12** B2
Village The SW11 . . **60** B4
Village Way SE21 . **63** C1
Villa Rd SW9 . . . . . . **62** C4
Villas On The Heath
NW3 . . . . **2** B1
Villa St SE17 . . . . . . **151** C1
Villiers Ct SW11 . . . **168** B4
Villiers Rd NW2 . . . . . **9** A2
Villiers St WC2 . . . . **120** B2
Vince Ct N1 . . . . **97** C3
Vincent Ct
Finsbury Pk N4 . . . . . . **5** A3
Marylebone W1 . . . . **102** C2
South Lambeth
SW9 . . . . **173** A3
Vincent Mews 1
E3 . . . . **26** C3
Vincent Rd W3 . . . . . **37** B3
Vincents Cl SE16 . . . **41** A4
Vincent St
Canning Town
E16 . . . . **35** B4
Westminster SW1 . . **147** C4
Vincent Terr N1 . . . . **86** B2
Vine Ct **6** E1 . . . . . . **111** C3
Vine Cl E5 . . . . **16** C4
Vine Ct E1 . . . . **111** C3
Vinegar St E1 . . . . . . **32** A1
Vinegar Yd SE1 . . . . **138** A4
Vine Hill EC1 . . . . **95** B1
Vine La SE1 . . . . **124** B1
Vine Rd SW13 . . . . . . **56** B4
Vine St Bridge EC1 . . **95** C1
Vine St
W14 . . . . **141** A1
Vine St
W1 . . . . **119** A3

Vine St continued
Whitechapel EC3 . . . **110** C1
Vineyard Path
SW14 . . . . **55** C4
Vineyard Prim Sch
The TW10 . . . . **54** A1
Vineyard The
TW10 . . . . **54** A2
Vineyard Wlk EC1 . . **95** B2
Viney Ct **9** SW4 . . . . **61** C1
Vine Yd SE1 . . . . **137** A4
Viney Rd SE13 . . . . . . **67** A4
Vining St SW2,
SW9 . . . . **62** C3
Vinson Ho N1 . . . . . . **87** C1
Vintners Ct EC4 . . . **123** A4
Viola Sq W12 . . . . . . **29** B2
Violet Cl **32** SE8 . . . . **51** B4
Violet Hill NW8 . . . . . **78** C1
Violet Hill Ho NW8 . . **78** C1
Violet Rd E3 . . . . **27** A1
Violet St E2 . . . . **25** A1
Virgil Pl W1 . . . . **102** C3
Virgil St SE1 . . . . . . **135** A2
Virginia Ct 7
SE16 . . . . **40** C4
Virginia Ho **3** E14 . **34** B2
Virginia Prim Sch 48
E2 . . . . **24** B2 **98** C3
Virginia Rd 19
E2 . . . . **24** B2 **98** C3
Virginia St E1 . . . . . **125** C3
Virginia Wlk SW2 . . **62** B1
Viscount Ct **9**
W11 . . . . **31** C3
Viscount St EC1 . . . **108** C4
Vision Coll of
Theology 9 E1 . . . **18** B2
Vista Bldgs **18** E3 . . **26** B2
Vitae Apartments 7
W6 . . . . **38** C3
Vittoria Ho N1 . . . . . **85** A3
Vittoria Prim Sch
N1 . . . . **85** B2
Vivian Comma Cl **3**
N4 . . . . **6** A1
Vivian Ho N4 . . . . **6** C4
Vivian Rd E3 . . . . **26** A3
Vivian Sq SE15 . . . . . **65** B4
Vogans Mill SE1 . . . **139** A4
Vogler Ho **6** E1 . . . . **32** B2
Vollasky Ho **5** E1 **111** B4
Voltaire
7 Camberwell
SE5 . . . . **49** B2
16 Richmond TW9 . **44** B2
Voltaire Ct 13
SW11 . . . . **169** C2
Voltaire Rd SW4 . . . . **61** C4
Volt Ave NW10 . . . . . **21** A2
Vorley Rd N19 . . . . . . **4** B2
Voss St E2 . . . . **24** C2 **99** C3
Voyager Bsns Est 10
SE16 . . . . **139** B2
Vulcan Cl SE4 . . . . . . **51** B1
Vulcan La E14 . . . . . . **41** C2
Vulcan Terr SE4 . . . . **51** B1
Vulcan Way N7 . . . . . **14** B2
Vyner Ct E5 . . . . **7** C2
Vyner Rd W3 . . . . **28** C2
Vyner St E2 . . . . **25** A4

W

Wadcroft Ct SE4 . . . . **66** B4
Wadding St SE17 . . . **151** B3
Waddington Rd
E15 . . . . **19** C2
Waddington St
E15 . . . . **19** C2
Wade Ho **16** SE1 . . . **139** B3
Wadeson St E2 . . . . . **25** A3
Wade's Pl E14 . . . . . . **34** A2
Wadham Gdns
NW3 . . . . **80** A4
Wadham Rd SW15 . . **58** A3
Wadhurst Rd W4 . . . . **37** C3
Wager St E3 . . . . **26** B1
Waghorn St SE15 . . . **64** C4
Wagner St SE15 . . . . **50** B3
Wainford Cl SW19 . . **69** C3
Wainwright Ho **3**
E1 . . . . **32** B1
Waite St SE15 . . . . . . **49** B4
Waithman St EC4 . . **108** A1
Wakefield Ho **8**
SE15 . . . . **49** C2
Wakefield Mews
WC1 . . . . **94** B3
Wakefield St WC1 . . **94** B3
Wakeford Cl SW4 . . . **61** B2
Wakeham St **9**
N1 . . . . **15** C2
Wakehurst Rd
SW11 . . . . **60** B2
Wakeling Ho **11**
SE27 . . . . **75** A1
Wakeling St **11**
E14 . . . . **33** A3
Wakelin Ho **11** N1 . . **15** A1
Wakeman Rd
NW10 . . . . **22** C2
Wakley St EC1 . . . . . **96** A4
Walberswick St
SW8 . . . . **162** B1
Walbrook EC4 . . . . . **123** B4
Walbrook Ct 19
N1 . . . . **24** A3
Walbrook Wharf
EC4 . . . . **123** B4
Walburgh St E1 . . . . **32** A3
Walcorde Ave
SE17 . . . . **151** A3
Walcot Gdns
SE11 . . . . **149** B4
Walcot Ho **5**
SE22 . . . . **64** A4
Walcot Sq SE11 . . . **149** C4
Walcott St SW1 . . . . **147** A4
Waldeck Gr SE27 . . . **75** A1
Waldeck Rd
Brentford W4 . . . . . . **44** C4
Mortlake SW14 . . . . . **55** B4
Waldeck Terr
SW14 . . . . **55** B4
Waldegrave Ho **5**
SW15 . . . . **57** B2
Waldemar Ave
SW6 . . . . **164** B2
Waldemar Avenue
Mans SW6 . . . . **164** A3
Walden Ct SW8 . . . **171** C4
Walden Ho
6 Clapham
SW11 . . . . **169** B2
SW1 . . . . **145** C3
Walden St E1 . . . . **32** A3

Waldo Cl SW4 . . . . . . **61** B2
Waldo Rd NW10 . . . . **22** A2
Waldorf Sch of S W
London SW16 . . . . . . **73** C2
Waldron Ho **17**
SW2 . . . . **62** B2
Waldron Mews
SW3 . . . . **157** C4
Waldron Rd SW18 . . **71** B1
Walerand Rd SE13 . . **52** B1
Waleran Flats
SE1 . . . . **152** A4
Wales Cl SE15 . . . . . . **50** A4
Wales Farm Rd
W3 . . . . **28** C4
Waley St **1** E1 . . . . . . **33** A4
Walford Ho **2** E1 . . . **32** A3
Walford Rd N16 . . . . **16** A4
Walham Ct **15**
NW3 . . . . **12** B2
Walham Gr SW6 . . . **155** B2
WALHAM
GREEN **156** A1
Walham Green Arc
SW6 . . . . **155** C2
Walham Yd SW6 . . . **155** B2
Walker Ho NW1 . . . . **83** B1
Walker Mews **9**
SW2 . . . . **62** C2
Walkerscroft Mead
SE21 . . . . **75** B3
Walker's Ct W1 . . . . **119** B4
Walkers Lo **9** E14 . . **42** B4
Walkers Pl **1** SW15 . . **58** A3
Walkinshaw Ct 1
N1 . . . . **15** B1
Walkynscroft **1**
SE15 . . . . **50** A1
Wallace Collection
W1 . . . . **103** B2
Wallace Ho N7 . . . . . **14** B2
Wallace Lo **1** SW1 . . **14** B2
Wallace No N1, N5 . . **15** B2
Wallbutton Rd
SE4 . . . . **51** A1
Waller Rd SE14 . . . . . **50** C1
Wallflower St W12 . . **29** B2
Wallgrave Rd
SW5 . . . . **142** A3
Wallingford Ave
W10 . . . . **30** C3
Wallis Alley SE1 . . . **137** A4
Wallis Cl SW11 . . . . . **59** C4
Wallis Ho **5** SE14 . . . **51** A2
Wallis Rd E9 . . . . **18** C2
Wallorton Gdns
SW14 . . . . **55** C3
Wallside EC2 . . . . . **109** A3
Wall St N1 . . . . **15** C2
Wallwood St E14 . . . **33** B4
Walmer Ho **31**
W10 . . . . **30** C3
Walmer Pl W1 . . . . . **102** C4
Walmer Rd
North Kensington
W10 . . . . **30** B3
W11 . . . . . **31** A2 **112** A3
Walm La NW2 . . . . **9** B2
Walney Wlk **8**
N1 . . . . **15** B2
Walnut Cl SE8 . . . . . . **51** B4
Walnut Ho **16** E3 . . . **26** B4
Walnut Tree Cl
SW13 . . . . **46** B2

Walnut Tree Ho
SW10 . . . . **156** B4
Walnut Tree Rd
Brentford TW8 . . . . . . **44** A4
Greenwich SE10 . . . . **43** A1
Walnut Tree Walk
Prim Sch SE11 . . . . **149** B4
Walnut Tree Wlk
SE11 . . . . **149** B4
Walpole Ave TW9 . . . **44** B1
Walpole Ct
7 Hammersmith
W14 . . . . **39** C3
South Hampstead
NW6 . . . . **11** B1
Walpole Gdns W4 . . **37** B1
Walpole Mews
NW8 . . . . **79** B3
Walpole St SW3 . . . **145** A2
Walsham Cl N16 . . . . . **7** C3
Walsham Ho
New Cross Gate
SE14 . . . . **50** C1
SE17 . . . . **151** B2
Walsham Rd SE14 . . **50** C1
Walsingham NW8 . . **79** C4
Walsingham Lo
SW13 . . . . **46** C2
Walsingham Mans
SW6 . . . . **156** B2
Walsingham Pl SW4,
SW11 . . . . **60** C1
Walsingham Rd E5 . . **7** C1
Walter Besant Ho **20**
E1 . . . . **25** C2
Walter Ct **3** W3 . . . . **28** B3
Walter Green Ho
SE15 . . . . **50** B2
Walter Ho SW10 . . . **157** B2
Walter Northcott Ho
2 NW6 . . . . **10** C3
Walters Cl SE17 . . . **151** A3
Walters Ho
5 Camberwell
SE5 . . . . **49** A1
Islington N1 . . . . **86** B4
13 Kennington
SE17 . . . . **150** B1
Walter Sickert Hall
N1 . . . . **86** C1
Walter St E2 . . . . **25** C2
Walters Way SE23 . . **65** C1
Walter Taylor Ct
SE4 . . . . **66** B3
Walter Terr E1 . . . . . . **32** C3
Walterton Rd W9 . . . **23** C1
Walter Green Ct
SW6 . . . . **156** A1
Waltham Ho
NW8 . . . . **78** C4
18 Stockwell SW9 . **173** A1
Walton Cl SW8 . . . . **162** B2
Walton Ho **24** E2 . . **99** A2
Upper Holloway N7 . . . **5** B1
Wandsworth SW18 . . **58** C1
Walton Pl SW3 . . . . **130** D1
Walton St SW3 . . . . **130** B1
Walton Way W3 . . . . **28** A4
Walt Whitman Cl 3
SE24 . . . . **63** A3
WALWORTH **151** C2
Walworth Acad
SE17 . . . . **152** B1
Walworth Pl SE17 . . **151** A1

Walworth Rd
SE17 . . . . **151** A2
Wanborough Dr
SW15 . . . . .69 A3
Wandle Ct **4** W12 . .38 A4
Wandle Ho
NW8 . . . . .102 A4
Wandsworth SW18 . .71 A4
Wandle Rd SW17 . . . .72 A2
Wandle Way SW18. .71 A3
Wandon Rd SW6 . . . .156 B1
WANDSWORTH 58 C1
Wandsworth Bridge
Rd SW6 . . . . .166 A3
Wandsworth Common
Sta SW12 . . . . .72 B4
Wandsworth Common
West Side SW18 . .59 B2
Wandsworth Gyratory
SW18 . . . . .59 A2
Wandsworth High St
SW18 . . . . .59 A2
Wandsworth Plain
SW18 . . . . .59 A2
Wandsworth Rd
SW8 . . . . .162 A1
Wandsworth Road Sta
SW4 . . . . .171 A1
Wandsworth Town Sta
SW18 . . . . .59 A3
Wangford Ho **13**
SW9 . . . . .63 A3
Wanless Rd SE24 . . .63 B4
Wanley Rd SE5 . . . . .63 C3
Wansbeck Rd E3,
E9 . . . . .18 B1
Wansdown Pl
SW6 . . . . .156 A2
Wandsworth Riverside
Quarter Pier
SW6 . . . . .58 C4
Wansey St SE17 . . . .151 A3
WAPPING 32 A1
Wapping Dock St **18**
E1 . . . . .32 A1
Wapping High St
E1 . . . . .32 A1
Wapping La E1 . . . . .32 A1
Wapping Sta E1 . . . .32 B1
Wapping Wall E1 . . .32 B1
Warbeck Rd W12 . . .39 A4
Warburg Ho
E2 . . . . .24 C2 **99** B3
Warburton Ct **7**
E8 . . . . .16 A2
Warburton Ct
SE15 . . . . .64 C4
Warburton Ho **5**
E8 . . . . .25 A4
Warburton Rd **8**
E8 . . . . .25 A4
Warburton St **8**
E8 . . . . .25 A4
Wardalls Ho **12**
SE8 . . . . .51 B4
Wardell Ho **7**
SE10 . . . . .52 B4
Warden Rd NW5 . . . .12 C2
Wardens Gr SE1 . . . .122 C1
Wardle St E9 . . . . . . .17 C3
Wardley St SW18 . . .71 A4
Wardlow NW5 . . . . . .13 A4
Wardo Ave SW6 . . . .164 A4
Wardour Mews
W1 . . . . .105 A1
Wardour St W1 . . . . .105 B1

Ward Point SE11 . . . .149 B3
Ward Rd
Camden Town N19 . . . . .4 B1
Mill Meads E15 . . . . . . .27 C4
Wardrobe Pl EC4 . . .108 B1
Wardrobe Terr
EC4 . . . . .122 B4
Wareham Ct **2**
E2 . . . . .16 A1
Wareham Ho
SW8 . . . . .162 C2
Warfield Rd NW10 . .22 C2
Warfield Yd **5**
NW10 . . . . .22 C2
Wargrave Ho **46**
E2 . . . . .24 B2 **98** C3
Warham Rd N4 . . . . . .5 C4
Warham St SE5 . . . . .48 A3
Waring Ho **6**
E2 . . . . .24 C2 **99** C3
Warley Ho N1 . . . . . .15 C2
Warley St E2 . . . . . . .25 C2
Warlock Rd W9 . . . . .23 C1
Warlters Cl N7 . . . . .14 A4
Warlters Rd N7 . . . . .14 A4
Warltersville Mans
N19 . . . . .5 A4
Warltersville Rd N4, N8,
N19 . . . . .5 A4
War Meml Homes
W4 . . . . .45 C3
Warmington Rd
SE24 . . . . .63 B1
Warmsworth NW1 . .82 C4
Warndon St SE16 . . .40 B2
Warneford St E9 . . . .25 A4
Warner Ho
4 Homerton E9 . . . . . .17 C2
Lewisham SE13 . . . . . . .52 A1
NW8 . . . . .88 C4
Warner Pl
E2 . . . . .24 C2 **99** C4
Warner Rd SE5 . . . . .48 B2
Warner St EC1 . . . . .95 B1
Warner Yd EC1 . . . . .95 B1
Warnford Ho
SW15 . . . . .56 A1
Warnham Ho **6**
SW2 . . . . .74 B4
Warple Mews W3 . . .38 A4
Warple Way W3,
W12 . . . . .38 A4
Warren Ave SW14,
TW10 . . . . .55 A3
Warren Cl SE21 . . . . .75 B4
Warren Ct N1 . . . . . .85 B2
Warren Gdns E15 . . .19 C3
Warren Ho **21** E3 . . .27 A2
Warren Mews W1 . . .92 C1
Warren St W1 . . . . . .92 C1
Warren Street Sta
NW1 . . . . .93 A2
Warriner Gdns
SW11 . . . . .169 B3
Warrington Cres
W9 . . . . .88 C2
Warrington Gdns
W9 . . . . .88 C1
Warspite Ho **3**
E14 . . . . .42 A2
Warton Rd E15 . . . . .27 B4
Warwick W14 . . . . . .141 A3
Warwick Ave W9 . . . .88 C1
Warwick Avenue Sta
W9 . . . . .88 C1

Warwick Bldg
SW8 . . . . .160 A3
Warwick Chambers
W8 . . . . .127 B2
Warwick Cres W2 . . .101 A4
Warwick Ct WC1 . . . .107 A3
Warwick Dr SW15 . . .57 A4
Warwick Gdns
W14 . . . . .141 A4
Warwick Ho
10 Brixton SW9 . . . . .173 B1
8 Putney SW15 . . . .69 B4
Stoke Newington N4 . . .6 B3
Warwick House St
SW1 . . . . .119 C2
Warwick La EC4 . . . .108 B1
Warwick Lo NW2 . . . .10 A3
Warwick Mans
SW5 . . . . .141 B4
Warwick Pas EC4 . . .108 B2
Warwick Pl W9 . . . . .100 C4
Warwick Pl N
SW1 . . . . .146 C3
Warwick Rd W14,
SW5 . . . . .141 A4
Warwick Row
SW1 . . . . .132 B2
Warwickshire Path
SE8 . . . . .51 B3
Warwick Sq
Holborn EC4 . . . . .108 B2
Pimlico SW1 . . . . .146 C2
Warwick Sq Mews
SW1 . . . . .146 C3
Warwick St W1 . . . . .119 A4
Warwick Way
SW1 . . . . .146 B4
Warwick Yd EC1 . . . .97 A1
Wasdale NW1 . . . . . .92 B3
Washbrook Ho
SW2 . . . . .62 C1
Washington Bldg **1**
SE13 . . . . .52 A2
Washington Cl **43**
E3 . . . . .27 A2
Washington Ho
SW1 . . . . .130 C3
Washington Rd
SW13 . . . . .46 C3
Watchfield Ct **7**
W4 . . . . .37 B1
Watcombe Cotts
TW9 . . . . .44 C4
Watercress Pl **12**
N1 . . . . .16 A1
Waterford Ho
W6 . . . . .156 A1
Waterford Way
NW10 . . . . .8 C3
Water Gardens The
W2 . . . . .102 B2
Watergate EC4 . . . . .122 A4
Watergate St SE8 . . .51 C4
Watergate Wlk
WC2 . . . . .120 B2
Waterhead NW1 . . . .92 C4
Waterhouse Cl
Hammersmith W6 . . . .39 C1
Hampstead NW3 . . . . .11 C3
Waterhouse Sq
EC1 . . . . .107 B3
Wateridge Cl E14 . . .41 C3
Water La
11 Camden Town
NW1 . . . . .13 A1
SE14 . . . . .50 B3

Waterloo Bridge SE1,
WC2 . . . . .121 A3
Waterloo Cl E9 . . . . .17 B3
Waterloo East Sta
SE1 . . . . .121 C1
Waterloo Gdns
20 Islington N1 . . . . .15 A1
South Hackney E2 . . . .25 B3
Waterloo Millennium
Pier SE1 . . . . .134 C4
Waterloo Pl
Kew TW9 . . . . .44 C4
9 Richmond TW9 . . .54 A3
SW1 . . . . .119 B2
Waterloo Rd SE1 . . .135 C4
Waterloo Sta SE1 . . .135 B4
Waterloo Terr **1**
N1 . . . . .15 A1
Waterlow Ct NW11 . .2 A4
Waterlow Rd N19 . . . .4 B3
Waterman Bldg **2**
E14 . . . . .41 C4
Watermans Arts Ctr
TW8 . . . . .44 A4
Watermans Ct **2**
TW8 . . . . .44 A4
Waterman St
SW15 . . . . .57 C4
Waterman Way E1 . .32 A1
Watermark Pl
EC4 . . . . .123 B3
Watermead Ho E9 . .18 B3
Watermeadow La
SW6 . . . . .166 C1
Water Mews SE15 . . .65 B3
Watermill Ct SE13 . . .67 A4
Watermint Quay
N16 . . . . .7 C4
Water's Edge SW6 . .47 B2
Waterside N1 . . . . . .86 C1
Waterside Cl
30 Bermondsey
SE16 . . . . .139 C3
Old Ford E3 . . . . .26 B4
Waterside Ct SE13 . .67 C3
Waterside Pl NW1 . . .81 C4
Waterside Point
SW11 . . . . .158 B2
Waterson St
E2 . . . . .24 B2 **98** C4
Waters Pl SW15 . . . .47 B1
Water St WC2 . . . . . .121 B4
Water Tower Pl
N1 . . . . .86 A3
Waterview Ho **19**
E14 . . . . .33 A4
Waterway Ave **2**
SE13 . . . . .67 A4
Waterworks Rd
SW2 . . . . .62 B1
Watford Cl SW11 . . .168 B4
Watford Rd E16 . . . . .35 C4
Watkins Ho **11** E14 . .42 B4
Watkinson Rd N7 . . .14 B2
Watling Ct EC4 . . . . .109 A1
Watling Gdns
NW2 . . . . .10 A2
Watling St
4 Camberwell
SE15 . . . . .49 A4
City of London EC4 . . .109 A1
Watney Cotts
SW14 . . . . .55 B4
Watney Mkt E1 . . . . .32 A3
Watney Rd SW14 . . .55 B4
Watney St E1 . . . . . . .32 A3
Watson Cl N16 . . . . .15 C3

Watson Ho **3**
SW2 . . . . .74 A4
Watsons Mews
W1 . . . . .102 B3
Watson's St SE8 . . . .51 C3
Watts Gr E3 . . . . .34 A4
Watts Ho **6** W10 . . .31 A4
Watts St
SE15 . . . . .49 B2
Wapping E1 . . . . .32 A1
Wat Tyler Rd SE10 . .52 C2
Wavel Ct
7 Streatham
SW16 . . . . .74 A1
7 Wapping E1 . . . . .32 B1
Wavel Mews NW6 . . .11 A1
Wavendon Ave
W4 . . . . .37 C1
Waveney Ave SE15 . .65 A3
Waveney Ho **20** E1 . .125 C2
Waveney Ho SE15 . . .65 A3
Waverley Ct
5 Brondesbury
NW6 . . . . .10 A1
W1 . . . . .103 C4
Waverley Pl
Finsbury Pk N4 . . . . . . .6 A3
St John's Wood
NW8 . . . . .79 B2
Waverley Rd N8 . . . . .5 A4
Waverley Sch NW3 . .12 B2
Waverton Ho **2**
E3 . . . . .26 B4
Waverton Rd
SW18 . . . . .71 B4
Waverton St W1 . . . .118 A2
Wavertree Ct **9**
SW2 . . . . .74 A3
Wavertree Rd
SW2 . . . . .74 B3
Waxham NW5 . . . . . .12 B3
Waxlow Rd NW10 . . .20 C3
Wayford St SW11 . . .168 B1
Wayland Ave E8 . . . .16 C3
Wayland Ho **5**
SW9 . . . . .173 B2
Waylett Ho SE11 . . .149 B1
Waylett Pl SE27 . . . .75 A1
Wayman Ct E8 . . . . .17 A2
Waynflete Sq
18 North Kensington
W10 . . . . .30 C3
5 Shepherd's Bush
W12 . . . . .30 C2
Waynflete St
SW18 . . . . .71 B2
Wayside
Golders Green
NW11 . . . . .1 A3
Mortlake SW14 . . . . . .55 B2
Weald Cl **16** SE16 . .40 A1
Weardale Ho N4 . . . . .6 B4
Weardale Rd SE13 . .67 C3
Wearmouth Ho **1**
E3 . . . . .33 B4
Wear Pl **13** E2 . . . . .25 A2
Wearside Rd SE13 . .67 A3
Weatherbury
W2 . . . . .31 C3
Weatherbury Ho **3**
N19 . . . . .4 C1
Weatherley Cl E3 . . .33 B4
Weaver Ct **2** E2 . . . .25 A1

Weaver Ho **12**
E1 . . . . 24 C1 **99** B1
Weaver's La SE1 . . . **124** B1
Weaver St
E1 . . . . 24 C1 **99** B1
Weavers Way
6 Camden Town
NW1 . . . . 13 C1
NW1 . . . . 83 B4
Webb Cl NW10 . . . . 22 B1
Webb Ct W3 . . . . . . 37 A4
Webber Row SE1 **136** A3
Webber St SE1 . . . **136** A3
Webb Est **5** 7 C3
Webb Ho SW8 . . . **161** C1
Webb Pl NW10 . . . 21 B2
Webb Rd SE3 . . . . . 53 B4
Webb's Rd SW11 . . . 60 B2
Webb St SE1 . . . . . **138** A1
Webheath **6** NW6 . . 10 B1
Webster Ho **16**
N16 . . . . 16 A3
Webster Rd SE16 . **139** C1
Weddell Ho **23** E1 . . 25 C1
Wedderburn Rd
NW3 . . . . 11 C3
Wedgewood Ho
SW1 . . . . **146** C1
Wedgewood Mews
W1 . . . . **105** C1
Wedgewood Wlk
NW3 . . . . 11 A3
Wedgwood Ho
17 Globe Town
E2 . . . . 25 C2
SE11 . . . . **135** B1
Wedlake St W10 . . . 23 A1
Wedmore Gdns
N19 . . . . 4 C2
Wedmore Mews
N19 . . . . 4 C1
Wedmore St N19 . . . 4 C1
Weech Rd NW6 . . . 10 C4
Weedington Rd
NW5 . . . . 12 C3
Weedon Ho W12 . . . 29 C3
Weekley Sq SW11 . . 59 C4
Weighhouse St
W1 . . . . **103** C1
Weimar St SW15 . . . 58 A4
Weir Ho **21** SW12 . . 73 B4
Weir Rd
Streatham SW12 . . . 73 B4
Wimbledon SW18,
SW19 . . . . 71 A1
Weiss Rd SW15 . . . 57 C4
Welbeck Ct W14 . **140** C4
Welbeck Mans **10**
NW6 . . . . 10 C3
Welbeck St W1 . . . **104** A2
Welbeck Way W1 . **104** A2
Welby Ct E8 . . . . . . 16 A1
Welby Ho N19 . . . . . 4 C4
Welby St SE5 . . . . . 48 A2
Weldon Ct SE18 . . . 51 C1
Welford Ct
12 Camden Town
NW1 . . . . 13 A1
7 Clapham SW8 . . **170** C1
Welland Ho SE15 . . 65 B3
Welland Mews **2**
E1 . . . . **125** C2
Welland St SE10 . . . 52 B4
Wellclose Sq E1 . . **125** C4

Wellclose St
E1 . . . . **125** C3
Well Ct EC4 . . . . . **109** A1
Wellday Ho **2** E9 . . 18 A2
Welldon Ct **1**
SE21 . . . . 75 C2
Weller Ho **23**
SE1 . . . . **139** B3
Weller St SE1 . . . . **136** C4
Welles Ct **8** E14 . . . 33 C2
Wellesley Ave W6 . . 39 A3
Wellesley Ct W9 . . . 88 C4
Wellesley Ho NW1 . 93 B3
Wellesley Pl
Camden Town
NW5 . . . . 12 C3
NW1 . . . . 93 B3
Wellesley Rd
Gospel Oak NW5 . . 12 C3
Gunnersbury W4 . . 37 A1
Wellesley St E1 . . . 32 C4
Wellesley Terr N1 . . 97 A4
Wellfit St **6** SE24 . . 63 A4
Wellgarth Rd NW11 . . 2 A3
Wellington Arch
SW1 . . . . **131** C4
Wellington Bldgs
18 Bow E3 . . . . 26 C2
SW1 . . . . **145** C1
Wellington Cl
Kensington W11 . . . 31 C3
New Cross Gate
SE14 . . . . 50 C2
Wellington Ct
Knightsbridge
SW1 . . . . **130** C3
St John's Wood
NW8 . . . . 79 C1
Strand WC2 . . . . . **120** A4
Wandsworth SW18 . 60 A2
Wellington Gr
SE10 . . . . 52 C3
Wellington Ho
NW3 . . . . 12 B2
Wellington Hospl The
NW8 . . . . 79 C1
Wellington Mans
N16 . . . . 16 B4
Wellington Mews
East Dulwich
SE22 . . . . 64 C3
3 Islington N7 . . . . 14 B2
Streatham SW16 . . . 73 C1
Wellington Prim NW8 **89** C4
Wellington Prim Sch
E3 . . . . 26 C2
Wellington Rd
Kensal Green
NW10 . . . . 22 C2
St John's Wood
NW8 . . . . 79 C1
Wimbledon SW19 . . 70 C2
Wellington Sq
Islington N1 . . . . . . 84 B4
SW3 . . . . **144** C2
Wellington St
WC2 . . . . **120** C4
Wellington Terr **2**
E1 . . . . 32 A1
Wellington Way
E3 . . . . 26 C2
Well La SW14 . . . . . 55 B2
Well Rd NW3 . . . . . . 2 C1

Wells Ct
21 Hampstead
NW3 . . . . 11 B4
1 Paddington
NW6 . . . . 23 C3
Stoke Newington
N1 . . . . 16 A3
Wells Ho
Finsbury EC1 . . . . . 96 A4
W10 . . . . 23 A1
New Cross Gate
SE4 . . . . 51 A1
8 Rotherhithe
SE16 . . . . 40 B3
Wells Ho The **7**
N1 . . . . 11 C4
Wells House Rd
NW10 . . . . 29 A4
Wellside Gdns
SW14 . . . . 55 B2
Wells Mews W1 . . **105** A2
Wells Pl SW18 . . . . 71 B4
Wells Rise NW8 . . . 80 C3
Wells Rd W12 . . . . . 39 B4
Wells Sq WC1 . . . . . 95 A3
Wells St W1 . . . . . **105** A2
Wells Terr N4 . . . . . . 5 C2
Wells Way
Brompton SW7 . . . **129** B2
Camberwell SE5 . . . 49 A4
Well Wlk NW3 . . . . . 2 C1
Wellwood Ct
SW15 . . . . 57 B3
Welmar Mews
SW4 . . . . 61 C3
Welsford St SE1 . . **153** B3
Welsh Ho **14** E1 . . . 32 A1
Welshpool Ho **22**
E8 . . . . 24 C4
Welshpool St **1**
E8 . . . . 25 A4
Welstead Ho **29**
E1 . . . . 32 A3
Welstead Way W4 . . 38 B2
Weltje Rd W6 . . . . . 38 C1
Welton Ct SE5 . . . . 49 A2
Welton Ho E1 . . . . . 32 C4
Welwyn St E2 . . . . . 25 B2
Wembury Mews N6 . . 4 B4
Wembury Rd N6 . . . . 4 A4
Wemyss Rd SE3 . . . 53 B1
Wendell Park Prim
Sch W12 . . . . 38 B4
Wendell Rd W12 . . . 38 B4
Wendle Ct SW8 . . **162** A3
Wendling NW5 . . . . 12 B3
Wendon St E3 . . . . 26 B4
Wendover SE17 . . . **152** A1
Wendover Ct
Acton W3 . . . . 20 A1
3 Becontree W3 . . . 20 B1
4 Child's Hill NW2 . . 1 C1
W1 . . . . **103** B3
Wendover Ho W1 . **103** B3
Wendover Rd
NW10 . . . . 21 B3
Wengham Ho W12 . 29 C2
Wenham Ho SW8 . **160** C1
Wenlake Ho EC1 . . . 96 C2
Wenlock Ct N1 . . . . 87 C1
Wenlock Rd N1 . . . . 87 A1
Wenlock St N1 . . . . 87 B1
Wennington Rd
E3 . . . . 25 C3

Wensdale Ho E5 . . . 7 C2
Wensleydale Ho **8**
N4 . . . . 6 B4
Wentworth Cres
SE15 . . . . 49 C3
Wentworth Ct
W6 . . . . **154** A3
Wandsworth SW18 . 59 A1
Wentworth Dwellings
E1 . . . . **110** C2
Wentworth Ho **4**
SE3 . . . . 53 B4
Wentworth Mews
E3 . . . . 26 B2
Wentworth St E1 . **111** A3
Werrington St
NW1 . . . . 83 A1
Werter Rd SW15 . . . 58 A3
Wesleyan Pl NW5 . . 13 A4
Wesley Ave NW10 . . 20 C2
Wesley Cl
Finsbury Pk N7 . . . . 5 B2
SE17 . . . . **150** B3
Wesley Ct W1 . . . . **103** C3
Wesley Ho SE24 . . . 63 C1
Wesley Rd NW10 . . 20 B4
Wesley Sq W11 . . . 31 A3
Wesley St W1 . . . . **103** C3
Wessex Ct SW11 . . . 57 C2
Wessex Gardens Prim
Sch NW11 . . . . 1 A3
Wessex Gdns NW11 . 1 A3
Wessex Ho
SE1 . . . . **153** A1
4 Tufnell Pk N19 . . . 4 C1
Wessex St E2 . . . . . 25 B2
Wessex Way NW11 . . 1 A3
West 12 Sh Ctr
W12 . . . . 39 C4
Westacott Cl N19 . . 4 C3
West Acton Prim Sch
W3 . . . . 28 A3
West Arbour St E1 . 32 C3
West Bank N16 . . . . 7 A4
Westbere Rd NW2 . 10 A4
West Block E1 . . . **152** B2
Westbourne Ave
W3 . . . . 28 C3
Westbourne Cres
W2 . . . . **115** B4
Westbourne Ct
W2 . . . . **100** C2
Westbourne Gdns
W2 . . . . **100** A2
Westbourne Gr
Notting Hill W2,
W11 . . . . 31 C3
W11 . . . . 31 B2 **113** A4
WESTBOURNE
GREEN **88** A2
Westbourne Gr Mews
7 W11 . . . . 31 C3
Westbourne Gr Terr
W2 . . . . **100** A1
Westbourne Ho
SW1 . . . . **146** A2
Westbourne Park Rd
Notting Hill W2 . . . 31 B3
Notting Hill W11 . . . 31 B3
Westbourne Park Sta
W11 . . . . 31 B4
Westbourne Park
Villas W2 . . . . . . **100** A3
Westbourne Rd
N7 . . . . 14 B2

Westbourne St
W2 . . . . **115** B4
Westbourne Terr
W2 . . . . **101** A2
Westbourne Terrace
Mews W2 . . . . . . **100** C2
Westbourne Terrace
Rd W2 . . . . **100** C3
Westbridge Cl
W12 . . . . 29 C1
Westbridge Prim Sch
SW11 . . . . **168** A4
Westbridge Rd
SW11 . . . . **168** A4
WEST
BROMPTON . . . **156** A4
West Brompton Sta
SW5 . . . . **141** C1
Westbrook Ho
5 Bethnal Green
E2 . . . . 25 B2
5 Clapham Pk
SW4 . . . . 61 B2
Westbury Ct SW4 . . 61 A1
Westbury Ho **6**
NW10 . . . . 8 A1
Westbush Ct **1**
W12 . . . . 39 A4
West Carriage Dr
W2 . . . . **116** B4
West Central St
WC1 . . . . **106** A2
Westchester Ho
W2 . . . . **102** C1
Westcliff Ho **13**
N1 . . . . 15 C2
Westcombe Ct **1**
SE3 . . . . 53 B3
Westcombe Hill SE3,
SE10 . . . . 53 C4
Westcombe Park Rd
SE3 . . . . 53 B3
Westcombe Park Sta
SE3 . . . . 53 A3
Westcott Ho **1**
E14 . . . . 34 A2
Westcott Rd SE17 . . 48 A4
West Cotts NW6 . . . 10 C3
Westcroft Cl NW2 . . 10 A4
Westcroft Ct **3**
W6 . . . . 38 C2
Westcroft Sq W6 . . 38 C2
Westcroft Way
NW2 . . . . 10 A4
West Cromwell Rd
W14 . . . . **141** A2
West Cross Route W10,
W11 . . . . 30 C2
Westdean Cl
SW18 . . . . 59 A1
Westdown Rd E15 . . 19 B4
WEST DULWICH . . 75 B2
West Dulwich Sta
SE21 . . . . 75 C3
West Eaton Pl
SW1 . . . . **145** B4
West Eaton Pl Mews
SW1 . . . . **145** B4
West Ella Rd NW10 . 8 A1
West End Ct NW6 . . 11 A1
West End La NW6 . . 11 A2
Westerdale Ct N5 . . 15 A4
Westerdale Rd **2**
SE10 . . . . 43 C1
Westerham NW1 . . . 82 C3

Westerham Ho
SE1 . . . . **137** C2
Western Ave W3 . . . . . **28** A3
Western Avenue Bsns
Pk W3 . . . . **20** C1
Western Beach Apts
E16 . . . . **35** C1
Western Ct 5
4 Dagenham W3 . . **28** C3
3 Kilburn W9 . . . . . **23** B3
Western Eye Hospl
The NW1 . . . . **102** C4
Western Gateway
E16 . . . . **35** C2
Western Ho 3 W9 . . **23** B1
Western La SW12 . . **72** C4
Western Mews
W9 . . . . **23** B1
Western Pl 12
SE16 . . . . **40** B4
Western Rd
Becontree NW10 . . . **20** B1
Brixton SW9 . . . . . . **62** C4
SW9 . . . . **62** C4
Western Terr 3
W6 . . . . **38** C1
Western Wharf 2
SE15 . . . . **49** C4
Westferry Cir E14 . . **33** C1
Westferry Rd E14 . . **41** C3
Westferry Sta E14 . **33** C2
Westfield NW3 . . . . . **10** C4
Westfield Cl
SW10 . . . . **156** C1
Westfield Ct 1
W10 . . . . **22** C2
Westfield Ho 8
SE16 . . . . **40** C2
Westfield London St
Ctr W12 . . . . **30** C1
Westfields Ave
SW13 . . . . **56** B4
Westfields Rd W3 . . **28** A4
Westfield Stratford
Ctr EH15 . . . . **19** B2
Westfield Way E1 . . **26** A1
West Garden Pl
W2 . . . . **102** B1
Westgate Bsns Ctr
2 Kensal Town
W10 . . . . **23** A1
North Kensington
W10 . . . . **22** C1
Westgate Ct 15
SW9 . . . . **62** C4
Westgate St E8 . . . . **25** A4
Westgate Terr
SW10 . . . . **156** B4
West Gdns E1 . . . . . **32** A2
West Gr SE10 . . . . . **52** C2
Westgrove La
SE10 . . . . **52** B2
West Halkin St
SW1 . . . . **131** B2
West Hall Rd TW9 . . **45** A2
WEST
HAMPSTEAD . . **10** C4
West Hampstead
Mews NW6 . . . . **11** A2
West Hampstead Sta
NW6 . . . . **10** C2
West Hampstead
Thameslink Sta
NW6 . . . . **10** C2
West Harding St
EC4 . . . . **107** C2

Westhay Gdns
SW14 . . . . **55** A2
West Heath Ave
NW11 . . . . 1 C3
West Heath Cl NW3 . . 1 C1
West Heath Ct
NW11 . . . . 1 C3
West Heath Dr
NW11 . . . . 1 C3
West Heath Gdns
NW3 . . . . 1 C1
West Heath Rd
NW3 . . . . 2 A1
WEST HILL **58** B1
West Hill SW15 . . . . **58** A1
Westhill Ct
W11 . . . . **31** B2 **113** A4
West Hill Ct N6 . . . . . . 3 C1
Westhill Pk
Dartmouth Pk N6 . . . 3 C2
Highgate N6 . . . . 3 C2
West Hill Prim Sch 17
SW18 . . . . **58** B2
West Hill Rd SW18 . . **58** B1
West Ho 9 SW12 . . **73** B4
Westhope Ho 29
E2 . . . . **24** C2 **99** C3
Westhorpe Rd
SW15 . . . . **57** B4
West House Cl
SW19 . . . . **70** A3
West India Ave
E14 . . . . **33** C1
West India Dock Rd
E14 . . . . **33** C2
West India Ho 11
E14 . . . . **33** C2
West India Quay Sta
E14 . . . . **33** C2
WEST
KENSINGTON . . **140** B3
West Kensington Ct
W14 . . . . **140** C2
West Kensington
Mans W14 . . . . **140** C1
West Kensington Sta
W14 . . . . **140** C3
WEST KILBURN . . **23** A2
Westla SE16 . . . . . . **40** A4
Westlake 12 SE16 . . **40** B2
Westland Pl N1 . . . . **97** B4
Westlands Terr 3
SW12 . . . . **61** B1
Westleigh Ave
SW15 . . . . **57** B2
Westly Ct NW2 . . . . . 9 C2
Westmacott Ho
NW8 . . . . **89** C1
West Mall
W11 . . . . **31** C1 **113** C2
Westmark Point 13
SW15 . . . . **69** A3
Westmead SW15 . . . **57** A1
West Mews SW1 . . **146** C3
Westmill Ct N4 . . . . . . **6** B2
WESTMINSTER . . **133** A1
Westminster Abbey
SW1 . . . . **134** A2
Westminster Abbey
Choir Sch SW1 . . **133** C2
Westminster Acad
W2 . . . . **31** C4
Westminster Acad
(Sch of English)
W1 . . . . **105** A2

Westminster Boating
Base SW1 . . . . . . **161** B4
Westminster Bridge
SE1, SW1 . . . . . . **134** B3
Westminster Bridge
Rd SE1 . . . . **134** C2
Westminster Cath
SW1 . . . . **132** C1
Westminster Cath
Choir Sch SW1 . . **132** C1
Westminster Cath RC
Prim Sch SW1 . . **147** C2
Westminster City Hall
SW1 . . . . **133** A2
Westminster City Sch
SW1 . . . . **133** A1
Westminster Coll
W1 . . . . **119** B4
Westminster St
22 Rotherhithe
SE16 . . . . **32** C1
5 Wandsworth
SW18 . . . . **58** C2
Westminster
Dragoons Mus
SW6 . . . . **58** A4
Westminster Gdns
SW1 . . . . **148** A4
Westminster
Kingsway Coll
(King's Cross
Centre) WC1 . . . . **94** C3
Westminster
Kingsway Coll
(Regent's Park Ctr)
NW1 . . . . **92** C2
Westminster
Kingsway Coll
(Victoria Centre)
SW1 . . . . **147** B4
Westminster
Millennium Pier
SW1 . . . . **134** B3
Westminster Pier
SW1 . . . . **134** B3
Westminster Sch
SW1 . . . . **134** A2
Westminster Sta
SW1 . . . . **134** B3
Westminster Under
Sch SW1 . . . . **147** B3
Westmore Ct
SW15 . . . . **58** A2
Westmoreland Ho
NW10 . . . . **21** C2
Westmoreland Pl
SW1 . . . . **146** B1
Westmoreland Rd
Barnes SW13 . . . . **46** C2
Camberwell SE17 . . **48** C4
Westmoreland St
W1 . . . . **103** C3
Westmoreland Terr
SW1 . . . . **146** B1
WEST NORWOOD . . **75** B1
West Norwood Sta
SE27 . . . . **75** A1
Westonbirt Ct 6
SE15 . . . . **49** B4
Weston Ct N4 . . . . . . **6** B1
West One Ho W1 . **104** C3
West One Sh Ctr
W1 . . . . **104** A1
Weston Ho
6 Brondesbury
NW6 . . . . **10** A1

Weston Ho continued
8 South Hackney
E9 . . . . **25** B4
Weston Rd W4 . . . . . **37** B3
Weston Rise N1,
WC1 . . . . **95** A4
Weston St SE1 . . . **137** C4
Weston Wlk 8 E8, . .
E9 . . . . **17** A1
Westover Hill NW3 . . 1 C2
Westover Rd
SW18 . . . . **59** B1
West Park Ave
TW9 . . . . **45** A2
West Park Rd TW9 . **44** C2
West Parkside
Greenwich SE10 . . . **43** B3
Greenwich SE10 . . . **43** C2
West Plaza E14 . . . . **34** A1
Westpoint SW15 . . **57** C1
West Point 2
SE1 . . . . **153** B2
Westpoint Trad Est
W3 . . . . **28** A4
Westport St E1 . . . . **32** C3
West Poultry Ave
EC1 . . . . **108** A3
West Quarters
W12 . . . . **29** C3
West Rd
Chelsea SW3 . . . . **159** A4
Clapham Pk SW4 . . **61** C2
Westrow SW15 . . . . **57** B1
West Row W10 . . . . . **23** A1
West Sheen Vale
TW9 . . . . **54** B3
Westside 11 W6 . . **38** C2
Westside
W9 . . . . **23** C1
West Silvertown Sta
E16 . . . . **35** C1
West Smithfield
EC1 . . . . **108** B3
West Sq SE11 . . . . **136** A1
West St 9
38 Bethnal Green
E2 . . . . **25** A3
Soho WC2 . . . . **105** C1
West Temple Sheen
SW14 . . . . **55** A2
West Tenter St
E1 . . . . **111** A1
Westvale Mews
W3 . . . . **38** A4
Westview Cl
North Kensington
W10 . . . . **30** B3
Willesden NW10 . . . . **8** B3
Westville Rd W12 . . **38** C4
West Warwick Pl
SW1 . . . . **146** C3
Westway W10,
W12 . . . . **29** C2
Westway (Elevated
Rd) W10 . . . . **31** B4
Westway Lo 55
W2 . . . . **31** C4
Westwell 4 NW5 . . **12** C2
Westwick Gdns
W14 . . . . **39** C4
Westwood Bsns Ctr
NW10 . . . . **21** A1
Westwood Gdns
SW13 . . . . **56** B4

Westwood Ho
6 Shepherd's Bush
W12 . . . . **30** B1
5 Stoke Newington
N4 . . . . **6** C4
Westwood Park Trad
Est W3 . . . . **20** A1
Westwood Rd
SW13 . . . . **56** B4
Wetherby Gdns
SW5 . . . . **142** C3
Wetherby Mans
SW5 . . . . **142** A2
Wetherby Mews
SW5 . . . . **142** B2
Wetherby Pl 3 SW7 **143** A3
Wetherby Prep Sch
SW11 . . . . . **33** C2 **113** A4
Wetherell Rd E9 . . . **25** C4
Wevco Wharf
SE15 . . . . **50** A4
Wexford Ho 11 E1 . **32** B4
Wexford Rd SW12 . . **72** B4
Weybourne St
SW18 . . . . **71** B2
Weybridge Ct 19
SE16 . . . . **40** A1
Weybridge Ho N4 . . . **6** B4
Weybridge Point 11
SW11 . . . . **169** A2
Weydown Cl SW19 . . **70** A3
Weyhill Ho 28 SE5 . **48** B1
Weyhill Rd 11 E1 . **111** C2
Wey Ho NW8 . . . . . . **89** C1
Weymouth Ct
5 Haggerston E2 . . **24** B3
16 Streatham SW2 . **74** B4
Weymouth Ho
Fitzrovia W1 . . . . . **104** B4
South Lambeth
SW8 . . . . **162** C2
Weymouth Mews
W1 . . . . **104** A4
Weymouth St W1 . **104** A4
Weymouth Terr
E2 . . . . **24** B3
Whadcoat St N4 . . . . **5** C2
Whaddon Ho
10 Camberwell
SE5 . . . . **64** A4
SW1 . . . . **131** A3
Wharfdale Rd N1 . **84** B2
Wharfedale Ct 5
E5 . . . . **17** C4
Wharfedale St
SW10 . . . . **142** A1
Wharf La 18 E14 . . **33** B3
Wharf Pl E2 . . . . **25** A4
Wharf Rd N1 . . . . . . **86** C1
Wharfside Rd E16 . . **35** A4
Wharf St E16 . . . . . . **35** A4
Wharf View Ct 18
E14 . . . . **34** B3
Wharncliffe Ho 3
SW15 . . . . **57** B2
Wharton Cl NW10 . . . **8** A2
Wharton Ho SE1 . . **138** C2
Wharton St WC1 . . . **95** A3
Whateley Rd SE22 . . **64** B2
Whatman Ho 10
E14 . . . . **33** B3
Wheatland Ho 7
SE22 . . . . **64** A4

Wheatlands Rd
SW17 . . . . **72** C1

Wheatley Ho
Gospel Oak NW5 . . . . **13** A4
🔲 Putney SW15 . . . . **68** C4

Wheatley St W1 . . . **103** C3

Wheat Sheaf Ct
E14 . . . . **42** A2

Wheatsheaf La
Fulham SW6 . . . . **47** B3
SW8 . . . . **162** B2

Wheatstone Ho
W10 . . . . **31** A4

Wheatstone Rd
W10 . . . . **31** A4

Wheeler Ct 🔲
SW11 . . . . **59** C4

Wheeler Gdns N1 . . **84** B4

Wheeler La E1 . . . . **110** C4

Wheelhouse The 🔲
E14 . . . . **42** A1

Wheelwright St
N7 . . . . **14** B1

Wheldon Ct SE1 . . **138** C4

Wheler Ho
E1 . . . . **24** B1 **98** C1

Wheler St
E1 . . . . **24** B1 **98** C1

Whellock Rd W4 . . . **38** A3

Whetstone Park
WC2 . . . . **106** C2

Whewell Rd N19 . . . . **5** A2

Whichcote St SE1 **121** B1

Whidborne Bldgs
WC1 . . . . **94** A3

Whidborne Cl SE8 . . **51** C1

Whidborne St WC1 . **94** B3

Whippingham Ho 🔲
E3 . . . . **26** B2

Whiskin St EC1 . . . . **96** A3

Whistler Mews 🔲
SE15 . . . . **49** B3

Whistlers Ave
SW11 . . . . **157** C1

Whistler St N5 . . . . . **15** A3

Whistler Twr
SW10 . . . . **156** C1

Whistler Wlk
SW10 . . . . **157** A2

Whiston Ho 🔢 N1 . . **15** A1

Whiston Rd E2 . . . . . **24** C4

Whitbread Ctr EC1 . **97** B1

Whitbread Rd SE4 . . **66** B3

Whitburn Rd SE13 . . **67** B3

Whitby Ave NW10 . . **20** A2

Whitby Ct 🔟 N7 . . . . **14** A4

Whitby Ho NW8 . . . . **78** C3

Whitby St
E1 . . . . **24** B1 **98** C2

Whitcher Cl SE14 . . . **51** A4

Whitcher Pl NW1 . . . **13** B2

Whitchurch Ho 🔢
W10 . . . . **30** C3

Whitchurch Rd
W11 . . . . **30** C2

Whitcomb St
WC2 . . . . **119** C3

Whitcome Mews
TW9 . . . . **45** A2

Whiteacre Mews
SE11 . . . . **149** C1

Whiteadder Way
E14 . . . . **42** A2

Whitear Wlk E15 . . . **19** C2

Whitebeam Cl
SW9 . . . . **163** A1

Whitebeam Ho 🔟
NW3 . . . . **12** B2

White Bear Pl 🔳 🔟
NW3 . . . . **11** C4

White Bear Yd EC1 . **95** B1

WHITECHAPEL . . . **110** C1

Whitechapel Gall . .

Whitechapel High St
E1 . . . . **111** A2

Whitechapel Mkt . .

Whitechapel Rd
E1 . . . . **111** C3

Whitechapel Sta
E1 . . . . **32** A4

Whitechapel Sta
E1 . . . . **32** A4

Whitechurch La 🔳
E1 . . . . **111** B2

Whitechurch Pas 🔟
E1 . . . . **111** B2

White City W10 . . . . **30** B3

White City Cl W12 . . **30** B2

White City Est
W12 . . . . **30** A2

White City Rd W12 . **30** B2

White City Sta
W12 . . . . **30** B2

Whitecliff Ho
SW18 . . . . **59** A1

White Conduit St
N1 . . . . **85** C2

Whitecross Pl
EC2 . . . . **109** C4

Whitecross St 🔢 E1 . **97** A1

Whitelock Ho 🔳
E9 . . . . **17** C2

White Lyon Ct
EC2 . . . . **108** C4

Whiteness Ho 🔞
SW9 . . . . **173** B4

White Post La E15 . **18** C2

White Post St SE14,
SE15 . . . . **50** B3

White Rd E15 . . . . . . **19** C1

White's Grounds
SE1 . . . . **138** B4

White's Grounds Est
SE1 . . . . **138** B4

White's Row E1 . . . **110** C3

White's Sq SW4 . . . . **61** C3

Whitestone La NW3 . **2** B1

Whitestone Wlk
NW3 . . . . **2** B1

Whitethorn St E3 . . . **33** C4

Whitfield Ct SW4 . . **172** A3

Whitfield Gdns
W1 . . . . **105** A4

Whitfield Ho NW8 . . **90** A1

Whitfield Pl W1 . . . . **93** A1

Whitfield St W1 . . . **105** A4

Whitgift Ho
Battersea SW11 . . . **168** A4
Lambeth SE11 . . . . . **148** C4

Whitgift St SE11 . . **148** C4

Whitington Ave
EC3 . . . . **110** A1

Whitley Ho SW1 . . **161** A4

Whitlock Dr SW19 . . **70** A3

Whitman Ho 🔞 E2 . **25** B2

Whitman Rd E3 . . . . **26** A1

Whitehead's Gr
SW3 . . . . **144** B3

White Ho
🔳 Battersea
SW11 . . . . **167** C2
🔳 Streatham SW4 . . **73** C4

Whitehorn Ho 🔟
E1 . . . . **32** B1

White Horse La
E1 . . . . **32** C4

Whitehorse Mews
SE1 . . . . **136** A2

Whitehorse Rd E1 . . **33** A4

White Horse Rd
E1 . . . . **33** A4

White Horse St
W1 . . . . **118** B1

White Horse Yd
EC2 . . . . **109** B2

White Ho The NW1 . **92** B3

White House Prep Sch
SW12 . . . . **73** C3

White Kennett St
E1 . . . . **110** B2

Whitelands Cres
SW18 . . . . **70** A4

Whitelands Ho
SW3 . . . . **145** A2

Whiteley Ho 🔳
SW4 . . . . **73** C4

Whiteleys Ctr 🔟
W2 . . . . **100** B1

White Lion Ct
EC3 . . . . **110** A1

White Lion Hill
EC4 . . . . **122** B4

White Lion St N1 . . **85** C1

White Lion Yd
W1 . . . . **118** A4

Whitelock Ho 🔳
E9 . . . . **17** C2

White Lyon Ct
EC2 . . . . **108** C4

Whitmore Gdns
NW10 . . . . **22** B3

Whitmore Ho 🔞
E1 . . . . **24** A4

Whitmore Prim Sch
E1 . . . . **87** C3

Whitmore Rd N1 . . . **24** A4

Whitnell Ct 🔳
SW15 . . . . **57** C2

Whitnell Way
SW15 . . . . **57** C2

Whitney Ho 🔳
SE22 . . . . **64** A4

Whitstable Ho 🔢
W10 . . . . **30** C3

Whitsters Ho SE1 . **138** C4

Whittaker Ct SW4 . **172** B3

Whittaker St SW1 . **145** B3

Whittaker Way 🔞
SE1 . . . . **153** C3

Whittingham Ct
W4 . . . . **46** A3

Whittingstall Mans
SW6 . . . . **165** A3

Whittingstall Rd
SW6 . . . . **165** A3

Whittington Hospl
The N19 . . . . **4** B2

Whittlebury Ho N4 . . **6** B4

Whittlesey St SE1 . **121** C1

Whitton NW3 . . . . . . **12** B1

Whitton Wlk E3 . . . . **26** C3

Whitworth Ho
SE1 . . . . **137** A1

Whitworth St SE10 . **43** A1

Whorlton Rd SE15 . . **65** A4

Whytlaw Ho 🔳 E3 . . **33** B4

Wicker St 🔠 E1 . . . . **32** A3

Wickfield Ho 🔢
SE16 . . . . **139** C3

Wickford Ho 🔳
E1 . . . . **25** B1

Wickford St E1 . . . . . **25** B1

Wickham Cl E1 . . . . . **32** B4

Wickham Gdns
SE4 . . . . **66** B4

Wickham Ho
SW1 . . . . **57** C1

Wickham Mews
SE4 . . . . **51** B1

Wickham Rd SE4 . . . **66** B4

Wickham St SE11 . **148** C2

Wick La
Hackney E3 . . . . **18** B1
Stratford Marsh E3 . . **26** C4

Wicklow Ho N16 . . . . **7** B3

Wicklow St WC1 . . . . **94** C4

Wick Rd
Hackney E9 . . . . **17** C2
Hackney E9 . . . . **18** A2

Wickstead Ho
TW8 . . . . **36** B1

Wicksteed Ho
SE1 . . . . **137** A1

Wick Village 🔳
E9 . . . . **18** B2

Wickway Ct 🔳
SE15 . . . . **49** B4

Wickwood St SE5 . . **48** A1

Widdenham Rd
N7 . . . . **14** B4

Widecombe Ho 🔞
SE5 . . . . **48** B1

Widegate St E1 . . . **110** B3

Widford 🔳 NW1 . . . . **13** A2

Widford Ho N1 . . . . . **86** A1

Widley Rd W9 . . . . . **23** C1

Widnes Ho 🔳 N7 . . . . **14** C1

Wigmore Hall W1 . **104** A2

Wigmore Pl W1 . . . **104** A2

Wigmore St W1 . . . **103** C2

Wigram Ct SW11 . . **168** A4

Wigram Ho 🔟 E14 . **34** A2

Wigton Pl SE11 . . . **149** C1

Wilberforce Ho 🔳
SW11 . . . . **59** C4

Wilberforce Mews 🔳
SW4 . . . . **61** C3

Wilberforce Prim Sch
W10 . . . . **23** A2

Wilberforce Rd
Finsbury Pk N4 . . . . . . **6** A2
Highbury N4, N5 . . . . . **6** B1

Wilbraham Ho
SW8 . . . . **162** A1

Wilbraham Pl
SW1 . . . . **145** B4

Wilby Mews
W11 . . . . **31** B1 **113** A2

Wilcox Cl SW8 . . . . **162** B2

Wilcox Ho 🔳 E3 . . . . **33** B4

Wilcox Pl SW1 . . . . **133** A1

Wilcox Rd SW8 . . . **162** A2

Wildcroft Manor
SW15 . . . . **69** B4

Wildcroft Rd
SW15 . . . . **69** B4

Wild Ct WC2 . . . . . **106** C2

Wilde Cl E8 . . . . **24** C4

Wilde Pl SW18 . . . . . **71** C4

Wilderness Mews
SW4 . . . . **61** A3

Wilderton Rd N16 . . . **7** A4

Wild Goose Dr
SE14 . . . . **50** B2

Wilding Ho 🔟 E9 . . . **17** C2

Wild's Rents SE1 . **138** A2

Wild St WC2 . . . . . . **106** C1

Wildwood Gr NW3 . . **2** C3

Wildwood Rd NW11 . **2** B4

Wildwood Rise
NW11 . . . . **2** B3

Wildwood Terr NW3,
NW11 . . . . **2** B3

Wilfred Fienburgh Ho
N7 . . . . **13** C4

Wilfred St SW1 . . . **132** C2

Wilfrid Gdns W3 . . . **28** B4

Wilkes Rd 🔳 TW8 . . **44** A4

Wilkie St E1 . . . . . . **111** A4

Wilkie Ho SW1 . . . **147** C2

Wilkin St Mews
NW1 . . . . **13** A2

Wilkins Ho SW1 . . **160** C4

Wilkinson Ho N1 . . . **87** C1

Wilkinson St SW8 . **162** C1

Wilkinson Way
W4 . . . . **37** C4

Wilkin St NW5 . . . . . **13** A2

Wilks Pl N1 . . . . **24** A3

Willan Wall E16 . . . . **35** B2

Willard St SW8 . . . . **61** A4

Willbury Ho 🔠 N7 . . **13** C3

Willcott Rd W3 . . . . **28** A1

Willenfield Rd
NW10 . . . . **20** B3

WILLESDEN **8** B1

Willesden Community
Hospl The NW10 . . . . . **8** C1

WILLESDEN
GREEN **22** A4

Willesden Green Sta NW2 . . . . 9 B2

Willesden Junction Sta NW10 . . . . 21 B2

Willesden La NW2, NW6 . . . . 9 C2

Willesden Sports Ctr W10 . . . . 22 A4

Willes Rd NW5 . . . . 13 A2

Willett Ho SW9 . . . . . . 62 A4

William Banfield Ho 10 SW6 . . . . 164 C2

William Blake Ho 2 SE15 . . . . 49 C1

William Bonney Est 10 SW4 . . . . 61 C3

William Booth Meml Training Coll SE5 . . . . 48 C1

William Brown Ct SE27 . . . . 75 A2

William Caslon Ho 28 E2 . . . . 25 A3

William Channing Ho 6 E2 . . . . 25 A2

William Cl SE13 . . . . . 67 B4

William Davis Prim Sch 10 E2 . . . . . . 24 C1 99 B2

William Dromey Ct NW6 . . . . 10 B1

William Dunbar Ho NW6 . . . . 23 B3

William Ellis Sch NW5 . . . . 3 C1

William Ellis Way SE16 . . . . 139 C1

William Evans Ho 8 SE8 . . . . 40 C2

William Gdns SW15 . . . . 57 A2

William Guy Gdns 4 E3 . . . . 27 A2

William Harvey Ho 1 SW19 . . . . 70 A3

William Hogarth Sch The 18 W4 . . . . 38 A1

William Hunt Mans SW13 . . . . 47 B4

William IV St WC2 . . . . 120 A3

William Margrie Cl 1 SE15 . . . . 49 C1

William Mews SW1 . . . . 131 A3

William Morris Acad W6 . . . . 39 C1

William Morris Ho W6 . . . . 47 C4

William Morris Way SW6 . . . . 166 C1

William Patten Prim Sch 5 N16 . . . . 7 B2

William Pl 2 E3 . . . . . . 26 B3

William Rathbone Ho 8 E2 . . . . 25 A2

William Rd NW1 . . . 92 C3

William Rushbrooke Ho 4 SE16 . . . . . 153 B4

William Saville Ho 2 NW6 . . . . 23 B3

William's Bldgs 1 E2 . . . . 25 B1

Williams Coll EC1 107 C3

Williams Ho 10 Bow E3 . . . . 26 C2

Williams Ho continued
9 Hackney E9 . . . . . . 25 A4
14 Streatham SW2 . . 74 C3

Williams La SW14 . . . 45 B1

Williamson Cl SE10 . . . . 43 B1

Williamson Ct SE17 . . . . 150 C1

Williamson St N7 . . . . 14 A4

William Sq 13 SE16 . . . . 33 A2

William St SW1 . . . . 131 A3

William Tyndale Prim Sch 20 N1 . . . . . . 15 A1

William Winter Ct 25 SW2 . . . . 74 C4

Willingham Cl 4 NW5 . . . . 13 B3

Willingham Terr NW5 . . . . 13 B3

Willington Rd SW9 . . . . 62 A4

Willis Ho 8 E14 . . . . . 34 A2

Willis St E14 . . . . 34 A3

Willoughby Ho EC2 . . . . 109 B3
20 Wapping E1 . . . . . 32 A1

Willoughby Rd NW3 . . . . 12 A4

Willoughby St WC1 . . . . 106 A3

Willoughbys The SW14 . . . . 56 A3

Willow Ave SW13 . . . 46 B1

Willowbank SW6 . . . . 58 A4

Willowbank Rd SE15 . . . . 49 B4

Willow Bridge Rd N1 . . . . 15 B2

Willow Cotts TW9 . . . 44 C4

Willow Ct
Brixton SW9 . . . . . . 173 B3
Chiswick W4 . . . . . . 46 A3
EC2 . . . . 24 A1 98 A2
Islington N7 . . . . . . 14 B3
8 Paddington W2 . . 31 C4
8 Streatham SW16 . . . . 74 B1

Willowdene
Highgate N6 . . . . 3 B4
1 Peckham SE15 . . . 50 A2
5 SE15 . . . . 50 A3

Willow Farm La SW15 . . . . 57 A4

Willow Hall NW3 . . . 11 C4

Willow Ho
9 Maitland Pk NW3 . . . . 12 B2
North Kensington W10 . . . . 22 C1

Willow Lo
Fulham SW6 . . . . . . 47 C2
Putney SW15 . . . . . 57 A4

Willow Lodge 10 SW8 . . . . 61 A4

Willowmere SE13 . . . 67 A2

Willow Pl SW1 . . . . 147 A4

Willow Rd
Ealing W5 . . . . 36 A4
Hampstead NW3 . . . 11 C4

Willow St EC2 . . . . . 24 A1 98 A2

Willows Terr NW10 . . . . 21 B3

Willow Tree Cl
10 Old Ford E3 . . . . 26 B4

Willow Tree Cl
continued
Wandsworth SW18 . . 71 A3

Willow Vale W12 . . . 29 C1

Willow Way 9 W11 . . . . 30 C2

Willow Wlk SE1 . . . . 152 C4
SE15 . . . . 49 B4

Wilman Gr E8 . . . . . . 16 C1

Wilmcote Ho W2 . . 100 A4

Wilmer Gdns 22 N1 . . . . 24 A4

Wilmer Ho 6 E3 . . . . 26 A3

Wilmer Lea Cl E15 . . 19 C1

Wilmer Pl N16 . . . . . . 7 B2

Wilmington Sq WC1 . . . . 95 B3

Wilmington St WC1 . . . . 95 B3

Wilmot Cl SE15 . . . . . 49 C3

Wilmot Pl NW1 . . . . . 13 B1

Wilmot St E2 . . . . 25 A1

Wilna Rd SW18 . . . . . 71 B4

Wilsham St W11 . . . . 31 A1 112 A2

Wilshaw Ho 10 SE8 . . . . 51 C3

Wilshaw St SE14 . . . . 51 C2

Wilson Gr SE16 . . . . . 40 A4

Wilson Ho
10 Clapham SW8 . . 171 B1
South Hampstead NW6 . . . . 11 B1

Wilson Rd SE5 . . . . . 49 A2

Wilson's Pl E14 . . . . . 33 B3

Wilson's Rd W6 . . . . . 39 C1

Wilson St EC2 . . . . . 109 C4

Wiltern Ct NW2 . . . . . 10 A2

Wilton Ave W4 . . . . . 38 A1

Wilton Cres SW1 . . . 131 B3

Wilton Ct
4 Richmond TW10 . . . . 54 A2
1 Stepney E1 . . . . . . 32 A3

Wilton Est E8 . . . . 16 C2

Wilton Ho 8 SE22 . . . 64 A4

Wilton Mews SW1 . . . . 131 C2

Wilton Pl SW1 . . . . . 131 B3

Wilton Rd SW1 . . . . 146 C4

Wilton Row SW1 . . . 131 B3

Wilton Sq N1 . . . . . . 87 B4

Wilton St SW1 . . . . . 132 A2

Wilton Terr SW1 . . . 131 B3

Wilton Villas N1 . . . . 87 B3

Wilton Way E8 . . . . . . 16 C2

Wiltshire Cl SW3 . . . 144 C3

Wiltshire Ct 2 N4 . . . . 5 B3

Wiltshire Rd SW9 . . . 62 C4

Wiltshire Row N1 . . . 87 C3

Wimbart Rd SW2 . . . . 74 B4

Wimbledon Lawn Tennis Mus SW19 . . . . 70 A2

Wimbledon Park Ct SW19 . . . . 70 B3

Wimbledon Park Montessori Sch SW18 . . . . 70 C2

Wimbledon Park Prim Sch SW19 . . . . . . 71 A2

Wimbledon Park Rd SW18, SW19 . . . . . 70 B3

Wimbledon Park Side SW19 . . . . 69 C3

Wimbledon Park Sta SW19 . . . . 70 C1

Wimbledon Stadium Bsns Ctr SW17 . . . 71 A1

Wimbledon Windmill Mus SW19 . . . . . . 69 B1

Wimbolt St E2 . . . . 24 C2 99 B4

Wimborne Ho
Canning Town E16 . . . . 35 B2
Marylebone NW1 . . . 90 B1
South Lambeth SW8 . . . . 163 A1
Upper Tooting SW12 . . . . 73 B1

Wimborne St N1 . . . . 87 B2

Wimbourne St N1 . . . 87 B2

Wimpole Mews W1 . . . . 104 A3

Wimpole St W1 . . . . 104 A3

Winans Wlk SW9 . . . 173 B1

Winant Ho 10 E14 . . . . 34 A2

Wincanton Rd SW18 . . . . 70 B4

Winchelsea Cl SW15 . . . . 57 C2

Winchelsea Ho 16 SE16 . . . . 40 B4

Winchelsea Rd NW10 . . . . 20 C4

Winchendon Rd SW6 . . . . 165 A4

Winchester Ave NW6 . . . . 10 A1

Winchester Cl SE17 . . . . 150 B3

Winchester Ct
Richmond TW9 . . . . . 54 B4
W8 . . . . 128 A4

Winchester Ho
Bayswater W2 . . . . 100 C1
Chelsea SW3 . . . . . 157 C3
24 Tower Hamlets E3 . . . . 26 B2

Winchester Pal SE1 . . . . 123 B2

Winchester Pl
6 Dalston E8 . . . . . . 16 B3
Highgate N6 . . . . 4 A3

Winchester Rd
Highgate N6 . . . . 4 A3
South Hampstead NW3 . . . . 11 C1

Winchester Sq SE1 . . . . 123 B2

Winchester St
Acton W3 . . . . 37 B4
SW1 . . . . 146 B2

Winchester Wlk SE1 . . . . 123 B2

Winchfield Ho SW15 . . . . 56 B1

Winch Ho
Isle of Dogs E14 . . . 42 A3
SW10 . . . . 157 A2

Winchilsea Ho NW8 . . . . 89 C3

Wincott St SE11 . . . 149 C3

Windermere NW1 . . . . 92 B4
12 Putney SW15 . . . 57 C1

Windermere Ave NW6 . . . . 23 A4

Windermere Ct SW13 . . . . 46 B4

Windermere Ho E3 . . . . 26 B1

Windermere Point 3 SE15 . . . . 50 B3

Windermere Rd N19 . . . . 4 B2

Winders Rd SW11 . . 168 A2

Windham Rd TW9 . . . 54 B4

Windlass Pl SE8 . . . . 41 A2

Windlesham Gr SW19 . . . . 69 C3

Windmill WC1 . . . . 106 C4

Windmill Alley 7 W4 . . . . 38 A2

Windmill Cl
1 Bermondsey SE1 . . . . 153 C4
6 Lewisham SE13 . . 52 B1

Windmill Ct NW2 . . 10 A2

Windmill Dr
Clapham SW4 . . . . . 61 A2
Cricklewood NW2 . . . 1 A1

Windmill Gdns SW2 . . . . 62 B1

Windmill Hill
1 Hampstead NW3 . . . . 11 B4
Hampstead NW3 . . . . 2 B1

Windmill Ho
4 Millwall E14 . . . . 41 C2
SE1 . . . . 121 C1

Windmill La E15 . . . . 19 C2

Windmill Pas 10 W4 . . . . 38 A2

Windmill Rd
Chiswick W4 . . . . . . 38 A2
Roehampton SW19 . . 69 A1
Wandsworth SW18 . . 59 C1

Windmill Row SE11 . . . . 149 B1

Windmill St W1 . . . 105 B3

Windmill Wlk SE1 . . 135 C4

Windrose Cl SE16 . . . 40 C4

Windrush Cl
Battersea SW11 . . . . 59 C3
Chiswick W4 . . . . . . 45 B3
4 Hackney E8 . . . . . 16 C1

Windrush Ho NW8 . . . . 101 C4

Windrush Rd NW10 . . . . 20 C4

Windrush Sq
Brixton SW9 . . . . . . 62 C3
SW2 . . . . 62 C3

Windsock Cl 8 SE16 . . . . 41 B2

Windsor Ct
Battersea SW11 . . . 167 C2
Bayswater W2 . . . . 114 A4
3 Clapham SW4 . . 144 B2
6 Clapham Pk SW4 . . . . 61 B3
Fulham SW6 . . . . . . 58 A4

Windsor Ho
E2 . . . . 25 C2
4 Wandsworth SW18 . . . . 58 C2

West Hampstead NW6 . . . . 10 C4

Windsor Gdns W9 . . 23 C1

Windsor Ho
4 Acton Green
W4 . . . . **37** B1
Brondesbury NW2 . . **10** A2
4 Globe Town E2 . . . **25** C2
Regent's Pk NW1 . . . . **92** B4
Shoreditch N1 . . . . . . **87** A2
Stoke Newington N4 . . **6** B3
Windsor Pl SW1 . . **147** A4
Windsor Rd
Richmond TW9 . . . . . . **44** B1
Upper Holloway N7 . . **5** A1
Willesden NW2 . . . . . . **9** A2
Windsor St N1 . . . . . **86** B4
Windsor Terr N1 . . . **97** A4
Windsor Way
W14 . . . . **140** A4
Windsor Wharf E9 . . **18** B3
Windsor Wlk SE5 . . **48** C1
Windspoint Dr
SE15 . . . . **50** A4
Windus Rd N16 . . . . . **7** B3
Windus Wlk N16 . . . . **7** B3
Wine Cl E1 . . . . **32** B2
Wine Office Ct
EC4 . . . . **107** C2
Winfield Ho 3
SW11 . . . . **167** C2
Winford Ct 18
SE15 . . . . **49** C2
Winford Ho E3 . . . . . **18** B1
Winforton St SE10 . . **52** B2
Winfrith Rd SW18 . . **71** B3
Wingate Ho
6 Bromley E3 . . . . . . **27** A2
8 Stoke Newington
N16 . . . . **15** C4
Wingate Rd W6 . . . . **39** A3
Wingfield Ct 5
E14 . . . . **34** C2
Wingfield Ho
Paddington NW6 . . . **78** A2
16 Spitalfields
E2 . . . . **24** B2 **98** C3
Wingfield Mews
SE15 . . . . **64** C4
Wingfield St SE15 . . **64** C4
Wingford Rd SW2 . . **62** A1
Wingham 3 NW5 . . **12** C2
Wingmore Rd
SE24 . . . . **63** B4
Wingrad Ho 3 E1 . . **32** B4
Wingrave SE17 . . . . **151** B3
Wingrave Rd W6 . . . **47** B4
Wingreen 16 NW8 . . **78** B4
Winicotte Ho W2 . . **101** C4
Winifrede Paul Ho 7
NW5 . . . . **13** A4
Winkley St 6 E2 . . . **25** A3
Winkworth Cotts 14
E1 . . . . **25** B1
Winnett St W1 . . . . **119** B4
Winnington Ho
16 Kensal Town
W10 . . . . **23** A1
8 SE5 . . . . **48** B3
Winscombe St N19 . . **4** A2
Winsham Gr SW11 . . **60** C2
Winsham Ho NW1 . . **93** C4
Winslade Rd SW2 . . **62** A2
Winsland Mews
W2 . . . . **101** B2
Winsland St W2 . . . **101** B2
Winsley St W1 . . . . **105** A2

Winslow SE17 . . . . **152** A1
Winslow Rd W6 . . . . **47** B4
Winstanley Rd
SW11 . . . . **59** C4
**Winston Churchill's
Britain at War
Experience** SE1 . . **124** A1
Winston Ho WC1 . . . **93** C2
Winston Ho N1 . . . . **15** C4
Winston Wlk 2
W4 . . . . **37** C2
Winterbourne Ho
W11 . . . . **31** A2 **112** A3
Winter Box Wlk
TW10 . . . . **54** B2
Winterbrook Rd
SE24 . . . . **63** B1
Winterfold Cl
SW19 . . . . **70** A2
Winterleys 7
NW6 . . . . **23** B3
Winter Lo 17
SE16 . . . . **153** C1
Wintersloe Ho 20
SE5 . . . . **48** B1
Winterton Ho 19
E1 . . . . **32** B3
Winterton Pl
SW10 . . . . **157** A4
Winterwell Rd
SW2 . . . . **62** A2
Winthrop Ho 14
W12 . . . . **30** A3
Winthrop St E1 . . . . **32** A4
Winton Prim Sch
N1 . . . . **84** C1
Wirrall Ho 15 SE26 . **76** C1
Wisbech 5 N5 . . . . . **5** B3
Wisden Ho SW8 . . . **163** A3
Wise Rd E15 . . . . . . **27** C4
Wiseton Rd SW17 . . **72** B3
Wisley Ho SW1 . . . **147** B2
Wisley Rd SW11 . . . **60** C2
Wisteria Ho SE4 . . . **66** A4
Wisteria Rd SE13 . . **67** C3
Wistow Ho 18 E2 . . **24** C4
Witanhurst La N6 . . . **3** C3
Witan St E2 . . . . **25** A2
Witchwood Ho 10
SW9 . . . . **62** C4
Witcombe Point 14
SE15 . . . . **49** C2
Witechapel Sp Ctr
E1 . . . . **32** B4
Witham Ct SW17 . . . **72** B1
Witham Ho 34 SE5 . . **48** B1
Witherington Rd
N5 . . . . **14** C3
Withers Pl EC1 . . . . **97** A2
Withycombe Rd
SW19 . . . . **69** C4
Withy Ho 4 E1 . . . . **25** C1
Witley Ct WC1 . . . . **94** A1
Witley Ho 2 SW2 . . **74** B4
Witley Point 8
SW15 . . . . **69** A3
Witley Rd N19 . . . . . **4** B2
Wittering Ho 9
SW11 . . . . **169** A2
Wivenhoe Cl SE15 . . **65** A4
Wix Prim Sch SW4 . **61** A3
Wix's La SW4 . . . . . **61** A3

Woburn Ct
32 Bermondsey
SE16 . . . . **40** A1
Richmond TW9 . . . . . . **54** B4
Woburn Pl WC1 . . . . **94** A1
Woburn Sq WC1 . . . **93** C1
Woburn Wlk WC1 . . . **93** C3
Wodeham Gdns 1
E1 . . . . **32** A4
Wodehouse Ave
SE15 . . . . **49** B2
Wodehouse Ct 10
W3 . . . . **37** B3
Woking Cl SW15 . . . **56** B3
Wolcot Ho NW1 . . . . **83** A1
Wolfe Cres 34
SE16 . . . . **40** C4
Wolfe Ho 16 W12 . . **30** A2
Wolfson Ct
Golders Green
NW11 . . . . **1** A4
SE1 . . . . **139** A4
Wolftencroft Cl
SW11 . . . . **59** C4
Wollaston Cl SE1 . . **150** C4
Wollotan Ho N1 . . . . **85** C2
Wolseley Ave
SW19 . . . . **70** C2
Wolseley Gdns
W4 . . . . **45** A4
Wolseley Rd W4 . . . **37** B2
Wolseley St SE1 . . . **139** A3
Wolsey Ct NW6 . . . . **11** B1
Wolsey Ho 3
NW5 . . . . **13** C2
Wolsey Mews
NW5 . . . . **13** B2
Wolsey Rd N1 . . . . . **15** C3
Wolsey St E1 . . . . . . **32** B4
Wolverley St E2 . . . . **25** A2
Wolverton SE17 . . . **152** A2
Wolverton Gdns
W6 . . . . **39** C2
Women's Liby The
EC2 . . . . **110** C2
Wontner Cl 3 N1 . . **15** B1
Wontner Rd SW12,
SW17 . . . . **72** B2
Woodall Cl 8 E14 . . **34** A2
Woodberry Down
N4 . . . . **6** B4
**Woodberry Down
Com Prim Sch** N4 . **6** B4
Woodberry Gr N4 . . . **6** B4
Woodberry Terr E9 . **17** B2
Woodborough Rd
SW15 . . . . **57** A3
Woodbourne Ave
SW16 . . . . **73** C1
Woodbourne Cl
SW16 . . . . **74** A1
Woodbridge Cl 10
N7 . . . . **5** B2
Woodbridge Ct N16 . **6** C1
Woodbridge St
EC1 . . . . **96** A2
Woodchester Sq
W2 . . . . **100** A4
Woodchurch Ho 15
SW9 . . . . **173** B4
Woodchurch Rd
NW6 . . . . **11** A1
Wood Cl E2 . . . . **24** C1 **99** B2
Woodcock Ho 4
E14 . . . . **33** C4

Woodcote Ho 4
SE8 . . . . **51** B4
Woodcott Ho 1
SW15 . . . . **68** C2
Woodcroft Mews
SE8 . . . . **41** A2
Wood Dene 6
SE15 . . . . **50** A2
Woodfall Rd N4 . . . . . **5** C2
Woodfall St SW3 . . **144** C1
Woodfarrs SE5 . . . . **63** C3
Wood Field NW3 . . . **12** B3
Woodfield Ave
SW16 . . . . **73** C1
Woodfield Ct
SW16 . . . . **73** C1
Woodfield Gr
SW16 . . . . **73** C1
Woodfield La
SW16 . . . . **73** C1
Woodfield Pl W9 . . . **23** B1
Woodfield Rd W9 . . . **31** A4
Woodford Ct 18
W12 . . . . **39** C4
Woodger Rd W12 . . **39** B4
Woodhall NW1 . . . . . **92** C3
Woodhall Ave
SE21 . . . . **76** B1
Woodhall Dr SE21 . . **76** B1
Woodhall Ho
SW18 . . . . **59** C1
Woodheyes Rd
NW10 . . . . **8** A3
Wood Ho
6 Clapham SW4 . . **171** C2
6 Paddington
NW6 . . . . **23** B3
Woodhurst Rd W3 . . **28** B2
Woodison St E3 . . . . **26** A1
Wood La W12 . . . . . . **30** B2
Woodland Cres
18 Rotherhithe
SE16 . . . . **40** C4
SE10 . . . . **53** A4
Woodland Gr SE10 . . **43** A1
Woodland Hts SE3 . . **53** A4
Woodland Mews
SW16 . . . . **74** A1
Woodlands SW4 . . . **61** A3
Woodlands Ave
W3 . . . . **28** A1
Woodlands Ct
NW10 . . . . **22** C4
Woodlands Gdns
SW15 . . . . **58** B2
Woodlands Park Rd
SE10 . . . . **53** A4
Woodlands Rd
SW13 . . . . **56** B4
Woodland St
E8 . . . . **16** B2
Woodlands The
Highbury N5 . . . . **15** B4
7 Hornsey N8 . . . . . . **5** A4
Woodlands Way
SW15 . . . . **58** B2
Woodland Wlk
9 Greenwich
SE10 . . . . **43** A1
NW3 . . . . **12** A3
Wood Lane High Sch
W12 . . . . **30** B3
Wood Lane Sta
W12 . . . . **30** B2
Woodlawn Cl
SW15 . . . . **58** B2

Woodlawn Rd
SW6 . . . . **47** C2
Woodlea Rd N16 . . . . **7** A1
Woodleigh Gdns
SW16 . . . . **74** A1
Woodman Mews
TW9 . . . . **45** A2
Woodmans Gr
NW10 . . . . **8** B3
Woodmans Mews
W12 . . . . **30** A4
Woodmere Cl 11
SW11 . . . . **60** C4
Woodpecker Mews
SE13 . . . . **67** C3
Woodpecker Rd 6
SE14 . . . . **51** A4
Wood Point 8
E16 . . . . **35** C4
Woodquest Ave
SE24 . . . . **63** B2
Woodruff Ho 12
SW2 . . . . **62** C1
Woodrush Cl 4
SE14 . . . . **51** A3
Woodseer St E1 . . . **111** A4
Woodsford SE17 . . . **151** B1
Woodsford Sq
W14 . . . . **126** B4
Woods Ho SW8 . . . **170** C4
Wood's Mews W1 . . **117** B4
Woodsome Rd NW5 . . **4** A1
Wood's Pl SE1 . . . . **138** B1
Woodspring Rd
SW19 . . . . **70** A2
Wood's Rd SE15 . . . **50** A2
Wood St
Chiswick W4 . . . . **38** A1
City of London EC2 . **109** A2
Woodstar Ho 3
SE15 . . . . **49** C3
Woodstock Ave
NW11 . . . . **1** A4
Woodstock Ct
SE11 . . . . **149** A2
Woodstock Gr
W12 . . . . **39** C4
Woodstock Ho 2
N5 . . . . **15** B4
Woodstock Mews
W1 . . . . **103** C3
Woodstock Rd
Bedford Pk W4 . . . . . **38** A3
Finsbury Pk N4 . . . . . . **5** C3
Golders Green NW11 . **1** B3
Woodstock St W1 . . **104** A1
Woodstock Studios 17
W12 . . . . **39** C4
Woodstock Terr
E14 . . . . **34** A2
Woodthorpe Rd
SW15 . . . . **57** A3
Woodview Cl 3
SW15 . . . . **68** B1
Woodville Ho SE1 . . **138** C2
Woodville Rd
Golders Green
NW11 . . . . **1** A4
Paddington NW6 . . . **23** B3
Stoke Newington
N16 . . . . **16** A3
Woodwarde Rd
SE22 . . . . **64** A1
Woodwell St
SW18 . . . . **59** B2

Wood Wharf SE10 . . 52 B4
Woodyard Cl NW5 . . .12 C3
Woodyard La SE21. .76 A4
Woolcombes Ct 4
  SE16. . . . . .32 C1
Wooler St SE17. . . 151 C2
Woolf Ct 7 W3. . . . .37 B3
Woolf Mews WC1 . . .94 A2
Woolley Ho SW9. . . .63 A4
Woollon Ho 8 E1 . . .32 B3
Woolmore Prim Sch
  14 E14 . . . . .34 B2
Woolmore St E14. . .34 B2
Woolneigh St
  SW6 . . . . 166 A1
Woolpack Ho 1
  E9 . . . . .17 B2
Wooldridge Way E9. .17 B1
Woolstaplers Way
  SE16 . . . . 153 B4
Woolstone Ho 7
  E2 . . . . .24 C4
Woolven Ho SE3. . .53 B4
Wooster Gdns E14. .34 C3
Wooster Pl SE1. . . 151 C4
Wootton St SE1 . . . 121 C1
Worcester Ct 44
  W2 . . . . .31 C4
Worcester Ho 4
  W2. . . . . .38 A4
Worcester Gdns
  SW11 . . . . .60 B2
Worcester Ho
  Bayswater W2 . . . . 100 C1
  3 Islington N1 . . . .15 B1
  Lambeth SE11 . . . 135 B1
  5 Putney SW15 . . .57 C2
Worcester Mews 2
  NW6 . . . . .11 A2
Wordsworth Ho
  NW6 . . . . .23 C2
Wordsworth Pl 11
  NW5. . . . . .12 B3
Wordsworth Rd
  Bermondsey SE1 . . 153 A3
  Stoke Newington
  N16. . . . . .16 A4
Worfield St SW11 . 158 B1
Worgan St
  Rotherhithe SE16. . .40 C2
  SE11 . . . . 148 C2
Working Men's Coll
  The NW1. . . . . . . .83 A2
World's End Pas
  SW10 . . . . 157 B2
World's End Pl
  SW10 . . . . 157 A2
World Trade Ctr
  London E14. . . . . .42 A4
Worlidge St W6 . . .39 B1
Worlingham Rd
  SE22 . . . . .64 B3
Wormholt Park Prim
  Sch W12 . . . . .29 C2
Wormholt Rd W12. .29 C1
Wormwood St
  EC2. . . . . 110 A2
Wornington Rd
  W10 . . . . .31 A4
Woronzow Rd
  NW8 . . . . .80 A3
Worple St SW14. . .55 C4

Worple Way TW10 . . .54 A3
Worship St
  EC2. . . . . . .24 A1 98 A1
Worsley Gr E5. . . . .16 C4
Worsopp Dr SW4 . . .61 B2
Worth Gr SE17. . . . 151 B1
Worthington Ho
  EC1. . . . . .95 C3
  16 Streatham SW2 . .74 C4
Wotton Ct 4 E14. . .34 C2
Wotton Rd 6 SE8. . .51 B4
Wouldham Rd E16. .35 B3
Wrayburn Ho 28
  SE16 . . . . 139 C3
Wray Cres N4 . . . . .5 B2
Wray Ct N4 . . . . . . .5 B2
Wray Ho 11 SW2 . . .74 A3
Wren Ave NW2 . . . . .9 B4
Wren Cl E16. . . . . . .35 B3
Wren Ho
  20 Bow E3. . . . . . .26 A3
  SW1 . . . . 147 B1
Wren Landing E14. .33 C1
Wrenn Ho SW13. . . .47 B4
Wren Rd SE5. . . . . .48 C2
Wren St WC1 . . . . . .95 A2
Wrentham Ave
  NW10. . . . . .22 C3
Wren View N6. . . . . .4 B3
Wrestlers Ct E3 . . . .27 B2
Wrexham Rd E3. . . .26 C3
Wrigglesworth St
  SE14. . . . . .50 C3
Wright Cl SE13. . . .67 C3
Wright Ho SW15. . . .57 A2
Wright's Gn SW4. . .61 C3
Wright's La W8. . . 128 A2
Wright's Rd E3. . . . .26 B3
Wrights Wlk SW14. .55 C4
Wrotham Ho SE1 137 C2
Wrotham Rd 19
  NW1. . . . . .13 B1
Wrottesley Rd
  NW10. . . . . .21 C3
Wroughton Rd
  SW11 . . . . .60 B1
Wroxton Rd SE15. . .50 B1
Wulfstan St W12. . .29 B3
Wyatt Cl SE16. . . . .41 B4
Wyatt Dr SW13. . . .47 A3
Wyatt Ho
  Blackheath Vale
  SE3. . . . . .53 B1
  NW8. . . . . .89 C1
Wyatt Park Mans 7
  SW2 . . . . .74 A2
Wyatt Park Rd
  SW2 . . . . .74 B2
Wyatt Rd N5 . . . . . .6 B3
Wybert St NW1. . . .92 C2
Wycherley Cl SE3. . .53 B3
Wychwood End N6. . .4 B4
Wychwood Ho N4 . . .6 B4
Wyclif Ct EC1. . . . . .96 A3
Wycliffe Ho 18
  W2 . . . . .31 C4
Wyclif St EC1. . . . . .96 A3
Wycombe Ho 1
  NW8 . . . . .90 A2

Wycombe Pl SW18 .59 B1
Wycombe Sq
  W8 . . . . . . .31 C1 113 B1
Wyersdale Ho N4. . . .6 B4
Wye St SW11. . . . . . .59 C4
Wyfold Rd SW6. . . 154 A1
Wyke Rd E3. . . . . . .18 C1
Wyldes Cl NW11. . . . .2 B3
Wyllifif E1. . . . . . . .25 B1
Wymering Mans 8
  W9 . . . . .23 C2
Wymering Rd W9. . .23 C2
Wymondham Ct
  NW8 . . . . .79 C4
Wymond St SW15 . .57 B4
Wynan Rd E14. . . . .42 A1
Wyndham Cres N19 . .4 B1
Wyndham Deedes Ho
  5 E2 . . . . .24 C3
Wyndham Ho
  SW1 . . . . 145 B3
Wyndham Mews
  W1 . . . . 102 C3
Wyndham Pl W1. . . 102 C3
Wyndham Rd SE5 . .48 B3
Wyndhams Ct 4
  E8 . . . . .16 B1
Wyndham St W1. . 102 C4
Wyndham Yd W1. . 102 C3
Wyneham Rd SE24. .63 C2
Wynford Rd N1. . . .85 A2
Wynne Ho SE14 . . . .50 C2
Wynne Rd SW9. . . 173 B1
Wynnstay Gdns
  W8 . . . . 127 C2
Wynter Ho 20
  SW9 . . . . 173 A1
Wynter St SW11 . . .59 B3
Wynton Pl W3. . . . .28 A3
Wynyard Ho SE11 149 A2
Wynyard Terr
  SE11 . . . . 149 A2
Wynyatt Ho EC1 . . . .96 A4
Wynyatt St EC1. . . .96 A4
Wytham Ho NW8 . . .89 C1
Wythburn Ct W1. . 102 C2
Wythburn Pl W1. . 102 C2
Wyvil Prim Sch
  SW8 . . . . 162 B2
Wyvil Rd SW8 . . . 162 A2
Wyvis St E14. . . . . .34 A4

Y

Yabsley St E14. . . . .34 B1
Yaldam Ho SE1 . . . 152 A3
Yalding Ho 20 E5. . .17 A3
Yalding Rd SE16. . 153 B4
Yale Ct NW6. . . . . . .11 A3
Yardley St WC1 . . . .95 B3
Yard The N1 . . . . . .84 B1
Yarmouth Pl W1 . . 118 A1
Yarnfield Sq 16
  SE15. . . . . .49 C2
Yarrow Ho
  12 Cubitt Town
  E14. . . . . .42 B3
  16 North Kensington
  W10 . . . . .30 B4
Yatesbury Ct E5 . . . .18 A3
Yates Ct NW2. . . . . . .9 C2

Yates Ho 22
  E2. . . . . . . .24 C2 99 C4
Yatton Ho 12 W10 . .30 B4
Yeadon Ho 14
  W10 . . . . .30 B4
Yearby Ho W10. . . .22 B1
Yeate St N1 . . . . . . .15 C1
Yeats Cl NW10. . . . . .8 A2
Yeldham Ho W6 . . . .39 C1
Yeldham Rd W6 . . . .39 C1
Yelverton Rd
  SW11 . . . . 167 C1
Yeoman Cl SE27. . .75 A1
Yeoman's Row
  SW3 . . . . 130 B1
Yeoman St SE8 . . . .41 A2
Yeoman's Yd E1. . 125 A4
Yeovil Ho
  Finsbury Pk N7. . . . .5 B2
  North Kensington
  W10 . . . . .22 B1
Yerbury Prim Sch
  N19. . . . . .4 C1
Yerbury Rd N19 . . . .4 C1
Yeshivo Horomo
  Talmudical Coll
  . . . . .6 C3
Yesodey Hatorah Jun
  Sch for Girls 7
  N16. . . . . .7 B4
Yesodey Hatorah Sec
  Sch for Girls 6
  . . . . .7 B4
Yet Lev Ct 5. . . . . .7 C3
Yewfield Rd NW10. . .8 B2
Yew Gr NW2. . . . . . .9 C4
Yew Tree Cl SE13. . .67 B4
Yew Tree Ct 3
  SE13. . . . . .67 B4
Yew Tree Cl 8 N16. . .6 A2
Yew Tree Rd W12. .29 B2
Yoakley Rd N16. . . .7 A2
Yoke Cl N7 . . . . . . .14 A2
Yonge Pk N4, N7 . . .5 C1
York Ave
  Mortlake SW14 . . . .55 B2
  Walworth SE17 . . . 151 A2
York Bldgs WC2 . . 120 B3
York Bridge NW1 . . .91 B2
York Cl 17 SE5. . . . .48 B1
York Gate NW1 . . . .91 C1
York Gr SE15 . . . . . .50 B2
York Hall L Ctr E2 . .25 B3
York Hill SE27,
  SW16 . . . . .75 A1
York Ho
  Acton W3 . . . . .28 B2
  Chelsea SW3 . . . . 145 A2
  Islington N5 . . . . . .14 C3
  Kensington W8 . . . 128 A4
  11 Kentish Town
  N7. . . . . .13 C2
  Kew TW9 . . . . .44 C2
  Lambeth SE1 . . . . 135 A1
  Marylebone W1 . . 102 C4
  Pentonville N1 . . . .84 C1
  Richmond TW10. . . .54 C2
York House Pl
  W8 . . . . 128 A4

Woo–Zof 289

Yorkley Ho 3
  W10 . . . . .22 B1
York Mans
  Battersea SW11. . . 169 C4
  Marylebone W1 . . 103 B4
  Walworth SE17. . . 151 A2
York Mews NW5 . . .13 A3
York Pl
  Battersea SW11. . . .59 C4
  WC2 . . . . 120 B3
York Place Mans
  NW1 . . . . 103 A4
York Rd
  Battersea SW11,
  SW18 . . . . .59 C4
  Dagenham W3 . . . .28 C3
  4 Richmond TW10 . .54 B2
  SE1 . . . . 135 A4
York Rise NW5 . . . . .4 A1
York Road Bsns Ctr
  SW11 . . . . 167 B1
York St Chambers
  W1 . . . . 102 C4
Yorkshire Cl N16 . . .7 A1
Yorkshire Grey Pl 13
  NW3. . . . . .11 B4
Yorkshire Grey Yd
  WC1 . . . . 106 C3
Yorkshire Rd E14. . .33 A3
York Sq 12 E14. . . .33 A3
York St W1. . . . . . 103 A4
York Terr E NW1 . . .91 C1
York Terr W NW1 . .91 B1
Yorkton St 2 . . . . .24 C3
York Water Gate The
  SW1 . . . . 120 B2
York Way
  Barnsbury N1, N7,
  NW1 . . . . .14 A1
  N1. . . . . .84 B3
York Way Ct
  Islington N1 . . . . . .84 C3
  Islington N1 . . . . . .84 B3
Young's Bldgs EC1. .97 A3
Young Ct SW11. . . 169 C3
Young St W8 . . . . 128 A3
Yoxall Ho 2 W10. . .22 B1
Yukon Rd SW12. . . .73 A4

Z

Zabludowicz
  Collection NW5 . . .12 C2
Zampa Rd SE16. . . .40 B1
Zander Ct
  E2. . . . . . . .24 C2 99 C4
Zangwill Ho NW6. . .23 B3
Zealand Ho 11 SE5. .48 B1
Zealand Rd E3 . . . .26 A3
Zennor Rd SW12 . . .73 B3
Zenoria St SE22 . . .64 B3
Zetland Ho W8 . . . 128 A2
Zetland St E14 . . . .34 B4
Zeus Ho N1 . . . . . . .97 B3
Zion Ho 8 E1 . . . . . .32 B3
Zoar St SE1 . . . . . 122 C2
Zodiac Ho 3 E3. . . .26 C1
Zoffany St N19 . . . . .4 C2

List of numbered locations

This atlas shows thousands more place names than any other London street atlas. In some busy areas it is impossible to fit the name of every place.

Where not all names will fit, some smaller places are shown by a number. If you wish to find out the name associated with a number, use this listing.

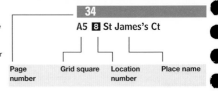

34

A5 **8** St James's Ct

Page number — Grid square — Location number — Place name

1
A2 **1** Talmud Torah Tiferes Shlomo
B1 **1** Mortimer Cl
2 Primrose Ct
3 Sunnyside Ho
4 Sunnyside
5 Prospect Pl
B4 **1** Berkeley Ct
2 Exchange Mans
3 Beechcroft Ct
4 Nedahall Ct
C1 **1** Portman Hts
2 Hermitage Ct
3 Moreland Ct
4 Wendover Ct

2
B1 **1** Hampstead Sq
2 Stamford Cl
3 Mount Sq The

4
B1 **1** Hunter Ho
2 Fisher Ho
3 Lang Ho
4 Temple Ho
5 Palmer Ho
6 Carlisle Ho
7 Durham Ho
8 Suffolk Ho
9 Lincoln Ho
10 Llewellyn Ho
11 Fell Ho
12 Aveling Ho
13 Merryweather Ct
14 Brennands Ct
15 St Christophers Ct
16 Francis Terrace Mews
17 Tremlett Mews
B2 **1** Flowers Mews
2 Archway Cl
3 Sandridge St
4 Bovingdon Cl
5 Cavell Ct
6 Torrence Ho
7 Rowan Wlk
8 Laurel Cl
9 Forest Way
10 Larch Cl
11 Pine Cl
12 Alder Mews

13 Aspen Cl
14 Hargrave Park Prim Sch
15 Middlesex Univ (Archway Campus)
B3 **1** Calvert Ct
2 Academy The
3 Whitehall Mans
4 Pauntley St
5 Archway Hts
6 Pauntley Ho
7 St Aloysius RC Coll
C1 **1** Melchester Ho
2 Norcombe Ho
3 Weatherbury Ho
4 Wessex Ho
5 Archway Bsns Ctr
6 Harford Mews
7 Opera Ct
8 Rupert Ho
9 All Saints Church
C2 **1** Bowerman Ct
2 Gresham Pl
3 Hargrave Mans
4 Church Garth
5 John King Ct
6 Ramsey Ct
7 St John's Upper Holloway CE Prim Sch
8 Byam Shaw Sch of Art
C3 **1** Louise White Ho
2 Levison Way
3 Sanders Way
4 Birbeck Ho
5 Scholars Ct
6 Mount Carmel RC Tech Coll for Girls
C4 **1** Eleanor Rathbone Ho
2 Christopher Lo
3 Monkridge
4 Marbleford Ct
5 High London
6 Garton Ho
7 Hilltop Ho
8 Caroline Martyn Ho
9 Arthur Henderson Ho
10 Margaret Mcmillan Ho
11 Enid Stacy Ho

12 Mary McArthur Ho
13 Bruce Glasier Ho
14 John Wheatley Ho
15 Keir Hardie Ho
16 Monroe Ho
17 Iberia Ho
18 Lygoe Ho
19 Lambert Ho
20 Shelbourne Ho
21 Arkansas Ho
22 Lafitte Ho
23 Shreveport Ho
24 Packenham Ho
25 Orpheus Ho
26 Fayetville Ho
27 Bayon Ho

5
A1 **1** Northview
2 Tufnell Park Mans
3 Fulford Mans
4 Tollington Ho
5 Grafton Prim Sch
A2 **1** Bracey Mews
2 Christie Ct
3 Ringmer Gdns
4 Kingsdown Rd
5 Cottenham Ho
6 St Paul's Ct
7 Rickthorne Rd
8 Stanley Terr
9 Arundel Lo
10 Landseer Ct
11 St Mark's Prim Sch
A3 **1** Beeches The
2 Lambton Ct
3 Nugent Ct
4 Lambton Mews
5 Mews The
A4 **1** Marie Lloyd Gdns
2 Edith Cavell Cl
3 Marie Stopes Ct
4 Jessie Blythe La
5 Barbara Rudolph Ct
6 Hetty Rees Ct
7 Leyden Mans
8 Brambledown
9 Lochbie
10 Lyngham Ct
11 High Mount
12 Woodlands The
13 St Gildas' RC Jun Sch

B1 **1** Pakeman Prim Sch
2 London Meridian Coll
3 American Univ in London The
4 South Eastern Univ in London The
5 Dean Coll of London
6 Montem Prim Sch
B2 **1** Berkeley Wlk
2 Lazar Wlk
3 Thistlewood Cl
4 Tomlins Wlk
5 Andover Ho
6 Barmouth Ho
7 Chard Ho
8 Christ the King RC Prim Sch
9 Methley Ho
10 Rainford Ho
11 Woodbridge Cl
12 Allerton Wlk
13 Falconer Wlk
14 Sonderburg Rd
15 St Mark's Mans
16 Athol Ct
17 Pooles Park Prim Sch
B3 **1** Lawson Ct
2 Wiltshire Cl
3 Fenstanton
4 Hutton Ct
5 Wisbech
6 Islington Arts & Media Sch
C2 **1** Brookfield
2 Churnfield
3 Cornwallis Sq

6
A1 **1** Hurlock Ho
2 Blackstock Ho
3 Vivian Comma Cl
4 Monsell Ct
A2 **1** Parkwood Prim Sch
2 Ambler Prim Sch
3 City & Islington Coll (Ctr for Life-long Learning)
B4 **1** Finmere Ho
2 Keynsham Ho
3 Kilpeck Ho
4 Knaresborough Ho

5 Leighfield Ho
6 Lonsdale Ho
7 Wensleydale Ho
8 Badminton Ct
C1 **1** Betty Layward Prim Sch
C2 **1** Chestnut Cl
2 Sycamore Ho
3 Lordship Ho
4 Clissold Ho
5 Beech Ho
6 Laburnum Ho
7 Ormond Ho
8 Yew Tree Ct
9 Oak Ho
C4 **1** Selwood Ho
2 Bnois Jerusalem Girls Sch
3 Mendip Ho
4 Ennerdale Ho
5 Getters Talmud Torah
6 Delamere Ho
7 Westwood Ho
8 Bernwood Ho
9 Allerdale Ho
10 Chattenden Ho
11 Farningham Ho
12 Oakend Ho

7
A1 **1** Gujarat Ho
2 Marton Rd
3 Painsthorpe Rd
4 Selkirk Ho
5 Defoe Ho
6 Edward Friend Ho
7 Sheridan Ho
8 Barrie Ho
9 Arnold Ho
10 Macaulay Ho
11 Stowe Ho
12 Carlyle Ho
13 Shaftesbury Ho
14 Lillian Cl
15 Swift Ho
16 Dryden Ho
17 Scott Ct
18 Kingsfield Ho
19 Uhura Sq
20 Hartopp Ct
A2 **1** Denman Ho

2 St Mary's Stoke Newington CE Prim Sch

A3
1 Godstone Ct
2 Farnham Ct
3 Milford Ct
4 Cranleigh Ct
5 Haslemere Ct
6 Belmont Ct
7 Hockworth Ho
8 Garratt Ho
9 Fairburn Ho
10 Thorndale Ho
11 Oakdene Ho
12 Briardale Ho

A4
1 Beis Rochel d'Satmar Girls Sch
2 Our Lady's Convent RC High Sch

B1
1 Lawrence Bldgs
2 Cottage Wlk
3 Batley Pl

B2
1 Garnham St
2 Garnham Cl
3 Sanford La
4 Sanford Wlk
5 Abney Gdns
6 Fleet Wood
7 Simon Marks Jewish Prim Sch
8 William Patten Prim Sch

B3
1 Stamford Hill Mans
2 Montefiore Ct
3 Berwyn Ho
4 Clent Ho
5 Chiltern Ho
6 Laindon Ho
7 Pentland Ho

B4
1 Regent Ct
2 Stamford Lo
3 Holmwood Ct
4 Bobov Foundation Sch
5 Yesodey Hatorah Sec Sch for Girls
6 Lubavitch Boys Prim Sch
7 Yesodey Hatorah Jun Sch for Girls
8 Lubavitch Girls Prim Sch
9 Lubavitch House Sch (Jun Boys)
10 Skinners Company Sch (Upper)

C1
1 Ravenscourt
2 Mellington Ct
3 Rendlesham Ho
4 Carroll Ct
5 St Scholastica's RC Prim Sch

C2
1 Cazenove Mans
2 Chedworth Ho
3 Aldergrove Ho
4 Abbotstone Ho
5 Briggeford Cl
6 Inglethorpe Ho
7 Ashdown Ho
8 Epping Ho
9 Cypress Cl

C3
1 Stamford Gr E
2 Stamford Mans
3 Grove Mans
4 Stamford Gr W
5 Talmud-Torah Yetev-Lev

8

A1
1 Beveridge Rd
2 Purcell Mews
3 George Lansbury Ho
4 Charles Hobson Ho
5 Reade Wlk
6 Westbury Ho
7 Bridge Ct
8 St Joseph's RC Prim Sch
9 Dixon Way
10 Armstrong Rd
11 Brittage Rd

A4
1 Grange Ct
2 Green Ct

C2
1 Regency Mews
2 Tudor Mews
3 Utopia Ho
4 Angel Ct
5 St Andrew & St Francis CE Prim Sch

9

A2
1 St Mary Magdelen's RC Jun Sch
2 Islamic Coll for Advanced Studies

B2
1 Rutland Park Gdns
2 Rutland Park Mans
3 Queens Par
4 Harcourt Ho
5 Solidarity Ho
6 Electra Ct
7 Cassandra Ct
8 Carlton Ct
9 Convent of Jesus & Mary RC Inf Sch

C4
1 Oaklands Mews
2 Acer Ct
3 Maple Ct
4 Argyle Mans

10

A1
1 Christ Church Ct
2 Paul Daisley Ct
3 Fountain Ho
4 Kingston Ho
5 Waverley Ct
6 Weston Ho
7 Mapes Ho
8 Athelstan Gdns
9 Leff Ho
10 Brondesbury Coll for Boys

B1
1 Alma Birk Ho
2 Brooklands Ct
3 Brooklands Court Apartments
4 Cleveland Mans
5 Buckley Ct
6 Webheath

C1
1 Linstead St
2 Embassy Ho
3 Acol Ct
4 Kings Wood Ct
5 Douglas Ct
6 King's Gdns
7 Carlton Mans
8 Smyrna Mans
9 New Priory Ct
10 Queensgate Pl
11 Brondesbury Mews
12 St Eugene de Mazenod RC Prim Sch

C2
1 Dene Mans
2 Sandwell Cres
3 Sandwell Mans
4 Hampstead West
5 Redcroft

C3
1 Orestes Mews
2 Walter Northcott Ho
3 Polperro Mans
4 Lyncroft Mans
5 Marlborough Mans
6 Alexandra Mans
7 Cumberland Mans
8 Cavendish Mans
9 Ambassador Ct
10 Welbeck Mans
11 Inglewood Mans
12 Dennington Park Mansions

C4
1 Parsifal Coll

11

A2
1 Beswick Mews
2 Worcester Mews
3 Minton Mews
4 Doulton Mews
5 Laurel Ho
6 Sandalwood Ho
7 Iroko Ho
8 Banyan Ho
9 Rosewood Ho
10 Ebony Ho
11 Rosemont Mans
12 Exeter Mews

B1
1 Harrold Ho
2 Glover Ho
3 Byron Ct
4 Nalton Ho

B2
1 Petros Gdns
2 Heath Ct
3 Imperial Twrs
4 Fairhurst
5 St John's Ct
6 New College Ct
7 Chalford
8 Rosslyn Mans
9 Sutherland Ho
10 Holy Trinity CE Prim Sch
11 Phoenix Sch The
12 North Bridge House Sch
13 Southbank International Sch

B3
1 Arkwright Mans
2 Hatstone Ct
3 Hampstead High Sch

B4
1 Windmill Hill
2 Highgrove Point
3 Gainsborough Ho
4 Holly Bush Hill
5 Heath Mans
6 Holly Bush Steps
7 Pavilion Ct
8 Holly Berry La
9 New Campden Ct
10 Holly Bush Vale
11 Benham's Pl
12 Prospect Pl
13 Yorkshire Grey Pl
14 Gardnor Mans
15 Ellerdale Cl
16 Monro Ho
17 Prince Arthur Mews
18 Prince Arthur Ct
19 Village Mount
20 Perrin's Ct
21 Wells Ct
22 Bakers Pas
23 Spencer Wlk
24 Bird In Hand Yd
25 Kings Well
26 New Ct
27 Streatley Pl
28 Mansfield Pl
29 Upper Hampstead Wlk
30 Hampstead Parochial CE Prim Sch
31 Univ Coll Jun Sch
32 Heathside Prep Sch
33 New End Prim Sch
34 Sisters of St Marcellina Sch

C1
1 New College Par
2 Northways Par
3 Noel Ho
4 Campden Ho
5 Centre Hts
6 Hickes Ho
7 Swiss Terr
8 Leitch Ho
9 Jevons Ho
10 Langhorne Ct
11 Park Lo
12 Avenue Lo
13 Frank Barnes Sch
14 Swiss Cottage Sch

C2
1 Belsize Park Mews
2 Baynes Mews
3 McCrone Mews
4 South Hampstead High Sch

C3
1 Belsize Court Garages
2 Roscommon Ho
3 Akenside Ct
4 Fitzjohns Prim Sch
5 St Christopher's Sch
6 St Anthony's Sch

C4
1 White Bear Pl
2 Wells Ho The
3 Boades Mews
4 Flask Cotts
5 Coach House Yd
6 Pilgrim's Pl
7 Rosslyn Mews
8 Royal Sch Hampstead The
9 Academy Sch The

12

A2
1 Banff Ho
2 Glenloch Ct
3 Havercourt
4 Holmefield Ct
5 Gilling Ct
6 Howitt Cl
7 Manor Mans
8 Straffan Lo
9 Romney Ct
10 Lancaster Stables
11 Eton Garages
12 Hampstead Coll of Fine Arts & Humanities

A3
1 Hampstead Hill Sch

B1
1 Hancock Nunn Ho
2 Higginson Ho
3 Duncan Ho
4 Mary Wharrie Ho

5 Rockstraw Ho
6 Cleaver Ho
7 Chamberlain St
8 Sharples Hall St
9 Primrose Mews
10 Rothwell St
11 St Georges Mews

B2
1 Alder Ho
2 Hornbeam Ho
3 Whitebeam Ho
4 Aspen Ho
5 Rowan Ho
6 Beech Ho
7 Chestnut Ho
8 Oak Ho
9 Willow Ho
10 Sycamore Ho
11 Maple Ho
12 Hazel Ho
13 Elaine Ct
14 Faircourt
15 Walham Ct
16 Stanbury Ct
17 Priory Mans
18 Wellington Ho
19 Grange The

B3
1 Cayford Ho
2 Du Maurier Ho
3 Isokon Flats
4 Palgrave Ho
5 Garnett Ho
6 Stephenson Ho
7 Park Dwellings
8 Siddons Ho
9 Mall Studios
10 Park Hill Wlk
11 Wordsworth Pl
12 Fraser Regnart Ct
13 St Pancras Almshouses
14 St Dominic RC Prim Sch
15 Fleet Prim Sch

C1
1 Bridge Ho
2 Hardington
3 Mead Ct
4 Rugmere
5 Tottenhall
6 Beauvale
7 Broomfield
8 Camden Coll of English

C2
1 Silverbirch Wlk
2 Penshurst
3 Wingham
4 Westwell
5 Chislet
6 Burmarsh
7 Shipton Ho
8 Stonegate
9 Leysdown
10 Headcorn
11 Lenham
12 Halstow
13 Fordcombe
14 Cannington
15 Langridge
16 Athlone Ho
17 Pentland Ho
18 Beckington
19 Hawkridge
20 Edington
21 Rhyl Prim Sch
22 Haverstock Sch

13

A1
1 Ferdinand Ho
2 Harmood Ho
3 Hawley Rd
4 Hawley Mews
5 Leybourne St
6 Barling
7 Tiptree
8 Havering
9 Candida Ct
10 Lorraine Ct
11 Donnington Ct
12 Welford Ct
13 Torbay Ct
14 Bradfield Ct
15 Torbay St
16 Water La
17 Leybourne Rd
18 Haven St
19 Stucley Pl
20 Lawrence Ho
21 Chalcot Sch
22 Holy Trinity & Saint Silas CE Prim Sch
23 Hawley Inf Sch

A2
1 Ashington
2 Priestley Ho
3 Leonard Day Ho
4 Old Dairy Mews
5 Monmouth Ho
6 Alpha Ct
7 Una Ho
8 Widford
9 Heybridge
10 Roxwell
11 Hamstead Gates
12 Kingsway Coll

A4
1 Denyer Ho
2 Stephenson Ho
3 Trevithick Ho
4 Brunel Ho
5 Newcomen Ho
6 Faraday Ho
7 Winifrede Paul Ho
8 Wardlow
9 Fletcher Ct
10 Tideswell
11 Grangemill
12 Hambrook Ct
13 Calver

B1
1 Cherry Tree Ct
2 Chichester Ct
3 Durdans Ho
4 Philia Ho
5 Bernard Shaw Ct
6 Foster Ct
7 Bessemer Ct
8 Hogarth Ct
9 Rochester Ct
10 Soane Ct
11 Wallett Ct
12 Inwood Ct
13 Wrotham Rd
14 St Thomas Ct
15 Caulfield Ct
16 Bruges Pl
17 Reachview Cl
18 Lawfords Wharf

B3
1 Eleanor Ho
2 Falkland Pl
3 Kensington Ho
4 Willingham Cl
5 Kenbrook Ho
6 Aborfield
7 Great Field
8 Appleford
9 Forties The
10 Maud Wilkes Cl
11 Dunne Mews
12 Dowdeny Cl
13 Kentish Town CE Prim Sch

B4
1 Benson Ct
2 Tait Ho
3 Manorfield Cl
4 Greatfield Cl
5 Longley Ho
6 Lampson Ho
7 Davidson Ho
8 Palmer Ho
9 Lambourn Cl
10 Morris Ho
11 Owen Ho
12 Eleanor Palmer Prim Sch

C1
1 Hillier Ho
2 Gairloch Ho
3 Cobham Mews
4 Bergholt Mews
5 Blakeney Cl
6 Weavers Way
7 Allensbury Pl

C2
1 Rowstock
2 Peckwater Ho
3 Wolsey Ho
4 Pandian Way
5 Busby Mews
6 Caledonian Sq
7 Canal Bvd
8 Northpoint Sq
9 Lock Mews
10 Carters Cl
11 York Ho
12 Hungerford Rd
13 Cliff Road Studios
14 Cliff Ct
15 Camelot Ho
16 Church Studios
17 Camden Terr
18 Brecknock Prim Sch
19 Hungerford Prim Sch

C3
1 Blake Ho
2 Quelch Ho
3 Lee Ho
4 Willbury Ho
5 Howell Ho
6 Holmsbury Ho
7 Leith Ho
8 Betchworth Ho
9 Rushmore Ho
10 Dugdale Ho
11 Horsendon Ho
12 Colley Ho
13 Coombe Ho
14 Ivinghoe Ho
15 Buckhurst Ho
16 Saxonbury Ct
17 Charlton Ct
18 Apollo Studios
19 Barn Cl
20 Long Meadow
21 Landleys Field
22 Margaret Bondfield Ho
23 Haywood Lo
24 Torriano Jun & Inf Schs

C4
1 Fairlie Ct
2 Trecastle Way

14

A2
1 Clock Tower Pl
2 Clock View Cres
3 Jim Veal Dr
4 Gower Sch The

A3
1 Kimble Ho
2 Saxonbury Ct
3 Poynder Ct
4 Pangbourne Ho
5 Moulsford Ho

A4
1 Arcade The
2 Macready Pl
3 Cardwell Ho
4 Mcmorran Ho
5 Crayford Ho
6 Whitby Ct
7 Prospect Pl
8 City & Islington Coll (Ctr for Bsns, Arts & Technology)

B1
1 Kerwick Cl
2 Rydston Cl
3 Skegness Ho
4 Frederica St
5 Ponder St
6 Kings Ct
7 Freeling St
8 Coatbridge Ho
9 Tilloch St

B2
1 Burns Ho
2 Scott Ho
3 Wellington Mews
4 Roman Ct
5 Piccadilly Ct
6 Knowledge Point Sch

B3
1 Culverin Ct
2 Garand Ct
3 Mount Carmel

B4
1 Buckmaster Ho
2 Cairns Ho
3 Halsbury Ho
4 Chelmsford Ho
5 Cranworth Ho
6 City & Islington Coll (Ctr for Health, Social & Child Care)

C1
1 Mountfort Terr
2 Avon Ho
3 Buckland Ho
4 Dovey Lo
5 Carfree Cl
6 Mitchell Ho
7 New College Mews
8 Lofting Ho
9 Brooksby Ho
10 Cara Ho
11 Thornhill Prim Sch
12 North London Science Ctr

C2
1 London Metropolitan Univ (Spring Ho)

C3
1 Slaney Pl
2 Eastwood Cl
3 Milton Ct
4 Hartnoll St

3 Dalmeny Avenue Est
4 Hyndman Ho
5 Carpenter Ho
6 Graham Ho
7 Tufnell Mans

5 St James School Flats
6 Widnes Ho
7 Tranmere Ho
8 Victoria Mans
9 Formby Ct
10 Mersey Ho
11 Birkenhead Ho
12 Drayton Park Mews
13 Drayton Park Prim Sch

15

A1
1 Islington Park Mews
2 Evelyn Denington Ct
3 Bassingbourn Ho
4 Cadmore Ho
5 Adstock Ho
6 Garston Ho
7 Flitton Ho
8 Datchworth Ho
9 Battishill St
10 Almeida St
11 Edward's Cotts
12 Hyde's Pl
13 Tyndale Terr
14 Spriggs Ho
15 Barratt Ho
16 Spencer Pl
17 Chadston Ho
18 Whiston Ho
19 Wakelin Ho
20 Tressel Cl
21 Canonbury St
22 Halton Ho
23 Shillingford St
24 Highbury Mans
25 Premier Ho
26 Waterloo Gdns
27 William Tyndale Prim Sch

A2
1 Hampton Ct
2 Salisbury Ho
3 Canonbury Prim Sch
4
5 Laycock Prim Sch

A3
1 De Barowe Mews
2 Fieldview Ct
3 Viewpoint
4 Ashurst Lo
5 Highbury Fields Sch
6 London Metropolitan Univ (Ladbroke Ho)
7 Robinswood Mews

A4
1 Chestnuts The
2 Bowen Ct
3 Peckett Sq
4 De Barowe Mews

B1
1 Astey's Row
2 Lincoln Ho
3 Worcester Ho
4 Melville Pl
5 Wontner Cl
6 Hedingham Ct
7 Laundry La
8 Base Apartments
9 Walkinshaw Ct
10 New Bentham Ct
11 Bentham Ct
12 Haslam Ho
13 Horsfield Ho
14 Riverside Ho
15 Eric Fletcher Ct

16 Annette Cres
17 Ashby Ho
18 Lindsey Mews
19 Cardigan Wlk
20 Red House Sq
21 Orchard Cl
22 Queensbury St
23 Raynor Pl

B2
1 Crowline Wlk
2 Upper Handa Wlk
3 Handa Wlk
4 Lismore Wlk
5 Bardsey Wlk
6 Walney Wlk
7 Upper Bardsey Wlk
8 Upper Lismore Wlk
9 Sark Ho
10 Guernsey Ho
11 Guernsey Rd
12 Sybil Thorndike Ho
13 Clephane Rd
14 Florence Nightingale Ho
15 Jersey Ho
16 Jethou Ho
17 Islay Wlk
18 Upper Caldy Wlk
19 Caldy Wlk
20 Alderney Ho
21 Gulland Wlk
22 Nightingale Rd
23 Upper Gulland Wlk
24 Church Rd
25 Oransay Rd
26 Canonbury Yd E

B3
1 Pearfield Ho
2 Larchfield Ho
3 Beresford Terr
4 Pondfield Ho
5 Ashfield Ho
6 Elmfield Ho
7 Highbury Grove Sch

B4
1 Fountain Mews
2 Woodstock Ho
3 Henson Ct
4 Taverner Sq

C1
1 Downham Ct
2 Trafalgar Point

C2
1 John Kennedy Ct
2 John Kennedy Lo
3 Ball's Pond Pl
4 Haliday Wlk
5 Queen Elizabeth Ct
6 Canonbury Hts
7 Pinnacle The
8 Threadgold Ho
9 Wakeham St
10 Saffron Ct
11 Callaby Terr
12 Tilney Gdns
13 Westcliff Ho
14 Ilford Ho
15 Ongar Ho
16 Greenhills Terr
17 Romford Ho
18 Bute Wlk
19 Upper Ramsey Wlk
20 Rona Wlk
21 Thorndike Rd
22 St Pauls Steiner Sch

C3
1 Newington Green Prim Sch

C4
1 Ledo Ho
2 Salween Ho
3 Prome Ho

4 Arakan Ho
5 Rangoon Ho
6 Mandalay Ho
7 Karen Ho
8 Wingate Ho
9 Jubet Ho
10 Orde Ho
11 Chindit Ho
12 Mabel Thornton Ho
13 Crawshay Ho
14 Avon Ho
15 Connaught Mans
16 Jonson Ho
17 Herrick Ho
18 Donne Ho
19 Thirlmere Ho
20 Grasmere Ho

16

A1
1 Dorchester Ct
2 Wareham Ho
3 Dorset Ct
4 Stratton Ct
5 Swanage Ct
6 Blandford Ct
7 Portland Ct
8 Oscar Faber Pl
9 Metropolitan Bsns Ctr
10 Lancaster Ct
11 Palazzo Apartments
12 Watercress Pl

A2
1 Kingsland Gn
2 Kingsland Pas
3 Metropolitan Benefit Societies Almshouses
4 Nimrod Pas
5 De Beauvoir Pl
6 Warburton Ct
7 Buckingham Mews
8 Aztec Ct
9 Kerridge Ct
10 Isabella Mews
11 St Jude & St Paul's CE Prim Sch
12 De Beauvoir Prim Sch
13 Our Lady & St Joseph RC Prim Sch
14 Childrens House Upper Sch

A3
1 Hewling Ho
2 Matthias Ho
3 Port Royal Pl
4 Cressington Cl
5 King Henry's Yd
6 Bronte Ho
7 Sewell Ho
8 Lydgate Ho
9 Patmore Ho
10 Congreve Ho
11 Elton Ho
12 Conrad Ho
13 Southwell Ho
14 Neptune Ho
15 Campion Ho
16 Webster Ho
17 Meredith Ho
18 Beckford Ho
19 Ashley Ct
20 Hayling Cl
21 Millard Cl
22 Lydford Cl
23 Salcombe Rd

24 Truman's Rd
25 Templeton Cl
26 John Campbell Rd
27 Gillett Pl
28 Bradbury St
29 Thomas Crowell Ct
30 Shellgrove Rd

A4
1 Londesborough Ho
2 Knebworth Ho
3 Knebworth Rd
4 Bransby Ct
5 Imperial Ave
6 Leonard Pl
7 Shakspeare Mews
8 Binyon Ho
9 Shelley Ho
10 Browning Ho
11 Burns Ho
12 Andrew Marvell Ho
13 Wycliffe Ho
14 Blake Ho
15 Marlowe Ho
16 Fletcher Ho
17 Chaucer Ct
18 St Matthias's CE Prim Sch

B1
1 Hilborough Rd
2 Shoreditch Ct
3 Evergreen Sq
4 Wyndhams Ct
5 Festival Ct
6 Fortune Ct
7 Rose Ct
8 Ability Plaza
9 Briar Ct
10 Lomas Dr
11 Queensbridge Inf Sch

B2
1 Prospect Ho
2 Woodland St
3 Crosby Wlk
4 Kirkland Wlk
5 Bowness Ho
6 Carlisle Wlk
7 Skelton Cl
8 Camerton Cl
9 Buttermere Wlk
10 Houghton Cl
11 Hayton Cl
12 Kingsland Sh Ctr
13 Springfield Ho
14 Parton Lo
15 Sanctuary Mews
16 Fenton Cl

B3
1 Miller's Terr
2 Chow Sq
3 Drysdale Flats
4 Gateway Mews
5 Birkbeck Mews
6 Winchester Pl

B4
1 Coronation Ave
2 Morris Blitz Ct
3 Shacklewell Ho
4 Alexandra Ct
5 Shacklewell Prim Sch
6 Princess May Prim Sch

C1
1 Aldington Ct
2 Bayton Ct
3 Rochford Wlk
4 Windrush Cl
5 Gayhurst Prim Sch

C2
1 Burdon Ct
2 Thomson Ct
3 Bruno Ct
4 Thackeray Mews

7 Madinah Rd

C3
1 Kingsdown Ho
2 Glendown Ho
3 Moredown Ho
4 Blakeney Cl
5 Beeston Cl
6 Benabo Ct
7 David Devine Ho
8 Kreedman Wlk
9 Hermitage Row
10 Grafton Ct
11 Lushington Terr
12 Aspen Ct
13 Pykewell Ct
14 Albion Works Studios

17

A1
1 Fortescue Ave
2 Pemberton Ct
3 Weston Wlk
4 Bayford St Ind Ctr
5 Bayford St
6 Sidworth St
7 Helmsley St
8 Cyntra Pl
9 Signal Ho
10 All Nations Ho
11 Vanguard Ho
12 Hacon Sq

A2
1 Bohemia Pl
2 Graham Mans
3 Marvin St
4 Boscobel Ho
5 Royal Oak Rd
6 Colonnades The
7 Sylvester Ho
8 Sylvester Path
9 Doctor Spurstowe Almshouses
10 Great Eastern Bldgs
11 Sojourner-Truth Cl

A3
1 Birchington Ho
2 Bicknor Ho
3 Boxley Ho
4 Adisham Ho
5 Cranbrook Ho
6 Marden Ho
7 Broome Ho
8 Crandale Ho
9 Cheriton Ho
10 Ditton Ho
11 Langley Ho
12 Dymchurch Ho
13 Elham Ho
14 Davina Ho
15 Pembury Pl
16 Downs Ct
17 Perrywood Ho
18 Staplehurst Ho
19 Pegwell Ho
20 Yalding Ho
21 Northbourne Ho
22 Monkton Ho
23 Milsted Ho
24 Athlone Cl
25 Clarence Pl
26 Gould Terr
27 Quested Ct
28 Brett Pas
29 Marcon Ct
30 Appleton Ct
31 Institute Pl

A4
1 Ross Ct
2 Downs La
3 Gaviller Pl
4 Robert Owen Lo

5 Apprentice Way
6 Arrowe Ct
7 Gilwell Ct
8 Sutton Ct
9 St Andrews Mans
10 Kinnoull Mans
11 Rowhill Mans
12 Sladen Pl
13 Mothers Sq The
14 Richborough Ho
15 Sandgate Ho
16 Sheppey Ho

B1
1 Pitcairn Ho
2 Lyme Grove Ho
3 Shakespeare Ho
4 Upcott Ho
5 Loddiges Ho
6 Parkinson Ho
7 Sloane Ho
8 Vanbrugh Ho
9 Cambridge Pas
10 Lyttleton Ho
11 Victoria Park Ct
12 Tullis Ho
13 Fairchild Ho
14 Forsyth Ho
15 Tradescant Ho
16 Mason Ho
17 Capel Ho
18 Cordwainers Ct
19 Bridgeman Ho
20 St Thomas's Pl
21 Barclay Ho
22 Clayton Ho
23 Danby Ho
24 Sherard Ho
25 Catesby Ho
26 Petiver Cl
27 Leander Ct
28 Philip Turner Est
29 Grendon Ho
30 Shore Mews
31 Shore Bsns Ctr
32 Kendal Ho
33 Classic Mans
34 Tudor Ho
35 Park Ho
36 Enterprise Ho
37 Alpine Gr
38 Clarendon Cl
39 Rotheley Ho
40 Bernie Grant Ho
41 Orchard Prim Sch
42 St John of Jerusalem CE Prim Sch

B2
1 Woolpack Ho
2 Elvin Ho
3 Thomas Ho
4 Hockley Ho
5 Retreat Ho
6 Butfield Ho
7 Brooksbank Ho
8 Cresset Ho
9 Brooksbank St
10 Lennox Ho
11 Milborne Ho
12 Collent Ho
13 Middlesex Pl
14 Elsdale Ho
15 Devonshire Hall
16 Brent Ho
17 Morningside Prim Sch
18 Hackney Free & Parochial CE Sec Sch

19 C1 293

B3
1 St John & St James CE Prim Sch

C1
1 Stuart Ho
2 Gascoyne Ho
3 Chelsfield Point
4 Sundridge Ho
5 Banbury Ho
6 Lauriston Ho

C2
1 Musgrove Ho
2 Cheyney Ho
3 Haynes Ho
4 Warner Ho
5 Gilby Ho
6 Gadsden Ho
7 Risley Ho
8 Baycliffe Ho
9 Sheldon Ho
10 Offley Ho
11 Latimer Ho
12 Ribstone Ho
13 Salem Ho
14 Fieldwick Ho
15 Lever Ct
16 Matson Ho
17 Wilding Ho
18 Rennell Ho
19 Dycer Ho
20 Granard Ho
21 Whitelock Ho
22 Harrowgate Ho
23 Cass Ho
24 Lofts on the Park
25 Heathcote Point
26 Ravenscroft Point
27 Vanner Point
28 Hensley Point
29 San Ho
30 Berger Prim Sch

C4
1 Cromford Path
2 Longford Ct
3 Overbury Ho
4 Heanor Ct
5 Wharfedale Ho
6 Ladybower Ct
7 Ilkeston Ct
8 Derby Ct
9 Rushmore Cres
10 Blackwell Cl
11 Belper Ct
12 Rushmore Prim Sch

18

A2
1 Chigwell Ct
2 Wellday Ho
3 Selman Ho
4 Vaine Ho
5 Trower Ho
6 St Dominics RC Prim Sch

B2
1 Mallard Ct
2 Merriam Ave
3 Gainsborough St
4 Palace Ct
5 St Anthony's Cl
6 Trowbridge Est

B3
7 Wick Village

19

C1
1 Service Route No 2
2 Service Route No 3
7 Newham Sixth Form Coll (Stratford Ctr)

C4
1 Mulberry Ct
2 Rosewood Ct
3 Gean Ct
4 Blackthorn Ct
5 Cypress Ct

20
C4 1 Carlyle Rd
2 Bernard Shaw Ho
3 Longlents Ho
4 Mordaunt Ho
5 Wilmers Ct
6 Stonebridge Ctr
7 Shakespeare Ave
8 Southcroft
9 Brent Adult Comm Education Service Coll

21
A3 1 Futters Ct
2 Barrett Ct
3 Elms The
4 Fairlight Ct
B3 1 New Crescent Yd
2 Harlesden Plaza
3 St Josephs Ct
4 Jubilee Cl
5 Ellery Cl

22
B1 1 Princess Alice Ho
2 Yoxall Ho
3 Yorkley Ho
4 Northaw Ho
5 Oakham Ho
6 Markyate Ho
7 Letchmore Ho
8 Pagham Ho
9 Quendon Ho
10 Redbourn Ho
11 Ketton Ho
12 Hillman Dr
C2 1 Westfield Ct
2 Tropical Ct
3 Chamberlayne Mans
4 Quadrant The
5 Queens Park Ct
6 Warfield Yd
7 Regent St
8 Cherrytree Ho
9 Artisan Mews
10 Artisan Quarter

23
A1 1 Sycamore Wlk
2 Westgate Bsns Ctr
3 Buspace Studios
4 Bosworth Ho
5 Golborne Gdns
6 Appleford Ho
7 Adair Twr
8 Gadsden Ho
9 Southam Ho
10 Norman Butler Ho
11 Thompson Ho
12 Wells Ho
13 Paul Ho
14 Olive Blythe Ho
15 Katherine Ho
16 Breakwell Ho
17 Pepler Ho
18 Edward Kennedy Ho
19 Winnington Ho
20 Queen's Park Prim Sch
21 Middle Row Prim Sch
22 St Mary RC Prim Sch
23 St Thomas' CE Prim Sch
A2 1 Selby Sq
2 Severn Ave
3 Stansbury Sq
4 Tolhurst Dr
5 John Fearon Wlk
6 Mundy Ho
7 Macfarren Ho
8 Bantock Ho
9 Banister Ho
10 Batten Ho
11 Croft Ho
12 Courtville Ho
13 Mounsey Ho
14 Bliss Mews
15 Symphony Mews
B1 1 Octavia Mews
2 Russell's Wharf
3 Western Ho
4 Kelly Mews
5 Queen Elizabeth II Jubilee Sch
B2 1 Boyce Ho
2 Farnaby Ho
3 Danby Ho
4 Purday Ho
5 Naylor Ho
6 St Judes Ho
7 Leeve Ho
8 Longhurst Ho
9 Harrington Ct
10 Mulberry Ct
11 Kilburn Ho
B3 1 Claremont Ct
2 William Saville Ho
3 Western Ct
4 Bond Ho
5 Crone Ct
6 Wood Ho
7 Winterleys
8 Carlton Ho
9 Fiona Ct
C1 1 Kilburn Park Sch
2 Westside Ct
3 Byron Mews
4 Sutherland Ct
5 Fleming Cl
6 Hermes Cl
7 St Peter's CE Prim Sch
C2 1 Pentland Rd
2 Nelson Cl
3 Pavilion Ct
4 Masefield Ho
5 Austen Ho
6 Fielding Ho
7 Argo Bsns Ctr
8 John Ratcliffe Ho
9 Wymering Mans
10 City of Westminster Coll, Queens Park Ctr
11 Essendine Prim Sch
C3 1 Wells Ct
2 Cambridge Ct
3 Ely Ct
4 Durham Ct
5 St Augustine's CE High Sch
6 Sch of the Islamic Republic of Iran The
7 Ryde Ho
8 Glengall Pass
9 Leith Yd
10 Daynor Ho
11 Varley Ho
12 Sandby Ho
13 Colas Mews
14 Bishopsdale Ho
15 Lorton Ho
16 Marshwood Ho
17 Ribblesdale Ho
18 Holmesdale Ho
19 Kilburn Vale Est
20 Kilburn Bridge
21 Coll of NW London
22 St Mary's Kilburn CE Prim Sch

24
A2 1 Pimlico Wlk
2 Aske Ho
3 Hathaway Ho
4 Haberdasher Pl
5 Fairchild Ho
6 Burtt Ho
7 Enfield Cloisters
8 McGregor Ct
9 Royal Oak Ct
10 Hoxton Mkt
11 Bath Pl
12 Chapel Pl
13 Standard Pl
14 Cleeve Workshops
15 Cleeve Ho
16 Printing House Yd
17 Perseverance Works
18 Crooked Billet Yd
19 Drysdale Ho
20 Castlefrank Ho
21 School App
22 Basing House Yd
23 Mail Coach Yd
24 St Monica's RC Prim Sch
25 Symister Mews
26 Hackney Com Coll
A3 1 Barret Ho
2 Scorton Ho
3 Fern Ct
4 Macbeth Ho
5 Oberon Ho
6 Buckland Ct
7 Crondall Ct
8 Osric Path
9 Caliban Twr
10 Celia Ho
11 Juliet Ho
12 Bacchus Wlk
13 Malcolm Ho
14 Homefield St
15 Crondall Pl
16 Blanca Ho
17 Miranda Ho
18 Falstaff Ho
19 Charmian Ho
20 Myrtle Wlk
21 Arden Ho
22 Sebastian Ho
23 Stanway Ct
24 Jerrold St
25 Rosalind Ho
26 Cordelia Ho
27 Monteagle Ct
28 John Parry Ct
29 James Anderson Ct
30 Ben Jonson Ct
31 Sara Lane Ct
32 Walbrook Ct
33 Burbage Sch
A4 1 Portelet Ct
2 Trinity Ct
3 Rozel Ct
4 St Helier Ct
5 Corbiere Ho
6 Kenning Ho
7 Higgins Ho
8 Cavell Ho
9 Girling Ho
10 Fulcher Ho
11 Francis Ho
12 Norris Ho
13 Kempton Ho
14 Nesham Ho
15 Crossbow Ho
16 Catherine Ho
17 Strale Ho
18 Horner Hos
19 Stringer Hos
20 Whitmore Ho
21 Nightingale Ho
22 Wilmer Gdns
23 Arrow Ho
24 Archer Ho
25 Meriden Ho
26 Rover Ho
27 Bowyer Ho
28 Tiller Ho
29 Canalside Studios
30 Kleine Wharf
31 Benyon Wharf
32 Quebec Wharf
33 Belvedere Ct
34 Portfleet Pl
B2 1 Gorsuch Pl
2 Strout's Pl
3 Vaughan Est
4 George Loveless Ho
5 Baroness Rd
6 James Brine Ho
7 Arthur Wade Ho
8 Robert Owen Ho
9 Sivill Ho
10 Georgina Gdns
11 Old Market Sq
12 Cuff Point
13 Bakers Rents
14 Leopold Bldgs
15 Dunmore Point
16 Wingfield Ho
17 Gascoigne Pl
18 Mandela Ho
19 Virginia Rd
20 Briggs Ho
21 Packenham Ho
22 Gowan Ho
23 Kirton Gdns
24 Chambord St
25 Ducal St
26 Strickland Ho
27 Alliston Ho
28 Gibraltar Wlk
29 Equity Sq
30 Shacklewell St
31 Rochelle St
32 Sonning Ho
33 Culham Ho
34 Hurley Ho
35 Palissy St
36 Taplow Ho
37 Chertsey Ho
38 Sunbury Ho
39 Sunbury Workshops
40 Datchett Ho
41 Hocker St
42 Coll Sharp Ct
43 Marlow Studio Workshops
44 Marlow Ho
45 Shiplake Ho
46 Wargrave Ho
47 Iffley Ho
48 Virginia Prim Sch
49 Bethnal Green Tech Coll
B3 1 Queensbridge Ct
2 Godwin Ho
3 Kent Ct
4 Brunswick Ct
5 Weymouth Ct
6 Sovereign Mews
7 Dunloe Ct
8 Cremer Bsns Ctr
9 James Hammett Ho
10 Allgood St
11 Horatio St
12 Cadell Ho
13 Horatio Ho
14 Shipton Ho
15 Haggerston Sch
16 Randal Cremer JMI Sch
B4 1 Hilborough Ct
2 Scriven Ct
3 Livermere Ct
4 Angrave Ct
5 Angrave Pas
6 Benfleet Ct
7 Belford Ho
8 Orme Ho
9 Clemson Ho
10 Longman Ho
11 Lowther Ho
12 Lovelace Ho
13 Harlowe Ho
14 Pamela Ho
15 Samuel Ho
16 Acton Ho
17 Loanda Cl
18 Phoenix Cl
19 Richardson Cl
20 Thrasher Cl
21 Mary Secole Cl
22 Canal Path
23 Pear Tree Cl
24 Hebden Ct
25 Charlton Ct
26 Laburnum Ct
27 Mansfield Ct
28 Garden Pl
29 Amber Wharf
30 Haggerston Studios
C1 1 Bentworth Ct
2 Hawksmoor Pl
3 Kerbela St
4 Fuller Cl
5 Kinsham Ho
6 Menotti St
7 Barnwell Ho
8 Grimsby St
9 Reflection Ho

12 Georgian Ct
13 Park Cl
14 Regency Ct
15 Norris Ho
C1 1 Raynham Ho
2 Pat Shaw Ho
3 Colmar Cl
4 Withy Ho
5 Stocks Ct
6 Downey Ho
7 Bay Ct
8 Sligo Ho
9 Pegasus Ho
10 Barents Ho
11 Biscay Ho
12 Solway Ho
13 Bantry Ho
14 Aral Ho
15 Pacific Ho
16 Magellan Ho
17 Levant Ho
18 Adriatic Ho
19 Genoa Ho
20 Hawke Ho
21 Palliser Ho
22 Ionian Ho
23 Weddell Ho
24 Carlyle Mews
25 Greencourt Ho
26 Sundra Wlk
C2 1 Stubbs Ho
2 Holman Ho
3 Clynes Ho
4 Windsor Ho
5 Gilbert Ho
6 Chater Ho
7 Ellen Wilkinson Ho
8 George Belt Ho
9 Ayrton Gould Ho
10 O'Brian Ho
11 Sulkin Ho
12 Jenkinson Ho
13 Bullards Pl
14 Sylvia Pankhurst Ho
15 Mary Macarthur Ho
16 Trevelyan Ho
17 Wedgwood Ho
18 Pemberton Ct
19 Leatherdale St
20 Walter Besant Ho
21 Barber Beaumont Ho
22 Brancaster Ho
23 Litcham Ho
24 Bradwell St
C3 1 Kemp Ho
2 Piggott Ho
3 Mark Ho
4 Sidney Ho
5 Pomeroy Ho
6 Puteaux Ho
7 Doric Ho
8 Modling Ho
9 Longman Ho
10 Ames Ho
11 Alzette Ho
12 Offenbach Ho
13 Tate Ho
14 Norton Ho
15 St Gilles Ho
16 Harold Ho
17 Velletri Ho
18 Bridge Wharf

19 Gathorne St
20 Bow Brook The
21 Twig Folly Cl
22 Palmerston Ct
23 Lakeview
24 Peach Walk Mews
25 Caesar Ct
26 Gatehouse Sch
C4 6 Lauriston Prim Sch

26
A1 1 Formosa Ho
2 Galveston Ho
3 Arabian Ho
4 Greenland Ho
5 Coral Ho
6 Anson Ho
7 Cambay Ho
8 Lindop Ho
9 Moray Ho
10 Azov Ho
11 Sandalwood Cl
12 Broadford Ho
A2 1 Imperial Ho
2 Newport Ho
3 Vassall Ho
4 Maurice Ct
5 Creed Ct
6 Christopher France Ho
7 Beaumont Ct
8 Pembroke Mews
9 Guardian Angels RC Prim Sch
10 Central Foundation Lower Girls Sch The
A3 1 Nightingale Mews
2 Bunsen Ho
3 Bunsen St
4 Beatrice Webb Ho
5 Margaret Bondfield Ho
6 Wilmer Ho
7 Sandall Ho
8 Butley Ct
9 Josseline Ct
10 Dalton Ho
11 Brine Ho
12 Ford Cl
13 Viking Cl
14 Stanfield Rd
15 Stoneleigh Mews
16 Ruth Ct
17 School Bell Cloisters
18 Schoolbell Mews
19 Medhurst Cl
20 Olga St
21 Conyer St
22 Diamond Ho
23 Daring Ho
24 Crane Ho
25 Exmoor Ho
26 Grenville Ho
27 Hyperion Ho
28 Sturdy Ho
29 Wren Ho
30 Ardent Ho
31 Senators Lo
32 Hooke Ho
33 Mohawk Ho
34 Ivanhoe Ho
35 Medway Mews
36 Chisenhale Prim Sch
B2 1 Olga Prim Sch
B2 1 Trellis Sq

2 Sheffield Sq
3 Howcroft Ho
4 Astra Ho
5 Frye Ct
6 Byas Ho
7 George Lansbury Ho
8 Regal Pl
9 Coborn Mews
10 Tredegar Mews
11 Cavendish Terr
12 Lyn Mews
13 Buttermere Ho
14 Coniston Ho
15 Tracy Ho
16 Hanover Ct
17 St Clair Ho
18 Longthorne Ho
19 Vista Bldgs
20 Verity Ho
21 Icarus Ho
22 Whippingham Ho
23 Hamilton Ho
24 Winchester Ho
25 Malmesbury Prim Sch
26 Phoenix Sec & Prim Sch
27 Central Foundation Upper Girls Sch The
B3 1 Roman Road Mkt
2 John Bond Ho
3 McKenna Ho
4 Dennis Ho
5 McAusland Ho
6 McBride Ho
7 Libra Rd
8 Dave Adams Ho
9 Regency Ct
10 Tay Ho
11 Sleat Ho
12 Brodick Ho
13 Ewart Pl
14 Lunan Ho
15 Cruden Ho
16 Anglo Rd
17 Mull Ho
18 Sinclairs Ho
19 Driftway Ho
20 Clayhall Ct
21 Berebinder Ho
22 Partridge Ho
23 Barford Ho
24 Gullane Ho
25 Gosford Ho
26 Dornoch Ho
27 Dunnet Ho
28 Enard Ho
29 Fraserburgh Ho
30 Forth Ho
31 Stavers Ho
32 Rosegate Ho
33 Crowngate Ho
34 Queensgate Ho
35 Towergate Ho
36 Ordell Ct
37 William Pl
38 Old Ford Prim Sch
B4 1 Hampstead Wlk
2 Waverton Ho
3 Elton Ho
4 Locton Gn
5 Birtwhistle Ho
6 Clare Ho
7 Magpie Ho
8 Hornbeam Sq
9 Rowan Ho

10 Barge La
11 Walnut Ho
12 Birdsfield La
13 Atkins Ct
14 Willow Tree Cl
15 Jasmine Sq
16 Tait Ct
17 Ranwell Ho
18 Ranwell Cl
19 Tufnell Ct
20 Pulteny Cl
21 Vic Johnson Ho
22 Lea Sq
23 Iceni Ct
24 Tamar Cl
25 Roman Rd
26 Valentine Ho
C1 1 Fairmont Ho
2 Healy Ho
3 Zodiac Ho
4 Buick Ho
5 Consul Ho
6 Bentley Ho
7 Cresta Ho
8 Daimler Ho
9 Riley Ho
10 Jensen Ho
11 Lagonda Ho
12 Ireton St
13 Navenby Wlk
14 Burwell Wlk
15 Leadenham Ct
16 Sleaford Ho
17 Bow Triangle Bsns Ctr
18 Clara Grant Prim Sch The
C2 1 Bow Ho
2 Denmark Pl
3 Marsalis Ho
4 Lovette Ho
5 Drapers Almshouses
6 Mallard Point
7 Creswick Wlk
8 Bevin Ho
9 Huggins Ho
10 Williams Ho
11 Harris Ho
12 Marina Ct
13 Electric Ho
14 Matching Ct
15 Wellington Bldgs
16 Grafton Ho
17 Berkeley Ho
18 Columbia Ho
19 Bow Sec Sch
20 Wellington Prim Sch
21 London Metrocity Coll
22 Cherry Trees Sch The
C3 1 Vincent Mews
2 Menai Pl
3 Heathfield Ct
4 Redwood Cl
5 Acorn Ct
6 Primrose Cl
7 Briar Ct
8 Springwood Cl
9 Lacey Mews
10 Matilda Gdns
C4 1 Ironworks
2 Juno Ho
3 Chariot Cl
4 Saturn Ho
5 Hadrian Cl

6 Mercury Ho
7 Forum Cl
8 Venus Ho
9 Vesta Ho
10 Tiber Cl
11 Gemini Ho
12 Crown Close Bsns Ctr

27
A1 1 Broxbourne Ho
2 Roxford Ho
3 Biscott Ho
4 Stanborough Ho
5 Hillstone Ct
6 Marner Prim Sch
A2 1 Bradley Ho
2 Prioress Ho
3 Alton Ho
4 Foxley Ho
5 Munden Ho
6 Canterbury Ho
7 Corbin Ho
8 Barton Ho
9 Jolles Ho
10 Rudstone Ho
11 Baxter Ho
12 Baker Ho
13 Insley Ho
14 Hardwicke Ho
15 St Agnes RC Prim Sch
16 Priory St
17 Sadler Ho
18 Ballinger Point
19 Henshall Point
20 Dorrington Point
21 Warren Ho
22 Fairlie Ct
23 Regent Sq
24 Hackworth Point
25 Priestman Point
26 Wingate Ho
27 Nethercott Ho
28 Thelbridge Ho
29 Bowden Ho
30 Kerscott Ho
31 Southcott Ho
32 Birchdown Ho
33 Upcott Ho
34 Langmead Ho
35 Limscott Ho
36 Northleigh Ho
37 Huntshaw Ho
38 Chagford Ho
39 Ashcombe Ho
40 Shillingford Ho
41 Patrick Connolly Gdns
42 Lester Ct
43 Franklin St
44 Taft Way
45 Washington Cl
46 Veronica Ho
47 William Guy Gdns
48 Denbury Ho
49 Holsworthy Ho
50 Padstone Ho
51 Old Palace Prim Sch
52 Ian Mikardo Sch
C1 1 Crescent Court Bsns Ctr
2 Ashmead Bsns Ctr
3 Forward Bsns Ctr
C4 1 Victoria Mills

2 Hallings Wharf Studios
3 Poland Ho
4 Peter Heathfield Ho
5 Burford Rd
6 John F Kennedy Specl Sch
7 Univ of East London (Duncan Ho)

28
A1
1 Lantry Ct
2 Rosemount Ct
3 Moreton Twr
4 Acton Central Ind Est
5 Rufford Twr
6 Narrow St
7 Mount Pl
8 Sidney Miller Ct
9 Mill Hill Terr
10 Cheltenham Pl
11 Mill Hill Gr
12 Benjamin Ho
13 Arlington Ct
14 Lombard Ct
15 Steyne Ho
16 Acton & West London Coll
B1
1 Rectory Rd
2 Derwentwater Mans
3 Market Pl
4 Hooper's Mews
5 Cromwell Pl
6 Locarno Rd
7 Edgecote Ct
8 Harleyford Manor
9 Coopers Ct
10 Avingdor Ct
11 Steyne Ho
B3
1 Avon Ct
2 Bromley Lo
3 Walter Ct
4 Lynton Terr
5 Acton Ho
6 Fells Haugh
7 Springfield Ct
8 Tamarind Ct
9 Lynton Ct
10 Aspen Ct
11 Pegasus Ct
12 Friary Park Ct
C3
1 Rosebank Gdns
2 Rosebank
3 Edinburgh Ct
4 Western Ct
5 Kilronan

30
A1
1 Arlington Ho
2 Lugard Ho
3 Shabana Ct
4 Sitarey Ct
5 Oaklands Ct
6 Davenport Mews
A2
1 Abercrombie Ho
2 Bathurst Ho
3 Brisbane Ho
4 Bentinck Ho
5 Ellenborough Ho
6 Lawrence Cl
7 Mackenzie Cl
8 Calvert Ho
9 Winthrop Ho
10 Auckland Ho

12 Blaxland Ho
13 Havelock Cl
14 Hargraves Ho
15 Hudson Cl
16 Phipps Ho
17 Lawson Ho
18 Hastings Ho
19 Wolfe Ho
20 Malabar Ct
21 Charnock Ho
22 Canning Ho
23 Cornwallis Ho
24 Commonwealth Ave
25 Champlain Ho
26 Grey Ho
27 Durban Ho
28 Baird Ho
29 Campbell Ho
30 Mitchell Ho
31 Denham Ho
32 Mackay Ho
33 Evans Ho
34 Davis Ho
A3
1 Holborn Ho
2 Clement Danes Ho
3 Vellacott Ho
4 O'Driscoll Ho
5 King Ho
6 Daley Ho
7 Selma Ho
8 Garrett Ho
B1
1 Linden Ct
2 Frithville Ct
3 Blomfield Mans
4 Poplar Mews
5 Hopgood St
6 Westwood Ho
7 Stanlake Mews
8 Stanlake Villas
9 Alexandra Mans
B3
1 Latimer Ind Est
2 Pankhurst Ho
3 Quadrangle The
4 Nightingale Ho
5 Gordon Ct
6 Ducane Cl
7 Browning Ho
8 Pavilion Terr
9 Ivebury Ct
10 Olympic Ho
B4
1 Galleywood Ho
2 Edgcott Ho
3 Cuffley Ho
4 Addlestone Ho
5 Rockliffe Ho
6 Sarratt Ho
7 Firle Ho
8 Sutton Est The
9 Terling Ho
10 Danes Ho
11 Udimore Ho
12 Vange Ho
13 Binbrook Ho
14 Yeadon Ho
15 Yatton Ho
16 Yarrow Ho
17 Clement Ho
18 Danebury
19 Coronation Ct
20 Calderon Pl
C1
1 St Katherine's Wlk
2 Dorrit Ho
3 Pickwick Ho
4 Dombey Ho

5 Caranday Villas
6 Mortimer Ho
7 Nickleby Ho
8 Stebbing Ho
9 Boxmoor Ho
10 Poynter Ho
11 Swanscombe Ho
12 Darnley Terr
13 Norland Ho
14 Hume Ho
15 Boundary Ho
16 Norland Rd
17 Helix Ct
C2
1 Frinstead Ho
2 Hurstway Wlk
3 Testerton Wlk
4 Grenfell Wlk
5 Grenfell Twr
6 Barandon Wlk
7 Treadgold Ho
8 St Clements Ct
9 Willow Way
10 Florence Ho
11 Dora Ho
12 Carton Ho
13 Agnes Ho
14 Marley Ho
15 Estella Ho
16 Waynflete Sq
17 Pippin Ho
18 Baseline Business Studios
19 St Francis of Assisi Prim Sch
20 Nicholas Rd
C3
1 Kelfield Ct
2 Downing Ho
3 Crosfield Ct
4 Robinson Ho
5 Scampston Mews
6 Girton Villas
7 Ray Ho
8 Walmer Ho
9 Goodrich Ct
10 Arthur Ct
11 Whitstable Ho
12 Kingsnorth Ho
13 Bridge Ct
14 Prospect Ho
15 St Marks Rd
16 Whitchurch Ho
17 Blechynden Ho
18 Waynflete Sq
19 Bramley Ho
20 Dixon Ho
21 Oxford Gardens Prim Sch
22 Bassett House Sch
C4
1 Treverton Twr
2 Raymede Twr
3 Bruce Ho
4 Balfour Ho
5 Burleigh Ho
6 Sion-Manning RC Sch for Girls
7 St Charles RC Prim Sch
8 St Charles RC Sixth Form Coll

31
A3
1 Malton Ho
2 Lancaster Lo
3 Manning Ho
4 Galsworthy Ho
5 Hudson Ho
6 Cambourne Mews

7 Upper Talbot Wlk
8 Kingsdown Cl
9 Lower Clarendon Wlk
10 Talbot Grove Ho
11 Clarendon Wlk
12 Upper Clarendon Wlk
13 Camelford Wlk
14 Upper Camelford Wlk
15 Camelford Ct
16 Thomas Jones Prim Sch
17 Notting Hill Prep Sch
A4
1 Murchison Ho
2 Macaulay Ho
3 Chesterton Ho
4 Chiltern Ho
5 Lionel Ho
6 Watts Ho
7 Wheatstone Ho
8 Telford Ho
9 Golborne Mews
10 Millwood St
11 St Columb's Ho
12 Norfolk Mews
13 Lionel Mews
14 Kensington & Chelsea Coll
15 Bevington Prim Sch
16 Sion-Manning RC Sch for Girls
17 Lloyd Williamson Sch
B3
1 Silvester Ho
2 Golden Cross Mews
3 Tavistock Mews
4 Clydesdale Ho
5 Colville Prim Sch
6 Melchester
7 Pinehurst Ct
8 Denbigh Ho
B4
1 Blagrove Rd
2 All Saints Ho
3 Tavistock Ho
4 Leamington Ho
C3
1 Shottsford
2 Tolchurch
3 Casterbridge
4 Sandbourne
5 Anglebury
6 Weatherbury
7 Westbourne Gr
8 Rosehart Mews
9 Viscount Ct
10 Hereford Mans
11 Hereford Mews
12 St Mary of the Angels RC Prim Sch
C4
1 Ascot Ho
2 Ashgrove Ct
3 Lockbridge Ct
4 Swallow Ct
5 Nightingale Lo
6 Hammond Lo
7 Penfield Lo
8 Harvey Lo
9 Hunter Lo
10 Barnard Lo
11 Falcon Lo
12 Johnson Lo
13 Livingstone Lo
14 Nuffield Lo

15 Finch Lo
16 Polesworth Ho
17 Oversley Ho
18 Derrycombe Ho
19 Buckshead Ho
20 Combe Ho
21 Culham Ho
22 Dainton Ho
23 Devonport Ho
24 Honwell Ho
25 Truro Ho
26 Sunderland Ho
27 Stonehouse Ho
28 Riverford Ho
29 Portishead Ho
30 Mickleton Ho
31 Keyham Ho
32 Moulsford Ho
33 Shrewsbury Mews
34 St Stephen's Mews
35 Westway Lo
36 Langley Ho
37 Brindley Ho
38 Radway Ho
39 Astley Ho
40 Willow Ct
41 Larch Ct
42 Elm Ct
43 Beech Ct
44 Worcester Ct
45 Union Ct
46 Leicester Ct
47 Kennet Ct
48 Oxford Ct
49 Fazerley Ct

32
A1
1 China Ct
2 Wellington Terr
3 Stevedore St
4 Portland Sq
5 Reardon Ho
6 Lowder Ho
7 Meeting House Alley
8 Farthing Fields
9 Oswell Ho
10 Park Lo
11 Doughty Ct
12 Inglefield Sq
13 Chopin's Ct
14 Welsh Ho
15 Hilliard Ho
16 Clegg St
17 Tasman Ho
18 Ross Ho
19 Wapping Dock St
20 Bridewell Pl
21 New Tower Bldgs
22 Tower Bldgs
23 Chimney Ct
24 Jackman Ho
25 Fenner Ho
26 Franklin Ho
27 Frobisher Ho
28 Flinders Ho
29 Chancellor Ho
30 Beechey Ho
31 Reardon Path
32 Parry Ho
33 Vancover Ho
34 Willoughby Ho
35 Sanctuary The
36 Dundee Ct

22 Grosvenor Ct
23 Lime House Ct
24 Swallow Pl
25 St Anne's Trad Est
26 Stepney Greencoat CE Prim Sch The
27 Sir William Burrough Prim Sch
28 Our Lady RC Prim Sch

B4 1 Wearmouth Ho
2 Elmslie Point
3 Grindley Ho
4 Stileman Ho
5 Wilcox Ho
6 Huddart St
7 Robeson St
8 Couzens Ho
9 Perley Ho
10 Whytlaw Ho
11 Booker Cl
12 Tunley Gn
13 Callingham Cl
14 Bowry Ho
15 Perkins Ho
16 Printon Ho
17 Tasker Ho
18 St Paul with St Luke CE Prim Sch

C2 1 West India Ho
2 Berber Pl
3 Birchfield Ho
4 Elderfield Ho
5 Thornfield Ho
6 Gorsefield Ho
7 Arborfield Ho
8 Colborne Ho
9 East India Bldgs
10 Compass Point
11 Salter St
12 Garland Ct
13 Bogart Ct
14 Fonda Ct
15 Welles Ct
16 Premier Pl
17 Kelly Ct
18 Flynn Ct
19 Mary Jones Ho
20 Cannon Dr
21 Horizon Bldg
22 Holy Family RC Prim Sch

C3 1 Landin Ho
2 Thomas Road Ind Est
3 Vickery's Wharf
4 Abbotts Wharf
5 Limehouse Ct
6 Charlesworth Ho
7 Gurdon Ho
8 Trendell Ho
9 Menteath Ho
10 Minchin Ho
11 Donne Ho
12 Old School Sq
13 Anglesey Ho
14 Gough Wlk
15 Baring Ho
16 Gladstone Ho
17 Hopkins Ho
18 Granville Ho
19 Overstone Ho
20 Pusey Ho
21 Russell Ho
22 Stanley Ho

C4 1 Bredel Ho

2 Linton Ho
3 Matthews Ho
4 Woodcock Ho
5 Limborough Ho
6 Maydwell Ho
7 Underhill Ho
8 Meyrick Ho
9 Ambrose Ho
10 Richardson Ho
11 Carpenter Ho
12 Robinson Ho
13 Bellmaker Ct
14 Lime Tree Ct
15 Bracken Ho
16 Bramble Ho
17 Berberis Ho
18 Bilberry Ho
19 Ladyfern Ho
20 Rosebay Ho
21 Invicta Cl
22 Phoenix Bsns Ctr
23 Metropolitan Cl
24 Busbridge Ho
25 St Paul's Way Com Sch
26 Stebon Prim Sch

34
A2 1 Westcott Ho
2 Corry Ho
3 Malam Gdns
4 Blomfield Ho
5 Devitt Ho
6 Leyland Ho
7 Wigram Ho
8 Willis Ho
9 Balsam Ho
10 Finch's Ct
11 Poplar Bath St
12 Lawless St
13 Storey Ho
14 Abbot Ho
15 Woodall Cl
16 Landon Wlk
17 Goodhope Ho
18 Goodfaith Ho
19 Winant Ho
20 Goodspeed Ho
21 Lubbock Ho
22 Goodwill Ho
23 Martindale Ho
24 Holmsdale Ho
25 Norwood Ho
26 Constant Ho
27 Tower Hamlets Coll

A3 1 Colebrook Ho
2 Essex Ho
3 Salisbury Ho
4 Maidstone Ho
5 Osterley Ho
6 Norwich Ho
7 Clarissa Ho
8 Elgin Ho
9 Shaftesbury Lo
10 Shepherd Ho
11 Jeremiah St
12 Elizabeth Cl
13 Chilcot Cl
14 Fitzgerald Ho
15 Vesey Path
16 Ennis Ho
17 Kilmore Ho
18 Cygnet House N
19 Cygnet House S
20 Lansbury Lawrence Prim Sch
21 Bygrove Prim Sch

22 Mayflower Prim Sch
23 Tower Hamlets Coll
A4 1 Sumner Ho
2 David Hewitt Ho
3 St Gabriel's Ct
4 Limehouse Cut
5 Colmans Wharf
6 Foundary Ho
7 Radford Ho
8 Manorfield Prim Sch
9 St Saviour's CE Prim Sch
10 Pioneer Cl

B1 1 Lumina Bldg
2 Nova Ct W
3 Nova Ct E
4 Aurora Bldg
5 Arran Ho
6 Kintyre Ho
7 Vantage Mews
8 Managers St
9 Horatio Pl
10 Concordia Wharf

B2 1 Discovery Ho
2 Mountague Pl
3 Virginia Ho
4 Collins Ho
5 Lawless Ho
6 Carmichael Ho
7 Commodore Ho
8 Mermaid Ho
9 Bullivant St
10 Anderson Ho
11 Mackrow Wlk
12 Robin Hood Gdns
13 Prestage Way
14 Woolmore Prim Sch

B3 1 Glenkerry Ho
2 Carradale Ho
3 Langdon Ho
4 Balfron Twr
5 St Frideswides Mews
6 Tabard Ct
7 Delta Bldg
8 Findhorn St
9 Kilbrennan Ho
10 Thistle Ho
11 Heather Ho
12 Tartan Ho
13 Sharman Ho
14 Trident Ho
15 Wharf View Ct
16 Culloden Prim Sch

B4 1 Mills Gr
2 St Michaels Ct
3 Duncan Ct
C2 1 Quixley St
2 Romney Ho
3 Pumping Ho
4 Switch Ho
5 Wingfield Ct
6 Explorers Ct
7 Sexton Ct
8 Keel Ct
9 Bridge Ct
10 Sail Ct
11 Settlers Ct
12 Pilgrims Mews
13 Studley Ct
14 Wotton Ct
15 Cape Henry Ct
16 Bartholomew Ct
17 Adventurers Ct

18 Susan Constant Ct
19 Atlantic Ct
C3 1 Lansbury Gdns
2 Theseus Ho
3 Adams Ho
4 Jones Ho
5 Sam March Ho
6 Arapiles Ho
7 Athenia Ho
8 Julius Ho
9 Jervis Bay Ho
10 Helen Mackay Ho
11 Gaze Ho
12 Ritchie Ho
13 Blairgowrie Ct
14 Circle Ho
15 Dunkeld Ho
16 Rosemary Dr
17 Sorrel La
18 East India Dock Road Tunnel

35
B3 1 Newton Point
2 Sparke Terr
3 Montesquieu Terr
4 Crawford Point
5 Rathbone Ho
6 George St
7 Emily St
8 Fendt Cl
9 Sabbarton St
10 St Luke Prim CE Sch
11 Briary Ct
12 Shaftesbury Ho
B4 1 Radley Terr
2 Bernard Cassidy St
3 Rathbone Mkt
4 Thomas North Terr
5 Mary St
6 Hughes Terr
7 Swanscombe Point
8 Rawlinson Point
9 Kennedy Cox Ho
10 Cooper St
C1 1 Capulet Mews
2 Pepys Cres
3 De Quincey Mews
4 Hardy Ave
5 Tom Jenkinson Rd
6 Kennacraig Cl
7 Charles Flemwell Mews
8 Gatcombe Rd
9 Badminton Mews
10 Holyrood Mews
11 Britannia Gate
12 Dalemain Mews
13 Bowes-Lyon Hall
14 Lancaster Hall
15 Victoria Hall
C2 1 Clements Ave
2 Martindale Ave
3 Balearic Apts
4 Marmara Apts
5 Baltic Apts
6 Coral Apts
7 Aegean Apts
8 Capital East Apts
C4 1 Odeon Ct
2 Edward Ct
3 Newhaven La
4 Ravenscroft Cl
5 Douglas Rd
6 Ferrier Point
7 Harvey Point

37 B3 299

8 Wood Point
9 Trinity St
10 Pattinson Point
11 Clinch Ct
12 Mint Bsns Pk
13 Keir Hardy Prim Sch

36
A1 1 Burford Ho
2 Hope Cl
3 Centaur Ct
4 Phoenix Ct
C1 1 Surrey Cres
2 Forbes Ho
3 Haining Cl
4 Melville Ct
5 London Stile
6 Stile Hall Par
7 Priory Lo
8 Meadowcroft
9 St James Ct
10 Rivers Ho

37
A1 1 Churchdale Ct
2 Cromwell Ct
3 Cambridge Rd S
4 Oxbridge Ct
5 Tomlinson Cl
6 Gunnersbury Mews
7 Grange The
8 Gunnersbury Cl
9 Bellgrave Lo
A2 15 Orchard House Sch
A4 1 Cheltenham Pl
2 Beaumaris Twr
3 Arundel Ho
4 Pevensey Ct
5 Jerome Twr
6 Anstey Ct
7 Bennett Ct
8 Gunnersbury Ct
9 Barrington Ct
10 Hope Gdns
11 Park Road E
B1 1 Arlington Park Mans
2 Sandown Ho
3 Goodwood Ho
4 Windsor Ho
5 Lingfield Ho
6 Ascot Ho
7 Watchfield Ct
8 Belgrave Ct
9 Beverley Ct
10 Beaumont Ct
11 Harvard Rd
12 Troubridge Ct
13 Branden Lo
14 Fromow's Cnr
15 Heathfield House Sch
B2 1 Chiswick Green Studios
2 Bell Ind Est
3 Fairlawn Ct
4 Dukes Gate
5 Dewsbury Ct
6 Chiswick Terr
7 Mortlake Ho
B3 1 Blackmore Twr
2 Bollo Ct
3 Kipling Twr

4 Lawrence Ct
5 Maugham Ct
6 Reade Ct
7 Woolf Ct
8 Shaw Ct
9 Verne Ct
10 Wodehouse Ct
11 Greenock Rd
12 Garden Ct
13 Barons Gate
14 Cleveland Rd
15 Carver Cl
16 Chapter Cl
17 Beauchamp Cl
18 Holmes Ct
19 Copper Mews
B4 1 Belgrave Cl
2 Buckland Wlk
3 Frampton Ct
4 Telfer Cl
5 Harlech Twr
6 Corfe Twr
7 Barwick Ho
8 Charles Hocking Ho
9 Sunninghill Ct
10 Salisbury St
11 Jameson Pl
12 Castle Cl
C1 1 Chatsworth Lo
2 Prospect Pl
3 Townhall Ave
4 Devonhurst Pl
5 Heathfield Ct
6 Horticultural Pl
7 Merlin Ho
8 Garth Rd
9 Autumn Rise
C2 1 Disraeli Cl
2 Winston Wlk
3 Rusthall Mans
4 Bedford Park Mans
5 Essex Place Sq
6 Holly Rd
7 Homecross Ho
8 Swan Bsns Ctr
9 Jessop Ho
10 Belmont Prim Sch

38
A1 1 Glebe Cl
2 Devonshire Mews
3 Binns Terr
4 Ingress St
5 Swanscombe Rd
6 Brackley Terr
7 Stephen Fox Ho
8 Manor Gdns
9 Coram Ho
10 Flaxman Ho
11 Thorneycroft Ho
12 Thornhill Ho
13 Kent Ho
14 Oldfield Ho
15 William Hogarth Sch The
A2 1 Chestnut Ho
2 Bedford Ho
3 Bedford Cnr
4 Sydney Ho
5 Bedford Park Cnr
6 Priory Gdns
7 Windmill Alley
8 Castle Pl

9 Jonathan Ct
10 Windmill Pas
11 Chardin Rd
12 Gable Ho
13 Chiswick & Bedford Park Prep Sch
14 Arts Educational Sch The
A3 1 Fleet Ct
2 Ember Ct
3 Emlyn Gdns
4 Clone Ct
5 Brent Ct
6 Abbey Ct
7 Ormsby Ct
8 St Catherine's Ct
9 Lodge The
A4 1 Longford Ct
2 Mole Ct
3 Lea Ct
4 Wandle Ct
5 Beverley Ct
6 Roding Ct
7 Crane Ct
B1 1 Miller's Ct
2 British Grove Pas
3 British Grove S
4 Berestede Rd
5 North Eyot Gdns
B2 1 Flanders Mans
2 Stamford Brook Mans
3 Linkenholt Mans
4 Prebend Mans
5 Middlesex Ct
B3 1 Stamford Brook Gdns
2 Hauteville Court Gdns
3 Ranelagh Gdns
C1 1 Chisholm Ct
2 North Verbena Gdns
3 Western Terr
4 Verbena Gdns
5 Montrose Villas
6 Hammersmith Terr
7 South Black Lion La
8 St Peter's Wharf
9 Eden High Sch
10 St Peter's CE Prim Sch
C2 1 Hamlet Ct
2 Derwent Ct
3 Westcroft Ct
4 Black Lion Mews
5 St Peter's Villas
6 Standish Ho
7 Chambon Pl
8 Court Mans
9 Longthorpe Ct
10 Charlotte Ct
11 Westside
12 Park Ct
13 London Ho
14 Latymer Upper Sch
15 Polish Univ Abroad
C3 1 Elizabeth Finn Ho
2 Ashchurch Ct
3 King's Par
4 Inver Ct
5 Ariel Ct
6 Pocklington Lo
7 Vitae Apartments
C4 1 Becklow Gdns
2 Victoria Ho

3 Lycett Pl
4 Kylemore Ct
5 Alexandra Ct
6 Lytten Ct
7 Becklow Mews
8 Northcroft Ct
9 Bailey Ct
10 Spring Cott
11 Landor Wlk
12 Laurence Mews
13 Hadyn Park Ct
14 Askew Mans
15 Malvern Ct

39
A1 1 Prince's Mews
2 Aspen Gdns
3 Hampshire Hog La
4 Blades Ct
A2 1 Albion Gdns
2 Flora Gdns
3 Lamington St
4 Felgate Mews
5 Galena Ho
6 Albion Mews
7 Albion Ct
8 King Street Cloisters
9 Dimes Pl
10 Clarence Ct
11 Hampshire Hog La
12 Marryat Ct
13 Ravenscourt Ho
14 Ravenscourt Theatre Sch
15 Cambridge Sch
16 Godolphin & Latymer Sch
17 Flora Gardens Prim Sch
A3 1 Ravenscourt Park Mans
2 Paddenswick Ct
3 Ashbridge Ct
4 Brackenbury Prim Sch
A4 1 Westbush Ct
2 Goldhawk Mews
3 Sycamore Ho
4 Shackleton Ct
5 Drake Ct
6 Scotts Ct
7 Raleigh Ct
8 Melville Court Flats
9 Southway Ct
B1 1 Bridge Avenue Mans
2 Bridgeview
3 College Ct
4 Beatrice Ho
5 Amelia Ho
6 Edith Ho
7 Joanna Ho
8 Mary Ho
9 Adela Ho
10 Sophia Ho
11 Henrietta Ho
12 Charlotte Ho
13 Alexandra Ho
14 Bath Ho
15 Elizabeth Ho
16 Margaret Ho
17 Peabody Est
18 Eleanor Ho
19 Isabella Ho
20 Caroline Ho
21 Chancellors Wharf

22 Sussex Pl
23 St Paul's CE Prim Sch
B2 1 Phoenix Lodge Mans
2 Samuel's Cl
3 Broadway Arc
4 Brook Ho
5 Hammersmith Broadway
6 Broadway Sh Ctr
7 Cambridge Ct
8 Ashcroft Sq
9 Sacred Heart High Sch
10 King Street Coll
B4 1 Verulam Ho
2 Grove Mans
3 Frobisher Ct
4 Library Mans
5 Pennard Mans
6 New Shepherd's Bush Mkt
7 Kerrington Ct
8 Granville Mans
9 Romney Ct
10 Rayner Ct
11 Sulgrave Gdns
12 Bamborough Gdns
13 Hillary Ct
14 Market Studios
15 Lanark Mans
16 Miles Coverdale Prim Sch
17 St Stephen's CE Prim Sch
18 London Coll of Fashion (Lime Grove)
C2 1 St Paul's Girls' Sch
2 Bute House Prep Sch
3 Jacques Prevert Sch
4 Larmenier & Sacred Heart RC Prim Sch
C3 1 Grosvenor Residences
2 Blythe Mews
3 Burnand Ho
4 Bradford Ho
5 Springvale Terr
6 Ceylon Rd
7 Walpole Ct
8 Bronte Ct
9 Boswell Ct
10 Souldern Rd
11 Brook Green Flats
12 Haarlem Rd
13 Stafford Mans
14 Lionel Mans
15 Barradell Ho
C4 1 Vanderbilt Villas
2 Bodington Ct
3 Kingham Cl
4 Clearwater Terr
5 Lorne Gdns
6 Cameret Ct
7 Bush Ct
8 Shepherds Ct
9 Rockley Ct
10 Grampians The
11 Charcroft Ct
12 Addison Park Mans
13 Sinclair Mans
14 Fountain Ct

15 Woodford Ct
16 Roseford Ct
17 Woodstock Studios
40
A1 1 Hockney Ct
2 Toulouse Ct
3 Lowry Ct
4 Barry Ho
5 Lewis Ct
6 Gainsborough Ct
7 Renoir Ct
8 Blake Ct
9 Raphael Ct
10 Rembrandt Ct
11 Constable Ct
12 Da Vinci Ct
13 Gaugin Ct
14 Michelangelo Ct
15 Monet Ct
16 Weald Cl
17 Jasmin Lo
18 Birchmere Lo
19 Weybridge Ct
20 Florence Ho
21 Gleneagles Cl
22 Sunningdale Cl
23 Muirfield Cl
24 Turnberry Cl
25 St Andrews Cl
26 Kingsdown Cl
27 St Davids Cl
28 Galway Cl
29 Edenbridge Cl
30 Birkdale Cl
31 Tralee Ct
32 Woburn Ct
33 Belfry Cl
34 Troon Cl
35 Holywell Cl
A2 1 Market Pl
2 Trappes Ho
3 Thurland Ho
4 Ramsfort Ho
5 Hambley Ho
6 Holford Ho
7 Pope Ho
8 Southwell Ho
9 Mortain Ho
10 Radcliffe Ho
11 Southwark Park Est
12 Galleywall Road Trad Est
13 Trevithick Ho
14 Barlow Ho
15 Donkin Ho
16 Landmann Ho
17 Fitzmaurice Ho
18 Dodd Ho
A3 1 Perryn Rd
2 Chalfont Ho
3 Prestwood Ho
4 Farmer Ho
5 Gataker Ho
6 Gataker St
7 Cornick Ho
8 Glebe Ho
9 Matson Ho
10 Hickling Ho
11 St Andrews Ho
12 Southwark Coll (Surrey Docks Ctr)
13 Southwark Park Prim Sch
A4 1 Butterfield Pl
2 Janeway Pl
3 Trotwood Ho

4 Station Mews Terr
5 Halstow Prim Sch
6 Holyrood Mews

44
A4 1 Ferry Sq
2 Watermans Ct
3 Wilkes Rd
4 Albany Par
5 Charlton Ho
6 Albany Ho
7 Alma Ho
8 Griffin Ct
9 Cressage Ho
10 Tunstall Wlk
11 Trimmer Wlk
12 Running Horse Yd
13 Mission Sq
14 Distillery Wlk
B2 1 Primrose Ho
2 Lawman Ct
3 Royston Ct
4 Garden Ct
5 Capel Lo
6 Devonshire Ct
7 Celia Ct
8 Rosslyn Ho
9 Branstone Ct
10 Lamerton Lo
11 Kew Lo
12 Dunraven Ho
13 Stoneleigh Lo
14 Tunstall Ct
15 Voltaire
C2 1 Clarendon Ct
2 Quintock Ho
3 Broome Ct
4 Lonsdale Mews
5 Elizabeth Cotts
6 Sandways
7 Victoria Cotts
8 North Ave
9 Grovewood
10 Hamilton Ho
11 Melvin Ct
12 Royal Par
13 Power Ho
14 Station Ave
15 Blake Mews
C4 5 Strand-on-the-
Green Schs

45
A2 1 Terrano Ho
2 Oak Ho
3 Aura Ho
4 Maple Ho
5 Cedar Ho
6 Saffron Ho
7 Lime Ho
8 Lavender Ho
9 Juniper Ho
A4 1 Falcons Pre Prep
school The

46
B1 1 Melrose Rd
2 Seaforth Lo
3 St John's Gr
4 Sussex Ct
5 Carmichael Ct
6 Hampshire Ct
7 Thorne Pas
8 Brunel Ct

9 Beverley Path

47
C4 1 Cobb's Hall
2 Dorset Mans
3 St Clements Mans
4 Bothwell St
5 Hawksmoor St
6 Melcombe Prim
Sch

48
A1 1 Langport Ho
2 Iveagh Ho
3 Newark Ho
4 Edgehill Ho
5 Hopton Ho
6 Ashby Ho
7 Nevil Ho
A2 1 Fairbairn Gn
2 Hammelton Gn
3 Foxley Sq
4 Silverburn Ho
5 Butler Ho
6 Dalkeith Ho
7 Turner Cl
8 Bathgate Ho
9 Black Roof Ho
10 Charles Edward
Brooke Sch (Den-
nen Site)
11 Charles Edward
Brooke Sch
A3 53 St Michael & All
Angels CE Acad
A4 1 Faunce Ho
2 Garbett Ho
3 Harvard Ho
4 Doddington Pl
5 Kean Ho
6 Jephson Ho
7 Cornish Ho
8 Bateman Ho
9 Molesworth Ho
10 Walters Ho
11 Cruden Ho
12 Brawne Ho
13 Prescott Ho
14 Chalmer's Wlk
15 Copley Cl
16 King Charles Ct
B1 1 Bergen Ho
2 Oslo Ho
3 Viking Ho
4 Jutland Ho
5 Norvic Ho
6 Odin Ho
7 Baltic Ho
8 Nobel Ho
9 Mercia Ho
10 Kenbury Gdns
11 Zealand Ho
12 Elsinore Ho
13 Norse Ho
14 Denmark Mans
15 Dane Ho
16 Canterbury Cl
17 York Cl
18 Kenbury Mans
19 Parade Mans
20 Winterslow Ho
21 Lilford Ho
22 Bartholomew Ho
23 Guildford Ho
24 Boston Ho
25 Hereford Ho
26 Weyhill Ho

27 Lichfield Ho
28 Lansdown Ho
29 Honiton Ho
30 Pinner Ho
31 Baldock Ho
32 Widecombe Ho
33 Nottingham Ho
34 Witham Ho
35 Barnet Ho
36 Empress Mews
B2 1 Bertha Neubergh
Ho
2 Mornington Mews
3 Badsworth Rd
4 Pearson Cl
5 Elm Tree Ct
6 Samuel Lewis Trust
Dwellings
7 Milkwell Yd
8 Keswick Ho
9 Mitcham Ho
10 Sacred Heart RC
Sec Sch
B3 1 Boundary Ho
2 Day Ho
3 Burgess Ho
4 Carlyle Ho
5 Myers Ho
6 Thompson Ave
7 Palgrave Ho
8 Winnington Ho
9 Brantwood Ho
10 Lowell Ho
11 Jessie Duffett Ho
12 Otterburn Ho
13 Crossmount Ho
14 Venice Ct
15 Bowyer St
16 Livingstone Ho
17 Gothic Ct
18 Coniston Ho
19 Harlynwood
20 Carey Ct
21 Finley Ct
22 Grainger Ct
23 Hayes Ct
24 Moffat Ho
25 Marinel Ho
26 Hodister Cl
27 Arnot Ho
28 Lamb Ho
29 Kipling Ho
30 Keats Ho
31 Kenyon Ho
32 New Church Rd
33 Sir John Kirk Cl
34 Comber Grove Prim
Sch
35 St Joseph's RC Inf
& Jun Schs
C1 1 Selborne Rd
2 Hascombe Terr
C2 1 Joiners Arms Yd
2 Butterfly Wlk
3 Cuthill Wlk
4 Colonades The
5 Artichoke Mews
6 Peabody Bldgs
7 Brighton Ho
8 Park Ho
9 Peabody Ct
10 Lomond Ho
11 Lamb Ho
12 Kimpton Ct
13 Belham Wlk
14 Datchelor Pl
15 Harvey Rd

C3 1 Masterman Ho
2 Milton Ho
3 Pope Ho
4 Chester Ct
5 Marvel Ho
6 Flecker Ho
7 Landor Ho
8 Leslie Prince Ct
9 Evelina Mans
10 Langland Ho
11 Drinkwater Ho
12 Procter Ho
13 Shirley Ho
14 Drayton Ho
15 Bridges Ho
16 Cunningham Ho
17 Hood Ho
18 Herrick Ho
19 Dekker Ho
20 Houseman Way
21 Coleby Path
22 Brunswick Park
Prim Sch
C4 1 Queens Ho
2 Arnside Ho
3 Horsley St
4 St Peter's Ho
5 St Johns Ho
6 St Marks Ho
7 St Stephens Ho
8 St Matthew's Ho
9 Red Lion Cl
10 Boyson Rd
11 Bradenham

49
A1 1 Springfield
2 Craston Ho
3 Walters Ho
4 Edgecombe Ho
5 Fowler Ho
6 Rignold Ho
7 Chatham Ho
A2 1 Barnwell Ho
2 Brunswick Villas
3 St Giles Twr
4 Bentley Ho
5 Dawson Ho
6 Dryden Ho
7 Mayward Ho
8 Longleigh Ho
9 Fairwall Ho
10 Bodeney Ho
11 Sandby Ho
12 Vestry Mews
13 Netley
14 Lakanal
15 Racine
16 Camberwell Coll of
Arts
A3 1 Tower Mill Rd
2 Tilson Cl
3 Granville Sq
4 Edgar Wallace Cl
5 Potters Cl
6 Dorton Cl
7 Samuel Jones Ind
Est
8 Dibden Ho
9 Marchwood Cl
10 Pilgrims Cloisters
11 Beacon Ho
12 Teather St
13 Stacy Path
14 Rumball Ho
15 Ballow Cl
16 Rill Ho

17 Southwark Coll
(Camberwell Ctr)
18 St George's CE
Prim Sch
A4 1 Downend Ct
2 Andoversford Ct
3 Pearse St
4 Watling St
5 Gandolfi St
6 Comfort St
7 Tower Mill Rd
B2 1 Colbert
2 Voltaire
3 Finch Mews
4 Charles Coveney Rd
5 Bamber Rd
6 Crane St
7 Curlew Ho
8 Mallard Ho
9 Tern Ho
10 Crane Ho
11 Falcon Ho
12 Bryanston Ho
13 Basing Ct
14 Marcus Ho
15 Sheffield Ho
16 Highshore Sch
17 St James The Great
RC Prim Sch
18 Oliver Goldsmith
Prim Sch
B3 1 Painswick Ct
2 Sharpness Ct
3 Mattingly Way
4 Hordle Prom N
5 Burcher Gale Gr
6 Calypso Cres
7 Hordle Prom S
8 Cinnamon Cl
9 Savannah Cl
10 Thames Ct
11 Shannon Ct
12 Amstel Ct
13 Danube Ct
14 Tilbury Cl
15 Hordle Prom E
16 Indus Ct
17 Oakcourt
18 Palm Ct
19 Rowan Ct
20 Blackthorn Ct
21 Pear Ct
22 Lidgate Rd
23 Whistler Mews
24 Boathouse Wlk
25 Camberwell Coll of
Arts
B4 1 Willsbridge Ct
2 Cam Ct
3 Quedgeley Ct
4 Saul Ct
5 Quenington Ct
6 Westonbirt Ct
7 Wickway Ct
C1 1 William Margrie Cl
2 William Blake Ho
3 Quantock Mews
4 Choumert Sq
5 Parkstone Rd
6 Atwell Rd
C2 1 Canal Head Public
Sq
2 Angelina Ho
3 Jarvis Ho
4 Richland Ho
5 Honeywood Ho
6 Wakefield Ho

7 Primrose Ho
8 Hardcastle Ho
9 Dunstall Ho
10 Springdale Cl
11 Purdon Ho
12 Flamborough Ho
13 Lambrook Ho
14 Witcombe Point
15 Yarnfield Sq
18 Winford Ct
19 Portbury Cl
20 Robert Keen Cl
C3 1 Thornbill Ho
2 Vervain Ho
3 Woodstar Ho
4 Tamarind Ho
5 Hereford Retreat
6 Haymerle Ho
7 Furley Ho
8 Thomas Milner Ho
9 Applegarth Ho
10 Freda Corbett Cl
11 Rudbeck Ho
12 Henslow Ho
13 Lindley Ho
14 Collinson Ho
15 Sister Mabel's Way
16 Timberland Cl
17 Hastings Cl
18 Sidmouth Ho
19 Budleigh Ho
20 Stanesgate Ho
21 Breamore Ho
22 Ely Ho
23 Gisburn Ho
24 Silkin Mews
25 Peckham Park
Prim Sch
26 St Francis RC Prim
Sch
C4 1 Bowles Rd
2 Western Wharf
3 Northfield Ho
4 Millbrook Ho
5 Denstone Ho
6 Deerhurst Ho
7 Caversham Ho
8 Battle Ho
9 Cardiff Ho
10 Bridgnorth Ho
11 Exeter Ho
12 Grantham Ho
13 Aylesbury Ho
14 Royston Ho
18 Haymerle Sch

50

A1 1 Walkynscroft
2 Ryegates
3 Hathorne Cl
4 Pilkington Rd
5 Russell Ct
6 Heaton Ho
7 Magdalene Cl
8 Iris Ct
9 St Mary Magdalene
CE Prim Sch
A2 1 Willowdene
2 Pinedene
3 Oakdene
4 Beechdene
5 Hollydene
6 Wood Dene
7 Staveley Cl
8 Carnicot Ho
10 Martock Ct
11 Cherry Tree Ct

12 Kendrick Ct
13 John Donne Prim
Sch
A3 1 Tortington Ho
2 Credenhill Ho
3 Bromyard Ho
4 Hoyland Cl
5 Willowdene
6 Ashdene
7 Acorn Par
8 Havelock Ct
9 Springall St
10 Harry Lambourn Ho
11 Grenier Apartments
B1 1 Honiton Gdns
2 Selden Ho
3 Hathway Ho
4 Hathway St
5 Station Ct
6 Symons Cl
7 Hollydale Prim Sch
B2 1 Trotman Ho
2 Boddington Ho
3 Heydon Ho
4 Boulter Ho
B3 1 Ambleside Point
2 Grasmere Point
3 Windermere Point
4 Roman Way
5 Laburnum Cl
6 Juniper Ho
7 Romney Cl
8 Hammersley Ho
9 Hutchinson Ho
10 Hammond Ho
11 Fir Tree Ho
12 Glastonbury Ct
13 Highbridge Ct
14 Filton Ct
15 Chiltern Ct
16 Cheviot Ct
B4 1 Penshurst Ho
2 Reculver Ho
3 Mereworth Ho
4 Camber Ho
5 Chiham Ho
6 Otford Ho
7 Olive Tree Ho
8 Aspen Ho
9 Lewis Silkin Ho
10 Richborough Ho
11 Dover Ho
12 Eynsford Ho
13 Horton Ho
14 Lamberhurst Ho
15 Canterbury Ind Pk
16 Upnall Ho
17 Sissinghurst Ho
18 Rochester Ho
19 Saltwood Ho
20 Leybourne Ho
21 Lullingstone Ho
22 Pilgrims Way Prim
Sch
C3 1 Richard Anderson
Ct
2 Palm Tree Ho
3 Edward Robinson
Ho
4 Antony Ho
5 Gerrard Ho
6 Palmer Ho
7 Pankhurst Cl
C4 1 Harrisons Ct
2 Grantley Ho
3 Sunbury Ct

4 Tilbury Ho
5 Graham Ct
6 Connell Ct
7 St Clements Ct
8 Henderson Ct
9 Jemotts Ct
10 Verona Ct
11 Heywood Ho
12 Francis Ct
13 Hind Ho
14 Donne Ho
15 Carew Ct
16 Burbage Ho
17 Newland Ho
18 Dobson Ho
19 Greene Ct
20 Redrup Ho
21 Tarplett Ho
22 Stunell Ho
23 Gasson Ho
24 Bryce Ho
25 Barnes Ho
26 Barkwith Ho
27 Bannister Ho
28 Apollo Ind Bsns Ctr

51

A2 1 Archer Ho
2 Browning Ho
3 Hardcastle Ho
4 Brooke Ho
5 Wallis Ho
A3 1 Batavia Ho
2 Marlowe Bsns Ctr
3 Batavia Mews
4 Woodrush Cl
5 Alexandra St
6 Primrose Wlk
7 Vansittart St
8 Granville Ct
9 Cottesbrook St
10 Ewen Henderson Ct
11 Fordham Ho
12 Deptford Green Sch
(Annex)
A4 1 Portland Ct
2 Phoenix Ct
3 Rainbow Ct
4 Hawke Twr
5 Chubworthy St
6 Woodpecker Rd
7 Hercules Ct
B3 1 Austin Ho
2 Exeter Way
3 Crossleigh Ct
4 Mornington Pl
5 Maple Ho
B4 1 Chester Ho
2 Lynch Wlk
3 Arlington Ho
4 Woodcote Ho
5 Cornbury Ho
6 Prospect Pl
7 Akintaro Ho
8 Mulberry Ho
9 Laurel Ho
10 Linden Ho
11 Ashford Ho
12 Wardalls Ho
13 Magnolia Ho
14 Howard Ho
15 Larch Cl
16 Ibis Ct
17 Merganser Ct
18 Wotton Rd
19 Kingfisher Sq

20 Sanderling Ct
21 Dolphin Twr
22 Mermaid Twr
23 Scoter Ct
24 Shearwater Ct
25 Brambling Ct
26 Kittiwake Ct
28 Diana Cl
29 Guillemot Ct
30 Marine Twr
31 Teal Ct
32 Lapwing Twr
33 Violet Cl
34 Skua Ct
35 Tristan Ct
36 Rosemary Ct
37 Cormorant Ct
38 Shelduck Ct
39 Eider Ct
40 Pintail Ct
41 Fulcher Ct
42 Grinling Gibbons
Prim Sch
C1 1 Ashmead Mews
3 St Stephen's CE
Prim Sch
C2 1 Admiralty Ct
2 Harton Lodge
3 Sylva Cotts
4 Pitman Ho
5 Heston Ho
6 Mereton Mans
7 Indiana Bldg
8 St John's Lodge
9 Dean's Gateway
10 Lucas Vale Prim
Sch
11 Addey & Stanhope
Sch
12 Lewisham Coll
(Deptford Campus)
C3 1 Sandpiper Ct
2 Flamingo Ct
3 Titan Bsns Est
4 Rochdale Way
5 Speedwell St
6 Reginald Pl
7 Fletcher Path
8 Frankham Ho
9 Cremer Ho
10 Wilshaw Ho
11 Castell Ho
12 Holden Ho
13 Browne Ho
14 Resolution Way
15 Lady Florence Ctyd
16 Covell Ct
17 Albion Ho
18 Maritime Green-
wich Coll
19 St Joseph's RC
Prim Sch
20 Tidemill Prim Sch
C4 1 Dryfield Wlk
2 Blake Ho
3 Hawkins Ho
4 Grenville Ho
5 Langford Ho
6 Mandarin Ct
7 Bittern Ct
8 Lamerton St
9 Ravensbourne
Mans
10 Armada St
11 Armada Ho
12 Benbow Ho
13 Oxenham Ho

52 B4 | **303**

14 Caravel Mews
15 Hughes Ho
16 Stretton Mans

52

A1 1 Morden Mount
Prim Sch
A2 1 Washington Bldg
2 California Bldg
3 Utah Bldg
4 Montana Bldg
5 Oregon Bldg
6 Dakota bldg
7 Idaho Bldg
8 Atlanta Bldg
9 Colorado Bldg
10 Arizona Bldg
11 Nebraska Bldg
12 Alaska Bldg
13 Ohio Bldg
14 Charter Bldgs
15 Flamsteed Ct
16 Friendly Pl
17 Dover Ct
18 Robinscroft Mews
19 Doleman Ho
20 Plymouth Ho
A3 1 Finch Ho
2 Jubilee The
3 Maitland Cl
4 Ashburnham
Retreat
B1 1 Ellison Ho
2 Pitmaston Ho
3 Aster Ho
4 Windmill Cl
5 Hertmitage The
6 Burnett Ho
7 Lacey Ho
8 Darwin Ho
9 Pearmain Ho
B2 1 Penn Almshouses
2 Jervis Ct
3 Woodville Ct
4 Darnall Ho
5 Renbold Ho
6 Lindsell St
7 Plumbridge St
8 Trinity Gr
9 Hollymount Cl
10 Cade Tyler Ho
11 Robertson Ho
B3 1 Temair Ho
2 Royal Hill Ct
3 Prince of Orange
La
4 Lambard Ho
5 St Marks Cl
6 Ada Kennedy Ct
7 Arlington Pl
8 Topham Ho
9 Darnell Ho
10 Hawks Mews
11 Royal Pl
12 Swanne Ho
13 Maribor
14 Serica Ct
15 Queen Elizabeth's
Coll
16 James Wolfe Prim
Sch
17 Greenwich Coll
B4 1 Crescent Arc
2 Greenwich Mkt

3 Turnpin La
3 Durnford St
5 Sexton's Ho
6 Bardsley Ho
7 Wardell Ho
8 Clavell St
9 Stanton Ho
10 Macey Ho
11 Boreman Ho
12 Clipper Appts
C4 **1** Frobisher Ct
2 Hardy Cotts
3 Palliser Ho
4 Bernard Angell Ho
5 Corvette Sq
6 Travers Ho
7 Maze Hill Lodge
8 Park Place Ho
9 Meridian Prim Sch

53
B1 **1** Heath House Prep Sch
B3 **1** Westcombe Ct
2 Kleffens Ct
3 Ferndale Ct
4 Combe Mews
5 Mandeville Ct
6 Pinelands Cl
C3 **1** Mary Lawrenson Pl
2 Bradbury Ct
3 Dunstable Ct
4 Wentworth Ho
C4 **1** Nethercombe Ho
2 Holywell Cl

54
A1 **1** Lancaster Cotts
2 Lancaster Mews
3 Bromwich Ho
4 Priors Lo
5 Richmond Hill Ct
6 Glenmore Ho
7 Hillbrow
8 Heathshott
9 Friars Stile Pl
10 Spire Ct
11 Ridgeway
12 Matthias Ct
13 Old Vicarage Sch
A2 **1** Lichfield Terr
2 Union Ct
3 Carrington Lo
4 Wilton Ct
5 Egerton Ct
6 Beverley Lo
7 Bishop Duppa's Almshouses
8 Regency Wlk
9 Clear Water Ho
10 Onslow Avenue Mans
11 Michels Almshouses
12 Albany Pas
13 Salcombe Villas
A3 **1** St John's Gr
2 Michel's Row
3 Michelsdale Dr
4 Blue Anchor Alley
5 Clarence St
6 Sun Alley
7 Thames Link Ho
8 Benns Wlk

55
A3 **1** Hershell Ct
2 Deanhill Ct
3 Park Sheen
4 Furness Lo
5 Merricks Ct
C4 **1** Rann Ho
2 Craven Ho
3 John Dee Ho
4 Kindell Ho
5 Montgomery Ho
6 Avondale Ho
7 Addington Ct
8 Dovecote Gdns
9 Firmston Ho
10 Glendower Gdns
11 Chestnut Ave
12 Trehern Rd
13 Rock Ave
14 St Mary Magdalen's RC Prim Sch

56
C2 **1** Theodore Ho
2 Nicholas Ho
3 Bonner Ho
4 Downing Ho
5 Jansen Ho
6 Fairfax Ho
7 Devereux Ho
8 David Ho
9 Leigh Ho
10 Clipstone Ho
11 Mallet Ho
12 Arton Wilson Ho

57
B2 **1** Inglis Ho
2 Ducie Ho

9 Waterloo Pl
10 Northumbria Ct
B1 **1** Chester Cl
2 Evesham Ct
3 Queen's Ct
4 Russell Wlk
5 Charlotte Sq
6 Jones Wlk
7 Hilditch Ho
8 Isabella Ct
9 Damer Ho
10 Eliot Ho
11 Fitzherbert Ho
12 Reynolds Pl
13 Chisholm Rd
B2 **1** Alberta Ct
2 Beatrice Rd
3 Lorne Rd
4 York Rd
5 Connaught Rd
6 Albany Terr
7 Kingswood Ct
8 Selwyn Ct
9 Broadhurst Cl
B3 **1** Towers The
2 Longs Ct
3 Sovereign Ct
4 Robinson Ct
5 Calvert Ct
6 Bedford Ct
7 Hickey's Almshouses
8 Church Estate Almshouses
9 Richmond International Bsns Ctr
10 Abercorn Mews

3 Wharncliffe Ho
4 Stanhope Ho
5 Waldegrave Ho
6 Mildmay Ho
7 Mullens Ho
C1 **1** Balmoral Ct
2 Glenalmond Ho
3 Selwyn Ho
4 Keble Ho
5 Bede Ho
6 Gonville Ho
7 Magdalene Ho
8 Armstrong Ho
9 Newnham Ho
10 Somerville Ho
11 Balliol Ho
12 Windermere
13 Little Combe Cl
14 Classinghall Ho
15 Chalford Ct
16 Garden Royal
17 South Ct
18 Anne Kerr Ct
19 Ewhurst
C2 **1** Geneva Ct
2 Laurel Ct
3 Cambalt Ho
4 Langham Ct
5 Lower Pk
6 King's Keep
7 Whitnell Ct
8 Whitehead Ho
9 Halford Ho
10 Humphry Ho
11 Jellicoe Ho
12 South Thames Coll (Putney Ctr)
C3 **1** Olivette St
2 Mascotte Rd
3 Glegg Pl
4 Crown Ct
5 Charlwood Terr
6 Percy Laurie Ho
7 Our Lady of Victories RC Prim Sch
C4 **1** Griffin Gate
2 Darfur St
3 John Keall Ho
4 Henry Jackson Ho
5 Felsham Ho
6 Ardshiel Cl
7 Ruvigny Mans
8 Star & Garter Mans
9 University Mans
10 Lockyer Ho
11 Princeton Ct
12 Kingsmere Ct
13 Kingsmere Cl
14 Felsham Mews
15 St Mary's CE Prim Sch

58
A2 **1** Claremont
2 Downside
3 Cavendish Ct
4 Ashcombe Ct
5 Carltons The
6 Espirit Ho
7 Millbrooke Ct
8 Coysh Ct
9 Keswick Hts
10 Avon Ct
11 Neild Ho The
B2 **1** Keswick Broadway
2 Burlington Mews
3 Cambria Lo

4 St Stephen's Gdns
5 Atlantic Ho
6 Burton Lo
7 Manfred Ct
8 Meadow Bank
9 Hooper Ho
10 Aspire Bld
C2 **1** Pembridge Pl
2 Adelaide Rd
3 London Ct
4 Windsor Ct
5 Westminster Ct
6 Fullers Ho
7 Bridge Pk
8 Lambeth Ct
9 Milton Ct
10 Norfolk Mans
11 Francis Snary Lo
12 Bush Cotts
13 Downbury Mews
14 Newton's Yd
15 Roche Sch The
16 St Joseph's RC Prim Sch
17 West Hill Prim Sch
18 St Michael Steiner Sch The

59
A2 **1** Fairfield Ct
2 Blackmore Ho
3 Lancaster Mews
4 Cricketers Mews
5 College Mews
6 Arndale Wlk
7 St Anne's CE Prim Sch
8 South Thames Coll (Wandsworth Ctr)
B2 **1** St Faith's CE Prim Sch
B4 **1** Molasses Ho
2 Molasses Row
3 Cinnamon Row
4 Calico Ho
5 Calico Row
6 Port Ho
7 Square Rigger Row
8 Trade Twr
9 Ivory Ho
10 Spice Ct
11 Sherwood Ct
12 Mendip Ct
13 Chalmers Ho
14 Coral Row
15 Ivory Sq
16 Kingfisher Ho
C3 **1** Burke Ho
2 High View Prim Sch
3 Centre Acad
4 Fox Ho
5 Buxton Ho
6 Pitt Ho
7 Ramsey Ho
8 Beverley Cl
9 Florence Ho
10 Linden Ct
11 Dorcas Ct
12 Johnson Ct
13 Agnes Ct
14 Hilltop
15 Courtyard The
16 Old Laundry The
17 Oberstein Rd
18 Fineran Ct
19 Sangora Rd
20 Harvard Mans

19 Plough Mews
C4 **1** Milner Ho
2 McManus Ho
3 Wilberforce Ho
4 Wheeler Ct
5 Sporle Ct
6 Holliday Sq
7 John Parker Sq
8 Carmichael Ct
9 Fenner Sq
10 Clark Lawrence Ct
11 Shaw Ct
12 Sendall Ct
13 Livingstone Rd
14 Farrant Ho
15 Jackson Ho
16 Darien Ho
17 Shepard Ho
18 Ganley Ct
19 Arthur Newton Ho
20 Chesterton Ho
21 John Kirk Ho
22 Mantua St
23 Heaver Rd
24 Candlemakers
25 Thames Christian Coll
26 Falconbrook Prim Sch

60
A4 **1** Kiloh Ct
2 Lanner Ho
3 Griffon Ho
4 Kestrel Ho
5 Kite Ho
6 Peregrine Ho
7 Hawk Ho
8 Inkster Ho
9 Harrier Ho
10 Eagle Hts
11 Kingfisher Ho
12 Lavender Terr
13 Temple Ho
14 Ridley Ho
15 Eden Ho
16 Hertford Ct
17 Nepaul Rd
B1 **1** Staplehurst Ct
2 Tepham Ct
3 Honeywell Jun & Inf Schs
B2 **1** Clapham Computer & Secretarial Coll
C1 **1** Rayne Ho
2 St Anthony's Ct
3 Earlsthorpe Mews
4 Nightingale Mans
C4 **1** Shaftesbury Park Chambers
2 Selborne
3 Rush Hill Mews
4 Marmion Mews
5 Crosland Pl
6 Craven Mews
7 Garfield Mews
8 Audley Cl
9 Basnett Rd
10 Tyneham Cl
11 Woodmere Cl
D1 **1** Broomwood Hall (Lower Sch)

61
A1 **1** Oliver House Prep Sch
A4 **1** Turnchapel Mews

C4 **1** Our Lady of Lourdes RC Prim Sch

68
C3 **1** Farnborough Ho
2 Rushmere Ho
3 Horndean Cl
4 Highcross Way
5 Timsbury Wlk
6 Foxcombe Rd
7 Ryefield Path
8 Greatham Wlk
9 Gosport Ho
10 Stoatley Ho
11 Milland Ho
12 Clanfield Ho
13 Fareham Ho
14 Grayswood Point
C4 **1** Woodcott Ho
2 Lyndhurst Ho
3 Wheatley Ho
4 Allbrook Ho
5 Bordon Wlk
6 Chilcombe Ho
7 Vicarage Ct
8 Shawford Ct
9 Eastleigh Wlk
10 Kings Ct
11 Somborne Ho

69
A3 **1** Ramsdean Ho
2 Purbrook Ho
3 Portsea Ho
4 Blentworth Point
5 Eashing Point
6 Hindhead Point
7 Hilsea Point
8 Witley Point
9 Buriton Ho
10 Grateley Ho
11 Hascombe Ho
12 Dunhill Point
13 Westmark Point
14 Longmoor Point
15 Cadnam Point
B4 **1** Cumberland Ho
2 Devonshire Ho
3 Cornwall Ho
4 Norfolk Ho
5 Leicester Ho
6 Warwick Ho
7 Sutherland Ho
8 Carmarthen Ho
9 Worcester Ho
10 Rutland Ho
11 Paddock Way
12 Putney Hill
C3 **1** Sandringham Cl
2 Eastwick Ct
3 Oatlands Cl
4 Banning Ho
5 Grantley Ho
6 Caryl Ho
7 Duncombe Ho
8 Chilworth Ct
9 Kent Lo
10 Turner Lo
11 Marlborough
12 Parkland Gdns
13 Lewesdon Cl
14 Pines Ct
15 Ashtead Ct
16 Mynterne Ct

17 Arden
18 Stephen Ct
19 Marham Ct
20 Doradus Ct
21 Acorns The
22 Heritage Ho
23 Conifer Ct
24 Spencer Ho
25 Chartwell
26 Blenheim
27 Chivelston
28 Greenfield Ho
29 Oakman Ho
30 Radley Lo
31 Simon Lo
32 Admirals Ct
33 Augustus Rd
C4 **1** Brett Ho
2 Brett House Cl
3 Sylva Ct
4 Ross Ct
5 Potterne Cl
6 Stourhead Cl
7 Fleur Gates
8 Greenwood
9 John Paul II Sch
10 Our Lady Queen of Heaven RC Prim Sch
11 Prospect House Sch

70
A3 **1** William Harvey Ho
2 Highview Ct
3 Cameron Ct
4 Galgate Cl
5 Green Ho The
6 King Charles Wlk
7 Florys Ct
8 Augustus Ct
9 Albert Ct
10 Hertford Lo
11 Mortimer Lo
12 Allenswood
13 Ambleside
14 Hansler Ct
15 Roosevelt Ct
16 Southmead Prim Sch
A4 **1** Douglas Gracey Ho
2 Aman Dalvi Ho
3 Andrew Reed Ho
4 Stoford Ct
5 Ronald Ross Prim Sch

71
B2 **1** Bremans Row
2 St Andrew's Ct
3 Townsend Mews
4 Sheringham Mews
5 Rainbow Sch
6 Garratt Park Sec Specl Sch

72
A2 **1** St Peters Cl
2 St Hildas Cl
3 St Edmunds Cl
4 St Hughes Cl
5 St Anthonys Cl
6 St Benets Cl
7 St Catherines Cl
8 Elsley Sch
C2 **1** Upper Tooting Park Mans

2 Cecil Mans
3 Marius Mans
4 Boulevard The
5 Elmfield Mans
6 Holdernesse Rd
7 Lumiere Ct
C3 **1** Heslop Ct
2 St James's Terr
3 Boundaries Mans
4 Station Par
5 Old Dairy Mews
6 Chestnut Grove Sch
7 Hornsby House Sch
8 Trinity St Mary's Prim Sch
C4 **1** Hollies Way
2 Endlesham Ct
3 Broomwood Hall Sch (Upper Sch)
4 Holy Ghost RC Prim Sch

73
A3 **1** Holbeach Mews
2 Hildreth Street Mews
3 Coalbrook Mans
4 Hub Buildings The
5 Metropolis Apartments
6 Hildreth St
A4 **1** Meyer Ho
2 Faraday Ho
3 Hales Ho
4 Frankland Ho
5 Graham Ho
6 Gibbs Ho
7 Dalton Ho
8 Ainslie Wlk
9 Rokeby Ho
10 Caistor Ho
11 Ivanhoe Ho
12 Catherine Baird Ct
13 Marmion Ho
14 Devonshire Ct
15 Blueprint Apartments
16 Royal Duchess Mews
17 Alderbrook Prim Sch
B3 **2** Henry Cavendish Prim Sch
3 Margaret Rutherford Pl
B4 **1** Limerick Ct
2 Homewoods
3 Jewell Ho
4 Glanville Ho
5 Dan Bryant Ho
6 Olding Ho
7 Quennel Ho
8 Weir Ho
9 West Ho
10 Neville Ct
11 Friday Grove Mews
12 St Bernadette RC Jun Sch
C3 **1** Sinclair Ho
2 MacGregor Ho
3 Ingle Ho
4 St Andrews Mews
5 Telferscot Prim Sch
C4 **1** Riley Ho
2 Bennett Ho
3 White Ho
4 Rodgers Ho

5 Dumphreys Ho
6 Homan Ho
7 Prendergast Ho
8 Hutchins Ho
9 Whiteley Ho
10 Tresidder Ho
11 Primrose Ct
12 Angus Ho
13 Currie Ho

74
A1 **1** De Montfort Ct
2 Leigham Hall Par
3 Leigham Hall
4 Endsleigh Mans
5 John Kirk Ho
6 Raeburn Ct
7 Wavel Ct
8 Homeleigh Ct
9 Howland Ho
10 Beauclerk Ho
11 Bertrand Ho
12 Drew Ho
13 Dowes Ho
14 Dunton Ho
15 Raynald Ho
16 Sackville Ho
17 Thurlow Ho
18 Astoria Mans
A2 **1** Wyatt Park Mans
2 Broadlands Mans
3 Stonehill's Mans
4 Streatleigh Par
5 Dorchester Ct
6 Picture Ho
A3 **1** Beaumont Ho
2 Christchurch Ho
3 Stapleford Cl
4 Chipstead Ho
5 Coulsdon Ho
6 Conway Ho
7 Telford Avenue Mans
8 Telford Parade Mans
9 Wavertree Ct
10 Hartswood Ho
11 Wray Ho
A4 **1** Picton Ho
2 Rigg Ho
3 Watson Ho
4 MacArthur Ho
5 Sandon Ho
6 Thorold Ho
7 Pearce Ho
8 Mudie Ho
9 Miller Ho
10 Lycett Ho
11 Lafone Ho
12 Lucraft Ho
13 Freeman Ho
14 New Park Par
15 Argyll Ct
16 Dumbarton Ct
17 Kintyre Ct
18 Cotton Ho
19 Crossman Ho
20 Cameford Ct
21 Parsons Ho
22 Brindley Ho
23 Arkwright Ho
24 Perry Ho
25 Brunel Ho
26 New Park Ct
27 Tanhurst Ho
28 Hawkshaw Cl

20 Richard Atkins Prim Sch
B1 **1** Carisbrooke Ct
2 Pembroke Lo
3 Willow Ct
4 Poplar Ct
5 Leigham Ct
6 Mountview
7 Spa View
B3 **1** Charlwood Ho
2 Earlswood Ho
3 Balcombe Ho
4 Claremont Cl
5 Holbrook Ho
6 Gwynne Ho
7 Kynaston Ho
8 Tillman Ho
9 Regents Lo
10 Hazelmere Ct
11 Dykes Ct
12 Hartwell Ct
13 Christ Church Streatham CE Prim Sch
14 Streatham Hill & Clapham High Sch
B4 **1** Archbishop's Pl
2 Witley Ho
3 Outwood Ho
4 Dunsfold Ho
5 Deepdene Lo
6 Warnham Ho
7 Albury Lo
8 Tilford Ho
9 Elstead Ho
10 Thursley Ho
11 Brockham Ho
12 Capel Lo
13 Leith Ho
14 Fairview Ho
15 Weymouth Ct
16 Ascalon Ct
17 China Mews
18 Rush Common Mews
C3 **1** Valens Ho
2 Loveday Ho
3 Strode Ho
4 Ethelworth Ct
5 Harbin Ho
6 Brooks Ho
7 Godolphin Ho
8 Sheppard Ho
9 McCormick Ho
10 Taylor Ho
11 Saunders Ho
12 Talcott Path
13 Derrick Ho
14 Williams Ho
15 Baldwin Ho
16 Churston Cl
17 Neil Wates Cres
18 Burnell Ho
19 Portland Ho
20 Fenstanton Prim Sch
21 St Martin-in-the-Fields High Sch
C4 **1** Ellacombe Ho
2 Booth Ho
3 Hathersley Ho
4 Brereton Ho
5 Holdsworth Ho
6 Dearmer Ho
7 Cherry Cl
8 Greenleaf Cl
9 Longford Wlk